THE
PRESIDENCY
A to Z

THE PRESIDENCY A TO Z

FOURTH EDITION

Gerhard Peters, Editor • John T. Woolley, Editor • Michael Nelson, Advisory Editor

CQ PRESS

A Division of Congressional Quarterly Inc.
Washington, D.C.

CQ Press
1255 22nd Street, NW, Suite 400
Washington, DC 20037

Phone: 202-729-1900; toll-free, 1-866-4CQ-PRESS (1-866-427-7737)

Web: www.cqpress.com

Cover design: Auburn Associates, Inc.
Interior design and composition: Auburn Associates, Inc.

Cover credits: White House: Photodisc; Lyndon B. Johnson and Abe Fortas: LBJ Library Photo by Yoichi R. Okamoto; John F. Kennedy: Associated Press; George Bush: Associated Press / J. Scott Applewhite; Abraham Lincoln: Library of Congress; Bill Clinton: Associated Press / Wilfredo Lee

⊚ The paper used in this publication exceeds the requirements of the American National Standard for Information Sciences—Permanence of Paper for Printed Library Materials, ANSI Z39.48-1992.

Printed and bound in the United States of America

11   10   09   08   07   1   2   3   4   5

The Library of Congress Cataloging-in-Publication data are available under LCCN: 2007031322.

CQ PRESS
AMERICAN GOVERNMENT A TO Z SERIES

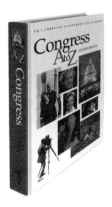

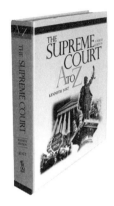

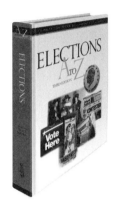

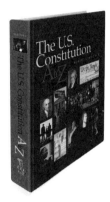

Congress A to Z, 4th Edition

No other volume so clearly and concisely explains the inner workings of the national legislature.

The Supreme Court A to Z, 4th Edition

This is the definitive source for information on the Court, its justices, and its impact on American democracy.

Elections A to Z, 3rd Edition

This single, convenient volume explores vital aspects of campaigns and elections, from voting rights to the current state of House, Senate, and presidential elections.

The U.S. Constitution A to Z

This is an ideal resource for anyone who wants reliable information on the U.S. Constitution and its impact on U.S. government and politics.

Contents

About the Authors / xiii
Preface / xv

A

Adams, Abigail / 1
Adams, John / 2
Adams, John Quincy / 4
Agnew, Spiro T. / 6
Agriculture Department / 7
Air Force One / 8

Appointment and Removal Power
   (Executive Branch) / 9
Arthur, Chester A. / 15
Article II / 16
Assassinations and Assaults / 19

B

Background of Presidents / 26
Barkley, Alben W. / 29
Bell, John / 30
Blaine, James G. / 30
Blair House / 31
Breckinridge, John C. / 32
Brownlow Committee / 33
Bryan, William Jennings / 33
Buchanan, James / 35

Buckley v. Valeo / 36
Budget Process / 37
Bureaucracy / 44
Burr, Aaron / 50
Bush, Barbara / 51
Bush, George H. W. / 52
Bush, George W. / 54
Bush, Laura / 56
Bush v. Gore / 57

C

Cabinet / 60
Calhoun, John C. / 66
Camp David / 67
Campaign Debates / 68
Campaign Financing / 71
Carter, Jimmy / 77
Carter, Rosalynn / 79
Central Intelligence Agency / 80
Cheney, Richard B. / 82
Chief of Staff / 84
Chief of State / 86
Civil Service / 91
Civil War / 95
Clay, Henry / 98
Cleveland, Grover / 99
Clinton v. Jones / 101
Clinton, Bill / 101

Clinton, George / 105
Clinton, Hillary Rodham / 106
Colfax, Schuyler / 108
Commerce Department / 109
Commissions, Presidential / 110
Congress and the Presidency / 111
Congressional Caucus
   (King Caucus) / 118
Constitutional Powers and
   Provisions / 119
Coolidge, Calvin / 125
Counsel to the President / 126
Court-Packing Plan / 127
Courts and the President / 128
Crawford, William Harris / 132
Curtis, Charles / 133

D

Daily and Family Life / 134
Dallas, George M. / 139
Davis, Jefferson / 140
Dawes, Charles G. / 141
Death of the President / 142
Debs, Eugene V. / 143
Defense Department / 144

Delegate Selection Reforms / 146
Dewey, Thomas E. / 148
Diplomatic Powers / 149
Disability Amendment / 154
Doctrines, Presidential / 155
Dole, Robert J. / 157
Douglas, Stephen A. / 158

E

Economic Advisers, Council of / 160
Economic Powers / 161
Education Department / 165
Eisenhower, Dwight D. / 167
Elections and Campaigns / 168
Elections Chronology / 174
Electoral College / 185
Emancipation Proclamation / 187
Emergency Powers / 188

Energy Department / 193
Environmental Protection Agency / 195
Ethics / 195
Executive Agreements / 198
Executive Office Buildings / 200
Executive Office of the President / 200
Executive Orders / 205
Executive Privilege / 206

F

Fairbanks, Charles W. / 208
Fair Deal / 209
Farewell Addresses / 210
Federal Bureau of Investigation / 211
Federal Election Commission / 212
Federalist Papers / 213
Federal Reserve System / 214

Ferraro, Geraldine A. / 216
Fillmore, Millard / 217
First Hundred Days / 218
First Ladies / 219
Ford, Betty / 223
Ford, Gerald R. / 224
Former Presidents / 226

G

Garfield, James A. / 229
Garner, John Nance / 231
Gerry, Elbridge / 232
Goldwater, Barry M. / 233
Gore, Albert, Jr. / 234

Grant, Ulysses S. / 235
Great Depression / 237
Great Society / 238
Group of Eight / 239

H

"Hail to the Chief" / 241
Hamdan v. Rumsfeld / 242
Hamilton, Alexander / 243
Hamlin, Hannibal / 244
Harding, Warren G. / 245
Harrison, Benjamin / 246
Harrison, William Henry / 248
Hayes, Rutherford B. / 249
Health and Human Services Department / 251
Hendricks, Thomas A. / 252

Historic Milestones of the
    Presidency / 253
Hobart, Garret A. / 259
Homeland Security Department / 260
Honeymoon Period / 262
Hoover, Herbert C. / 263
Hoover Commissions / 264
Housing and Urban Development
    Department / 266
Hughes, Charles Evans / 267

Humphrey, Hubert H. / 268
Humphrey's Executor v. United States / 269

Hurricane Katrina / 269

I

Immigration and Naturalization Service v. Chadha / 272
Impeachment / 273
Impoundment / 280
Inauguration / 282
Independent Counsel / 284
Independent Executive Agencies / 286

Independent Regulatory Agencies / 287
Interest Groups and the Presidency / 290
Interior Department / 293
Iran-Contra Affair / 294
Iraq War (Operation Iraqi Freedom) / 296

J

Jackson, Andrew / 300
Japanese American Internment / 303
Jefferson, Thomas / 304
Johnson, Andrew / 307
Johnson, Lady Bird / 308

Johnson, Lyndon B. / 309
Johnson, Richard M. / 311
Joint Chiefs of Staff / 312
Justice Department / 313

K

Kennedy, Jacqueline / 317
Kennedy, John F. / 318
Kerry, John / 320

King, William R. / 321
Kitchen Cabinet / 322
Korean War / 323

L

La Follette, Robert M. / 326
Labor Department / 327
Lame Duck / 328
Landon, Alfred / 329
Law Enforcement Powers / 330
Legislative Veto / 333

Libraries / 335
Lincoln, Abraham / 336
Lincoln, Mary Todd / 339
Line-Item Veto / 340
Louisiana Purchase / 341

M

McCarthy, Eugene J. / 343
McClellan, George B. / 345
McGovern, George S. / 346
McKinley, William / 347
Madison, Dolley / 349
Madison, James / 350
Management and Budget, Office of / 352
Marshall, Thomas R. / 353
Martial Law / 354
Media and the Presidency / 355

Memorials, Presidential / 360
Mexican-American War of 1846 / 361
Midterm Elections / 363
Milligan, Ex parte / 364
Mondale, Walter F. / 365
Monroe, James / 366
Monroe Doctrine / 368
Morton, Levi P. / 369
Myers v. United States / 370

N   National Archives and Records
Administration / 371
National Bank / 372
National Economic Council / 373
National Intelligence, Office of
the Director of / 374
National Party Conventions / 375
National Security Adviser / 380

National Security Council / 381
Neutrality Proclamation of 1793 / 382
New Deal / 383
New Freedom / 385
New Frontier / 386
Nixon, Pat / 387
Nixon, Richard / 388
Nuclear Command Procedures / 391

O   Oath of Office / 393

P   Pardon Power / 395
Party Leader / 396
Patronage / 398
Perot, H. Ross / 400
Persian Gulf War (Operations Desert Shield
and Desert Storm) / 401
Personnel Management, Office of / 403
Pierce, Franklin / 404
Political Action Committees (PACs) / 405

Political Parties / 407
Polk, James K. / 411
Presidential Greatness / 413
Presidential Medal of Freedom / 415
Press Conferences / 416
Press Secretary, Presidential / 418
Primaries and Caucuses / 420
Proclamations and Endorsements / 426
Public Opinion and the Presidency / 427

Q   Qualifications of the President
and Vice President / 432

Quayle, Dan / 433

R   Reagan, Nancy / 435
Reagan, Ronald / 437
Reconstruction / 439
Religion and the Presidency / 441
Rockefeller, Nelson A. / 443

Roosevelt, Eleanor / 444
Roosevelt, Franklin D. / 445
Roosevelt, Theodore / 448
Rumsfeld, Donald H. / 450

S   Salary and Perquisites / 453
Seals of Office / 456
Secret Service / 457
Senate Election of the Vice President / 458
Senatorial Courtesy / 459
Separation of Powers / 460
Sherman, James S. / 462
Signing Statements / 463
Smith, Alfred E. / 464
Spanish-American War of 1898 / 465

Speeches and Rhetoric / 466
Square Deal / 471
Staff / 471
State Department / 478
State of the Union Address / 479
Stevenson, Adlai E. / 480
Stevenson, Adlai E., II / 481
Stewardship Theory / 482
Succession / 483
Summit Meetings / 487

T

Taft, William Howard / 490
Taylor, Zachary / 492
Teapot Dome Scandal / 493
Tennessee Valley Authority / 494
Term of Office / 495
Third Parties / 498
Thurmond, J. Strom / 502
Tilden, Samuel J. / 503
Titles of the President and Vice President / 504
Tompkins, Daniel D. / 504
Tonkin Gulf Resolutions / 505

Trade Policy / 506
Trade Representative,
   Office of the U.S. / 509
Transition Period / 510
Transportation Department / 511
Travel / 513
Treasury Department / 514
Treaty Power / 515
Truman, Harry S. / 519
Tyler, John / 521

U

Unitary Executive Theory / 524
United Nations / 525
United States v. Curtiss-Wright Export Corp. / 528

United States v. Nixon / 528

V

Van Buren, Martin / 530
Veterans Affairs Department / 532
Veto Power / 533

Vice President / 539
Vice Presidential Residence / 546
Vietnam War / 546

W

Wallace, George C. / 550
Wallace, Henry A. / 552
War of 1812 / 553
War on Terrorism / 554
War Powers / 555
War Powers Act of 1973 / 560
Warren Commission / 562
Washington, George / 564
Washington, Martha / 566
Watergate Affair / 567
Weaver, James B. / 570

Wheeler, William A. / 571
Whiskey Rebellion / 572
Whiskey Ring Scandal / 573
White House / 573
Whitewater Investigation / 578
Willkie, Wendell L. / 581
Wilson, Edith / 581
Wilson, Henry / 582
Wilson, Woodrow / 583
World War I / 586
World War II / 588

Y

Youngstown Sheet and Tube Co. v. Sawyer / 591

Z

Zapruder Film / 593

REFERENCE MATERIAL

U.S. Presidents and Vice Presidents / 597
Backgrounds of U.S. Presidents, 1789–2007 / 599
Summary of Presidential Elections, 1789–2004 / 602
Party Affiliations in Congress and the Presidency / 607
Presidential Cabinets, 1789–2007 / 610
U.S. Government Organizational Chart / 626
Federal Internet Gateways and Search Engines / 627
Constitution of the United States / 629

Selected Bibliography / 642
Index / 649

About the Authors

Gerhard Peters is the co-creator and director, along with John T. Woolley, of the American Presidency Project at the University of California, Santa Barbara, and is a professor of political science at Citrus College in Glendora, California. Peters is a frequent contributor to the media on questions regarding the presidency and has appeared as a guest on Voice of America and National Public Radio in southern California. He was a coauthor with Deborah Kalb and John T. Woolley in the CQ Press volume *State of the Union: Presidential Rhetoric from Woodrow Wilson to George W. Bush.*

John T. Woolley is a professor of political science and department chair at the University of California, Santa Barbara. One of the creators of the American Presidency Project, Woolley has written extensively on presidents' management of the economy, presidential vetoes, and the study of change in the presidency. Along with Gerhard Peters, he was a coauthor in *State of the Union: Presidential Rhetoric from Woodrow Wilson to George W. Bush.*

About the Book

The Presidency A to Z is part of CQ Press's five-volume American Government A to Z series, which provides essential information about the history, powers, and operations of the three branches of government, the election of members of Congress and the president, and the nation's most important document, the Constitution. In these volumes, CQ Press's writers and editors present engaging insight and analysis about U.S. government in a comprehensive, ready-reference encyclopedia format. The series is useful to anyone who has an interest in national government and politics.

The Presidency A to Z offers accessible information about the historical foundations of the American presidency, the institution's development over time, the organization of the executive branch, presidential elections, the balance of power between the executive and legislative branches, and the lives of presidents and vice presidents. The volume also includes a detailed index, reference materials about presidential backgrounds, elections, and cabinet members, and a bibliography.

The fourth edition of *The Presidency A to Z* has been thoroughly updated to incorporate contemporary events that have shaped the presidency of George W. Bush, including developments in Iraq and the aftermath of Hurricane Katrina. In addition, new controversies related to the nature of presidential power and the executive's relationship to Congress are discussed in new entries on signing statements and the unitary executive theory. Presented in a new and engaging design, this edition contains a wealth of stimulating side-bar material, such as memorable quotations from the history of presidential rhetoric, and numerous other features inviting the reader to explore issues in further detail.

Preface

When George W. Bush assumed office in January 2001, it seemed that he had, like his predecessors in the post–World War II era, succeeded in obtaining from the American people the badge of legitimacy. This was especially important because his electoral college triumph was the climax of arguably the most bitterly contested vote in presidential election history, and a rare instance in which a newly elected chief executive received fewer popular votes than his major opponent. Once the Supreme Court halted the manual recount of ballots in Florida by way of its 5–4 decision in *Bush v. Gore,* effectively assuring Bush of a narrow electoral college victory, questions arose as to whether the president-elect would be able to govern effectively.

Americans, however, tend to set aside a certain degree of partisanship each four to eight years. Since the era of reliable public opinion polling on presidential job approval was begun by George Gallup in the 1930s, surveys have revealed that new presidents enjoy public approval from a percentage of Americans greater than that which elected them. Although the public's final opinion of Presidents Eisenhower, Kennedy, Nixon, Carter, Reagan, George H. W. Bush, and Clinton vary, each of these men enjoyed a short "honeymoon" period following their inaugurations in which public approval of their job performances hovered well above 50 percent, and more commonly as high as two-thirds of those polled. George W. Bush was no exception, as he enjoyed support from more than half of the country in early 2001, effectively integrating support from some of those citizens who had voted for Al Gore the previous November.

Presidential honeymoon periods do come to an end as a combination of many forces, some beyond the president's control and others wholly within the president's grasp, begin to shape the president's ability to lead the nation. Expectations of sweeping changes, as promised by the new president on the campaign trail, usually collide with America's separated system of government. The promise of substantial new public policies are regularly tempered by the reality that in a system of pluralism, only incremental change may become immediately possible.

Independent events also start to drive perceptions of presidential leadership. Ronald Reagan, who saw his job approval rating reach almost 70 percent during his first months in office, experienced a protracted decline to the mid-30s over the next two years, as the nation suffered through one of the deepest recessions since the Great Depression. Although Reagan, like all presidents before and after him, could not immediately solve the problems of unemployment through executive order or other forms of unilateral action, Americans' confidence in his leadership mirrored their financial situation. Fortunately for the president, the economy rebounded, and a robust expansion came just in time for his 1984 reelection campaign.

As the year 2001 progressed, there were many indications that the Bush administration would continue to press for implementation of Bush's "compassionate conservative" domestic agenda, including tax cuts, education reform, and promotion of "faith-based" initiatives. His legacy, and prospects for reelection, appeared to hinge on many of the same forces affecting his predecessors: the state of the economy and his ability to forge a bipartisan coalition in Congress and among the electorate by following presidential scholar Richard Neustadt's advice to use persuasion as a tool.

Then, on September 11, the most serious attack against the United States since Pearl Harbor served as a tectonic moment in American history that would irreversibly alter the course of the Bush presidency. The public rallied behind its commander in chief as it has done throughout history when American interests are threatened by foreign actors. In the days that followed, the president's job approval ratings reached the highest point any president had ever enjoyed, topping out at 90 percent. The country was united behind Bush, and he faced virtually no political opposition in retaliating against the al Qaeda terrorist network and its state sponsor, the Taliban government in Afghanistan. As further evidence of the consequence of war, in the 2002 midterm congressional election, the Republicans gained seats in both houses of Congress, bucking a decades-long trend in which an incumbent first-term president's party loses seats. As Bush said in a 2004 interview on the Sunday morning news program *Meet the Press,* he had become a "war president."

Later that year, with the nation still concerned with its security, Bush won reelection in a relatively close race, this time squeaking out a narrow majority of popular votes over his rival, John Kerry, a Vietnam War–decorated junior senator from Massachusetts. Although Bush's victory can hardly be considered a landslide similar to the reelection triumphs of Reagan in 1984, Nixon in 1972, Johnson in 1964, Eisenhower in 1956, or Franklin Roosevelt's multiple successes in 1936, 1940, and 1944, it was perceived by the president as a mandate, one that he claimed earned him "political capital."

As Bush's second term began, the effects of war appeared to have greatly enhanced his ability to dominate the political agenda. Even in wartime, however, the president's ability to lead is still dependent on public approval, congressional support, and the complexities of America's separated system. When James K. Polk, another war president, explained in an annual message to Congress that "the war with Mexico has thus fully developed the capacity of republican governments to prosecute successfully a just and foreign war with all the vigor usually attributed to more arbitrary forms of government," in essence what he declared was that representative government had historically been perceived as too weak and complex to respond effectively to emergencies. Popular sentiment and checks and balances might constrain an executive at the very moment when rapid unilateral decision making is essential.

In the case of President Bush, Congress continued to support operations in Iraq during the first two years of his second term, partially in deference to his role as commander in chief. As the occupation of Iraq seemed to continue with no apparent end in sight, however, the public's overall perception of the president's job performance steadily eroded, and his "political capital" rapidly evaporated. The result was the Republican 109th Congress's rejection of Bush's plan for Social Security reform. Following the Republicans' defeat in the 2006 midterm congressional elections, which was partially a result of the public's frustration with progress in Iraq, the now Democratic 110th Congress rejected immigration reform in 2007, with opposition this time coming from the GOP minority. President Bush's political base was crumbling, in large part because of his inability to persuade the nation and thus other actors in the policymaking infrastructure.

Until about 1960 research on the presidency examined the role of the chief executive as defined in Article II of the Constitution. This narrower, often descriptive, body of research looked at formal roles and powers such as veto use, executive orders, and the position of the president as administrative head of the nation. In addition, much of this research was oriented toward using philosophical foundations such as *The Federalist Papers,* as well as legal precedents regarding executive power and an examination of delegated authority.

The "strict constructionist" model of presidential leadership, as articulated by William Howard Taft, provides an example. Taft's attitude toward the use of noninstitutional and potential presidential power was limited and strict. Ironically, Taft was also a chief justice of the United States following his single-term presidency (1909–1913). As a jurist who used restraint in interpreting the Constitution, Taft noted:

> The true view of the Executive functions is, as I conceive it, that the President can exercise no power which cannot be fairly and reasonably traced to some specific grant of power or justly implied and included within such express grant as proper and necessary to its exercise. Such a specific grant must be either in the Federal Constitution or in an act of Congress passed in pursuance thereof. There is no undefined residuum of power which he can exercise because it seems to him to be in the public interest.[1]

Although Taft's philosophic contribution is significant, it is worth noting that his treatise, faithfully implemented in practice when he sat in the White House, was written during the administration of Democrat Woodrow Wilson, who was elected, arguably, because of the intraparty challenge Theodore Roosevelt thrust on American politics with his Progressive Party challenge of, among other issues, Taft's restrained view of leadership. Taft's static attitude toward the use of presidential power, while a central contribution to the state of scholarship during the first half of the twentieth century, was already being undermined by developing changes in leadership style practiced by the men who served as president immediately before and after his term.

In the evolution of presidential scholarship, this strict approach to studying presidential power in the first half of the twentieth century typically excluded or downplayed variables such as interest group politics, public opinion, and bargaining, which have been well integrated into contemporary scholarship. Other variables such as economic conditions and foreign crises or, borrowing

---

1. William H. Taft, *Our Chief Magistrate and His Powers* (New York: Columbia University Press, 1916), Ch. 6.

from psychological studies, the distinct personalities of presidents, were essentially absent from this earlier body of knowledge.

Beginning with Clinton Rossiter's *American Presidency* (1960), and especially with Richard Neustadt's landmark *Presidential Power* (1960), presidency scholarship significantly shifted its coverage and understanding of the office. Keeping with the basic approach of traditional presidency research, Rossiter's landmark work considered the formal roles of the presidency—including chief of state, chief executive, diplomat, and legislator—yet it moved beyond to highlight five prominent "informal roles" increasingly portrayed by modern presidents—chief of party, voice of the people, protector of the people, manager of prosperity, and world leader. With one foot in the original paradigm and one foot examining newer and more explicitly political and behavioral roles, Rossiter signaled a shift toward a different theoretical framework for understanding and studying the nation's highest office.

Neustadt's seminal work on presidential persuasion and behavior, *Presidential Power*, placed the president squarely at the center of the political system. Unlike the constitutional approach, which grew in part from a historical tradition of weak executives and a reflexive antagonism toward strong chief executives, this new approach advocated an aggressive leader who, from the center of the government, would be the undisputed architect and executor of foreign policy and, especially, a wide-ranging set of domestic policies. To operate successfully from this strategic position, a president would have to utilize "personal," not formal constitutional, power. This is commonly known as the "power of persuasion," which is dependent on interpersonal skill and organization and the president's reputation as an able leader.

Returning to the administration of George W. Bush: Bush's service to the nation as a "war president," is being tested during his last months in office. Only time will tell whether he was able to maintain the political capital needed to dominate Washington or if he has already assumed "lame duck" status and thus had lost the ability to persuade.

Gerhard Peters
John T. Woolley
The American Presidency Project
University of California, Santa Barbara

Adams, Abigail

Source: Library of Congress

Abigail Smith Adams (1744–1818) was the wife of John Adams, the second president of the United States. Of all the early first ladies, she was the most politically active and influential.

Abigail was the daughter of a New England minister. She had no formal schooling, yet she acquired a considerable education from the private library of her family. Her intelligence, sharp wit, and willingness to speak out impressed those who knew her. One such person was John Adams. After overcoming the objections of her parents, who did not consider him to be in her social class, John and Abigail married on October 25, 1764. They had five children, including John Quincy Adams, who would become the sixth president of the United States.

Abigail ran the family farm in Massachusetts largely on her own while John was pursuing his legal and political careers and serving as an American diplomat abroad. In 1784, after a six-year separation, she sailed to London to rejoin her husband, who was then the first American minister to England. They spent four years in London and Paris before returning to the United States in 1788. After eight years as vice president, Adams was elected president in 1796.

Abigail was a prolific letter writer, and over two thousand of her letters still exist. They provide evidence of her active interest in politics. She had urged her husband in 1775 to support independence and later to back the abolition of slavery and more education for women. She repeatedly asked her husband to "remember the ladies" in government matters. Her husband had a high regard for her judgment and intelligence, and her influence on him was evident to her contemporaries.

In 1800 Abigail supervised the move from Philadelphia to the new presidential mansion on the Potomac. Unfortunately, the building was still unfinished when she arrived, and only a few rooms were habitable. As a practical New Englander she hung laundry in the East Room. The new nation's capital, Washington, was in no better condition with its collection of mud roads and half-built buildings, and Abigail was privately unhappy at having left Philadelphia for it. Nevertheless, she spent her time laying the foundations of a social life for the new capital.

John Adams served only one term as president before retiring to Massachusetts in 1801. Abigail died of typhoid fever at the age of seventy-four on October 28, 1818. John outlived her by almost eight years.

More on this topic:

Adams, John, below

Adams, John Quincy, p. 4

First Ladies, p. 219

Adams, John

John Adams

Source: William Winstanley, Adams National Historic Site

John Adams (1735–1826) was the second president of the United States and a leading patriot during the American Revolution. He also served as the first vice president of the United States, under George Washington. Adams's single term as president saw the intensification of partisan politics and the rise of the rival Democratic-Republican Party, which would dominate American government during the early nineteenth century.

Adams was born on October 30, 1735, in Braintree (now Quincy), Massachusetts. His parents were well-established farmers whose ancestors had immigrated to Massachusetts from England a century before his birth. Adams enrolled in Harvard University in 1751, intending to become a Congregational minister. However, before he graduated in 1755 he had decided on a career in either law or medicine. After briefly teaching school in Worcester, Adams began studying law. By 1758 he had been admitted to the Massachusetts bar and was practicing law in Braintree.

Adams soon became recognized throughout Massachusetts as an outspoken advocate of colonial causes. He wrote Braintree's protest against the British Stamp Act of 1765 and published a series of anonymous letters in the *Boston Gazette* in which he said that the rights of English citizens were derived solely from God, not from the British monarchy or Parliament. In 1770 Adams demonstrated his commitment to due process of the law when he defended the British soldiers on trial for the murder of colonial citizens at the Boston Massacre. His reputation withstood the unpopularity of his action, and the following year he was elected by a large margin to the Massachusetts legislature.

In 1774 Adams became a delegate to the First Continental Congress. He was an early and influential advocate of separation from Britain and was appointed to the committee assigned to draft a declaration of independence. Adams retired from Congress in November 1777. Within a month, however, Congress appointed him to the American commission in France. He set sail to join Benjamin Franklin and Arthur Lee in Paris on February 13, 1778, but a treaty of alliance had already been concluded by the time he arrived. Adams returned to America in the summer of 1779. Upon his arrival he was elected as a delegate to the Massachusetts constitutional convention. He wrote the first draft of the new state constitution, which the convention adopted with only minor changes. He returned to Europe in 1780 and spent the next eight years in various diplomatic posts, including minister to Holland and minister to Great Britain. He signed the armistice ending war with the British in 1783 and negotiated several loans and commercial treaties with the European powers.

After returning to Boston in 1789, Adams was elected vice president in the first presidential election. Adams dutifully presided over the Senate in accordance with the Constitution. Because the original Senate had only twenty-two members, the vice president was often in a position to break tie votes as prescribed by the Constitution. During Adams's two terms he had twenty-nine opportunities to decide issues with his tie-breaking vote, more than any later vice president. However, he was seldom consulted by Washington on important issues and complained that the vice presidency was an insignificant and mechanical job. Nevertheless, Adams's relations with Washington remained cordial.

After eight years as vice president, Adams was elected president when Washington retired. The most important and contentious issue of Adams's presidency was an impending war with France. French vessels had been preying on U.S. shipping since 1795, and just before Adams's inauguration Paris issued a decree legitimizing the seizure of virtually any American ship. Adams faced political pressure from pro-British Hamiltonians who believed that the United States should join Britain in fighting to prevent French domination of Europe and to preserve American dignity. Jefferson's Democratic-Republicans opposed a war with France, but they did not have the votes in Congress to stop a declaration of war if Adams had wanted one. Adams chose to strengthen the nation's military, particularly the navy, while continuing negotiations with the French.

He dispatched a delegation to Paris in the summer of 1797 to seek an agreement that would avoid war and end French attacks on American shipping. But the diplomatic mission failed when the U.S. representatives were greeted with demands for a bribe for French foreign minister Charles Maurice Talleyrand, a loan to France, and an official apology for Adams's criticisms.

In April 1798 Adams's release of documents relating to the incident (which came to be known as the XYZ affair) aroused American opinion against France and rallied public support behind Adams. By this time an undeclared naval war between the two nations had already begun. But Adams resisted calls to declare war against France, even though he could have bolstered his own political fortunes by yielding to the public's militant sentiment.

In early 1799 France began sending conciliatory signals, which prompted Adams to send another peace commission before the year was over. Increased taxes to support war preparations had diminished public enthusiasm for military adventurism. By May the immediate danger of a land war with France had passed, and Adams ordered a drastic reduction in the army. In November word reached the United States that the American delegation had successfully concluded a treaty of peace and commerce with France.

By this time the Democratic-Republicans had taken control of the state legislatures of several pivotal states, setting the stage for Adams's defeat in the 1800 presidential election. One of the reasons for the growing disaffection with the Federalist Party was its support of the Alien and Sedition Acts. In 1798 the Federalist majority in Congress attempted to put an end to the attacks on Federalist members of Congress and cabinet members in the Democratic-Republican press. The Sedition Act provided for imprisonment and fines for individuals who wrote, published, or uttered anything false or malicious about federal government officials. The Sedition Act, together with the Alien Act of the same year, which gave the president broad authority to deport aliens suspected of subversive activity, suppressed freedom of expression. Adams signed these bills into law but was not active in enforcing them. Despite the disunity of the Federalist Party and the unpopularity of the Alien and Sedition Acts, the 1800 election was close. Adams received sixty-five electoral votes, eight fewer than Jefferson, who became president, and Aaron Burr, who became vice president.

Before leaving office Adams appointed more than two hundred new judges, attorneys, clerks, and marshals. Some of these "midnight appointments" were removed by Jefferson, but many retained their offices. Adams also appointed John Marshall chief justice of the United States, a selection Adams was especially proud of in his later years.

When Adams's term ended, he returned to his farm in Massachusetts without attending Jefferson's inauguration. Adams spent much of his retirement writing his autobiography and corresponding with former colleagues. In December 1811 he wrote a letter of reconciliation to his once close friend Thomas Jefferson at the insistence of their mutual friend Dr. Benjamin Rush. Jefferson replied immediately, and they established a lasting correspondence. Adams died in Quincy on July 4, 1826, the fiftieth anniversary of the Declaration of Independence. His last words reportedly were "Thomas Jefferson still lives." Adams had no way of knowing that Jefferson had died only a few hours before.

Adams had married Abigail Smith in 1764. One of their sons, John Quincy Adams, became a prominent diplomat, congressman, and the sixth president of the United States. In 2001 Congress passed legislation creating the Adams Memorial Foundation as the first step to create a memorial for John Adams and his family in Washington.

In 1770 Adams demonstrated his commitment to due process of the law when he defended the British soldiers on trial for the murder of colonial citizens at the Boston Massacre.

More on this topic:

Adams, Abigail, p. 1

Adams, John Quincy, below

Adams, John Quincy

John Quincy Adams

Source: Gilbert Stewart and Thomas Sully, Harvard University Art Museums

John Quincy Adams (1767–1848) was a son of John Adams, the second president of the United States. They were one of two father-son teams who both served as president, the other being George H.W. Bush and George W. Bush.

John Quincy was born on July 11, 1767, in Braintree (now Quincy), Massachusetts. He was educated at schools in France and the Netherlands and learned to speak several languages. When he was just fourteen, he served as secretary and translator for Francis Dana, the first U.S. ambassador to Russia. Adams graduated from Harvard University in 1787. He passed the bar in 1790 and established a law practice in Boston.

Adams's distinguished diplomatic career began in 1794 when George Washington appointed him ambassador to the Netherlands. Three years later, after his father assumed the presidency, Adams became minister to Prussia, a post he held throughout his father's term.

When Thomas Jefferson defeated John Adams in his try for reelection in 1800, John Quincy returned to the United States where he embarked on a legislative career as a Federalist. In 1802 he was elected to the Massachusetts senate, which sent him to the U.S. Senate the following year. Adams, however, angered his fellow Federalists by supporting President Jefferson's Embargo Act in 1807.

When the Massachusetts legislature elected his successor six months before his term expired, Adams resigned in protest and returned to Massachusetts to practice law and teach at Harvard University.

Despite Adams's Federalist background, President James Madison, a Democratic-Republican, appointed him minister to Russia in 1809. In 1814 Adams was sent to Ghent to negotiate an end to the War of 1812. The treaty negotiated by Adams and his delegation and signed on December 24, 1814, extricated the United States from the embarrassing war without making significant concessions. Adams was then sent to London where he served as minister to Great Britain until 1817.

President James Monroe called Adams home from London in 1817 to become secretary of state. Adams distinguished himself in this post by concluding the Adams-Onís Treaty with Spain on February 22, 1819. It provided for the transfer of East and West Florida to the United States and the establishment of a border between Spanish and U.S. territory running from the Gulf of Mexico to the Rocky Mountains and along the forty-second parallel to the Pacific Ocean. Historians regard the treaty as a brilliant act of diplomacy, and Adams himself called its conclusion "the most important event of my life." Adams also was the mind behind the Monroe Doctrine, which warned that the United States would oppose any European interference in the internal affairs of an American nation or further European colonization of territory in the Western Hemisphere.

The 1824 presidential election was one of the most confused in U.S. history. The remnants of the Federalist Party had faded away during Monroe's presidency, leaving the Democratic-Republican Party the only significant party in existence. The Democratic-Republican congressional caucus nominated W. H. Crawford of Georgia as the party's candidate, but several state caucuses refused to be guided by the judgment of this group. Consequently, John Quincy Adams, Andrew Jackson, and Henry Clay were nominated as regional candidates. The four-candidate race split the electoral vote, and no one received the majority required to be elected. Jackson led Adams, 99–84, with Crawford and Clay receiving 41 and 37 votes, respectively. This stalemate threw the election into the House of Representatives. There Henry Clay, a powerful member of the House, gave his support to Adams, who emerged victorious despite having received less than one-third of the popular vote. When Adams selected Clay to be his secretary of state, the new president's opponents charged him with making a "corrupt bargain."

Despite the absence of an electoral mandate and the disadvantage of a Congress set to oppose him, Adams proposed a program of public improvements. To stimulate the economy he advocated construction of a federally funded system of roads and canals and the implementation of high protective tariffs. He also called for federal funding of a national university, a national observatory, and scientific expeditions. However, the president's proposals failed to attract significant support. Adams gained respect from certain groups for his antislavery and Indian rights stands, but he was out of step politically with the majority of the American public, especially in the South and West. When he ran for reelection in 1828 against Andrew Jackson, he did well in his native New England but lost the South and West, and therefore the election, by a landslide.

In 1830 the Twelfth District of Massachusetts elected the former president to the U.S. House of Representatives. Adams wrote, "No election or appointment conferred upon me ever gave me so much pleasure." Although not a radical abolitionist, Adams won respect for his conscientious opposition to slavery. His role as defense counsel in the *Amistad* case in 1841 demonstrated his convictions. In 1839 a group of Africans was abducted, sold in Cuba to Spaniards, and put aboard the Spanish schooner *Amistad*. The Africans revolted, killing the ship's master and a crewman. The ship was seized off Long Island, New York, and the Africans imprisoned. The Spaniards and those who saved the schooner argued that, under the law of salvage, the Africans were property. The case was appealed to the Supreme Court, which upheld lower-court rulings that the Africans were free men and women.

Adams also was a leading congressional critic of the annexation of Texas and the Mexican-American War. His life of public service ended in February 1848 when he became ill at his desk in the House chamber, fell into a coma, and died two days later, on February 23, in the Capitol.

More on this topic:

Adams, Abigail, p. 1

Adams, John, p. 2

Elections Chronology, p. 174

1824 PRESIDENTIAL ELECTION: POPULAR AND ELECTORAL VOTE RESULTS

Candidate	Home State	Electoral Votes	Popular Vote	State Delegations Won in House Balloting
Andrew Jackson	Tennessee	99	41.3%	13
John Quincy Adams (winner)	Massachusetts	84	30.9	7
William Harris Crawford	Georgia	41	11.2	4
Henry Clay	Kentucky	37	13.0	N/A

Agnew, Spiro T.

Source: Library of Congress

Spiro Theodore Agnew (1918–1996) served as vice president under Richard Nixon from 1969 to 1973. Agnew functioned as a hard-line spokesman for the administration by frequently attacking Nixon's opponents. After he was implicated in a bribery scheme, however, Agnew became one of only two vice presidents to resign from office (the other was John C. Calhoun).

Agnew served as an army officer during World War II, and he saw combat in France and Germany. After the war he earned a law degree from the Baltimore Law School and opened a law office in Towson, Maryland, a Baltimore suburb. Agnew had been a Democrat, but he switched to the Republican Party in the late 1940s and actively supported local Republican candidates. In 1962 he was elected executive of Baltimore County, a post with responsibilities similar to those of a mayor.

Agnew ran for governor of Maryland in 1966. During the campaign he acquired a reputation as a liberal, in part because his Democratic opponent, George Mahoney, was a segregationist, whereas Agnew supported some civil rights initiatives. Substantial support from blacks and liberal Democrats helped him to defeat Mahoney decisively, despite the Democratic Party's three-to-one advantage over the Republicans among Maryland's registered voters.

With the cooperation of the Maryland legislature, Agnew reformed the state's tax code, increased aid to the poor, passed an open housing law, repealed the ban on racial intermarriage, liberalized the abortion law, and enacted strict regulations to reduce water pollution. In 1968, however, Agnew appeared to shift to the right. In particular, his uncompromising response to race riots in Baltimore after the assassination of civil rights leader Martin Luther King Jr. in April 1968 caused observers to question his liberal image.

On August 7, 1968, Agnew placed Richard Nixon's name in nomination for president at the Republican national convention in Miami. After Nixon won the nomination, he surprised many observers by choosing Agnew as his running mate. Agnew was virtually unknown outside Maryland, but Nixon hoped that he would appeal to southern voters who might be drawn to the third-party candidacy of former Alabama governor George C. Wallace.

During the 1968 campaign Agnew made several political blunders that betrayed his lack of national political experience. His claim that the Democratic presidential candidate, Vice President Hubert H. Humphrey, was "squishy soft on communism" rekindled memories of Nixon's extreme anticommunist rhetoric during the 1940s and 1950s. Agnew also used the derogatory term *Polack* in a statement referring to a person of Polish ancestry and remarked in an interview that "if you've seen one city slum, you've seen them all." Despite these mistakes, Nixon and Agnew defeated Democrats Humphrey and Maine senator Edmund S. Muskie in the Electoral College vote 301–191.

As vice president, Agnew had little influence on policy decisions, but he became the president's mouthpiece against liberal members of the news media, Vietnam War protesters, and other groups perceived by the administration as enemies. In 1972 Nixon, with Agnew as his running mate, defeated the Democratic nominee, Sen. George McGovern of South Dakota, in a landslide.

In August 1973 the U.S. attorney in Baltimore disclosed that Agnew was under investigation for having received bribes from contractors during his years as Baltimore County executive and governor of Maryland. Agnew claimed he was innocent, but his lawyers worked out a plea bargain in which the vice president agreed to resign, to plead "no contest" to income tax evasion, and to pay a $10,000 fine and $150,000 in back taxes. In return, the Justice Department agreed not to prosecute Agnew for taking bribes. He resigned the vice presidency on October 10, 1973. Two days later Nixon nominated Gerald R. Ford to replace him.

Early in 1974 Agnew was disbarred. He decided to write a novel to pay his debts, and in 1976 he published *The Canfield Decision,* a story about a U.S. vice president who becomes involved with Iranian militants. He also established a profitable international consulting business for companies doing business in the Middle East. In 1980 he published his autobiography, *Go Quietly... or Else,* in which he claimed he was innocent of the crimes that forced his resignation. In 1994, two years before he died of acute leukemia, Agnew revealed that he had not spoken with Nixon since his resignation from the vice presidency.

> *In the United States today, we have more than our share of nattering nabobs of negativism. They have formed their own 4-H club—the hopeless, hysterical hypochondriacs of history.*
>
> **Spiro Agnew,** Speech at the California Republican convention, San Diego, September 11, 1970.

More on this topic:

Nixon, Richard, p. 388

Vice President, p. 539

Agriculture Department

The U.S. Department of Agriculture (USDA) assists the nation's farmers through a variety of programs, including subsidies, credit, and rural development loans. The department also oversees the nation's food quality through inspections of processing plants, and it establishes quality standards for every major agricultural commodity. It provides nutrition education programs as well.

USDA's research facilities investigate a variety of subjects, such as animal and crop production, plant and animal diseases, pest controls, food safety, and forestry. The department supports environmental protection through conservation programs for energy, soil, water, and forest resources.

Other responsibilities of the department include administering programs for school lunches, food stamps, food for the needy, and overseas food aid distribution; managing national forests and parklands; and helping developing nations improve food production.

The department was established in 1862 and elevated to cabinet status in 1889. By the early 1890s it had become known as one of the world's premier agricultural research institutions. It was given oversight of the national forests and additional regulatory authority over meat inspection and food and drugs (the latter authority was transferred to the Food and Drug Administration in 1940). The department soon became active in establishing standards and grades for various agricultural products.

In the 1920s agriculture was swept into the general economic decline that was to culminate in the Great Depression. Several significant programs were created in the 1930s to aid farmers, including the basic system of price supports and production control that is still in existence. In addition, USDA joined the welfare agencies in aiding the poor in rural and urban areas through programs designed to distribute food surpluses to the needy.

Responding to overseas food needs after World War II, USDA urged U.S. farmers to expand their production. When this policy resulted in surpluses and falling farm prices in the 1950s, the government instituted programs to expand markets.

During the 1960s the Food Stamp Program was passed, and programs for school lunches, school milk, and other types of food donation were expanded. At the same time, international "Food for Peace" activities were increased. All of these programs assisted farmers as well as the recipients of the programs.

Ronald Reagan's administration launched a drive in the 1980s to end many of the depression-era programs and eliminate the assumption that the federal government was directly responsible for farmers' well-being. But the worsening economic climate in the rural community forced the administration to drop many of its plans.

USDA underwent a major reorganization in 1994 as part of President Bill Clinton's "Reinventing Government" initiative; many field offices were closed and staff and agencies were significantly reduced. But these events were overshadowed by the resignation of Clinton's first agriculture secretary, Mike Espy, in late 1994 over allegations that he had accepted gifts from businesses regulated by USDA, including a large poultry conglomerate owned by a prominent Clinton supporter in Arkansas. In 1996 Clinton signed into law the Federal Agriculture Improvement and Reform Act (FAIR), which cut production subsidies as a step toward phasing them out and giving farmers more latitude in responding to market needs.

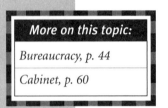

More on this topic:

Bureaucracy, p. 44

Cabinet, p. 60

In May 2002 President George W. Bush signed into law a new six-year farm bill that reestablished federal support payments based on crop prices. In early 2003 two units of USDA—the Animal and Plant Health Inspection Service and the Plum Island Animal Disease Center—became part of the new Department of Homeland Security.

Air Force One

A small fleet of air force jets is at the disposal of the president, and whichever one the president is aboard becomes *Air Force One*. The official *Air Force One* that the president uses most often is one of two Boeing 747-200Bs, jets that superseded the aging Boeing 707 as the president's official airplane during George H. W. Bush's presidency.

The new *Air Force One* carries seventy passengers and a crew of twenty-three. On board, the president has an office and a private bedroom for an occasional shower or nap. The jet also has a conference room, a guest area, several work stations equipped with computers, space for reporters, medical facilities, and a kitchen. Amenities include a stereo system, televisions, movie screens, and playing cards embossed with the presidential seal and the words "Aboard Air Force One."

Air Force One was designed to be both luxurious and secure. It was built with special protection against electromagnetic pulses from a nuclear explosion. The plane also has an elaborate communications system that allows the president to contact anyone anywhere. And somewhere aboard *Air Force One* is a compartment for the "black box" that contains the secret codes for the president's use in the event of a military crisis.

When presidents first became airborne, the Army Air Corps, the predecessor of the U.S. Air Force, took its rightful place as air chauffeur to the commander in chief. The air force has continued to be in charge of selecting and piloting presidential planes. The first official presidential plane, used by Franklin D. Roosevelt for one trip in 1945, was a U.S. Air Corps Douglas C-54 Skymaster cargo plane. President Harry S. Truman flew often in this plane, which was nicknamed *Sacred Cow* by reporters. In 1947 the official presidential plane was upgraded to a Douglas Aircraft DC-6 passenger liner. Named the *Independence* after Truman's hometown in Missouri, the plane was equipped with weather radar, long-range flight capability, and a teletype system that allowed the president to stay in touch with Washington even when he was 3,000 miles away.

President Dwight D. Eisenhower's first official plane was a Lockheed Constellation 749 named *Columbine II* after his personal military craft during World War II and the state flower of his wife's home state, Colorado. Because of rapidly advancing aviation technology, the plane was replaced in 1954 by *Columbine III*, a Lockheed 1049C Super-Constellation. On a whirlwind, eighteen-day tour of eleven countries in 1959, Eisenhower chose not to use *Columbine III* and became the first president to travel by jet.

The distinction of becoming the first president to travel regularly by jet went to John F. Kennedy. Assigned a propeller-driven Douglas Viscount VC-118A by the air force, Kennedy preferred the new, and much faster, Boeing 707, which he received in 1962.

Previous presidential aircraft had been military in appearance, but famed industrial designer Raymond Loewy, together with First Lady Jacqueline Kennedy, created an elegant blue and white exterior motif for the president's new plane. It, along with a newer 707 added in the early 1970s, remained the president's official aircraft into George H.W. Bush's presidency.

CLOSER LOOK

Air Force One is the designation given to an aircraft only when the president is on board. The designation was created in 1953 when President Eisenhower's plane entered the same airspace as a commercial airliner with the same call sign. Today the presidential fleet consists of two Boeing 747 jets with tail numbers 28000 and 29000 that were placed in service during the administration of George H.W. Bush.

> **More on this topic:**
> *Travel, p. 514*

Amnesty *See* PARDON POWER.

Appointment and Removal Power (Executive Branch)

No president can make all the important policy and administrative decisions necessary to carry out the functions of the U.S. government. As the size of the federal government has grown, presidents have been forced to delegate more and more of their responsibilities to a growing number of political executives.

Consequently, one of the most important administrative powers that presidents have is their ability to recruit and appoint people to fill high-level positions in their administration. Effective use of the appointment process is vital to the functioning of any administration. Presidents who pay inadequate attention to it may wind up with appointees who are incompetent, unqualified, corrupt, or at odds with the president's philosophy.

Background

Article II, Section 2, of the Constitution gives the president the power to appoint principal officers of the government—"Ambassadors, other public Ministers and Consuls, Judges of the Supreme Court, and all other Officers of the United States, whose Appointments are not herein otherwise provided for, and which shall be established by Law...."

The Constitution separates the appointment process into a two-step procedure shared by the president and the Senate. The president recruits and nominates appointees, and the Senate either confirms or rejects them. The Constitution also gives Congress the authority to place other appointments within the prerogative of the president (such as the White House STAFF), of the courts (such as an INDEPENDENT COUNSEL), or of the department heads without Senate confirmation.

The president has the power under the Constitution to make "recess appointments"—that is, to fill vacancies when the Senate is in recess. These appointments expire at the end of the next session of Congress.

Although the Constitution gives the president the responsibility for selecting the approximately 2.7 million civilian employees (as of the early 2000s) in the federal BUREAUCRACY, over the years the chief executive has given up much direct participation in the process to the federal CIVIL SERVICE system.

Until the 1880s most executive branch jobs were apportioned through PATRONAGE, the system of granting favors and filling jobs as political rewards. Nineteenth-century presidents placed their friends and allies in federal government positions. But with the passage of the Pendleton Act in 1883, creating a merit system for government employment, most agencies began to choose their employees according to their qualifications and ability to do the job.

Because the vast majority of executive branch jobs are merit system positions, only the most senior executive positions are filled by presidential appointees. Among these are the White House staff and other officials in the EXECUTIVE OFFICE OF THE PRESIDENT, CABINET department heads, members of the so-called subcabinet (policy-making officers immediately subordinate to the cabinet officer and at the level of under secretary, deputy secretary, and assistant secretary), and ambassadors. Agency and department heads make additional appointments within their agencies. Of the 5,200 or so appointments they and their subordinates make, presidents are most interested in a few hundred top political executive posts—cabinet secretaries, under secretaries, assistant secretaries, and bureau chiefs.

The question of the president's power to dismiss these appointees once they are in office has generated much controversy over the years. Although the Constitution makes clear that the appointment process is a joint responsibility of the president and the Senate, it is silent on the issue of removals, except for Article II's IMPEACHMENT provisions.

Debate over the removal issue began in the early days of the Republic and continued intermittently into the twentieth century. Several Supreme Court cases have defined the legal and constitutional authority of presidents to remove government officials. Some of these decisions have given the chief executive considerable authority to fire executive branch officials appointed by the president and confirmed by the Senate; other decisions have placed limits on presidential removal authority over agencies that exercise quasi-legislative or quasi-judicial functions, such as independent regulatory agencies.

Appointment Process

The power to recruit and appoint top officials in the executive branch is critical to a president's ability to control the federal government.

Factors Considered

To ensure effective leadership, presidents look for competence and loyalty in appointees. Major sources of staff for new presidents include close associates, people already serving in the government, business leaders, academic figures, and representatives of the constituencies served by the various departments.

Presidents must consider other factors as well. Most presidents have accumulated political debts on their way to the White House. Numerous groups and individuals have contributed both money and votes to their victories, and presidents look for ways to reward their chief supporters with political appointments. Although these selections usually do not constitute the majority of a president's appointments, rewarding supporters is an important consideration in presidential appointments.

Presidents also make appointments for purely political reasons. For example, to increase the number of members of minorities in the federal government, Lyndon B. Johnson in 1966 appointed Robert C. Weaver, the first black cabinet member, as secretary of the Housing and Urban Development Department.

A president's very first personnel selections are the most important politically. In fact, the appointments that presidents make as they establish their administrations generally set the tone and priorities of their presidencies. These selections serve as symbols and are subject to very close public scrutiny.

In addition, presidents consider how future political relationships will be affected by their early choices. An administration's success often depends on the ability of the president to forge political alliances and broaden the president's base of support. Indeed, presidents may be able to expand their universe of political allies through the appointment process. In addition to rewarding those who have supported them in the past, presidents often use appointments to get on the good side of their own political party, interest groups whose support they seek, and often members of Congress. But this strategy can sometimes backfire. William Howard Taft, quoting Thomas Jefferson, used to lament, "Every time I make an appointment I create nine enemies and one ingrate."

Another consideration in presidential appointments is the presidency's managerial needs. As the bureaucracy has become more technologically complex, presidents have had to choose appointees who possess managerial and administrative capabilities. The larger the department or agency, the greater is the need for management expertise. Departments such as Defense and Health and Human Services and agencies such as the U.S. Postal Service are examples of large government organizations requiring administrative competence in their appointed leaders.

Yet, more often than not, the ability to manage becomes one of the last factors in evaluating a potential appointee. Political considerations often outweigh managerial skill. Characteristics such as an appointee's geographic or ethnic background are often much more obvious and easy to evaluate than his or her administrative ability.

Constraints

The postelection rush to fill vacancies in a new administration places constraints on the appointment process. Presidents have the largest number of appointments to make and the least amount of time to consider them. At this point in their administrations, presidents are unable to take full advantage of one of their greatest administrative powers.

Between the election and the inauguration, presidents work to establish the policy objectives of their administrations. But while they are still formulating these objectives, presidents or their subordinates must make the vast majority of their most important appointments. There is little time to match appointees with administration policies. Once in office, appointees may change their attitudes as a result of their new responsibilities, or some may become rigidly wedded to the views of the interest groups with which they have the most contact.

Presidents often find it difficult to persuade potential nominees to give up high-paying positions in the private sector and move to Washington, D.C. Potential nominees may be reluctant to disclose their financial background and income, as required by law.

Presidents occasionally must pass up a potential nominee because of the person's involvement with a past administration, a scandal, or even the appearance of wrongdoing. After Bill Clinton's surgeon general, Joycelyn Elders, was asked to resign because of her outspoken support for sex education in schools and for legalizing some narcotics, Clinton's next nominee, Henry Foster, quickly became entangled with antiabortion interests over the number of abortions he had performed. Even after the Senate Labor and Human Resources Committee approved his nomination, abortion opponents were able to muster enough votes in the full Senate to place his nomination in doubt, and he withdrew his name in June 1995.

Senate Role

The Senate serves as one of the most important limits to the presidential appointment privilege. Constitutionally, presidents share the appointment of many political executives with the Senate, and the Senate must confirm most of the president's major appointments. As a result, the Senate has come to view the appointment procedure as one in which its members should have a considerable say. Senators see it as both a constitutional responsibility and a political opportunity to influence government policy.

The number of presidential nominations sent to the Senate for confirmation is staggering. In addition to the high-profile political appointments made by the president, the Senate also processes thousands of other executive nominations each year.

For example, in 1989, the first year of George H. W. Bush's presidency, the Senate received more than 48,000 nominations, although fewer than 600 involved high-level positions that might invite Senate scrutiny. Almost all—about 45,000—consisted of routine military commissions and promotions. Action on these types of nominations is perfunctory, as compared with the careful consideration given to appointments to top-level positions in the executive branch or to the federal judiciary. (See COURTS AND THE PRESIDENT.)

Like most other matters before Congress, the nomination process is handled mostly by standing committees. Although each committee has different sets of procedures for managing appointments referred to it, most committees have developed their own standard proceedings. Usually, these require additional background checks and financial disclosures, other than those already required by the president's personnel director and the Ethics in Government Act of 1978, and extensive hearings.

The average length of time required by the Senate to confirm presidential nominees during Ronald Reagan's administration was nearly fifteen weeks. One result of this rigorous and lengthy investigative process has been an increase in demands on potential appointees.

Political and ethical issues frequently have dominated consideration of nominations to the cabinet. Reagan adviser Edwin Meese III was confirmed as attorney general in 1987 after a bitter thirteen-month battle that turned on his ethical conduct and fitness for office. Confirmation came only after a special prosecutor appointed to review the matter found "no basis" for criminal prosecution.

In 1989 the Senate rejected Bush's nomination of former senator John Tower of Texas to be secretary of defense—the first rejection of a cabinet nomination since 1959. Democratic opponents of the nomination questioned Tower's personal conduct. Republicans insisted that the personal questions about Tower, a longtime member and former chairman of the Senate Armed Services Committee, were merely a screen for a Democratic power grab. The defeat of the Tower nomination marked only the ninth time that the Senate had turned down a cabinet nominee. It was the first time it had denied a president a cabinet nominee at the start of his first term.

In the early days of his administration Bill Clinton went through a prolonged and embarrassing search for an attorney general. His first two choices withdrew after controversies erupted over their hiring of undocumented domestic workers. At the beginning of Clinton's second term, Anthony Lake, his nominee for director of the Central Intelligence Agency, withdrew his name from Senate consideration after allegations that he was not forthcoming about certain investments and objections by conservative critics to some of his previous foreign policy activities. Lake had served as national security adviser.

Confirmation debates that center on political opinions often involve appointments to independent boards and commissions. Usually created by act of Congress and not subordinate to any executive department, such agencies frequently are viewed as arms of Congress, and members of Congress expect to play a major role in the selection process. Typically, the act of Congress creating an independent agency may require a bipartisan membership or impose geographic or other limitations on the president's flexibility of selection. Contests with the Senate over these nominations have been frequent.

Outright rejection of presidential nominees is rare. All presidents have been successful in getting the vast majority of their nominees confirmed. However, the occasions on which the Senate has rejected a presidential nominee, and the thoroughness of its investigations, indicate that the Senate does exert some control over the president's appointments.

The Senate also exercises influence through the custom of SENATORIAL COURTESY, whereby the Senate refuses to confirm a nomination to an office within a particular state unless the nominee has been approved by the senators of the president's party from that state.

In some cases the Senate may use its confirmation power as a political bargaining chip. Often it keeps the nominee in limbo until the president agrees to support a political position. For example, during the 1980s and 1990s Sen. Jesse Helms of North Carolina repeatedly held up nominations because he found them politically unacceptable or wished to force political opponents to compromise on policy issues. In 1997 Helms refused to schedule a Foreign Relations Committee hearing for William Weld, Clinton's nominee as ambassador to Mexico, because of several of Weld's liberal positions. In the Weld case Clinton's support for his nominee was tepid, because he did not want to antagonize Helms and thereby stalemate more pressing foreign policy issues.

Personnel System

The presidential appointment process remained relatively unchanged throughout the first 150 years of U.S. history. Presidents had little, if any, staff to help them make their appointments; political parties usually controlled personnel selection for the president.

Even when chief executives did become actively involved in the selection process, they often used the existing political party structure. Other nominees were usually suggested to the president by party leaders or members of Congress from the president's party. Too often this dependence on the party resulted in administrations filled with top-level appointees who had little loyalty to presidential objectives.

Since Franklin D. Roosevelt's administration, however, newly elected presidents have needed significant staff support and a centralized procedure for choosing personnel because of the large number of appointments that must be made in a short time. Perhaps more important, a centralized appointment process under the president's control helps to ensure loyalty to White House policies and objectives.

Nevertheless, until the 1960s the selection of presidential appointments was haphazard and unfocused. Presidential personnel operations relied heavily on chance to place the right people in the right positions. During the 1940s Roosevelt attempted to alleviate the problem by introducing government reforms that removed presidential patronage from the national political parties. For example, he appointed an assistant to handle personnel matters. Specific recommendations by the BROWNLOW COMMITTEE and the two HOOVER COMMISSIONS helped to centralize power in the presidency.

President Harry S. Truman appointed the first full-time staff member responsible only for personnel matters. President Dwight D. Eisenhower used special assistants for executive appointments to screen potential appointees.

Because there was still no systematic appointment operation, John F. Kennedy's personnel director, Dan Fenn, concluded that the most important jobs in the federal government were being filled by an unsophisticated "Whom do you know?" system—a process he called BOGSAT, a "bunch of guys sitting around a table."

To remedy this and create a systematic approach to appointments, significant changes were made during the administrations of Kennedy and Lyndon B. Johnson. As a result, a full-time personnel staff has become a regular component of the White House Office. Presidents have attempted to maintain their independence from the traditional pressures of political parties by recruiting their own candidates. Each administration has developed and followed routine procedures for scrutinizing the background, competence, integrity, and political loyalty of each potential appointee.

Presidents also have found that their active involvement in the selection process is crucial to its success. President Richard Nixon, for example, ran into personnel difficulties partly because he was not attentive enough to appointments at the beginning of his administration. Jimmy Carter's initial insistence that cabinet heads be given almost total discretion in choosing their subordinates diminished his ability to control his administration.

In contrast, Reagan and his staff devoted much energy to controlling the selection process, with special emphasis on recruiting officials who agreed with Reagan's political philosophy. As a result, Reagan was able to exercise greater control over the bureaucracy than any other modern president. George H. W. Bush began planning for staffing his administration while running for the presidency, and when he won the presidential election, his personnel management team moved rapidly into action.

Clinton's personnel team, operating under the dictum that they were to go to Washington to change things, chose executive branch staffers who were largely inexperienced in Washington politics. Clinton's personnel system was slow, stemming in part from his desire for racial and gender diversity and in part from the system he used that required White House approval for executive branch appointments. George W. Bush—who because of the contested 2000 presidential election had a short transition period to make his appointments—was somewhat more successful than his predecessors in getting personnel appointments made in a timely fashion. Even so, by the end of his first year in office one-third of the senior-level posts in his administration had not been filled. Bush, like Clinton, made an effort to appoint minorities and women to high-level posts.

Removal Power

The ability of presidents to control their administrations is often dependent on their authority to remove subordinates from office. This issue is central to the chief executive's power over the bureaucracy. But the power of presidents to remove officials who are not doing their jobs properly or who disagree with presidential goals and programs is controversial and has been significantly limited by the Supreme Court. Because the Constitution does not explicitly grant presidents power to remove officials from office, the legitimacy of the power often has rested on court interpretations of specific presidential actions.

Johnson Impeachment

The question of removal has been a major concern of several presidents, especially Andrew Johnson. When Johnson tried to suspend and then remove Secretary of War Edwin M. Stanton in violation of the Tenure of Office Act of 1867, he was subjected to a vote of impeachment in the House and a trial in the Senate.

The tenure act, which had been enacted over Johnson's veto, provided for Senate involvement in the removal of executive officials. After a presidential-congressional clash over the Senate's involvement in removal during the Grover Cleveland administration, the Tenure of Office Act was repealed.

Court Decisions

Preferring to avoid the removal question as long as possible, the Supreme Court refused to make a definitive ruling on the issue until 1926. In MYERS V. UNITED STATES the Court ruled that a law of 1876 that limited the president's removal power over postmasters was unconstitutional. The Court held that presidents could not effectively administer the executive branch unless they could control their subordinates with the threat of removal for political and other reasons.

The Court modified this position in 1935. At issue was Franklin Roosevelt's attempt to remove a commissioner of the Federal Trade Commission for political reasons. In HUMPHREY'S EXECUTOR V. UNITED STATES, the Court denied the president the power to remove members of independent regulatory agencies without the consent of Congress and limited the president's removal power to purely executive officers. In this case, the Court ruled, the Federal Trade Commission was not an executive arm but rather an administrative body created by Congress to carry out legislative policies.

In 1958 the Supreme Court further clarified the removal power of presidents. In *Wiener v. United States,* the Court held that if officials are engaged in adjudicative functions presidents may not remove them for political reasons.

More on this topic:
Cabinet, p. 60
Constitutional Powers and Provisions, p. 119
Myers v. United States, *p. 370*
Patronage, p. 398

Approval Rating *See* PUBLIC OPINION AND THE PRESIDENCY.

Arms Control *See* DIPLOMATIC POWERS.

Arthur, Chester A.

Cheoter A. Arthur

Source: Library of Congress

Chester Alan Arthur (1830–1886) was the fourth vice president to succeed to the presidency after the death of the incumbent. The only office to which he ever was elected was the vice presidency.

Arthur was born on October 5, 1830, in Fairfield, Vermont. His father was a Baptist minister. In 1845 at the age of fifteen Arthur enrolled in Union College in Schenectady, New York, where he studied Greek and Latin. He graduated three years later and was elected to the Phi Beta Kappa national honor society. Arthur then settled in North Pownal, Vermont, where he taught school at the North Pownal Academy. While teaching, Arthur studied law, and in 1853 he joined a New York City law firm as a clerk. The next year he passed the bar and became a member of the firm. As a lawyer he often defended fugitive slaves and free blacks. On October 25, 1858, he married Ellen Lewis Herndon. She died in 1880 before her husband was nominated for the vice presidency.

In 1856 Arthur became an active supporter of the Republican Party. New York Republican governor Edward D. Morgan rewarded Arthur's political work by appointing him state engineer in chief in 1860 with the military rank of brigadier general. During the Civil War Arthur served the troops of New York as assistant quartermaster general, inspector general, and finally quartermaster general. He excelled in these administrative posts, spending state funds efficiently and keeping the books scrupulously. He resigned his commission at the beginning of 1863 and returned to his law practice when Democrat Horatio Seymour became governor. He continued his rise in the New York Republican Party, however, and by the time Ulysses S. Grant was elected president in 1868, Arthur was Sen. Roscoe Conkling's principal lieutenant in the state's Republican machine.

In 1871, with Conkling's support, President Grant appointed Arthur to one of the most coveted offices in government—collector of the port of New York. In this post Arthur oversaw almost one thousand officials, was in charge of collecting about two-thirds of the country's tariff revenue, and earned an income that averaged about $40,000 per year. Despite Arthur's basic honesty, President Rutherford B. Hayes fired him from the post in 1878 as part of his fight against the spoils system.

On January 16, 1883, Arthur signed the Pendleton Civil Service Reform Act, which set up a commission to administer tests for many federal jobs previously filled through patronage.

The Republican national convention of 1880 pitted Senator Conkling and his party faction known as the Stalwarts against James G. Blaine and the Half-Breed faction. Conkling supported former president Ulysses S. Grant for the nomination, but after thirty-six ballots the convention turned to a dark-horse candidate, James A. Garfield of Ohio. In an effort to appease the Stalwarts and unify the party, Republican leaders offered the vice presidency to Levi P. Morton, one of Conkling's associates. Conkling, however, was in no mood to be appeased, and he convinced Morton to reject the offer. When the same offer was made to Arthur, he gratefully accepted the nomination despite Conkling's objections. Garfield and Arthur defeated the Democratic ticket of Winfield Scott Hancock and William H. English by fewer than 10,000 votes but won in the Electoral College, 214–155.

Garfield served only 199 days of his presidential term. On July 2, 1881, he was shot by an assassin, Charles J. Guiteau, in Washington, D.C. Garfield initially survived his wounds but died on September 19. Guiteau identified himself as a Stalwart, and although Arthur had no connection to Guiteau, he was sensitive to charges that he and the Stalwarts might have been involved in Garfield's death. Therefore, once Arthur assumed the presidency he broke his ties to Conkling. The new president demonstrated his independence by backing the investigations of post office scandals in which several Stalwarts were implicated. On January 16, 1883, Arthur signed the Pendleton Civil Service Reform Act, which set up a commission to administer tests for many federal jobs previously filled through patronage.

In economic policy Arthur sought to reduce the government's continuing budget surplus that took money out of the economy. He proposed reducing tariffs, building up the navy, and cutting the federal debt with the surplus. Arthur succeeded in making moderate improvements to the navy and reducing the national debt, but Congress rejected his proposals to cut tariffs.

Upon leaving office Arthur returned to New York City to practice law. In February 1886 a medical examination revealed that he had Bright's disease, a life-threatening kidney ailment. He died on November 18 of that year in New York City.

More on this topic:

Civil Service, p. 91

Garfield, James A., p. 229

Succession, p. 484

Article II

Article II of the U.S. Constitution provides the basis for the executive power of the U.S. government. Consisting of a co-equal and distinct branch of government, executive power is granted explicitly to a single individual called the president of the United States. Debates at the Constitutional Convention over whether the executive power of government should consist of a plural executive, a council of advisors sharing some degree of power with a single executive, or one person were settled with the language that opens Article II: "The executive Power shall be vested in a President of the United States of America. He shall hold his Office during the Term of four Years, and, together with the Vice President, chosen for the same Term, be elected…."

Article II plays a vital role in preserving the delicate balance of powers between the legislative and executive branches of government. At the time of the Constitutional Convention in 1787, many of the framers were suspicious of executive authority and were careful not to create an institution that could supersede the authority of Congress, but they also understood the dangers of creating an institution wholly subservient to Congress, a branch intended to reflect the passions of public opinion.

Section 1, Clause 1, of Article II begins by establishing the unitary nature of the chief executive and the four-year term of office. Clauses 2 through 5 are devoted to the rules governing qualifications for office and the procedure for presidential and vice-presidential selection, specifically the design of the Electoral College. Over time, states have delegated the power of elector selection to the people through the popular vote. Article II explicitly grants the power of choosing electors to the various state legislatures. So that states can maximize the importance of their electoral votes in the overall Electoral College voting, all states except Maine now use a "winner-take-all" system in which the candidate receiving a plurality of the popular vote in a presidential election wins that state's entire slate of electors. Clause 3 gave the runner-up presidential candidate the vice presidency (each elector cast two votes; the top vote-getter became president, and the candidate with the next highest number of votes became vice president). After political parties emerged in the election of 1796, the flaw in this system became apparent. John Adams garnered the most electoral votes and was named president, but his political rival, Thomas Jefferson, with the second most electoral votes, became vice president. The Twelfth Amendment (1804) was adopted to prevent this situation in the future by creating a "ticket" system in which each party nominates separate presidential and vice-presidential candidates, and electors vote separately for the president and vice president. Clause 4 empowers Congress to set a national election date for selection of electors. Currently this is the Tuesday after the first Monday in November in the year before the president's term is to expire. Finally, Clause 5 defines qualifications for office. At the time the constitutionally prescribed oath is taken (Section 1, Clause 8), a person must be 35 years of age, must have lived in the United States for 14 years, and must be a "natural born" citizen of the United States. This latter qualification is what prevents naturalized citizens, such as Austrian-born California governor Arnold Schwarzenegger, from becoming president. Many people assume mistakenly that a person must be born in the United States to meet this qualification, but children of American citizens born abroad, for example, would qualify as long as they have resided in the United States for 14 years before running for president. No court has yet interpreted the language of this clause.

The sixth clause of Section 1 provoked some controversy in the early nineteenth century. Explaining what should occur if the presidency becomes vacant, Clause 6 states, "In Case of the Removal of the President from Office, or of his Death, Resignation, or Inability to discharge the Powers and Duties of the said Office, the same shall devolve on the Vice President." When President William Henry Harrison died shortly after taking office in 1841, a debate ensued as to whether his vice president, John Tyler, would become president, or merely "acting" president with the same powers as if he had been elected in his own right. Because the language in Clause 6 was not clear enough to settle the debate, Tyler took the oath of office and set a precedent that allowed future vice presidents to assume the office when presidents died or resigned.

The final clause of Section 1, Clause 8, provides the verbatim oath that presidents must take upon assuming office: "Before he enter on the Execution of his Office, he shall take the following Oath or Affirmation: 'I do solemnly swear (or affirm) that I will faithfully execute the Office of President of the United States, and will to the best of my Ability, preserve, protect and defend the

Source: U.S. Senate

Constitution of the United States.'" Controversy regarding the meaning of these words has sparked debate as to whether the oath is a simple affirmation of loyalty to the Constitution, or whether taking such an oath empowers the president to take measures beyond his explicit powers, if such actions are in defense of the Constitution. Andrew Jackson, explaining his veto of the renewal of a national bank's charter, implied that presidents may choose to ignore laws they believe violate the Constitution. More recently, George W. Bush has asserted that the presidential oath allows him to take actions, not necessarily prescribed in the Constitution, in defense of the United States. The presidential oath is unique; no other officers of the United States, including the vice president, take the same oath.

Section 2 of Article II grants the president a number of explicit powers, all of which may be countered by Congress, except his power to grant pardons, a vestige of British monarchy that allows the president a reactive check on the judiciary in criminal matters. According to Clause 1 of this section, the president is assigned the role of "Commander in Chief" of the armed forces; however, Article I (Section 8) stipulates that Congress alone is authorized to declare war. More important, Congress is empowered to raise and spend money and can use that power to rescind funding for a military operation of which it no longer approves. In Clause 2 the president is empowered to "make treaties," but two-thirds of the Senate must concur. As early as George Washington's administration, this clause caused controversy because it remained unclear whether the president should seek congressional input during the treaty negotiation process or if it simply meant that the president's role as chief diplomat allowed him to "make" treaties, with the Senate simply ratifying them. Today it is generally accepted that the president shall "make" or negotiate treaties, but Congress, and the Senate in particular, regularly exercises its right to conduct inquiry and opposition. The most noteworthy example of this was the Senate's rejection of the Treaty of Versailles, which included a provision establishing the League of Nations following World War I. By refusing to include influential senators such as Henry Cabot Lodge in the negotiations, President Wilson ensured that his efforts to reshape American foreign policy were defeated when the Senate rejected the treaty.

The president may make appointments to various federal offices—including judges, ambassadors, and other officers such as the heads of the executive departments and agencies—but the Senate must confirm such nominations. Clause 3 does give the president power to make temporary appointments while the Senate is in recess and allows those officers to remain in office until the end of the Senate's session. Presidents have sometimes taken advantage of this provision by appointing more controversial persons during recess. For example, George W. Bush appointed John Bolton as ambassador to the United Nations not long after his failed nomination bid in the Senate. An ambiguity contributing to the impeachment of Andrew Johnson, and not clarified until 1926 in the case *MYERS V. UNITED STATES*, was the issue of whether a president can dismiss officers without Senate approval. Although Article II does not mention the issue of removing officers of the United States, Congress in 1867 passed the Tenure of Office Act to require presidents to obtain the advice and consent of the Senate when dismissing officers whose appointments required the same. When President Johnson removed Secretary of War Edwin M. Stanton and attempted to replace him, he was impeached and narrowly acquitted.

More on this topic:

Appointment and
Removal Power, p. 9

Pardon Power, p. 395

Succession, p. 484

Veto Power, p. 533

War Powers, p. 555

Section 3 defines presidential responsibilities. The president is required "from time to time" to give Congress information on the state of the union, a responsibility that has evolved into the modern tradition of presidents addressing Congress near the beginning of each session. Washington clarified the phrase "from time to time" by delivering annual addresses. The president may call Congress into extraordinary session but is not empowered to enforce such proclamations. He shall receive foreign ambassadors, make sure the laws are "faithfully executed," and commission all officers of the military.

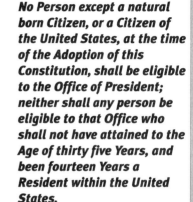

No Person except a natural born Citizen, or a Citizen of the United States, at the time of the Adoption of this Constitution, shall be eligible to the Office of President; neither shall any person be eligible to that Office who shall not have attained to the Age of thirty five Years, and been fourteen Years a Resident within the United States.

—Article II, Section 1, Clause 5 of the U.S. Constitution

Section 4 provides a mechanism for removing the president (or other executive officers or judges) through impeachment for committing acts of treason, bribery, or other "high crimes and misdemeanors." The House of Representatives may impeach the president by formally presenting charges to the Senate, which has the power to try the president and, if he is convicted, remove him from power. Debate over the phrase "high crimes and misdemeanors" exists to this day. In 1998 President Clinton was impeached but later acquitted by the Senate. Many people felt that Clinton's actions did not warrant impeachment in the first place.

PRESIDENCY-RELATED AMENDMENTS

Amendment	Year Ratified	Details
Twelfth Amendment	1804	Created "ticket" system election of president and vice president, replacing former rule whereby the presidential candidate receiving the second most votes for president would become vice president.
Twentieth Amendment	1933	Established noon on January 20 as the date and time at which a presidential term is to commence, beginning in 1937.
Twenty-second Amendment	1951	Limits presidents to two full terms in office. In instances where a president has served 2 years or less in office after assuming the office from someone previously elected, the limit is 10 years.
Twenty-third Amendment	1961	Grants to the District of Columbia a number of electoral votes equivalent to the number it would have if it was a state.
Twenty-fifth Amendment	1967	Clarifies that the vice president shall become president (as opposed to acting president) in the event the office of president becomes vacant. Establishes procedures for presidential succession in the event the president is incapacitated. Provides a method for appointment of a vice president if that office becomes vacant.

Assassinations and Assaults

Four times in the history of the United States the nation has been stunned by the assassination of a president. Abraham Lincoln, James A. Garfield, William McKinley, and John F. Kennedy were killed by assassins' bullets.

The assassination of a president is an even greater national disaster than the death of a president by natural causes. An assassination not only can cause governmental confusion but also may send the country into shock because people perceive an attack upon the president, the symbol of the United States, as an attack upon the nation itself.

The presidency is a highly personal office, and power ultimately resides in the person who occupies it, not that person's political party. Assassinations, therefore, always alter the course of government, sometimes dramatically. Even if a president is succeeded by a vice president who shares the slain leader's political philosophy, an assassination of a president undermines the democratic process. Yet unlike in some cultures where assassination is used by factions as a political tool, in the United States assassins and potential assassins of presidents have more often been motivated by delusion, personal grievances, or a desire for fame or attention.

In addition to the presidents who were assassinated, four other presidents have been the target of a total of five unsuccessful assassination attempts. In all, presidents, presidents-elect, and presidential candidates have been attacked thirteen times. All but three of these attacks occurred in the twentieth century. Moreover, threats against the president's life and attempts by individuals to enter the White House grounds illegally have become increasingly frequent.

There are few common characteristics among the four presidential assassinations except that in each case the assassin used a gun and took advantage of inadequate security measures. All four of the assailants were caught, although in the case of Kennedy's assassination, suspicions linger that the killer was part of a larger conspiracy.

Abraham Lincoln

On April 14, 1865, President Lincoln and his wife attended a play at Ford's Theatre in Washington, D.C. The end of the Civil War had put the capital in a festive mood. Just five days before, Gen. Robert E. Lee had surrendered to Gen. Ulysses S. Grant. While watching a performance of *Our American Cousin,* President Lincoln was shot by John Wilkes Booth, an actor and Confederate sympathizer. Booth, who had been plotting for months to either kidnap or kill the president, learned that the president would be at the theater that evening and so set his plan in motion. His conspiracy entailed assassinating the president, Vice President Andrew Johnson, and Secretary of State William H. Seward.

Source: Corbis-Bettmann

Booth's target was to be the president, while fellow conspirator George Atzerodt was to kill Johnson and Lewis Thornton Powell was to kill Seward. Powell succeeded in stabbing Seward at his home, but the secretary survived. Johnson escaped attack when Atzerodt decided not to carry out his part of the conspiracy.

Booth, who was well known at Ford's Theatre as an actor, had no trouble gaining access to the building. He also had no difficulty entering the president's box, because the president's guard had left his post to watch the play. Holding his gun less than six inches from the president, Booth fired. The single bullet struck the president behind the left ear and came to rest behind the right eye. Booth then vaulted the railing of the theater box, declaring, "Sic semper tyrannis" (ever thus to tyrants). He landed on the stage, breaking a bone in his leg, and ran out a rear exit, where he mounted his waiting horse and escaped. Booth was killed by a gunshot wound after being cornered by soldiers on a Virginia farm on April 26.

President Lincoln was carried across the street to a private home where he died at 7:22 on the morning of April 15. Later that morning the presidential oath of office was administered to Vice President Johnson by Salmon P. Chase, chief justice of the United States.

The outpouring of national grief at Lincoln's death was unprecedented. The funeral services, held in Washington, took the better part of a week. Lincoln's body was then placed on a train for transport to Springfield, Illinois, for burial. For twenty days and more than sixteen hundred miles the funeral train carrying Lincoln's body crept through Baltimore, Harrisburg, Philadelphia, New York City, Albany, Buffalo, Cleveland, Columbus, Indianapolis, Michigan City, and Chicago, on its way to Springfield. Thirty million people attended religious services or watched the train or the hearse pass by.

James A. Garfield

Four months after his inauguration President Garfield began a tour of New England. On the morning of July 2, 1881, as the president and Secretary of State James G. Blaine walked through a Washington train depot, the president was shot twice. One shot grazed his arm and the other lodged in his spinal column. The would-be assassin was captured immediately and identified as Charles J. Guiteau, a disappointed office-seeker. Although present-day psychiatrists suspect Guiteau was insane, he was judged by his contemporaries to be competent. He was tried, found guilty, and executed on June 30, 1882.

Upon being taken into custody Guiteau declared: "I did it and will go to jail for it. I am a Stalwart; now Arthur is president!" In his pocket were two letters. The first, addressed to the White House, maintained that "the President's tragic death was a sad necessity, but it will unite the Republican Party and save the Republic.... His death was a political necessity." The second, addressed to Vice President Chester A. Arthur, informed him of the assassination and his succession to the presidency. It went on to recommend cabinet appointments. At first, these letters led investigators to suspect that Guiteau was part of a conspiracy, and they even cast suspicion on Vice President Arthur. The conspiracy notion was quickly discarded, but the attack placed Arthur in a difficult political position in dealing with the president's disability.

In the weeks after the shooting, Garfield's health underwent a series of gains and setbacks. In early September the president asked to be moved from the White House to a cottage on the New Jersey shore at Elberon. After making the trip on September 6 the president seemed to improve. On the night of September 19, however, Garfield died of what was probably blood poisoning.

For the eighty days during which Garfield was disabled almost no executive functions were carried out. The vice president never saw or spoke with the president after the assassination attempt. Arthur spent most of this period in New York at his home. It was there that he received on September 20, 1881, the telegram informing him of the president's death. The same day he took the oath of office from Judge John R. Brady of the New York Supreme Court.

William McKinley

Six months after his second inauguration President McKinley traveled to the Pan-American Exposition in Buffalo, New York, to deliver a speech. The president participated as well in a public reception held at the Temple of Music on the afternoon of September 6, 1901. Even though the president was accompanied by a contingent of Secret Service agents, as well as four special guards and some soldiers, he was shot as he greeted people in a receiving line. Leon Czolgosz, the assassin and an anarchist, fired two bullets at McKinley. One bounced off a button and the other hit the president in the stomach. The assassin was subdued quickly. He was tried, convicted, and executed within fifty-three days.

An operation to remove the bullet was attempted immediately, but the bullet could not be located. The wounds were then bathed, and the president seemed to be on the road to recovery. On September 10 Vice President Theodore Roosevelt, who had come to Buffalo, was told that the president's condition had dramatically improved. Roosevelt departed for a vacation with his family in Vermont. During the next three days fever, gangrene, and infection set in, weakening the president. Once again Roosevelt was summoned to Buffalo. President McKinley died in the early morning hours on Friday, September 14, 1901. Roosevelt was sworn in as the new president the following afternoon.

John F. Kennedy

Unlike the other slain presidents, Kennedy was killed by rifle fire from a distance. On the morning of Friday, November 22, 1963, he was traveling through Dallas, Texas, in an open car that was part of a motorcade. The president and the first lady, Jacqueline Bouvier Kennedy, as well as Texas governor John B. Connally and his wife, were in the lead car. Vice President Lyndon B. Johnson and his wife, Lady Bird, were in the following car.

As the cars rolled past the Texas School Book Depository a series of short, sharp noises startled everyone. Kennedy was hit by two shots, one in the head and one in the neck and upper torso. The president's car raced for the nearest hospital.

Word of the shooting went out over the wire services. Military forces in the Washington, D.C., area were put on special alert. A plane with half the cabinet aboard, including Secretary of State Dean Rusk, received word while in midflight to Japan, and it immediately returned to Washington.

Medical efforts made at the hospital in Dallas were futile. In another hospital room security personnel and staff convinced Vice President Johnson to leave Dallas as soon as possible. Fears of a larger conspiracy prompted them to return the new president to the kind of security that could be found only in Washington.

At 2 p.m. the television networks interrupted their regular programming to bring word to a stunned nation that President Kennedy was dead. (The president was pronounced dead officially at 1:15 p.m.)

Vice President Johnson was whisked back to the airfield where he boarded *Air Force One*. There the mournful party awaited the arrival of Jacqueline Kennedy and the president's casket. Meanwhile, the Dallas police had identified and apprehended the suspected assassin, Lee Harvey Oswald, a maladjusted worker at the book depository who had Marxist leanings. Before the plane took off, a brief swearing-in ceremony was held; local federal district judge Sarah T. Hughes administered the oath of office to Johnson.

On Sunday, November 24, shortly before Kennedy's funeral procession in Washington was scheduled to begin, Lee Harvey Oswald was shot and killed as he was being transferred to a different jail. Jack Ruby, a Dallas club owner, had elbowed through the crowd of security officers and reporters, pointed a .38 revolver at Oswald, and pulled the trigger, shouting, "You killed the president, you rat!" The event was caught on film and was broadcast repeatedly.

At 1 p.m. that same day the president's funeral began. It was estimated that 95 percent of the adult U.S. population was following television or radio accounts of the funeral. The entire country and much of the world were mesmerized by the ceremony of mourning for the slain president.

Within days of the funeral President Johnson appointed Chief Justice Earl Warren to head an independent investigatory commission into the assassination. Ten months later the Warren Commission report declared that Oswald was the sole assassin and dismissed the possibility that he was part of a conspiracy. Many independent investigators found the report unconvincing, and decades after Kennedy's death speculation about possible conspiracy plots continues.

Other Assaults

In addition to the four presidents who have died at the hands of assassins, four other sitting presidents have withstood five assassination attempts. Andrew Jackson, Harry S. Truman, Gerald R. Ford, and Ronald Reagan, who was wounded, each survived assassination attempts. In addition, president-elect Franklin D. Roosevelt was attacked three weeks before his first inauguration. Three presidential candidates, Theodore Roosevelt, Robert F. Kennedy, and George C. Wallace, were shot—with Kennedy being killed.

On January 30, 1835, while Jackson was attending the funeral of South Carolina representative Warren Davis in the rotunda of the Capitol, house painter Richard Lawrence attempted to shoot him. This was the first presidential assassination attempt. Aiming from a distance of only seven feet, Lawrence fired two pistols at the president at point-blank range. Both guns misfired, however, and Lawrence was captured. He was later found to be insane.

Franklin Roosevelt was the only president-elect ever to be the target of an assassin. On February 15, 1933, in Miami, Florida, Roosevelt narrowly escaped shots fired by Joseph Zangara, an apparent anarchist who hated rulers and capitalists. Roosevelt's companion in the car, Chicago mayor Anton J. Cermak, was fatally wounded.

President Truman was the next target of an assassination attempt. On November 1, 1950, two Puerto Rican nationalists tried to shoot their way into Blair House, where Truman was staying while the White House was being renovated. One of the assailants was killed and the other was wounded. A White House policeman was killed in the attack, but the president was not harmed.

Andrew Jackson, a controversial president, was said to have been threatened with assassination many times before a deluded young man tried it. Richard Lawrence, who claimed Jackson was preventing him from assuming the British throne, was later committed to an insane asylum.
Source: The Historical Society of Pennsylvania

In September 1975 two attempts were made on President Gerald Ford's life, both in California. In each instance protective actions by Secret Service agents and others succeeded in deflecting the attack. On September 5, 1975, in Sacramento, Lynette (Squeaky) Fromme emerged from the crowd and pointed a gun at the president from two feet away. A Secret Service agent walking behind the president saw the gun, grabbed it, and wrestled the would-be assassin to the ground. Fromme had been a member of the extremist "Manson family." Approximately two weeks later, on September 22, 1975, a single gunshot rang out as the president was walking from his hotel to his car in San Francisco. Two Secret Service agents and presidential assistant Donald H. Rumsfeld pushed the president down beside his car, then onto the floor of the back seat, shielding him with their bodies until the motorcade could make a hasty departure for the airport. The individual who had fired the gun, Sara Jane Moore, was quickly identified and apprehended. Her apparent motive for the deed was her revolutionary ideology.

On March 30, 1981, Ronald Reagan became the first president to be wounded by an assassin and survive. John W. Hinckley Jr. fired a series of shots at the president with a handgun outside a Washington, D.C., hotel. The shots wounded Reagan, seriously injured his press secretary, James Brady, and also wounded a Secret Service agent and a District of Columbia police officer. The twenty-five-year-old assailant was arrested at the scene of the shooting. Hinckley was judged insane and confined to a mental hospital. He suggested that his need to impress a teenage movie actress was his motive for shooting the president.

President Reagan was rushed to the hospital with a chest wound and a bullet lodged in his left lung. The operation to remove the bullet lasted two hours, and the president remained hospitalized until April 11.

In 1994 President Bill Clinton experienced four separate threatening incidents. A Maryland truck driver was killed September 12 when he crashed a small Cessna plane just outside the president's White House bedroom. The Clintons were staying at nearby Blair House while renovations were under way at the executive mansion, and they were unhurt. On October 29, while Clinton was in the White House watching a televised basketball game, a Colorado hotel worker sprayed the building's facade with bullets from a range of fifty yards. On December 17 several bullets were fired at the building's south facade from the Ellipse, but no one was apprehended. Three days later, a knife-wielding homeless man was shot and killed by police on the Pennsylvania Avenue sidewalk in front of the White House. As a result of these abortive attacks and the car bombing of a federal building in Oklahoma City in April 1995, Clinton accepted a Secret Service recommendation that the two blocks of Pennsylvania Avenue on which the executive mansion sits be closed to vehicular traffic and converted to a more easily secured pedestrian mall.

After the terrorist attacks of September 11, 2001, protective measures in and around the White House became stricter still. White House tours were suspended—although selected groups, including student ones, later were allowed to return—and vehicular traffic was temporarily banned from a section of E Street south of the building.

Presidential Security

In the years after President Garfield's assassination in 1881, the need for greater protection of the president began to be recognized. For example, SECRET SERVICE agents accompanied President Grover Cleveland to his summer vacation home in Buzzard's Bay, Massachusetts. Such protection was used more regularly during the McKinley administration, when the president requested that an agent accompany him on formal outings. Indeed, because of prior threats three agents were with President McKinley when he was mortally wounded in Buffalo, New York, in 1901.

Secret Service protection for presidents was formally authorized by Congress in 1906, with two agents normally assigned to presidential guard duty. Eight agents provided twenty-four-hour coverage when the president was on extended vacation. In 1908 such protection was extended to the president-elect and in 1945 to the vice president. After the 1950 attempted attack on President Truman, the Secret Service limited public access to the president by varying the time and location of the president's leisure activities and by restricting access to the presidential residence and its vicinity. Until the mid-1960s the essential protective strategy of the Secret Service was to increase security personnel and to restrict public access to the president.

The assassination of President Kennedy in Dallas in 1963 prompted closer cooperation between the Secret Service and other agencies, particularly the Federal Bureau of Investigation (FBI). It was discovered that although the FBI was aware of Lee Harvey Oswald as a communist supporter with revolutionary views, this information was not provided to the Secret Service before the Dallas trip. The Secret Service and FBI drew up joint guidelines for the communication of FBI reports to the Secret Service.

The threat of assassination and the cumbersome security measures necessary to ensure the president's safety have forced changes in the way presidents approach public appearances. No longer are presidents expected to wade unprotected into a crowd of citizens to shake hands. Reagan commented that he would have liked to have gone to see a college football game between Army and Navy as many other presidents had done, but he did not because "nobody wants to run 75,000 people through a magnetometer." Reagan even justified his lack of church attendance on the grounds that security measures would disrupt the congregation.

Orchestrated events in front of carefully screened groups and televised speeches and press conferences have become the usual methods by which presidents communicate with the American people. This development has contributed to the isolation of presidents. Now, when they spontaneously place themselves before a crowd, as Jimmy Carter did when he left his limousine and walked up Pennsylvania Avenue after his inauguration in 1977, it is considered a brave and confident gesture.

PRESIDENTIAL ASSASSINATIONS AND ASSASSINATION ATTEMPTS

President	Description
Andrew Jackson	On January 30, 1835, Richard Lawrence, an out-of-work and delusional house painter, took two shots at President Jackson at a congressional funeral in the Capitol building, but both of his guns misfired. Lawrence was quickly overpowered and spent the remainder of his life in asylums and jails. This marked the first assassination attempt against a U.S. president.
Abraham Lincoln	John Wilkes Booth, a prominent actor and ardent southern sympathizer, shot President Lincoln at Ford's Theater in Washington on April 14, 1865, in an apparent attempt to decapitate the leadership of the recently victorious Union government and revive the Confederacy. The president died the next day. Booth escaped but was shot and killed while hiding in a Virginia barn on April 26, 1865.
James A. Garfield	Charles Julius Guiteau, a disgruntled office seeker who had been repeatedly passed over in the political patronage system of the era, shot President Garfield as he walked through a Washington train depot on July 2, 1881. Garfield's condition gradually worsened until his death on September 19, 1881. Guiteau was convicted and hanged on June 30, 1882.
William McKinley	Anarchist Leon Czolgosz, distraught over economic injustice in the United States, shot President McKinley at the Pan-American Exposition in Buffalo, New York, on September 6, 1901. Doctors were unable to find the second bullet, and McKinley died from his wounds on September 14, 1901. Czolgosz was tried, convicted, and executed by electric chair on October 29, 1901.
Harry S. Truman	Oscar Collazo and Griselio Torresola, Puerto Rican pro-independence activists, attempted to storm the Blair-Lee House and assassinate President Truman on November 1, 1950. Torresola was killed during the ensuing gunfight with police. Collazo was convicted and sentenced to death. The sentence was commuted to life imprisonment by President Truman. President Carter later commuted the sentence again and freed Collazo.
John F. Kennedy	Lee Harvey Oswald shot and killed President Kennedy in his motorcade through Dealey Plaza in Dallas, Texas, on November 22, 1963. While in police custody, Oswald was shot and killed by Jack Ruby on November 24, 1963.
Gerald R. Ford	Lynette "Squeaky" Fromme, a member of the notorious "Manson family," attempted to assassinate President Ford at Capital Park in Sacramento, California, on September 5, 1975. The gun's firing chamber was empty, and Secret Service guards restrained Fromme. She was convicted and is currently serving a life term.
Gerald R. Ford	Sara Jane Moore, apparently inspired by counterculture ideology, attempted to assassinate President Ford on September 22, 1975, just seventeen days after the attempt by Lynette "Squeaky" Fromme. A bystander grabbed Moore's arm, causing her gun to misfire and preventing a second shot. Moore was convicted and is currently serving a life term.
Ronald Reagan	On March 30, 1981, John Hinckley Jr., obsessed with actress Jodie Foster and the film *Taxi Driver*, shot President Reagan outside the Washington Hilton hotel in the nation's capital. The president was injured from a ricocheted bullet but recovered quickly following emergency surgery. Hinckley was found not guilty by reason of insanity and has been institutionalized ever since.

B

Background of Presidents

The Constitution requires only that a president be at least thirty-five years of age, a natural-born citizen or a citizen at the time of the adoption of the Constitution, and a resident within the United States for fourteen years. Although these constitutional requirements disqualify few Americans, the forty-two persons who have served as president since 1789 have come from a relatively narrow slice of American society.

Similarities of Background

All presidents have shared several important characteristics. First, all have been white men.

Second, all forty-two presidents have had northern European ancestors. Only five could trace their roots to continental Europe. The ancestors of Martin Van Buren, Theodore Roosevelt, and Franklin D. Roosevelt were Dutch; Herbert C. Hoover's were Swiss; and Dwight D. Eisenhower's were German. The forebears of the other thirty-seven presidents came to America primarily from the British Isles.

Third, no president has reached the presidency without significant experience as a public servant or military officer. Most presidents have served in at least one elective office at the national or state level. Twenty-four presidents have been members of Congress; seventeen have been governors of a state (including George W. Bush); and fourteen have been vice presidents. Presidents also have served as cabinet members, diplomats, state legislators, mayors, judges, sheriffs, and prosecutors on their way to higher office. Because George Washington was the first president, he did not have the opportunity to run for Congress, but he served the nation as a general, a delegate to the Continental Congress, and president of the Constitutional Convention. Three presidents—Zachary

Taylor, Ulysses S. Grant, and Eisenhower—were career generals without civilian political experience. Two others, William Howard Taft and Hoover, had never been elected to a national political office or a governorship but had served the nation as cabinet officers. Taft was Theodore Roosevelt's secretary of war; Hoover was secretary of commerce under Warren G. Harding and Calvin Coolidge.

Beyond these three characteristics common to all of the first forty-two persons who have served in the office, two characteristics have been shared by all but two of them: marriage and Protestantism. James Buchanan was the only president who never married. Five others entered the presidency without a wife: Grover Cleveland did not marry until after he became president, and Thomas Jefferson, Van Buren, Andrew Jackson, and Chester A. Arthur took office as widowers. Not until the election of Ronald Reagan in 1980, however, did the American people elect a president who had been divorced.

Until John F. Kennedy became the first Catholic president in 1961, all chief executives had come from Protestant backgrounds, with the Episcopalian, Presbyterian, and Unitarian denominations predominating. Although all presidents have professed their belief in God, they have varied widely in their religious convictions and practices. Jefferson's political opponents accused him of being an atheist—a charge he denied. Although Abraham Lincoln frequently quoted the Bible in his speeches, he belonged to no specific denomination and felt compelled early in his political career to make a statement declaring his belief in God.

The 1872 Republican campaign called voters' attention to the humble backgrounds of presidential candidate Ulysses S. Grant and his running mate, Henry Wilson.
Source: Currier & Ives, Library of Congress

A few presidents have been outwardly religious men. James A. Garfield was a lay preacher for the Disciples of Christ before beginning his congressional career. Jimmy Carter described himself as a born-again Christian during the 1976 presidential campaign, as did Ronald Reagan in 1980 and George H. W. Bush in 1988. Bill Clinton, a Southern Baptist, often used religious references in his speeches, as did George W. Bush, a Methodist.

If one considers all these characteristics, a distinct profile of the American president emerges. A typical president is an American-born, married man who is at least forty-two years old (Theodore Roosevelt was the youngest to hold office), is descended from northern European, Protestant ancestors, and has some type of public service career at the state or national level.

Differences in Background

From this well-defined societal group, presidents have come into office from a variety of economic, educational, professional, and geographic backgrounds.

Some presidents have been descended from the American aristocracy, including Jefferson, James Madison, John Quincy Adams, John Tyler, William Henry Harrison and his grandson Benjamin Harrison, the Roosevelts, Taft, Kennedy, George H. W. Bush, and George W. Bush. These

PRESIDENTS' BACKGROUNDS

President	Occupation
George Washington	Farmer/surveyor
John Adams	Farmer/lawyer
Thomas Jefferson	Farmer/lawyer
James Madison	Farmer
James Monroe	Farmer/lawyer
John Quincy Adams	Lawyer
Andrew Jackson	Lawyer
Martin van Buren	Lawyer
William Henry Harrison	Military officer
John Tyler	Lawyer
James K. Polk	Lawyer
Zachary Taylor	Military officer
Millard Fillmore	Lawyer
Franklin Pierce	Lawyer
James Buchanan	Lawyer
Abraham Lincoln	Lawyer
Andrew Johnson	Tailor
Ulysses S. Grant	Military officer
Rutherford B. Hayes	Lawyer
James A. Garfield	Educator/lawyer
Chester A. Arthur	Lawyer
Grover Cleveland	Lawyer
Benjamin Harrison	Lawyer
William McKinley	Lawyer
Theodore Roosevelt	Lawyer/author
William H. Taft	Lawyer
Woodrow Wilson	Educator
Warren G. Harding	Newspaper editor
Calvin Coolidge	Lawyer
Herbert Hoover	Engineer
Franklin D. Roosevelt	Lawyer
Harry S Truman	Clerk/store owner
Dwight D. Eisenhower	Military officer
John F. Kennedy	Lawyer
Lyndon B. Johnson	Educator
Richard Nixon	Lawyer
Gerald R. Ford	Lawyer
Jimmy Carter	Farmer
Ronald Reagan	Actor
George H. W. Bush	Businessman
Bill Clinton	Lawyer
George W. Bush	Businessman

SOURCE: Ragsdale, Lynn, *Vital Statistics on the Presidency* (Washington, D.C.: CQ Press, 1998), 21–22.

presidents had the advantage of wealth and family connections when building their political careers. Other presidents, including Jackson, Lincoln, Andrew Johnson, and Garfield, were self-made men from poor, sometimes destitute circumstances. Several presidents, such as Hoover, Richard Nixon, Reagan, and Clinton, did not grow up in poverty but received little financial support from their families as they started their careers.

The educational background of presidents ranges from that of Woodrow Wilson, who earned a Ph.D. from Johns Hopkins University, to that of Andrew Johnson, who never attended a school of any type. Other presidents, such as Washington and Lincoln, received only a rudimentary formal education. Thirty-two presidents attended college, including every twentieth-century president except Harry S. Truman.

Presidents have worked in all types of professions before entering public service. The most common profession among presidents has been law; twenty-five were admitted to the bar. Only three of the last eleven presidents—Gerald R. Ford, Nixon, and Clinton—have practiced law. More than half the presidents had some experience in agriculture, either as a plantation owner, dirt farmer, rancher, field worker, or son of a farming family. Eight presidents were teachers. Several others were professional soldiers, merchants, surveyors, or journalists. Andrew Johnson was a tailor who learned his trade as an apprentice; Hoover studied engineering at Stanford University and became a successful mining engineer; and Reagan's engaging personality led to a career as a Hollywood actor.

Presidents have come from a variety of regions, but until the Civil War most came from only a few states. Virginia boasts being home to the most presidents, with eight born in the "Old Dominion" and seven of the first fifteen chief executives hailing from there. Due to the westward expansion of the United States, by the late nineteenth century the Midwest had become the home to many commanders in chief. Ohio produced seven of the eleven different men who served in the White House from 1869 to 1923. By the mid-twentieth century, specific regional bias had disappeared, and post–World War II presidents have called states such as Texas, California, and Arkansas their homes. However, since the narrow victory of

Massachusetts' John F. Kennedy in 1960, all Democratic presidents have come from Texas, Georgia, or Arkansas.

Given their differences in wealth, education, and profession, it is not surprising that presidents have taken their political strides toward the White House at different times in their lives. Jackson and Nixon, for example, began their political careers with election to the U.S. House of Representatives at the ages of twenty-nine and thirty-three, respectively. In contrast, Wilson and Reagan were not elected to their first political offices—governor of New Jersey and governor of California, respectively—until they were in their mid-fifties. No one could have foreseen in 1922 that Truman, then the owner of a failing haberdashery who had never gone to college or run for public office, would be president in twenty-three years at the age of sixty. In contrast, twenty-three years before John Quincy Adams became president at the age of fifty-seven, he already had graduated Phi Beta Kappa from Harvard, served as minister to Holland and Prussia, been elected to the Massachusetts senate, and narrowly lost election to the U.S. House of Representatives.

The backgrounds from which presidents have risen to power demonstrate that humble beginnings or nontraditional professions do not exclude a candidate from being elected president. Recent presidential elections have shown that candidates who are divorced, Catholic, or descended from southern European ancestors have a much better chance of being nominated for and elected to the presidency than in the past. The race and sex of a candidate, however, remain powerful factors in the selection of presidents. Through the 2004 election no woman or non-Caucasian had even been nominated for president by a major political party, although the Democratic Party nominated Geraldine Ferraro for vice president in 1984. History may be made in 2008, however, as in early 2007 the two front-runners for the Democratic presidential nomination in terms of popularity and fund-raising are New York senator Hillary Clinton and Illinois senator Barack Obama, an African American.

> **More on this topic:**
>
> *Qualifications of the President and Vice President, p. 432*
>
> *Religion and the Presidency, p. 441*

Barkley, Alben W.

Source: Library of Congress

Alben William Barkley (1877–1956) served as vice president under Harry S. Truman. Barkley brought much legislative experience to the office, having held a seat in Congress for thirty-six consecutive years before attaining the vice presidency. He served in Congress longer than any other vice president or president.

A native of Kentucky, Barkley graduated in 1897 from Marvin College in Clinton, Kentucky. He studied law for a year at Emory University, which was then located in Oxford, Georgia. After working in a Paducah, Kentucky, law office, he was admitted to the bar in 1901.

Barkley served as a prosecuting attorney and a county administrative official before winning a seat in the U.S. House of Representatives in 1912 as a Democrat. He held the seat continuously until he became a senator in 1927. He remained in the Senate until he became vice president in 1949.

In Congress Barkley supported President Woodrow Wilson's decision to enter World War I and voted for the Versailles treaty. Although he backed most liberal causes, he gained a reputation as a political compromiser. He also was renowned for his speaking ability, which combined a formal style with homespun humor. He delivered the keynote addresses at the 1932, 1936, and 1948 Democratic national conventions.

In 1937, with the support of the White House, Barkley was elected majority leader of the Senate. He backed both Franklin D. Roosevelt's New Deal social programs and the president's aid to Britain before World War II. Barkley remained majority leader until 1946, when the Republicans gained control of the Senate and he became minority leader.

Barkley had long wanted to be president, but Roosevelt's four-term grip on the Democratic presidential nomination prevented him from running. In 1948, at the age of seventy, Barkley decided that he wanted the Democratic nomination for vice president. Truman agreed to support his candidacy, and he was nominated by acclamation. Although opinion polls indicated that the Democrats would lose, Truman and Barkley campaigned tirelessly around the country and defeated Republicans Thomas E. Dewey and Earl Warren.

Barkley, at seventy-one, was the oldest vice president ever to take office, but he served an active term. He lobbied Congress to support the administration's programs and made many ceremonial appearances. His grandson called him the "Veep," a title that stuck with the office of vice president even after Barkley had left it.

In 1952 Barkley announced his interest in the presidential nomination, but he received little support because of his advanced age. He retired briefly but was elected to the Senate in 1954 by the voters of Kentucky. He died in 1956 from a heart attack suffered during a speaking engagement.

> **More on this topic:**
>
> Truman, Harry S., p. 519
>
> Vice President, p. 539

Bell, John

John Bell (1797–1869) of Tennessee was the presidential nominee of a short-lived political party formed in 1860 with the sole aim of preventing civil war over slavery. As the presidential candidate of the Constitutional Union Party, Bell competed for southern votes with the candidate of the pro-slavery Democrats, John C. Breckinridge of Kentucky. The election was won by Republican Abraham Lincoln of Illinois, whose principal rival in the four-man race was Stephen A. Douglas, also of Illinois. For Bell, running on a platform that did not mention slavery, the only hope had been as a compromise candidate in case the election was so close it had to be decided in the House of Representatives. Bell correctly warned that if Lincoln were elected, civil war would follow.

Bell's career reflected the political instability of his time. An Andrew Jackson Democrat when he was first elected to the House in 1827, Bell joined the Whigs, a party that developed in opposition to Jackson. Bell particularly objected to Jackson's "spoils system" under which the president rewarded his political supporters by appointing them to government positions. While Bell was in the Senate during the 1850s, the Whig Party broke apart over slavery. He then briefly joined an anti-Catholic, anti-immigrant splinter party called the American Party, or Know-Nothings. Although he had campaigned in 1860 to preserve the Union and the Constitution, Bell supported the Confederacy during the Civil War.

> **More on this topic:**
>
> Breckinridge, John. C., p. 32
>
> Douglas, Stephen A., p. 158
>
> Elections Chronology, p. 174
>
> Jackson, Andrew, p. 300
>
> Lincoln, Abraham, p. 336

Blaine, James G.

James G. Blaine (1830–1893), a Republican from Maine, was one of the most powerful American politicians of the late nineteenth century. He ran unsuccessfully for president in 1884 and served as secretary of state under James A. Garfield and Benjamin Harrison.

Blaine rose to political prominence as an influential newspaper editor who helped to establish the Republican Party in Maine. In 1863 he became a member of the U.S. House of Representatives. He stepped up to the position of Speaker of the House in 1869 and remained in that post for six years.

While Blaine was Speaker, he was accused of having received bribes from Crédit Mobilier of America, a holding company set up by the director of the Union Pacific Railroad. Blaine was implicated in the scandal by a series of letters that indicated he had done legislative favors for the railroad in return for gifts of stock. The scandal severely damaged but did not destroy Blaine's political career.

Blaine left the House in July 1876, when he was appointed to an unexpired Senate term. He later was elected to a full term, but he relinquished his seat in 1881 to become secretary of state for the newly elected president, James Garfield. Blaine was walking through a Washington, D.C., railroad station with the president on July 2, 1881, when Garfield was shot by an assassin. Garfield died of complications caused by his wounds on September 19. Blaine resigned from the cabinet before the end of the year.

The Republican Party chose Blaine as its presidential candidate in 1884. His opponent was Democrat Grover Cleveland. Blaine's campaign was one of the dirtiest in American history, misrepresenting Cleveland's policy proposals and attempting to stir fears that the South would reassert its rebel ways if Cleveland were elected. Blaine's campaign also tried to make a major scandal out of Cleveland's fathering of a child out of wedlock years before. But Blaine's involvement in the railroad bribery scandal damaged his own candidacy, and he lost one of the closest presidential elections in U.S. history. Cleveland received 219 electoral votes and 4.9 million popular votes to Blaine's 182 and 4.8 million. Cleveland defeated Blaine by just a thousand votes in New York, a state that would have given Blaine the election.

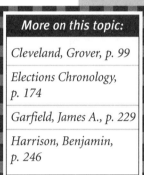

More on this topic:

Cleveland, Grover, p. 99

Elections Chronology, p. 174

Garfield, James A., p. 229

Harrison, Benjamin, p. 246

Blaine returned to public life in 1889 when Benjamin Harrison appointed him secretary of state. He served in that post until 1892. His health deteriorated, and he died in Washington on January 27, 1893.

Blair House

Blair House, an official guest residence owned by the federal government, stands across Pennsylvania Avenue from the White House. The simple, white brick house was acquired by the government in 1942. Along with the adjacent Blair-Lee House to which it is connected, Blair House serves as a free private hotel for distinguished state visitors to the capital city and for some recent presidents-elect and their families at inauguration time. Built in 1824, Blair House was named for Francis Preston Blair, a journalist and politician who bought it in 1836. Blair built the adjoining house for his daughter, Elizabeth Blair Lee.

Before the Civil War, representatives of both the North and South met at Blair House to discuss the political crisis. In the years after the war, presidents often crossed the street to visit the prominent families who owned the house. After Blair House became government property President Harry S. Truman and his family lived there for more than three years while the White House underwent extensive renovations. On November 1, 1950, two Puerto Rican nationals attacked Blair House with automatic weapons, hoping to fight their way inside to kill the president. Truman was not harmed, but one Secret Service agent and one of the would-be assassins were killed.

More on this topic:

Assassinations and Assaults, p. 19

Truman, Harry S., p. 519

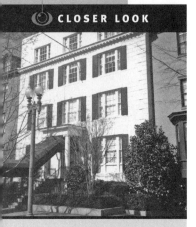

Source: Library of Congress

Blair House is actually larger than the White House. At first glance, Blair House looks like a single town home. However, it also comprises two neighboring homes. It totals 70,000 square feet with 119 rooms. Among these are 35 bathrooms, 14 guest bedrooms, a hair salon, and a flower shop. With a dedicated staff, Blair House has served a diplomatic task for the president by providing foreign heads of state an honorable residence while visiting Washington. The guest book contains the names of Charles de Gaulle, Jawaharlal Nehru, Margaret Thatcher, Queen Elizabeth II, Vladimir Putin, and Dr. Chaim Weizmann.

Breckinridge, John C.

John Cabell Breckinridge (1821–1875) was the youngest person ever to serve as vice president. He was elected as James Buchanan's running mate at the age of thirty-six. As vice president he worked for a compromise that would avert civil war. When war came shortly after he had left office, he gave his loyalty to the South.

Descended from a prominent Kentucky family, Breckinridge graduated from Centre College in Danville, Kentucky, in 1839. After studying law he was admitted to the bar in 1841. By 1845 he had established a successful law partnership in Lexington, Kentucky.

In 1849 Breckinridge was elected to the Kentucky legislature as a Democrat. Two years later, in a race for a seat in the U.S. House of Representatives, he upset the

Source: Library of Congress

Whig candidate from Henry Clay's former district. In 1855, after two terms, Breckinridge left Congress to resume his law practice in Kentucky. That year he also turned down President Franklin Pierce's offer of the ambassadorship to Spain.

The 1856 Democratic national convention nominated Pennsylvanian James Buchanan for president and Breckinridge for vice president. Buchanan easily defeated John C. Fremont of the new Republican Party, whose election many Americans feared would bring civil war. Breckinridge was a capable presiding officer of the Senate. The handsome and eloquent vice president was so popular in his home state that sixteen months before his vice-presidential term was to expire he was elected to a term in the U.S. Senate, which was to begin when he left the vice presidency.

In 1860 southern Democrats nominated Breckinridge for the presidency, while Illinois senator Stephen A. Douglas was nominated by Democrats in the North. Breckinridge declared that he favored preserving the Union but opposed outlawing slavery in the territories. He finished second with seventy-two electoral votes from eleven southern states. Abraham Lincoln received less than 40 percent of the popular vote, but with three other candidates splitting the rest of the votes—Breckinridge, Douglas, and John Bell of the Constitutional Union Party—Lincoln won a clear majority of 180 electoral votes and the presidency.

After Lincoln's inauguration, Breckinridge favored secession for Kentucky, but he accepted the state's declaration of neutrality. When Congress reconvened on July 4, 1861, he took his seat in the Senate. Throughout the summer he defended the right of southern states to secede and opposed Lincoln's efforts to raise an army.

Later in 1861 Breckinridge accepted a commission as a brigadier general in the Confederate army and was indicted for treason by the federal government. In February 1865 Confederate president Jefferson Davis appointed him secretary of war. When

More on this topic:

Bell, John, p. 30

Buchanan, James, p. 35

Elections Chronology, p. 174

Pardon Power, p. 395

the South surrendered in April 1865, Breckinridge fled to Europe. For three and a half years he lived in Europe and Canada while he waited for the treason charge against him to be dropped.

On Christmas Day 1868 President Andrew Johnson declared an amnesty for all who had taken part in the rebellion. The following March, Breckinridge returned to Kentucky, where crowds greeted him as a hero. He settled in Lexington and practiced law there until he died in 1875.

Brownlow Committee

One of the important turning points in the development of the institutional presidency came with the appointment of the Brownlow Committee by Franklin D. Roosevelt in March 1936. Its purpose was to study the administration of the White House and the executive branch. The committee's recommendations helped to bring about administrative reform within the government and gave the president greater authority and responsibility over the executive branch.

Seeking to establish a line of command that ran directly from the White House through the departmental secretaries to their subordinates, Roosevelt appointed the Committee on Administrative Management to plan the overhaul of the executive branch. To fill the panel he selected three of the nation's foremost scholars of public administration, including Louis D. Brownlow, who served as committee chairman.

In its 1937 report the Brownlow Committee concluded that the executive branch had become so complex that "the president needs help" in managing it. The panel proposed creating six new positions, presidential assistants, who would be assigned at the president's discretion. The staff of the White House Office, the report said, should be loyal and energetic aides with "a passion for anonymity." In addition, it recommended that discretionary funds be put at the president's disposal to allow him to acquire more help as needed. Related to this, the committee called for the extension of the merit system "upward, outward, and downward." It was critical of the Civil Service Commission's policy of encouraging a narrow, specialized federal workforce; it called instead for hiring administrators with broad, general skills.

The purpose of making Federal administrative management modern and businesslike is to make American democracy efficient. It is the view of the Committee that self-government cannot long survive even in this country unless it can do its work efficiently.

—Preamble to the *Summary of the Report of the Committee on Administrative Management*, January 12th, 1937

The report also said that the president should be involved in both discharging existing policies and taking the initiative for creating new ones. It called for inclusion of a long-term planning board within the Executive Office of the President and a strengthened Bureau of the Budget.

Overall, the aim of the Brownlow Committee's report was to centralize the powers and responsibilities of the president, blurring the distinction between politics and administration that had previously been established by reformers most concerned with efficiency and the elimination of patronage.

Roosevelt won approval from Congress in 1939 for most of the Brownlow Committee's recommendations. An exception was the suggestion to place the Civil Service Commission under the control of the White House, which did not gain approval. Although the final bill was a compromise and some of the provisions of the report had to be dropped because of congressional opposition, the main thrust of the panel's recommendations was preserved, in terms of both structural proposals and its overall desire to strengthen the president's control over the administration.

More on this topic:

Civil Service, p. 91

Roosevelt, Franklin D., p. 445

Bryan, William Jennings

William Jennings Bryan (1860–1925), one of the most dramatic orators in the history of U.S. presidential elections, championed "the common man" in three losing campaigns for president. Bryan

Source: Library of Congress

was defeated twice by Republican William McKinley, in 1896 and 1900, and a third time by Republican William Howard Taft, in 1908. A religious and moralistic man, Bryan led a crusade for free coinage of silver, a policy he believed would improve the economic welfare of farmers and industrial workers by increasing the supply of money. He never was able to unite the Democrats behind his reformist banner, or to match the financial power of the Republicans.

Bryan's famous "Cross of Gold" speech electrified the 1896 Democratic national convention and won him the nomination. He was only thirty-six years old, a newspaper editor from Omaha who had previously represented Nebraska during two terms in the House of Representatives. Bryan had adopted much of the free silver platform of the Populist splinter party that fielded a presidential candidate in 1892. In the often quoted climax of his speech, Bryan railed against the gold standard, which he saw as a tool of the business class to keep the less prosperous from advancing. "You shall not press down upon the brow of labor this crown of thorns," he thundered. "You shall not crucify mankind upon a cross of gold."

Bryan's losing campaign of 1896 was memorable not only for his stirring convention speech but also for the way he campaigned. Abandoning a tradition of public restraint on the part of presidential candidates, Bryan barnstormed the country in a style that would become the rule rather than the exception in the next century. McKinley's more sedate and well-financed campaign was able to convince a substantial majority of voters—including the industrial workers to whom Bryan had appealed—that conservative economic policies were in their interests. McKinley won not only the East but also many of the small cities and towns in Bryan's western belt of support.

Economic prosperity, a popular war with Spain, and the strenuous campaigning of vice-presidential nominee Theodore Roosevelt helped McKinley to defeat Bryan even more decisively in 1900. Bryan's flamboyance and populism having worn thin, the Democrats nominated an obscure conservative, Alton B. Parker, in 1904. In the wake of Parker's crushing defeat by Theodore Roosevelt, the Democrats nominated Bryan for a third time in 1908 to face Republican William Howard Taft. Bryan called for a host of liberal reforms—including government ownership of railroads, a lower tariff, a graduated income tax, and stronger enforcement of antitrust laws. But the progressive programs of Roosevelt and Taft were enough to satisfy most voters, and Taft won easily.

More on this topic:

Elections Chronology,
p. 174

McKinley, William,
p. 347

Bryan's support helped Woodrow Wilson to win the Democratic nomination in 1912, for which President Wilson rewarded him with the post of secretary of state. Bryan resigned in 1915 because, as a pacifist, he could not support Wilson's strong stand against Germany. As Bryan's political influence waned, he took up crusades in favor of prohibition and against the teaching of evolution. As a witness for the prosecution in the notorious Scopes "monkey trial" of 1925, Bryan was subjected to a humiliating grilling by the legendary defense attorney Clarence Darrow. Although Darrow lost the case, he managed to steal Bryan's thunder and to make his religious beliefs appear weak-minded and inconsistent. Bryan died in his sleep just days after the trial ended.

Buchanan, James

Source: National Archives

James Buchanan (1791–1868) was president during the four years preceding the Civil War. He held a narrow conception of presidential power that hindered his efforts to find a solution to growing sectional tensions. Despite his diplomatic skill, which he honed during his years as secretary of state and an ambassador, he was unable to construct a compromise to postpone or avert war.

Buchanan was born on April 23, 1791, in Stony Batter, Pennsylvania. He grew up working in the family's thriving frontier trading post. Buchanan graduated with honors in 1809 from Dickinson College in Carlisle, Pennsylvania. In 1812 he was admitted to the bar, and the next year he was appointed assistant prosecutor for Lebanon County, Pennsylvania.

In 1814, after serving briefly in the War of 1812, Buchanan returned to Pennsylvania where he was elected to the state assembly. He served two terms before leaving politics to establish a successful law practice.

Buchanan began his national political career in 1820 with his election to the U.S. House of Representatives as a Federalist. He served in the House for ten years. He was a staunch opponent of John Quincy Adams and in 1828 gave his allegiance to Andrew Jackson and the Democratic Party. Jackson appointed Buchanan minister to Russia in 1831. He returned home in 1833 and was elected to the U.S. Senate by the Pennsylvania legislature the following year. He quickly became a leading conservative Democrat and chairman of the Foreign Relations Committee. Buchanan chose to stay in the Senate despite President Martin Van Buren's offer of the post of attorney general and President John Tyler's offer of a seat on the Supreme Court. When President James K. Polk offered Buchanan the post of secretary of state, however, he accepted. As secretary of state, Buchanan took a leading role in the negotiations with Britain that produced a compromise on fixing the boundary of the Oregon Territory.

After losing the 1848 Democratic presidential nomination to Lewis Cass, Buchanan retired to Lancaster. In 1853, however, he accepted an appointment from President Franklin Pierce as minister to Great Britain.

Upon returning from Britain in 1856, Buchanan was nominated for president by the Democrats. His absence from the country during the bloody fighting in Kansas precipitated by the Kansas-Nebraska Act made him a more acceptable nominee than either President Pierce or Sen. Stephen A. Douglas, both of whom had supported the act. Buchanan faced John Fremont of the newly formed Republican Party and former president Millard Fillmore of the right-wing American (Know-Nothing) Party. Buchanan received only 47 percent of the popular vote but won every southern state in defeating Fremont 174–114 in the Electoral College.

Buchanan's presidency was dominated by the slavery issue. Although he considered slavery to be unjust, he believed people in the southern states had the constitutional right to own slaves. He was a committed Unionist who tried to steer a middle course between the forces for and against slavery, but most of his policies appeared to northerners to favor the South. He enforced the Fugitive Slave Act, tried to quell northern antislavery agitation, and supported the Supreme Court's *Dred Scott* decision. That decision denied that slaves could be citizens, recognized the right of slave owners to take their slaves into free states and territories, declared unconstitutional the Missouri Compromise restricting slavery to below 36°30′ latitude, and implied that neither Congress nor the territorial governments created by Congress had the authority to exclude slavery from the territories.

In 1858 Buchanan split his party when he sent to Congress a pro-slavery constitution written by the minority southern faction in Kansas and recommended that Kansas be admitted as a slave state. Many Democratic leaders, including Stephen Douglas, denounced the constitution and distanced themselves from Buchanan. The Senate approved the plan to admit Kansas under the pro-slavery constitution, but the House rejected it. Kansas continued to inspire conflict between North and South until it became a state in 1861.

The 1860 election brought the secession crisis that Buchanan had hoped to prevent. When Abraham Lincoln of the antislavery Republican Party was elected, southerners began to debate secession. Buchanan supported compromise solutions, but none of the plans were acceptable.

After Lincoln's election, secessionists seized most federal forts in the South without much resistance. Buchanan considered secession to be unconstitutional, but he refrained from responding with force to the acts of rebellion. He did request the power to call out the militia and increase the size of the armed forces, but Congress refused. By the time Buchanan's term ended, seven states had seceded, and the nation was headed toward civil war.

After Lincoln's inauguration, Buchanan retired to his home in Lancaster, Pennsylvania. During his retirement the northern press criticized him for failing to prevent the Civil War and accused him of allowing federal forts to remain vulnerable. In an attempt to justify his actions and the policies of his administration, he published his memoirs, *Mr. Buchanan's Administration on the Eve of the Rebellion*, in 1866. Buchanan died in Lancaster on June 1, 1868. He was the only president never to marry.

> **More on this topic:**
>
> *Civil War, p. 95*
>
> *Constitutional Powers and Provisions, p. 119*
>
> *Presidential Greatness, p. 414*

Buckley v. Valeo

In 1974 Congress passed the most sweeping reform of the CAMPAIGN FINANCING system up to that time. The legislation was intended to curb the kinds of electoral abuses that President Richard Nixon's 1972 campaign organization perpetrated—abuses that led to the WATERGATE AFFAIR and Nixon's eventual resignation from office. But in trying to curb abuses, the law ran afoul of the Supreme Court.

The 1974 law established limits on the amount individuals, parties, and political action committees could donate to presidential and congressional elections. The law's restrictions on the use of candidates' personal money included a $50,000 limit on the amount presidential candidates could contribute to their own campaign. The statute also limited the amount candidates could spend in both the nominating process and the general election. Public financing of presidential general elections was extended to cover prenomination campaigns and national nominating conventions. The law also created the FEDERAL ELECTION COMMISSION (FEC) to enforce the campaign financing laws and established several disclosure and reporting procedures.

As soon as the law took effect, it was challenged in court by an array of plaintiffs, including James L. Buckley, the Conservative senator from New York; former Democratic senator Eugene J. McCarthy of Minnesota; the New York Civil Liberties Union; and the American Conservative Union.

They argued that the law's new limits on campaign contributions and expenditures curbed the freedom of contributors and candidates alike to express themselves in the political marketplace. They also contended that the provisions discriminated against third-party and lesser-known candidates in favor of the major parties and better-known candidates.

The Supreme Court handed down its decision in *Buckley v. Valeo* in January 1976. The Court upheld limits on the amount that individuals, parties, and political action committees could contribute to candidates. It also ruled that public financing of presidential primary and general election campaigns was constitutional. And it upheld spending limits for presidential candidates who accepted public financing.

The Court ruled that other limits on campaign spending were unconstitutional restrictions of the freedom of expression and association guaranteed by the First Amendment. Although it had upheld the limits on contributions others could make to candidates, it struck down the limits on how much federal candidates could contribute to their own campaigns. "The use of personal funds reduces the candidate's dependence on outside contributions," the Court wrote. In dissent Justice Thurgood Marshall wrote that "it would appear to follow that the candidate with a substantial personal fortune at his disposal is off to a significant 'head start.'" However, for those presidential candidates who participated in the public financing program, the personal spending ceiling was still the $50,000 limit set by the original law.

'Your honor, my client believes that campaign spending limitations are a curb on free speech because everybody knows money talks!'

The Court also ruled that the FEC was unconstitutional. It held that the method for appointing FEC commissioners violated the Constitution's separation-of-powers and appointments clauses because some members were named by congressional officials but exercised executive powers. The justices refused to accept the argument that the commission, because it oversaw congressional as well as presidential elections, could have congressionally appointed members.

The 1976 election campaign was already under way, but the Court said that the FEC could not continue to disburse public funds to presidential candidates so long as some commission members were congressional appointees. A law enacted in May 1976 reconstituted the FEC as a six-member panel appointed by the president and confirmed by the Senate. The new FEC immediately voted to approve all previous actions.

More on this topic:

Campaign Financing, p. 71

Elections and Campaigns, p. 168

Federal Election Commission, p. 212

Budget Process

The federal budget is the nation's fiscal blueprint. It tells how much money can be spent in a year by the federal government, how much money must be raised, and how far into debt the government can go.

The process by which this budget is reached is long and complicated, involving both the executive and the legislative branches. It is usually a politically divisive process that pits Democrat against Republican and the White House against Capitol Hill. Political battles increased as the government, beginning in the 1960s, routinely spent more than it took in, creating budget deficits.

Frustrations with the budget process have sent Congress to the drawing board several times in recent decades. After repeated clashes with the Nixon administration over its refusal to spend

Federal Budget Deficits and Surpluses, Eisenhower to George W. Bush (billions)

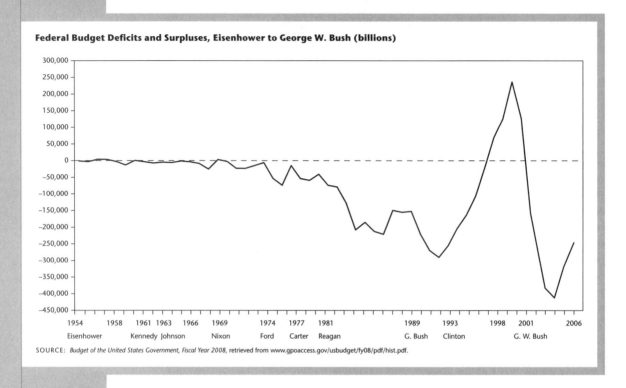

SOURCE: *Budget of the United States Government, Fiscal Year 2008,* retrieved from www.gpoaccess.gov/usbudget/fy08/pdf/hist.pdf.

money approved by Congress, the legislative branch in 1974 designed a whole new budget system. Aware that its haphazard way of dealing with the president's budget left it no match for the executive branch in budget battles, Congress centralized its budget procedures and greatly increased its technical support.

Budget battles intensified under President Ronald Reagan as he and congressional Democrats blamed each other for the growing deficits of the 1980s. In 1985 Congress decided on a new approach to controlling federal spending: automatic spending cuts if Congress and the president did not agree on a budget that met specific targets. In 1990, as the budget deficit seemed to be rapidly growing out of control, Congress once again revised its budget procedures. Budget battles nevertheless continued in the 1990s and into the 2000s. By the late 1990s, as the economy boomed, a budget surplus greeted lawmakers, but it vanished rapidly in the early 2000s as the George W. Bush administration used tax cuts to stimulate the economy and sought to finance its war on terrorism.

How the Process Works

To keep track of its revenues (government income from taxes and other sources) and expenditures in an orderly way, the federal government has established a twelve-month period known as the fiscal year. For many years the government's fiscal year ran from July 1 through June 30. To give itself more time to consider the budget during its annual sessions, which begin in January, Congress in 1974 pushed back the start of the fiscal year to October 1 and set a timetable for itself to meet that deadline.

President's Budget

Each year the executive branch prepares a financial plan for the U.S. government. It is the most important annual document produced by the Executive Office of the President. It specifies how government funds have been raised and spent and outlines the president's plans for the fiscal year ahead. The president's budget provides for both discretionary and mandatory expenditures. Discretionary funds are those actually approved, or appropriated, by Congress each year. Mandatory spending is for entitlement programs, such as Social Security and Medicare, that must provide benefits to all eligible persons who seek them. Such programs generally are permanently authorized and are not subject to annual appropriations.

The president's budget also serves as an important tool in setting fiscal policy, which is the coordinated use of taxes and expenditures to influence the levels of inflation, unemployment, and economic growth. Moreover, it is a good indicator of the president's priorities and therefore affects political and social programs as much as fiscal policy.

The White House works for months to prepare its budget. It first must evaluate all agency budget requests and decide which to accept or reject before submitting the budget to Congress. The director and staff of the OFFICE OF MANAGEMENT AND BUDGET play the major roles in this process, setting guidelines for each department, holding hearings on departmental requests, conferring with other members of the administration, and finally deciding how much to request from Congress. These decisions can be appealed, but presidents rarely reverse their budget director's decisions.

Congress receives the first official hint of the president's plans in the STATE OF THE UNION ADDRESS at the end of January. Details are provided in the president's budget request and economic forecast, which must be submitted to Congress by the first Monday in February.

Congressional Role

The president's budget is sent to the House and Senate Budget Committees. With the aid of the Congressional Budget Office's expert staff and technical support services, the committees study the president's budget and recommend changes. The committees draw up a concurrent resolution outlining a tentative alternative federal budget.

The budget resolution sets target totals for budget authority (amounts the federal agencies are allowed to obligate or lend), outlays (amounts actually paid out by the government during the year), revenues, the deficit, and the federal debt. It includes spending caps and five-year budget projections.

Once it has been approved, the budget resolution guides Congress as it acts on the separate appropriations bills and other measures providing budget authority for spending on federal programs. The budget resolution uses "reconciliation" instructions to direct committees to change existing law to meet the new levels.

If Congress does not finish its work on the appropriations bills by the October 1 start of the fiscal year, funds can be provided through passage of a continuing appropriations resolution.

Executive Influence

Once the White House submits its budget to Congress, the executive branch does not simply sit back and wait; it has an ongoing involvement in the process. Executive branch officials testify in support of the budget proposals before committees of Congress. Members of the legislative liaison staff lobby Congress for the president's proposals. The president may lobby Congress personally and, if things are not going as desired, may threaten to veto funding bills. (See CONGRESS AND THE PRESIDENCY.)

Sometimes the White House and congressional leaders use high-level "summit" meetings to negotiate a compromise agreement on reducing the budget deficit. Many on Capitol Hill dislike this arrangement because it shuts most members of Congress out of the process of making the most important decisions of the session. Budget summits were used by President George H. W. Bush in

1989 and again in 1990—until the House staged a revolt and handed its leadership a humiliating, bipartisan defeat of a budget agreement. The White House and Congress were unable for several agonizing weeks to reach an agreement to resolve the budget impasse. At one point, the government shut down for three days when Bush vetoed a stopgap spending bill. Another budget agreement was finally hammered out, this time with input from a much larger group of members of Congress.

Background

The formulation of a comprehensive federal budget is a relatively modern development in the nation's history. In fact, the federal government has operated under a budget only since 1921.

Ratification of the Constitution cleared the way for establishment of a government financial system. In September 1789 Congress enacted a law establishing the Treasury Department and requiring the secretary of the Treasury "to prepare and report estimates of the public revenues, and the public expenditures." But attempts to establish an executive budget failed because of party divisions and Congress's concern for its prerogatives.

Throughout the nineteenth century, the federal government relied on customs duties for most of its revenues. Because there was an abundance of such revenues, there was no need to weigh expenditures against revenues. Consequently, the budget-making process deteriorated.

By the end of World War I, however, the diffuse system that had grown up in place of a centralized budget procedure could no longer meet the needs of an increasingly complex government. Congress decided it had to reform the government's financial machinery. In the Budget and Accounting Act of 1921, Congress established two important offices—the Bureau of the Budget and the General Accounting Office. The former was created to centralize fiscal management of the executive branch directly under the president; the latter was designed to strengthen congressional oversight of spending and is now called the Government Accountability Office.

With passage of the 1921 act, Congress ended the right of federal agencies to decide for themselves how much money to request from Congress. The Budget Bureau, under the president's direction, was to act as a central clearinghouse for budget requests. In 1935 President Franklin D. Roosevelt broadened this clearance function to include legislative as well as appropriation requests.

In 1970 President Richard Nixon restructured the Bureau of the Budget. The new Office of Management and Budget was given sweeping authority to coordinate the implementation of government programs, and it assumed the Budget Bureau's old role of advising the president on agency funding requests.

Although the executive branch streamlined its budget process, responsibility for congressional budget decisions remained dispersed among various committees. Because they represented different regions and economic interests, members of Congress had always had mixed feelings about budget control. The few times the House and Senate voted for overall budget restraints, they were unable or unwilling to cut enough from individual programs to meet those goals. In the first thirty years after World War II the momentum of those separate spending decisions sooner or later overwhelmed whatever devices Congress used to try to keep the budget in check.

Budget Reforms

The spending issue came to a head in the late 1960s and early 1970s, when funding for President Lyndon B. Johnson's Great Society social programs, combined with military outlays for the Vietnam War, increased the budget deficit. Repeated clashes between the White House and Capitol Hill finally led to major reform of Congress's budget process.

When members of Congress failed to set effective spending limits, President Nixon did it for them. The president's campaign to curb federal spending brought to the surface long-simmering differences over whether the government must spend all the money that Congress appropriates.

Continuing a practice that many presidents had followed, Nixon in the early 1970s impounded billions of dollars that Congress had provided—despite the president's objections—for certain government programs. By withholding the funds, Nixon set off a legal and political struggle over the issue of whether the executive or the legislature held final authority over how the government spent its money. (See IMPOUNDMENT.) Frustrated by the impoundment battle and aware that its own haphazard budget process was causing its problems, Congress passed the Congressional Budget and Impoundment Control Act of 1974. The new act set limits on the president's impoundment powers, but it went far beyond that. The act created a timetable to force congressional action on the budget, changed the fiscal year to give Congress more time to consider the budget, and established procedures for Congress to evaluate it as a whole rather than as a group of unconnected spending bills.

The legislation also created the House and Senate Budget Committees to centralize congressional budget making and the Congressional Budget Office to provide Congress with an expert staff to analyze the budget. It required Congress to vote each year to set specific spending, tax, and deficit limits and to adhere to those limits or make adjustments.

The process seldom worked as intended. Deadlines were rarely met, Congress's budgetary restraint was weak, and federal deficits ballooned. In the early years of the process, congressional budget making still was largely a process of accommodation. House and Senate leaders, anxious to keep the process going, proposed budget resolutions that left room for new programs and additional spending. As long as Congress remained in an expansive mood, the House and Senate were able to construct budgets in a piecemeal fashion that satisfied the particular interests of various committees and groups.

When Congress tried to adopt more austere budgets beginning in 1979, it encountered difficulty. While acknowledging the need to hold down spending, members of Congress sought to avoid cuts in programs important to their constituents. That goal became harder to achieve as the competition for federal dollars increased.

Budget battles with the White House consumed Congress during the administration of President Ronald Reagan. Upon taking office in 1981 Reagan seized control of the congressional budget machinery to carry out sweeping spending and tax cuts that he had promised in his election campaign. In subsequent years Congress routinely dismissed Reagan's budgets, but it had trouble developing plans of its own that also were acceptable to the president. Each year the two branches battled over the federal deficit, which more than doubled during Reagan's first term.

In the mid-1980s the federal deficit spiraled to more than $200 million a year, and Congress—stalemated over Reagan's opposition to more tax increases, demands for additional cuts in domestic spending, and pressure for a larger defense budget—seemed unable or unwilling to do anything about it. In 1985 reformers, with Reagan's approval, pushed through antideficit legislation that provided for the biggest change in the congressional budget process and in budget politics since 1974. The new law was properly called the Balanced Budget and Emergency Deficit Control Act of 1985, but most people knew it as Gramm-Rudman-Hollings, or just Gramm-Rudman, after its congressional sponsors.

The law set a goal of achieving a balanced budget by 1991. It mandated specific deficit targets each year and established a procedure for automatic across-the-board spending cuts—called a sequester—if the president and Congress could not agree on a budget that met the targets. It accelerated the budget timetable and strengthened procedures to make Congress meet its schedule. One of the measure's sponsors, Sen. Warren B. Rudman, R-N.H., called it "a bad idea whose time has come."

Budget deficits dipped only slightly in the late 1980s before resuming their rapid climb. During this time there were mixed results from the Gramm-Rudman law. Only once, in fiscal 1986, did the automatic ax of Gramm-Rudman actually do its job. After that, Congress chose for the most part to use "blue smoke and mirror" techniques, such as sales of assets and manipulation of the government pay calendar, to avoid making hard choices.

Congress revised Gramm-Rudman in 1987. The new measure promised a balanced budget by fiscal 1993, two years later than required in the original law. It also revised the procedure for automatic spending cuts to meet objections raised by the Supreme Court the previous year.

By 1990 the budget deficit seemed to be rapidly growing out of control, thanks to a slowdown in the economy coupled with the huge cost of the bailout of the savings and loan industry. The goal of a balanced budget was dismissed as impossible, and the Gramm-Rudman law was criticized as leading to accounting gimmickry rather than true deficit reduction. After the spectacle of the House defeat of a budget summit agreement and a government shutdown, the White House and Congress settled on a five-year package of tax increases and spending reductions. As part of the deficit reduction law, Congress once again revised its budget procedures.

In a major change in budget policy, the Budget Enforcement Act of 1990 played down the sheer size of the deficit. The law set revised deficit targets, but the targets were designed to be adjusted in the future for economic conditions or errors in technical forecasts. The new law also revised the budget process timetable and set appropriations caps. It replaced the scheme of across-the-board spending cuts under Gramm-Rudman that took effect October 1 with a set of three sequesters that would kick in fifteen days after Congress adjourned. The first would offset discretionary appropriations for the coming fiscal year that exceeded statutory limits; it affected only discretionary spending. The second would be triggered if Congress enacted entitlement spending increases or revenue decreases during the year and would affect only entitlements that had not been exempted. The third would offset an increase in the deficit above the limit set in the law, if the first two sequesters had not eliminated the excess deficit; it would cover all nonexempt spending.

In 1993 President Bill Clinton set yearly targets for entitlement spending and issued an executive order requiring the president to propose a remedy if the limit was breached. The House changed its rules to require that it act on any such proposal.

Although his party was in control of both houses of Congress, Clinton found enactment of his budget priorities difficult. Congressional Republicans attacked the proposal as a typical "tax and spend budget" that shortchanged deficit reduction. Even after some modifications, not a single Republican in either house voted for it. The budget passed by a 218–216 vote in the House, and Vice President Al Gore had to cast a tie-breaking vote in the Senate to end a 50–50 stalemate. The budget contained little new investment, but it did shift some tax burden from the poor to the wealthiest taxpayers. It was estimated to achieve $496 billion in budget savings over five years, with about half the savings coming from tax increases, half from spending cuts. The rancorous debate over its passage created hard feelings between Clinton and GOP leaders in Congress that would result in the historic budget impasse of 1995–1996.

The election of a Republican majority in Congress in 1994 set off a contentious debate with President Clinton about the size and role of government in American life, and the budget was at its center. Clinton cast his first veto in rejecting a GOP plan to cut $16.6 billion from the 1995 budget, defending traditionally liberal programs for education, the environment, crime prevention, and housing. Over the course of the year he vetoed ten additional spending bills, as the new GOP majority sought to make good on its election year promise of a balanced budget, an important provision of its "Contract with America."

Late in 1995 Republicans in the House and Senate united around a plan to balance the budget by 2002. A controversial part of the plan was to cut the growth of Medicare spending. Clinton's opposition to the GOP plan led to one of the worst budget standoffs in the nation's history. On November 20 Congress passed the fiscal 1996 budget reconciliation bill, which was estimated to balance the budget within seven years. It would achieve this by cutting nearly $900 billion from projected spending in entitlements and discretionary programs over that period and also included a $245 billion tax cut. Clinton vetoed the bill, saying the cuts hurt the most vulnerable Americans. Because less than half of the fiscal 1996 appropriations bills had been passed, funding for many government agencies had expired and Congress had to pass continuing resolutions to keep the government functioning. Meanwhile, both sides played for the public relations advantage while engaging in furious off-stage bargaining.

The result was two partial government shutdowns—the longest in history to date. While Clinton agreed in principle to balance the budget by 2002, he held fast on his budget priorities, a position that, polls showed, the public favored. By April 1996 Clinton and Congress compromised on the final 1996 appropriations bill, a measure that cut $22 billion in domestic spending and preserved many of the president's programs.

For the next several years the Republicans proved reluctant to challenge the president's budget leadership. Consequently, when the budget achieved balance and then surpluses by 1998, the White House received most of the political credit.

In 1997 Congress and the president avoided some of the angry partisanship that had characterized the past year's budget struggle by agreeing to compromise on taxes and spending and by mutually endorsing the idea that annual deficits should be brought to zero by 2002. By adopting some of the GOP proposals as his own, Clinton angered the liberal wing of the Democratic Party, whose spokespersons said he had all but abandoned traditional Democratic constituencies.

The later years of the Clinton administration featured a healthy, booming economy, which increased revenues. By 1998 the Clinton White House was enjoying credit for a balanced budget and the surpluses achieved. In 1999 Clinton vetoed a huge $792 billion Republican-backed tax cut, but the GOP-controlled Congress and the Democratic president agreed on a $385 billion omnibus spending bill in November. During the last years of Clinton's presidency the surpluses contributed to a weakening of fiscal restraint among politicians.

In 2001 newly sworn-in President George W. Bush pushed Congress to pass a substantial tax cut, which ended up totaling $1.35 trillion over ten years. But the economy had begun to slow down, and the terrorist attacks of September 11, 2001, had a devastating effect on the country's financial situation. The "war on terrorism" and a new focus on homeland security—a Department of Homeland Security was created in late 2002—also heightened the strain on the economy, as did preparations in 2002 for war with Iraq. The stock market, which had surged during the boom times, faltered. By fiscal 2002 budget deficits had returned.

In 2002 the Senate, for the first time since the modern budget process came into effect in 1974, failed to adopt a budget resolution. With the Senate narrowly controlled by Democrats and the House under a small GOP majority, Congress, riven by partisan battles, managed to pass only two of thirteen fiscal 2003 appropriations bills, leaving the work for the new Congress that convened in January 2003. Meanwhile, the Bush administration proposed in early 2003 a $674 billion, ten-year package, including tax cuts, to stimulate the economy; many Democrats assailed the plan, charging that it favored the wealthy. The Democratic-controlled 110th Congress promises to alter the course of federal fiscal policy that has dominated the first six years of the Bush administration. Many tax cuts passed during Bush's first term are set to expire without extension, and reigning in the federal budget deficit was a top priority of Democratic congressional candidates during the 2006 midterm elections.

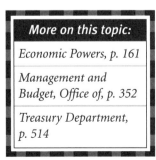

More on this topic:

Economic Powers, p. 161

Management and Budget, Office of, p. 352

Treasury Department, p. 514

Bureaucracy

The U.S. government organizations that carry out public policy are collectively referred to as the federal bureaucracy. There is no mention of the bureaucracy in the Constitution, yet it is one of the most powerful elements of modern American government. In fact, the bureaucracy is often called the "fourth branch" of government because of its prominence in contemporary politics. Presidents quickly discover that they can accomplish little without help from the bureaucracy; therefore, their relationship with it is one of the most important aspects of any administration.

For many people the word *bureaucracy* conjures up images of red tape, impersonality, and rigidity. Opposition to "big government" has become almost synonymous with opposition to bureaucracy. Political candidates from both major political parties regularly decry the evils of the growing U.S. bureaucracy, denouncing it for removing Americans from the decision-making process of their federal government. Presidents often have been among the vocal critics, but they have a variety of powers they can use in their attempts to work with—and control—the bureaucracy.

Structure of the Bureaucracy

Federal government agencies can be sorted into five categories: departments, independent agencies, government corporations, presidential and congressional agencies, and various other agencies.

Departments

The executive departments make up the first layer of bureaucracy under the president. The heads of these departments, who are also known as secretaries, are members of the president's CABINET. Department secretaries and their immediate subordinates are appointed by the president with Senate approval. The departments conduct some of the bureaucracy's most important business and employ about two-thirds of all federal workers.

In 2002 there were fourteen executive departments: Agriculture, Commerce, Defense, Education, Energy, Health and Human Services, Housing and Urban Development, Interior, Justice, Labor, State, Transportation, Treasury, and Veterans Affairs. In late 2002 a fifteenth department, for homeland security, was approved and opened its doors in March 2003. A proposal to raise the Environmental Protection Agency to a cabinet-level department also has been considered. (For more information, see the individual entries for these departments.)

Congress determines the number and jurisdiction of cabinet-level departments, but the president can request changes. The departments of State, Treasury, and War (now Defense) were established in 1789 to meet immediate national needs, and other departments were created in response to problems or political pressures as the nation developed.

Some departments, such as Justice and Interior, serve the general needs of the entire country. Others, such as Agriculture, Commerce, Labor, and Veterans Affairs, mostly serve particular segments of society. Each of the fifteen executive departments is broken down into smaller units—offices, administrations, services, and bureaus—that administer the department's programs.

Independent Agencies

About sixty independent agencies and corporations operate within the federal bureaucracy.

Many of these are either INDEPENDENT REGULATORY AGENCIES or INDEPENDENT EXECUTIVE AGENCIES. These agencies are roughly equivalent to the department subunits in size and influence, but they exist outside of and independent from the executive departments.

Agencies are made independent for several reasons. First, independent agencies are less tied to tradition and therefore can be more innovative than the executive departments. Second, these agencies are in theory less susceptible to outside pressures. Third, some agencies are independent because their missions do not fall naturally within any of the departments.

Independent regulatory agencies are designed to regulate parts of the private economic sector to protect the public interest. Such agencies include the Federal Communications Commission, Federal Trade Commission, and Securities and Exchange Commission.

Independent executive agencies perform a single primary function and report directly to the president. Among these agencies are the National Aeronautics and Space Administration, Central Intelligence Agency, General Services Administration, and Environmental Protection Agency.

Government Corporations

When confronted with tasks similar to those carried out by private business, the federal government can form GOVERNMENT CORPORATIONS to take advantage of the rights enjoyed by private corporations.

Government corporations, which are run like businesses, have greater freedom of operation than most other government agencies. For example, they can buy and sell property, borrow money, bring suit, and be sued. Some of the best-known government corporations are the U.S. Postal Service, Tennessee Valley Authority, Federal Deposit Insurance Corporation, and Amtrak.

Presidential and Congressional Agencies

The presidency has its own supporting bureaucracy within the EXECUTIVE OFFICE OF THE PRESIDENT. This includes the White House Office, where the presidents place their closest, most trusted staff members, as well as other offices that assist presidents primarily with policy issues. One of the most notable is the OFFICE OF MANAGEMENT AND BUDGET (OMB), which constructs the federal budget and assesses legislation and regulations.

Congress also has its supporting bureaucracy, which includes members' personal staffs, committee staffs, and research agencies such as the Library of Congress and the Congressional Budget Office. The Government Accountability Office acts as congressional watchdog over federal programs. Other congressional agencies, such as the Government Printing Office, fulfill responsibilities not directly related to policy making. (See CONGRESS AND THE PRESIDENCY.)

Other Agencies

Operating within the federal government are hundreds of advisory committees and other minor boards. Advisory committees, which can be either temporary or permanent, give expert advice on a wide range of subjects. Some presidents are fond of such committees because their creation demonstrates to the public that the administration cares about the problems being examined and because they provide an opportunity to pay political debts with committee appointments.

Other agencies include PRESIDENTIAL COMMISSIONS and minor boards. These groups usually have no permanent staff and can only make recommendations.

Growth of the Bureaucracy

In the early 2000s civilian employees in these various federal departments and agencies numbered about 2.7 million. Some 8 percent work in the Washington, D.C., metropolitan area.

These numbers are a far cry from the several hundred workers employed in George Washington's three executive departments. The bureaucracy has exploded in size and scope in the intervening centuries because of the ever increasing demands placed on government. The bureaucracy has had to keep up with rapid technological changes, the growth in government regulation, major national crises, and political pressure for more government services.

Beginnings

The modern federal bureaucracy had humble beginnings. George Washington's administration began with only three executive departments—State, Treasury, and War—and very few federal workers. Creation of the U.S. Post Office in 1792 caused a small surge in federal employment, but the entire government workforce still numbered only about three thousand in 1801.

The early system of administration was highly informal and remained so until one of Andrew Jackson's appointees decided to make some changes. Amos Kendall, the new head of the Post Office, replaced informality with routines by setting up clear lines of authority, specifying job descriptions, and establishing strict accounting practices. At that point, the bureaucracy began to take on the formal character it has today.

Jackson also instituted the "spoils system," in which election winners rewarded their supporters with federal government jobs. Although Jackson was not the first president to give public jobs to friends and allies, his openness and unapologetic attitude were new. His behavior was not entirely partisan, however, because it was based on his belief that a regular change of public officials made the government more democratic and prevented the rise of a bureaucratic elite that was unrepresentative of the general public.

Growth and Reforms

In the 1860s the Civil War caused tremendous growth in the bureaucracy but also revealed some of the system's weaknesses. While there undoubtedly had been corruption and inefficiency before the war, wartime pressures exposed the problems. Proposals for reform of the bureaucracy soon surfaced and then intensified as scandals over government employment practices arose in the postwar period.

Rapid industrial growth and expansion of government activities placed additional strains on the bureaucracy. New executive agencies and departments, such as the Departments of Agriculture and Labor, were formed to help meet the increasing demands by powerful interest groups for government service.

The reform movement received its biggest push from the assassination of President James A. Garfield by a disappointed federal job seeker. Public outrage at the killing focused attention on the problems of the spoils system and spurred passage of the Pendleton Act in 1883. The law reformed the CIVIL SERVICE by mandating that many federal jobs be granted to the most qualified applicants, rather than those with the best political connections. It also provided those employees with job security, thus ending the mass rotation that had occurred with every new president.

The Twentieth Century

The first few decades of the twentieth century brought further sizable increases in the bureaucracy. Many new agencies, such as the Forest Service and the Food and Drug Administration, were created to carry out new tasks assigned to government during the Progressive era. Similarly, America's entry into World War I resulted in more government activity and therefore more bureaucracy.

Franklin D. Roosevelt's New Deal program to combat the economic depression of the 1930s resulted in the formation of more than sixty new bureaucratic agencies. It also brought about a fundamental shift in the role of government. The federal government was now expected to take an active role in fighting the nation's problems, a role that would require adding to the bureaucracy.

America's participation in World War II also led to growth in the bureaucracy, most noticeably in the military. Another important consequence of the war was the dramatic increase in the amount of money raised and spent by the federal government. From 1940 to 1945 total federal tax collections skyrocketed from approximately $5 billion to almost $44 billion, an increase that also enlarged the influence of bureaucracy. Taxes did not fall after the war ended; instead, resources were directed to continued military readiness and domestic social programs.

By the early 1950s the number of federal civilian employees had leveled off at about 2.6 million, and that figure has changed by only about a third of a million since then. But the importance of bureaucracy has continued to grow.

Presidents and the Bureaucracy

Traditionally, presidents have viewed the federal bureaucracy as one of their biggest political headaches. Rather than a system of compliant agencies faithfully executing the president's will, the bureaucracy is more often—especially from the president's perspective—the source of many difficult problems. Presidents may feel a variety of emotions toward the bureaucracy—frustration, anger, disappointment, disdain, boredom, distrust, or despair—but rarely do they feel complete satisfaction. As Jimmy Carter once put it, "Before I became president, I realized and was warned that dealing with the federal bureaucracy would be one of the worst problems I would have to face. It has been worse than I had anticipated."

Bureaucratic Power

The federal bureaucracy wields considerable power. Depending on the situation, it can be one of the president's primary allies or one of the president's chief rivals in government and politics. There are several reasons for the agencies' considerable power.

First, agencies usually have the expertise needed to deal with technically complex issues. Citizens and their political leaders look to the bureaucracy for expertise and advice on policy, a role that enhances the credibility, prestige, and power of the agencies.

Second, agencies have the information needed to make policy. The information and recommendations passed along by the agencies affect what comes out of the political decision-making process by shaping what goes into it.

Third, the size and complexity of the federal bureaucracy increase its power and autonomy by making it difficult for the president, Congress, and the courts to exert control over it. Moreover, bureaucracies have a certain inertia that makes outside management extremely difficult. It is hard to spur bureaucracies to take new action and equally difficult to stop bureaucratic routines once they have begun. Bureaucratic inertia frustrates presidents, who have a limited time in office and generally want to act quickly and effectively. But the deliberate movement of a bureaucracy can sometimes benefit the president by providing time to reconsider possibly rash decisions.

Another factor in the power of the bureaucracy is the quality of its leadership. More than any other individual, an agency's leader affects that agency's power. The best example of this is J. EDGAR HOOVER, who molded the FEDERAL BUREAU OF INVESTIGATION into a potent political force during his nearly fifty-year reign as its director.

The clout of an agency also depends on the extent of support—or opposition—it has from the president, other agencies, Congress, interest groups, and the public.

Presidential Power

Although presidents find it difficult to exert control over the bureaucracy, they are far from powerless in their relationship with this sector of the federal government.

The Constitution and subsequent statutes grant presidents many powers over federal agencies. Although these powers are legally available to all presidents, they cannot be used successfully in every situation: political and personal considerations constrain presidential actions. Presidents have varying degrees of leadership skills, and these skills are crucial in either winning the support of the bureaucracy or doing battle with it.

Through the APPOINTMENT AND REMOVAL POWER the president can exercise considerable influence. Presidents can appoint bureaucrats who share their own political philosophy and are likely to support their goals as well. And the president may remove or, as is more often the case, ask for the resignation of appointed officials who fail to perform their duties satisfactorily or who clash with the president on policy matters.

Presidential staffs help to manage the bureaucracy. Recent presidents have given their staffs authority over bureaucratic programs and have required that OMB or other entities that serve the president approve agency decisions.

Presidents also exercise control through reorganization of the bureaucracy. They can abolish or create agencies, merge agencies, or move them within departments or to other departments.

Presidents can influence how much money agencies receive, particularly during the BUDGET PROCESS. Although Congress actually appropriates the money that government spends, the president wields power at both the beginning and the end of the budget process. Moreover, all agency requests for legislation, even those not requiring additional funding, must be cleared with OMB before going to Congress.

The expansion of the Executive Office of the President in recent years has given the president an important alternative and a thoroughly loyal source of information that can be used to make policy and counter the bureaucracy. Presidents have other sources of information as well, including the news media, interest groups, the private sector, and academia.

Presidents also set the nation's agenda, which can be a powerful political tool for influencing the bureaucracy. They decide what issues will be considered and which agencies will handle them, and then use their position to generate public support for the proposals.

Presidents have the power to issue EXECUTIVE ORDERS, which are presidential proclamations that carry the force of law. Executive orders may be used to enforce the Constitution or treaties, implement legislation, or direct bureaucratic agencies. Richard Nixon tried to use, and sometimes succeeded in using, executive orders to abolish bureaucratic programs and agencies established by Congress. He also used them to strengthen certain agencies. Executive orders were used as well by Ronald Reagan to curb the bureaucracy's role in promulgating regulations for the private sector.

Presidents are also able to exercise authority over the bureaucracy through their powers as commander in chief and in times of national crisis.

Presidential Limits

All of these presidential powers have their limits, and unfortunately for presidents there are other limits as well.

For one thing, presidents are subject to time constraints. Longevity is one of the bureaucracy's strongest weapons; many problems facing it diminish after enough time passes. But presidents cannot afford to wait indefinitely. Their relatively short terms in office, as well as their desire to be reelected and then to make a mark on history, demand quick, dramatic action. The passage of time generally works to the advantage of the bureaucracy and to the disadvantage of the president. Moreover, presidents and their staffs are faced with tremendous daily demands that leave them little time to devote to controlling the vast bureaucracy.

Even with the expansion of the Executive Office of the President, presidents still are at a disadvantage when it comes to information. The expertise and specialization of the bureaucracy, perhaps largely because of its size, give it the advantage in information gathering.

At times, presidents face formidable opposition from so-called iron triangles, which are alliances among federal agencies, interest groups, and congressional committees or subcommittees with stakes in a particular issue. Each member of the alliance, or each point of the triangle, has a mutually beneficial relationship with the other two members, and all members work together to pursue common goals. The power of iron triangles limits presidential control of the bureaucracy because agencies always can turn to their congressional and interest group allies for help against the president.

Presidential control also can be frustrated by what political scientist Hugh Heclo has called "issue networks," coalitions of individuals and groups who want to influence particular areas of executive policy. These networks draw more people—most of them independent of the president and holding diverse views—into the policy-making process, which then becomes more difficult to control. Moreover, the networks may supply Congress and the bureaucracy with information and political backing they can use to pursue their own objectives and to thwart presidential intervention.

Probably the most important restraint on presidential control stems from bureaucratic preferences. Presidents usually find it difficult to get the bureaucracy to do what it does not want to do. Federal agencies generally want to survive and, if possible, to expand. If a presidential proposal runs counter to those goals, it is almost certain to draw opposition. Not surprisingly, then, Reagan's effort to abolish the Education and Energy Departments drew vigorous resistance from them.

And then agencies may simply disagree with a president when they believe a presidential decision is ill-advised or unworkable. Disagreement also may spring from ideological differences.

Finally, the goals of civil servants working within agencies may hamper presidential control of the bureaucracy. Permanent civil servants are committed to their careers and their agencies. Their preferences for stability and regularity inevitably clash with those of presidents, who typically want rapid, bold action from the bureaucracy.

Even though they are selected by the president, political appointees too have goals that often conflict with those of the president. Because most appointees serve in government for only a short time, they want to establish their reputations quickly. But their attempts to do so may entail taking actions that clash with the president's wishes. A conflict of goals also may result when political appointees adopt the positions and attitudes of their agencies and become primarily representatives of the agencies to the president rather than the reverse—a phenomenon known as "marrying the natives."

Presidential Control

Although presidents cannot control everything the bureaucracy does, they can indeed exert significant influence over it. Influencing the bureaucracy is by no means an easy job, however. It is a skill, and presidents who develop and use that skill effectively enjoy more success with the bureaucracy than those who do not. To do this, they must call on many of the powers of their office.

John F. Kennedy took primary control of foreign policy making by relying more on White House assistants than on the State Department. Lyndon B. Johnson used his budgetary powers to sway the military bureaucracy. Richard Nixon took advantage of reorganization and other management techniques to achieve some control over the welfare system. Jimmy Carter appointed like-minded people to help achieve his objective of deregulating numerous private sector industries.

But none of these presidents achieved the success that Ronald Reagan did in controlling the bureaucracy. Reagan was especially careful to appoint managers who shared his political ideology. He also used his staff and budget powers effectively. As a result, the federal bureaucracy began working for policies—items on Reagan's conservative agenda—that were radically different from those put forth by previous presidents. Reagan accomplished this feat by using constitutional and statutory powers that have been available to presidents for decades.

Bill Clinton followed Reagan's lead: to ensure that White House policies were faithfully executed, he demanded that cabinet secretaries seek administration approval before making any subcabinet appointments. Clinton had publicly decried the inefficiency of the federal bureaucracy during the 1992 campaign and promised, if elected, to "reinvent government." In 1993 Vice

President Al Gore was charged with the task and after six months of examinations released the National Performance Review, an initiative that sought to make the bureaucracy more efficient by injecting market forces into it. Among the objectives were cutting red tape, reducing spending, decentralizing authority, empowering employees, using incentives, and assessing outcomes. Gore claimed the plan, if enacted, would save more than $100 billion over a five-year period and cut some 252,000 federal jobs. Many of the initiatives have since been carried out and were particularly successful at the Agriculture Department. But critics felt that truly significant change would require a measure of congressional support. Yet members of Congress were likely to object to individual parts of the plan that would have an effect on them or their constituencies.

Congress generally approves presidential reorganization requests, but presidents make such requests infrequently. In the wake of the terrorist attacks of September 11, 2001, George W. Bush opted to ask Congress to create a new Department of Homeland Security (DHS). Congress authorized the creation of the department, its operations officially began in November 2002, and department status was conferred on January 24, 2003. Charged with the mission of securing the territory of the United States against terrorist attacks and responding to natural disasters, DHS is today the third largest federal department in terms of its number of personnel. The creation of DHS involved a massive reorganization of the federal bureaucracy as many agencies were transferred to its control, including the Coast Guard (formerly part of the Commerce Department), the Secret Service (formerly under Treasury), and the Federal Emergency Management Agency (once an independent agency).

> **More on this topic:**
>
> *Independent Executive Agencies*, p. 286
>
> *Independent Regulatory Agencies*, p. 287

Burr, Aaron

Source: Library of Congress

Aaron Burr (1756–1836) served as vice president during Thomas Jefferson's first term, from 1801 to 1805. He was the first vice president who was not eventually elected president in his own right. Burr was one of the most colorful and complex political figures of his era. While vice president he killed Alexander Hamilton in a duel and began to develop a treasonous plot to create a vast empire in western North America.

Burr graduated with honors from Princeton University in 1772. He began studying law but joined the continental army in 1775 after receiving a commission. He served until 1779, rising to the rank of lieutenant colonel.

Burr was admitted to the bar in 1782. After practicing law in New York City, he was elected to the New York legislature in 1784 as a Democratic-Republican. He was appointed the state's attorney general in 1789, and two years later he was elected to the U.S. Senate. Burr served in the Senate until 1797. His reputation for political intrigue and romantic affairs made him a controversial figure, but his intelligence, charm, and service to the Democratic-Republicans led to his nomination for vice president by that party in 1800.

Under the electoral procedure in effect through the 1800 election, the candidate who received the second highest number of electoral votes for president became vice president. Each elector voted for two candidates, with no distinction made between a vote for president and a vote for vice president. Although the parties named presidential and vice-presidential candidates, nothing prevented a vice-presidential candidate from being elected president if he received more electoral votes than his presidential running mate.

In the election of 1800 this voting procedure resulted in a tie between the Democratic-Republican Party's presidential candidate, Thomas Jefferson, and his vice-presidential running mate, Burr. Both men received seventy-three electoral votes, and the ambitious Burr refused to concede the election. The responsibility for selecting a president then fell to the House of Representatives, where the Federalist Party had a majority. After a week and thirty-six ballots, the weary representatives elected Jefferson president. (The confusion of the 1800 election led to the Twelfth Amendment to the Constitution, ratified in 1804, which separated the voting for president and vice president.)

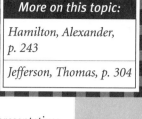

More on this topic:

Hamilton, Alexander, p. 243

Jefferson, Thomas, p. 304

Because of Alexander Hamilton's reputation as one of the most important framers of the U.S. Constitution and the unusual circumstance of a vice president killing a man while in office, Burr will always be remembered as the man who shot Hamilton in a duel on July 11, 1804, at Weehawken, New Jersey. Burr had challenged Hamilton for making negative remarks about him during the 1804 New York gubernatorial campaign, which Burr lost to Hamilton's candidate. After mortally wounding Hamilton, Burr fled south to avoid the warrants that had been issued for his arrest in New York and New Jersey. Because federal law did not yet provide for the extradition of wanted criminals from the District of Columbia, Burr returned to the capital. Incredibly, he resumed his duties as presiding officer of the Senate as if nothing had happened.

Before he left office in 1805 Burr had begun working on a plot to incite a rebellion in the western regions of the United States, conquer Mexico, and then establish a vast western empire with New Orleans as its capital. While vice president he had asked the British for financial backing of the scheme. The British rejected his proposal, but Burr raised money through other means. He assembled a small force in the summer of 1806 and was preparing to move against Mexico when one of his partners, James Wilkinson, revealed the plot.

Burr was arrested and tried for treason in 1807, with Chief Justice John Marshall personally presiding over the case. President Jefferson urged that Burr be convicted. Despite evidence that Burr had planned the conspiracy, he was acquitted because he had not yet committed an overt act of treason.

After the trial Burr went to Europe to live. There he continued to seek means to gain a North American empire. He tried unsuccessfully to convince Napoleon to help him conquer Florida. In 1812 he gave up his plots and returned to New York City, where he spent the rest of his years practicing law.

Bush, Barbara

Barbara Pierce Bush (1925–) was born into a wealthy family in Rye, New York, on June 8, 1925. Her father was publisher of *McCall's* magazine. She attended school at prestigious Ashley Hall in South Carolina. Barbara met George H. W. Bush at a Christmas dance in 1942 and became engaged to him a year later. Their marriage was delayed, however, while George served in the U.S. Navy. In 1945 Barbara dropped out of school after two years at Smith College to marry him.

After George graduated from Yale University in 1948, the Bushes moved to Odessa, Texas, where he entered the oil business. Between 1946 and 1959 Barbara gave birth to six children, the oldest of whom, George

Source: The White House

More on this topic:

First Ladies, p. 219

W. Bush, became president of the United States in 2001. The second child, Robin, died of leukemia just before her fourth birthday.

After succeeding in oil, George became active in politics, serving as a member of Congress from Texas, U.S. ambassador to the United Nations, chairman of the Republican National Committee, U.S. representative to China, director of the Central Intelligence Agency, and finally vice president and president.

Barbara Bush was widely praised as one of the most effective and most popular contemporary first ladies. A strong believer in volunteerism, she donated much of her time to helping less fortunate people. Her primary charitable undertaking was combating illiteracy in the United States. And, in addition to her charitable work, Barbara Bush displayed a generous and unflappable style that made her a favorite of the press.

Bush, George H. W.

Source: The White House

After holding many top government positions and serving as vice president under Ronald Reagan for eight years, George Herbert Walker Bush (1924–) was elected president in 1988. He became the first sitting vice president to be elected president since Martin Van Buren in 1836.

Bush was born on June 12, 1924, in Milton, Massachusetts. His father, Prescott Bush, was a wealthy Wall Street banker who represented Connecticut in the U.S. Senate from 1952 to 1963. George graduated from Phillips Academy in Andover, Massachusetts, in 1942 and joined the navy, becoming the youngest bomber pilot in that branch of the service. On September 22, 1944, Bush was shot down near the Japanese-held island of Chichi Jima. He parachuted safely into the Pacific Ocean and after four hours was rescued by a submarine. He received the Distinguished Flying Cross.

After the war Bush enrolled in Yale University, where he majored in economics and was captain of the baseball team. He graduated Phi Beta Kappa in 1948. Bush then moved to Texas, where he gradually became successful in the oil business.

In 1964 Bush ran unsuccessfully for the Senate as a Republican against Democratic incumbent Ralph Yarborough. In 1966, when reapportionment gave Houston another House seat, Bush ran for it and won. He served on the Ways and Means Committee and became an outspoken supporter of Richard Nixon. Bush was reelected to the House in 1968 when Nixon captured the presidency. Two years later Bush followed Nixon's advice and abandoned his safe House seat to run for the Senate. He was defeated by conservative Democrat Lloyd M. Bentsen Jr., who was later the Democratic vice-presidential nominee in 1988 on the ticket opposing Bush.

After the 1970 election Nixon appointed Bush ambassador to the United Nations. When Nixon was reelected in 1972, he asked Bush to leave that post to take over as chair of the Republican National Committee. Bush served in that capacity during the difficult days of the Watergate affair. At first he vigorously defended President Nixon. In 1974, however, as the evidence against Nixon mounted, he privately expressed doubts about the president's innocence. On August 7, 1974, Bush joined other party leaders in asking Nixon to resign, which he did two days later.

When Vice President Gerald R. Ford succeeded to the presidency upon Nixon's resignation, Bush was a leading candidate to fill the vice-presidential vacancy. Bush wanted the job, but he was passed over in favor of Gov. Nelson A. Rockefeller of New York. Ford tried to make up the disappointment to Bush by offering him the ambassadorship to Britain or France. Instead, Bush chose the post of chief of the U.S. Liaison Office in the People's Republic of China.

In 1975 Ford called Bush back to the United States to become director of the Central Intelligence Agency (CIA). As CIA chief, Bush's primary goal was restoring the reputation of the agency, which had been damaged by revelations of its illegal and unauthorized activities during the 1970s.

After being replaced as CIA director when Democrat Jimmy Carter became president in 1977, Bush returned to Houston. On January 5, 1979, he declared his intention to seek the presidency. He campaigned full time during 1979 and established himself as the leading challenger to Republican front-runner Ronald Reagan when he won the Iowa caucuses on January 21, 1980. Reagan, however, prevailed in the primaries and secured the nomination.

Former president Ford declined Reagan's offer to be the vice-presidential nominee, and Reagan offered the nomination to Bush in an attempt to unify the party. Bush accepted, and the Republican ticket defeated President Jimmy Carter and Vice President Walter F. Mondale in a landslide.

Despite Bush's differences with Reagan during the campaign, as vice president he was extremely loyal to the president. Bush frequently made diplomatic trips overseas, visiting more than seventy countries during his vice presidency. Reagan and Bush won a second term in 1984 by easily defeating the Democratic ticket of Walter F. Mondale and Geraldine Ferraro.

During Reagan's second term Bush launched his campaign for the presidency and secured the nomination before the end of the primary season.

Bush faced Gov. Michael S. Dukakis of Massachusetts in the general election. Bush attacked his opponent for liberal policies that Bush said were out of touch with American sentiments, and he promised to continue Reagan's economic policies and diplomacy with the Soviet Union. Bush also pledged not to raise taxes. He overcame speculation about his role in the Reagan administration's IRAN-CONTRA AFFAIR and criticism of Dan Quayle, his vice-presidential choice, and defeated Dukakis. Bush won the election decisively in the Electoral College 426–111.

World events during the Bush administration were tailor-made for a president whose strong suit was foreign affairs. His presidency saw the dissolution of the Soviet Union and the end of the cold war. His biggest triumph came in the 1991 Persian Gulf War, when he marshaled congressional and allied support for driving Iraqi forces out of Kuwait. The overwhelming rout of the Iraqis was accomplished with comparatively few American casualties, and Bush's prestige as a world leader rose dramatically.

But by the time of his 1992 reelection campaign, domestic concerns were foremost on American minds. Bush already had lost considerable political capital when in 1990 he went back on his 1988 "no new taxes" pledge. And in 1992 the economy went into what even Bush called a "free fall," and there was not much the White House could do to revitalize either the economy or the president's political standing. Voters wanting change turned to Democrat Bill Clinton. Clinton won the presidency with 370 electoral votes, compared with 168 for Bush.

After Bush left office he made a triumphant trip to Kuwait in 1993 and was hailed as a liberator. Intelligence reports that Iraqi agents planned to assassinate the former president during the visit led President Clinton to launch a missile strike against Iraq shortly after the visit.

In 1994 two of George H. W. Bush's sons, George W. Bush and Jeb Bush, campaigned for the governorships in Texas and Florida, respectively. George beat incumbent Democrat Ann Richards, who had mocked his father's elitist background when she delivered the keynote address at the Democratic national convention in 1988. Jeb lost a close election but won in 1998.

More on this topic:

Iran-Contra Affair, p. 294

Perot, H. Ross, p. 400

Reagan, Ronald, p. 437

George W. Bush was reelected governor of Texas in 1998, but he resigned from that office two years later after defeating Vice President Al Gore for the presidency in the 2000 election. Bush thus became only the second son of a president to win the office (John Quincy Adams was the first).

Bush, George W.

George W. Bush
Source: The White House

George Walker Bush (1946–), the forty-third president, was born in New Haven, Connecticut, the eldest child of George H. W. Bush, who would later serve as the forty-first president, and Barbara Pierce Bush. The family eventually moved to Midland, Texas, where George attended public schools.

When the Bushes moved to Briarwood, a Houston suburb, young George was sent to Phillips Academy in Andover, Massachusetts. George was not an exceptional student, but he quickly became a popular figure at the exclusive all-male school, noted for his gregariousness and quick-witted (and sometimes sarcastic) nature. He would become the school's head cheerleader.

After graduation George attended Yale University, as his father, his father's three brothers, and his grandfather (by now a Yale trustee) had before him. At Yale he was tapped for the secretive Skull and Bones society and was elected president of the Delta Kappa Epsilon fraternity. Bush was arrested twice while an undergraduate, both times for fraternity-related pranks. He graduated in 1968, but in later years he would downplay his Ivy League roots.

While a senior at Yale, George had been accepted into the Texas National Guard. The move seemed likely to limit the chance that he would be sent to fight in the Vietnam War, and some critics have charged that Bush and other sons of prominent Texas families received preferential treatment from Guard leaders. George moved to Texas and spent his first summer there in basic training. He then began to learn to fly F-102 jets, becoming a pilot as his father had before him. His service hitch lasted two years.

After completing his military duty, Bush worked in Texas on his father's unsuccessful 1970 Senate bid and in Alabama on an unsuccessful GOP Senate race in 1972 before returning to school. He graduated in 1974 from Harvard Business School with a master's in business administration and returned to Midland to start an oil company, Arbusto Energy (later, Bush Exploration). His personal net worth at the time was about $50,000. Despite his less-than-successful experiences with oil-well drilling and a drastic fall-off in crude oil prices, Bush would leave Midland in the late 1980s with a net worth of more than $1 million.

In 1977 Bush married Laura Welch, a Midland native whom he had known briefly as a child. (They would have twin girls, Barbara and Jenna, in 1981.) A year after the wedding, breaking his promise to her that she would never have to make a political speech, Bush ran for Congress when the incumbent retired. In the general election Democrat Kent Hance played incessantly on Bush's elitist roots in the East and the fact that nearly half of Bush's campaign contributions had come from out of the district. Hance won the election 53 percent to 47 percent.

Bush left the oil business in 1986 when his failing company was acquired by a larger one. In 1987 Bush went to Washington and spent eighteen months immersed in his father's successful presidential campaign. He took little interest in policy questions and positions; rather, he served more as the family watchdog over the professional campaign staffers.

In 1989, with $600,000 he borrowed, Bush bought a 2 percent stake in the Texas Rangers baseball team from another old friend of his father and became the team's managing general partner.

Bush and his aides gradually built the team into a contender that won the American League's Western Division title in 1994, which was Bush's last year with the Rangers. He sold his share for some $15 million.

Early Political Career

When his father lost the 1992 presidential election to Bill Clinton, Bush decided to run on his own for the Texas governorship. With high name recognition for his work with the Texas Rangers, Bush was well placed to mount a challenge to Democratic incumbent Ann Richards, who had been elected in 1990. Bush campaigned on educational reform and school accountability, and he pulled an upset win in 1994, taking 53 percent of the vote to Richards's 46 percent.

Working with key Democratic legislative leaders, Bush succeeded in getting much of his program enacted into law. Among the measures were tort reform and a reworking of the state's welfare program, which limited the payment of benefits and mandated job training for recipients. He also pushed his education agenda, which included state-run testing of public school students and tougher accountability standards for education officials. Bush opposed gun control measures and during his first term signed into law a bill that allowed Texans to carry concealed weapons. He also sided with industry on environmental measures, even as pollution problems in some of the state's larger cities mounted.

Bush was easily reelected in 1998 with 68 percent of the vote, becoming the first Republican governor of Texas to be reelected to a second term.

Presidential Nomination and Campaign

Bush's generous margin of victory in the 1998 governor's race, high popularity ratings, and name recognition made him a leading contender for the 2000 Republican presidential nomination. Anti-Clinton sentiment among some Republicans was so strong that Bush quickly raised a record sum of about $70 million to finance his primary campaigns. He had to spend most of it fending off a strong challenge from maverick Republican John McCain, Arizona's senior senator. Bush was chosen the party's nominee at its Philadelphia convention in August.

The Texas Republican, who called himself a "compassionate conservative," chose Richard B. Cheney, a former representative from Wyoming and defense secretary during the presidential administration of his father, as his running mate.

Bush promised to propose a $1.3 trillion income tax cut if elected and said he favored a Social Security reform allowing private accounts. On the environment, he favored voluntary cleanups instead of action mandated by the Environmental Protection Agency. Most important for the party faithful and others disenchanted with the Clinton administration, he vowed that he and Cheney would restore "honor and decency" to the White House.

In the November election Bush and Cheney faced the Democratic ticket of Vice President Al Gore and Sen. Joseph Lieberman of Connecticut. The presidential vote was one of the closest in history. Florida's twenty-five electoral votes, which were the key to victory for both tickets, were hotly disputed over several weeks. After numerous legal challenges in state and federal courts, including the U.S. Supreme Court, over the legitimacy of Florida's final tally, Bush finally won Florida and the Electoral College vote. (See BUSH V. GORE.)

Presidency

After his inauguration on January 20, 2001, Bush faced a country split by the bitter election of 2000. He had to move quickly to staff his White House team because the disputed election took over a month to resolve, leaving him little transition time. But once in office, he succeeded in pushing through a $1.35 trillion tax cut and a bipartisan education reform bill.

Bush faced a crisis on September 11, 2001, when terrorists struck the United States. His popularity skyrocketed, from 51 percent before the attacks to an unprecedented 90 percent shortly after. Bush was credited with pulling the country together behind a new "war on terrorism." He and his foreign policy team quickly prosecuted a war in Afghanistan, installing new leadership in that country, and in late 2002 Bush won congressional and United Nations approval for the possible use of force against Saddam Hussein's regime in Iraq if it failed to destroy its weapons of mass destruction. Bush's success in the immediate aftermath of the September 11 attacks, and in building support for his wartime policies, led to electoral success for his party. In the 2002 midterm elections Bush campaigned hard for GOP congressional candidates and scored a triumph. The Republican Party won additional House seats and regained control of the closely divided Senate—an unusual midterm success for a sitting president's party.

Bush's determination to remove Hussein from power by any means necessary grew in early 2003, despite increasing international pressures to employ ongoing UN inspections and other means short of war. In March 2003 Bush ordered the invasion of Iraq, and on May 1, following the fall of the Hussein regime and surrender of the Iraqi army, Bush declared that major combat operations in Iraq had ended with the United States victorious.

Although Hussein was captured in December 2003, tried for various crimes as dictator, and hanged three years later, the United States was still occupying Iraq and struggling to maintain civil order when Bush faced reelection. In November 2004 Bush was able to keep the White House against a challenge by Massachusetts senator John Kerry, squeaking out 286 electoral votes, the lowest percentage of the Electoral College vote for an incumbent president since Woodrow Wilson won reelection in 1916 with 52.2 percent of the electoral votes cast.

George W. Bush's second term began with his assumption of a sweeping electoral mandate. One of his first priorities was a failed proposal to privatize Social Security. In the late summer of 2005, Bush faced one of the greatest natural disasters to affect the United States when Hurricane Katrina struck the Gulf Coast, almost devastating the city of New Orleans. Over one thousand persons lost their lives, and although the storm could not be blamed on the administration, television news networks devoted almost 24-hour coverage of what appeared to the nation to be an inadequate federal response to the storm-ravaged areas. Many Americans began to question the readiness of the Department of Homeland Security in responding to urban crises although it was formed for such a purpose.

More on this topic:
Hurricane Katrina, p. 270
Signing Statements, p. 463
Unitary Executive Theory, p. 524
War on Terrorism, p. 554

Bush's political fortunes took a turn for the worse when his party lost a significant number of seats in the 2006 midterm congressional elections after a year in which his job approval sank to and settled into the low 30s. Although the party of most two-term presidents usually loses seats in the second midterm election, the Republicans' preelection majorities were relatively narrow, and the Democrats were able to take control of both houses of Congress. The unpopularity of the war in Iraq and disapproval of Bush's war leadership contributed to the voters' rebuke. In 2007 Bush entered a political environment promising to veto congressional attempts to oversee management of the war and limit his administration's attempt to strengthen executive authority and unilateral presidential action.

Bush, Laura

Laura Welch (1946–) was born in Midland, Texas, in the center of the state's oil industry. The only child of Harold and Jenna Welch, she grew up in a stable, middle-class environment. Her father was a building contractor, and her mother kept his account books and maintained the household.

Source: The White House

Jenna Welch read to her daughter as soon as "she could open her eyes," instilling a lifelong passion for books and reading in her child.

She and her husband-to-be, George W. Bush, who also grew up in Midland, attended different elementary schools but had a nodding acquaintance when they were in the same seventh-grade class. She graduated from Southern Methodist University in Dallas with an education degree in 1968. Then for three years she taught in racially mixed public elementary schools in Dallas and Houston. At one point during her time in Houston she and her husband-to-be lived in the same apartment complex, but neither recalled seeing the other during their stay.

In 1973 Laura received a master's degree in library science from the University of Texas in Austin and soon found a position in Austin as an elementary school librarian. While on a trip home to Midland to see her family and friends in 1977, she and George became reacquainted after mutual friends invited both to a backyard cookout. George, following in his father's footsteps, was now in the oil business in Midland. He invited Laura out the next night for a game of miniature golf. Shortly thereafter he asked her to marry him, and they wed just months later, on November 6, 1977.

Before they married, George had promised Laura that she would never have to make a political speech. But the very next year he broke that vow when he asked her to help him campaign for Midland's congressional seat, a close race that he lost.

During their early marriage Laura tamed the frequently rambunctious George, setting some new standards for him in terms of neatness. She also was instrumental in getting her husband to give up drinking when he turned forty.

> **More on this topic:**
>
> *First Ladies, p. 219*

In 1981 Laura gave birth to twin daughters, named Barbara and Jenna after their paternal and maternal grandmothers, respectively.

In 1988 the couple moved to the Dallas area when George, after quitting the oil business, became the managing general partner and a minority owner of the Texas Rangers baseball team. With greater name recognition because of his father, who served as vice president under Ronald Reagan from 1981 to 1989 and as president from 1989 to 1993, and his own high visibility with the Rangers, George ran for governor of Texas and was elected in 1994.

During George's first term as governor, Laura put her teaching and librarian skills to public use, organizing the Texas Book Festival, a fund-raiser for the state's public libraries. She also worked with her mother-in-law on a family literacy program; the senior Mrs. Bush, during her years as first lady, had begun the Barbara Bush Foundation for Family Literacy.

During her husband's 2000 presidential campaign, Laura avoided making speeches about policy and instead concentrated on promoting literacy and education, her longtime interest. She disliked the limelight, yet made public appearances to push her causes. As first lady, Bush hosted national book festivals in the capital and met with literary figures at the White House.

Bush v. Gore

After the polls closed on election night 2000, Vice President Al Gore, a Democrat, clearly had defeated his Republican opponent, Texas governor George W. Bush, in the popular vote for presi-

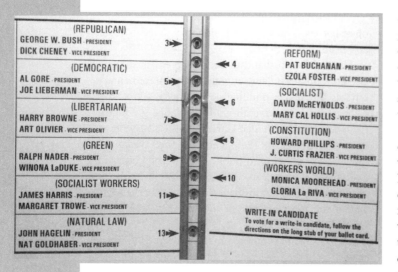

(REPUBLICAN)	
GEORGE W. BUSH · PRESIDENT	3▶
DICK CHENEY · VICE PRESIDENT	
(DEMOCRATIC)	
AL GORE · PRESIDENT	5▶
JOE LIEBERMAN · VICE PRESIDENT	
(LIBERTARIAN)	
HARRY BROWNE · PRESIDENT	7▶
ART OLIVIER · VICE PRESIDENT	
(GREEN)	
RALPH NADER · PRESIDENT	9▶
WINONA LaDUKE · VICE PRESIDENT	
(SOCIALIST WORKERS)	
JAMES HARRIS · PRESIDENT	11▶
MARGARET TROWE · VICE PRESIDENT	
(NATURAL LAW)	
JOHN HAGELIN · PRESIDENT	13▶
NAT GOLDHABER · VICE PRESIDENT	

◀4 (REFORM)
PAT BUCHANAN · PRESIDENT
EZOLA FOSTER · VICE PRESIDENT

◀6 (SOCIALIST)
DAVID McREYNOLDS · PRESIDENT
MARY CAL HOLLIS · VICE PRESIDENT

◀8 (CONSTITUTION)
HOWARD PHILLIPS · PRESIDENT
J. CURTIS FRAZIER · VICE PRESIDENT

◀10 (WORKERS WORLD)
MONICA MOOREHEAD · PRESIDENT
GLORIA La RIVA · VICE PRESIDENT

WRITE-IN CANDIDATE
To vote for a write-in candidate, follow the
directions on the long stub of your ballot card.

The "butterfly" ballot used in Palm Beach, Florida, confused some voters, who, intent on voting for Al Gore, punched out the second hole from the top, recording a vote instead for Reform Party candidate Patrick J. Buchanan (right-hand side). The confusion probably cost Gore votes—enough to swing the state, and thus the Electoral College majority, to George W. Bush.
Source: AP

dent. But neither Bush nor Gore had garnered enough electoral votes to claim victory. The outcome of the election would be determined by the twenty-five electoral votes of the state of Florida, whose popular vote tally was in dispute.

As required by Florida law in a close election, an automatic state-wide machine recount took place on November 10. It revealed a minuscule lead for Bush. Claiming that machines had failed to count all his votes and thus thwarted the will of the people, Gore called for a hand count in four counties that had voted strongly Democratic and that were controlled by Democratic election commissions. The core of Gore's legal challenge, supported by the state supreme court, was that Florida's voting machines, and therefore its official ballots, were flawed, especially in Democratic counties.

Meanwhile, Bush's lawyers appealed to the U.S. Supreme Court to stop the recount. They argued that the Florida court decision violated both the Constitution's provision that the state legislature must determine how a state's electors will be chosen and the 1887 Electoral Count Act's requirement (passed in the wake of the disputed 1876 Hayes-Tilden election) that electors be chosen according to state laws enacted by the legislature before election day. Bush's lawyers also claimed that the recount violated the Equal Protection Clause of the Fourteenth Amendment.

As he pursued legal channels, Bush was able to take comfort in knowing that the state legislature, which arguably had the power to appoint a slate of electors if all other approaches failed, was heavily Republican. Furthermore, the Republican governor of Florida was his brother Jeb, who was responsible for informing the National Archives and Records Administration which slate of electors had been chosen by the state.

On December 12 the Supreme Court ruled 7–2 in *Bush v. Gore* that the recount process ordered by the Florida supreme court, which required manual recounts of every undervote in Florida (that is, every ballot in the state for which a machine failed to register a vote for president), was unconstitutional. By failing to establish a standard by which counties across the state would judge the voters' intention, the Florida court had violated the Fourteenth Amendment's assurances of equal protection and due process of the law for all citizens.

In the second, decisive part of its ruling, the Court ruled 5–4 that the Florida court also had violated the Constitution in overruling the state's legislature, which had indicated its desire to take advantage of a federal law that insulates a state's electors from challenge so long as they are certified by December 12. The Court argued that "any recount" that would meet Fourteenth Amendment standards would frustrate the constitutional prerogative of the state legislature to determine how electors are chosen. Therefore, it reversed the judgment of the Supreme Court of Florida ordering the recount to proceed.

In a dissent, Justice John Paul Stevens decried the Court's majority for emphasizing the need to certify votes by December 12 instead of enforcing Florida's obligation to determine the intention of voters. In the interest of "finality," Stevens charged, "the majority effectively orders the disenfranchisement of an unknown number of voters whose ballots reveal their intent—and are therefore legal votes under state law—but were for some reason rejected by ballot-counting machines." The endorsement of that position, Stevens concluded, privileged the will of the state legislature over that of the voters.

As a result of the Court ruling the recount was halted and Gore conceded the election. Many of Gore's Democratic supporters criticized *Bush v. Gore,* calling the decision a crude power play by the Court's most reactionary members to make the Republican candidate president.

More on this topic:

Elections and Campaigns, p. 168

Electoral College, p. 185

Gore, Albert, Jr., p. 234

C

Cabinet

The cabinet is one of the most unusual institutions of the presidency. Although not mentioned in the Constitution or provided for by any law, it has become an institutionalized part of the presidency. The modern cabinet consists of the president, vice president, the heads (usually known as secretaries) of the executive departments, several officials who have been given cabinet rank, and any others the president might wish to invite.

Because the cabinet is solely a product of tradition and custom, presidents use it as they see fit. Cabinet members serve at the pleasure of the president and can be removed at any time. The president is also free to ignore recommendations made by the cabinet.

In theory, the cabinet meets regularly, debates major issues, and acts as the president's primary advisory group. The cabinet room's location just a few feet away from the Oval Office and its impressive view of the White House Rose Garden seem to affirm the cabinet's importance in forming national policy. But, in reality, it rarely works that way. The cabinet does carry out important political functions, but policy making usually is not one of them.

Cabinet's Role

Presidential attempts to use the cabinet as a meaningful decision- and policy-making body have almost always failed. Yet virtually every presidential candidate and president-elect pledges to give the cabinet real policy-making power in the new administration, and the public generally approves of that idea.

The failure of such attempts stems from a variety of reasons. First, presidents are rarely willing to delegate the decision-making power needed to make the cabinet an effective advisory board.

Many presidents feel that a strong, institutionalized cabinet with its own staff might be in a position to challenge their power. Most presidents want advice when they ask for it, but they want to reserve the right either to disregard it or not even to seek it. They also fear that a vigorous cabinet system might reduce their control of resources and information. Few presidents want to feel they are not in control of the flow of information in the White House.

Second, cabinet members often prefer to save their suggestions for private conversations with the president, in part because they are competing with the other cabinet members for the president's time and support and for funds, and in part because they would rather not air private or sensitive topics in a crowded cabinet meeting. Indeed, some department heads see cabinet meetings as nothing more than opportunities for their peers to take potshots at their departments' programs.

A third reason why the cabinet has no policy-making role is that presidents frequently have good reason to wonder where the ultimate loyalties of their cabinet members lie. The secretaries of state, defense, and Treasury, and the attorney general—a group that presidential scholar Thomas E. Cronin has called the "inner cabinet"—are usually chosen on the basis of personal friendships, loyalty, and views similar to those of the president. But many of the other secretaries in the so-called outer cabinet are selected more on the basis of geographic, ethnic, or political representation. Because they have weaker ties to the president, they often adopt an advocacy position for their departments. Such a development is not too surprising given that the secretaries spend much more time with their subordinates in the department and with interest group leaders than they do with the president. Self-interest also prompts secretaries to protect and expand the departments they head.

Presidents have tended to rely mainly on the advice of the inner cabinet, as well as their own staff. Since the establishment of the EXECUTIVE OFFICE OF THE PRESIDENT and the White House STAFF in 1939, the White House staff has threatened the cabinet's role as a policy-making institution. With their closer proximity to the Oval Office, White House staff members have more access to the president than do cabinet members. Moreover, these staff people often are longtime personal friends of the president.

The principal role of the cabinet is to give the president informal advice on matters brought before it. Because its members represent diverse groups, the cabinet is able to provide a broad spectrum of viewpoints, possibly including some not yet presented to the president. Yet cabinet discussions of issues that do not affect all the departments—and few issues do—can be a waste of time. Cronin quotes Richard Nixon, a veteran of many cabinet meetings, as remarking that the day had "long since passed when it was useful to take an hour and a half to have the Secretary of Defense and the Secretary of State discuss the Secretary of Transportation's new highway proposal."

The cabinet also plays an important symbolic role. The image of the president sitting down at the meeting table with the cabinet in attendance to ponder the important issues of the day is comforting. It symbolizes the president's commitment to listening to and consulting with representatives of the major social, economic, and political groups in American society.

Elevation of a government agency to the cabinet signifies the nation's commitment to that agency's goals. For example, the two new cabinet departments created during the Carter administration, Energy and Education, demonstrated Jimmy Carter's commitment to those issues. To show his high regard for the nation's veterans, Ronald Reagan supported the creation of a Department of Veterans Affairs. George W. Bush, after the September 11, 2001, terrorist attacks on the Pentagon and New York City's World Trade Center, worked with Congress in 2002 to approve a Department of Homeland Security.

Origins

The idea of some kind of advisory council for the president was discussed at the Constitutional Convention. Although advocates of a cabinet kept the idea alive throughout most of the convention, the concept failed to win enough support among the convention's delegates. The majority of the framers apparently feared that the presidency might become too overburdened with unnecessary advisory councils. Alexander Hamilton explained the framers' concerns in the *Federalist* No. 70: "A council to a magistrate, who is himself responsible for what he does, are generally nothing better than a clog upon his good intentions; are often the instruments and accomplices of his bad, and are almost always a cloak to his faults."

Consequently, all that remained of the idea when the Constitution was drafted was the authorization that the president "require the Opinion, in writing, of the principal Officer in each of the executive Departments, upon any Subject relating to the duties of their respective Offices" (Article II, Section 2).

When George Washington was inaugurated in 1789, he laid the foundation of the modern cabinet. Early in his administration, Washington took the view that department heads should be assistants to the president and not to Congress. Seeking both administrative and advisory help in his new administration, Washington asked Congress to create three executive departments to oversee, respectively, foreign affairs, military affairs, and fiscal concerns. Similar departments had existed under the Articles of Confederation.

For more than two months Congress debated the establishment of the three departments. The lawmakers' primary concern was the relationship of each department to Congress. The laws that were finally passed reflected members' preference for the foreign affairs and war departments to rest primarily under the control of the executive and for the Treasury to be more under the control of Congress.

Yet it did not turn out that way. As Washington's Treasury secretary, Hamilton greatly increased the prestige and independence of the cabinet. He assumed an office that Congress had intended as an extension of its own authority and made it a stronghold of executive power.

Washington initially had believed that the Senate would fill the role of an advisory council, but that hope faded in August 1790 when Washington went to the Senate floor to seek advice on an Indian treaty. The senators made it clear that they were uncomfortable meeting with the president and that they would not serve as an advisory council. As a result, Washington gradually began to rely on the advice of members of his own administration.

At first, Washington consulted with each individually. By 1792 he was holding frequent meetings with his secretaries of the Treasury, state, and war, and his attorney general (the Justice Department was not established until 1870). The next year James Madison applied the term *cabinet* to these conferences. The name stuck, and the cabinet became a permanent addition to the executive branch.

Like many presidents after him, Washington had hoped that his advisers would consult with one another and work together harmoniously. Early cabinet meetings, however, were marred by a growing rift between Hamilton and Secretary of State Thomas Jefferson, who detested each other and differed on important policy positions. After his experience with this cabinet and its successor, which was composed of men of cooler heads but lesser talents, Washington apparently abandoned his hopes of the cabinet serving as an advisory board. This disillusionment and uncertainty surrounding the proper role of the cabinet have afflicted almost every administration since Washington's.

President John Adams, in fact, was even more disillusioned with his cabinet than his predecessor had been. He had important differences of opinion with his department heads, and he found them more loyal to Hamilton, who had left government during Washington's presidency, than they were to him. Yet the formal cabinet remained Adams's principal official advisory unit.

Nineteenth Century

The cabinet gradually declined in importance in the first part of the nineteenth century. Few cabinets got along all that well, and few presidents relied on their cabinets as advisory groups. As the selection of cabinet members came to be dictated by political and geographic considerations, presidents increasingly appointed cabinet members they did not know personally and did not necessarily trust. Indeed, many times presidents had to struggle to maintain control over their cabinets. If a president failed to prepare an agenda for a cabinet meeting, the secretaries would take the initiative.

Andrew Jackson was the first president to largely ignore his cabinet. During his first two years in office he did not even meet with the cabinet, and he convened it only sixteen times during his entire eight years as president. Instead of the formality of his official cabinet, Jackson preferred the intimacy of his so-called KITCHEN CABINET, a group of close personal advisers, many of whom were newspapermen who kept him in touch with public opinion.

Abraham Lincoln appointed to his cabinet strong political leaders, many of them his political antagonists. Lincoln's strong leadership, however, allowed him to retain control of the cabinet and use it for his own ends. Indeed, as the story goes, when seeking advice on one critical decision, Lincoln polled his entire cabinet, only to be overwhelmingly outvoted. He then proclaimed: "Seven nays and one aye, the ayes have it."

During the latter part of the nineteenth century an attempt was made to move responsibility for the cabinet from the White House to Congress, thereby giving Congress considerable access to information on the executive branch. Legislation to allow department secretaries to occupy seats on the House floor was introduced and debated several times but was never voted into law.

Early in the twentieth century the cabinet grew in size but continued to play only a modest role as an advisory body. As the federal government became more complex and the power of the presidency began to expand, the size of the cabinet expanded as well.

In 1913, during Woodrow Wilson's administration, the cabinet swelled to ten members. Wilson, however, rarely met with his cabinet. During World War I Wilson relied instead on the advice of his Council of National Defense, composed of the secretaries of war, navy, interior, agriculture, commerce, and labor.

WASHINGTON AND HIS CABINET.

George Washington, elected in 1789, selected four cabinet members. Depicted by Currier & Ives in 1876 are, left to right, Washington, Secretary of War Henry Knox, Secretary of the Treasury Alexander Hamilton, Secretary of State Thomas Jefferson, and Attorney General Edmund Randolph.
Source: Library of Congress

Modern Cabinets

Under Franklin D. Roosevelt cabinet meetings continued to be more of a forum for discussion than a decision-making body. Roosevelt downplayed the importance of the cabinet and often intervened in the activities of his cabinet members.

President Harry S. Truman boasted of reviving the cabinet system, which he believed should be similar to a board of directors. He actually asked his cabinet to vote on some major issues, but toward

SIZE OF EXECUTIVE DEPARTMENTS, SELECTED YEARS

Executive department	Year established	Paid civilian employees 1980	2004
Agriculture	1889	126,139	112,071
Commerce[a]	1913	48,563	37,863
Defense[b]	1947	960,116	651,415
Education	1980	7,364	4,578
Energy	1977	21,557	15,021
Health and Human Services[c]	1980	155,662	63,413
Homeland Security	2002	n/a	162,294
Housing and Urban Development	1965	16,964	10,059
Interior	1849	77,357	77,557
Justice	1870	56,327	102,898
Labor	1913	23,400	15,807
State	1789	23,497	23,977
Transportation	1966	72,361	57,130
Treasury	1789	124,663	110,600
Veterans Affairs[d]	1989	228,285	236,180
TOTAL		1,942,255	1,680,863

SOURCE: Office of Personnel Management, "Federal Civilian Workforce Statistics. The Fact Book. 2005 Edition." Retrieved from www.opm.gov/feddata/factbook/2005/factbook2005.pdf.
a. Originally the Department of Commerce and Labor, established in 1903 and split in 1913.
b. Originally the Department of War, established in 1789.
c. Originally the Department of Health, Education, and Welfare, established in 1953.
d. Originally Veterans Administration.

the end of his administration he backed away from that approach and relied instead on an informal group of advisers. Throughout his administration Truman reserved the most difficult decisions for himself.

Dwight D. Eisenhower took his cabinet more seriously than most other twentieth-century presidents. He established a cabinet secretariat (one of the cabinet secretaries set the agenda and served as liaison with the president), and he charged his cabinet with advising him on major issues and seeing that every decision was carried out. He also expanded cabinet meetings to include important aides in his administration. Although vice presidents had served in cabinets since Franklin Roosevelt's first administration, Eisenhower was the first president to make effective use of his vice president in the cabinet. He made the vice president chairman of several cabinet committees and his acting chairman of the cabinet if he was unable to attend a meeting. Yet even under Eisenhower the cabinet functioned mainly as an advisory body and took no part in making final policy decisions.

Although he spent time with his department heads individually, John F. Kennedy held cabinet meetings as seldom as possible. Lyndon B. Johnson used his cabinet much more than Kennedy, but cabinet meetings were mostly for show and contained little in the way of substantive discussion. Johnson, in fact, used cabinet meetings to create the impression of consensus within his administration.

Richard Nixon announced his intention to use a cabinet system, but he held few cabinet meetings and relegated the cabinet to a position of lesser importance than that of most of his White House staff.

Both Gerald R. Ford and Jimmy Carter pledged to use their cabinets as decision-making bodies. Both held regular cabinet meetings at the beginning of their administrations, but only Ford came close to making his cabinet a meaningful advisory group. Convinced that the Watergate affair had resulted from Nixon's carelessness in allowing his personal aides to gain too much power at the expense of his cabinet, Ford restored the cabinet secretariat established by Eisenhower but abandoned by subsequent presidents. Like Eisenhower, he asked a cabinet secretary to draw up formal agendas for cabinet meetings, which often were used to gauge the views of his department heads on different issues. Carter, on the other hand, went from weekly cabinet meetings in his first year in office to only sporadic meetings in his last year. Major decisions were reserved for high-level White House staff.

Similarly, Ronald Reagan met less frequently with his cabinet as his term in office progressed. His administration was much more successful, however, in using the cabinet as an advisory group. Reagan divided the cabinet into councils dealing with specific areas so that its members could concentrate on matters of importance only to them and not to the cabinet as a whole.

When George H.W. Bush came into office, he put some of his oldest and most trusted friends in his cabinet and

President George W. Bush meets with his cabinet in the Cabinet Room of the White House, in April 2001. Bush is flanked by Secretary of State Colin L. Powell (left), Secretary of Defense Donald Rumsfeld, and Secretary of Commerce Donald Evans.
Source: AP

turned to well-respected figures in Washington for several other cabinet slots. He gave his cabinet a greater policy role than Reagan had done with his. But major policy decisions still were made by the president and a few senior advisers.

Bill Clinton selected a mix of old friends, political allies, members of Congress, and professional experts for his cabinet. But an overriding concern in the selection process was diversity—Clinton named more women and minorities to his cabinet than ever before. As in previous administrations, major policy decisions were made by Clinton and a few close advisers.

George W. Bush also chose a diverse cabinet, naming minorities and women to some key positions. After the September 11, 2001, terrorist attacks on the United States, some cabinet officials exerted institutional authority over foreign and domestic affairs, notably the Bush administration's first attorney general, John Ashcroft, whose public profile rose in the days following September 11, as did his mandate to investigate and prosecute potential terrorists living in the United States. Defense Secretary Donald Rumsfeld, who held the post through 2006, was also given a large amount of discretion to transform the military into a lighter, more mobile force geared toward responding to small intensity twenty-first-century conflicts.

Cabinet Members

By 2002 the number of cabinet departments had grown to fourteen: Agriculture, Commerce, Defense, Education, Energy, Health and Human Services, Housing and Urban Development, Interior, Justice, Labor, State, Transportation, Treasury, and Veterans Affairs. The new Department of Homeland Security was approved in late 2002, making it fifteen.

Other officers with cabinet rank in the Bush administration included the heads of the national drug program and the Office of Homeland Security (before it became a cabinet department). The vice president also participated in cabinet meetings, as well as other officials the president chose to invite to particular discussions.

More on this topic:

Appointment and Removal Power, p. 9

Executive Office of the President, p. 200

Kitchen Cabinet, p. 322

Staff, p. 471

Presidential appointments of cabinet department heads must be submitted to the Senate for majority confirmation. For some nominees Senate confirmation is gained easily, but for others it can be a long, grueling process. Nominees must prove to the Senate and the American public that they have the managerial skills necessary to administer a large public bureaucracy, as well as some knowledge of the subject area of their departments. The personal lives of appointees also are subject to scrutiny. Former Texas senator John Tower, President George H. W. Bush's nominee for secretary of defense in 1989, saw his nomination defeated on the Senate floor after allegations of drunkenness and other improprieties. (See AP-POINTMENT AND REMOVAL POWER; see the appendices for a complete list of cabinet members.)

Calhoun, John C.

John C. Calhoun.
Source: National Portrait Gallery, Smithsonian Institution

John Caldwell Calhoun (1782–1850) served as vice president under John Quincy Adams and Andrew Jackson from 1825 to 1832. Calhoun was an important player in many of the greatest political controversies of his era. He also was the first vice president to resign and the only incumbent vice president to run for reelection on a ticket opposing the president he had just served.

Calhoun was born into a family of wealthy South Carolina planters. He graduated from Yale University in 1804 and passed the South Carolina bar in 1807. The next year he won a seat in the state legislature, and in 1811 he was elected to the U.S. House of Representatives as a Jeffersonian Democratic-Republican.

During the War of 1812 Calhoun was a leader of the War Hawks, a group of expansionist members of Congress who had helped push the United States toward war with Britain. He served three terms in the House and chaired the Foreign Relations Committee. In 1817 President James Monroe appointed Calhoun secretary of war, a post that he held throughout Monroe's presidency.

In 1824 Calhoun maneuvered for the vice presidency, an office he hoped would lead to the presidency. He courted the two main candidates, Andrew Jackson and John Quincy Adams, and received the support of both men for his vice-presidential candidacy. Calhoun became vice president when Adams was elected president by the House of Representatives, since neither Adams nor Jackson had received a majority of electoral votes.

Relations between Calhoun and Adams quickly became strained. Calhoun shared few political goals with Adams, and as vice president Calhoun worked to foil many of the president's programs. By 1828 Calhoun's break with Adams was complete. The vice president threw his support behind Democratic presidential candidate Andrew Jackson, who in turn backed Calhoun's nomination for a second vice-presidential term. The Jackson-Calhoun ticket easily defeated Adams and Richard Rush.

Like Adams, Jackson soon became dissatisfied with his vice president. The split between the two men was first opened in early 1829 by the refusal of Calhoun's wife to accept the wife of Secretary of War John H. Eaton into Washington society. This was a small matter, however, compared with Calhoun's increasingly radical opinions on states' rights. During his early career Calhoun had been known as a nationalist. He had not only called for war with the British in 1812 but also supported the national bank, internal improvements, and a high tariff that many of his fellow southerners opposed. By 1827, however, Calhoun had begun to believe that the southern states needed protection from high tariffs and from the growing antislavery movement in the North. He wrote anonymously in support of nullification, a concept that allowed a state to nullify a federal law within its borders. Jackson rejected nullification as unconstitutional.

On April 13, 1830, at a Jefferson Day dinner, Jackson resolved to find out whether his vice president's first loyalties were to his country or to his state. The president stared directly at Calhoun as he delivered the toast: "Our Union—it must be preserved." When the vice president replied, "The Union, next to our liberties, most dear," he finally committed himself to South Carolina and the South.

In 1832 South Carolina declared that federal tariffs had no force in the state, triggering what was called the nullification crisis. However, South Carolina leaders agreed to a compromise tariff after Jackson threatened to send 200,000 troops to that state to enforce the law.

Two months before his term was to expire, Calhoun resigned the vice presidency in response to Jackson's actions and accepted an appointment to a vacant Senate seat from South Carolina. He remained in that office until 1844, when he resigned to become secretary of state during John Tyler's last year in office. He then returned to the Senate in 1845 and served there until his death in 1850. After leaving the vice presidency Calhoun made no efforts to conceal his southern partisanship. He was celebrated in the South for his advocacy of slavery and states' rights.

> **More on this topic:**
>
> *Jackson, Andrew, p. 300*

Camp David

Most modern presidents have had a favorite vacation spot far from the capital. But when presidents want to get away without going far, they have Camp David, a retreat only fifty miles northwest of Washington, D.C., in the Catoctin Mountains of Maryland. Since 1942, when the retreat was built for Franklin D. Roosevelt, presidents have gone off to Camp David for solitude, relaxation, and an opportunity to work in a peaceful atmosphere. Occasionally, the retreat has been the site of important diplomatic negotiations.

Camp David is perched on the highest point in Catoctin Mountain Park, a location recommended by Roosevelt's doctor for its altitude and cool temperatures. Nestled in a hardwood forest, it offers trails for

President George W. Bush receives a briefing in September 2001 at Camp David from, clockwise, CIA director George Tenet, Chief of Staff Andrew H. Card Jr., and national security adviser Condoleezza Rice.
Source: Reuters

hiking and creeks for trout fishing. Over the years the compound has been expanded and updated to include a well-appointed lodge for the president, guest cabins, a dining hall, conference rooms, and elaborate sports facilities. The amenities include a heated swimming pool, a bowling alley, archery and skeet ranges, riding stables, tennis courts, a small golf course, and a movie theater.

More on this topic:

Diplomatic Powers,
p. 149

Salary and Perquisites,
p. 453

Travel, p. 513

Most Americans were not aware of this mountain retreat, which Roosevelt named Shangri-La, until after his death. His successor, Harry S. Truman, did not use it much, but Dwight D. Eisenhower went often and convalesced there after he suffered a heart attack. Eisenhower renamed the compound Camp David after his grandson. John Kennedy preferred Cape Cod, but all of the presidents after him—with the exception of Bill Clinton, who suffered from allergies—used Camp David extensively.

At times presidents have used Camp David as a secluded spot in which to conduct sensitive negotiations with foreign dignitaries. In 1959 Eisenhower invited Soviet premier Nikita Khrushchev to Camp David for informal discussions on foreign affairs. These talks inspired the phrase "spirit of Camp David," connoting a serious intent to negotiate and compromise. Probably the most notable diplomatic negotiations ever to take place at Camp David came in September 1978, when President Jimmy Carter met with Egyptian president Anwar Sadat and Israeli prime minister Menachem Begin. This meeting produced the Camp David peace accords and led to Egypt's historic recognition of Israel's right to exist and the return of Israeli-occupied land to Egypt.

Campaign Debates

Debates between presidential contenders have become a mainstay of political campaigns, both in the fall campaigns and in the primary season, for presidential nominees and for vice-presidential nominees.

The first televised debate between the two parties' presidential nominees occurred during the 1960 campaign between Richard Nixon and John F. Kennedy. Nixon is widely considered to have lost the first debate to Kennedy, in part because of his poor makeup and haggard appearance.

Incumbent presidents and front-runners—before 1960 but more so afterward—resisted agreeing to debates because they feared they would give their opponents a boost in stature by appearing on the same stage with them. They also feared that a less than perfect performance might undermine their advantages in the polls or give opponents ammunition for the campaign trail.

In 1976, however, President Gerald R. Ford decided to challenge Jimmy Carter to a series of televised debates as part of a "no campaign" campaign strategy. Far behind in the polls, Ford was generally perceived to be a poor stump performer but well prepared for debates. Ford and his advisers calculated that he had little to lose and much to gain from his participation.

In 1960 Vice President Richard Nixon, right, is at the podium during the first televised presidential debate, while his opponent, Sen John F. Kennedy, left, takes notes. The moderator is in the center. Since 1976 televised debates have become a regular part of each presidential campaign.
Source: UPI/Bettmann Newsphotos

The outcome of the debates was mixed. Surveys taken immediately after the second debate indicated that viewers, by almost a two-to-one margin, thought that Ford had won. However, media attention to Ford's misstatement that Eastern Europe was not dominated by the Soviet Union dramatically reversed that opinion within three days.

In recent years front-runners have been obliged to take part in debates to avoid the charge that they are "hiding" from their opponents. President Ronald Reagan agreed to debate Democrat Walter F. Mondale in 1984 despite Reagan's huge leads in the polls. The chairs of the Democratic and Republican national committees secured commitments from their candidates to participate in debates the year before the 1988 campaign.

Although debates are a vehicle for the transmission of policy positions, viewers often seem to be more impressed by the style of the debaters than by their stands on the issues. Nixon's appearance in 1960 is a case in point. Likewise, Ronald Reagan won against Jimmy Carter in 1980 largely because of his style. He conveyed a warm image through his use of folksy anecdotes, his rejoinders to the president ("There you go again..."), and his answers, which were structured in easy-to-understand terms.

The importance of style was illustrated by the 1992 debates in which Republican George H.W. Bush, Democrat Bill Clinton, and independent candidate H. Ross Perot participated. There were three debates, each with different rules and format—each favoring one of the candidates' speaking styles. The inclusion of Perot in the 1992 debates worked to the detriment of President Bush, whose economic policies Perot continually attacked and whose tentative responses hurt his performance. Perot's attacks on Bush gave Democratic candidate Bill Clinton the chance to appear above the fray and focused on policy. Less formal debates on television talk shows also worked to Clinton's benefit. By 1996 Clinton had gained even more confidence as a debater and displayed a reassuring and competent image in his two debates with Republican candidate Robert J. Dole.

The 2000 campaign debates between Republican George W. Bush and Democrat Al Gore ended up helping Bush, although it was Gore who entered the series of three debates with a reputation as a skilled debater. Gore was criticized for appearing to change his demeanor from one debate to the next, and Bush, who had been trailing by about five percentage points in the polls, came out of them with about a five-point lead. In the weeks leading up to the debates the Bush team had downplayed the candidate's abilities as a debater, which allowed him to exceed expectations and helped him achieve positive results. The 2004 campaign also included a series of three debates, including one in the town-hall format in which citizens had the opportunity to ask questions. While most respondents to a Gallup poll after the first event felt Senator Kerry won the debate, similar polls conducted after the second and third debates indicated that voters were about evenly split on their perceptions of who ultimately prevailed.

The effect of debates is hard to measure, especially because—as in the 1976 Ford-Carter match—they are quickly followed by a barrage of media commentary and speculation over who won. Nevertheless, it appears that debates usually do not significantly alter voters' perceptions of the candidates.

Vice-Presidential Debates

The vice-presidential debates might have a greater, if longer-range, impact. Experts closely watch those debates because the vice president could become president by SUCCESSION, and also because the vice-presidential nominees could be future party leaders regardless of the election outcome.

Debates between vice-presidential nominees have occurred regularly since 1976 when Republican Robert Dole faced Democrat Walter Mondale. Both men were highly partisan, but some experts thought that Dole's acerbic style damaged the Republican ticket, perhaps enough to lose the close election. Republican Dan Quayle, George H.W. Bush's running mate in 1988, did not fare well against the rhetoric of Democratic senator Lloyd M. Bentsen Jr. When the youthful

TELEVISED PRESIDENTIAL DEBATES

Year	Democrat	Republican	Other	Date and Location
1960	John F. Kennedy	Richard Nixon		September 26, 1960, Chicago
	John F. Kennedy	Richard Nixon		October 7, 1960, Washington, D.C.
	John F. Kennedy	Richard Nixon		October 13, 1960, New York and Los Angeles
	John F. Kennedy	Richard Nixon		October 21, 1960, New York
1964	No debate			
1968	No debate			
1972	No debate			
1976	Jimmy Carter	Gerald R. Ford		September 23, 1976, Philadelphia
	Jimmy Carter	Gerald R. Ford		October 6, 1976, San Francisco
	Jimmy Carter	Gerald R. Ford		October 22, 1976, Williamsburg, Virginia
1980		Ronald Reagan	John Anderson (Independent)	September 21, 1980, Baltimore, Maryland
	Jimmy Carter	Ronald Reagan		October 28, 1980, Cleveland, Ohio
1984	Walter Mondale	Ronald Reagan		October 7, 1984, Louisville, Kentucky
	Walter Mondale	Ronald Reagan		October 21, 1984, Kansas City, Missouri
1988	Michael Dukakis	George H. W. Bush		September 25, 1988, Winston-Salem, North Carolina
	Michael Dukakis	George H. W. Bush		October 13, 1988, Los Angeles
1992	Bill Clinton	George H. W. Bush	H. Ross Perot (Independent)	October 11, 1992, St. Louis, Missouri
	Bill Clinton	George H. W. Bush	H. Ross Perot (Independent)	October 15, 1992, Richmond, Virginia
	Bill Clinton	George H. W. Bush	H. Ross Perot (Independent)	October 19, 1992, East Lansing, Michigan
1996	Bill Clinton	Bob Dole		October 6, 1996, Hartford, Connecticut
	Bill Clinton	Bob Dole		October 16, 1996, San Diego
2000	Al Gore	George W. Bush		October 3, 2000, Boston
	Al Gore	George W. Bush		October 11, 2000, Winston-Salem, North Carolina
	Al Gore	George W. Bush		October 17, 2000, St. Louis, Missouri
2004	John Kerry	George W. Bush		September 30, 2004, Coral Gables, Florida
	John Kerry	George W. Bush		October 8, 2004, St. Louis, Missouri
	John Kerry	George W. Bush		October 13, 2004, Tempe, Arizona

Quayle sought to compare his experience in Congress with that of John Kennedy, Bentsen flatly declared that Quayle was "no Jack Kennedy."

James Stockdale, independent candidate Perot's running mate, was included in the 1992 vice-presidential debate, but was often reduced to the role of bystander as Quayle and Al Gore bickered. In the 1996 debates Gore's strong familiarity with the issues sometimes made Jack Kemp look tentative and unprepared.

In the 2000 vice-presidential debate between Republican Richard B. Cheney and Democrat Joseph Lieberman, both candidates discussed the issues reasonably and amicably. But Cheney, a rusty campaigner, had more to gain in the minds of voters than did the better-known Lieberman, and the debate redounded to the benefit of the Bush-Cheney ticket. In 2004, while running for reelection, Vice President Cheney debated Democratic senator John Edwards in Cleveland in front of a television audience almost as large as that for the presidential debates. Cheney succeeded in enhancing his reputation as a possible commander-in-chief. A postelection poll by Survey USA showed that 47 percent of Americans felt Cheney was qualified to assume the presidency whereas only 25 percent had the same opinion of Edwards.

Prenomination Debates

Prenomination debates have become common since the number of presidential primary races increased in the 1970s. These debates may be the most useful in helping voters and political pundits sort out and get to know the candidates of each party. Especially in the early stages of a campaign, debates are important because they offer the only large event at which candidates can be judged.

Debates among party contenders have been prominent parts of every presidential campaign since 1980. Debates in Iowa and New Hampshire that year were considered crucial turning points in the Republican nomination process. Ronald Reagan became vulnerable in Iowa when he refused to debate his opponents; he fell from 50 percent to 26 percent in the opinion polls between December and the day after the January 5 debate.

Just weeks later, Reagan's posturing in the Nashua, New Hampshire, debate gave his campaign an important lift. Reagan invited other Republican candidates to join the one-on-one debate he had scheduled with George Bush. When Bush resisted the inclusion of the others and the debate moderator ordered Reagan's microphone cut off, Reagan declared angrily, "I paid for this microphone." The self-righteous declaration won applause for Reagan and made Bush appear stiff and uncompromising.

The 1984 Democratic debates first chipped away at former vice president Mondale's status as front-runner, then dealt a devastating blow to Gary Hart's candidacy. Mondale's mocking of Hart's "new ideas" campaign with an allusion to a popular television commercial ("Where's the beef?") left the Colorado senator on the defensive in a major Atlanta debate.

Republicans vying for their party's 2000 presidential nomination squared off in debates that often were seen as a battle between the two strongest candidates in the field: George W. Bush, the front-runner, and his dark-horse challenger, John McCain. The 2008 presidential election cycle is anticipated to produce some of the earliest prenomination debates in history. With more states opting to hold their primary elections earlier than ever, the first debate between Democratic candidates took place in Nevada in February 2007.

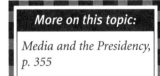

More on this topic:

Media and the Presidency, p. 355

Campaign Financing

Running for president is expensive and becoming more so by the campaign.

In the 2000 presidential race Republican candidate George W. Bush spent $187 million and Democrat Al Gore spent $120 million on their primary and general election campaigns. Nearly $354 million more was spent by other presidential hopefuls in 2000. And these totals do not begin to take into account the additional millions spent by political parties, corporations, labor unions, political actions committees, individuals, and other interested parties to influence the outcome of the presidential contest.

A system to publicly finance presidential elections was implemented in the 1970s to curtail the flow of money in presidential contests. But other avenues for outside money were soon discovered, and the cost of presidential elections continued to mount.

The influx of massive amounts of unregulated money—known as soft money—led to the enactment in 2002 of a new law to overhaul the system. The law was immediately challenged in the courts, and in the meantime outside interests went to work to find ways around it.

Mining magnate and financier Mark Hanna (standing at the far right between president and Mrs. McKinley) raised millions of dollars for McKinley's 1896 and 1900 campaigns. His fund-raising practices sparked the first major effort toward campaign finance reform.
Source: Library of Congress

Public Money

Concerns about the financing of elections are not a modern phenomenon. Wealthy donors have been playing a role in politics since long before the Civil War, and from the beginning citizens have debated whether that money strengthens or undermines democracy.

Campaign money traditionally comes from individual donors and interest groups. Ideally, they contribute to a particular candidate because they believe the candidate has the skill and experience to run the government and the values and political beliefs to lead the nation in a positive direction. Viewed this way, political contributions are an important way in which people can participate in political life.

But acceptance of campaign contributions can lead to charges that the candidate has promised something in return—support for the contributor's interests in a particular area. The links between contributions and the positions that candidates take on issues are usually indirect. Contributors say they only want their views on the issue to be heard. But few dispute that these contributors are buying access to decision makers that many other citizens will never have. Moreover, if the candidate rejects their views too often, contributors may abandon him or her—a prospect that candidates are not likely to forget.

In part to minimize the influence of wealthy donors and reduce this potential for corruption, Congress in 1971 provided for public funding of presidential general election campaigns. It also was hoped that the program would relieve candidates of some fund-raising burdens and level the playing field so that qualified candidates would not be shut out by the spiraling costs of campaigns. The plan gave each taxpayer the option of designating $1 of his or her annual federal income tax payment for a general campaign fund to be divided among eligible presidential candidates. Couples filing joint returns could designate $2. (The income tax "checkoff" is now up to $3 for an individual and $6 for a couple.)

Democrats, whose party was $9 million in debt after the 1968 presidential election, contended that the voluntary tax checkoff was needed to free presidential candidates from obligations to their wealthy campaign contributors. Republicans, whose party treasury was well stocked, charged that the plan was a device to rescue the Democratic Party from financial difficulty. President Richard Nixon reluctantly signed the measure but forced a change in the effective date of the fund from the 1972 election to 1976.

Then in 1974 Congress extended public funding for presidential campaigns to include not only general election campaigns but also prenomination contests and national nominating conventions. Eligible candidates seeking a party's presidential nomination would receive public funds matching their privately raised money within prescribed limits. Eligible candidates in a general election would each receive $20 million in public funding (to be adjusted for inflation each election). Eligible political parties would receive grants of $2 million (to be adjusted for inflation) to conduct their nominating conventions. The Supreme Court upheld these public financing provisions in its 1974 ruling in BUCKLEY V. VALEO.

The public funding program for primaries was designed specifically to encourage candidates to seek out numerous small contributions from individual donors. And in the general election campaign, if a candidate accepted public funding no outside contributions were permitted. But this attempt to put an end to the dominant role of wealthy donors—the so-called fat cats—would soon be circumvented.

In the late 1970s the campaign finance equation changed dramatically. First, the FEDERAL ELECTION COMMISSION (FEC), the agency charged with overseeing compliance with federal campaign finance laws, allowed state and local parties to use the so-called soft money that was not permitted under the law—in this case, corporate and labor union contributions—to pay for a portion of grass-roots and generic party activities, even if those activities indirectly aided federal candidates. Next, Congress passed a law encouraging greater participation of these parties in presidential election campaigns. It allowed them to spend unlimited amounts of regulated money, known as hard money, on things such as get-out-the vote drives and campaign materials.

The combination of these actions by the FEC and Congress triggered a surge in soft money. Once the national political parties determined that they, too, could use soft money for certain expenses, they began raising millions of dollars for their nonfederal accounts. Soon the money was being spent not only for get-out-the-vote drives and the like but also for major advertising campaigns, which the parties claimed were designed to promote party issues but which critics branded as thinly veiled political ads for or against specific federal candidates. The use of soft money for certain party expenses had the added advantage of freeing up more hard dollars for direct aid to federal candidates, further fueling the upward spiral of campaign spending.

By the 1990s soft money had inundated the campaign finance system. The national parties reported receiving $86 million in soft money in the 1992 election, $262 million in the 1996 election, and $495 million in the 2000 election. Not all of that money was raised or spent in the presidential races in those years, but enough of it was. Indeed, the fund-raising tactics of the Bill Clinton White House set off a major scandal and energized the movement to ban soft money from federal elections.

Money in Primaries

Contenders for a presidential nomination face a variety of challenges. They need to hire staff, buy ads, travel to key states, commission polls, pay for mailings—and they need to raise a lot of money if they hope to do all those things. If they are successful at fund-raising, they not only will have a better chance of getting their message out but also will have a more substantial image in the press and then attract more campaign contributors.

The eighteen candidates running in the 2000 primary campaign reported receipts of nearly $347 million and expenditures of more than $326 million. The biggest spender by far was George W. Bush, who set a record with his $89 million in expenditures. Bush opted not to participate in the public funding program during the primaries and therefore was not bound by the program's spending limits. The Texas governor took in more than $94 million in contributions.

To be eligible for federal money during the primary season, a candidate must raise $100,000 from individual contributors. At least $5,000 of that total must come from each of twenty states. Because only $250 of each contribution counts toward this threshold, there must be more than twenty individual donors in each of those states. This requirement encourages candidates to seek relatively small donations from many people rather than to appeal to a few wealthy contributors, and thereby show that they have broad popular support. Under the 1974 campaign finance law, individual contributors could give only $1,000 to a candidate's nomination drive. However, the 2002 campaign finance law raised the contribution level for individuals to $2,000.

In return for the matching funds, a candidate must agree to a total national spending limit, as well as state-by-state limits. A candidate also must agree to limit personal spending on the campaign to $50,000. For those who decline public funds, there are no limits. For example, publishing magnate Steve Forbes spent about $38 million of his own money on his unsuccessful 1996 prenomination campaign and then came back in 2000 and gave his primary campaign another $39 million. He was unsuccessful then, too.

Almost $62 million of the $347 million candidates took in during the 2000 primary campaign came from the federal matching fund program. Ten of the eighteen candidates participated. Taking into account postelection repayments, about $23.6 million in federal money was given to candidates meeting the eligibility requirements in 1976, $29.6 million in 1980, $35.6 million in 1984, $66.3 million in 1988, $42.6 million in 1992, and almost $58 million in 1996. In 2004 the sum was less than $30 million because George W. Bush did not face a renomination challenge.

To continue to be eligible for the federal matching funds, primary candidates must demonstrate their popularity with the voters. Matching funds are limited to candidates who receive at least 10 percent of the vote in two consecutive primaries. However, they can maintain their eligibility by notifying the FEC that they would like to exclude certain primaries from the 10 percent requirement.

This "threshold" has been a crucial factor contributing to the high dropout rate early in the primary season. Poor primary performance not only costs candidates the federal matching funds, but private contributions tend to dry up as well.

Since the federal matching fund program began, most presidential candidates have accepted public funding and the spending limits that come with it. Bush in 2000 became the first candidate to win a major-party nomination after refusing public funding for the primary campaign.

The major political parties now are entitled to receive $4 million, plus a cost-of-living adjustment, for their national presidential nominating conventions, up from the $2 million plus adjustment allowed in the original public funding law. A qualified minor party may receive funding based on its nominee's share of the popular vote in the previous presidential election.

The two major political parties each received $13.5 million and the Reform Party $2.5 million for their 2000 conventions. This was the first time a third party received public funds for its convention.

Party convention committees in theory cannot spend more than their public funding allotment. However, the FEC has permitted contributions and spending by a variety of other sources, which has added tens of millions to the conventions' final price tags.

Money in the General Campaign

The official campaigns of the major-party nominees for president are financed entirely by the federal government, if they choose to participate. Occasionally a minor-party candidate is eligible for partial public funding because of the party's total popular vote in the preceding election. A candidate of a new party may become eligible for public funds after the current election if he or she receives a certain percentage of the vote.

Major-party nominees who are eligible for public funding in the general election receive a grant of $20 million, plus the cost-of-living adjustment. The first campaign underwritten by public money was the 1976 race. In that year, both candidates were given $22 million. Because of inflation, funding rose to $29 million in 1980, $41 million in 1984, $46 million in 1988, $55.2 million in 1992, $60 million in 1996, $67.5 million in 2000, and $74.6 million in 2004.

Federal financing of presidential elections did not eliminate private interests from the election. Some of the money has been redirected to independent groups, such as POLITICAL ACTION COMMITTEES (PACs), which can spend unlimited amounts of money on favorite candidates, so long as they do not coordinate their actions with the candidate's campaign. In 2000 PACs reported $6 million in independent expenditures in the presidential race. Issue ad spending by certain political groups known as 527s (for the section of the tax code that governed their existence) and other nonprofits may also indirectly benefit a candidate.

But the real story was the soft money moving through the system. Through the use of soft money contributions to national party committees, big donors continued to be major players in presidential politics. By the 2000 presidential campaign, it was becoming commonplace for corporations, labor unions, and wealthy individuals to make donations of $100,000 or more to party soft money accounts.

In theory, presidential candidates no longer had to spend time raising money for their general election campaigns because of public funding. In reality, they were devoting more and more time and energy to raising funds for their parties' soft money accounts, which when spent on issue ads would indirectly benefit their campaigns along with congressional races.

The parties' enthusiasm for soft money in the 1996 election campaign helped to produce the most significant campaign finance scandal since Watergate. At the root of the scandal were allegations that foreign money—particularly Chinese—had made it into the campaign in violation of federal law and that the parties' pursuit and use of soft money may have crossed the line into illegal activity.

Much of the focus was on the Democrats. As the scandal unfolded it was revealed that the Democratic National Committee (DNC) had accepted nearly $3 million in illegal or suspect contributions, money the DNC said it would return. The fund-raising tactics of President Clinton and Vice President Gore were central to the scandal. The news media provided accounts of the Clintons entertaining large donors at private White House coffees and inviting some contributors to stay overnight in the Lincoln bedroom or to go along on government foreign trade missions. Gore was accused of making fund-raising calls from his office and attending a controversial fund-raiser at a Buddhist temple in California.

Hearings in the Senate and the House on the alleged campaign finance abuses occupied the center of Washington's political stage in the fall of 1997, but the Republican-led committees did little more than embarrass the Democrats for their fund-raising excesses. Investigators came up with no proof of allegations that the Chinese govern-

GENERAL ELECTION CAMPAIGN FINANCING

Year	Republicans	Democrats
1860	100,000	50,000
1864	125,000	50,000
1868	150,000	75,000
1872	250,000	50,000
1876	950,000	900,000
1880	1,100,000	355,000
1884	1,300,000	1,400,000
1888	1,350,000	855,000
1892	1,700,000	2,350,000
1896	3,350,000	675,000
1900	3,000,000	425,000
1904	2,096,000	700,000
1908	1,665,518	629,341
1912	1,071,549	1,134,848
1916	2,441,565	2,284,590
1920	5,417,501	1,470,371
1924	4,020,478	1,108,836
1928	6,256,111	5,342,350
1932	2,900,052	2,245,975
1936	8,892,972	5,194,741
1940	3,451,310	2,783,654
1944	2,828,652	2,169,077
1948	2,127,296	2,736,334
1952	6,608,623	5,032,926
1956	7,778,702	5,106,651
1960	10,128,000	9,797,000
1964	16,026,000	8,757,000
1968	25,402,000	11,594,000
1972	37,624,278	13,041,661
1976	21,820,000	21,820,000
1980	29,400,000	29,400,000
1984	40,400,000	40,400,000
1988	46,100,000	46,100,000
1992	55,200,000	55,200,000
1996	61,800,000	61,800,000
2000	67,560,000	67,560,000
2004	74,620,000	74,620,000

SOURCE: 1860–1996 data: Lynn Ragsdale, *Vital Statistics on the Presidency* (Washington, D.C.: CQ Press, 1998), 146; 2000–2004 data: compiled by Gerhard Peters (www.presidency.ucsb.edu/data/financing.php).

ment had conspired to influence U.S. elections through large campaign contributions or that the White House had knowingly accepted illegal foreign contributions or that the Clinton administration had ever changed policy in exchange for campaign contributions. And along the way, Democrats managed to reveal that a Republican National Committee (RNC) think tank also had accepted foreign money that may have been passed on to the RNC.

Several requests were made for the appointment of an independent counsel to look into alleged Clinton-Gore fund-raising abuses, but Democratic attorney general Janet Reno declined, stating that the allegations did not meet the standard for such an appointment. A Justice Department task force investigated other allegations of wrongdoing by various contributors and fund-raisers, most of whom were Democrats. The investigations resulted in some guilty pleas and convictions. The FEC later imposed civil penalties for some abuses in the 1996 election.

Campaign Finance Overhaul

Advocates of banning soft money hoped the 1996 scandal would galvanize support for reform measures, but an overhaul of the system was still a few years off. The House twice in the late 1990s passed legislation to restrict soft money and issue ads, but action on Senate proposals was stymied by filibusters.

One campaign finance loophole was closed in 2000, however, when a law was enacted to require disclosure of contributors to and spending by the growing number of Section 527 groups. Sen. John McCain, R-Ariz., a leader on this issue as well as broader campaign finance overhaul, had been targeted by a 527 group during his unsuccessful bid for the Republican presidential nomination in 2000. Two backers of Texas governor George W. Bush had formed a group called Republicans for Clean Air, which ran about $2.5 million worth of television ads attacking McCain's environmental record.

McCain had made campaign finance reform the centerpiece of his presidential campaign. Although he failed to win his party's nomination, he vowed to continue to battle on the Senate floor to change the system. The bill on the 527 groups was the opening skirmish.

The prominence of the issue in the presidential campaign, a realignment of the Senate and new support in that chamber, and public disgust with corporate scandals combined to push campaign finance reform legislation to the forefront and ultimately to final passage in 2002. McCain, along with Wisconsin Democrat Russell D. Feingold in the Senate, and Connecticut Republican Christopher Shays and Massachusetts Democrat Martin T. Meehan in the House, led the effort.

The new law—known as the Bipartisan Campaign Reform Act of 2002 or by the more popular name of McCain-Feingold—made changes in campaign finance law, but the most far-reaching provisions dealt with soft money and issue ads. The measure banned the national parties and federal candidates from raising and spending soft money. It also broadened the definition of issue ads to include any ad that referred to a specific federal candidate sixty days before a general election and thirty days before a primary. It barred the use of corporate or union money for such ads and required that the names of major backers of the ads be disclosed.

As soon as the law was signed, opponents went to court to challenge various provisions as an infringement of their First Amendment right to free speech. Led by then Senate majority whip Mitch McConnell (R-Ky.), the plaintiffs included a diverse set of interests ranging from the California Democratic Party to the National Rifle Association. In a 5–4 decision announced in December 2003, the Supreme Court eventually ruled in *McConnell v. F.E.C.* that most of the provisions of the law were constitutional. Many of the provisions upheld included limits on the use of state party funds in national elections and limits on hard money contributions.

Sponsors of the law soon were unhappy as well. They sharply attacked the FEC's regulations for implementing the law as weak and loophole-ridden. During the 2004 presidential election cycle, many of the campaign strategies financed by soft money were taken on by 527 groups, resulting in negative campaign ads outside the control of the candidates they were supposed to support. In 2004 this problem manifested itself in negative ads by the independent group "Swift Boat Veterans for Truth," which claimed Democratic nominee for president John Kerry's awards for valor in Vietnam were based on fabricated stories of his heroism. Other groups attacked President Bush's record as a stateside reservist during the war. Both the Bush and the Kerry campaigns publicly distanced themselves from these attacks claiming that 527 groups act independently of their campaigns. One highly visible effect of the new regulations is that in official campaign commercials, candidates now state, usually at the end of the advertisement, that they "support this message," implying that other commercials are sponsored by groups not officially affiliated with their campaign organizations.

Comparative Party Strength

When it comes to hard dollars, the Republican Party has had a distinct advantage over the Democrats. Since the FEC first began tracking political party finances in the mid-1970s, Republican national party committees have consistently raised and spent more federal money than their Democratic Party counterparts.

In the 2000 election cycle, for example, Democratic national party committees raised about $275 million and spent nearly $266 million in hard money. But the Republicans raised almost $466 million and spent $427 million.

The gap between the parties' fund-raising prowess, however, narrowed considerably when they got into the business of raising and spending unregulated soft money. Statistics since the 1992 election cycle, when the parties first began reporting their nonfederal activity to the FEC, indicate that the Democrats even managed to outspend the Republicans in one election. Democratic national party committees reported $50 million in soft money expenditures in the 1994 midterm election, compared with $48 million by the Republicans.

In the 2000 election Democrats took in about $245 million in soft money and spent nearly all of it. Republicans raised almost $250 million and spent close to $253 million. In the 1996 presidential election cycle Democrats took in nearly $124 million and spent about $122 million, while Republicans raised $138 million and spent almost $150 million. Yet the Democrats were at the center of the 1996 scandal, thanks to their aggressive tactics for raising soft money.

Because soft money gave them the opportunity at long last to compete with the Republicans in raising funds for their party, voting to ban it was not easy. Nevertheless, Democrats provided a majority of the votes for the 2002 campaign finance law.

Campaigns *See* ELECTIONS AND CAMPAIGNS.

Candidates *See* ELECTIONS AND CAMPAIGNS.

Carter, Jimmy

James Earl Carter Jr. (1924–) became president after he defeated several better-known Democrats for the 1976 presidential nomination and incumbent Republican president Gerald R. Ford in the general election. As an inexperienced, one-term governor from a southern state, Carter had been

---

CLOSER LOOK

Major-party nominees who are eligible for public funding in the general election receive a grant of $20 million, plus the cost-of-living adjustment. The first campaign underwritten by public money was the 1976 race. In that year both candidates were given $22 million. Because of inflation, funding rose to $29 million in 1980, $41 million in 1984, $46 million in 1988, $55.2 million in 1992, $60 million in 1996, $67.5 million in 2000, and $74.6 million in 2004.

More on this topic:

Buckley v. Valeo, *p. 36*

Federal Election Commission, p. 212

Political Action Committees (PACs), p. 405

a long shot for the presidency. The public liked his unpretentious image, but his popularity dwindled during the second half of his term as the nation suffered through economic troubles and the Iran hostage crisis. He lost his bid for reelection in 1980 to Ronald Reagan.

Carter was born on October 1, 1924, in Plains, Georgia. From childhood on, he preferred to be called Jimmy instead of James. His father was a storekeeper, farmer, and insurance broker who believed in segregation. His mother held more progressive views on social and racial issues. Carter graduated from the U.S. Naval Academy number 59 in his class of 820 in 1946. He married eighteen-year-old Rosalynn Smith on July 7 of that year.

In 1948 Carter was accepted for submarine duty. After two and a half years as a crew member on a submarine in the Pacific, he was selected to work in the navy's nuclear submarine program. He became an engineering officer on the *Sea Wolf,* a nuclear submarine under construction. After his father died in 1953, however, he decided to retire from the navy.

Carter returned to his home in Plains, where he successfully managed and expanded the family peanut farm. As Carter's wealth grew he became involved in local politics. In 1962 he ran for the Georgia senate as a Democrat. He lost the primary election but challenged the results because he had personally witnessed a ballot box being stuffed by a supporter of his opponent. His protest was upheld, and he became the Democratic nominee. He was elected and served two terms.

In 1970 Carter surprised political observers when he was elected governor. He openly denounced racial segregation and became a symbol of the "new South." He also reorganized the state government, supported measures to protect the environment, and opened government meetings to the public. Georgia law prohibited a governor from running for two consecutive terms, so Carter set his sights on the presidency. One month after leaving the Georgia statehouse he announced he was running for president.

Carter campaigned tirelessly during 1975 and 1976 and gained national attention by winning the Democratic caucuses in Iowa on January 19, 1976. When he won again in the New Hampshire primary on February 24, he suddenly became the Democratic front-runner. Before the June 1976 Democratic national convention in New York he had earned enough delegates to secure the nomination.

Carter emerged from the convention with a solid lead in public opinion polls over the Republican incumbent, Gerald Ford, whose candidacy suffered from several years of economic troubles and his pardon of former president Richard Nixon. This gap narrowed as the election approached, but Carter won 297–240 in the Electoral College.

One of Carter's early presidential goals was to make the presidency more responsive to the people. He conducted frequent press conferences, held public meetings in towns across the country, and projected a common-man image. Despite the president's open, informal style, he could not sustain his initial popularity.

In the late summer of 1977 investigators disclosed that Carter's budget director, Bert Lance, had engaged in questionable financial practices during his career as a banker before he joined the Carter administration. Carter defended Lance, who was a close friend, but on September 21, 1977, Lance resigned under the weight of the charges. He was acquitted of bank fraud charges in 1981, but the Lance affair appeared to contradict Carter's claim that he was holding his advisers to a higher ethical standard than that held by previous presidents.

The state of the economy did even more damage to Carter's presidency. During the 1976 campaign Carter had criticized President Ford for the high inflation and unemployment afflicting the country. Under Carter, however, the economy worsened. Prices and interest rates continued to rise, and the unemployment level was higher than most Americans would accept.

In foreign policy Carter achieved several notable successes. In 1978 he won Senate approval of treaties granting control of the Panama Canal to Panama as of December 31, 1999. He also mediated negotiations between Prime Minister Menachem Begin of Israel and President Anwar Sadat of Egypt. The talks produced the 1979 Camp David Accords, which established peace between those two countries. On January 1, 1979, he formalized relations with the People's Republic of China.

The last two years of Carter's term brought several foreign policy failures. On June 18, 1979, Carter and Soviet leader Leonid Brezhnev signed a treaty in Vienna to limit strategic nuclear weapons, but the Senate was hesitant to approve this agreement, known as SALT II. In 1980 Carter withdrew the SALT II treaty after the Soviet Union invaded Afghanistan. In response to the Soviet invasion, Carter imposed a grain embargo and refused to allow the U.S. team to participate in the 1980 Olympic Games in Moscow.

> *The threat is nearly invisible in ordinary ways. It is a crisis of confidence. It is a crisis that strikes at the very heart and soul and spirit of our national will. We can see this crisis in the growing doubt about the meaning of our own lives and in the loss of a unity of purpose for our Nation.*
>
> *Jimmy Carter, Address to the Nation on Energy and National Goals, July 15, 1979*

On November 4, 1979, Iranian militants stormed the U.S. embassy in Tehran, taking American embassy personnel as hostages. Carter's efforts to free the hostages—including a failed helicopter raid in April 1980 in which eight soldiers died—proved ineffective. The hostage crisis cast a shadow over the last year of Carter's presidency, and the hostages were not released until January 20, 1981, minutes after Carter had left office.

Despite these problems, Carter fought off a challenge for the 1980 Democratic presidential nomination from Sen. Edward M. Kennedy of Massachusetts. Carter's opponent in the general election was Ronald Reagan, the conservative former governor of California. Reagan defeated Carter 489–49 in the Electoral College, with Carter winning only six states and the District of Columbia.

After leaving the presidency, Carter returned to his home in Plains. He lectured and wrote about world affairs; monitored elections in several developing countries; established the Carter Center, located near Emory University in Atlanta, to be used to examine important public policy issues; and won praise for his efforts on behalf of several voluntary service programs. In 1994 Carter brokered an agreement in Haiti that restored the exiled president, Jean-Bertrand Aristide, to office and averted a full-scale invasion by U.S. troops. Since leaving office, Carter has risen steadily in the public's esteem; a Gallup poll found Americans give higher marks for Carter's conduct as a former president than for any other president's.

In 2002 Carter won the Nobel Peace Prize for his international peacemaking efforts, including his involvement in the Camp David agreement between Israel and Egypt, and his continuing focus on democracy and human rights.

More on this topic:

Former Presidents, p. 226

Libraries, p. 335

Carter, Rosalynn

Rosalynn Smith Carter (1927–) was born and grew up about three miles from Plains, Georgia, home of the man who would be her future husband. In sharp contrast to most modern first ladies, she openly participated in White House policy making.

Rosalynn was the valedictorian of her high school class. She attended Georgia Southwestern Junior College so that she could remain near home. She married Jimmy, who was a naval officer at the time, on July 7, 1946. They had four children.

Rosalynn Carter
Source: White House

In 1953 Jimmy's father died, and he resigned his commission to run the family peanut business. Rosalynn helped with the business and became active in local organizations. She overcame an acute fear of public speaking so that she could help Jimmy when he ran unsuccessfully for governor of Georgia in 1966, an office to which he was elected in 1970. When he decided to run for the presidency in 1976, Rosalynn set off separately to campaign for him.

Few first ladies have achieved the prominence that Rosalynn Carter attained between 1977 and 1981. Her activism and influence were frequently compared to those of First Lady Eleanor Roosevelt. In her first two years as first lady, Rosalynn made 248 speeches or public comments, gave 154 press interviews, attended 641 briefings, and visited 36 foreign countries. She fought for better treatment of the mentally ill and appeared before congressional subcommittees to put forward her views. Among the causes she took up were problems of the aged, refugee camps in Thailand, and equality for women. Rosalynn also traveled abroad on the president's behalf, most notably to Latin America in 1977. She frequently sat in on cabinet meetings and even participated in President Carter's Camp David negotiations between Egyptian president Anwar Sadat and Israeli prime minister Menachem Begin.

Burdened by an economic downturn and his failure to obtain the release of American diplomats being held hostage in Iran, Jimmy Carter was defeated in his bid for reelection in 1980. He and Rosalynn retired to Plains, where they wrote separate accounts of their years in the White House. Critics found her 1984 book, *First Lady from Plains,* a memoir of her White House years, to be more insightful in some ways than her husband's. In 1987 they also published *Everything to Gain,* a book on retirement. She also has written two other books, about care-giving and mental illness. The Carters' ongoing humanitarian and charitable efforts in support of causes such as low-income housing have been widely praised.

More on this topic:

First Ladies, p. 219

Central Intelligence Agency

Presidents serve as the commander in chief of the nation's armed forces, and they also serve as the commander of the numerous agencies involved in gathering and interpreting foreign intelligence and carrying out covert missions. These agencies are known collectively as the "intelligence community."

At the heart of the intelligence community is the Central Intelligence Agency (CIA), an independent agency established in 1947. The person chosen to fill the CIA directorship is scrutinized closely by the Senate, which must confirm the appointment.

The CIA is responsible for collecting and analyzing foreign intelligence information. The CIA also conducts covert activities abroad in support of U.S. foreign policy objectives. These actions are designed so that the role of the U.S. government is not apparent or acknowledged publicly.

Only the president can authorize covert actions. Usually covert operations involve spying on the activities of foreign governments or groups, but some operations are intended to aid foreign insurgent groups, destabilize unfriendly governments, encourage defections, spread disinformation, or achieve other goals. For example, it was reported in late 2002 that the George W. Bush administration had authorized the CIA to kill certain terrorist leaders if necessary.

The CIA has no law enforcement or security functions either at home or abroad. It is expressly prohibited from spying on U.S. citizens in the United States. This prohibition can be lifted only under extraordinary conditions of concern for the national welfare and only with the approval of the U.S. attorney general.

In addition to the CIA, the intelligence community consists of the National Security Agency, the Defense Intelligence Agency, the FEDERAL BUREAU OF INVESTIGATION (FBI), the intelligence units within the four military branches, and the State Department's Bureau of Intelligence and Research. The new HOMELAND SECURITY DEPARTMENT also plays a role in intelligence work. It works with the CIA, FBI, National Security Agency, Drug Enforcement Administration, Defense Department, and other sources to analyze intelligence. After the 9/11 Commission concluded that the CIA and FBI had failed to properly communicate with one another in sharing intelligence that may have prevented the September 11, 2001, terrorist attacks, steps were taken to overhaul the intelligence bureaucracies, including the CIA. The Intelligence Reform and Terrorism Prevention Act of 2004 was passed, creating an Office of the Director of National Intelligence (DNI), sometimes referred to as the "Intelligence Czar," who reports directly to the president. The director of the CIA now reports to the DNI.

Twentieth director of the Central Intelligence Agency, General Michael Hayden
Source: National Security Agency

Most foreign intelligence information is not gathered through spying by agents. Instead, it is collected by spy satellites that peer down on foreign countries and by electronic eavesdropping stations that listen in on foreign communications signals. Many professional employees of the CIA and other intelligence agencies are not engaged in gathering information, but in interpreting the large quantity of information that these technologies obtain.

The majority of foreign policy decisions, particularly those that involve the use of force, cannot be made wisely without access to intelligence information. For example, President John F. Kennedy decided to blockade Cuba during the Cuban missile crisis after he and his advisers had carefully analyzed all intelligence information. Similarly, President George H. W. Bush's decisions to send U.S. troops to Saudi Arabia in 1990 and to attack Iraqi forces occupying Kuwait in early 1991 were based in part on intelligence information collected by satellite photos, surveillance aircraft, electronic eavesdropping, and human sources.

The president's access to intelligence has provided a rationale for presidential primacy in foreign policy. Congress's recognition of this executive branch advantage contributed to its frequent willingness to accept presidential leadership in foreign affairs after World War II. Since the Vietnam War, however, Congress has more actively sought access to intelligence and has been more reluctant to accept presidential evaluations of international issues.

Several congressional investigations, especially the one headed by Democratic senator Frank P. Church of Idaho in 1975 and 1976, revealed that both the FBI and the CIA had illegally investigated

Americans (mostly anti–Vietnam War protesters) in the late 1960s and early 1970s at the behest of the Nixon administration. The investigations also revealed that the CIA had played a role in the overthrow of the popularly elected Allende regime in Chile. These activities raised fundamental questions about the misuse of the intelligence community.

In 1975 President Gerald R. Ford created a special commission to examine CIA activities. The commission found that the CIA had plotted to assassinate Fidel Castro of Cuba and other heads of governments who were deemed unfriendly. Based on the commission's findings, Ford directed the CIA to refrain from engaging in assassination plots.

In an attempt to curtail intelligence abuses, each house of Congress created a permanent Select Committee on Intelligence. These committees were designed to oversee the activities of the CIA and other intelligence agencies. In 1980 Congress passed the Accountability for Intelligence Activities Act. This law provided that the two intelligence committees would be the sole funnels for information about covert operations, and it required the committees to be fully informed of all intelligence activities.

In 1994, with the arrest of Aldrich Ames, a high-level CIA officer, for selling classified information to the Soviet Union and later to Russia—actions that compromised important intelligence operations and likely resulted in the assassinations of several U.S. double agents—the inadequacies of the agency's internal security measures were exposed, and Congress intervened. The Clinton administration argued that intelligence matters should be dealt with by the executive branch, but issued a directive incorporating many of the reforms being proposed in Congress. Despite this action, Congress passed a bill that overhauled the process of internal investigations, increased the level of external oversight, and called for a review of missions, procedures, and structure of the intelligence services in the post–cold war era.

CIA leaders also came under criticism for weak or nonexistent intelligence-gathering operations involving hostile governments and terrorist groups, particularly those operating in vital spheres of U.S. interest such as the Middle East and Central America. Although expensive technology such as spy satellites provided some useful information to CIA analysts, the lack of "human intelligence" resources on the ground in Iran, Iraq, Libya, Syria, and rogue states such as North Korea had left a gaping hole in the CIA's ability to present to America's leaders a coherent and complete analysis of developments in these volatile nations and any potential dangers to U.S. interests.

This hole took on greater significance in the aftermath of the terrorist attacks on the United States on September 11, 2001. The attacks prompted a much broader review of American spy agencies, specifically whether the CIA had adjusted from a cold war mentality to address the murkier danger of a stealth network of anti-American terrorists. Heeding the advice of several blue-ribbon presidential commissions, Congress in the months after the attacks sought to bolster the agency's ability to infiltrate terrorist groups, improve communications with other government agencies, and hire more linguists to decipher intercepted clues.

More on this topic:

Federal Bureau of Investigation, p. 211

Homeland Security Department, p. 260

Cheney, Richard B.

Richard Bruce Cheney (1941–), George W. Bush's vice president (2001–), was born in Lincoln, Nebraska. When he was thirteen, his father, a soil conservation agent for the federal government, moved the family to Casper, Wyoming. Cheney met his future wife, Lynne, at Natrona County High School, where he was senior class president and co-captain of the football team. He flunked out of Yale University as a sophomore because he "goofed off," he said. He eventually earned bachelor's and master's degrees in political science at the University of Wyoming.

Richard B. Cheney
Source: White House

While in a political science doctoral program at the University of Wisconsin at Madison, Cheney married Lynne. In 1968 he left Wisconsin without completing his doctoral dissertation to become a congressional fellow in the office of Wisconsin Republican William A. Steiger. Cheney's ideas about reorganizing the Office of Economic Opportunity (OEO) caught the eye of Donald H. Rumsfeld, then a Republican representative from Illinois. Rumsfeld later was President Gerald R. Ford's chief of staff, and he brought Cheney to the White House as his deputy. When Rumsfeld became Ford's defense secretary in 1975, Cheney, age thirty-four, took the chief of staff's job and was called a "boy wonder" by veteran Washington observers.

After Ford lost his bid to stay in the White House in 1976, Cheney returned to Wyoming and won its one at-large House seat in 1978. Early in the House race, he suffered a mild heart attack and was unable to campaign actively. His wife, Lynne—who later became the head of the National Endowment for the Humanities—took over the campaigning in the final weeks, and Cheney won with 59 percent of the vote. He would go on to serve five terms, despite suffering two more heart attacks (he later would have quadruple bypass surgery). He served in the Republican House leadership and eventually was elected House minority whip.

While in Congress, Cheney amassed a conservative voting record. He opposed the 1987 reauthorization of the Clean Water Act, the Endangered Species Act, funding for Head Start, and all gun control legislation. Despite his conservatism, though, Cheney made friends among his Democratic colleagues, who respected him as a scrupulous and ethical adversary with whom they could work.

In 1988 President George H. W. Bush tapped Cheney to become defense secretary. Cheney had little experience with defense issues, but he studied military matters diligently and ably managed the huge department during the U.S. invasion of Panama in 1989. Later Cheney was highly instrumental in ensuring American military success in the 1991 Persian Gulf War. With the end of the cold war, Cheney also orchestrated a stringent cut in the military budget. He frequently clashed with entrenched military and congressional interests on issues such as base closings and weapons systems.

Cheney briefly flirted with the idea of making his own presidential run in 1996 but decided against entering a race in which domestic policies, and not security matters, were the primary issues. Instead he joined the Halliburton company, a Texas-based international oil services and construction company, as chairman and chief executive.

When he resigned in 2000 to be on the ticket with George W. Bush, then governor of Texas, the $20 million or more in stock options that Halliburton granted him raised ethical questions about whether Cheney, if elected, could distance himself from the oil business. This perception also dogged Bush, who had strong ties to the industry. In 2002, amid a wave of corporate accounting scandals, the Securities and Exchange Commission investigated accounting practices at Halliburton while Cheney was chief executive officer.

In the 2000 presidential campaign many political observers noted that Cheney appeared to lend weight to the candidacy of the two-term governor who had never served in national office and lacked experience in foreign affairs. Laconic and unexciting as a speaker, Cheney was a well-seasoned Washington veteran whose long and varied experience as a leader in two branches of government was an invaluable asset to the ticket.

As vice president, Cheney had to answer many questions about his health, and in June 2001 he received a cardiac pacemaker after tests showed an occasional irregular heartbeat. In August 2002 Cheney declared himself fit for a second term if invited by President Bush. Bush said in November 2002 that he wanted Cheney on his ticket in the 2004 election.

Cheney was instrumental in the Bush administration, serving as a trusted adviser, chairing an energy task force, and traveling on important missions abroad. Cheney's energy task force became the center of a legal battle between Congress and the administration after congressional investigators demanded records from task force meetings.

After the September 11, 2001, terrorist attacks, Cheney often was described as being in an "undisclosed location" for security purposes, and he rarely appeared at events with Bush. Relying on his background as a former defense secretary, Cheney played an important advisory role in the Bush administration's war on terrorism, including the war in Iraq.

Cheney's second term as vice president was not short of controversy. In February 2006 Cheney accidentally shot a friend during a hunting trip in Texas. Although the vice president was cleared of any wrongdoing, Cheney was criticized for not reporting the incident sooner to President Bush or the media, creating a public relations problem for the administration.

A more serious scandal arose in 2005, developing from Cheney's intimate involvement in the Bush administration's Iraq policy. On October 28, 2005, the vice president's chief of staff Lewis "Scooter" Libby was indicted on charges related to false statements he is alleged to have made to a federal grand jury regarding how he knew about the identity of a covert CIA agent, Valerie Plame Wilson. Her identity had been exposed to the press, effectively ending her covert career. A Justice Department investigation was launched to determine who leaked the information. It was widely speculated that her identity was revealed to the press in an attempt to punish her husband, Ambassador Joe Wilson, for questioning the administration's rationale for going to war in Iraq. Questions have been raised regarding whether Cheney may have ordered the leaking of Plame's identity. Libby was found guilty on three counts in early 2007.

More on this topic:

Bush, George W., p. 54

Ford, Gerald R., p. 224

Vice President, p. 539

Chief of Staff

The chief of staff is the most important member of the White House STAFF, serving as manager, traffic controller, gatekeeper, adviser, and shield for the president. The chief is responsible for the smooth operation of the White House, which is no small task. Materials must be made available to the president in a timely manner, and the president's requests and directives must be acted on and implemented quickly. The swift and accurate flow of business is a primary goal.

As head gatekeeper to the president, the chief reviews all papers and visitors—and routes as many as possible around the president. This function provides chiefs of staff with a great deal of influence, because anyone wishing to bring an issue before the president must obtain their approval. Sherman Adams in the Eisenhower administration and H.R. Haldeman in the Nixon administration were very effective in this role.

Chief of Staff Josh Bolten is joined by outgoing chief of staff Andrew Card as Bolten is sworn-in by Deputy Chief of Staff Joe Hagin, right, Friday, April 14, 2006, in the Roosevelt Room of the White House.
Source: The White House

Although most chiefs of staff have denied a role in policy making, the position has acquired a policy function as well. Most chiefs have a close working relationship with the president, so it is only natural for the president to seek and heed their opinions. Hamilton Jordan, who served as Jimmy Carter's chief of staff, was an important policy adviser, as were James A. Baker III and Donald Regan to Ronald Reagan and John H. Sununu to George H. W. Bush. Sometimes, the chief also has to be a partisan defender of the administration; Leon Panetta and John Podesta tended to function that way for Bill Clinton.

Another important function of the chief is presidential hatchet wielder. All presidents have jobs that they would like to avoid. Many turn over to the chief of staff the difficult task of reprimanding or dismissing members of their administration.

Finally, the chief often shoulders the blame for the president. Performing unpleasant jobs such as dismissals, which may have political significance, and accepting responsibility for misstatements or other errors in fact made by the president are two types of cases in which the chief may act as presidential shield.

The role of the chief of staff has evolved over the years. President Harry S. Truman in 1946 created the position of assistant to the president to serve as a link with the domestic agencies and to resolve many of their problems and disputes. The position was a direct forerunner of the post of chief of staff. But Truman's choice for the job, John Roy Steelman, proved not very effective at shielding Truman from the everyday problems of his administration.

The position gained strength in the hands of Sherman Adams. Believing in hierarchy and not

CHIEFS OF STAFF, 1932–2006

President	Chief of staff	Years
F. Roosevelt	None	—
Truman	John R. Steelman[a]	1946–1952
Eisenhower	Sherman Adams[a]	1953–1958
	Wilton Persons[a]	1958–1961
Kennedy	None	—
L. Johnson	None	—
Nixon	H. R. Haldeman	1969–1973
	Alexander M. Haig Jr.	1973–1974
Ford	Donald H. Rumsfeld	1974–1975
	Richard B. Cheney	1975–1977
Carter	Hamilton Jordan	1979–1980
	Jack H. Watson Jr.	1980–1981
Reagan	James A. Baker III	1981–1985
	Donald T. Regan	1985–1987
	Howard H. Baker Jr.	1987–1988
	Kenneth Duberstein	1988–1989
G. H. W. Bush	John H. Sununu	1989–1991
	Samuel Skinner	1991–1992
	James A. Baker III	1992–1993
Clinton	Thomas F. McLarty III	1993–1994
	Leon Panetta	1994–1996
	Erskine Bowles	1997–1998
	John Podesta	1998–2001
G. W. Bush	Andrew H. Card Jr.	2001–2006
	Joshua B. Bolten	2006–

SOURCE: Michael Nelson, ed., *Congressional Quarterly's Guide to the Presidency,* 3d ed. (Washington, D.C.: CQ Press, 2002); updated by the author.
a. These aides carried the title of "assistant" rather than "chief of staff."

wanting to be bothered with unnecessary details, Eisenhower sought an aide to manage the White House much as the general's chief of staff had managed his headquarters staff in the army. As the president's gatekeeper and chief administrator, Adams possessed a degree of influence unprecedented for a member of the White House staff.

Neither the Kennedy nor the Johnson administration had a formal chief of staff, but the position was resurrected under President Richard Nixon. H. R. Haldeman was ruthlessly effective in the job.

In the wake of the Watergate affair Gerald R. Ford tried to downplay the role of chief of staff, and Jimmy Carter tried to eliminate it altogether. But when these presidents became overwhelmed with details and problems, each turned to a chief of staff. The position continued to gain influence under Ronald Reagan and George H. W. Bush.

Bill Clinton chose his boyhood friend Thomas F. "Mack" McLarty III as his first chief of staff. In contrast to his predecessors, McLarty operated more behind the scenes during Clinton's first year in office, serving as a valuable envoy and sounding board for the president and presiding over a loosely run, collegial-style White House.

More on this topic:

Executive Office of the President, p. 200

Staff, p. 471

But this relaxed style of management was blamed for much of the perceived confusion that seemed to dog the early days of the Clinton presidency. In 1994 Leon Panetta, the former budget director and acknowledged Washington insider, replaced McLarty. Panetta reinstituted the stronger chief of staff function and greatly tightened White House administration. At the start of Clinton's second term, with the staff functioning efficiently, Panetta resigned and North Carolina businessman Erskine Bowles took the job. John Podesta was Clinton's last chief of staff.

Andrew H. Card Jr., a veteran of the Reagan and George H. W. Bush administrations, served as George W. Bush's chief of staff from 2001 to 2006. After resigning, he was replaced by Joshua B. Bolten. In recent years, because of the increasing size of the White House Office, the chief of staff has had two deputy chiefs of staff. One oversees policy development and implementation and the other is in charge of operations.

Chief of State

Every government must have a chief of state who presides over ceremonial functions. In many countries this responsibility is fulfilled by a monarch with little government authority or by an official whose post was created to shelter the chief executive from ceremonial drudgery. In the United States, however, the president performs this task.

Like monarchs, U.S. presidents are the living symbol of the nation. They symbolize the country's history, liberty, and strength. Presidents can delegate ceremonial tasks to their representatives, but while they are in office they cannot escape their role as chief of state. At every moment they represent the United States at home and abroad.

As chief of state, presidents preside over an endless series of ceremonies that range in tone from the solemnity of the inauguration to the informality of a White House barbecue. They greet foreign ambassadors, dedicate monuments, pin medals on war heroes, buy Easter seals and Girl Scout cookies, visit schools, throw out the first ball on opening day of the baseball season, and hold state dinners for foreign chiefs of state. These and other ceremonies create shared symbols and emotional sentiments that comfort, motivate, and unify the American people.

Ceremonial Duties

The Constitution designates several ceremonial duties that presidents are obliged to perform. They are required to take an oath of office, periodically inform Congress of the state of the union, and receive "Ambassadors and other public Ministers." These constitutional ceremonial duties supported the assumption of the chief of state role by George Washington and his successors because they made the president appear as the leader of the entire nation.

Both the oath of office ceremony (inauguration) and the State of the Union address physically place the president out in front of other government officials and focus the nation's attention on the president's opinions and recommendations. In addition, the president's duty to receive ambassadors implies that foreign governments are to regard the president as the official representative of the United States. Given that the international community sees the president as chief of state, no one but the president could gracefully assume the domestic responsibilities of chief of state.

As chief of state the president also performs numerous functions that do not have their origins in the Constitution. Some of these activities have been established as annual events by a succession of presidents. A president who claimed to be too busy to light the national Christmas tree or congratulate the World Series baseball champions would waste valuable opportunities to score political points. Like the three ceremonial functions based on the Constitution, these informal activities emphasize the president's role as the leader of the nation; in addition, they serve to humanize the president and symbolically to bridge the gap between the president and the people.

As the nation's chief of state, the president serves as its ceremonial spokesperson. A presidential proclamation or dedication is a national stamp of approval for cultural events, national monuments, public works projects, charity drives, and special weeks and days. In accordance with their role as national spokesperson, presidents are expected to give out national awards and convey congratulations. Presidents routinely invite citizens to the White House, where they congratulate them on their accomplishments and present them with an award or memento of their visit.

Presidents also frequently lead the nation's observance of a holiday. In addition to lighting the national Christmas tree, they deliver a patriotic address on the Fourth of July and lay a wreath at the Tomb of the Unknowns on Memorial Day.

When a prominent American dies the president is expected to lead the nation in mourning. The White House issues state-

Since president William Howard Taft threw out the first baseball of the 1910 major league season in Washington, D.C., most presidents have observed the tradition.
Source: Library of Congress

ments eulogizing well-known Americans who have died. Presidential attendance at funerals, however, generally is reserved for those of former presidents, high government officials, or people who had a close personal or political relationship with the president. When presidents do attend funerals in the United States in their role as chief of state, they usually address the mourners. President Richard Nixon delivered the eulogy at former president Dwight D. Eisenhower's state funeral at the U.S. Capitol on March 30, 1969. President Bill Clinton delivered a eulogy at Nixon's funeral in California on April 27, 1994.

Presidents also must comment on the deaths of Americans who died while serving their country. Perhaps the most famous of all presidential speeches, Abraham Lincoln's Gettysburg Address, was delivered during the president's visit to the site of the great battle where thousands of Union and Confederate troops lost their lives.

Finally, presidents often honor Americans whose deaths capture the attention of the nation. President George W. Bush proclaimed September 14, 2001, a national day of "prayer and remembrance" for the victims of the September 11 terrorist attacks. He eulogized the dead at a nationally televised multifaith service held at Washington's National Cathedral.

Enhancement of Power

The ceremonial and symbolic aspects of the presidency appear less important than the responsibilities that come with the president's other powers. When presidents veto bills, sign treaties, nominate Supreme Court justices, issue pardons, or order military actions, it is obvious that they have exercised presidential power. As chief of state, however, the president acts neither as a commander nor as an administrator. The effects of ceremonial leadership are less observable. Consequently, the duties of chief of state are seldom described as a power and are sometimes denounced as a waste of the president's time.

Although the president's right to dedicate a monument or congratulate an astronaut may mean little, the symbolism of the role constitutes a real power because it enhances presidential authority and legitimizes and magnifies other presidential powers. As political scientist Clinton Rossiter explained, "No President can fail to realize that all his powers are invigorated, indeed are given a new dimension of authority, because he is the symbol of our sovereignty, continuity, and grandeur." The presidency, therefore, is elevated above other offices and institutions not just by its legal authority but also by its symbolic and historic mystique.

Effective government requires more than rational deliberation and action. Hearts are stirred and ranks are closed more easily by symbols than by reasoned arguments. Consequently, every government that hopes to provide effective leadership must provide symbols that unify, inspire, and reassure the people. The most powerful symbols are human symbols. In the United States the president, as chief of state, is the dominant political symbol for most Americans.

This symbolic stature enables presidents to exercise inspirational leadership from the stage of the White House. Americans want more from a leader than efficiency and honesty. They want a dramatic leader who can articulate their goals, motivate them, and even amuse them. Skillful presidents can use their symbolic assets to build the nation's morale and confidence and call on patriotic sentiments in a crisis. When, for example, a truck bomb exploded outside a federal building in Oklahoma City on April 19, 1995, killing 169 people and wounding hundreds more, fear of other terrorist acts virtually paralyzed the nation. President Bill Clinton's strong speech condemning the act and the political climate that he blamed for producing it helped to calm fears and reassure the nation of its safety and ultimate security. President George W. Bush, who, like President Clinton after the Oklahoma City bombing, played a reassuring role in the aftermath of the September 11, 2001, terrorist attacks, received the approval of 90 percent of Americans polled ten days after the attacks. That rating represented an amazing jump of thirty-nine percentage points over the rating he had held the week before the attacks.

Presidents benefit from occupying an office that is identified with the continuity of the United States and the stability of its political institutions. The American people see the president simultaneously as the current national leader and also as the latest in a long line of presidents who have guarded the freedom and laws of the United States. Consequently, when political rivals challenge the president they are in the uncomfortable position of confronting the defender of the Constitution and the heir of Washington, Jefferson, Lincoln, and the Roosevelts.

In the United States power has always been transferred peacefully from one president to the next. The unbroken chain of presidents has survived assassinations, civil war, impeachment proceedings, election fraud, and a presidential resignation. Even before the presidency faced any of these trials, its continuity impressed Martin Van Buren, who wrote, "The President under our system, like the king in a monarchy, never dies."

Role in Foreign Policy

As chief of state the president is the ceremonial representative of the United States before the international community. Presidents make ceremonial visits to foreign countries and greet foreign dignitaries who visit the United States. Whether presidents are receiving visitors in the White House or touring the world, they are expected to fulfill both their diplomatic and ceremonial responsibilities. When U.S. presidents visit Great Britain, for example, they usually have a ceremonial meeting with the reigning monarch and a policy meeting with the prime minister.

The international role of chief of state cannot be neatly separated from the president's role as the architect of U.S. foreign relations. State visits and other international ceremonies that the president undertakes as chief of state are tools of foreign policy. They are a means of communicating the intentions and attitudes of the administration and improving the relationships of the United States with foreign governments and peoples.

Partisan Politics

When a political system separates the role of chief of state from that of the chief executive, the chief of state can transcend partisanship. The British monarch takes no official position in the political struggles between British political parties. But such nonpartisanship is impossible for U.S. presidents, who must function as their PARTY LEADER as well as chief of state.

Although presidents may genuinely promote a nonpartisan atmosphere on some occasions, they frequently exploit their standing as chief of state for partisan purposes. Virtually everything the president does in public as chief of state has political significance. Given that the presidency itself is more consistently popular than any particular incumbent can hope to be, presidents benefit from activities as chief of state because these make them appear "presidential." Formal ceremonies, such as the State of the Union address or a state dinner for a foreign head of state, appeal to public patriotism and allow the president to stand forth as the nation's leader and guardian. They also underscore the president's links with the past glories of the office. Activities as chief of state can be staged to make presidents appear patriotic, amiable, concerned, skilled, and noble. Because such activities are built into the president's job description, the role allows presidents to campaign subtly throughout their term without having to appear overly political or self-serving. The dignity and status given presidents as the nation's symbolic leader increase their popularity with the American public and their bargaining advantages over other government officials.

Burdens of Chief of State

One of the justifications of the British monarchy offered by its contemporary proponents is that it shelters the prime minister from many ceremonial duties. Prime ministers can devote their time and energies to formulating policy and dealing with Parliament and foreign governments while the royal family presides at ceremonial functions and absorbs media and public attention. Presidents have no shield against ceremonial activities equivalent to the British monarchy. Although family members, vice presidents, cabinet secretaries, and other presidential associates can lighten the president's ceremonial burden, the president fills innumerable ceremonial functions. Between lobbying a member of Congress to support a bill and meeting with the National Security Council to discuss an international situation, the president may have to pause to greet Olympic athletes or officials of the United Way. The president's duties as chief of state may interrupt or even interfere with the president's duties as chief executive.

Calvin Coolidge, who as president refused to overcrowd his schedule, warned:

> The duties of the Presidency are exceedingly heavy. The responsibilities are overwhelming. But it is my opinion that a man of ordinary strength can carry them if he will confine himself very strictly to a performance of the duties that are imposed upon him by the Constitution and the law. If he permits himself to be engaged in all kinds of outside enterprises, in furnishing entertainment and amusement to great numbers of public gatherings, undertaking to be the source of inspiration for every worthy public movement, for all of which he will be earnestly besought with the inference that unless he responds civilization will break down and the sole responsibility will be on him, he will last in office about 90 days.

Few presidents, however, have been able or have wanted to limit their activities the way Coolidge did, and several have driven themselves to exhaustion.

Because the duties of chief of state increase the presidential workload, one may argue that they are an unnecessary burden. In addition to the drain on a president's time and energy, the role of

Source: Library of Congress

Performing their role as chief of state, presidents have been throwing out the ceremonial "first pitch" at professional baseball games for almost a century. William Howard Taft was the first to do so and has been followed by every president since. George H. W. Bush, who played baseball for Yale while in college, holds the record for a single-term president by throwing out the ball eight times in four years. Although he was a presidential candidate at the time, Franklin D. Roosevelt threw out the first pitch during the World Series at Wrigley Field in Chicago on October 1, 1932, the same game in which Babe Ruth famously "called his shot," by pointing to where he would hit a home run on the next pitch. More recently, in a show of support for New Yorkers reeling from the September 11 terrorist attacks, George W. Bush threw out the first pitch at Yankee Stadium prior to Game 3 of the 2001 World Series.

chief of state may make the president more vulnerable to assassination attempts and reinforce unreasonable public expectations of the president.

Dangers of Deference

Because presidents are partisan political leaders, they are routinely attacked by their political opponents and scrutinized by a combative press. Yet because they are the chief of state, the symbol of the unity and majesty of the United States, they also are treated with deference.

Presidents are provided with a mansion, guards, aircraft, and custom-made automobiles and are waited upon by a host of servants. They are addressed as "Mr. President" even by close friends they have known for many years. The strains of "Hail to the Chief" greet them when they enter the scene of an important occasion. Journalists constantly seek their thoughts on any subject, no matter how mundane or irrelevant to national policy. Despite the democratic origins of the presidency, the president enjoys the luxury and attention usually reserved for monarchs. (See SALARY AND PERQUISITES.)

The intoxicating effects of the deference given to presidents are reinforced by the historic significance of the presidency and the White House. Newly elected presidents become members of an extremely elite club. No matter how ordinary their political careers might have been, as soon as they take the oath of office they become major historical figures. They know historians will rate them on lists with Lincoln, Washington, and other immortal figures. Election to the presidency ensures that many books will be written about their lives. Presidential libraries will be constructed to hold their official papers, and when they die their graves will become national landmarks.

The mythic atmosphere surrounding the presidency may ennoble some presidents by imbuing them with a sense of destiny or historic duty. The royal trappings of the office, however, also can contribute to the development of an "imperial presidency"—one in which the president is insulated from the public, resistant to constructive criticism, and tolerant of almost any activity that furthers cherished policies or political goals.

In the Nixon administration the well-being of the president and the presidency were seen as more important than obedience to the law. The respect given to Nixon as chief of state and the privileges of the presidency, which he relished, undoubtedly enabled Nixon and his staff to justify more easily to themselves violations of the law and unethical political tactics.

In addition, if the deference shown presidents may cause them to believe they are always right and above criticism, meaningful debate on presidential policies may be squelched. Presidents who become overconfident of their own judgment may feel resentment toward staff members who disagree with their opinions.

The duties of the Presidency are exceedingly heavy. The responsibilities are overwhelming. But it is my opinion that a man of ordinary strength can carry them if he will confine himself very strictly to a performance of the duties that are imposed upon him by the Constitution and the law.

—Calvin Coolidge

Presidents accustomed to being treated like monarchs inside the White House grounds also may develop a deep resentment of criticism from outside the White House. Such a president may then rely exclusively on a small group of loyal advisers. Even if the president permits disagreement and frank discussion within this group, an isolated decision-making process will deprive the president of valuable sources of insight and information.

More on this topic:
Party Leader, p. 396
Salary and Perquisites, p. 453
Titles of the President and Vice President, p. 504

Civil Service

The way in which jobs are filled in the federal government has been a volatile issue throughout much of U.S. history. A merit-based system of employment has evolved in response to widespread criticism of the political favoritism that dominated federal hiring at one time.

In the nineteenth century most federal jobs were filled through PATRONAGE—that is, presidents awarded jobs to their supporters. In what was known as the spoils system—from the maxim "to the victor belong the spoils of the enemy"—jobs were seen as political rewards, a view that led to tremendous turnover in personnel after almost every presidential election.

The spoils system came under increasing attack after the Civil War, and support grew for some type of merit system that would make the federal government less susceptible to political manipulation. The assassination of President James A. Garfield in 1881 by a disappointed office-seeker was the final impetus for the creation of a merit-based civil service.

The Pendleton Act of 1883 provided for, among other things, creation of a bipartisan commission to help the president make rules for filling government positions. The commission was given two crucial powers—control of examinations and authority to investigate enforcement of its rules. The 1883 act served as the basis for the merit system, until it was modified by reform legislation in 1978.

In the beginning, only about 10 percent of all federal employees were covered by the merit system. From this small base the merit concept grew steadily, so that today about 90 percent of federal employees are covered by a merit system.

Civil Service Today

Most federal bureaucrats today work under one of several merit systems. These include the career civil service

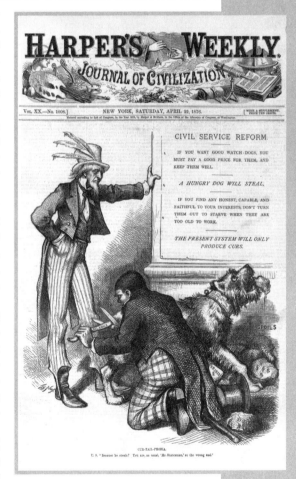

This 1876 cartoon by Thomas Nast shows "Mr. Statesman" cutting the tail off a hungry dog. The tail represents "salaries," and the dog, "the spoils system." Uncle Sam leans against a poster with civil service reform guidelines, which recommended better salaries and working conditions.
Source: Library of Congress

system, which is managed by the Office of Personnel Management (OPM); the excepted service, which does not come under the authority of OPM; and the Senior Executive Service, which is also outside of OPM. (See PERSONNEL MANAGEMENT, OFFICE OF.)

Competitive Civil Service

The career civil service system managed by OPM is the largest merit system, covering about three-fifths of federal employees. There were about 2.7 million civilian federal employees as of the early 2000s.

Each federal agency is responsible for classifying its own positions, but all agencies follow specific OPM guidelines. This standardization allows the civil service to maintain a coherent personnel system for most of the executive branch and to follow uniform procedures for recruitment, examination, and pay.

OPM ensures this uniformity by classifying positions for most of the civil service within what is called the General Schedule (GS). Positions are ranked according to their difficulty and are assigned a specific GS grade running from GS-1, the lowest, to GS-15, the highest. OPM also administers the Wage Grade schedule for blue-collar positions.

OPM acts as a recruiting agency for the federal BUREAUCRACY. Its primary tools for recruitment are the federal job information centers located throughout the country to provide information and application forms to anyone seeking federal employment. The centers also send out information about federal jobs to college and university placement offices. When a job opens up in a federal agency, OPM applies the "rule of three" and refers a list of three eligible candidates to the agency, which must hire someone from that list.

OPM administers competitive examinations and approves selection criteria formulated by other agencies covered by OPM policies. Most examinations are written and are designed to measure both aptitude and competence. Occasionally consideration is given to education and experience, which sometimes substitute for test taking. OPM also uses a veterans' preference system, which provides veterans with additional points on their examination scores. Another part of the examination process is a personal investigation conducted by OPM into the applicant's reputation, character, and loyalty to the United States.

About half of all federal government workers are under the General Schedule for white-collar positions. They are paid according to their grade, or level, within the schedule. Each October the president may change the pay rate, corresponding to rate changes in the private sector for comparable jobs. Workers who fall under the Wage Grade schedule are paid the prevailing wage in their geographic location for their type of work.

Federal government employees at the GS-13, GS-14, or GS-15 level may be rewarded for meritorious service under the Merit Pay System. The amount of the salary increases for these grades depends entirely on performance appraisals, unlike employees at lower grades who advance through the salary grades on the basis of length of service and continued adequate performance.

Appeals of OPM personnel actions are heard and adjudicated by the Merit Systems Protection Board, an independent quasi-judicial agency composed of three members, no more than two of whom may be from the same political party. Cases may include removals, suspensions, demotions, denials of periodic pay raises, and merit system violations. In addition, the board has the authority to review rules and regulations issued by OPM to see if they meet merit system standards.

The board also protects employee rights and interests and enforces provisions of the law that forbid certain personnel practices, including reprisals against so-called whistle-blowers (civil servants who expose possible wrongdoing). Within the board the Office of Special Counsel investigates alleged personnel violations and recommends corrective action if there is evidence of a violation.

Separate Merit Systems

Some federal agencies have their own merit personnel systems, independent of OPM control. About 30 percent of federal employees work under these systems. Although the specific procedures of the separate systems vary from agency to agency, they were created for some of the same reasons: to make recruitment of professionals easier, to give the agency more freedom in hiring and firing than allowed under the civil service system, and to enable close screening and supervision of applicants and employees.

Separate systems also add credibility to the notion that employment in these agencies is a career rather than just a job. Agencies that operate their own personnel systems include the U.S. Postal Service (which has the largest system by far), Department of State (for foreign service officers), Federal Bureau of Investigation, Department of Veterans Affairs, and U.S. Public Health Service.

Excepted Service

Two categories of federal jobs, Schedule A and Schedule B, are excepted from competitive hiring and other merit-based procedures, but as a rule they are not political appointments. Schedules A and B apply to non-policy-making positions that cannot be filled using normal civil service system methods. The difference between the two schedules is that applicants for Schedule B jobs must take an exam, and those for Schedule A need not. Many Schedule A employees are lawyers. Treasury Department bank examiners, among others, fall under Schedule B.

Less than 3 percent of the excepted employees are appointed on a basis other than, or in addition to, merit. These include presidential appointments (such as cabinet members, judges, and ambassadors), Schedule C positions (policy-making positions), and noncareer executive assignments (high-ranking members of the civil service who are involved in high-level policy making, such as subcabinet positions). The Bush administration in 2002 opted to give bonuses to political appointees, an approach that the Clinton administration had discontinued.

Senior Executives

About eight thousand senior-level positions in the federal government, known as the Senior Executive Service (SES), also are outside OPM's competitive civil service. These positions were moved out of what had been the top three GS grades, GS-16 through GS-18, and into SES in 1978 in an effort to make top-level federal employees more productive and more responsive to the president's policy goals.

Incentives for SES officials include higher pay and eligibility for financial bonuses, but there are disadvantages as well. For example, SES employees have less job security than other federal employees and can be transferred comparatively easily.

Background

As political parties developed in the early days of the Republic, so too did partisan appointments to government jobs. It was soon the pattern for new presidents to replace some government employees with their own appointees.

One of the most outspoken early defenders of this spoils system was President Andrew Jackson. Although many people attribute the spoils system and its bleak consequences to Jackson, it is probably more accurate to say that Jackson's actions reflected his desire to democratize the U.S. public service rather than a lack of commitment to the merit system.

Although Jackson instituted a large-scale system of spoils, he in fact removed only a few more persons from office than his predecessors had. But his public advocacy of the system made it easier for later presidents to manipulate patronage to strengthen their political parties and gain congressional support for their programs.

The spoils system reached its peak during Abraham Lincoln's presidency. In an effort to consolidate the federal government behind his program and war effort, Lincoln made a more thorough house cleaning of federal employees than any president before him.

The problems and misbehavior of patronage appointees in the administrations of Andrew Johnson and Ulysses S. Grant focused attention on the spoils system, and civil service reform became a popular concern among legislators and critics.

Pendleton Act

Meaningful civil service reform came only after President James A. Garfield's assassination by Charles J. Guiteau, who had been turned down for a job in the Garfield administration and apparently thought he would fare better under Garfield's successor. Many newspapers ran editorials deploring Guiteau's actions and the spoils system in general.

The Civil Service Act of 1883, also known as the Pendleton Act for its main sponsor, Democratic senator George H. Pendleton of Ohio, created within the executive branch a bipartisan commission of three members, known as the Civil Service Commission, to help the president make rules for filling government positions. To ensure a certain amount of neutrality, not more than two members of the commission could be from the same political party. The act required that government employees be chosen "from among those graded highest" in competitive examinations. In addition, it prohibited assessments of federal employees for money to help party candidates.

The act did not immediately end the massive turnover of personnel at the beginning of each presidential administration. In fact, it initially affected only about fourteen thousand positions, or about 10.5 percent of federal employees. Under the provisions of the act, however, the president could issue an executive order extending the coverage to other appointees. As succeeding presidents exercised their option to extend merit coverage, almost all federal employees eventually came under a merit system.

Extension of Merit System

The Pendleton Act built on the tradition of egalitarianism and equal opportunity that prevailed during the early period of public employment. The authors of the act did not abandon the Jacksonian belief in widespread access to jobs in the federal government. Instead they provided for "practical" entrance tests that would ensure that the applicants would be able to do their jobs.

The merit system under the new Civil Service Commission experienced slow but steady growth, as reformers put pressure on presidents and Congress to bring as many federal employees as possible under the jurisdiction of the commission.

The Pendleton Act originally placed only clerical and technical employees under the protection of the civil service. As presidents increased the number of positions covered, they not only tended to place more clerical positions under the civil service but also to include more and more policy-making positions shortly before they left office. Because only new appointees had to take examinations, these presidents were able to "blanket in" their political appointees and ensure that agencies would be staffed with their supporters for some time to come.

1978 Reform Act

The Civil Service Reform Act of 1978 represented the most sweeping reform of the civil service since 1883. Recognizing the conflict between being both manager of civil servants and watchdog of the merit system, the act abolished the ninety-five-year-old Civil Service Commission. In its place the act set up the Office of Personnel Management and the Merit Systems Protection Board. The act also created the Senior Executive Service, a reform originally proposed by the Second Hoover Commission in 1955.

Hatch Act

The number of classified positions in the merit system soared to new heights during Franklin D. Roosevelt's administration. By 1948 nearly 84 percent of all civil service employees were in classified positions.

Roosevelt's extension of merit had a twofold purpose: he attempted to increase the efficient administration of his New Deal programs by putting a large number of positions in the protected category, and by doing so he also intentionally blanketed in thousands of Democrats who were in patronage jobs.

As Roosevelt's Democrats were blanketed in, many reformers began to be concerned that the principle of political neutrality would be violated. Because the majority of those who worked in federal agencies owed their jobs to President Roosevelt and the Democratic Party, it seemed normal for them to campaign for the Democratic Party.

In the election of 1938, however, a coalition of Republicans and conservative Democrats seized control of Congress and passed the Political Activities Act of 1939, known as the Hatch Act for coalition leader Carl Hatch, a Democratic senator from New Mexico.

The original Hatch Act prohibited federal workers from taking an active role in the political management of campaigns. Federal workers could vote, attend political rallies, and talk privately about politics. But they were prohibited from participating in partisan voter registration drives, endorsing candidates, or working for or against a candidate in any way. In addition, the Hatch Act made illegal the use of rank to force federal employees to support certain candidates or to make political contributions.

The courts resisted attempts to weaken the Hatch Act, reaffirming the desire to have a nonpartisan federal civil service. Attempts by Congress to lift some of the restrictions on government employees were vetoed by Presidents Gerald R. Ford and George H. W. Bush. But in 1993, with President Bill Clinton's backing, a law was enacted to tighten on-the-job restrictions and ease off-duty limits on most federal and postal employees. Most could now hold office in a political party, participate in political campaigns and rallies, publicly endorse candidates, and raise political funds from within their agency's political action committee. But they were barred from soliciting such funds from the general public or running for partisan elective offices.

> **More on this topic:**
>
> *Bureaucracy, p. 44*
>
> *Patronage, p. 398*
>
> *Personnel Management, Office of, p. 403*

Civil War

The Civil War (1861–1865) between the North and the South was the major event of nineteenth-century U.S. history. More than 600,000 soldiers were killed and almost 400,000 were wounded during the four years of fighting. The war resulted in the abolition of slavery and the preservation of the Union. It also brought a vast expansion of presidential power.

Road to Conflict

For several decades tensions had flared between the northern states, where slavery was prohibited, and the southern states, where it was part of the social and economic fabric of life. Abolitionists in the North called for an end to slavery, while southern politicians resisted federal intrusions into the affairs of their states. The admission of new states into the Union was a particularly contentious issue. Both regions feared that the entry of new states with slavery laws the opposite of their own would alter the balance of political power between the two regions. As a result, compromises were constructed in 1820 and 1850 that attempted to balance the competing interests of the two regions as states were admitted to the Union.

Matthew Brady photographed Union general Ulysses S. Grant in April 1865. Because of Grant's spectacular war record, he was idolized by the American people, who elected him president in 1868.
Source: National Portrait Gallery

Despite efforts by many leaders to resolve the interregional dispute over slavery and states' rights, by the 1850s southern leaders frequently talked of secession—leaving the Union. Such a step was likely to lead to war between the North and the South.

The election of Abraham Lincoln as president in 1860 sparked the secession crisis that had been threatening the nation. Lincoln's Republican Party opposed any further extension of slavery. Despite his assertion that he would not "interfere with the institution of slavery where it already exists," he was the first president whom the supporters of slavery viewed as a serious threat to their cause. Lincoln won only 39 percent of the popular vote, but he won eighteen northern states accounting for 180 out of the total 303 electoral votes.

On December 20, 1860, South Carolina seceded. Within months a total of eleven slave states had seceded. These states formed the Confederate States of America and elected Jefferson Davis president. Reconciliation proposals failed as both sides prepared for war.

Lincoln's War Powers

President Lincoln's extraordinary exercise of WAR POWERS during the Civil War demonstrated how far the authority of the presidency could be expanded in wartime. Lincoln believed he faced a choice between preserving the Union and adhering to a strict interpretation of the Constitution. He feared that if he carefully observed the law he would not be able to prevent the destruction of the nation. In April 1864 he explained his reasoning in a letter to his friend Albert Hodges:

> Was it possible to lose the nation and yet preserve the Constitution? By general law, life and limb must be protected, yet often a limb must be amputated to save a life; but a life is never wisely given to save a limb. I felt that measures otherwise unconstitutional might become lawful by becoming indispensable to the preservation of the nation. Right or wrong, I assumed this ground and now avow it.

On April 12, 1861, the Civil War began when Confederate forces attacked the Union garrison at Fort Sumter in South Carolina. Recognizing that Congress might object to emergency measures he thought necessary to deal with the crisis, Lincoln delayed the convocation of Congress until July 4. He used this three-month period to order a series of executive actions to meet the military emergency.

On May 3, 1861, he called for the mobilization of 75,000 state militia members who were subject to his orders. Although this step was considered within the powers of the president, most of Lincoln's actions during the early months of the war had no constitutional or congressional sanction. He increased the size of the regular army and navy, ordered nineteen vessels added to the navy, and directed the secretary of the Treasury to advance $2 million to authorized persons to pay for military requisitions. Lincoln also ordered a blockade of southern ports, suspended the writ of

habeas corpus (the constitutional guarantee against illegal detention and imprisonment) in some areas, restricted "treasonable correspondence" from being carried by the Post Office, and directed the military to arrest and detain persons "who were represented to him" as contemplating or participating in "treasonable practices."

When Congress finally convened on July 4, Lincoln asked the members to ratify the actions he had taken in their absence. During the summer Congress debated a joint resolution that sanctioned Lincoln's acts. Nagging doubts about the legality of his suspension of habeas corpus and blockade of ports prevented a vote. Near the end of the session, however, Congress approved the president's emergency measures.

Throughout the war Lincoln continued to expand his power as commander in chief beyond its constitutional limits. In 1862 Lincoln ordered a militia draft. The same year he extended his suspension of the writ of habeas corpus to persons throughout the entire nation who were "guilty of any disloyal practice." He also declared that these persons could be tried by military courts. On January 1, 1863, Lincoln issued the Emancipation Proclamation freeing "all persons held as slaves within any State or designated part of a State, the people whereof shall then be in rebellion against the United States." Lincoln maintained that his power as commander in chief gave him the authority to issue the proclamation because the liberation of slaves reduced the labor force of the South, thus hindering its war effort.

> [T]he writ of habeas corpus is suspended in respect to all persons arrested, or who are now or hereafter during the rebellion shall be imprisoned in any fort, camp, arsenal, military prison, or other place of confinement by any military authority or by the sentence of any court-martial or military commission.
>
> —**Abraham Lincoln**, Proclamation—Suspending the Writ of Habeas Corpus

Although the Supreme Court eventually objected to Lincoln's order that civilians could be tried in military courts, it did sanction his prosecution of a total war against the South. When hostilities began, the president had ordered a blockade of Confederate ports. The owners of four vessels seized by the blockade sued on the grounds that the seizures were illegal because Congress had not declared war against the South. They argued that Lincoln's duty to suppress the insurrection was not equivalent to the power to wage war. Therefore, an act of war such as a blockade could not legally be ordered by the president in the absence of a declaration of war.

In 1863 the Supreme Court rejected these arguments in its 5–4 decision in the *Prize Cases*. The decision supported Lincoln's interpretation that the South was without sovereign rights, while the North possessed all rights of a belligerent in wartime. Advocates of a strong presidency have often cited this case when arguing in favor of a broad interpretation of presidential war power.

Union Victory

In the early years of the war, superior generalship led to many southern victories, particularly by the army of Virginia under Gen. Robert E. Lee. However, the North held a vast advantage in population and industrial production that wore down the South.

By July 1863 Union forces had gained control of the Mississippi River and repelled a southern invasion of Pennsylvania at the Battle of Gettysburg. Under the command of Gen. Ulysses S. Grant, the Union army launched in 1864 a relentless campaign to destroy Lee's army. In that year Lincoln ran for reelection against Gen. George B. McClellan, a Democrat and a former commander of Union forces whom Lincoln had fired for being ineffective and overly cautious.

Lincoln's reelection appeared in doubt during the spring of 1864 as Grant's army suffered heavy casualties during an indecisive campaign in Virginia. But in September, Union forces under Gen. William T. Sherman captured Atlanta and began laying waste to large swaths of Georgia and South Carolina. Northern voters, sensing that victory was inevitable, reelected the president. Lincoln's victory ensured that the North would continue to prosecute the war. On April 9, 1865, Lee surrendered to General Grant.

More on this topic:

Lincoln, Abraham, p. 336

War Powers, p. 555

Lincoln had proposed a lenient Reconstruction plan for the South that was intended to reunify American society. The chances that Lincoln's plan would be implemented were destroyed when Lincoln was shot by assassin John Wilkes Booth on April 14, 1865. The president died the next day and was succeeded by Andrew Johnson, who favored Lincoln's Reconstruction plan but did not have the political power to implement it. Instead the Radical Republicans who controlled Congress imposed a harsh Reconstruction program on the South.

Clay, Henry

Henry Clay
Source: Library of Congress

Henry Clay (1777–1852) was one of the most powerful public figures of the first half of the nineteenth century. An eloquent speaker and skilled politician, Clay was known as the Great Compromiser for his efforts to defuse sectional disputes over slavery. He was a congressional leader, a secretary of state, and a frequent presidential candidate who never attained the presidency.

Born in Virginia, Clay moved in 1797 to Kentucky where he practiced law and served in the state legislature. His congressional career began in the Senate when he was appointed to fill unexpired Senate terms in 1806–1807 and 1809–1810. In 1810 he was elected to the House of Representatives, where he served for most of the next fifteen years. Clay was chosen as Speaker the day he took office in 1811, and he remained Speaker as long as he was in the House. He joined with other young "War Hawks" in Congress to push the nation toward war with Great Britain. Clay resigned his seat twice—in 1814, to serve on the delegation sent to Europe to negotiate an end to the War of 1812, and again in 1820. He was reelected Speaker as soon as he returned to the House in 1815 and 1823. He left the chamber for good in 1825.

In that year Clay became secretary of state after what many of his contemporaries charged was a "corrupt bargain" with incoming president John Quincy Adams. Because of the disintegration of the Federalist Party during the presidency of James Monroe, the Democratic-Republican Party was left without an opponent in the 1824 election. The Democratic-Republican caucus nominated W. H. Crawford of Georgia, but he did not receive wide backing within the party. As a result, Clay, Adams, and Andrew Jackson were nominated as regional candidates by their home state legislatures, although they all belonged to the Democratic-Republican Party. These four prominent men split the vote, preventing anyone from gaining the majority of electoral votes necessary to win. In accordance with the Constitution, the election was thrown into the House of Representatives. As fourth-place finisher Clay was not eligible for the election in the House. Had Clay finished third he would have been in a strong position to win because the election was being decided by a body that he dominated.

Instead Clay could only endorse one of the other candidates. He gave his support to Adams, who emerged victorious. Adams then appointed Clay his secretary of state in what looked like a political payoff. The supporters of Jackson, who had received the most electoral votes of the four candidates, were especially angry.

In 1830 Clay was elected to the Senate, where he played a leading role in the ongoing debates on slavery and the national bank. He left the Senate in 1842 but returned in 1849.

Clay ran for president on the National Republican ticket in 1832. He was defeated by incumbent Andrew Jackson by an electoral vote of 219–49. The central issue of the campaign was the rechartering of the national bank, which Clay favored and Jackson opposed. Clay was again nominated for president in 1844, this time by the Whig Party. He faced a dark-horse Democratic nominee, James K. Polk. Clay lost a close election—Polk received 170 electoral votes to Clay's 105. Had Clay taken New York's thirty-six electoral votes—he lost the state by five thousand votes—he would have defeated Polk.

After losing the Whig nomination to Zachary Taylor in 1848, Clay was reelected to the Senate. There he participated in the debates that led to the Compromise of 1850, which attempted to head off civil war by making concessions to both the South and the North on the issue of slavery. Clay served in the Senate until his death in 1852.

<table>
<tr><td>More on this topic:</td></tr>
<tr><td>Adams, John Quincy, p. 4</td></tr>
<tr><td>Electoral College, p. 185</td></tr>
</table>

Cleveland, Grover

Source: Library of Congress

Grover Cleveland (1837–1908) was the only president to serve two nonconsecutive terms. He also was the only Democrat to be elected president between James Buchanan (1857–1861) and Woodrow Wilson (1913–1921).

Cleveland was born on March 18, 1837, in Caldwell, New Jersey. His father was a Presbyterian minister who died when Grover was sixteen. In 1855 the young man set out for Cleveland, Ohio, in search of work. On the way he stopped in Buffalo, New York, where he went to work for his uncle, Lewis F. Allen, as a farmhand. A few months later Cleveland went to work as an apprentice clerk in a local law firm, and in 1859 he was admitted to the bar.

Cleveland was drafted to fight in the Civil War, but in accordance with the law he hired a substitute for $300 so that he could continue to help support his family. In 1863 Cleveland accepted an appointment as assistant district attorney of Erie County, New York. Two years later he was defeated in an election for district attorney. With the exception of a two-year term as sheriff of Buffalo from 1871 to 1873, he practiced law for the next sixteen years.

In 1881 Cleveland was elected mayor of Buffalo and immediately took action to reform the city administration. His well-deserved reputation as a reformer earned him the Democratic nomination for governor of New York in 1882. He easily won the election and assumed office on January 3, 1883. As governor, Cleveland combated corruption and the spoils system.

The governor's reform principles made him an attractive presidential candidate in 1884. The Republicans nominated James G. Blaine, a Republican senator from Maine, who had been linked to several scandals. Cleveland's supporters argued that if the Democratic Party nominated the reform governor, the reform-minded Republicans, known as Mugwumps, might desert their party. The Democratic delegates at the national convention in Chicago agreed with this strategy, and

Cleveland was nominated on the second ballot. Cleveland's election hopes were damaged when a newspaper report disclosed that he had fathered an illegitimate child, whom he continued to support. Cleveland admitted his paternity and instructed his campaign workers to "tell the truth." Cleveland also was attacked for not serving in the Civil War, although Blaine had avoided service as well. In the end, Cleveland received just sixty thousand more votes than Blaine and defeated him by a vote of 219–182 in the Electoral College.

During his first term Cleveland attempted to bring his reformist principles to the presidency. He implemented the Pendleton Civil Service Act, signed into law by Chester A. Arthur, which shifted thousands of government jobs from patronage to a merit system of hiring. He also vetoed numerous private pension bills for individual Civil War veterans. Cleveland was unsuccessful, however, in lowering the tariff, which he considered to be unfair to farmers and workers and unnecessary given the large federal budget surplus.

Cleveland, who was a bachelor when he entered office, married Frances Folsom, the twenty-one-year-old daughter of his former law partner, on June 2, 1886, in a White House ceremony.

In 1888 Cleveland ran for reelection against Indiana Republican Benjamin Harrison. Despite defeating Harrison by 100,000 votes, Cleveland lost to Harrison in the Electoral College, 233–168. Cleveland moved to New York City, where he practiced law. Four years later he was again nominated for president by his party. The 1892 election featured a rematch between Cleveland and President Harrison. This time Cleveland easily defeated Harrison in the Electoral College 277–145 but received only 46.3 percent of the popular vote because of the third-party candidacy of James Baird Weaver of the People's Party, which drew over one million votes.

Soon after Cleveland took office for the second time, the Panic of 1893 touched off a deep economic depression. Hundreds of banks failed, and unemployment rose sharply. Cleveland believed the depression was caused by inflation and an erosion of business confidence. With the support of many congressional Republicans, he convinced Congress in 1893 to repeal the mildly inflationary Sherman Silver Purchase Act. He also authorized the purchase of several million ounces of gold from private holders to replenish the government's shrinking gold reserves. Cleveland's policies, however, did not ease the depression.

In 1894 the economic situation worsened when a local strike at the Pullman Palace Car Company near Chicago led to a railroad strike throughout the Midwest. When violence erupted in Chicago, Cleveland sent federal troops there to break the strike despite the protests of Illinois governor John P. Altgeld.

The depression had greeted Cleveland as he entered office, but he received much of the blame for the nation's economic troubles. As a result, the 1896 Democratic convention nominated William Jennings Bryan for president, and many Democratic candidates distanced themselves from Cleveland.

In foreign affairs Cleveland withdrew in March 1893 from a treaty negotiated by the Harrison administration that would have annexed Hawaii as U.S. territory. He considered the treaty unfair and blocked any further attempt to annex the islands. He also resisted the temptation to yield to public pressure and go to war with Spain over its suppression of a rebellion in Cuba that began in 1895.

Upon leaving office for the second time, Cleveland settled in Princeton, New Jersey. He devoted his time to fishing, delivering lectures, and writing books and articles. In 1907 Cleveland was elected president of the Association of Presidents of Life Insurance Companies. He died of a heart attack in Princeton on June 24, 1908.

More on this topic:

Economic Powers, p. 161

Electoral College, p. 185

Harrison, Benjamin, p. 246

Clinton v. City of New York   *See* LINE-ITEM VETO

Clinton v. Jones

The Supreme Court case of *Clinton v. Jones* began in 1994 as a sexual harassment lawsuit against President Bill Clinton, alleging that while he was governor of Arkansas, Clinton made crude sexual advances on a state employee, Paula Corbin Jones. Besides tarnishing President Clinton's image, the case set a landmark precedent that sitting presidents are not immune from having to answer to civil lawsuits brought against them while in office.

The case was originally heard in the U.S. District Court for the Eastern District of Arkansas by Judge Susan Webber Wright, a former law school student of Clinton's when he taught at the University of Arkansas Law School. Wright allowed pretrial discovery to take place but ruled that a civil suit against a sitting president must be postponed until the defendant leaves office. Jones appealed her case to the Eighth Circuit Court of Appeals, which overturned Wright's decision on the grounds that a sitting president is subject to the same laws that govern all citizens, including other government officials. President Clinton then appealed the Eighth Circuit's decision to the U.S. Supreme Court.

In a unanimous decision the Supreme Court ruled in affirmation of the Eighth Circuit Court of Appeals. Writing the opinion of the majority, Associate Justice John Paul Stevens rejected Clinton's position that forcing a sitting president to answer to civil charges while in office was a violation of the constitutional doctrine of separation of powers, in this instance between the executive and the judiciary. In a concurring opinion, Associate Justice Stephen Breyer maintained that a civil lawsuit could be deferred if the suit interfered with the president's official duties. But the Court did not see a connection between this lawsuit and Clinton's ability to execute his presidential functions.

Although a common law precedent affecting all future presidents was established in *Clinton v. Jones*, the case had a more immediate impact on the Clinton administration. Because the Supreme Court allowed the case to continue in district court as *Jones v. Clinton*, the plaintiffs sought to illustrate a similar pattern of behavior they claimed Clinton engaged in with other government employees. One of the witnesses in the case, White House intern Monica Lewinsky, denied having an affair with the president. Clinton, too, denied that he had "sexual relations" with Ms. Lewinsky. When Lewinsky's friend Linda Tripp tape recorded Lewinsky privately contradicting their sworn testimony, Tripp gave the tape to Kenneth Starr, an independent counsel who had already been investigating other alleged misconduct by Clinton, including the Whitewater affair. Armed with this information, Starr expanded his investigation of Clinton, eventually forcing the president to testify before a federal grand jury, which in turn led to Starr's report to the House of Representatives suggesting that the president committed acts of perjury and obstruction of justice. The House of Representatives impeached President Clinton on two counts related to these charges, but the president was eventually acquitted after a trial in the Senate.

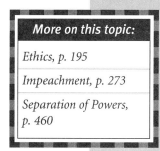

More on this topic:

Ethics, p. 195

Impeachment, p. 273

Separation of Powers, p. 460

Clinton, Bill

William J. "Bill" Clinton (1946–), the forty-second president, was born in Hope, Arkansas. He originally was named William Jefferson Blythe, after his father, who died in an automobile accident before his son was born. When Clinton was four, his mother married Roger Clinton, a car salesman who legally adopted him.

Clinton grew up in Hot Springs, Arkansas, where he excelled in public schools and played saxophone in the band. In 1968 he graduated from Georgetown University in Washington, D.C., with

William J Clinton

a degree in foreign service. He earned a Rhodes scholarship and attended Oxford University for two years. He returned to the United States in 1970 and entered Yale University Law School, earning his law degree in 1973. While at Yale he met Hillary Rodham, whom he married on October 11, 1975. Their daughter, Chelsea, was born in 1980.

Political Career

Politics had been Clinton's lifelong ambition, and he became one of the most polarizing politicians in U.S. history, inspiring great affection as well as strong dislike. In 1972 he managed the Texas campaign of Democratic presidential nominee George McGovern. After a brief stint as a staff member of the House Judiciary Committee, he began teaching law at the University of Arkansas in 1973. The next year he ran unsuccessfully for a U.S. House seat. Although he lost, his strong showing established his position in Arkansas politics.

In 1976 Clinton was elected attorney general of Arkansas. Then in 1978, at age thirty-two, he defeated a crowded field of Democratic contenders for the gubernatorial nomination and easily won the general election. Two years later, however, Clinton was defeated for reelection.

After his defeat, Clinton went to work for the Little Rock law firm Wright, Lindsay, and Jennings, but spent much of his time preparing for another run. He won in 1982 and was reelected in 1984 to two-year terms and in 1986 and 1990 to four-year terms.

At the 1988 Democratic national convention, Clinton delivered an overly long nominating speech for Michael S. Dukakis that was widely criticized. Nevertheless, during the late 1980s and early 1990s Clinton achieved national prominence as a reform governor and was often mentioned as a future presidential candidate. He served two terms as chairman of the National Governors Association. In 1990 and 1991 he also headed the Democratic Leadership Council, a national organization of Democrats who favored the party's realignment to more moderate positions.

In 1991 Clinton announced he would seek the Democratic presidential nomination and quickly emerged as one of the front-runners. The campaign was jeopardized, however, by allegations of marital infidelity and avoidance of military service during the Vietnam War. Without denying either charge, Clinton and his wife, Hillary, appealed for understanding in a notable television appearance on *60 Minutes*. Clinton outlasted rivals Paul Tsongas and Jerry Brown to win the nomination.

In the general election Clinton faced incumbent George H. W. Bush and billionaire populist H. Ross Perot, who ran as an independent. Bush's support had been weakened by a stagnant economy and a widespread belief that he had little interest in domestic policy. Clinton promised to make economic policy and the middle class his top priorities, promoting himself as a fiscally conscientious agent of change who would reform the country's health care, welfare, and education systems. He chose as his running mate Sen. Al Gore of Tennessee, another southern Democrat in his mid-forties. Clinton won the election with 43 percent of the popular vote and 370 electoral votes. Bush finished second with 37 percent and 168 electoral votes. Perot won nearly twenty million votes, almost half of Bush's total.

First Term

Clinton's first hundred days in office were a mixed bag of successes and setbacks. His first two choices for attorney general had to withdraw their names after revelations that they had employed illegal immigrants as nannies; he was forced to compromise on his campaign pledge to lift the ban on gays in the military; and his economic stimulus bill was defeated by a Republican filibuster in the Senate. But Clinton succeeded in passing family leave legislation and a long-stalled motor-voter bill. Later that year he scored major legislative successes with his deficit-reduction program, the North American Free Trade Agreement, and the Brady bill, which mandated a five-day waiting period for the purchase of a handgun.

In 1994, however, Clinton was less successful. With First Lady Hillary Clinton serving as the head of Clinton's task force on health care, the administration attempted to advance a comprehensive reform plan. Republicans at-

As a high school youth and member of Boys Nation, Bill Clinton shook President John F. Kennedy's hand at a Rose Garden ceremony in 1963.
Source: © 1991 W. H. Owen, Black Star

tacked it as overly complex, expensive, and bureaucratic. By early fall, lacking sufficient congressional, industry, or public support, the bill was withdrawn without coming to a final vote in either house. Clinton's disappointment was tempered somewhat by passage of a major crime bill and revisions to the General Agreement on Tariffs and Trade.

The 1994 congressional elections stunningly realigned Washington. Republicans gained control of both houses of Congress for the first time in four decades. The highly partisan Congress also reinvigorated a lingering ethics investigation arising from investments Clinton and his wife had made in an Arkansas land development deal known as "Whitewater" during his time as governor, establishing a charged political climate in Washington that would later lead to Clinton's impeachment and trial.

During 1995 Clinton blocked many Republican priorities with adept use of the veto, a weapon he did not have to use during his first two years in office. Most notably, Clinton vetoed Republican legislation to balance the budget in seven years, terming the proposed cuts in health care, education, the environment, and welfare as draconian. The vetoes led to two shutdowns of government services and bitter partisan accusations as the two parties sought political advantage. With the polls showing strong support for his position, Clinton was able to keep a firm hand in the budget negotiations, and by April 1996 his stubborn style was proving successful. The final 1996 fiscal spending bill reflected his priorities, not the deeper cuts sought by congressional Republicans.

As he had promised during his campaign, Clinton deemphasized foreign policy to focus on domestic problems, but world events soon altered this approach. Clinton actively promoted a broadening of the accord signed earlier between Israel and the Palestine Liberation Organization on achieving peace, and he advanced negotiations between warring factions in Ireland. Clinton also expanded the humanitarian mission in Somalia that had been launched during the Bush administration. But when U.S. military units began experiencing casualties, Clinton withdrew American troops. In 1994 Clinton also sent American forces to Haiti to reestablish the deposed government of Jean-Bertrand Aristide.

But Clinton's largest foreign policy endeavor during his first term was in the Balkans. In 1995 he sent twenty thousand U.S. troops to a North Atlantic Treaty Organization (NATO) peacekeeping mission in war-torn Bosnia. The deployment followed the signing of a complex U.S.-brokered peace agreement in Dayton, Ohio.

During the second half of 1996 Clinton moved to the political center, a policy called "triangulation," in preparation for his November reelection bid. He signed, despite opposition from liberal Democrats, a landmark welfare reform bill pushed by the Republican Congress.

Reelection and Second Term

Clinton faced former Senate majority leader Robert J. Dole in the 1996 presidential election. Despite several embarrassing White House ethics questions and the ongoing inquiries into the Whitewater affair, Clinton led Dole in the polls throughout the campaign. He benefited from a strong economy, low inflation and unemployment, and the perception of many voters that congressional Republicans had been too strident in pursuit of their conservative agenda. Clinton received 49 percent of the popular vote and defeated Dole 379–159 in the Electoral College.

In 1997 Clinton and the Republican majority in Congress struck a historic agreement to balance the federal budget in five years. However, with a strong economy boosting federal tax receipts, a $70 billion surplus—the first government surplus in twenty-nine years—was attained just a year later. The debate in Washington quickly turned from how to balance the budget to how to spend the surplus.

Years of rancorous animosity toward Clinton from conservatives in and out of Washington culminated in December 1998 in the president's impeachment by the House of Representatives. The impeachment grew out of an investigation by independent counsel Kenneth W. Starr into reports that Clinton had covered up a sexual relationship with a one-time White House intern, Monica Lewinsky. The relationship had come to light because of a sexual harassment suit brought against Clinton by a former Arkansas state employee, Paula Corbin Jones, and Clinton's efforts to conceal his relationship with Lewinsky from Jones's attorneys, some of whose legal fees were paid by anti-Clinton conservatives.

Clinton acknowledged "an inappropriate relationship" with Lewinsky in a televised address on August 17, 1998, and Starr, on September 9, turned over to the House what he termed was "substantial and credible information that may constitute grounds" for impeaching the president.

Despite his televised admission, Clinton's standing in public opinion polls held strong; the majority of those polled indicated a distrust of Republican motives. In the elections on November 3 the GOP lost five House seats, marking the first time in sixty-four years that the party holding the presidency registered such a gain in a midterm election. Still, the House leadership went forward with the impeachment process, and on December 19 the full House, voting almost along strict party lines, approved two articles of impeachment that charged Clinton with giving false and misleading testimony and with obstructing justice. Clinton thus became the second president in U.S. history to be impeached.

Beginning on January 7, 1999, Chief Justice William H. Rehnquist presided over Clinton's trial in the Senate. The trial's outcome was never in doubt as the Republicans held only fifty-five seats and a two-thirds vote of members (or sixty-seven votes) was needed for conviction. On February 12 the Senate found the president not guilty on both counts, with the votes following party lines.

Although he weathered the political proceedings of impeachment and a trial, the threat of criminal legal action for perjury and obstruction of justice would dog Clinton until his next-to-last day in office. On January 19, 2001, Clinton reached a plea agreement with independent counsel Robert W. Ray. Ray would drop further legal action in return for a $25,000 fine, Clinton's public acknowledgment that he had made false statements under oath, and suspension of his Arkansas law license for five years.

In foreign policy during his second term, Clinton increased U.S. involvement in the turbulent Balkans after reports of widespread atrocities in Serbia's "ethnic cleansing" campaign against ethnic Albanians, many of whom were Muslims, in the Serbian province of Kosovo. After the failure of negotiations with Serbian president Slobodan Milosevic in 1999, NATO nations began an extensive bombing campaign against Milosevic's Yugoslavia. After eleven weeks of bombing, Milosevic finally pulled out of Kosovo, allowing NATO peacekeepers in and giving Clinton a foreign policy triumph.

Clinton spent much of his last year in office trying to broker a historic peace agreement between Israel and the Palestinians. Despite encouraging progress, discord over the status of Jerusalem and the eruption of violence in the Middle East in September and October 2000 brought the talks to a halt.

As Clinton's second term drew to a close, his wife, Hillary, began her own political career. Mrs. Clinton was elected to the U.S. Senate from New York in 2000, the first time a first lady had sought and won elective office.

Acrimony and allegations of unethical behavior trailed the president into retirement. On his last day in office, Bill Clinton issued presidential pardons or commutations to 176 individuals, some of them highly controversial. Among those pardoned was Marc Rich, a fugitive from justice who had been indicted in 1983 for evading $48 million in taxes and for trading illegally with Iran. Rich's former wife, Denise Rich, had donated about $1 million to the Democratic Party and its candidates and $450,000 to Clinton's presidential library fund. Many of the pardons had not gone through normal channels, and two of the pardons were issued to clients of attorney Hugh Rodham, the brother of Sen. Hillary Rodham Clinton. The pardons scandal largely overshadowed a smaller tempest over the Clintons' acceptance of gifts valued at about $200,000. The Clintons returned some gifts that the National Park Service believed were intended for the White House's permanent collection.

As an ex-president, Clinton spends much time traveling and delivering lectures, and in 2004 released his autobiography, *My Life.* He located his post-presidential office in New York's Harlem, contributing to a revitalization of the historic African American neighborhood. After undergoing a successful quadruple coronary bypass surgery in September 2004, Clinton continues to stay involved in public policy through the William J. Clinton Foundation, which seeks to promote international understanding of issues arising out of globalization and interdependence, including combating AIDS. In January 2005 Clinton, along with former president George H. W. Bush, was appointed by President George W. Bush to coordinate an international relief campaign to assist nations suffering from the devastating effects of the December 26, 2004, tsunami in the Indian Ocean.

> **We are fortunate to be alive at this moment in history. Never before has our Nation enjoyed, at once, so much prosperity and social progress with so little internal crisis and so few external threats.**
>
> —**Bill Clinton,** Address Before a Joint Session of the Congress on the State of the Union, January 27, 2000

More on this topic:

Clinton v. Jones, *p. 101*

Elections Chronology, p. 174

Former Presidents, p. 226

Impeachment, p. 273

Pardon Power, p. 395

Clinton, George

George Clinton (1739–1812) was a powerful New York governor who was elected to two terms as vice president, the first under Thomas Jefferson and the second under James Madison. In 1812 he became the first vice president to die in office.

Clinton's father was a poor Irish immigrant who could not afford to send his son to college. George went to sea at age eighteen, returning home after a year. After service in the French and Indian War, he studied law in New York City and was admitted to the bar. In 1765 he became district attorney of his native Ulster County, New York. Three years later he was elected to the New York assembly. He remained in that body until 1775, when he was elected to the Second Continental Congress.

George Clinton
Source: Library of Congress

During the Revolutionary War Clinton served as a brigadier general in the New York militia and the Continental army until he was chosen governor of New York. He assumed the office on July 30, 1777, and served six successive terms, until 1795. Clinton became known for his harsh treatment of New Yorkers who supported Great Britain during the war. In 1795 he declined to run for a seventh term, because his public support had declined. In 1801, however, he won another term as governor with the help of his powerful nephew DeWitt Clinton, who manipulated his aging uncle during his last term in office.

Clinton's nomination as the Democratic-Republican candidate for vice president in 1804 stemmed from the new Twelfth Amendment, which linked the fates of a party's presidential and vice-presidential candidates. Vice-presidential nominees were chosen according to their ability to attract votes for their running mates. The Democratic-Republicans hoped that Clinton would deliver many New York votes and provide geographic balance to the ticket with Virginian Thomas Jefferson. Despite his declining faculties, Clinton accepted the vice-presidential nomination in the hope that it would be a stepping-stone to the presidency. The Jefferson-Clinton ticket won easily over Federalists Charles Cotesworth Pinckney and Rufus King.

Clinton was a poor presiding officer of the Senate, and his forgetfulness caused much parliamentary confusion. Complaining that his vice-presidential duties were tiresome, he spent most of his time in New York.

Clinton declared his availability for the presidency in 1808, but he was widely regarded as senile. The Democratic-Republican Party, as expected, nominated James Madison. Clinton bitterly accepted the consolation of yet another vice-presidential nomination. After Madison and Clinton were elected, Clinton refused to attend Madison's inauguration and openly opposed the new president's policies.

In 1811 the vote on the bill to recharter the Bank of the United States, which Madison favored, was tied in the Senate. Clinton, as vice president, cast the deciding vote against rechartering the bank. On April 20, 1812, at the age of seventy-two, Clinton died, leaving the vice presidency vacant.

More on this topic:

Jefferson, Thomas, p. 304

Madison, James, p. 350

National Bank, p. 372

Vice President, p. 539

Clinton, Hillary Rodham

Hillary Rodham Clinton (1947–) was born in Chicago and raised in the Chicago suburb of Park Ridge. She attended public high school in Chicago and then went to Wellesley College, where her political views became more liberal. She delivered her class commencement address, punctuating it with an attack on the day's guest speaker, Massachusetts senator Edward Brooke, as a representative of establishment politics. The verbal fireworks earned her national publicity in *Life* magazine.

After graduating from Wellesley, Hillary attended Yale Law School. There she became interested in children's rights issues. She also met and began dating Bill Clinton, a fellow law student.

After her graduation from Yale in 1973, Hillary worked at the Children's Defense Fund for a brief time and then, in January 1974, joined the Impeachment Inquiry staff of the House of Representatives Judiciary Committee, which was grappling with legal questions surrounding the possible impeachment of President Richard Nixon. Her work with the committee led to several prestigious job offers after Nixon's resignation, but she decided to join Bill in Arkansas. She taught law at the University of Arkansas in Fayetteville and married Bill on October 11, 1975, in a house he had purchased there for them.

In 1976 Bill was elected attorney general of Arkansas, and the Clintons moved to Little Rock, where Hillary joined a prominent law firm, working in family law, commercial litigation, and criminal law. She quickly established herself as one of the city's best lawyers. Two years later Bill became governor. During this time Hillary founded the Arkansas Advocates for Children and Families, was appointed by President Jimmy Carter to chair the Legal Services Corporation, and served on the board of the Children's Defense Fund. But as first lady of Arkansas, Hillary's high profile, outspokenness, and "liberal" ideas—such as continuing to use her maiden name—made her a lightning rod for criticism and con-

Senators Hillary Rodham Clinton, D-N.Y., and Don Nickles, R-Okla., talk to reporters in the Senate Daily Press Gallery about the first bill passed in the 108th Congress. The law authorizes thirteen weeks of federal aid to unemployed workers after their twenty-six weeks of state benefits end.
Source: Congressional Quarterly, Scott J. Ferrell

tributed to Bill's reelection defeat in 1980. Also in 1980 their daughter, Chelsea, was born.

In 1982 Bill Clinton rebounded and was reelected governor of Arkansas. He held the office for the next decade. Finally adjusting to Arkansas realities, Hillary changed her image while remaining prominent and became one of the state's more popular first ladies. In the meantime she spearheaded education reform by serving as head of the Arkansas Education Standards Committee. And, not least, she served as an adviser to her husband, evincing political skills good enough to earn her mention as a gubernatorial candidate in her own right. Her law practice and her reputation also grew, and by 1989 the *National Law Journal* had cited her as one of the nation's one hundred most powerful lawyers.

In the 1992 presidential campaign, her intelligence and proven abilities, which sometimes led the campaign to claim the public would be getting "two for the price of one" in a Clinton presidency, proved to be a double-edged sword. It won many supporters, some of whom thought her better qualified than her husband to be president, but it also left her open to attacks from political opponents, particularly the Republican right, who claimed that she had too much influence with her husband and that her views were "antifamily." Similar charges plagued her as first lady.

Once the Clintons were in the White House, Hillary was appointed by the president to head the commission established to create a health care reform program. When after eight months the commission produced a plan, Hillary became its foremost advocate, lobbying behind the scenes and appearing publicly before five different congressional committees to explain and defend it. Republican opponents and interest groups mounted a heavily financed campaign against the plan, casting it as complex and dangerous "social engineering." Before the reform plan even came to a vote in Congress, public support dropped precipitously and the plan was withdrawn.

More on this topic:

First Ladies, p. 219

Hillary also served as one of her husband's most important informal advisers on almost every topic. "Ask Hillary" was the watchword in the White House.

While first lady, Hillary continued to address issues involving women and children, and she attended the United Nations conference on women in Beijing, China, in 1995. She also wrote a weekly newspaper column and published the book *It Takes a Village.*

As in Arkansas, the first lady's prominence led to controversy. Legal and ethical questions arose about her role in the 1993 firing of the White House Travel Office staff and in the handling of the Clintons' Whitewater real estate venture dating from the late 1970s. In the latter case she responded to questions from a Senate investigation committee and in February 1996 became the first sitting first lady to be subpoenaed by, and to testify before, a grand jury. In 2000, after an exhaustive six-year probe, the independent counsel's office announced there was insufficient evidence against the Clintons in both matters.

During Bill Clinton's successful 1996 reelection bid against Republican Robert J. Dole, Hillary maintained a visible but secondary role in the campaign. Throughout Clinton's second term she also took a lower profile while working on women's and children's issues. When Bill Clinton's sex scandal exploded in January 1998, she was quick to rally support behind her husband. The president's admission in August that he had misled her and the nation caused her a great deal of pain, but she remained stoically with him.

In 1999 the Clintons bought a house in Chappaqua, New York, to establish residency in the state. That year, Hillary toured the state to test the waters for a Senate run in 2000. After deciding to run, she won the Democratic primary in September 2000. In the general election she decisively defeated Republican Rick Lazio, a representative from Long Island. For the first time in history, a first lady won elective office. Further, Hillary was the first woman to represent New York in the U.S. Senate.

Hillary's political career continues to develop, leading to ambitions for even higher office. In 2006 she easily won reelection to a second term in the Senate. After years of speculation, and having amassed a significant war chest of money left over from her Senate campaign, Hillary Clinton on January 20, 2007, announced the formation of a presidential campaign "exploratory committee," an official initial step allowing her to raise money for the 2008 presidential election campaign.

Colfax, Schuyler

Schuyler Colfax.
Source: Library of Congress

Schuyler Colfax (1823–1885) was Ulysses S. Grant's first vice president, serving from 1869 to 1873. During Colfax's rise in government he became known as the "Smiler" and "Great Joiner" for his propensity to join any organization that would accept him. Abraham Lincoln had called Colfax a "friendly rascal." Events would show, however, that Colfax was not just an opportunistic politician but a corrupt one.

Colfax began working as a newspaper reporter at age sixteen. In 1845 he became part owner of the *South Bend Free Press.* He changed its name to the *St. Joseph Valley Register* and used it to support Whig candidates. Colfax ran unsuccessfully for the U.S. House of Representatives in 1851. When the Republican Party was formed, he became a member and helped build a Republican organization in Indiana. In 1855 he finally was elected to the House, where he served for the next fourteen years until he became vice president in 1869. During his last five and a half years in the House, he held the office of Speaker.

At the 1868 Republican national convention Colfax emerged from a crowd of favorite-son candidates to receive the vice-presidential nomination. Republican presidential nominee Ulysses S. Grant and Colfax easily defeated Democrats Horatio Seymour and Francis P. Blair Jr. 214–80 in the Electoral College. Like most nineteenth-century vice presidents, Colfax did not play a significant role in his running mate's administration.

A September 1872 newspaper exposé implicated Colfax in a bribery scandal. In 1867 Congress had provided funds for the construction of the Union Pacific Railroad. The director of the railroad, Oakes Ames, a Republican House member from Massachusetts, set up a holding company, Crédit Mobilier of America, in which he deposited millions of dollars appropriated for the railroad. He proceeded to bribe other members of Congress not to expose his corruption and to support legislation favorable to the railroad. While Speaker of the House, Colfax had taken a bribe of twenty shares of Crédit Mobilier stock.

Some members of Congress considered impeaching Colfax, but because his term as vice president was about to expire they dropped the matter. Colfax claimed he had been exonerated, but his political reputation was ruined. After he left office he made a good living by touring the country delivering lectures. He died of a stroke on January 13, 1885, during a lecture tour.

More on this topic:

Ethics, p. 195

Grant, Ulysses S., p. 235

Vice President, p. 539

Commerce Department

The Commerce Department promotes international trade, economic growth, and technological advancement. In international trade the department's programs are aimed at increasing U.S. competitiveness in the world economy and preventing unfair foreign trade competition. In the area of economic growth the Commerce Department provides various statistics and analyses for business and government planners and promotes domestic economic development and the growth of minority businesses. Finally, in the area of technological advancement the department supports the increased use of scientific, engineering, and technological developments, including the development of telecommunications and information services. The department also studies the earth's physical environment and oceanic resources and forecasts the weather, and it grants patents and registers trademarks.

The Department of Commerce and Labor was established in 1903 in response to the demands for business representation at the highest levels of government fueled by the nation's rapid economic growth between 1850 and 1900.

The new cabinet department was one of the largest and most complicated in the federal government; within five months of its creation it had more than ten thousand employees. Its responsibilities included foreign and domestic commerce; the mining, manufacturing, shipping, and fishery industries; labor interests; and transportation.

As the nation's manufactured exports continued to expand and workers moved from farms to industry, pressures built up on both sides to separate labor and commerce into independent departments. In March 1913 the two were established as separate departments. (See LABOR DEPARTMENT.)

The Commerce Department came into the limelight during Herbert C. Hoover's tenure as its secretary in the 1920s. Hoover was determined to make it the most powerful department in the government. Under his stewardship the department promoted a great expansion of U.S. exports, acquired several new divisions (including the Patent Office), expanded its statistical functions, and developed safety codes for industry and transportation.

In the wake of the Great Depression the department's role and budget were substantially reduced. Some thought was even given to abolishing the department. But World War II and the years that followed ushered in a new role for the Commerce Department. The National Bureau of Standards gained importance for its efforts to ensure interchangeability of weapons parts, while the Civil Aeronautics Administration significantly expanded its pilot-training programs. Various transportation programs were moved to the Commerce Department, and it remained the principal overseer of such programs until the TRANSPORTATION DEPARTMENT was established in 1967.

Although the Commerce Department has remained an important source of economic information, its responsibilities in international economics have been taken over increasingly by special presidential advisers, the TREASURY DEPARTMENT, and the OFFICE OF THE U.S. TRADE REPRESENTATIVE.

The commerce secretary is assisted by a deputy secretary, as well as under secretaries for oceans and atmosphere, international trade, export administration, economic affairs, travel and tourism, and technology.

The department includes several well-known entities, including the National Oceanic and Atmospheric Administration, the Bureau of the Census, the National Institute of Standards and Technology, and the Patent and Trademark Office. In 2003 the Critical Infrastructure Assurance Office moved to the new DEPARTMENT OF HOMELAND SECURITY.

More on this topic:

Trade Representative, Office of the U.S., p. 509

Commissions, Presidential

Since the founding of the United States, presidents have been appointing commissions to probe subjects that normally are beyond the daily scope of presidential advisory organizations.

Modern presidents have relied on commissions to gather information and to focus public attention on specific problems in a variety of policy areas. Recent commissions have investigated business regulation, tariffs, government waste, defense spending, the space program, Social Security, the Iran-contra affair, government reorganization, ocean policy, energy policy, and security failures such as the Kennedy assassination and the September 11, 2001, terrorist attacks.

Although some critics claim that presidents appoint commissions to avoid confronting an issue, to delay action on it, or to divert attention from it, research indicates that most presidents heed and act favorably on the reports they receive from their commissions.

Theodore Roosevelt introduced the use of commissions for substantive policy advice to the president. Inspired by the royal commissions used extensively in Great Britain to investigate policy questions, Roosevelt appointed several commissions during his administration, including the Aldrich Commission, whose recommendations led to establishment of the Federal Reserve System.

Herbert C. Hoover significantly expanded the use of presidential commissions by appointing sixty-two during his first sixteen months in office. After his retirement from the presidency, Hoover headed two important commissions—the HOOVER COMMISSIONS—on government reorganization.

Presidential commissions also have been sent overseas to supervise national elections and investigate the stability of foreign governments. In 1917, for example, President Woodrow Wilson sent a special commission to Russia to look into the new regime that came to power after the overthrow of the czar.

In a few cases presidential commissions have been organized to investigate failures in preparation or security after tragic events. President Lyndon Johnson established the Warren Commission and charged it with investigating the assassination of President Kennedy. Headed by Chief Justice Earl Warren and including then-representative Gerald R. Ford, the commission concluded that Lee Harvey Oswald was the sole assailant and that no larger assassination conspiracy existed. More recently the National Commission on Terrorist Attacks Upon the United States (the 9/11 Commission) was approved by President George W. Bush after intense public pressure for a nonpartisan investigation into possible security lapses leading up to the terrorist attacks. The 9/11 Commission found that both the CIA and the FBI were not aggressive enough to prevent the attacks.

Although the objectives of presidential commissions have varied, most have been important to presidential decision making, and many have contributed significantly to the development of government policy. For example, Franklin D. Roosevelt's most notable commission, the President's Committee on Administrative Management (BROWNLOW COMMITTEE), developed the blueprint for the Executive Office of the President.

Although it is generally recognized that presidents have the power to establish presidential commissions, they often seek congressional approval anyway. One reason may be to obtain the funds needed to operate and staff a presidential commission. Presidents often seek public funds for financing commission activities through legislation, which Congress routinely passes. Some presidential commissions, however, are created by EXECUTIVE ORDERS of the president and are financed by emergency, executive, or special projects funds, which are spent at the president's discretion.

Presidential commissions fall into three broad categories: permanent federal advisory organizations, ad hoc or "blue ribbon" commissions, and White House conferences.

More on this topic:
Brownlow Committee, p. 33
Hoover Commissions, p. 264
Warren Commission, p. 562

Congress and the Presidency

Conflict and cooperation characterize the relationship between the White House and Capitol Hill. Examples can be seen in the newspaper headlines and on the evening news nearly every day—one day members of the two branches are patting each other on the back at a White House meeting, and the next day they are angrily berating each other's positions and policies. While some of this contention is posturing for public consumption, there is indeed tension between the two branches. And it was put there by design.

When the framers of the Constitution met in Philadelphia in 1787, they faced a serious dilemma: how to reconcile their fear of powerful executives with their equal dread of unchecked legislative power.

After much give-and-take, they came up with a system of SEPARATION OF POWERS under which three branches of government—the executive, legislature, and judiciary—each would perform different governing functions. But at the same time they introduced a web of checks and balances, which required that each branch cooperate with the others to make the system work. The result of their efforts was aptly described by political scientist Richard E. Neustadt in his book *Presidential Power* as a system of "separated institutions *sharing* powers."

Congress, for example, passes laws, but these laws cannot be enacted until they cross the president's desk for a signature or veto. The president sets the administration's

The president's contact and personal relationship with Congress vary with each president. Here Lyndon B. Johnson (right) converses intimately with Senate leaders Mike Mansfield (left) and Everett McKinley Dirksen (center) during the Vietnam War.
Source: LBJ Library

policies, but those policies almost always have to be funded by Congress. The president chooses nominees to important administrative and judicial positions, but they must be approved by the Senate. Likewise, the president has the power to negotiate treaties with other nations, but before treaties can be ratified they need the Senate's approval. The president serves as commander in chief of the military, but Congress declares war and regulates the armed forces.

In other words, Congress and the presidency need each other. No matter how divergent their views or how bitter the rhetoric, they will eventually have to reach some kind of compromise for the system to work.

Legislative Leader

The writers of the Constitution gave all legislative powers to Congress but said little about the executive's role. The few legislative powers given to the president included the powers to "from time to time give to the Congress Information of the State of the Union, and recommend to their Consideration such Measures as he shall judge necessary and expedient," as well as to veto legislation. The president also was given authority to negotiate treaties and the little used power to convene one or both houses of Congress. The brevity of these passages in the Constitution masks the considerable influence that presidents have come to wield over legislative matters.

Today the president is considered to be the nation's chief legislator. Presidents send an extensive legislative program to Capitol Hill and have a vast array of powers and tools at their disposal to persuade a majority in Congress to approve it. Presidents lobby Congress directly and through their aides. They seek to influence Congress indirectly by appealing to public opinion and special interest groups for support. Government jobs, federal contracts, and other forms of patronage serve as presidential bargaining tools with members of Congress. Presidents also provide legislators with constituent services, campaign aid, and social courtesies to build goodwill and loyalty. The ultimate presidential tool in dealing with Congress is the veto. Sometimes, however, just the threat of a veto is effective in achieving the president's legislative objective.

Obviously, this growth in the president's powers did not happen overnight. More than two hundred years of history have seen an enormous expansion of the powers and resources that presidents can use to influence public policy, far beyond the president's "express" powers specifically named in the Constitution.

Some of the president's powers were "implied" in the Constitution, awaiting only time and, perhaps, judicial interpretation to emerge. Others were delegated by Congress to meet changing economic or social circumstances and demands, such as the requirement that the president send Congress an annual budget with the administration's plans for taxes and spending.

Still other presidential powers have arisen from new technologies, such as television, or new international responsibilities of the United States, such as the defense of Western Europe after World War II.

Historical Development

George Washington rapidly discovered the difficulties of influencing Congress. He was the first—and last—president ever to attend Congress during an actual floor debate. Washington had expected to win quick approval of an Indian treaty he personally presented to the Senate in the summer of 1789, but Congress declined to cooperate and seemed uneasy about his presence. After that, the first president stayed away from the Capitol, except to deliver annual messages. Instead, he sent Secretary of State Thomas Jefferson and Treasury Secretary Alexander Hamilton for private talks on foreign and fiscal matters. Hamilton became so influential that the House established its Committee on Ways and Means to defend against him.

When Jefferson became president, he avoided personal lobbying and went so far as to suspend the fledgling tradition of personally delivering an annual STATE OF THE UNION ADDRESS. But Jefferson was no passive chief executive. He carefully maintained the forms of separation of powers and congressional supremacy, but relied heavily on cabinet members and his strong party caucus organization, which held the majority in Congress, to initiate and dominate legislative activity.

After Jefferson, however, power flowed back to the legislative branch, and strong congressional leaders such as Henry Clay and John C. Calhoun actively set the agenda of government through the 1820s. At the same time, as presidents came and went Congress began to develop its own power centers—the standing committees, in particular—for making policy.

President Andrew Jackson in the 1830s briefly renewed the role of the political party in setting the national agenda. But Jackson's legislative strategy was largely negative, relying pri-

President George W. Bush enters the House chamber to deliver the State of the Union address in January 2003. Accompanying him are House minority leader Nancy Pelosi, D-Calif., and House majority leader Tom Delay, R-Texas, left.
Source: Congressional Quarterly, Scott J. Ferrell

marily on the veto. The idea that the president should actively propose and shepherd legislation through Congress was still controversial, and the increasing power of the standing committees prevented Jackson from dominating Congress through his political party.

Aside from the actions of a few presidents, notably Abraham Lincoln's emergency actions during the Civil War, nineteenth-century legislation generally was a congressional affair. The federal government had little involvement in international politics and concerned itself largely with domestic matters, such as post offices and public works projects. Except in time of crisis, little was done on a national scale, and the president therefore played a secondary role in policy formation.

But in the late 1880s industrial growth began to transform the country. The United States went from a self-sufficient farm economy to an urban manufacturing one, from largely local business concerns to huge national corporations. The issues of the day became more national in scope and often overlapped with questions of international trade and diplomacy. Calls for more active executive leadership on legislation began to be heard as Congress increasingly found itself ill-equipped to handle broad national questions.

Theodore Roosevelt took the first steps in transforming the presidency to meet the growing demands of a modern society. He was keenly aware that his was the only purely national voice, and he saw the Oval Office as a "bully pulpit" for stimulating public opinion and pushing legislation through Congress. And he did just that, leaving a legacy of energetic presidential leadership.

Roosevelt's successor, William Howard Taft, was the first president to present draft legislation formally to Congress. Woodrow Wilson, the first president since John Adams to deliver his State of the Union address in person before a joint session of Congress, used the annual message to present his legislative agenda. Wilson used cabinet members to influence Congress and established his own direct ties to important congressional leaders.

But the presidency for the most part remained a largely negative force in opposition to Congress, instead of the source of initiative and leadership Americans know today. It was not until the 1930s, under Franklin D. Roosevelt, that the office underwent major, permanent changes that led to the contemporary presidency.

Roosevelt came to office in 1933 as the nation faced unprecedented economic and social pressures. The Great Depression devastated the national economy, forcing millions into unemployment and weakening public faith in government. The emergency required major action and gave Roosevelt the opportunity to take the lead in ways no other peacetime president ever had. Congress, which had been unable to resolve the crisis, awaited strong direction.

The New Deal and Roosevelt's actions during World War II redefined the role of the national government and thoroughly altered the presidency as an institution. By the time Roosevelt died in 1945, the executive branch had grown dramatically in size and in responsibilities. The presidency was no longer a single person but an institution, one that was increasing in size and potency as Congress gave the president more staff and more tools.

Aside from Franklin Roosevelt, Lyndon B. Johnson probably had more success in dealing with Congress than any other president. With the assistance of an overwhelmingly Democratic Congress (the famous eighty-ninth Congress of 1965–1967), he succeeded in enacting an enormous volume of legislation known as the GREAT SOCIETY program. But the good fortune of his administration was soon reversed as the country became more deeply involved in the Vietnam War.

The political troubles that accompanied the Vietnam War not only interrupted Johnson's programs but also ushered in a period of deadlock between the two branches. Congress was anxious to reassert itself in the face of presidential dominance. Opposing political parties often controlled the executive and legislative branches. The economy was stagnating, and more and more people questioned the government's ability to solve national problems. Yet despite these difficulties, the president remained at the center of the legislative process.

In recent years presidents often have faced a Congress controlled by members of the opposite party, leading to stalemates over stalled legislation and nominations. Bill Clinton battled with a Republican congressional majority for most of his time in the White House. The partisan divisions and animosities contributed to the chain of events that led to Clinton's impeachment by the House in 1998. George W. Bush faced a Democratic-controlled Senate for most of the first two years of his presidency, resulting in battles over judgeships and other issues. After the 2006 midterm congressional elections, both houses of Congress came under the control of Democrats, who vowed to force Bush to compromise on a variety of issues, perhaps most notably Bush's Iraq policy.

President's Program

No longer do presidents maintain the fiction of separation from the legislative process. Contemporary presidents often are judged by the quality and timing of their legislative programs. In fact, Congress and the public demand that presidents initiate legislation and will criticize any presidents who do not.

Presidents lay out most of their program in the annual State of the Union address. These priorities are then translated into specific pieces of legislation, which are sent to Capitol Hill for consideration.

The executive branch also submits to Congress hundreds of other presidential reports, messages, and communications. Many of these are required by law. The Budget and Accounting Act of 1921, for example, requires the president to present Congress with an annual budget message as part of the BUDGET PROCESS. The Employment Act of 1946 calls for presidential submission of an annual economic report as well.

Modern presidents are aided in these tasks by an immense executive institution of hundreds of special assistants, personal aides, policy experts, and clerical staff distributed among several specialized agencies. The EXECUTIVE OFFICE OF THE PRESIDENT (EOP) is the president's personal bureaucracy, designed expressly to help the president oversee department and agency activities, formulate budgets and monitor spending, craft legislation, lobby Congress, and above all ensure that the president's priorities are promoted. Within EOP the OFFICE OF MANAGEMENT AND BUDGET plays the "central clearance" role, reviewing legislative proposals and assessing bills passed by Congress.

Executive Lobbying

To win enactment of important—and therefore usually controversial—legislation, the president cannot simply submit legislation and wait for the finished product.

Specialized coalitions often must be built in Congress. Presidents and their staff must understand the legislative process and the significance of the timing of legislative maneuvers. They must consult with pivotal members of Congress. They must know how to use the variety of resources available to them for winning congressional support.

Presidents whose political party controls both houses of Congress begin with an immediate advantage, although, as some presidents have discovered, it does not guarantee success. Most of those who have had the greatest success with Congress—among them Jefferson, Theodore Roosevelt, Wilson, Franklin Roosevelt, and Lyndon Johnson—have used party ties to chamber and committee leaders to cement support for important programs.

Even presidents whose party is not in control of Congress find ways of dealing with partisan differences. President Ronald Reagan amassed a series of major successes during his first year in office by relying on the Republican majority in the Senate and a working House majority composed of minority Republicans and "Boll Weevil" Democrats (conservative southern Democrats who were sympathetic to many of Reagan's objectives).

In lobbying for their legislative programs, presidents themselves can play a pivotal role. One of the president's most important legislative resources is a personal appeal. Although not always successful, a phone call to or face-to-face meeting with a member of Congress is usually an effective means of winning support.

Presidents often use the vice president to lobby on behalf of the administration's policies. The vice president also serves as president of the Senate, a largely ceremonial position that takes on significance on those rare occasions when the vice president's vote is needed to break a tie so that the vote goes in favor of the administration.

Presidents today also have a large STAFF to persuade and bargain with Congress. Presidents have always maintained informal relations with congressional leaders. Wilson was the first president in the twentieth century to lobby personally on Capitol Hill. Franklin Roosevelt inaugurated or perfected many of the lobbying techniques used by contemporary presidents, but legislative liaison remained an informal process.

Harry S. Truman in 1949 set up a small legislative liaison office, but the staff was inexperienced and the real lobbying was still done by Truman and a few top advisers. In 1953 his successor, Dwight D. Eisenhower, appointed full-time senior staff to the task. With the establishment of the Congressional Relations Office, Eisenhower became the first president to openly operate a congressional liaison staff and to give it a formal place in the White House.

The liaison office grew to maturity during the Kennedy and Johnson administrations, when many modern legislative liaison practices were adopted. Staff members were assigned to work with virtually every faction and bloc in Congress, and they consequently spent much of their time roaming the halls of the Capitol building. The liaison office prepared weekly reports for the president and made projections about the week to come.

The office also became a focal point for the liaison activities of the executive agencies and departments. The federal departments have maintained liaison staffs since 1945, when the War

Department created the office of assistant secretary for congressional liaison, centralizing congressional relations that had been handled separately by the military services.

There are some legal limits on executive lobbying. The executive branch has been prohibited by a 1919 criminal statute from spending money to influence votes in Congress. It has generally been understood that direct pressure by the executive on Congress is acceptable, but that spending money to solicit outside pressure on Congress is not.

Public Appeals

Because direct lobbying of Congress does not always work, every president has found it necessary on occasion to turn to the people to recruit support. Public pressure can be a potent weapon against a recalcitrant Congress.

The potency of public appeals grew enormously with the advent of radio and television. Franklin Roosevelt entered the White House as radio reached its heyday, and he used the medium not only to reassure the nation but also to move Congress into action on his legislative program. In 1933, at the end of his first week in office, Roosevelt went on the radio to urge support for his banking reforms. He also addressed a joint session of Congress. His reforms were passed that very day. In later radio broadcasts, which became known as "fireside chats" because of their intimate, my-house-to-your-house tone, Roosevelt continued to win public and congressional support.

Television further revolutionized the art of public appeals. Lyndon Johnson, for example, made masterful use of a televised address in 1965 to move the nation and Congress to support the most sweeping voting rights bill in ninety years.

Ronald Reagan, a former movie and television actor, quickly displayed his skill in using the media to his political advantage. He relied heavily on his rhetorical talents to whip up massive support for his dramatic budget and tax policy victories in 1981. Particularly powerful was Reagan's May 1981 appeal to a joint session of Congress for support on his budget package, his first public appearance since the March 1981 assassination attempt. So massive was the outpouring of public support for the president that the Democratic-dominated House passed his package a few days after the speech. (See MEDIA AND THE PRESIDENCY.)

Patronage

Presidents readily rely on PATRONAGE as a means of winning support. Although the civil service limits the extent to which federal jobs may be filled by presidential appointment, presidents nevertheless have the authority to fill thousands of federal positions, including judgeships and federal marshal and attorney positions. Such appointments can be used to curry favor among members of Congress.

Presidents also can exercise substantial personal patronage by, for example, making campaign trips to the home district of a member of Congress, extending White House invitations to legislators, and even providing tickets to the president's box at the John F. Kennedy Center for the Performing Arts. Such favors can have an effect on those of either party whose support is sought by the president.

Presidents also have a large say in the distribution of so-called pork-barrel projects. They may reward friends and punish enemies by throwing their support to or withholding support from public works projects, construction projects, defense contracts, agricultural subsidies, and the like.

Veto

When personal appeals, lobbying, public pressure, White House parties, free concert tickets, army bases, and jobs all fail to move Congress, presidents may resort to their most powerful defensive weapon: the veto.

Presidents use the veto to kill bills they find unacceptable as well as to dramatize policies and to try to force compromises on Capitol Hill. Although the Constitution allows Congress to override a veto by a two-thirds vote in each chamber, this rarely happens.

Short of an actual veto, a presidential threat to veto legislation is a powerful form of lobbying. (See VETO POWER.)

Executive Order

The framers of the Constitution gave presidents potentially far-reaching power when they granted them "executive power" and authority to "take Care that the Laws be faithfully executed."

One result of this vague constitutional wording is the EXECUTIVE ORDER, a significant weapon in the president's arsenal. Although it is not defined in the Constitution, an executive order generally is a presidential directive that becomes law without prior congressional approval. It is based either on existing laws or on the president's other constitutional responsibilities.

Executive orders have become critical to the legislative role of modern presidents precisely because Congress frequently finds itself unable or unwilling to pass highly detailed laws. Instead Congress legislates in broad language and leaves it to the executive branch to hammer out the details.

Executive orders are often controversial because of their great potential for overuse by presidents who are unwilling to work with Congress, frustrated by opposition, or overeager to impose strict secrecy.

Congressional Role

Congress plays an important role in the functioning of the executive branch, just as the president does for the legislative branch.

The Constitution provides that Congress will count electoral votes for president and vice president; if candidates fail to win a majority, the House will choose the president and the Senate will choose the vice president. (See ELECTORAL COLLEGE.) The Senate has the power to confirm executive appointments and approve treaties. (See APPOINTMENT AND REMOVAL POWER and TREATY POWER.) Both the House and the Senate can conduct investigations into activities of the executive branch and play significant parts in any IMPEACHMENT attempts. Congress also shares with the executive important WAR POWERS. But Congress exercises its greatest influence over executive branch activities through its power of the purse and the role it plays in the budget process. Through its authorizations and appropriations (approval and actual funding of programs), Congress helps to formulate and carry out executive policies. It may use its taxing power both to raise money and to regulate government activities.

Congress also has the important responsibility of oversight of executive branch activities to ensure that its legislative intent is being carried out and to remedy the situation if it is not.

In the 1970s Congress used these various tools to counter what it saw as an inordinate increase in presidential power. It enacted a wide range of limitations on executive discretion, including a revision of the budget process, increased reliance on the LEGISLATIVE VETO, short-term authorization for federal programs to ensure more frequent review, greater use of provisions in appropriations bills to dictate how funds are spent, freedom-of-information rules, and additional reporting requirements for the executive branch.

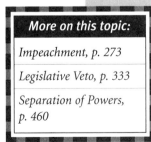

More on this topic:

Impeachment, p. 273

Legislative Veto, p. 333

Separation of Powers, p. 460

Congress also dramatically expanded its own ability to oversee the executive branch by hiring thousands of additional staff and by creating or expanding congressional support agencies, such as the General Accounting Office (now called the Government Accountability Office) and Congressional Budget Office.

Congressional Caucus (King Caucus)

CAUCUS CURS in full YELL, or a WAR-WHOOP to saddle on the PEOPLE, a PAPPOOSE PRESIDENT.

This 1824 political cartoon criticizes Andrew Jackson's treatment by the hostile press and the practice of nominating candidates, especially Democratic-Republican nominee William Crawford, by congressional caucus. The snarling dogs are labeled with the names of critical newspapers.
Source: Library of Congress

From 1796 until 1824 most presidential nominees were chosen by their party's members of Congress. The congressional caucus—or "King Caucus," as its detractors called it—eventually gave way to a more open, democratic method of candidate selection. Its demise was ensured by the controversial election of 1824, in which the Democratic-Republican Party was splintered over who would be its presidential nominee and the House ultimately chose John Quincy Adams over popular front-runner Andrew Jackson.

The congressional caucus system was far from what the framers of the Constitution had in mind. Delegates to the Constitutional Convention of 1787 had hoped political parties would be kept out of the selection process, and during George Washington's two terms in office this was mostly the case. But strong political parties soon developed and took over the nominating process. (See ELECTIONS AND CAMPAIGNS.)

The congressional caucus system first appeared in the election of 1796. A caucus of Democratic-Republican senators attempted, though unsuccessfully, to reach agreement on a running mate for their uncontested presidential candidate, Thomas Jefferson. The Federalists held what historian Roy F. Nichols described as a "quasi caucus" of the party's members of Congress to choose their candidates.

The election of 1800 was the first in which both parties used congressional caucuses to nominate presidential candidates. Neither party, however, wanted that fact publicized. They deliberated in secret, and few details were made known. But by the next election the Democratic-Republicans were willing to report their deliberations publicly.

The Federalists dropped the congressional caucus as their nominating method in 1804, but the Democratic-Republican Party continued to use the caucus system for two decades. Not everyone within the party liked the system, however. To quiet the opposition, the caucuses often passed resolutions lauding and defending themselves.

By 1816 the Federalist Party was nearly extinct. Although the collapse of the Federalists ensured Democratic-Republican rule, it also increased friction among the Democratic-Republicans and spurred further attacks on the caucus system. Its opponents claimed that presidential nomination should not be a function of Congress and that the caucus system encouraged presidential candidates to curry the favor of Congress.

At the same time there was a growing democratization of the political system. Many of the states were choosing their presidential electors by popular vote, mass participation in presidential elections was increasing dramatically, and there was a trend toward expansion of the right to vote. The caucus system was a holdover from an age that distrusted mass democratic sentiments.

Against this backdrop came the election of 1824. When the Democratic-Republican caucus met, only 66 of 261 members of Congress were present, and three-quarters of those were from only four states. The caucus chose William H. Crawford as its presidential nominee from among five serious candidates. Three of the other candidates—Adams, Henry Clay, and Jackson—refused to withdraw. In the ensuing election, Jackson received the most popular and the most electoral votes, but not a majority of either. Because there was no majority in the Electoral College, the election was thrown to the House of Representatives, which elected Adams, who had come in second.

The caucus's selection of Crawford over Jackson and the House election of Adams over Jackson proved to be the kiss of death for the congressional caucus.

> **More on this topic:**
>
> *Party Leader, p. 396*

Constitutional Powers and Provisions

The powers and duties of the president are outlined in Article II of the Constitution. Although the Constitution grants far fewer explicit powers to the president in Article II than it does to Congress in Article I, the ambiguity and vagueness of Article II have made it possible for presidents to expand their authority greatly beyond that specifically listed in the Constitution.

The two passages in the Constitution that have provided the basis for the expansion of presidential authority are Article II, Section 1, which grants "the executive Power" to the president, and Section 3, which makes the president responsible for the enforcement of federal laws: "he shall take Care that the Laws be faithfully executed."

The Constitution lays out the powers and duties of the president. Here the founders take turns signing their names.
Source: Library of Congress

The uncertainty in the Constitution about the president's powers reflects the ambivalence of the framers of the Constitution over the office they were creating. On one hand, the framers saw the president as a nonhereditary, elected official responsible to the people, while, on the otherhand, they were concerned about the effects of too much democracy and the possibility that the president would respond to popular demands in ways that hurt minority rights. Similarly, the Constitution gives the president sweeping powers over the administration of the federal government, while also subjecting it to congressional constraints.

The following brief descriptions cover the chief categories of presidential powers created by the Constitution.

Chief Executive

Although the founders placed a high priority on the president's executive duties, the Constitution provides very few instructions about the president's tasks as head of the executive branch. Specific presidential administrative powers have evolved as the presidency has matured.

The Constitution does not make direct provision for the vast administrative structure that the president must oversee. It does, however, authorize the president to demand written reports from the "principal Officer in each of the executive Departments, upon any Subject, relating to the Duties of their respective Offices." This clause implies a division of labor within the executive branch and clearly establishes a hierarchy with the president as the chief administrative officer.

Appointment and Removal Power

One of the most important administrative powers of the president is to appoint people to fill high-level positions in the administration. Article II, Section 2, gives the president the power to select top officials, subject to Senate approval.

In the nineteenth century presidents and Congress had much greater appointment powers, sharing in the use of the patronage system to distribute all types of government jobs to their friends and political supporters. The enactment of civil service laws largely put an end to that practice, so that today about 90 percent of executive branch positions are covered by the merit systems, leaving only the most senior positions to be filled by presidential appointees. Nevertheless, presidents' powers to choose personnel for these positions enable them to help set the direction for the bureaucracy. The Constitution does not explicitly authorize the president to remove federal officeholders, even though that power with respect to top officials would seem to be a major aspect of the president's administrative control. The president's removal power was not confirmed by the Supreme Court until 1926, and the Court has since limited this power over certain federal agencies. (See APPOINTMENT AND REMOVAL POWER.)

Budgeting

The Constitution does not clearly establish a budgetary process or spell out the presidency's role in such a process. Because of this ambiguity, presidents have been able to bring much of the process under their control. Article I of the Constitution gives Congress power over taxes and spending, while Article II, Section 3, gives presidents the power to recommend fiscal policies.

The power to control the BUDGET PROCESS is one of the most important administrative prerogatives of the presidency. Often, it is the president who decides where and how money should be spent. In the last part of the twentieth century, the presidency assumed an increasingly important role in determining federal spending.

Law Enforcement

The president's role in law enforcement rests on the constitutional requirement that the president "take Care that the Laws be faithfully executed." The president serves as chief executive of what has become a vast law enforcement apparatus. Should assistance be needed, the president can invoke the authority of "commander in chief" and deploy the armed forces, including units of state militias, to enforce the law.

Presidential LAW ENFORCEMENT POWERS have grown in rough proportion to enlargements in the responsibilities and power of the national government itself. Over the years Congress has added greatly to the law enforcement duties of the president. One dramatic example of this use of presidential power came in 1962, when John F. Kennedy ordered U.S. marshals and regular army troops to quell riots protesting a court order that required the University of Mississippi to integrate its student body by admitting a black student, James Meredith.

Clemency

The Constitution gives the president the "Power to grant Reprieves and Pardons for Offences against the United States, except in Cases of Impeachment." The framers specifically included this power to enable the president to make well-timed offers of pardon to those in domestic rebellion against the government, when such a move might help restore order.

The clemency authority of the president is extensive. It applies to any federal process or offender, except officials who have been impeached. The best-known use of the clemency power in recent decades was Gerald R. Ford's pardon of Richard Nixon for offenses committed during the Watergate affair. In addition, Ford and Jimmy Carter issued amnesties, which are pardons covering a whole group of people, for draft evaders during the Vietnam War. Bill Clinton ran into controversy when he issued 140 pardons and 36 commutations on January 20, 2001, his last day in office.

Legislative

The Constitution is reticent about the president's role in legislating, yet the relationship between Congress and the executive is the most important aspect of the U.S. system of government. More than two hundred years of history have seen an immense and fundamental expansion in the array of resources the president can use to influence public policy.

Veto

Perhaps the chief legal weapon presidents have in their relationship with Congress is the VETO POWER, which enables presidents to prevent all but the most popular pieces of legislation from becoming law against their wishes.

Under the Constitution, presidents may respond to a bill passed by Congress in one of three ways. They may sign it, veto the bill by returning it to Congress, or do nothing. If they do nothing, the bill becomes law after the passage of ten days, excluding Sundays. If Congress adjourns sooner than ten days after the bill passed, however, the bill dies, under the "pocket veto" provision. If the president vetoes a bill, Congress can still enact it into law by repassing the measure with two-thirds majorities in both chambers. Such overrides are relatively rare, however; from 1789 through 2002, only 106 of 2,551 presidential vetoes were overridden, about 4 percent.

Legislative Proposals

The Constitution also authorizes the president to "recommend to [Congress's] Consideration such Measures as he shall judge necessary and expedient." Unlike the veto, which is a limited and somewhat negative instrument for stopping legislation, the duty to recommend legislation has over time become the primary mechanism by which chief executives influence the nation's political agenda. Given the presidency's relatively weak array of formal devices for mandating government policy, no other facet of the office today is as critical to presidential success or failure. The ability to shape the agenda of government—to decide what is or is not a priority—is in essence the power to influence what government will or will not do.

Throughout most of the nineteenth century, the president had little power to define the national agenda. Congress dominated government, and presidents were not expected to formulate legislative proposals. The turning point in the transformation of the presidency into the chief initiator of major legislation came in 1933, when Franklin D. Roosevelt responded to the crisis of the Great Depression with a flood of legislative proposals, known as the "FIRST HUNDRED DAYS," that both dominated the congressional agenda and brought about a historic change in the role of the federal government in national life. Although few presidents since have been as successful as Roosevelt, his tenure has become the model for the office.

Executive Orders

The section of the Constitution that allots to the president "executive power" is one of the least specific but potentially most important in the document. When paired with the provision requiring presidents to take care that laws are faithfully executed, the executive power clause provides for a range of implied powers whose extent and potency have grown beyond anything the framers could have foreseen.

An offshoot of the implied powers doctrine is the EXECUTIVE ORDER. This critical instrument of active presidential power is nowhere defined in the Constitution but generally is construed as a presidential directive that becomes law without prior congressional approval. It is based either on existing statutes or on the president's other constitutional responsibilities. Executive orders usually pertain specifically to government agencies and officials, but their effects often reach to the average citizen. For example, in 1965 Lyndon B. Johnson issued Executive Order 11246, which required companies that win federal government contracts to create programs for hiring more minorities, significantly affecting private sector employment practices. For the most part, presidents issue executive orders to establish executive branch agencies, to modify bureaucratic rules or actions, to change decision-making procedures, or to give substance and force to statutes.

Emergency Powers

In times of crisis presidents often lay claim to extraordinary powers to preserve the nation. Such EMERGENCY POWERS are neither granted expressly to the president nor delegated to Congress by the Constitution. Instead, they are judged to reside purely in the need for leaders to protect national sovereignty and domestic order. The mandate in Article II that the president "preserve, protect and defend" the Constitution and uphold its provisions is considered to contain implicitly the notion of emergency powers.

The most significant use of presidential emergency powers was made by Abraham Lincoln during the Civil War. Faced with the secession of the southern states, Lincoln claimed numerous emergency war powers to save the Union, in the process becoming what some have called a "constitutional dictator." The most controversial use of the emergency power in the twentieth century came in 1951 when Harry Truman, who had put the nation on emergency footing after North Korea invaded South Korea, ordered the seizure of strike-threatened steel mills to avoid potential shortages. Truman based his action on the president's inherent authority to meet national emergencies. However, the Supreme Court later ruled that the seizure was unconstitutional.

In November 2001, in the wake of the September 11, 2001, terrorist attacks on the United States, George W. Bush authorized the use of military tribunals for trying foreigners accused of terrorist acts against the United States. Bush said that emergency powers under the commander-in-chief clause gave him the latitude to put these measures into place.

Foreign Affairs

The Constitution grants few foreign affairs powers to the president. Although it gives the president authority to make treaties and appoint ambassadors, it allots Congress a range of powers in the area that are at least equal to those of the president. Indeed, the constitutional division of foreign affairs power has been described as "an invitation to struggle."

Nevertheless, presidents in recent decades have won interbranch struggles for primacy in foreign relations. Although Congress sometimes can block or modify presidential foreign policy initiatives, the president has dominated the formulation and initiation of foreign policy.

Treaty Powers

Article II, Section 2, Clause 2, gives the president power to make treaties with other countries, subject to ratification by a two-thirds majority of the Senate. This provision sets up a classic division of power between the legislative and executive branches. The primary responsibility for conducting treaty negotiations lies with the president, but the president cannot bring about a final agreement without the concurrence of most senators.

Nevertheless, the executive branch has established itself as the dominant branch in treaty making. As the sole organ of communication with foreign countries, as the commander in chief, and as the head of the foreign policy bureaucracy, presidents are equipped with the means needed to control most phases of the treaty-making process. Presidents can stop the process at any time, if they think the pact would be voted down on a full Senate vote, or if they dislike any changes the Senate has made. In 1980, for example, Jimmy Carter withdrew the SALT II treaty with the Soviet Union from Senate consideration after Soviet troops invaded Afghanistan.

Executive Agreements

An EXECUTIVE AGREEMENT is a pact other than a treaty made by the president with a foreign government. Presidents have asserted that their constitutional powers give them authority to make these pacts without Senate approval. For presidents, the executive agreement is a particularly powerful foreign policy tool because it allows them to act without seeking congressional backing. The chief limitation on executive agreements is that, unlike treaties, they do not supersede any U.S. laws with which they might conflict.

The executive agreement power was used as early as 1803, when Thomas Jefferson arranged for the Louisiana Purchase without congressional approval. Throughout the nineteenth century presidents made little use of the power, concluding on average only one executive agreement per year. The use of such agreements grew dramatically in the twentieth century. Between 1945 and 1996 only 6 percent of all international agreements entered into by the United States were treaties. Executive agreements are now used to conduct business once reserved for treaties. For example, trade agreements, the annexation of territory, military commitments, and arms control pacts have all been concluded through executive agreements.

Recognition and Appointment Powers

Although the Constitution does not explicitly grant presidents the power to recognize foreign governments, it is generally accepted that they have this power as a result of their authority to send and receive ambassadors. Because the acts of sending an ambassador to a country and receiving its representative imply recognition of the legitimacy of the foreign government involved, presidents have successfully claimed exclusive authority to decide which foreign governments will be recognized by the United States. It follows, then, that they have the power to terminate relations with another nation as well.

The constitutional power to appoint ambassadors is also important because the success of a president's foreign policy depends somewhat on the personalities and abilities of the people who fill important diplomatic posts. Many ambassadorships are given to foreign service officials with years of experience, but presidents also take advantage of this power of appointment for various purposes. For many years, ambassadorships to small countries, preferably those with pleasant climates, have been used as rewards for major financial contributors or political allies of the president. Presidents also have used high-visibility appointments to make political statements, such as when Jimmy Carter appointed civil rights activist Andrew Young to be ambassador to the United Nations, or when Ronald Reagan picked conservative foreign policy analyst Jeane Kirkpatrick for the same post.

Commander in Chief

Reflecting the clear consensus at the Constitutional Convention that the nation's highest civilian officer should have charge of the military, the Constitution states that the president "shall be

⊙ **CLOSER LOOK**

The framers were hoping that the first president, George Washington, would bring to office a high standard of conduct and set precedents to clarify some of the ambiguities in the Constitution. Perhaps the most noteworthy was Washington's decision not to seek a third term in office, a precedent followed until 1940. A lesser known precedent important in cementing the president's role as chief diplomat was his refusal to turn over papers to the House of Representatives related to the negotiations over Jay's treaty with Great Britain. In 1796 Washington sent a message to the House stating in part,

> The nature of foreign negotiations requires caution, and their success must often depend on secrecy.... To admit, then, a right in the House of Representatives to demand and to have as a matter of course all the papers respecting a negotiation with a foreign power would be to establish a dangerous precedent.

—George Washington, *Message to the House of Representatives Regarding Documents Relative to the Jay Treaty*

Commander in Chief of the Army and Navy of the United States, and of the Militia of the several States, when called into the actual Service of the United States." That is the only statement in the document about the president's war-making power. Because the precise authority of the office of commander in chief is left undefined, presidents have been able to argue that they possess any power needed to improve the nation's defenses in peacetime or to help it prevail over an enemy in wartime, without usurping the power of the other branches or violating the law.

The Constitution does not give the president complete domination over the war-making function. The power to declare war is reserved for Congress, as is the ability to raise and maintain an army. Nevertheless, presidential use of the power to order U.S. forces into combat without a congressional declaration of war increased greatly during the twentieth century. Particularly during the half-century of cold war conflict between the United States and the Soviet Union, presidents claimed the right to deploy military forces on their own initiative. Presidents also had the support of congressional resolutions authorizing them to use force, such as the Tonkin Gulf resolution which Lyndon Johnson claimed as his legal authority for carrying out the war in Vietnam.

In 1973 Congress responded to Richard Nixon's continuing prosecution of the Vietnam War by passing the WAR POWERS ACT over Nixon's veto. The most important and controversial provisions of the law outlined the situations under which presidents could commit troops, permitted Congress at any time to order the president to disengage troops involved in an undeclared war, and required the president to withdraw armed forces from a conflict within sixty to ninety days unless Congress specifically authorized its continuation. The law has failed to substantially change presidential war-making prerogatives, however. Presidents since Nixon have strongly refused to invoke the law, and only once—in speeding the removal of U.S. forces from Lebanon in 1982—has the law forced a compromise over the use of military power. In 1991 George H. W. Bush allowed a dramatic debate and vote in Congress over authorization of his use of force in the Persian Gulf without admitting that his actions were subject to the War Powers Act. In the fall of 2002, George W. Bush sought, and eventually received, congressional authorization to use military force against Saddam Hussein's regime.

Chief of State

The president also serves as the CHIEF OF STATE of the United States, presiding over ceremonial functions. This office, which in countries with constitutional monarchies is carried out by the king or queen, serves as a symbol of the permanence of the national state. The president's role as chief of state as described in the Constitution includes the obligation to take the oath of office, deliver an annual State of the Union message, and receive ambassadors from other countries. Although the president's ceremonial functions do not constitute a major source of power, they elevate the office above other offices and institutions and create a leadership mystique that can be of great help to a president in achieving policy goals.

More on this topic:
Article II, p. 16
Emergency Powers, p. 188
Law Enforcement Powers, p. 330
Veto Power, p. 533
War Powers, p. 555

Conventions *See* NATIONAL PARTY CONVENTIONS.

Coolidge, Calvin

Source: Library of Congress

Calvin Coolidge (1872–1933) became a symbol of honest and efficient but passive stewardship in the White House. During his five and a half years in office, he was fondly called "Silent Cal" by the public because of his quiet, almost sphinx-like demeanor. Presidential scholars have judged him less kindly.

Coolidge was born on July 4, 1872, in Plymouth Notch, Vermont. His parents farmed and owned a general store. He was originally named John Calvin after his father, but he dropped his first name when he became an adult. In 1895 Coolidge graduated with honors from Amherst College in Amherst, Massachusetts. He then moved to nearby Northampton, where he found a job as a law clerk. He was admitted to the bar in 1897, started his own law practice, and became involved in Northampton politics as a Republican. He served as a member of the city council, city solicitor, and chairman of the county Republican committee. He suffered his only political defeat in 1905 when he was beaten for a seat on the Northampton school board. That year he married Grace Goodhue.

In 1906 Coolidge was elected to the Massachusetts house of representatives. After two terms, he returned to Northampton and in 1910 was elected mayor. In 1911 Coolidge won a seat in the state senate. After four one-year terms he was elected lieutenant governor in 1915.

Coolidge became a political figure of national importance when he was elected governor of Massachusetts by a slim margin in 1918. In September 1919 the Boston police staged a strike that opened the way for a criminal rampage. When Governor Coolidge called out the state militia to keep order in Boston, Samuel Gompers, head of the American Federation of Labor, accused Coolidge of acting unfairly. Coolidge replied with a wire declaring, "There is no right to strike against the public safety by anybody, anywhere, any time." The statement made Coolidge famous across the country.

At the 1920 Republican national convention in Chicago, a deadlock led to the presidential nomination of a compromise candidate, Sen. Warren G. Harding of Ohio. Party leaders expected their choice for vice president, Wisconsin senator Irvine Lenroot, to be similarly ratified by the convention. When Coolidge's name was put into nomination for vice president after Lenroot's, however, the convention unexpectedly threw its support behind the popular governor, who was nominated on the first ballot.

During the 1920 campaign Harding and Coolidge promised to raise tariffs to protect U.S. industry and to keep the nation out of war and entangling alliances. They won more than 60 percent of the popular vote on their way to a 404–127 victory in the Electoral College over Democrats James M. Cox and Franklin D. Roosevelt.

In 1923 Vice President Coolidge was spending the summer in Vermont when a telegraph messenger arrived at his home after midnight on August 3 with the news that President Harding had suddenly died in San Francisco. Coolidge's father, who was a notary public, administered the oath of office.

Coolidge retained Harding's cabinet, but when the scandals that pervaded the Harding administration were revealed, he asked for the resignations of those involved. Coolidge dutifully prosecuted the former Harding administration officials who had committed crimes.

Coolidge ran for a term of his own in 1924 against John W. Davis. Despite the scandals of the Harding administration, Coolidge's personal honesty and national prosperity carried him to victory. He defeated Davis in the Electoral College vote 382–136.

During his second term Coolidge was successful in decreasing the national debt and cutting income taxes. These policies put more money into the hands of consumers and helped stimulate investment. Coolidge's hands-off policies toward business activities, however, put off needed reforms of the financial industry and encouraged overspeculation which contributed to the stock market crash of 1929 and the subsequent Great Depression. In foreign relations, Coolidge reestablished diplomatic relations with Mexico, which had been severed under Woodrow Wilson, and improved relations with other Latin American nations, which had been strained since the turn of the century.

> *I no longer fit in with these times.... When I read of the newfangled that are now so popular, I realize that my time in public affairs is past. We are in a new era to which I do not belong, and it would not be possible for me to adjust myself to it.*
>
> **—Calvin Coolidge**

After leaving office Coolidge returned to Northampton, Massachusetts. During his short retirement he wrote newspaper columns and served on the board of directors of the New York Life Insurance Company. On January 5, 1933, less than four years after leaving the White House, Coolidge died of a heart attack in Northampton.

More on this topic:
Elections Chronology, p. 174
Harding, Warren, p. 245

Counsel to the President

Alberto Gonzales
Source: Library of Congress

The counsel to the president, or special counsel as the position is often called, is the White House's lawyer, but does not act as the president's personal lawyer. This staff member provides legal advice on an assortment of topics, reviews legislation before it is sent to Congress, and may even check draft treaties for legal problems.

In addition, the counsel's office helps to arrange for background checks on possible appointees to the executive branch and oversees security clearances for those who are appointed. The office also is involved in the selection of new federal judges and works with the Justice Department and with counsel offices in other federal agencies.

The counsel's office tracks compliance with conflict-of-interest measures for workers in the Executive Office of the President and, since the Watergate affair, also has been responsible for ensuring the proper behavior of the presidential staff. An additional duty that the counsel undertook in the Clinton administration was assisting the president's defense against impeachment (Charles F. C. Ruff assumed that role).

Beyond these duties, the office often has served as a place to put valuable aides. In creating the position, Franklin D. Roosevelt argued that the White House needed its own lawyer because the attorney general was too busy to give the White House the necessary time. In reality, he envisioned a bigger role for his counsel. His primary purpose was to create a place for Samuel I. Rosenman, who served him as an adviser and a speechwriter.

Clark Clifford filled a similar function while occupying the same post under Harry S. Truman. John F. Kennedy named Theodore Sorensen special counsel; Sorensen also served as a speechwriter and domestic policy adviser. Under Jimmy Carter, the office was used in two different ways: Robert J. Lipshutz confined himself to legal matters; his successor, Lloyd Cutler, advised the president on a wide range of issues, both foreign and domestic. Bill Clinton tapped Cutler to return temporarily to his old post, after Clinton's first counsel, Bernard Nussbaum, resigned amid criticism that he lacked the political sensitivity needed for the job. Nussbaum was later questioned by a congressional committee about charges that he had interfered with investigators probing the suicide of deputy White House counsel Vincent Foster. Other White House counsels under Clinton were Abner J. Mikva, Lanny J. Davis, Jack Quinn, Ruff, and Beth Nolan. George W. Bush appointed Alberto R. Gonzales to be his special counsel. Gonzales thus became the highest-ranking Hispanic ever to serve in the White House Office and later became attorney general. Bush's failed Supreme Court nominee Harriet Miers held the position from 2005 to 2007 and was replaced by former Reagan special counsel Fred Fielding.

> **More on this topic:**
>
> *Executive Office of the President, p. 200*
>
> *Staff, p. 471*

Court-Packing Plan

During his first term Franklin D. Roosevelt won extraordinary support from Congress for his New Deal programs. Designed to lead the country out of the Great Depression, these programs gave new and existing federal agencies extensive powers to regulate the nation's economic activities.

It was inevitable that such revolutionary uses of federal power would be tested before the Supreme Court and almost as certain that a majority of the Court would be unreceptive. In Roosevelt's first term four of the nine justices were staunch conservatives opposed in principle to government economic regulation. They needed only one additional vote to prevail in a given case and often were able to obtain it.

Between January 1935 and June 1936, the Supreme Court ruled against the Roosevelt administration in eight of the ten cases involving major New Deal measures. The Court also held that the president did not have any inherent power to fire members of federal regulatory agencies.

Roosevelt grew increasingly frustrated as the Court overturned one New Deal measure after another. After he won a landslide victory in the 1936 election, he decided to take action. On February 5, 1937, the president proposed a judicial "reorganization" to Congress. The measure would have increased the number of Supreme Court justices to

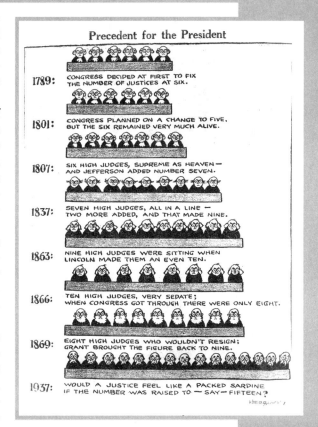

Precedent for the President

1789: CONGRESS DECIDED AT FIRST TO FIX THE NUMBER OF JUSTICES AT SIX.

1801: CONGRESS PLANNED ON A CHANGE TO FIVE, BUT THE SIX REMAINED VERY MUCH ALIVE.

1807: SIX HIGH JUDGES, SUPREME AS HEAVEN— AND JEFFERSON ADDED NUMBER SEVEN.

1837: SEVEN HIGH JUDGES, ALL IN A LINE— TWO MORE ADDED, AND THAT MADE NINE.

1863: NINE HIGH JUDGES WERE SITTING WHEN LINCOLN MADE THEM AN EVEN TEN.

1866: TEN HIGH JUDGES, VERY SEDATE; WHEN CONGRESS GOT THROUGH THERE WERE ONLY EIGHT.

1869: EIGHT HIGH JUDGES WHO WOULDN'T RESIGN; GRANT BROUGHT THE FIGURE BACK TO NINE.

1937: WOULD A JUSTICE FEEL LIKE A PACKED SARDINE IF THE NUMBER WAS RAISED TO — SAY— FIFTEEN?

Source: Herblock

More on this topic:

*Appointment and
Removal Power, p. 9*

*Courts and the President,
below*

New Deal, p. 383

*Roosevelt, Franklin D.,
p. 445*

as many as fifteen, creating one new seat for each sitting justice who, upon reaching the age of seventy, declined to retire. Six of the nine justices were seventy or over.

Although Roosevelt attempted to portray his proposal as a way to ease the judicial workload, the public saw it for what it was—a Court-packing plan—and many vigorously opposed it. People might have supported the president and his policies, but by and large they criticized his scheme as perverting the Constitution and destroying judicial integrity and independence.

The Court itself dealt the death blow to the Court-packing plan. In a series of decisions announced between late March and late May 1937, the Court upheld several New Deal measures, three of them by 5–4 votes. In each of these cases, the deciding vote was cast by Owen J. Roberts, who abandoned the four conservatives with whom he had voted in previous terms.

"A switch in time saves nine" was the popular saying of the day, and Roberts's vote was long assumed to be a direct response to the Court-packing threat. Later evidence suggests that Roberts may have decided to switch his vote before the Court-packing plan was announced. In any event, Roosevelt's plan never emerged from Congress.

The president may have lost the battle, but he eventually won the war. After 1937 the Court gradually repudiated its earlier New Deal decisions. In cases involving labor relations, manufacturing, agriculture, and federal spending the Court struck down most of the limits it had placed on the exercise of federal power.

Courts and the President

The framers of the Constitution built checks and balances into the relationship between the federal courts and the president. The president is responsible for appointing all federal judges and enforcing judicial decisions, while the judiciary—most notably the Supreme Court—defines the limits of presidential authority.

For the most part, the judiciary has allowed presidential powers to develop with few checks. The Supreme Court has legitimized significant claims of presidential diplomatic, war, and economic powers. It also has rebuffed various attempts by Congress and the states to limit presidential powers. Nevertheless, the judiciary has from time to time curbed the exercise of presidential authority. Among the most dramatic rulings in the twentieth century were the short-lived series of anti–New Deal rulings, the 1952 *Steel Seizure* decision, and the 1974 Watergate tapes decision that resulted in Richard Nixon's early departure from the White House. A major decision in 1997 was *Clinton v. Jones,* which helped to provide a legal backdrop for Bill Clinton's impeachment, and in 2000 was *Bush v. Gore,* in which the Court, amid great controversy, resolved the prolonged 2000 presidential election in favor of the Republican candidate, George W. Bush.

Two factors contribute to the infrequency of Supreme Court rulings on the authority of the chief executive. First, the constitutional language describing the powers of the president is general: the president is vested with the executive power, is commander in chief, and is directed to take care that the laws are faithfully executed. That language leaves courts with a great deal of latitude in determining whether presidents are exercising their powers appropriately.

Second, the aura that surrounds the office of the president tends to insulate its occupant from court challenges. The president is better able than the other two branches of government to capture the public eye and gain political support, which makes the task of curbing presidential power ever more difficult. In light of these characteristics, the Supreme Court has been cautious in locking horns with the chief executive.

Presidents themselves have held strikingly different views on the limits of presidential powers. William Howard Taft, the only president who also sat on the Supreme Court, viewed executive power as limited to the specific powers granted in the Constitution. "The President," Taft wrote, "can exercise no power which cannot be fairly and reasonably traced to some specific grant of power or justly implied and included within such grant as proper and necessary."

Theodore Roosevelt viewed the presidential office differently. He envisioned an active president acting responsibly on behalf of the public welfare. "My belief," Roosevelt wrote, "was that it was not only [the president's] right but his duty to do anything that the needs of the nation demanded unless such action was forbidden by the Constitution or by the laws."

Another assertion of executive authority was made by Franklin D. Roosevelt, who took steps to cope with the Great Depression and World War II. Roosevelt's argument that extraordinary times demanded extraordinary measures was not immediately accepted by the Supreme Court. Between January 1935 and June 1936 the Court ruled against the administration in eight out of ten cases involving New Deal statutes. Roosevelt counterattacked with his COURT-PACKING PLAN to get liberal justices appointed by himself onto the bench to reverse its anti–New Deal stance. Although the president's scheme failed, the Court in 1937 began to uphold New Deal measures. Soon retirements from the Court allowed Roosevelt to appoint new justices whom he considered to be more in tune with his political philosophy.

President Ronald Reagan fulfilled a campaign promise to name a woman to the Supreme Court when he nominated Sandra Day O'Connor in 1981. She was confirmed unanimously by the Senate.
Source: AP/Wide World Photos

Defining the Limits

The Court has generally upheld the president's right to exercise sweeping power in foreign and military matters. In the midst of its rulings denying the president's authority to cope with the economic crisis at home, the Court in 1936 upheld his inherent and virtually unlimited authority to conduct the nation's foreign affairs.

Justice George Sutherland's opinion in this case, UNITED STATES V. CURTISS-WRIGHT EXPORT CORP., claimed that the foreign affairs powers emanated from sources different from those of other presidential powers. This reasoning provided the basis for Sutherland's view that the president could act entirely alone in matters of foreign relations. Although Sutherland's historical analysis has been criticized, the Court has not modified the broad grant of executive power sanctioned by this ruling.

Yet the Court has denied the president broad inherent power in domestic affairs. When a potential strike threatened to interrupt production of steel during the Korean War, President Harry S. Truman seized the mills and kept them running. The Court rejected the president's claim of the power to take this action, in part because Congress some years earlier had decided not to grant the president the power he now sought to exercise.

In 1974 the Court denied Richard Nixon an absolute EXECUTIVE PRIVILEGE to withhold White House tapes sought for use as evidence in a trial related to the Watergate affair. However, the ruling recognized the need for a limited privilege to protect documents and information related to foreign affairs.

In 1997 the Court ruled that Paula Corbin Jones's sexual harassment lawsuit against President Bill Clinton could proceed while Clinton was in office, denying that such a trial was likely to "impose an unacceptable burden on the President's time and energy." Instead, the decision had far greater consequences than anyone had anticipated. In laying the background for Jones's sexual harassment charges, attorneys questioned Clinton, and he denied having had sexual relations with White House intern Monica Lewinsky. That denial later resulted in his impeachment by the House of Representatives on charges of perjury and obstruction of justice and his acquittal by the Senate.

It is always possible in confrontations with the Court that the president will ignore or defy it. Both Andrew Jackson and Abraham Lincoln did so. When the Court in 1832 ruled that Georgia had no jurisdiction, as the state claimed, over the Cherokees and their lands that lay within the state, Jackson refused to act to enforce the ruling. "Well, [Chief Justice] John Marshall has made his decision, now let him enforce it," Jackson is said to have declared.

Lincoln refused to abide by the Court's decision that his suspension of the privilege of the writ of habeas corpus during the Civil War was unconstitutional. Maintaining that wartime emergency measures superseded constitutional niceties, Lincoln continued to suspend or ignore habeas corpus requirements for those persons suspected of aiding the Confederate cause.

Early in the nation's history presidents realized that they held the strongest possible position against judicial challenge when they acted in conjunction with Congress. Joint action by the two political branches of government has consistently provided insulation from Court challenge. When presidents act without the backing of Congress, supported only by their claim of inherent power, they run a high risk of rejection by the Court. The unanimous ruling against Nixon in the tapes case came at a time when Congress—far from supporting the president's claim—was considering articles of impeachment against Nixon.

Appointments to the Court

The major way a president exerts influence over the Supreme Court's work is through the power to select its members. All presidents attempt to nominate justices—usually from their own political party—whose views coincide with their own. This effort has met with varying degrees of success. Presidents Thomas Jefferson, Andrew Jackson, Abraham Lincoln, Franklin Roosevelt, Richard Nixon, and Ronald Reagan have been the most successful in influencing the Court's conduct through judicial appointments.

Presidents also have attempted to influence the Court by turning the judiciary or the Court's earlier decisions into a campaign issue. To win the White House in 1980 and 1984, Ronald Reagan said what many of the nation's most conservative voters wanted to hear: that he would work for the reversal of the Supreme Court's decision permitting abortion and its earlier rulings forbidding officially prescribed prayers in public schools. Reagan had only limited success until 1988, when a retirement allowed him to name his third conservative justice to the Court. (In 1986 Reagan had also named sitting justice William H. Rehnquist as chief justice.) Half a year after Reagan left office, the Supreme Court for the first time since 1973 upheld a state law imposing significant restrictions on a woman's right to have an abortion.

A vacancy on the Supreme Court occurs, on average, about every two years. But at times the Court seems to defy the actuarial tables, and its membership may remain unchanged for a much longer period. Jimmy Carter was the first full-term president denied the opportunity to name anyone to the Supreme Court; no vacancy occurred during his four years in the White House.

President Nixon, by contrast, had an opportunity to appoint a new chief justice during his first year in office. Nixon then made three more appointments to the Court during his first term.

Presidents are sometimes disappointed in those whom they appoint to the Court. Nixon appointed Warren E. Burger chief justice because, apart from his judicial qualifications, Burger had been outspoken in his criticism of the Court's earlier rulings limiting prosecutors' efforts to convict criminals. Later, Burger wrote the Court opinion that forced Nixon to resign or face impeachment and trial for his role in the Watergate affair.

Thomas Jefferson made several appointments to the bench that he hoped would counteract Chief Justice John Marshall's control over the Court's decisions. Jefferson's efforts to reduce Marshall's effectiveness with his judicial colleagues failed, however.

Dwight D. Eisenhower nominated Earl Warren as chief justice in 1953 to repay the California governor for helping Eisenhower to win the presidential nomination in 1952. Years later, looking at the Warren Court's liberal record, Eisenhower called the appointment "the biggest damn-fool mistake I ever made."

SUPREME COURT NOMINATIONS REJECTED BY THE SENATE		
Year	Nominee	Nominated by
1795	John Rutledge	Washington
1811	Alexander Wolcott	Madison
1844	John C. Spencer	Tyler
1845	George W. Woodward	Polk
1861	Jeremiah S. Black	Buchanan
1869	Ebenezer R. Hoar	Grant
1893	William B. Hornblower	Cleveland
1894	Wheeler Hazard Peckham	Cleveland
1930	John J. Parker	Hoover
1969	Clement Haynsworth	Nixon
1970	G. Harrold Carswell	Nixon
1987	Robert H. Bork	Reagan

NOTE: In addition, eight nominees have withdrawn their nominations before Senate action, and in six instances, the Senate took no action on a president's nominee, allowing the nomination to expire when the president's term ended.

Presidents sometimes appoint their friends to the Court. Perhaps the most famous friendship between a president and a justice was that of Franklin Roosevelt and Felix Frankfurter. Friends since undergraduate days at Harvard, Roosevelt and Frankfurter maintained a lively correspondence throughout most of their careers. After Roosevelt appointed Frankfurter to the Court in 1939, the two men communicated freely, offering each other advice and criticism on politics and legal matters.

Lyndon B. Johnson appointed his longtime adviser Abe Fortas to the Supreme Court and later nominated him for chief justice to replace Earl Warren. The ensuing congressional investigation revealed that Johnson and Fortas had continued an active political association after Fortas had joined the Court. Public disapproval of this relationship compounded by political concerns eventually forced Johnson to withdraw the nomination.

Politics and ideology have always been primary factors in a president's selection of a Supreme Court nominee. But other factors also are important. The idea of a "Roman Catholic" seat and a "Jewish" seat on the Court developed as a way of acknowledging the role of these religious minority groups in the nation. Chief Justice Roger Taney was the first Catholic named to the Court; with one brief exception between 1949 and 1956, a Catholic has sat on the Court since 1894. The Jewish seat was established in 1916 with the appointment of Louis D. Brandeis. By the late twentieth century, however, the importance of reserving slots for religious minorities had faded. As of 2003 there were three Catholic and two Jewish justices.

As the Court began its third century, two other political constituencies—blacks and women—seemed to be guaranteed permanent slots on the Supreme Court. In 1967 President Johnson nominated Thurgood Marshall as the first black justice. When Marshall retired in 1991, President George H. W. Bush nominated another black, Clarence Thomas, to succeed him. During the 1980 campaign Reagan pledged that he would name a woman to the Court, and within his first year in office he made good on that pledge. In July 1981 he named Arizona judge Sandra Day O'Connor as the first woman justice. Bill Clinton named the second woman justice, Ruth Bader Ginsburg, in 1993. Amid specula-

More on this topic:

Appointment and Removal Power, p. 9

Court-Packing Plan, p. 127

Executive Privilege, p. 206

United States v. Curtiss-Wright Export Corp., p. 528

tion that he would yield to political pressure and appoint the first Hispanic to the Court after Justice Harry Blackmun's 1994 retirement, Clinton instead named an appeals court judge and former Harvard Law School professor, Stephen G. Breyer, to the seat.

Political and ethical issues frequently have dominated the Senate's consideration of nominations to the Court. As of 2002, twenty-nine Supreme Court nominations (including one person who was nominated twice) had been rejected by the Senate or dropped because of Senate opposition. Among the better-known rejected candidates was Robert H. Bork, nominated to the Court by Reagan. Bork lost his confirmation battle in 1987 at least in part because a majority of senators believed that his judicial views on subjects such as civil rights and privacy were so conservative as to be outside the "mainstream" of American legal philosophy.

Presidents also are responsible for nominating judges to federal appeals and district courts. They tend, however, to be much less involved in the selection process for these courts, mainly because of the number of appointments. Typically, the attorney general and Justice Department associates play a critical role in the recruitment process. The long-standing practice known as senatorial courtesy also comes into play in these judicial nominations. Under this tradition, senators of the president's party from the state in which the nominee is to serve—or from which a Supreme Court nominee comes—have effective veto power over that nomination. Therefore, presidents or their agents usually consult the relevant senators before making the nomination. (See APPOINTMENT AND REMOVAL POWER.)

Although partisanship has always played a role in the nomination process, in recent years it has assumed even greater importance. From 1995 to 2000 Clinton forwarded to the Republican-controlled Senate eighty-four nominees for federal appellate court seats. Of those, only forty-six were confirmed. In many cases, Republican opponents simply halted or delayed consideration of nominees. When George W. Bush faced a Democratic-controlled Senate during part of his first term, Republicans charged Democrats with slowing down the approval process.

The power to nominate federal judges from the Supreme Court down is important because new appointments influence the development of precedent. As new appointees replace older judges, the precedents of the past are questioned and may be qualified or discarded. The values of a continually changing society, as reflected by a new president and new judges, become part of the law. The appointment power has its limitations, however, because the president can make nominations only when judges leave a court or Congress creates new positions.

Crawford, William Harris

William Crawford (1772–1834) was a presidential candidate in 1816 and 1824 as a member of the Democratic-Republican Party. Crawford was born in Virginia and lived in Virginia, South Carolina, and Georgia in his youth. He was a schoolteacher and then a lawyer in Georgia. He was elected to the state legislature in 1803. His political career advanced quickly; in 1807 he was elected to the U.S. Senate as a Jeffersonian Republican.

In 1813 Crawford accepted President James Madison's offer to become minister to France. After he returned to the United States in 1815, Madison appointed him secretary of war. While heading the War Department, Crawford clashed with Gen. Andrew Jackson over terms of a treaty with the Creek Indians.

As the 1816 elections approached, Crawford was urged by supporters to run for president, but he deferred to James Monroe. Madison named Crawford Treasury secretary that same year, and Monroe, after being elected president, kept Crawford in the post. He remained there through 1825.

The 1824 elections were among the most confused in the nation's history. Crawford, John Quincy Adams, Henry Clay and Jackson were the leading presidential candidates for the Democratic-Republican Party. By this point, the opposition Federalist Party had begun to fade away, and nomination by the Democratic-Republicans was seen as similar to actual victory. Although Crawford was viewed as the front-runner, he suffered an illness, possibly a stroke, in the fall of 1823 that affected his sight and mobility. The Democratic-Republican congressional caucus nominated him as their candidate, but most state parties refused to fall in line, and Adams, Jackson, and Clay were nominated as regional candidates. No one won the electoral vote, and the stalemate threw the election into the House of Representatives. Clay gave his support to Adams, who emerged victorious.

Crawford later served as a judge in Georgia, from 1827 through 1834.

> **More on this topic:**
>
> *Elections Chronology, p. 174*
>
> *Electoral College, p. 185*

Curtis, Charles

Charles Curtis
Source: Library of Congress

Charles Curtis (1860–1936) served one term as vice president under Herbert C. Hoover, from 1929 to 1933. Curtis and Hoover were the first president–vice president team to run for a second term and lose since Martin Van Buren and Richard M. Johnson in 1840.

Curtis was born on January 25, 1860, in North Topeka, Kansas. His mother died when he was a young child. His father, a cavalry officer, left Charles in Kansas with his two grandmothers, who took turns raising him. He graduated from high school in 1879. He then clerked for a Topeka lawyer and was admitted to the bar in 1881.

In 1892 Curtis was elected to the first of seven consecutive terms in the U.S. House of Representatives. In 1907 he shifted from the House to the Senate when he was chosen by the Kansas legislature to fill several months of an unexpired term. The legislature elected him to a term of his own that year, and he served until 1913, when he was defeated for reelection. In 1914 he won a seat in the Senate in the first election in which senators were chosen by popular vote under the new Seventeenth Amendment. Curtis remained in the Senate until 1929, when he became vice president. He supported Prohibition, voting rights for women, and bills helping farmers and Indians.

In 1928 Republican Party leaders chose Curtis for vice president because he was a political conservative from a farm state who could balance the ticket with Hoover, a liberal Californian. The nation was prospering after eight years of Republican presidential leadership, and Hoover and Curtis had little trouble defeating Democrats Alfred E. Smith and Joseph T. Robinson.

As vice president, Curtis faithfully supported Republican policies. Hoover and Curtis were renominated in 1932, but the Great Depression had turned voters against the Republicans. They were defeated by Franklin D. Roosevelt and John Nance Garner 472–59 in the Electoral College.

After leaving office, Curtis practiced law in Washington, D.C. He died of a heart attack on February 8, 1936.

> **More on this topic:**
>
> *Hoover, Herbert, p. 263*
>
> *Vice President, p. 539*

Daily and Family Life

Candidates for president work hard to persuade voters that they are ordinary folks who understand the daily cares of average citizens. Yet once a candidate becomes president, life changes dramatically. Guarded around the clock by Secret Service agents, the president and the first family leave the White House only under carefully planned and controlled circumstances. In fact, for them the WHITE HOUSE becomes a sort of prison. But it is a luxurious one, with a large staff to meet their every need, a movie theater and sports facilities for relaxation, and opulent surroundings furnished with valuable art works and antiques.

Staff

The 132-room White House is run by a staff of about one hundred permanent, full-time employees who take great pride in their work. The most important member of this staff is the chief usher, who coordinates everything from social events to redecoration projects. Under him are butlers, maids, cooks, engineers, electricians, carpenters, plumbers, painters, and others. In recent years the total for staff salaries has averaged almost $4 million a year.

In addition to the regular White House staff, the first family is allowed to hire a small number of full- and part-time personal servants at government expense. These have included the president's valet, personal cook, and barber, and the first lady's personal secretary and maids.

The President's Workday

A television commercial aired by Jimmy Carter during his 1980 reelection campaign captures the modern expectation of how a president spends his time. The ad pictures the White House late at night with one light shining from the window of an office in which Carter is at his desk, burning the midnight oil to solve the nation's problems. The president who works long hours to meet crushing demands is a relatively recent development, however. Before 1930 most presidents were not expected to work too hard or long. Congress dominated the federal government, and most governing was done by states and localities in any case.

In 1890 a schedule such as that of Benjamin Harrison was typical. He arrived at the office at about nine in the morning, worked for two or three hours, and took the rest of the day off. In the early years of the twentieth century Theodore Roosevelt did government business in the morning, exercised in the afternoon, and read in the evening. In the 1920s Calvin Coolidge spent little time working as president because he believed the government should do little. There

President Dwight D. Eisenhower plays golf at a club in Newport, Rhode Island, while onlookers watch and take pictures.
Source: Courtesy Dwight D. Eisenhower Library

were exceptions such as James K. Polk, who worked so compulsively that he ruined his health and died at age fifty-three, but most presidents did not find the job overly taxing.

The president's workload began to grow in the 1930s as the nation confronted problems that seemed too large for the states and the private sector to solve—problems such as the Great Depression and World War II. As the federal government grew in importance, the public looked to the president for direction, and the presidency became a very demanding job.

Herbert C. Hoover spent many more hours in the Oval Office than had most of his predecessors. Franklin D. Roosevelt spent all day at work and often combined strategy sessions with meals. Harry S. Truman arose at 5:30 in the morning, exercised, ate breakfast, and went straight to work. Among recent presidents, Lyndon B. Johnson, Richard Nixon, Gerald R. Ford, Jimmy Carter, George H. W. Bush, and Bill Clinton all followed the pattern of long hours and demanding schedules.

Dwight D. Eisenhower and Ronald Reagan were criticized for their more relaxed work habits but were enormously popular nevertheless. Eisenhower, who believed that proper rest and relaxation made him more effective, often tried to finish his work in the morning so he could play golf in the afternoon. Like Eisenhower, Reagan delegated much of the detail work of the presidency to his staff and kept relatively short hours. George W. Bush, like Reagan, sees his role as providing broad direction for the government, and thus there was no reason to spend hours mastering innumerable details of policy. In his mind, a workload like Clinton's was counterproductive. President John F. Kennedy did not keep long hours either and consistently took weekends off. Kennedy worked through the morning; paused in the afternoon for a swim, lunch, and a nap; and returned to his office for a time in the late afternoon.

Rest and Recreation

The presidency is a demanding and stressful job, and presidents need to pace themselves with periods of relaxation and recreation. Within the White House, presidents have at their disposal a

WEDDINGS IN THE WHITE HOUSE

	Presidential Weddings	Bride/Groom	Location
1886	Grover Cleveland	Frances Folsom	Blue Room
	Presidential Children's Weddings		
1820	Maria Monroe	Samuel Gouverneur	East Room
1828	John Adams (son of John Q. Adams)	Mary Catherine Hellen	Blue Room
1842	Elizabeth Tyler	William Nevison Waller	East Room
1874	Nellie Grant	Algernon Sartoris	East Room
1906	Alice Roosevelt	Nicholas Longworth	East Room
1913	Jessie Wilson	Frances Bowes Sayer	East Room
1914	Eleanor Wilson	William Gibbs McAdoo	Blue Room
1967	Lynda Bird Johnson	Chuck Robb	East Room
1971	Tricia Nixon	Edward Cox	Rose Garden

Note: One president and nine presidential daughters or sons have been married in the White House. Four members of the families of first ladies have been married at the White House as well as three other close presidential associates or relatives.

heated swimming pool, a small gymnasium, a tennis court, a one-lane bowling alley, a movie theater, and a library stocked with the reading material of their choice. For weekend getaways the president and the first family can take a short helicopter ride to CAMP DAVID, a retreat in the Catoctin Mountains of Maryland.

For longer vacations most recent presidents have had at least one personal retreat, a kind of alternate White House equipped with communications and security facilities paid for with public funds. Franklin Roosevelt withdrew to his family estate in Hyde Park, New York, or to Warm Springs, Georgia, where he received physical therapy for polio. Truman went home to Independence, Missouri, and Eisenhower had a farmhouse in Gettysburg, Pennsylvania. Kennedy retreated to his family's compound at Cape Cod, Massachusetts, his father's estate in Palm Beach, Florida, or the country home of a friend in Virginia. George H. W. Bush and his family vacationed at their house in Kennebunkport, Maine. Before he was elected president, Clinton spent many years living in the Arkansas statehouse, and so the Clintons had no permanent home of their own to which they could retreat. They borrowed houses on Martha's Vineyard, Massachusetts, and Jackson Hole, Wyoming, for family vacations. George W. Bush's preferred retreat is his ranch near the small town of Crawford, Texas.

Presidents' choice of a vacation spot can influence the way they are viewed by the public. Carter, for example, emphasized his simplicity and frugality by returning to his modest home in the small town of Plains, Georgia, for vacations. In contrast, Nixon maintained luxurious homes in San Clemente, California, and Key Biscayne, Florida, and was criticized for making extensive renovations to both at public expense. Reagan, Lyndon Johnson, and George W. Bush played the role of rancher on their picturesque spreads in the southern California hills (Reagan), in the hill country outside Austin, Texas (Johnson), and near Waco, Texas (Bush).

As the public has become increasingly fascinated by the personal lives of famous people, the president's leisure activities have become more than a way of escaping the cares of office: they help to shape the president's image. Theodore Roosevelt was the first president whose athletic exploits contributed significantly to his public profile. He hiked, jogged, rode horses, hunted, swam in the

Potomac River, and played tennis with political figures who accepted his challenge. He also enjoyed fencing, boxing, and wrestling.

Theodore Roosevelt's tireless pursuit of sports has a parallel in a recent president, George H.W. Bush, whose jogging, speed boating, and games of tennis, baseball, and horseshoes exhausted the reporters assigned to follow in his wake. Bush's relentless pace gave him an aura of vitality, as did Roosevelt's. But unlike Roosevelt, who spent long hours reading, Bush sometimes seemed as if he could not slow down. His son George W. Bush, a jogger until he suffered a knee injury, ran three miles a day on the White House track. Subsequently he took up mountain biking. Bush also enjoys reading, lifting weights, and working outdoors at his Texas ranch. His greatest passion

While living in the White House, Theodore Roosevelt's six children were boisterous and active, often disrupting their father's meetings and social events. Here, two of his sons pose with White House guards.
Source: Library of Congress

was baseball. An avid fan, he was part owner of the Texas Rangers baseball team for several years.

Some recent presidents have experienced the pitfalls of public recreation. Jimmy Carter, a determined jogger, felt faint during a race and had to be helped off the course, projecting an image of physical weakness at a time when his presidency was faltering. Gerald Ford, an avid skier, reinforced his reputation for ineptness by occasionally tumbling down the slopes. His willingness to laugh at himself helped to offset this failing.

Joggers Bill Clinton and Al Gore gave the image of a youthful, vigorous team. This picture was further burnished in 1997 when Clinton and his wife, Hillary, like many other proud yet anxious American families engaging in a familiar ritual of autumn, escorted their only child, daughter Chelsea, to Palo Alto, California, where she enrolled as a freshman at Stanford University. The Clintons suddenly found themselves "empty nesters," even if the nest was the White House, and soon procured a chocolate Labrador puppy, "Buddy," to keep them company.

Family and Friends

The presidency has been called the loneliest job in the world, yet presidents rarely have been alone in the White House. Only two bachelors, James Buchanan and Grover Cleveland, have been elected president, and Cleveland married while in office. A president's spouse, children, relatives, and close friends are able to provide support and advice. Their symbolic function is important as well, especially in the modern media age. Family and friends often improve a president's image by showing off a personal side, but they also can be liabilities.

Some presidents, such as Reagan and George H.W. Bush, arrive at the White House after their children are grown. Those with younger families often have benefited politically from the charm and human interest of small children. Perhaps the most famous presidential family was that of Theodore Roosevelt, who in 1901 brought his six small children to the White House. They arrived just as press coverage and interest in the president's family were beginning to grow, and their exploits were soon the talk of the nation. At the White House they slid down banisters, rode bicycles and roller skated on the hardwood floors, climbed the trees, swam in the fountains, and leapfrogged over the furniture. Their father often joined in their play.

The most celebrated of recent White House children were Caroline Kennedy and John F. Kennedy Jr., who were ages three and one, respectively, when their father became president in 1961. Like the Roosevelt children, Caroline and "John John" were regularly photographed and chronicled. Images of the pair are part of American lore: running to meet their father, walking with their mother, dancing in the Oval Office, Caroline holding her mother's hand at her father's funeral as John-John saluted the coffin. Amy Carter was another appealing White House child, a wholesome, freckled girl of nine when her father became president in 1977. Although their own children were grown when he became president in 1987, George and Barbara Bush filled the White House with their small grandchildren.

Life in the White House is more difficult for older children, who may enjoy the excitement but resent the restrictions of Secret Service protection and the glare of publicity. The public learned all about Susan Ford's eighteenth birthday, her senior prom, how much she charged for babysitting, and the rides she preferred at Disney World. Nixon's younger daughter, Julie, handled the spotlight well, but her older sister, Tricia, shrank from attention and faced the publicity of a White House wedding with trepidation. Lynda Bird and Lucy Baines Johnson, President Johnson's two teenage daughters, also endured close press scrutiny and seemed relieved to escape into adulthood. The Clintons carefully shielded their daughter, who was twelve when they moved into the White House. George W. Bush and his wife, Laura, tried to keep their college-age twin daughters, Barbara and Jenna, out of the spotlight, but the girls faced some negative publicity for underage drinking.

A relative can be an asset to the president. Milton Eisenhower never held an official position in the administration of his brother Dwight, but he was a close confidant on whom the president could try out ideas and rely for honest advice. Robert F. Kennedy, the most prominent presidential brother in U.S. history, was attorney general in the Kennedy administration, but his role went far beyond that job. Robert Kennedy was his brother's closest adviser, a kind of alter ego whose hard-driving passion complemented the president's easygoing style.

Some brothers of presidents have been less helpful. Sam Houston Johnson struggled with alcoholism and lived in the White House under virtual house arrest during his brother Lyndon's administration. Apprehensive about the image Sam projected, Lyndon Johnson kept him far from reporters and closely monitored his doings. The business activities of Richard Nixon's younger brother, Donald, were a continuing embarrassment in Nixon's political career. A loan Donald had accepted from the wealthy industrialist Howard Hughes and never repaid became an issue in Richard Nixon's 1960 presidential bid. When Nixon was elected president in 1968 he watched Donald carefully, even going so far as to order his brother's telephone to be tapped.

A more public problem was caused by Jimmy Carter's younger brother, Billy, a folksy, beer-drinking southerner, who became an instant celebrity when Carter was elected in 1976. Billy wore out his welcome in the ensuing years with his crude public behavior, off-color comments, and efforts of questionable propriety to cash in on the presidency. The worst embarrassment came in 1980 when it was revealed that Billy had accepted more than $200,000 in "loans" from Libya. But President Carter refused to disavow his errant sibling, declaring, "He's my brother, and I love him." Bill Clinton's younger half-brother, Roger, an aspiring rock-and-roll singer, made news with some inappropriate public actions, and the president made a public statement much like Jimmy Carter's in support of his kin.

Presidents are surrounded every day by people who have a cause to promote or a personal interest to protect. This sharpens their need for at least one confidant who has no ax to grind, a need often filled by one or two old and trusted friends. The relationship of Woodrow Wilson and his friend Col. Edward M. House, a wealthy man who enjoyed the excitement of politics, came to symbolize the closeness that may exist between president and adviser. House advised Wilson throughout his presidency and even represented Wilson in European negotiations over World War I. He was known to be so close to Wilson that people came to House to appeal for access to the president.

Franklin Roosevelt, a president who tapped the expertise of a wide range of advisers, had two particularly close associates. Louis McHenry Howe, a newspaperman who had advised Roosevelt since the early days of his career, was able to point out errors and speak more bluntly to the president than other advisers could. Harry Hopkins, who advised Roosevelt on the conduct of World War II, lived at the White House.

While presidential friends and cronies often have been valuable sources of advice, some have proved dishonest and corrupt. The administrations of Ulysses S. Grant and Warren G. Harding both suffered from this problem. Grant, who came to the White House in 1869 as an army officer with no political experience, appointed many old friends to fill positions, setting in motion one of the most scandal-plagued administrations in history. Harding, elected in 1920, could not resist the company of friends who turned out to be trouble. The biggest of the numerous scandals of the Harding administration was the TEAPOT DOME SCANDAL, which involved the illegal sale of oil leases in the western states.

Other presidents have suffered from the shady dealings of friends, although few to the extent of Grant and Harding. In 1945 Truman brought to Washington several of his old cronies from Missouri, some of whom turned out to be associated with an influence-peddling scandal. And Carter was hurt by allegations of financial wrongdoing made against his old friend and budget director Bert Lance. Webster Hubbell was a Little Rock law partner of First Lady Hillary Rodham Clinton and close friend of the president. Hubbell, who was appointed to a high post in the Justice Department, pleaded guilty in 1994 to embezzling $400,000 from his old law firm, to mail fraud, and to income tax evasion and went to prison as a result.

> **More on this topic:**
>
> Camp David, p. 67
>
> Teapot Dome Scandal, p. 493
>
> White House, p. 573

Dallas, George M.

George M. Dallas, vice president under James K. Polk
Source: National Oceanic and Atmospheric Administration

George Mifflin Dallas (1792–1864) served as vice president under James K. Polk from 1845 to 1849. He brought wide political and diplomatic experience to the vice presidency but did not play a large role in Polk's administration. Despite presidential ambitions, Dallas received little support for his party's nomination in 1848.

Dallas was born into a wealthy Philadelphia family. His father, Alexander Dallas, had served as secretary of the Treasury under James Madison. George graduated from Princeton University in 1810 and was admitted to the bar in 1813. During Dallas's political career he served as mayor of Philadelphia, U.S. district attorney for eastern Pennsylvania, Pennsylvania state attorney general, minister to Russia, and U.S. senator.

In 1844 the Democratic national convention, meeting in Baltimore, chose Dallas as James Polk's vice-presidential running mate after Sen. Silas Wright of

New York refused to accept the nomination. Polk and Dallas defeated Whigs Henry Clay and Theodore Frelinghuysen by a vote of 170–105 in the Electoral College.

Dallas believed that a vice president should support the administration's policies even when he disagreed with them. In 1846 he demonstrated his devotion to this principle by breaking a tie vote in the Senate on a low tariff bill supported by Polk, in spite of his state's strong protectionist sentiment. The vice president's action was attacked so bitterly in Pennsylvania that he arranged to move his family to Washington, D.C., because he feared for their safety.

By voting for the low tariff bill, Dallas had hoped to win support in the South and West for his own presidential candidacy in 1848. At the Democratic national convention that year he received only a handful of votes on the first ballot. The convention chose instead Sen. Lewis Cass of Michigan, and Dallas retired from politics. In 1856 President Franklin Pierce appointed Dallas minister to Great Britain, a post he retained under James Buchanan. In 1861 he returned to Philadelphia, where he resided until his sudden death on the last day of 1864.

> **More on this topic:**
>
> *Polk, James K., p. 411*
>
> *Vice President, p. 539*

Davis, Jefferson

Jefferson Davis, President of the Confederate States of America, 1861–1865
Source: U.S. Army

In 1861, two weeks before Abraham Lincoln was inaugurated in Washington, D.C., as the sixteenth president of the United States, another president was inaugurated in Montgomery, Alabama. On February 18 Jefferson Davis (1808–1889) became the first and only president of the Confederate States of America.

Davis was born in Kentucky on June 3, 1808. His family moved to a small Mississippi plantation when he was a boy. In 1828 he graduated from the U.S. Military Academy at West Point. He saw action in the Black Hawk War during the early 1830s. In 1835 he left the army and married the daughter of his commanding officer, Zachary Taylor, who became the twelfth president of the United States. Davis and his new wife, Sarah, settled on a thousand-acre plantation in Mississippi, but she died of malaria just three months after their wedding. For several years Davis devoted himself to developing his land and accumulating wealth.

In 1845 Davis remarried and was elected to the U.S. House of Representatives. When the MEXICAN-AMERICAN WAR began, he gave up his seat to accept a commission as a colonel. He served heroically until leaving the army in 1847. He was elected to the U.S. Senate that year and served until he gave up his seat in 1851 to run for governor of Mississippi. He lost that election but returned to Washington in 1853 when President Franklin Pierce appointed him secretary of war.

In 1857 Davis was reelected to the Senate. Although he became a leading spokesman for the South, he did not advocate secession until 1860, when it had become inevitable. Davis hoped to be appointed commander in chief of the Confederate army, but instead he was chosen as president by a convention of the seceding states.

Davis believed that his first priority as president was to preserve southern independence. He tried to secure French and British support for the Confederacy but was largely unsuccessful. Like Lincoln, he helped to develop military strategy and on occasion interfered with the plans of his generals. Davis was in a difficult position from which to manage the Confederate war effort. By most accounts, the South could fight most effectively as a unified nation run by the central government in Richmond, but the southern states had seceded in part to preserve their rights as independent states. Davis took actions, including the suspension of habeas corpus and the establishment of a draft, that were criticized by many southerners.

When the Union was on the verge of victory in early 1865, Davis fled south from Richmond and was captured by federal troops. He was indicted for treason and imprisoned for two years, but he never stood trial. After being released he lived in Canada and Europe for several years before retiring to Mississippi. He died in New Orleans on December 6, 1889.

> **More on this topic:**
>
> *Civil War, p. 95*
>
> *Mexican-American War, p. 361*

Dawes, Charles G.

Charles G. Dawes.
Source: Library of Congress

Charles Gates Dawes (1865–1951) served as vice president under Calvin Coolidge from 1925 to 1929. Dawes had a successful career as a banker, businessman, administrator, and public official before coming to the vice presidency, his first elective office.

Dawes was born into a prominent Ohio family. His great-great-grandfather was William Dawes, who on April 18, 1775, rode with Paul Revere to alert the people near Boston that British troops were approaching. Charles graduated from Marietta College in Marietta, Ohio, in 1884. He then earned a law degree from the Cincinnati Law School and joined a firm in Lincoln, Nebraska. In 1894 he moved to Chicago after purchasing two nearby utility companies. He eventually organized the Central Trust Company of Illinois and became its president. The bank's success made him one of the nation's leading financiers.

During his rise in the financial world Dawes had been active in public service and the Republican Party. He served as comptroller of the currency from 1897 until 1902, when he ran unsuccessfully for an Illinois Senate seat. During World War I Dawes was the chief purchasing agent for the American army. In this role he oversaw the purchase and transportation of millions of tons of supplies to U.S. troops in Europe.

In 1921 Dawes accepted a one-year appointment from President Warren G. Harding as the first director of the new Bureau of the Budget. In 1923 he was appointed chairman of the Allied Reparations Commission, formed to develop a plan for restructuring payments of Germany's World War I reparations. He helped to develop the "Dawes Plan," which trimmed Germany's reparation payments and provided for a loan to stimulate the German economy. For his efforts he was awarded the Nobel Peace Prize in 1925.

In 1924 the Republican Party nominated Dawes as vice president on the ticket with President Coolidge. Coolidge and Dawes easily defeated Democrats John W. Davis and Charles W. Bryan. As vice president, Dawes became active in Senate politics, where he worked behind the scenes for naval appropriations, banking reform, and farm relief programs. When President Coolidge announced that he would not run for another term, Dawes also declined to run.

> **More on this topic:**
>
> *Coolidge, Calvin, p. 125*
>
> *Vice President, p. 539*

After leaving the vice presidency, Dawes served as ambassador to Great Britain from 1929 to 1932. He died in 1951 at the age of eighty-five. Dawes was a talented amateur composer, whose "Melody in A Major" became a popular song in 1951, when it was set to lyrics and retitled "It's All in the Game."

Death of the President

IN MEMORY OF

PRESIDENT

WM. H. HARRISON,

WHO DEPARTED THIS LIFE, APRIL 4, 1841, AGED 68,

Deeply lamented by 16 Millions of people.

Within a mere month of his inauguration, William Henry Harrison became the first president to die in office. In his memory, many Americans wore armbands like this one.
Source: Library of Congress

Eight presidents have died in office, four from assassination and four from natural causes. All were succeeded by their vice presidents. Only two presidents—William Henry Harrison in 1841 and Zachary Taylor in 1850—died in the White House.

Abraham Lincoln was shot on April 14, 1865, while attending a performance at Ford's Theatre in Washington, D.C., and died the next morning in a private house across the street from the theater. James A. Garfield was shot in a Washington, D.C., train station on July 2, 1881, and died September 19 in Elberon, New Jersey, where he had gone to recover. William McKinley was shot at a public reception in Buffalo, New York, and died several days later, on September 14, 1901. John F. Kennedy was shot and killed while riding in a presidential motorcade in Dallas on November 22, 1963.

Warren G. Harding died on August 2, 1923, in a San Francisco hotel. Although the actual cause of death was uncertain, it was most likely related to the president's high blood pressure. Franklin D. Roosevelt died on April 12, 1945, from a massive cerebral hemorrhage, in Warm Springs, Georgia, where he had gone to rest after the Yalta Conference.

Seven of the eight presidents lay in state in the East Room of the White House; Garfield was the exception. Several of the presidents, including Harrison, Lincoln, and Kennedy, also lay in state in the Capitol rotunda, where members of the public could pay their respects. Only Kennedy was buried in the national capital area. A veteran, Kennedy was interred at Arlington National Cemetery, where his grave is marked by an eternal flame. The bodies of Harrison and Taylor were buried temporarily in the capital, but later were moved for permanent burial in their home states of Ohio and Kentucky, respectively.

The train carrying Lincoln's body to its final resting place took twenty days, stopping in Baltimore, Harrisburg, Philadelphia, New York City, Albany, Buffalo, Cleveland, Columbus, Indianapolis, Michigan City, and Chicago on its way to Springfield, Illinois. At each city the president's coffin was moved off the train to lie in state, allowing the American people to bid Lincoln farewell. A million Americans actually walked past his coffin. Thirty million attended religious services or watched the train or the hearse pass by.

Immense crowds also came out to watch the train carrying Harding's body back to the capital. An estimated 1.5 million people lined the rails in Chicago alone, and people placed pennies on the track to be flattened by the passing funeral train and retrieved as souvenirs.

An estimated 250,000 mourners filed past Kennedy's coffin as it lay in state at the U.S. Capitol, but television brought Kennedy's funeral services to millions more, both in the United States and abroad. It was estimated that 95 percent of the adult U.S. population followed television or radio accounts of the funeral. Networks canceled virtually all other programming, including commercials, weather reports, news, and sportscasts. For three days much of the world was mesmerized by the ceremony of mourning for the youthful assassinated president.

<table>
<tr><td>More on this topic:</td></tr>
<tr><td>Assassinations and Assaults, p. 19</td></tr>
<tr><td>Succession, p. 483</td></tr>
</table>

Debates   *See* CAMPAIGN DEBATES.

Debs, Eugene V.

Eugene V. Debs.
Source: Library of Congress

Eugene V. Debs (1855–1926) ran for president five times as the candidate of the Socialist Party. A railroad union leader from Indiana, Debs won 6 percent of the popular vote in the election of 1912, the highest ever for a Socialist candidate. That year, Theodore Roosevelt ran as a Progressive, splitting the Republican vote with incumbent William Howard Taft, and Democrat Woodrow Wilson was elected president. The outcome, including the Socialists' relatively strong showing, was considered a sign of a leftward drift in Americans' political views. Debs also ran for president in 1900, 1904, 1908, and 1920. His last campaign was conducted from a federal penitentiary in Atlanta, where he had been imprisoned for speaking against the government's wartime policies.

Debs left high school in Terre Haute, Indiana, for railroad work, eventually taking the difficult and dangerous job of railroad fireman. He became a national official of the Brotherhood of Locomotive Firemen and in 1884 was elected to the Indiana legislature. Believing that an industrywide union would have more impact than a collection of trade unions, Debs founded the American Railway Union in 1893, a time of severe economic depression. After a successful strike against the Great Northern Railroad, Debs's union participated in one of the most divisive labor disputes in U.S. history, the 1894 Pullman strike. To support striking Pullman workers in Chicago, more than fifty thousand railway workers across the nation boycotted Pullman cars, which at that time were found on most trains. Democratic president Grover Cleveland responded forcefully, directing his attorney general to seek an injunction against the strike. When violence continued despite the injunction, and the courts requested intervention, Cleveland ordered federal troops into Chicago to protect U.S. property and keep the mail moving. The troops clashed with strikers, blood was shed, and Debs was arrested. The Supreme Court upheld the injunction and Debs's six-month prison sentence.

In his first run for president in 1900 Debs represented a group he had helped to found in 1898, the Social Democratic Party. He had the support of the moderates of another left-wing group, the Socialist Labor Party. In 1901 Debs's supporters united to form the Socialist Party, calling for government ownership or control of essential industries. The Socialists favored a gradual shift to a socialist economy rather than a revolution as envisioned by the Socialist Labor Party. For a time, Debs attracted members and gave socialism more respectability than it had ever enjoyed in the

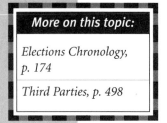

More on this topic:

Elections Chronology,
p. 174

Third Parties, p. 498

United States. But the party's influence and strength waned during World War I, a war it refused to support.

In 1918 Debs, a pacifist, received a ten-year sentence for speaking against the Espionage Act of 1917, a law designed to stifle antiwar sentiment. He ran his 1920 presidential campaign from prison and received close to 920,000 votes. Pardoned by President Warren G. Harding and released after serving almost three years, Debs left prison in poor health. His political career was over, but he was respected by many for his dedication to his beliefs.

Defense Department

The Defense Department has primary responsibility for protecting the national security of the United States. It is made up of three military services—the army, navy, and air force—and numerous agencies, offices, and unified multiservice commands, all under the leadership of the secretary of defense. The secretary serves as the president's top adviser on national security matters and is a statutory member of the NATIONAL SECURITY COUNCIL. The secretary sometimes is also considered to be the deputy commander in chief, and the president's military orders are transmitted through the secretary. The secretary is sixth in the line of succession to the presidency.

The Defense Department is by far the largest cabinet department in terms of personnel. In 2002 the department was made up of some 1.4 million active-duty members of the military, backed by 1 million reservists. About 650,000 civilians also work for the Department of Defense. The 2003 defense appropriations bill totaled $355.1 billion, an increase over the 2002 total of $333 billion, and President George W. Bush's proposed fiscal year 2004 defense budget totaled about $380 billion. In the wake of the terrorist attacks of September 11, 2001—during which a hijacked plane struck the Pentagon—defense spending rose in priority, a shift from the post–cold war era focus on reductions.

Creation of the Department

Before 1947 the War and Navy Departments functioned independently; each had its own cabinet-level secretary, military command structure, and procurement operations. The National Security Act of 1947 created the post of secretary of defense, but its occupant was not given a staff or significant power over the individual services. The defense secretary functioned as the coordinator among the loose confederation of the Departments of the Army (the old War Department) and Navy (which includes the Marine Corps), and the new Department of the Air Force. A 1949 amendment to the National Security Act created the Defense Department and recognized the primacy of the defense secretary, but in practice the individual services retained authority over their budgets and were administered autonomously by the service secretaries. The three services were not unified into one military organization because reformers believed such an organization could more easily threaten civilian primacy over the military.

Finally, in 1958 the Department of Defense Reorganization Act placed the secretary of defense at the top of the military command structure, second only to the president. The act gave the secretary the means to centralize authority over defense operations and planning within the Office of the Secretary of Defense (OSD). The secretaries of the individual services remained, but they were subordinated to the defense secretary.

In 2003 two units of the Defense Department—the National BW (biological weapons) Defense Analysis Center and the National Communications Center—moved to the new Department of Homeland Security.

Presidential Command

As commander in chief the president is positioned at the top of a large, complex defense establishment. In addition to the secretary of defense, the president is advised on military matters by the JOINT CHIEFS OF STAFF (JCS). The JCS consists of a chairman appointed from any of the services, a vice chairman, the chiefs of staff of the army and the air force, the chief of naval operations, and the commandant of the Marine Corps. The president appoints all of these top military officers with the advice and consent of the Senate. The chairman is considered the president's senior military adviser.

Presidents do not always dominate the military. Like any government organization, the Defense Department has its own organizational objectives

Aerial view of the Pentagon, headquarters of the Department of Defense. Designed by its architects to fit the site, which is bounded by five roads, the building is made up of five pentagons and a center courtyard of five acres. Source: Eddie McCrossan, Department of Defense

and is capable of resisting policies it dislikes. Military leaders have been particularly successful in cultivating friends in Congress who pressure the administration to accept the military's perspective on certain issues. In 1993, for example, Gen. Colin L. Powell, JCS chairman, vigorously opposed President Bill Clinton's policy of allowing homosexuals to serve in the military. Powell found a strong ally in Congress, Sen. Sam Nunn of Georgia, the Democrat who headed the Armed Services Committee. Their unyielding opposition to the proposed policy effectively killed it. Congress also has pushed the military for fuller disclosure and internal reform over some troubling issues. One such issue was the sex scandals that beset the services in the mid-1990s; another was the department's inept handling of service personnel who became ill after serving in the first Persian Gulf War, in 1990–1991.

In addition to the military's political clout, presidential control over the Defense Department is limited by the president's dependence on military expertise. Estimates about the force requirements and prospects for success of a combat operation can be supplied only by the military. Presidents also depend on the military to implement their military orders. While presidential initiatives in other areas, such as diplomacy, can be accomplished through several channels, only the military can carry out a combat operation.

Presidents are the final judge of disputes over Defense Department budgets. Every year the executive branch must submit a defense budget that proposes both defense spending levels and the specific military programs on which funds will be spent. The level of spending is a highly visible political issue, one on which most Americans have an opinion and presidential candidates must announce their intentions. JCS chairman Powell raised serious objections in 1993 to Clinton's budget, which sought to provide taxpayers a "peace dividend" by cutting the defense budget. Powell publicly called Clinton's proposed cuts "dangerously excessive," and many were taken off the table. George W. Bush gave an extraordinary amount of leeway to Defense Secretary Donald Rumsfeld in shaping the department's budget for the twenty-first century and for fighting terrorist organizations. Although large increases in

More on this topic:

Joint Chiefs of Staff, p. 312

National Security Council, p. 381

defense spending have been authorized by Congress for the purposes of modernization and to maintain the occupation of Iraq, Rumsfeld's decision to use a "lighter" force in Iraq combined with the privatization of many roles traditionally performed by the U.S. military, has drawn criticism.

Decisions about the specific programs to be funded, however, must be determined through a complex process of conflict and compromise among the president, Congress, the Defense Department's civilian leadership, and the individual armed services, all under the lobbying pressure of defense contractors and public interest groups.

Delegate Selection Reforms

Since 1968 the presidential nomination process has undergone a major transformation. A proliferation of presidential primaries has vastly increased the influence of rank-and-file voters in choosing the party's nominee and greatly diminished the influence of party leaders.

This reform movement had its roots in the tumultuous Democratic national convention of 1968. That convention nominated Vice President Hubert H. Humphrey over antiwar activist Sen. Eugene J. McCarthy, even though Humphrey had not participated in a single primary. State delegations that opposed Humphrey felt excluded from the process. They complained that the delegate selection process was unfair and that party leaders had manipulated the outcome of the convention.

As a result, in February 1969 the party established the Commission on Party Structure and Delegate Selection, chaired by Sen. George S. McGovern and later by Rep. Donald Fraser. (The commission came to be known as the McGovern-Fraser Commission.) A little more than a year later the commission issued eighteen detailed guidelines to be followed in the state delegate selection process.

The mandatory guidelines condemned discrimination based on race, color, creed, sex, or age and required that affirmative steps be taken to give delegate slots to women, minorities, and young people in proportion to their population in each state. They also barred restrictive fees and petition requirements for delegate candidates. The guidelines banned the "unit rule," under which all delegates had to vote as the majority of the delegation voted. They also limited the influence of party committees in the selection of convention delegates.

In addition, the guidelines urged a move toward "proportional representation." Under this system, delegates are assigned in proportion to the percentage of the total that each presidential candidate receives in the primary. The major alternative is a winner-take-all system, in which the candidate who wins the plurality of the popular vote receives all of the delegate votes.

These reforms had a considerable impact: they substantially democratized the process. At the same time, they greatly reduced the power of Democratic Party leaders, prompting some to complain that the party itself had been dismantled.

Although states were largely in compliance with the guidelines by 1972, there was considerable resistance to the reforms. To address these concerns the Democrats created commissions in 1972 and again in 1976. But neither commission changed the McGovern-Fraser rules significantly, and the notion of fair representation became generally accepted.

Concern that the reforms had gone too far in reducing the influence of party leaders still ran high. So in 1980 the party created yet another commission, this one chaired by North Carolina governor James B. Hunt Jr. The main recommendation made by the Hunt Commission was to increase the number of delegate slots reserved at the national convention for party leaders and elected officials—or superdelegates, as they have come to be called. Every state is now guaranteed enough slots to accommodate its "core" Democratic officials, defined as the governor, members of Congress, and mayors of cities with populations of more than 250,000.

As a result of the reforms, the number of primaries ballooned. Most state party leaders thought that the adoption of a presidential primary was the easiest and surest way to conform to

PRESIDENTIAL PRIMARIES, 1912–2004

Year	Democratic Party			Republican Party		
	Number of primaries	Votes cast	Percentage of delegates selected through primaries	Number of primaries	Votes cast	Percentage of delegates selected through primaries
1912	12	974,775	32.9	13	2,261,240	41.7
1916	20	1,187,691	53.5	20	1,923,374	58.9
1920	16	571,671	44.6	20	3,186,248	57.8
1924	14	763,858	35.5	17	3,525,185	45.3
1928	16	1,264,220	42.2	15	4,110,288	44.9
1932	16	2,952,933	40.0	14	2,346,996	37.7
1936	14	5,181,808	36.5	12	3,319,810	37.5
1940	13	4,468,631	35.8	13	3,227,875	38.8
1944	14	1,867,609	36.7	13	2,271,605	38.7
1948	14	2,151,865	36.3	12	2,653,255	36.0
1952	16	4,928,006	38.7	13	7,801,413	39.0
1956	19	5,832,592	42.7	19	5,828,272	44.8
1960	16	5,687,742	38.3	15	5,537,967	38.6
1964	16	6,247,435	45.7	16	5,935,339	45.6
1968	15	7,535,069	40.2	15	4,473,551	38.1
1972	21	15,993,965	65.3	20	6,188,281	56.8
1976	27	16,052,652	76.0	26	10,374,125	71.0
1980	34	18,747,825	71.8	34	12,690,451	76.0
1984	29	18,009,217	52.4	25	6,575,651	71.0
1988	36	22,961,936	66.6	36	12,165,115	76.9
1992	39	20,239,385	66.9	38	12,696,547	83.9
1996	35	10,996,395	65.3	42	14,233,939	84.6
2000	40	14,045,745	64.6	43	17,156,117	83.8
2004	38	16,397,871	83.2	27[a]	7,936,894	56.9

Note: Only those primaries in which delegates are selected and bound by the primary results are included in the above counts.

a. Republican primaries in five states (Connecticut, Florida, Mississippi, New York, and South Dakota), with 309 delegates, were canceled because only George W. Bush qualified for the primary. Consequently, these five are not included in the primary count, and the delegates from these states (12.3 percent of the total) are not included in the percentage of delegates selected through primaries.

Sources: 1912–2000: *Congressional Quarterly's Guide to U.S. Elections,* 4th ed. (Washington, D.C.: CQ Press, 2001), 307ff.; 2004: derived by the editors from "The Rhodes Cook Letter," August 2004, 4 (http://www.rhodescook.com), as of June 5, 2005; Federal Election Commission, "2004 Presidential Primary Election Results" (http://www.fec.gov), as of June 5, 2005; "Democratic Delegate Vote Allocation" and "Republican Delegate Allocation" (http://www.thegreenpapers.com), as of June 5, 2005.

the rules and prevent challenges to their convention delegations. The reforms also transformed the national convention itself. Many thought that the use of proportional representation would enhance the role of the convention by creating a situation in which there would be many candidates but no front-runners. That has not happened, however. Instead the convention has become a rubber stamp, formally adopting a decision that has already been made by the popular vote of the rank and file.

Although the proliferation of primaries that accompanied the Democratic reforms also affected the Republican Party, it did not experience the same kind of wrenching pressures to reform that

More on this topic:

Elections and Campaigns, p. 168

Elections Chronology, p. 174

affected the Democratic Party. For one thing, the Republicans were a smaller, more ideologically cohesive party than the Democrats. The Republican Party also had far fewer minority members, which meant there was less demand for equal representation of minorities within its ranks. Furthermore, the Republicans already had instituted several of the reforms sought by the Democrats. For example, use of the unit rule had been banned at Republican conventions since the mid-nineteenth century.

Democratic Party *See* POLITICAL PARTIES.

Depression *See* GREAT DEPRESSION.

Dewey, Thomas E.

Thomas E. Dewey.
Source: New-York Historical Society

Gov. Thomas E. Dewey (1902–1971) of New York represented the Republicans in two losing presidential campaigns, against Franklin D. Roosevelt in 1944 and Harry S. Truman in 1948. A liberal Republican and strong leader in his three terms as governor of New York (1943–1955), Dewey stood only a small chance against Roosevelt during wartime. But his defeat by Truman came as one of the biggest surprises in the history of U.S. elections, defying the confident predictions of pollsters and the press.

Dewey came to prominence in the mid-1920s as a young special prosecutor appointed to clean up racketeering in New York City. As a Republican and former assistant district attorney, Dewey was well equipped to take advantage of the public's weariness with a Democratic-controlled city government that had tolerated corruption for years. His highly publicized prosecution and conviction of mobster Lucky Luciano made Dewey a national hero. Other gangster prosecutions followed when Dewey was elected New York district attorney in 1937. The prosecutor with the bottlebrush moustache was known as a ruthlessly hard-working, brilliant man with more than a touch of arrogance.

After battling the party's 1940 candidate, Wendell L. Willkie, in the primaries, Dewey won the 1944 Republican nomination at the convention. His running mate was Gov. John Bricker of Ohio. Dewey called for new leadership without questioning the premises of the New Deal. In his convention acceptance speech he criticized "stubborn men grown old and tired and quarrelsome in office." But the war effort was going well, and Roosevelt's calls for wartime unity helped him win the fourth term he was never to complete. Dewey received 45.9 percent of the popular vote to Roosevelt's 53.4 percent.

Dewey's second presidential bid, with Gov. Earl Warren of California as his running mate, against Roosevelt's successor, Harry S. Truman, looked from the start like a Republican victory in the making. Truman was unpopular, and the Democrats were badly divided, with splinter candidates on the right and left. Early polls showed Dewey with a strong lead, and Dewey ran as if he were an incumbent, speaking in restrained, diplomatic tones and refusing throughout most of the campaign to answer Truman's feisty challenges. The *Chicago Tribune*'s headline the morning after the election, "Dewey Defeats Truman," told the story: the polls and the press had been wrong to the end. Truman won 49.5 percent of the popular vote to Dewey's 45.1 percent. It appeared that the Democratic splinter candidates might have helped Truman by positioning him in the center. His support among farmers also was important. The Republicans had alienated farmers by proposing cuts in agricultural subsidies and by failing to put a midwesterner on the ticket.

> **More on this topic:**
>
> *Elections Chronology,*
> *p. 174*

Diplomatic Powers

John F. Kennedy expressed the importance of foreign affairs to the presidency when he observed, "The big difference [between domestic and foreign policy] is that between a bill being defeated and the country [being] wiped out." Most contemporary presidents would have agreed with Kennedy's appraisal of the importance of foreign affairs. In the nineteenth century, when U.S. foreign interests were limited primarily to trade and to disputes about western expansion, presidents often could concentrate on domestic policy. Today the dangers of the international environment and the wide array of U.S. economic, political, and military commitments virtually ensure that presidents will spend at least half of their time on foreign affairs.

Distribution of Diplomatic Power

The Constitution specifically grants few foreign affairs powers to the president. It states: "He shall have Power, by and with the Advice and Consent of the Senate, to make Treaties, provided two-thirds of the Senators present concur; and he shall nominate and, by and with the Advice and Consent of the Senate, shall appoint Ambassadors, other public Ministers and Consuls." And it calls on the president to "receive Ambassadors and other public Ministers." The Constitution also bestows upon the president the related responsibilities of serving as commander in chief of the nation's military and executing the laws of the United States:

> The Constitution assigns to Congress the powers "to ... provide for the common Defence and general Welfare of the United States; ... to regulate Commerce with foreign Nations; ... to define and punish Piracies and Felonies committed on the high Seas, and Offences against the Law of Nations; to declare War ... and make Rules concerning Captures on Land and Water; to raise and support Armies; ... to provide and maintain a Navy; ... to make all Laws which shall be necessary and proper for carrying into Execution the foregoing Powers."

At a glance, the congressional powers in foreign affairs appear at least as broad as those granted to the president. The president commands the armed forces, but Congress declares war; the president makes treaties, but not without the advice and consent of the Senate; the president appoints ambassadors, but they must be confirmed by the Senate. Only the power to receive ambassadors, a seemingly ceremonial function, is left unchecked by a corresponding congressional power. (See CHIEF OF STATE.) In contrast, Congress has several specific foreign affairs powers, including the important responsibility of regulating foreign commerce. More important, the legislative branch's general power to make laws, control appropriations, and "provide for the common Defence and general Welfare of the United States" gives it broad authority to become involved in any foreign policy decision or action not reserved for the president by the Constitution.

The affirmative grants of power in the Constitution do not begin to answer all the questions about how foreign policy decisions shall be made and implemented. For example, the Constitution does not say how the president is to receive Senate advice on treaties, whether the president can make international agreements without using the treaty process, whether the president needs congressional approval to sustain military action that might commit the United States to war, or what foreign policy actions the president can take under the general executive authority of the office. The authors of the Constitution set up a very ambiguous distribution of shared foreign policy powers between the president and Congress, which could be sorted out only by events. In the famous words of presidential scholar Edward S. Corwin, the Constitution is "an invitation to struggle for the privilege of directing American foreign policy."

Presidential Dominance of Foreign Policy

Addressing members of the Jewish War Veterans in 1948, President Harry S. Truman stated, "I make foreign policy." Most historians and political scientists would agree that although Truman's assessment of presidential power was an exaggeration, it reflects modern presidents' relative autonomy over foreign policy compared with their more limited authority in domestic affairs.

The ambiguity of the Constitution ensured that customs and precedents would be developed that would fill in the gaps left by its brief treatment of diplomatic powers. The branch most capable of asserting its own interests and demonstrating its ability to make foreign policy would emerge as the more powerful. This branch proved to be the executive. Although Congress has retained an important role in foreign affairs, its actions almost always have been responses to presidential policies. On many occasions Congress has been able to delay or modify presidential foreign policy, but the president has dominated the formulation and initiation of foreign policy.

Theodore Roosevelt (center) won the Nobel Peace Prize for his efforts in ending the war between Russia and Japan. In 1905 he met with delegates from both sides in Portsmouth, New Hampshire.
Source: Theodore Roosevelt Collection, Harvard College Library

The president has several advantages over Congress in the area of foreign relations. First, as head of the foreign policy bureaucracy, the diplomatic corps, the intelligence agencies, and the military, the president controls information that is vital to decision making in foreign policy. Second, because only one person occupies the office of the president, whereas 535 make up the Congress, the president is able to work with speed and secrecy—two capabilities that are indispensable in many diplomatic crises. Third, because communication with foreign governments through treaty negotiations and diplomatic channels is the responsibility of the presidency, the president can most easily formulate policy that is consistent with negotiating positions and official statements. Fourth, as chief executive and commander in chief, the president is in the best position to judge whether the U.S. government can carry out a given foreign policy initiative. Fifth, because presidents are elected every four years, they can provide more continuity to foreign policy than Congress, which must sustain an election every two years. Sixth, because presidents, unlike members of Congress, are elected by a national constituency, they are usually more inclined than Congress to focus on international problems that affect the entire nation. Finally, the president is the most identifiable leader and visible symbol of the nation and is, therefore, the most capable of rallying national support in a crisis.

In spite of presidential advantages, presidents do not completely control U.S. foreign policy. At times Congress has refused to follow the president's leadership and has attempted to legislate its own policy course. Even when presidents have dominated foreign policy, Congress has demonstrated that no chief executive can sustain a foreign policy program for long without its support. Cooperation between the two branches, therefore, has been crucial to establishing effective foreign policies.

Power of Communication

The Constitution's separation of powers between independent branches created a question that was unique to the United States: Who has the power to receive communications from foreign countries and to speak for the nation? Under the Articles of Confederation these responsibilities belonged to Congress. The presidency created by the Constitution, however, had strong claims to the communication power. Negotiating treaties and sending and receiving ambassadors, two communications powers, were specifically assigned to the president. Perhaps more important, communications was a function better suited to an office occupied by a single person with executive power than to a legislature.

George Washington was anxious to establish the presidency as the only organ of government empowered to communicate officially with foreign governments. He recognized that if both the president and Congress presumed to speak for the nation, diplomacy would be impossible, and foreign governments might try to exploit the confusion. During the first year of his administration, Washington received a letter from King Louis XVI of France. Washington told Congress that he had received the letter and that he would send a reply to France. The president informed the king that "by the change which has taken place in the national government of the United States, the honor of receiving and answering your Majesty's letter of the 7th of June to 'the President and Members of Congress' has devolved upon me."

In 1793 Washington's secretary of state, Thomas Jefferson, echoed this assertion when he explained to the French ambassador, Edmond Genêt, that because the president is "the only channel of communication between this country and foreign nations, it is from him alone that foreign nations or their agents are to learn what is or has been the will of the nation; and whatever he communicates as such, they have the right, and are bound to consider, as the expression of the nation."

Washington's conception of the president's role as national communicator was accepted without serious challenge. In 1799 John Marshall reaffirmed the president's position as the instrument of communication with foreign governments when, as a member of the House of Representatives, he declared, "The President is the sole organ of the nation in its external relations, and its sole representative with foreign nations."

The president's authority to communicate with other nations is not merely a ceremonial power. From Washington's day to the present, presidents have found they can make foreign policy simply by making a statement. Presidents have used their communications power to make commitments, formalize decisions, or institutionalize broad policy goals.

Because only the president can speak for the United States, Congress often is forced to choose between supporting a presidential decision it had no part in making or undermining that decision, which the world has accepted as U.S. policy. How a president expresses U.S. interests and intentions, therefore, can shape U.S. foreign policy. Kennedy's famous speech at the Berlin Wall in 1963, for example, encouraged the people of Berlin to expect U.S. protection, thereby committing the United States to its defense.

Treaty Power

Article II, Section 2, Clause 2, of the Constitution declares that the president "shall have the Power, by and with the Advice and Consent of the Senate, to make Treaties, provided two-thirds of the Senators present concur." This concise statement splits the power to make formal agreements with foreign nations between the president and Senate. Presidents conduct treaty negotiations, but the Senate must approve the document before it becomes law.

In practice, however, the president has come to dominate the treaty-making process. The president decides what agreements to pursue and how to pursue them. Senate power is limited to voting on the completed document. (See TREATY POWER.)

Presidents also have developed the practice of concluding EXECUTIVE AGREEMENTS. These are pacts between the president and other governments that have the force of law but are not subject to congressional approval. Presidents have maintained that their position as chief executive, commander in chief, and sole organ of foreign policy gives them the legal authority to make these pacts without obtaining the specific approval of the Senate. The executive agreement is a particularly powerful foreign policy tool because presidents can make agreements with foreign governments without congressional consent. Executive agreements do not supersede U.S. laws with which they conflict, but in every other respect they are binding.

Recognition Power

Although the Constitution does not explicitly grant presidents the power to recognize foreign governments, it is generally accepted that they have this power as a consequence of the authority to send and receive ambassadors. Article II, Section 2, of the Constitution says the president "shall appoint Ambassadors," and Section 3 of the same article grants the president the power to "receive Ambassadors and other public Ministers" of foreign nations. Because the acts of sending an ambassador to a country and receiving its ambassador imply recognition of the legitimacy of the foreign government involved in the exchange, presidents have successfully claimed exclusive authority to decide which foreign governments will be recognized by the United States. It follows, then, that they also have the power to end relations with another nation.

This extension of presidential power was not taken for granted at the beginning of the Republic. In the *Federalist Papers,* Alexander Hamilton did not appear even to notice the potential connection between the ceremonial power to receive ambassadors and the recognition of nations. James Madison wrote that the president's power to receive ambassadors "is more a matter of dignity than of authority. It is a circumstance which will be without consequence in the administration of the government; and it was far more convenient that it should be arranged in this manner than that there should be a necessity of convening the legislature, or one of its branches, upon every arrival of a foreign minister."

The first use of the president's power of recognition occurred in 1793 when Washington agreed to receive Edmond Genêt, the ambassador of the new French Republic. Because most of the members of Congress who were inclined to resist the growth of executive power into areas not specifically granted in the Constitution were also supporters of the new republican regime in France, this expansion of the president's power to receive ambassadors was not questioned. All later presidents have assumed the right to make recognition decisions. Congress has no role in the recognition process other than to approve the president's nominees for ambassadorships.

In 1913 President Woodrow Wilson set a precedent by refusing to recognize the Mexican regime of Victoriano Huerta on the grounds that it was immoral and did not represent the will of the Mexican people. Since then the ideology and morality of a foreign regime have become accepted factors in determining whether a government should be recognized.

A decision to recognize or not to recognize a nation can be a major policy statement that expresses the attitudes and intentions of the United States toward the nation in question, and sometimes toward an entire region. In 1836 Andrew Jackson realized that the act of recognizing the Republic of Texas could have the effect of a declaration of war against Mexico, which regarded Texas as a Mexican territory.

The president's power to sever diplomatic relations has been used as an ultimate sanction to protest another country's behavior. Severance of relations is usually reserved for situations in which the differences between the two nations are so great that there is no hope they may be resolved through normal diplomacy. It is customary to break diplomatic ties with a country before declaring war against it, but many events short of war have prompted presidents to terminate relations. In 1979, for example, President Jimmy Carter ended diplomatic relations with Iran in response to the taking of U.S. diplomats as hostages by the Iranians.

Appointing Diplomatic Personnel

Article II, Section 2, of the Constitution states that the president shall "nominate, and by and with the Advice and Consent of the Senate, shall appoint Ambassadors, other public Ministers and Consuls." As the president was to be the sole organ of foreign communications, the power to appoint those individuals who would be communicating directly with foreign leaders was properly a presidential duty. The success of a president's foreign policy program depends greatly on the personalities and abilities of the people who fill important diplomatic posts.

Although the president appoints officials, Congress has the constitutional power to create offices. Nevertheless, presidents have used executive orders to create government bodies that required them to make appointments. John Kennedy established the Peace Corps in this manner, and Gerald R. Ford unilaterally created the Committee on Foreign Intelligence and the Intelligence Oversight Board.

Many presidents also have used personal emissaries not subject to Senate confirmation to conduct foreign policy. Often such presidential representatives have been employed to carry out specific diplomatic missions. The use of personal envoys allows presidents to inject their own ideas and proposals directly into negotiations without having to go through the State Department or other official channels.

The use of presidential envoys is not discussed in the Constitution. The practice contradicts the apparent intention of the Constitution, because the president is supposed to appoint ambassadors "with the Advice and Consent of the Senate." The use of personal envoys, therefore, is a means by which presidents have evaded the Senate's check on their diplomatic appointment power.

As chief diplomat, presidents can conduct diplomacy themselves. Meetings between the president and other heads of state are known as SUMMIT MEETINGS. Such meetings have come to be regarded as an established and useful method of negotiation.

The Constitution does not specifically sanction the president's authority to meet with other world leaders, but the power to appoint, send, and receive ambassadors and to negotiate treaties clearly establishes the president's right to conduct diplomatic negotiations personally.

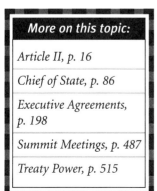

More on this topic:
Article II, p. 16
Chief of State, p. 86
Executive Agreements, p. 198
Summit Meetings, p. 487
Treaty Power, p. 515

CLOSER LOOK

Eisenhower terminated diplomatic relations with Cuba on January 3, 1961 three weeks before leaving office. He said "there is a limit to what the United States in self-respect can endure" (from *Statement by the President on Terminating Diplomatic Relations with Cuba* —January 3, 1961).

This began a U.S. policy of isolating Cuba, prohibiting the import of Cuban products and the export of American food, medical supplies, and capital to Cuba. In 1977 "interest sections," unofficial consular offices, were opened up in each country's capital—in the respective embassies of Switzerland.

Disability Amendment

Presidential disability was a minor concern at the Constitutional Convention. Since then it has been a recurring inconvenience during much of U.S. history, and a potentially grave crisis during the nuclear age.

The original Constitution provided that "[i]n Case of … Inability [of the president] to discharge the Powers and Duties of the said Office, the Same shall devolve on the Vice President … until the Disability be removed, or a President shall be elected." No debate or explanation accompanied the enactment of this clause, so it is impossible to determine what the delegates meant by "inability" or "disability." Nor was any procedure created to determine whether a president was disabled.

Not until the Twenty-fifth Amendment was adopted in 1967 did such a procedure exist, even though eleven presidents who served before 1967 were disabled during at least part of their administrations. The most seriously afflicted were James A. Garfield, who hovered near death for eighty days in 1881 before succumbing to an assassin's bullet, and Woodrow Wilson, who suffered a stroke in 1919 that incapacitated him during most of his final year and a half in office.

President Lyndon B. Johnson signing the Twenty-fifth Amendment, which authorized the president to nominate a new vice president when a vacancy occurred and provided for an orderly transition of authority should the president become disabled. With the vice presidency vacant, if Johnson had died or become disabled, seventy-four-year-old Speaker John McCormack (far right) would have been president. Next in line was the president pro tempore of the Senate, eighty-eight-year-old Carl Hayden (third from left, standing).
Source: Lyndon Baines Johnson Library

Discussions took place within both presidents' cabinets about transferring power to the vice president. The absence of constitutional guidance, however, made the cabinets reluctant to act. "I am not going to seize the place and then have Wilson—recovered—come around and say 'Get off, you usurper,' " Vice President Thomas R. Marshall confided to his secretary.

Presidential disability became a pressing issue after the development of nuclear weapons in World War II. There was a growing awareness that the nation no longer could afford to be leaderless even for brief periods, since the president might be called upon at a moment's notice to make a decision that could literally destroy the world.

After a series of severe health problems in the mid-1950s, President Dwight D. Eisenhower improvised an arrangement with Vice President Richard Nixon under which Eisenhower, by letter, would temporarily transfer the powers and duties of the presidency to Nixon if he again were disabled. The arrangement also provided that Nixon could simply assume those powers if the president were unable to transfer them voluntarily. Presidents John F. Kennedy and Lyndon B. Johnson made similar arrangements with their vice presidents.

These arrangements hardly solved the problem of presidential disability. For one thing, they lacked the force of law. For another, they made no provision to relieve a president who was disabled but who refused to admit it. The Twenty-fifth Amendment, offered by Democratic senator

Birch Bayh in the aftermath of the Kennedy assassination, provided at least a partial solution to the problem.

The amendment addresses two different situations. In the first, the president recognizes—say, before or after surgery—that he is unable to discharge his duties. A letter from the president to the Speaker of the House and the president pro tempore of the Senate is sufficient to make the vice president acting president. A subsequent letter declaring that the disability is ended restores the president's powers.

In the second situation, the president is unable—perhaps having lost consciousness—or unwilling, owing perhaps to a mental disability, to declare himself disabled. In that event the vice president and a majority of the heads of the executive departments may declare the vice president to be acting president. Again, a letter from the president to the leaders of Congress would restore the president to power.

If the vice president and a majority of the cabinet were to disagree with the president's claim that the disability was ended, Congress would have to decide who was right. In the meantime, to prevent the president from simply firing the cabinet, Congress could substitute another body for it. Unless two-thirds of both the House and Senate sided with the vice president and the cabinet, the president's claim would prevail. Because the amendment transfers power to the vice president for only as long as the president is disabled, a subsequent claim of restored health by the president would set the whole process in motion again.

Interestingly, the Twenty-fifth Amendment does not actually define *disability*. It is clear from the congressional debate that disability is not to be equated with incompetence, laziness, unpopularity, or impeachable conduct. As to what does constitute disability, Congress thought that any definition it might write into law would likely be rendered obsolete by later changes in medical technology.

George H. W. Bush was the first vice president to become acting president under the Twenty-fifth Amendment. Ronald Reagan and his aides were criticized for not transferring the powers and duties of the presidency to Bush when Reagan was shot in 1981 in an assassination attempt. While Bush was on a plane returning to Washington from Texas, Secretary of State Alexander M. Haig Jr. created a bit of stir by announcing to reporters that he was in control "here in the White House, pending the return of the vice president." Haig then went on to misstate the line of succession to the presidency: "Constitutionally, gentlemen, you have the president, the vice president, and the secretary of state."

In 1985 Reagan transferred his powers to Bush before undergoing intestinal surgery and signed papers reclaiming them less than eight hours later. Bush spent his eight hours as acting president at home, playing tennis and chatting with friends.

Specifically citing Section 3 of the Twenty-fifth Amendment, George W. Bush in 2002 transferred presidential powers to his vice president, Richard B. Cheney, before undergoing a colonoscopy. Bush resumed power more than two hours later.

> **More on this topic:**
>
> *Assassinations and Assaults, p. 19*
>
> *Succession, p. 483*

Doctrines, Presidential

A presidential foreign policy doctrine is an important, wide-ranging goal or strategy announced by a president that becomes closely associated with that president. The most famous and durable of these doctrines is the MONROE DOCTRINE announced by James Monroe. Presidential doctrines often reflect a president's particular vision of the world or draw attention to a region that has increased in importance.

These foreign policy declarations are not always accepted by Congress, and they have no force of law. However, because presidents function as commander in chief and chief diplomat, they have substantial power to implement foreign policy strategies on their own. (See DIPLOMATIC POWERS.)

Almost no president ever referred to his own policy principles as a "doctrine." An exception is Richard Nixon, who referred to the Nixon Doctrine on 33 occasions. The Nixon Doctrine was first enunciated in a press conference on July 25, 1969, and then discussed in more detail in an address to the nation concerning Vietnam on November 3, 1969. The Nixon Doctrine was related to the policy of "Vietnamization," in which the South Vietnamese were asked to take up a greater share of the burden fighting the North Vietnamese and reflected the American people's growing weariness with the war. Nixon identified the crux of the doctrine in his November address stating, "[w]e shall look to the nation directly threatened to assume the primary responsibility of providing the manpower for its defense."

In 1823 President Monroe announced in his annual message to Congress that the United States would resist any attempt by a European power to interfere in the affairs of a nation in the Western Hemisphere that was not already a European colony. Monroe did not consult Congress before his announcement, and some of its members believed the president had overstepped his authority. Henry Clay proposed a joint resolution supporting the president's policy, but his proposal was never acted on. Not until 1899 did the Monroe Doctrine receive a congressional endorsement. Yet it became a cornerstone of U.S. foreign policy that continues to be observed.

Theodore Roosevelt built on the Monroe Doctrine in 1904 when he announced what came to be known as the Roosevelt Corollary in his annual message to Congress. Roosevelt claimed for the United States the right to act as the Western Hemisphere's policeman if "chronic wrongdoing or impotence" in a country required U.S. intervention.

Many contemporary presidents have been associated with foreign policy doctrines. In 1947 President Harry S. Truman asked Congress for $400 million in aid for Greece and Turkey, nations that were threatened by communist insurgents. Truman declared that "it must be the policy of the United States to support free peoples who are resisting attempted subjugation by armed minorities or outside pressures." This theme became known as the Truman Doctrine. Under the doctrine, successive administrations opposed the expansion of international communism.

The Eisenhower Doctrine, which was supported by a joint resolution, built upon the Truman Doctrine. After the Suez crisis of 1956, Dwight D. Eisenhower claimed for the United States the right to intervene militarily in the Middle East to protect legitimate governments from attacks by communist forces. In accordance with this doctrine, he sent troops to Lebanon in 1958 when the Lebanese government requested help fighting insurgents.

Reacting to the unpopularity of U.S. involvement in the Vietnam War, President Richard Nixon announced the Nixon Doctrine (also known as the Guam Doctrine). It proposed continuing to give allies military and economic aid while encouraging them to reduce their reliance on U.S. troops.

In his State of the Union address on January 23, 1980, President Jimmy Carter warned that "an attempt by any outside force to gain control of the Persian Gulf region will be regarded as an assault on the vital interests of the United States of America, and such an assault will be repelled by any means necessary, including military force." This statement came to be known as the Carter Doctrine. It was a direct response to the Soviet invasion of Afghanistan a month earlier. Subsequently, Presidents Ronald Reagan and George H. W. Bush reaffirmed the Carter Doctrine.

Reagan also announced his own presidential doctrine. He declared that he would oppose international communism by providing support to insurgents fighting against communist governments around the globe. Under the Reagan Doctrine, aid was sent to anticommunist rebels in Afghanistan, Angola, and Nicaragua.

A year after the September 11, 2001, terrorist attacks on New York City and Washington, D.C., the George W. Bush administration announced a new strategy known as the "Bush Doctrine." It called for preemptive strikes on terrorists and states with weapons of mass destruction that could pose threats to the United States. Although the September 11 attacks had stimulated the development of this new doctrine, elements of it had been under way before that point. This doctrine was not formulated in opposition to a specific enemy; unlike cold war foreign policy, which was geared mostly toward combating communism, the Bush Doctrine

More on this topic:

Diplomatic Powers,
p. 149

Monroe Doctrine, p. 368

focused more broadly on national security threats, particularly terrorism. In early 2003 Bush put the doctrine into action in a war against Iraq aimed at toppling its leader, Saddam Hussein, with the intention of promoting political and economic freedom in the Middle East. By 2007, with the U.S. military still consumed with promoting stability in Iraq, the Bush doctrine has given way to a more diplomatic approach in dealing with nations such as North Korea and Iran.

Dole, Robert J.

Robert Joseph Dole (1923–), a career politician and consummate Washington insider, was the Republican Party's choice to run against President Bill Clinton in the 1996 campaign. His campaign, weakened by a series of divisive and expensive primary battles, the candidate's long-standing image as an unimaginative political operative, and his failure to project to the electorate what he stood for and what his national agenda would be, resulted in his defeat.

Bob Dole was born in Russell, Kansas, to a hard-working but poor family. A star athlete in high school, Dole entered the University of Kansas with plans to become a doctor. World War II intervened, however, and he enlisted in the army a year after Pearl Harbor. Assigned to the elite 10th Mountain Division, he was severely wounded in a battle in Italy just three weeks before the war in Europe was over. His recovery took more than three years, and he never regained the use of his right arm.

His wound, he would later wryly recount, led to his political career. A Kansas Republican politician told him, "You got shot; we can get you elected." After studying law, Dole first won a county prosecutor's job, then a seat in Congress in 1960, followed by election to the

Sen. Robert J. Dole and his wife, Elizabeth Hanford Dole, on the campaign trail during the 1996 presidential primaries. His wife and Hillary Rodham Clinton, the wife of his opponent in the 1996 race, were both elected to the Senate in 2000.
Source: Jeff Christensen, Reuters

Senate in 1968. He became the Senate Republican leader in 1985. As a sign of his popularity with his fellows as an expert consensus builder and deal maker, Dole would become the longest-serving Republican leader in Senate history.

In the 1976 presidential election, President Gerald R. Ford chose Dole to be his running mate. Dole's caustic and highly partisan style of campaigning was later blamed, many said unfairly, for the GOP's loss. Dole tried unsuccessfully in 1980 and 1988 to win his party's presidential nomination.

Dole was seventy-three in 1996 as he made his last try for the presidency. Even though he seemed to be the acknowledged party favorite, he lost three of the first four primaries before securing enough victories to win the nomination. The divisive and expensive primary process was a harbinger of things to come.

His choice of Jack Kemp, a fervent advocate of supply-side economics, as his running mate and his call for an across-the-board 15 percent income tax cut, helped raise Dole's standing in the polls. However, the tax cut represented a sea change for a long-professed "deficit hawk" and quickly drew charges of opportunism.

More on this topic:

Elections Chronology, p. 174

Presidential Medal of Freedom, p. 415

Social conservatives in the party remained unconvinced of Dole's commitment to banning abortion; party moderates worried that Dole would give in to the party's conservative extremists, abandoning his pragmatic approach. The party's 1996 platform, dictated by its right wing, was exceedingly conservative, alienating many moderates.

Despite a vigorous campaign, Dole never overcame the uneasiness that most voters felt about his reputation as a political "hatchet man." The irony was that only when the race appeared to be out of reach did Dole decide to attack Clinton on character issues, and this tactic succeeded in cutting the gap in the polls to 7 percent. But it was not enough, and Clinton won easily in November, with 49.2 percent of the popular vote and 379 electoral votes to Dole's 40.7 percent and 159 electoral votes. Reform Party candidate H. Ross Perot took 8.4 percent of the vote and received no electoral votes.

After the election President Clinton presented his defeated opponent with the PRESIDENTIAL MEDAL OF FREEDOM, honoring him for his military heroism and his long years of congressional service. Dole joined a private Washington, D.C., law firm.

Douglas, Stephen A.

Stephen A. Douglas.
Source: Mathew Brady, Bettmann Archive

The name Stephen Arnold Douglas (1813–1861) is linked forever with that of an Illinois politician of greater fame, Abraham Lincoln. The two were rivals in a Senate race in 1858 that is remembered more for Lincoln's eloquence in a series of debates than for Douglas's victory. They became rivals again in 1860 when Lincoln defeated Democrat Douglas and two other candidates to win the presidency. But Lincoln and Douglas were allies in the larger political cause of preventing the United States from breaking up over slavery.

Douglas, who was five feet, four inches tall, was called the "Little Giant" by his admirers. He was born in Vermont and moved to Illinois as a young man. With a sketchy education and no money but plenty of ambition, Douglas studied law and became a force in his state's Democratic Party. After holding a series of state and local offices, Douglas was elected to the U.S. House of Representatives in 1843. He served three terms before his election to the Senate, where he remained from 1847 until his death fourteen years later. Douglas unsuccessfully sought the Democratic presidential nomination twice, in 1852 and 1856, before winning it in 1860.

The struggle that dominated Douglas's political career, to preserve the Union through compromise, was lost in the end. Still, historians have speculated that his efforts helped stave off civil war for a decade. As chairman of the Senate Committee on Territories, Douglas was at the center of the most explosive issue of the pre–Civil War years: whether slavery should be allowed in the territories. Douglas championed what he called "popular sovereignty"—the idea that the territories should be allowed to decide the slavery question for themselves. He had hoped to hold the Democratic Party together and resolve the slavery issue through legislative compromise; as those hopes faded, Douglas broke with the southern Democrats who favored slavery.

The Democratic convention that nominated Douglas as its presidential candidate in 1860 reflected the party's irreconcilable divisions. The convention had first met in Charleston, South Carolina, but adjourned in deadlock after fifty-seven ballots and a walkout by southern delegates. The convention reconvened in Baltimore the next month and nominated Douglas without the support of the pro-slavery southerners. The Democratic defectors nominated their own presidential candidate, Vice President John C. Breckinridge, to run on a pro-slavery platform. A fourth candidate, John Bell, represented the Constitutional Union Party, a group of southerners who opposed Breckinridge.

In the four-way race for president, Douglas was Lincoln's principal opponent, because the South had too few electoral votes to give the other two candidates a chance. Lincoln won the election easily with Douglas in second place in the popular vote. Breaking with the tradition that presidential candidates remained above the campaign fray, Douglas had campaigned hard—first to reunite his party, and when that appeared futile, to save the Union. He spent the last months of his life fighting for the policies of President Lincoln as the nation prepared for war.

More on this topic:
Civil War, p. 95
Elections Chronology, p. 174
Lincoln, Abraham, p. 336

E

Economic Advisers, Council of

President George W. Bush stands with Ed Lazear of the Council of Economic Advisers, left, and Al Hubbard of the National Economic Council, in the Rose Garden Friday, April 28, 2006
Source: The White House

The Council of Economic Advisers (CEA) is a three-member body appointed by the president and subject to Senate confirmation. It is headed by a chair who oversees the council's small staff, reports to the president, and represents the CEA before the rest of the executive branch and Congress.

The main purpose of the CEA is to provide the president with expert economic advice. The Employment Act of 1946, which established the CEA, states that each member of the council "shall be a person who, as a result of his training, experience and attainments, is exceptionally qualified to analyze and interpret economic developments ... and to formulate and recommend national economic policy."

Because the CEA does not represent a large government agency and has no responsibilities in running the government except preparing the president's annual economic report, Congress hoped that the council would have the time and independence to give the president nonpartisan, expert advice on the

More on this topic:

Economic Powers, p. 161

Executive Office of the President, p. 200

Staff, p. 472

economy. Traditionally the CEA has been most concerned with promoting economic growth and managing the trade-off between inflation and unemployment.

The CEA's influence depends on the president. If the president values its advice and includes it in policy making, the CEA can have great power because of its economic expertise. However, if the CEA approaches problems from a perspective that ignores the president's political needs or is too theoretical, it may lose influence. Often the CEA's role has depended simply on whether the president liked working with the chair.

Economic Powers

The authors of the Constitution seem to have intended Congress to be the branch of government most concerned with the economic affairs of the nation. Article I, Section 8, of the Constitution grants Congress numerous economic powers, including the authority to "lay and collect Taxes, Duties, Imposts and Excises, to pay the Debts and provide for the common Defence and general Welfare of the United States …; [t]o borrow Money on the credit of the United States; [t]o regulate Commerce with foreign Nations, and among the several States …; [t]o coin Money, regulate the Value thereof, and of Foreign coin."

In contrast, the Constitution grants the president no specific economic powers. Nevertheless, the framers expected the president to have significant influence over the economy. The president would, after all, oversee the implementation of Congress's spending and taxing decisions, suggest economic legislation in the State of the Union address and other communications to Congress, negotiate commercial treaties with foreign nations, and have the power to veto legislation on economic matters.

Presidential economic power, however, has developed beyond these constitutional powers. Presidents have effectively used their visibility and their prerogatives over the execution of policy to promote their own economic programs. In addition, as management of the economy became more complex during the twentieth century, Congress passed laws giving presidents greater economic power.

Over time the American people have come to associate the presidency—the nation's most powerful and identifiable political office—with the performance of the federal government. As a result, they have come to expect presidents to produce economic prosperity for the United States just as presidents are expected to enforce its laws and ensure its security. As political scientist Clinton Rossiter observed near the end of the Eisenhower administration, "The people of this country are no longer content to let disaster fall upon them unopposed. They now expect their government, under the direct leadership of the President, to prevent a depression or panic and not simply wait until one has developed before putting it to rout. Thus the President has a new function which is still taking shape, that of Manager of Prosperity."

Limitations

Despite the expectations of the American public and the president's pivotal role in economic policy making, the president's ability to influence economic conditions does not measure up to his responsibility for them in the eyes of the public. When unemployment, inflation, and budget deficits rise, presidents receive most of the blame. Herbert C. Hoover, Gerald R. Ford, Jimmy Carter, and George H. W. Bush all lost their reelection bids in large part because of the poor economic conditions that prevailed during their presidencies.

Four factors combine to limit the president's control over the U.S. economy. First, the chief executive must share power with other individuals and government bodies. As the enumeration of congressional economic powers shows, Congress has the constitutional authority to frustrate virtually any presidential economic initiative. Most important, the president cannot levy taxes or appropriate money without the consent of Congress. The independence of the Federal Reserve Board also limits presidential power over monetary policy.

A second factor is the highly complex and theoretical nature of the discipline of economics. Even if presidents trust the judgment of their economic advisers, there often is little agreement among economists about which theory or theories should guide economic policy.

A third factor limiting presidential economic control is the imprecision of economic information. When presidents attempt to adjust the economy, they assume that they have accurate information about how the economy is performing. Economic statistics and indicators, however, do not measure the immediate conditions of the economy; rather, they measure the conditions that prevailed between one and four months earlier, depending on the particular economic statistic. Consequently, presidents who take action on the basis of incoming economic information may be reacting to a problem that no longer exists or is now much worse than believed. In such cases presidential economic policies may destabilize the economy.

Finally, presidential control over the economy is limited by forces outside the reach of the federal government. The economic policies of state and local governments, the price of oil, bad weather, low consumer confidence, and the decisions of large corporations may undercut presidential economic policy. A president making all the right decisions will not, therefore, necessarily produce a thriving economy; nor will an economically inexperienced or inept president inevitably bring on a national economic disaster or even a recession.

Yet, in spite of these limitations, no one has more influence over the U.S. economy than the president. As chief executive the president oversees the government's economic and regulatory functions and appoints members of the cabinet and Federal Reserve Board, who make many economic decisions; as chief legislator the president proposes spending, tax, and other economic legislation and can use the veto to influence what legislation becomes law; as commander in chief the president oversees the multibillion-dollar purchases of the Defense Department; as chief diplomat the president negotiates with foreign governments about trade and currency issues; and as chief of state the president helps to shape the morale, attitudes, and expectations of the American people.

Economic Management

From the beginning of the Republic, presidents understood that promoting the nation's prosperity was as much a part of their job as ensuring its security and enforcing its laws. Presidents did not, however, attempt to affect the performance of the economy through spending and taxing decisions until the Great Depression of the 1930s. Before then the classical theory of economics prevailed, a theory associated with the writings of Adam Smith, the eighteenth-century Scottish economist. This theory held that a laissez-faire approach to government economic activity—one that allowed farmers, merchants, and manufacturers to operate unencumbered by government intervention and regulation—would result in the most prosperous economic conditions. If the economy was running smoothly, the president's economic responsibilities would then be limited primarily to executing the spending and revenue measures passed by Congress, promoting a balanced budget, and working with business leaders and foreign governments to expand industrial development and trade.

The U.S. economy did not always run smoothly, however. As the nation became industrialized in the late nineteenth and early twentieth centuries, fluctuations in employment became more frequent and severe. The growth of industry also made new demands on the nation's financial system and forced the government to protect consumers and workers from the power of monopolies. Society came to believe that government should work to prevent crises and create a stable and fair business environment. Consequently, presidents in the late nineteenth and early twentieth centuries occasionally abandoned their laissez-faire stance and proposed or supported solutions to obvious economic problems.

Indeed, the public increasingly looked to the president, the symbol and most visible leader of the government, for economic direction. By the time the Great Depression struck in the 1930s, laissez-faire attitudes toward the executive's economic role had already given way to more activist conceptions of governmental and presidential power. The human suffering of the Depression convinced the American public and its leaders that the government should intervene to relieve and prevent periods of economic trauma. By the time World War II ended, a national consensus had developed that the government, and especially the president, should use every means available to produce the best economic conditions possible even if the economy was not depressed.

The Civilian Conservation Corps, part of President Franklin D. Roosevelt's New Deal program, not only provided relief for jobless young men during the Great Depression but helped protect and conserve the nation's resources. Roosevelt visited one of the camps in Big Meadows, Virginia, in August 1933.
Source: AP

Post-Depression presidents have attempted to create the best economic conditions possible through their stabilization policies. The U.S. economy, like all capitalist economies, experiences cyclical patterns of expansion and contraction in which the levels of inflation, unemployment, and economic growth vary. During periods of contraction, businesses lose sales, investment decreases, unemployment grows, and prices tend to increase at a slower rate or even to fall. During periods of expansion, consumers spend more, investment increases, unemployment declines, and prices tend to increase at a faster rate. The objective of stabilization policy is to smooth out the natural swings in the economy so that unemployment does not become too severe during periods of contraction and inflation does not run out of control during times of expansion. Ideally, an administration should achieve these goals while maintaining a steady rate of economic growth and balancing the federal budget, or at least running manageable deficits that can be corrected during periods of prosperity.

Stabilization policy can be accomplished through fiscal policy and monetary policy. Fiscal policy refers to the government's taxing and spending decisions. Presidents make fiscal policy in cooperation with Congress, which passes spending and tax bills. Monetary policy refers to decisions about the supply of money in the economy. Presidents do not have legal control over monetary policy, which is determined by the independent Federal Reserve Board. However, presidents appoint the members of the Federal Reserve Board and have some informal influence over its decisions.

We had a bad banking situation. Some of our bankers had shown themselves either incompetent or dishonest in their handling of the people's funds. They had used the money entrusted to them in speculations and unwise loans.... It was the Government's job to straighten out this situation and do it as quickly as possible. And the job is being performed.

—Franklin D. Roosevelt, First Fireside Chat, March 12, 1933

Fiscal Policy

Fiscal policy is the body of spending and taxing decisions made by the government in pursuit of economic stabilization. The government can choose to combat unemployment and stagnant economic growth by stimulating the economy through tax cuts or increased spending. It can choose to fight inflation by contracting the economy through tax increases or reduced spending.

Although Congress must pass legislation approving every taxation and spending decision, presidents and their advisers initiate most fiscal policy proposals and greatly influence congressional debate. Congress rarely has rubber-stamped presidential fiscal policies. Consequently, any president hoping to exercise control over fiscal policy must persuade Congress to accept the plan of the executive branch.

When presidents formulate fiscal policy, they must consider not only what is economically best but also what is politically feasible. A president's fiscal policies depend as much on the chief executive's ability to present them to the American people and to bargain with Congress as on the ability of the president's economic team to understand the economic situation and to formulate effective fiscal responses.

Budget Making

The budget is the most important annual document produced by the EXECUTIVE OFFICE OF THE PRESIDENT. It spells out the funding decisions of the president and the president's advisers and is also an important fiscal policy tool. As Gerald R. Ford said, "The budget reflects the President's sense of priorities. It reflects his best judgment of how we must choose among competing interests." (See BUDGET PROCESS.)

Since the late 1960s the budget-making process has been for the most part a struggle to limit budget deficits in the face of erratic economic growth and dramatic increases in funding for entitlements and social programs. Yet for a brief period during Bill Clinton's second term, budget deficits seemed to be a thing of the past as the economy boomed. The government experienced budget surpluses from 1998 through 2001. But by 2002 the economy had turned sour and the government faced a budget deficit again.

The American people consistently indicate in surveys that they believe government spending should be reduced. They also say they do not want higher taxes. Yet this desire for less government spending is not accompanied by a willingness to sacrifice funding for specific programs. The public believes the government spends too little on most things and too much in only a few policy areas, such as foreign aid and welfare. Thus the budget is one of the most persistent political dilemmas facing presidents. They must try to reduce overall spending (or convince the electorate that they are trying to reduce it) while funding the programs that the American public has come to expect.

Tax Power

Traditionally presidents have exerted less influence over tax policy than over spending matters. Presidents are required to submit an executive budget to Congress outlining their spending proposals each year, but tax laws do not require the executive to make major annual revisions.

Legislators, especially members of the powerful House Ways and Means Committee, have historically regarded tax policy as a special province of Congress. Nevertheless, presidential influence over tax policy is significant and has grown since World War II. As Congress and the nation have become used to looking to the president for economic initiatives, the chief executive has taken over much of the burden of proposing and campaigning for changes in the tax code.

In addition to proposing tax legislation, presidents influence tax policy by standing ready to veto tax bills passed by Congress that they believe are unfair, excessive, or harmful to the economy. Since World War II, presidents rarely have had to veto tax bills, because the threat to veto them usually has been enough to stop the legislation in its tracks. One exception was in Clinton's second term, when the GOP-controlled Congress sent the president a series of large and small tax cut bills. Clinton vetoed almost all the measures, and the Republicans did not come close to overriding his vetoes.

Using tax policy as a tool of fiscal policy is complicated by the government's need for revenue. Although some tax cuts have generated greater revenues, most notably the Kennedy tax cut of 1964, tax cuts usually generate less revenue and higher deficits than would have resulted had they not been enacted. Conversely, raising taxes may increase revenues in the short term but also may contract the economy, resulting in higher unemployment. The supply-side economic theory, which says that cutting tax rates generates higher revenues, became popular in the early 1980s, but the budget deficits that followed Ronald Reagan's 1981 tax cut diminished enthusiasm for this concept among the public and economists.

George W. Bush's narrow victory in the 2000 presidential election was viewed by Republicans as a mandate for their tax cut plans, and Bush succeeded in pushing through a massive multiyear tax cut bill in 2001.

International Economic Role

As the sole negotiator with foreign governments, the president dominates international economic policy. The president's international economic powers have become increasingly important as nations have become more economically interdependent. Because of high volumes of trade, integrated financial markets, multinational corporations, and other factors that bind together the world's economies, prosperous conditions in the United States cannot be sustained if other large economies, especially those of Western Europe and Japan, are ailing.

In view of this shared economic destiny between industrial nations, presidents must function not just as national economic managers but also as international economic coordinators. They dispatch the U.S. trade representative to international talks aimed at reducing trade barriers, oversee the Treasury Department's negotiations with other finance ministries about the value of major currencies, and announce U.S. economic policies to the international community. Since 1975 presidents also have attended annual economic summits where the leaders of the once seven, and now eight, major industrial nations have met to confer on broad issues of economic policy. (See TRADE POLICY.)

But presidents also have faced tensions when international trade agreements have clashed with domestic concerns. The North American Free Trade Agreement (NAFTA) between Canada, Mexico, and the United States was approved and signed into law by Clinton in late 1993 after a concerted White House effort to sway undecided members of Congress to support the agreement. Unions and other opponents voiced fears about the potential loss of American jobs, while supporters contended that the elimination of Mexican trade barriers would open completely a large and increasingly prosperous market to U.S. businesses. In an example of how political considerations can play a role in trade decisions, President George W. Bush, generally a supporter of free trade, decided in 2002 to impose tariffs of up to 30 percent over three years on most steel imports—a move viewed as helping Republicans in steel-producing states.

> **More on this topic:**
>
> *Budget Process, p. 37*
>
> *Executive Office of the President, p. 200*
>
> *Trade Policy, p. 506*

Education Department

The Department of Education administers most federal assistance to education. The federal government provides aid for preschool, elementary, secondary, and postsecondary education, as well as for education of handicapped children and disabled adults, and vocational and adult education. Through the department the government also funds research and demonstration projects.

One responsibility of the department is to ensure that educational institutions comply with federal civil rights laws that prohibit discrimination in programs and activities receiving federal financial assistance from the department.

One responsibility of the department is to ensure that educational institutions comply with federal civil rights laws that prohibit discrimination in programs and activities receiving federal financial assistance from the department.

The department distributes most of its program funds directly to the states as formula grants. The amounts of the grants are based on the number of students in various special categories. The states then distribute the money to local districts under plans approved by the Education Department.

The cabinet-level department is a fairly recent addition to the federal government. Unlike many other countries for which a centralized educational system was a vital component of nation building, the United States traditionally has avoided a strong federal role in education. A federal education agency—called the Department of Education but not represented in the cabinet—was not established until 1867.

The first Department of Education was downgraded quickly to the status of a bureau in the Interior Department. For the next seventy years it limped along as a small record-keeping office, collecting information on the modest federal educational efforts. Proposals for a separate department were made periodically but went nowhere. In 1939 the bureau, renamed the Office of Education, was transferred to the Federal Security Agency, which became the Department of Health, Education, and Welfare (HEW) in 1953.

With the tremendous expansion of federal educational programs in the post–World War II period, arguments for a separate department grew more persuasive. In 1972 Congress established an Education Division within HEW, headed by an assistant secretary for education.

Hundreds of educational programs remained spread across federal agencies, and supporters still pushed for a separate department. Political obstacles had to be overcome, however, including opposition from some of the departments that would lose programs and from a coalition of labor and civil rights groups that feared their influence would be reduced in a department dominated by professional educators. With the strong support of teachers' groups and President Jimmy Carter, Congress approved creation of the new department in 1979.

The department's existence was precarious during its first years. In 1982 President Ronald Reagan, who rode into office on a wave of voter dissatisfaction with what was seen as widespread federal intervention in local affairs, proposed abolishing the Education Department. But Congress ignored the suggestion, and the proposal gradually faded from view. Instead a 1983 report commissioned by the secretary of education, Terril H. Bell, entitled *A Nation at Risk* dramatically set the agenda for future policy discussions. The commission wrote, "The educational foundations of our society are presently being eroded by a rising tide of mediocrity that threatens our very future as a Nation and a people." When Republicans took over both houses of Congress after the 1994 elections, some in the House GOP also sought to abolish four departments, including Education, but they were unsuccessful.

More on this topic:

Bureaucracy, p. 44

Cabinet, p. 60

The department is divided into offices that handle programs for various types and levels of education. In addition to departmental responsibilities, the secretary of education performs certain functions related to five federally aided corporations: American Printing House for the Blind in Kentucky; Gallaudet University (for the deaf) in Washington, D.C.; Howard University in Washington, D.C.; National Institute for Literacy in Washington, D.C.; and National Technical Institute for the Deaf (part of Rochester Institute of Technology) in New York.

Eisenhower, Dwight D.

Source: Library of Congress

Dwight David Eisenhower (1890–1969), like presidents Zachary Taylor and Ulysses S. Grant, became president on the strength of his popularity gained as a war hero. He had never held elective office before taking up residence in the White House in 1953. His presidency is associated with peace and stability, although the cold war with the Soviet Union continued and the United States began to openly confront divisive civil rights issues during Eisenhower's two terms in office.

Eisenhower was born on October 14, 1890, in Denison, Texas, but his family lived there for only a short period. When Dwight was still a baby, they returned to Kansas, where they had lived before he was born. They settled in Abilene, and Dwight's father worked as a mechanic in a creamery.

Eisenhower lacked the money to pay for college, but he was nominated to the U.S. Military Academy at West Point. He played football and graduated number 65 in his class of 164 in 1915. Eisenhower married Marie (Mamie) Doud, the daughter of a wealthy Denver businessman, on July 1, 1916.

When the United States entered World War I in 1917, Eisenhower served as a troop instructor in the United States Army. In 1925 he received an appointment to the Army General Staff School in Leavenworth, Kansas. The next year he graduated first in his class of 275. He then served on the staff of the assistant secretary of war and as an aide to the army chief of staff, Gen. Douglas MacArthur.

When the United States entered World War II in 1941, Eisenhower was a brigadier general. During the next three years he was promoted above hundreds of senior officers. In February 1942 he took command of the War Plans Division of the War Department's general staff. Eisenhower's skill as a tactician and his reputation as a soldier who could unify military leaders holding diverse points of view led to his appointment in June 1942 as the commanding general of the European Theater of Operations. In November 1942 he directed the successful Allied invasion of North Africa. The next year he attained the rank of full general and oversaw the Allied invasions of Sicily and Italy. In December 1943 President Franklin D. Roosevelt named him supreme commander of all Allied forces in Europe and instructed him to develop a plan for an invasion of France. On June 6, 1944, Allied forces landed in Normandy in the largest amphibious invasion ever undertaken. The troops gained a beachhead and began driving toward Germany. Eisenhower accepted the surrender of the German army on May 7, 1945.

When the war was over, Eisenhower was one of America's most prominent war heroes. After serving as commander of the U.S. occupation zone in Germany, Eisenhower was appointed army chief of staff in November 1945. In 1948 he retired from the military to become president of Columbia University. That year he was approached by both the Democrats and the Republicans as a possible presidential candidate. Eisenhower, however, declined all offers to run for office.

In 1950 President Harry S. Truman asked Eisenhower to become supreme commander of the North Atlantic Treaty Organization (NATO) forces in Europe. During his time in Europe, Eisenhower was again courted by both major political parties. Finally, in January 1952, he announced that he would accept the Republican nomination for president if it were offered. He resigned his NATO command in May and was nominated by the Republicans in July. His opponent was Gov. Adlai E. Stevenson II of Illinois. During the campaign Eisenhower avoided detailed discussions of issues, relying instead on his outgoing personality and his popularity to win votes. He won the election with a landslide, defeating Stevenson by a vote of 442–89 in the Electoral College.

When Eisenhower became president in 1953, a settlement of the Korean War, which had begun in 1950, was within reach. In December 1952, after the election, he had fulfilled a campaign promise to go to Korea to survey the situation. On July 27, 1953, an armistice was signed ending the war.

Although international tensions eased somewhat with the death of Soviet leader Joseph Stalin in March 1953 and the Korean War settlement, the cold war continued. Eisenhower continued Truman's policy of containing communist expansion but sought to avoid conflict when possible.

In 1956 Eisenhower protested the attack on Egypt by Great Britain, France, and Israel after Egypt nationalized the Suez Canal. After the Suez crisis, he announced the Eisenhower Doctrine, a commitment by the United States to use force to stop communist aggression in the Middle East. In accordance with this doctrine, he sent U.S. troops to Lebanon in 1958 when the Lebanese government requested assistance fighting insurgents.

On September 24, 1955, Eisenhower suffered a heart attack that limited his activity for several months. In June 1956 he had an operation for an attack of ileitis, an inflammation of the small intestine. Eisenhower's illnesses raised questions about his fitness for a second term. In November 1956, however, the voters reelected him over Democrat Adlai Stevenson by an even larger margin than he had enjoyed in 1952. Eisenhower was confined to bed a third time in 1957 after suffering a stroke.

In domestic policy Eisenhower favored anti-inflation policies over measures to stimulate economic growth. He produced budget surpluses in three of the eight years of his presidency, a feat that became even more noteworthy in the three decades after his retirement, when the federal budget was balanced only once. He also warned of the dangers inherent in the development of a "military-industrial complex" and sought to limit defense spending. He signed bills that paid farmers for taking land out of production and that initiated the national interstate highway system. Although he was not a leading opponent of racial segregation, he enforced existing civil rights laws. In 1957 he sent troops to Little Rock, Arkansas, when local citizens and officials tried to block integration of public schools.

Eisenhower held several summits with Soviet leaders. He met with Soviet premier Nikolai Bulganin and Allied leaders in 1955 at Geneva and with Soviet premier Nikita Khrushchev in 1959 at Camp David, Maryland. However, Eisenhower's plans for a 1960 summit soured when the Soviets shot down an American U-2 spy plane over the Soviet Union on May 1 of that year. Khrushchev protested the U-2 overflights and refused to attend a summit in Paris with Allied leaders later that month. Eisenhower took responsibility for the missions and defended them as vital to the security of the United States.

More on this topic:

Korean War, p. 323

World War II, p. 588

Eisenhower left office at the age of seventy, the oldest person to serve as president up to that time. He retired to his 230-acre farm near Gettysburg, Pennsylvania, where he enjoyed a quiet retirement. In November 1965 he suffered two heart attacks but recovered. During the spring and summer of 1968 he had a series of heart attacks that confined him to a hospital. He died of a final heart attack on March 28, 1969, in Washington, D.C.

Elections and Campaigns

Every four years U.S. voters elect a president whose awesome job it is to protect and nurture the well-being of the nation and all its citizens. Just as the responsibilities of the presidency have evolved to accommodate an ever broader and more diverse array of domestic and international interests, so has the election process evolved to encompass a greatly expanded electorate, shifting power structures, and changing technologies.

Presidential nominees are no longer chosen solely or even primarily by party leaders, but through a series of primary elections and open party caucuses, where rank-and-file party members have an opportunity to express their preference. Once forums for determining who would head the presidential ticket, national nominating conventions today are little more than ratifying assemblies. The candidates' personal contact with the voters is still important, but equally important is how those campaign events are portrayed to the millions more voters watching on television.

Campaigns for primaries and for the general election are carefully orchestrated exercises designed to appeal to the most voters and offend the fewest. That has always been the rule, but the existence of mass communications means that any missteps are likely to have major consequences.

As a result, presidential election campaigns have become complicated organizations made up of the candidate, the candidate's family, a running mate, political allies, campaign strategists, media consultants, advertising experts, fund-raisers, pollsters, schedulers, and issues experts. Campaign strategy must be managed carefully if the candidate is to move successfully through the primary season, the nominating convention, and the general election campaign.

Who Runs for President

All presidential and vice-presidential candidates must meet certain constitutional requirements. Candidates must be at least thirty-five years old and natural-born citizens who have "been 14 years a Resident within the United States."

Just as important are several unwritten, informal requirements. Americans demand that their chief executive meet standards of political and managerial expertise as well as moral and social standing. Sometimes, however, the voters are willing to soften those demands if the candidate has compensating appeal. Voters regularly list foreign policy expertise as an important consideration, yet the only experience several recent presidents have had were their efforts as governors to attract foreign trade to their states.

Failure to meet moral standards has been troublesome for recent would-be presidents. In 1987 former senator Gary Hart's front-runner status collapsed within a week after the appearance of newspaper reports alleging that he had committed adultery. Soon after, media reports that Sen. Joseph R. Biden Jr. of Delaware had plagiarized a law school paper and parts of campaign speeches led to his early exit from the campaign. But Bill Clinton overcame questions about his character to win the presidency in 1992 and 1996.

The decision to seek the presidency is a difficult one. In one respect it is a matter of logic. The candidates must make complicated calculations about financial and time requirements. They must sort out the tangle of party and state rules and the makeup of the electorate in each state. And they must assess their own ability to attract endorsements, recruit a competent staff, and develop an "image" suitable for media presentation. They also must consider the effect a campaign will have on their families, the psychological demands of the office, and possible revelations about their personal lives that might hinder a campaign.

The Exploratory Stage

Candidates have always maneuvered for position long before the election year. In the past, however, the positioning took place behind the scenes and was intended to impress party leaders. Candidates usually did not formally announce their intentions until late in the year before the election. After 1976, when Jimmy Carter won the presidency after a two-year campaign, many candidates began to announce their intentions earlier, in part to have time to build a strong public profile and in part because early fund raising can be crucial to a campaign.

Candidates routinely establish POLITICAL ACTION COMMITTEES (PACS) to broaden their visibility and to test their appeal and fund-raising ability. After all, they cannot hope to survive the primary season without adequate CAMPAIGN FINANCING. Candidates also establish "exploratory committees" to undertake a sober analysis of their prospects. The members of an exploratory committee consider possible campaign themes and strategies, write speeches and position papers, line up major endorsements, recruit professional and volunteer staff, assemble campaign organizations in key primary and caucus states, hire pollsters and campaign consultants, and develop media appeals.

The Primary and Caucus Schedule

Candidates who decide to vie for the presidency must then enter their party's series of PRIMARIES AND CAUCUSES, where delegates to the Democratic and Republican national conventions are selected. This sequence of electoral contests has become the heart of the nominating process. Indeed, since 1956 these contests have determined the likely winner of the party's presidential nomination. Today front-runners must hold on to the coalition they build before the national nominating convention rather than continue building at the convention.

The states and the parties have a wide variety of rules for ballot qualifications and allocation of delegates. Candidates must follow legal requirements to qualify for state contests, and they also have to adapt their campaign strategies to each state's particular circumstances. The complexity can be daunting.

New Hampshire has long held the first primary and Iowa the first caucus—a tradition that has given the two states extraordinary influence over the selection process. Critics have complained that the system is unrepresentative because both states are predominantly rural, with largely white, Anglo-Saxon, Protestant populations.

The early primaries have grown in importance, and in recent years more states have chosen to hold their primaries in the first months of the calendar year. Especially when the campaign does not have an obvious front-runner, the early contests single out a possible leader. After several early tests, the field of candidates shrinks. Lack of adequate funding is often a deciding factor in many of these early dropouts. Not surprisingly, contributors tend to back only those candidates who appear to have the best chance of winning the nomination.

After the initial flurry of primaries, the goal of the candidates who have not already dropped out of the race is to attract media attention by winning, or performing "better than expected," in the next contests. Candidates who do not perform as well as expected typically withdraw.

After most of the primaries have been held, attention begins to turn to the questions of which candidate leads in the delegate race and how many delegates are needed for a first-ballot convention victory. A candidate who enjoys a delegate lead late in the race usually focuses attention more on accumulating as many delegates as possible in the remaining primaries and caucuses than on actually winning the contests.

The Presidential Nomination

The primary season culminates in the national conventions of the two major parties, usually held in late July or August. Since 1936 the party holding the White House has convened after the party not in power holds its convention. At these conventions, attended by thousands of delegates and even more guests and reporters, the presidential and vice-presidential nominees are formally selected, and a party platform, setting out the party's goals for the next four years, is approved. In recent elections the convention also has become an important occasion for showcasing party unity after the sometimes divisive primary battles.

The first national convention was held in 1831, and for the next 130 years or so, state party leaders had the ultimate say in deciding who the presidential nominee would be. As direct primaries took hold in the twentieth century, this influence began to wane. Then in the 1970s and 1980s the Democrats initiated a series of DELEGATE SELECTION REFORMS that opened the nominating process. The reforms were expected to result in more open conventions, but instead they led to even more primaries. Today the national conventions do little more than ratify the choice the voters made during the primary season.

This does not mean that the primary leader faces no opposition at the convention. Other candidates may stay in the race because they hope to benefit if the leader falters, or they may use the bloc of delegates committed to them to bargain for specific planks in the party platform or to influence the selection of the vice-presidential nominee.

Nominating speeches mark the beginning of the formal selection process. These are usually followed by a series of short seconding speeches, and all of these speeches are accompanied by floor demonstrations staged by delegates supporting the candidate. For many years a good deal of convention time was taken up by the nomination of "favorite sons," candidates nominated by their own state's delegation. Such nominations were seldom taken seriously, and since 1972 both parties have instituted rules that have effectively stopped them.

In recent years the balloting for the presidential nominee has been virtually anticlimactic. Since 1952 neither party has required more than one ballot to confirm its presidential nominee. More attention focuses on whom the presidential nominee will select as a running mate. Even then, much of the suspense has been removed from the process, because the leading presidential candidate may have named a likely running mate before the convention began, as George W. Bush did in 2000 when he named Richard Cheney his choice prior to the Philadelphia convention in early August.

Often the choice of the vice-presidential candidate has been motivated by an effort to "balance the ticket." For years a balanced ticket was one that boasted an easterner and a midwesterner. More recently the balance shifted so that the split has more often been between a northerner and a southerner. Ideological considerations also have played a part in the balance. A liberal presidential candidate may be paired with a more conservative running mate to attract a broader base of votes. Or the choice of the vice-presidential candidate may be used to appease factions of the party that are unhappy with the presidential candidate. Governors generally choose senators or other Washington hands. With the increasing number of vice presidents who go on to be president, more attention is given to the abilities of the person who is chosen (and more prominent figures are willing to accept the nomination).

The method for nominating the vice-presidential candidate mirrors the procedure for presidential nominations. The climax of the convention then occurs with the two nominees' acceptance speeches and their first appearance together, with their families, on the podium.

General Election Campaign

The traditional opening of the presidential election campaign is Labor Day, just two months before the general election on the first Tuesday after the first Monday in November. In recent years, however, candidates have been unwilling to wait until Labor Day to campaign.

The period between the end of the convention and Labor Day also is used for any mending of fences that the nominees may have to undertake with rivals from their own party. It is also the time for the nominees to develop strategy with their close aides and solidify the campaign organization.

The issues that must be considered include whether to concentrate their appeals on certain sections of the country, how many issues to stress throughout the campaign, how many and what kinds of broadcast commercials to buy, what kinds of collaboration to undertake with groups interested in helping the campaign, and how to organize state and local campaign efforts. With every decision the nominees must try to anticipate the opposition's likely response.

The campaign organization for the general election is usually an extension of the nomination organization, and it is separate from the national and state party organizations. The Federal Election Commission (FEC) is charged with administering the public financing of the presidential campaign process. In exchange for federal funding, the campaign must agree not to spend more than it receives from the FEC. Since 1976, when federal funding of elections began, all nominees have chosen to accept the government funds. In 2004 the major-party nominees received $74.6 million in federal funds, compared with $67.5 million in 2000 and $21.8 million in 1976.

Although the presidential campaign is limited in its expenditures, allied organizations may supplement the campaign with more or less independent efforts. State and local party organizations, political action committees, independent committees established to help specific candidates, and labor unions contribute time, money, and volunteers to assist the nominee of their choice. A landmark campaign finance law passed in 2002 tightened the regulations on some sources of campaign contributions.

An incumbent president running for reelection has inherent advantages. The incumbent already has the stature of the presidency and is able to influence media coverage with official presidential actions and to use pork-barrel politics to appeal to specific constituencies. The incumbent also benefits from the public's reluctance to reject a tested national leader for an unknown quantity.

Even though the candidates and their advisers map out a campaign strategy before Labor Day, the campaign inevitably shifts its tactics according to polls, political events, and each nominee's instincts about which approaches will be successful. One element of campaign strategy that usually remains intact is the decision about where to campaign. Under the winner-take-all Electoral College system, the leading vote-getter in a state wins all that state's electoral votes (except in Maine and Nebraska, each of which gives two votes to the candidate who wins the statewide vote and allocates the remaining votes according to which candidate wins each congressional district). The winner-take-all system encourages nominees to win as many large states as possible rather than build up strength in states in which they are weak. Nominees generally spend most of their time in closely contested states and just enough time in "likely win" states to ensure victory. Appearances in unfavorable states are usually symbolic efforts to show that the candidate is not conceding anything.

The ideological tone of the presidential campaign usually moderates once the parties have determined their nominees. To win the nomination, Democrats must appeal to the more liberal sections of their party; Republicans, to the more conservative sections of theirs. But during the general election campaign the nominees must try to attract independents and voters from the other party. Because the candidates usually can depend on the support of the most ideological members of their own party, they are able to shift their sights in the fall.

The exceptions arise when a third-party candidate appeals to the conservative or liberal elements of one or both parties, or when a major-party nominee has suffered a bruising nomination battle and must persuade the backers of the defeated candidates to go to the polls.

Whether to highlight specific issue stances or adopt a "fuzzy" ideological stance is a major question in every campaign. Campaign consultants often advise against being too specific. Democrat Walter F. Mondale's pledge in 1984 to raise taxes shows both the opportunity and the risk associated with adopting a specific position. For a while, the proposal put Republican president Ronald Reagan, who presided over historic budget deficits, on the defensive, but Mondale's strategy backfired when Reagan regained the offensive and charged Democrats with fiscal and taxing irresponsibility.

The electronic and print media—television, radio, newspapers, and magazines—are important elements of presidential elections. For a variety of reasons, they have come to perform many of the functions that party leaders once did in the presidential selection process. Indeed, the media are the primary source of information about candidates and elections for most Americans. As a result the media have helped to change the type of candidate who is likely to succeed. Increasingly the emphasis has been on style, image, and an ability to communicate well on television.

To take advantage of news coverage, daily campaign activities are geared to getting impressive visual and sound bites on national and local news programs. Strategists try to adapt the day's "news" events to reinforce the campaign's overall themes and advertising appeals. The candidates use television and radio throughout the fall to advertise their campaigns, and the pace quickens at the end of October, when many voters first begin to pay close attention to the race. Depending on their standing in the polls, and on whether they are running for or against the party in power, the candidates switch back and forth between appeals to bolster their own image and appeals to undermine their opponent's credibility.

CAMPAIGN DEBATES between the presidential and the vice-presidential candidates have become a mainstay of the fall election campaign since 1976. Although political pundits are quick to declare a winner at the end of each debate, most debates have not fundamentally changed the voters' perceptions of the candidates.

All of the campaign hoopla culminates on election day, when Americans go to the polls. In recent years

Campaign buttons are symbolic of the U.S. electoral process.
Source: General Dynamics

about 100 million Americans have voted for president, about half the number eligible to register.

Although ballots are tallied electronically in most parts of the United States, the major television networks have developed ways to make their own counts of the election in all states and report the results as soon as they come in. In 1980 the three major broadcast networks declared Ronald Reagan the winner before the polls had closed on the West Coast. This spurred complaints that the premature announcement discouraged westerners from voting. Since then the networks have refrained from projecting a winner until all the polls have closed. The networks again faced controversy in the 2000 election when they had to reverse themselves repeatedly over which candidate, Democrat Al Gore or Republican George W. Bush, had won the pivotal state of Florida.

Electoral College

Even though the winner has declared victory and the loser conceded defeat, at least two more steps must take place before a president-elect is officially declared. The first step occurs on the first Monday after the second Wednesday in December. On that day electors meet in their respective state capitals to cast their votes for president. The framers of the Constitution devised the ELECTORAL COLLEGE as a compromise between those who wanted direct election of the president by the people and those who thought Congress should select the president.

Each state has as many electors as it has members of Congress, and the District of Columbia has three, for a total of 538. States may select their electors in any way they see fit. Typically slates of electors are pledged to each of the presidential nominees. When voters cast their ballot for a particular presidential nominee, they are actually voting for the electors pledged to that nominee. The presidential nominee who wins the state wins that state's electors, although the Constitution does not require electors to remain faithful to their pledge of support for a particular candidate.

The second step occurs when the ballots of the electors of all the states are opened and counted before a joint session of Congress in early January. The candidate who wins a majority of the vote (270) is declared the president-elect and is inaugurated three weeks later, on January 20.

In the rare event that no presidential candidate receives a majority of the Electoral College vote, the election is thrown into the House of Representatives. If no vice-presidential candidate receives a majority of the Electoral College vote, the Senate makes the final selection. In 2004 Sen. Barbara Boxer, joined by Rep. Stephanie Tubbs Jones, made an official objection to the counting of Ohio's electoral votes, invoking a procedural requirement in electoral law. Ultimately both the House and the Senate voted overwhelmingly to accept the Ohio electoral votes as reported.

More on this topic:
Campaign Debates, p. 68
Campaign Financing, p. 71
National Party Conventions, p. 375
Political Action Committees (PACs), p. 405
Primaries and Caucuses, p. 420

I'm the one who won't raise taxes. My opponent now says he'll raise them as a last resort, or a third resort. When a politician talks like that, you know that's one resort he'll be checking into. My opponent won't rule out raising taxes. But I will. The Congress will push me to raise taxes, and I'll say no, and they'll push, and I'll say no, and they'll push again, and I'll say to them, "Read my lips: no new taxes."

—George H.W. Bush, Republican National Convention, August 18, 1988

Elections Chronology

The presidential selection process has changed significantly since George Washington was elected to his first term in 1789. One reason for the changes is that the constitutional provisions for presidential selection are so vague.

There are no provisions in the Constitution for organizing political parties, for nominating candidates, or for campaigning for office. Indeed, the framers assumed—incorrectly—that the selection process would transcend petty partisanship. Furthermore, the original provision for balloting by the Electoral College was flawed and had to be superseded by the Twelfth Amendment in 1804.

As a result of the Constitution's ambiguities, the procedure for choosing presidential and vice-presidential candidates has evolved with each election. What follows are brief descriptions of those elections that proved to be turning points in the development of presidential elections.

Election of 1789

In 1789 there was no formal nomination of candidates. It had been obvious since the close of the Constitutional Convention that Washington would be president, even though he was not eager to serve. The only real question was who his vice president would be. Most Federalist leaders ultimately decided to support John Adams of Massachusetts.

Federalist leader Alexander Hamilton disliked Adams and so plotted to siphon votes away from him. When the electoral votes were counted, Washington had been elected president unanimously, with all sixty-nine votes. Adams was elected vice president, but he received only thirty-four electoral votes; the others were divided among several candidates.

The First Contest: 1796

Washington won a second term in 1792 but chose not to run again in 1796. With Washington out of the race, the United States witnessed its first partisan contest for president. And once again the defects of the Electoral College system were evident.

Under the system in effect at that time, each member of the Electoral College was to cast two votes, each for a different person. The person who won

After riding his horse for a full week, Charles Thompson, secretary of the Continental Congress, arrived at Mount Vernon on April 14, 1789, with the official news of Washington's election as the first president of the United States.
Source: New York Public Library

the most votes would become president; the person with the second highest number of electoral votes would be named vice president. Because no distinction was made between balloting for president and vice president, it was possible for the two top candidates to receive the same number of votes, which would throw the election into the House of Representatives. It was also possible that the candidate for vice president—through fluke or machination—could end up with the most votes and thus be elected president.

The two presidential candidates were Federalist John Adams and Democratic-Republican Thomas Jefferson. Hamilton once again sought to thwart Adams's ambitions by urging northern electors to divide their votes between Adams and his running mate, Thomas Pinckney of South Carolina. Because Adams was unpopular in the South, Hamilton expected that Pinckney would win more votes there, and with northern electors divided, Pinckney would win the election.

Hamilton's plot backfired, however, when eighteen northern electors voted not for Pinckney but for other Federalist candidates. As a result, Adams was elected president with seventy-one electoral votes, and Thomas Jefferson was named vice president with sixty-eight votes. Pinckney came in third.

Neither the Federalists nor the Democratic-Republicans seemed unduly concerned that the president and vice president were of opposing parties. Both sides felt that they had prevented the opposition from gaining total victory.

The Jefferson-Burr Contest: 1800

The election of 1800 was notable for two reasons. It was the first in which both parties used congressional caucuses to nominate candidates for their tickets, and it was the first presidential election to be decided in the House of Representatives.

The Federalists named Adams and Maj. Gen. Charles Cotesworth Pinckney, older brother of Thomas Pinckney, to their ticket. Jefferson and Aaron Burr were the nominees of the Democratic-Republicans. Hamilton again sought to use the defect of the Electoral College system to defeat Adams and give Pinckney the presidency. But when the votes were counted, it turned out that Jefferson and Burr were tied for first place. The election was thrown into the Federalist-controlled House of Representatives.

Some Federalists felt that Burr was the lesser of two evils and plotted to elect him president instead of Jefferson. Hamilton helped to squelch that idea, but thirty-six ballots were taken before

Jefferson received a majority. The crisis—which could have fatally wounded the new nation by calling into question the legitimacy of the president—was over.

The near disaster led to passage of the Twelfth Amendment to the Constitution in September 1804. It called for electors to vote for president and vice president on separate ballots, thus eliminating the possibility of a tie between the principal candidate and the candidate's running mate.

The Death of King Caucus: 1824

With Jefferson's election the Federalist Party began to fade away, leaving only the Democratic-Republicans. Nomination by the Democratic-Republican caucus, or King Caucus as it was known, was therefore tantamount to election. In 1824 the Democratic-Republicans were still the only party, but several candidates within it were seeking the presidential nomination: Secretary of State John Quincy Adams, Sen. Andrew Jackson, Secretary of War John C. Calhoun, House Speaker Henry Clay, and Secretary of the Treasury William H. Crawford.

Crawford was the early leader, and it was assumed that he would win the nomination if a congressional caucus were held. So supporters of the other candidates refused to attend a caucus. When it was finally convened, only sixty-six members of Congress were present, virtually all of them Crawford supporters. Although Crawford was suffering from the debilitating effects of a stroke, he won the nomination. The other candidates immediately criticized the caucus as being unrepresentative of the party and refused to abide by its results.

That put an end to the caucus as a mechanism for naming presidential nominees. But it did not end the drama of the 1824 election. Calhoun dropped his race to join forces with Crawford, but Adams, Clay, and Jackson all continued to campaign. When none of the four received a majority of the electoral votes, the names of the top three candidates—Jackson, Adams, and Crawford—were placed before the House. Clay, who came in fourth, helped tip the balance when he announced that he would support Adams. Adams narrowly won the House election, even though Jackson had won the most popular votes and the most electoral votes. Rumor had it that Adams had promised to name Clay secretary of state, as in fact he did. The events of 1824 kindled the flame of popular democracy and set the stage for a rematch between Adams and Jackson in 1828.

Jackson's Rise: 1828

The hold of the so-called Virginia dynasty on U.S. politics was loosened in 1828, when Jackson's broad appeal among farmers and common laborers, especially in the West, gave him an easy victory. As the nation expanded economically and geographically, Jackson's appeal for democratic processes to replace elite maneuverings was bound to receive a sympathetic hearing.

Under the tutelage of Vice President Martin Van Buren of New York, Jackson developed a strong national Democratic Party based on patronage. Strict party organization soon became a prerequisite for competition in national politics. The Whigs' 1836 presidential campaign was the last in which a party eschewed a unified national ticket. Van Buren easily defeated the Whigs that year.

The Fateful Election of 1860

The regional differences that had torn the nation apart for decades reached their peak in 1860. Four major candidates sought the presidency. None could compete seriously throughout the nation, and it was probable that a candidate from the North would win because that region had the most electoral votes.

The two northern candidates were Abraham Lincoln, a former U.S. representative from Illinois, and Stephen A. Douglas, a Democrat who had defeated Lincoln for the Illinois Senate seat in 1858. Southern Democrats who had defected from the party nominated Vice President John C. Breckinridge of Kentucky as their candidate for president. The Constitutional Union Party—

which developed as an attempt, albeit an unsuccessful one, to repair the nation's geographic divisions—nominated John Bell of Tennessee.

Lincoln was the consensus compromise choice of the Republican Party, which had developed in the 1850s out of disgruntled elements from several parties. Above all else the Republicans stood against the extension of slavery into new territories. By accepting slavery where it already existed but warning against nationalization of the system, the Republicans divided the Democrats and picked up support from an array of otherwise contentious factions—abolitionists, moderate abolitionists, and whites who feared for their position in the economy.

Lincoln won easily, with 40 percent of the popular vote and 180 electoral votes. Although Douglas came in second with the electorate, winning 29.5 percent, he won only 12 electoral votes. Breckinridge received 72, Bell 39.

Southerners had vowed to secede from the Union if Lincoln won the presidency. After the election South Carolina, Louisiana, Mississippi, Alabama, Georgia, Texas, and Florida did just that and in February 1861 formed the Confederate States of America. After a protracted standoff between the Union soldiers who held Fort Sumter in Charleston, South Carolina, and the Confederate soldiers who controlled the state, the Confederates fired on the fort. Soon after, Virginia, Arkansas, North Carolina, and Tennessee joined the Confederacy, and the Civil War began.

The Compromise of 1876

Little more than ten years after the Civil War ended, disputed election results in the contest between Republican Rutherford B. Hayes and Democrat Samuel J. Tilden created a constitutional crisis and raised fears that another civil war was imminent.

Hayes, the three-time governor of Ohio, lost the popular vote and had a questionable hold on the Electoral College vote, but he managed to win the presidency when the election was settled by a special commission created by Congress. (Hayes won 4.0 million votes to Tilden's 4.3 million.)

The problem arose when the vote tallies in Florida, South Carolina, and Louisiana were called into question. There was good reason to be suspicious of any vote count in these and other southern states. Republicans controlled the balloting places and mounted vigorous drives to get newly enfranchised blacks to the polls, but Democrats used physical intimidation and bribery to keep blacks away.

When state election board recounts and investigations did not settle the issue, Congress appointed a commission to do so. It was composed of five senators, five representatives, and five Supreme Court justices; eight commission members were Republican, seven Democratic. The crisis was resolved after weeks of bargaining that gave the Republicans the presidency in exchange for a pledge to pull federal troops out of the states of the Confederacy and to commit federal money to making internal improvements in the South.

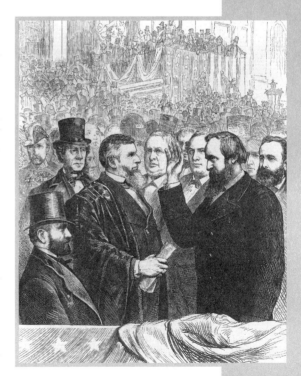

Chief Justice Morrison R. White administers the oath of office to Rutherford B. Hayes on March 4, 1877. The results of the Hayes-Tilden election were settled by a special commission made up of five senators, five representatives, and five members of the Supreme Court.
Source: Library of Congress

The compromise did more than settle the partisan dispute between Hayes and Tilden; it also es-tablished a rigid alignment of political interests that would dominate U.S. politics for the next half-century. Although Democrats won occasional victories, the Republican, eastern, conservative, business-oriented establishment held sway over the system until Franklin D. Roosevelt's election in 1932. At the same time, southern politics was left in the hands of many of the same figures who led or, later, honored the Confederacy. Within months southern states were erecting a powerful edifice of racial discrimination that would last until the 1960s.

The Republicans Self-Destruct: 1912

Between 1860 and 1932 only two Democrats won the presidency—Grover Cleveland in 1884 and 1892, and Woodrow Wilson in 1912.

In Wilson, a former university professor and governor of New Jersey, the Democrats nominated a true liberal. During his presidency Wilson left a lasting legacy in domestic and foreign affairs and also in the style of presidential leadership. But Wilson probably would not have won the general election in 1912 without a battle in the Republican Party that pitted incumbent William Howard Taft against popular former president Theodore Roosevelt.

The Taft-Roosevelt feud stemmed largely from Roosevelt's feeling that Taft had betrayed the trust-busting, conservation, and foreign policies that Roosevelt had pursued between 1901 and 1908. Roosevelt was a proud advocate of the "bully pulpit," and Taft was ill-suited to the rough-and-tumble nature of public controversies.

While Roosevelt challenged Taft in the Republican primaries—the first instance of a popular campaign for the nomination—Wilson plotted and plodded his way to the Democratic nomina-tion. He won the nomination on the forty-sixth ballot. Wilson then took to the podium, urging Americans to seek a moral awakening and to approve a program of liberal reforms.

But Wilson's campaigning alone might not have been enough to win him the presidency. The margin of victory was provided when Roosevelt bolted the Republican Party to run his own Progressive ("Bull Moose") Party campaign. Wilson won the election with 41.8 percent of the vote. Roosevelt finished second with 27.4 percent, and the incumbent, Taft, brought up the rear with 23.2 percent. It was a most unusual result, with a newly created third party outpolling the incum-bent and both losing to a candidate with little political experience.

Dawn of the New Deal: 1932

After three years of Republican Herbert C. Hoover's uncertain leadership following the stock mar-ket crash of 1929, Democrat Franklin Roosevelt won the presidency and oversaw the greatest shift in political alignments in U.S. history.

Roosevelt, who won the Democratic nomination on the fourth ballot, was the first candidate to appear before the convention that nominated him. In his acceptance speech he made passing ref-erence to a "new deal" that his administration would offer Americans. After an active fall campaign, Roosevelt won 57.4 percent of the vote, 42 of the 48 states, and 472 of 531 electoral votes.

The Democratic coalition that began to form during that election brought together a disparate group of interests. Until the New Deal the party's base in the North had consisted of laborers and the poor, immigrants and Catholics; in the South the Democrats were the party of white su-premacy and agricultural interests. In 1932 blacks moved en masse to the Democratic Party from their traditional position in the "Party of Lincoln," partly because of Hoover's failure, but also be-cause of the inclusive rhetoric of the New Deal. Jews, who had traditionally voted Republican, turned to the Democrats as they became the more liberal party.

Political scientist Samuel Beer has argued that with the New Deal, the Democratic Party was able to combine its traditional concern for local, individual interests with a national vision. By bringing "locked out" groups into the system, the Democrats contributed both to the building of the nation and to individual freedoms.

The political genius of the New Deal was not just that it offered something to everyone but also that it created a situation in which everyone's interest lay in growth. The potentially divisive competition over restricted and unequally distributed resources was avoided with a general acceptance of growth as the common goal. When there was growth, everyone could get a little more. That public philosophy remained part of American political discourse.

Roosevelt's coalition and leadership were so strong that he became the only president to win more than two elections. Roosevelt's four electoral triumphs caused Republicans to fume about his "imperial" presidency.

In his second run for the White House, Roosevelt won 60.8 percent of the popular vote and increased the number of Democrats in both the House and the Senate. His percentages dropped in the next two elections—to 54.7 percent in 1940 and 53.4 percent in 1944—but in neither election did his Republican challenger receive more than ninety-nine electoral votes.

Franklin D. Roosevelt shakes hands with supporters as he campaigns in West Virginia on October 19, 1932.
Source: FDR Library

Harry S. Truman, who succeeded to the presidency when Roosevelt died less than two months after his fourth inauguration, had a much tougher time of it in 1948. Truman ran against not only Republican Thomas E. Dewey, who had lost to Roosevelt in 1944, but also two candidates backed by the left and right wings of his own party. The Dixiecrats, under the leadership of South Carolina's governor J. Strom Thurmond, left the Democratic convention to run a states' rights campaign in the South. Henry Wallace was the candidate of the Democratic left, campaigning against Truman's Marshall Plan, military buildup, and confrontational stance toward the Soviet Union. Truman squeaked by with 49.5 percent of the vote to Dewey's 45.1 percent. Each of the breakaway Democrats won 2.4 percent.

Truman's political fortunes worsened after the 1948 election, and he belatedly decided against seeking a second full term. In 1952, for the first time in twenty-four years, neither party had an incumbent president as its nominee.

Eisenhower's Victory: 1952

In Dwight D. Eisenhower the Republicans were able to recruit a candidate with universal appeal who was coveted by both parties. Eisenhower, who had just left the presidency of Columbia University to take charge of the forces of the North Atlantic Treaty Organization, won the Republican nomination on the first convention ballot. He selected as his running mate Sen. Richard Nixon of California, a young conservative who had won national recognition for his role in the controversial House Committee on Un-American Activities.

The eventual Democratic nominee was Adlai E. Stevenson II, governor of Illinois and the son of Grover Cleveland's second vice president. Stevenson's campaign was an eloquent call to arms for liberals and reformers. Years later Democrats would recall how the campaign inspired the generation that would take the reins of power under John F. Kennedy. But Stevenson did not stand a chance against the popular Eisenhower.

> *That's what we have and that's what we owe. It isn't very much but Pat and I have the satisfaction that every dime that we've got is honestly ours. I should say this— that Pat doesn't have a mink coat. But she does have a respectable Republican cloth coat. And I always tell her that she'd look good in anything.*
>
> —*Richard Nixon,* "Checkers Speech," September 23, 1952

The campaign's biggest controversy developed when newspaper reports alleged that Nixon had used a "secret fund" provided by California millionaires to pay for travel and other expenses. Nixon admitted the existence of the fund but maintained that he used the money solely for travel and that his family had not accepted personal gifts.

Eisenhower refused to back his running mate, and Nixon decided to confront his accusers with a television speech, even though campaign aides told him he would be dropped from the ticket if public reaction was not favorable. The speech was remarkable. Nixon denied that he had accepted gifts, such as a mink coat for his wife, Pat, saying that she wore a "Republican cloth coat." Nixon acknowledged receiving a pet dog named Checkers from a Texas admirer: "And you know, the kids love that dog, and I just want to say this right now, that regardless of what they say about it, we're going to keep it." His folksy message and appeal for telegrams created a wave of sympathy, which Eisenhower rewarded with a pledge of support. The crisis was over.

Eisenhower swept into office in a personal victory, since surveys showed that the nation still favored the programs of the New Deal and simply wanted to put the cronyism of the Truman years and the Korean War behind it. Ike won 442 electoral votes and 55.1 percent of the popular vote.

Kennedy and the Politics of Change: 1960

The periodic national desire for change took its toll on the Republicans in 1960, when Sen. John F. Kennedy of Massachusetts became the youngest person elected president. Kennedy defeated Vice President Nixon in one of the tightest elections in history.

The presidential election took shape in the 1958 midterm election. The Democrats made impressive gains in Congress, which gave them 64 of 98 Senate seats and 283 of 435 House seats. A recession and the election of several younger and more liberal Democrats to Congress created the first major shift toward liberalism since the administration of Franklin Roosevelt.

Running against senior party leaders such as Sens. Lyndon B. Johnson of Texas, Hubert H. Humphrey of Minnesota, and Stuart Symington of Missouri, Kennedy seemed more likely to win the vice-presidential nomination. Well-financed and backed by a skilled campaign staff headed by his younger brother Robert, Kennedy used the primaries to allay fears both that he was too conservative and that his Catholic religion would affect his loyalty to the nation. With primary victories over Humphrey in the crucial states of Wisconsin and West Virginia, Kennedy was able to win the nomination on the first ballot. His surprise choice of Johnson for a running mate raised doubts even among Kennedy supporters, but the selection of the southerner was a classic ticket-balancing move.

Vice President Nixon was the overwhelming choice for the Republican nomination, and he selected United Nations ambassador Henry Cabot Lodge as his running mate.

Nixon's campaign stressed the need for experience in a dangerous world and tried to portray Kennedy as an inexperienced upstart. Kennedy's campaign was based on a promise to "get the nation moving again" after eight years of calm Republican rule. The high point of the campaign came on September 26, 1960, when the candidates debated on national television before seventy million viewers. It was the first nationally televised debate in the nation's history, and the last until 1976. Kennedy was well rested and tan. Nixon was tired from two solid weeks of campaigning. His five o'clock shadow reinforced the political cartoonists' image of him as darkly sinister. Polls found that Nixon had "won" the debate in the minds of radio listeners, but that Kennedy had captured the TV audience. "It was the picture image that had done it," wrote historian Theodore H. White, "and in 1960 it was television that had won the nation away from sound to images, and that was that."

The candidates held three more debates, but none of them had the effect of the first, which had neutralized Nixon's incumbency advantage. Nor was Nixon greatly helped by President Eisenhower, who did not stump for his vice president until late in the campaign.

The election results were so close that Nixon did not concede his defeat until the afternoon of the day after the election. Just 115,000 votes separated Kennedy from Nixon in the popular vote tally. A shift of 11,000–13,000 votes in just five or six states would have given him the electoral vote triumph. As it was, Kennedy won 303 electoral votes to Nixon's 219. (Democratic senator Harry F. Byrd of Virginia attracted 15 electoral votes.)

Johnson and the Great Society: 1964

Kennedy's presidency was cut short by his assassination on November 22, 1963. Lyndon Johnson, his vice president, faced no serious opposition for the 1964 Democratic nomination. The Republicans, however, were bitterly divided between the conservatives, led by Sen. Barry Goldwater of Arizona, and the liberal wing of the party, led by New York governor Nelson A. Rockefeller. Goldwater had lined up most of the delegate support he needed even before the primaries began, and key primary victories, including his defeat of Rockefeller in California, ensured that he would receive the nomination.

There was never a real contest between the two presidential nominees in the fall campaign. Johnson's landslide was the largest in U.S. history. He won 61 percent of the popular vote to Goldwater's 38 percent and won 486 Electoral College votes to Goldwater's 52.

The Breakup of Consensus: 1968

A long period of uncertainty in U.S. politics began after Johnson's landslide victory in 1964. There was rising opposition to the Vietnam War, combined with a conservative reaction to Johnson's Great Society programs and to the riots in many of the nation's cities. These issues seriously divided the nation and the Democratic Party. After Sen. Eugene McCarthy of Minnesota ran surprisingly well against Johnson on an antiwar platform in the New Hampshire primary, the beleaguered president withdrew from the campaign. Vice President Hubert Humphrey became the administration's candidate but decided not to enter any primaries. New York senator Robert F. Kennedy entered the race as an antiwar candidate and appeared to be leading McCarthy when he was assassinated in a Los Angeles hotel the night of his victory in the California primary.

The Democratic national convention in Chicago was marred by skirmishes on the convention floor and bloody confrontations between police and antiwar and civil rights demonstrators outside. Democrats nominated Humphrey on the strength of endorsements from state party organizations. The nomination of a candidate who had not entered a single primary led to major changes in the way Democrats selected their delegates and ultimately to the proliferation of presidential primaries.

The Republicans united behind Richard Nixon. The former vice president's fall campaign was well financed and well organized, and the Republican candidate capitalized on the national discontent. Alabama governor George C. Wallace also made use of national sentiment, mounting one of the strongest third-party campaigns in U.S. history. Wallace ran as an antiestablishment conservative, railing at desegregation, crime, taxes, opponents of the Vietnam War, social programs, and "pointy head" bureaucrats. Wallace's campaign stirred fears that neither major-party candidate would receive a majority of the Electoral College votes and that the election would be thrown into the House of Representatives.

The election was one of the closest in U.S. history. Nixon attracted 31.8 million votes, to Humphrey's 31.3 million and Wallace's 9.9 million. But Nixon won 301 electoral votes, a clear majority. Humphrey picked up 191, and Wallace won only 46. President Nixon and his vice president, Spiro T. Agnew, were nominated in 1972 with barely a peep out of other Republicans. On the Democratic side, though, twelve serious contenders announced their candidacy. Senator George S. McGovern of South Dakota led the pack at the end of a grueling primary season and was nominated at the convention.

Under the best of circumstances, the liberal Democrat would have been an underdog in the race against Nixon. But McGovern was badly damaged when his choice for vice president, Thomas F. Eagleton of Missouri, withdrew from the ticket after it was revealed that he had been treated for nervous exhaustion. McGovern replaced Eagleton with R. Sargent Shriver but never overcame the appearance of confusion that surrounded the Eagleton affair.

Nixon won all but Massachusetts and the District of Columbia in the fall election, garnering 520 electoral votes to McGovern's 17.

Effects of the Watergate Affair: 1976

Revelations that people associated with Nixon's campaign committee had been arrested for breaking into Democratic headquarters in the Watergate Hotel in June 1972 had little effect on the 1972 election. Eventually the investigation of the burglary and the subsequent cover-up by President Nixon and his aides drove the president from office in August 1974. Less than a year earlier, Vice President Agnew had resigned after pleading no contest to charges that he had accepted bribes while he was governor of Maryland and vice president. Nixon had named House minority leader Gerald R. Ford, a longtime Republican Party stalwart, to become vice president under the Twenty-fifth Amendment. When Nixon resigned, Ford became the first president in U.S. history who had never run in a presidential election.

Although he started out with the support of the American public, Ford soon ignited a firestorm of criticism when he granted Nixon a full pardon for any crimes he might have committed as president. Combined with nagging economic problems and a stubborn, but losing, primary campaign waged by California governor Ronald Reagan, the pardon left Ford and the Republican Party vulnerable in the 1976 election.

I want you all to remember what Adlai Stevenson said: "You have to vote like a Democrat if you want to live like a Republican." Right?

—*Jimmy Carter*, Remarks at a Voter Registration Rally, Chicago, Illinois, October 6, 1980

The Democrats appeared headed for a long and bitter nomination struggle for the third time in a row. But former Georgia governor Jimmy Carter, whose support as measured by national polls was extremely low when the campaign began, executed a brilliant campaign strategy. He was elected on the first ballot and went on to defeat Ford by a slim margin, winning 297 electoral votes to Ford's 240.

The 1976 election was notable in two ways. For the first time the presidential campaigns were partially financed with public funds. And for the first time since 1960 the presidential nominees took part in televised debates. (See CAMPAIGN DEBATES; CAMPAIGN FINANCING.)

The Reagan Revolution: 1980

Carter's presidency was troubled by inflation and unemployment, his own inability to work with a Democratic Congress, an energy crisis, and the Iran hostage crisis. He nonetheless managed to win renomination on the first ballot, putting down a serious challenge from Massachusetts senator Edward M. Kennedy. But the Democratic ticket garnered little enthusiasm from the rank and file.

The Republicans united early behind the conservative Ronald Reagan. By the time of the convention Reagan was the consensus candidate, and he improved party unity by adding George H.W. Bush, his only serious primary challenger, to the fall ticket. Rep. John B. Anderson of Illinois, a moderate who dropped out of the Republican race, ran an independent campaign.

Although polls before election day predicted a close race, Reagan won all but six states and took the White House in an electoral landslide, 489–49. The Republicans also gained control over the Senate.

The extraordinarily popular former movie actor was able to parlay his claims of an electoral mandate into wide-ranging changes in tax, budget, and defense policies. Although Reagan's popularity fell during

President Reagan and Mrs. Reagan receiving a concession phone call from Walter Mondale, Los Angeles, California, November 6, 1984
Source: University of Texas

a recession early in his first term, he recovered, and there was no serious challenge to his renomination in 1984.

Jimmy Carter's vice president, Walter F. Mondale of Minnesota, was the early front-runner for the Democratic nomination and won the nomination on the first ballot. Mondale named Rep. Geraldine A. Ferraro as his running mate, the first woman ever to receive a major-party nomination for national office. Ferraro's nomination was probably a drag on the ticket, not because of her gender but because of her lack of government experience and the controversy that surrounded her husband's finances. The Mondale-Ferraro campaign never caught fire, and Reagan rolled to an easy victory, winning 525 electoral votes to the Democrats' 13.

Clinton Victory: 1992

Democrat Bill Clinton broke what seemed like a Republican lock on the White House when he defeated incumbent president George H.W. Bush in 1992. Republicans had won five of the six previous presidential elections. And for a while it did not seem as if 1992 would be any different.

Just a year before the campaign began, Bush seemed poised for one of the smoothest reelections in White House history. After leading the nation to victory in the brief 1991 Persian Gulf War, Bush's popularity soared. But in the months that followed, the economy went into what even the president called a "free fall." So, too, did Bush's popularity. And not much the White House did before or during the campaign helped to revitalize either the economy or the president's political standing.

A majority of American voters listened to Clinton's call for change and turned Bush out of office. Clinton carried thirty-two states and the District of Columbia, won 370 of 538 electoral votes, and outscored Bush in the popular vote 43 percent to 38 percent.

Clinton was only the second Democrat to win the White House in the nearly three decades since Lyndon Johnson's lopsided victory in 1964. Clinton's win was especially important to the

Democratic Party; it had made dismal showings in the three national elections since Democrat Jimmy Carter was in office in the late 1970s. With the election of Clinton, forty-six, and his vice-presidential running mate, Tennessee senator Al Gore, forty-four, Americans for the first time chose a president and a vice president who were both born after World War II.

The widespread desire for change in government also benefited independent candidate H. Ross Perot, a Texas billionaire who spoke bluntly of the need to reduce the federal budget deficit. Perot won 19 percent of the popular vote, the largest vote total for an independent candidate in presidential election history and the biggest vote share since 1912, when Theodore Roosevelt ran under the Progressive Party banner.

Election of 2000: Bitter to the End

Partisanship was at fever pitch even before the elections of November 2000. Relations between congressional Democrats and Republicans were chilly, and relations between the GOP-controlled Congress and the Democratic administration of Bill Clinton had been rancorous.

Congressional Republicans objected not only to Clinton's priorities and programs—the normal fodder of partisan debate—but also to what they viewed as his moral (and legal) lapses. A six-year investigation by the Office of Independent Counsel into the Clintons' involvement in a questionable Arkansas land deal, known as Whitewater, was closed in September 2000, having found insufficient evidence of any wrongdoing. But the investigation by independent counsel Kenneth W. Starr into allegations that Clinton had maintained a sexual relationship with a White House intern, Monica Lewinsky, and lied about it under oath in an unrelated sexual harassment lawsuit, ended in Clinton's impeachment by the House of Representatives on December 19, 1998, and acquittal in the Senate on February 12, 1999, largely along party lines. The investigation and impeachment proceedings further poisoned relations between Democrats and Republicans.

Vice President Al Gore, the Democratic nominee, faced the difficult task of linking himself to some of the positive elements of the Clinton-Gore administration—the booming economy, for one—while distancing himself from Clinton's ethical lapses. Texas governor George W. Bush, the Republican nominee, meanwhile, portrayed himself as a "compassionate conservative"—one without the hard edge of the congressional Republicans.

Political observers had expected a close race and were proven correct. Bush and Gore ran neck and neck. Gore won Iowa by 4,144 votes of 1,315,563 cast in the state (a margin of 0.003 percent); he won New Mexico by 366 votes of 589,605 cast. Nationwide, Gore outpolled Bush by 537,179 votes, yet won only twenty states and the District of Columbia to Bush's thirty states. In the Electoral College, Bush prevailed 271–266, receiving one more vote than the minimum 270 required for election. (One elector, from the District of Columbia, did not vote.)

That outcome, however, hung in the balance for more than a month after the polls had closed because of a variety of election day problems in Florida centering around ballots, voting equipment, and voter registration. As a result, Florida's twenty-five electoral votes became ensnared in a messy tangle of lawsuits and appeals. The Democratic campaign and its supporters filed suits to force certain counties to conduct manual recounts and also filed challenges to absentee ballots, which tended to favor the Republican candidate. On December 8 the Florida Supreme Court ordered a statewide manual recount of disputed ballots, handing Al Gore's campaign a major victory. The Bush campaign appealed to the U.S. Supreme Court, which the next day ordered a temporary halt to the Florida recounts. By a 5–4 decision in BUSH V. GORE issued December 12, the Court ruled that the recount must not resume because the absence of statewide guidelines based in law for evaluating the ballots undermined the equal protection of all Florida voters. In the end Bush was awarded Florida by a margin of 537 votes out of almost six million votes cast.

In the Senate, Democrats scored a net gain of five seats to even the partisan split at 50–50, a major accomplishment but short of the party's goal of taking control. However, the even division meant the tie-breaking vote would be cast by the vice president, in this case Republican Richard B. Cheney. This situation lasted only half a year, until Vermont Republican James Jeffords left the party over a variety of issues to become an independent. He gave his support to the Democrats, however, allowing them a one-vote majority and the ability to take control of the chamber.

The Democratic Party also made gains in the House, to narrow the already slim Republican majority. Many individual congressional races were as close as the presidential contest. In Florida's Twenty-second Congressional District, Clay Shaw (R), a ten-term House incumbent, defeated challenger Elaine Bloom by 599 votes; Rush Holt (D) retained his House seat in New Jersey's Twelfth Congressional District with a 651-vote victory over challenger Dick Zimmer (R).

Election of 2004

In 2004 George W. Bush campaigned as a wartime president defending U.S. security against the forces of terror, while his opponent, John Kerry, attempted to focus more narrowly on the management of the war in Iraq. Bush reminded voters repeatedly of the September 11, 2001, terrorist attacks and spoke of his determination to keep America secure. Kerry attempted without much success to focus attention on the management of the war in Iraq, which had been launched in May 2003 and resulted in the swift overthrow of the government of Saddam Hussein. Bush fashioned himself as a steady and determined leader as opposed to Kerry, whom he accused of "flip-flopping." The ultimate outcome again hinged on the Electoral College as a close vote in the state of Ohio kept voters in suspense for another day after the election. Following his victory Bush claimed that he had "political capital" and he intended to use it.

Exit polls at the time of the election suggested that "moral issues" (gay marriage, abortion rights) were key to the Bush success. However, subsequent analysis showed that concerns about terrorism and unemployment were far more important to most voters than were these so-called moral issues. Bush voters overwhelmingly believed that the economy was improving, that the Iraq war was worth the cost, and that a unilateral U.S. approach to terrorism was justified. Whereas national security and Iraq had once proved hallmarks of Bush's administration, these same issues dogged the latter years of his presidency as the war in Iraq seemed to slide toward civil war and popular approval for the war and the president plummeted in the United States.

> **More on this topic:**
>
> *Campaign Debates, p. 68*
>
> *Delegate Selection Reforms, p. 146*
>
> *National Party Conventions, p. 375*

Electoral College

For more than two centuries Americans have been choosing their presidents indirectly through what is known as the Electoral College system. The framers of the Constitution conceived the system as a compromise between selection by Congress and election by direct popular vote. Few decisions of the framers have been criticized more than the one on the Electoral College. Thomas Jefferson called it "the most dangerous blot on our Constitution," and people have been calling for reform ever since.

When citizens vote for a particular presidential candidate, they are in fact voting for a slate of electors pledged to that candidate. Each state is allocated as many electors as it has representatives and senators in Congress. The winning electors in each state then meet in their state capital on the first Monday after the second Wednesday in December to cast their votes for president and vice president. A statement of the vote is sent to Washington, D.C., where Congress counts the votes on January 6. A majority of electoral votes (270 out of a total of 538) is needed to elect.

Counting the electoral votes is usually a ceremonial function, unless no candidate for president wins a majority of electoral votes. The House of Representatives must then choose the president. Each state delegation in the House has one vote, and a majority of states is required for election. (The Senate chooses the vice president in the event no candidate wins a majority of the Electoral College vote.) The House has chosen the president only three times, although several campaigns have been designed deliberately to throw elections into the House.

Originally no distinction was made between Electoral College ballots for president and vice president. That caused confusion when national POLITICAL PARTIES emerged and began to nominate party tickets for the two offices. All the electors of one party tended to vote for their party's own two nominees. But with no distinction between the presidential and vice-presidential nominees there was danger of a tie vote. That happened in the election of 1800. The election was thrown into the House of Representatives, which was forced to choose between running mates Thomas Jefferson and Aaron Burr. (See ELECTIONS CHRONOLOGY.) In 1804 the Twelfth Amendment was added to the Constitution, requiring separate votes for the two offices.

The Constitution stipulates that each state shall specify how its electors are to be chosen. Initially, the norm was for state legislatures to appoint electors, although a handful of states used direct popular election. After the first three presidential elections, popular vote increasingly became the preferred method for choosing electors. Since 1860 only Colorado, in 1876, has used legislative appointment.

After 1832 electors also came to be chosen by what is known as the general ticket. Electors for each party are grouped together on a general ticket for each party and are elected as a bloc. In all but a few states, electors' names do not even appear on the ballot. Instead voters cast their ballot for a particular party's presidential ticket, and the winner of the popular vote wins all of the state's electors, in what is known as winner-take-all. Maine and Nebraska are exceptions. They allocate their electors by special presidential-elector districts. The electors pledged to the presidential nominee who wins the popular vote in the district are elected. Under the Constitution, electors are free to vote as they please in the official Electoral College vote, but electors who do so are rare and are known as "faithless electors."

The Constitution does not say what to do if there are disputes about electors' ballots. That became a critical concern after the 1876 election when, for the first time, the outcome of the election had to be determined by decisions on disputed electoral votes. The 1876 campaign pitted Republican Rutherford B. Hayes against Democrat Samuel J. Tilden. Tilden led in the popular vote by more than 250,000 votes but trailed by one vote in the Electoral College; the votes of three southern states were in dispute. After Republicans agreed to withdraw federal troops from the South, a special commission awarded the disputed electoral votes to Hayes.

In 1887 Congress passed permanent legislation for the handling of disputed electoral votes. The 1887 law, still in force, gives each state final authority in determining the legality of the choice of electors. Majorities of both the House and the Senate are needed to reject any disputed electoral votes.

Critics of the Electoral College system point out several possible sources of an electoral crisis. For one thing, a candidate who loses the popular vote may still be elected president. That has happened four times in the nation's history. John Quincy Adams in 1824, Hayes in 1876, Benjamin Harrison in 1888, and George W. Bush in 2000 won the presidency even though they lost the popular vote.

The elections of Adams and Hayes were decided in the House—the only two elections the House has been called upon to decide since it elected Jefferson over Burr in 1800. Corrupt deals allegedly thwarted the will of the people in both cases, raising serious concerns about the legitimacy of the elections. Harrison won about 100,000 fewer votes (of almost 12 million cast) than President Grover Cleveland, but he won the Electoral College vote by 233–168. In the election of 2000 Vice President Al Gore led Texas governor Bush 48.4 percent to 47.9 percent in the nationwide popular vote. The Electoral College vote was just as close, with Bush at 271 electoral votes to Gore's 266. (When the electors met in their respective state capitals on December 18, 2000, to cast their ballots, one elector in the District of Columbia withheld her vote for Gore to protest the District of Columbia's lack of voting rights in Congress. When Congress certified the electoral vote on January 6, 2001, Gore received 266 votes.)

Concern also has been expressed about a possible deadlock in the Electoral College if the election involves more than two candidates. If a third-party candidate won one or two states in a close race, he or she could try to play an important "broker" role either in the Electoral College or, if one candidate did not receive a majority in the Electoral College, in the House.

George C. Wallace's candidacy on the American Independent Party ticket in 1968 presented such a threat. Republican Richard Nixon and Democrat Hubert H. Humphrey ran one of the closest races in history. Despite earlier hopes of winning the whole South, Wallace won only five states and forty-six electoral votes. If Nixon had lost just California or two or three smaller states that were close, he would have been denied an electoral majority.

Numerous reforms have been proposed to alter both the fundamental structure of the Electoral College system and some of its obsolete and odd features. These proposals include direct election of the president, bonus electors for the winner of the popular vote in each state, and proportional allocation of a state's electoral vote, which would lead to more frequent congressional selection of the president. The most recent proposal is for states controlling a majority of the votes in the Electoral College to pledge to cast their electoral votes for the plurality winner in the popular vote. This approach would guarantee that the plurality popular vote winner would be the Electoral College winner, unlike the case in 2000. None of the reforms has been adopted.

While the Electoral College vote and the popular vote are strongly correlated, the Electoral College magnifies the plurality winner's vote share. Since 1824, 37 percent of elected presidents received less than a majority in the popular vote but got a majority of the Electoral College votes.

POPULAR VOTE WINNERS AND ELECTORAL COLLEGE LOSERS

Year	Winning Candidate	Electoral Vote Margin	Popular Vote Margin
1824	John Quincy Adams[a]	−5.7%	−10.4%
1876	Rutherford B. Hayes	0.2%	−3.0%
1888	Benjamin Harrison	16.2%	−0.8%
2000	George W. Bush	1.0%	−0.5%

Note: The Electoral College sometimes produces a president who lost the popular vote. In four elections the winning candidate's popular vote margin was less than that of his major opponent.
a. Because no candidate received the majority of electoral votes, the election was decided by the House of Representatives in Adams's favor.

More on this topic:

Bush v. Gore, p. 57

Elections Chronology, p. 174

Political Parties, p. 407

Emancipation Proclamation

Abraham Lincoln issued the Emancipation Proclamation freeing the slaves on January 1, 1863. It was perhaps his single most important action during the Civil War. The proclamation decisively changed the character of the Union's war against the Confederacy and ensured Lincoln's standing among the greatest of presidents.

Before he could issue the historic proclamation, however, Lincoln had to find a way to carry out his desire to free the slaves while still maintaining the integrity of the Constitution. Lincoln had argued consistently that the emancipation of the slaves in the existing states was beyond the constitutionally given powers of Congress.

President Abraham Lincoln gave the first reading of the Emancipation Proclamation to his cabinet in July 1862. Seated (left to right) are Secretary of War Edwin M. Stanton, Lincoln, Secretary of the Navy Gideon Welles, Secretary of State William H. Seward, and Attorney General Edward Bates. Standing (left to right) are Secretary of the Treasury Salmon P. Chase, Secretary of the Interior Caleb B. Smith, and Postmaster General Montgomery Blair.
Source: Library of Congress

But, he reasoned, the duties of the commander in chief allowed the president to assume extra powers in war. So Lincoln decided to base his proclamation solely on his "war power," arguing that emancipation was "a fit and necessary war measure for suppressing rebellion." Freeing the slaves would undermine the ability of the Confederacy to carry on the war, by depriving it of an essential labor force, while providing a new pool of recruits to the Union army. To uphold the military rationale, however, Lincoln was forced to limit the effects of the proclamation to the states then in rebellion. The proclamation therefore did not free slaves in border states that had remained in the Union; it freed slaves only in regions that were then beyond the reach of the government and the Union army.

By adopting a cautious measure, Lincoln pursued a plan that was more limited than members of his cabinet or the Radical Republicans in Congress had wanted. Lincoln did not proclaim a comprehensive policy of emancipation, and in fact he pronounced unauthorized and void declarations by two of his generals that went that far.

Lincoln was also cautious in waiting until the Union army had achieved a major victory in combat against the Confederates. When the Confederate general, Robert E. Lee, retreated from his invasion of the North after the battle of Antietam, Lincoln had the victory he felt he needed to act. The announcement that the war was for freeing the slaves rather than just preserving the Union helped to ensure that the European powers would not intervene on behalf of the Confederacy.

As an act based on "military necessity," the Emancipation Proclamation had an important practical effect. More than 100,000 men were taken from slave labor and added to the Union soldiery. Yet the proclamation included neither a moral attack on slavery nor any guarantee that the institution of slavery would be abolished entirely once the war was over. Lincoln believed that such a comprehensive strike at the institution of slavery could come only through a constitutional amendment. In 1865 Lincoln pressed the Thirteenth Amendment banning slavery nationwide through a reluctant Congress, believing as he did so that such a sweeping social reform was incompatible with the existing framework of the U.S. Constitution.

More on this topic:

Civil War, p. 95

Lincoln, Abraham, p. 336

Proclamations and Endorsements, p. 426

CLOSER LOOK

What is Juneteenth?

Although Lincoln signed the emancipation proclamation on January 1, 1863, many southern slaves did not know about it until June 19, 1865, when Union major general Gordon Granger read General Order #3 to the people of Galveston, Texas. African Americans continue to celebrate "Juneteenth" as emancipation day.

Emergency Powers

During times of crisis—war, economic upheaval, domestic unrest, or a natural disaster—the public looks to the president to take charge. Presidents often do exactly that through the use of "emergency" powers—that is, extraordinary powers to preserve the nation, to promote the general welfare, or to provide for the common good of the people.

During a war, the severest kind of crisis, presidents have the greatest freedom of action. They can freeze prices, create new agencies, allocate jobs, and even censor the press. Presidents have even restricted fundamental civil liberties—for example, Abraham Lincoln suspended habeas corpus during the Civil War and Franklin D. Roosevelt ordered the internment of Japanese Americans during World War II. In the midst of a crisis presidents find that they can do almost anything in the name of national security.

Similarly, during the economic crisis of the GREAT DEPRESSION in the 1930s, Franklin Roosevelt was able to obtain virtually everything he wanted from Congress during his first one hundred days in office.

Many cases of presidential leadership are less dramatic, especially when the crises are less severe. For example, Lyndon B. Johnson directed the effort to rebuild Alaska in the wake of a devastating earthquake in 1964, and Jimmy Carter declared fuel emergencies during the fierce winters of 1976 through 1979.

Powers in Wartime

The United States has entered into five declared wars, a civil war, and numerous undeclared hostilities in its history. In each instance presidents have relied on assorted emergency powers to deal with the threat. (See also WAR POWERS.)

In the early years of the Republic most presidential claims of war powers involved the deployment of U.S. forces against pirates abroad or Indian uprisings at home to protect American citizens and their property. Their actions usually were based on some specific congressional grant of authority.

Early presidents exhibited a great deal of restraint in using their responsibilities as commander in chief. But restraint was abandoned during the single greatest threat to national unity yet encountered by the United States, the CIVIL WAR.

Lincoln's War Powers

Faced with secession by the southern states in 1861, Lincoln claimed numerous emergency war powers to save the Union and in the process used remarkable, often unconstitutional, means to quell the rebellion.

Congress was not in session when the hostilities began. Lincoln unilaterally proclaimed a blockade of southern ports, mobilized state militias, increased the size of the army and navy, sent weapons to Unionists in Virginia (who established the state of West Virginia), authorized construction of ships for the navy, and appropriated funds for purchases of war material.

Lincoln conveniently failed to call Congress back into session for eleven weeks; when he did, he claimed that his actions were justified by the inherent powers of the presidency, especially his role as commander in chief. Congress ultimately gave Lincoln retroactive authority for his actions, even though some of them (such as expanding the army and spending unappropriated funds) clearly were unconstitutional. Legal nuances paled before the emergency at hand, and Lincoln continued to assume and exercise independent war powers even with Congress in session.

This same sense of emergency led the courts to support many of Lincoln's claims. In 1863 in the *Prize Cases,* the Supreme Court upheld Lincoln's blockade of southern ports without a congressional declaration of war. A state of war already existed, the majority said, and the president was obligated "to meet it in the shape it presented itself, without waiting for Congress to baptize it with a name."

But some of the president's actions provoked clashes with the judiciary. To meet problems behind Union lines Lincoln, among other things, declared MARTIAL LAW and suspended habeas corpus, which is the right of prisoners to have the legality of their detention or imprisonment reviewed by the courts and to be released upon a court's order. In 1861 in *Ex parte Merryman,* Chief Justice Roger B. Taney, sitting as a circuit trial judge, ruled that Lincoln had usurped the sole right of Congress to suspend writs of habeas corpus during an emergency. Lincoln flagrantly ignored the ruling, and Congress later affirmed his actions.

In 1866 in *Ex Parte Milligan,* the Supreme Court ruled that Lincoln lacked the constitutional authority to use military courts behind northern lines so long as the civil judicial system remained intact. By the time the Court ruled, however, Lincoln was dead and the Civil War over, so *Milligan* joined a group of judicial decisions that create doubts about whether the courts would challenge a sitting president during national crises.

World Wars

Unlike Lincoln, who disregarded the Constitution to preserve the nation, both Woodrow Wilson and Franklin Roosevelt fought foreign wars based largely on powers at least broadly delegated to them by Congress.

Legislation passed by Congress empowered Wilson during WORLD WAR I to seize defense-related facilities; regulate manufacturing, mining, and food production; fix prices on commodities; raise an army; restrict exports; and regulate and censor all external communications. Wilson also received broad authority to monitor the actions of resident aliens, regulate or operate transportation and communications facilities, and reorganize executive branch agencies where necessary.

In effect, Wilson was granted almost free rein to conduct the war and to maintain the domestic economy—a pattern that recurred two decades later, although on a larger scale, when Congress delegated broad discretionary powers to Roosevelt during WORLD WAR II.

Moreover, neither Wilson nor Roosevelt overlooked his constitutional prerogatives as commander in chief. Both claimed the right to create wartime executive agencies, to enforce "voluntary" press censorship, and to coordinate private industry beyond the scope of congressional authorization. Roosevelt in particular claimed emergency powers to sidestep congressional declarations of neutrality as Europe fell into war. Although he usually tried to cloak his actions to prepare the country for war in existing statutory powers, he dropped even the pretense of delegated powers once war was declared.

Limits on Powers

Neither Woodrow Wilson nor Franklin Roosevelt made sweeping claims to inherent emergency powers during either world war. Later presidents operated differently, however, as the United States in the late 1940s began a period of prolonged confrontation with the Soviet Union.

The nature of war changed—from total conventional war to indeterminate potential thermonuclear war at one extreme and localized wars of containment at the other. Boundaries between war and peace no longer were clear, and the sheer scope of the meaning of national security (defense, intelligence, economic health, and scientific advances, to name just a few factors) gave presidents greater potential power than ever before in virtually every aspect of national affairs. Presidential influence over both civil liberties and congressional authority had never seemed so extensive.

The debate about the use of inherent powers reached a crescendo in 1952. Harry S. Truman had put the nation on emergency war footing in 1950 in response to China's decision to come to the aid of North Korea during the KOREAN WAR. In late 1951 Truman ordered the seizure of strike-threatened steel mills to avoid potential shortages.

Truman first based his actions on authority given him by the Constitution and the laws of the United States, and on his authority as president and commander in chief. When challenged on this rationale, Truman argued simply that the president has vast inherent powers to meet national emergencies. But in 1952 the Supreme Court in *YOUNGSTOWN SHEET AND TUBE CO. V. SAWYER* declared the seizure of the steel mills unconstitutional because in the 1947 Taft-Hartley Labor Act Congress had explicitly decided *not* to give presidents the right to take over industrial facilities shut down by strikes.

Although the majority opinion implied that the president did not possess inherent powers in times of emergency, and that the role of commander in chief did not grant special domestic powers, four of the five justices concurring in the majority decision did not reject these concepts outright. Their concurring opinions suggested that emergency prerogatives may exist when presidents act in accordance with the express or implied will of Congress or in the absence of congressional action. Congressional opposition places the presidency in its weakest constitutional position, and Truman's action could not be supported because it so clearly violated congressional intent.

War on Terrorism

After terrorists attacked the United States in 2001, there was little debate about whether the president should have broad authority to act against a real threat to the country. Indeed, George W. Bush quickly expanded the authority of the executive branch to fight the war on terrorism by creating the Office of Homeland Security by executive order and giving that office the authority to coordinate domestic antiterrorism efforts. Congress quickly approved $20 billion for domestic security. The military phase of the antiterrorism campaign, Operation Enduring Freedom, began on October 7, 2001. The U.S. military attacked terrorist training camps in Afghanistan and sought to seize suspected terrorists in the al Qaeda network, including its elusive leader, Osama bin Laden. In November 2001 the president issued an executive order that set forth procedures for detaining, and then trying in military tribunals, noncitizens suspected of terrorist activities. In late 2002 Congress approved the creation of a Department of Homeland Security, and the president signed the bill into law, marking the biggest reorganization of the federal government in decades.

Great controversy emerged over two particular claims Bush made relating to the war on terror. First was Bush's claimed authority to hold "enemy combatants" indefinitely without any rights to ordinary judicial processes. Second was Bush's assertion of the right to engage in warrantless electronic surveillance of American citizens who were suspected of being in contact with terror-related organizations. In both instances the President argued that his inherent authority and responsibility as commander in chief in wartime was extensive and further that congressional authorization for the use of military force in Iraq provided specific authority he needed to carry out his actions.

Economic Crises

Outside of wartime, presidents may wield emergency powers when the nation's economic system is seriously unstable. In economic crises it appears that such power is based exclusively on statutes, although presidents have shown ingenuity in stretching the boundaries of that authority.

The 1917 Trading with the Enemy Act gave Woodrow Wilson the authority to impose diverse economic measures in times of war or national emergency. This law, passed on the eve of U.S. entry into World War I, was intended as a wartime measure, but its authority was never revoked after the war ended. Later presidents used it to justify emergency actions to manage a faltering economy.

In 1933, when faced with the imminent collapse of the nation's financial system, Franklin Roosevelt declared a national state of emergency and closed the banks, basing his action on the Trading with the Enemy Act. This interpretation of the wartime statute was dubious but reflected Roosevelt's desire to cloak his action in legal authority.

Congress sanctioned his move in legislation passed three days later. In the following months it also granted Roosevelt a wide range of new powers to address the economic emergency. In fact, the single greatest outpouring of major legislation in peacetime U.S. history took place between March 9 and June 16, 1933.

Richard Nixon in August 1971 declared a national emergency over a growing imbalance in the U.S. balance of payments. Based on the 1970 Economic Stabilization Act, Nixon's actions devalued the dollar, drove down the prices of American goods overseas, and temporarily halted inflation.

Domestic Unrest

Presidential emergency powers also include the authority to call out federal troops or take control over state national guards (descendants of the state militias) to quell domestic unrest or to deter violence. Such authority has been used in the United States to put down illegal labor strikes, to ensure delivery of the mail, to impose order during natural disasters and urban riots, and to prevent other volatile situations from exploding.

Before the 1940s, and particularly during the late nineteenth century, presidents became involved in domestic disorders most often during labor strikes. Until passage of the Wagner Act of 1935, which ensured the right of collective bargaining and established procedures for negotiations, strikes usually were considered illegal and often resulted in violent clashes between strikers and companies' security forces. Use of troops to break the 1894 Pullman strike in Chicago is one of several well-known examples of a practice that virtually ended by the 1950s.

Presidential emergency powers include the authority to call upon the military in times of crisis. Here a soldier from the Houston National Guard unit searches for debris from the explosion of the space shuttle Columbia, February 2003.
Source: Reuters

During the 1950s and 1960s presidents relied on federal troops or state national guards to ensure calm in situations involving racial desegregation. The first and perhaps most notable instance was in 1957 when Dwight D. Eisenhower sent troops into Little Rock, Arkansas, to enforce desegregation of the public schools in the face of resistance from state officials.

During the late 1960s troops were used more frequently to quell urban riots and to control demonstrations against U.S. involvement in Vietnam. Most noteworthy was the use of some 55,000 troops to deal with the widespread rioting sparked by the April 1968 assassination of civil rights leader Martin Luther King Jr.

In 1970 Richard Nixon responded to a postal strike in New York, which threatened to cripple the postal service nationally, by declaring a state of national emergency and calling out federal troops to take over the New York postal system and keep mail deliveries flowing.

Natural Disasters

Presidents by statute have the authority to declare states of emergency in areas of the country hit by hurricanes, floods, earthquakes, or other natural disasters. By declaring a natural disaster area the president sets in motion the government machinery that can provide immediate aid, such as food, shelter, and police protection.

Furthermore, the president can help victims of the disaster recover faster and with less financial hardship by ensuring longer term assistance such as federally guaranteed home and business loans at interest rates significantly lower than those commercial banks might offer. Responding to the damage inflicted by Hurricane Katrina, which struck the Gulf Coast in 2005, President Bush requested and Congress agreed to emergency supplemental appropriations of billions of dollars in disaster aid. In addition, Bush enlisted the help of former presidents George H.W. Bush and Bill Clinton to assist in organizing additional private fund-raising efforts.

Congressional Limits

Both world wars, as well as the Civil War, pointed up the problems of ending a national emergency. Duties and new responsibilities delegated to the president remained in the president's hands long after hostilities had ended and national emergencies were over.

In 1947 Congress terminated certain temporary emergency and war powers involving about 175 statutory provisions, some of which dated back to World War I. But other war or emergency statutes remained in effect.

Congressional concern with the continuing existence of national emergencies led to the creation of a special Senate committee to study the matter. The committee found four existing states of national emergency it said should be ended. It also released a catalog of some 470 provisions of law that taken together, according to the committee, conferred enough authority "to rule the country without reference to normal constitutional processes."

As a result, Congress in 1976 approved legislation ending as of 1978 the four emergencies—Roosevelt's 1933 declaration because of the Depression, Truman's 1950 declaration during the Korean War, Nixon's 1970 declaration at the time of the postal strike, and Nixon's 1971 economic declaration. The legislation also provided for congressional oversight and review of future declarations of emergency.

> *On great occasions, every good officer must be ready to risk himself in going beyond the strict line of the law, when the public preservation requires it; his motives will be a justification.*
>
> **— Thomas Jefferson** to W.C.C. Claiborne in 1807, *The Writings of Thomas Jefferson*

In 1977 Congress curbed executive authority to impose economic controls during presidentially declared states of emergency by amending the 1917 Trading with the Enemy Act and by confining the act's broader authority to wartime. The 1977 law also defined economic controls that presidents could employ without calling a state of national emergency, including the ability to regulate foreign currency transactions, to institute embargoes against other nations, and to freeze foreign assets. These powers would be more restricted than might be the case during wartime.

In October 2001 Congress passed the USA Patriot Act (Public Law 107-56), intended to improve the ability of law enforcement to address threats of terrorism. In addition to making domestic terrorism a separate class of crime, the Patriot Act increased authority of the government to engage in surveillance of suspected terrorists (for example, examining telephone and library records) without having to notify the suspects. The act also provided strengthened ability to track financial transactions. In early 2006 the Patriot Act was renewed, making permanent several sunsetting provisions in the antiterror law, extending two provisions until 2009, and incorporating a number of new rights protections. Nonetheless, many observers, including Arlen Specter, then chair of the Senate Judiciary Committee, argued that civil liberties protections needed to be enhanced.

More on this topic:
Hamdan v. Rumsfeld, *p. 242*
Martial Law, *p. 354*
War Powers, *p. 555*

Energy Department

The Department of Energy coordinates and administers the energy policies and programs of the federal government. It is responsible for research on and development of energy technology; the

Aerial photograph of the administration building at Los Alamos National Laboratory. Los Alamos was the site of the ultrasecret Manhattan Project during World War II that developed America's first atomic bombs.
Source: Los Alamos National Laboratory

marketing of federal power; renewable energy programs; a nuclear weapons program; and a central program for collection and analysis of energy data.

The 1973–1974 Arab oil embargo provided dramatic evidence that the U.S. government needed to formulate a more coherent and comprehensive energy policy to centralize its energy-related programs, which at that time were scattered among various federal agencies. The initial federal response to this need was the creation in 1974 of the Energy Research and Development Administration (ERDA) and the Federal Energy Administration (FEA), as requested by President Richard Nixon.

It soon became clear that additional steps were needed. Before President Gerald R. Ford left office, he submitted a plan to Congress for reorganizing the energy bureaucracy into a Department of Energy. The plan was similar in many respects to a proposal Jimmy Carter submitted a few months later.

In 1977 Congress passed legislation creating a cabinet-level Department of Energy. The new department assumed the powers and functions of the FEA, ERDA, the Federal Power Commission, and the four regional power commissions. The department also absorbed energy-related programs formerly administered by the Departments of the Interior, Defense, Commerce, and Housing and Urban Development, and by the Interstate Commerce Commission. The department assumed as well the role of consultant to the Department of Transportation and the Rural Electrification Administration.

During the 1980 presidential campaign Ronald Reagan contended that federal actions had caused, rather than alleviated, the nation's energy problems. With the support of conservatives who viewed the Energy Department as an unneeded instrument for federal meddling in energy matters, Reagan vowed to abolish the department. But the department remained intact during the Reagan presidency.

President George H.W. Bush in 1989 appointed as Energy Department secretary James D. Watkins, a former nuclear submarine skipper and chief of naval operations. It was hoped that Watkins's expertise in nuclear energy would lead to solutions for problems with the nation's nuclear weapons reactor complex. By 1993, when Bill Clinton came into office, the department was trimming its nuclear facilities, but enormously expensive and technically challenging cleanup and disposal problems remained. George W. Bush's energy secretary, Spencer Abraham, pushed for an energy policy centered on increasing domestic oil and gas exploration and production—including drilling in the Arctic National Wildlife Refuge—to reduce energy prices.

Programs within the Energy Department include energy research, fossil energy, nuclear energy, and civilian radioactive waste management. The department's Energy Information Administration collects, analyzes, and publishes data on en-

More on this topic:

Bureaucracy, p. 44

Cabinet, p. 60

ergy. An independent, five-member commission within the department, the Federal Energy Regulatory Commission, oversees the interstate transmission of electricity, natural gas, and oil.

In 2003 four units of the Energy Department moved to the new Department of Homeland Security. They were the Nuclear Incident Response Team, CBRN Countermeasures Program, Environmental Measurements Laboratory, and Energy Security and Assurance Program.

Environmental Protection Agency

The Environmental Protection Agency (EPA) is the regulatory agency responsible for implementing federal laws to protect the environment. It has the job of controlling and abating pollution in the areas of air, water, solid waste, pesticides, radiation, and toxic substances.

The EPA was created in 1970 through an executive reorganization plan that consolidated components of five executive departments and agencies into a single unit, one of several INDEPENDENT EXECUTIVE AGENCIES. Proposals to make it an executive department were resisted at that time because lawmakers were reluctant to add another layer of government bureaucracy.

The EPA's responsibilities have steadily increased since its creation. Most notably, passage of the federal "superfund" law in 1980 and the reauthorizations of the Clean Water Act in 1987 and the Clean Air Act in 1990 boosted the agency's regulatory authority. The laws gave the agency sweeping responsibility to order cleanups of hazardous waste, to fund construction of wastewater treatment plants, and to control emissions of nearly two hundred chemicals.

The EPA's reputation had suffered a setback in the early 1980s, when an appointee of President Ronald Reagan proposed deregulation, going so far as to suggest repealing restrictions on lead in gasoline and on the dumping of toxic wastes into unlined landfills. Only after a few years did Congress and environmentalists begin to trust the agency once again. In the Clinton administration, with Vice President Al Gore serving as the driving force, the EPA reasserted itself, promulgating stringent new regulations on clean air in 1997.

The EPA is directed by an administrator and a deputy administrator appointed by the president with Senate confirmation. They are appointed to no fixed term and serve at the pleasure of the president.

The agency enforces its regulations through compliance promotion, administrative money penalties, negotiated compliance schedules, and judicial enforcement entailing criminal proceedings.

> **More on this topic:**
>
> *Independent Executive Agencies, p. 286*

Ethics

Instances of questionable or unethical behavior of public officials can be found throughout American history. In some instances full-blown scandals resulted, irrevocably linking presidents with the corruption that occurred during their administrations. Ulysses S. Grant's presidency will always be tied to the WHISKEY RING SCANDAL. Warren G. Harding's administration will be associated with the TEAPOT DOME SCANDAL. The accomplishments of Richard Nixon will be overshadowed by the abuses of power that were at the heart of the WATERGATE AFFAIR, and he will go down in history as the first president to resign from office. Bill Clinton was impeached by the House over issues connected to his affair with White House intern Monica Lewinsky; he later was acquitted by the Senate.

Fortunately for the institution of the presidency, there have been few ethics scandals of this magnitude. But other presidents have been embarrassed or hurt politically when members of their administration were caught up in controversies over alleged conflicts of interest or improper behavior.

President Harry S. Truman, for example, brought to Washington some of his old Missouri cronies, several of whom turned out to be associated with an influence-peddling scandal. This situation helped to undercut his chances of running in 1952.

Dwight D. Eisenhower's chief of staff, Sherman Adams, was accused of accepting gifts from a businessman who was seeking favorable treatment from federal agencies. In the aftermath Adams resigned.

Allegations about improper banking practices before he entered government brought about the resignation of Bert Lance, Jimmy Carter's director of the Office of Management and Budget, and damaged the administration in its early days. The selection and tenure of Edwin Meese III as Ronald Reagan's attorney general were marred by controversy over Meese's ethical conduct and fitness for office. Meese was the subject of two investigations by an INDEPENDENT COUNSEL. Allegations of influence peddling and political favoritism at the Department of Housing and Urban Development during the Reagan era sparked several investigations.

Campaign finance violations during the 1996 presidential election sparked Justice Department inquiries into the actions of several senior Clinton administration officials, including Vice President Al Gore, forcing Attorney General Janet Reno to consider appointment of a special prosecutor in each of the cases. Earlier, in 1994, Clinton agriculture secretary Mike Espy resigned, and in 1997 was indicted on charges of receiving gifts from businesses over which his department had jurisdiction. He pled guilty to one charge and was acquitted of all others.

The Clinton administration faced other ethical questions during its eight years. Even as Clinton was leaving office, he was hit with a storm of criticism for the 140 pardons and 36 commutations he issued his last day as president.

Although George W. Bush campaigned in 2000 that he would restore integrity to the Oval Office, early in his administration critics began to raise concerns about whether Bush and his vice president, Richard B. Cheney, both formerly involved in the oil business, had overly close ties to that industry. In 2002, during a period of corporate accounting scandals, the Securities and Exchange Commission investigated accounting practices at the oil services company Halliburton while Cheney was chief executive officer. More salient to the public were ethical issues that emerged during Bush's second term. One particular episode was the scandal involving the conviction of Vice President Cheney's chief of staff, I. Lewis "Scooter" Libby. Libby was convicted on charges of perjury related to misstatements he made to federal prosecutors and a grand jury about alleged attempts by the White House to punish the wife of a former diplomat who publicly criticized the administration's rationale for going to war in Iraq. In 2007 the White House faced additional criticism over speculation that pressure was put on the Justice Department to fire eight U.S. attorneys for political reasons.

Scandals both in the executive branch and on Capitol Hill have focused special attention on the issue of ethics in recent decades and led to a series of reforms to require public disclosure of the finances of government officials and to reduce conflicts of interest. In late 1995 the House Ethics Committee found that the Republican Speaker of the House, Newt Gingrich of Georgia, had misused public funds to benefit his own business interests, and that in taking a large book advance from a publisher who had an interest in pending legislation had created "the impression of exploiting one's office for political gain." Gingrich was fined $300,000 and censured.

Until modern times, ethics guidelines in the federal government were contained in a patchwork of federal statutes, agency rules, and congressional practices. The first federal antibribery statutes went on the books in the 1860s. And the growth of the civil service system brought more regulations.

In 1958 Congress approved a code of ethics for all government employees, in part in reaction to the 1957–1958 investigation of Sherman Adams. The code, however, had no legal force. In 1962 Congress enacted legislation consolidating existing federal bribery and conflict-of-interest laws, but the new law did not give agency heads the authority to issue ethics standards or to take disciplinary action, which President John F. Kennedy had requested, nor were there any financial disclosure provisions.

President Lyndon B. Johnson issued an executive order in 1965 requiring presidential appointees to file confidential financial statements with the chairman of the Civil Service Commission. And in 1968, in response to several ethics investigations on Capitol Hill, the House and the Senate adopted new rules requiring for the first time that members of Congress file reports of their financial interests and avoid conflicting outside employment.

The 1970s brought historic changes in the rules and regulations governing public officials. For the first time the law required comprehensive disclosure of federal candidates' campaign receipts and expenditures. Members of Congress and top officers of the executive and judicial branches also were required to publicly disclose their financial holdings. (See ELECTIONS AND CAMPAIGNS.)

The 1972–1974 Watergate affair and a series of scandals in Congress in the 1970s focused renewed attention on ethics. Both the House and the Senate in 1977 adopted new codes of ethics, which, among other things, required disclosure of substantial financial information about members, their immediate families, and key employees.

In 1978 Congress enacted the Ethics in Government Act, which wrote into law the financial disclosure requirements of the 1977 House and Senate ethics codes and required the same public disclosures by high-ranking members of the executive and judicial branches. The act contained other strong conflict-of-interest provisions covering officials who left top government positions for high-paying jobs lobbying their former agencies (known as "revolving door" restrictions). The law set civil penalties for violations.

President Jimmy Carter had given impetus to these new precautions even before he assumed the presidency. As president-elect he required his appointees to meet guidelines for financial disclosure, divestiture of holdings that could create conflicts between private and government interests, and postgovernment employment restrictions. He asked Congress to enact these requirements into law.

As a direct outgrowth of the Watergate investigations, the Ethics in Government Act established procedures for court appointment of an independent counsel to substitute for Justice Department prosecutors whenever a high-ranking federal official was accused of criminal action. The new law set forth a step-by-step process for initiating and carrying out such an investigation. The independent counsel statute expired in 1999, and it was not renewed.

The act also established an Office of Government Ethics, which initially was part of the Office of Personnel Management but later became a separate agency. The office develops rules and regulations on government conflicts of interest and other ethical problems, and monitors and investigates compliance with federal ethics laws.

The 1978 revolving-door provisions were weakened the next year because of fears that there would be a mass exodus of high-level federal officials before the conflict-of-interest restrictions went into effect.

Ethics laws and rules were revised again in 1989. In another attempt to clamp down on the revolving-door problem, the 1989 Ethics Reform Act incorporated new restrictions on lobbying by government officials and members of Congress after they left office. The tighter restrictions followed the conviction of two high officials in the Reagan White House—Michael K. Deaver and

We cannot tolerate conflicts of interest or favoritism—or even conduct which gives the appearance that such actions are occurring.

—Lyndon B. Johnson, Statement by the President Upon Issuing Order Prescribing Standards of Ethical Conduct for Government Officers and Employees, May 9, 1965

Let me just say this, and I want to say this to the television audience: I made my mistakes, but in all of my years of public life, I have never profited, never profited from public service—I have earned every cent. And in all of my years of public life, I have never obstructed justice. And I think, too, that I could say that in my years of public life, that I welcome this kind of examination, because people have got to know whether or not their President is a crook. Well, I am not a crook. I have earned everything I have got.

—Richard Nixon, Question-and-Answer Session at the Annual Convention of the Associated Press Managing Editors Association, Orlando, Florida, November 17, 1963

More on this topic:

Independent Counsel,
p. 284

Teapot Dome Scandal,
p. 493

Watergate Affair, p. 567

Whiskey Ring Scandal,
p. 573

Lyn Nofziger—for their lobbying activities after they left the administration. Nofziger's conviction was subsequently overturned.

Cabinet secretaries and other top White House officials were banned from lobbying any other senior executive branch officials for a year after leaving office. The law imposed a one-year ban on lobbying by former high-level executive employees and military officers at the agency they had served. Former employees also were barred from "representing, aiding or advising" foreign governments or foreign political parties for a year and from using confidential information on trade and treaty negotiations to advise clients for a year.

The law retained a lifetime ban on lobbying by all former executive branch employees on matters in which they were "personally and substantially involved" while in office and a two-year ban on lobbying on matters that were "under their official responsibility within the year preceding termination of government service."

Executive Agreements

An executive agreement is a pact other than a treaty made by the president or representatives of the president with a foreign leader or government. Presidents have asserted that their power to execute the laws, command the armed forces, and function as the sole organ of foreign policy gives them the legal authority to make these pacts without obtaining congressional approval.

The executive agreement is a particularly powerful foreign policy tool because it allows the president to conclude an agreement with a foreign government without obtaining the two-thirds majority in the Senate required to ratify a treaty. Executive agreements have the force of law. Unlike treaties they do not supersede U.S. laws with which they conflict, but in every other respect they are binding. Most executive agreements are routine extensions of existing treaties or are based upon broad legislative directives. (See TREATY POWER.)

Some executive agreements have been supported by congressional joint resolutions. Presidents occasionally have chosen to seek the approval of a majority of both houses of Congress for executive agreements when they did not have the support of two-thirds of the Senate but wanted some type of congressional consent. John Tyler was the first president to use this method when he received the approval of both houses for an executive agreement annexing Texas in 1845.

A small percentage of executive agreements are "pure" executive agreements, which are not accompanied by any congressional approval. These are usually the most important and controversial pacts made under the president's authority.

Since World War II the number of executive agreements has skyrocketed. Contemporary presidents can accomplish virtually anything through an executive agreement that can be accomplished through a treaty.

Constitutional Dilemma

The power of the president to make agreements without their approval worries members of Congress. Although the Constitution does not prohibit executive agreements, the framers' careful division of the treaty power in the Constitution must be interpreted as an attempt to ensure that Congress has a direct voice in making international commitments. The growing use of executive agreements by recent presidents to avoid the advice and consent of the Senate has been widely regarded by constitutional scholars and members of Congress as a weakening of constitutional checks and balances in the area of foreign policy.

The development of the United States into a world power with security commitments and economic interests in every corner of the world has made it desirable that there be some degree of executive flexibility in making executive agreements. Presidents are sometimes faced with an international situation that calls for making commitments with speed and secrecy. Also, executive agreements often provide a simpler method of transacting international business that would overload the already tight legislative schedule if treaties were used. For example, the North Atlantic Treaty Organization (NATO) was based on a short treaty that pledged the signatories to maintain and improve their collective defense capabilities. Upon this foundation the contracting parties used additional executive agreements to build an organization with an integrated command structure, detailed battle plans, and extensive transportation and communications facilities.

The problem, however, is that some important international agreements may warrant Senate approval, but there are no clear guidelines to indicate which agreements need Senate consent and which can be handled simply by executive agreement. Numerous presidents, faced with the prospect of fighting for two-thirds approval in the Senate, have used executive agreements to skirt the treaty requirements imposed by the Constitution rather than abandon a diplomatic initiative. For example, Franklin D. Roosevelt sent destroyers to the British in 1940 under an executive agreement rather than put the action to an uncertain vote in Congress, which was disposed to take an isolationist stance toward the worsening war in Europe.

Despite the use of executive agreements to avoid the treaty ratification process, the Supreme Court has repeatedly upheld (most notably in 1936 in *United States v. Belmont*) the president's power to make international agreements without the consent of the Senate.

Attempts to Limit Executive Agreements

Since the end of World War II, Congress has made two major attempts to limit the president's power to make executive agreements without the advice and consent of the Senate. The first was a constitutional amendment proposed by Sen. John W. Bricker, a Republican from Ohio, in 1953. The Bricker amendment would have made executive agreements subject to the approval and regulation of Congress and would have required them to be accompanied by implementing legislation. As a result, the ability of presidents to make foreign policy through executive agreements and to negotiate treaties without involving Congress would have been severely curtailed. The amendment did not pass.

The second attempt to control the president's power to make executive agreements occurred in the early 1970s and culminated in the Case Act of 1972. The act obligates the executive branch to inform Congress of all executive agreements within sixty days of their conclusion. The House Foreign Affairs Committee and the Senate Foreign Relations Committee must be informed of any executive agreements that the president has decided must be kept secret to ensure national security.

After several years Congress found that many executive agreements were not being reported under the provisions of the Case Act because executive branch officials did not define them as executive agreements. Congress reacted by passing legislation in 1977 that required Congress to be informed of any verbal or informal understanding made by any representative of the U.S. government that might constitute a U.S. commitment.

Although the Case Act does not limit the president's power to make executive agreements, legislators are more likely to be able to check this executive branch power if they know what sort of agreements the president is making. Given that Congress can conduct investigations, issue resolutions, pass laws, and control appropriations, it does have tools with which to challenge the executive agreements it believes are unwise or improper.

More on this topic:
Constitutional Powers and Provisions, p. 119
Mexican-American War of 1846, p. 361
Treaty Power, p. 515

Executive Branch   *See* BUREAUCRACY.

Executive Office Buildings

The large, pale gray building next to the White House that reminds many people of a wedding cake is the Old Executive Office Building. Built in the post–Civil War period, this example of French Second Empire architecture is unique in the capital city. The wedding cake effect comes from its four tiers of columns. Its elaborate dormer windows, mansard roof of copper that has turned a light green with time, and more than two dozen chimneys topped with oversized chimney pots make the building a curious companion to the simply designed White House next door. In 1999 the building was renamed the Eisenhower Executive Office Building.

President Harry S. Truman, expressing the sentiments of many, called the building "the greatest monstrosity in America." But it has survived proposals to remodel or demolish it and is now a historic landmark. Originally built to house the Departments of State, War, and Navy, the building in recent years has contained most of the White House Office, the National Security Council, the Office of Management and Budget, the Council of Economic Advisers, and the vice president's office.

When completed in 1880 the Old Executive Office Building was the largest office building in Washington and among the largest in the world. It is still one of the largest granite buildings, with exterior walls that are four and a half feet thick and many eighteen-foot-high ceilings. The building has 553 rooms connected by two miles of black-and-white tiled corridors. A thorough restoration was undertaken in 1981.

Source: The White House

In 1939 the White House began moving some of its offices into the building. Ten years later the original tenants had moved out, leaving the building for the expanding EXECUTIVE OFFICE OF THE PRESIDENT. Less than twenty-five years after moving into the building, the Executive Office of the President again needed more space. The solution became known as the New Executive Office Building, a ten-story, contemporary red-brick building completed in 1968, one block from the original building at Seventeenth and H streets, N.W.

More on this topic:

Executive Office of the President, below

Executive Office of the President

In contrast to the early days of the presidency, when presidents had little or no staff to help them, the modern presidential establishment is a bureaucracy with thousands of employees, all of whom work for the president. The Executive Office of the President (EOP) is the president's tool for coping with Congress and the far-flung executive branch. The EOP helps the president oversee department and agency activities, formulate budgets and monitor spending, craft legislation, and lobby Congress. Above all, it ensures that the president's priorities are promoted.

Despite its name the EOP is in no real sense an office; rather, it is a collection of agencies whose only tie is their direct responsibility to the president. The components of the EOP have changed many times in response to the changing needs of the presidency. Today some of the major elements of the EOP are the White House Office, Office of Management and Budget,

National Security Council, Council of Economic Advisers, and Office of Policy Development.

Although EOP organizations serve the president directly, their staff members may or may not have daily access to the Oval Office. The heads of EOP organizations, like the president's closest White House advisers, are appointed by the president. Unlike the president's personal staff, however, the top positions in the EOP are subject to Senate approval.

Only modern presidents have enjoyed the increased management and control that the EOP provides. Based on the recommendations of a special presidential commission and with congressional authorization, President Franklin D. Roosevelt established the EOP in 1939 to help him manage the burgeoning bureaucracy resulting from his New Deal programs.

EXCOMM meeting, Cuban Missile Crisis, October 29, 1962.
Source: Kennedy Library

In the beginning the EOP consisted of five units, the most important of which were the Bureau of the Budget and the White House Office. As federal programs proliferated and the bureaucracy grew even larger, the EOP grew into a more specialized and complex organization.

EOP Components

The composition and organization of the EOP have changed many times since it was established. Over the years nearly fifty different boards, offices, and councils have been established within the EOP. Congress created some of these, but many others were set up by executive order. Many no longer exist as separate units within the EOP because their missions have been accomplished, transferred, consolidated, or abolished. For example, in the aftermath of the September 11, 2001, terrorist attacks against the United States, President George W. Bush moved quickly to create an Office of Homeland Security within the EOP. The office helped to coordinate domestic antiterrorism strategy. By 2002, though, the Bush administration opted to push for a cabinet-level Department of Homeland Security; legislation to create the new department was signed into law late that year.

White House Office

Of all the offices within the EOP, the White House Office may be the most important. Presidents usually place their closest and most trusted advisers on the White House staff because much of their success in managing the federal bureaucracy, working with Congress, and retaining the support of the American people will depend on the skills, loyalty, and political know-how of these staff members. (For details, see STAFF.)

Management and Budget

The Office of Management and Budget (OMB), previously known as the Bureau of the Budget, is one of the oldest and certainly one of the most powerful components of the EOP. The budget bureau, created in 1921 to act as a central clearinghouse for all budget requests, was incorporated into the EOP at its inception in 1939. The bureau was renamed and given increased responsibilities in 1970. Today OMB has broad influence over how much the government spends, how the funds are spent, and how the states disburse what they are allocated. Among other duties, it advises the president on fiscal and economic policies, helps the president to oversee budget preparations, evaluates federal programs, and coordinates and clears with the president legislative proposals submitted to Congress. (See MANAGEMENT AND BUDGET, OFFICE OF.)

National Security

The NATIONAL SECURITY COUNCIL (NSC) was established in 1947 to help the president coordinate the actions of government agencies into a single cohesive policy for dealing with other nations. It is the highest advisory body to the president on military and diplomatic issues. Presidents value advice from the NSC because of its loyalty and its independence. The NSC is subject to little effective control from Congress and lacks the institutional loyalties frequently evident in departments such as State and Defense.

Policy Development

The Office of Policy Development, originally called the Domestic Policy Staff, was established in 1977 to advise the president on long-range domestic and economic policy. The office supports the operations of the Domestic Policy Council and the National Economic Council. (For details, see POLICY DEVELOPMENT, OFFICE OF.)

Economic Advisers

The three-member COUNCIL OF ECONOMIC ADVISERS was created in 1946 to advise the president on wide-ranging issues concerning the nation's economic future. The council and its staff work closely with the White House, OMB, and congressional committees to advocate the administration's view of economic trends and policies, to identify problems and opportunities that lie ahead, and to suggest what the federal government might do to avoid or promote them. The council prepares the president's annual economic report to Congress.

Trade Office

The Office of the U.S. Trade Representative was established in 1963 and given its present name in 1980. It is headed by a cabinet-level official with the rank of ambassador, who is the president's chief adviser on international trade policy and is responsible for developing this policy and coordinating its implementation. The trade representative is the nation's chief negotiator for international trade agreements. (For details, see TRADE REPRESENTATIVE, OFFICE OF.)

Science and Technology

Although it was not formally established until 1976, the president's Office of Science and Technology Policy dates back to World War II, when the government recognized that science and technology were vital to the nation's military capabilities. Since that time science advisers and advisory panels have been a part of the president's support staff. A science and technology office was established within the EOP in 1962 but was abolished during the presidency of Richard Nixon.

When the present office was created, its director was designated as the chief policy adviser to the president on science and technology for major national policies, programs, and issues. In this capacity the director advises the chief executive on how science and technology will affect the nation's economy, national security, foreign relations, health, energy, environment, and resources. The director also assists the president in coordinating the government's research and development programs, evaluates existing science and technology efforts, and reviews pertinent budget items.

In recent decades the office has addressed topics such as a national aeronautics policy, agricultural research, Arctic research, health issues surrounding the use of the defoliant Agent Orange during the Vietnam War, biotechnology, basic research in defense and space policy, the nation's scientific and technological competitiveness in national security matters, emergency preparedness planning, energy policy issues, and international scientific cooperation.

Environmental Quality

The Council on Environmental Quality was established in 1969 to advise the president on national policies to improve the quality of the environment. The council was given a support staff the following year, with the creation of the Office of Environmental Quality.

The council and its staff were created in response to the nation's growing concern about declining air and water quality and a general deterioration of the environment. An oil well accident off the coast of California in 1969, which resulted in extensive damage to beaches and wildlife, focused public attention on the seriousness of environmental problems. Dissatisfied with the Nixon administration's response to the issue, Congress passed in 1969 the National Environmental Policy Act, which made environmental protection a matter of national policy and created the Council on Environmental Quality. The ENVIRONMENTAL PROTECTION AGENCY was created in 1970.

The council provides the president with expert opinion and policy advice on environmental issues and prepares an annual report for the president on the state of the environment. The council also is responsible for interagency coordination of environmental policies.

Drug Control

The Office of National Drug Control Policy was created by Congress in 1988 to help combat the nation's drug abuse problem. It replaced three existing boards that dealt with the drug issue.

The office coordinates federal, state, and local efforts to control illegal drug abuse and devises national strategies to carry out anti–drug abuse activities. It also makes recommendations to the president on changes in the operations and budgets of federal departments and agencies engaged in drug enforcement.

Executive Residence

The Executive Residence at the White House is considered a unit of the EOP. The staff ranges from domestic workers, skilled laborers, and groundskeepers to curators, florists, and calligraphers.

Vice President

The Office of the Vice President and the Official Residence of the Vice President are two other units within the EOP.

The vice president's office was not listed in *The United States Government Manual* as part of the EOP until 1972. The listing highlighted the vice presidency's advance in stature and resources. In contrast to the scarce resources of the years before the 1960s, the vice president today has offices in the White House's West Wing and in the Eisenhower Executive Office Building, adjacent to the White House. Vice presidents appoint their own staff, which has been expanded and reorganized to resemble the White House staff. The ability to hire a skilled staff has enhanced the vice president's value as a policy adviser to the president. (For details, see VICE PRESIDENT.)

In the 1970s the vice president was for the first time given an official residence, the Admiral's House on the grounds of the U.S. Naval Observatory in Washington, D.C. The cost of providing security systems and protection for the house of each new vice president had become greater than the cost of establishing and maintaining a single residence.

Administrative Support

As the scope and activities of the Executive Office of the President expanded over the years, it became apparent that the support functions of all EOP offices needed to be centralized in a single agency. The Office of Administration was established in 1977 to meet this need.

The office provides the EOP with administrative support services such as personnel management; financial management; data processing; library services, record-keeping, and information services; and various routine office services and operations.

Background

The modern executive establishment dates to the presidency of Franklin Roosevelt. Roosevelt came to the White House in 1933, the fourth year of a world economic crisis that raised grave doubts about the U.S. political system, even about the future of the Western world. Fifteen million Americans were unemployed, and banks in thirty-two states had been closed by state government edict. There was a sense of national despair.

In response, Roosevelt launched his New Deal recovery program. He succeeded in rebuilding the nation's economic system and also in reestablishing national trust and confidence. The nation came to look to the White House as the preeminent source of moral leadership, legislative guidance, and public policy.

The modern executive establishment dates to the presidency of Franklin Roosevelt.

Because of the mushrooming responsibilities of the executive office, the president needed more staff support. The presidency, previously an office with a very modest staff, developed after the 1930s into a major institution.

In 1936 Roosevelt made a significant contribution to the development of the presidential establishment when he named three of the country's foremost scholars of public administration—Louis Brownlow (chairman), Charles E. Merriam, and Luther Gulick—to a President's Committee on Administrative Management. The committee was directed to study the staffing needs of the presidency.

The next year the BROWNLOW COMMITTEE declared, "The President needs help." It proposed that an Executive Office of the President be established, including a White House Office staffed by loyal and energetic aides who were to have "a passion for anonymity."

Immediately endorsing its findings, with which he completely agreed and over which he had had significant influence, Roosevelt forwarded the committee's report to Congress for authorization to implement the recommendations. Congress, however, was angry over Roosevelt's ill-fated attempts to pack the Supreme Court, and it refused to act on the report. Not until April 1939 did Congress agree to most of the Brownlow Committee's proposals. On September 8, 1939, Roosevelt issued Executive Order 8248, creating the Executive Office of the President.

Since its creation the EOP has been a constantly changing, fluid entity. Offices come and go, depending on the issues of the day, the needs of the country, and the interests and style of the president.

The first EOP had five units: the White House Office, Bureau of the Budget (the predecessor of OMB), National Resources Planning Board, Office of Government Reports, and Office of War Mobilization. A Committee for Congested Production Areas and a War Refugee Board were added later by Roosevelt.

During the presidency of Harry S. Truman, the Council of Economic Advisers, National Security Council, Office of Defense Mobilization, and Office of Director for Mutual Security, among others, were added to the EOP. Dwight D. Eisenhower was the first president to appoint a special assistant for national security affairs.

The White House EOP complex expanded considerably under President John F. Kennedy, with establishment of the Office of the Special Representative for Trade Negotiations, Office of the Food for Peace Program, and others. Lyndon B. Johnson's Great Society programs resulted in a further expansion of the EOP, including the addition of the Office of Consumer Affairs and Office of Economic Opportunity.

Richard Nixon also established several EOP offices during his presidency, including the Council for Urban Affairs, Office of Intergovernmental Relations, Council on Environmental Quality, Council for Rural Affairs, Council on International Economic Policy, Special Action Office for Drug Abuse Prevention, and Office of Telecommunications Policy. At the same time he abolished or shifted the functions of other offices.

Gerald R. Ford replaced Nixon's anti–drug abuse office with an Office of Drug Abuse Policy. Jimmy Carter eliminated seven of the seventeen units in the EOP during his presidency. Ronald Reagan further streamlined the office, although he also created several new units, including the Office of National Drug Control Policy, National Space Council, and National Critical Materials Council. The latter two were abolished under Clinton. In addition to creating the Office of Homeland Security, George W. Bush established an Office of Faith-Based and Community Initiatives.

> **More on this topic:**
>
> *Staff, p. 471*
>
> *Vice-Presidential Residence, p. 546*

Executive Orders

Executive orders are presidential proclamations that carry the force of law. The president's power to issue executive orders is essentially a legislative one because the orders may require agencies or individuals to perform acts not necessarily mandated by Congress. Executive orders may be used to enforce the Constitution or treaties with foreign countries, implement legislative statutes, or direct bureaucratic agencies.

Although the Constitution does not explicitly grant the power to issue executive orders, it does require the president to "take Care that the Laws be faithfully executed." Occasionally presidents must act quickly and decisively to fulfill this directive, and the executive order is one way of doing so.

In addition, modern presidents have maintained that Article II of the Constitution grants them inherent power to take whatever actions they judge to be in the nation's best interests so long as those actions are not prohibited by the Constitution or by law. Presidents therefore view executive orders as perfectly acceptable exercises of presidential power, and the Supreme Court generally has upheld this interpretation.

Modern presidents have issued executive orders for a wide range of purposes. At one extreme, executive orders have been used to restrict liberties during time of war. Franklin Roosevelt issued Executive Order 9066 on February 19, 1942, authorizing the secretary of war to prescribe military areas in the United States from which Japanese Americans could be excluded. On the other hand, presidents have used executive orders to safeguard or promote the civil rights of minorities and women. Many orders were applied to executive branch agencies; others altered federal programs after Congress proved unable or unwilling to act. Harry S. Truman used an executive order to integrate the armed forces, John F. Kennedy issued one to bar racial discrimination in federally subsidized housing, and Lyndon B. Johnson used one to require firms that win federal government contracts to create minority hiring programs.

Presidents also have used executive orders to mold and control the federal bureaucracy. Roosevelt used an executive order to centralize budget-making authority in the Executive Office of the President. Richard Nixon and Ronald Reagan used executive orders to increase the authority of the OFFICE OF MANAGEMENT AND BUDGET over bureaucratic actions.

Perhaps the most controversial modern use of executive orders has been to create a system for classifying government documents or other information in the name of national security. Executive orders were used to establish, extend, and streamline the classification system.

More on this topic:

Japanese American Internment, p. 303

Management and Budget, Office of, p. 352

For many years executive orders were issued without any system of publication or recording. The numbering of executive orders began only in 1907, with numbers assigned retroactively to the time of Abraham Lincoln. Because of haphazard reporting and record-keeping throughout much of U.S. history, scholars estimate that many more executive orders were issued than were actually recorded.

To respond to growing concerns that these lax conditions created serious problems for governing and democratic accountability, Congress mandated in 1946 that the number and text of all executive orders be published in the *Federal Register,* the official U.S. government record of all executive branch announcements, proposals, and regulations. The exception to this rule applies to "classified" executive orders—those pertaining directly to sensitive national security matters, which are entered into the *Register* by number only.

Executive Privilege

The term *executive privilege* was coined during the administration of President Dwight D. Eisenhower, but the idea that the president has a right to withhold sensitive information from Congress or the courts has been around since the beginning of the presidency. George Washington drew on the idea when he refused to disclose information to Congress about the Jay Treaty with Britain.

The extent and nature of executive privilege have long been debated. Presidents have argued that it is an important component of executive power, allowing them to conduct sensitive business, such as negotiations that affect national security, without disruption. In rebuttal, Congress has argued that it has an equally legitimate right to know about executive business, especially when such business relates to its authority to oversee the administration of laws. (See CONGRESS AND THE PRESIDENCY.)

When presidents have come into conflict with Congress over executive privilege, the differences usually have been resolved through compromise. An exception was the conflict that arose between Congress and the courts on one side and President Richard Nixon on the other over tape recordings of Nixon's conversations with aides. An independent counsel assigned to investigate the WATERGATE AFFAIR subpoenaed the tapes. Nixon refused to release them, citing executive privilege. In 1974 the Supreme Court settled the dispute by ruling that although executive privilege did exist, it was limited rather than absolute in coverage. The Court then forced Nixon to surrender his tapes, but it recognized a president's "need for complete candor and objectivity from advisers" and need "to protect military, diplomatic, or sensitive national security secrets." (See UNITED STATES V. NIXON.)

Another interesting court case unfolded in 2002, during George W. Bush's administration, when the Government Accountability Office, a congressional agency, sued Vice President Richard B. Cheney in an ef-

The Supreme Court's decision in **United States v. Nixon (1974) cost President Richard Nixon his job. Cartoon by Le Pelley.**
Source: Library of Congress

More on this topic:

Congress and the
Presidency, p. 111

Diplomatic Powers,
p. 149

United States v. Nixon,
p. 528

fort to obtain information about meetings of Cheney's energy task force in 2001. In December 2002 a federal district judge ruled that the congressional office lacked the standing to compel disclosure of the information from the executive branch—a victory for the Bush administration. In 2004 in a related case, this time brought by Judicial Watch and the Sierra Club, Cheney appealed to the Supreme Court, arguing that the court was overstepping its power (*Cheney v. U.S District Court*). The Supreme Court sent the case back to the U.S. Court of Appeals for the D.C. Circuit for further adjudication. The issue in the case was whether the Federal Advisory Committee Act of 1972 applied to the Cheney advisors drawn from industry. In May 2005 the U.S. Court of Appeals ruled 8–0 that the Act did not apply to the Energy Task Force because only federal employees were officially members of the task force, rejecting the claim of the plaintiffs that industry officials were so deeply involved that they were de facto members of the task force. In 2004 both President Bush and Vice President Cheney agreed to be questioned by the congressionally established 9/11 commission, albeit without testifying under oath and on the agreement that no transcript of their comments would be made. Still, some observers felt this was a substantial concession to the principle of executive privilege and separation of powers.

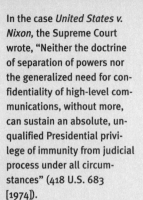

CLOSER LOOK

In the case *United States v. Nixon,* the Supreme Court wrote, "Neither the doctrine of separation of powers nor the generalized need for confidentiality of high-level communications, without more, can sustain an absolute, unqualified Presidential privilege of immunity from judicial process under all circumstances" (418 U.S. 683 [1974]).

F

Fairbanks, Charles W.

Charles W. Fairbanks.
Source: Library of Congress

Charles Warren Fairbanks (1852–1918) served as vice president under Theodore Roosevelt from 1905 to 1909. The two prominent Republican leaders did not get along well. Fairbanks held presidential ambitions, but he never actually ran for the higher office.

Fairbanks rose from a humble background to graduate from Ohio Wesleyan University and become a respected Indianapolis attorney specializing in railroad litigation. While accumulating a fortune from his law practice, Fairbanks became involved in politics. By 1896 he was one of Indiana's leading Republicans, although he had never held public office. That year his keynote address at the Republican national convention brought him national acclaim. In 1897 he was elected to the U.S. Senate.

In the Senate, Fairbanks was one of President William McKinley's most consistent supporters. Republican leaders considered Fairbanks for the vice-presidential nomination in 1900, but he decided to remain in the Senate. Theodore Roosevelt was nominated instead.

Fairbanks had planned to run for the presidency after McKinley served out his second term, but McKinley's assassination in 1901 elevated Roosevelt to the presidency and eliminated any chance that Fairbanks would receive the presidential nomination in 1904. Instead Fairbanks settled for the vice-presidential nomination. Roosevelt would have preferred someone else, but he accepted Fairbanks, who was the choice of the party's conservative wing. Roosevelt and Fairbanks easily defeated Democrats Alton B. Parker and Henry G. Davis.

Roosevelt made no effort to involve Fairbanks in his administration. He had a low opinion of Fairbanks and was disdainful of his vice president's persistent maneuverings to set himself up as the Republican presidential nominee in 1908. Roosevelt's endorsement of Secretary of War William Howard Taft ensured that Fairbanks would not receive the nomination.

After finishing his vice-presidential term, Fairbanks never again held public office, but he remained a powerful figure in national and state politics. In 1916 he was again nominated by the Republicans for vice president. Woodrow Wilson and Thomas Marshall, however, defeated Charles Evans Hughes and Fairbanks in the electoral college 277–254. After the defeat Fairbanks retired from politics. He died in 1918 at the age of sixty-six after undertaking a speaking tour in support of the U.S. effort in World War I.

More on this topic:

Roosevelt, Theodore, p. 448

Vice President, p. 539

Fair Deal

When Harry S. Truman assumed the presidency in April 1945 after the death of Franklin D. Roosevelt, he was determined both to extend FDR's New Deal and to put his own stamp on the presidency. On September 6, 1945, Truman presented to Congress a twenty-one-point program for postwar reconversion that became the Fair Deal, his domestic policy agenda.

A major goal of the program was to return the nation's economy to a peacetime footing after the all-out national mobilization for World War II. Among its other provisions were an extension of Social Security, an increase in the minimum wage, national health insurance, urban development, a full employment bill, and what Truman called a "national reassertion of the right to work for every American citizen able to." The agenda was one of the longest ever sent to Congress by a president up to that time.

Conservative critics of the New Deal had expected Truman to roll back many of its provisions and engineer "a return to normalcy" when the war was over. His progressive proposals for continuation and expansion of Roosevelt's program under the new rubric drew heated opposition, and the 1946 congressional election, which for the first time in sixteen years gave the Republicans control of Congress, seemed to be a dramatic rejection of the Fair Deal and its spiritual predecessor, the New Deal.

Truman fought back and cast more than two hundred vetoes to turn back the Eightieth Congress's determined campaign to bury the New and Fair Deals. Although Congress overrode his veto of the 1947 Taft-Hartley bill, a measure viewed as strongly anti-union, Truman's stand brought him increased support among labor and middle-class liberals. That bloc of voters proved crucial to Truman's upset victory in the 1948 presidential race, which he turned into a referendum on the domestic policies of the FDR and Truman administrations. In

The strength of our Nation must continue to be used in the interest of all our people rather than a privileged few. It must continue to be used unselfishly in the struggle for world peace and the betterment of mankind the world over. This is the task before us. It is not an easy one. It has many complications, and there will be strong opposition from selfish interests. I hope for cooperation from farmers, from labor, and from business. Every segment of our population and every individual has a right to expect from our Government a fair deal.

—Harry S. Truman, State of the Union Address, January 5, 1949

More on this topic:

Economic Powers, p. 161

New Deal, p. 383

Truman, Harry S., p. 519

January 1949 Truman said memorably in his State of the Union address that "Every segment of our population and every individual has a right to expect from our Government a fair deal...." Since the 1948 election returned control of Congress to the Democrats, Truman was able to push through some of the Fair Deal's components, most notably the Social Security, minimum wage, and public housing proposals. His assertiveness with Congress also strongly reconfirmed the modern president's leadership role in legislative affairs.

Farewell Addresses

George Washington writing his farewell address with the assistance of Alexander Hamilton
Source: Architect of the Capitol

The farewell address is an important ceremonial speech given by the president upon leaving office. It not only can help set the tone for the next administration but also can shape the nation's memory and assessment of that particular presidency. The farewell can be an emotional time for the president and the public, and for the president's political allies.

When moving from active leader to historical figure, presidents are not subject to the same political pressures as they were while in office, nor are they able to exert the same influence. The farewell address may be very influential over time, but it is not likely to have much effect on immediate politics. Rather it is intended to leave the nation with a lasting statement of principles.

Perhaps the most historically significant farewell address was that of George Washington. In it, he set both substantive policy and rules of etiquette for subsequent presidents. Although he never delivered it in person, the message was widely circulated in the press and helped to ensure that there would be no effort to reelect him to a third term. In the message, Washington warned in particular of the potential threat to national unity posed by political parties, which were just then emerging in an organized form. He also urged the new nation not to become entangled in the political quarrels of Europe.

Another important farewell address was given by Dwight D. Eisenhower. The speech is remembered mostly for its warning against the power of what Eisenhower called the "military-industrial complex" formed by the armed services and defense industries during the cold war. "In the councils of government, we must guard against the acquisition of unwarranted influence, whether sought or unsought, by the military-industrial complex," he said, in a warning that had special importance because it came from a man who had spent most of his career in the military.

> **In the councils of government, we must guard against the acquisition of unwarranted influence, whether sought or unsought, by the military-industrial complex.**
>
> —**Dwight D. Eisenhower,** *Farewell Address,* January 17, 1961

More on this topic:

Speeches and Rhetoric, p. 466

Other important farewell addresses were delivered by Andrew Jackson, Grover Cleveland, Richard Nixon, Jimmy Carter, and Ronald Reagan.

Federal Bureau of Investigation

The Federal Bureau of Investigation (FBI) is part of the U.S. Department of Justice. The FBI can trace its origins to 1908, when Attorney General Charles J. Bonaparte appointed a group of special agents to work as the Justice Department's investigative force. That group later evolved into the FBI. Its most famous director, J. Edgar Hoover, ran the bureau for almost fifty years (1924–1972) and shaped it into a modern, professional, and semiautonomous law enforcement agency.

FBI director J. Edgar Hoover
Source: University of Texas

The bureau was celebrated in the 1930s for catching or killing well-known criminals, such as John Dillinger. Hoover and his agents retained a favorable image during World War II and the cold war, as they apprehended enemy spies. But the FBI's mystique began to crumble in the 1960s, when critics charged Hoover with being insensitive to civil rights issues and refusing to commit enough resources to the fight against organized crime.

The bureau faced more controversy in the wake of the Watergate affair, when its acting director, L. Patrick Gray, admitted destroying documents important to the initial investigation and when high bureau officers were convicted and imprisoned for illegal activities.

In 2001 it was revealed that in the 1960s the FBI, with the full knowledge and consent of Hoover, had fabricated a legal case against an innocent man for alleged organized crime activity.

After the terrorist attacks on the United States of September 11, 2001, the FBI, along with the Central Intelligence Agency (CIA), faced criticism that it had not done enough to protect the country. The attacks sparked a reorientation in the bureau, which previously had devoted its resources mainly to ordinary crime, leaving large-scale terrorism threats to the CIA and the Department of Defense. But after September 11 the FBI began to distribute some of its ordinary crime responsibilities to other agencies, such as the Drug Enforcement Agency (DEA) and the Bureau of Alcohol, Tobacco, Firearms and Explosives (ATF), and to focus more of its resources on counterterrorism activities.

The bureau also was affected by other actions taken after September 11. The USA Patriot Act, passed and signed in late October 2001, broadened the federal government's powers of surveillance. In November 2002 President George W. Bush signed into law a bill creating a new federal Department of Homeland Security; the FBI works with the department on domestic security and antiterrorism efforts. In fact, two units of the FBI—the National Domestic Preparedness Office and the National Infrastructure Protection Center—were moved to the new department.

The 9/11 Commission in July 2004 blamed the CIA and the FBI jointly for intelligence failures that might have prevented the attacks. The report included a number of recommendations for reforms that have guided the FBI in subsequent years. The FBI as of 2007 defined its major tasks as counterterrorism and counterintelligence.

The FBI is headed by a director who is appointed by the president for a ten-year term and must be confirmed by the Senate. The bureau's Washington, D.C., headquarters gives direction and support to other units, including fifty-six field offices and over four hundred satellite offices. As of early 2007 the FBI had over twelve thousand special agents and about eighteen thousand professional support personnel.

> ### More on this topic:
>
> *Justice Department,*
> *p. 313*
>
> *Law Enforcement Powers,*
> *p. 330*

Federal Election Commission

The Federal Election Commission (FEC), one of the government's INDEPENDENT REGULATORY AGEN-CIES, was created in 1975 to administer and enforce the provisions of the Federal Election Campaign Act (FECA) of 1971, as amended. It is responsible for the Bipartisan Campaign Reform Act of 2002 as well.

Campaign finance law requires the disclosure of sources and uses of funds in campaigns for any federal office, sets limits on the size of contributions, and provides for partial public financing of presidential elections.

Any candidate for federal office and any political group or committee formed to support one or more candidates must, once they cross a certain threshold, register with the FEC and file periodic reports on their campaign receipts and expenditures. Individuals and committees contributing to or making independent expenditures on behalf of, or against, a candidate must also file reports. The FEC makes these reports available to the public at the agency and online at the FEC Web site (*www.fec.gov*).

FEC staff members review the reports for omissions, and if any are found, the FEC requests additional information from the candidate or committee. If the FEC discovers what it believes to be a violation of campaign finance law, it has the authority to seek a conciliation agreement, including a civil penalty. If a conciliation agreement cannot be reached, the FEC may sue for enforcement in U.S. district court. The commission may refer any matters involving willful violations to the Justice Department.

The commission also administers provisions of the law covering the public financing of presidential primaries, national party conventions, and presidential general elections. These amounts undergo periodic adjustment for inflation. In addition the FEC maintains a clearinghouse for information on federal election administration.

There had been several attempts to reform campaign financing before the 1971 statute. In the early 1900s Theodore Roosevelt recommended a ban on corporate contributions and public financing of federal elections. A ban on contributions by corporations and national banks was enacted in 1907, but it would be more than a half-century before public funding for presidential elections would be approved. A series of Corrupt Practices Acts attempted to regulate the system, but enforcement was difficult.

The campaign finance system remained riddled with loopholes until passage of the 1971 act. The revelations of the WATERGATE AFFAIR, which involved the role of money in politics, spurred further reforms. Congress passed in 1974 the most significant overhaul of campaign finance legislation in the nation's history, which, among other things, created the FEC in 1975.

In 1976 the Supreme Court in *Buckley v. Valeo* declared several features of the 1974 amendments unconstitutional, including the method for selecting members of the FEC. The Court said the method violated the Constitution's clauses on separation of powers and appointments because four commissioners were appointed by congressional officials but exercised executive powers. Amendments passed in 1976 reconstituted the FEC as a six-member panel appointed by the president and confirmed by the Senate.

The commissioners serve staggered six-year terms. Beginning in 1998, new commissioners were limited to a single term. No more than three commissioners may be members of the same political party. The clerk of the House and secretary of the Senate served as nonvoting members until 1993, when a federal court ruled the practice unconstitutional. The Supreme Court let the ruling stand.

Another landmark campaign finance law was enacted in 2002 to ban national party committees and federal candidates from raising and using "soft money"—money raised in amounts and from sources prohibited in federal elections but allowed for some state party activities. The bill also barred the use of soft money for certain political ads, known as "issue ads," if they mention a specific federal candidate and run in the weeks immediately preceding an election. Other provisions in the measure included changes in some of the existing contribution limits.

The FEC regulations implementing the 2002 law outraged the bill's principal congressional sponsors, Sens. John McCain and Russell Feingold, who accused the agency of creating loopholes that would allow federal candidates to continue raising soft money. Reps. Christopher Shays and Martin Meehan successfully sued the FEC concerning its failure to regulate so-called 527 groups engaged in independent campaign spending. In 2006 federal district court ruled that the agency had "failed to present a reasoned explanation" for not issuing regulations.

More on this topic:

Buckley v. Valeo, *p. 36*

Campaign Financing, p. 71

Federalist Papers

The *Federalist Papers* are among the most important documents of U.S. constitutional history. In them, three men who had played major roles in the development of the Constitution—James Madison, Alexander Hamilton, and John Jay—explained the thinking that had led to the different aspects of the founding charter and sought to persuade the American people to adopt it as the cornerstone of a new nation.

The *Federalist Papers* were originally published as a series of eighty-five newspaper articles that appeared under the pseudonym "Publius." We now know that Hamilton wrote about fifty of them, Madison twenty-five, Jay five, and Hamilton and Madison jointly three. They were reprinted and disseminated widely through the states as the debate raged over ratification of the product of the Constitutional Convention.

The presidency as it was established in Article II of the Constitution posed a major political problem to Federalists seeking its adoption. Not only was the presidency the most obvious innovation in the new plan of government, but it raised fears of the worst thing many citizens could imagine—a return to an all-powerful monarchy like the British one they had overthrown only a few years before. Moreover, Anti-Federalists opposed to adoption of the Constitution did their best to encourage fears that the new chief executive would soon become a king.

Proponents of the Constitution at the state ratifying conventions emphasized both the virtues of the presidency and the restraints that the Constitution placed on the office. In doing so, they frequently relied on the arguments put forward in the *Federalist Papers*. The presidency is covered in Nos. 69–77, which were written by Hamilton.

THE

FEDERALIST:

ADDRESSED TO THE

PEOPLE OF THE STATE OF NEW-YORK.

NUMBER I.

Introduction.

AFTER an unequivocal experience of the inefficacy of the subsisting federal government, you are called upon to deliberate on a new constitution for the United States of America. The subject speaks its own importance; comprehending in its consequences, nothing less than the existence of the UNION, the safety and welfare of the parts of which it is composed, the fate of an empire, in many respects, the most interesting in the world It has been frequently remarked, that it seems to have been reserved to the people of this country, by their conduct and example, to decide the important question, whether societies of men are really capable or not, of establishing good government from reflection and choice, or whether they are forever destined to depend, for their political constitutions, on accident and force. If there be any truth in the remark, the crisis, at which we are arrived, may with propriety be regarded as the æra in which that

A copy of the first Federalist Paper published.
Source: Senate Historical Office

In his articles Hamilton squarely addressed the charge that the presidency could become a monarchy. He tried to show how far a president would be from a king by contrasting the office with

the British monarchy. Unlike the British king, who serves for life, the president serves for a limited term. The president can be impeached by the legislative branch, but the king cannot. Moreover, Hamilton pointed out, the king has an absolute power to veto legislation approved by Parliament, while the president's veto can be overridden by a two-thirds majority of Congress.

In developing those and other contrasts Hamilton was not always entirely accurate, because his picture of the British monarchy was in some ways already out of date. Nevertheless, his arguments proved effective in countering the Anti-Federalists' threatening picture of the presidency.

Hamilton also praised the virtues of the presidency. He argued that the office would have "energy," a crucial element of good government. Energy, he said, "is essential to the protection of the community against foreign attacks; it is not less essential to the steady administration of the laws; to the protection of property against those irregular and high-handed combinations which sometimes interrupt the ordinary course of justice; to the security of liberty against the enterprises and assaults of ambition, of faction, and of anarchy."

Hamilton believed that the presidency could provide energy because it is held by only one person at a time and therefore can have "decision, activity, secrecy, and dispatch … vigor and expedition." A committee or multimember executive, by contrast, could be split by disagreements that would make it slow to act and would be liable to create factional strife. The nation also would find it hard to hold a multimember executive responsible for failure, Hamilton argued, because each member of the executive could blame the others.

Hamilton also defended the presidency as having other qualities that are indispensable to energy. The presidential four-year term, for example, gives the president enough time to act with firmness and courage but is not so long as "to justify any alarm for the public liberty," Hamilton wrote.

Another important aspect of the presidency, Hamilton contended, was the incumbent's eligibility for reelection. He argued that eligibility for more than one term acknowledges that "the desire of reward is one of the strongest incentives of human conduct." Without the prospect of another term, Hamilton said, presidents might either neglect their duties or be tempted to seize power violently.

"Adequate provision for its support," Hamilton noted, is yet another quality of the presidency that ensures its energy in governing. The Federalist author argued that the constitutional prohibition against Congress's raising or lowering an incumbent president's salary was a vital protection, because without it Congress could "reduce him by famine, or tempt him by largesse," and thus "render him as obsequious to their will as they might think proper to make him."

> *Of all the cares or concerns of government, the direction of war most peculiarly demands those qualities which distinguish the exercise of power by a single hand. The direction of war implies the direction of the common strength; and the power of directing and employing the common strength, forms a usual and essential part in the definition of the executive authority.*
>
> —*Alexander Hamilton,* Federalist No. 74

• • • • • • • • • • • • • • • • •

> *In framing a government which is to be administered by men over men, the great difficulty lies in this: you must first enable the government to control the governed; and in the next place oblige it to control itself.*
>
> —*James Madison,* Federalist No. 51

More on this topic:
Hamilton, Alexander, p. 243
Madison, James, p. 350

Federal Reserve System

The Federal Reserve System, often known simply as the Fed, is an independent regulatory and monetary policy-making agency established by the Federal Reserve Act in 1913. As the nation's central bank, it is charged with making and administering policy for the nation's credit and monetary affairs. It also supervises certain banks.

The operations of the Fed are conducted through a nationwide network of twelve Federal Reserve banks and twenty-five branches. Each Federal Reserve bank is an incorporated institution with its own board of directors.

The Fed is administered by a board of seven governors who are nominated by the president and confirmed by the Senate. Governors are appointed to a single fourteen-year term. One member is designated by the president to serve as chair for a four-year, renewable term. The chair of the Federal Reserve is considered one of the most powerful posts in government. Alan Greenspan, thought to be among the most powerful Fed chairs, took office in 1987 and occupied the post until 2006, when his term expired and Benjamin Bernanke was appointed to the post.

The board's primary function is to formulate monetary policy—that is, to manipulate interest rates, using its own studies and forecasts, for the purpose of improving or stabilizing the economy. The goals of monetary policy include low inflation, low unemployment, and strong economic growth.

The Fed can change the rate of growth of the supply of money through several means. First, it can require commercial banks to keep a greater or smaller proportion of deposits on reserve. If this reserve requirement is lowered, banks have more money to lend, and the money supply grows faster. If the reserve requirement is raised, banks have less money to loan, and the growth of the supply of money slows. Second, the Fed can slow or accelerate the growth of the money supply by decreasing or increasing the rate at which banks may borrow funds from the Federal Reserve System. When this rate, known as the discount rate, increases, banks cannot afford to borrow as much from the Fed and therefore will have less money to loan. A lower discount rate will put more money in the hands of banks by making it cheaper for them to borrow from the Fed. Finally, the Fed can alter the growth of the money supply by buying and selling U.S. securities. This process, known as open market operations, is by far the most commonly used method for affecting the money supply. When the Fed buys securities, it pumps money into the banking system. Selling securities to banks brings money into the Fed that banks could have loaned, thereby slowing the growth of the money supply.

The Fed's manipulations of the money supply affect the performance of the economy through their impact on interest rates. If the Fed increases the money supply, interest rates fall because banks have more funds available to loan. The lower interest rates induce firms to borrow more money to invest in the expansion and modernization of their operations. This increase in investment creates jobs and causes the economy to expand. Consumers also find borrowing cheaper, and so they are better able to finance the purchase of expensive items such as homes and cars. If the Fed slows the growth of the money supply, banks have less money to loan, and the competition for these limited funds forces interest rates up. Firms and consumers respond to more expensive rates of interest by borrowing less money for investment and purchases, so the economy contracts.

FEDERAL RESERVE BANKS

District	Location	Letter on Currency
1	Boston	A
2	New York	B
3	Philadelphia	C
4	Cleveland	D
5	Richmond	E
6	Atlanta	F
7	Chicago	G
8	St. Louis	H
9	Minneapolis	I
10	Kansas City	J
11	Dallas	K
12	San Francisco	L

CLOSER LOOK

The letter in the middle of the seal to the left of Washington's portrait on U.S. paper currency indicates which of the various Federal Reserve System district banks issued the note. The example in this photograph indicates the banknote was issued by the San Francisco district "L".

More on this topic:

Independent Regulatory Agencies, p. 287

National Bank, p. 372

The primary role of monetary policy in the economy has been to fight inflation. Monetary policy has two advantages over fiscal (taxing and spending) policy as an inflation-fighting tool. First, the time required to decide on and execute a strategy is much shorter for monetary policy than for fiscal policy. After an economic problem has been recognized, the Fed can reach a monetary policy decision within days.

Second, the Fed's relative insulation from politics makes its fight against inflation simpler than the president's. Fiscal policy remedies for inflation—tax increases and expenditure cuts—are seldom popular with voters. Because the members of the Fed are not elected, they do not have to worry constantly that growing unemployment or declining economic growth brought on by anti-inflationary monetary policy may anger constituents or cause them to lose an election. Nevertheless, the Fed does not work in a political vacuum. It must contend with pressure from the president and Congress to implement particular monetary policies.

Ferraro, Geraldine A.

1984 Democratic vice-presidential nominee Geraldine Ferraro
Source: bioguide.congress.gov

Geraldine A. Ferraro (1935–) blazed a trail in 1984 when she became the first woman ever chosen for a national ticket by a major political party. Hoping to energize his uphill battle against Republican president Ronald Reagan, Democratic nominee Walter F. Mondale chose Ferraro as his running mate. A three-term House member from New York City, Ferraro campaigned effectively. Yet controversies over her husband's business practices and her own position on abortion and lack of government experience hurt the Democratic ticket. Political experts differed on whether Ferraro's overall contribution was negative or positive, but the question seemed insignificant in light of Reagan's overwhelming reelection victory.

Mondale's choice of Ferraro reflected his responsiveness to the lobbying of women's groups as well as his theory that demographic, rather than geographic, forces would determine the election. Mondale's strategists hoped that even though both candidates were northern liberals, Ferraro would attract women and the young, independent voters who had supported Sen. Gary Hart of Colorado in the primaries. Ferraro also brought symbolic value to the ticket, as a woman and as the daughter of Italian immigrants.

During the campaign Ferraro worked hard to moderate her witty, fast-talking manner, which sometimes seemed abrasive, especially on television. She appeared knowledgeable and competent, if a bit stiff, during a debate with Republican vice-presidential nominee George H. W. Bush, and she often drew large and enthusiastic crowds. Her energies, and those of the campaign, were diverted when the press forced her husband into an embarrassing public accounting of the details of his lucrative real estate business that led to the revelation of some legal infractions. Another distraction came from antiabortion militants. Ferraro had walked a fine line on the issue as a Catholic feminist: She personally opposed abortion but did not favor making it illegal. Abortion opponents dogged her campaign, and she became embroiled in a lengthy public dispute on the issue with Catholic archbishop John O'Connor.

Ferraro's rise to political prominence was inspirational to many women. The daughter of working-class immigrants, she was a housewife with three children who went on to build a private law practice. In 1974 Ferraro became an assistant district attorney in the New York City borough of Queens, specializing in crimes such as child abuse and domestic violence. In the House, where she served from 1978 to 1984, Ferraro quickly became a leader among a new generation of female politicians who successfully combined feminism with an ability to work within the traditional male-dominated power structure. Supported by House Speaker Thomas P. "Tip" O'Neill, she won a seat on the important Budget Committee and took on various Democratic Party assignments that increased her visibility and influence.

Ferraro relinquished her House seat after the 1984 campaign and was expected to seek a New York Senate seat. But her political career was derailed at least temporarily by the well-publicized problems of her family. Her husband, John A. Zaccaro, pled guilty in 1985 to a misdemeanor charge of fraud.

Ferraro sought a Senate seat in 1992 but was defeated in the primary.

More on this topic:

Mondale, Walter F., p. 365

Fillmore, Millard

Millard Fillmore signature

Source: Library of Congress

Millard Fillmore (1800–1874) was the second vice president to succeed to the presidency after the death of the incumbent. He supported the Compromise of 1850, which temporarily defused tensions between the North and the South, but he did not attempt to address the passionate disagreements over slavery that led to the Civil War.

Fillmore was born to a poor farm couple on January 7, 1800, in Cayuga County, New York. When Millard was fourteen he was apprenticed to a clothmaker, but he bought his freedom from apprenticeship and took a job teaching school. While teaching, he studied law with a county judge and was admitted to the bar in 1823.

Fillmore began his political career as a member of New York's Anti-Masonic Party, which opposed secret societies in the United States. In 1828 Fillmore was elected to the New York assembly as a member of that party. After being reelected twice, he left the legislature to establish a lucrative law practice in Buffalo. From 1833 to 1835 and 1837 to 1843 Fillmore served in the U.S. House of Representatives.

In 1834 he shifted to the Whig Party and soon became a prominent member of its northern wing and a close ally of Sen. Henry Clay of Kentucky. In 1844 Fillmore was defeated narrowly for the governorship of New York. The Whigs nominated Mexican-American War hero Zachary Taylor as their presidential candidate in 1848. The party's search for a vice-presidential candidate to balance the ticket with the slave-owning Taylor led to Fillmore, who had impressed many party leaders with his personal bearing and political skills. The Taylor-Fillmore ticket narrowly defeated Democrats Lewis Cass and William Butler.

As vice president, Fillmore was excluded from policy making in the Taylor administration, but he dutifully presided over the Senate as that body struggled with the slavery issue. Fillmore was a staunch opponent of slavery, but he believed a moderate course was necessary to preserve the Union.

He therefore supported the Compromise of 1850 devised by Clay. The plan sought to make concessions to both the North and the South. President Taylor, however, opposed the compromise and was prepared to veto it and use force to put down any rebellions in the South that might result. Fillmore foresaw a close vote in the Senate and informed the president that if a tie vote should occur, his conscience obliged him to vote for the compromise despite Taylor's opposition. Before the Senate could vote on the plan, Taylor died suddenly on July 9, 1850, and Fillmore succeeded to the presidency.

Because Fillmore believed Taylor's cabinet was against the compromise, he accepted the resignations of all seven men and appointed a new cabinet that supported the measure. With Taylor dead, the threat of a presidential veto of Clay's plan was removed, and work on the compromise moved forward. In September 1850 Fillmore signed the series of bills that made up the Compromise of 1850. Under the compromise, California was admitted to the Union as a free state, the territories of Utah and New Mexico were established without mention of slavery, and Texas was paid $10 million for surrendering its claim to New Mexico. Other provisions made federal officials responsible for capturing and returning runaway slaves and outlawed the slave trade in the District of Columbia while affirming the right to own slaves there.

Many southerners objected to the compromise because it set a precedent that allowed the federal government to pass legislation on slavery rather than leaving the issue to the states. Abolitionists, however, thought the compromise favored the South. They especially detested the Fugitive Slave Law, which Fillmore felt obligated to enforce. The president believed the compromise would work only if the federal government upheld all of its provisions.

No one was entirely satisfied with the Compromise of 1850, but it resulted in a few years of relative calm. During this period Fillmore oversaw the modernization of the White House, worked to secure federal funds for railroad construction, and opposed the efforts of private U.S. citizens to overthrow Spanish rule in Cuba. Before Fillmore left office in 1853 he sent Commodore Matthew Perry on a cruise across the Pacific to open up Japan to U.S. trade.

Fillmore attempted to secure the Whig presidential nomination in 1852, but the convention chose a popular Mexican-American War hero, Gen. Winfield Scott, instead. Scott then lost to Democrat Franklin Pierce in a landslide.

After the election of 1852 the Whig Party disintegrated. Its most visible leaders, Daniel Webster and Henry Clay, had died in 1852, and Fillmore's enforcement of the Fugitive Slave Act had disaffected many northern Whigs, who helped to form the new Republican Party in 1854. Fillmore declined to join the Republicans and instead accepted the 1856 presidential nomination of the anti-Catholic, anti-immigrant American, or Know-Nothing, Party. The Know-Nothings were named for their practice of responding "I know nothing" to questions about their rituals. In the election Fillmore received more than 800,000 popular votes but just eight electoral votes. He finished a distant third behind Democrat James Buchanan and Republican John Fremont.

After this defeat Fillmore retired from politics. His first wife, Abigail Powers, had died shortly after he left the presidency. In 1858 he married Caroline McIntosh. Fillmore died of a stroke on March 8, 1874, in Buffalo, New York.

> **More on this topic:**
>
> *Death of the President,*
> *p. 142*
>
> *Succession, p. 484*
>
> *Taylor, Zachary, p. 492*

Financing   *See* CAMPAIGN FINANCE.

First Hundred Days

Most presidents experience what is known as a HONEYMOON PERIOD during their first weeks in office, when they enjoy a high level of public support and trust. During this period, which may last

for a few weeks or a few months, Congress and the public are likely to be the most receptive to a president's legislative initiatives. The president who had the most successful honeymoon period was Franklin D. Roosevelt. His legislative achievements during his first hundred days in the Oval Office are unsurpassed.

Roosevelt entered the White House in March 1933 as the nation faced unprecedented economic and social pressures. The Great Depression had devastated the national economy, forcing millions into unemployment and crippling public faith in government. Many blamed President Herbert C. Hoover for their hardships, and he suffered a humiliating defeat in the 1932 election. Congress, which had been unable to resolve the crisis, was now controlled by Democrats for the first time since 1919 and was looking for strong direction.

The emergency gave Roosevelt the opportunity to take the lead in ways no earlier peacetime president ever had. And take the lead he did. On March 5, one day after he was sworn in, Roosevelt issued the Bank Holiday Proclamation. On March 9 Congress, convened in special session, passed the president's Emergency Banking bill after just eight hours of debate.

The bill, coupled with the president's March 13 broadcast speech, or "fireside chat," ended the banking crisis and began the New Deal. Roosevelt at first thought about sending Congress back home after passage of the banking reform act. But the momentum attained seemed too valuable to waste. As historian Arthur M. Schlesinger Jr. later wrote, "In the three months after Roosevelt's inauguration, Congress and the country were subjected to a presidential barrage of ideas and programs unlike anything known to American history."

Between noon on March 9 and 1 a.m. on June 15, 1933, a willing Congress passed dozens of laws dealing with the nation's economic crisis. These included the Agricultural Adjustment Act establishing a national agricultural policy, the National Industrial Recovery Act, the Farm Credit Act reorganizing federal farm credit programs, the Emergency Farm Mortgage Act refinancing farm mortgages, the Tennessee Valley Authority Act, the Civilian Conservation Corps, the Federal Emergency Relief Act setting up a national relief system, and the Glass-Steagall Banking Act separating commercial from investment banking functions and setting up federal insurance for bank deposits.

Most observers believe that it would take another crisis of the same proportions as the depression to prompt another president and Congress to enact so much important legislation in so little time. Even at that, the president would have to be a forceful leader, and a majority of Congress would have to be willing to cooperate—requirements that might not easily be met. As presidential scholar Clinton Rossiter said of Roosevelt, "In the first Hundred Days he gave Congress a kind of leadership it had not known before and still does not care to have repeated."

> *After the adjournment of the historical special session of the Congress five weeks ago I purposely refrained from addressing you for two very good reasons. First, I think that we all wanted the opportunity of a little quiet thought to examine and assimilate in a mental picture the crowding events of the hundred days which had been devoted to the starting of the wheels of the New Deal.*
>
> **—Franklin D. Roosevelt**, Fireside Chat, July 24, 1933

More on this topic:

Great Depression, p. 237

Honeymoon Period, p. 262

New Deal, p. 383

Roosevelt, Franklin D., p. 445

First Ladies

The president's spouse (and all presidents so far have been men) holds no official position and earns no salary. The Constitution does not mention her. Yet she is a prominent public figure who can, and often does, influence the president's political decisions and shape public perceptions of his administration.

In the early days of the Republic, the first lady fulfilled public expectations if she was a gracious hostess and ran the White House efficiently. Although she still manages the daily domestic affairs of the White House and acts as hostess at social functions, a modern first lady is expected to be a public figure as well. To succeed, she must appear to be articulate, well informed, and self-assured.

Early First Ladies

If the first ladies of the eighteenth and early nineteenth centuries had political views and ambitions, most were careful to keep them under wraps. In those days, women were expected to conform to an ideal of passive purity that did not include participation in the less-than-pure world of politics. ABIGAIL ADAMS, the nation's second first lady and a pioneering feminist, illustrates this limitation. She took an active interest in politics and occasionally expressed her views openly, for which she was widely criticized as being unladylike. Her well-known influence as a political adviser to her husband, John Adams, was viewed with suspicion and alarm.

DOLLEY MADISON, another memorable early first lady, avoided politics and instead poured her considerable intelligence and energy into entertaining. Her social grace and charm offset the public aloofness of her husband, James Madison. Dolley Madison excelled as a hostess, but she was tough as well. During the War of 1812 when British soldiers marched on Washington and burned the White House, she displayed her courage by staying behind until the last possible moment to supervise the removal of documents and valuables. Thanks to her presence of mind, a full-length portrait of George Washington painted by Gilbert Stuart was saved from the fire and still hangs in the White House.

Julia Tyler, second wife of John Tyler, followed in Dolley Madison's footsteps. During her brief stay in the White House in 1844, she entertained lavishly, received guests while seated on a raised platform, and hired her own press agent. MARY TODD LINCOLN also caused a stir, but for negative reasons. President Abraham Lincoln called her his "child wife" because of her emotional instability. Her compulsive shopping and other erratic behavior drew widespread public attention and did not help Lincoln's image during the difficult days of the Civil War.

In the second half of the nineteenth century public interest in first ladies grew. More people, especially more women, could read and had some leisure time to do so. The spread of mass-circulation newspapers and magazines made more material available. First ladies became celebrities on a par with actresses, sports figures, and society women. At the same time, the image of women as passive, delicate creatures began to fade with the onset of the woman's suffrage movement. (Women did not win the right to vote until 1920.)

Julia Grant was the first president's wife to become a truly national figure and the first to be called "first lady of the land." During Ulysses S. Grant's two terms in the post–Civil War period, Julia redecorated the White House at great expense and entertained lavishly. The public loved her flamboyance. The elegant Frances Folsom, who married Grover Cleveland in a well-publicized White House wedding in 1886, attained even greater public celebrity. Her hairstyle and clothing became national fads, and her White House parties and receptions had great social cachet.

Modern First Ladies

Edith Roosevelt, the second wife of Theodore Roosevelt, was first lady at the start of the twentieth century. Her handling of the job was distinctly modern. For the first time, a first lady hired her own staff to answer mail and reporters' questions instead of relying on the president's staff. She showed a new sophistication in her dealings with the press, carefully managing news about her boisterous family of six children in order to project a positive image. Edith Roosevelt was not a political activist, but it was well known that she gave advice to her husband and that he listened to her. Unlike Abigail Adams, she was not criticized for her influence.

First ladies who came after Edith Roosevelt found other new possibilities in the job. It was widely believed that William Howard Taft would not have become president without the driving ambition of Helen Taft, who participated energetically in her husband's political decisions and had little patience for social events. President Woodrow Wilson's first wife, Ellen, became the first president's wife to support publicly social legislation pending before Congress, when she openly pushed for a bill to improve housing in the poor neighborhoods of the capital city.

Wilson's second wife, EDITH WILSON, showed little interest in politics until her husband suffered a stroke in 1919. Then she took on many of his responsibilities and was thought by many to be running the government while he recovered. Lou Hoover, wife of President Herbert C. Hoover, was a serious intellectual who spoke five languages. As first lady, she commented on social issues and headed the Girl Scouts of America.

First Lady Eleanor Roosevelt was one of Franklin Roosevelt's most important emissaries to interest groups such as blacks and labor. Here she speaks to members of the CIO, AFL, and unaffiliated unions in West Park, New York.
Source: FDR Library

ELEANOR ROOSEVELT, wife of Franklin D. Roosevelt, is judged by many to have been the most remarkable first lady in the nation's history. She held the job from 1933 until 1945 and set a daunting example. A woman of great energy and intellect, she traveled extensively and fought openly for a variety of liberal causes, chief among them women's rights and an end to racial discrimination. During World War II she visited soldiers at the front and served as deputy director of the Office of Civilian Defense. While earlier first ladies usually had settled for behind-the-scenes influence, Eleanor Roosevelt was in some ways an independent political force. She held regular press conferences, to which only women reporters were invited; gave lectures; made radio broadcasts; and wrote a daily newspaper column. When her own arguments failed to persuade the president, she sometimes invited an advocate of her position as a surprise dinner guest. Eleanor Roosevelt's activism made her enemies as well as friends, and she sometimes was ridiculed in the press. But she broadened her husband's outlook and base of support as she earned a place in history alongside him.

In sharp contrast to Eleanor Roosevelt, Bess Truman and Mamie Eisenhower, her immediate successors, chose to remain in the background. Two more recent first ladies, LADY BIRD JOHNSON and ROSALYNN CARTER, followed in the Eleanor Roosevelt tradition of independence and serious involvement in political causes.

By the time her husband, Lyndon B. Johnson, became president at the death of John F. Kennedy in 1963, Lady Bird Johnson was an experienced political wife as well as the owner of a prosperous broadcast empire in Austin, Texas. In 1964 she set a precedent by campaigning on her own in the South for her husband, who faced serious opposition there because of his support for civil rights legislation. A tough but gracious southern woman, Lady Bird was able to win over audiences that might have shunned her husband. She pioneered what has become a role for many first ladies and candidates' wives, that of political surrogate. As first lady, Lady Bird took an interest in education policy and housing, but she is best known for her enthusiasm for national beautification. Her idea that planting trees and flowers and cleaning up unsightly areas would improve the quality of national life was integral to the environmental movement. Lady Bird traveled and gave speeches tirelessly to drum up public and private support for her program. Her lobbying efforts led to passage of the Highway Beautification Act of 1965.

Rosalynn Carter of Plains, Georgia, campaigned extensively for her husband Jimmy Carter, who was elected president in 1976. She became one of the most active and influential first ladies since Eleanor Roosevelt. Rosalynn Carter spoke and lobbied on behalf of her own interests, which included care of the mentally ill and elderly, the Equal Rights Amendment for women, and the plight of refugees. Beyond that, she was an adviser to her husband, meeting with him regularly to discuss policy, sitting in on cabinet meetings, and occasionally representing him on trips abroad. The extent of Rosalynn Carter's involvement in her husband's administration tested the limits of the first lady's role and provoked considerable public criticism.

One of the most glamorous and popular first ladies in history, JACQUELINE KENNEDY, steered clear of politics. Her youth, beauty, and aristocratic poise made her a media star during the administration of John F. Kennedy in the early 1960s. Known popularly as Jackie, she invited accomplished performers, such as cellist Pablo Casals, to the White House and worked to restore the historical authenticity of the mansion's decor. Her nationally televised White House tour in 1962 showed off both her refurbishing efforts and her charm. Jackie Kennedy was a constant object of media attention. Women all over the country copied her bouffant hairdo, pillbox hats, and tailored suits. She guarded her privacy and sometimes refused to attend official social events to spend time with her small children, but she attracted large crowds whenever she appeared in public.

NANCY REAGAN, another first lady who projected glamour, received a more mixed reaction from the public. At the beginning of Ronald Reagan's two-term presidency in the early 1980s, Nancy Reagan was criticized frequently for her expensive wardrobe, wealthy friends, and lavish entertaining. She became more popular after she took up drug abuse prevention as her special cause. Nancy Reagan did not campaign alone and emphasized her role as a loyal and adoring wife. Behind the scenes, however, she was known as a fierce protector of her husband's interests, who fired aides she did not like and occasionally tried to arrange the president's schedule to coincide with astrological forecasts.

Two recent first ladies who won wide popularity by projecting warmth and honesty as well as seriousness of purpose were BETTY FORD and BARBARA BUSH. Betty Ford, who had not always enjoyed the life of a political wife, came into her own as first lady, a job she assumed in 1974 when her husband, Gerald R. Ford, replaced Richard Nixon as president. Her willingness to speak frankly brought her considerable attention, and what she said was sometimes controversial. She strongly endorsed the Equal Rights Amendment for women and personally lobbied state legislators to pass it. Although that effort failed, Betty Ford also pressed for more women in high government positions and supported programs for the arts, the handicapped, and the mentally retarded. Her views generally were more liberal than those of her husband, yet her influence on him was considerable. The courage and openness Betty Ford displayed during her bout with breast cancer, which resulted in a radical mastectomy, won her admirers and helped focus attention on the problem.

Barbara Bush brought a cheerful, homey style to the White House when George H. W. Bush became president in 1989. The mother of five grown children, she filled the White House with her small grandchildren and made it clear that she was comfortable with the role of supportive wife. She had been active in volunteer programs for years, however, and she made literacy her chief cause. She spoke frequently on behalf of literacy programs and urged parents to read aloud to their children. Although she steered clear of political controversy, Barbara Bush campaigned effectively for her husband and showed grace under pressure. When President Bush became ill at a state dinner in Japan and had to leave abruptly, she quickly stepped in with a humorous toast that put the guests at ease and reassured the public about her husband's health.

The impact HILLARY RODHAM CLINTON had during her husband's first year in office was often likened to that of Eleanor Roosevelt. And like that activist first lady, Mrs. Clinton made enemies and incurred resentment. An intelligent and well-educated wife, mother, and successful attorney, to some Hillary Clinton epitomized the modern woman. She wrote a well-received book, *It Takes a Village,* about nurturing children, one of her causes as first lady. But she also wielded great influence as one of her husband's closest political advisers and headed the task force that drew up his health care reform proposal, a top priority for the first Clinton administration. In that role she traveled around the country meeting with health care professionals, interest groups, and ordinary people to hear their views on the nation's health care system. She consulted with members of Congress and testified before congressional committees on the president's plan, a rare occurrence for a first lady. In conjunction with the Whitewater investigation, in February 1996 she became the first sitting first lady to be subpoenaed by, and to testify before, a grand jury. Earlier she had answered questions from Senate probers about the 1978 land deal in Arkansas. In 2000, as the curtain fell on her husband's political career, Hillary Clinton began her own, becoming the first first lady to seek political office. She defeated Republican Rick Lazio for the U.S. Senate in New York.

LAURA BUSH took a less outspoken stance as first lady. Bush, a former teacher and librarian, focused on reading and education issues on the campaign trail and later in the White House. She disliked the limelight yet made public appearances to promote her causes. As first lady, Bush met with literary figures at the White House and in 2001 she initiated the first National Book Festival, which attracted 30,000 attendees. She followed up in 2002 with another festival. Laura Bush has continued to travel widely during her husband's second term. She maintained high approval ratings and often seemed to take positions more moderate than her husband's, for example, urging that a woman be appointed to replace Sandra Day O'Connor, and advising politicians that same-sex marriage issues should be treated with "a lot of sensitivity."

> **More on this topic:**
>
> *Daily and Family Life,*
> *p. 134*
>
> *White House, p. 573*

Ford, Betty

Elizabeth Bloomer Warren Ford (1918–), called "Betty," was the wife of President Gerald R. Ford. She grew up in Grand Rapids, Michigan, but moved to New York City in 1939, where she worked as a dancer and model. She returned to Grand Rapids in 1941, and the next year she married William Warren, a local salesman. Their marriage ended in divorce after five years. Betty met Gerald Ford in 1947 and married him on October 15, 1948. They had four children. Three weeks after their wedding Ford was elected to Congress for the first time.

Betty took on the role of political wife, but the strain of the demands on her forced her to seek psychiatric counseling in 1970. The Fords agreed that Gerald should soon retire from politics. In 1973, however, President Richard Nixon named Ford to replace Spiro T. Agnew as vice president.

By the time Ford took office, Nixon's role in the Watergate scandal was under scrutiny. When he resigned from the presidency on August 9, 1974, Ford became president. Betty Ford's outspoken honesty quickly brought her considerable attention as first lady. She strongly endorsed the Equal Rights Amendment, which was receiving faltering support in the (ultimately unsuccessful) drive for its ratification, and she personally lobbied state legislators for its passage. She also worked to increase the number of women in high government positions and backed other causes in the area of women's rights. She supported increased funding for the arts and for programs for the

Betty Ford was one of the most popular first ladies. By the 1976 campaign, buttons began to appear saying, "Betty's Husband for President" and "Keep Betty in the White House."
Source: Gerald R. Ford Library

physically and mentally handicapped. Her endorsement of the Supreme Court's position on abortion, her discussion of a hypothetical affair by her daughter, and her comments on her children's experimentation with drugs all caused controversy.

The courage and openness she displayed in her bout with breast cancer, which ended in a radical mastectomy, won her admirers and helped to focus public attention on that disease. Her influence on President Ford was considerable. He acknowledged the value he placed on her opinions, while she referred to the importance of the "pillow talk" she had with him over issues.

The Fords left the White House in 1977 and retired to Palm Springs, California. By that time Betty had become one of the more popular and respected modern first ladies. She was praised when she acknowledged publicly her dependency on drugs and al-

cohol (caused in part by pain from an inoperable pinched nerve and arthritis) and told of her struggle to overcome it. She received awards for her work in behalf of women's rights and against cancer, and she helped to establish the Betty Ford Center for Drug and Alcohol Rehabilitation in Rancho Mirage, California.

> **More on this topic:**
>
> First Ladies, p. 219
>
> Ford, Gerald R., below

Ford, Gerald R.

Gerald R. Ford (signature)

Source: Gerald R. Ford Library

Gerald Rudolph Ford (1913–2006) was the first person to become president without being elected either president or vice president. He served the unexpired term of Richard Nixon, who had resigned in 1974 over the WATERGATE AFFAIR. Ford was narrowly defeated for a term of his own by Jimmy Carter in 1976.

Ford was born on July 14, 1913, in Omaha, Nebraska. He was originally named Leslie Lynch King Jr., but his parents divorced when he was two. His mother gained custody of the child and moved to Grand Rapids, Michigan, where she married Gerald R. Ford in 1916. Ford, a paint salesman, adopted young Leslie, who was renamed Gerald Rudolph Ford Jr.

In 1931 Gerald Jr. enrolled in the University of Michigan. There he studied economics and political science and played center on the football team, earning his team's "most valuable player" honors in 1934. After he graduated in 1935, several professional football teams recruited him, but he accepted a position as boxing coach and assistant football coach at Yale University. In

1938 he was admitted to Yale's law school. He continued to coach to support himself and finished his law degree in 1941.

Ford practiced law in Grand Rapids for less than a year before joining the navy early in 1942. He was commissioned as an ensign and served as a gunnery officer on an aircraft carrier in the Pacific. He fought in several major battles and achieved the rank of lieutenant commander by the end of the war.

Ford returned to his Grand Rapids law practice in late 1945. He ran for the U.S. House of Representatives in 1948. With the support of Michigan's powerful Republican senator Arthur H. Vandenberg, Ford defeated an isolationist Republican incumbent, Bartel Jonkman, in the primary. Ford's district was solidly Republican, so he had little trouble beating the Democratic candidate in the general election. A few weeks before the election, Ford married Elizabeth (Betty) Bloomer Warren, a thirty-year-old divorcee.

Ford won thirteen consecutive terms in the House, always with at least 60 percent of the vote. In 1964 President Lyndon B. Johnson appointed him to the Warren Commission, which investigated the assassination of John F. Kennedy. The next year Ford was elected House minority leader, a post he held for nine years.

In 1973 Vice President Spiro T. Agnew resigned after being accused of evading income taxes and accepting bribes. When the vice presidency is vacant, under the terms of the Twenty-fifth Amendment, ratified in 1967, the president nominates a new vice president, who then must be confirmed by both houses of Congress.

I believe that truth is the glue that holds government together, not only our government but civilization itself. That bond, though strained, is unbroken at home and abroad. In all my public and private acts as your President, I expect to follow my instincts of openness and candor with full confidence that honesty is always the best policy in the end. My fellow Americans, our long national nightmare is over.

—Gerald R. Ford, Remarks on Taking the Oath of Office, August 9, 1974

Because the credibility of the administration had been damaged by Agnew and the unfolding Watergate affair, President Richard Nixon chose Ford, who had gained a reputation for honesty during his years in the House. Nixon announced Ford's appointment on October 12, 1973. After two months of scrutiny by Congress, Ford's nomination was approved 92–3 by the Senate and 387–35 by the House. He was sworn in as vice president on December 6.

The Watergate affair forced President Nixon to resign under threat of impeachment on August 9, 1974. Later that day Ford took the oath of office and declared that "our long national nightmare is over." He nominated former New York governor Nelson A. Rockefeller to be vice president. Rockefeller was sworn into office on December 19, 1974.

Ford's reputation for honesty, his friendly relations with Congress, and the public's desire for a return to normalcy led to an initial honeymoon with the American public. But Ford's honeymoon lasted only one month. On September 8 he announced that he was granting Nixon an unconditional pardon. Ford explained that the pardon was needed to heal the political and social divisions caused by the Watergate scandal. Although no evidence of a secret bargain with Nixon came to light, the pardon severely damaged Ford's popularity.

The most pressing domestic problems facing Ford during his term were persistent inflation and a sluggish economy. The president initially attempted to fight inflation by vetoing spending bills. In 1975, however, unemployment had become the more serious problem, and Ford compromised with Congress on a tax cut and a spending plan designed to stimulate the economy. Although inflation and unemployment remained high, the nation experienced an economic recovery during late 1975 and 1976.

In foreign affairs Ford continued Nixon's policy of seeking improved relations with the Soviet Union and China. Congressional restrictions on U.S. military involvement in Southeast Asia prevented Ford from giving military assistance to South Vietnam, which North Vietnam conquered in 1975. But when the U.S. merchant ship *Mayaguez* was seized by Cambodia that year, he ordered

More on this topic:

Pardon Power, p. 395

Succession, p. 483

Watergate Affair, p. 567

marines to rescue the crew. The operation freed the crew, but forty-one of the rescuers were killed.

In September 1975 Ford was the target of two assassination attempts. On September 5 Lynette "Squeaky" Fromme pointed a pistol at the president in Sacramento. A Secret Service agent disarmed her before she could fire. Fromme, a follower of mass murderer Charles Manson, was convicted of attempted assassination and sentenced to life in prison. Two weeks later, on September 22, political activist Sara Jane Moore fired a handgun at Ford as he was leaving a hotel in San Francisco. The bullet struck a taxi driver, who received a minor wound. Moore was apprehended before she could fire a second shot. She, too, was convicted of attempted assassination and sentenced to life imprisonment.

In early 1976 Ronald Reagan, the conservative former governor of California, made a strong bid for the Republican presidential nomination, but Ford collected enough delegates at the party's convention to edge out Reagan. Jimmy Carter, the Democratic presidential candidate, was favored to defeat Ford in the general election, and he did, even though Ford made up ground during the fall campaign. The Electoral College vote was 297–240 in favor of Carter.

After leaving the presidency, Ford retired to Palm Springs, California. In 1980 Republican candidate Reagan approached Ford about becoming his vice-presidential running mate, but the former president turned down Reagan's offer. After hospitalization in early 2006 for pneumonia, Ford's health began a gradual decline, and on December 26, 2006, he died at his home in Rancho Mirage, California. At the time of his death, Ford had lived longer than any other person to serve as president, living 93 years and 165 days.

Former Presidents

When George H. W. Bush left office in 1993, he became the nation's fifth living ex-president, joining Richard Nixon, Gerald R. Ford, Jimmy Carter, and Ronald Reagan. Their ranks were reduced to four with Nixon's death on April 22, 1994; again increased to five with the end of Bill Clinton's second term on January 20, 2001; and were reduced again to four with Ford's death on December 26, 2006. Only once before had as many former presidents been alive at one time: between March 1861 and January 1862. The five were Martin Van Buren, John Tyler, Franklin Pierce, Millard Fillmore, and James Buchanan.

Almost from the beginning, former presidents have been uncertain about what they should and should not do. Some, especially in the nineteenth century, remained in politics. The sixth president, John Quincy Adams, served eighteen years in the House of Representatives after one term as chief executive. Some ex-presidents have tried to return to the White House, but only one, Grover Cleveland, succeeded.

Some former presidents retired from politics but took on other government posts when duty called. Herbert C. Hoover accepted several assignments for President Harry S. Truman after World War II, including the direction of two special commissions to reorganize the federal government. One former president, William Howard Taft, became chief justice of the United States. Some ex-presidents, like George Washington and Dwight D. Eisenhower, enjoyed peaceful retirements. For others, contentment was marred by financial troubles. Presidents Jefferson, Madison, Monroe, and Jackson all died in debt. Ulysses S. Grant attempted to avoid that plight by engaging in shady business ventures.

Former presidents received no federal pension until Truman moved Congress to act in 1958. Truman, who bought his own train ticket to Missouri when he left the White House in 1953, complained that it cost him $30,000 a year just to answer mail and respond to requests for speeches and public appearances. He said he had turned down many business offers, but that if the government did not help out, he would be forced to "go ahead with some contracts to keep ahead of the hounds." The Former Presidents Act of 1958 gave ex-presidents (unless impeached and removed) a pension of $25,000 a year; a generous allowance to hire staff, office space, and furnishings in a federal building of their choice; free postage for nonpolitical mail; and a pension for their widows.

As time passed, Congress added more benefits. Ex-presidents who visited the capital could stay in a Victorian townhouse about a block from the White House set aside especially for them. And the federal government generously supported the LIBRARIES former presidents set up to house their papers and memorialize their years in office. By fiscal 2001

Attending the funeral for Richard Nixon in Yorba Linda, California on April 27, 1994, were President Bill Clinton and his wife, Hillary, and all the living former presidents and their wives: George and Barbara Bush, Ronald and Nancy Reagan, Jimmy and Rosalynn Carter, and Gerald and Betty Ford.
Source: AP

the total allowance for all former presidents and widows came to about $2.3 million a year. Secret Service protection was provided to ex-presidents for their entire lives, to their widows unless remarried, and to their children under sixteen. A last-minute directive by Bill Clinton before he left office extended Secret Service protection to his almost twenty-one-year-old daughter, Chelsea, and to outgoing vice president Al Gore.

Some of these benefits inspired some public grumbling during the 1970s, as expenses for presidential libraries and Secret Service protection skyrocketed. Americans wanted their former chief executives to operate with dignity but not to deplete the federal treasury. "They can make a million dollars or so a year going around and being ornaments and making dull speeches," said one member of Congress. "Let them pay their own office rent and let them pay for their own secretaries."

Although ex-presidents in recent years have mostly spent their time raising funds and planning for their libraries and writing their memoirs, beyond that their conduct of the "office of ex-president" has been as different as their presidencies.

Richard Nixon, who resigned in 1974 to avoid a Senate trial after the House voted a bill of impeachment over the WATERGATE AFFAIR, suffered ill health, financial reverses, and ignominy in the aftermath of his departure from the White House. He sold his homes in Florida and California, settling for a while in New York, then moving to other locations. The author of several books on international affairs as well as a best-selling memoir, Nixon began to emerge from seclusion cautiously during the 1980s. He gave reporters his views on the political scene from time to time and advised Republican politicians, including Presidents Reagan and Bush, on strategy.

Gerald Ford, Nixon's appointed successor, lost his bid to be elected president in 1976 and spent the next four years working toward a political comeback. When that failed, he set about making more money than he ever had before by accepting lucrative offers to serve on corporate boards of directors, giving lectures, and investing in real estate. He was criticized for endorsing a commercially produced series of presidential medals. Ford, who moved from his home state of

More on this topic:

Libraries, p. 335

Salary and Perquisites, p. 453

Michigan to California after his retirement from the White House, was often seen on ski slopes and golf courses.

Jimmy Carter, the one-term Democrat who defeated Ford, did not pursue business or politics after the presidency. He returned to his modest home in Plains, Georgia; resumed teaching Sunday school; and wrote a memoir and a collection of poetry. Carter also wrote books on the Middle East, on fishing, and, with his wife, on retirement. He volunteered his services for a wide range of public service projects, including building and repairing homes for the poor and monitoring the fairness of several Latin American and African elections. But his principal interest remained the Carter Center, which he established in Atlanta for the analysis of international public policy. In 2002 Carter traveled to Cuba, a country whose communist government the United States does not recognize diplomatically. Also in 2002 he won the Nobel Peace Prize for his efforts toward international peacemaking.

After leaving the White House, Ronald Reagan went back to California and George H. W. Bush returned to Texas. Both former presidents worked on books—Reagan, his memoirs, and Bush, a book on foreign policy with his former national security adviser, Brent Scowcroft. During his first year out of office, Bush traveled extensively, giving speeches throughout the United States and abroad. In 1994, in an open letter to the American people, Reagan revealed that he had Alzheimer's disease.

Whereas most former presidents left Washington, D.C., at the end of their terms, Bill Clinton followed in the footsteps of Woodrow Wilson, taking up residence in the capital. The relatively youthful and vigorous ex-president Clinton and his wife, Sen. Hillary Rodham Clinton, purchased a house near the vice president's mansion, along so-called Embassy Row; they also maintained a home in Chappaqua, New York. Clinton secured office space in New York City's Harlem district, after a small public tempest over his plans to rent in a more expensive area. As a result of the lawsuits and investigations that marked the Clinton administration, the Clintons carried millions of dollars in unpaid legal fees into their post–White House years. Clinton embarked on a busy speaking schedule, which took him to thirty countries during his first fourteen months out of office. He earned $9.2 million in speaking fees in 2001. Clinton also devoted considerable time and energy to planning and raising funds for his presidential library in Little Rock, Arkansas, and to writing his memoirs.

Fourteen Points   *See* WILSON, WOODROW; WORLD WAR I.

G

Garfield, James A.

James A. Garfield.

Source: Library of Congress

James Abram Garfield (1831–1881) brought impressive credentials to the presidency, having served as an educator, a general, and a prominent legislator. His presidency was cut short, however, when he became the second president to die at the hands of an assassin.

Garfield was born on November 19, 1831, in a log cabin on a farm near Orange, Ohio. When he was one, his father, Abram, died, leaving his mother, Eliza, to raise James and his three older siblings. In 1851 James enrolled in the Western Reserve Eclectic Institute (later Hiram College). After a semester the school hired him as an English teacher. He taught and studied there until September 1854, and then used the money he had saved to enroll at Williams College in Williamstown, Massachusetts. He graduated with honors in 1856 and returned to Ohio, where he became president of Western Reserve Eclectic Institute with its five-member faculty.

While presiding over the school, Garfield studied law and became known as an eloquent public speaker and preacher. On November 11, 1858, he married

229

Lucretia Rudolph. He was elected to the Ohio Senate as a Republican in 1859 and was admitted to the bar in 1860.

As a colonel in the Civil War, Garfield led a brigade to a dramatic victory over a superior number of Confederate troops at the battle of Middle Creek, Kentucky, on January 10, 1862. Garfield's success brought him a promotion to brigadier general. He participated in the Battle of Shiloh on April 7, 1862, before falling ill and returning to Ohio in July. In September Garfield was elected to the U.S. House of Representatives, but he declined to retire from military service. After the Battle of Chickamauga in September 1863, he was promoted to major general for his bravery.

Garfield resigned his commission in December to take his seat in the House. There his leadership on important committees made him a prominent Republican member of Congress. Garfield dramatically demonstrated his rhetorical skills on April 15, 1865, the day after President Lincoln was assassinated. When a mob threatened to avenge Lincoln's death by destroying the headquarters of the *New York World,* a newspaper that had been a severe critic of Lincoln, Garfield quieted the crowd with a short speech given from the balcony of the New York Stock Exchange. It concluded: "Fellow citizens, God reigns and the government of Washington still lives."

Garfield served in the House until 1880. During this time he supported the harsh Reconstruction policies of the radical wing of his party. While the Democrats controlled the House during the presidency of Rutherford B. Hayes, Garfield held the post of Republican minority leader.

At the 1880 Republican national convention the party was sharply divided over whom to nominate for president. The Stalwart faction of the Republican Party, headed by New York senator Roscoe Conkling, supported former president Ulysses S. Grant, while the Half-Breed faction backed Sen. James G. Blaine of Maine. The convention eventually nominated Garfield as a compromise candidate on the thirty-sixth ballot. In a gesture to the Stalwarts, the convention nominated Chester A. Arthur, a Conkling associate, for vice president.

Garfield faced Democrat Winfield Scott Hancock of Pennsylvania, a hero of the battle of Gettysburg, in the general election. During the campaign the Democrats tried to capitalize on Garfield's role in the Crédit Mobilier bribery scandal that had occurred during the Grant administration. The scandal had ruined several other politicians, but Garfield's relatively minor role had not crippled his career. Despite his unpopularity in the South, where he lost every state, Garfield won in the Electoral College 214–155. In the popular vote, however, Garfield received just ten thousand more votes than Hancock.

More on this topic:

Arthur, Chester A., p. 15

Assassinations and Assaults, p. 19

Death of the President, p. 142

Succession, p. 453

Once Garfield took office, his broad-based appointments and support for anticorruption measures angered Stalwarts. But Garfield had little time to pursue reform measures. On July 2, 1881, as he walked through the Baltimore and Potomac railroad station in Washington, D.C., on his way to deliver the commencement address at his alma mater, Williams College, he was shot in the back by Charles J. Guiteau.

Garfield was taken to the White House, where he remained for two months while doctors unsuccessfully probed for the bullet that was lodged near his spine. On September 6 the president asked to be moved to Elberon, New Jersey, in the hope that the sea air would help him recover. He died in Elberon on September 19.

Guiteau had been captured at the time of the assault and was put on trial in Washington two months after the president's death. At the time of the attack the assassin had shouted, "I am a Stalwart; now Arthur is president!" Guiteau, however, was not an associate of Arthur or the Stalwarts. The assassin believed his distribution of pro–Republican Party literature entitled him to a diplomatic appointment. Repeated rejections by the White House angered him, and he claimed to have received a divine vision instructing him to kill the president. Guiteau was hanged in Washington on June 30, 1882.

Garner, John Nance

John Nance Garner.
Source: Library of Congress

John Nance Garner (1869–1967) served as vice president during Franklin D. Roosevelt's first two terms. Garner aspired to the presidency, but Roosevelt's decision to seek an unprecedented third term in 1940 cut Garner off from his chance at the nation's highest office.

The son of a Confederate soldier, Garner grew up in Texas. He enrolled in Vanderbilt University when he was eighteen but dropped out soon afterward when he realized he was not scholastically prepared for college. Instead he studied law under local attorneys and was admitted to the bar in 1890. He opened a practice in Clarksville, Texas, but after two years he relocated to Uvalde, Texas. Through shrewd investing, he gradually acquired thousands of acres of land, three banks, and numerous businesses that made him a millionaire.

Garner served as a judge of Uvalde County and a member of the Texas House of Representatives before winning a seat in the U.S. House in 1902. He served in the House continuously until 1933, becoming minority leader in 1928 and Speaker on December 7, 1931.

In 1932 Garner ran for the Democratic presidential nomination. More than half of the delegates favored Franklin D. Roosevelt, but he could not muster the two-thirds needed for nomination. Garner, who was running a distant third behind Roosevelt and Alfred E. Smith, released his ninety delegates in an effort to end the deadlock that was dividing the party. Garner's move allowed Roosevelt to secure the necessary two-thirds majority. Roosevelt then supported Garner for the vice-presidential nomination. Roosevelt and Garner denied that they had made a swap, but they convinced few political observers. Nevertheless, they were swept into office by a landslide victory over President Herbert C. Hoover and Vice President Charles Curtis.

As vice president, Garner used his congressional contacts and experience to help push Roosevelt's New Deal legislation through Congress. Roosevelt and Garner were reelected easily in 1936, but during their second term their relationship soured. Garner was alarmed by the enhancement of executive power under Roosevelt and opposed the president's plan to increase the number of Supreme Court justices in 1937. Garner also believed that deficit spending on Roosevelt's New Deal social programs should be cut back. As a result, the president excluded Garner from many White House meetings.

More on this topic:

Roosevelt, Franklin D.,
p. 445

In December 1939 Garner announced he would run for president in 1940. When Roosevelt announced he would seek a third term, Garner denounced the president's decision. Roosevelt was nominated for a third term by acclamation.

After this disappointment, Garner quit politics and retired to Uvalde. He died on November 7, 1967, two weeks before his ninety-ninth birthday. He lived longer than any other vice president or president.

Gerry, Elbridge

Elbridge Gerry.
Source: Library of Congress

THE GERRY-MANDER.

A new species of *Monster*, which appeared in *Essex South District* in Jan. 1812.

" *O generation of* VIPERS *! who hath warned you of the wrath to come ?*"

THE horrid Monster of which this drawing is a correct representation, appeared in the County of Essex, during the last session of the Legislature. Various and manifold have been the speculations and conjectures, among learned naturalists respecting the genus and origin of this astonishing production. Some believe it to be the real *Basilisk*, a creature which had been supposed to exist only in the poet's imagination. Others pronounce it the *Serpens Monocephalus* of Pliny, or single-headed *Hydra*, a terrible animal of pagan extraction. Many are of opinion that it is the *Griffin* or

Classic cartoon of the gerrymander of Essex County, Massachusetts, from 1812.
Library of Congress

Elbridge Gerry (1744–1814) was a powerful political figure in Massachusetts who served as James Madison's vice president from 1813 until his death in 1814. Gerry was a signer of the Declaration of Independence, and he is remembered as the person from whose name the term *gerrymander* was derived.

Gerry graduated from Harvard and entered his father's importing and shipping business. His resentment of British efforts to tax American commerce drew him into revolutionary circles. From 1776 to 1781 Gerry served in the Continental Congress. After the war Gerry represented Massachusetts in Congress under the Articles of Confederation from 1783 to 1785. At the Constitutional Convention in Philadelphia in 1787 Gerry advocated strengthening the federal government but refused to back the plan that the convention produced because he thought it gave the federal government too much power over the states. After the Constitution was ratified by Massachusetts, Gerry put his objections aside and supported it. He was elected to two terms in the House of Representatives (1789–1793).

In 1797 President John Adams sent Gerry, along with John Marshall and Charles C. Pinckney, to France to negotiate a treaty that would head off war with that country. The talks were abandoned by the American side when the French demanded a bribe for French foreign minister Charles Maurice Talleyrand, a loan for the French government, and an apology for Adams's recent criticisms. Marshall and Pinckney left for home, but Gerry stayed in Paris until the next year. The bribery incident, which came to be known as the "XYZ affair," outraged Americans and ushered in several years of undeclared naval warfare with France. Gerry's Federalist opponents accused him of conducting an accommodating diplomacy with an enemy nation, but his reports of France's desire to avoid war contributed to Adams's decision to send another delegation to France in 1799.

When Gerry returned to the United States, he ran for the governorship of Massachusetts for four consecutive years (1800–1803) without winning—he was a Democratic-Republican in a traditionally Federalist state. Finally, in 1810 and 1811 Gerry was elected to consecutive terms as governor.

Before the Massachusetts elections of 1812 Gerry left a lasting mark on U.S. political culture. He signed a bill that redrew the senatorial districts of his state so that his party, the Democratic-Republicans, would be likely to win more seats than their actual numbers warranted. Because observers noticed that the outline of one of the new districts resembled that of a salamander, the unfair redistricting tactic was dubbed a *gerrymander*. The term continues to be used to describe a redistricting plan designed to benefit one party. Gerry had not sponsored the bill, but Federalists were quick to blame him for it. That year he failed to win reelection to his third term as governor.

Despite Gerry's advanced age and his defeat in his home state, his political career was not over. In 1812 the Democratic-Republicans nominated him as vice president on the ticket with President James Madison. He and Madison defeated DeWitt Clinton and Jared Ingersoll, who had formed a coalition of Federalists and maverick Democratic-Republicans.

Gerry fulfilled his constitutional duty of presiding over the Senate despite his declining health. During his vice presidency he was an outspoken proponent of the War of 1812. He narrowly missed becoming president in 1813 when Madison was stricken by a severe fever. Madison recovered and lived twenty-three years longer, but Gerry died on November 23, 1814, while still in office.

> **More on this topic:**
>
> *Madison, James, p. 350*
>
> *Vice President, p. 539*

Goldwater, Barry M.

Sen. Barry M. Goldwater accepting his party's nomination for president in 1964.
Source: Library of Congress

Sen. Barry M. Goldwater (1909–1998) of Arizona was the Republican candidate on the losing end of the largest presidential landslide in U.S. history. His overwhelming defeat by Democratic president Lyndon B. Johnson in 1964 appeared a certainty from the start. In the face of nearly impossible odds, Goldwater waged an uncompromising crusade for his conservative principles. "Extremism in defense of liberty is no vice; moderation in pursuit of justice is no virtue," Goldwater declared in his acceptance speech at the 1964 Republican national convention. The Democrats turned that and similar statements against Goldwater with devastating results, portraying him as a rash ideologue who should not have his finger near the nuclear button. He won 38 percent of the popular vote to Johnson's 61 percent and won only 52 electoral votes to Johnson's 486. Goldwater never ran for president again. By the time he ended his thirty-year Senate career in 1987, he had become an elder statesman of the Republican Party, respected for the forthrightness, if not always the content, of his views.

In retrospect, it seemed to many that the Johnson campaign had exaggerated the danger Goldwater posed to the nation. Johnson had run as the "peace" candidate, and yet he escalated the war in Vietnam and became so unpopular he did not run for reelection. Another reason for Goldwater's improved image

> *Those who seek absolute power, even though they seek it to do what they regard as good, are simply demanding the right to enforce their own version of heaven on earth. And let me remind you, they are the very ones who always create the most hellish tyrannies. Absolute power does corrupt, and those who seek it must be suspect and must be opposed.*
>
> —*Barry M. Goldwater,* Republican National Convention, San Francisco, CA, July 16, 1964

> **More on this topic:**
>
> *Elections Chronology, p. 174*

was his willingness to speak out during the Watergate scandal, urging President Richard Nixon to tell the truth and admitting that the scandal was damaging to the Republican Party.

Gore, Albert, Jr.

Al Gore.
Source: White House

Albert Gore Jr. (1948–) was elected as vice president in 1992 and 1996 on the ticket with Bill Clinton. Previously he had served eight years in the Senate and eight years in the House. During his service in Congress, which began in 1977, the Tennessee Democrat gained a reputation as a moderately liberal, detail-oriented lawmaker. He became an expert on the environment and many defense issues.

Gore was born in Washington, D.C., where his father, Albert Gore Sr., was serving in the House of Representatives. After seven terms in the House, Gore Sr. was elected in 1952 to the Senate, where he served until he lost reelection in 1970. The younger Gore graduated from Harvard and was an army journalist during the Vietnam War. From 1971 to 1976 he worked as a reporter for the Nashville *Tennessean,* writing investigative pieces and covering local politics.

In 1976 he won his father's former seat in the House, and he was easily reelected by the heavily Democratic district three more times. In 1984 Gore successfully jumped to the Senate, receiving more than 60 percent of the vote despite Republican Ronald Reagan's landslide reelection as president. Gore began to pursue the White House after settling into the Senate. In the 1988 presidential primaries he demonstrated appeal among his native southerners and among party moderates, and did well on "Super Tuesday," March 8. But he was unable to find a breakthrough state above the Mason-Dixon line, and eventually he suspended his campaign.

Gore was reelected to the Senate in 1990. He raised eyebrows in January 1991 when he broke with his party to authorize the use of military force against Iraq. His votes on national security matters positioned him at his party's rightward edge, but his overall pattern was decidedly liberal, particularly for a southerner.

A respected voice on technology development, the environment, and defense issues, Gore published in 1992 the book *Earth in the Balance: Ecology and the Human Spirit.* It reached the *New York Times* bestseller list.

Gore seemed an unlikely running mate for Clinton in 1992. He was—like Clinton—young, moderate, Baptist, and southern. He did not, therefore, bring demographic, ideological, religious, or regional balance to the ticket. Putting aside the traditional formula for picking vice-presidential candidates, Clinton chose instead to redefine the image of the national Democratic Party. Some thought Clinton's choice was a political risk, but in the end the voters opted for what Gore called a "new generation of leadership" and elected for the first time a president and a vice president born after World War II.

Although Clinton and Gore had had relatively few dealings with each other prior to the 1992 campaign, the two ran well together and won a sweeping electoral victory. During the first year of the Clinton administration Gore came to be one of Clinton's closest advisers. Clinton tapped Gore to oversee science, technology, and environmental issues, and used his expertise in dealing with

Congress. Gore headed a multiagency review that led to an administration proposal, known as the Reinventing Government initiative, for a major overhaul of the federal government. The vice president also unveiled the administration's plan to deregulate the telecommunications industry. His participation in a debate with H. Ross Perot, an outspoken opponent of the North American Free Trade Agreement (NAFTA), gave an important boost to the Clinton administration's campaign for congressional approval of the trade pact.

Gore's politically clean image was tarnished slightly in 1997 by unproven charges of misconduct in his campaign fund raising for the 1996 presidential election. He demonstrated his loyalty to Clinton by remaining steadfast in his support of the president during his impeachment investigation and trial in 1998–1999.

Gore was the widely acknowledged front-runner for the Democratic nomination for president in 2000. He defeated his rival, former senator Bill Bradley of New Jersey, in the Democratic primaries and faced Republican nominee George W. Bush, the Texas governor, in the general election. In an extremely close contest Gore won the popular vote, but he lost the electoral vote after the Supreme Court intervened and stopped the vote counting in Florida's disputed presidential election. (See BUSH V. GORE for more details.) Florida's twenty-five electoral votes went to Bush, who then became president-elect. Gore, who had been embroiled in legal wrangling with Bush for more than a month after the November election, retreated to private life.

Gore began to reemerge gradually in the later part of 2002, sparking discussion about whether he would challenge Bush in 2004. But in a surprise move in December 2002, Gore announced he would not seek the 2004 Democratic presidential nomination. Most recently, Gore resumed his work on environmental issues by promoting awareness of global warming in his Oscar award–winning documentary film *An Inconvenient Truth*.

More on this topic:

Bush v. Gore, *p. 57*

Clinton, William J., p. 101

Grant, Ulysses S.

Source: Library of Congress

Ulysses S. Grant (1822–1885) was the most celebrated Union general of the Civil War. His popularity led the voters to elect him president in 1868 and again in 1872. However, Grant's presidency was much less successful than his military career. His two terms were marred by corruption and scandal.

Grant was born to a tanner and his wife on April 27, 1822, in Point Pleasant, Ohio. Grant received an appointment to the U.S. Military Academy at West Point in 1839 through the efforts of his father. Grant's name at birth was Hiram Ulysses, but when he enrolled at West Point he reversed the order of these two names. The school, however, officially recorded his name as Ulysses S. Grant. Rather than correct the mistake, Grant adopted West Point's version of his name without expanding his new middle initial. In 1843 Grant graduated twenty-first in his class of thirty-nine.

Grant fought in most of the major battles of the MEXICAN-AMERICAN WAR under Gen. Zachary Taylor. He was recognized for his bravery and promoted to first lieutenant after the capture of Mexico City in September

1847. After returning to the United States in July 1848, Grant married Julia Boggs Dent on August 22 in St. Louis. In 1852 he reluctantly left his wife and children behind in St. Louis when he was transferred to California. Grant hated being separated from his family and drank heavily to ease his loneliness. In 1854, after a drinking episode, he was forced to resign his commission.

The next few years were difficult for Grant. He returned to his family in Missouri where he failed as a farmer and as a real estate broker. In 1860 his younger brother offered him a job as a clerk in their father's hardware and leather store in Galena, Illinois. With no better options, Grant accepted the salary of $800 a year and moved his family to Galena.

Civil War

Grant had worked in the store only eleven months when, in April 1861, President Abraham Lincoln called for volunteers to put down the insurrection in the South. Because of his military experience, Grant was commissioned as a colonel in June. He impressed his superiors and in August was promoted to brigadier general. Grant led a military campaign into the South in January 1862. On February 6 Grant's troops defeated Confederate forces at Fort Henry, Tennessee. Ten days later he won the first major Union victory of the war, when his forces captured Fort Donelson in Tennessee. In that battle Grant captured fifteen thousand Confederate soldiers. He gained a promotion to major general and achieved a national reputation.

In July 1862 Grant was placed in charge of all Union forces in the West. During the next twelve months Grant slowly maneuvered to capture the imposing Confederate fortifications at Vicksburg, Mississippi. On July 4, 1863, the Confederate commander at Vicksburg and twenty thousand troops surrendered to Grant. The victory gave the Union control of the Mississippi River and split the South in two.

In March 1864 President Lincoln promoted Grant to lieutenant general and appointed him general in chief of the army. Grant used his army's numerical superiority to fight a battle of attrition in Virginia against the main body of the Confederate army under Gen. Robert E. Lee. After a year of heavy fighting in which tens of thousands of troops on both sides were killed or wounded, Lee surrendered to Grant at Appomattox Court House in Virginia on April 9, 1865.

After the war Grant toured the South and issued a report advocating a lenient Reconstruction policy. In 1866 he was promoted to the newly established rank of general of the army of the United States. In 1868 the Republican Party nominated him as its candidate for president. Grant, whose war record had made him the most idolized person in America, received 52.7 percent of the popular vote and defeated Democrat Horatio Seymour 214–80 in the electoral college.

Presidency

When Grant took office, rebuilding the South was the primary issue confronting his administration. Grant supported the Reconstruction laws enacted by Congress after the war and the Fifteenth Amendment giving blacks the right to vote, which was ratified on March 30, 1870. Although Grant opposed blanketing the South with troops to guarantee the rights of blacks, he did respond with force to violations of the law. As Grant's term progressed, however, many northerners came to believe that federal attempts to keep southern whites from controlling state governments could not go on forever and were causing southern whites to use terror to achieve their ends. Grant, therefore, was less willing and able to rally support for an activist Reconstruction policy.

Grant pursued a conservative financial course. In March 1869 he signed the Public Credit Act, which pledged the government to redeem its debts in gold rather than paper money.

In foreign affairs Grant and Secretary of State Hamilton Fish successfully negotiated the Treaty of Washington with Great Britain. The treaty, signed in May 1871, provided for the settlement of U.S. claims against Great Britain for destruction caused during the Civil War by the *Alabama* and other ships built in Britain for the Confederacy. Grant was unsuccessful, however, in his attempts to annex Santo Domingo.

Grant retained his popularity during his first term and in 1872 won an overwhelming victory over Horace Greeley, editor of the *New York Tribune*. Greeley had been nominated by the Democratic Party and the Liberal Republican Party, a faction of former Republicans pledged to fight corruption and implement a conciliatory policy toward the South.

Like his former commander Zachary Taylor, Grant had no political experience before becoming president. Although he was honest, many of his appointees were not. Grant's administration, particularly his second term, is remembered for its scandals.

Before Grant's second inauguration, the Crédit Mobilier scandal was revealed. Grant's outgoing vice president, Schuyler Colfax, and incoming vice president, Henry Wilson, were implicated in the bribery scheme, which involved skimming profits from the construction of the transcontinental railroad. In 1875 a Treasury Department investigation revealed that several prominent Republicans, including Orville Babcock, Grant's personal secretary, were involved in the Whiskey Ring. This group had used bribery to avoid taxes on liquor. In 1876 Grant's secretary of war, William Belknap, resigned just before being impeached by the House of Representatives for accepting bribes. In his last annual message to Congress in 1876, Grant acknowledged that he had made mistakes but said that "failures have been errors of judgment, not of intent."

Retirement

Upon leaving office, Grant traveled in Europe, Africa, and Asia for two and a half years. In 1880 he was the preconvention favorite for the Republican presidential nomination. On the first ballot at the Republican convention in Chicago, Grant received 304 of the 378 votes necessary for nomination. But the anti-Grant factions had enough strength to prevent the former president's nomination on subsequent ballots. The convention remained deadlocked until finally a compromise candidate, James A. Garfield, was nominated.

After the convention, Grant retired from politics and moved to New York City. In May 1884 a brokerage firm in which he was a silent partner failed, and he was forced to sell much of his property to pay his debts. In August of that year he was diagnosed with cancer. He began writing his memoirs in an attempt to give his family financial security before his death. Although suffering extreme pain, Grant lived longer than his doctors had predicted and finished his memoirs four days before he died on July 23, 1885, in Mt. McGregor, New York. The two-volume *Personal Memoirs of U.S. Grant* sold 300,000 copies and earned Grant's widow nearly $500,000 in royalties.

> **More on this topic:**
>
> *Civil War, p. 95*
>
> *Ethics, p. 195*
>
> *Whiskey Ring Scandal, p. 573*

Great Depression

The Great Depression, which lasted from 1929 until the early 1940s, was both the worst economic crisis in U.S. history and a major turning point in the development of the presidency. It brought down one president, Herbert C. Hoover, and provided another, Franklin D. Roosevelt, with an opportunity to display the greatness of leadership that elevated him to the first rank among presidents. By the time the Great Depression was over, the presidency, along with much of the nation, had been profoundly transformed.

Hoover had the bad luck to be president when the economic boom of the 1920s reached its catastrophic conclusion in the great stock market crash of 1929. First described by economists as a temporary interruption in good times, the crash led to a wave of business and bank failures, joblessness, and a crisis of political leadership. But Hoover, who had once proclaimed that the end of

Breadlines became symbolic of the Great Depression. Shown here are people queued up in New York, beside the Brooklyn Bridge.
Source: Library of Congress

poverty was near, did not know how to cope with the crisis. Holding the conventional belief in the need for government economy and a balanced budget, he was unwilling to take the steps needed to aid the economy or even to show people that the government cared about their suffering. His popularity plunged, and he was defeated by Roosevelt in a landslide election in 1932.

Roosevelt actually had campaigned on a platform of government economy and a balanced budget. Once in office, however, he proved himself a master pragmatist, willing to consider almost any idea if it had a chance of helping the economy and restoring people's confidence in the future.

Roosevelt's first months in the White House were perhaps the most crucial. Taking office at a time when the financial system seemed on the verge of complete collapse, he moved quickly to stabilize the banking system and spoke directly to Americans with a message of reassurance. Within a few weeks he had worked a remarkable and enduring change in the spirit of the nation, banishing the despair and political paralysis of the Hoover years and replacing them with an ebullient national mood and a refashioned presidency. Almost overnight the presidency was transformed from a passive entity to the vivid focal point of national attention.

During a session of Congress known as the FIRST HUNDRED DAYS, Roosevelt also pushed through a series of bills aimed at dealing with the national emergency. In the years that followed, his New Deal program brought about massive economic and social changes, such as the Social Security program for the elderly and federal aid for the unemployed, disabled, and poor children. His program sought to help individuals and to counter the economic and social problems of the depression by, for example, helping workers to form unions to resist the relentless economic pressures on them.

Yet despite the government's efforts, the depression continued throughout the 1930s. When, after modest improvements, the economy began to turn down again in 1937, Roosevelt also brought about an important change in the government's economic philosophy. Drawing on the work of the British economist John Maynard Keynes, who advocated government spending to counter unemployment, Roosevelt and his advisers began using deficit spending as a way of stimulating the economy. The new approach to economic management, which in one form or another has guided federal budget policies ever since, helped bring about a reduction in unemployment. The Great Depression itself did not fully end, however, until the United States began massive military spending after its entry into World War II.

More on this topic:

Hoover, Herbert C., p. 263

New Deal, p. 383

Roosevelt, Franklin D. p. 445

Great Society

The domestic program enacted under the name of the Great Society by Lyndon B. Johnson and Congress in the mid-1960s represents one of the outstanding legislative achievements of the twen-

tieth century. A political backlash against the concept took place some years later, and some of the smaller and more controversial programs were eliminated, but the core of the Great Society in areas such as health care, education, and civil rights has endured and enjoys broad acceptance more than forty years later.

Johnson began his presidency determined to complete the New Frontier program of his predecessor, John F. Kennedy. His first accomplishment was passage of the Civil Rights Act of 1964, which was passed by the Senate only after an intense struggle. While Johnson was winning praise from liberals for his civil rights effort, he quickly made clear that this was only the beginning. In a May 1964 speech he outlined his plans for a "Great Society" embodying a reform vision of extraordinary scope. The term itself was borrowed from a book by a British socialist, Graham Wallas.

Johnson's landslide victory in the 1964 election gave him a "mandate for change" and an overwhelming Democratic majority in Congress. Backed by his unchallenged political strength, he quickly outlined a comprehensive program aimed at fighting poverty, ignorance, disease, and other social problems.

The Great Society rests on abundance and liberty for all. It demands an end to poverty and racial injustice, to which we are totally committed in our time. But that is just the beginning.

—President Lyndon B. Johnson, Remarks at the University of Michigan, May 22, 1964

Johnson and the Eighty-ninth Congress, which began in 1965, left an unparalleled record. In that year alone Congress passed eighty of Johnson's proposals, denying him only three. The measures passed included important policy departures such as Medicare, the health insurance program for the elderly; Medicaid, a federal-state health program for the poor; the Voting Rights Act, which sought to protect the voting rights of blacks and other minorities; the Elementary and Secondary Education Act, which provided federal funds for the education of disadvantaged children; and the War on Poverty, which sought to encourage social and community participation by the poor.

But the high tide of the Great Society did not last long. Opinion soon began to shift against poverty programs such as Model Cities and the Community Action Program, which often were badly organized. Rising crime rates and the great urban riots of the period made many people less sympathetic to the needs of the poor. Moreover, the growing strain over the war in Vietnam and the economic problems caused by Johnson's refusal to propose a tax increase to pay for the war and the Great Society eroded the president's support.

More on this topic:

Johnson, Lyndon B., p. 309

New Frontier, p. 386

Group of Eight

Since 1975 presidents have attended an annual summit meeting with leaders from other important industrialized countries. Each year a different member nation hosts the meeting. Until the May 1998 summit, held in Birmingham, England, the nations represented—Canada, France, Germany, Great Britain, Italy, Japan, and the United States—were known collectively as the Group of Seven or G-7. In 1994, 1995, and 1996 Russia met with the G-7 after each summit, an event known as the Political Eight or P-8. The 1997 Denver Summit of the Eight marked the first instance of Russia's full participation in everything except discussions of some financial and economic issues. At the 1998 annual summit Russia was confirmed as the eighth member, and the G-7 became the Group of Eight or G-8.

The purpose of these meetings is to give the leaders of the major industrial nations an opportunity to confer on broad issues of economic policy and to resolve their differences. The summits have focused attention on the international component of economic policy, forced politicians to develop a better understanding of international economic issues, created a justification for frequent meetings between finance ministers, and provided a forum where economic

MEMBERS OF THE GROUP OF EIGHT (BY SIZE OF GROSS DOMESTIC PRODUCT IN 2005)

Country	Date Joined
	Original "G-6": 1975
United States	1975
Japan	1975
Germany	1975 (west until 1991)
United Kingdom	1975
France	1975
Italy	1975
	Original "G-7": 1976–1997
Canada	1976
	Current "G-8"
Russia	1998

matters can be discussed in the broader context of allied relations.

Because the annual meetings compel the leaders to face one another, they have had a somewhat positive influence on free trade. The leader of a country that has erected protectionist trade barriers or taken other measures contrary to the interests of the group must justify those measures to the others and face their collective pressure to reverse the action.

Although the meetings usually concentrate on international economic issues such as trade and currency values, they often are used to discuss urgent political and security matters as well. In recent years the finance ministers also have called ad hoc meetings to address pressing issues, such as assistance to Russia in 1993 and terrorism in 1996. At the 2002 meeting, held less than a year after the terrorist attacks on the United States of September 11, 2001, terrorism was among the topics under discussion. The meeting was held amid tight security at a resort in Alberta, Canada. The remote location also hindered antiglobalization protestors, who had disrupted other recent international meetings.

More on this topic:

Economic Powers, p. 161

Summit Meetings, p. 487

H

"Hail to the Chief"

Sheet Music for "Hail to the Chief"
Source: Library of Congress

"Hail to the Chief" is the ceremonial march played to accompany the president's presence at most public events. Made the official presidential anthem in 1954 by a Defense Department regulation, the music is universally known as an announcement to the audience that the president has arrived.

The song has its origins not in politics but in literature. Around 1810, British composer James Sanderson set music to the words of Sir Walter Scott's poem "The Lady of the Lake" for a stage adaptation of Scott's work. The music used by Sanderson is believed to possibly have its origins as a folk melody used for rowing in the lochs of the Scottish Highlands. Scott's poem was popular, and after its 1812 debut in a theater in New York featuring Sanderson's melody, many versions of the tune proliferated through society, making it quite well-known.

MILITARY BAND.

Published by JOHN F. STRATTON, New-York.

HAIL TO THE CHIEF.

"Hail to the Chief" also includes lyrics by Albert Gamse that are rarely sung

Hail to the Chief we have chosen for the nation,
Hail to the Chief! We salute him, one and all.
Hail to the Chief, as we pledge cooperation
In proud fulfillment of a great, noble call.
Yours is the aim to make this grand country grander,
This you will do, That's our strong, firm belief.
Hail to the one we selected as commander,
Hail to the President!
Hail to the Chief!

Although the music did not become the official anthem of the president until the mid-twentieth century, it was performed as early as 1815 to honor former president George Washington's birthday. It was first played informally in a sitting president's presence in 1828 when it was heard at a ceremony attended by John Quincy Adams at the opening of the C&O Canal. Presidents Jackson and Van Buren had it played during their presidencies, and beginning in 1845 it was first used to announce the new president at James Polk's inauguration. Since that time it is common that immediately upon completing the constitutional Oath of Office, the newly sworn-in president is greeted with four "ruffles and flourishes" and the playing of "Hail to the Chief," usually by the Marine Corps Band. The tradition of regularly using the music to ceremonially introduce the president has its beginnings with the recommendations of First Lady Julia Tyler during her husband's presidency.

Hamdan v. Rumsfeld

The balance of powers among the three branches of government is the bedrock principle of the U.S. Constitution. In June 2006 the Supreme Court upheld that principle in *Hamdan v. Rumsfeld* (three conservative justices dissenting, Chief Justice Roberts not participating). The Court struck down a military tribunal system erected unilaterally by President George W. Bush, because it violated congressional legislation governing military justice: the Uniform Code of Military Justice (UCMJ) and Common Article 3 of the Geneva Conventions, a U.S. treaty obligation.

Hamdan was a driver and bodyguard for Osama bin Laden, the leader of al Qaeda, the group responsible for the terrorist attacks on the World Trade Center and the Pentagon on September 11, 2001. In the subsequent U.S. military action in Afghanistan, Hamdan was taken into custody by local militia forces, handed over to the U.S. military, and transferred to Guantanamo Bay for holding. In July 2003 Hamdan was charged with conspiracy to "commit ... offenses triable by military commission." Hamdan filed writs of mandamus and habeas corpus to challenge his prosecution by military tribunal. The Supreme Court granted certiorari, "[r]ecognizing, as we did over a half-century ago, that trial by military commission is an extraordinary measure raising important questions about the balance of powers in our constitutional structure."

The military commissions were established unilaterally by President Bush in a military order on November 13, 2001, to govern the "Detention, Treatment, and Trial of Certain Non-Citizens in the War Against Terrorism." Under the order the president retained exclusive control over the commissions within the executive branch, with no oversight by Congress or appeal to the judiciary. The procedures for the commissions, such as evidentiary rules and access to counsel, differed from those in the UCMJ and violated Common Article 3 of the Geneva Conventions.

The *Hamdan* case established that Congress has the authority to define the system of justice applicable to the military, even in times of war. The president could not establish alternative military tribunals, except in compliance with the congressional system enacted in the UCMJ.

The Bush tribunals violated the UCMJ, which requires procedural uniformity across different military courts "*insofar as practicable*," but the Bush administration failed to show that it would be impracticable to apply court-martial rules in *Hamdan*.

The UCMJ extends the president's authority to convene military commissions only to "offenders or offenses" that "by statute or by the law of war may be tried by" such military commissions.

The "law of war" includes the Geneva Conventions, which require a trial by "regularly constituted court affording all the judicial guarantees which are recognized as indispensable by civilized peoples." Since at a minimum a military commission "can be 'regularly constituted' only if some practical need explains deviations from court-martial practice, the Bush order establishing military tribunals violated congressional mandates. Although it did include the Geneva Conventions in its analysis, the Court did not address other judicial guarantees "recognized as indispensable by civilized peoples" or recognized in the U.S. Constitution, but chose to base its decision on the narrowest statutory analysis of the UCMJ.

Following the Supreme Court's constitutional check on the president's powers as executive and commander in chief in *Hamdan v Rumsfeld*, the Republican Congress acted quickly to pass new legislation, the Military Commission Act of 2006 (MCA), authorizing military commissions structured substantially in line with the president's previous orders. President Bush signed the act into law on October 17, 2006; thus the *Hamdan v Rumsfeld* result has been circumvented by Congress and the president. On remand from the Supreme Court's decision, Hamdan's case has already been dismissed under the MCA by a federal district court.

> **More on this topic:**
>
> *Rumsfeld, Donald H., p. 451*

> **"Trial by military commission raises separation-of-powers concerns of the highest order. Located within a single branch, these courts carry the risk that offenses will be defined, prosecuted, and adjudicated by executive officials without independent review.... Concentration of power puts personal liberty in peril of arbitrary action by officials, an incursion the Constitution's three-part system is designed to avoid. It is imperative, then, that when military tribunals are established, full and proper authority exists for the Presidential directive."**
>
> —*Justice Anthony Kennedy*, Concurring opinion in Hamdan v. Rumsfeld

Hamilton, Alexander

Alexander Hamilton.
Source: Library of Congress

Alexander Hamilton (1755–1804) was never elected to the presidency or any other office, but he did much to establish and solidify the office of the presidency. A veteran of the Revolutionary War, he attended the convention at which the Constitution was drafted and helped to persuade the states to ratify it. He was a leader among those who wanted their new nation to have a strong central government and a powerful president. As George Washington's Treasury secretary and most influential adviser, Hamilton was able to impose his Federalist views on the government during its formative years. His influence continued throughout Washington's two terms as president and the subsequent administration of John Adams; it declined when Thomas Jefferson, Hamilton's chief political rival, was elected president in 1800. Hamilton's life ended dramatically when he was shot by a political foe, Vice President Aaron Burr, in a duel instigated by Burr.

Hamilton was born in the British West Indies, the illegitimate son of a Scotsman. He made his way to New York as a teenager, fought in the Revolutionary War, and at the age of twenty-one won a command under Gen. George Washington.

Hamilton married into a wealthy and established New York family, the Schuylers, and became a wealthy New York lawyer and banker himself. Although he was instrumental in setting up the Constitutional Convention of 1787, Hamilton had little influence at the Convention. His arrogant, impatient manner was ill-suited to cooperative deliberation, and his views were too elitist. After the convention, however, Hamilton recruited James Madison and John Jay to help him write a series of eighty-five newspaper articles urging ratification of the Constitution. The articles, the majority of them by Hamilton, later were published as the *Federalist Papers* and became a classic of American political philosophy.

As President Washington's Treasury secretary, Hamilton presented Congress with a series of proposals designed to strengthen the economy of the new nation. This, Hamilton believed, would be the most effective way to establish a government that was respected by other nations and by its own citizens, many of whom still felt stronger loyalty to their home states than to their nation. Hamilton proposed that the federal government assume the Revolutionary War debts of the states, that tariffs and excise taxes be instituted to raise revenues, and that a national bank be created to exert control over the economy. His proposals were supported by northern commercial interests but opposed by agrarians and those who feared giving too much power to the federal government. In spite of this opposition, Washington backed Hamilton's economic plan, and Congress approved it.

Washington feared the development of political parties and tried to prevent it, yet before his presidency ended two factions had emerged: the Federalists, led by Hamilton, and the Democratic-Republicans, led by Washington's secretary of state Thomas Jefferson. Jefferson resisted Hamilton's efforts to strengthen the federal government at the expense of the states and opposed his preference for Great Britain over France in foreign policy. Hamilton and Jefferson were enemies, but Hamilton respected Jefferson. He did not respect Aaron Burr of New York, who was elected vice president under Jefferson in 1800. Hamilton had paved the way for Jefferson's election by the House of Representatives when Jefferson and Burr had accidentally received the same number of electoral votes. In 1804 Hamilton blocked Burr's attempt to be elected governor of New York. Charging that Hamilton had slandered him, Burr challenged Hamilton to a duel and on July 11, 1804, fatally shot him on the cliffs above the Hudson River in Weehawken, New Jersey. The Federalist leader felt compelled to defend his honor even though his son had died in a duel and he was opposed to the practice.

> **More on this topic:**
>
> *Burr, Aaron, p. 50*
>
> *Federalist Papers, p. 213*
>
> *National Bank, p. 372*

Hamlin, Hannibal

Hannibal Hamlin (1809–1891) was Abraham Lincoln's first vice president, serving from 1861 to 1865. He was dropped from the ticket by the Republicans in 1864 in favor of Andrew Johnson, who would succeed to the presidency after Lincoln's death.

Hamlin worked as a surveyor, printer, schoolteacher, and farmer before deciding to study law. He was admitted to the bar in 1833 and established a lucrative law practice in Hampden, Maine. In 1836 he was elected as a Democrat to the Maine House of Representatives. During his five years in that body he served three one-year terms as Speaker.

In 1843 Hamlin was elected to the U.S. House of Representatives, where he served two terms. Then in 1847 he was elected to the U.S. Senate. While in the Senate, Hamlin became an outspoken opponent of slavery. In 1856 his abolitionist sentiments caused him to defect to the new Republican Party.

The 1860 Republican national convention nominated Abraham Lincoln of Illinois for president. Republican leaders knew that Lincoln had little chance to win electoral votes in the South. Consequently, giving the ticket geographic balance meant choosing a northeasterner for vice president. The convention settled on Hamlin. Lincoln and Hamlin faced a divided

Hannibal Hamlin.
Source: Library of Congress

Democratic Party and won the election with less than 40 percent of the popular vote but a clear majority in the Electoral College.

Hamlin, who criticized the president's careful approach to emancipation, had little influence in the Lincoln administration. Hamlin disliked the vice presidency, not only because of his lack of power but also because the office did not allow him to dispense any patronage. Routinely, he presided over a new session of the Senate only until it chose a president pro tempore, after which he returned to Maine.

Despite Hamlin's misgivings about the vice presidency, he wanted a second term. Lincoln, however, believed that Hamlin's view toward the South had become too radical and did not support his candidacy. The 1864 National Union convention, a coalition of Republicans and pro-Union Democrats, nominated Tennessee Democrat Johnson to run with Lincoln.

In 1868 Maine again elected Hamlin to the Senate. He served two terms during which he sided with the Radical Republicans who advocated harsh Reconstruction policies toward the South. Hamlin retired from politics in 1881 but secured an appointment as minister to Spain. In late 1882 he returned to Maine, where he enjoyed a quiet retirement. He died of heart failure on July 4, 1891, at the age of eighty-one.

> **More on this topic:**
>
> *Lincoln, Abraham, p. 336*

Harding, Warren G.

Source: Library of Congress

Warren Gamaliel Harding (1865–1923), the first president elected after women received the right to vote, presided over a period of tranquility after World War I. His brief administration, however, was tarnished by scandal.

Harding was born on November 2, 1865, in Corsica (now Blooming Grove), Ohio. His father was a farmer. He graduated in 1882 from Ohio Central College in Iberia. He then taught in a country school, sold insurance, and worked briefly as a reporter. In 1884 he and two friends bought the *Marion Star,* a bankrupt, four-page newspaper. Harding bought out his friends in 1886 and gradually made the paper a financial success.

In 1899 Harding won the first of two terms in the Ohio Senate. He was elected lieutenant governor in 1903 but after two years returned to manage his paper in Marion rather than run for reelection. Harding gained national prominence in June 1912 when he delivered the speech nominating William Howard Taft for president at the Republican national convention in Chicago. Two years later, Harding was elected to the U.S. Senate.

More on this topic:

Presidential Greatness,
p. 414

Teapot Dome Scandal,
p. 493

As a senator, Harding followed the party line and avoided controversy. He frequently missed roll calls and did not introduce any important legislation. He voted for Prohibition and women's suffrage but against the Versailles treaty. Much of his time in the capital was spent drinking and playing poker. Despite his marriage to Florence Kling de Wolfe in 1891, he carried on a secret affair with Nan Britton, with whom he had a child.

At the 1920 Republican national convention in Chicago, Harding was one of many dark-horse candidates entered into nomination for president. After four ballots, none of the front-runners could muster a majority of support. Fearing a deadlock that would threaten party unity, Republican leaders decided to give the nomination to Harding, who possessed good looks, an amiable personality, and a willingness to take directions.

During a "front porch" campaign reminiscent of William McKinley's 1896 campaign, Harding promised a "return to normalcy" after the Woodrow Wilson years. This promise appealed to Americans, who had lived through a difficult period during World War I and were skeptical of outgoing president Wilson's internationalist idealism. Harding defeated James M. Cox in a landslide, receiving 404 electoral votes, while Cox managed to win just eleven states, all in the South, for a total of 127 electoral votes.

In 1919 and 1920 the Senate had rejected Wilson's Versailles treaty ending World War I because that body objected to U.S. membership in the League of Nations. Consequently, a separate agreement was needed to formalize the end of the war. In 1921 the Harding administration concluded treaties with Germany, Austria, and Hungary, officially making peace with those nations. In 1921 Harding also called the Washington Disarmament Conference. This meeting, masterminded by Secretary of State Charles Evans Hughes, produced a treaty that reduced the navies of the United States, Great Britain, France, Germany, Japan, and Italy.

In domestic policy Harding cut taxes on high incomes and signed the Fordney-McCumber Act, which raised tariff rates that had been lowered during the Wilson administration.

Harding's administration is known mainly for the scandals that were revealed after his death. He appointed to high government posts many cronies who used their positions for personal enrichment. Harding is not known to have participated in the crimes committed by his associates, but he did little to prevent the corruption. One of the most notorious scandals involved Secretary of the Interior Albert Fall, who leased government oil reserves at TEAPOT DOME, Wyoming, and Elk Hills, California, to private interests for a bribe. Fall was later imprisoned for his actions. Secretary of the Navy Edwin Denby, Attorney General Harry Daugherty, and Charles Forbes, head of the Veterans Bureau, also were found to have engaged in corruption.

In 1923, before the scandals were disclosed, Harding went on a speaking tour. In Seattle he was stricken with pains that were diagnosed as indigestion but may have been a heart attack. Harding improved, but on August 2 he died suddenly in San Francisco. His doctors suspected that a blood clot in the brain might have killed him, but his wife refused to permit an autopsy. The absence of conclusive evidence about his death and the later revelations of scandals led to public speculation that he might have committed suicide or been poisoned, but no evidence of an unnatural death exists. The news of Harding's death brought an outpouring of public grief. As details of the scandals of his administration became known in 1923 and 1924, Harding's reputation declined.

Harrison, Benjamin

Benjamin Harrison (1833–1901), a Republican descended from a prominent family, served one term as president before being defeated for a second term by former president Grover Cleveland. Harrison's grandfather, William Henry Harrison, was the ninth president of the United States, but

Source: Library of Congress

he died after just one month in office. Benjamin's great-grandfather, Benjamin Harrison, had been a signer of the Declaration of Independence and governor of Virginia.

Benjamin was born on August 20, 1833, in North Bend, Ohio. He graduated with honors from Miami University in Oxford, Ohio, in 1852. There he met his future wife, Caroline Lavinia Scott, who eventually died in the White House in 1892. After studying law at a firm in Cincinnati, Harrison moved to Indianapolis in 1854, where he soon became a respected lawyer.

In 1862, during the Civil War, Harrison was commissioned as a colonel. He gained a reputation as a disciplinarian and was unpopular with many of his troops. His unit fought well, however, and he was promoted to brigadier general in 1865.

When the war ended, Harrison returned to Indianapolis, where his legal skill, war record, and speeches on behalf of Republican causes made him one of the best-known men in Indiana. In 1876 Harrison received the Republican nomination for governor but lost a close race to James D. Williams. He presided over the Indiana Republican convention in 1878 and was chairman of his state's delegation to the Republican national convention in 1880.

In 1881 Harrison was elected to the U.S. Senate, where he chaired the committee on territories. In this capacity he defended the interests of homesteaders and Indians against the railroads. Harrison also was a strong advocate of Civil War veterans. He ran for reelection in 1886, but the Democrats, who had gained control of the Indiana legislature two years before, voted him out of office.

At the 1888 Republican national convention in Chicago, Harrison was nominated on the eighth ballot to run for president against incumbent Grover Cleveland. The primary issue of the campaign was the tariff, which Harrison promised to raise if elected. Harrison lost the popular vote but won in the Electoral College 233–168, with the help of a narrow victory in New York that gave him that state's thirty-six electoral votes.

Harrison was able to implement much of his economic program because both houses of Congress were in Republican hands. In July 1890 he signed the Sherman Antitrust Act and the Sherman Silver Purchase Act. The former outlawed trusts and business combines that restrained trade, while the latter required the Treasury to purchase large quantities of silver with notes that could be redeemed in gold. The silver purchase was inflationary and strained the nation's gold reserves, but Harrison and the Republicans resisted the more damaging proposal of free coinage of silver desired by many farmers and silver miners from the South and West. Harrison also signed the McKinley Tariff Act, which sharply raised tariffs as Harrison had promised during the campaign, providing protection to some U.S. industries but raising prices for consumers.

In foreign policy Harrison enjoyed several successes. His secretary of state, James G. Blaine, presided over the Inter-American Conference in Washington, D.C., in 1889 and 1890, which led to the formation of the Pan American Union. Blaine also secured an agreement in 1889 with Britain and Germany to preserve the independence of the Samoan Islands under a tripartite protectorate. He failed, however, in his attempt to annex Hawaii as a U.S. territory late in his term.

In 1892 Harrison again faced Grover Cleveland in the presidential election. Cleveland avenged his loss to Harrison four years earlier. The former president

More on this topic:

Electoral College, p. 185

beat Harrison by a vote of 277–145 in the Electoral College. Harrison returned to Indianapolis, where he resumed his lucrative law practice. Three years after he left office, on April 6, 1896, Harrison, now a widower, married thirty-seven-year-old Mary Scott Lord Dimmick, a niece of his first wife. He died in Indianapolis on March 13, 1901, from pneumonia.

Harrison, William Henry

Source: Library of Congress

William Henry Harrison (1773–1841) was a famous Indian fighter and the first Whig president, but he is best known as the first president to die in office and the president who served the shortest term—just one month.

Harrison was born on February 9, 1773, in Berkeley, Virginia. His father was Benjamin Harrison, a prosperous Virginia planter who was a member of the Continental Congress, a signer of the Declaration of Independence, and governor of Virginia. When William was fourteen his parents sent him to Hampden-Sydney College in his home state. Before graduating, however, he left for Philadelphia to study medicine under Dr. Benjamin Rush.

When his father died in 1791, Harrison left the field of medicine to join the army. He was commissioned as a lieutenant and assigned to Fort Washington near Cincinnati. Harrison was promoted to captain in March 1795 and was given command of Fort Washington late that year.

In 1798 President John Adams appointed Harrison secretary of the Northwest Territory. The next year Harrison traveled to Washington, D.C., as the delegate of the Northwest Territory to Congress. There he worked successfully for legislation that separated the Indiana Territory from the Northwest Territory. In 1800 Adams appointed Harrison governor of the Indiana Territory, a post he held until 1812. In November 1811 Harrison led the Indiana militia in a battle fought near Tippecanoe Creek against a confederation of Indians under the Shawnee chief Tecumseh. The battle was inconclusive, but it made Harrison a nationally famous Indian fighter and earned him the nickname "Tippecanoe."

During the War of 1812 Harrison was appointed brigadier general in command of the U.S. Army in the Northwest. Two years after the Battle of Tippecanoe, Harrison again met Tecumseh, who had formed an alliance with the British. At the battle of Thames River in Ontario, Harrison's troops decisively defeated the Indians. Tecumseh was killed, and the federation of Indians was broken.

After the war Harrison was elected first to the U.S. House of Representatives, then to the Ohio Senate. Finally, he became a member of the U.S. Senate. In 1828 Andrew Jackson appointed him ambassador to Colombia, but Harrison served there only eight months before returning to North Bend, Ohio, to manage his farm.

After witnessing the ease with which Democrat Andrew Jackson won two presidential elections, leaders of the Whig Party decided that they needed a candidate like Jackson, who was a war hero from the West. In the 1836 presidential election the Whigs ran Harrison, along with several other regional candidates, against Jackson's chosen successor, Martin Van Buren. Van Buren won the election, but Harrison won seven states.

Harrison's strong showing made him the natural choice for Whig candidate in 1840. Van Buren's hold on the presidency was vulnerable because of an economic depression that had begun

LONGEST AND SHORTEST INAUGURAL ADDRESSES

Longest Inaugural Addresses			Shortest Inaugural Addresses		
Year	President	Words	Year	President	Words
1841	William Henry Harrison	8,444	1793	George Washington (second term)	135
1909	William Howard Taft	5,428	1945	Franklin D. Roosevelt (fourth term)	556
1845	James K. Polk	4,800	1865	Abraham Lincoln (second term)	699
1821	James Monroe (second term)	4,461	1905	Theodore Roosevelt	983
1889	Benjamin Harrison	4,386	1849	Zachary Taylor	1,088

in 1837. The Whig campaign of 1840 was a study in political manipulation. Party leaders promoted "Tippecanoe" as a champion of the common people and war hero who was raised in a log cabin and liked to drink hard cider. Meanwhile, they portrayed Van Buren as the rich person's candidate who lived like a king in the White House. The Whigs buried political issues under a mountain of slogans, songs, picnics, stump speeches, and parades. The strategy worked, and Harrison received 234 electoral votes to Van Buren's 60.

Harrison's inaugural address, delivered on March 4, 1841, while hardly the most memorable in presidential history, was probably the most fateful. A driving rainstorm soaked Harrison as he rode hatless to the Capitol on a white horse, and the rain continued throughout his address, which was the longest inaugural speech ever delivered. Harrison caught a severe cold from his long exposure to the elements. On March 27 his condition deteriorated, and he was confined to his bed with what doctors diagnosed as pneumonia. He died on April 4, exactly one month after his inauguration. His vice president, John Tyler, became the first vice president to succeed to the presidency.

Harrison had married Anna Symmes on November 25, 1795, while he was an army lieutenant stationed in Ohio. They had six daughters and four sons. One of their sons, John Scott, was the father of Benjamin Harrison, who became the twenty-third president.

> **More on this topic:**
>
> *Death of the President,*
> *p. 142*
>
> *Tyler, John, p. 522*

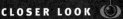

CLOSER LOOK

Harrison's inaugural address, the longest ever by a president, was 8,444 words, or over three times longer than the average inaugural address, and went on for almost two hours on a miserably cold and damp winter day. Harrison's address was over 3,000 words longer than the next longest inaugural address, delivered in 1909 by William Howard Taft. It is thought that Harrison's intention in delivering such a long address was to quell skepticism regarding his intellect and sophistication. Coincidentally, Harrison's grandson, Benjamin Harrison, delivered the fifth longest inaugural address at 4,386 words.

Hatch Act *See* CIVIL SERVICE.

Hayes, Rutherford B.

Rutherford Birchard Hayes (1822–1893) became president as a result of one of the most disputed elections in presidential history. He also was the second candidate to be elected despite losing the popular vote.

Hayes was born on October 4, 1822, in Delaware, Ohio. His father, a merchant who died two months before his birth, left a substantial estate. When he was sixteen, Hayes enrolled at Kenyon College in Gambier, Ohio, and graduated four years later in 1842 as the valedictorian of his class. He studied law for a year at a law firm in Columbus, Ohio, before enrolling in Harvard Law School. In 1845 he graduated and was admitted to the Ohio bar.

In 1846 Hayes began practicing law in Lower Sandusky (now Fremont), Ohio, but moved in 1850 to Cincinnati, where he established a thriving law office whose clients included several fugitive slaves. In Cincinnati, Hayes married Lucy Ware Webb on December 30, 1852. He joined the Republican Party when it was formed in the mid-1850s.

When the Civil War began, Hayes was commissioned as a major and given command of a regiment. He was promoted to lieutenant colonel in October 1861 and to colonel in September 1862 after he led a charge at the Battle of South Mountain, Maryland, despite being shot in the arm. In August 1864 he was nominated for the U.S. House of Representatives. When Ohio Republican leaders suggested that he take a furlough to campaign, Hayes replied, "An officer fit for duty, who at this crisis would abandon his post to electioneer for a seat in Congress, ought to be scalped." Hayes's devotion to duty impressed voters more than any campaign speech he could have made.

After being elected, Hayes still refused to leave the army until the war was over. In October 1864, after the battle of Cedar Creek, Virginia, where he was wounded for the fourth time, he was promoted to brigadier general. On June 8, 1865, Hayes finally resigned from the army to take his seat in Congress.

Hayes served two terms in the House before being elected governor of Ohio in 1867. He was re-elected two years later but declined to run for a third term. In 1872 he was defeated in his try for a House seat and turned down an offer from President Ulysses S. Grant of the post of assistant Treasury secretary. He retired to Fremont in 1873 and a year later inherited a large estate from his uncle, Sardis Birchard. Although Hayes did not seek the 1875 Republican nomination for a third term as governor of Ohio, he accepted his party's draft and was elected.

In March 1876 Hayes was put forward as a "favorite son" presidential candidate by the Ohio delegation at the Republican national convention. James G. Blaine of Maine received the most votes on the first ballot but fell short of the number required for nomination. Blaine's opponents recognized they had to unite behind a single candidate. They chose Hayes primarily because he was uncontroversial and free of scandal. Hayes was nominated on the seventh ballot.

Hayes's chances for election were weakened by the scandals of the Grant administration and poor economic conditions. When the votes had been counted, Democrat Samuel J. Tilden had beaten Hayes by about 260,000 votes in the popular election and, it seemed, by a vote of 203–166 in the electoral college. Republican leaders, however, challenged the results in Florida, Louisiana, and South Carolina on the grounds that blacks had been intimidated from going to the polls. If the nineteen electoral votes of these three states were given to Hayes he would narrowly win, 185–184. Republican election officials from the three disputed states disqualified votes from Democratic precincts and declared Hayes the winner. Democratic leaders from these states accused the Republicans of corruption and sent rival sets of electoral votes to Congress, which was left to deal with the mess. With no apparent way to determine who deserved the electoral votes, members of Congress struck a deal. Democratic members agreed to the formation of an election commission that favored the Republicans in return for secret assurances that federal troops would be withdrawn from the South. The commission voted 8–7 for Hayes, who was officially declared president on March 4, 1877.

As president, Hayes honored the agreement made with the Democrats to withdraw federal troops from the South. This move ended the Reconstruction era and enabled white Democrats to reestablish their political control over the southern states.

Hayes was well intentioned, but the stigma of the deal that had made him president, his quarrels with conservatives in his party, and Democratic control of the House from 1877 to 1879 and of the Senate from 1879 to 1881 limited his ability to push legislation through Congress. When Congress tried to stimulate the economy by minting overvalued silver coins, Hayes, an advocate of sound money, vetoed the inflationary measure. Congress passed the bill over Hayes's veto. The president's calls for civil service reform also had little effect. In 1877, however, Hayes demonstrated his ability to take decisive action when he dispatched federal troops to stop riots that had broken out in several cities as a result of a nationwide railroad strike.

> **More on this topic:**
>
> *Electoral College, p. 185*

When his term expired, Hayes retired to Fremont, Ohio, where he promoted humanitarian concerns and managed several farms he had bought. He suffered a heart attack while aboard a train and died three days later, on January 17, 1893, in Fremont.

Health and Human Services Department

The Department of Health and Human Services (HHS) is the cabinet department most involved in the health, safety, and well-being of U.S. citizens. The department's broad responsibilities include programs such as Medicare for the elderly and disabled, assistance to needy families, medical research, and food and drug inspection.

HHS was established in 1979 as the successor to the Department of Health, Education and Welfare (HEW). HEW had evolved in a series of presidential reorganization plans and laws that became effective between 1939 and 1953.

In 1939 President Franklin D. Roosevelt sent Congress his first presidential reorganization plan, creating a new federal office, the Federal Security Agency. Several existing programs were transferred to the new agency, among them the Public Health Service from the Treasury Department, the Office of Education from the Interior Department, and the independent Social Security

President Johnson, former president Harry S. Truman, and others at Medicare signing on July 30, 1965
Source: Truman Library

Board. In later years other programs were transferred to the agency, such as the Food and Drug Administration from the Department of Agriculture. In 1953 President Dwight D. Eisenhower submitted to Congress a reorganization plan that transformed the Federal Security Agency into the cabinet-level Department of Health, Education and Welfare.

Over the years the responsibilities of HEW increased significantly, especially when President Lyndon B. Johnson initiated his Great Society programs. Certainly the most dramatic development was the enactment of the Medicare program in 1965 to provide hospital insurance for the elderly, financed through the Social Security system. Also in 1965 a Medicaid program of aid to the poor for medical expenses was enacted. Existing programs were broadened as well.

HEW grew into one of the government's largest bureaucracies, triggering several reorganization efforts. The broadest of these occurred in 1979 when Congress voted to consolidate the education functions of HEW and several other departments in a separate EDUCATION DEPARTMENT, with the remaining HEW responsibilities vested in the renamed Department of Health and Human Services.

HHS has four operating divisions. The Administration for Children and Families advises the secretary on family support programs and human development services. Its programs include family assistance, community services, refugee resettlement, and child support enforcement.

The Public Health Service administers a variety of programs to protect and advance the nation's physical and mental health. Agencies within the Public Health Service include the Food and Drug Administration, Centers for Disease Control and Prevention, National Institutes of Health, Agency for Toxic Substances and Disease Registry, Indian Health Service, and the Health Resources and Services Administration.

More on this topic:

Bureaucracy, p. 44

The Centers for Medicare and Medicaid Services, formerly known as the Health Care Financing Administration, oversees the Medicare and Medicaid programs.

The Administration on Aging develops programs to promote the welfare of older people and advises the secretary and other federal departments on senior citizens' issues.

Hendricks, Thomas A.

Marble bust of Thomas A. Hendricks by Ulric Stonewall Jackson Dunbar
Source: U.S. Senate

Thomas Andrews Hendricks (1819–1885) was elected vice president in 1884 on the Democratic ticket with Grover Cleveland. Hendricks, an Indiana politician who had served as a governor, a U.S. senator, and a member of the U.S. House of Representatives, died less than nine months into his vice-presidential term.

Hendricks graduated from Hanover College near Madison, Indiana, in 1841. He passed the bar in 1844 and established a successful law practice in Shelbyville, Indiana. After serving in the Indiana legislature, Hendricks was elected to the U.S. House of Representatives in 1851. While in the House, he aligned himself with Democratic senator Stephen A. Douglas of Illinois. After Hendricks lost reelection to the House in 1854, President Franklin Pierce appointed him commissioner of the general land office, a post he held until 1859.

Hendricks ran for governor of Indiana in 1860 but was defeated. In 1863, at the height of the Civil War, he was elected to the U.S. Senate. During his single term, he was a leading critic of Abraham Lincoln. Hendricks supported appropriations to pay for troops, weapons, and supplies, but he opposed the Emancipation Proclamation, the draft, and many other wartime measures. After the war he worked against the Thirteenth Amendment, which abolished slavery, and the Fourteenth Amendment, which gave blacks the rights of U.S. citizens. Hendricks claimed that the black slave was "inferior and no good would come from his freedom."

In 1868 Hendricks again lost an election for governor of Indiana. In 1872 he ran for governor for the third time and was finally elected by a narrow 1,148-vote margin.

In 1876 the Democrats nominated Hendricks as Samuel J. Tilden's vice-presidential running mate. The presence of Hendricks on the ticket helped Tilden to carry Indiana and seemingly the election. The Republicans, however, disputed the vote in several southern states. An election commission that favored the Republicans gave the election to the Republican presidential candidate, Rutherford B. Hayes.

Hendricks was nominated again for vice president in 1884 to balance the ticket with New Yorker Grover Cleveland. Cleveland and Hendricks defeated Republicans James G. Blaine and John A. Logan by a vote of 219–182 in the Electoral College. As vice president, Hendricks presided over only a one-month session of the Senate called to consider Cleveland's cabinet nominations. Hendricks died in his home in Indianapolis on November 25, 1885, two weeks before the Senate was scheduled to resume its business.

More on this topic:

Cleveland, Grover, p. 99

Historians' Ratings of the Presidents

See PRESIDENTIAL GREATNESS.

Historic Milestones of the Presidency

During its two hundred plus years of existence, the U.S. presidency has been a constantly changing institution. Over the years its power and prestige have regularly risen and fallen in long cycles that reflect broader currents in the nation's politics and social and governmental needs. Within this ever shifting current, however, several turning points have helped to define the office for future years. These "milestones" of the presidency have been shaped by the personalities and abilities of the presidents and other leaders involved—and by the specific political situations of the day—as well as by long-term trends.

Creation of a Strong Presidency

One of the most significant decisions made by the Constitutional Convention was to create a relatively strong executive office with substantial powers. Because of their great fear of creating a new king to replace the one they had only recently overthrown, many of the delegates to the convention were initially inclined toward a weak executive office that would be subordinate to Congress.

During the convention a group of committed and talented delegates came together in opposition to the initial consensus on behalf of an executive office that was unquestionably subservient to Congress. This group worked diligently and effectively to persuade the other framers of the Constitution to strengthen the constitutional power of the presidency. The group was led by James Wilson, who envisioned the executive as a "man of the people," and by Gouverneur Morris, who regarded the executive as "the general guardian of the national interests."

The pro-executive group won on many issues during the months of debate. Among its victories were the decisions to make the executive a unitary office held by a single person rather than a committee, and to ensure that the president would not be bound by an executive council with power to control his actions. In addition, the president was to be chosen through an independent system, the Electoral College, rather than by Congress, and he was given the right to run for reelection. Moreover, the presidency was assigned a detailed list of powers, including those of military command, involvement in the legislative process, pardon, execution of laws, and control of appointments and treaty making, subject to Senate approval.

Washington Defines the Office

As the unanimous choice to be the first holder of the new presidency, George Washington was in a position to resolve many unsettled questions about the office by setting precedents for his successors on many issues.

The paradox of Washington's presidency was that while his awe-inspiring personality and popularity were an indispensable source of legitimacy and unity for the new government, they also were the source of great concern for those who feared that the presidency could evolve into a monarchy or tyranny. Many of the conflicts of Washington's presidency revolved around efforts to make strong executive power compatible with representative democracy.

But while he was careful to respect the rights of the legislative branch in many areas, Washington and his administration also established a critical precedent in favor of the view that the executive authority was held solely by the president. This view prevailed against competing philosophies of public administration, according to which either the Senate or individual cabinet officers would share fully in executive operations.

Washington's administration also saw the first full exposition of the view, advocated by Secretary of the Treasury Alexander Hamilton, that foreign policy was properly the domain of the president. Although that idea was bitterly criticized at the time, it became a main point in many twentieth-century views of the presidency.

Washington was less successful, however, in trying to create a precedent for the political nature of his office. He felt that the presidency should be a nonpartisan office, with the chief executive rising above the "factions" at that time forming in the nation. Since then, open party conflict has been a central aspect of the presidency.

Revolution of 1800

The partisan struggles that Washington had hoped the nation might avoid came to a crisis in the presidential election of 1800. In that year Thomas Jefferson and the nascent Democratic-Republican Party carried a majority of votes in the Electoral College. Unfortunately, under the system for vice-presidential selection then in force, Jefferson and his running mate, Aaron Burr, received the same number of votes, rather than one less for Burr as had been planned. As a result, the election was thrown into the House, where the Federalist Party still held sway. The Federalist leadership threw its support behind Burr, creating a stalemate that lasted for months before Jefferson was elected.

One major consequence of the deadlock was the approval of the Twelfth Amendment governing vice-presidential selection. In place of the clearly unworkable system in the Constitution—which had given the vice presidency to the candidate with the second highest number of votes—the amendment provided for a technically separate election of the president and vice president. By allowing two candidates to run together as a "ticket," the amendment effectively institutionalized the party system in presidential elections.

Jefferson's triumph also marked a critical realignment of forces in U.S. politics, resulting in the dominance of the Democratic-Republicans until 1824. Although Jefferson's party was opposed to the idea of a strong national government espoused by the Federalists, during its long reign it did not bring about any fundamental changes in the concept and institutions of the executive branch developed by Jefferson's predecessors. Perhaps the most important shift was a philosophical one, from the Federalists' view that the president's power derived mainly from constitutional authority to the Jeffersonian belief that the strength of the presidency also derived from its public support.

Jackson: Tribune of the People

The election of Andrew Jackson in 1828 marked a turning point in the nation's political alignment, governmental structure, and ideas about the presidency. The lines were clearly drawn between two factions of the old Democratic-Republican Party: the "new" Republicans, who espoused national development, and the traditional advocates of states' rights and a strict interpretation of the national government's powers. Jackson's victory represented the political triumph of "self-made" men from the South and West over the commercial and financial interests of the East.

The philosophy of the Jacksonians resulted in a much more strident assault on national institutions and programs than the generally more flexible Jeffersonians had undertaken. Jackson forcefully withdrew the federal government from the field of internal improvements, kept military power to a minimum, and focused fiscal policy on holding down expenditures. Jackson also dismantled the Bank of the United States.

Jackson's view of the presidency, however, was an expansive one. The Jacksonians had a concept of the president as the "tribune" of the people, a view that invested the executive with tremendous influence. Jackson's presidency marked an effort to establish a direct relationship between the executive and the people, challenging the status of Congress as the principal representative institution.

> *Many of our rich men have not been content with equal protection and equal benefits, but have besought us to make them richer by act of Congress. By attempting to gratify their desires we have in the results of our legislation arrayed section against section, interest against interest, and man against man, in a fearful commotion which threatens to shake the foundations of our Union.*
>
> **—Andrew Jackson,** Veto Message to the Senate, July 10, 1832

Tyler and the Succession Issue

The death of William Henry Harrison in 1841 after only a month in office provided the first opportunity to settle some of the ambiguities in the Constitution about the vice-presidential succession in the event of the death or removal of the president. When Harrison died, there was uncertainty about whether the Constitution provided that the vice president would become president and serve out the full term of the departed president, or whether it intended him to serve only as acting president until a special election could be held. But the vice president, John Tyler, quickly made clear that he considered himself to be a president in all respects, and the precedent has stood.

Polk Reasserts Presidential Power

The administration of James K. Polk represented a major assertion of presidential power, which enabled Polk to assume for his office kinds of authority that had been denied to his predecessors. Through a combination of shrewd political maneuvering and forceful statesmanship, Polk was able to overcome the centrifugal forces that were beginning to dominate U.S. politics during the late 1840s.

Polk asserted vigorously and effectively executive functions that reinforced, even expanded, the Jacksonian concept of presidential power. He was the first president to assume a routine and consistent influence over the major departments of the executive branch. Polk obtained the first presidential authority over the previously independent Treasury Department and took the first steps to coordinate the formulation of budgetary policy. In addition, during the Mexican-American War he forcefully assumed the role of commander in chief, showing for the first time that a president could run a war.

Lincoln's Wartime Powers

Abraham Lincoln made the last important contribution to the theory and institutions of the presidency during the nineteenth century. In the role of commander in chief he established important precedents that demonstrated the great potential of the executive to assume extraordinary powers during a national emergency. In some ways Lincoln even became a kind of benevolent dictator. He took many actions of highly questionable constitutionality, including suspending the writ of habeas corpus and establishing martial law in many areas.

Lincoln defended his actions on the basis of a conception of the Constitution and executive power that, while respectful of procedural regularity and formal legality, was concerned above all with the need to uphold the principles that were the foundations of the U.S. constitutional order. His regard for maintaining the integrity of the Constitution was clearly revealed by his cautious handling of the Emancipation Proclamation. He based it solely on his power as commander in chief to use it as a "war measure" to weaken the South: It freed the slaves only in the states in rebellion.

Impeachment of Andrew Johnson

The first time a president was impeached came in 1868, when the leaders of the Republican majority in Congress attempted to remove Andrew Johnson from office. (See IMPEACHMENT.) The move, which was formally based on charges of having violated a law prohibiting the president from removing officials who had been confirmed by the Senate, actually reflected the severe conflicts between Johnson and the Radical faction over Reconstruction policy toward the defeated Confederacy. The House passed a bill of impeachment, but Johnson was acquitted by one vote in the Senate.

Gutzon Borglum honored George Washington, Thomas Jefferson, Theodore Roosevelt, and Abraham Lincoln by sculpting their faces into Mount Rushmore in South Dakota.
Source: National Park Service

The impeachment trial threatened not only Johnson's presidency but also the independence of the executive office. The Republican leadership did all it could to bring public pressure on senators to vote to convict Johnson, despite fears that removing him from office would destroy the constitutional system of checks and balances. If Johnson had been convicted under such conditions, the presidency might have suffered irreparable damage to its power and prestige.

Hayes's Battle over Patronage

By the end of the corruption-ridden administration of Ulysses S. Grant, the presidency had reached a low ebb. The Senate seemed to have achieved a secure mastery over the power of the executive. But the administration of Rutherford B. Hayes was marked by a persistent and effective defense of the prerogatives of presidential power for the first time since the Civil War.

The pivotal incident in Hayes's battle to reassert presidential authority came in a dispute with the Senate over patronage—the power to appoint holders of federal offices, including such potentially lucrative positions as customs inspectors. For more than a year Hayes's attempt to replace three customs officials in New York City was blocked by powerful senators, notably Roscoe Conkling of New York. During this time the president was virtually helpless as the administrative head of government. Hayes finally won in the Senate, however, and his triumph restored some of the executive powers that had been lost since Lincoln.

Theodore Roosevelt and the Expansion of Executive Power

The next major shift in thinking about presidential authority and responsibility came under Theodore Roosevelt. In both foreign and domestic matters Roosevelt extended executive authority as far as the Constitution would allow. He also believed that the president possessed a special mandate from the people. But

Theodore Roosevelt speaking at Carnegie Hall
Source: Library of Congress

unlike Andrew Jackson, who had developed a similar view, Roosevelt advocated the unprecedented expansion of the national government's responsibility to secure the social and economic welfare of the people.

Roosevelt's determination to use the executive office to serve the interests of the people brought about significant changes in the conduct of the executive office. Arguably, the most important of these changes was the advancement of the president's role as the leader of public opinion. Roosevelt's administration marked the advent of the "rhetorical presidency," or the use of public speeches as a tool of presidential governing.

The rise of the rhetorical presidency under Roosevelt went hand in hand with an expansion of the executive's responsibility to provide guidance in the formation of public policy. Roosevelt's presidency resulted in a fundamental shift of federal power from Congress to the White House. In addition, Roosevelt took action to assert the primacy of the president's role in foreign affairs over that of the legislature in executing such policy. He engineered a revolution in Panama that cleared the way for construction of the Panama Canal and helped to negotiate an end to the Russo-Japanese War of 1905.

Wilson and Popular Leadership

Woodrow Wilson came into office with a well-developed theory about presidential power. Although he agreed with Theodore Roosevelt that the president must focus more attention on national problems, he also believed that such leadership would be ineffective or dangerous unless accompanied by a fundamental change in government arrangements. This change would be marked by combining the usually separated branches of government. Thus presidential leadership and practices had to be recast so as to lower the wall between the executive and legislative branches in the formulation and adoption of public policy. Most significantly, it was necessary to strengthen the role of the president as party leader so that the executive as the leader of national opinion could fuse the executive and legislative branches in his own person.

As president, Wilson acted both to perfect the methods of popular leadership already developed by Roosevelt and to apply them so as to establish leadership of Congress and achieve mastery over the Democratic Party. Wilson was not completely successful, but historians believe that his expansion and perfection of presidential powers were his most lasting contribution. Symbolic of his effort to exert greater leadership over Congress was his decision to deliver his annual State of the Union address in person before both houses of Congress, instead of sending a written message as every president since Jefferson had done.

By the end of his term Wilson had largely transformed the U.S. presidency. His leadership consolidated and extended Roosevelt's achievements. The Constitution had not been formally amended, but its powers as they pertained to the presidency had new meaning.

Franklin D. Roosevelt's "First Hundred Days"

Franklin D. Roosevelt achieved one of the most dramatic and successful displays of presidential leadership during the first few weeks of his administration. Coming into office in the midst of a financial panic caused by the Great Depression, he managed through a series of policy moves and public speeches to stabilize the banking industry and change the public mood from despair to optimism. Almost overnight the office of the chief executive was transformed from the passive entity it had been since Wilson to a vivid focal point of national attention. At the same time, Roosevelt pushed through Congress an unprecedented string of reform and economic revival bills during a session that became known as the FIRST HUNDRED DAYS.

Roosevelt's subsequent years in office brought about a fundamental expansion of the role of the federal government in American life and a basic transformation in the office of the presidency. With its greatly increased responsibilities as the source of moral leadership, legislative guidance, and public policy, the White House needed much greater resources in terms of staffing and budgets. The White House organization that developed under Roosevelt became the institutional basis of the modern presidency.

Roosevelt's tenure also represented a major, but only temporary, change in thinking about the proper length of a president's time in office. As his second term was ending in 1940, when World War II was already under way and most people thought the United States might be drawn into the conflict, Roosevelt decided to try to break the precedent set by George Washington and to seek a third term. He won both a third and a fourth term, but the nation decided a few years after his death that two terms would be enough for any president in the future. The Twenty-second Amendment was adopted in 1951.

Kennedy and "Camelot"

Although his presidency lasted less than three years before he was assassinated in 1963, John F. Kennedy found a lasting place in U.S. history. His presidency became part of a myth embraced by many people, as reflected in the use of the name Camelot, location of the legendary King Arthur's court, to describe Kennedy's White House. The persistence of Kennedy's popularity is due in part to his tragic death and in part to his inspirational qualities as president. His inaugural address set the tone for his administration with its stirring call to Americans, "Ask not what your country can do for you; ask what you can do for your country."

Kennedy's administration also marked a revolutionary advance in the use of television in politics. Particularly in televised press conferences, of which he was a master, Kennedy used the electronic media as a way of reaching the public over the heads of Congress and the print media. Moreover, his use of the "personal" presidency, in which his own family played a major role, undercut the traditional party structure and helped to bring about a greater concentration of policy responsibility in the executive office.

Watergate Brings Nixon Down

The low point in the history of the modern presidency came during the Watergate crisis. In its aftermath Richard Nixon became the first president in U.S. history to resign his office. The efforts of Nixon and his aides to block an investigation of a break-in at the offices of the Democratic National Committee in the Watergate complex in Washington, D.C., led to the most severe political crisis of the postwar era. Nixon's impeachment was ensured when the Supreme Court in a landmark case rejected Nixon's sweeping claims of executive privilege and forced him to release Oval Office tapes revealing that the president had known all along about the cover-up. Before he could be impeached, Nixon resigned, bringing his office to a nadir of public respect and trust.

Reagan, the Great Communicator

After the problems of diminished presidential power faced by Nixon's successors, Gerald R. Ford and Jimmy Carter, Ronald Reagan brought about a renewal of the prestige and popularity of the presidency. Using his unrivaled ability to reach the American people through televised speeches—he was dubbed the Great Communicator—Reagan was able to push much of his initial legislative program through Congress, easily win reelection, and retire as the most popular president in a half-century.

The Reagan presidency marked the resumption of the trend in modern presidential leadership to concentrate power in the White House, a trend that had been suspended in the wake of the Vietnam War and the Watergate scandal. Moreover, Reagan dramatically confirmed the acceptance by conservatives of the need to centralize power in order to carry out their objectives. Although the White House's attempt to circumvent congressional restrictions on foreign policy, in the Iran-contra affair, was a major political embarrassment to the administration, Reagan in many other areas was able to strengthen the "administrative presidency" begun by Nixon as a way of bypassing the Democratic-controlled Congress.

The crew of the space shuttle Challenger *honored us by the manner in which they lived their lives. We will never forget them, nor the last time we saw them, this morning, as they prepared for their journey and waved goodbye and "slipped the surly bonds of Earth" to "touch the face of God."*

—*Ronald Reagan,* Address to the Nation on the Explosion of the Space Shuttle Challenger, January 28, 1986

Impeachment of Bill Clinton

Bill Clinton, a Democrat elected in 1992 and 1996, was a gifted politician who created strong feelings, positive and negative, among the public. Presiding at a time of increased economic prosperity, Clinton nevertheless became one of the more controversial recent presidents. He was impeached by the Republican-controlled House in 1998 but acquitted in 1999 by the GOP-controlled Senate of charges that he committed perjury and obstructed justice in an effort to cover up an affair with a young White House intern, Monica Lewinsky. Clinton's detractors criticized him for demeaning the office of the presidency, while his supporters railed against the Republicans in Congress for pushing the impeachment process forward.

> **More on this topic:**
>
> *Impeachment, p. 273*

Hobart, Garret A.

Garret Augustus Hobart (1844–1899) was the last vice president of the nineteenth century, serving under William McKinley from 1897 until his death in 1899. Although he had never held national office before becoming vice president, Hobart had a keen understanding of national political issues and became one of McKinley's closest friends and advisers. The press often referred to Hobart as the "Assistant President."

Hobart graduated with honors from Rutgers College in New Jersey in 1863. He taught school briefly before moving to Paterson, New Jersey, to work in a law office. In 1869 he was admitted to the bar.

After serving as Paterson city counsel in 1871, Hobart entered state politics and in 1872 was elected to the state assembly as a Republican. He became Speaker in 1874 at the age of thirty. Two years later he won election to the state senate, where he served two three-year terms. Hobart left the state senate in 1882 but continued to be a leading figure in New Jersey politics.

Despite Hobart's involvement in politics, most of his energies were devoted to his legal and business careers. He served as president of the Passaic, New Jersey, water company and was director of several banks. By the time he entered national politics he had amassed a fortune.

Marble bust of Garret A. Hobart by Frank Edwin Elwell
Source: U.S. Senate

In 1896 the Democrats nominated William Jennings Bryan for president. The Republicans countered with William McKinley of Ohio and announced a conservative platform that advocated the gold standard. Republican Party leaders wanted for vice president a candidate from the East who was a known supporter of gold. They found their man in Hobart. In his acceptance speech at the Republican national convention in St. Louis, Hobart uttered one of the most famous political statements of his era: "An honest dollar, worth 100 cents everywhere, cannot be coined out of 53 cents of silver, plus a legislative fiat." The Republicans won the 1896 election by a vote of 271–176 in the Electoral College.

As vice president, Hobart became a respected national Republican leader and a major player in Washington politics. He was said to preside over the Senate with energy and fairness. In the spring of 1899, however, he became ill. He left the capital to recuperate in New Jersey but died at his home in Paterson in November with more than fifteen months left in his term. Hobart received moving eulogies in the nation's newspapers, and his funeral was attended by President McKinley and many other top government officials.

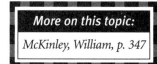

More on this topic:

McKinley, William, p. 347

Homeland Security Department

When President George W. Bush signed a bill in late 2002 creating a Department of Homeland Security (DHS), it marked the biggest reorganization of the federal government since the late 1940s. The new department was conceived in the wake of the terrorist attacks on the United States of September 11, 2001, when government leaders decided a more coordinated effort was needed to protect the country.

Bush had called for the creation of the department in June 2002. Likening his plan to the 1947 National Security Act, which authorized President Harry S. Truman to create the National Security Council and the Department of Defense, Bush asked Congress to create "a single, permanent department with an overriding and urgent mission: securing the homeland of America, and protecting the American people."

The president at first had resisted the idea of creating another department of government, opting instead to create a White House Office of Homeland Security, headed by former Pennsylvania governor Thomas J. Ridge. Ridge was to identify priorities in homeland security and direct the agencies responsible for solving problems. This approach, as the administration first saw it, was preferable to creating a new department to take over the work of existing agencies.

Bush, facing criticism about whether his administration did everything possible to avoid the September 11 attacks and had taken adequate measures to avoid future ones, eventually embraced the idea of a new cabinet department. Ridge's Office of Homeland Security appeared to have inadequate control over the budgets and activities of agencies he was responsible for coordinating. The president's plan, which placed a huge swath of the executive branch, including the Customs Service, Secret Service, Coast Guard, Immigration and Naturalization Service, Federal Emergency

Management Agency (FEMA), and Transportation Security Administration in the new department, aimed to endow a cabinet secretary with more authority to coordinate the activities of agencies that share responsibility for protecting the homeland.

The new department, which began operations March 1, 2003, is divided into four major directorates. Border and Transportation Security brings together the major border security and transportation operations. Among other agencies it includes the U.S. Customs Service, formerly part of the Treasury Department. The Customs Service collects revenue from imports and enforces customs and related laws. It also administers the 1930 Tariff Act. As the principal border enforcement agency, the service's mission has been extended over the years to assisting in the administration and enforcement of safety standards on be-

President George W. Bush greets Thomas J. Ridge, secretary of the new Department of Homeland Security, during a welcome ceremony for the employees on February 28, 2003.
Source: Reuters

half of other government agencies. The Transportation Security Administration, a relatively new agency created as a result of the plane hijackings of September 11, 2001, oversees airport baggage screening. It was transferred to DHS from the Department of Transportation. Also within this directorate is the Immigration and Naturalization Service, formerly part of the Department of Justice. It is now known as the Bureau of Citizenship and Immigration Services (BCIS).

The Emergency Preparedness and Response directorate oversees domestic disaster preparedness training and coordinates government disaster response. Among other agencies, it includes FEMA, which has responsibility for "responding to, planning for, recovering from and mitigating against disaster." Its mandate was soon put to the test. In August and September 2005, FEMA, facing its first major crisis under the new department, suffered heavy criticism for the way it responded to Hurricane Katrina, especially its refusal to allow private relief efforts, its slow response, and poor coordination practices. Particularly singled out for rebuke was FEMA director Michael Brown and Ridge's successor, Secretary of Homeland Security Michael Chertoff. Both men were widely perceived to be oblivious to the refugee problem in New Orleans. This incident made many Americans question whether the new department was truly prepared to manage another terrorist attack on a major city.

The other two directorates are Science and Technology, which seeks to utilize all scientific and technological advantages in protecting the United States, and Information Analysis and Infrastructure Protection, which analyzes intelligence and information from other agencies (including the Central Intelligence Agency and the Federal Bureau of Investigation) involving threats to homeland security and evaluates vulnerabilities in the nation's infrastructure.

The U.S. SECRET SERVICE was created to halt counterfeiting operations. Reporting directly to the secretary of DHS, it continues to pursue that goal, but its best-known function is executive protection, which it assumed after the assassination of President

More on this topic:

Hurricane Katrina, p. 269

William McKinley in 1901. The Federal Law Enforcement Training Center, located in Georgia, is an interagency training facility serving federal law enforcement organizations both within and outside the Treasury Department.

The U.S. Coast Guard, among other things, conducts search and rescue missions, enforces U.S. maritime laws, and investigates and cleans up oil spills. After September 11, the Coast Guard took on a larger role in ensuring port security. It too reports directly to the DHS secretary.

Honeymoon Period

New presidents begin their tenure in office with a high level of public support and trust. For a few weeks or months the president and the public are joined in the hope that the new administration can bring peace and prosperity to the nation. This period of good feeling is referred to as the "honeymoon."

For a new administration the honeymoon period may be the best time to pass difficult legislation. No other president is likely to match the achievements of Franklin D. Roosevelt's FIRST HUNDRED DAYS, when Congress approved dozens of New Deal measures that Roosevelt proposed in response to the crisis of the Great Depression.

Other presidents have enjoyed significant victories during their first months in office. Ronald Reagan experienced a two-stage honeymoon. During the first stage in the very earliest days of his first administration, his presidency was widely perceived as a personal success. This stage began with the release of fifty-two U.S. hostages from Iran just as Reagan was taking the oath of office. The second stage followed the assassination attempt on March 30, 1981, and helped Reagan to push his proposals for massive cuts in spending and taxes through Congress.

Although a nation in mourning did not call it a honeymoon period, in the months after John F. Kennedy's assassination Lyndon B. Johnson was able to win enactment of some Kennedy initiatives as a memorial to the slain leader. Most notable was the Civil Rights Act of 1964, which was considerably stronger than the Kennedy bill that had stalled in Congress before his death.

Elected in his own right in 1964, Johnson succeeded in having many of the most important elements of his Great Society enacted in 1965 and 1966 before the growing unpopularity of the Vietnam War undermined his effectiveness with Congress and the public.

Gerald R. Ford learned just how fickle public opinion could be. Ford succeeded to the presidency when Richard Nixon resigned in 1974 to escape almost certain impeachment and removal from office. Ford was the first president who was not elected as either president or vice president. His honest reputation, his friendly relations with Congress, and the public's desire for a return to normalcy led to an initial honeymoon with the public. But the honeymoon ended when he pardoned Nixon for any crimes that the former president might have committed in connection with the Watergate affair and offered conditional amnesty to Vietnam draft evaders and war deserters.

HONEYMOON PERIOD EFFECTS ON JOB APPROVAL RATING

President	Popular Vote	Poll Dates	Approval	Gain
Eisenhower	55.1	Feb. 20, 1953	66.9	11.8
Kennedy	49.7	Feb. 10–15, 1961	71.6	21.9
Nixon	43.4	Feb. 20–25, 1969	59.5	16.1
Carter	50.1	Feb. 15, 1977	71.2	21.1
Reagan	50.7	Feb. 13–16, 1981	55.4	4.7
Bush	53.4	Feb. 24–27, 1989	60.7	7.3
Clinton	43.0	Feb. 18–19, 1993	56.7	13.7
GW Bush	47.9	Feb. 19–21, 2001	61.7	13.8

NOTE: Difference between presidents' popular vote percentage and approval in Gallup surveys in mid-February following January inauguration.

Bill Clinton's honeymoon period was extremely brief, exacerbated by negative media coverage of his decision to allow gays and lesbians to serve in the military and by revelations that his first two choices for attorney general had employed illegal aliens as child care workers. Clinton's job approval rating for his first hundred days in office was the worst for any president in polling history.

The length of the honeymoon period has a great effect on whether the new president can be a decisive and strong leader in the first term. But sooner or later the president's popularity inevitably begins to decline as the public realizes that the president cannot meet its expectations (which were almost certainly set too high in the first place) and as the president's specific policy decisions adversely affect some segments of society.

George W. Bush—who took office in 2001 after a controversial, disputed election—succeeded in pushing a large tax cut through Congress in the early months of his presidency. Bush experienced a variation on the typical pattern of presidential popularity. He saw his approval ratings gradually decline from 57 percent in January to 51 percent in early September. After the terrorist attacks on the United States of September 11, 2001, Bush's approval rating skyrocketed to an unprecedented high of 90 percent.

> **More on this topic:**
>
> *Public Opinion and the Presidency, p. 427*

Hoover, Herbert C.

Source: Library of Congress

Herbert Clark Hoover (1874–1964) was one of the most qualified and accomplished persons ever to become president. However, he was unable to find a remedy to the Great Depression, which greeted him soon after he took office in 1929. As a result, he became closely associated in the public mind with the suffering and economic hardship of the depression era.

Hoover was born in West Branch, Iowa, on August 10, 1874. His father, a blacksmith and farm implement merchant, died of typhoid when Herbert was six. When his mother died of pneumonia two years later, he was sent to Oregon to live with an aunt and uncle.

Despite an uneven education, Hoover's impressive math skills earned him a place in Stanford University's first freshman class in 1891. He worked his way through college and earned his degree four years later. In 1897 an international mining company hired him as an engineering assistant. During the next seventeen years Hoover managed mines in Africa, Asia, Europe, Australia, and the United States. Before the age of forty he was a millionaire. Hoover married Lou Henry, a fellow student at Stanford, on February 10, 1899.

During World War I, Hoover served as U.S. food administrator. In this post he was responsible for stimulating food production and distributing food supplies. In 1918 he was appointed chairman of the Allied Food Council, which distributed food to millions of Europeans left impoverished by the war. Hoover also attended the Versailles Conference as an adviser to President Woodrow Wilson.

Hoover's relief activities made him one of the most admired Americans of his day. But his political stance was unclear because he had supported Republican Theodore Roosevelt's third-party candidacy in 1912 and had worked closely with Wilson, a Democrat. In 1920 Hoover declared that he was a Republican and received some support for the party's presidential nomination, which went to Warren G. Harding.

When Harding was elected president, he appointed Hoover secretary of commerce. Hoover remained in this post for eight years. He reorganized the department and helped to solidify the progress toward an eight-hour workday and a prohibition against child labor. He also became a close economic adviser to both Harding and Calvin Coolidge.

Hoover was the popular choice of Republicans for the party's presidential nomination in 1928. In the election he easily defeated Democrat Al Smith 444–87 in the Electoral College. Hoover had run on a Republican platform that took credit for the prosperity achieved during the 1920s. Seven months after Hoover's inauguration the October 1929 stock market crash began the Great Depression, which left about one-quarter of the work force unemployed. Although Hoover had not created the conditions that caused the depression, many Americans blamed him for it.

Hoover tried to fight the depression through public works projects, increased government loans to banks and businesses, cuts in the already low income tax, and personal appeals to industry to maintain wages and production levels. But these measures did little to ease the country's economic problems. Hoover's preoccupation with balancing the budget and his belief that federal relief violated the American principle of self-reliance prevented him from taking more sweeping actions. He opposed federal benefit programs to help the poor and unemployed and deficit spending that would have created jobs. He reluctantly signed the Smoot-Hawley Act of 1930, which dramatically raised tariff rates to protect U.S. industries, thereby starting a trade war that hurt the American and world economies.

Hoover was nominated by the Republicans for a second term, but the nation, desperate for relief from the depression, elected Democrat Franklin D. Roosevelt in a landslide. Hoover returned to his home in Palo Alto, California. During Roosevelt's presidency Hoover criticized the New Deal programs and the U.S. alliance with the Soviet Union during World War II.

In 1946 President Harry S. Truman tapped Hoover's experience in famine relief by naming him chairman of the Famine Emergency Commission, which was charged with preventing starvation in post–World War II Europe. Between 1947 and 1955 Hoover chaired two commissions on executive branch organization. The Hoover Commissions recommended hundreds of organizational changes to make the executive branch more efficient, many of which were adopted. Hoover died on October 20, 1964, in New York City at the age of ninety. Until that time he was the country's second longest living president (John Adams lived 136 days longer).

> **More on this topic:**
>
> *Great Depression, p. 237*

Hoover Commissions

Because the president and Congress often find themselves opposing each other for control of the BUREAUCRACY, presidents frequently look to reorganization as a means of gaining the upper hand and increasing their ability to manage their administrations. Presidents have attempted countless reorganization plans, only to find that the affected agencies are strongly protected by their sponsoring congressional committees. Yet without the cooperation of Congress, presidents find it extremely difficult to reorganize the executive branch.

Every president wants to coordinate policy-making efforts as much as possible, but because the number of federal programs has increased rapidly, coordination of the many agencies and departments is difficult. Overlap among agencies means that the executive branch often wastes time and effort trying to manage the development and implementation of public policy.

The first real effort at administrative reorganization took place during Franklin D. Roosevelt's administration. Acting on the recommendations of the BROWNLOW COMMITTEE, Roosevelt established in 1939 the EXECUTIVE OFFICE OF THE PRESIDENT (EOP) with the Bureau of the Budget as its centerpiece.

The next two major reorganizations resulted from the work of commissions chaired by former president Herbert C. Hoover. Their recommendations further increased the administrative power of the presidency by giving it more control over the vast federal bureaucracy and substantial authority over the appointment process.

First Hoover Commission

The first Hoover Commission was created during the presidency of Harry S. Truman. After large gains in the congressional elections of 1946, Republicans anticipated the end of the Truman presidency in 1949. The Republican-controlled Congress voted to set up a Commission on the Organization of the Executive Branch of the Government to help a new president grapple with the problems of executive branch organization. Truman appointed Hoover as chairman in 1947.

Hoover set about the task of evaluating the effectiveness of executive branch organization with much enthusiasm. Truman, who could have viewed the commission as a means of criticizing his administration, also was enthusiastic about the project and gave it his full cooperation. In the end, Truman was the one to benefit from the Hoover Commission's efforts when the Republicans failed to capture the presidency in the 1948 election.

The commission's report charged that the executive branch was unmanageable; its lines of communication and authority were confusing; and there were too few tools at the top for the development of effective policy. The commission recommended that the major authority within the executive departments be centralized in the department heads rather than continue to reside in the bureau chiefs. The commission proposed more coherent grouping of executive branch agencies and suggested that the EOP be strengthened by giving the president a stronger staff. The commission said the president should have absolute freedom in dealing with his staff, giving it shape and appointing its members.

Truman supported the commission's recommendations, and Congress supported most of them as well. Recommendations for increased presidential staff and discretion in the use and organization of the EOP were implemented. Following the commission's proposals, the Post Office and the Departments of the Interior, Commerce, and Labor were reorganized. The National Security Council and several independent agencies, including the Civil Service Commission and the Federal Trade Commission, also were reorganized.

By and large, the success of the reforms reflected the nonpartisan nature of the report. Hoover and his commission approached the presidency solely in managerial terms without engaging in political ideology.

Second Hoover Commission

When Dwight D. Eisenhower came to office in 1952 he faced a bureaucracy that had grown tremendously since the last Republican—Hoover himself—had been in the White House. After twenty years of Democratic control of the presidency, few Republicans had experience in running the federal government. In fact, after years of opposing big government and big spending, Republicans now found themselves in charge of the same "bloated" government they had criticized. A further complication for Eisenhower was a bureaucracy composed mostly of Democrats appointed under Democratic presidents.

Searching for a way to make the executive branch more responsive to his leadership, Eisenhower called once more on Hoover, now seventy-nine years old, to head the second Commission on the Organization of the Executive Branch of Government, or the Second Hoover Commission.

Whereas the First Hoover Commission had been interested primarily in improving the administrative management of the executive branch, the second commission centered on issues of policy and function. At the heart of its recommendations was the idea that the executive branch should reduce its scope, thereby saving money, reducing taxes, and eliminating competition with the private sector. Ideologically, the commission had a conservative agenda that aimed at reducing the size of the government, which had been growing since the time of the New Deal. The commission was more concerned with prescribing what government should do than how it should be organized and managed.

In its study of the executive branch, the Commission has been impressed by the size and complexity of our Government. This fact alone has led to the conclusion that only through good management can we weld the governmental organization into a mechanism for carrying on efficiently the public business.

— Harry S. Truman, Statement by the President Upon Receiving the Final Report of the Hoover Commission, **May 26, 1949**

Most of the commission's recommendations were of only indirect value to the Eisenhower administration as it wrestled with the problems of a massive executive bureaucracy. For the first time, however, a major reorganization report dealt with the relations between political appointees and career public servants. Among its specific recommendations was the creation of a "Senior Civil Service" of upper-level career executives serving in administrative positions, who would constitute a personnel pool that would be rotated regularly to improve management quality. The idea finally became incorporated into general personnel practices in the executive branch with the establishment of the Senior Executive Service in 1978.

More on this topic:

Commissions, Presidential, p. 110

Housing and Urban Development Department

The Department of Housing and Urban Development (HUD) is the federal agency concerned with the nation's housing needs, fair housing opportunities, and the development and preservation of communities.

HUD offers, among other things, Federal Housing Administration (FHA) mortgage insurance to help families become homeowners and to facilitate the construction and rehabilitation of rental units; rental assistance for low-income families; Government National Mortgage Association mortgage-backed securities that help to ensure an adequate supply of mortgage credit; programs to combat housing discrimination and promote fair housing; assistance for community and neighborhood development and preservation; and programs that protect home buyers in the marketplace.

In 1965 Congress elevated the federal government's role in housing to cabinet-level importance when it voted to replace the existing federal House and Home Finance Agency with HUD. The action came after four years of lobbying by Presidents John F. Kennedy and Lyndon B. Johnson.

HUD was created in response to the urgent problems arising from the shift of the U.S. population from the country to cities and suburbs. More than 70 percent of the U.S. population lived in cities and suburbs, a percentage that was growing rapidly. Programs intended to deal with the problems of urban and suburban living—housing shortages, pollution, lack of mass transit, urban decay, inadequate roads—were in disarray, scattered among federal, state, and local governments. As a result, a new public housing project or hospital might be located far from public transportation, while slums might be replaced by parking lots or new high-rent dwellings.

The department opened its doors in 1966 and was thrust immediately into the fray of administering controversial and extremely complex housing laws.

Among the program areas under HUD's jurisdiction are some Indian and Alaskan Native programs, small and disadvantaged business utilization, contract appeals, and administrative and judicial proceedings. In addition, the Office of Federal Housing Enterprise Oversight oversees the financial soundness and safety of the Federal National Mortgage Association (Fannie Mae) and the Federal Home Loan Mortgage Corporation (Freddie Mac), and the Office of Healthy Homes and Lead Hazard Control directs the department's lead-based paint activities.

The Government National Mortgage Association (GNMA), also known as Ginnie Mae, is a government corporation within HUD. Funds from investors are channeled into the mortgage industry through GNMA, thus increasing the money available for housing loans.

> **More on this topic:**
>
> *Bureaucracy, p. 44*
>
> *Cabinet, p. 60*

Hughes, Charles Evans

Charles Evans Hughes.
Source: Library of Congress

Charles Evans Hughes (1862–1948) was one of the most prominent public officials of the early twentieth century. He served as governor of New York, secretary of state, and chief justice of the United States, but he failed to win election to the presidency by a narrow margin in 1916.

Hughes was born to an abolitionist minister and his wife on April 11, 1862, in Glens Falls, New York. After graduating from Brown University in 1881, he taught school and clerked for a Wall Street firm before entering Columbia law school. He graduated in 1884 and spent most of the next twenty-two years practicing law in New York City.

In 1906 Hughes, running as a Republican, defeated William Randolph Hearst for governor of New York. He won reelection two years later. President William Howard Taft appointed Hughes to the Supreme Court in 1910. The nomination was greeted with approval by the press, Congress, and the Court.

In 1916 Hughes resigned from the Court to run for president against President Woodrow Wilson. Hughes was a poor campaigner, but his candidacy did unify the Republican Party. In 1912 Theodore Roosevelt had broken with the Republicans and run under the banner of the Progressive Party. This had split the Republicans and allowed Wilson to be elected. In 1916, despite Roosevelt's endorsement, Hughes was beaten by Wilson in one of the closest elections up to that time. The president received 9.1 million popular votes and 277 electoral votes to Hughes's 8.5 million and 254. After his defeat, Hughes joined a New York law firm.

When Republican Warren G. Harding became president in 1921, he appointed Hughes secretary of state, a post he held until 1925. Hughes was the leading organizer of the Washington Armament Conference of 1921, which was attended by the major powers. The conference produced an agreement that reduced tensions in the Pacific and established limits on naval forces.

President Herbert C. Hoover appointed Hughes chief justice in 1930. Although Hughes was criticized for having provided legal representation to large corporations during the period after he left the State Department, he was confirmed in the Senate by a 52–26 vote. Hughes retired from the Court in 1941 because of failing health. He died on August 27, 1948.

Humphrey, Hubert H.

Hubert H. Humphrey.
Source: Library of Congress

Hubert Horatio Humphrey Jr. (1911–1978) served as vice president under Lyndon B. Johnson from 1965 to 1969. Humphrey attempted to succeed Johnson as president, but he was defeated by Republican Richard Nixon in a close election.

The son of a druggist, Humphrey was licensed as a registered pharmacist in 1933. He managed the family drugstore when his father, who had been active in politics as a Democrat, won a seat in the South Dakota legislature. In 1937 Humphrey enrolled at the University of Minnesota. He graduated in 1939 with a degree in political science and was elected to the Phi Beta Kappa honor society. He then earned a master's degree in 1940 from Louisiana State University.

Color blindness and a double hernia disqualified Humphrey from military service during World War II. Instead he served as Minnesota's director for war production training and later became assistant director of the state's War Manpower Administration.

In 1945 Humphrey was elected mayor of Minneapolis as a Democrat, in his second try at the office. He gained a reputation as a reformer and won a second term in 1947. A year later he was elected to the U.S. Senate, where he became a leading proponent of civil rights legislation and welfare programs. He was reelected in 1954 and 1960.

In 1964 President Lyndon B. Johnson chose Humphrey as his running mate, after Humphrey promised that he would remain loyal to Johnson even if he disagreed with the president's policies. Johnson and Humphrey defeated Republicans Barry M. Goldwater and William E. Miller by a huge landslide. As vice president, Humphrey was not one of Johnson's close advisers. Nevertheless, he worked to push the president's Great Society social programs through Congress and made several tours of foreign nations, including two trips to Vietnam.

Johnson declined to seek another term, and Humphrey received his party's nomination for president in 1968. His nomination was secure after his chief rival, Robert F. Kennedy, was assassinated in Los Angeles on June 5. Humphrey's campaign was burdened by the unpopularity of the Vietnam War, which the public associated with Johnson's presidency. He was defeated 301–191 in the Electoral College but received only a half-million fewer popular votes than Richard Nixon (31.3 million and 31.8 million, respectively). Third-party candidate George C. Wallace received 9.9 million votes.

In 1970 Humphrey returned to the Senate after winning the seat vacated by retiring Democrat Eugene J. McCarthy. Humphrey was a late entry in the 1972 presidential race, and the Democratic nomination went instead to Sen. George S. McGovern of South Dakota.

In August 1976 doctors found cancer in Humphrey's prostate gland and bladder. Despite his illness, the voters of Minnesota reelected him to the Senate in 1976. Humphrey's high spirits during the year preceding his death won him the nation's admiration. He died at his Minnesota home on January 13, 1978. Humphrey's wife, Muriel, was appointed to her husband's Senate seat and served until January 3, 1979.

More on this topic:

Johnson, Lyndon B.,
p. 309

Humphrey's Executor v. United States

The controversial issue of whether a president may remove officials from office has come before the Supreme Court several times.

The Supreme Court first sided squarely with the president in the 1926 decision MYERS V. UNITED STATES, in which it upheld President Woodrow Wilson's dismissal of a postmaster. The Court ruled that the president's removal authority was extensive and came directly from the Constitution. Restrictions placed on this authority by Congress were invalid, the Court held.

President Franklin D. Roosevelt interpreted this ruling to mean that he could fire a member of the Federal Trade Commission (FTC) at will. Although the law creating the FTC limited such firings to "inefficiency, neglect of duty, or malfeasance in office," Roosevelt fired William E. Humphrey solely because he and Humphrey disagreed about FTC policy. Humphrey died in 1934, never having agreed to his removal. The executor of his estate sued the United States to recover the wages Humphrey would have been paid had he continued in office. The estate won.

The Supreme Court in 1935 ruled that Congress could restrict the ability of the president to fire officers of the executive branch when those officers exercised nonexecutive powers delegated to them by Congress. Because commissioners of the FTC were given extensive rule-making and adjudicatory powers by Congress, neither of which was considered executive in nature, the Court concluded that Roosevelt's firing of Humphrey was unlawful.

The Court did not overrule *Myers v. United States.* Instead, it distinguished the facts in *Myers* by pointing out that postmasters did not exercise nonexecutive powers.

In 1958 the Supreme Court further clarified the removal power of presidents in *Wiener v. United States.* After being dismissed as a member of the War Claims Commission for political reasons, Myron Wiener claimed that President Dwight D. Eisenhower was without legal authority to fire him and sued to recover the wages he would have earned had he remained a commission member. The case differed from the *Humphrey* case in that the law setting up the War Claims Commission made no provision for the removal of commissioners. This left open the question of whether, if Congress was silent, the removal power is vested exclusively in the president. Without dissent, the Court said that it is not. The Court held that if officials are engaged in adjudicative functions, presidents may not remove them for political reasons.

> **More on this topic:**
>
> *Appointment and Removal Power (Executive Branch),* p. 9
>
> Myers v. United States, p. 370

Hurricane Katrina

One of the greatest crises to affect the presidency of George W. Bush came as a result of the perceived inadequate government response to the devastation created by Hurricane Katrina. On August 29, 2005, the storm, once a "category 5" hurricane, made landfall along the southern Gulf Coast of the United States near the Louisiana-Mississippi border. By the time the storm dissipated a few days later, more than 1,800 people had lost their lives, over $81 billion in damage had been recorded, 80 percent of the city of New Orleans had flooded, and tens of thousands of people had been dislocated. In terms of dollars, it was the most costly natural disaster in American history.

For days after the storm had passed, the American people witnessed almost constant media coverage of its effects and the resulting humanitarian crisis. Although a mandatory evacuation order was issued by New Orleans mayor Ray Nagin on August 28 and a million residents fled the city, thousands remained either in their homes, most of which were flooded when the city's levee system was overwhelmed, or at the Louisiana Superdome, a designated shelter. Because local and state

Satellite image of Hurricane Katrina over the Gulf Coast.
Source: AP

emergency services were overwhelmed by the scale of the unfolding crisis, looting and violence soon broke out throughout New Orleans. In addition, lacking adequate supplies of drinking water and baking in the summer heat, many people succumbed to exhaustion and thirst.

The Department of Homeland Security's "National Response Plan" was invoked for the first time in response to Hurricane Katrina. Under that scheme, local officials are the first to respond to natural disasters. If they are overwhelmed by the scope of the disaster, they are to request assistance from their county, then state, and if needed the federal government. Because local Louisiana authorities did not have the resources to respond to the crisis, Homeland Security secretary Michael Chertoff invoked the plan on August 30, effectively accepting responsibility for managing the crisis.

Blame for the inadequate response to the storm has been placed on many actors ranging from Mayor Nagin to Louisiana governor Kathleen Blanco, Federal Emergency Management Agency (FEMA) director Michael Brown, Homeland Security secretary Chertoff, and President Bush. A CNN/*USA Today*/Gallup poll taken about a week after the hurricane struck found that 13 percent of Americans blamed the president, 18 percent blamed federal agencies, 25 percent blamed state and local authorities, and 38 percent thought nobody was to blame.

Although less than one-fifth of the country placed the blame squarely on President Bush's shoulders, the public's perception of his ability to manage crisis events—thought to be his strongest quality since the September 11, 2001, terrorist attacks—seemed forever tarnished. On vacation at his ranch in Crawford, Texas, when the storm hit, the president chose not to alter his schedule; and on August 30, while New Orleans was flooding, he attended a V-J Day ceremony in San Diego, California, instead of attending to the disaster. A famous image taken by an Associated Press photographer at the San Diego event showed Bush merrily playing a presidential seal–embossed guitar while country music singer Mark Wills looked on. Many critics of the president began to draw parallels between Bush's response and Roman emperor Nero, who "fiddled while Rome burned."

Although some observers questioned Bush's intentions, the historical record indicates that the president and other federal officials suffered partly from bad information and partly from strict adherence to statutes designed to protect the sovereignty of state and local governments from undo encroachment by the federal government.

Illustrating the problem of poor information, the president simply did not watch the television news images broadcast to millions of Americans. So that the president would understand the gravity of the situation, White House counsel Dan Bartlett made a DVD of news coverage for the president to view on September 1 while en route to the disaster zone on *Air Force One*. The next day, amid the controversy surrounding FEMA's response, the president publicly praised Brown

---

More on this topic:

Public Opinion and the Presidency, p. 427

but then replaced his on-site command eight days later. On September 12, Brown resigned as head of FEMA. Critics later charged that Bush appointed Brown to the FEMA post more for political reasons than for his experience, arguing that Bush overlooked the fact that Brown had no real crisis management experience and that Brown had spent eleven years prior to his appointment overseeing horse shows.

Again, I want to thank you all for—and Brownie, you're doing a heck of a job. The FEMA director is working 24—they're working 24 hours a day.

—George W. Bush, *Remarks on the Aftermath of Hurricane Katrina in Mobile, Alabama, September 2, 2005*

The problem of jurisdiction also hampered the timeliness of federal assistance. Because states are technically sovereign, under the Posse Comitatus Act, federal troops may not participate in domestic law enforcement unless a domestic insurrection is declared by the president. Governors must request federal troops, and offers of aid from National Guard units of other states must first be approved by officials in Washington. A governor may instead activate a compact among neighboring states, but this is something the Louisiana governor did not do.

In the end the failures in responding to Hurricane Katrina in Louisiana were distributed throughout many levels of government, including state and local jurisdictions. The crisis had a lasting effect on the Bush administration. The president appeared to be out of touch with the urgency of the situation; questions arose as to whether the president had filled important emergency management positions with political friends; and the public began to question whether the emergency management apparatus of the federal government, reorganized under the new Department of Homeland Security, would be functional in future crises.

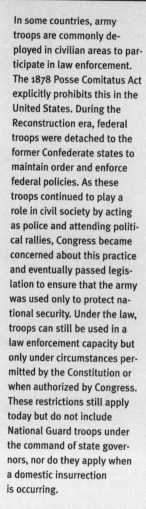

CLOSER LOOK

In some countries, army troops are commonly deployed in civilian areas to participate in law enforcement. The 1878 Posse Comitatus Act explicitly prohibits this in the United States. During the Reconstruction era, federal troops were detached to the former Confederate states to maintain order and enforce federal policies. As these troops continued to play a role in civil society by acting as police and attending political rallies, Congress became concerned about this practice and eventually passed legislation to ensure that the army was used only to protect national security. Under the law, troops can still be used in a law enforcement capacity but only under circumstances permitted by the Constitution or when authorized by Congress. These restrictions still apply today but do not include National Guard troops under the command of state governors, nor do they apply when a domestic insurrection is occurring.

Immigration and Naturalization Service v. Chadha

Congress began in the 1930s to use a device called the LEGISLATIVE VETO to review and possibly reject executive branch regulations and policies.

The legislative veto took a variety of forms, but essentially it allowed Congress to delegate to the executive departments and agencies authority to implement legislation, subject to veto by one or both houses of Congress or sometimes even a committee or subcommittee. Congress usually exercised its legislative veto through passage of a concurrent or simple resolution, neither of which required the president's signature (although the original bill authorizing the legislative veto would have been signed into law).

From the beginning, presidents of both parties protested the legislative veto as an infringement on executive prerogatives. Congress's increased use of the device in the 1970s fanned the controversy surrounding it and strained already tense relations between the executive and legislative branches. Once the issue reached the Supreme Court, it declared in 1983 in *INS v. Chadha* that certain legislative vetoes were unconstitutional.

The case had begun in 1974 when Jagdish Rai Chadha, an East Indian born in Kenya who had overstayed his student visa, persuaded the Immigration and Naturalization Service (INS) to suspend his deportation. But Congress had amended the Immigration and Nationality Act of 1952 to give either of its chambers the power to veto an INS decision to suspend an individual's deportation. In December 1975 the House exercised its power to veto Chadha's stay of deportation. Its reasons, however, were never clear; no debate or recorded vote occurred.

Chadha contested the House veto, arguing that it was unconstitutional. In 1980 the U.S. Court of Appeals for the Ninth Circuit agreed. The case was then appealed to the Supreme Court. (Chadha, in the meantime, had married an American, fathered a child, and settled down in the United States.) On June 23, 1983, the Supreme Court held, 7–2, the one-house legislative veto unconstitutional. The majority found the device violated the separation of powers between the executive and legislative branches and ran counter to the "single, finely wrought and exhaustively considered procedure" the Constitution prescribes for the enactment of legislation: approval by both chambers and presentation to the president for signature.

Chief Justice Warren E. Burger wrote for the majority that in only four specific situations had the framers of the Constitution authorized one chamber to act alone with the force of law, not subject to a presidential veto: in initiating an impeachment, in trying a person who had been impeached, in approving presidential appointments, and in approving treaties.

With this decision, invalidating a device included in one form or another in more than two hundred laws enacted since 1932, the Court struck down at one time more provisions in more federal laws than it had previously invalidated in its entire history.

The Constitution sought to divide the delegated powers of the new Federal Government into three defined categories, Legislative, Executive, and Judicial, to assure, as nearly as possible, that each branch of government would confine itself to its assigned responsibility. The hydraulic pressure inherent within each of the separate Branches to exceed the outer limits of its power, even to accomplish desirable objectives, must be resisted.

—**Chief Justice Warren Burger,** Immigration and Naturalization Service v. Chadha Opinion of the Court

The Court reinforced its decision a month later when it upheld two lower-court rulings striking down one- and two-house legislative vetoes.

In 1987, in *Alaska Airlines v. Brock,* the Court held unanimously that in most of the laws containing legislative vetoes only the veto provision itself had been nullified by the *Chadha* ruling. The remainder of the law could stand, unless the inclusion of the veto was critical to Congress's decision to pass the law in the first place, the Court ruled.

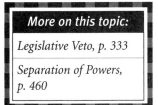

More on this topic:

Legislative Veto, p. 333

Separation of Powers, p. 460

Impeachment

Congress's power of impeachment is the ultimate check on executive and judicial authority. The Constitution grants Congress the power to remove from office the president, vice president, "and all civil Officers of the United States," upon impeachment for and conviction of "Treason, Bribery, or other high Crimes and Misdemeanors."

The House of Representatives is the prosecutor in impeachment proceedings. The Senate chamber is the courtroom, and the Senate—with the chief justice of the United States presiding over a presidential impeachment—is judge and jury. The penalty for conviction is removal from office and, if senators so decide, disqualification from holding government office in the future. There is no appeal of a conviction.

Impeachment is a rarely used power. Only three presidents—Andrew Johnson in 1868, Richard Nixon in 1974, and Bill Clinton in 1998–1999—have faced the serious possibility of being removed from office through impeachment. Johnson and Clinton were impeached by the House but survived Senate trials and completed their terms of office; Nixon avoided the possibility of removal through impeachment by becoming the first president in U.S. history to resign from office. Since

1789 only seventeen government officials have been impeached; seven of these, all lower-court judges, were convicted.

Constitutional Origins

The impeachment process dates from fourteenth-century England, when the fledgling Parliament wanted to gain authority over the king's advisers. The monarch was considered incapable of wrongdoing and was therefore immune, but ministers and judges who were believed guilty of breaking the law or of carrying out unpopular orders of the king could be impeached by Parliament. By the late eighteenth century, however, ministers had become accountable to Parliament, so that parliamentary impeachments were considered unnecessary.

As impeachment was dying out in England, the framers of the U.S. Constitution were embracing it "as a method of national inquest into the conduct of public men," in the words of Alexander Hamilton.

American colonial governments had adopted the English system under which impeachment charges were brought by the lower house of the legislative body while the upper house sat in judgment. Despite these precedents the Constitutional Convention debated whether the Senate was the appropriate site for trials on impeachment charges. James Madison and Charles Pinckney opposed that role for the Senate, arguing that it would make presidents too dependent on the legislative branch. Suggested alternatives included the Supreme Court or a convocation of the chief justices of the state supreme courts. In the end, however, the Senate was selected as the trial arena.

The Constitutional Convention also debated the definition of impeachable crimes. Initially, it was proposed that the president be subject to impeachment and removal for "mal or corrupt conduct" or for "malpractice or neglect of duty." There were several other versions, which some viewed as too narrow and others as too broad, before agreement was reached on "Treason, Bribery, or other high Crimes and Misdemeanors." Treason and bribery are easily defined, but what exactly was meant by the phrase "high Crimes and Misdemeanors" has never been clear. Debate over its meaning has resumed during every serious impeachment inquiry, pitting broad constructionists, who view impeachment as a political weapon, against narrow constructionists, who regard impeachment as limited to offenses for which a person may be indicted under the criminal code. Generally, "high Crimes and Misdemeanors" has come to mean anything the prosecution has wanted it to mean. As Rep. Gerald R. Ford, R-Mich., put it in 1970: "An impeachable offense is whatever a majority of the House of Representatives considers it to be at a given moment in history."

Impeachment Procedures

Since 1789 impeachment proceedings have been initiated in a variety of ways. In modern times they have started in the House Judiciary Committee, which investigates and holds hearings on the charges. If its investigation supports the charges, the committee reports an impeachment resolution, which usually includes articles of impeachment. The resolution then goes to the House floor for consideration. The accused official is impeached if the resolution and articles of impeachment are approved by a majority vote of the House.

House managers are then selected to present the case of impeachment to the Senate. They will act as prosecutors in the Senate trial. They are chosen by a resolution fixing the number of managers and empowering the Speaker to appoint them, by a resolution establishing the number and naming the appointees, or by a resolution that fixes the number but empowers the House to elect the managers later. An odd number—ranging from five to eleven—has traditionally been selected. Any House member may attend the trial, but the House managers are the official representatives in the Senate proceedings.

The Senate trial is similar to any criminal proceeding. Both sides may present evidence and witnesses, and the defendant is allowed counsel and has the right to testify and to cross-examine witnesses.

If the president or vice president is on trial, the Constitution stipulates that the chief justice of the United States must preside. There is no constitutional specification about the presiding officer for other defendants, but in the past it has been either the vice president or the president pro tempore of the Senate. An impeachment case normally is tried before the full Senate. In 1986 the Senate broke with tradition by using a special committee to collect and hear evidence in a judge's impeachment trial. The shortcut procedure had been authorized since 1935 but had never before been used. By 1994 the procedure had been used three times. Former U.S. district judge Walter L. Nixon Jr. challenged the procedure in court, claiming his 1989 conviction was unconstitutional because the full Senate did not conduct an important part of the proceedings. But the Supreme Court in 1993 upheld the Senate's authority to carry out impeachment trials as it sees fit.

At the end of the hearing the Senate goes into closed session to debate the guilt or innocence of the accused. Each senator is limited to fifteen minutes of debate. The Senate votes separately on each article of impeachment, and the Constitution requires a two-thirds vote for conviction. If no article is approved by two-thirds of the senators present, the impeached official is acquitted. If any article receives two-thirds approval, the person is convicted. The Senate may vote separately to remove the person from office. This is not necessary, however, because the Constitution provides that federal officials shall be removed from office upon impeachment and conviction. The Senate also may vote to disqualify the person from holding future federal office, but disqualification is not mandatory. Only two of the seven Senate convictions have been accompanied by disqualification, which is decided by majority vote.

Impeachment of Andrew Johnson

Andrew Johnson has the dubious distinction of being one of only two presidents impeached by the House and tried by the Senate. Technically, the main charge against Johnson was that he had violated a federal statute, the Tenure of Office Act. But in essence the impeachment grew out of a profoundly political struggle between Johnson and an overwhelmingly Republican Congress. Questions such as control of the Republican Party, the future of the South after the Civil War, and the treatment of the freed slaves, as well as monetary and economic policy, all weighed heavily in the proceedings.

Johnson had been the only member of the U.S. Senate from a seceding southern state (Tennessee) to remain loyal to the Union in 1861. Abraham Lincoln later made him military governor of Tennessee and chose him as his running mate in 1864.

When Johnson succeeded to the presidency in 1865 after Lincoln was assassinated, he was an outsider without allies or connections in the Republican Party. His ideas on what should be done to reconstruct and readmit the southern states to the Union clashed with the wishes of the Republican majority in Congress.

The scene was set for repeated legislative battles, with Johnson vetoing important Republican bills and Congress often easily overriding those vetoes. The Tenure of Office Act was one of those passed over Johnson's veto. The act, which barred the president from removing civil officers (appointed with the consent of the Senate) without the approval of the Senate, was aimed at protecting incumbent Republican officeholders from executive retaliation if they did not support the president.

The first attempt to impeach Johnson was overwhelmingly defeated by the House on December 6, 1867. Most members recognized the general charges leveled against Johnson—usurpation of power and corrupt use of the appointment, pardon, and veto powers, constituting "high Crimes and Misdemeanors"—as basically political grievances instead of illegal acts. But another attempt was soon made.

In 1868 the House of Representatives impeached President Andrew Johnson. This sketch depicts Johnson's trial in the Senate, where by one vote he was acquitted and allowed to remain in office.
Source: Library of Congress

Johnson had long wanted to get rid of Secretary of War Edwin M. Stanton, who was a close ally of the more extreme Radical Republicans. After repeatedly trying to get Stanton to resign, Johnson suspended him on December 12, 1867. In January 1868 the Senate refused to concur, thereby, under the terms of the Tenure of Office Act, reinstating Stanton. Apparently flushed by his victory on the earlier impeachment issue, Johnson decided to force the issue. He dismissed Stanton on February 21, citing the power and authority vested in him by the Constitution.

This action enraged Congress, driving conservative Republicans into alliance with the Radical Republicans. An impeachment resolution was reported out of committee on February 22, and two days later the House voted to impeach Johnson on a party-line vote of 126–47. A week later the House approved eleven articles of impeachment. Eight of the articles concerned Johnson's removal of Stanton; the others alleged violation of another law and seditious libel against Congress.

The Senate trial opened March 30. During the weeks of argument and testimony, Johnson's lawyers insisted that the Tenure of Office Act was unconstitutional, that it did not apply to Johnson anyway because Stanton had been appointed by Lincoln, and that Stanton had not actually been removed from office because he remained physically barricaded in his office at the War Department.

At the same time, some conservative Republicans were beginning to have second thoughts. Their main concern was fiery Ben Wade of Ohio, president pro tempore of the Senate and, under the succession law then in effect, next in line for the presidency. One of the most radical of the Radical Republicans, he had taken a hard line on Reconstruction and favored monetary expansion.

On May 16 the Senate took a test vote on a general, catch-all article of impeachment, one that House managers thought most likely to produce a vote for conviction. The drama of the vote has become legendary. With thirty-six votes needed for conviction, the final count was thirty-five, guilty, to nineteen, not guilty.

Ten days later, Johnson was acquitted on two more charges by identical 35–19 votes. The Senate abandoned the remaining articles and adjourned, abruptly ending the trial. President Johnson had been acquitted of impeachment charges by a single vote.

The Tenure of Office Act was virtually repealed during the administration of Ulysses S. Grant and entirely repealed in 1887. In the 1926 *Myers v. United States* decision, Chief Justice William Howard Taft referred to the act and said it had been invalid.

Case of Richard Nixon

The effort to impeach Richard Nixon marked only the second time in U.S. history that Congress has seriously considered removing an incumbent president from office. The process of impeachment did not move beyond its first stage, yet it realized its purpose. Ten days after the House Judiciary Committee recommended that Nixon be impeached for obstruction of justice, abuse of power, and contempt of Congress, Nixon resigned. In the face of certain impeachment by the House and removal by the Senate, he chose to leave the White House voluntarily.

The impeachment inquiry stemmed from a chain of events that began on June 17, 1972, with a burglary at the offices of the Democratic National Committee in the Watergate complex in Washington, D.C. The burglary was carried out by individuals associated with Nixon's reelection committee and was later covered up by members of Nixon's White House staff. It was only one example of the extraordinary, and illegal, steps taken to ensure that Nixon's victory in 1972 would be a resounding one, as indeed it was. These activities would come to be known as the WATERGATE AFFAIR.

Nixon precipitated an impeachment inquiry with his firing on October 20, 1973, of the first Watergate independent counsel, Archibald Cox. Cox had been persisting in his effort to force Nixon to release tape recordings of certain of his conversations in the White House that, Cox suspected, concerned the Watergate break-in.

Charging that Cox had exceeded his authority and had deliberately challenged presidential authority, Nixon ordered his firing. But both the attorney general and deputy attorney general chose to resign rather than carry out the order. Finally, Solicitor General Robert H. Bork fired Cox. This sequence of events, which came to be known as the Saturday night massacre, aroused immediate adverse public reaction. In the firestorm of protest that followed, House Democratic leaders introduced impeachment resolutions.

On February 6, 1974, the House, by a 410–4 vote, authorized its Judiciary Committee to investigate the charges.

While the investigation was still under way, the Supreme Court on July 24 unanimously rejected Nixon's claim of executive privilege to withhold evidence sought by the Watergate special prosecutor. The Court ruled that Nixon must turn over the requested tapes.

That evening, on nationwide television, the Judiciary Committee began the final phase of its inquiry. For the first time all thirty-eight members spoke publicly on the evidence, and by the end of the evening it was clear that there would be a bipartisan majority in favor of impeachment.

On July 27 the committee approved, 27–11, the first article of impeachment, charging Nixon with obstructing justice. The second article, charging abuse of power, was approved July 29 by a margin of 28–10. The third, charging contempt of Congress, was approved July 30 by a 21–17 vote. Two other proposed articles were rejected.

On August 5 Nixon released transcripts of the subpoenaed tapes that the Supreme Court ruling had forced him to turn over to the special prosecutor. Included in these was the so-called "smoking gun" tape of June 23, 1972, which revealed that Nixon had knowingly participated in the cover-up of White House involvement in the Watergate burglary.

Faced with this new evidence, even the members of the Judiciary Committee who had continued to defend Nixon called for his resignation or impeachment. Republican leaders told Nixon he had no more than ten supporters in the House and fifteen in the Senate. On August 8 Nixon told the nation he would resign the presidency the next day.

Despite the president's resignation, the Judiciary Committee prepared its report, explaining the basis for its decisions to recommend impeachment. The report was accepted by the House on August 20 by a 412–3 vote. By "accepting" rather than "approving" the report, the House took official notice of the com-

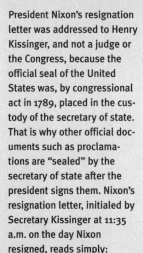

CLOSER LOOK

President Nixon's resignation letter was addressed to Henry Kissinger, and not a judge or the Congress, because the official seal of the United States was, by congressional act in 1789, placed in the custody of the secretary of state. That is why other official documents such as proclamations are "sealed" by the secretary of state after the president signs them. Nixon's resignation letter, initialed by Secretary Kissinger at 11:35 a.m. on the day Nixon resigned, reads simply:

> Dear Mr. Secretary:
>
> I hereby resign the Office of President of the United States.
>
> Sincerely,
> Richard Nixon

Dear Mr. Secretary:

I hereby resign the Office of President of the United States.

Sincerely,

Richard Nixon

Presidents and First Ladies Nixon and Ford as the Nixons prepare to board a helicopter upon leaving the White House on August 9, 1974
Source: Nixon Presidential Materials

mittee's recommendations and authorized the printing of the report without adopting the articles of impeachment and thereby setting a Senate trial in motion.

Impeachment of Bill Clinton

President Bill Clinton was impeached in 1998 and acquitted in 1999 of charges that he committed perjury and obstructed justice in an effort to cover up an affair with a young White House intern, Monica Lewinsky. Clinton was never in any real danger of being removed from office, in part because his job approval rating in public opinion polls remained high. But the historical record will forever note the president's adamant denials of wrongdoing, his grudging apologies, and, finally, on his last full day in office, his admission that he had indeed lied under oath.

The Lewinsky scandal was pursued by Kenneth W. Starr, who had been appointed as independent counsel in August 1994 to investigate Clinton and his wife, Hillary Rodham Clinton, in connection with their involvement in a complicated Arkansas land deal known as Whitewater. A former solicitor general with close ties to conservative Republicans, Starr soon expanded his operation to look into several other events connected to the Clinton White House, including the abrupt firing of White House Travel Office personnel in 1993.

Clinton also was the defendant in a sexual harassment suit brought against him in February 1994 by Paula Corbin Jones. She had accused Clinton of requesting oral sex from her when he was governor of Arkansas and she was a state employee. Clinton's attorneys had fought off the case until May 1997, when the Supreme Court ruled that a sitting president is not immune to a civil suit for a personal action that allegedly occurred before he took office. Lewinsky's name appeared on a list, compiled by Jones's lawyers, of women whose names had been linked to Clinton's.

Although Lewinsky filed a sworn affidavit on January 7, 1998, denying having had sexual relations with Clinton, she had confided in several friends about an affair with the president. One of these confidantes, former White House employee Linda Tripp, had taped several conversations with Lewinsky in which she described her affair and said that Clinton had urged her to lie about it. Lewinsky was recorded urging Tripp, herself a witness in the Jones case, to lie to the court about her knowledge of Lewinsky's affair with the president.

Tripp turned the tapes over to the independent counsel's office on January 12, 1998, and Starr subsequently sought, and was granted, permission to investigate the Lewinsky affair from a three-judge panel overseeing independent counsels.

Clinton denied several times in January 1998 that he had had sexual relations with Lewinsky. Throughout that spring and summer, Starr called Clinton aides and Lewinsky friends before a federal grand jury in Washington. Clinton himself testified on August 17 before the grand jury on closed-circuit television from the White House. He was the first president to give evidence to a grand jury investigating his own alleged criminal conduct. Clinton later that day admitted on national television that he had had a relationship with Lewinsky but denied he had done anything illegal.

On September 9 Starr delivered a report to Congress containing what he described as "substantial and credible evidence" that Clinton had committed impeachable offenses in trying to cover up his relationship with Lewinsky. The so-called "Starr Report" charged Clinton with committing perjury, obstructing justice, tampering with a potential witness, and acting in a manner inconsistent with his constitutional duty to faithfully execute the laws.

Republican leaders, already at political loggerheads with Clinton, pushed ahead with an impeachment inquiry. The House Judiciary Committee, after holding an inquiry into Clinton's actions, approved four articles of impeachment against him in December 1998: two counts of perjury, obstruction of justice, and abuse of power. The first article charged Clinton with committing perjury during his August 17 testimony. The second article said he committed perjury in his deposition in Paula Jones's sexual harassment suit. The third article charged him with obstruction of justice for efforts to try to find Lewinsky a job in New York, possibly in return for her silence, and for alleged witness tampering directed at his secretary, Betty Currie. The fourth article dealt with abuse of power, charging, among other things, that Clinton provided misleading statements to the Judiciary Committee.

Formal debate on the proposed articles of impeachment began on the House floor on December 18. The House voted on December 19 on the four articles, approving two—the perjury article dealing with his August 17 testimony and the obstruction of justice article—and voting down two others. Then the House authorized the appointment of thirteen Republican members of the Judiciary Committee to prosecute the case in the Senate. Democratic members refused to participate as prosecutors.

The Senate began the trial on January 7, with Chief Justice William H. Rehnquist presiding, and it continued into February. On February 12 the Senate voted to acquit Clinton on both counts of impeachment. On the first article, accusing Clinton of perjury, the Senate voted 45–55 against conviction, twenty-two votes short of the two-thirds vote necessary for conviction. On the second article, which accused the president of obstructing justice, the Senate voted 50–50.

Clinton's legal troubles continued after his acquittal. Even in the last months of his presidency, a grand jury investigation into whether Clinton had lied under oath to cover up his relationship with Lewinsky was pending. On January 19, 2001, Clinton's last full day as president, the White House announced that he had reached a settlement with Robert W. Ray, Starr's successor. Clinton admitted he had given false testimony under oath and agreed to give up his right to practice law for five years in return for avoiding the possibility of indictment.

Other Impeachment Cases

Impeachment proceedings have been initiated in the House about sixty times in the nation's history, but very few officials have actually been impeached and even fewer convicted.

The overwhelming majority of impeachment proceedings since 1789 have been directed against federal judges, who hold lifetime appointments "during good behavior." They cannot be removed by any other method, and only by impeachment can their salary be taken away while in office.

In addition to Andrew Johnson and Bill Clinton, the list of those who have actually been impeached includes one cabinet officer, one senator, and thirteen federal judges. Of these sixteen cases, fifteen were sent to the Senate for trial (the other resigned before impeachment articles were drafted and sent to the Senate). Seven officials were convicted, and six were acquitted. Two other cases were dismissed before a trial could begin because the officials had left office.

In addition to the presidential impeachments, the case of a Supreme Court justice, Samuel Chase, in 1804–1805, stands out. Chase was acquitted by the Senate after a trial in which intense partisan politics was the major factor. Chase, a Federalist, was a victim of attacks on the Supreme Court by Jeffersonian Democrats, who planned to impeach Chief Justice John Marshall, also a Federalist, if Chase was convicted.

Secretary of War William W. Belknap, the only cabinet member to be impeached and tried by the Senate, was acquitted in 1876 largely because some senators questioned their authority to try Belknap after he had resigned from the cabinet. Belknap had been one of many high officials tainted by widespread corruption and incompetence in the Grant administration.

Proceedings against the only senator to be impeached, William Blount of Tennessee, were dismissed by the Senate in 1799 for lack of jurisdiction since the Senate had already expelled him.

Although few officials have been impeached, calls for impeachment of federal officials are frequently made by disgruntled and disaffected members of Congress. Such calls seldom advance beyond rhetoric. For example, in 1843 the House rejected a resolution to investigate whether there was cause to initiate impeachment proceedings against John Tyler, who became president after the death of William Henry Harrison. Tyler had become a political outcast, ostracized by the Democrats and his own Whig Party, but a majority of the House apparently felt that impeachment was too drastic a measure to use against him.

More on this topic:

Watergate Affair, p. 567

One member of the House twice attempted to launch impeachment proceedings against President Herbert C. Hoover during the Great Depression in 1932 and 1933, but the House overwhelmingly rejected both attempts.

A move was made in 1872 to impeach Schuyler Colfax, Grant's first vice president, because of his involvement in the Crédit Mobilier scandal. Crédit Mobilier was a dummy corporation set up by several members of Congress to pocket public funds intended to be used for the building of the Union Pacific Railroad, and Colfax owned some of the stock. The Judiciary Committee recommended against impeachment on the grounds that he obtained his stock before becoming vice president.

Timing was on Vice President Aaron Burr's side in 1804 when he shot and killed former Treasury secretary Alexander Hamilton in a duel. Because Burr's term was set to expire less than eight months later, the House never launched impeachment proceedings against him, even though he was indicted for murder in New York and New Jersey. Burr was never arrested and prosecuted.

Impoundment

Refusal to spend money voted by Congress, a practice known as impoundment, was at one time a potent tool of the president in countering Congress's spending power. But its frequent use in the late 1960s and 1970s prompted Congress to set limits.

The Constitution does not spell out whether presidents are required to promptly spend funds appropriated by Congress or whether they can make independent judgments on the timing of such spending and on whether appropriated funds should be used at all. Some presidents took advantage of this gap to impound appropriated funds they believed were unnecessary or wasteful. In effect, then, impoundment gave them a second veto over appropriations, because they could withhold funds Congress intended to be spent for programs and even for entire agencies.

Impoundment for the most part was used infrequently and without a great deal of controversy until the presidency of Richard Nixon, who refused to spend billions of dollars of appropriated funds. Nixon argued that he was withholding the money to combat inflation, but opposition Democrats contended the president was using impoundment primarily to enforce his own spending priorities in defiance of the will of Congress.

Frustrated by the impoundment battle, Congress acknowledged that it had forfeited control of the budget through the haphazard way it dealt with presidential spending requests. In 1974 Congress set up a new BUDGET PROCESS. The new system set limits on the president's power to delay spending temporarily (called a deferral) or to cancel it altogether (a rescission).

The practice of impoundment dated to the presidency of Thomas Jefferson, but presidents seldom used it, largely because they wanted to avoid major fights with Congress over control of the purse. Congress gave impoundment a statutory basis by passing the Anti-Deficiency Acts of 1905 and 1906. These laws allowed presidents to withhold funds for a period of time to prevent deficits or overspending in an agency.

In the New Deal, President Franklin D. Roosevelt occasionally used impoundments for budgetary or policy purposes. In some cases the president acted with at least the implied consent of Congress. During the Great Depression, for example, spending bills were sometimes treated as ceilings, allowing Roosevelt to refuse to spend money when he believed it to be unnecessary. During World War II Roosevelt argued that his war powers gave him the power to cut spending that was not essential to national security.

Presidents Harry S. Truman, Dwight D. Eisenhower, and John F. Kennedy all used impoundments to cut military spending. Kennedy, for example, refused to spend funds appropriated to build an air force bomber, much to the irritation of Congress.

President Lyndon B. Johnson, on the other hand, used impoundments to curtail domestic spending during the Vietnam War. As the war continued and inflation rose, Johnson impounded funds designated for agriculture, conservation, education, housing, and transportation. These impoundments were usually temporary, and the funds eventually were released. Although Johnson did not use the power of impoundment to cripple congressionally appropriated programs (many of them were his own), his actions did set a precedent for the use of impoundment to combat inflation—a power later adopted and expanded by Nixon.

Both Johnson and Nixon used impoundment to control spending, but Nixon's use was unprecedented in its scope and effects. While Johnson relied on temporary deferrals rather than permanent cuts and worked personally with Congress to soothe tempers, the Nixon administration's impoundments seemed designed to eliminate or to curtail particular programs favored by the Democratic Congress.

Between 1969 and 1974 the administration attempted to rearrange Congress's budget priorities. When Congress overrode Nixon's veto of a bill to control water pollution, Nixon handicapped the program by impounding half the money allotted for it. The Nixon administration also made major changes through impoundment of funds for construction of low-rent housing, mass transit, food stamps, and medical research programs. By 1973 Nixon had impounded more than $20 billion, and his budget for the next year included more planned reductions.

Pressure began to build for Congress to do something about Nixon's use of the impoundment power. At first, individual members attempted to intervene personally with the president in an effort to restore funds to certain projects. Many subcommittees became concerned about the pattern of impoundment that was beginning to emerge—a pattern they feared threatened their control of the policy-making process. Congress began inserting language in certain spending bills mandating that funds be spent.

In 1974 Congress adopted the Congressional Budget and Impoundment Control Act, creating a whole new budget process. Included in the legislation were new procedures to prevent a president from impounding appropriations against the will of Congress.

Under the act, presidents must notify Congress when they decide to permanently impound appropriated funds. Rescissions require positive action by Congress: Unless Congress enacts a law

Q: Mr. President, how do you respond to criticism that your impoundment of funds abrogates power or authority that the Constitution gave to Congress?

THE PRESIDENT: The same way that Jefferson did, and Jackson did, and Truman did.... The constitutional right for the President of the United States to impound funds—and that is not to spend money, when the spending of money would mean either increasing prices or increasing taxes for all the people—that right is absolutely clear.

—Richard Nixon, News Conference, January 31, 1973

More on this topic:

Budget Process, p. 37

Immigration and Naturalization Service v. Chadha, p. 272

Separation of Powers, p. 460

Veto Power, p. 533

approving the rescission within forty-five days, presidents must spend the funds. Deferrals work in the opposite way: Once presidents notify Congress of their intention to defer spending appropriated funds, the deferral will take effect automatically unless Congress enacts a law forbidding the delay in spending. Congress may act on a deferral at any time. The original 1974 act permitted either chamber of Congress to overrule deferrals, but the one-house legislative veto by which either chamber could reject an executive branch action was declared unconstitutional by the Supreme Court in 1983. (See IMMIGRATION AND NATURALIZATION SERVICE V. CHADHA.) One question that remained unresolved was whether presidents could defer spending for policy reasons. In 1986 and 1987 the federal courts ruled that deferrals could be used only for management reasons, such as unanticipated delays in federal construction projects. Legislation passed by Congress in 1987 affirmed the court decisions and limited the president to deferrals for reasons of management, not policy.

Inauguration

The presidential inauguration, at which a new or reelected president formally assumes office, is an important event in the life of the nation; it serves as a grand, ceremonial conclusion to the election process. Such ceremonies are overt political rituals that instill patriotism, unite the nation behind its leader, and provide for an orderly transfer of power.

Most of the current practice of inaugurations has evolved by way of tradition. The only part prescribed in the Constitution is the requirement that the president take the OATH OF OFFICE. Traditions have grown up around the oath itself, in particular the practice of the president taking the oath with one hand on the Bible. George Washington was the first to do so, and since the mid-nineteenth century almost all presidents have done likewise. The Bible used is sometimes a family heirloom, and at times it has been opened to a particular passage that the new president hopes will symbolize his administration. The oath, which has been taken outdoors since 1817 with one exception (Ronald Reagan's inauguration in 1985), is administered by the chief justice of the United States.

From the beginning, inaugurations have involved far more than just the swearing in of the president. To take the first oath of office, Washington traveled from Mount Vernon to New York City, hailed by great crowds of enthusiastic citizens along the way. In New York, Washington was greeted by even more frenzied rejoicing. He took the oath of office on the balcony of Federal Hall in front of a huge crowd before going inside to deliver the first inaugural address to the Senate.

Since then, inaugurations have usually been a time for pomp and circum-

President Kennedy taking the oath of office
Source: National Archives

stance. It is now customary for the president-elect to come to the White House and make the trip to the Capitol with the incumbent president—an awkward moment if the outgoing and new presidents are political opponents. Another feature is the inaugural parade, which originally proceeded to the Capitol for the swearing in, but for the past century has followed Pennsylvania Avenue from Capitol Hill to beyond the White House after the oath-taking.

Today inaugural parades are elaborate events that are broadcast live on television, with presidents watching the proceedings from behind bullet-proof glass. The parades include thousands of people and dozens of marching bands and floats, at a cost that had reached $25 million by 1993 when Bill Clinton and Al Gore were sworn into office. Additional expenses for police and public safety measures pushed the figure over $36 million. The government recouped two-thirds of the costs through ticket and souvenir sales and television broadcast rights to inaugural events. George W. Bush's 2001 inaugural committee raised almost $40 million to pay for elaborate celebrations that drew tens of thousands of Bush supporters to Washington, D.C.

Coming as they do in mid-January, inaugurations sometimes have to struggle with inclement weather. In 1961 John F. Kennedy's inaugural parade was made possible only by an all-out mobilization of snow-clearing equipment to plow through the drifts left by a major snowstorm that had hit the city. In 1985 Ronald Reagan's outdoor inaugural ceremony was canceled because of extremely cold weather; the swearing in was held inside the Capitol. Even in the nineteenth century, when the presidential term still began in March, Washington's unpredictable weather could have serious, even tragic, consequences. In 1841 William Henry Harrison, who insisted on attending the event and delivering his inaugural address, the longest in history, without an overcoat despite a cold, heavy rain, contracted pneumonia and died a month after taking office.

Actions taken during an inaugural ceremony are often highly symbolic. To the dismay of his Secret Service protectors, in 1977 Jimmy Carter chose to walk down Pennsylvania Avenue with his wife and family. His action, taken as a symbolic reaffirmation of his promise to reduce the imperial pomp of the presidency, also harked back to the nineteenth century, when presidents mingled much more easily with the people and the public was freely invited to enter the White House and have refreshments and shake the new president's hand. But sometimes these events became unruly, such as when a huge crowd virtually ransacked the White House at the celebration for Andrew Jackson in 1829.

Another common feature of inaugurations is the inaugural balls that end the day's festivities. To accommodate the large numbers of people who want to attend, many balls are held throughout the city, and the newly inaugurated president appears at all the official parties. Ronald and Nancy Reagan visited nine balls in 1985, Bill and Hillary Clinton stopped in at eleven in 1993, and George and Laura Bush attended eight in 2001.

Perhaps the most memorable and historically significant aspect of inaugurations is the inaugural address, which has supplied some of the most dramatic instances of presidential oratory. After the divisiveness of the presidential election, the inaugural address is an opportunity to bind up wounds by stressing unity and nonpartisanship. After having defeated Gerald R. Ford in 1976, for example, Carter began his speech with these conciliatory words, which acknowledged Ford's role in restoring a sense of trust in his office after the Watergate crisis: "For myself and for our nation, I want to thank my predecessor for all he has done to heal our land."

In troubled times an inaugural address is a chance to offer the people reassurance. Taking office in the midst of a financial panic, Franklin D. Roosevelt told the nation, "The only thing we have to

> *Let the word go forth from this time and place, to friend and foe alike, that the torch has been passed to a new generation of Americans—born in this century, tempered by war, disciplined by a hard and bitter peace, proud of our ancient heritage—and unwilling to witness or permit the slow undoing of those human rights to which this nation has always been committed, and to which we are committed today at home and around the world.*
>
> —*John F. Kennedy,* Inaugural Address, January 20, 1961

More on this topic:

Oath of Office, p. 393

Speeches and Rhetoric, p. 466

fear is fear itself." In the final weeks of the Civil War, Lincoln promised to act "with malice toward none, with charity for all, with firmness in the right as God gives us to see the right" in the effort to "bind up the nation's wounds."

Optimism is another common theme of inaugural addresses, one that was perhaps best represented by Kennedy's inaugural speech in 1961. The address, which seemed to many to sum up the idealistic aspirations of a generation, contained these memorable words: "And so, my fellow Americans: ask not what your country can do for you; ask what you can do for your country."

Every inaugural address since Harry S. Truman's in 1949 has been carried live on television. Such instant communication is taken for granted today, but early in the nation's history the distribution of the president's remarks to all parts of the country took a long time. In 1841 a record was set when the text of President William Henry Harrison's address was carried by train from Washington to New York in only ten hours. Four years later, Samuel Morse stood on the platform and transmitted an account of the proceedings to Baltimore as James K. Polk was sworn in. Calvin Coolidge's 1925 inaugural address was the first to be broadcast by radio.

Independent Counsel

The president is the chief law enforcement officer of the United States. But what happens if the president, or someone close to the president, is suspected of a crime? Who can be trusted to investigate and, if necessary, to prosecute? This was the question that faced the nation when President Richard Nixon and some of his top aides were implicated in the WATERGATE AFFAIR.

Watergate

The scandal was touched off in 1972 by a burglary at the Democratic Party national headquarters at the Watergate complex in Washington, D.C. The burglars turned out to be employees of the Nixon White House and the Committee to Re-elect the President, or CREEP, as it became known. After evidence emerged that the administration had attempted to cover up the burglary, Congress called on the president to appoint an independent counsel (also called a special prosecutor) to conduct all future investigations free of White House influence. The president agreed, and Harvard law professor Archibald Cox was appointed to the position.

Cox pursued his job too aggressively for the beleaguered president. When Cox demanded that Nixon relinquish tape recordings of conversations that had taken place in the Oval Office, Nixon ordered that Cox be fired. But neither Attorney General Elliot Richardson nor Deputy Attorney General William Ruckelshaus would agree to fire Cox, and both resigned. The next official in line, Solicitor General Robert H. Bork, fired Cox on Saturday night, October 20, 1973, completing the chain of events that became known as the Saturday night massacre.

After a public and congressional outcry, another independent counsel, Leon Jaworski, was appointed. Jaworski, a well-known trial lawyer from Texas, pursued the disputed tapes in the courts and eventually won. (See UNITED STATES V. NIXON.) Nixon turned over the tapes and resigned in disgrace.

The Independent Counsel Law: Never Popular

The Watergate affair inspired Congress to establish guidelines for future special prosecutors that would guarantee their independence. A provision of the 1978 Ethics in Government Act created an office of independent counsel to investigate and prosecute criminal allegations against high-ranking members of the executive branch, including the president. In 1988 the Supreme Court upheld the legality of the independent counsel law.

The independent counsel is appointed to investigate and prosecute a specific case, such as the IRAN-CONTRA AFFAIR or the Arkansas Whitewater land deal. The counsel is named at the request of the attorney general, after a preliminary investigation by the Justice Department, by a special panel of judges appointed by the chief justice of the United States. The attorney general, who serves at the pleasure of the president, is a pivotal figure in the independent counsel process. Some attorneys general have been political associates of the president and have acted as legal "bodyguards" for the president in matters warranting consideration of the naming of an independent counsel. The attorney general can delay, subvert, or derail the process by slipshod investigations or narrow interpretations of the law allegedly being violated by executive branch members.

In late 1997 Janet Reno, the Clinton administration's attorney general, faced sustained congressional and media pressure to appoint independent counsels in cases involving the president, vice president, and past and present cabinet officers in alleged violations of campaign finance laws during the 1996 election. Reno, saying she had no "solid evidence" that the laws had been broken, was accused of being manipulated and influenced by the White House for its own political advantage. She nevertheless refused to appoint an independent counsel to look into these matters. The issue of Vice President Al Gore's activities during the 1996 campaign reemerged during his 2000 presidential bid.

The law always had its detractors. In the 1980s Republicans were unhappy with its implementation against Republican presidents and their administrations. Officials in the administrations of Ronald Reagan (1981–1989) and George H. W. Bush (1989–1993) faced eleven independent counsel probes, including the highly charged investigation into the so-called Iran-contra affair. Lawrence E. Walsh, a former federal judge, was appointed on December 19, 1986, to look into the matter, and his investigation lasted until 1992. The only major convictions to come out of that expensive six-year investigation—those of Lt. Col. Oliver L. North and Adm. John M. Poindexter—were overturned on appeal. The independent counsel statute lapsed on December 15, 1992, after Senate Republicans blocked action on reauthorization.

The Democratic-controlled 103d Congress revived the law on June 30, 1994, and President Bill Clinton signed it into law. Little more than a month later, the panel of judges appointed Kenneth W. Starr as independent counsel to look into the president's and first lady's involvement with the failed Whitewater Development Corporation in Arkansas. Starr replaced special prosecutor Robert B. Fiske Jr., whom Attorney General Reno had appointed on January 20, 1994, at a time when the independent counsel law was in abeyance. With the permission of the court, Starr had expanded the investigation into the firing of White House Travel Office personnel and a White House aide's

This subpoena, issued by Watergate special prosecutor Archibald Cox on July 23, 1973, ordered President Richard Nixon to appear before the federal grand jury and to bring taped conversations relevant to the Watergate affair.

Source: National Archives.

More on this topic:

Clinton v. Jones, *p. 101*

Iran-Contra Affair, p. 294

Watergate Affair, p. 567

use of confidential Federal Bureau of Investigation files on past Republican appointees.

In January 1998 Starr received approval to expand his investigation even further, to determine whether President Clinton had attempted to suborn perjury to cover up an alleged sexual affair with a White House intern, Monica Lewinsky. Starr's investigation led directly to Clinton's impeachment by the House on December 19, 1998. The president was acquitted in the Senate on February 12, 1999. Acquittal in that political venue, however, did not end the criminal investigation. Under Starr's replacement, Robert W. Ray, the Office of Independent Counsel continued its investigation until Clinton's penultimate day in office, when Clinton concluded a settlement with Ray.

Independent counsels also had been appointed to investigate several Clinton cabinet secretaries. By the time the independent counsel statute lapsed for the second time on June 30, 1999, neither Democrats nor Republicans were enthusiastic about it. In lieu of that law, the Justice Department unveiled guidelines on July 1 for how special prosecutors would assume their responsibilities, thereby returning the country to a system similar to that in place before enactment of the first independent counsel law in 1978. Whether to appoint a counsel, whom to appoint, and the areas for inquiry would be dictated exclusively by the attorney general. In a bid to prevent an administration from quashing worthy inquiries, attorneys general may fire a special prosecutor only for "good cause."

Independent Executive Agencies

Independent executive agencies exist outside of and independent from the executive departments. However, they are normally considered to be part of the presidential hierarchy, and presidents exert considerable influence over them.

These agencies perform a single function and report directly to the president. They usually are headed by one person who serves at the pleasure of the president—that is, someone who is appointed by the president and can be dismissed by the president as well.

Prominent among such agencies are the National Aeronautics and Space Administration (NASA), the General Services Administration, the Environmental Protection Agency (EPA), and the Central Intelligence Agency.

Many of these agencies were created in an effort to avoid bureaucratic inertia, often resulting from the failure of existing agencies to accomplish their objectives. In 1964, for example, President Lyndon B. Johnson created the Office of Economic Opportunity to help implement his Great Society pro-

President George W. Bush meets with NASA officials and crew members of the space shuttle and the International Space Station in the Oval Office on January 15, 2003.
Source: Reuters

grams. By locating the office in the Executive Office of the President and not in a specific department, the White House was able to exert more control over its operation and ensure that the administration's antipoverty objectives were carried out.

Similarly, NASA was located outside the control of a specific department to help expedite its formation and operation, free from the traditional demands of departmental control. In addition, it was set apart from the Defense Department to demonstrate that the U.S. space program would be controlled by civilians rather than the military.

Other independent agencies are born out of vested interests. Members of Congress and interest groups want to guarantee that these agencies are responsive to their wishes. Moreover, presidents and Congress often want these agencies to remain free of the traditional constraints and methods of old-line departments. For example, in an effort to challenge actions detrimental to the environment, EPA was made independent of departments that might have had traditional environmental interests.

Because of their independent status, these agencies can pursue their objectives more freely and maneuver more openly than departments. This kind of freedom, however, often means that independent agencies will have few allies in the executive branch, possibly diminishing their overall influence on the development of executive policy. Executive independence also may result in overlapping jurisdictions and conflicts between the independent agencies and existing executive organizations.

Some agencies have been quite successful in their independent status by developing new coalitions with groups not traditionally represented by executive departments. For example, the Civil Rights Commission, established in 1957 as a six-member, bipartisan, independent agency, used its autonomous organizational status to become a constructive critic of federal civil rights policies. Between 1959 and 1970, by forging coalitions outside the executive branch, the commission was able to achieve having more than two-thirds of its recommendations either enacted into law or included in executive orders.

Independent Regulatory Agencies

Independent regulatory agencies regulate various parts of the economy to protect the public interest. As the name indicates, they are designed to operate independently of all three branches of government.

These agencies are usually headed by a bipartisan group—often called a commission or a board—rather than an individual. Commission members are appointed by the president and approved by the Senate, but they do not report directly to either.

Prominent examples of independent regulatory agencies are the Federal Reserve Board (FRB), National Labor Relations Board (NLRB), Federal Communications Commission (FCC), Federal Trade Commission (FTC), Federal Election Commission (FEC), and Securities and Exchange Commission (SEC).

Although regulatory agencies oversee a wide range of activities, they are alike in some ways. For example, all of these agencies have substantial authority to carry out various regulatory functions. They are sometimes called "quasi-agencies" because they can perform quasi-legislative, quasi-executive, and quasi-judicial functions. They can issue rules that govern certain sections of the economy, oversee implementation of those rules, and adjudicate disputes over interpretation of the rules.

Congress has attempted to protect the independence of these organizations. Commissioners serve overlapping fixed terms, usually four to seven years. Even though they are political appointees, presidents cannot simply fire them.

In 1935 the Supreme Court ruled that President Franklin D. Roosevelt had unconstitutionally fired a member of the FTC. In *HUMPHREY'S EXECUTOR V. UNITED STATES* the Court held that presidents cannot remove regulatory commission members for ruling in ways that might displease the president or members of Congress. Commissioners usually can be removed only for inefficiency, neglect of duty, or misconduct.

In a further attempt to ensure political independence from the president, Congress made these commissions bipartisan and placed limits on the number of appointees from any single political party. Generally, neither political party may have a majority of more than one.

Still, presidents always have been able to name board or commission members who share their views regardless of political party affiliation. Many conservative Democrats share the same policy beliefs as Republicans, and many liberal Republicans have policy beliefs similar to those of Democrats. Although commissioners serve long overlapping terms, presidents often have the opportunity to place a majority of their appointees in any given agency. By appointing agency heads and commissioners who share their philosophical views, presidents are able to leave their imprint on the government.

Whether regulatory commissioners should come from the industries that they are supposed to regulate is one of the controversial questions confronting such appointments. The logical place to turn for experts on the interest to be controlled is that interest itself. But appointing someone who has such an association leaves the commissioner open to a charge of conflict of interest.

Presumably, appointees to regulatory commissions should be experts in the policy area they have been chosen to oversee and also objective parties who would not favor one side over another in a policy dispute. In practice, however, regulatory agencies tend to develop reciprocal relationships with the interests they are supposed to regulate.

In addition to the traditional independent commissions, there are regulatory agencies within the executive branch. The Environmental Protection Agency (EPA), for example, is one of the IN-DEPENDENT EXECUTIVE AGENCIES whose administrator serves at the pleasure of the president and with the approval of the Senate.

There also are regulatory agencies within the executive departments, such as the Food and Drug Administration (FDA) in the Health and Human Services Department and the Occupational Safety and Health Administration (OSHA) within the Labor Department. These agencies serve under the authority of the department in which they are located. Heads of these agencies, like the EPA director, are subject to presidential appointment and also to presidential dismissal. Presidents may appoint and dismiss these agency heads either personally or through their department secretaries.

Growth of Regulation

At first, regulatory activity primarily involved economic matters, but modern regulatory agencies have moved more and more into the area of social concerns. Although these social concerns usually are related to economic activities, their scope is different from traditional regulation in that they touch on issues that are of importance to individual consumers.

Economic Regulation

In 1887 the federal government undertook its first major regulation of a private sector of the economy when Congress, exercising its constitutional right to regulate interstate commerce, created the Interstate Commerce Commission (ICC). Congress initially did not intend to make the ICC independent of the control of the executive branch. During the original congressional debate on its creation, matters of independence and presidential control were never considered. Congress first placed the ICC in the Interior Department but two years later gave the ICC control over its own affairs. Gradually the ICC became politically and organizationally independent as Congress increased its regulatory powers.

When it became evident that the ICC could not handle the regulation of all commerce, Congress created a network of new regulatory agencies patterned after the ICC. In 1913, for example, the Federal Reserve System began to govern banking and regulate the supply of money. The next year the Federal Trade Commission was created to regulate business practices and control monopolistic behavior. Between 1915 and 1933, the beginning of Franklin Roosevelt's administration, Congress set up seven other regulatory agencies, including the Tariff Commission (1916), Commodities Exchange Authority (1922), Customs Service (1927), and Federal Power Commission (1930).

After the Great Depression and beginning with Roosevelt's New Deal, an extraordinary flood of regulatory programs passed Congress. Between 1932 and 1938 eight major regulatory agencies were set up to handle problems created by the economic crisis of the depression. These included several agencies that became mainstays in the American way of life, including the Federal Home Loan Bank Board (abolished in 1989), Federal Deposit Insurance Corporation, Securities and Exchange Commission, and National Labor Relations Board.

Social Regulation

The New Deal was the true beginning of large-scale federal regulation of the economy, and it also provided the foundation for many social regulatory agencies that characterized the 1960s and 1970s. As New Deal programs expanded the scope of the federal government, use of the federal government to solve the nation's economic and social problems became accepted. By the mid-1960s the federal government was providing medical care, educational aid, nutritional help, urban renewal, and job training, among other services.

Social activism grew to such an extent that many consumer and environmental groups were calling for a new wave of regulation to achieve certain social goals, such as clean air and consumer protection. Congress responded in the 1970s with the creation of several new regulatory agencies, including the National Highway Traffic Safety Administration in the Department of Transportation, the EPA, OSHA, the Consumer Product Safety Commission, and the Nuclear Regulatory Commission.

Methods of Regulation

Regulatory agencies use a variety of techniques to carry out their mandates. Sometimes the method that an agency uses is set by Congress in the legislation creating the agency. Congress may find an issue of such importance that it tells the agency exactly how to regulate the area of concern. For issues of lesser importance Congress may give the agency a free hand to use whatever regulatory methods it believes appropriate.

One of the commonest methods of regulation is the required disclosure of consumer information. Requirements that food product labels list the product's ingredients, that household products come with safety instructions, or that cigarette packages bear health warnings are some of the best-known examples.

The most extreme form of regulation is mandatory licensing, which requires specific professions and businesses to obtain licenses to practice their trade, to take certain actions, or to own certain goods. Various federal agencies and commissions license everything from radio and television stations to nuclear power plants.

More on this topic:

Federal Election Commission, p. 212

Federal Reserve System, p. 214

Humphrey's Executor v. United States, *p. 269*

Independent Executive Agencies, p. 286

When information about certain products cannot be conveniently provided to consumers or a product's potential for harm is very great, agencies often set standards with which companies must comply. Failure to maintain the standards may result in legal penalties. Some agencies have the power to recall consumer products that could harm their users.

Interest Groups and the Presidency

Beginning with Alexis de Tocqueville, the French author who wrote about his impressions of the United States in the 1830s in the classic study *Democracy in America,* observers have noted the strong tendency of Americans to form private associations to pursue their social and political ends. These organizations or interest groups, which may be defined as a set of people who join together to promote ideals or material benefits, are one of the most important elements of the U.S. political scene and one of the major elements with which any president must deal.

Interest groups form to protect a group's material interests in budget, tax, and regulatory proceedings in Washington, D.C., or in state capitals, to express a group's ideology and desires, or to provide services and standards to a group. Because the assistance sought by interest groups usually is available only from the public sector, they frequently take their claims to government at all levels, including the president.

Although interest groups have existed throughout the history of the United States, their power and importance increased greatly with the New Deal. Today thousands of interest groups exist across the nation, with hundreds active in Washington. Interest groups play a larger role in national politics because of the decline of the political parties, the fragmentation of Congress, the complexity of many government issues, and changes in the style of political campaigning.

For the president, mastering interest group politics is an important key to success. Presidents need to line up interest group support to mobilize both the general public and political leaders in difficult policy battles. Chief executives look to interest groups for votes from their members at election time, support in lobbying Congress, expertise on difficult issues, and funds for political campaigns and other causes.

In seeking to reach out to interest groups and use their support in political and policy battles, presidents must have a strategy that takes a variety of factors into account. Perhaps the most important consideration is which interests have supported the president during previous political campaigns and government initiatives. As when dealing with public opinion, the president must maintain the steady

Members of the prominent public interest group Common Cause rally outside the Capitol in March 2002, before the Senate vote on Bipartisan Campaign Reform Act.
Source: Common Cause

backing of a basic core of supporters. Republican presidents traditionally have aligned themselves with interests such as business, oil companies, conservative social groups, and some farm organizations. Democratic chief executives usually have looked for support from labor, environmental groups, minorities, and developers.

Sometimes, however, the president's relationship with interest groups develops issue by issue. Because most such groups are concerned with advancing the interests of their members rather than putting forward a broad, ideological view of government and society, they often are willing to work together with other organizations on one particular matter even though they may disagree with those groups on most other points. For example, business and labor groups may be in alliance on issues relating to economic growth or foreign trade, but they may strongly oppose each other on workplace issues. A president must be sensitive to the opportunities for putting together disparate alliances, while also remaining aware of the danger that one of his proposals might lead to the formation of a coalition in opposition. Bill Clinton ran into interest group opposition in the early years of his presidency as he tried to push his health care reform plan. Environmental groups fought George W. Bush's plans to dismantle some environmental regulations, and liberal interest groups fought some of his more conservative judicial nominations.

Presidential policies and programs may have an important impact on the broad array of interest groups. Using public opinion, budget priorities, and White House staff, the president can help some groups and undercut others. A textbook example of presidential influence over interest group alignment was provided by Franklin D. Roosevelt, who brought together groups such as the elderly, labor, blacks, and the poor into the New Deal coalition, which was to dominate the Democratic Party for a generation. Similarly, Lyndon B. Johnson's Great Society programs in housing, community development, and health care led to the creation of many new interest groups.

The Reagan administration also acted skillfully to transform the interest group balance of power. Reagan gave greater visibility to many groups, such as southern white evangelical Christians, and encouraged them to move into the political sphere. His policies also helped to unite groups, such as conservative Protestants and Catholics, that previously had been divided but now for the first time found common ground on abortion and other "moral" issues. At the same time, the administration helped to widen the differences between business and labor and ensure that the two interests did not unite in opposition to elements of its program.

In addition to such broad questions of strategy, presidents have an array of methods for maximizing their influence on interest groups. Traditionally, the most important means has been the federal departments. The White House was less likely in the past to have direct ties to

President Ronald Reagan's support of interest groups such as southern white evangelical Christians gave television evangelist Pat Robertson the visibility he needed to enter the 1988 contest for the Republican presidential nomination.
Source: AP

Presidents have always had to maintain good relationships with various interests for political support. This is especially true in contemporary American politics, where the number of organized interest groups has exploded yet expectations remain high that presidents will support certain interests that provide electoral support. Presidents can appease interests through the use of unilateral action such as executive orders, which do not require the time and negotiation required of the legislative process. In taking credit for promoting diversity in education, for example, President Clinton assured the American Council on Education, while addressing them in 1994,

groups; instead, the cabinet served as the main link between the administration and such organizations. Cabinet officials tend to have strong ties to the groups whose affairs their department oversees, and in some cases entire departments—notably Agriculture, Commerce, Labor, Education, and Veterans Affairs—were created to serve the interests of specific groups. Appointed positions within the departments also give presidents an opportunity to reach out to groups by naming prominent members to important posts.

Indeed, for many interest groups the focus of attention in Washington has always been much more the departments and Congress than the White House. Lobbying organizations tend not to concentrate on the White House for several reasons, not least of which is that it is far easier to arrange to talk with a member of Congress or department official than with the tightly scheduled chief executive and top aides. Presidents come and go every few years, but bureaucrats and the members and staff of congressional committees—which together with the interest groups form the so-called "iron triangle" of Washington lobbying—tend to stay around much longer. Moreover, interest groups in many cases are concerned with regulatory and technical questions that might seem insignificant from the lofty position of the White House but can have a vital impact on the economic health of the groups' members.

Even if interest groups favor the predictability of agencies and committees, many have a relationship with the presidency. Since World War II the presidency has developed regular channels for interest groups to make and receive appeals. The size of the White House staff has increased greatly, with many officials assigned in some way to keep track of interest groups. The formal mechanism for dealing with interest groups is the Office of Public Liaison, which was created in the administration of Gerald R. Ford.

White House aides assigned to interest groups have several responsibilities. They must keep track of the president's debts to particular groups and attempts to help those groups, while also monitoring the current concerns of such organizations. In addition, the White House must work to build coalitions behind specific proposals, and then help to mediate conflicts within the coalitions to ensure that the president's support does not fragment.

Another effective tactic available to the White House in managing interest groups is to appoint their representatives to a commission to study a problem that concerns them. By doing so, a president can send a message to the groups that their opinions are valued, without making commitments to adopt the policies they favor. The commissions can work behind closed doors, which encourages interest groups that are at odds to resolve their differences without public controversy. When the commission finally produces its report, the administration has the option of acknowledging and publicizing its conclusions if it agrees with them or thinks they would be politically helpful. If, however, it finds the commission's work not to its advantage, it can simply ignore that work, usually at little political cost.

Although the White House has many resources in its ongoing campaign to bend and shape interest group politics to its advantage, the relationship is by no means one-sided. Interest groups can take a variety of actions to bring pressure on a president and direct policy decisions to their benefit. One of the most important of these actions is campaign promises. Despite the cynical view that candidates forget campaign promises as soon as they

More on this topic:

Elections and Campaigns, p. 168

Public Opinion and the Presidency, p. 427

enter office, studies have found that presidents at least attempt to honor most of their pledges. Presidents usually target those pledges to specific interest groups. Jimmy Carter, for example, pushed through Congress a bill to create a separate Department of Education in order to fulfill a commitment he had made to the National Education Association during his 1976 campaign.

Most interest group pressure on an administration is brought through the customary channels of politics and behind-the-scenes relationships with executive agencies. In addition, organizations have the option of using public demonstrations. In recent years, interest groups have used modern telecommunications to make their point, sending petitions to the White House via mass e-mail. Many groups that are not part of the secure federal establishment must find more dramatic and visible ways to influence the president. Sometimes such efforts are successful, as when antiwar protesters in the 1960s helped bring about a shift in public opinion and ultimately in presidential policy toward a withdrawal from Vietnam. But presidents may choose to defy such public pressure, as Reagan did in the face of massive demonstrations against his nuclear weapons policies.

> *Later today, I will sign another Executive order to advance educational excellence for Hispanic-Americans. I believe we now live in a Nation with way over 150 ethnic and racial groups. In a global economy with shrinking distances, instantaneous communication, and blurred borders, this can give us an advantage in the 21st century unlike that enjoyed by any other nation, but only if we have a genuinely deep commitment to universal education and the development of the capacities of all Americans.*
>
> *—Bill Clinton,* Remarks to the American Council on Education, February 22, 1994

Interior Department

As the nation's principal conservation agency, the U.S. Department of the Interior is responsible for more than 500 million acres of federal land, or about one-fifth of the total U.S. land area. The department also oversees the conservation and development of natural resources, including minerals, water, and fish and wildlife. (The Department of Agriculture oversees the nation's forests.)

Other responsibilities include preservation and administration of the nation's scenic and historic areas, reclamation of arid lands in the West through irrigation, and management of hydroelectric power systems.

The department also administers programs providing services to Native Americans. It acts as trustee for over 50 million acres of land that the United States holds in trust and that consists mostly of Indian reservations. Interior is responsible as well for other territories under U.S. administration.

During the nation's early years, functions that would be carried out by an "interior," "home," or "internal affairs" department were apportioned by Congress among other agencies. To

The Beehive Geyser at Yellowstone National Park
Source: National Park Service

streamline these activities, proposals to establish a home office were made as early as 1789, but to no avail.

In the late 1840s advocates of a separate cabinet-level department won over a majority in Congress. It was argued that the Treasury Department already was burdened by increasing fiscal duties and could not handle management of the vast domain acquired through the Louisiana Purchase of 1803, the Mexican-American War of 1846–1848, and the 1848 treaty with Great Britain by which the United States acquired the Oregon Territory.

Legislation to create the Interior Department was approved in early 1849. Congress transferred to the new department the General Land Office from Treasury, the Patent Office from the State Department (it was later moved to the Commerce Department), and the Bureau of Indian Affairs and Pension Office from the War Department. Other responsibilities were assigned as well.

For a long time Interior's policy mirrored the general public sentiment that natural resources were the limitless foundation on which a powerful nation could be built. As a result, public policy on the exploitation of resources was extremely permissive.

> **More on this topic:**
>
> *Cabinet, p. 60*

Gradually, however, Americans realized that their natural resources were not inexhaustible. The environmental movement of the late 1960s and 1970s heightened this awareness and led to the creation of additional agencies and programs to share responsibility with the Interior Department for overseeing the nation's resources.

The major bureaus within the department are the U.S. Geological Survey, Bureau of Indian Affairs, U.S. Fish and Wildlife Service, Bureau of Land Management, Office of Surface Mining Reclamation and Enforcement, Bureau of Reclamation, Minerals Management Service, and National Park Service.

Iran-Contra Affair

The Iran-contra affair, which was uncovered in late 1986, was the most significant political scandal since the Watergate affair was exposed during the early 1970s. Investigations revealed that members of President Ronald Reagan's staff had secretly sold U.S. weapons to Iran and then illegally diverted some of the profits from the sales to help contra rebels in Nicaragua. No hard evidence was found that Reagan knew about the diversion of funds, but the scandal weakened his presidency and called into question his detached management style.

Covert Activities

The scandal grew out of the Reagan administration's desire to help the Nicaraguan contras overthrow the communist Sandinista government of Nicaragua. The Democratic-controlled Congress, however, doubted the wisdom of providing U.S. aid to the contras. It enacted a series of "Boland amendments" (named after Rep. Edward P. Boland, a Massachusetts Democrat who was then chairman of the House Intelligence Committee) that restricted aid to the contras. Reagan administration officials—including Central Intelligence Agency director William Casey, successive national security advisers Robert C. MacFarlane and Adm. John M. Poindexter, and National Security Council staff member Lt. Col. Oliver L. North (U.S. Marine Corps)—secretly explored ways to skirt the congressional ban on aid. Through private agents, North helped the contras to buy covert shipments of arms and provided them with advice on military tactics. North also worked closely with a group of conservative fund-raisers who solicited money for the contras from wealthy Americans.

In early 1986, despite a U.S. embargo on direct arms sales to Iran and an aggressive campaign to halt arms exports by all countries to Iran, the Reagan administration authorized the secret sale of military equipment to Iran. Iran was in the midst of a long war with neighboring Iraq and was desperate for weaponry. Reagan and his advisers hoped that the arms sales would improve relations with the Iranians and secure the release of American hostages held captive in Lebanon by pro-Iranian kidnappers.

In the spring of 1986 Reagan staffers developed a scheme to use the profits from the secret Iranian arms sales to fund the contras. About $3.5 million was devoted to this purpose. In November 1986, however, the sale of arms to Iran was revealed. Later that month Attorney General Edwin Meese III announced that profits from the Iranian sale had been diverted to the contras. Initial probes of the affair revealed that North and other officials had lied to Congress and shredded documents to cover up their activities.

Investigations

In an effort to assure Congress and the public that his administration wanted a full disclosure of the facts surrounding the developing scandal, Reagan appointed a board of inquiry chaired by former senator John Tower, a Texas Republican. Under political pressure, the Reagan administration also requested appointment of an independent counsel, and retired federal judge Lawrence E. Walsh, an Oklahoma Republican, was selected. Meanwhile, the Senate and House voted to establish select Iran-contra investigating committees, headed by Sen. Daniel K. Inouye of Hawaii and Rep. Lee H. Hamilton of Indiana, both Democrats.

The Tower Commission report, issued on February 26, 1987, was highly critical of Reagan. It maintained that Reagan delegated too much authority to the National Security Council staff without monitoring its activities. Reagan, the report said, had not paid close attention to what his aides were doing and had not asked the kinds of questions that would have revealed problems in time to correct them.

The Senate and House investigating committees worked throughout much of 1987. Joint hearings of the committees drew large national television audiences. For the American public, the focal point of the hearings was the combative and articulate North, who portrayed himself as a loyal soldier who had done only what was authorized and who had sought merely to serve his country. North's forceful and sometimes emotional presentation—aided by his appearance in his Marine Corps uniform adorned with medals—created a public sensation.

The committee's majority report, issued on November 18, 1987, concluded that members of the National Security Council and others (including private businesspeople) had consciously attempted to circumvent the law prohibiting aid to the contras. Although some members of the committee expressed their amazement that Reagan could have been kept in the dark about his staff's illegal activities, no hard evidence came to light to show that he was aware of the diversion. Admiral Poindexter claimed that he had authorized the diversion without telling the president.

Doubts remained about the president's involvement, but his presidency survived the scandal. Although the public was troubled by Reagan's detachment from and apparent mismanagement of his staff, he remained popular. An overhaul of White House personnel, Reagan's status as a president late in his second term, and continuing economic prosperity combined to dampen the political effects of the scandal.

Independent Counsel

The Iran-contra affair did not fade away with Reagan's departure from the White House. The probe by independent counsel Walsh continued to capture headlines during George H. W. Bush's

President Reagan receives the Tower Commission Report in the Cabinet Room with John Tower and Edmund Muskie, February 26, 1987

presidency. Walsh's final report on the affair was issued in early 1994, more than seven years after the scandal first became public. The probe produced indictments of Iran-contra participants both within and outside of government, but Walsh's efforts in the major cases ultimately proved unsuccessful.

North and Poindexter were tried and convicted of felony charges, but their convictions were overturned on the grounds that their trials may have been tainted by their earlier immunized testimony before Congress. Several other participants pleaded guilty or were found guilty of various charges.

Caspar W. Weinberger, Regan's secretary of defense, was scheduled to go on trial in early 1993 on charges of lying to Congress and concealing the existence of his personal notes that detailed the Reagan administration's decision to approve arms sales to Iran. But on Christmas Eve 1992, a few weeks before he was to leave office, Bush pardoned Weinberger and five others who had been accused of withholding information or lying to Congress about the Iran-contra affair.

Walsh's probe, estimated to have cost about $38 million, came to an end on January 18, 1993, with the release of his final report. In it, Walsh exonerated Reagan of criminal culpability in the affair even as he bluntly accused the former president of creating a climate in which his senior aides felt free to violate the law. Walsh sharply disputed Bush's repeated assertions that, as Reagan's vice president, he had been "out of the loop" during the arms-for-hostages dealings with Iran. But Walsh also said he found no evidence of criminal wrongdoing by Bush.

In contrast to the conclusion reached by the select congressional committees that the scheme had been carried out largely by a mid-level "cabal of zealots," Walsh said Reagan and his entire foreign policy team knowingly pursued secret programs that directly contravened the U.S. embargo on arms sales to Iran and the congressional restrictions on aid to the contras.

In the scorching written responses to Walsh's findings included in the final report, Reagan and Bush denied wrongdoing and denounced the investigation, as did most of the other former officials named by Walsh.

> **More on this topic:**
>
> *National Security Council, p. 381*
>
> *Reagan, Ronald, p. 437*

Iraq War (Operation Iraqi Freedom)

Following the successful 1991 Persian Gulf War led by President George H. W. Bush, Iraqi president Saddam Hussein remained in power but with a greatly reduced military capability. As a condition of the Gulf War ceasefire, Iraq had agreed to a number of constraints on its ability to wage war. These included economic sanctions, United Nations inspections of the country's weapons stockpiles to ensure that Hussein was not developing weapons of mass destruction, and two "no-fly" zones over the northern and southern portions of the country, imposed to limit Hussein's ability to use air power to threaten the ethnic Kurds in the north and Shiites in the south. For over a decade the United States and the United Kingdom, acting to enforce various UN Security Council resolutions related to the ceasefire, were engaged in low-level conflict with Hussein's regime when Iraq refused cooperation with weapons inspectors. One such instance was the December 1998 bombing of military sites known as Operation Desert Fox. Earlier that year President Bill Clinton also signed the "Iraq Liberation Act" to aid groups in opposition to the Hussein Regime.

September 11 and the "Axis of Evil"

The September 11, 2001, terrorist attacks on New York and Washington, D.C., produced a sea-change in American foreign policy toward Iraq. A centerpiece of President George W. Bush's strategy for combating threats to the United States was unveiled in his January 2002 State of the Union address. Suggesting the United States would take preemptive action against "rogue" states such as Iraq, Iran, and North Korea that were seeking to acquire nuclear weapons, Bush stated, "This [Iraq] is a regime that agreed to international inspections, then kicked out the inspectors. This is a regime that has something to hide from the civilized world. States like these and their terrorist allies constitute an *axis of evil,* arming to threaten the peace of the world." Operation Enduring Freedom in Afghanistan, launched in October 2001 and aimed at toppling the al-Qaeda-friendly Taliban government, appeared to be a resounding success, and the Bush administration then turned its sights on Iraq.

In 2002 and early 2003 Bush pushed for action to disarm Hussein, at times focusing on his alleged weapons of mass destruction and at times linking him to the al Qaeda terrorist network that had struck the United States on September 11, 2001. Bush succeeded in winning congressional approval in the fall of 2002 for military action against Iraq.

The Bush administration also won unanimous approval that fall from the UN Security Council for a resolution calling for tough UN weapons inspections in Iraq and providing Hussein with a last chance to disarm. In March 2003, citing Hussein's noncompliance, the administration opted for military action against the Iraqi dictator. It decided, however, not to seek another vote in the United Nations, this time to authorize war, because it was clear such a resolution would not pass. Although some countries, most notably Britain, agreed with Bush that military action was necessary, and joined Bush's "coalition of the willing," others, including France, Russia, and China, argued that the weapons inspectors should be given more time. (See also UNITED NATIONS.)

Invasion and "Mission Accomplished": March–May 2003

On March 19, 2003, Bush announced the start of the war, after Hussein and his sons did not meet a deadline to leave Iraq. After some three weeks the regime fell, Hussein went into hiding, and the United States sought to restore order to the country by establishing the Coalition Provisional Authority (CPA) headed by L. Paul Bremer. In addition, the Iraq Survey Group was formed with the mission of finding weapons of mass destruction, but none were ever found, thus damaging the credibility of the administration and American intelligence agencies.

Announcing the coalition's triumph in toppling the Hussein regime, President Bush made a highly publicized and dramatic speech to the nation on May 1. He appeared in a flight suit after arriving on the aircraft carrier USS *Abraham Lincoln.* In his infa-

Major combat operations in Iraq have ended. In the battle of Iraq, the United States and our allies have prevailed. And now our coalition is engaged in securing and reconstructing that country.

—*George W. Bush,* Address to the Nation on Iraq from the USS Abraham Lincoln, May 1, 2003

President George W. Bush walks across the tarmac with NFO Lt. Ryan Phillips to Navy One, an S-3B Viking jet, at Naval Air Station North Island in San Diego, May 1, 2003
Source: AP

mous address from the flight deck he asserted that "major combat operations in Iraq have ended." Behind him a large banner on the ship's bridge proclaimed, "Mission Accomplished." While it was true at the time that the Ba'ath regime was deposed and the Iraqi army was disbanded, remnants of the former regime had to be eliminated. Only then could the operation in Iraq turn to managing the occupation and building the foundation for a democratic government.

A part of Iraq in particular need of pacification is known as the Sunni Triangle, an area extending northwest from the capital and made up of the provinces of Baghdad, Anbar, and Salah. Throughout that region, remnants of the Ba'ath regime, radical religious elements, and some average Iraqis opposed to the U.S. occupation began to take advantage of the tens of thousands of tons of ammunition stocks left behind by the defeated Iraqi army, transforming the conflict into an anti-occupation insurgency. In July 2003, while responding to a reporter's question about the U.S. military's ability to maintain order in Iraq, President Bush replied, "Bring them on. We've got the force necessary to deal with the security situation."

Insurgency, Nation Building, and Civil War: 2004–2006

The years 2004 through 2005 saw an evolution in the domestic security situation in Iraq. After Hussein's two sons were killed on July 22, 2003, and the former dictator was captured on December 13, 2003, remnants of the Ba'ath regime were somewhat pacified, but foreign insurgents and elements of al Qaeda began to enter the country to battle the occupation. Power was eventually passed on from the CPA to the interim Iraqi government, but the insurgency began targeting Iraqi forces as well, putting additional pressure on an already fragile domestic ruling coalition.

The year 2004 was characterized by a number of historic battles for control of cities in the notoriously violent Sunni Triangle. Two of these battles took place in the city of Fallujah, west of Baghdad. American soldiers and marines captured their objectives, but the security situation in the country continued to deteriorate. Another complication was the inability of coalition forces to hold many cities and neighborhoods that had been cleared of insurgents. Further, underequipped and inadequately trained Iraqi security forces were unable to prevent insurgents from reoccupying cleared areas.

Despite the continuing violence, on January 31, 2005, Iraq's first democratic elections took place for the new Iraqi transitional government, which was set to replace the interim Iraqi government. Unfortunately, in May of that year, the violence in Iraq began to transition from an insurgency against the coalition occupation to a wider ethnically based struggle for control over the country's destiny after a swarm of mainly Sunni suicide bombers began to target Shiite civilians. On October 15 the constitution of Iraq was ratified and on December 15 the first election was held to elect members to the permanent Iraqi National Assembly. The violence then appeared to move toward civil war when on February 22, 2006, several men believed to be members of al Qaeda in Iraq entered the cherished Shiite Al Askari Mosque and detonated bombs that destroyed its famous "golden dome." Many Shiites retaliated by attacking Sunni mosques. Religious leaders pleaded for calm, but the bloodshed, often dubbed "sectarian violence," continued throughout 2006 and into 2007.

Domestic Discontent and Troop Surge

By late 2006 over 3,000 American service personnel had lost their lives in Iraq, the overwhelming majority of whom were killed by insurgents after the fall of the Hussein regime. Public opinion in the United States had also moved decidedly against the war. Bush suffered a major setback to his war strategy when his party lost both houses of Congress to the Democrats in the November 2006 midterm elections. Reasons for the Republican election loss included public dissatisfaction with Congress's overall job performance and various corruption scandals, but the vote was largely seen as a vote of no-confidence on the war in Iraq. Bush then began to alter his ongoing "stay the course" rhetoric, promising a change in strategy. One possible avenue for a change in direction came with the release of the bipartisan Iraq Study Group report in December. Included among its recommendations to the president was a proposal to open a dialogue with neighboring Syria and Iran for help in establishing order, and a phased pullback of U.S. forces from the country. Although the president announced that he would take the report seriously, he chose instead to embark on an escalation announced the following month. Finally, in December the Iraqi government carried out the death sentence on Saddam Hussein.

On January 10, 2007, President Bush addressed the nation to announce a course change recognizing, "The situation in Iraq is unacceptable to the American people, and it is unacceptable to me." The hallmark of this new strategy was a "surge" of additional forces in an attempt to restore order to the country, especially in Baghdad. With the American people wary of escalating the war and skeptical of the prospects for success, a historic showdown began to take shape between Bush and the new Democratic majority in Congress. On February 16, 2007, the House of Representatives completed debate on a nonbinding resolution opposing the "surge" and voted 246–182 in opposition to the president. As the president began to lose Republican support in Congress, the ongoing war in Iraq left open the possibility that unless events in Iraq changed for the better, Congress might begin to use its "power of the purse" to force the Bush administration to accept conditions in exchange for continued funding of the war.

More on this topic:

Persian Gulf War, p. 401

United Nations, p. 525

War on Terrorism, p. 554

Item Veto *See* LINE-ITEM VETO.

J

Jackson, Andrew

Andrew Jackson

The election of Andrew Jackson (1767–1845) as president in 1828 was a watershed in American politics. Jackson was the first westerner to be elected president and the first president to have been elected with the overwhelming support of the masses of farmers and citizens who recently had been enfranchised in most states.

Jackson was born on March 15, 1767, in Waxhaw, South Carolina. He was the youngest of the three sons of Andrew and Elizabeth Jackson, poor farmers who had emigrated from Ireland. Andrew's father died a few days before Andrew was born.

When he was just thirteen, Andrew and his older brother Robert joined the militia. Their older brother, Hugh, had already been killed in the Revolutionary War, and Andrew and Robert were wounded and captured by the British in 1781. While a prisoner, Andrew was scarred on the hand by a British officer who struck him with a saber. Based on his experiences during the war, Andrew developed a hatred of the British. Robert died two days after being released by the British, and his mother died later that year. Andrew was then left in the care of his mother's relatives.

In 1784 Jackson moved to Salisbury, North Carolina, where he studied law. He was admitted to the bar and began practicing law in 1787. In 1788 he moved to the new settlement of Nashville, where he became the prosecuting attorney of the Western District of North Carolina, which became the state of Tennessee.

In that same year Jackson met his future wife, Rachel Donelson Robards, who was separated from her husband, Lewis Robards. She and Jackson were married in 1791, believing that Rachel's divorce from Robards had already been obtained. After learning in late 1793 that Rachel's divorce had only recently become final, the couple repeated their wedding ceremony in January 1794 to avoid legal difficulties. Rachel Jackson died in 1828, after Jackson had been elected president but before his inauguration.

In 1796 Jackson was elected without opposition as Tennessee's first member of the U.S. House of Representatives. Although Jackson declined to run for reelection and returned to Tennessee when his term ended, within months he was elected to fill a vacant U.S. Senate seat. He served in the Senate from November 1797 to April 1798, when he resigned. He then returned to Tennessee because of financial difficulties and his dislike of being separated from his family. In November of that year he was appointed to a seat on the Tennessee Superior Court. He served there until 1804.

Jackson possessed a violent temper. During his years in Tennessee he was involved in several duels and fights. In 1806 Jackson fought a duel with Charles Dickenson, who had questioned the propriety of Jackson's marriage. Dickenson fired first, wounding Jackson in the chest. The athletic Jackson shrugged off his wound, straightened himself, and mortally wounded Dickenson with his volley. Because Dickenson's bullet was lodged near Jackson's heart, it could not be removed and caused Jackson periodic pain for the rest of his life.

Military Career

Beginning in 1802 Jackson held the rank of major general in the Tennessee militia. After the United States declared war on Great Britain in 1812, Jackson was sent to fight the Creek Indians, who were allied with the British. Jackson, whose troops had earlier nicknamed him "Old Hickory" in tribute to his toughness, engineered a five-month campaign that culminated in the decisive defeat of the Creeks at the Battle of Horseshoe Bend, Alabama, on March 27, 1814. Soon after, he was commissioned as a brigadier and then major general in the U.S. Army.

After a brief campaign in which Jackson's forces captured Pensacola, Florida, from the British, the general was ordered west to defend New Orleans. When the British attacked on January 8, 1815, Jackson's motley army of U.S. regulars, Tennessee backwoodsmen, free blacks, friendly Indians, and pirate Jean Lafitte's crew members laid down a deadly fire that left more than two thousand British troops killed or wounded. Only about forty of Jackson's men were killed, wounded, or missing. The decisive victory at New Orleans raised the morale of the nation, which had suffered many embarrassing military defeats during the war, and made Jackson a folk hero.

After the war Jackson remained military commander of the Southern District of the United States. In late 1817, acting on vague orders to defend the frontier near Spanish Florida from Indian attacks, Jackson launched an invasion of Florida that led to the capture of several Spanish posts. Secretary of State John Quincy Adams defended Jackson's actions as increasing pressure on the Spanish to cede the territory to the United States. President James Monroe stated his qualified support of Jackson's campaign, and in 1819 Adams concluded a treaty in which Spain renounced its claims to the Floridas.

Presidency

Although Jackson denied any interest in seeking the presidency, his supporters in Tennessee maneuvered to make him a candidate. In 1823 Jackson was elected to the U.S. Senate by the Tennessee legislature, which sent him back to Washington as an obvious contender for the presidency.

The 1824 election was a confusing affair in which all the candidates were Democratic-Republicans and no one received a majority of electoral votes. A total of 133 electoral votes were needed for election, but Jackson, who came in first, received only 99. John Quincy Adams finished second with 84, and William Crawford and Henry Clay received 41 and 37 votes, respectively. The election was thrown into the House of Representatives. Jackson lost the election when the House elected Adams after Clay gave his support to the second-place finisher.

In 1828, however, Democrat Jackson easily defeated incumbent Adams. Tens of thousands of rowdy citizens descended on Washington for Jackson's inauguration. The jubilant throngs at the White House broke furniture and china, muddied carpets, and forced Jackson to evacuate the premises for his own safety.

Jackson, like many presidents of his era, faced sectional tensions. In 1832 Congress had passed a high tariff despite the opposition of many southern states. Southerners objected to high tariffs because they protected the manufacturing interests in the North, while trade reprisals from Europe denied the South markets for its agricultural products. In response to the tariff law the South Carolina legislature declared that the federal tariff was null in that state. Jackson met the challenge to the Constitution by denouncing nullification and requesting authority from Congress to send troops to South Carolina if needed to enforce the tariff. Congress granted this authority, which helped to convince South Carolina to accept a compromise tariff bill backed by Jackson. The episode led to the estrangement of Jackson from his vice president, John C. Calhoun, who had supported his home state of South Carolina.

Although Jackson was a strong defender of the primacy of the federal government, he did not support all its activities. In 1832 Jackson vetoed the bill that would have rechartered the Second Bank of the United States, on the grounds that the bank was unconstitutional and a monopoly that benefited the rich. Jackson's political opponents hoped to turn the issue against him in the 1832 election, but the popular president easily defeated Whig Henry Clay. Unfortunately, the lack of a central bank weakened controls over state and local banks and contributed to inflation and overspeculation, which were partially responsible for the severe depression that began in 1837 after Jackson left office.

On January 30, 1835, Jackson became the first president to be the target of an assassination attempt. As Jackson was emerging from the Capitol, Richard Lawrence fired two pistols at him at point-blank range. Miraculously, both misfired. Jackson went at his assailant with his walking stick as onlookers seized Lawrence. The deluded man, who claimed Jackson was preventing him from assuming the British throne, later was committed to an insane asylum.

When Jackson's second term expired, he retired to the Hermitage, his estate near Nashville. Although he never again sought public office and suffered from several ailments that left him weak, he retained his avid interest in politics. His support was important to the presidential victories of Martin Van Buren in 1836 and James K. Polk in 1844. Jackson died on June 8, 1845, at the Hermitage.

> *I consider, then, the power to annul a law of the United States, assumed by one State, incompatible with the existence of the Union, contradicted expressly by the letter of the Constitution, unauthorized by its spirit, inconsistent with every principle on which it was founded, and destructive of the great object for which it was formed.*
>
> —**Andrew Jackson,** Proclamation, December 10, 1832

More on this topic:

War of 1812, p. 553

Japanese American Internment

Japanese Americans arriving at the Alien Reception Center in California in 1942. More than 100,000 people, labeled "potential enemies," were evacuated from their homes after the Japanese attack on Pearl Harbor. They spent the rest of the war behind barbed wire in relocation camps.
Source: AP

President Franklin D. Roosevelt's decision to relocate Japanese Americans to internment camps at the outset of World War II is often cited to show how far presidents can go in exercising EMERGENCY POWERS during wartime.

After the Japanese attack on Pearl Harbor on December 7, 1941, Roosevelt ordered several controversial measures to increase security on the West Coast, including Executive Order 9066, authorizing the designation of "military areas" which certain people would have no rights to enter or to leave. Following "exclusion orders" issued under the authority of the executive order, 120,000 Japanese descendants were excluded from the Pacific Coast except for "war relocation centers." Congress passed legislation validating the president's directive in 1942, and it was upheld by the Supreme Court, 6–3, in *Korematsu v. U.S.* in December 1944. In that case, Justice Felix Frankfurter pointed out that war conditions justified internment orders, even though "like action in times of peace would be lawless."

The relocation applied to persons of Japanese ancestry regardless of their citizenship or loyalty. Men, women, and children were forcibly removed from their homes and placed in camps surrounded by barbed wire and armed troops. Many lost the homes and businesses they left behind.

The order later came to be viewed as a gross violation of the civil liberties of U.S. citizens, but at the time it was defended as a safeguard against potential sabotage. Although some Italians and Germans were detained, their numbers were far fewer than the numbers of Japanese Americans. No citizen of Japanese descent ever was convicted of espionage or sabotage.

In *Korematsu,* writing for the majority, Justice Hugo Black explained, "Compulsory exclusion of large groups of citizens from their homes, except under circumstances of direct emergency and peril, is inconsistent with our basic governmental institutions. But when under conditions of modern warfare our shores are threatened by hostile forces, the power to protect must be commensurable with the threatened danger."

In a bitter dissenting opinion, Justice Francis Murphy rejected the premise of the Court's decision that the emergency on the West Coast warranted the exclusion from there of all persons of Japanese ancestry. "Such exclusion," he wrote, "goes over 'the very brink of Constitutional power' and falls into the abyss of racism."

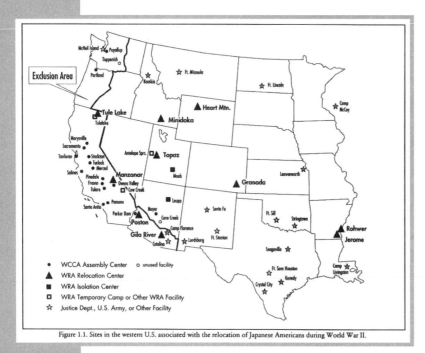

Figure 1.1. Sites in the western U.S. associated with the relocation of Japanese Americans during World War II.

Sites in the western United States associated with the relocation of Japanese Americans during World War II
Source: National Park Service

Although *Korematsu* is now generally regarded as an embarrassing moment in Supreme Court history, it reinforced the prerogative of the president and Congress jointly to take almost any emergency action in time of war, even if that action violates the basic rights of U.S. citizens.

In 1983, based on the fact that the government had suppressed evidence that Japanese Americans posed no security threat, the conviction of *Korematsu* was vacated. The judge in that case, Marilyn Hall Patel, warned that "the shield of military necessity and national security must not be used to protect governmental actions from close scrutiny and accountability."

In the Civil Liberties Act of 1988, forty-six years after the Japanese American internment, Congress formally apologized to the sixty thousand surviving internees and set up a $1.25 billion trust fund to provide them with tax-free payments of $20,000 apiece. The fund also was to be used to support further historical study and education about the events that surrounded the internment.

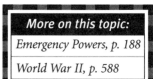

More on this topic:

Emergency Powers, p. 188

World War II, p. 588

Jefferson, Thomas

Thomas Jefferson (1743–1826) is remembered as the third president of the United States and the author of the Declaration of Independence. He also was a powerful political leader, who was largely responsible for founding the Democratic-Republican Party. As president his actions invigorated the powers of the office even as he insisted that presidents should interpret their powers narrowly.

Jefferson was born into a family of wealthy plantation owners on April 13, 1743, in Goochland (now Albemarle) County, Virginia. As a boy, Thomas received instruction in Latin, Greek, French, mathematics, and philosophy from local scholars. In 1760, at the age of seventeen, he entered the College of William and Mary in Williamsburg, Virginia. There he studied for two years before leaving the college in the spring of 1762 without taking a degree. Jefferson then studied law in Williamsburg for five years under the well-respected lawyer George Wythe. In 1767 Jefferson was admitted to the Virginia bar and began a successful legal practice. Two years later he took a seat in Virginia's House of Burgesses. During his six years in that body, Jefferson distinguished himself as a powerful literary stylist.

Jefferson married Martha Wayles Skelton, a wealthy twenty-three-year-old widow, on January 1, 1772. On September 6, 1782, Martha Jefferson died at the age of thirty-three. Jefferson never remarried.

In 1775 Jefferson brought his reputation as a gifted writer to the Continental Congress. The next year, at the age of thirty-three, he was appointed by Congress to the committee charged with writing the Declaration of Independence. His fellow committee members chose him to draft the document. Although minor changes were made to Jefferson's original draft, the Declaration of Independence was largely Jefferson's work. Jefferson returned to Virginia in 1776 to a seat in the state legislature. In 1779 he became governor, serving until 1781.

Diplomat and Secretary of State

In 1784 Congress sent Jefferson to Paris as its minister to France. During his five years at this post Jefferson witnessed the French Revolution. His assignment to Europe caused him to miss the drafting of the Constitution.

In 1789 Jefferson returned to the United States to become the country's first secretary of state. In this capacity he was more than just the nation's leading diplomat. Like the other members of

Source: Library of Congress

George Washington's cabinet, Jefferson served as an adviser to the president on a wide range of policies. Washington often preferred to have his cabinet debate issues while he listened dispassionately to their reasoning. In these debates Jefferson was usually pitted against Treasury Secretary Alexander Hamilton. Hamilton, who was closer ideologically to Washington than Jefferson, was the most influential member of the cabinet. On July 31, 1794, Jefferson announced that he would resign at the end of the year because of his disagreements with Washington's policies. In particular, Jefferson objected to Hamilton's creation of a national bank and Washington's strict neutrality toward the conflict between Britain and France, despite the 1778 treaty of alliance with France.

By 1796 the Democratic-Republican Party, which opposed the Federalists, had begun to emerge with Jefferson as its leader. That year he lost the presidential election to John Adams by three electoral votes; according to the original election rules of the Constitution, his second-place finish earned him the vice presidency. In this office he actively opposed the policies of Adams and the Federalists.

Presidency

In 1800 Jefferson was elected president despite the problems that occurred when his vice-presidential running mate, Aaron Burr, received as many electoral votes as Jefferson. When Burr refused to concede the election, the tie gave the House of Representatives, in which the Federalists were still in the majority, the responsibility of electing the president. To Alexander Hamilton's credit, he worked for the election of Jefferson, his longtime political rival, whom he thought less dangerous and more reasonable than Burr. The tie-breaking process took thirty-six ballots before Jefferson was elected.

Jefferson entered office preaching national reconciliation. He immediately freed all persons who had been jailed under the Alien and Sedition Acts enacted during the Adams administration. The Alien Act had given the president the authority to jail or deport aliens in peacetime, and the Sedition Act had allowed federal authorities to prosecute persons who criticized the government.

He also worked with Congress, which had come under the control of his party after the 1800 election, to cut the government's budget and federal taxes.

Jefferson's most important act during his first term as president was the Louisiana Purchase. In 1803 the French owned the port of New Orleans as well as a vast area that stretched from New Orleans to present-day Montana, known as the Louisiana Territory. Jefferson, fearing that the French could block U.S. navigation of the Mississippi River and threaten American settlements in the West, sent ambassadors to France in the hope of purchasing New Orleans. The French instead offered to sell the entire Louisiana Territory. The U.S. representatives, James Monroe and Robert Livingston, saw the opportunity to create an American empire and improve the security of the western frontier. They struck a deal with French emperor Napoleon to buy all of the Louisiana Territory for $15 million.

> *The enlightened Government of France saw, with just discernment, the importance to both nations of such liberal arrangements as might best and permanently promote the peace, friendship, and interests of both; and the property and sovereignty of all Louisiana, which had been restored to them, have on certain conditions been transferred to the United States....*
>
> **—Thomas Jefferson,** *Third Annual Message, October 17, 1803*

Jefferson recognized that to support the agreement he would have to ignore his own principles of strict constructionism, because the Constitution did not specifically authorize the president to acquire territory and Congress had not appropriated money for the purchase. However, he feared that the offer from Napoleon might be withdrawn if he hesitated. Therefore, Jefferson approved the deal and urged Congress to appropriate funds for it. In the fall of 1803 Congress bowed to his wishes and appropriated the $15 million. With the addition of the 828,000 square miles of the Louisiana Territory, the area of the United States nearly doubled.

In 1804 Jefferson, who was at the height of his popularity, easily won reelection. He lost only two states and defeated Charles C. Pinckney in the Electoral College by a vote of 162–14.

Jefferson's second term was troubled by war between Britain and France. In 1806 both powers were blockading each other's ports and seizing U.S. sailors and cargo. Jefferson was determined not to become involved in the war. He persuaded Congress to pass the Embargo Act of 1807, which prohibited the shipping of U.S. products to other nations. Jefferson hoped that by ending all foreign trade he would prevent provocations on the seas that could lead to war.

The Embargo Act was a total failure. It hurt American businesses and farmers by denying them export markets. Many merchants defied the embargo, causing Jefferson to order harsh enforcement measures that led to abuses of civil rights. On March 1, 1809, three days before the end of his term, Jefferson signed the Non-Intercourse Act, which ended the embargo against nations other than Britain and France and made provisions to lift the embargo against those two nations if they stopped violating U.S. neutrality. Despite the unpopularity of the Embargo Act, Jefferson's chosen heir and secretary of state, James Madison, won the 1808 presidential election.

More on this topic:

Historic Milestones of the Presidency, p. 253

Louisiana Purchase, p. 341

When his second term expired, Jefferson retired to Monticello, his home outside Charlottesville, Virginia, which he had designed himself. He devoted his time to entertaining visitors, corresponding with former colleagues, founding the University of Virginia, and pursuing his many intellectual interests. Jefferson died at Monticello on July 4, 1826, the same day John Adams died and the fiftieth anniversary of the Declaration of Independence. Jefferson is buried at Monticello beneath a gravestone that bears an epitaph of his own wording: "Here was buried Thomas Jefferson, Author of the Declaration of American Independence, of the Statute of Virginia for Religious Freedom, and the father of the University of Virginia."

Johnson, Andrew

Andrew Johnson (1808–1875) was thrust into the presidency after the assassination of Abraham Lincoln. He became the first president to be impeached by the House of Representatives; Bill Clinton was the second. The Senate vote to remove Johnson from office, however, fell one vote shy of the required two-thirds majority.

Johnson was born on December 29, 1808, in Raleigh, North Carolina. Neither of his parents could read or write, and Johnson received no formal education. At the age of thirteen he was apprenticed to a tailor in Raleigh. His fellow workers taught him to read, although he did not learn to write until several years later. In 1824, after two years as an apprentice, Johnson ran away from his master and worked as a journeyman tailor in Laurens, South Carolina. In 1826 he moved west to Greeneville, Tennessee, where he opened a tailor shop. He married sixteen-year-old Eliza McCardle on May 17, 1827.

In 1828 the people of Greeneville elected the young tailor alderman. After two years on the city council Johnson was chosen mayor at the age of twenty-one. In 1835 he was elected as a Democrat to the Tennessee legislature. He espoused the ideals of Andrew Jackson and became an advocate of small farmers and business owners. In 1837 he was defeated for a second term in the Tennessee legislature, but he won reelection in 1839. Two years later he was elected to the state senate, and in 1843 his congressional district sent him to the U.S. House of Representatives.

In Washington, Johnson supported the Mexican-American War and the Compromise of 1850. He served four terms in the House, then won two terms as governor of Tennessee. In 1857 the Tennessee legislature sent him back to Washington to serve in the Senate.

In 1860, after Abraham Lincoln was elected president, Johnson surprised many southerners by declaring his loyalty to the Union. When his state seceded in June 1861, he was the only southerner to remain in the Senate. In 1862, after Union forces had captured most of Tennessee, Lincoln appointed Johnson as military governor of his state. At Johnson's urging, Tennessee became the only seceding state to outlaw slavery before the 1863 Emancipation Proclamation.

Johnson's loyalty to the Union was rewarded with a vice-presidential nomination in 1864. Delegates to the National Union convention in Baltimore (the Republican nominating convention expanded to include Democrats loyal to the Union) hoped that having a southern Democrat on the ticket would attract support from northern Democrats and voters in border areas. Lincoln and Johnson defeated Democrats George McClellan and George Pendleton by an electoral vote of 212–21.

Johnson had served as vice president only six weeks when Lincoln died on April 15 from a gunshot wound inflicted by assassin John Wilkes Booth. The new president faced the problem of reconstructing a broken South, which had surrendered six days before. Johnson tried to implement Lincoln's lenient Reconstruction program, but he was blocked by Radical Republicans in Congress who were intent on punishing the region and limiting the influence of white southerners in national politics. Johnson successfully vetoed several harsh Reconstruction bills early in his presidency, but in the 1866 congressional elections the Radical Republicans gained firm control of Congress.

VOTES ON ARTICLES OF IMPEACHMENT AGAINST ANDREW JOHNSON

State	Convict	Acquit
California	2	0
Connecticut	1	1
Delaware	0	2
Illinois	1	1
Indiana	1	1
Iowa	1	1
Kansas	1	1
Kentucky	0	2
Maine	1	1
Maryland	0	2
Massachusetts	2	0
Michigan	2	0
Minnesota	1	1
Missouri	1	1
Nebraska	2	0
Nevada	2	0
New Hampshire	2	0
New Jersey	2	0
New York	2	0
Ohio	2	0
Oregon	2	0
Pennsylvania	1	1
Rhode Island	2	0
Tennessee	0	2
Vermont	2	0
Wisconsin	1	1
West Virginia	1	1
Total	35	19

Note: Thirty-six votes needed to convict.

On March 2, 1867, Congress passed the first Reconstruction Act over Johnson's veto. It established martial law in the South, granted universal suffrage to blacks, and limited the voting rights of southern whites. The same day Congress overrode Johnson's veto of the Tenure of Office Act, which prohibited the president from removing without Senate approval any presidential appointee who had been confirmed by the Senate. Johnson's defiance of the act in 1867 led to a showdown between the president and Congress. On February 24, 1868, the House voted 126–47 to impeach the president.

Johnson's fate was then in the hands of the Senate, which could remove him from office with a two-thirds vote. On March 13 Johnson's trial began in the Senate chambers with Chief Justice Salmon P. Chase presiding. The Senate voted 35–19 for the impeachment articles, one vote short of the two-thirds needed for conviction. Although Johnson's Radical Republican opponents controlled the Senate, seven believed that the charges against Johnson did not warrant his removal and voted against conviction despite the consequences for their careers. The decisive vote belonged to freshman senator Edmund G. Ross, a Republican from Kansas, whose not-guilty vote acquitted Johnson.

Although Johnson's presidency was dominated by Reconstruction and his battles with Congress, he and his secretary of state, William H. Seward, achieved a notable foreign policy success in 1867 when they negotiated the purchase of Alaska from Russia for only $7.2 million.

When Johnson's term expired in 1869 he returned to Tennessee. In 1874 the Tennessee legislature elected him to the Senate.

More on this topic:

Reconstruction, p. 439

He returned to Washington, where he resumed his fight for more lenient Reconstruction policies. Johnson served only five months of his Senate term before he died of a stroke on July 31, 1875, while visiting his daughter at Carter's Station, Tennessee.

Johnson, Lady Bird

Claudia Alta Taylor (1912–2007) was the wife of President Lyndon B. Johnson. While she was still an infant a nursemaid nicknamed her "Lady Bird," and she carried that name for the rest of her life.

Lady Bird attended the University of Texas, where she finished in the top ten of her class with degrees in liberal arts and journalism. In 1934 she met Lyndon Johnson, then a secretary to a member of Congress, and married him on November 17 after a courtship of only two months. The couple had two daughters.

Lady Bird proved to be an astute businesswoman. In 1943 she bought a nearly bankrupt Austin radio station. She and Lyndon expanded the station into a multimillion-dollar broadcasting empire known as the Texas Broadcasting Corporation. Although the extent of her active management of the corporation varied over the years, she always maintained some involvement in its operation.

Lady Bird had virtually no experience in politics, but she quickly became a capable political wife. She borrowed from her inheritance to provide money for Lyndon's first race for Congress in 1937, and when he volunteered for active duty at the beginning of World War II, she ran his congressional office by herself for a few months. According to some observers, she was so capable that she could have won elected office herself. Lyndon Johnson moved to the Senate in 1949, and after only four years he was elected minority leader. In January 1955, when the Democrats took control of the Senate, he was elected majority leader. He was defeated for the Democratic presidential nomination in 1960 by Sen. John F. Kennedy of Massachusetts, but accepted Kennedy's offer of the vice-presidential slot.

Source: LBJ Library

In 1963 Vice President Johnson became president upon Kennedy's assassination. During her husband's 1964 election campaign, Lady Bird delivered forty-seven speeches across the South, where Johnson faced opposition for his pro–civil rights stance. After he was elected she turned her attention to her national "beautification" project, which she saw as symbolic of improving the quality of life in both urban and rural areas. Lady Bird traveled 200,000 miles to make speeches in its behalf and personally lobbied Congress for passage of the Highway Beautification Act of 1965. She took an interest in education policy as well. In all, despite her avoidance of highly controversial issues, such as the war in Vietnam, she was the most active first lady since Eleanor Roosevelt. She also was an excellent manager. Observers have claimed that she ran her wing of the White House much more efficiently than the president ran his.

President Johnson decided not to seek reelection in 1968, and the couple retired to their Texas ranch. After Lyndon's death in 1973 Lady Bird largely withdrew from public life. But she continued to manage her business interests successfully and to pursue her interest in natural resources. In 1988 her book, *Wildflowers across America*, was published.

More on this topic:

First Ladies, p. 219

Johnson, Lyndon B.

Lyndon Baines Johnson (1908–1973) succeeded to the presidency after the assassination of John F. Kennedy in 1963. After being elected to a term of his own in 1964, he pressed Congress to enact his Great Society programs, which were designed to fight poverty, ignorance, disease, and other social problems. By 1968, however, his expansion of U.S. involvement in the Vietnam War had weakened his popularity, and he declined to run for another term.

Johnson was born in Stonewall, Texas, on August 27, 1908. Both of his parents were teachers, and his father and grandfathers had served in the Texas legislature. Johnson enrolled in Southwest Texas State Teachers College in San Marcos in 1927. He graduated in 1930 and taught high school in Houston for a year before Richard Kleberg, a newly elected member of the U.S. House of Representatives, asked him to come to Washington, D.C., as an aide. Johnson worked for Kleberg from 1931 until 1935. During this period he became an ardent supporter of President Franklin D.

Roosevelt. Johnson married Claudia Alta Taylor (known as "Lady Bird"), the daughter of a storekeeper and rancher, on November 17, 1934.

In 1935 Roosevelt appointed Johnson as Texas director of the National Youth Administration. This program sought to help the nation's unemployed youth find jobs and go to school. Two years later Johnson was given the opportunity to run for Congress when James P. Buchanan, the House member from Johnson's Texas district, died. Johnson won the House seat by campaigning on a pro-Roosevelt platform.

Johnson won reelection to the U.S. House of Representatives in 1938 and 1940 but was narrowly defeated when he ran for a Senate seat in 1941. After the Japanese attacked Pearl Harbor, Johnson was the first House member to volunteer for active duty in the armed forces. He was commissioned as a lieutenant commander in the navy and sent to the South Pacific. Johnson's service was short, however, because in July 1942 President Roosevelt ordered all members of Congress in the military to return to Washington.

Johnson served in the House until January 1949 and then moved to the Senate to take the seat he had won the previous November. After just four years his Democratic colleagues elected him minority leader. In January 1955 he was elected majority leader when the Democrats gained control of the Senate. During his six years as majority leader, Johnson became known as one of the most skilled legislative leaders in congressional history. He was renowned for his ability to use flattery, coercion, and compromise to get legislation passed.

Johnson wanted to run for president in 1960, but he was defeated for the Democratic nomination by Sen. John F. Kennedy of Massachusetts. Johnson accepted Kennedy's offer of the vice-presidential nomination. Kennedy and Johnson defeated Republicans Richard Nixon and Henry Cabot Lodge in a close election. Many political observers believed Kennedy might not have won without Johnson on the ticket. Johnson's presence helped Kennedy win five southern states, including Texas.

Although Johnson was not an insider in the Kennedy administration, the president frequently sought his advice, especially on legislative matters. Kennedy was assassinated while he rode in a motorcade through Dallas on November 22, 1963; Johnson was riding in a car behind the president. After Kennedy was pronounced dead, Johnson decided to take the oath of office immediately, rather than wait until he returned to Washington. While *Air Force One* sat on the runway, federal judge Sarah T. Hughes administered the oath of office to Johnson, who became the thirty-sixth president.

In the days following the assassination Johnson declared his intention to carry out Kennedy's programs. Recognizing that public sentiment for the slain president improved his chances of enacting Kennedy's program, Johnson vigorously lobbied Congress to pass a civil rights bill and a tax cut. Congress passed both bills in 1964. The tax cut succeeded in stimulating the economy, and the Civil Rights Act of 1964 protected black voting rights, established the Equal Employment Opportunity Commission, and forbade discrimination on account of race or sex.

In 1964 Johnson ran for a presidential term of his own against Republican senator Barry Goldwater of Arizona. Many Americans believed that Goldwater's conservative positions were too extreme. Johnson outpolled Goldwater by more than fifteen million votes and defeated him 486–52 in the Electoral College.

Johnson regarded his landslide victory as a mandate to enact the Great Society social programs that he had outlined in his campaign. During his second term he guided numerous bills through Congress establishing federal programs that provided expanded aid for medical care, housing, welfare, education, and urban renewal.

Although Johnson had intended to focus his administration on his Great Society programs, the involvement of the United States in Southeast Asia soon came to dominate his presidency. The government in North Vietnam and guerrillas in South Vietnam were attempting to unify the country under communist rule by force of arms. Since Vietnam had been split into North and South Vietnam in 1954, the United States had supported South Vietnam with weapons, U.S. military advisers, and economic aid. In 1965 Johnson increased the U.S. commitment by sending American combat troops to South Vietnam.

> **But we are not about to send American boys 9 or 10,000 miles away from home to do what Asian boys ought to be doing for themselves.**
>
> **—Lyndon B. Johnson,** Remarks in Memorial Hall, Akron University, October 21, 1964

Johnson continued to enlarge U.S. involvement in the war in response to the inability of the South Vietnamese government to defend its country. Meanwhile, the growing war was diverting attention and dollars away from Johnson's domestic programs. He hoped that each increase in U.S. troop strength would produce a breakthrough on the battlefield that would lead to a negotiated settlement. The communists, however, refused to give up their goal of reunification.

By early 1968 public opinion had swung decisively against both the war and Johnson. He recognized that there was a good chance that he might not be renominated by his party. On March 31, 1968, Johnson delivered a television address in which he announced a partial halt to U.S. air attacks on North Vietnam. He then stunned the nation by saying that he would not seek or accept the Democratic nomination for president.

More on this topic:

Great Society, p. 238

Kennedy, John F., p. 318

Vietnam War, p. 546

After leaving office in January 1969, Johnson retired to his ranch near Johnson City, Texas. On January 22, 1973, Johnson was stricken by a heart attack and was pronounced dead on arrival at Brooke Army Medical Center in San Antonio.

Johnson, Richard M.

Marble bust of Richard M. Johnson by James Paxton Voorhees.
Source: U.S. Senate

Richard Mentor Johnson (1780–1850) served as Martin Van Buren's vice president from 1837 to 1841. Like Andrew Jackson, Johnson was a westerner who had become a military hero during the War of 1812. Born in Kentucky, he was the first vice president who was not from one of the original thirteen states.

Johnson studied law at Transylvania University in Lexington, Kentucky, and was admitted to the bar in 1802. After briefly practicing law, he was elected to the Kentucky legislature in 1804. Two years later he was elected to the U.S. House of Representatives, where he served until 1819.

Before the War of 1812 Johnson joined with other War Hawks from the South and West in calling for war with Great Britain. When the fighting began, he left the capital without resigning his seat to take command of a regiment of Kentuckians. In 1813 he fought at the battle of Thames River, where U.S. forces defeated the

British and their Indian allies. Johnson, who was seriously wounded in the battle, gained national fame for allegedly killing the Indian chief Tecumseh. When his wounds healed, Johnson returned to Congress. In 1819 he was elected to an unexpired Senate seat. He served in that body until 1829, when he was again elected to the House after losing reelection to the Senate.

Johnson developed close political ties with Democrat Andrew Jackson, who became president in 1829. As a member of Congress, Johnson voted for the president's tariff policies and supported Jackson's stand against the Second Bank of the United States. Before the 1836 presidential election Andrew Jackson endorsed Martin Van Buren as the Democratic Party's presidential nominee and pushed for Johnson to be Van Buren's running mate. The Kentuckian gave the ticket geographical balance and a more heroic image. The lore surrounding Johnson's Indian-fighting exploits helped to offset the popularity of William Henry Harrison, one of the Whig candidates, who had been his commanding general at the battle of Thames River.

The presence of three other vice-presidential candidates in the 1836 race prevented Johnson from receiving a majority of electoral votes. In accordance with the Constitution, the selection of the vice president was left to the Senate, which chose Johnson. Despite his close ties to Andrew Jackson, Johnson exercised little influence in the Van Buren administration.

Johnson's political standing was damaged by his keeping a succession of black mistresses, a practice that was reviled by his fellow politicians. He had two daughters by his first mistress, Julia Chinn, a mulatto slave he had inherited from his father. Johnson's attempts to introduce his daughters into society offended many powerful southern slaveowners.

When it came time to select Van Buren's running mate in 1840, Andrew Jackson refused to support Johnson's candidacy, saying it would cost "thousands of votes." The Democrats chose to allow individual states to nominate vice-presidential candidates. Enough states nominated Johnson to place his name on the ballot, but Van Buren and Johnson were beaten by the Whig candidates William Henry Harrison and John Tyler. The economic depression that had plagued Van Buren's presidency and a shrewd Whig campaign based on catchy slogans contributed to the outcome.

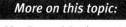

More on this topic:

Van Buren, Martin, p. 530

After leaving the vice presidency in 1841 Johnson returned to Kentucky, where he again served in the state legislature until 1842. Sixty-nine years old and in failing health, Johnson was elected to the Kentucky legislature for a final time in 1850, but he died of a stroke before he could take up his legislative duties.

Joint Chiefs of Staff

The Joint Chiefs of Staff (JCS) is the body of top military officers responsible for planning unified military strategy and advising the president on military matters. Created in 1947, the JCS consists of a chairman appointed from any of the services, a vice chairman, the chiefs of staff of the army and the air force, the chief of naval operations, and the commandant of the Marine Corps. The chairman is considered the nation's highest-ranking military officer.

All of the chiefs are appointed by the president with the advice and consent of the Senate. Since 1967 the chairman has been appointed for a two-year term, which can be renewed by the president. The four service chiefs serve one nonrenewable four-year term. The JCS is served by the joint staff, which is composed of officers from all of the services.

Presidents can nominate several types of officers to the JCS. Most often, presidents simply choose the officer recommended by a particular service to be its chief. But despite the goodwill engendered by such a choice, presidents will have little political control over these nominees. Sometimes presidents look beyond the service's candidates and choose officers whose professional reputation has come to their attention.

In 1986 President Ronald Reagan signed a bill reorganizing the JCS. The reorganization was a response to long-standing criticism of the JCS by many observers, including influential members of the JCS and blue-ribbon panels commissioned to study its organization.

These critics had identified several problems with the JCS. First, its members had been given the conflicting tasks of being service chiefs responsible for the welfare of their military branches and at the same time members of the JCS responsible for developing unbiased military plans and proposals for the president. The chiefs seldom were able to do both and usually put the interests of their branches first. Second, the entire JCS was consid-

Secretary of Defense Donald Rumsfeld, President George W. Bush, and General Peter Pace, Chairman of the Joint Chiefs of Staff, at Rumsfeld's Farewell Parade on December 15, 2006
Source: U.S. Department of Defense

ered to be the president's military adviser, yet it usually could not agree on anything but uncontroversial compromise plans of little value to the president. Third, although the JCS was supposed to develop military plans, it was an advisory body that lay outside the military's chain of command. Consequently, JCS proposals often were unrelated to the needs of the commanders in the field.

The 1986 reorganization bill sought to solve these problems by making the chairman of the JCS the president's supreme military adviser and placing the chairman in the chain of command. The bill's advocates hoped that the chairman would be free to develop advice and options independent of service biases. The bill created the post of vice chairman to assist the chairman and placed the joint staff under the chairman's direct control. The vice chairman became a full voting member of the JCS after passage of the National Defense Authorization Act of 1992. To ensure that the service chiefs would continue to have an advisory role, the chairman is required to forward their dissenting views to the president and secretary of defense upon the request of any of the chiefs.

> **More on this topic:**
>
> *Defense Department,*
> *p. 144*

Judiciary *See* COURTS AND THE PRESIDENT.

Justice Department

The Justice Department, one of the smallest cabinet departments, is the national government's law firm, and the attorney general is its chief counsel and law enforcement officer. Together they are responsible for enforcing federal law in the public interest. Through its thousands of lawyers, investigators, and agents, the department investigates violations of federal law ranging from tax evasion to criminal syndicates. Some functions that had been under Justice, including the oversight of legal and illegal aliens and domestic preparedness against subversive threats, were transferred from Justice to the new Department of Homeland Security, created in late 2002.

Among its responsibilities, the department polices narcotics trafficking and advises the president and other government agencies on legal matters. Through the office of the solicitor general, the department also conducts all suits in the Supreme Court to which the U.S. government is a party. The attorney general supervises and directs these activities, as well as those of the U.S. attorneys and U.S. marshals in the nation's ninety-four judicial districts. Finally, included among its various units is the FEDERAL BUREAU OF INVESTIGATION.

Background

The U.S. attorney general was one of the first positions to be established, with cabinet rank, in the federal government. The Judiciary Act of September 24, 1789, made the attorney general the chief legal officer of the federal government. At that time the nation's top law officer was a part-time official assisted by one clerk.

The Department of Justice was established in 1870, with the attorney general as its head. Through nearly the first century of its existence, the department's mission was perceived as primarily one of prosecuting violations of the Internal Revenue Code, instituting some antitrust suits, and keeping watch over "subversives" and "public enemies."

In the 1960s the Justice Department became intimately involved with major domestic issues, such as racial violence, mass demonstrations, riots, resistance to the draft during the Vietnam War, and rising crime rates, among others. To cope with its increased responsibilities, the department created new divisions.

At the same time, the increase in crime became an emotionally charged political issue. Richard Nixon was elected president in 1968 on a tough law-and-order platform, and more and more federal dollars were spent on law enforcement. In a peculiar twist on the law-and-order theme of the Nixon administration, the crimes that drew national attention in its last years were those committed by or charged against some of its highest officials, including the president himself and his attorney general, John N. Mitchell, in the WATERGATE AFFAIR. As a direct result of the scandal, in 1978 Congress created the INDEPENDENT COUNSEL system, under the Ethics in Government Act, to investigate and possibly prosecute high-level executive officers accused of serious crimes. The law provided that, in such instances, upon the application of the attorney general a special court appointed by the chief justice of the United States may appoint a special prosecutor. After the law's enactment, independent counsels became important factors in determining the legal and ethical ramifications of matters such as the IRAN-CONTRA AFFAIR and the Whitewater investigation.

In a peculiar twist on the law-and-order theme of the Nixon administration, the crimes that drew national attention in its last years were those committed by or charged against some of its highest officials, including the president himself and his attorney general, John N. Mitchell, in the Watergate affair.

Other law-related issues emerged in succeeding administrations. Gerald R. Ford emphasized that law enforcement should focus more on the needs of the victims of crime than on the criminal. Access to justice, rather than a war on crime, was the theme of President Jimmy Carter's law enforcement program.

For the most part, crime was mentioned little during Ronald Reagan's first years in office, even though the nation appeared more concerned about the issue than it had been during Carter's administration. The work of Reagan's second attorney general, Edwin Meese III, was overshadowed by personal and ethical problems and by the political tension that characterized his fights with Congress. Meese himself was the subject of a probe because of allegations of wrongdoing. After a fourteen-month investigation, an independent counsel concluded in 1988 that although he would not indict Meese for criminal wrongdoing, the attorney general had "probably violated" the law. Meese's resignation brought to an end a particularly fractious era in relations between the Justice

Department and Congress. His successor, Richard Thornburgh, concentrated on setting high ethical standards for the Justice Department, restoring morale, and improving the department's relationships with Congress.

In the late 1980s criminal law enforcement was again a hotly debated political issue. With the nation's drug abuse problem a primary concern of the American people, an omnibus anti–drug abuse bill was passed providing more money, programs, and human resources for the war against the misuse of drugs.

When the crime issue heated up again in the 1990s, the Clinton White House and members of Congress from both parties pushed for tougher anticrime measures. Clinton's attorney general, Janet Reno, found herself in the middle of controversies ranging from the standoff between federal law enforcement agents and the Branch Davidian religious sect near Waco, Texas, to the case of a young Cuban boy, Elián González, and the fight over whether he should remain in the United States or return to Cuba.

George W. Bush's first attorney general, John Ashcroft, a conservative former Missouri senator, overcame a tough confirmation battle to gain his post. After the September 11, 2001, terrorist attacks, he became one of the Bush administration's most prominent cabinet officials. Ashcroft pushed for passage of the USA Patriot Act, which gave new powers to law enforcement officials in their fight against terrorism. The Bush administration later, through executive orders, expanded the attorney general's power to investigate suspected terrorists and their accomplices. The powers, which faced sharp criticism on civil liberties grounds, included the ability to detain material witnesses for an indefinite period. Alberto R. Gonzales, former counsel to the president, was sworn in as Bush's second attorney general in February 2005. Gonzales had been central to White House articulation of an expansive concept of executive power. In early 2007 Gonzales found himself in the center of a controversy involving the firing of eight U.S. attorneys on December 7, 2006. Although U.S. attorneys can be replaced at will by the president, critics claim that they were fired for political reasons, or to make room for attorneys loyal to the Republican Party. When evidence surfaced that Gonzales may have been more involved in the decision to fire these attorneys than he previously claimed, calls for his resignation were voiced by members of Congress from both political parties.

Organization

The office of the attorney general provides overall policy and program direction for the offices, divisions, bureaus, and boards of the department. The office represents the United States in legal matters generally; it also makes recommendations to the president about appointments to federal judicial positions. The attorney general is assisted by a deputy attorney general, an associate attorney general, and assistant attorneys general.

Among the highest officers in the Justice Department is the solicitor general, who represents the U.S. government before the Supreme Court. Cases in which the United States is a party make up about two-thirds of all cases the Court decides each year. The solicitor general, often called the "tenth justice" of the Court, determines which cases the government will take before the Court and what the government's position will be.

The solicitor general, often called the "tenth justice" of the Supreme Court, determines which cases the government will take before the Court and what the government's position will be.

The Justice Department advises the president and the other executive departments. Various offices also deal with legislative affairs, policy development, pardon requests, community relations, professional responsibility, national security matters, U.S. attorneys, bankruptcy cases, and departmental management and conduct. Much of the legal work of the department is han-

Paul D. Clement, forty-third solicitor general of the United States
Source: U.S. Department of Justice

dled by its divisions: antitrust, civil, civil rights, criminal, environment and natural resources, and tax. An office within Justice investigates and prosecutes cases of unfair employment practices toward immigrants.

The department also includes specialized bureaus. The best known is the Federal Bureau of Investigation (FBI). Established in 1908 the FBI is the principal investigative arm of the department. It is charged with gathering and reporting facts, locating witnesses, and compiling evidence in cases involving federal jurisdiction. The FBI became a powerful and influential agency under J. Edgar Hoover, who served as its director for forty-seven years (1924–1972).

More on this topic:

Law Enforcement Powers, p. 330

K

Kennedy, Jacqueline

Jacqueline Kennedy
Source: Library of Congress

Jacqueline Lee Bouvier Kennedy (1929–1994), called "Jackie," was the wife of President John F. Kennedy. Her youth and glamour helped to create the perception of the Kennedy presidency as a romanticized "Camelot."

Jackie was the daughter of a New York stockbroker. Her parents divorced in 1940, and her mother later married the very wealthy Hugh Auchincloss. Intelligent and strikingly attractive, Jackie grew up in high social circles. She attended Vassar College, the Sorbonne in Paris, and George Washington University, graduating in 1951 with a degree in art. She worked as a writer on the *Washington Times-Herald* and had a daily feature in the newspaper. Jackie met John Kennedy at a dinner party in 1951 when he was a member of the House of Representatives. After an off-and-on romance, they married on September 12, 1953.

When Kennedy became president in 1961, Jackie was just thirty-one. She made the White House a center for promoting culture and the arts, and she worked to obtain authentic antiques to furnish the mansion. As part of these efforts she led a televised tour of the White House in February 1962.

Women throughout the country began copying her fashions and hairstyle. Citing the needs of her two small children, Jackie stubbornly insisted on a restricted official social schedule. Her independent streak also showed when she took vacations separately from the president.

Despite its fairy-tale appearance, life was not always easy for Jackie. Childbirth proved traumatic: her first child was stillborn, the next two were difficult Caesarean births, and her last child, Patrick, died after only two days. Moreover, shadowing her marriage were the extramarital affairs of her husband, which were hushed up at the time.

On November 22, 1963, during one of the infrequent political trips that she took with the president, he was assassinated as she rode next to him through the streets of Dallas. Later in the day, while still wearing a suit stained with her husband's blood, she witnessed the swearing in of Vice President Lyndon B. Johnson.

More on this topic:

First Ladies, p. 219

After leaving the White House, Jackie tried to maintain a more private life, despite constant pressure by inquisitive reporters. In 1968 she married Aristotle Onassis, a Greek shipping tycoon, but his death in 1975 left her a widow for a second time. She then pursued a career in publishing as a senior editor for a New York book publisher. She died of cancer on May 19, 1994.

Kennedy, John F.

Source: Library of Congress

John Fitzgerald Kennedy (1917–1963) was the youngest person ever to be elected president, although Theodore Roosevelt was younger than Kennedy when he succeeded to the presidency after William McKinley's death. Kennedy's youth, idealism, and attractive family made him one of the most popular presidents of the twentieth century. His administration came to be known as "Camelot" because of its romantic image. The nation went into mourning when he was shot to death by an assassin after less than three years in office.

Kennedy was born on May 29, 1917, in Brookline, Massachusetts. His father, Joseph Kennedy, was a millionaire who had made his fortune in banking and real estate. In 1937 Franklin D. Roosevelt appointed Joseph Kennedy as ambassador to Great Britain, a position he resigned in December 1940 when he became pessimistic about Britain's chances for survival during World War II. He returned to the United States, where he advocated isolationism.

In 1940 John graduated with honors from Harvard University; he studied economics and political science. In 1941 he tried to enter the army, but he was rejected because of a bad back, the result of a football injury. He strengthened his back through exercise and passed the navy's physical exam later that year. While he was serving as the commander of a patrol torpedo boat in the South Pacific in August 1943, his vessel was rammed and sunk by a Japanese destroyer. Eleven of his thirteen crew members survived, and Kennedy led them on a four-hour swim to a nearby island where they were eventually rescued by Allied personnel. After the ordeal Kennedy was sent back to the United States, where he was hospitalized for malaria. In 1944 he underwent a disk operation and was discharged from the navy the next year.

After working briefly as a reporter for the International News Service, Kennedy decided to run for Congress from his Massachusetts district. He was elected in 1946 and served three terms before being elected to the Senate in 1952. Kennedy married Jacqueline Lee Bouvier on September 12, 1953.

In 1956 Kennedy tried to secure the Democratic vice-presidential nomination on the ticket with Adlai Stevenson, but he narrowly lost the nomination to Sen. Estes Kefauver of Tennessee. In 1958 he won reelection to the Senate by a record margin in Massachusetts.

By 1960 Kennedy was the leading candidate for the Democratic presidential nomination. He was nominated on the first ballot at the Democratic national convention in Los Angeles in July 1960 and convinced Sen. Lyndon B. Johnson of Texas, who had finished second, to be his running mate. Kennedy's opponent was Vice President Richard Nixon. Kennedy and Nixon engaged in a series of four televised debates, the first in presidential election history. Out of almost 69 million popular votes cast, Kennedy received only 120,000 more than Nixon. Kennedy won in the Electoral College, 303–219.

Soon after entering office, Kennedy endorsed a plan developed by the Central Intelligence Agency during the Eisenhower presidency to arm, train, and land 1,400 Cuban exiles in Cuba in an attempt to overthrow the communist regime of Fidel Castro. The operation on April 17, 1961, which came to be known as the Bay of Pigs invasion, was a complete failure because 1,200 of the Cuban exiles were captured. The president accepted responsibility for the blunder.

Cuba may have been the site of Kennedy's greatest foreign policy failure, but it also was the site of his most memorable foreign policy success. In October 1962 aerial photography revealed that the Soviet Union was building offensive missile bases in Cuba. The president demanded that the Soviets dismantle the bases, and he imposed a naval blockade of the island. The confrontation brought the United States and Soviet Union to the brink of nuclear war, but the Soviets backed down and agreed to remove the missiles.

Tensions decreased after the Cuban missile crisis, but the incident spurred the Soviet Union to undertake a military buildup. In 1963 Kennedy concluded an arms control treaty with Great Britain, France, and the Soviet Union that banned nuclear tests in the atmosphere, in outer space, and under water.

Outside of superpower relations, Kennedy increased U.S. involvement in international development. In 1961 he established the Peace Corps, an agency that sent skilled volunteers overseas to assist people of underdeveloped countries. He also initiated the Alliance for Progress, an aid program devoted to Latin American development.

In domestic policy Kennedy made substantial progress in furthering the cause of civil rights. He advocated school desegregation, established a program to encourage registration of black voters, issued rules against discrimination in public housing built with federal funds, and appointed many blacks to public office. He also sent federal troops and officials to oversee the integration of the University of Mississippi in 1962 and the University of Alabama in 1963. That year he proposed a sweeping civil rights bill, but it did not come to a vote during his lifetime.

Kennedy also tried unsuccessfully to convince Congress to cut taxes. The president's advisers convinced him that a tax cut would stimulate the economy and bring growth without large budget deficits or inflation. After Kennedy's death, President Lyndon Johnson was able to secure passage of the Kennedy tax cut and civil rights legislation.

In late November 1963 Kennedy traveled to Texas on a trip intended to build political support. While riding through Dallas in an open car on November 22, Kennedy was killed by rifle shots. He died at a nearby hospital without regaining consciousness. Vice President Johnson was sworn in as president later in the day.

Police quickly apprehended the alleged assassin, Lee Harvey Oswald. Initial investigations concluded that Oswald had shot Kennedy from a sixth-story window of the Texas School Book Depository building. Three days after the shooting, Oswald was murdered in front of millions of tel-

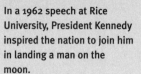

CLOSER LOOK ⊙

In a 1962 speech at Rice University, President Kennedy inspired the nation to join him in landing a man on the moon.

But why, some say, the moon? Why choose this as our goal? And they may well ask why climb the highest mountain. Why, 35 years ago, fly the Atlantic? Why does Rice play Texas? We choose to go to the moon in this decade and do the other things, not because they are easy, but because they are hard, because that goal will serve to organize and measure the best of our energies and skills....

During the Kennedy administration the first Americans visited space and orbited the Earth. After Kennedy's death the space program continued in earnest with NASA making good on Kennedy's commitment to land a man on the moon by the end of the 1960s: Neil Armstrong set foot on the lunar surface on July 20, 1969.

evision viewers by Jack Ruby, owner of a Dallas nightclub. The WARREN COMMISSION, a seven-member panel appointed by President Johnson to investigate the assassination, determined that Oswald had acted alone. But certain unresolved questions surrounding the assassination have led to speculation that Oswald might have been part of a conspiracy. (See ZAPRUDER FILM.)

Kennedy's speeches are among the most memorable given by modern presidents—starting with his inaugural pledge that the United States would "pay any price, bear any burden, meet any hardship, support

Astronaut Edwin E. Aldrin Jr. poses for a photograph beside the deployed flag of the United States on the surface of the moon on July 20, 1969
Source: National Aeronautic and Space Administration

any friend, oppose any foe to assure the survival and the success of liberty."

Well after Kennedy's assassination, scholars began to disclose the details of his extensive health problems and heavy use of prescription drugs. Kennedy had been diagnosed with Addison's disease (among other things) in the 1940s, but his health problems and treatment were not disclosed publicly. An important area of speculation has to do with how Kennedy's medical condition affected his performance as president.

More on this topic:
Assassinations and Assaults, p. 19
New Frontier, p. 386
Warren Commission, p. 562
Zapruder Film, p. 593

Kerry, John

Senator John Kerry (D-MA)
Source: AP

John Forbes Kerry (1943–), Democratic candidate for president in 2004, was defeated by George W. Bush. Kerry was elected four times (most recently in 2002) to the U.S. Senate from Massachusetts, beginning in 1984. In the presidential contest, Kerry won 48 percent of the national popular vote and 251 electoral votes. Kerry's campaign did not contest the electoral outcome despite allegations of irregularities in voting in Ohio and Florida, which were narrowly decided.

Kerry, born December 11, 1943, was the son of Richard John Kerry, a Foreign Service officer, and Rosemary Forbes Kerry. Rosemary Forbes Kerry was a member of the wealthy Forbes family. As a result of these two connections, young John Kerry was well-traveled and familiar with Forbes family estates in France and Massachusetts.

Kerry attended private schools in Massachusetts and New Hampshire where he became involved in politics, formed a debating society, played ice hockey and lacrosse, and played bass in the school band. At Yale College, Kerry majored in political science. He also participated in intercollegiate sports and was inducted into Skull and Bones, the famous "secret society." While at Yale, Kerry joined the Naval Reserves. Upon graduation, Kerry began active duty with the navy, serving until 1970 in Vietnam. He received several medals including the Silver Star, Bronze Star, and three Purple Hearts.

After returning from Vietnam, Kerry joined the Vietnam Veterans Against the War and was prominent in antiwar activities. In 1971, in testimony before the Senate Foreign Relations Committee, Kerry described veterans' reports of war crimes they had committed, and he said that soldiers had been sent "to die for the biggest nothing in history." The following day, Kerry participated in a widely televised demonstration in which Vietnam veterans threw their medals over the front steps of the U.S. Capitol. Kerry became highly visible in the media at this time.

In 1972 Kerry ran unsuccessfully for an open U.S. House seat in Lowell, Massachusetts. He entered Boston College law school in 1973 and while in law school served as executive director of Mass Action, an advocacy group, and was a student prosecutor in the office of the District Attorney of Middlesex County. Following his graduation in 1976 Kerry joined the office as a full-time prosecutor.

Kerry left the district attorney's office in 1979 to enter private practice. He returned to public service in 1982 when he ran successfully for lieutenant governor of Massachusetts, serving with Governor Michael Dukakis. In 1984 incumbent senator Paul Tsongas announced his resignation for health reasons, and Kerry ran successfully for the U.S. Senate. Kerry took office in January 1985.

As a senator, Kerry played an important and visible role in early investigations of the Iran-contra scandal. Kerry staked out a leadership position among liberal Democrats and was active on a variety of issues including health insurance, education, and the environment. Kerry also served as cochairman, with senator John McCain (R-Ariz.), of the Senate Select Committee on POW/MIA affairs.

The 2004 presidential campaign focused extensively on the conduct of the war in Iraq. Kerry had initially voted for the congressional resolution authorizing the use of military force in 2003 but later criticized the Bush administration for misleading the nation at the outset of the conflict. In the 2004 campaign, Kerry had a difficult time shaking Bush's criticism of him as a "flip-flopper" on Iraq and other issues. Kerry also found it difficult to successfully contrast his heroic wartime service with George W. Bush's dubious record in the Texas National Guard. Kerry's wartime record was called into question by right-wing critics, and his clear-cut antiwar rhetoric from the Vietnam era was recalled to portray him as antimilitary extremist. Nonetheless, the Kerry campaign effectively identified itself as the choice for citizens concerned about or opposed to the war in Iraq.

More on this topic:

Elections Chronology, p. 174

King, William R.

William Rufus Devane King (1786–1853) served briefly as Franklin Pierce's vice president. King was ill when he was nominated, and he died just twenty-five days after taking the oath of office.

King graduated from the University of North Carolina in 1803 and was admitted to the bar in 1806. A year later he won a two-year term in the North Carolina House of Commons. In 1810 he was elected to the U.S. House of Representatives, where he sided with the War Hawks, who supported the War of 1812 with Great Britain. He resigned from the House in 1816 to undertake a diplomatic mission to Italy and Russia.

Early-generation photographic portrait of William R. King
Source: Library of Congress

When he returned to the United States in 1818, King moved to Alabama and bought a plantation. He was elected to the U.S. Senate in 1820 as one of Alabama's first senators. During his twenty-four-year career in the Senate, King was a strong supporter of Andrew Jackson's policies. He served as president pro tempore of the Senate from 1836 to 1841.

In 1844 King left the Senate when President John Tyler appointed him minister to France. While in Paris he helped secure French approval for the U.S. annexation of Texas. He returned to Alabama in 1846. Two years later he was appointed to fill an unexpired Senate seat.

During King's time in Washington, D.C., he was surrounded by an air of personal scandal. His lack of a wife and his close friendship with James Buchanan, with whom he shared an apartment while the two men served in the Senate, gave rise to speculation that he was a homosexual. King also was ridiculed for his fastidious dressing habits and his insistence on wearing a wig long after they had gone out of style. Andrew Jackson referred to him as "Miss Nancy."

In 1852 the Democrats chose King to balance the ticket with their dark-horse presidential candidate, Franklin Pierce of New Hampshire. King, however, was sick with tuberculosis when he received the nomination. His condition did not raise much concern among voters, however, as the Pierce-King team overwhelmed Whigs Winfield Scott and William Alexander Graham.

After the election King traveled to Cuba in the hope that the Caribbean climate would heal him. There on March 24, 1853, with the special permission of Congress, he became the only executive officer of the United States to take the oath of office on foreign soil. On April 18, a day after returning to his home in Alabama, he died.

More on this topic:

Pierce, Franklin, p. 404

Kitchen Cabinet

"Kitchen cabinet" is the name given to close friends and associates of presidents who are important but unofficial advisers.

Many members of the president's official CABINET are appointed for reasons other than friendship or compatibility; they may have expertise in the subject area of the cabinet department, or the appointment may be made in light of political necessities. Once named, cabinet appointees frequently develop a loyalty to the department in which they serve that overrides their loyalty to the president.

Presidents look to old friends to provide the additional advice that the cabinet may not give. Most presidents have had one or two, and sometimes several, such advisers.

The first kitchen cabinet was created by President Andrew Jackson. Jackson's official cabinet was a relatively weak body, several of whose members had been appointed to satisfy factions within the Democratic Party, most notably one led by Vice President John C. Calhoun. Jackson therefore tended to rely on his unofficial advisers.

Most members of Jackson's kitchen cabinet had been important in his 1828 presidential campaign. Some were old Tennessee associates, such as Maj. John H. Eaton and Andrew J. Donelson;

others, such as Amos Kendall, Isaac Hill, and Francis P. Blair, were important members of the press. Finally, there were political figures, such as Roger B. Taney and Martin Van Buren. Several of these men remained in the background, but others occupied important places in the government.

Not every kitchen cabinet has been as large as Jackson's. From 1913 to 1920 Woodrow Wilson had a one-person advisory board, Col. Edward M. House. A wealthy man who entered politics for the excitement of it, Colonel House met Wilson in 1911 and became his closest confidant throughout much of his presidency. House also represented the president in Europe in efforts to mediate World War I and later helped to lay the foundations of the Paris peace conference that ended the war. Although House and Wilson eventually had a falling out and never spoke to each other after 1919, their relationship became the symbol of the closeness that can exist between president and adviser.

President Wilson with Edward M. House
Source: Yale Library

Another president who had a particularly close relationship with his unofficial advisers was Franklin D. Roosevelt. Although Roosevelt had some people of notable ability in his cabinet, he drew on many sources for information. One of the most important in the early days of the New Deal was the brain trust, a group of academicians led by Rexford G. Tugwell, Raymond Moley, and Adolph A. Berle Jr. Each formally held a minor post in government.

Of greater importance was the influence of two longtime associates of Roosevelt, Louis Howe and Harry Hopkins. Howe was a journalist and Roosevelt's closest political adviser throughout the early years of the New Deal. Harry Hopkins, who lived at the White House, had been part of Roosevelt's New York state administration. He was a major adviser during World War II and served as an important figure in the war effort.

> **More on this topic:**
>
> *Cabinet, p. 60*
>
> *Daily and Family Life, p. 134*

Korean War

The Korean War was the first conflict after World War II and the development of the atomic bomb in which large numbers of U.S. soldiers engaged in combat. In the Korean War a United Nations (UN) force led by the United States supported South Korea against North Korea and its ally, communist China. The war began when, on June 25, 1950, North Korea launched a massive attack against South Korea. The war continued for three years and resulted in the death or injury of more than 150,000 Americans.

After the invasion President Harry S. Truman believed he had to act to save South Korea and discourage further communist aggression. The next day the United States called an emergency session of the UN Security Council, which passed a resolution condemning the invasion and asking UN members to "render every assistance" to South Korea. By coincidence, the Soviets were boycotting the Security Council to protest the exclusion of the new communist government of China from the UN. Consequently, the Soviet representative was not present to veto the resolution. That evening Truman authorized Gen. Douglas MacArthur to evacuate Americans from South Korea, transport supplies to the South Koreans, and bomb North Korean forces in South Korea.

Members of Congress overwhelmingly supported Truman's decision to commit U.S. forces. A few Republicans, however, protested Truman's failure to involve Congress in the decision. Truman had asked Secretary of State Dean Acheson and the chairman of the Senate Foreign Relations Committee, Texas Democrat Tom Connally, if his armed response to the invasion required a declaration of war or other congressional action. Both men advised Truman that his commander-in-chief power and the UN Security Council resolution gave him ample authority to use the armed forces.

After Truman announced his intention to defend South Korea, the UN Security Council passed a second resolution explicitly calling on members to give military assistance to South Korea. By June 30 Truman had authorized General MacArthur to use U.S. ground forces and to bomb targets in North Korea. Truman could easily have secured a congressional resolution approving his use of military forces in Korea, but the president wished to avoid an appearance of dependence on Congress.

During the fall of 1950 the public continued to support the war effort as UN troops drove the North Koreans up the peninsula. By November MacArthur's forces had driven North Korean forces out of the south and were occupying most of North Korea. In November and December, however, communist China entered the war and pushed UN forces back across the thirty-eighth parallel into South Korea.

By April 1951 UN forces had recaptured most of South Korea, and the fighting had bogged down along the thirty-eighth parallel that separated the two Koreas. Meanwhile, the inconclusive and bloody war was weakening Truman's popularity. On April 11, 1951, the president fired General MacArthur for insubordination. The popular general had repeatedly called for a wider war against communist China and had denounced Truman's Korean War strategy as "Die for [a] Tie." The firing caused Truman's already low public approval rating to slip to just 24 percent.

> *I believe that we must try to limit the war to Korea for these vital reasons: to make sure that the precious lives of our fighting men are not wasted; to see that the security of our country and the free world is not needlessly jeopardized; and to prevent a third world war.*
>
> *A number of events have made it evident that General MacArthur did not agree with that policy. I have therefore considered it essential to relieve General MacArthur so that there would be no doubt or confusion as to the real purpose and aim of our policy. It was with the deepest personal regret that I found myself compelled to take this action. General MacArthur is one of our greatest military commanders. But the cause of world peace is much more important than any individual.*
>
> **—Harry S. Truman,** *Radio Report to the American People on Korea and on U.S. Policy in the Far East, April 11, 1951*

President Harry S. Truman pinning a medal on Gen. Douglas MacArthur at their October 15, 1950, meeting on Wake Island. Truman called the meeting to discuss MacArthur's strategy in Korea, but six months later he fired the general for insubordination.
Source: Library of Congress

The Truman administration was able to draw attention away from MacArthur's patriotic appeals to focus on the general's insubordination and the constitutional principle of civilian control of the armed forces. Truman also received the crucial support of the military. The chairman of the Joint Chiefs of Staff, Omar Bradley, told the Senate Foreign Relations and Armed Services committees that MacArthur's Korean strategy "would involve us in the wrong war, at the wrong place, at the wrong time, and with the wrong enemy." Talk of impeaching Truman subsided, and Congress took no action against the president. However, little progress was made toward peace in Korea.

Finally on July 27, 1953, newly elected president Dwight D. Eisenhower fulfilled his 1952 campaign promise to conclude an armistice. The peace agreement created a demilitarized zone near the thirty-eighth parallel that previously had separated the two Koreas. Critics of the agreement charged that the United States had fought the war for nothing, but most Americans supported the armistice and believed the war demonstrated that the United States would oppose communist aggression. In 1997 talks began at Columbia University in New York City among representatives of the United States, China, North Korea, and South Korea with the aim of securing a formal peace agreement.

Truman's actions during the Korean War set the stage for a period of unquestioned presidential primacy in foreign and national security policy. In 1952 Truman did suffer a setback, however, when the Supreme Court ruled that he did not have the authority to take over steel mills to prevent a strike that would damage the Korean War effort. Still, as historian Arthur M. Schlesinger Jr. wrote in his book *The Imperial Presidency,* "By bringing the nation into war without congressional authorization and by then successfully defending his exercise of independent presidential initiative, Truman enormously expanded assumptions of presidential prerogative."

More on this topic:

Eisenhower, Dwight, p. 167

Truman, Harry S., p. 520

United Nations, p. 525

War Powers, p. 555

L

La Follette, Robert M.

Robert M. La Follette.
Source: Library of Congress

Sen. Robert M. "Fighting Bob" La Follette of Wisconsin (1855–1925) carried the banner of militant liberalism through a long political career that included service in the House, the governorship of Wisconsin, and almost twenty years in the Senate. A man of strong beliefs and impressive oratorical ability, La Follette sought the Republican presidential nomination three times without success. He finally left the party to run as the Progressive Party candidate in 1924, the year Americans elected conservative Republican Calvin Coolidge to the presidency. La Follette, who said democracy was his religion, fought with uncompromising zeal for a wide range of reforms, including greater citizen participation in elections, higher taxes for the wealthy, and the strict regulation of railroads and other large corporations.

As governor of Wisconsin from 1901 to 1906, La Follette gained national recognition for his progressive reform program, especially a law providing for primaries so that all voters, rather than just party insiders, could elect delegates to national party conventions. When La Follette was elected to the Senate in 1906, Republican Theodore Roosevelt was in the White House promoting his own more pragmatic set of progressive reforms. These two intense leaders clashed more often than they cooperated, most notably in 1912 over the Republican presidential nomination. When William Howard Taft, the Republican president elected in 1908, proved too cautious for many liberal Republicans, they chose La Follette as their candidate under the banner of the National Progressive Republican League. La Follette's appeal was limited primarily to the Midwest, and the splinter group dumped him when Roosevelt agreed to lead them. After losing the nomination to Taft at the Republican convention that year, Roosevelt ran in the general election as the candidate of a new progressive splinter group, the Bull Moose Party. La Follette supported the winning Democratic candidate, Woodrow Wilson.

After two more unsuccessful bids for the Republican presidential nomination in 1916 and 1920, La Follette left the party in 1924 to run as the presidential candidate of the Conference for Progressive Political Action, another in a series of short-lived progressive parties that had formed in support of specific candidates. Charging that powerful monopolies controlled the nation, La Follette called for nationalization of the railroads, increased taxes on the rich, pro-labor laws, and government reforms such as direct election of presidents. With conservative Democrat John W. Davis running against conservative Republican Coolidge, the Republicans warned that La Follette could attract enough liberal votes to deadlock the election. Their anti–La Follette slogan, "Coolidge or Chaos," proved effective. Coolidge won easily, with 54.1 percent of the popular vote to Davis's 28.8 percent and La Follette's 16.6 percent. La Follette carried his home state of Wisconsin and ran second in eleven western states. The Progressive Party, lacking an organizational base, did not outlive La Follette, who died within a year of the election. His son Robert La Follette Jr. took over his Senate seat and served until 1947; another son, Philip Fox La Follette, was elected governor of Wisconsin.

> **More on this topic:**
>
> *Third Parties, p. 498*

Labor Department

The Labor Department is responsible for enforcing a wide range of federal laws affecting the well-being of workers, including unemployment insurance and workers' compensation, minimum wage and overtime pay, occupational health and safety, antidiscrimination policies in employment, protection of pension rights, job training, and the strengthening of free collective bargaining.

The department compiles statistics on prices, employment, and other appropriate subjects and strives to solve the employment problems of minorities, youth, older workers, women, and the disabled.

The department has its roots in the labor movement of the late 1800s. After the Civil War, as labor unions grew in strength, pressures increased to create a federal office that represented workers. Proponents argued that existing federal departments were closely tied to wealthy businesses, and there was no federal agency that concentrated solely on the interests of labor.

In 1884 Congress passed legislation establishing a Bureau of Labor in the Interior Department, but pressure continued for a cabinet-level department. Four years later an independent Department of Labor was created but without cabinet status. In 1903 a combined cabinet-level Department of Commerce and Labor was established, over the objections of Democrats who argued that mutual distrust between business and labor would paralyze the department and that the powers of the existing independent Department of Labor would be weakened.

Finally, in 1913, Commerce and Labor were divided into separate cabinet-level departments.

During its early years the department experienced difficulties: Business distrusted it, and conservative members of Congress slashed at its funds and functions. For many years Labor was the smallest and least influential cabinet department. But under President Franklin D. Roosevelt's labor secretary, Frances Perkins (the first woman named to the cabinet), the department's authority

The first woman ever to hold a cabinet position, Frances Perkins was appointed secretary of labor by President Franklin D. Roosevelt.
Source: Library of Congress

and stature grew considerably. Thereafter, other responsibilities were given to the department with the passage of significant labor relations legislation and Supreme Court decisions upholding these acts and workers' rights in general. From the viewpoint of organized labor, the administration of Lyndon B. Johnson was one of the most fruitful legislative periods in U.S. history with the enactment of Johnson's Great Society programs and a far-reaching wage law.

Labor Department functions that most affect the lives of American workers include those administered by the Employment and Training Administration, whose responsibilities include employment services, job training, and unemployment insurance programs. The Pension and Welfare Benefits Administration helps to protect the economic future and retirement security of American workers.

The Employment Standards Administration deals with minimum wage and overtime standards and attempts to achieve nondiscrimination in employment by federal contractors.

The Office of the American Workplace works with government, business, and labor to encourage cooperative labor-management relations and the adoption of high-performance work practices. Worker safety and health concerns are the responsibility of the Occupational Safety and Health Administration and the Mine Safety and Health Administration. The Veterans' Employment and Training Service directs the department's veterans programs through a nationwide field staff. The Bureau of Labor Statistics is the government's principal agency for collecting data on various aspects of labor.

> **More on this topic:**
>
> *Bureaucracy, p. 44*
>
> *Cabinet, p. 60*

Lame Duck

Presidents who have been defeated for reelection (such as Jimmy Carter in 1980 and George Bush in 1992), who have announced that they will not seek another term (Lyndon B. Johnson in 1968), or who are nearing the completion of their second and final term in office (Dwight D. Eisenhower in 1960, Ronald Reagan in 1988, and Bill Clinton in 2000) are often called lame ducks. Originally a British term, the label was applied to bankrupt businessmen. By the 1830s, however, it was being used in the United States to describe politicians who were running low on political capital. (The same term is applied today to members of Congress who will not be returning when a new Congress convenes.)

During a president's lame-duck period, Congress is least likely to respond to presidential initiatives. Legislators are already looking ahead to the next administration and their own reelections. Moreover, a president's administration has run its course by the time the president becomes a lame duck. Presidents who attempt new initiatives at this late stage find it difficult to arouse the interest, much less obtain the resources, necessary to ensure enactment.

A president who has been defeated for reelection in November remains the chief executive until noon on January 20 of the following year, when the new president is inaugurated. Until the Twentieth Amendment was ratified in 1933, new presidents were not sworn in until March 4, a full four months after the election. (See TERM OF OFFICE.)

The dangers of that long a delay were demonstrated even while the amendment was in the process of being ratified. After the 1932 election, president-elect Franklin D. Roosevelt was not able to take over from defeated incumbent Herbert C. Hoover for four months. During that period the nation, deep in the grip of the Great Depression and nearly leaderless, veered to the edge of economic catastrophe.

Some presidential observers have suggested that an outgoing president's lame-duck status has been made worse by the Twenty-second Amendment, which limits the president to two four-year terms. The possibility of a third term, it is sometimes argued, would help keep each presidency a more vigorous institution in its final days. Evidence indicates that the lame-duck effect on presidential persuasion is real. Since World War II, the party of all but one two-term president has lost seats in both the House and the Senate during the latter of the two MIDTERM ELECTIONS (i.e., after six years in office). The only exception was in 1998, during the Clinton administration's second term, when the Democrats gained eight House seats and lost none in the Senate.

> *My great ambition on January 20, 1941, is to turn over this desk and chair in the White House to my successor, whoever he may be, with the assurance that I am at the same time turning over to him as President, a Nation intact, a Nation at peace, a Nation prosperous. . . .*
>
> —*Franklin D. Roosevelt,* Address at the Democratic Victory Dinner, Washington, D.C., March 4, 1937

More on this topic:

Farewell Addresses, p. 210

Midterm Elections, p. 363

Landon, Alfred

Alfred Landon.
Source: Library of Congress

Alfred Mossman Landon (1887–1987), a two-term Republican governor of Kansas, ran unsuccessfully against Franklin D. Roosevelt in 1936, the first of Roosevelt's three winning campaigns for reelection. Landon's defeat was overwhelming. He won just 36.5 percent of the popular vote to Roosevelt's 60.8 percent and carried only two states, Maine and Vermont. After his defeat Landon never again ran for public office, although he remained active in the Republican Party for many years. The magnitude of his loss, combined with his longevity, made Landon an almost legendary figure by the time of his death at the age of one hundred.

Alf Landon was born in Pennsylvania on September 9, 1887, and later moved to Kansas with his parents. After graduating from law school in Kansas he worked in a bank just long enough to raise the funds he needed to start his own oil company, which eventually made him a millionaire. Landon became involved in Republican politics and, as a young man, supported Theodore Roosevelt's short-lived attempt to form a progressive splinter group, the Bull Moose Party. During the 1920s Landon became a force in Kansas Republican politics and also lobbied the state and federal governments on behalf of independent oil producers. An effective campaigner with strong support from business and the press, Landon won the governorship of Kansas in 1932 as a Republican, despite worsening economic conditions that favored Democrats.

As governor, Landon took bold actions to save his state from economic disaster and was reelected in 1934 in the midst of a Democratic landslide. Landon's reputation as "Frugal Alf," the politician who balanced his state's budget during the depression, helped bring him to the fore when the Republicans looked around for someone to take on the daunting task of challenging Roosevelt. Landon was nominated at the 1936 Republican national convention with no serious opposition. His running mate was Frank Knox, publisher of the *Chicago Daily News* and later secretary of the navy in Roosevelt's wartime cabinet.

Landon had always been a liberal Republican, but in 1936 he voiced his party's strong opposition to every aspect of the New Deal. Polls became a memorable feature of the campaign when a magazine, the *Literary Digest,* predicted a landslide for Landon. Unfortunately, the *Digest* poll had included an inordinate number of well-to-do citizens who happened to be Republicans. Pollster George Gallup boosted his reputation by calling the election correctly. In the end, Landon's well-organized and well-financed campaign, and his folksy but uninspired speeches, was no match for Franklin Roosevelt's popularity and powerful rhetoric. Landon returned to his oil business and continued to attend Republican conventions for many years. His daughter, Nancy Landon Kassebaum, was elected to the Senate from Kansas in 1978. She served three terms before retiring in 1997.

Law Enforcement Powers

In 1894 President Grover Cleveland sent federal troops to Chicago to prevent striking railroad workers from blocking trains. In 1962 President John F. Kennedy sent the army into Oxford, Mississippi, to protect James Meredith from rioters as he became the first black student to enroll at the state university. In 1975 President Gerald R. Ford issued a full pardon to Richard Nixon, protecting the former president from the possibility of criminal prosecution for his part in the Watergate affair.

These actions were unusual and dramatic demonstrations of the president's law enforcement powers. Most of the time the president's role in law enforcement is less obvious. The president's powers are limited by Congress, the courts, and public opinion. Still, as chief executive in charge of the vast law enforcement bureaucracy of the federal government, the president exerts considerable influence.

Sources of Law Enforcement Powers

The Constitution sets out the president's law enforcement powers in four areas:

1. Article II, Section 1, states that "the executive Power shall be vested in a President of the United States of America." This, along with another section of Article II, authorizes the president to appoint many of the nation's law enforcement officials.

2. Article II, Section 2, states that the "President shall be Commander in Chief of the Army and Navy of the United States, and of the Militia of the several States, when called into actual Service of the United States." Article IV, Section 4, provides that the federal government will protect states from "domestic Violence" when states request such help. These articles authorize the president to use force if necessary to uphold the law, as Cleveland did during the railroad strike and Kennedy did to desegregate the University of Mississippi. Although presidents rarely resort to force, its availability strengthens their position as chief law enforcement officer of the nation.

3. Article II, Section 2, gives the president the power to "grant Reprieves and Pardons for Offenses against the United States, except in Cases of Impeachment." (See PARDON POWER.)

4. Article II, Section 3, states that the president "shall take Care that the Laws be faithfully executed." As interpreted by the Supreme Court, this clause gives the president a broad range of discretionary powers.

Many of the laws the president executes and enforces have been enacted by Congress, drawing on its constitutionally granted powers. Others are the result of court rulings, treaties, executive orders, and regulations issued by government agencies. President Kennedy's actions in 1962 to desegregate the University of Mississippi, for example, were based on his constitutional powers, on laws written by Congress that delegated authority to the president, and on a 1954 Supreme Court decision outlawing segregation in public schools.

In 1957 a federal court ordered the integration of Central High School in Little Rock, Arkansas, but local authorities and segregationist mobs prevented nine black students from entering the school. Here, Arkansas National Guard troops, federalized by President Dwight D. Eisenhower, escort the students as they arrive in a U.S. Army station wagon during the first week of integration.
Source: AP

The Law Enforcement Bureaucracy

When people think of federal law enforcement, usually they think of the Federal Bureau of Investigation (FBI), the agency that posts mug shots of wanted criminals in post offices. The FBI is just one element in a vast federal law enforcement bureaucracy made up of scores of departments and agencies. As chief law enforcement officer of the nation, the president oversees this bureaucracy.

The FBI is a division of the JUSTICE DEPARTMENT, the foremost law enforcement agency of the federal government. The department is headed by the attorney general, who serves as the president's chief legal adviser. The attorney general supervises a large force of U.S. attorneys in Washington and throughout the country who represent the federal government in court.

Many other federal departments also have had responsibility for enforcing federal laws, including the Treasury Department, the Labor Department, and the Defense Department. The new federal Department of Homeland Security, created in late 2002, also has taken on a law enforcement role. Independent agencies, such as the Federal Trade Commission and the Securities and Exchange Commission, have enforced laws as well.

The federal law enforcement bureaucracy investigates cases, enforces federal laws, prosecutes violators, and takes custody of convicted criminals. An FBI investigation of an alleged national security violation, for example, may require months of work as agents gather evidence. U.S. attorneys do most of the federal government's work in court, prosecuting alleged lawbreakers. Anyone convicted of breaking federal laws and sentenced to prison is put in the custody of the U.S. Bureau of Prisons, the Justice Department's agency in charge of the federal prison system. In addition to the arrest and conviction of criminals, federal law enforcement involves monitoring compliance with federal regulations, such as when Agriculture Department inspectors visit meat-packing plants to see whether health and safety regulations are being followed.

The president's oath of office includes the phrase that he shall "faithfully execute the office of President of the United States." When combined with language in Article II, Section 3, which states, "he shall take Care that the Laws be faithfully executed," a president finds himself under a legal and constitutional mandate to enforce federal law, even if he personally does not agree with the law in question. On April 22, 2000, federal agents from the Immigration and Naturalization Service stormed the Miami home of the relatives of Elián González, a young boy who fled Cuba on a small boat with his mother and others. Elián's mother was one of many who died during the journey, and after the boy was placed in the custody of his relatives in Miami, his father demanded that he be returned to his custody in Cuba. Federal courts decided that Elián had to be returned to the custody of his father, and federal agents acting on orders from Attorney General Janet Reno, herself acting under the authority of President Clinton, forcibly returned Elián to his father's custody.

Growth of Law Enforcement Powers

When the nation was young, the federal government's role in law enforcement was limited. It collected customs taxes, suppressed domestic rebellions, enforced court orders, controlled the mail, and ran the army and navy. Over the years Congress has extended federal regulation to more and more aspects of life and has given the government more enforcement powers. The courts have upheld and sometimes expanded these powers.

Franklin D. Roosevelt's New Deal programs, designed to lift the nation out of economic depression, greatly expanded the federal government's law enforcement powers. The banking industry, Wall Street, civilian aviation, and labor practices all came under federal regulation. The trend continued after World War II, with new federal agencies and powers to regulate employment practices, housing, transportation, consumer credit, product safety, and environmental pollution. Despite the reduction or elimination of some regulations starting in the 1970s, the regulatory and police powers of the federal government continue to grow. The president, as the nation's chief executive and chief law enforcement officer, becomes more powerful as a result.

The terrorist attacks of September 11, 2001, led to greater law enforcement powers for the federal government. The USA Patriot Act, quickly passed and signed into law in October 2001, broadened the government's surveillance powers, facilitated greater sharing of confidential information from grand juries and financial institutions, and mandated cooperation between various law enforcement agencies. But the law sparked controversy among some lawmakers, who complained that Congress was unable to oversee it effectively because of Justice Department secrecy. And some lower courts ruled that the government had to release the names of certain people detained during its investigations.

One important way the president influences law enforcement policy is through the power to appoint and in some cases to fire officials who enforce laws. A president tries to choose leaders who have similar values and priorities, and who will in turn influence their subordinates to follow the president's agenda. When a new president takes office, it is common for him to replace most, if not all, U.S. attorneys just as he replaces thousands of other executive branch officials who occupy non-civil-service positions. This privilege sparked controversy in early 2007, however, when it was alleged that in December 2006, in the middle of George W. Bush's second term, the Justice Department fired and replaced eight federal prosecutors with persons more sympathetic to the Republican Party. The fired prosecutors had performed competently while in office, and the newly elected 110th Congress, controlled by the Democrats, began hearings to determine if political motives were the driving force behind the dismissals. Although U.S. attorneys serve at the pleasure of the president, this controversy underscored the political limitations of presidential appointment power on matters related to law enforcement. (See APPOINTMENT AND REMOVAL POWER.)

It is for this reason that I must tell those who fail to report for duty this morning they are in violation of the law, and if they do not report for work within 48 hours, they have forfeited their jobs and will be terminated.

—**Ronald Reagan,** Statement and a Question-and-Answer Session with Reporters on the Air Traffic Controllers Strike, August 3, 1981

The president appoints the attorney general and the principal officers of the Justice Department, as well as the heads of federal departments and agencies involved in law enforcement. Most of these appointees require Senate confirmation, and most receive it. The president is free to fire any appointee at any time and for any reason.

The president appoints other high-ranking law enforcement officials who have some protection against removal. The FBI director, for example, serves for a ten-year term and cannot be fired without cause. The heads of independent regulatory agencies such as the Federal Trade Commission and the Securities and Exchange Commission also are appointed by the president, but Congress has placed limits on the president's power to fire them.

A vacancy on the Supreme Court gives a president the chance to affect law enforcement policy at the highest level. A president's nominee for justice of the Supreme Court must be confirmed by the Senate. If confirmed, the justice cannot be removed except by impeachment. The same is true for federal judges: They are nominated by the president, confirmed by the Senate, and serve for life unless impeached. (See COURTS AND THE PRESIDENT.)

> **More on this topic:**
>
> *Article II, p. 16*

Legislative Powers   *See* CONGRESS AND THE PRESIDENCY; VETO POWER.

Legislative Veto

The legislative veto is a device that gives Congress the power to review and reject executive branch decisions implementing laws. It has permitted Congress to write broad legislation and then let the executive branch develop the regulations and policies to carry out the law, subject to later congressional reaction.

For Congress the legislative veto has been a way to restrain the executive branch. Most presidents have seen it as an unconstitutional intrusion by Congress into their executive prerogatives. Presidents in the past found it particularly frustrating that most legislative vetoes were accomplished through resolutions that did not have to be sent to the White House for the president's signature or veto. The president could do nothing to prevent them.

More than two hundred legislative veto provisions were enacted into law before the Supreme Court in 1983 ruled that most legislative vetoes were unconstitutional. Since that decision, Congress has continued to devise other ways to influence executive actions.

The legislative veto has taken several different forms. It was invoked sometimes by a vote of both houses of Congress (usually through a concurrent resolution), at other times by a vote of one house (through a simple resolution), and at still other times through the actions of a single congressional committee or subcommittee. None of these methods required the president's signature, although the original legislation authorizing the legislative veto would have had to cross the president's desk. All of these procedures allowed the federal departments or agencies to implement certain rules or programs unless Congress moved to block them, usually within a period of thirty to sixty days.

The legislative veto was first used during the presidency of Herbert C. Hoover. In 1930 Hoover asked Congress to enact legislation for reorganization of the executive branch. When Congress failed to do so, he asked for the authority to do it himself, subject to congressional review. Congress went along, and in 1932 Hoover was allowed to reorganize by executive order, but each order had to be sent to Congress and could be rejected by either house within sixty days. The device was used the very next year to disapprove a reorganization plan.

The legislative veto became a standard provision in reorganization legislation and appeared in other types of legislation as well. Its use increased during the 1940s as a way of checking the vast war-making and emergency powers Congress delegated to Franklin D. Roosevelt's administration during World War II.

Use of the legislative veto declined in the 1950s and 1960s but mushroomed in the 1970s as Congress attempted to reassert itself against a presidency weakened by the Vietnam War and Watergate. Legislative vetoes were incorporated into the War Powers Resolution of 1973, the Congressional Budget and Impoundment Control Act of 1974, the Federal Election Campaign Act of 1974, and the International Security Assistance and Arms Control Act of 1976.

Although presidents of both parties strongly objected to the legislative veto, most of them chose not to confront the issue directly. In 1976, however, President Gerald R. Ford dramatized his opposition by vetoing an environmental bill because it contained a legislative veto provision. And Ronald Reagan in 1982 had his solicitor general urge the Supreme Court to declare the legislative veto unconstitutional.

Critics argued that the legislative veto infringed on the executive's constitutional duty to carry out the laws because it allowed Congress to direct administrative action. Some argued that it violated the Constitution's requirement that binding actions taken by the legislature be presented to the president for a signature or veto (known as the presentment clause). Opponents also claimed that the legislative veto reversed the normal relationship between the two branches, because the president or an agency could take an action unless Congress "vetoed" the action.

Proponents pointed out that Congress delegates rule-making authority to the executive branch all the time and should have the power to set some limits on that delegated power through the use of a legislative veto. Moreover, although the legislative veto itself was not subject to White House approval, the law authorizing the veto was. Supporters of the device also argued that it had become an important political tool for Congress at a time when Congress needed such tools to make its oversight more effective.

The Supreme Court agreed with the critics. In *IMMIGRATION AND NATURALIZATION SERVICE V. CHADHA* (1983), the Court ruled that a legislative veto provision attached to an immigration law violated the constitutional doctrine of separation of powers and the presentment clause. If Congress wished to prevent the executive branch from undertaking some action, the majority ruled, it had to either legislate in greater detail to begin with or pass a regular bill—subject to presidential review—to stop an action it found unacceptable.

Despite the sweeping nature of the *Chadha* decision, the legislative veto is still employed through devices such as informal agreements, reliance on arcane bill language, and use of internal congressional rules. Congress also now uses more explicit language in bills. Furthermore, it is writing provisions into appropriations bills forbidding funding for some specific bureaucratic or presidential actions—language that provides the functional equivalent of a legislative veto if the president accepts the appropriations bill as a whole.

> **[A]t any time that United States Armed Forces are engaged in hostilities outside the territory of the United States, its possessions and territories without a declaration of war or specific statutory authorization, such forces shall be removed by the President if the Congress so directs by concurrent resolution.**
>
> —**Joint Resolution Concerning the War Powers of Congress and the President,** Public Law 93-148, 93d Congress, H. J. Res. 542, November 7, 1973

> **House Joint Resolution 542 would attempt to take away, by a mere legislative act, authorities which the President has properly exercised under the Constitution for almost 200 years.**
>
> —**Richard Nixon,** Veto of the War Powers Resolution, October 24, 1973

More on this topic:

Immigration and Naturalization Service v. Chadha, p. 272

War Powers Act of 1973, p. 560

Lewinsky, Monica *See* CLINTON, WILLIAM J.; IMPEACHMENT.

Libraries

Abraham Lincoln, Rutherford B. Hayes, William McKinley, Woodrow Wilson, and every president since Calvin Coolidge has had a library established in his honor. These libraries are not only depositories for presidential papers but also memorials complete with museums, attracting tourists as well as scholars. With the opening of the William J. Clinton Presidential Library and Museum in 2004, there were twelve libraries administered by the NATIONAL ARCHIVES AND RECORDS ADMINISTRATION, and five maintained by private organizations or local governments. The National Archives is responsible for all libraries beginning with the Hoover administration, with the exception of the Nixon Library. Nixon's presidential materials are held by the National Archives at College Park, Maryland, but the Richard Nixon Library and Birthplace in Yorba Linda, California, is privately held.

Franklin D. Roosevelt was the first president to come up with the idea of an official presidential library; he used the Hayes library as a model. Roosevelt organized a private committee to fund and construct the library in his hometown of Hyde Park, New York, and donated its contents to the federal government. It opened in 1948 and was run by the National Archives with federal funds.

In 1955 Congress passed a law making the Roosevelt arrangement general: Presidential libraries would be built with private funds and then run by the National Archives with public funds. But by the mid-1980s the eight existing presidential libraries were costing the government about $15 million a year to operate. Critics complained that the libraries were primarily tourist attractions rather than research archives and should not be run at public expense. In 1986 Congress passed a law requiring that private endowments supplement the expenses of operating future presidential libraries. Congress made an exception for Ronald Reagan's library. Richard Nixon's library, also completed after 1986, was an entirely private endeavor.

Presidential libraries house a president's papers as well as films, photographs, and clippings that document his administration. Some papers are considered so sensitive that they are kept secret for a period of years before being opened for researchers. The libraries also feature museums that depict the president's life and display his memorabilia in carefully designed settings. Negative aspects of an administration, such as scandals, are downplayed or ignored, while accomplishments are displayed. An exception is the Nixon library, which devotes an entire room to the WATERGATE AFFAIR, although efforts have been made to present Nixon's inten-

Visitors to the Jimmy Carter Library may enjoy a stroll around the Carter Center grounds. The site contains a Japanese garden with an imitation landscape of deep mountains and secluded valleys, including two symbolic waterfalls.
Source: Jimmy Carter Library

U.S. Postal Service Presidential Libraries Stamp
John F. Kennedy Library

tions in a favorable light. As the director of the Reagan library observed, "A presidential library tells history through the eyes of a president."

The presidential libraries in order of the presidents' service are as follows:

Libraries Administered by the National Archives

- Herbert Hoover Presidential Library and Museum, West Branch, Iowa
- Franklin D. Roosevelt Presidential Library and Museum, Hyde Park, New York
- Harry S. Truman Presidential Museum and Library, Independence, Missouri
- Dwight D. Eisenhower Presidential Library and Museum, Abilene, Kansas
- John F. Kennedy Presidential Library and Museum, Boston, Massachusetts
- Lyndon Baines Johnson Presidential Library and Museum, Austin, Texas
- Nixon Presidential Materials, College Park, Maryland
- Gerald R. Ford Presidential Library and Museum, Ann Arbor, Michigan
- Jimmy Carter Presidential Library and Museum, Atlanta, Georgia
- Ronald Reagan Presidential Library and Museum, Simi Valley, California
- George Bush Presidential Library and Museum, College Station, Texas
- William J. Clinton Presidential Library and Museum, Little Rock, Arkansas

Privately Managed Libraries

- Abraham Lincoln Presidential Library and Museum, Springfield, Illinois
- Rutherford B. Hayes Memorial Museum and Library, Fremont, Ohio
- William McKinley Presidential Library and Museum, Canton, Ohio
- Woodrow Wilson Presidential Library, Staunton, Virginia
- Calvin Coolidge Presidential Library and Museum, Northampton, Massachusetts
- Richard Nixon Library and Birthplace, Yorba Linda, California

In 2001 American taxpayers paid over $43 million to operate presidential libraries. Bill Clinton's library in Little Rock, Arkansas, opened in 2004, and a state-supported Abraham Lincoln library, in Springfield, Illinois, opened in 2005. On December 22, 2006, it was announced that George W. Bush's library will be built in Texas at Southern Methodist University (SMU), but controversy surrounds this decision. A coalition of historians and archivists are urging SMU to reject the library unless the Bush administration reverses Executive Order 13233, which allows presidents to keep their papers secret for an indefinite period of time.

> **More on this topic:**
>
> *Former Presidents, p. 226*
>
> *National Archives and Records Administration, p. 371*

Lincoln, Abraham

Abraham Lincoln (1809–1865) guided the nation through the Civil War, greatly expanding the powers of the presidency in the process. His election as president in 1860 provoked the war. Shortly after his inauguration to a second term, he became the first president to be assassinated.

Abraham Lincoln was born on February 12, 1809, in a one-room log cabin near Hodgenville, Kentucky. His father, Thomas Lincoln, was a poor farmer who also did carpentry work. Abe's younger brother died in infancy, and his mother, Nancy, died when he was nine.

During Abe's childhood the Lincolns lived on farms in Kentucky and Indiana. The boy attended country schools sporadically, learning to read, write, and do elementary math. He worked at numerous odd jobs while in his teens, including as a farmhand, grocery store clerk, and ferry boat rower. In 1828 and 1831 he took trips down the Mississippi River to New Orleans as a flatboat deckhand. While in New Orleans during the second trip he is said to have witnessed the maltreatment of slaves and developed a hatred of slavery.

Upon returning to Illinois from New Orleans in 1831, Lincoln settled in New Salem. In 1832 he volunteered to fight Sauk Indians led by Chief Black Hawk. After serving several months in the army, he was discharged without participating in any combat. He returned from his military service to New Salem, where he failed in business as keeper of a general store before becoming a postmaster and surveyor.

Source: Library of Congress

Early Political Career

In 1834 Lincoln won a seat in the Illinois legislature. He began studying law by reading borrowed law books and was licensed to practice shortly after being reelected to a second term in 1836. He also won third and fourth terms, serving for a time as Whig floor leader. On November 4, 1842, he married Mary Todd, the well-educated daughter of a prominent Lexington, Kentucky, businessman and his wife. Their marriage was a stormy one, complicated by her lavish spending, superstitious nature, and bouts with depression.

In 1846 Lincoln was elected to the U.S. House of Representatives. Despite the popularity of the Mexican-American War in his district, he joined fellow Whigs in denouncing the war as unjust. Lincoln also opposed the extension of slavery into the territories, but he did not advocate the abolition of slavery where it already existed. Lincoln had promised Illinois Whig Party leaders that he would serve only one term. He spent the next several years in Springfield, Illinois, reading widely and developing his successful law practice.

In 1854 Lincoln ran for the Senate but backed out of the race when his candidacy threatened to split the antislavery vote. Two years later he joined the new Republican Party, formed in 1854. The Illinois Republican Party nominated Lincoln for senator in 1858. He faced incumbent Democrat Stephen A. Douglas, author of the Kansas-Nebraska Act of 1854, which was favored by many proslavery Democrats. The act gave the people in the territories of Kansas and Nebraska the option to permit slavery. Lincoln challenged Douglas to a series of seven debates that were attended by huge crowds. In the debates Lincoln questioned the morality of slavery and argued strongly against its expansion. In the end, the state legislature elected Douglas over Lincoln, 54–46, but the debates made Lincoln famous nationally. During the next two years he made several highly publicized speaking tours, including one to the East. The 1860 Republican national convention in Chicago nominated him for president on the third ballot.

The Democratic Party split into two factions at its 1860 convention. Stephen Douglas was nominated by northern Democrats, and Vice President John C. Breckinridge of Kentucky was nominated by southern Democrats. The southern remnants of the Whig and Know-Nothing Parties further complicated the election by joining to nominate Tennessean John Bell as the candidate of their new Constitutional Union Party. Lincoln won the four-candidate race with less than 40 percent of the popular vote. He captured eighteen northern states with 180 of 303 electoral votes. Breckinridge, Bell, and Douglas followed with 72, 39, and 12, respectively.

Presidency

Lincoln's election precipitated the secession crisis that the nation had feared for several decades. In December 1860 South Carolina left the Union, followed by six more states early in 1861. The rebelling states formed a confederacy and elected Jefferson Davis as their president.

Lincoln declared in his first inaugural address that he had no intention or authority to "interfere with the institution of slavery where it already exists." But he warned the southern states that he did not recognize their secession and would enforce federal law and defend the Union. He declared, "In your hands, my dissatisfied fellow-countrymen, and not in mine, is the momentous issue of civil war." War came in April 1861 when rebels attacked and captured Fort Sumter in Charleston harbor. The attack on the federal fort signaled the South's unwillingness to return to the Union. On April 15 Lincoln called for 75,000 volunteers to put down the rebellion. Soon after, four more southern states seceded, raising the number of states in the Confederacy to eleven.

During the next three months Lincoln refused to call Congress into special session, while he took extraordinary actions to prepare for war, many of which violated the Constitution. He blockaded the South, doubled the size of the armed forces, suspended the writ of habeas corpus in some areas, and spent Treasury funds, all without congressional approval. Finally, on July 4, he convened Congress, which ratified most of his war measures.

Lincoln and the North hoped that the rebellion could be put down quickly, but the war turned into a protracted and bloody conflict. The Union won victories in the West under Gen. Ulysses S. Grant, but in the East Union generals were repeatedly outmaneuvered by Robert E. Lee and other Confederate leaders. On January 1, 1863, Lincoln issued the Emancipation Proclamation, which declared that the slaves in the rebellious states were free. So that the proclamation would have greater credibility, Lincoln issued it only after the Union had won a victory, which came at the battle of Antietam in September 1862.

With malice toward none, with charity for all, with firmness in the right as God gives us to see the right, let us strive on to finish the work we are in, to bind up the nation's wounds, to care for him who shall have borne the battle and for his widow and his orphan, to do all which may achieve and cherish a just and lasting peace among ourselves and with all nations.

—**Abraham Lincoln,** *Second Inaugural Address*, March 4, 1865

In July 1863 the Union victory in the battle of Gettysburg, Pennsylvania, put the Confederacy on the defensive. Lincoln traveled to Gettysburg on November 19, where he delivered his famous Gettysburg Address during a ceremony to dedicate the battlefield's cemetery. The address began, "Four score and seven years ago our fathers brought forth on this continent, a new nation, conceived in Liberty, and dedicated to the proposition that all men are created equal." It ended with the stirring words of commitment that "government of the people, by the people, for the people, shall not perish from the earth."

In 1864 Lincoln took an important step toward winning the war when he ordered General Grant east to take command of all Union armies. That year Lincoln ran for reelection against Democratic candidate George B. McClellan, one of his former generals. Lincoln had relieved McClellan of his command of the Union army in 1862 because the general was overcautious and ineffective.

During the spring of 1864 Lincoln's reelection was in doubt as Grant's army fought a series of indecisive and costly battles in Virginia. But by September, Union general William T. Sherman had captured Atlanta, and Grant had besieged Petersburg, Virginia. Voters sensed that the Union was close to victory and reelected the president. Lincoln won all but three states and defeated McClellan by a vote of 212–21 in the Electoral College.

On April 9, 1865, Lee surrendered to Grant at Appomattox Courthouse in Virginia, ending the war. In his second inaugural address, delivered on March 4, 1865, Lincoln proposed a magnanimous peace, saying, "With malice toward none, with charity for all, with firmness in the right as God gives us to see the right, let us strive on to finish the work we are in, to bind up the nation's wounds…"

Lincoln, however, was not able to implement his generous Reconstruction plans. On April 14, 1865, while watching a production of the play *Our American Cousin* at Ford's Theatre in Washington, D.C., he was shot in the back of the head at close range by actor John Wilkes Booth. After shooting Lincoln, Booth jumped from the presidential box to the stage, fled the theater, and rode south. On April 26 federal troops surrounded and killed him at a farm in Virginia. Booth, who had sympathized with the Confederacy, was part of a conspiracy to kill several government officials, including Vice President Andrew Johnson. With the exception of Secretary of State William H. Seward, who received a nonfatal stab wound at his home, the other targets of assassination escaped harm.

Lincoln was treated by a doctor at the theater, then carried across the street to a house where he died the next morning, April 15, without regaining consciousness. Vice President Andrew Johnson took the oath of office later that day. Lincoln's body lay in state in the Capitol and White House before being carried back to Illinois on a train that made stops in many towns so that the president's body could be viewed by millions of mourners.

More on this topic:
Assassinations and Assaults, p. 19
Civil War, p. 95
Emancipation Proclamation, p. 187
Memorials, Presidential, p. 360
War Powers, p. 555

Lincoln, Mary Todd

Mary Todd Lincoln.
Source: Library of Congress

Perhaps the most controversial of the first ladies, Mary Todd Lincoln (1818–1882) was the wife of President Abraham Lincoln. Mary was attractive, intelligent, and witty, but she was troubled by deep insecurity and a mercurial personality that would burden her husband's presidency.

Mary was the well-educated daughter of a prominent businessman of Lexington, Kentucky. At the age of twenty-one she went to live with a sister in Springfield, Illinois. There she met Abraham Lincoln, whom she married on November 4, 1842. The couple had four sons.

By the time Lincoln was elected president in 1860, the death of their son Edward at age four had combined with Mary's moody temperament to leave her emotionally unstable. Lincoln called her his "child wife." She was extremely nervous and prone to blinding headaches. Her insecurity often led to displays of irrational jealousy.

During Mary's stay at the White House she was the target of unceasing criticism. Despite the strain placed on the national budget by the Civil War, she fought with Congress for more money to renovate the White House. Her family's ties to the Confederacy led many to call her a traitor, and she was investigated by a congressional committee. When she held White House receptions, she was criticized for her inappropriate frivolity during a crisis, yet if she did not host social functions, she was attacked for "adding to the gloom" of the day.

When the Lincolns' son Willie died of typhoid in 1862, Mary's unrestrained grief was condemned as excessive in a time of national tragedy. She refused to enter the rooms where the boy had died and was embalmed. She also banned flowers and music from the White House and conducted seances in an attempt to make contact with his spirit. Mary compulsively bought clothes without Lincoln's knowledge, and her clothing bills soon exceeded his yearly salary. She fearfully awaited the returns of the 1864 elections, knowing that a loss would force her to face creditors she could not pay. When Lincoln won, she bought more clothes.

Mary was forty-seven when Lincoln was assassinated in 1865. She did not attend his funeral and stayed in mourning in the White House for five weeks. After leaving the White House she developed a delusion that she was poor, although Lincoln's estate left her $35,000 after settling debts. Mary petitioned Congress for a pension, but she was so clumsy in her appeals that she alienated most members of Congress as well as the public. To escape the criticism she traveled to Europe with her favorite son, Tad, and did not return until Congress granted her a small pension in 1870. But when Tad died of typhoid in 1871, she developed symptoms of paranoia and kept her money and securities sewn into her coat. In May 1875 her erratic behavior caused her remaining son, Robert, to commit her to a mental hospital.

> **More on this topic:**
>
> *First Ladies, p. 219*
>
> *White House, p. 573*

After one of her sisters arranged her release from the sanitarium a few months later, Mary moved to France and lived there alone until 1879. Sick, unhappy, and estranged from her son, Mary returned to Springfield and died there of a stroke in 1882. She was buried next to her husband and children in Springfield.

Line-Item Veto

For more than a hundred years, presidents have sought the power to veto parts or items of a specific bill. Democratic president Bill Clinton was granted the line-item veto by a Republican-controlled Congress in 1996 and, before the Supreme Court declared it unconstitutional, used it more than eighty times during 1997 and 1998.

Congress often has attached controversial proposals or "riders" to popular or urgent legislation as a way of avoiding, or sometimes inviting, for political reasons, a president's veto. Until the enactment of the Line Item Veto Act, the president had the authority to veto only a whole bill and often had to sign into law a bill with provisions he disliked or veto a bill he favored that contained provisions he did not want.

That a congressional cession of power is voluntary does not make it innocuous. The Constitution is a compact enduring for more than our time, and one Congress cannot yield up its own powers, much less those of other Congresses to follow.

—*Justice Anthony Kennedy,* Concurring Opinion in the Case of Clinton v. City of New York, *No. 97-1374,* June 25, 1998

The line-item veto was a prominent part of the "Contract with America," a list of ten agenda items that Republican candidates for the House of Representatives pledged to enact should they gain control of Congress in 1994. And the Republicans were true to their word, passing the line-item veto primarily as a tool to control federal spending. The 1996 law gave the president the right to "cancel" in any appropriations bill a single spending item, any newly approved mandatory entitlement provision, and certain limited tax benefits. More specifically, under the act a president could cancel any of these three types of provisions within five days of signing a bill into law. Should Congress want to force the president to approve the expenditure, it would have to pass a "disapproval" bill and send it to the president. If he vetoed that measure, two-thirds majorities in both houses were required to override the veto. Under the law's "lockbox" provision, any savings generated by the cancellation had to go toward deficit reduction. Under a "sunset" provision, the law was to expire after eight years, on January 1, 2005.

Supporters of the law contended it discouraged members of Congress from inserting money for pet projects or for constituency-specific measures that benefited a few special interests (that is, so-called pork-barrel measures) into appropriations bills. They also contended that the law gave the president needed control over such expenditures and therefore helped to eliminate wasteful programs. This, in turn, conservatives argued, would reduce the size of government.

Criticism of the line-item veto law fell into three basic categories:

- The amount of money saved was modest in terms of the entire budget. Analysts of the forty-three state governments that have a line-item veto law say the state laws have had little effect on state spending levels. At the national level, modest savings of less than $1 billion a year were predicted by some opponents in Congress.
- The law was unconstitutional because it infringed on Congress's constitutional power over federal spending and it permitted a president to amend a law, a legislative function that cannot be transferred to the president by an ordinary statute.
- The law gave presidents a political weapon in that they could trade dollars for votes. For example, they could threaten to cancel a pet project of a member of Congress unless the member voted their way on an issue.

After its passage, the law was immediately challenged in court by three senators, one former senator, and two representatives, who claimed that it infringed on their constitutional responsibilities. The Supreme Court quickly issued a ruling that the lawmakers did not have legal standing to challenge the law in court before it had even been used. But the next year, in 1998, the Court accepted an appeal from New York City and ruled in *Clinton v. City of New York* that the line-item veto violated Article I, Section 7, of the Constitution, the presentment clause. The law was unconstitutional, said the Court, because it allowed the president to rewrite bills already passed by Congress, thereby creating a new law with language that had not been approved by the House and Senate. Such a change in the president's role, if sought, would have to come about by constitutional amendment and not by legislation, Justice John Paul Stevens wrote for the Court.

Calls to give the president line-item veto authority have resurfaced during the administration of George W. Bush. At a press conference following his reelection in 2004, Bush introduced his desire to have a "constitutional" line-item veto. He made a specific request in his 2006 State of the Union address, followed by a message to Congress outlining a plan for a new version that he argued would not violate the notion of separation of powers. In the new proposal, the various line-item vetoes in legislation would be returned to Congress for it to approve of the president's actions. Although the House of Representatives passed Bush's proposed legislation in 2006, it was defeated in the Senate on January 24, 2007.

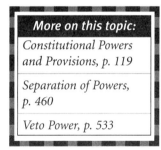

More on this topic:

Constitutional Powers and Provisions, p. 119

Separation of Powers, p. 460

Veto Power, p. 533

Lobbying   *See* INTEREST GROUPS AND THE PRESIDENCY.

Louisiana Purchase

Thomas Jefferson's most important act during his first term as president was the Louisiana Purchase. In 1803 the French owned the port of New Orleans as well as a vast area that stretched from New Orleans to present-day Montana, known as the Louisiana Territory. Fearing that the French could block U.S. navigation of the Mississippi and threaten American settlements in the West, Jefferson sent negotiators to France in the hope of purchasing the port of New Orleans. The French instead

This early-nineteenth-century French map of the United States shows the vast lands acquired when President Thomas Jefferson authorized the Louisiana Purchase.
Source: Library of Congress

CLOSER LOOK

The United States expanded during its history through a combination of military conquest (Mexico, in 1846; Spain, in 1898), presidential proclamation (West Florida, in 1810), treaties (Texas Annexation, in 1845), and purchase. Other notable acquisitions of land through purchase were the 1853 Gadsden Purchase from Mexico of almost 30,000 square miles of land comprising southern Arizona and parts of southwestern New Mexico at a cost of $10 million; the 1867 Alaska Purchase from Russia of approximately 600,000 square miles at a cost of $7.2 million; and the U.S. Virgin Islands (although not a state) from Denmark in 1917 for $25 million.

offered to sell the entire Louisiana Territory. The U.S. representatives, James Monroe and Robert Livingston, saw the opportunity to create an American empire as well as to improve the security of the western frontier. They struck a deal with French emperor Napoleon to buy all of the Louisiana Territory for 60 million francs (approximately $15 million), or about 4 cents an acre.

Jefferson recognized that to support the agreement he would have to ignore his own principles of strict adherence to the Constitution, which did not specifically authorize the president to acquire territory. Congress had not appropriated money for the deal. He believed that the purchase would greatly benefit the nation and that the offer from Napoleon might be withdrawn if he hesitated. Jefferson did not want to risk the possibility that Great Britain might take control of the area or that Napoleon might sell the land to the British while the Senate debated the purchase. Therefore, Jefferson concluded the deal, dispatched the money to France, and later urged Congress to ratify the purchase and appropriate funds to pay for it.

In the fall of 1803 Congress approved the purchase and appropriated the $15 million. On December 20 the United States took formal control of its new possession. With the addition of the 828,000 square miles of the Louisiana Territory, the area of the United States nearly doubled. William C.C. Claiborne was formally installed as territorial governor. In 1812 the state of Louisiana became the first to be admitted from the territory.

Historians view the Louisiana Purchase as an example of presidential flexibility. The Louisiana Purchase also has been cited as the first time a president concluded a major international agreement without obtaining congressional approval in advance. Pacts with foreign governments made independently by the president came to be called EXECUTIVE AGREEMENTS. Because Jefferson eventually obtained Senate approval, historians generally do not consider the Louisiana Purchase to be the first executive agreement, but it clearly presaged the use of executive agreements by future presidents.

More on this topic:

Constitutional Powers and Provisions, p. 119

Executive Agreements, p. 198

Jefferson, Thomas, p. 304

M

McCarthy, Eugene J.

Eugene J. McCarthy.
Source: Judith Barry Smith

Sen. Eugene Joseph McCarthy (1916–2005) of Minnesota changed the course of U.S. history during the tumultuous presidential election of 1968. His strong showing in the New Hampshire Democratic primary that year as an anti–Vietnam War candidate helped to convince Sen. Robert F. Kennedy of New York to enter the Democratic race—and President Lyndon B. Johnson to bow out. McCarthy's protest candidacy galvanized thousands of college students into what became known as a "children's crusade" to end the war. A low-key campaigner, McCarthy avoided the heated rhetoric of many antiwar activists and appealed to voters to make a "reasoned judgment" on whether the war was worth the cost in lives and money. Kennedy was assassinated after defeating McCarthy in the California primary. Johnson's vice president, Hubert H. Humphrey, went on to win the nomination and lose a close election to Republican Richard Nixon.

Success in the presidential primary season depends on a candidate's ability to accomplish two important goals: exceeding expectations and gaining momentum. For this reason, it is not necessary to win early primary elections like the perennially first New Hampshire primary but rather to at least meet and hopefully exceed expectations. When expectations are exceeded in early contests, a candidate then gains momentum that brings more media attention and campaign contributions, paving the way for future success in the remaining primaries. McCarthy's near-win in New Hampshire against the incumbent president Johnson had the opposite effect for the president in 1968. Other notable instances where candidates exceeded expectations in New Hampshire include Estes Kefauver, who defeated incumbent president Harry S. Truman in 1952, and Bill Clinton, who in 1992 amidst a scandal involving an alleged extra-martial affair came in second in New Hampshire when many in the media expected that he would have to drop out of the race. In his speech after the vote count, a jubilant Clinton announced that "New Hampshire tonight has made Bill Clinton the comeback kid."

Tall and athletic with a sculpted profile and silver hair, McCarthy looked like a presidential candidate. By temperament, however, he was an unlikely choice to lead a political movement. A philosophical former economics teacher, who wrote poetry as well as books on public policy, McCarthy had earned a reputation in the Senate as a loner. He was described variously as witty, cynical, aloof, and arrogant.

Raised on a farm in Minnesota, he attended and later taught at Catholic schools. Although influenced by a liberal strain of Catholicism, McCarthy did not emphasize his religion in the political arena. He began his political career in local Democratic politics in St. Paul, where he taught at a Catholic college after World War II. In the House of Representatives (1949–1959), McCarthy was a founder of the Democratic Study Group, an alliance of House liberals, and served on the important Ways and Means Committee. He seemed less comfortable in the Senate (1959–1971), where he sat on the Finance and Foreign Relations Committees. Not content with the political life, McCarthy studied twentieth-century poetry, formed a friendship with the eminent American poet Robert Lowell, and struggled to become a poet himself.

McCarthy announced his candidacy for the Democratic presidential nomination in November 1967 at the urging of antiwar Democrats, some of whom had failed to convince Kennedy to join the race. Johnson seemed invulnerable then, but public sentiment against his conduct of the war mounted after the North Vietnamese in January 1968 launched a military operation, the Tet offensive, which resulted in unexpectedly large U.S. casualties. McCarthy volunteers poured into New Hampshire, while Democratic Party regulars waged a last-minute write-in campaign for the president.

Johnson won the March 12 primary with 49.6 percent of the vote to McCarthy's 41.9 percent, but the challenger's unexpectedly strong showing in a conservative state made headlines, and Johnson was seen as the loser. McCarthy's achievement in New Hampshire brought Kennedy into the race within days. With another victory for McCarthy predicted in the Wisconsin primary, Johnson went on television March 31 to make the stunning announcement that he would not seek or accept his party's nomination for a second term.

Both McCarthy and Kennedy wanted to end the war, but their battles in the primaries were bitter. McCarthy and his supporters resented Kennedy's entry into the race after McCarthy had paved the way. Kennedy was strong among black and Hispanic voters, while McCarthy's support came largely from liberal, upper-middle-class whites. Just before Kennedy was killed, his narrow victory over McCarthy in the California primary appeared to have given him the edge. McCarthy therefore went to the Democratic national convention lacking the delegates to defeat Humphrey, his former Senate colleague from Minnesota, who had the support of Johnson and traditional Democrats. In the end, at the divisive convention in Chicago an antiwar plank went down to defeat along with McCarthy.

After he left the Senate in 1971 McCarthy kept his eye on the presidency as he wrote and lectured on his often novel ideas for reforming the political system. In 1976 he ran for president as an independent, hoping to energize his 1968 supporters. He successfully challenged many state ballot access laws but won slightly less than 1 percent of the popular vote. In 1982 McCarthy lost a primary bid to regain his Senate seat. McCarthy died in Washington, D.C., on December 10, 2005, from complications of Parkinson's disease. He was eulogized by former president Bill Clinton.

More on this topic:

Delegate Selection Reforms, p. 146

Elections Chronology, p. 174

McClellan, George B.

George B. McClellan (1826–1885) was a Union general and the Democratic presidential nominee who challenged President Abraham Lincoln in 1864. The election was held during the Civil War and was considered by many to be a referendum on the war. Lincoln decisively defeated McClellan, but the outcome of the election was not obvious during the preceding months.

McClellan was a highly professional general and West Point graduate, who was reputed to be an expert at building and supplying an army. In July 1861 he was appointed commanding general of the Union's Army of the Potomac.

Fired by President Abraham Lincoln during the Civil War, Gen. George B. McClellan (foreground, center) later ran against Lincoln in the presidential race of 1864. The incumbent president defeated the former commanding general of the Union Army.

Despite McClellan's strengths, he was an extremely cautious military commander. On numerous occasions he refused to take the fight to the outnumbered Confederates or to seize on battlefield advantages. Frustrated with McClellan's caution, Lincoln once remarked that the general used his army "like a bodyguard." In November 1862 Lincoln relieved him of his command.

By 1864 the North was growing weary of the war, and the leaders of the Democratic Party thought they could win an election if their candidate promised to end the war. McClellan seemed to be the logical candidate. He could be presented as a victim of Lincoln's injustice—a general who had accomplished much and would have accomplished more if he had been fairly treated. McClellan's campaign was built around a call for a cease-fire and a convention to restore the Union.

McClellan's acceptance of the nomination placed him in an awkward situation. He had always supported the war and had recently reaffirmed this position in a speech at West Point. His campaign themes, therefore, were often inconsistent. He was conciliatory toward the Confederacy, yet he also sought the votes of Union soldiers.

McClellan's fate as a candidate, however, had less to do with his own campaign than with the progress of the war. In the spring and summer of 1864 the North clearly had the upper hand in the conflict, but its progress had been stalled. In Virginia Gen. Ulysses S. Grant had laid siege to the Confederate army at Petersburg, and in Georgia Gen. William T. Sherman was maneuvering to capture Atlanta. Both forces were making little progress and had sustained large numbers of casualties. Without a major Union victory on one of the two fronts, voters might have decided to cast their votes for McClellan and a negotiated peace. In early September, however, Sherman's forces broke Confederate defenses and marched into Atlanta. Most voters in the North came to believe that the South would soon be defeated.

> **By direction of the President, it is ordered that Major-General McClellan be relieved from the command of the Army of the Potomac, and that Major-General Burnside take the command of that army....**
>
> **—Abraham Lincoln,** *Executive Order— Relieving General G. B. McClellan and Making Other Changes,* November 5, 1862

More on this topic:
Civil War, p. 95
Lincoln, Abraham, p. 336

On election day McClellan resigned his commission in the army. The returns showed that he had carried only New Jersey, Delaware, and Kentucky, giving him 21 electoral votes against Lincoln's 212. Lincoln garnered 2.2 million popular votes (55 percent) to McClellan's 1.8 million (45 percent). After the defeat McClellan retired from national politics, although he served as governor of New Jersey from 1878 to 1881.

McGovern, George S.

George McGovern
Source: McGovern Library

Sen. George Stanley McGovern (1922–) of South Dakota led the Democrats to a crushing defeat in the 1972 presidential race in which Richard Nixon was elected to a second term. Against all predictions, McGovern's grass-roots anti–Vietnam War campaign had upset traditional forces in the Democratic Party to win him the nomination. But only Massachusetts and the District of Columbia went for McGovern in November; the Nixon camp had successfully portrayed him as a dangerous extremist. While McGovern was frantically crossing the country calling for an end to the war, Nixon had spent most of the campaign in the White House, assuring the public through a series of spokesmen that he was winding down the war with statesmanlike deliberation. The result was a landslide that Nixon called "one of the greatest political victories of all time."

McGovern's success in the 1972 Democratic primaries was a memorable political victory. His announcement came earlier than that of any other candidate, but his standing in the polls remained low on the eve of the primary season, and he was perceived as having little chance of success. McGovern traveled around the country in 1971 and early 1972 building up an efficient grass-roots network of thousands of volunteers inspired by his stand against the war. The campaign was managed by Gary Hart, a Denver lawyer who went on to become a senator and make his own bid for the Democratic presidential nomination in 1984.

McGovern's organizing was bolstered by new rules that opened the Democratic Party to more women, minorities, and young people while reducing the power of party leaders. McGovern had led the push for those changes as chairman of the Commission on Party Structure and Delegate Selection in the years after the divisive Democratic national convention of 1968. As the 1972 primaries progressed, McGovern defeated two political heavyweights favored by the party establishment: first Sen. Edmund S. Muskie of Maine, and then Sen. Hubert H. Humphrey of Minnesota, the party's losing presidential candidate in 1968 who had served as vice president under Lyndon B. Johnson.

But McGovern never managed to broaden his appeal significantly beyond his original base of antiwar liberals. His campaign started out with a distracting blunder and never recovered. Within weeks of the convention, McGovern's running mate, Sen. Thomas Eagleton of Missouri, was forced off the ticket after he admitted having been treated for psychiatric problems. R. Sargent Shriver, the former head of the Peace Corps and a Kennedy in-law, agreed to take Eagleton's place after others turned down the nomination. Nixon and his spokesmen attacked McGovern's plans to end the war quickly and to cut the defense budget as threats to the national security, and they dismissed his domestic proposals as unrealistic. McGovern tried to strike a populist note, saying the Vietnam War had been prosecuted in secret and promising to "restore the government to the people." Nixon, fresh from history-making trips to China and the Soviet Union, undercut McGovern's antiwar message decisively in October when his secretary of state, Henry Kissinger, announced that "peace is at hand." McGovern's charge that the Nixon administration was "the most corrupt in history" had little impact, although the postelection revelations of the Watergate scandal eventually forced Nixon to resign.

The populist antiwar message McGovern preached in 1972 had its roots in his background. The son of a Methodist minister and his wife from rural South Dakota, McGovern flew thirty-five bombing missions over Europe during World War II, was decorated for bravery, and concluded that war was an abomination. As a graduate student after the war, he was briefly drawn to Henry Wallace, the presidential nominee of the left-wing Progressive Party in 1948. McGovern taught history and political science at Dakota Wesleyan University from 1949 to 1953 and then took on the job of rebuilding South Dakota's decimated Democratic organization.

McGovern won election to the U.S. House of Representatives in 1956 and again in 1958, but was defeated in his first run for the Senate in 1960, having supported presidential candidate John F. Kennedy against the advice of his advisers. In 1961 President Kennedy appointed McGovern head of Food for Peace, an idealistic program aimed at reducing world hunger.

More on this topic:

Delegate Selection Reforms, p. 146

Elections Chronology, p. 174

In 1962 and 1968 McGovern's skillful grass-roots campaigning helped him to win two Senate elections, even though he was far more liberal than most voters in South Dakota. In the Senate, McGovern was an early and outspoken opponent of U.S. involvement in Vietnam and a supporter of programs to help the poor. McGovern mounted an ineffective campaign for the 1968 Democratic presidential nomination after the assassination of his friend and political ally, Sen. Robert F. Kennedy.

McKinley, William

Source: Library of Congress

William McKinley (1843–1901) was the last president of the nineteenth century. He presided over an economic recovery and the U.S. victory in the Spanish-American War. Six months after beginning his second term, he became the third president to be assassinated.

McKinley was born on January 29, 1843, in Niles, Ohio. His father was an iron founder. He enrolled in Allegheny College in Meadville, Pennsylvania, when he was sixteen, but he dropped out the next year because of illness and financial problems. McKinley returned to Ohio, where he taught school and worked in a post office.

When the Civil War began in 1861, McKinley enlisted as a private. He worked his way through the ranks, becoming an officer in September 1862 after the battle of Antietam. When the war ended he was a twenty-two-year-old major who had been decorated for bravery.

McKinley chose to leave the army to study law. He worked for two years in the law office of a Youngstown, Ohio, attorney and then polished his legal skills for a

term at Albany Law School in New York. He was admitted to the bar in 1867 and opened a practice in Canton, Ohio. There he married Ida Saxton, the daughter of a banker, on January 25, 1871.

In 1876, when his old commanding officer, Rutherford B. Hayes, was elected president, McKinley won a seat in the U.S. House of Representatives. He served seven consecutive terms in the House until 1891. As a member of Congress, McKinley supported civil service reform and voting rights for blacks. But he was best known for his support of high tariffs as a means of protecting U.S. industries. While serving as the chairman of the House Ways and Means Committee, he sponsored the McKinley Tariff of 1890, which raised tariff rates to new highs. The tariff brought higher prices for consumers and contributed to voters' disaffection for the Republican Party. McKinley was voted out of Congress along with many other Republicans in 1890.

> *Spanish rule must be replaced by a just, benevolent, and humane government, created by the people of Cuba, capable of performing all international obligations, and which shall encourage thrift, industry, and prosperity and promote peace and good will among all of the inhabitants, whatever may have been their relations in the past.*
>
> —**William McKinley,** *Second Annual Message,* December 5, 1898

McKinley returned to Ohio, where he was elected governor and served two two-year terms. In 1892 he was chairman of the Republican national convention in Chicago. President Benjamin Harrison was nominated on the first ballot, and McKinley came in second. Four years later McKinley was nominated on the first ballot at the Republican national convention in St. Louis.

Although McKinley had favored the coinage of silver, he renounced his former position and supported the gold standard in order to win conservative Democrats away from the Democratic nominee, William Jennings Bryan, who was a silver advocate. McKinley waged his campaign from his front porch, speaking to crowds of people who came to Canton by railroad. In the end, McKinley received the strong support of business leaders, who feared that Bryan's presidency would bring inflation. In winning the election, McKinley defeated Bryan in the Electoral College, 271–176.

McKinley's top priority upon entering office was the economy, which had been mired in a depression during much of Grover Cleveland's second term. Congress quickly passed the Dingley Tariff Act of 1897 in response to McKinley's requests. Thereafter, the economy began to improve. Although the tariff bill may not have been the cause of the recovery, McKinley took credit for it.

McKinley's first term was dominated by the Spanish-American War and its results. Americans were disturbed by press accounts of atrocities committed by Spanish colonialists against Cuban natives. McKinley responded to public pressure for war by sending a war message to Congress on April 11, 1898. Congress declared war two weeks later, on April 25. By August U.S. forces had won the war. Spanish control of Cuba was broken, and the U.S. Asiatic squadron under Commodore George Dewey destroyed the Spanish Pacific fleet in the battle of Manila Bay. On December 10, 1898, Spain signed a treaty freeing Cuba and ceding the Philippines, Puerto Rico, and Guam to the United States. McKinley decided to take possession of the Philippines rather than grant it independence. He resolved to "uplift and civilize and Christianize" the Filipinos. Many Filipinos, however, were determined to gain their independence. In 1899 they launched a guerrilla war against the U.S. occupying force, which ended in 1902 with the defeat of the insurgents.

McKinley took several important steps in other parts of Asia and the Pacific. He oversaw the annexation of Hawaii in 1898 and the partition of the Samoan Islands with Germany in 1899. Secretary of State John Hay negotiated an agreement with European nations in 1900 that established an "open door" policy toward China, under which all nations would enjoy equal trading rights in that country.

McKinley was renominated without opposition in 1900. His close friend and first-term vice president, Garret A. Hobart, had died in 1899, and the Republican national convention chose Theodore Roosevelt as his running mate. The Democrats again ran William Jennings Bryan, but the economic recovery gave the Republicans a strong election issue. McKinley improved upon the victory he had enjoyed in 1896, defeating Bryan in the Electoral College, 292–155.

After Roosevelt's nomination the national chairman of the Republican Party, Mark Hanna, who regarded the vice-presidential candidate as an unpredictable reformer, wrote McKinley, saying, "Your duty to the country is to live for four years from next March." McKinley was unable to carry out this charge. In September 1901 he traveled to Buffalo, New York, to deliver a speech at the Pan-American Exposition, a fair celebrating friendship in the Western Hemisphere. The next day the president greeted the thousands of people who were waiting in line to shake his hand at a reception. Among them was Leon Czolgosz, an anarchist disturbed by social injustice. When it was his turn to shake McKinley's hand, Czolgosz shot McKinley twice with a concealed revolver.

Doctors initially thought the president would recover. Vice President Roosevelt, who had cut short his vacation and rushed to Buffalo upon hearing that the president had been shot, even resumed his holiday. After a week, however, gangrene set in, and McKinley's condition deteriorated. He died early on the morning of September 14 in Buffalo, and Roosevelt became president.

> **More on this topic:**
>
> *Assassinations and Assaults, p. 19*
>
> *Spanish-American War of 1898, p. 465*

Madison, Dolley

Dolley Madison.
Source: Library of Congress

Perhaps the most popular of the early first ladies, Dorothea (Dolley) Payne Todd Madison (1768–1849) was the wife of President James Madison. She consolidated the first lady's role as hostess of the White House and the center of Washington society.

Dolley was born into a Quaker family that owned a Virginia plantation. When she was five, her father freed their slaves and moved the family to Philadelphia. There, in 1790, Dolley married a young Quaker lawyer named John Todd. The couple had two children. They had been married for three years when a yellow fever epidemic killed Dolley's husband and younger son.

Shortly after Todd's death Dolley met James Madison and married him within a year, on September 15, 1794. The Madisons had no children of their own. For the indiscretion of marrying outside her faith, Dolley was expelled from the Quaker church. She discarded her plain gray Quaker garments for bright clothing and elegant turbans.

When Madison took office as president in 1809, the White House became a festive place. Dolley delighted in giving large, formal dinner parties. She was greatly admired as a hostess, especially for her good memory for names and her ability to put everyone at ease. In this, she was a particular asset to Madison's political career, for he was generally withdrawn among crowds. So popular was Dolley that even her habit of taking snuff, which was considered very unladylike, was overlooked.

As a Quaker, Dolley was a well-educated woman for her time. But she downplayed her intelligence and strong will in deference to her husband's position. During the War of 1812 when the British threatened Washington, she stayed behind in the White House until the last possible moment to supervise the removal of documents. Before leaving, she retrieved the portrait of George Washington by American painter Gilbert Stuart and took it with her for safekeeping.

More on this topic:

First Ladies, p. 219

Madison, James, below

White House, p. 573

When Madison's second term expired in 1817, he and Dolley retired to their Virginia estate, Montpelier. She still entertained, but the Madisons were plagued by financial problems. After Madison died in 1836, Dolley had to sell first his well-known papers on the Constitutional Convention and then Montpelier itself to pay her debts.

Eventually she returned to Washington, where she spent the rest of her life. As she grew older, she remained a leading figure in Washington society, admired by every president through James K. Polk. She was even granted a lifetime seat on the floor of the House of Representatives. She died on July 12, 1849, and was buried in Washington. Later she was removed to rest beside Madison at Montpelier.

Madison, James

Source: David Edwin, National Portrait Gallery

James Madison (1751–1836), who is known as the "Father of the Constitution" for his efforts in creating the Constitution and promoting it during the ratification process, served two terms as president. During Madison's eight years in office the United States fought the inconclusive War of 1812 with Great Britain.

Madison was born to plantation owners on March 16, 1751, at Port Conway, Virginia. He graduated from the College of New Jersey (now Princeton University) in 1771 and spent an extra six months studying theology. In 1772 he returned to Virginia to continue his study of law and religion. Like John Adams, he considered entering the ministry, but the lure of a political career and the urgency of the patriot cause led him into public service.

In 1775 Madison assumed his first government office, a slot on the committee of public safety of his native Orange County. By the spring of 1776 he was well enough known and respected to be elected as a delegate to Virginia's constitutional convention. He served on the committee that drafted a declaration of rights and was primarily responsible for the constitutional article on religious freedom. As a member of the state constitutional convention, Madison automatically became a state legislator in the new Virginia government. There he met Thomas Jefferson, who became his close friend and political mentor. He served as an adviser to Jefferson when the latter was governor.

Father of the Constitution

In 1780 Madison was chosen to serve in the Continental Congress. During this period he began to believe that the Articles of Confederation had to be strengthened if the government was to survive. Congress had no means of implementing its decisions and was completely dependent on the goodwill of the states.

At the end of 1783 Madison returned to Virginia, where he was reelected to the state legislature. He served there until 1786. Between sessions he studied the history of politics and began to form ideas about how to strengthen the national government.

In 1787 a national convention was scheduled for Philadelphia to amend the Articles of Confederation. Madison led a group of nationalists who wanted to establish a broad mandate for the convention. The group urged all thirteen states to send delegates, obtained a congressional endorsement of the convention, and enhanced the prestige of the gathering by convincing George

Washington to attend. After the convention began, delegates decided that the weak government set up by the Articles had to be replaced, and they immediately set out to write a new constitution that would establish a strong central government.

At the Constitutional Convention, Madison was able to make full use of his extensive study of political theory. More than any other person, he was responsible for the content of the Constitution produced by the convention. The "Virginia Plan," which served as the basis of the Constitution, was submitted to the convention by Virginia governor Edmund Randolph, but it was largely Madison's work.

After the convention Madison wrote a series of essays, known as the *Federalist Papers*, with Alexander Hamilton and John Jay. These essays explained and defended the new Constitution, which had to be ratified by the states before it could become law. Madison also led the successful fight for ratification at Virginia's own ratifying convention in 1788. He won election to the first U.S. House of Representatives. There he proposed nine amendments to the Constitution, which became the basis for the Bill of Rights.

While serving in the House, Madison legislated according to a strict interpretation of the Constitution—that is, he opposed the government's exercising any powers not specifically granted in the Constitution. He fought unsuccessfully against Treasury Secretary Alexander Hamilton's plans to establish a national bank and have the federal government assume the war debts of the states. He also wrote, under the name "Helvidius," a series of articles that argued against the expansion of presidential power and attacked as unconstitutional Washington's unilateral proclamation of neutrality toward warring Britain and France in 1793.

From his position in Congress, Madison assumed a leading role, second only to Thomas Jefferson, in the formation of the Democratic-Republican Party. On September 15, 1794, at the age of forty-three, Madison married widow Dorothea (Dolley) Payne Todd. In 1797, after four terms, he retired from Congress.

In 1801 newly elected president Thomas Jefferson appointed Madison secretary of state. He served in this post for all eight years of Jefferson's presidency. With Jefferson's backing, Madison was nominated for president by the Democratic-Republicans in 1808. Although he lost five northern states, Madison received 122 electoral votes to the 47 received by Federalist Charles C. Pinckney.

Presidency

Madison's presidency was focused on issues related to the war between Great Britain and France. Members of Congress known as the War Hawks—a group that included Henry Clay and John C. Calhoun—urged Madison to declare war on the British. The War Hawks, most of whom were from the South and West, also wanted to stop British seizures of U.S. ships, to launch military ventures into Canada, and to halt Indian attacks in the West, which they believed were encouraged by the British. On June 1, 1812, Madison asked Congress for a declaration of war. The declaration passed on June 18, by votes of 19–13 in the Senate and 79–49 in the House. That fall, Madison ran for reelection against DeWitt Clinton of New York, the nominee of an anti-Madison faction of the Democratic-Republican Party. The Federalists, who did not nominate a candidate, threw their support to Clinton. Madison defeated Clinton 128–89 in the Electoral College.

The United States was not prepared for war. Its navy was small compared with the British fleet, and throughout the war the army had great difficulty in fulfilling its recruitment goals. Moreover, the nation was not united behind the war effort. Many citizens in the Northeast opposed the war,

> *Liberty is to faction what air is to fire, an aliment without which it instantly expires. But it could not be less folly to abolish liberty, which is essential to political life, because it nourishes faction, than it would be to wish the annihilation of air, which is essential to animal life, because it imparts to fire its destructive agency.*
>
> —*James Madison,* Federalist No. 10

favoring the British in their fight with the French. Northeast merchants preferred the occasional seizure of their neutral vessels by the British to a war that could end trade completely. Indeed, some New England Federalists openly discussed secession during the war.

The United States prevailed in several sea battles, and frontier generals William Henry Harrison and Andrew Jackson won decisive victories over Britain's Indian allies, but overall the war went badly for the United States. The worst humiliation occurred in August 1814 when the British occupied Washington, D.C., and burned government buildings, including the Executive Mansion and Capitol. On December 24, 1814, Britain and the United States signed the Treaty of Ghent, which ended the war without resolving the issues over which it had been fought. For example, Britain gave no guarantees that it would allow U.S. ships safe passage in the future.

In spite of the many defeats suffered by the United States, the end of the war brought a resurgence of nationalism. The Treaty of Ghent and Andrew Jackson's overwhelming victory over the British at the battle of New Orleans on January 8, 1815, two weeks after the peace treaty had been signed, convinced many Americans that the war had been won. The Federalists' opposition to the war crippled their party, leaving Madison's Democratic-Republicans in a commanding position.

Madison's last two years in office were fruitful. Congress backed the president's proposal to appropriate funds to strengthen the armed forces. Madison also supported the establishment of the Second Bank of the United States and increased tariffs to protect U.S. industries.

> **More on this topic:**
>
> *Federalist Papers, p. 213*
>
> *Madison, Dolley, p. 349*
>
> *War of 1812, p. 553*

After leaving office Madison returned to Montpelier, his estate in Virginia. He remained a close friend of Thomas Jefferson, who lived thirty miles away. Madison died peacefully at Montpelier on June 28, 1836, at the age of eighty-five.

Management and Budget, Office of

The Office of Management and Budget (OMB) analyzes the merits of budget requests and recommends to the president what funding should be cut, preserved, or expanded. Its director is one of the president's most important advisers.

Before 1921 no system existed in the executive branch for unified consideration or control of federal spending policy. The various departments simply sent their spending requests to the secretary of the Treasury, who forwarded them to Congress. This practice did not allow the White House to implement spending priorities.

In 1921 Congress created the Bureau of the Budget (BOB) to coordinate and modify the budget estimates of the executive departments. It was originally located within the Treasury Department but was moved to the newly created Executive Office of the President in 1939. With the creation of BOB, federal departments and agencies no longer determined for themselves how much funding to seek from Congress. In 1970 President Richard Nixon expanded BOB's staff and duties and renamed it the Office of Management and Budget.

The office serves to pull together the president's national budget plan. To do this, OMB must estimate the size of the annual budget deficit or surplus and analyze spending proposals made by the executive departments. Because OMB's mission centers on developing an efficient budget with as little waste as possible, its institutional bias has often been to limit spending. In addition to its budgetary duties, OMB also reviews the organization and management procedures of the executive branch and evaluates the performance of federal programs.

The post of budget director has become highly politicized since the Nixon administration. The director is appointed by the president and, since 1973, confirmed by the Senate. Budget directors frequently testify before Congress, and they help shape the president's social agenda through their budget recommendations. If they have a close relationship to the president their duties and influence may extend far beyond preparation of and advice on the budget. For example, President George H. W. Bush's budget director, Richard Darman, was considered to be a member of Bush's inner circle of advisers with power to shape the budget and many aspects of domestic policy.

Perhaps the most famous budget director was David Stockman, who served under Ronald Reagan from 1981 until 1985. Reagan gave him broad power to cut items from the budget in order to reduce budget deficits. In the first six months of the Reagan administration, Stockman came to symbolize Reagan's domestic budget and tax cuts and the president's goal of reducing the size of government. However, Stockman became disillusioned with Reagan's policies, which he believed contributed to growing budget deficits. As a result, he resigned in 1985.

In 2001 George W. Bush's choice to head OMB was Mitchell E. Daniels, Jr. A former Reagan administration political adviser and senior executive at the pharmaceutical firm Eli Lilly, Daniels was seen as a conservative foe of big government. Presiding over OMB at a time when the economy had turned sour, Daniels had a difficult relationship with Congress, as he criticized the lawmakers as big spenders. On April 18, 2006, Bush nominated Rob Portman to become the 35th director. Following confirmation by the Senate, he was sworn in on May 29, 2006.

More on this topic:

Budget Process, p. 37

Bureaucracy, p. 44

Congress and the Presidency, p. 111

Executive Office of the President, p. 200

Marshall, Thomas R.

Source: Library of Congress

Thomas Riley Marshall (1854–1925) served as vice president under Woodrow Wilson from 1913 to 1921. He was the first vice president since Daniel D. Tompkins to serve two full terms. Marshall is remembered as much for his witticisms as for his accomplishments in government.

An Indiana native, Marshall graduated Phi Beta Kappa in 1873 from Wabash College in Crawfordsville, Indiana. After college he studied law and was admitted to the bar in 1875. He then embarked on a successful legal career in Columbia City, Indiana.

Marshall ran for office for the first time when he was nominated for governor of Indiana in 1908. Indiana had not elected a Democratic governor since 1892, but he won the election by more than ten thousand votes. As governor, Marshall opposed capital punishment (he issued many pardons), Prohibition, and voting rights for women.

Marshall was prepared to leave politics in 1912 because Indiana barred a governor from seeking two consecutive terms. But that year he received the Democratic nomination for vice president on the ticket with Woodrow Wilson. Wilson and Marshall faced a Republican Party divided by Theodore Roosevelt's third-party candidacy. The Democrats received less than 42 percent of the popular vote but won 435 electoral votes to Roosevelt's 88 and President William Howard Taft's 8 votes.

While serving as vice president, Marshall gained a national reputation for his dry humor. After listening to Sen. Joseph L. Bristow, a Republican from Kansas, deliver a long speech on the needs of the country, Marshall remarked in a voice loud enough for many in the Senate chamber to over-

hear, "What this country needs is a really good five-cent cigar." This line was reported in newspapers and became his most famous utterance. During his political career he declined to run for Congress on the grounds that he "might be elected." He also told a story about two brothers, one of whom "ran away to sea; the other was elected vice president. And nothing was ever heard of either of them again."

Both President Wilson and Vice President Marshall were renominated for a second term. In the 1916 election they were opposed by a Republican Party united behind Charles Evans Hughes and former vice president Charles W. Fairbanks. Wilson and Marshall narrowly defeated Hughes and Fairbanks by a vote of 277–254 in the Electoral College.

Marshall's most significant action as vice president may have been something he did *not* do. When President Wilson suffered a stroke in 1919 many people advised Marshall to assume the presidency. At that time, however, there was no provision in the Constitution for the replacement of an incapacitated president by the vice president. Marshall refused to replace Wilson because he believed such a move would set a bad precedent and might divide the nation.

When Marshall's second term expired in 1921 he retired to Indianapolis. He occupied his time by writing syndicated articles, delivering lectures, and traveling. Just before his death at the age of seventy-one, he finished writing *Recollections,* a book containing many of his humorous stories.

> *As a testament to his dry humor, Marshall once told a story about two brothers, one of whom "ran away to sea; the other was elected vice president. And nothing was ever heard of either of them again."*

More on this topic:
Disability Amendment, p. 154
Vice President, p. 539
Wilson, Woodrow, p. 583

Martial Law

> *Now, therefore, be it ordered, first, that during the existing insurrection, and as a necessary measure for suppressing the same, all rebels and insurgents, their aiders and abettors, within the United States, and all persons discouraging volunteer enlistments, resisting militia draft or guilty of any disloyal practice affording aid and comfort to rebels against the authority of the United States, shall be subject to martial law and liable to trial and punishment by courts-martial or military commissions....*
>
> **—Abraham Lincoln,** Proclamation—
> Suspending the Writ of Habeas Corpus,
> September 24, 1862

A declaration of martial law is the most extreme wartime emergency measure a president can take. Under such a declaration, civilian government is temporarily replaced by military rule.

Substitution of military for civilian authority may be absolute, or it may involve the military taking over only a specific civil function. But even cases of limited martial law invariably result in the curbing of individual rights.

The Constitution does not provide for a power to declare martial law, although it does mention the suspension of habeas corpus under Article I, which outlines Congress's powers. Habeas corpus is the right of prisoners to be brought before the courts to determine the legality of their detention or imprisonment and to be released upon a court's order.

The declaration of martial law is usually presumed to be a presidential function flowing from the president's powers to command the armed forces and execute the laws. Because there is no specific constitutional basis for martial law, presidents must justify their decision to proclaim it on the grounds that the welfare and security of the nation require them to govern through military force rather than established laws. (See WAR POWERS and EMERGENCY POWERS.)

No president has ever declared a condition of absolute martial law that applied to the entire country. And not since President Abraham Lincoln placed several areas of the nation under martial law during the Civil War has any president directly proclaimed martial law on behalf of the national government.

Martial law has been declared by presidential agents or military officers, often with the explicit or implied approval of the president. For example, Gen.

Andrew Jackson declared martial law in New Orleans before his battle with the British there in 1814; the commander of federal troops sent to Idaho in 1899 to quell labor unrest declared martial law with President William McKinley's approval; and after the Japanese attack on Pearl Harbor on December 7, 1941, the territorial governor of Hawaii declared martial law on the islands with the support of President Franklin D. Roosevelt.

> ### More on this topic:
> *Emergency Powers, p. 188*
> *Milligan, Ex parte, p. 364*
> *War Powers, p. 555*

Although the courts may reject the president's assessment of the need for martial law, historically they have done so only after the emergency has passed. In 1866 the Supreme Court ruled in *Ex parte Milligan* that Lincoln's suspension of the civil court system in Indiana during the Civil War was illegal. (See MILLIGAN, EX PARTE.) Similarly, in 1946 the Court declared in *Duncan v. Kahanamoku* that the establishment of martial law in Hawaii by the governor during World War II, carried out with Roosevelt's approval, had been unlawful. Yet neither decision had any effect on either president's ability to abrogate civil liberties during the wars.

Media and the Presidency

Modern presidents must be effective communicators. To promote their programs and policies, they must be able to forge a bond with the electorate and earn its trust and confidence. Presidents do this largely by "going public" and by managing the news media.

Communication has become an important part of politics and the governing process. Because of the great changes in the media and mass communications, presidents have had to change their political styles and the way they govern.

Television in particular has enhanced presidents' ability to project their message and mobilize public sentiment. On the other hand, television's close scrutiny of presidents has tended to magnify their defects, diminishing to some extent the aura of power that surrounds the office. In general, however, the modern media have provided presidents with a marked advantage over their critics.

Today's president is the prime news personality in the country, and virtually everything the president does in an official capacity is reported to millions of readers and television viewers. In a sense, the presidency has evolved into a form of theater in which the chief executive is the most visible and compelling actor on the American stage. The media age has contributed to the making of a more visible and personalized presidency.

All presidents have had relations with the press of one kind or another, ranging at different times from friendliness to hostility. The present large press corps has its base of operations inside the White House, a fact that symbolizes the great importance American leaders place on reaching the public through the mass media.

Throughout the history of president-press relations, one continuing theme has been the frustration presidents have felt over their inability to control the media. This inability exposes presidents' vulnerability and often seems to mock the grandeur of their office.

All presidents at some point have become angry at what they feel is their unfair treatment by the press. How individual presidents have responded when they feel mistreated by the press, however, has varied according to their personal temperaments, current thinking about the role of the press, and the overall state of their presidency.

The contradictory strains in the presidential attitude toward the media were evident in the nation's first chief executives. While recognizing the need to use the press to inform public opinion and mobilize support, they kept their distance from it and frequently complained of being unfairly abused and slandered by opposition journals.

To an extent the early presidents were justified in their feelings, because the press of that time was largely a propaganda tool. The idea that the press should be an independent, objective carrier of information did not develop until much later. Most newspapers and other publications were vehicles designed to advance the interests of various political factions. In the face of press criticism, presidents responded by supporting newspapers that advanced their own and their party's interests.

Early Presidents

One president who took a serious misstep in this area was John Adams, who felt so maligned by the press and other critics that he supported the Sedition Act, which served in part as a gag rule on the press and led to the imprisonment of editors. The unpopular law contributed to the decline of Adams's Federalist Party. The law expired in 1801.

Subsequent presidents actively used the partisan press of the day to advance their interests. Thomas Jefferson exalted freedom of the press as "one of the great bulwarks of liberty"; he also encouraged the founding of the *National Gazette,* which served as the voice of his Democratic-Republican Party. Members of Andrew Jackson's "kitchen cabinet" founded the *Washington Globe,* which grew fat on lucrative government printing contracts.

By the time Abraham Lincoln came into office the partisan press had declined, and the idea of objective reporting was beginning to take hold. As a wartime president, Lincoln displayed a contradictory attitude toward the press. He fully understood its role and dealt with newspapers and journalists on a more intimate basis than any of his predecessors. At the same time, he ordered censorship and suppression of antiwar newspapers on a scale not seen since the founding of the Republic. Lincoln's successor, Andrew Johnson, became the first president to grant interviews with reporters on a regular basis.

By the time William McKinley was elected, the press had assumed its modern role as the people's watchdog over government affairs. McKinley allowed reporters to wait in the White House to interview people coming out of important meetings, and his staff distributed advance copies of his speeches. But McKinley generally avoided direct contact with journalists.

The Media Come of Age

The first president to appreciate fully the influence of the press and to cultivate journalists was Theodore Roosevelt. The beginnings of the White House press corps occurred during his administration, and his dynamic personality and rhetorical flair made him a favorite subject of the press. Roosevelt was a strong advocate of press freedom, but he was often critical of specific newspaper accounts and coined the term *muckraking* for what he saw as irresponsible investigative journalism.

Theodore Roosevelt gave reporters unprecedented access to the White House, while seeking to retain control over what was published. But the presidential relationship with the press remained largely on an ad hoc basis and was not institutionalized until Woodrow Wilson established the first formal news conferences, at which reporters were required to submit their questions in written form.

Although Wilson had an aide, Joseph P. Tumulty, who served as his press adviser, the first formally designated presidential press secretary was George Akerson, who served under Herbert C. Hoover. The modern concept of the office was established by Stephen T. Early, Franklin D. Roosevelt's press secretary, who is generally credited with making the position into a permanent part of the White House staff.

The Media in the Age of the Modern Presidency

Franklin Roosevelt exerted a great impact on White House press relations in other ways as well. He established a habit of frequent, informal meetings with reporters, holding a total of 998 news conferences during his twelve years in office. Perhaps even more important, he became the first president to use the electronic media—in his case, radio—to bypass the press establishment and reach out directly to the public.

The next major development in presidential press relations came under Dwight D. Eisenhower, who was the first chief executive to hold a televised news conference. The film was edited by his press secretary to delete unflattering segments before being shown to the public. Eisenhower generally enjoyed good relations with the media, but the White House decision to lie to the press after the downing of a U-2 spy plane over the Soviet Union in 1960 led to disillusionment among many people about the government's credibility.

Indeed, the decades following World War II were marked by a growing adversarial relationship between the White House and the press corps. Journalists, who were becoming more conscious of their professional standards and skeptical of government claims, became more intent on discovering and writing the truth even if it led to conflict with government officials.

With his youth, wit, and telegenic good looks, John Kennedy was able to make effective use of the media and build good relationships with much of the journalistic establishment. He held the first "live" presidential press conference. Relations between the White House and the press grew increasingly sour, however, under Lyndon B. Johnson and Richard Nixon. Nixon developed a strong resentment of the "establishment" press, and he even included several journalists on his "enemies list." He also sought unsuccessfully to block the publication of the secret Pentagon Papers detailing U.S. policy in Vietnam. Journalists in turn played a pivotal role in his eventual downfall, in particular Bob Woodward and Carl Bernstein of the *Washington Post*, whose reporting helped reveal the Watergate conspiracy and cover-up.

Ronald Reagan's rise to the White House was viewed by many as the culmination of the dominance of politics by image makers and media consultants. No president in modern history, except perhaps Franklin Roosevelt, was more successful in presenting himself through the media than Reagan, who had polished his skills during a lifetime as a movie actor and television performer.

The Reagan White House was extremely adept at managing media events and staging presidential appearances, while at the same time protecting the president from inquisitive reporters. The Reagan administration also stepped up its efforts to control the flow of all government information, sometimes using lie-detector tests to trace news leaks by government employees and clamping down on the release of sensitive material.

George H. W. Bush fared less well as the media took to picking on his sometimes tangled locutions and verbal shorthand. Bill Clinton proved an adept, articulate communicator, but his relations with the media got off to a rocky start. Instead of holding news conferences, Clinton continued to

Dwight D. Eisenhower was the first president to hold a televised press conference. However, his press secretary ensured that any unflattering moments were edited out of the tape before it was shown to the public.
Source: AP/Wide World Photos

To promote his "Healthier U.S." initiative, in June 2002 President George W. Bush participated in a three-mile run at nearby Fort McNair, while his wife, Laura, number two, led the 1.5-mile walk.
Source: The White House

appear on some of the nontraditional media outlets he had used during the campaign. Clinton's press relations improved midway through his first term when he asked Michael McCurry to replace Dee Dee Myers as his press secretary. When McCurry decided to leave in 1999, Joe Lockhart was selected for the post and remained in it through the fall of 2000.

George W. Bush's relations with the press were sharply colored by the terrorist attacks of September 11, 2001, less than a year into his presidency. Facing a national—and international—crisis, Bush relied on the media to help rally the nation and its allies behind his war on terrorism and later against Iraqi dictator Saddam Hussein. As the war dragged on into Bush's second term, the president found less support for his policies from the media. In addition, political scandals such as the conviction of Vice President Cheney's former chief of staff, I. Lewis "Scooter" Libby, combined with the media's perception of administrative failure in responding to Hurricane Katrina, contributed to a more critical media. To more effectively communicate administration policy to the media, the president appointed *Fox News Sunday* host Tony Snow as press secretary in April 2006.

Managing the President's Image

Modern presidents have had varying degrees of success in dealing with the press, but several common elements define the White House–media relationship throughout different administrations. The first of these is the presidential press secretary who generally is, except for the president himself, the most important element in the current system. Never far from the president's side, privy to most White House decisions, and mentioned in the media almost every day, the modern presidential press secretary is a figure of national standing.

The press secretary serves as a conduit of news from the president and major administration figures to the press, as the creator and protector of the presidential image, as an adviser in the art of communications, and as administrator of the White House press–public relations section. During the first year and a half of the George W. Bush administration, however, counselor Karen Hughes, a longtime Bush confidante, managed almost every facet of his communications with the people, including oversight of press secretary Ari Fleischer's office.

On the other side of the relationship, the second common element is the Washington press corps and especially the elite group of full-time White House correspondents. Although the administration on different occasions must deal with many of the thousands of journalists who are based in the nation's capital, at the core of the press relationship are the seventy or so reporters who cover the White House from day to day. The members of this group, who represent major daily newspapers, television networks, wire services, national news magazines, and other publications, hold a highly visible and coveted assignment. Print and television reporters who have this beat are assured of almost daily exposure in their publications and broadcasts, greatly enhancing their careers.

The White House press corps, and Washington journalists in general, represent a major arena for presidents' efforts to manage the flow of information and to direct news coverage in a way that is favorable to their policy goals. Prohibited by the First Amendment from controlling the press, presidents and their aides seek to manipulate it to their advantage.

White House officials sometimes resort to questionable or unethical tactics in that effort, such as the Eisenhower administration's misleading account of the U-2 incident or Nixon's attempt to block investigations of the Watergate affair. In general, however, they are able to manage the news by using conventional techniques that have evolved over the years and are constantly being refined along with advancements in communications technology. Prominent among these techniques are daily press briefings, background briefings, formal televised news conferences, exclusive interviews, news releases, and public announcements.

The most common and possibly the most effective tactic of White House news management is the daily briefing conducted by the presidential press secretary. Shortly after noon each weekday, the press secretary appears before the press corps and television cameras to make a series of announcements and answer questions. In doing so, the White House attempts to set the news agenda for the day and in effect compel the press to carry its message to the public. A more subtle tactic involves the use of the "background" interview in which an unnamed administration official seeks to steer the direction of coverage on sensitive points. On occasion, these interviews can be used to float a trial balloon—a policy proposal the administration is considering but, before committing itself formally, wants to test for the public's reaction.

White House aides also can use access to the president as a way of influencing coverage. The granting of an exclusive interview frequently leads to a favorable piece in an important publication or television news program. But there are ways to ensure that the president receives daily visual exposure on television—a "photo opportunity"—without being subjected to probing questions by reporters. Reagan, for example, frequently was shown boarding the presidential helicopter, his hand cupped to his ear to show that he could not hear reporters' shouted questions.

The summit of presidential-press relations is the televised news conference, in which millions of viewers have an opportunity to observe the president responding directly to reporters' questions. Such events are extremely useful to the administration because they provide an opportunity to cast the president in a positive light regardless of the type of questions asked. Friendly or neutral questions give the president a chance to explain the administration's ideas and show command of the issues. Hostile or probing inquiries can be turned around to show the public how the president is being unfairly badgered by biased reporters.

FREQUENCY OF PRESS CONFERENCES BY PRESIDENT

President	Months in Office	Total Conferences	Average per Month
Truman	93	303	3.26
Eisenhower	96	192	2.00
Kennedy	34	64	1.88
Johnson	62	135	2.18
Nixon	66	39	0.59
Ford	30	40	1.33
Carter	48	59	1.23
Reagan	96	46	0.48
George H. W. Bush	48	142	2.96
Clinton	96	193	2.01
George W. Bush	72	151	2.10

SOURCE: For Johnson through Clinton: Martha Joynt Kumar, "Source Material: 'Does This Constitute a Press Conference?' Defining and Tabulating Modern Presidential Press Conferences," *Presidential Studies Quarterly,* 33 (March 2003): 230. For Truman through Kennedy and George W. Bush: Gerhard Peters, The American Presidency Project.

More on this topic:

Honeymoon Period, p. 262

Press Conferences, p. 416

Press Secretary, Presidential, p. 418

Speeches and Rhetoric, p. 466

For all the usefulness of those and other techniques, however, presidents and their aides in recent decades have had only limited success in altering what appears to be an almost inevitable cycle in their dealings with the media. Typically, the relationship goes through a series of stages from early acceptance and cooperation to mutual tolerance and, finally, suspicion and thinly cloaked hostility. At the heart of this predictable pattern are the media's natural tendency to want to know virtually everything going on inside the White House and the White House's predisposition to manage the news and release only information that is favorable to the president.

The first phase of the relationship is the so-called honeymoon, during which both sides have high hopes and a willingness to cooperate. Presidential aides are accessible, press conferences are frequent, and the president vows publicly to have an "open" administration.

The next phase begins with political conflicts over issues and policies. Administration opponents criticize the president and release information that reflects unfavorably on the administration. In retaliation, the White House closes regular avenues of journalistic access and becomes more manipulative in its handling of information. Reporters deemed to be overly critical may find themselves cut off from sources of information. Tempers may flare at the daily news briefings.

In the twilight years of an administration the relationship with the press becomes more detached. Reporters are kept at arm's length, and press conferences are few. More and more the president attempts to bypass the working press by using radio and television addresses and public speeches to get the administration's message across.

Still, it is generally conceded that in the United States the president—especially one who is a skilled communicator—enjoys the upper hand in dealing with the press.

Memorials, Presidential

President Bill Clinton and First Lady Hillary Rodham Clinton view the statue of Franklin D. Roosevelt and his dog, Fala, at dedication ceremonies for the FDR Memorial on May 2, 1997. Clinton was recovering from knee surgery.
Source: Reuters

Among the national memorials honoring past presidents, six are in the District of Columbia, one is in New York City, and one, Mount Rushmore, is in the Black Hills of South Dakota. Mount Rushmore honors four presidents. All the memorials are administered by the National Park Service, a bureau of the Interior Department.

Four of the presidents memorialized in the capital—George Washington, Thomas Jefferson, Abraham Lincoln, and Franklin D. Roosevelt— also rank at the top of historians' lists of great presidents. (See PRESIDENTIAL GREATNESS.) The Washington Monument, the towering obelisk that dominates the capital's skyline, was begun in 1848 and opened to the public in 1888. The Lincoln Memorial was dedicated in 1922. The

Workmen carving the face of George Washington on Mount Rushmore, circa 1932
Source: Library of Congress

Jefferson Memorial was dedicated on April 12, 1934, the two hundredth anniversary of Jefferson's birth. The newest addition, the Franklin D. Roosevelt Memorial, opened in 1997. Also within the District of Columbia, an island in the Potomac River is maintained in honor of Theodore Roosevelt. Nearby is the Lyndon B. Johnson Grove on the Potomac (1973) with a view of the river and Capitol.

Grant's Tomb on Riverside Drive in New York City (1897) houses the remains of Ulysses S. Grant and his wife, Julia. Historians have generally rated Grant as an outright failure as a chief executive but outstanding as a Civil War general. His final resting place was financed by $600,000 in donations from private citizens. Most of the other memorials have been built with public funds.

In South Dakota the likenesses of Washington, Jefferson, Lincoln, and Theodore Roosevelt are carved into the side of Mount Rushmore. The memorial was dedicated in 1925.

In 2001, as historian David McCullough's biography of the second president hit the bestseller lists, a new law authorized construction of a monument to John Adams on federal land in the District of Columbia or its environs.

More on this topic:

Presidential Greatness,
p. 413

More on this topic:
Presidential Greatness, p. 413

CLOSER LOOK

One of the most spectacular presidential memorials is Mount Rushmore located in the Black Hills of South Dakota. The memorial covers over 1,200 acres and draws almost three million visitors per year. Sculptor Gutzon Borglum and a crew of 400 began carving in 1927 and finished the last of the 60 foot tall faces in 1939 with the dedication of Theodore Roosevelt's head. The entire cost of the project was just under $1,000,000. The original plan called for the depictions to include the entire torso down to the waist, but there was not enough funding for it, and the project ended in 1941. An interesting fact is that Jefferson's head was originally started on Washington's right side, but after 18 months the rock was deemed unsuitable and it was dynamited, only to be recarved on Washington's left.

Mexican-American War of 1846

The Mexican-American War fought between the United States and Mexico is regarded by many historians as the first presidential war. President James K. Polk took action that led to the outbreak of fighting, and he used the war to accomplish his goal of acquiring California and other territory in the present-day southwestern United States.

The central issue leading to the war was the status of Texas. In 1836 Texas had declared its independence from Mexico and indicated that it was interested in becoming part of the United States. Although most Americans supported the principle of expansion, the slavery issue made annexation of a new state a tricky political problem for any president. Texas allowed slavery. Presidents Andrew Jackson and Martin Van Buren avoided action on the Texas issue that would anger voters in the

U.S. and Mexican forces clash at the Battle of Buena Vista in 1847. In an effort to secure territory occupied by Mexico but claimed by Texas, President James K. Polk maneuvered the country into a "defensive" war after U.S. soldiers were attacked by Mexican forces.
Source: Library of Congress

North who were opposed to an extension of slavery.

President John Tyler, however, secretly concluded an agreement with the Texans on annexation. When the needed two-thirds of the Senate refused to approve the annexation treaty produced by the negotiations, Tyler sidestepped the Constitution by asking Congress to validate the agreement with a majority vote of both Houses. The joint resolution was passed, thereby establishing a new type of congressionally approved executive agreement.

Annexation had been achieved, but the boundaries of Texas were uncertain, and Mexico had warned that it regarded U.S. annexation of Texas as a hostile act. In the spring of 1846 President Polk ordered Gen. Zachary Taylor to deploy his army in a strip of disputed territory near the Rio Grande that was claimed by Texas but occupied exclusively by Mexicans. Polk had decided to ask Congress for a declaration of war even before Mexican forces attacked Taylor's army, killing some American soldiers. The clash ensured the passage of a declaration of war, since Polk could claim that Mexico was the aggressor. He told Congress, "Now, after reiterated menaces Mexico has invaded our territory and shed American blood on American soil." On May 13, 1846, Congress recognized "a state of war as existing by act of the Republic of Mexico." Polk's successful maneuvering to place the country in a "defensive" war demonstrated the power of presidents to initiate hostilities through their responsibility to defend the nation.

During the entire Mexican-American War, U.S. forces did not lose a major battle. Mexican forces often fought bravely, but they faced an army that was better equipped, better organized, better commanded, and better armed. Forces under General Taylor won several victories in northern Mexico that made him an American hero and a leading presidential candidate. An army under the command of Gen. Winfield Scott occupied Mexico City in 1847.

Despite the overwhelming military success, the war was not universally popular in the United States. Democrats generally supported the war, which was closely associated with their president. But many members of the Whig Party, including a young Abraham Lincoln (then a member of Congress), denounced the war as immoral and aggressive. Other citizens feared that the territory acquired would lead to the extension of slavery.

On February 2, 1848, negotiators concluded the Treaty of Guadalupe Hidalgo, which set down the terms for the end of the war. Under the treaty, Mexico relinquished its claims to 522,568 square miles of territory stretching from Texas to California. In return, the United States paid Mexico the modest sum of $15 million and assumed the claims of U.S. citizens against Mexico, which amounted to another $3 million. Congress ratified the treaty on May 30, 1848.

Polk had demonstrated that a president without previous military experience could control and dominate the military. During the war he insisted on being the decisive authority on all military matters.

As he had promised, Polk did not run for a second term in 1848. Taylor, the Whig candidate, won the election on the strength of his war record, despite the opposition of most of his party to the war that had brought him glory.

More on this topic:

Polk, James K., p. 411

Midterm Elections

The congressional elections that fall in the middle of presidential terms are called midterm elections. Since the beginning of the twentieth century, in every midterm election except 1934, 1998, and 2002, the president's party lost seats in the House of Representatives. Because only one-third of the Senate is elected every two years, the results of its midterm election are a less accurate gauge of the mood of the country than are those for House seats.

To some extent, midterm elections are perceived as referenda on the president's performance during the previous two years. The number of seats lost by the president's party is related to the state of the economy and the president's popular standing. When those indicators turn down, it is more difficult for the president's party to raise money and to field strong candidates for office. If the opposition party is not strongly challenged in a congressional race, the likelihood that the president's party will suffer is even greater.

An example of this phenomenon was the 1974 midterm election. Elected in a landslide in 1972, Republican Richard Nixon suffered precipitous drops in public standing by 1974 because of the damaging revelations of the WATERGATE AFFAIR. Voters also were disgruntled by an economic downturn, and Republicans had trouble raising money and persuading strong candidates to run for office. Democrats were roused to action by the Watergate scandal, in part because the offenses were directed against Democratic Party leaders. As a result, Democrats at all levels were motivated to run for office, donate money, and work to defeat Republicans.

At the same time, an unusually large number of legislators, most of them Republicans, decided to retire in 1974, opening up more seats and enhancing the Democratic challengers' chances. The result for the Democrats was a gain of forty-nine seats in the House and four in the Senate.

In the 1994 midterm elections the Republicans gained control of both houses of Congress for the first time since the Eighty-third Congress (1953–1955). It looked as though the voters had sent a strong message of disapproval of President Bill Clinton's performance in his first two years as chief executive. The decisive defeat led many political analysts to write off Clinton as a one-term president.

LOSS AND GAIN OF SEATS IN CONGRESS BY PRESIDENT'S PARTY IN MIDTERM ELECTIONS

Year	President	Party	Seats Gained/Lost House	Senate
1950	Harry S. Truman	D	−29	−6
1954	Dwight D. Eisenhower	R	−18	−1
1958	Dwight D. Eisenhower	R	−48	−13
1962	John F. Kennedy	D	24	3
1966	Lyndon B. Johnson	D	−47	−4
1970	Richard Nixon	R	−12	2
1974	Gerald R. Ford (*Nixon*)	R	−48	−5
1978	Jimmy Carter	D	−15	−3
1982	Ronald Reagan	R	−26	1
1986	Ronald Reagan	R	−5	−8
1990	George Bush	R	−8	−1
1994	William J. Clinton	D	−52	−8
1998	William J. Clinton	D	5	0
2002	George W. Bush	R	8	2
2006	George W. Bush	R	−30	−6

But the newly resurgent GOP majority, particularly in the House, misread the election results as a mandate for substantial, primarily conservative, changes in many national policies. This miscalculation enabled the president to position himself as a bulwark against the GOP's "extremism," best displayed in the political maneuvering over the 1996 federal budget in late 1995 that resulted in several highly unpopular government shutdowns. Clinton's refusal to back down and accept the Republican budget was, many believe, the single most important factor in his political rehabilitation and subsequent reelection in 1996.

In 1998, with Clinton's impeachment looming, he became the first president since Franklin D. Roosevelt in 1934 to see his party gain House seats in a midterm election. The Democrats scored a net gain of five House seats while holding steady in the Senate.

Even though the president's party is almost certain to lose seats in the midterm House elections, modern presidents are expected to campaign actively for their party's congressional candidates. Such campaigning appears to be more an effort to minimize losses than to maximize gains.

Leading up to the 2002 midterm elections, George W. Bush campaigned across the country for Republican candidates and appeared to be a key factor in the GOP's history-defying pickups of both House and Senate seats. Republicans retained control of the House and won back control of the narrowly divided Senate.

The 2006 election was much different for the president, however. Following a pattern of many lame-duck presidents entering their seventh year, Bush's party suffered significant losses amounting to thirty seats in the House and six in the Senate. Control of both houses went to the Democrats amid mounting criticism of the president's Iraq War policies.

> **More on this topic:**
>
> *Public Opinion and the Presidency, p. 427*
>
> *Watergate Affair, p. 567*

Midterm campaigning may harm the president's ability to work later with Congress, especially a Congress controlled by the opposition party. Campaigning that inflames partisan opposition may make the president's subsequent bipartisan appeals less effective. In some situations, some presidents have found members of the opposition party to be more supportive than their own partisans. As a result, they have naturally been reluctant to campaign against those members. To avoid these situations, presidents may delegate some midterm campaign chores to their vice presidents.

Milligan, Ex parte

During the Civil War, President Abraham Lincoln instituted several emergency measures that infringed on personal liberties. The most notable was his suspension of habeas corpus (the constitutional guarantee against illegal detention and imprisonment) in some areas vital to the war effort. Although Congress passed legislation approving Lincoln's suspension of habeas corpus, one measure that it never approved was his subjection of civilians to military courts.

It was for Congress to determine the question of expediency. And Congress did determine it. That body did not see fit to authorize trials by military commission in Indiana, but, by the strongest implication, prohibited them.

—*Chief Justice Salmon P. Chase,*
Opinion of the Court—71 U.S. 2—Ex parte
Milligan, April 3, 1866

Lambdin P. Milligan, a citizen of Indiana, was arrested in 1864 by military authorities who charged him with aiding a Confederate raid into Indiana from across the Ohio River. On May 9, 1865, he was found guilty and sentenced to death. Milligan's case eventually came before the Supreme Court.

The Court held 9–0 in *Ex parte Milligan* (1866) that the president did not have the authority to subject civilians to military courts in an area where civilian courts were functioning. The Court also ruled 5–4 that even the president and Congress together lacked power to authorize trials of civilians by military courts outside of a war zone. The majority opinion, written by Justice David Davis, admitted that if civilian courts are closed and the only power maintaining order is the military, then civilians may be tried in military courts. The Court rejected the idea that such conditions existed in Indiana—hundreds of miles from the front—where civilian courts were functioning normally.

More on this topic:

Emergency Powers, p. 188

Martial Law, p. 354

War Powers, p. 555

Beyond their verdict, the justices used this case to defend the inviolability of the Constitution. Davis wrote, "The Constitution of the United States is a law for rulers and people, equally in war and in peace, and covers with the shield of its protection all classes of men, at all times, and under all circumstances. No doctrine involving more pernicious consequences was ever invented by the wit of man than that any of its provisions can be suspended during any of the great exigencies of government."

Milligan is regarded as significant by legal scholars for demonstrating that even during the most dire military emergency there are constitutional limits to presidential power.

Mondale, Walter F.

Walter Frederick Mondale (1928–) served as vice president under Jimmy Carter from 1977 to 1981. After Carter and Mondale failed to win reelection in 1980, Mondale received the Democratic nomination for president in 1984. However, he was defeated in a landslide by popular Republican president Ronald Reagan.

Mondale, who was nicknamed "Fritz," grew up in Minnesota. His father was a Methodist minister. After graduating with honors from the University of Minnesota in 1951, he enlisted in the army. He was discharged after two years with the rank of corporal. Mondale returned to the University of Minnesota, where he earned his law degree in 1956. That same year he was admitted to the Minnesota bar and began practicing law.

Mondale became a follower of Democrat Hubert H. Humphrey in 1946 when Humphrey was mayor of Minneapolis. In 1948 Humphrey ran successfully for the Senate, with Mondale managing Humphrey's campaign in one of Minnesota's congressional districts. Mondale worked as campaign manager for Gov. Orville Freeman's successful bid for reelection in 1958, and Freeman appointed him special assistant to Minnesota's attorney general. When the attorney general resigned in 1960, Mondale served out the remaining eight months of the term. He was elected to the post in 1960 and reelected in 1962.

When Humphrey resigned from the Senate in 1964 after being elected vice president, Mondale was appointed to Humphrey's seat. He was elected to a term of his own in 1966 and reelected in 1972. In the Senate Mondale compiled a liberal voting record. He became a leading advocate of civil rights, Lyndon B. Johnson's Great Society social programs, and bills

Raising an enormous photograph of Walter Mondale at the 1976 Democratic National Convention, New York City
Source: Library of Congress

benefiting farm workers, Indians, children, and the elderly. He supported U.S. military involvement in Vietnam until 1968. He then sided with those members of Congress who sought to limit U.S. participation in the war.

Mondale campaigned for the 1976 Democratic presidential nomination, but he abandoned his candidacy when he failed to attract early, significant support. Jimmy Carter, the eventual Democratic presidential nominee, selected Mondale to be his running mate. Carter and Mondale defeated President Gerald R. Ford and Robert J. Dole 297–240 in the Electoral College.

As vice president, Mondale was deeply involved in the Carter administration's policy making. He helped to choose cabinet officers and draft policy proposals. He also met alone with Carter at least once a week and had an open invitation to attend any White House meeting. In 1980 Carter and Mondale were renominated, but a sagging economy and the Iran hostage crisis weakened their chances for reelection. They were easily defeated by Republicans Ronald Reagan and George Bush.

In 1984 Mondale was the front-runner of a pack of Democrats seeking the party's presidential nomination. He overcame early primary successes by Sen. Gary Hart of Colorado to win the nomination. Mondale chose Rep. Geraldine A. Ferraro of New York as his running mate. She was the first (and so far the only) woman to be nominated for vice president by a major political party. Mondale faced Reagan, who was running for reelection during a period of economic prosperity. The Democrats won only Minnesota and the District of Columbia in an election that was a forty-nine-state Republican landslide. After the election, Mondale retired from politics and returned to Minnesota. In 1993 he was appointed U.S. ambassador to Japan. He resigned from that post in late 1996 to return to private life.

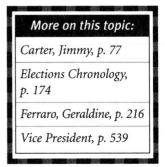

More on this topic:

Carter, Jimmy, p. 77

Elections Chronology, p. 174

Ferraro, Geraldine, p. 216

Vice President, p. 539

In the fall of 2002 Mondale was drafted into a whirlwind Senate campaign after Democratic senator Paul Wellstone of Minnesota, in the midst of a heated reelection battle, was killed in a plane crash. Mondale lost the election to Republican Norm Coleman.

Monetary Policy *See* FEDERAL RESERVE SYSTEM.

Monroe, James

James Monroe (1758–1831), the fifth U.S. president, presided over eight years of relative political tranquility, a period that became known as the "era of good feelings." Like his predecessors Thomas Jefferson and James Madison, he was a Democratic-Republican from Virginia who served two full terms.

Monroe was born on April 28, 1758, in Westmoreland County, Virginia. He was the eldest child of a Virginia planter of modest means. Monroe entered the College of William and Mary in Williamsburg, Virginia, when he was sixteen but left two years later to join the Continental Army. As a lieutenant the young man fought at Trenton, Brandywine, Germantown, and Monmouth. At Trenton he was wounded and promoted to captain for his bravery by Gen. George Washington.

Monroe left the army in 1780 to study law under Thomas Jefferson, then governor of Virginia. Monroe quickly developed a close personal and professional relationship with his mentor. In 1782 Monroe was elected to the Virginia legislature, and a year later he was chosen along with Jefferson to represent Virginia at the Continental Congress in New York City, where he served three terms. In 1786 Monroe married Elizabeth Kortright, whom he had met in New York.

Monroe was not a delegate to the Constitutional Convention of 1787, and his belief that the Constitution gave the president and Senate too much power led him to oppose the document at

James Monroe

Source: Library of Congress

Virginia's ratifying convention in 1788. Nevertheless, soon after Virginia ratified the Constitution he adopted a national political perspective.

Monroe was appointed to a vacant Senate seat in 1790. During this period he worked against Treasury Secretary Alexander Hamilton's fiscal policies and helped Jefferson and James Madison to establish the foundations of the Democratic-Republican Party.

In 1794 President Washington appointed Monroe ambassador to France. In Paris, however, his outspoken support of the French conflicted with Washington's careful policy of neutrality in the Franco-British war. Washington recalled him in 1796. Monroe was elected governor of Virginia in 1799 and served effectively for three years.

Thomas Jefferson was elected president in 1800, ushering in a period of Democratic-Republican dominance over national affairs. In January 1803 Jefferson asked Monroe to go to France to negotiate the purchase of New Orleans. When Napoleon offered to sell not just New Orleans but the entire Louisiana Territory, Monroe and Ambassador Robert Livingston closed the deal for $15 million. The purchase added 828,000 square miles to the United States.

Monroe accepted President James Madison's offer to become secretary of state in 1811. That year Monroe backed Madison's request for a declaration of war against the British. The United States was ill prepared for the War of 1812. The first two years of fighting brought several humiliating defeats, including the capture and burning of Washington, D.C., by the British in August 1814. In September Madison appointed Monroe secretary of war in addition to his duties as secretary of state. Monroe then worked tirelessly to reorganize the nation's defenses and to end the confusion that had prevailed in the War Department. In March 1815, three months after the war ended, an exhausted Monroe resigned as secretary of war but stayed on as secretary of state.

With Madison's backing, Monroe was nominated as the Democratic-Republican presidential candidate in 1816. He easily defeated the Federalist candidate, Sen. Rufus King of New York, by a vote of 183–34 in the Electoral College. Less than three months after taking office, Monroe followed Washington's example and toured the Middle Atlantic and New England states, where he received an enthusiastic reception. In 1820 Monroe ran for reelection unopposed and received all but one electoral vote.

Monroe's presidency was not without its problems. When Missouri sought admission to the United States as a slave state, sectional tensions over the slavery issue erupted. Monroe was a slaveholder who believed that the institution should eventually be abolished. He also believed that new states entering the Union had the constitutional right to determine for themselves if they would permit slavery. In 1820 Congress passed the Missouri Compromise. The plan allowed Missouri to enter the Union as a slave state simultaneously with the admission of Maine as a free state. The compromise also prohibited slavery north of latitude 36°30′ in the territory acquired in the Louisiana Purchase. Monroe doubted the constitutionality of the plan, but he approved it because he considered it the best way to avoid sectional conflict.

In foreign policy Monroe's administration had several notable successes. The Rush-Bagot Agreement signed with Great Britain in 1817 limited the number of warships each country could deploy on the Great Lakes and led to the demilitarization of the Canadian frontier. In 1819

More on this topic:

Doctrines, Presidential, p. 155

Louisiana Purchase, p. 341

Monroe Doctrine, below

White House, p. 573

Secretary of State John Quincy Adams concluded a treaty in which Spain transferred control of the Floridas to the United States and agreed to a border dividing the United States from Spanish territory in western North America.

Monroe's administration is best known for the foreign policy doctrine that bears his name and continues to influence U.S. policy toward Latin America. In October 1823 Great Britain suggested that the United States join it in resisting European intervention in Latin America. Monroe, however, was swayed by the arguments of Secretary of State Adams, who advocated an independent U.S. declaration against European intrusion into the Western Hemisphere. In his annual message to Congress in 1823, Monroe announced that the United States intended to stay out of European conflicts and would not interfere in the existing Latin American colonies of the European powers. Monroe warned the Europeans that any attempt to establish new colonies in the Western Hemisphere or to interfere in the affairs of independent American nations would be regarded by the United States as an "unfriendly" act. At the time the Monroe Doctrine was issued, it had little force because the United States did not possess the military strength to defend Latin America. As the nation developed, however, the Monroe Doctrine became a cornerstone of U.S. foreign policy.

On July 4, 1831, in New York City, Monroe became the third president, along with John Adams and Thomas Jefferson, to die on Independence Day.

Monroe Doctrine

President James Monroe announced the Monroe Doctrine in 1823, declaring the intention of the United States to resist European intervention in the affairs of the independent nations of the Western Hemisphere. The Monroe Doctrine became one of the most durable foreign policy principles in U.S. history, and it continues to influence U.S. policy toward Latin America. It also reinforced the constitutional right of the president to take the initiative in setting foreign policy.

Monroe was motivated to announce the policy by two circumstances: a Russian claim to land along the Pacific coast, from the Bering Strait south to an unspecified location along the shore of the Oregon Territory; and rumors of European plans to recolonize the newly independent nations of previously Spanish South America.

In October 1823 Great Britain suggested that the United States join it in resisting European intervention in Latin America, where several revolutions had succeeded in overthrowing Spanish colonial rule. Former presidents James Madison and Thomas Jefferson advised Monroe to accept the proposal. Monroe, however, followed the advice of his secretary of state, John Quincy Adams, who favored an independent U.S. declaration opposing European intrusion in Latin America.

In his seventh annual message to Congress on December 2, 1823, Monroe announced his intention to keep the United States out of European conflicts and avoid interfering in existing European colonies in Latin America. However, Monroe said, any attempt to establish new colonies in the Western Hemisphere or interfere in the affairs of independent American nations would be regarded by the United States as an "unfriendly" act.

At the time of its declaration, the Monroe Doctrine had little force because the United States did not possess the military strength to defend Latin America.

We owe it, therefore, to candor and to the amicable relations existing between the United States and those powers to declare that we should consider any attempt on their part to extend their system to any portion of this hemisphere as dangerous to our peace and safety.

—**James Monroe,** Seventh Annual Message, December 2, 1823

As it turned out, European states had no intention of recolonizing Latin America. Meanwhile, the Russians continued for a time their efforts to claim parts of the Pacific Northwest.

In 1899 the Monroe Doctrine was officially endorsed by Congress. President Theodore Roosevelt expanded on the doctrine in 1904 when he declared in his annual message to Congress that the United States had the right to intervene if "chronic wrongdoing or impotence" in a country of the Western Hemisphere seemed to require such intervention. Protest from Latin America led to the withdrawal of the Roosevelt Corollary in 1928.

The Monroe Doctrine has remained a cornerstone of national foreign policy. Presidents have invoked the doctrine on several occasions to justify intervention in Latin America, and the doctrine has contributed to the perception that Latin America is a U.S. sphere of influence.

More on this topic:
Adams, John Quincy, p. 4
Diplomatic Powers, p. 149
Doctrines, Presidential, p. 155
Monroe, James, p. 366
State of the Union Address, p. 479

Morton, Levi P.

Twenty-second vice president of the United States Levi Morton
Source: Library of Congress

Levi Parsons Morton (1824–1920) served as vice president under Republican Benjamin Harrison from 1889 to 1893. Morton, a New York businessman and banker, entered politics after amassing a personal fortune. He began his climb in the business world as a store clerk. By 1855 he owned a wholesale business in New York City. In 1863 he established a Wall Street banking firm, Morton, Bliss & Company, which became one of the most powerful financial institutions in the country.

In 1878 Morton won a seat in the U.S. House of Representatives from Manhattan's wealthy Eleventh District. Two years later he was offered the Republican vice-presidential nomination on the ticket with James A. Garfield. The offer was a gesture to Morton's political mentor, Republican senator Roscoe Conkling of New York, who had lost his battle to have Ulysses S. Grant nominated for president. Morton refused on the instructions of Conkling. Instead, the nomination went to another of Conkling's allies, Chester A. Arthur, who defied similar instructions from Conkling.

Despite Morton's refusal of the vice-presidential nomination, Garfield appointed him minister to France, where for four years he threw lavish parties for European royalty. He returned to the United States in 1885 hopeful of winning a Senate seat, but his election campaigns for the Senate in 1885 and 1887 were unsuccessful.

In 1888 Morton was offered the vice-presidential slot on the Republican ticket with Benjamin Harrison. Although Harrison and Morton lost the popular election by ten thousand votes to President Grover Cleveland and Allen G. Thurman, they won in the Electoral College, 233–168.

Morton conscientiously fulfilled his duties as presiding officer of the Senate. During one Democratic filibuster in late 1890 and early 1891, he refused to cooperate with Republican attempts to end it. His decision to side with the Democrats in this case damaged his standing in the Republican Party. In 1892 President Harrison ran for reelection, but Republican leaders dropped Morton from the ticket.

More on this topic:

Harrison, Benjamin,
p. 246

Vice President, p. 539

In 1895 Morton was elected governor of New York. In this office he angered the New York Republican machine by advocating civil service reform. Morton hoped to be his party's presidential nominee in 1896, but William McKinley was the clear choice of the convention.

When Morton's term as governor ended in January 1897, he retired from politics. He died at his estate in Rhinebeck, New York, in 1920 on his ninety-sixth birthday. Of all the vice presidents, only John Nance Garner lived longer.

Mount Rushmore   *See* MEMORIALS, PRESIDENTIAL.

Myers v. United States

The power of presidents to remove from office officials who are not doing their jobs properly or who disagree with presidential goals and programs has been surrounded by controversy and debate. Because the Constitution does not explicitly grant presidents removal power, it has been left to the courts to decide how and when a president may exercise such power.

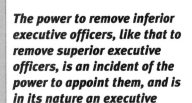

The issue first reached the Supreme Court in 1926. In *Myers v. United States* the Court ruled that an 1876 law that limited the president's removal power over postmasters was unconstitutional.

In 1917 President Woodrow Wilson had appointed Frank Myers to be a postmaster in Portland, Oregon, for a term of four years. Attempting to make his administration responsive to his policy goals, Wilson removed Myers from office in 1920 without consent of the Senate, although the 1876 statute provided that postmasters should be appointed and removed by the president by and with the advice and consent of the Senate. Myers sued for his salary in the U.S. Court of Claims. When he received an adverse judgment, he took his case to the Supreme Court.

In delivering the opinion of the Court, Chief Justice William Howard Taft, a former president, strongly argued that presidents cannot administer the executive branch effectively unless they can control their subordinates with the threat of removal for political and other reasons. He stated that the power of removal is implied in Article II of the Constitution, which gives the president the responsibility to see that the laws are faithfully executed. Furthermore, Congress cannot constitutionally restrain or limit that power. Taft contended that presidents cannot carry out their constitutional responsibilities if Congress interferes with their ability to control the executive branch.

> *The power to remove inferior executive officers, like that to remove superior executive officers, is an incident of the power to appoint them, and is in its nature an executive power.*
>
> —**Chief Justice William Howard Taft,** *Opinion of the Court—272 U.S. 52—Myers v. United States, October 25, 1926*

The *Myers* case arguably gave presidents sweeping authority to remove executive appointees. However, the scope of the case was sharply limited in 1935, when the Supreme Court in HUMPHREY'S EXECUTOR V. UNITED STATES denied the president the power to remove members of independent regulatory agencies without the consent of Congress. (See APPOINTMENT AND REMOVAL POWER.)

More on this topic:

Appointment and Removal Power, p. 9

Humphrey's Executor v. United States, *p. 269*

National Archives and Records Administration

The National Archives and Records Administration is responsible for identifying, preserving, and making available to the federal government and the American people all forms of government records not restricted by law that have been determined to have sufficient historical, informational, or evidential value to warrant being preserved.

Holdings of the archives date from the Revolution to the present time and range from the Constitution of the United States to the Watergate affair tapes of President Richard Nixon.

The National Archives was established as an independent agency in 1934. In 1949 it was incorporated into the newly established General Services Administration and renamed the National Archives and Records Service. In 1984 Congress once again established the archives as one of the INDEPENDENT EXECUTIVE AGENCIES, renaming it the National Archives and Records Administration.

The agency is headed by the archivist of the United States, who is appointed by the president, with Senate confirmation, to no fixed term. The archivist can be removed only for cause.

Most of the agency's historically valuable records are maintained in the Washington, D.C., area. There also are twelve regional archives located throughout the country.

The National Archives is responsible as well for making available to the public the official text of laws, administrative regulations, and presidential documents. Its Office of the Federal Register publishes the *Federal Register, Code of Federal Regulations, U.S. Government Manual, Weekly Compilation of Presidential Documents, Public Papers of the Presidents,* and *Codification of the Presidential Proclamations and Executive Orders.* The office also is responsible for publication of slip laws (pamphlets containing the text of a bill as enacted and a summary of its legislative history), the *U.S. Statutes at Large,* and the *Privacy Act Compilation,* and it ensures the accuracy of the official count of Electoral College votes for president and vice president.

As of 2006 the National Archives maintained eleven presidential LIBRARIES or presidential materials projects dedicated to preserving and displaying records of presidents from Herbert C. Hoover through Bill Clinton. President Nixon's library is privately operated, but the National Archives maintains a collection of materials from the Nixon presidency.

The holdings of the National Archives as of the early 2000s included about 21.5 million cubic feet of original textual materials; nearly 300,000 reels of motion picture film; over 5 million maps, charts, and architectural drawings; more than 200,000 sound and video recordings; over 9 million aerial photographs; almost 14 million still pictures and posters; and about 7,600 computer datasets.

> **More on this topic:**
>
> *Independent Executive Agencies, p. 286*
>
> *Libraries, p. 335*

Weekly Compilation of

PRESIDENTIAL DOCUMENTS

Monday, August 2, 1965

Volume 1 · Number 1
Pages 1–25

Source: Author

Before the National Archives began compiling public presidential documents in 1934, these papers were the private property of the outgoing presidents, and many are now lost or in various private collections. The *Public Papers of the Presidents* series began printing in 1957 and includes the administration of Herbert Hoover through the present, with the exception of Franklin D. Roosevelt's papers, which were privately printed. In 1965 the National Archives also began publication of the *Weekly Compilation of Presidential Documents,* which includes all of the papers that will eventually be included in the *Public Papers* series plus executive orders, proclamations, and various statements. Executive orders and proclamations are also codified and numbered by the National Archives. As of early 2007, there are a total of 13,424 numbered executive orders and 8,105 numbered proclamations.

National Bank

President George Washington's Treasury secretary, Alexander Hamilton, hoped to enhance the financial credibility and stability of the new United States by establishing a national bank. In December 1790 Hamilton asked Congress to charter a national bank to assist in the financial operations of the United States. It was to be run primarily by private directors and funded by private capital.

The proposal aroused opposition. Many of the bank's opponents feared granting more influence to the federal government. Others, including James Madison, argued that the bank was unconstitutional because the Constitution did not explicitly give government the power to charter a bank. In spite of opposition, the bill passed. On February 25, 1791, Washington signed it after being convinced by Hamilton that it was both constitutional and beneficial.

The First Bank of the United States functioned well for twenty years, but in 1811 Congress refused by one vote to recharter it. Because the bank was the brainchild of Hamilton, who was a Federalist, many members of the Democratic-Republican Party, which dominated U.S. politics in the early nineteenth century, opposed renewing its charter. Some party members agreed with Democratic-Republican leaders Thomas Jefferson and Madison that the bank was unconstitutional.

> *I consider the foundation of the Constitution as laid on this ground: That "all powers not delegated to the United States, by the Constitution, nor prohibited by it to the States, are reserved to the States or to the people." To take a single step beyond the boundaries thus specially drawn around the powers of Congress, is to take possession of a boundless field of power, no longer susceptible of any definition. The incorporation of a bank, and the powers assumed by this bill, have not, in my opinion, been delegated to the United States, by the Constitution.*
>
> —**Thomas Jefferson,** *Opinion on the Constitutionality of a National Bank,* 1791

After experiencing difficulties with national finance during the War of 1812, Congress chartered the Second Bank of the United States in 1816. President Andrew Jackson vetoed the bill that would have rechartered the bank in 1832, and its charter expired in 1836. Jackson opposed the central control of finance and claimed that the bank was a monopoly benefiting wealthy citizens in the East. The lack of a national bank weakened federal control over state and local banks and contributed to inflation and overspeculation that led to a depression in 1837.

Jackson's veto was significant because it left the country without a national bank and because it set a precedent that greatly strengthened the president's VETO POWER. Before the veto the prevailing view was that presidents should veto only bills they considered to be unconstitutional. In 1819 the Supreme Court had ruled in *McCulloch v. Maryland* that Congress could establish a national bank. But Jackson attacked the bank as bad public policy and asserted that the president and Congress had as much right to interpret the Constitution as the Court did.

Between 1836, when the charter of the Second Bank of the United States was allowed to expire, and 1914 the United States did not have a central bank. The nation had experienced several banking panics between 1873 and 1907 that prompted Congress to establish the National Monetary Commission to study the U.S. banking system and its problems. In 1912 the commission concluded that the nation needed a central bank to regulate credit conditions and provide stability to the U.S. banking system. With these goals in mind, Congress passed the Federal Reserve Act in 1914, which created the FEDERAL RESERVE SYSTEM. Unlike the First and Second Banks of the United States, Congress gave the Federal Reserve System a permanent charter to avoid the type of political fight that had prevented the first two national banks from being rechartered.

More on this topic:
Federal Reserve System, p. 214
Hamilton, Alexander, p. 243
Jackson, Andrew, p. 300
Veto Power, p. 533

National Economic Council

The National Economic Council (NEC), created by President Bill Clinton by executive order 12835 in January 1993, is the central mechanism for coordinating executive branch economic policy. In organizational terms, the council is located within the Executive Office of the President as part of the White House Office of Policy Development. Parallel to the NEC in the Office of Policy Development is the Domestic Policy Council.

The NEC has eighteen principal members including the president and the vice president, eight heads of major executive agencies, and other top presidential advisers including the chairman of the Council of Economic Advisers. The NEC is directed by the assistant to the president for economic policy. Under George W. Bush, starting in 2005 this position was held by Allan Hubbard, a businessman with law and business degrees from Harvard. The NEC director is assisted by a number of special assistants to the president.

As set forth in the Clinton executive order, the NEC has four principal functions: to coordinate policy making for domestic and international economic issues, to coordinate economic policy advice for the president, to ensure that policy decisions and programs are consistent with the president's economic goals, and to monitor implementation of the president's economic policy agenda.

The Clinton proposal to create the NEC reflected a Clinton campaign promise to elevate the stature of economic policy in the White House to equal that of foreign and defense policy. To that end, Clinton proposed to create an economic organization equivalent to that of the National Security Council.

All executive departments and agencies, whether or not represented on the Council, shall coordinate economic policy through the Council.

—*Bill Clinton*, Executive Order 12835— Establishment of the National Economic Council, January 25, 1993

In prior administrations, similar functions to those of the NEC were performed by an organization known as the Economic Policy Council, which was located within the White House Office of Policy Development and chaired by the Treasury secretary.

The first director of the NEC was Robert Rubin, who later became secretary of the Treasury. The first NEC director in George W. Bush's administration was economist Lawrence Lindsey, a former member of the Board of Governors of the Federal Reserve System. Lindsey resigned abruptly from the Bush administration in 2002 as controversy swirled around his estimate that the cost of the Iraq war would be $200 billion. Lindsey's estimate was far higher than the $50–$60 billion estimate then endorsed by Defense Secretary Donald Rumsfeld.

In the Clinton years, the NEC issued a steady stream of major policy documents on key economic policy issues ranging from energy and education to technology and transportation. However, in the Bush administration, the NEC generally had a very low profile and released no reports that received any public attention.

Critics have complained that the NEC is essentially an unnecessary extra layer of bureaucracy. Often, it has been alleged, this layer only complicates the work of traditional economic agencies like the Treasury Department and the Council of Economic Advisers.

> **More on this topic:**
>
> *Economic Powers, p. 161*

National Intelligence, Office of the Director of

First director of national intelligence John Negroponte speaking in 2004
Source: Department of State

For decades following the establishment of the Central Intelligence Agency (CIA) in 1947 there was debate as to whether a unified office should exist to coordinate all of the nation's intelligence efforts for the president. One congressionally commissioned study in 1955 recommended that the CIA director should play such a role with a deputy overseeing the CIA's day-to-day operations. After the September 11, 2001, terrorist attacks on New York and Washington, D.C., a renewed call for a national director of intelligence took center stage in debates as to how better to protect the United States from future attacks.

Investigations into the cause of the September 11 attacks took place both in Congress and through the independent National Commission on Terrorist Attacks Upon the United States (9/11 Commission). In particular, the 9/11 Commission determined that the terrorist attacks may have been avoided if there had been better coordination of response measures and communication of intelligence between the various agencies, especially the Federal Bureau of Investigation (FBI) and the CIA. When the Commission's report was released in July 2004, one of its key recommendations was the establishment of a Director of National Intelligence (DNI), sometimes referred to as the "intelligence czar."

Soon afterward, President George W. Bush issued a series of four executive orders to facilitate change in the intelligence community. Because new legislation was needed for a major overhaul, both houses of Congress passed their own revisions to the National Security Act of 1947. To reconcile differences between the two pieces of legislation, the Intelligence Reform and Terrorism Prevention Act of 2004 was negotiated in conference and overwhelmingly passed by both houses of Congress. President Bush signed the bill into law on December 17, 2004. After John Negroponte was confirmed by the Senate as the first DNI, the office began operations on April 22, 2005.

For intelligence matters related to national security, the DNI functions as the principal adviser to the president, the National Security Council, and the Homeland Security Council. In addition, the director oversees the national intelligence program, which is described as "all programs, projects, and activities of the intelligence community, as well as any other programs of the intelligence community designated jointly by the DNI and the head of a United States department or agency or by the President." Finally, the DNI is the head of the sixteen-member United States Intelligence Community, which includes the CIA, the various Department of Defense intelligences services such as the National Security Agency, and the FBI's Directorate of Intelligence.

Wishing to return to the business of diplomacy, Negroponte resigned the office in 2007 to join the State Department as deputy secretary of state and was replaced by Mike McConnell on February 13. Negroponte's almost two years in office were primarily hailed as a success. Former deputy director of central intelligence John McLaughlin once wrote in an article in the *Washington Post* that "Negroponte must be credited with bringing a reassuring and confident demeanor to a community that had been rocked by controversy." *Newsweek* offered additional praise by explaining, "Under Negroponte, the intel czar's office was praised by both congressional and executive-branch officials for greatly improving ... the sharing among relevant agencies of intelligence reports about terror threats."

> *A key lesson of September the 11th, 2001, is that America's intelligence agencies must work together as a single, unified enterprise. The Intelligence Reform and Terrorism Prevention Act of 2004 creates the position of Director of National Intelligence, or DNI, to be appointed by the president with the consent of the Senate.*
>
> **—George W. Bush,** Remarks on Signing the Intelligence Reform and Terrorism Prevention Act of 2004, December 17, 2004

More on this topic:

Central Intelligence Agency, p. 80

Independent Executive Agencies, p. 286

National Security Council, p. 381

National Party Conventions

Perhaps nothing symbolizes the presidential election process so much as the parties' nominating conventions. Every four years Republican and Democratic delegates who have been selected by state PRIMARIES AND CAUCUSES gather at their party's national convention to select the two people who will carry their party's banner into the fall election and, if successful in November, into the White House.

The convention delegates also agree on a statement of party principles and issue stances, or platform, on which the party's nominees can run. The gathering serves as a massive party rally, where rival factions can be conciliated and unified, and enthusiasm generated, in preparation for the fall election campaign.

Since the adoption of DELEGATE SELECTION REFORMS by both major parties in the 1970s, national conventions have been more media events than deliberative bodies. Much of the once spontaneous enthusiasm is now carefully orchestrated to appeal to the television audience. Seldom does the balloting hold any real suspense. Since 1952 every Democratic and Republican nominee for president has been nominated on the first ballot. Nevertheless, a stirring keynote or acceptance speech can still inspire party regulars and television viewers. The convention gives the presidential and vice-presidential nominees a forum in which to kick off the general election campaign and to demonstrate their leadership qualities to the party and the public.

In the nineteenth century, state representation at the national convention followed the Electoral College formula, which itself was based on the Constitutional Convention's Great Compromise on congressional apportionment. In the bicameral Congress, the House of Representatives is appor-

Delegates jammed the aisles in the Chicago Stadium after President Franklin D. Roosevelt was nominated for a third term at the Democratic national convention on July 17, 1940. Chicago has hosted twenty-four major-party conventions since 1860.
Source: AP

tioned according to population, with varying numbers of representatives for the states, and the Senate according to state, with two senators for each state. Under this arrangement, delegate seats at the nominating convention were allocated in proportion to each state's representation in Congress—a mixture of representation according to population and state equality.

In the twentieth century both major parties adopted formulas that also weight representation according to the states' previous electoral support for the party. For example, in the 1980s the Republicans assigned each state a core of delegates based on the size of its congressional delegation. Each state also received a specified number of at-large delegates. Additional delegates were given to those states that had Republican governors, senators, and a party majority in their congressional delegations. A final bonus provision gave a state more representation if its electoral votes had gone to the Republican nominee in the previous presidential election.

The Democrats in recent years have embraced two principles. First, they have systematically sought through affirmative action to give representation to a variety of population groups, including women and racial minorities. Second, the Democrats have seated hundreds of ex officio superdelegates, party officeholders chosen apart from the normal delegate selection process.

Over the years the conventions have grown dramatically in size. Early conventions drew fewer than three hundred delegates. In contrast, contemporary Democratic national conventions bring together more than four thousand delegates, while Republican conventions assemble about two thousand. Altogether, convention delegates, alternate delegates, guests, the candidates and their staffs, and thousands of journalists and broadcast technicians from around the world put the number of people attending a convention at about twenty thousand. Twenty-one cities have been convention sites, some more than once.

Convention Events

Both parties follow a similar schedule of convention events. In recent years the schedule has been streamlined to hold the attention of the national television audience.

Three major committees carry out the work of the national conventions of both parties: credentials, platform, and rules. These committees have traditionally met before the start of the national convention—usually in the week before it begins. More recently the Democrats have begun holding committee sessions several weeks before the convention.

The credentials committee reviews all disputes arising over delegates to the convention. The committee holds hearings on each challenge to delegates' credentials and then makes its recommendations as to whether or not to seat the disputed delegate to the full convention, which makes the final decision on the matter.

The rules committee is responsible for determining the operating rules of the convention. Actions on proposed rule changes can influence the outcome of a convention. In 1976 Ronald Reagan announced his intention to nominate Pennsylvania senator Richard Schweiker as his running mate if he won the Republican presidential nomination. He then proposed a rule change to force his opponent, Gerald R. Ford, to name his own choice. Reagan hoped that Ford's choice might alienate enough delegates to give Reagan the 110 delegate votes he needed to clinch the nomination. But Ford supporters voted down the rule change, and Ford went on to win the nomination.

The platform committee is responsible for preparing a statement of party principles for the convention's approval. Because party leaders are eager to mute conflict within the party and to appeal to as wide a base as possible, platforms are seldom controversial. Nevertheless, their adoption sometimes causes bitter fights. The passage of a strong civil rights plank in the 1948 Democratic platform provoked opposition from southern states. Some of the disgruntled southerners then formed their own party, which ran South Carolina governor J. Strom Thurmond for president under the States' Rights banner.

National party conventions are called to order by the national committee chair, who presides until a temporary convention chair is appointed. The temporary chair then presides until the convention acts on the recommended slate of permanent officers. The permanent chair presides over the nomination process and therefore may be in a position to use strategic rulings to help or hinder particular candidates. Indeed, the permanent chair is often described as the most important officer of the convention. Beginning in the 1930s, it became customary for the party's leader in the House of Representatives to serve as the permanent chair. In 1972 the Democrats undermined that custom by requiring that the position alternate every four years between men and women.

The keynote address is the first major speech of the convention. Because their job is to whip up enthusiasm among the delegates, keynote speakers usually are chosen for their oratorical skills. Before the actual nominations begin, committee reports have been read and any disputes resolved.

SITES OF MAJOR PARTY CONVENTIONS, 1832–2008

	Total Conventions	Number	Democratic Conventions Last Hosted	Number	Republican Conventions Last Hosted
Chicago	25	11	1996	14	1960
Baltimore	10	9	1912	1	1864
Philadelphia	8	2	1948	6	2000
New York	6	5	1992	1	2004
St. Louis	5	4	1916	1	1896
San Francisco	4	2	1984	2	1964
Cincinnati	3	2	1880	1	1876
Kansas City	3	1	1900	2	1976
Miami Beach	3	1	1972	2	1972
Cleveland	2	0	—	2	1936
Houston	2	1	1928	1	1992
Denver	2	2	2008	0	—
Atlanta	1	1	1988	0	—
Atlantic City	1	1	1964	0	—
Charleston	1	1	1860	0	—
Dallas	1	0	—	1	1984
Detroit	1	0	—	1	1980
Los Angeles	2	2	2000	0	—
Minneapolis	1	0	—	1	1892
New Orleans	1	0	—	1	1988
San Diego	1	0	—	1	1996
Boston	1	1	2004	0	—
St. Paul	1	0	—	1	2008

Nominating speeches mark the beginning of the formal selection process. Over the years these speeches had lengthened and were joined by numerous seconding speeches, punctuated with floor demonstrations by delegates supporting the candidate. In 1936 Franklin Roosevelt was seconded fifty-six times.

With the advent of television, however, convention managers began to encourage shorter speeches and fewer seconding speeches. For example, Arkansas governor Bill Clinton was given fifteen minutes to nominate Michael S. Dukakis at the 1988 Democratic convention. Yet Clinton carried on for half an hour through all manner of signals to desist.

Once all the nominating and seconding speeches are completed, the roll call begins. Typically states are called in alphabetical order. When the name of each state is called, the chair of the state's delegation rises and gives the vote of that delegation. Until 1972 the Democrats permitted use of the unit rule, which meant that the entire delegation voted as the majority willed. In recent years individual delegates have been able to vote as they see fit. (Republicans banned use of the unit rule in the mid-nineteenth century.)

After the nomination of the presidential candidate, the convention chooses a vice-presidential nominee. Formerly the presidential candidate had little say in naming his running mate. For example, the 1920 Republican convention ignored Warren G. Harding's preference for Sen. Irvine L. Lenroot of Wisconsin and chose Massachusetts governor Calvin Coolidge instead. Sometimes presidential candidates did not even bother to indicate a preference. The choice was the prerogative of the party leaders.

This practice changed in 1940 when Franklin Roosevelt threatened not to run unless the convention accepted his vice-presidential choice, Secretary of Agriculture Henry A. Wallace. Conventions now routinely approve the presidential nominee's choice. In recent years likely nominees sometimes have selected their running mates before the convention begins. The method for nominating the vice-presidential candidate mirrors the procedure for presidential nominations, with nominating and seconding speeches, demonstrations, and balloting.

The climax of the convention occurs with the two nominees' acceptance speeches. Acceptance speeches were not a part of conventions until 1932, when Franklin Roosevelt flew from Albany to Chicago to address the Democratic national convention. New York governor Thomas E. Dewey in 1944 became the first Republican nominee to deliver an acceptance speech. The drafting of acceptance speeches is now a major endeavor, often involving the work of many writers and designed to satisfy specific voting blocs and interest groups as well as to appeal to the millions of television viewers.

In recent years convention speeches have been supplemented with films extolling the virtues of the candidates and former party greats. These films are virtual campaign commercials beamed free of charge across network television. Since 1980, however, the networks have been more restrictive in their coverage of these films. In 1988, for example, NBC refused to show the Republican film until it had been cut down from twenty minutes to slightly more than seven minutes.

Development of Party Conventions

The national party conventions for selecting presidential nominees developed in reaction to the nation's first system, the King Caucus. Under this early system, congressional caucuses, or meetings of top party leaders, were responsible for the selection of candidates. The closed nature of the caucus system soon came under attack, and the caucus was abandoned after the 1824 election. (See ELECTIONS CHRONOLOGY.)

The Anti-Masonic Party held the first party convention in September 1831. Delegates from thirteen states nominated William Wirt for president. The National Republican, or Whig, Party held a convention that December and nominated Henry Clay. The following May, Democrats convened to nominate Andrew Jackson.

Although they were a repudiation of the framers' dislike for partisanship, conventions still were in accord with the nation's federalist ideals. States could decide on their own how they wished to select delegates. But once they met with other states' representatives, they were forced to bargain and consider more than their own parochial concerns.

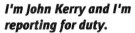

I'm John Kerry and I'm reporting for duty.

—**John Kerry,** Acceptance Speech at the 2004 Democratic National Convention, July 29, 2004

The convention system was open and deliberative. Party leaders often met without any idea which candidates would head the national ticket or how the party would stand on major issues. Those matters were subject to debate and bargaining. Conventions were sufficiently open to allow the occasional emergence of a dark-horse candidate. James K. Polk, who won the Democratic nomination in 1844, is considered the first true outsider to lead a party.

Some conventions were so badly divided that party leaders were forced to stay in session longer than they had planned. In 1860 the Democrats disbanded their convention after fifty-seven ballots; no candidate was able to muster the required two-thirds majority after forty-five delegates walked out to protest the moderate stance on slavery the party had adopted. The next month the convention reconvened and nominated Stephen A. Douglas of Illinois on the second (or fifty-ninth) ballot.

The 1924 Democratic convention went through seventeen days, 103 ballots, and sixteen candidates in New York's sweltering Madison Square Garden before rejecting the two major contenders, New York governor Alfred E. Smith and William Gibbs McAdoo of California, and settling on a third, John W. Davis of New York.

Divisions in the Republican Party led to the rejection of Ulysses S. Grant for a third term in 1880 and the nomination in 1940 of Wendell L. Willkie, who had no political experience.

A genuine draft of a reluctant candidate at a convention is very rare. The first was New York governor Horatio Seymour, who was nominated by the Democrats in 1868. Upon learning of his nomination, Seymour cried, "Pity me! Pity me!" Since then, there have been two other drafts of reluctant candidates: the selection of Supreme Court justice Charles Evans Hughes by the Republicans in 1916 and the selection of Illinois governor Adlai E. Stevenson II by the Democrats in 1952. None of these draft candidates won the general election.

The development of state presidential primary elections at the beginning of the twentieth century gradually made conventions more responsive to the will of the electorate. Party leaders increasingly referred to the importance of public opinion rather than their duty to use their independent political judgment. By the end of World War II conventions were losing control over the nomination process.

In 1952 the convention battle between Dwight D. Eisenhower and Sen. Robert A. Taft was important, but the outcome was shaped by results from Republican primaries. The last open bargaining for the national ticket was the jockeying for the Democratic vice-presidential nomination in 1956. Since then, front-runners for the nomination have had to hold on to the coalition they built before the convention rather than continue building at the convention. The nomination victories of Democrats John F. Kennedy (1960) and Jimmy Carter (1976) and Republican Gerald R. Ford (1976) were secured when the front-runners avoided an erosion of support in early convention votes. In recent years, largely due to party rules having evolved so that more delegates are pledged to support candidates consistent with primary election results, the selection of the eventual nominee is largely predetermined before the nominating convention begins.

More on this topic:

Delegate Selection Reforms, p. 146

Elections Chronology, p. 174

Primaries and Caucuses, p. 420

National Security Adviser

Condoleezza Rice made history in 2001 when she became the first female national security adviser
Source: Department of State

The national security adviser, one of the most important members of the president's personal staff, oversees the functions of the NATIONAL SECURITY COUNCIL (NSC) staff and performs whatever foreign policy duties the president designates. The official name of the post is assistant to the president for national security affairs, but it has been known as national security adviser since the Nixon administration.

The national security adviser is not confirmed by the Senate and does not have the legal authority of a cabinet member. Rather, the power of the national security adviser within the administration depends entirely on the president.

The post of national security adviser was created during Dwight D. Eisenhower's presidency and was originally intended to fill an administrative function. The national security adviser was to be responsible for overseeing the NSC staff, coordinating NSC meetings, and managing the flow to and from the White House of documents relating to foreign policy. Given the central location of the national security adviser in the policy process, however, it was natural that presidents began turning to this official for advice as well as coordination. As a result, national security advisers have become important policy-making figures who often rival cabinet members in stature.

The best-known example of a national security adviser who was the top foreign policy adviser to his president is Henry A. Kissinger, who served President Richard Nixon. During Nixon's first term, Kissinger functioned as the administration's principal foreign policy spokesperson, negotiator, and strategist. Kissinger was far more powerful than Secretary of State William P. Rogers, whose activities were confined primarily to ceremonial tasks and administration of the State Department. In 1973 Kissinger became secretary of state, occupying the office that traditionally went with the power he already possessed.

Zbigniew Brzezinski, who served as national security adviser under Jimmy Carter, and Brent Scowcroft, who served under Gerald R. Ford and George H. W. Bush, are also cited as particularly powerful national security advisers. Anthony Lake, once a special assistant to Kissinger, oversaw the office in Bill Clinton's first term, restructuring it to stress the economic thrust of Clinton's post–cold war national security policy. Lake was nominated to be Central Intelligence Agency (CIA) director when Clinton won reelection in 1996; his deputy, Samuel R. (Sandy) Berger, succeeded him as national security adviser. Lake withdrew his name from consideration for the CIA post when the nomination ran into difficulties with the Senate Intelligence Committee. In 2000 George W. Bush selected as his national security adviser trusted friend and Stanford professor Condoleezza Rice, a Russia specialist on his father's NSC staff. She was the first woman to hold the position. Beginning with Bush's second term in 2005, Rice became secretary of state and was replaced as national security adviser by Stephen Hadley.

More on this topic:

Executive Office of the President, p. 200

National Security Council, p. 381

Staff, p. 472

National Security Council

The 1947 National Security Act established the National Security Council (NSC). The NSC is a presidential advisory body consisting of the president, vice president, and secretaries of defense and state. In addition to these statutory members, the director of the Central Intelligence Agency and the chairman of the Joint Chiefs of Staff are designated as statutory advisers to the NSC.

The NSC was established to help the president to coordinate the actions of government agencies into a coherent foreign policy. The action was taken by the Republican-dominated Eightieth Congress after four terms of Democratic presidents, partly to ensure that the president would listen to advisers. How and when the NSC was to function was left completely to presidents to decide. They could convene the NSC as often or as seldom as they liked and invite anyone they wanted to attend in addition to the council's statutory participants.

President George W. Bush making remarks during a National Security Council meeting on June 29, 2005
Source: The White House

Although presidents could call cabinet meetings to consider national security matters, the cabinet was a large and unwieldy body that included heads of departments unrelated to national security policy. The NSC gave presidents a smaller and more focused forum than the cabinet that would allow them to draw together their top defense, diplomatic, economic, and intelligence advisers to consider broad issues of national security.

The National Security Act stated that the NSC's responsibility was "to advise the President with respect to the integration of domestic, foreign, and military policies relating to the national security so as to enable the military services and other departments and agencies of the government to cooperate more effectively in matters involving the national security." Some presidents have used the NSC as a forum for bringing up and discussing policy options; others have made decisions outside the NSC and then asked the council to approve them. The NSC occasionally has been used as a decision-making forum during crises, such as the North Korean invasion of South Korea in 1950, the Soviet invasion of Czechoslovakia in 1968, and the *Mayaguez* incident in 1975. The NSC also has been used for less dramatic functions, such as policy planning and budget review.

In addition to creating the National Security Council, the National Security Act established an NSC staff independent of other departments and agencies. This staff, intended to serve the president and the NSC members, has become a major player in foreign policy making. At times it has rivaled or eclipsed the State Department in influence, as presidents have used it to implement their personal visions of foreign policy.

> *The passage of the National Security Act by the Congress at its last session was a notable step in providing for the security of this country.*
>
> *—Harry S. Truman, Annual Message to the Congress on the State of the Union, January 7, 1948*

The NSC staff is headed by the assistant to the president for national security affairs, a post established by Dwight D. Eisenhower. Since the administration of Richard Nixon, it has commonly been referred to as the NATIONAL SECURITY ADVISER. The role of the NSC staff has depended greatly on the personal influence of the national security adviser. When the national security adviser has been a relatively weak figure, the NSC staff has had little power. With a strong adviser, however, the NSC staff has been the dominant institutional force in the setting of foreign policy. The most notable example of a strong national security adviser is Henry A. Kissinger, who served under Nixon. Condoleezza Rice, picked by George W. Bush to be his national security adviser, was the first woman to hold the post.

Because the national security adviser and most NSC staff owe their position and status to the president, they have few competing loyalties. The NSC staff is made up of policy experts who specialize in analyzing foreign policy issues. Although the NSC staff sometimes is referred to simply as the "NSC," staff members are distinct from the formal members of the National Security Council.

Some NSC staff members are borrowed from other departments and agencies, but most do not belong to any other body. Even those who are on loan are responsible only to the president during their tenure on the NSC staff. In addition, the NSC staff is virtually beyond the reach of the legislative branch because it has no statutory responsibility to report to Congress. Because of the staff's lack of competing loyalties and responsibilities, presidents have tended to rely heavily on it when they wish to avoid the bureaucratic pitfalls of the formal policy process.

Many observers have criticized presidential reliance on the NSC staff, contending that the president should not use it to bypass the State Department, the Defense Department, or Congress. During the administration of Ronald Reagan, NSC staff members, including Lt. Col. Oliver L. North, played important roles in carrying out secret plans to sell arms to Iran and to divert the proceeds to guerrillas fighting the leftist government of Nicaragua. The so-called IRAN-CONTRA AFFAIR was a major political embarrassment for Reagan, and it fueled the ongoing debate over the role of the NSC staff.

Some experts in government organization argue that the NSC staff should be limited to managing the flow of information and policy options from the departments to the president. They contend that the State Department was intended to be preeminent in foreign affairs, and that its foreign policy expertise, accountability to Congress, and network of embassies in foreign capitals make it the best choice to run the president's foreign policy-making system.

But other experts, including some former national security advisers, argue that the NSC staff should have considerable authority to define the president's overall policy and ensure that it is carried out. Although a foreign policy-making system coordinated by the NSC staff denies the State Department its traditional role as the manager of foreign policy, they argue, the NSC has a better chance of succeeding as a referee between competing departments and agencies and ensuring that the president remains in control of foreign policy. This argument is based on the NSC's being answerable to the president and having no institutional mission beyond serving the president.

> **More on this topic:**
>
> *Executive Office of the President, p. 200*
>
> *Iran-Contra Affair, p. 294*
>
> *National Security Advisor, p. 380*
>
> *Staff, p. 472*

Neutrality Proclamation of 1793

In 1793 President George Washington was trying to keep the United States out of a war between Great Britain and France. Although he was skeptical of exercising power without accompanying congressional action, he unilaterally declared that the United States would not take sides in the war. This proclamation helped to keep the young nation out of war, and it set an important precedent that enhanced presidential power.

The treaty of alliance with France signed in 1778 was still in effect, and most Americans favored the French. Washington feared, however, that U.S. involvement in the conflict between the British and French would disrupt the strengthening of the U.S. economy and political institutions. On

April 22, 1793, he issued what came to be known as the Neutrality Proclamation of 1793. It stated that the United States would be "friendly and impartial" toward Great Britain and France.

The proclamation carefully avoided using the word *neutrality* in deference to Secretary of State Thomas Jefferson, who had opposed the proclamation. Among other objections, Jefferson was not convinced that the president's action was constitutional. Jefferson reasoned that because only Congress could declare war, the president did not have the power to decide unilaterally that the nation would not fight a war. Although the proclamation was unpopular with many pro-French Americans, Congress followed Washington's lead by passing the Neutrality Act of 1794, which endorsed the president's policy. Washington had shown that the president could make foreign policy through executive power, even without the prior consent of Congress.

Washington's action set off a famous debate between Treasury Secretary Alexander Hamilton and James Madison—then a member of the House of Representatives from Virginia—on the subject of presidential power. In a series of articles printed in the *Gazette of the United States,* a Federalist newspaper published in Philadelphia, Hamilton defended Washington's authority to issue the proclamation. Writing under the pseudonym "Pacificus," Hamilton argued that the "executive power" granted to the president by the Constitution empowers the president to conduct all facets of foreign policy that do not usurp the powers specifically granted to Congress.

This expansive view of presidential power alarmed the pro-French Democratic-Republicans led by Secretary of State Jefferson. Jefferson was a member of Washington's cabinet, and he felt it would be improper for him publicly to refute Hamilton's article. He therefore urged Madison to "take up your pen, select the most striking heresies and cut him [Hamilton] to pieces in face of the public."

Writing as "Helvidius," Madison stated that Congress's authority to declare war and its role in the treaty-making process made it the branch of government properly entrusted to make foreign policy, including declarations of neutrality. He rejected Hamilton's broad interpretation of the president's power by claiming that "the natural province of the executive magistrate is to execute laws, as that of the legislature is to make laws. All his acts, therefore, properly executive, must presuppose the existence of the laws to be executed." Thus, according to Madison, the president's role in foreign affairs was restricted to executing the laws, treaties, and declarations of war made by Congress and performing those duties specifically enumerated in the Constitution.

Over time, Hamilton's conception of presidential power has triumphed. Presidents have almost always prevailed when the Constitution is silent on foreign affairs. Indeed, many presidents have behaved as if they had a general, comprehensive power to conduct foreign affairs.

> *Whereas it appears that a state of war exists between Austria, Prussia, Sardinia, Great Britain, and the United Netherlands of the one part and France on the other, and the duty and interest of the United States require that they should with sincerity and good faith adopt and pursue a conduct friendly and impartial toward the belligerent powers.*
>
> **—George Washington,** Proclamation of Neutrality, April 22, 1793

More on this topic:

Diplomatic Powers, p. 149

Washington, George, p. 564

New Deal

The New Deal created by Franklin D. Roosevelt to counter the GREAT DEPRESSION was one of the turning points of twentieth-century U.S. history and of the presidency. Within less than a decade, Roosevelt's New Deal created the foundations for many of the social programs that continue to help the elderly, the poor, and workers today, while also transforming the political landscape and giving the Democratic Party a firm hold on power for many years.

During FDR's first three months in office in 1933, which came to be known as the First Hundred Days, he pushed a series of proposals through Congress. Among the legislation enacted were bills to reform the national banking system, legalize alcohol, create public works, and establish various relief programs.
Source: FDR Library

We are told by the opposition that we must have a change, that we must have a New Deal. It is not the change that comes from normal development of national life to which I object or you object, but the proposal to alter the whole foundations of our national life....

—**Herbert Hoover,** *Address at Madison Square Garden in New York City,* October 31, 1932

The New Deal also brought about a profound change in the federal government. More than sixty new executive agencies were established, and there was a fundamental shift in the role of government in American society. Most people came to believe that the federal government had to take an active role in the nation's problems. To manage the growing federal bureaucracy, the presidency itself also changed, both in the prominent position of the president himself and in the increasing size of the White House staff.

Roosevelt probably did not have such a radical transformation in mind when he ran for president in 1932. Although he used the phrase "new deal" in his speech to the Democratic convention that year, he campaigned on a traditional platform of government economy and the need for a balanced budget. Only after he was elected did he begin pushing drastic steps to alleviate the nation's misery. An incomparable pragmatist, he kept trying things until he found some that worked.

Roosevelt began his legislative program in a burst of activity. In his first three months in office in the spring of 1933—an extraordinary period that became known as the FIRST HUNDRED DAYS—he pushed through Congress an unprecedented series of proposals. Among the major pieces of legislation enacted during that short time were bills to reform the national banking system, legalize the sale of alcoholic beverages, create public works and relief programs, establish the Tennessee Valley Authority, and reorganize farm credit programs.

But the centerpiece of the New Deal was the Social Security Act of 1935, which initiated a comprehensive federal system of insurance for the elderly and unemployed. To sell the plan to the American people, who were initially skeptical and uncertain about the idea, Roosevelt had to undertake a major effort of moral persuasion and civic education. By the time he had finished, the act was law and the nation had adopted the basic concept that government had an obligation to provide some measure of economic security to its citizens.

The New Deal program sought not only to secure the economic welfare of individuals but also to remedy the economic problems of the Great Depression. Programs were established to provide aid to the handicapped and to fatherless children and to provide work-relief projects.

Moreover, for the first time the national government fostered unionization. When Roosevelt took office few factory workers belonged to unions. By the time he died in office, industrial unionism was firmly established. The cornerstone of that change was the National Labor Relations (Wagner) Act of 1935, which guaranteed the right of workers to form unions and gave government officials the authority to enter factories to conduct elections to determine if the workers wished to be represented by a union.

The New Deal also added greatly to the regulatory power of the federal government. The Banking Act of 1933 expanded regulation of that industry, while the Securities Acts of 1933 and 1934 placed the sale of stocks under direct federal supervision. The Civil Aeronautics Act of 1938 established federal control of aviation; wages and hours of employment became the subject of extensive federal regulation with passage of the Fair Labor Standards Act of 1938. By the time the New Deal ended, the regulatory jurisdiction and power of the federal government had been made more inclusive, intensive, and extensive. Regulating the general welfare of the nation had become a major activity of the federal government.

With the opposition Republicans reduced to a small minority in Congress during the height of the New Deal, the federal courts became the chief obstacle to the implementation of Roosevelt's program. This was particularly true of the Supreme Court, where four justices were adamantly opposed to government regulation of business and were frequently able to bring a majority to their point of view. Although the Supreme Court did not invalidate the president's legislative agenda as a whole, it did strike down important parts, including the National Industrial Recovery Act and the Agricultural Adjustment Act of 1933.

Several other pieces of New Deal legislation were headed toward the Court, and many feared that these too would be killed. In response, Roosevelt came up with a plan to "pack" the Supreme Court by adding more members, in the hopes that the new members he would appoint would provide a majority willing to support the New Deal. The COURT-PACKING PLAN was seen by many as a poorly disguised attempt to evade the Supreme Court's power of judicial review of laws, and it did not pass Congress. Nevertheless, retirements soon cleared the way for Roosevelt to appoint justices friendlier to the New Deal.

While the New Deal program was changing the federal government, it also was bringing about a major shift in politics. Roosevelt put together the New Deal coalition of disparate groups united behind his program. Included in the coalition were southerners, blacks, immigrants, farmers, liberals, capital-intensive producers, international business leaders, city dwellers, trade unionists, Catholics, and Jews. The elements of the coalition were not always in harmony—the conflict between conservative southern Democrats and liberals was sharp—but together they provided the building blocks for national political dominance.

The New Deal coalition gave Roosevelt his unique four-term presidency and allowed the Democratic Party, except for the Eisenhower years, to keep a strong hold on the White House until the late 1960s. Although the coalition was finally shattered by racial tensions, the Vietnam War, and other factors, the dream of restoring it continued to be an important aspect of Democratic Party politics.

More on this topic:
Court-Packing Plan, p. 127
Economic Powers, p. 161
First Hundred Days, p. 218
Great Depression, p. 237
Roosevelt, Franklin D., p. 445

New Freedom

Following a tradition begun by Theodore Roosevelt and continued by most subsequent presidents, Woodrow Wilson developed a catchy phrase to sum up his domestic agenda. He called it the "New Freedom," a slogan that stood for a progressive program that included an antitrust campaign and reform of tariffs and the currency.

Wilson felt that his New Freedom, outlined in his 1912 presidential campaign, expressed the progressive tradition as rooted in the Democratic Party's traditional hostility to centralized authority. The program was developed in opposition to the campaign of one of his electoral opponents in 1912, former president Theodore Roosevelt, whose New Nationalism

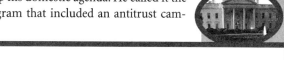

There was a time when corporations played a very minor part in our business affairs, but now they play the chief part, and most men are the servants of corporations.

—**Woodrow Wilson,** *The New Freedom: A Call for the Emancipation of the Generous Energies of a People,* 1913

program accepted the development of great corporations as inevitable. Wilson, by contrast, called for an attack on the power of monopolies and the stranglehold that giant corporations in many cases had on the economy.

As the leader of the Democratic Party, Wilson promised remedial policies, such as reform of the tariff system on imported goods, an overhaul of the banking and monetary system, and a vigorous antitrust program that would "disentangle" the "colossal community of interest" in the United States and restore fair competition to the economy.

To the astonishment of many, Wilson was able to get much of his New Freedom program through Congress. Indeed, most of the elements of the program were achieved within two years of his election. Tariff reform legislation was enacted in October 1913, and the Federal Reserve Act, which reconstructed the national monetary system, passed a few months later. Finally, the Clayton Anti-Trust Act and the Federal Trade Commission Act strengthened the government's authority to prevent unfair competition.

> **More on this topic:**
>
> *Federal Reserve System, p. 214*
>
> *Wilson, Woodrow, p. 583*

The scope of Wilson's legislative achievements was remarkable. In a few short months he turned the fractious Democratic Party in Congress into a disciplined body able to pass landmark bills that in some cases still form the framework of national policy. He enacted many programs that progressives had been demanding for two decades.

New Frontier

John F. Kennedy addresses delegates to the 1960 Democratic national convention
Source:

John F. Kennedy, the youngest elected president, came to office in 1960 determined to shake the nation out of the complacency that had developed during the two terms of his predecessor, Republican Dwight D. Eisenhower. Doubts about the country's future had proliferated because of a stalled economy, a simmering civil rights controversy, and threats to U.S. interests abroad from a bellicose Soviet Union.

Kennedy's New Frontier program sought to inspire the American people to meet the challenges of the postwar era. It drew on elements of Franklin D. Roosevelt's NEW DEAL and Harry S. Truman's FAIR DEAL in advocating medical insurance for all and federal aid to education. The themes of social justice and national service that Kennedy had emphasized during his presidential campaign were echoed later in initiatives such as the Peace Corps and civil rights legislation, which, in Kennedy's words, held out "the promise of more sacrifice instead of security." His inspirational inaugural speech challenged his fellow citizens to "ask not what your country can do for you—ask what you can do for your country."

But Kennedy's stunning rhetoric was not matched by similar legislative achievement, and many of the promises he made were unfulfilled. Foreign policy troubles such as the failed Bay of Pigs in-

vasion, the Berlin crisis, and the Cuban missile crisis diverted the administration from full attention to domestic legislation. The Peace Corps was enacted into law, but Congress rejected many of the young president's other New Frontier bills.

On civil rights, the Kennedy administration advocated school desegregation, increased registration among black voters, and issued rules against discrimination in public housing built with federal funds. Kennedy appointed an unprecedented number of blacks to high public office. He sent federal troops to oversee integration at the state universities in Mississippi and Alabama, but the civil rights legislation he proposed in 1963 was stalled in Congress by a conservative coalition and never came to a vote in his lifetime.

After Kennedy's assassination in November 1963, many of the elements of the New Frontier were pushed through Congress by his successor, Lyndon B. Johnson. Invoking the memory of the nation's fallen leader, Johnson used his considerable skill and experience in legislative politics to persuade Congress to pass, among other bills, the Civil Rights Act of 1964. Passage of this landmark bill broke the back of the conservative coalition that had long resisted such legislation.

But I tell you the New Frontier is here, whether we seek it or not. Beyond that frontier are the uncharted areas of science and space, unsolved problems of peace and war, unconquered pockets of ignorance and prejudice, unanswered questions of poverty and surplus.

—**John F. Kennedy,** Accepting the 1960 Democratic presidential nomination, July 15, 1960

> **More on this topic:**
>
> *Fair Deal, p. 209*
>
> *Great Society, p. 238*
>
> *Kennedy, John F., p. 318*
>
> *New Deal, p. 383*

News Conferences *See* PRESS CONFERENCES.

1968 Democratic Convention (Chicago) *See* DELEGATE SELECTION REFORMS.

Nixon, Pat

Thelma Catherine Ryan Nixon (1912–1993) was the wife of President Richard Nixon. Her father, an Irish miner and farmer, nicknamed her "Pat" because she was born the day before St. Patrick's Day.

In 1932 Pat entered the University of Southern California. After graduating cum laude she took a teaching job in Whittier, California. There she met Richard Nixon while both were acting in a local theater production. He proposed to her on the night of their first meeting. Startled, Pat at first refused, but she eventually changed her mind. They married two years later, on June 21, 1940. The couple had two daughters.

Nixon became successful as a small-town lawyer, and he entered politics after World War II. Pat did not relish the constant public exposure that political life brought, and as Nixon sought higher offices and the campaigns became more intense and vicious, she came to dislike politics.

In September 1952 rumors about financial misconduct forced Nixon to make what later became known as his "Checkers speech" in an effort to save his vice-presidential candidacy. While for him it was a great triumph, for Pat it was humiliating to have the family finances opened to public scrutiny. As early as 1950 she extracted a pledge from her husband not to seek office again, but he broke the promise repeatedly. As she gradually adjusted to life as a politician's wife, Pat's lively personality was replaced by a stiff and formal public demeanor.

First Lady Pat Nixon
Source: Library of Congress

In 1969 Nixon became president. As first lady, Pat sought out authentic antiques to refurnish the White House, and she tried to make the mansion more accessible to the public. She also traveled more widely than any other first lady, visiting eighty-three countries.

Pat attempted to embrace various social projects, but her efforts largely failed. This stemmed in part from her own difficulties in dealing with the public and in part from the White House staff's insistence that she maintain a low public profile. She seemed to have little influence on her husband's political business and was left out of many important decisions, including his decision to run for president in 1968.

As the Watergate scandal intensified during 1973, Pat urged her husband to destroy the White House tapes that contained evidence of his complicity in the cover-up. She argued that the tapes were a private diary, not a public record. Nixon ignored her warning, and he eventually was forced to make the tapes public. Under threat of impeachment he resigned from the presidency in August 1974.

The Nixons retired to San Clemente, California, and later moved several times. In 1976, while at home in California, Pat suffered a stroke and had to undergo several months of physical therapy; she had a milder stroke in 1983. She died on June 22, 1993.

More on this topic:

First Ladies, p. 219

Nixon, Richard, below

Nixon, Richard

Source: The White House

Richard Milhous Nixon (1913–1994) was the only president ever to resign from the presidency. During his five and a half years in office he presided over a volatile economy, domestic social upheaval, and a reduction in tensions with the Soviet Union and the People's Republic of China. But his presidency is best remembered for the WATERGATE AFFAIR, which drove him from office under the threat of certain impeachment.

Nixon was born on January 9, 1913, in Yorba Linda, California. His parents managed a combination gas station and general store. Nixon graduated from Whittier College in 1934 with a degree in history. He earned a tuition scholarship to Duke University law school, from which he graduated in 1937, third in his class. He returned to California, where he practiced law. Nixon married Thelma Catherine (Pat) Ryan, a high school typing teacher, on June 21, 1940.

During World War II Nixon worked in the Office of Price Administration in Washington, D.C., before receiving a navy commission. He served for over a year in the

Pacific theater. When he left active duty in 1946, he had attained the rank of lieutenant commander.

Political Career

In 1945 Nixon was persuaded by California Republican leaders to run for Congress. He won the election after putting his Democratic opponent on the defensive by accusing him of being a socialist. Nixon was reelected in 1948. In the House he gained a national reputation as an anticommunist crusader. In August 1948 he was appointed chairman of a subcommittee of the House Un-American Activities Committee. His subcommittee investigated charges that several government employees were communists, including Alger Hiss, a former State Department official. In his testimony Hiss denied that he was a communist. Nixon pressed the investigation and found discrepancies that led to Hiss's conviction for perjury.

Nixon impressed Republican leaders in 1950 when he won a Senate seat by a huge margin. He became an early supporter of Gen. Dwight D. Eisenhower for the 1952 Republican presidential nomination and was chosen as the party's vice-presidential candidate when Eisenhower was nominated. In September 1952 Nixon's candidacy was threatened by accusations that he had used for personal expenses secret funds provided by California business interests. In an emotional televised speech on September 23 that was viewed by sixty million people, Nixon denied any wrongdoing and said he and his family lived a simple life without luxuries. The address became known as the "Checkers speech" because after admitting that he had accepted the gift of a dog his daughter had named Checkers, Nixon asserted that he would not give it back. The address aroused an outpouring of support from Americans and saved Nixon's candidacy.

Eisenhower's status as a war hero and his pledge to find a settlement to the Korean War brought victory to the Republican ticket. Four years later Eisenhower and Nixon were reelected easily. As vice president, Nixon chaired several domestic policy committees and made numerous trips overseas, including a 1959 visit to Moscow where he engaged in a famous spontaneous debate with Soviet premier Nikita Khrushchev on the merits of capitalism versus communism.

Nixon received the Republican nomination for president in 1960. He and his Democratic opponent, Sen. John F. Kennedy of Massachusetts, engaged in the first televised presidential debates in history. Nixon is considered to have lost the important first debate, partly because he appeared tired on camera. Kennedy defeated Nixon by a slim margin of 120,000 popular votes but won solidly, 303–219, in the Electoral College. After the defeat Nixon returned to California to practice law. In 1962 he ran for governor but lost to Edmund G. Brown. After the election he told reporters they would not "have Dick Nixon to kick around anymore."

Nevertheless, Nixon remained politically ambitious, and he was nominated again for president in 1968 by the Republican Party. In an election that was almost as close in the popular vote as his 1960 loss, Nixon defeated his Democratic opponent, Vice President Hubert H. Humphrey, by a vote of 301–191 in the Electoral College.

Presidency

Nixon's first priority as president was achieving "peace with honor" in Vietnam. He proposed a plan to "Vietnamize" the war by providing the South Vietnamese with upgraded training and weaponry, while slowly withdrawing

Let historians not record that when America was the most powerful nation in the world we passed on the other side of the road and allowed the last hopes for peace and freedom of millions of people to be suffocated by the forces of totalitarianism. And so tonight — to you, the great silent majority of my fellow Americans — I ask for your support.

—**Richard Nixon,** Address to the Nation on the War in Vietnam, November 3, 1969

Always remember, others may hate you, but those who hate you don't win unless you hate them, and then you destroy yourself.

—**Richard Nixon,** Remarks on Departure from the White House, August 9, 1974

Richard Nixon experienced both agonizing defeats and resounding victories in his political career. After narrowly losing to John F. Kennedy in the 1960 presidential election, Nixon returned to California where in 1962 he ran for governor as the Republican nominee against incumbent governor Edmund "Pat" Brown. After losing that election, it appeared as though Nixon's political career was over. In a press conference offering his concession, he stated to the press, "You won't have Dick Nixon to kick around any more." Six years later and in private practice as an attorney, he then orchestrated one of the greatest comebacks in American political history when he won the Republican nomination for president and went on to defeat Democratic nominee Hubert H. Humphrey to become the thirty-seventh president. In 1972 Nixon won reelection capturing 520 electoral votes, the third most ever (behind the 525 won by Ronald Reagan in his 1984 reelection and the 523 won by Franklin Roosevelt in his 1936 reelection). Nixon's 60.7 percent of the popular vote was also the third highest.

U.S. troops. Nixon ordered several controversial military operations, including an invasion of Cambodia in 1970 that increased domestic protest against the war. Nevertheless, the majority of Americans supported Nixon's slow withdrawal. In January 1973 the Nixon administration finally concluded an agreement that ended direct U.S. participation in the Vietnam War and provided for an exchange of prisoners. Nixon secretly promised South Vietnamese president Nguyen Van Thieu that the United States would not allow his regime to be overthrown by the communists—a commitment that was not met. The communists conquered the South in 1975 after Nixon had left office and Congress had placed strict limits on U.S. military activities in Southeast Asia.

Nixon's most notable successes were the improvement of relations with China and the Soviet Union. In 1972 he became the first U.S. president to travel to communist China. His summit meeting with Chinese leaders signaled a new beginning for U.S.-Chinese relations, which had been hostile since the communists came to power in 1949. In 1972 Nixon also became the first incumbent president to travel to Moscow. His summit with Soviet leader Leonid Brezhnev was the result of a relaxation of tensions between the superpowers known as détente. In Moscow, Brezhnev and Nixon signed agreements limiting nuclear weapons and antiballistic missile systems. The Soviet leader returned Nixon's visit in June 1973, when he came to Washington, D.C., for a summit meeting.

Nixon's most significant domestic policy action was his imposition of wage and price controls on August 15, 1971. The controls initially slowed inflation, but their removal late in Nixon's presidency, combined with a jump in the price of oil caused by an Arab oil embargo, led to sharp increases in inflation. Prices rose 6.2 percent in 1973 and 11.0 percent in 1974.

The 1971 wage and price controls allowed Nixon to stimulate the economy in 1972 without fear that inflation would skyrocket. With unemployment falling, peace at hand in Vietnam, and the memory of Nixon's dramatic 1972 trips to China and the Soviet Union fresh in the minds of voters, the president was reelected in a landslide. Democratic challenger Sen. George McGovern of South Dakota won only Massachusetts and the District of Columbia.

Despite Nixon's overwhelming election victory, his second term soon became consumed by the Watergate affair. On June 17, 1972, during the presidential campaign, five men with connections to the Committee to Re-elect the President were arrested while breaking into the

TOP 10 ELECTORAL COLLEGE VICTORIES AND POPULAR VOTE PERCENTAGES

Top 10 Electoral College Vote Winners

Election	President	Electoral Votes
1984	Ronald Reagan	525
1936	Franklin D. Roosevelt	523
1972	Richard Nixon	520
1980	Ronald Reagan	489
1964	Lyndon B. Johnson	486
1932	Franklin D. Roosevelt	472
1956	Dwight D. Eisenhower	457
1940	Franklin D. Roosevelt	449
1928	Herbert Hoover	444
1952	Dwight D. Eisenhower	442

Top 10 Popular Vote Percentages

Election	President	Popular Vote
1964	Lyndon B. Johnson	61.1%
1936	Franklin D. Roosevelt	60.8
1972	Richard M. Nixon	60.7
1920	Warren G. Harding	60.3
1984	Ronald Reagan	58.8
1928	Herbert Hoover	58.2
1932	Franklin D. Roosevelt	57.4
1956	Dwight D. Eisenhower	57.4
1904	Theodore Roosevelt	56.4
1828	Andrew Jackson	56.1

Democratic National Committee headquarters in the Watergate complex in Washington, D.C. Investigation of the burglary and the White House's attempt to cover up its ties to the burglars led to disclosure of numerous crimes and improprieties committed by members of the administration. Nixon claimed he was innocent of any wrongdoing, but evidence showed that he had participated in the cover-up. In July 1974 the House Judiciary Committee recommended to the full House that Nixon be impeached for obstruction of justice, abuse of presidential powers, and contempt of Congress.

On August 9 Richard Nixon resigned from office rather than be impeached. Vice President Gerald R. Ford became president. Nixon had chosen Ford to replace his first vice president, Spiro T. Agnew, who had resigned in 1973 because of a scandal unrelated to Watergate. Nixon did not have to face criminal charges because on September 8 President Ford granted him a "full, free, and absolute pardon."

After leaving the presidency Nixon wrote several books about his time in office and world affairs. Although he remained tainted by the Watergate affair, he came to be regarded as an elder statesman by many Americans because of his successes in foreign policy. Nixon died on April 22, 1994, after suffering a stroke several days earlier.

More on this topic:

Elections Chronology,
p. 174

Nixon, Pat, p. 387

United States v. Nixon,
p. 528

Vice President, p. 539

Vietnam War, p. 546

Watergate Affair, p. 567

Nominating Process

See NATIONAL PARTY CONVENTIONS; PRIMARIES AND CAUCUSES.

Nuclear Command Procedures

One of the president's most important duties since World War II has been commanding the nation's nuclear forces. For most of the period since World War II, the United States has maintained a huge arsenal of nuclear bombs and warheads that can be delivered by bombers, land-based missiles, and submarine-based missiles. During the cold war this arsenal was primarily intended to deter nuclear attacks by the Soviet Union, which had built a similar nuclear arsenal. The United States warned that a nuclear attack against it would provoke a retaliatory nuclear response against the aggressor. Because of the horrible consequences of nuclear war, both the United States and the Soviet Union, despite their global competition and the arms race, avoided conflict that could have led to nuclear war.

The nature of nuclear weapons necessitated that one person be in charge of the U.S. nuclear arsenal. If a foreign power launched a nuclear attack, the missiles could begin striking U.S. territory within a half-hour or less of their launch. The president would not have time to make a tentative decision to retaliate and then consult Congress. As commander in chief, the president has sole authority over the decision to launch nuclear weapons in response to an attack. Yet, if the president ordered a surprise nuclear attack during peacetime when no crisis existed, it is likely those orders would be questioned and resisted by civilian advisers and military officers. (See WAR POWERS.)

Because the decision to launch nuclear weapons in response to an attack must be made quickly under conditions of extreme stress, nuclear planners provided the president with the Single Integrated Oper-

ational Plan (SIOP). This highly classified document contains the possible U.S. nuclear responses to a variety of possible attacks. Its purpose is to familiarize the president and other top defense officials with nuclear attack options from which they can quickly choose in a crisis.

If the North American Aerospace Defense Command (NORAD)—the underground post in Colorado charged with processing early warning information from an elaborate network of satellites and radars—detects evidence of a possible nuclear attack against the United States, it and other defense units begin steps to verify the authenticity of the attack. If NORAD commanders believe the attack is real, they notify the president. The president then consults with defense officials and considers SIOP options.

If a nuclear attack option is chosen, the president transmits launch codes to officers in charge of nuclear weapons. These codes unlock the nuclear weapons and assure the officers that the launch order is authentic. The launch codes are carried in an ordinary black bag, known as the "football," by a military officer who is always near the president. The exact procedures for ordering nuclear forces to launch their weapons are highly classified and probably change depending on the incumbent president's preferences.

If the president is killed by a nuclear attack or is unable to communicate with nuclear forces, nuclear command is transferred to the president's successors as specified in the Twenty-fifth Amendment and the Presidential Succession Act of 1947. Presidents, however, may give authority to launch nuclear weapons to specified military commanders rather than depend on the survival of presidential successors.

More on this topic:

War Powers, p. 555

Oath of Office

Article II, Section 1, Clause 8, of the Constitution requires the president-elect to recite the following oath before assuming the office: "I do solemnly swear (or affirm) that I will faithfully execute the Office of President of the United States, and will to the best of my Ability, preserve, protect, and defend the Constitution of the United States."

The presidential oath in the Constitution is unique because the presidency is the only office for which swearing-in language is spelled out. Other government officials are required to swear to defend the Constitution, but the wording of their oaths is not specified.

I do solemnly swear (or affirm) that I will faithfully execute the Office of President of the United States, and will to the best of my Ability, preserve, protect and defend the Constitution of the United States.

—**Constitution of the United States of America,** *Article II, Section 1, Clause 8*

At the Constitutional Convention there was little debate over the presidential oath, although some changes were made in the language of the oath as the convention went on. The most important substantive decision made by delegates was to bar the imposition of religious oaths on the president and other government officials. Recognizing that the beliefs of some Christian sects prohibit their members from swearing, the Constitution also allows presidents to "affirm" their oath. Only Franklin Pierce in 1853 affirmed, rather than swore, to execute his office faithfully.

The wording of the presidential oath is brief and straightforward, but the swearing in of each holder of the office represents one of the dramatic high points of each presidency.

On April 30, 1789, at Federal Hall in New York City, George Washington took the first oath of office. By adding the words "so help me God" at the end of the oath, Washington set a precedent for future inaugurals. This drawing of the celebration appeared in Harper's Weekly one hundred years later.

Source: H.A. Ogden, *Harper's Weekly*

Whether taken on the Capitol steps in front of a huge inaugural crowd or in some lonely or unexpected spot after the sudden death of a president, the taking of the oath is always memorable.

George Washington established a precedent for many future presidents by taking his oath of office as the first president with his left hand placed on a Bible and his right hand raised. Although not required by the Constitution, the practice of taking oaths on the Bible was deeply ingrained in British and colonial American history. It has also become standard practice for presidents to add the words, "so help me God" at the end of the oath, though it is unclear when this tradition began. Some historians claim Washington was the first, while research into contemporary accounts of various inaugurals suggests that Chester A. Arthur in 1881 was the first to utter these words, and Warren Harding the second, but not until 1921.

There is no definite record of a Bible being used again at a swearing-in ceremony until James K. Polk's inauguration in 1845. Since James Buchanan assumed office in 1857, every president but one has taken the oath with his hand on the Bible. The exception was Theodore Roosevelt, who was hastily sworn in after the assassination of William McKinley. The oldest inaugural Bible was the one used by Franklin D. Roosevelt; it had been in his family since the seventeenth century.

The page that the Bible is opened to when the president takes the oath is sometimes chosen to symbolize the aspirations of the new chief executive. Taking office in 1969 in the middle of the Vietnam War, for example, Richard Nixon swore with his hand on the passage from Isaiah that reads, "They shall beat their swords into plowshares, and their spears into pruning hooks."

With rare exceptions, the oath of office has been administered by the chief justice of the United States, although the Constitution does not require this. At regular inaugurations it is easy to arrange to have the chief justice present. Other judges have administered the oath in times of unexpected presidential succession. But such times raise several questions. For example, can someone assume the presidency without having taken the oath? When William Henry Harrison died in office in 1841, Vice President John Tyler thought he did not need to take the presidential oath, because he had sworn to defend the Constitution when he became vice president. Tyler soon decided to take the oath anyway, just to be sure, and later, suddenly elevated presidents have done so as well.

Still, the period between the death of a president and the swearing in of his successor remains a gray area. After John F. Kennedy was killed in Dallas in 1963, there was some question whether Lyndon B. Johnson should take the oath immediately in Dallas or wait until he arrived in Washington. After Attorney General Robert F. Kennedy advised that it would be better to take the oath immediately, Johnson was sworn in aboard the presidential aircraft by a federal district judge.

> **More on this topic:**
>
> *Article II, p. 16*
>
> *Inauguration, p. 282*

Oval Office   See WHITE HOUSE.

PACs *See* POLITICAL ACTION COMMITTEES (PACS).

Pardon Power

Article II, Section 2, of the Constitution gives the president "Power to grant Reprieves and Pardons for Offenses against the United States, except in Cases of Impeachment." As it has been interpreted by the courts, the pardon power is one of the few constitutional powers of the president that does not require the agreement of Congress or allow for congressional interference.

A reprieve reduces the severity of a legal penalty without removing the guilt. President Dwight D. Eisenhower reprieved a person sentenced to death by a military court, commuting the sentence to life imprisonment without parole. A pardon wipes out guilt and punishment, restoring the person pardoned to the legal status he or she enjoyed before the crime was committed.

Presidents can issue pardons at any time after a crime or alleged crime has been committed: before trial, during trial, or after trial and conviction. President Gerald R. Ford's unconditional pardon of former president Richard Nixon after the WATERGATE AFFAIR came before Nixon had been indicted for any crime. Although most reprieves and pardons are granted to individuals, a president can grant either form of clemency to a specific group of people by signing an "amnesty," as President Andrew Johnson did for southerners after the Civil War.

The framers of the Constitution reasoned that the pardon power would help the president to maintain law and order in the new nation. As Alexander Hamilton explained in the *Federalist Papers,* "in seasons of insurrection or rebellion, there are often critical moments when a well-timed

offer of pardon to the insurgents or rebels may restore the tranquillity of the commonwealth." Not long after the Constitution was ratified, President George Washington used his pardon power to help quell the WHISKEY REBELLION, a revolt of farmers who objected to an excise tax on whiskey.

The framers could not have guessed that the pardon power would one day be used to heal the wounds of a devastating civil war or of a divisive foreign war. Amnesties signed by Presidents Abraham Lincoln and Andrew Johnson restored voting and office-holding rights to Confederates after the Civil War. These measures helped to "restore the tranquillity of the community" as Hamilton had hoped. Presidents Ford and Jimmy Carter had similar aims a century later when they signed amnesties for those who had evaded the military draft or left the country to avoid serving in the Vietnam War.

The most famous—some would say infamous—presidential pardon of modern times was the "full, free and absolute" pardon granted to Nixon by his successor, Ford. The pardon came one month after Nixon's resignation because of the Watergate affair and related misdeeds in which he was implicated. Some of Nixon's top aides and associates served time in prison for their part in the scandals, but the pardon protected Nixon from criminal prosecution for all federal offenses he might have committed during his presidency.

Ford argued that Nixon had suffered enough and that the pardon would spare the nation the painful spectacle of a former president brought to trial. The pardon provoked a storm of controversy, however, and eroded Ford's popularity. Some critics charged that Ford had agreed to pardon Nixon in exchange for his resignation, an accusation that was never substantiated and that Ford denied in an unprecedented appearance before the House Judiciary Committee.

> *Now, therefore, I, Gerald R. Ford, President of the United States, pursuant to the pardon power conferred upon me by Article II, Section 2, of the Constitution, have granted and by these presents do grant a full, free, and absolute pardon unto Richard Nixon for all offenses against the United States which he, Richard Nixon, has committed or may have committed or taken part in during the period from January 20, 1969 through August 9, 1974.*
>
> —*Gerald R. Ford,* Proclamation 4311— Granting Pardon to Richard Nixon, *September 8, 1974*

More on this topic:
Article II, p. 16
Clinton, William J., p. 101
Ford, Gerald R., p. 224
Whiskey Rebellion, p. 572

Among other controversial gestures of clemency were some of the 140 pardons and 36 commutations that Bill Clinton issued on January 20, 2001, his last day in office. Among those, none was more questionable than the pardon of fugitive financier Marc Rich, whose former wife, Denise Rich, had made appeals for the pardon after she contributed generously to the Democratic Party, the Clinton reelection campaign, and the Clinton presidential library. Clinton's actions were the subject of congressional probes and a Justice Department investigation. During his first term, George W. Bush used the pardon power less often, granting his first pardons to seven people in December 2002. By early 2007 Bush had pardoned slightly more than 100 people.

Parties *See* POLITICAL PARTIES.

Party Leader

In the United States, presidents fill many roles: chief executive, chief of state, commander in chief, legislative leader, chief economic manager—and leader of their political party.

Presidential party leadership can be controversial. The president is, after all, president of all the people and not just a particular segment of the population. Therefore, it is rare for presidents to act mainly as a party leader. But it is equally rare for presidents to perform their other roles without regard for their political party.

The presidential role of party leadership was not envisioned by the framers of the Constitution, largely because they did not anticipate the development of POLITICAL PARTIES. Thomas Jefferson, the third president, is generally considered to be the founder of presidential party leadership, which he exercised primarily through his relations with Congress. By working for his program through fellow Democratic-Republicans in Congress, Jefferson had more success than he would have had simply as a chief executive asking the national legislature to consider his program.

You know, Harry Truman's old saying has never been more true, "If you want to live like a Republican, you better vote for the Democrats."

—**Bill Clinton,** Remarks to the Democratic National Convention in Los Angeles, California, August 14, 2000

The tactics Jefferson developed were to become standard practice. He participated in recruiting candidates for congressional office. He enlisted members of Congress as his agents and worked through them in pursuit of his legislative objectives, he deployed members of his cabinet as emissaries on Capitol Hill, and he established personal relationships with Democratic-Republican legislators.

By the time Andrew Jackson became president in 1828, two important developments were taking place in the relations between president and party: the growth of national party organizations and the emergence of mass parties. Ordinary citizens began to identify with political parties and to provide electoral support for the party's candidates.

These developments significantly enhanced the president's role as party leader. The national nominating convention linked the president to both the national party organization and state and local party organizations throughout the country. Furthermore, under Jackson, a popular military and political hero, the presidency became the focus of popular attention. Meanwhile, under the astute direction of Jackson's vice president and successor, Martin Van Buren, presidential PATRONAGE (the spoils system) extended and strengthened party organizations.

The next important shift in president-party relations occurred in the aftermath of the Civil War. Congressional Republicans reacted to Abraham Lincoln's assertive wartime leadership by restraining his successors. Also, party leaders at the state and local levels—fortified by patronage resources of their own and by strong party identifications and loyalties in the electorate—increased their role in national politics. By the late nineteenth century, these party bosses were dominating the presidential nominating process.

After the turn of the century the balance of power began to shift again, this time in favor of the president. Strong, assertive occupants of the White House, such as Theodore Roosevelt and Woodrow Wilson, invigorated the presidency. An increasing world role for the United States enhanced the visibility and power of the office. At the same time, advancing communications technology focused more popular attention on the president.

Franklin D. Roosevelt ushered in the modern era in president-party relations with his long tenure in the White House. In responding to the Great Depression and World War II, Roosevelt dramatically increased the size and scope of the federal executive. This expansion had important implications for party relations, because Roosevelt came to rely on executive branch personnel to perform many of the political and social service roles that traditionally had been the province of the political party.

Since then, further advances in communications technology, especially television, have served to connect the president even more directly with the public. This stronger connection has, in turn, weakened the party's traditional position as intermediary between the two. In addition, and indeed in response, voters' allegiance to a particular party has been declining. Party reforms have reduced the power of the party organization in the presidential nominating process.

Although presidents no longer work primarily through the party organization, they are clearly still the focal point and leader of their political party. Through their White House aides, presidents maintain ties with the party organization, members of their party in Congress, and supportive

More on this topic:

Congressional Caucus (King Caucus), p. 118

Patronage, below

Political Parties, p. 407

members of the public. The president's ability to wield influence within his party, especially among his party's congressional caucus, depends on his job approval ratings and whether he is nearing the end of his term. Jimmy Carter, suffering from low job approval on issues related to the economy, was less successful in commanding Democrats in Congress than was Ronald Reagan, a Republican. Beginning with the 110th Congress in 2007, George W. Bush, suffering from job approval ratings in the mid-30s for a protracted period of time, and with a vice president not seeking to extend Bush's legacy by running for president in 2008, has seen his base of support among Republicans in Congress erode.

Patronage

Patronage is the filling of jobs as political rewards. A patronage system for filling federal jobs became institutionalized in the U.S. government in the nineteenth century. As a CIVIL SERVICE system based on merit was extended to more and more federal jobs, patronage all but died out in the twentieth century. Today, then, presidents are confined to filling only certain high-level policy positions through patronage.

Background

As the first president, George Washington had the initial responsibility of filling subordinate positions within the executive branch. Ostensibly, partisanship played no role in his decisions, since at the outset of his administration political parties had not yet appeared on the scene. Washington deplored even the idea of partisan division and put forward instead the criterion of fitness of character for consideration as a presidential appointee. Nevertheless, the great majority of the fit characters receiving appointments during his administration turned out to be followers of the policies advocated by one of Washington's closest advisers, Secretary of the Treasury Alexander Hamilton.

By the time Thomas Jefferson entered the presidency in 1801, the executive branch was filled with his partisan adversaries. For the most part, Jefferson did not so much clean house as make new and replacement appointments with partisan considerations in mind.

Charles Guiteau, a disgruntled office seeker, was arrested on July 2, 1881, after shooting President Garfield. The assassination led Congress to pass the Civil Service Reform Act, legislation that sought to replace patronage with merit as the basis for hiring government workers.
Source: Library of Congress

Andrew Jackson, the seventh president, enthusiastically embraced what came to be called the "spoils system"—from the ancient Roman saying "to the victor belong the spoils of the enemy." Under the spoils system, appointed positions within the federal executive were viewed as rewards of electoral victory, to be doled out to the supporters of the winning presidential candidate.

The emerging national party organizations of the post-Jacksonian era quickly asserted claims on the distribution of federal patronage. They had assembled and directed the campaign support essential to electoral victory, and patronage was the means by which they could reward the party faithful.

Within the federal government the post office offered a harvest of available jobs, establishing a long-standing connection between the post office and party politics. Presidents usually retained personal control over the high-level appointments in the executive branch, but they customarily delegated responsibility for the vast number of lesser appointments to the party managers.

In time, the spoils system became entangled in allegations of incompetence and scandal. Increasingly, reformers called for its abolition in favor of a system of civil service based on merit.

Decline of Patronage

The 1881 assassination of President James A. Garfield by Charles Guiteau, who was angry at not being appointed as U.S. consul to Paris, led Congress in 1883 to pass the Pendleton Act, also known as the Civil Service Reform Act. This landmark legislation sought to replace partisanship with merit as the essential standard for low-level positions within the executive branch.

Initially only a small minority, about 10 percent, of the total number of executive branch positions came under the merit civil service. The majority remained in the hands of the president and continued to be allocated through the party as spoils.

Gradually the number and proportion of civil service positions increased. Under the guise of reform, presidents would extend civil service classification to large groups of their partisan appointments. Subsequent presidents would find their discretion in making appointments severely limited by the "blanketing in" of their predecessors' appointees.

The Hatch Act, passed in 1939, continued the process of removing the executive establishment from politics. The law stemmed from a series of newspaper reports that Franklin D. Roosevelt's administration was improperly using the Works Projects Administration to bolster the reelection campaign of a Senate ally. Passed by a coalition of Republican and anti–New Deal Democrats, the act banned federal employees from taking part in organized national political activity. In 1993 a new law tightened on-the-job restrictions, but loosened off-duty limits on most federal and postal workers.

The last major blow to the patronage system was dealt in 1969, when Richard Nixon decided to remove 63,000 postmaster and rural carrier appointments from politics. Special boards were set up to select candidates for these positions. The Postal Reorganization Act of 1970, which established the U.S. Postal Service, put an end to patronage in the post office.

Today more than 90 percent of government jobs are under a merit system, a rough reversal of the percentage distribution at the outset of civil service reform little more than a century earlier.

At the beginning of a new administration, Congress publishes *Policy and Supporting Positions,* known as the "plum book." This publication lists the top executive branch positions available for direct presidential appointment, many of which require Senate confirmation. Each new administration appoints approximately 200 members of the White House staff, 14 cabinet department heads (15 with the addition of the Department of Homeland Security), 400–500 members of the subcabinet, and approximately 150 ambassadors. In addition, agency and department heads appoint 600–800 members of the Senior Executive Service and about 1,800

More on this topic:
Appointment and Removal Power, p. 9
Civil Service, p. 91
Historic Milestones of the Presidency, p. 253

special aides in Schedule C positions, which are exempt from the testing and qualification requirements of the civil service merit system. Altogether, presidents and their subordinates must appoint some 5,200 people to the executive branch. (See also APPOINTMENT AND REMOVAL POWER.)

Presidents can use their appointment power to curry favor among members of Congress, especially through their appointments to posts such as federal judgeships and federal marshal and attorney positions.

Pendleton Act *See* CIVIL SERVICE; PATRONAGE.

Perot, H. Ross

The 1992 election produced some firsts, not the least of which was the role played by independent candidate H. Ross Perot. The Texas billionaire achieved the largest vote total for an independent in presidential history as well as the biggest vote share—18.9 percent—since 1912.

Cartoon from June 1, 1992, parodying Perot's run for president
Source: Library of Congress

Perot's on-again, off-again candidacy often overshadowed the campaigns of George H. W. Bush and Bill Clinton. He campaigned on the premise that politicians in the major parties lacked the will to address the pressing issues facing the nation, particularly the budget deficit. If the voters wanted to get down to business, then they should vote for Perot, he often said. But if all they wanted was talk and slow dancing, then they should vote for Bush or Clinton.

Perot's plain talk and call for change struck a chord among many of the nation's voters. His supporters joined Perot's volunteer organization, United We Stand, America, and worked to get him on the ballot in all fifty states and the District of Columbia. Perot's withdrawal from the race in July 1992 and reentry in October raised questions about his ability to withstand the pressures of a presidential campaign, but he still garnered an unprecedented number of votes (nearly twenty million) for an independent candidate, and, by most accounts, his presence in the race forced the two major political party candidates to address issues they would have rather ignored.

In the fall of 1995 Perot announced formation of a third party, the Reform Party, to appeal to disaffected voters. Perot promised an open nominating process, but actively discouraged any rival. His attitude rankled many former supporters, and throughout the campaign polls showed his support in the single digits. As a result, he was not invited to participate in the two debates between President Clinton and the Republican candidate, Robert J. Dole. The widespread wave of voter anger that sustained the 1992 Perot campaign had ebbed greatly by November 1996, and he received 8.4 percent of the vote, less than half of his 1992 total.

Perot was born on June 27, 1930, in Texarkana, Texas. He graduated from the U.S. Naval Academy in 1953. Perot built his fortune in the computer business.

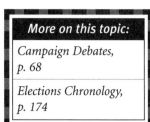

More on this topic:

Campaign Debates,
p. 68

Elections Chronology,
p. 174

Persian Gulf War (Operations Desert Shield and Desert Storm)

The Persian Gulf region, in just over a decade, has produced two wars that featured the same principal participants, the United States and Iraq. The first war, known as the Persian Gulf War, started on August 2, 1990, when Iraqi troops invaded neighboring Kuwait. The invasion and subsequent annexation of Kuwait by Iraqi president Saddam Hussein set in motion an international crisis that led to war between Iraq and a U.S.-led coalition determined to undo the Iraqi annexation. That military operation was successful within its specific objectives. Iraqi forces were expelled from Kuwait and much of Iraq's military capacity was destroyed, but Hussein was not removed from power. As part of the effort to lessen his grip on Iraq, the United Nations imposed armament inspections and sanctions on the Iraqi government, which, over the next decade, Hussein worked continually to avoid, eventually leading to the Iraq War, which started in 2003.

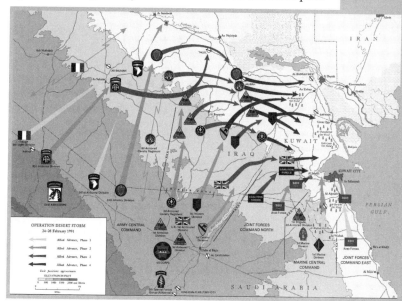

Map of troop movements from Operations Desert Shield and Desert Storm
Source: U.S. Army

At the forefront of the opposition to Saddam Hussein's invasion of Kuwait was President George H. W. Bush. He believed that Iraq's conquering of Kuwait set an international precedent that had to be reversed. Bush and his advisers contended that Hussein could not be allowed to control Kuwait's vast oil reserves or threaten the even larger oil reserves of neighboring Saudi Arabia. The Bush administration also claimed that Iraq's progress toward building a nuclear bomb had to be stopped. If Hussein's aggression went unopposed, the administration said, the Middle East would likely see a larger, more destructive war in the future.

Operation Desert Shield

Bush sent U.S. forces to Saudi Arabia to prevent further aggression by Iraq. He then built an international military coalition of more than thirty nations, including Egypt, France, Great Britain, Saudi Arabia, and Syria. The Bush administration also rallied international support for a harsh economic blockade of Iraq that was designed to force Hussein to give up Kuwait by completely cutting off his country's economy from the world.

During August and September the international coalition continued economic sanctions against Iraq while fortifying eastern Saudi Arabia against an Iraqi invasion. By the end of August the United States and its allies had enough forces in Saudi Arabia to deter an Iraqi attack. Recognizing this, the Iraqis began to fortify Kuwait against a possible coalition assault. Multinational consultation led by President Bush succeeded in isolating Iraq economically and

Demolished vehicles line Highway 80, the route fleeing Iraqi forces took as they retreated from Kuwait during Operation Desert Storm
Source: Department of Defense

diplomatically. In November Bush began to send more U.S. troops to Saudi Arabia, raising the number to about 450,000 from 230,000, to give the coalition the option of attacking Iraq. On November 29, at Bush's urging, the United Nations Security Council passed a resolution authorizing the use of force against Iraq if it did not withdraw from Kuwait by January 15, 1991. Further diplomatic efforts and international pressure failed to convince Saddam Hussein to withdraw.

Operation Desert Storm

On January 17, 1991, just after Bush's deadline had passed, coalition warplanes and ships began a devastating bombardment of Iraq. The bombing campaign seriously weakened Iraqi forces. Iraq launched missiles carrying explosive warheads against Israel in an attempt to draw the Israelis into the war. The Iraqis hoped to place the Arab members of the coalition in the awkward position of fighting beside Israel, their traditional enemy. Although Israel sustained some damage, it declined to enter the fight.

On February 24 the coalition launched an attack that overran Iraqi defenses and quickly liberated Kuwait. The ground phase of the war lasted just a hundred hours until February 28 when Bush gave the order to cease fire. Much of Iraq's most sophisticated military equipment was destroyed or captured. The six-week military operation, which was dubbed Operation Desert Storm, resulted in the deaths of about 125 American soldiers.

Despite the destruction of much of his military forces and uprisings by two Iraqi ethnic groups, Saddam Hussein remained in power in Iraq. The international community maintained economic sanctions on Iraq aimed at preventing Hussein from rebuilding his army and ultimately at forcing him from power.

Although Bush's handling of the crisis was praised by most experts and his public approval rating swelled to around 90 percent, critics charged that his administration had made some serious mistakes before the crisis began and at its conclusion. They said that the Bush administration had sent ambiguous diplomatic signals to Hussein that may have contributed to the Iraqi leader's belief that the United States would take no significant action against Iraq if it invaded Kuwait. Some critics also attacked Bush for not pressing the offensive at the end of the war to ensure that Hussein was removed from power. After the war the United Nations instituted a disarmament inspection process in Iraq. The process proved difficult over the years as inspectors often had trouble gaining Iraqi cooperation.

Mr. President, it is customary at joint sessions for the Chair to present the President to the Members of Congress directly and without further comment. But I wish to depart from tradition tonight and express to you on behalf of the Congress and the country, and through you to the members of our Armed Forces, our warmest congratulations on the brilliant victory of the Desert Storm Operation.

—House Speaker Tom Foley, *Address before a Joint Session of the Congress on the Cessation of the Persian Gulf Conflict, March 6, 1991*

Several years after the war ended, a large number of American military personnel who served in it complained of a debilitating illness, which became known as Gulf War Syndrome. The symptoms were thought to be caused by the fallout from the destruction of Iraqi chemical warfare stores. The Defense Department, which was castigated for its slowness in reacting to the illness, later agreed, but grudgingly. The Pentagon also was criticized for claiming higher success rates for the effectiveness of its "smart" weapons used in the January 1991 bombardment than were actually achieved.

Although problems persisted in the Persian Gulf, Bush had achieved his primary goals: protecting Middle East oil reserves, forcing Iraqi forces out of Kuwait, and weakening Saddam Hussein's capacity to threaten his neighbors militarily. He had demonstrated the capacity of the U.S. president to lead the international community in time of crisis.

But Bush had not toppled Saddam Hussein, and Bush's son, President George W. Bush, aimed to do just that. In 2003, in the wake of heightened domestic anxiety following the September 11 terrorist attacks, and claiming that Saddam Hussein possessed weapons of mass destruction that might be used against the United States, the junior Bush launched a new military campaign to topple the Hussein regime. (See IRAQ WAR).

> **More on this topic:**
>
> *Bush, George H. W., p. 52*
>
> *Iraq War, p. 296*
>
> *United Nations, p. 525*
>
> *War Powers Act of 1973, p. 560*

Personnel Management, Office of

The Office of Personnel Management (OPM) is an independent agency that sets and carries out personnel policies for the federal workforce. OPM was created by the Civil Service Reform Act of 1978, replacing the U.S. Civil Service Commission, which had been established in 1883 by the Pendleton Act. (See also CIVIL SERVICE and APPOINTMENT AND REMOVAL POWER.)

OPM has its headquarters in Washington, D.C., and maintains five regional offices as well as area offices in key locations nationwide. In 2003, OPM personnel policies covered a workforce of about 1.8 million federal employees. The director of OPM is appointed by the president with Senate confirmation and serves as chief adviser on personnel policies governing civilian employment in executive branch agencies and some legislative and judicial agencies. The director is appointed to a four-year term and can be removed only for cause. An incoming president may appoint a new director at any time.

As the U.S. government's central personnel agency, OPM is responsible for recruiting and examining federal employees under a merit system based on their knowledge and skills. Other responsibilities include providing development and training programs, classifying jobs, investigating personnel to support its selection and appointment processes, evaluating agency personnel programs, and overseeing pay administration.

OPM covers the federal civil service (General Schedule grades one through fifteen and Wage Grade, or blue-collar, positions) and also administers the Qualifications Review Board, an examining process for career Senior Executive Service appointments.

OPM oversees retirement and insurance programs for federal employees and enforces government policies on labor relations and affirmative action. It administers incentive awards for suggestions, inventions, and special acts, as well as the Presidential Rank Awards program for recognition of sustained outstanding accomplishment of career members of the Senior Executive Service.

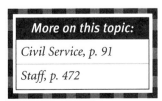

> **More on this topic:**
>
> *Civil Service, p. 91*
>
> *Staff, p. 472*

OPM initially included the Office of Government Ethics, which directs executive branch policies toward preventing conflicts of interest by executive branch personnel, but the ethics office became a separate executive agency in 1989.

Pierce, Franklin

Source: Library of Congress

Franklin Pierce (1804–1869) served as president from 1853 to 1857. His term was dominated by the brewing tensions over the slavery issue that led to the outbreak of the Civil War four years after he left office. His signing of the Kansas-Nebraska Act in 1854 provoked the first large-scale violence over slavery.

Pierce was born on November 23, 1804, in Hillsboro, New Hampshire. He graduated third in his class from Bowdoin College in Brunswick, Maine, in 1824. After college he studied law and was admitted to the bar in 1827. Two years later he was elected to the New Hampshire legislature while his father was governor.

Pierce left the New Hampshire legislature when he was elected to the U.S. House of Representatives in 1833 as a Jacksonian Democrat. In 1836 the New Hampshire legislature elected him to the U.S. Senate. When his term was up in 1842, he retired from the Senate at the urging of his wife, Jane Means Appleton Pierce, and returned to New Hampshire to practice law. In 1844 President James K. Polk appointed Pierce U.S. attorney for New Hampshire.

As U.S. attorney and chairman of the Democratic Party in New Hampshire, Pierce remained a powerful political figure, but he refused a series of high-level political appointments, partly because his wife did not want to move back to Washington, D.C. In 1845 Pierce declined an appointment to a vacant Senate seat and the New Hampshire Democratic gubernatorial nomination. In 1846 Polk offered him the U.S. attorney generalship, but Pierce again refused.

After the United States declared war on Mexico in 1846, Pierce accepted a commission as a colonel. Before he sailed for Mexico in May 1847, he was promoted to brigadier general. Pierce saw little action during his five and a half months in Mexico because of an intestinal ailment and an injury sustained when his horse fell. Nevertheless, in January 1848 he returned to a hero's welcome in Concord.

Pierce's rise to the presidency was sudden and unexpected. The 1852 Democratic nominating convention produced a stalemate among James Buchanan, Lewis Cass, William Marcy, and Stephen A. Douglas. Because none of these candidates was able to garner a majority of the votes, the convention began searching for a fifth candidate. On the forty-ninth ballot the Democrats nominated Franklin Pierce. As a northerner with southern sympathies and a spotless record, Pierce was an acceptable compromise candidate, although he had not served in an elective office since 1842. His Whig opponent was Gen. Winfield Scott, a hero of the Mexican-American War. Scott's campaign was crippled by the defection of many northern Whigs to the Free Soil Party. As was customary in the nineteenth century, Pierce remained in New Hampshire during the months before the election, letting his fellow Democrats campaign for him. The uncontroversial

Democratic platform of strict observance of the Compromise of 1850 gained Pierce a 254–42 victory in the Electoral College.

Pierce advocated tranquility at home and the extension of U.S. territories and commercial interests abroad. Most of his domestic policies favored the South. In his inaugural address he declared his belief that slavery was constitutional and that "states where it exists are entitled to efficient remedies" to enforce it. In 1854 Pierce signed the Kansas-Nebraska Act into law. It repealed the 1820 Missouri Compromise that had outlawed slavery north of 36°30′, thereby enabling Kansas to declare itself a slave state if its citizens favored that course. Pierce, who believed that each state should decide for itself whether to permit slavery, strongly supported the act, which had been sponsored by Illinois senator Stephen A. Douglas. The act, however, turned Kansas into a war zone. Pro-slavery southerners and abolitionist northerners raced into Kansas hoping to seize control of the territory's government for their side. Many atrocities were committed by both groups, causing the territory to be called "Bleeding Kansas."

In international affairs Pierce supported Millard Fillmore's initiative of sending Commodore Matthew Perry to Japan to open that country's ports to Western trade. Perry negotiated a treaty that gave U.S. ships access to two ports and guaranteed humane treatment of U.S. sailors shipwrecked off Japan's coast.

After leaving the presidency in 1857, Pierce never again sought public office. He and his wife traveled in Europe from 1857 to 1859 and then retired to their Concord, New Hampshire, home. Pierce died in Concord on October 8, 1869.

> **More on this topic:**
>
> *Oath of Office, p. 393*

Political Action Committees (PACs)

Political action committees (PACs) are organizations that raise and distribute campaign contributions to candidates for president, Congress, and other offices. Because of their explosive growth in numbers and influence, PACs for a time were one of the most controversial aspects of the CAMPAIGN FINANCING system. But by the mid-1990s the limited and well-disclosed activities of PACs seemed far less threatening than the massive amounts of unregulated money flooding the campaign system.

Organizations commonly thought of as PACs fall into two main categories. The first and largest category includes those PACs that are connected with specific economic interests in society, such as businesses, trade and professional associations, and labor unions. The Business-Industry Political Action Committee (BIPAC) and the AFL-CIO's Committee on Political Education are examples of this type of PAC.

PACs that are not connected to a labor organization or an incorporated entity make up the second category. These are the PACs of ideological and single-issue groups. They include the National Rifle Association's Political Victory Fund and EMILY's (Early Money Is Like Yeast) List, which donates to Democratic women candidates who support abortion rights.

This nonconnected category also includes a small but influential group of PACs within Congress called "leadership PACs" or "politicians' PACs." These PACs, which are separate from members' campaign committees, are set up by members to raise funds to achieve political goals other than reelection to Congress. The focus is usually on Congress; members contribute to other congressional candidates to win election to a leadership position, appointment to a prestigious committee, support for the party leadership, and the like. But members also may use such PACs as building blocks for a run for the White House. Besides widening their support with direct PAC contributions to election campaigns, they might use PAC money to defray the cost of such things

Top 10 Political Action Committees (PACs) by Contributions to Candidates and Other Committees (January 1, 2005–June 30, 2006)

Rank	Organization Managing the PAC	Contributions
1	National Association of Realtors	$2,363,505
2	National Beer Wholesalers Association	2,035,000
3	Association of Trial Lawyers of America	2,033,500
4	International Brotherhood of Electrical Workers	2,025,000
5	Credit Union National Association	1,790,939
6	National Auto Dealers Association	1,737,600
7	American Bankers Association	1,716,564
8	National Association of Home Builders	1,700,750
9	United Parcel Service	1,696,359
10	American Federation of State/County/Municipal Employees	1,532,601

SOURCE: Federal Election Commission; www.fec.gov/press/press2006/20060828pac/top_50_pac_contrib .pdf.

as polling or travel to early primary states.

Sometimes the term *political action committee* is used more broadly to refer to other types of political groups formed to influence elections. Such groups—nicknamed "stealth PACs"—were set up under Section 527 of the tax code and initially were not subject to regulation under federal campaign finance law. Legislation requiring that these groups register with the Internal Revenue Service and disclose most of their receipts and expenditures was enacted in 2000.

Although PACs date back to the 1940s, their significance in political campaigns began with the passage in 1971 and 1974 of laws to reform campaign financing. The laws, along with FEDERAL ELECTION COMMISSION (FEC) and Supreme Court rulings, allowed PACs to become a major factor in the financing of elections. In 1974 only about six hundred PACs were registered, and PACs gave about $12.5 million to House and Senate candidates. By 2000 there were more than 3,800 PACs registered with the FEC, and nearly $248 million in PAC money went to federal candidates running for office in 2000.

But for several reasons only a fraction of that $248 million went into the presidential campaign—$2.6 million, to be exact. PACs may contribute up to $5,000 to presidential primary candidates, but only relatively small contributions from individuals are eligible for matching with federal funds. Most candidates in the primaries therefore spend their time courting individual donors instead of PACs. In the general campaign, PACs may contribute another $5,000 to the presidential nominees, unless the candidates accept public funding, as most do. Publicly funded candidates are barred from accepting nearly all private contributions to their campaigns.

PACs also may make independent expenditures for or against candidates, so long as they do not coordinate their activities with a presidential campaign. About $43.5 million in PAC money went for independent expenditures in the 2004 presidential race.

Nevertheless, the money of corporations, labor unions, and other special interests found its way into presidential campaigns. Indeed, the 1996 and 2000 presidential elections were awash in it, but at the time that money was beyond the reach of federal campaign finance law. It was the excesses of those campaigns that sparked the 2000 law to shine a light on the activities of Section 527 groups, as well as the Bipartisan Campaign Reform Act of 2002 (also known as the McCain-Feingold bill), a law intended to root out unregulated "soft money" from the federal election process.

More on this topic:

Campaign Financing, p. 71

Elections and Campaigns, p. 168

Federal Election Commission, p. 212

Political Parties

Political parties are the link between citizens and their leaders. In the broadest sense a political party is a coalition of people who join together to try to gain government power by winning elections. Members of a party supposedly share a loosely defined set of common beliefs, although wide differences of opinion and outlook may exist among members of the same party. Citizens rely on political parties to define issues, to support or oppose candidates on the basis of those issues, and then to carry out the agreed-upon policies when the party is in power.

The main role of the political parties is to nominate candidates for president, vice president, and members of Congress and then to work for their election. Congress itself is organized along party lines; the party that has a majority of seats in each chamber controls all positions of authority. Parties also put forward candidates for most state and local elected offices and help elected leaders at all levels of government to mobilize support for their programs.

Political parties do not claim the allegiance of voters as they once did. Presidents and the public now interact through the media, public opinion polls, and interest groups, with less reliance on political parties.

The organizational connections between the presidency and parties have largely eroded. This erosion can be attributed to changes in presidential selection procedures and practices, the structure of the presidential offices, and the decline of PATRONAGE.

Nevertheless, presidential aspirants still seek the party nomination to authorize and legitimize their candidacies, and they run for office under the party label and the symbolism it evokes. Once elected, the president, more than any other individual, embodies the political party in the eyes of the general public. Indeed, the president serves as PARTY LEADER.

Emergence of Parties

The framers never envisioned how important political parties would become and did not mention them in the Constitution. However, the Constitution, especially the Bill of Rights, made possible a permanent role for parties by giving citizens civil liberties and the right to organize. At the same time it erected safeguards against partisan excesses by creating a system of checks and balances within the government.

National parties emerged soon after the adoption of the Constitution. Those who favored the strong central government embodied in the Constitution came to be called Federalists. Led by Treasury Secretary Alexander Hamilton, they were drawn mostly from merchants and bankers of the Northeast, who favored strong government action to foster economic development. They were opposed by a group that later became known as the Democratic-Republicans. Led by Thomas Jefferson and James Madison, the Democratic-Republicans were largely southern and western farmers who opposed a strong central government and favored government policies to make it easier to borrow money.

In the 1790s these two parties were government factions. By 1800, however, they were developing organizational means to appeal to the electorate to support the parties' candidates for public office. They also had a profound effect on the framers' design for choosing presidents.

The Constitution originally called for each member of the Electoral College to cast a single ballot with two names on it. The person receiving the most votes would become president, and the person receiving the second largest number of votes would become vice president. In the election of 1800 supporters of Thomas Jefferson openly sought the selection of electors committed to both Jefferson and his running mate, Aaron Burr. When the votes were counted, it turned out that Jefferson and Burr were tied for first place. The election was thrown into the House, which selected

Presidential candidate John F. Kennedy (left) and running mate Lyndon B. Johnson (right) talk with Eleanor Roosevelt at a Democratic Party rally in New York City, November 5, 1960.
Source: Library of Congress

Jefferson as president. In the aftermath, Congress passed the Twelfth Amendment to the Constitution, which was ratified in 1804. It provided that electors would cast two separate ballots, one for president and one for vice president.

For the next twenty years the Democratic-Republicans dominated the national government. The party caucus selected the presidential ticket and exercised a great deal of power over Congress's operations. With the demise of the Federalist Party in the 1816 elections the Democratic-Republicans became the only national political party.

The development of internal factions soon began to pull the party apart. By the mid-1820s two groups had emerged: the National Republicans, who favored internal economic development projects and a protective tariff against foreign imports, and the Democrats, who represented agrarian interests from the South and West and held that the common people, not the rich, should have the dominant voice in government.

Development of the Two-Party System

The Democrats, led by Andrew Jackson, won the White House in 1828 and were to remain the dominant party in Congress for the next three decades. The National Republicans, who soon took the name of Whigs, twice won the presidency and always held a substantial number of seats in Congress. But the slavery issue split the Whigs badly, and the party ceased to exist in 1856. The Republican Party took its place, and the rivalry between the Democratic and Republican parties has endured ever since.

The Republicans lost their first national campaign in 1856, but won the White House in 1860 when a former Whig, Abraham Lincoln, defeated the divided Democratic Party. After the Union won the Civil War, the Republicans dominated U.S. politics for seventy years with little opposition. Between 1860 and 1932 the Democrats won the presidency only in 1884 and 1892, with Grover Cleveland on the ticket, and in 1912 and 1916, with Woodrow Wilson.

The Republicans maintained their leadership through vigorous pursuit of a national economic policy. The federal government aided economic expansion with a high tariff system, funding of exploration and transportation, limitations on labor unions, and tight money policies. Even under Democrat Grover Cleveland the nation followed conservative policies. Particularly on labor relations and monetary policy, the most important issues of the time, Cleveland pursued basically Republican politics.

Republican dominance ended with the stock market crash of October 29, 1929, when Herbert C. Hoover was in the White House. Hoover was regarded with such enmity by so many voters that nearly any Democrat would have been elected in 1932. After Democrat Franklin D. Roosevelt won the White House that year, he proceeded to change the face of U.S. politics. Under the coalition that Roosevelt built, the Democrats were the dominant party for the next three decades. The New Deal coalition included southerners, blacks, organized labor, some business leaders and bankers, urbanites, Catholics, and Jews. The Democrats won seven of the next nine presidential elections. The only Republican winner between 1932 and 1964 was Dwight D. Eisenhower (in 1952 and 1956), who was wooed by the Democrats before he decided to run as a Republican. But Republicans won seven of the ten presidential elections held from 1968 to 2004. Significant defections from the

Democrats among white southerners, the middle class, and blue-collar workers contributed to the Republican presidential successes.

In Congress neither party has consistently held the upper hand since 1968. With the exception of the Senate during the first six years of Republican Ronald Reagan's administration, the Democrats controlled Congress until 1994, when Republicans won control of both houses of Congress for the first time since the Eisenhower administration. The Democrats took back narrow control of the Senate in mid-2001, when a Republican senator left the party to become an independent but voted with the Democrats, giving them a majority. But the Democrats lost control of the Senate again in the 2002 midterm elections. The 2006 election was a watershed, however, as the Republicans lost control of both houses of Congress for the first time since 1994, resulting in the election of Nancy Pelosi (D-Calif.) as the first female Speaker of the House.

The Democrats had dominated governorships and legislatures in most states since the Roosevelt revolution, but the Democratic Party's hold on statehouses slipped in the 1990s before recovering after the 2006 elections. In 1998 thirty-two governors were Republican, seventeen were Democrats, and one was an independent. The 2006 midterm elections, however, resulted in a lead for the Democrats: twenty-eight Democratic governors to twenty-two Republicans.

Studies have shown that the high degree of loyalty voters once felt to a particular party is waning. Straight-ticket voting once prevailed, but in recent years voters have shown an increasing inclination to split their tickets, leading some commentators to conclude that Americans prefer divided government.

Party Decline

The decline of the dominant role of parties in American political life can be attributed to several developments. One is the explosion of the mass media. In the 1800s and early 1900s the voting public depended on political parties as a guide in choosing among candidates and understanding political issues. Today television, radio, newspapers, magazines, and the Internet communicate an abundance of information on politics and politicians directly to the voters.

Another development is the decline of patronage. The spoils system, which allowed the victorious party to install loyal followers in government jobs, all but disappeared by the late 1900s. No longer could the parties establish and maintain ties with citizens by holding out prospects of jobs and the status associated with them.

Yet another factor is the growth of the welfare state. Before the New Deal of the 1930s neither the federal government nor the states provided much in the way of help to the needy. Political parties, particularly the urban political machines, began to fill that void. At times, the party machine provided food, clothing, and shelter directly. More often, the parties enabled new immigrants to take part in the political process. Newcomers looked to the parties when problems arose that involved government. Since the New Deal, however, government in general—and the federal government in particular—has supplied many of these services, supplanting the urban political machines in the process.

A change in the way candidates are nominated also has contributed to the decline of political parties. For much of the nineteenth and twentieth centuries the party organization exercised tight control over this process. Aspirants to the presidency and other elected offices had to receive the endorsement of the party organization to pursue their electoral ambitions. The reforms of the late 1960s and early 1970s that opened the presidential nominating system to wider popular participation diminished the role of the party. The proliferation of presidential primaries strengthened the direct relationship between the candidates and the public. At the same time, primaries open the party's nomination to candidates not necessarily approved by the party organization and perhaps even antagonistic to it.

Presidents Gerald R. Ford and Ronald Reagan stand at the podium at the 1976 Republican national convention, Kansas City, Missouri.
Source: Library of Congress

Still, the party system is not dead. Some political scientists suggest that the country is in a period of political "dealignment"—that is, a breakup of traditional alliances without an obvious set of new ones.

The Democrats' victories in 1992 and 1996 added to the uncertainty. Bill Clinton, who portrayed himself as a different kind of Democrat, made deep inroads into Republican strongholds in the suburbs. He made the best showing for a Democrat among independents and among white voters since 1964, and he reclaimed some traditionally Democratic blue-collar areas that recently had voted Republican. In 2001 the Republicans returned to the White House when their presidential nominee, Texas governor George W. Bush, narrowly prevailed in a disputed election against Vice President Al Gore. At the outset of the twenty-first century, then, the two major parties were highly competitive in presidential politics, with neither holding a decisive advantage. Minor parties continue to lurk on the periphery, but the electoral arrangements preclude prospects for their winning the White House. These parties can and do, however, affect outcomes in the states by drawing enough support away from the major parties to determine the winner.

Party Organization

The formal machinery of the parties parallels government organization in the United States. At every level of government—national, state, and local—there is a corresponding unit of party organization.

Party organization at the national level dates back to the time of Andrew Jackson, when the first nominating conventions were held. Replacing the discredited congressional caucus as a nominating device, the quadrennial convention brought together state delegations to name the party's presidential ticket.

An institution convening for a few days every four years can hardly exercise power and authority within a political party. Early on, in the 1840s, the Democratic national convention established a national committee to oversee the conduct of the presidential campaign and to guide the party's fortunes between conventions. When the Republican Party was formed a few years later, it adopted a similar arrangement.

These national committees consisted of representatives of the state and local parties, chosen by the state parties according to party rules and state law. The national committees are run by a chair, with support from a headquarters staff. By recent custom the national committee has deferred to the party's presidential nominee in electing its chair. Usually the chair has been a state party leader, a member or former member of Congress, or a political associate of the presidential nominee. State and local parties are structured along varying but roughly parallel lines.

Although the party organization developed largely to support the process of nominating and electing a president, in recent years it has become increasingly superfluous to presidential politics. National committees that used to play a significant role in organizing the presidential campaign have been replaced by the candidates' personal campaign staffs. National party chairs were once important political advisers to presidents, keeping them in touch with state and local elected leaders. Today presidents rely for that advice on aides within the White House and on polling organizations that provide an abundance of data about public opinion.

State and local party bosses virtually controlled the presidential selection process until the 1960s. Conventions featured "smoke-filled rooms" where party leaders gathered to wheel and deal for the presidential nomination. Astute presidential candidates sought the support of these grass-roots leaders and were beholden to those bosses who backed them at the convention and mounted get-out-the-vote campaigns to elect them. Modern presidential candidates use the medium of television to appeal directly to the voters.

Outside the arena of presidential politics, however, the national party staffs make significant contributions, primarily in campaign assistance and other services to state and local parties. The national parties actively engage in candidate recruitment. They offer training sessions and make available information and expertise for the benefit of the parties' nominees, particularly those running for Congress. They may provide research, polling, data processing, direct mail, consultants, and money in vast quantities.

More on this topic:
Congressional Caucus (King Caucus), p. 118
National Party Conventions, p. 375
Party Leader, p. 396
Patronage, p. 398
Third Parties, p. 498

Polk, James K.

Source: Library of Congress

Many historians have called James Knox Polk (1795–1849) the best president who served in the interval between Andrew Jackson and Abraham Lincoln. He also was the first "dark-horse" presidential candidate of a major party.

Polk was born on November 2, 1795, in Mecklenburg County, North Carolina. He was the eldest of ten children born to a prosperous North Carolina farmer and his wife. When Polk was ten his family moved to Duck River, Tennessee, a settlement on the edge of the frontier. As a boy he was frail and often ill. When he was seventeen he survived an operation to remove gallstones; his health improved dramatically after the surgery.

In 1818 Polk graduated with honors from the University of North Carolina. He then moved to Nashville, Tennessee, where he studied law for two years before being admitted to the bar. He married Sarah Childress on January 1, 1824.

Polk began his political career in the Tennessee legislature in 1823 at the age of twenty-seven. Two years later he was elected to the U.S. House of Representatives from Andrew Jackson's former district. Polk rose quickly to positions of power in the House, becoming chairman of the Ways and Means Committee, majority leader, and finally Speaker in 1835. He earned the nickname "Young Hickory" because of his unswerving support for Andrew Jackson.

In 1839 Polk left the House when the Democratic Party in Tennessee drafted him as its candidate for governor. He won that election and served a two-year term. He ran for reelection in 1841 and 1843, but was defeated both times by the Whig candidate.

At the 1844 Democratic national convention in Baltimore, Polk's political career was resurrected dramatically from the gubernatorial defeats. Martin Van Buren was favored to receive the Democratic presidential nomination, but neither he nor his chief rival, Lewis Cass, could muster the two-thirds vote required to secure the nomination. With the balloting deadlocked, the con-

vention turned unanimously to Polk as a compromise candidate. In the general election campaign Polk stood on a party platform that advocated annexation of Texas and a settlement with Britain that would fix the northern boundary of Oregon at latitude 54°40'. He also received the endorsement of Andrew Jackson. In the election Polk defeated his better-known Whig opponent, Henry Clay, by a vote of 170–105 in the Electoral College, but the race was closer than the electoral vote indicates. Polk received only forty thousand more popular votes than Clay, and he won New York's thirty-six electoral votes—which would have given Clay a 141–134 victory—by just five thousand votes.

In further vindication of our rights and defense of our territory, I invoke the prompt action of Congress to recognize the existence of the war, and to place at the disposition of the Executive the means of prosecuting the war with vigor, and thus hastening the restoration of peace.

—*James K. Polk,* Message to Congress, May 11, 1846

The most important issue confronting the new president was westward expansion. Polk and most of the nation wished to resolve the Oregon boundary question with Great Britain, acquire California and other lands in the Southwest from Mexico, and annex Texas. An agreement signed in 1818 provided for joint U.S.-British ownership of the Oregon Territory, which extended north of California to above the fifty-fourth parallel. Although Polk had campaigned on the slogan "54°40' or fight"—the battle cry of those who wanted all of the Oregon Territory—he offered to divide Oregon with the British at the forty-ninth parallel. When Great Britain refused, Congress, at Polk's request, terminated the joint ownership agreement on April 23, 1846. Realizing that lack of a settlement could mean war, the British accepted the president's original offer.

Three days before Polk's inauguration President John Tyler had signed a joint resolution annexing Texas, as Polk had advocated during his campaign. The southern border of Texas, however, remained in dispute. In 1846 Polk sent U.S. troops under Gen. Zachary Taylor into the territory between the Nueces River and the Rio Grande. The action was provocative because the area was claimed by both Mexico and Texas but occupied by Mexicans. Polk had already decided to ask Congress for a declaration of war when news reached Washington that Mexican forces had attacked the U.S. contingent. The president then claimed that Mexico was the aggressor. Congress declared war despite opposition from some northern lawmakers. U.S. forces under Taylor and Gen. Winfield Scott won major victories over the Mexican army and eventually occupied Mexico City. In 1848 Mexico agreed to the Treaty of Guadalupe Hidalgo, which ceded California and New Mexico to the United States in return for $15 million and recognized the Rio Grande as the boundary of Texas.

In domestic policy Polk also achieved his major goals. With his backing, Congress narrowly passed the Walker Tariff Act in 1846, which greatly reduced tariffs. Although the bill was opposed in the North, it stimulated free trade and the U.S. economy. Polk also persuaded Congress to pass an independent treasury bill in 1846, which reestablished the system of federal subtreasuries first set up under Van Buren to handle government funds. Before Polk reestablished the subtreasuries, these funds were deposited in state banks.

More on this topic:

Historic Milestones of the Presidency, p. 253

Mexican-American War of 1846, p. 361

At the beginning of his term Polk reputedly told a friend that his four main goals as president were resolution of the territorial dispute over Oregon, acquisition of California and New Mexico, a lower tariff, and reestablishment of a subtreasury system. He achieved all four goals.

Upon entering office, Polk had declared that he would not run for a second term. He kept his promise in 1848 by not seeking the Democratic presidential nomination. After attending Zachary Taylor's inauguration, the former president left Washington for his recently purchased home in Nashville. Polk, who worked long hours and almost never took a day off during his presidency, did not enjoy a lengthy retirement. The stress of his work schedule may have weakened his health. He died in Nashville on June 15, 1849, at the age of fifty-three, only three and a half months after leaving office.

Polls   *See* PUBLIC OPINION AND THE PRESIDENCY.

President of the Senate   *See* VICE PRESIDENT.

Presidential Greatness

One approach to the presidency taken by historians has been to rate each chief executive's performance in office, then rank the presidents in relation to one another. In doing so, historians are participating in a favorite American pastime, listing and ranking everything from the ten best movies of the year to the top forty songs. But historians also hope to learn from their ratings by determining the qualities and circumstances that make a president great, average, or a failure.

Perhaps the best-known ratings of presidents are those of the Harvard University historian Arthur M. Schlesinger Sr., who conducted the first presidential rating survey in 1948 and repeated his poll in 1962. In his first poll Schlesinger asked fifty-five distinguished historians to evaluate each president as great, near great, average, below average, or a failure. The only yardstick Schlesinger offered was that the evaluations had to be based solely on the president's performance in office, not on what he did either before or after.

Schlesinger's survey found a high degree of consensus among historians about which presidents belonged in each of the categories. Six presidents were judged great— Abraham Lincoln, George Washington, Franklin D. Roosevelt, Woodrow Wilson, Thomas Jefferson, and Andrew Jackson, in that order. Theodore Roosevelt, Grover Cleveland, John Adams, and James K. Polk were rated as near great. All the others were rated as average or below average, except for Ulysses S. Grant and Warren G. Harding, who were branded failures.

In 1962 Schlesinger polled a somewhat wider group and obtained similar results. The only significant changes were that Jackson slipped to near great, and Harry S. Truman, who had been in office during the first poll, was placed in the same category.

Assessing the results of his two polls, Schlesinger sought to draw some conclusions about the qualities that cause a president to be ranked high, low, or in between. He concluded that the great presidents were those who, among other things, were "lucky in their times: they are all identified with some crucial turning point in our history." Washington and the birth of the Republic,

Despite criticisms that surveys of scholars produce inherently biased results, a degree of consistency exists in terms of which presidents are ranked as great or near great, and which are failures, or close to being labeled as failures. This consistency spans over half a century, includes large and small sample sizes of respondents, and exists among polls including respondents from a wide range of ideological predispositions. Washington, Lincoln, and Franklin Roosevelt are identified as great presidents in the five major surveys examined. In addition, Harding is consistently listed as a failure. Grant, James Buchanan, and Franklin Pierce all fall either into the failure category or near the bottom of those considered below average. Interestingly, the Gallup Organization, known for its public opinion surveys, regularly queries the public's rating of presidents. Since 1999, John F. Kennedy and Reagan consistently emerge as two of the public's greatest presidents.

COMPARISON OF PRESIDENTIAL RANKINGS

	Schlesinger		Maranell	Murray -Blessing	Wall Street Journal
Year	1948	1962	1968	1981	2000
Sample size	55	75	571	953	78
Top rankings					
Washington	2	2	2	3	1
Lincoln	1	1	1	1	2
Franklin Roosevelt	3	3	3	2	3
Bottom rankings					
Pierce	27	28	28	31	37
Buchanan	26	29	30	33	39
Grant	28	30	32	35	32
Harding	29	31	33	36	38
Total ranked	**29**	**31**	**33**	**36**	**39**

Jefferson and the opportunity for national expansion, Jackson and the rise of agrarian democracy, Lincoln and the Civil War, Wilson and World War I, Franklin Roosevelt and the Great Depression and World War II—the times provided each of these presidents with a real chance for presidential leadership.

The great presidents also shared some personal and political qualities, Schlesinger observed. Notable among these were moral strength and the desire for power. Each left the office of the presidency stronger than when he assumed it, and each knew how to get his way with Congress. On the other hand, Schlesinger noted, the great presidents were somewhat inattentive to the responsibilities for administering the federal departments and frequently had to endure harsh criticism from the press.

The near-great presidents, Schlesinger continued, shared many of the qualities of the greats but had less opportunity for greatness and were not as forceful as leaders. Average presidents tended to be overshadowed by Congress, and the administrations of the two presidential failures, Grant and Harding, were marked by extensive corruption.

The Schlesinger polls inspired many later surveys. The numbers of historians and others surveyed have increased in later polls, but the results have not changed significantly, although there have been some minor shifts. In 1981, for example, two scholars at Pennsylvania State University surveyed nearly one thousand historians and found that Lincoln, Franklin Roosevelt, Washington, and Jefferson remained in the first rank of presidents, and that Roosevelt had passed Washington for second place, behind Lincoln.

A poll conducted in 1996 by Schlesinger's son, Arthur M. Schlesinger Jr., contained few surprises: Lincoln, Washington, and Franklin Roosevelt were listed as great, and Jefferson, Jackson, Theodore Roosevelt, Wilson, Truman, and Polk were listed as near great. Dwight D. Eisenhower, who had fared poorly in the 1962 poll, had risen to tenth, leading the high average list.

In late 2000 Northwestern University law professors James Lindgren and Steven G. Calabresi conducted a poll of scholars for the *Wall Street Journal*. In this study Washington was ranked as the greatest of the great presidents—the other two considered great were Lincoln and Franklin Roosevelt—and Ronald Reagan was ranked eighth, between Truman and Eisenhower in the near-great category.

Some scholars have criticized the effort to assess presidents through such surveys. The historian Thomas A. Bailey, for example, has argued that the ratings tend to reflect the "brainwashing" of historians, who, like every other American, are subjected from an early age to images of certain presidents as great, whether on coins or on monuments in the nation's capital or on Mount Rushmore. Moreover, Bailey contended, historians and other academics tend on average to be more liberal than many other Americans, and their lists sometimes give higher ratings to Democratic presidents and lower rankings to Republicans. Yet when Bailey did his own poll, with forty-three yardsticks measuring presidential greatness included in his questionnaires, his final rankings virtually mirrored those of Arthur Schlesinger Sr.

In addition to bias, Bailey argued that the ratings were flawed because they reflected the circumstances into which a president was thrust more than his response to them. Presidents in the nineteenth century frequently had little chance to seem great because strong presidential leadership was not valued in that era.

As critics of the historians' polls suggest, surveys that rate the presidents may reveal as much about the scholars who assign the ratings as about the presidents. At the least, such surveys demonstrate the standards by which historians most often evaluate presidents—notably, moral strength and the desire for power.

Presidential Medal of Freedom

Source: File photo

Created by President John F. Kennedy in 1963, the Presidential Medal of Freedom is the cultural equivalent of the Congressional Medal of Honor, the nation's highest award for heroism on the battlefield.

Shortly after he took office in 1961, Kennedy decided to use the award to infuse the nation with a new sense of energy, idealism, and pride in its achievements. The White House used the idea of an older medal, the Medal of Freedom, created in 1945 by President Harry S. Truman to reward contributions to the country's national security. Kennedy's executive order renamed the medal and established new, broad-based criteria for awarding it to individuals who had made "especially meritorious contributions to (1) the security or national interests of the United States, or (2) world peace, or (3) cultural or other significant public or private endeavors."

The first awards ceremony was scheduled for December 6, 1963. Kennedy was assassinated in November, but his widow, Jacqueline, who had helped to design the medal, and Kennedy's successor, Lyndon B. Johnson, decided the ceremony should be held as scheduled to promote national healing.

The president decides who gets the medal, a highly coveted honor, and only about 400 had been awarded as of early 2007. The winners have come from diverse backgrounds: scientists, writers and journalists, artists, government officials, movie stars, and sports figures. It also has been awarded to a few foreign dignitaries, including a posthumous medal to the slain Egyptian leader Anwar el-Sadat.

Richard Nixon conceived of the idea of giving the award to people in the same discipline and holding a group ceremony. The April 1970 gala produced an unintended irony, however. Nixon awarded the medal to eight leading journalists; a few years later, the relentless media coverage of the Watergate scandal would drive him from office.

President Bill Clinton revived the idea of grouping recipients, presenting medals to five noted social reformers, including two former justices of the Supreme Court, in a 1993 ceremony. After his 1996 reelection Clinton chose his defeated opponent, Sen. Robert J. Dole, as a 1997 recipient, honoring Dole's military heroism and distinguished legislative career.

Through 2006 George W. Bush had honored sixty-four people including B. B. King, Muhammad Ali, Pope John Paul II, and Nancy Reagan. In December 2004 Bush presented the award to former Central Intelligence Agency director George

More on this topic:

Chief of State, p. 86

Tenet, Iraq Coalition Provisional Authority head L. Paul Bremer, and General Tommy Franks, three key players in the Iraq War. This action stirred controversy among critics of the intelligence used to justify the war and of the failures of the initial stages of the occupation.

Press Conferences

President George W. Bush speaks to the press at Barksdale Air Force Base in Louisiana shortly after the September 11, 2001, terrorist attacks.
Source: Reuters

With the possible exception of election campaign debates between presidential candidates, televised news conferences provide the American people with the best opportunity to see their president in the act of thinking and speaking. Much more than presidential speeches, which are written in advance and presented in a carefully managed setting, the press conference gives a picture of how the president grapples with the issues of the day.

Indeed, some analysts have elevated the press conference almost to the status of an important institution of government, although press conferences are neither mentioned in the Constitution nor required by an act of Congress. Students of government suggest that the conferences have become a way of holding presidents accountable and forcing them to explain their policies, in much the same way that question-and-answer sessions in the British parliamentary system bring prime ministers to task.

Since Woodrow Wilson began the practice of holding presidential press conferences, chief executives have reacted differently to the need to appear before reporters, depending on their personalities, communication strengths and weaknesses, and political situations.

In keeping with the long-standing tradition of presidential aloofness to the press, Wilson and his immediate successors sought to control press appearances. Questions had to be submitted in writing, and reporters often were prohibited from quoting the president directly. The first president to have a knack for easy verbal give-and-take with reporters was Franklin D. Roosevelt, who made his answers to spontaneous questions into an important method of communicating his message to the public. Roosevelt proved to be a master of the informal press conference, holding nearly a thousand during his twelve years in office. Other presidents have not excelled in the art. For example, Dwight D. Eisenhower, who introduced televised press conferences, often seemed ill at ease and tended to answer questions in a garbled syntax that confused listeners.

John F. Kennedy found the televised news conference an ideal forum. His youth, good looks, and comfortable rapport with reporters came across perfectly on television. His press conferences attracted large audiences, and viewers responded favorably to his polished persona.

◉ **CLOSER LOOK**

The most famous White House correspondent is Helen Thomas, who served United Press International and Hearst News Service before resigning in 2000 to become an independent correspondent. In 1960 she began covering John. F. Kennedy's campaign for president and in 1961 began regularly covering presidential press conferences. Thomas has been a fixture at the White House for almost fifty years and has sometimes been referred to as the "First Lady of the Press." Her reputation has earned her the respect of presidents to the degree that, until the presidency of George W. Bush, she was seated in

continued

For some chief executives, the combination of an instantaneous command of a wide range of policy issues and a telegenic personality has often proved elusive. Richard Nixon, for example, had a solid grasp of the issues but tended to avoid televised sessions because of his strong distrust of the press. Ronald Reagan was adept at reaching the voters through televised speeches, but he tended to stumble or misstate the facts when forced to give impromptu answers.

Although many presidents have not been particularly well equipped to deal with press conferences, the institution itself provides them with powerful advantages. Basically, press conferences belong to the president, who, in fact, controls them.

The president decides when a press conference will be held, sets the ground rules, selects the reporters who will ask questions, and decides what information may be divulged. Sometimes presidents may evade a question by making a joke or pleading inability to reply because of national security concerns. They can decline to answer a question without giving a reason, and they may abruptly change the tone and direction of the questions by calling on a friendly reporter.

Presidents enjoy still other, invisible advantages in press conferences. By scheduling conferences at long intervals, they can ensure that reporters will ask a wide range of relatively superficial questions. Because so many reporters attend press conferences, there is little chance that any one journalist will be able to probe deeply into the president's thinking. Reporters traditionally have been allowed to ask only one question apiece, although the Reagan administration instituted the policy of allowing a follow-up question.

The biggest danger to presidents is that they will make a misstatement or inadvertently give away some information they had not wanted revealed. Presidents must be meticulous and cautious, yet informative and affable. A single wrong word or gesture can send tremors around the world or acutely embarrass the administration.

For members of the news media, presidential press conferences offer a chance to assert themselves as the "fourth branch of government" in the limelight of national television. Washington reporters today have almost equal billing with the president within the theatrics of the press conference, and their performance is scrutinized almost as closely as that of the president.

Yet the press's role at these events is full of contradiction. On the one hand, reporters are faulted for asking soft questions that presidents can exploit to their advantage; on the other hand, they are sometimes accused of being rude and unnecessarily hostile.

> **More on this topic:**
>
> Media and the
> Presidency, p. 355
>
> Speeches and Rhetoric,
> p. 466

Defenders of the press maintain that asking presidents to justify their policies is a critical function in a democracy. As the format and function of press conferences have changed, however, there is a sense that they have declined in significance. Presidential press conferences have become more confrontational than informational, more choreography and theater than legitimate news, more of a personal exhibition than an opportunity to understand the president's actions. Some observers wonder whether the press conference may soon outlive its usefulness either to the president or to the press.

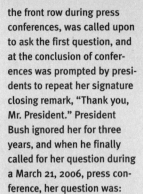

CLOSER LOOK

the front row during press conferences, was called upon to ask the first question, and at the conclusion of conferences was prompted by presidents to repeat her signature closing remark, "Thank you, Mr. President." President Bush ignored her for three years, and when he finally called for her question during a March 21, 2006, press conference, her question was:

Q: I'd like to ask you, Mr. President, your decision to invade Iraq has caused the deaths of thousands of Americans and Iraqis, wounds of Americans and Iraqis for a lifetime. Every reason given, publicly at least, has turned out not to be true. My question is, why did you really want to go to war? From the moment you stepped into the White House, from your Cabinet officers, intelligence people, and so forth—what was your real reason? You have said it wasn't oil, quest for oil—it hasn't been Israel, or anything else. What was it?

THE PRESIDENT: I think your premise—in all due respect to your question and to you as a lifelong journalist—is that—I didn't want war. To assume I wanted war is just flat wrong, Helen, in all due respect. . . .

—*George W. Bush*, *News Conference*, March 21, 2006

Press Secretary, Presidential

The White House press secretary is one of the most visible officials in the government. As the presidency has grown in power and visibility since the early twentieth century, and with the advent of modern communication media such as radio, television, and the Internet, the White House press secretary has become a household name, frequently seen on nightly newscasts promoting the administration's agenda. The press secretary is never far from the president's side and is kept informed of virtually all policy decisions by the president and top White House aides.

The press secretary serves as the principal conduit of news and messages from the president and major agencies to the press, creator and protector of the president's image, contact for representatives of the print and broadcast media, and adviser in the art of communication. In addition, the press secretary can help to keep a president informed about trends in public opinion.

The press secretary also serves as administrator of the White House press–public relations office. With the increased emphasis on media politics, this office has become one of the largest divisions of the presidential complex, with roughly fifty employees in recent administrations.

The press secretary's first and overriding obligation is to the president, not the press. The chief job of the press secretary is to show the president in the best possible light and to attract public support for the president's programs. Although the press secretary has a general obligation to provide the truth to the public, many have sought to stretch or bend the facts to aid the president, and some have later admitted that they lied outright.

While nineteenth-century presidents had little direct dealings with reporters, some chief executives had aides who acted as the guardians of their public image and managers of their press relationships. The position of press secretary did not begin to evolve until the administration of Woodrow Wilson. His aide, Joseph P. Tumulty, coordinated his schedule and served as his adviser on the press. The first formally designated presidential press secretary was George Akerson, who served under Herbert C. Hoover.

The modern concept of the position stems from Franklin D. Roosevelt's aide, Stephen T. Early, a former Associated Press reporter. Early was the first press secretary whose name became familiar to the public, and it was during his tenure that the press secretary's function became permanently established.

The pattern for modern White House media operations was set by James C. Hagerty, a former *New York Times* reporter who served for eight years as Dwight D. Eisenhower's press secretary. Hagerty, who enjoyed the confidence of both Eisenhower and White House journalists, was highly effective in creating organizational and operational techniques that became models for later press secretaries. Hagerty's talent was particularly evident on the three occasions when Eisenhower became seriously ill.

Subsequent press secretaries have had to deal with the political and other problems facing their presidents. Pierre Salinger, for example, had to face White House reporters during the Cuban missile crisis, when John F. Kennedy's confrontation with the Soviet Union brought the world to the brink of nuclear war. Lyndon B. Johnson's three press secretaries had to deal with his resentment of what he thought was his unfair treatment by the press over Vietnam.

The press secretary position may have reached a low point under Richard Nixon. Nixon appointed Ronald L. Ziegler to oversee a press operation that he had restructured to control the flow of information. But Ziegler was never included fully in the decision-making process, so his effectiveness was severely diminished. During the Watergate scandal, White House relations with the press became strained to the breaking point, and Ziegler and the press corps faced each other amid great tension and mistrust. Ziegler later conceded that some of the information he gave out during the crisis was incorrect, but he claimed that he had not been told by the president or his top aides what the facts really were.

Ronald Reagan's first press secretary, James S. Brady, served in his post for only two months before he was seriously wounded during an assassination attempt on the president. Brady kept his title but never returned to work, and his duties were assumed by Larry Speakes. Speakes, who was generally not included in the highest ranks of presidential aides, created considerable controversy after he left office by admitting in his memoirs that on more than one occasion he had fabricated quotes of the president.

Jody Powell, who served under Jimmy Carter, was a different sort of press secretary. Along with chief of staff Hamilton Jordan, Powell was Carter's closest aide and adviser and was widely recognized as having the complete confidence of the president and full access to information. Powell faced a difficult test in the spring of 1980 during the Iran hostage crisis. Asked directly whether the United States was preparing an attempt to rescue the hostages, Powell said it was not— even though he had been informed shortly before by Carter that a raid would begin soon. Although the rescue attempt later ended in disaster, Powell insisted afterward that he had done the right thing by lying in order to preserve the secrecy of the mission.

President George W. Bush and outgoing press secretary Scott McClellan introduce the new White House press secretary, Tony Snow, to the press.
Source: The White House

Because of the structure of the communications office in the Clinton administration, his first press secretary, Dee Dee Myers, the first woman to hold the post, was not part of the information loop of the president's top advisers. The media felt Myers was not fully informed, and, as a result, some hostility existed that reflected in negative coverage for Clinton. Michael McCurry, who replaced Myers in 1994, was made an integral part of the information loop, which helped mollify the media. He also proved masterly at managing the information flow from the White House. McCurry and his deputy, Joe Lockhart, who succeeded him in the fall of 1998, faced a difficult situation during the Monica Lewinsky scandal and subsequent presidential impeachment. McCurry deliberately took himself "out of the loop" so that he could truthfully plead ignorance of the affair between Clinton and Lewinsky.

George W. Bush's first press secretary, Ari Fleischer, was somewhat eclipsed by Karen Hughes, a longtime Bush aide who held the title of counselor to the president. Hughes, who left the White House after the first year and a half of Bush's tenure, managed the president's communications, including oversight of Fleischer's office. After Fleischer resigned in 2003, Scott McClellan served Bush until 2006 when Fox News anchor Tony Snow assumed the position.

Some observers were surprised that Bush chose Snow who, as a reporter, had sometimes harshly criticized the administration. Snow was concerned that the exclusion of Bush's previous press secretaries from administration policy debates led to briefings where the press thought the secretary was ill informed. As a result, Snow insisted on being included in White House internal deliberations. After a year in his position, Snow has been a particularly colorful press secretary, known for his unusual candor and willingness to research matters about which he is not knowledgeable. His future as press secretary became uncertain in 2007. Snow is a colon cancer survivor, but in March of that year he announced that the disease had returned, this time in his liver. Snow returned to his post in April 2007 after taking leave to undergo treatment; his deputy, Dana Perino, held press briefings in his absence.

More on this topic:

Executive Office of the President, p. 200

Media and the Presidency, p. 355

Staff, p. 472

Primaries and Caucuses

Surrounded by family and other supporters, Arizona senator and presidential hopeful John McCain celebrates his victory over Texas governor George W. Bush in both the Michigan and Arizona primaries, February 22, 2000. The Michigan primary was a crucial victory for McCain, but Bush won a cluster of primaries on March 7, Super Tuesday, to clinch the Republican presidential nomination.
Source: Reuters

In recent years no presidential candidate in either major party has won the nomination without first winning a majority of his party's primary elections. Primaries allow the party's registered voters to express their preference for the party's nominee. Most of them also serve as the mechanism for choosing the party's delegates to the NA- TIONAL PARTY CONVENTIONS. Other delegates are chosen at meetings of party regulars, known as caucuses.

Before the Democratic Party initiated a series of DELEGATE SELEC- TION REFORMS in the early 1970s, state and national party leaders often chose the nominee without much regard for the wishes of rank-and-file party members. To win the nomination, the presidential candidates had to woo these officials, not the voters.

Primaries did not exist before the twentieth century, and their use in presidential races developed slowly. Even in the 1950s and 1960s presidential candidates often entered only a few primaries, to demonstrate that they could win votes. Vice President Hubert H. Humphrey won the Democratic nomination in 1968 without entering a single primary.

Not all states hold presidential primary elections, but most have done so in recent years. The remaining states have selected delegates to the national conventions through caucus procedures, and several states have used both methods.

Primaries

There are two basic types of presidential primaries. One is the presidential preference primary, in which people vote directly for the person they wish to be nominated for president. In the other type the voters select delegates to the national conventions. States may use various combinations of these methods:

- A state may have a preference vote but choose delegates at party conventions. The preference vote may or may not be binding on the delegates.
- A state may combine the preference and delegate selection primaries by electing delegates pledged to or favorable to a candidate named on the ballot. Under this system, however, state party organizations may run unpledged slates of delegates.
- A state may have an advisory preference vote and a separate delegate selection vote in which delegates may be listed as pledged to a candidate, favorable to a candidate, or unpledged.
- A state may have a mandatory preference vote with a separate delegate selection vote. In these cases the delegates are required to reflect the preference primary vote.

Most primary states hold presidential preference votes, in which voters choose among the candidates who have qualified for the ballot in their states. Although preference votes may be binding or nonbinding, in most states the vote is binding on the delegates, who either are elected in the primary itself or are chosen outside of it by a caucus process, a state committee, or the candidates who have qualified to win delegates. Delegates may be bound for as short a time as one ballot or for as long as a candidate remains in the race.

Primaries may be closed, which means that only registered voters of the party may vote. A few states continue to maintain open primaries, in which registered voters may vote in whichever primary they choose.

Systems for determining the number of delegates that a candidate receives in a primary or caucus are complicated and, if neglected, can deal major setbacks to a strong candidate. Party members in states with binding presidential preference systems vote directly for candidates, and delegates are allocated to the candidates in several ways. "Beauty contest" states use the vote simply as a measure of popular preferences for the candidates; the selection of delegates takes place later. Delegates are allocated at different levels. Some states require candidates to recruit delegates to run in each congressional district. Other states allow delegates to be recruited from anywhere in the state. In some states delegates are allocated proportionally according to each candidate's share of the popular vote. A number of states use "bonus proportional representation" systems in which candidates receive delegate bonuses for winning congressional districts, in addition to a proportional allocation of delegates based on their overall share of the vote. Winner-take-all primaries are now largely obsolete. Candidates in some states compete at the congressional district level under a "loophole" winner-take-all system—so called because it avoids bans on statewide winner-take-all primaries. In these states, a candidate who wins a plurality in every congressional district ends up winning all of the delegates in the state.

In nearly half the primary states, major candidates are placed on the ballot by the secretary of state or a special state nominating committee. Elsewhere, candidates must take the initiative to place themselves on the ballot. The filing requirements range from sending a letter of candidacy to election officials to filing petitions signed by a specified number of registered voters and paying a filing fee.

By tradition, the first primary has been New Hampshire's, in recent years scheduled for late January or February. The last primaries have been held in several states during the first week in June. The trend in recent elections has been to front-load primaries—that is, to move them up to give a state a greater influence on the party's choice. In 2000 twenty-five states held primaries in January through March, and several more held caucuses.

The 2008 primary season is shaping up to be the most front-loaded ever. To encourage diversity the Democrats have scheduled a January 19 caucus in Nevada between the Iowa caucus (January 14) and the New Hampshire primary (January 22). This change is causing more states to move their election dates even farther forward. California, a large state that in recent years had moved its primary from June to March, is considering moving it as far forward as February 5. Other delegate-rich states such as Illinois, Michigan, and Pennsylvania are considering an early February primary as well. This earlier nomination process means that the major-party nominees will likely be decided before March 2008, causing the candidates to begin campaigning and amassing funds almost as soon as the 2006 midterm elections were over.

Caucuses

Caucuses represent a middle ground between open primary elections, dominated by the voters, and state conventions, dominated by party professionals. Before the 1970s state conventions had been the center of nomination battles.

Senator Barack Obama campaigning in early 2007
Source: BarackObama.com

Compared with a primary, the caucus system is complicated. Instead of focusing on a single primary election ballot, the caucus is a multitiered system that involves meetings scheduled over several weeks, or even months.

The operation of the caucus varies from state to state, and each party has its own set of rules. Most begin with precinct caucuses or some other type of local mass meeting open to all party voters. These meetings often last several hours and attract only the most enthusiastic and dedicated party members. Participants debate the merits of the candidates before voting for them; backers of candidates try to persuade other caucus-goers to change sides. At the end of the debate and deal making the precinct meeting votes on which delegates it will send to the next stage of the process.

In small states delegates are elected directly to a state convention, where the national convention delegates are chosen. In larger states there is at least one intervening step. Most frequently, delegates are elected at the precinct caucuses to county conventions, where the national convention delegates are chosen.

Voter participation, even at the first level of the caucus process, is much lower than in the primaries. Caucus participants usually are local party leaders and activists. Many rank-and-file voters find a caucus complex, confusing, or intimidating.

In a caucus state the focus is on individual campaigning. Time, not money, is the most valuable resource. Because organization and personal campaigning are so important, a candidate's early start is far more critical in a caucus state than in most primaries. Only a small segment of the electorate is targeted in most caucus states, so candidates commonly use little media advertising.

Although the basic steps in the caucus process are the same for both parties, the rules that govern them are vastly different. Democratic rules have been revamped substantially since 1968, establishing national standards for grass-roots participation. Republican rules have remained largely unchanged, with the states given wide latitude in the selection of delegates.

Development of Primary System

Presidential primaries grew out of the Progressive movement at the turn of the century. The most persistent complaints of Progressives concerned the undemocratic way in which urban and state political machines selected party leaders. The idea of the primary was to bypass completely the vested interests that controlled presidential nominations and thereby limited the people's choices in the general election.

Florida passed the nation's first primary law in 1901. In 1910 Oregon established the first "beauty contest," a primary election in which voters merely expressed a preference for the candidates themselves. By 1916 twenty-five states had passed presidential primary laws.

But resistance to primaries persisted. The combination of World War I, the political apathy of the 1920s, and the struggle for economic survival during the Great Depression brought about the collapse of the system. By 1935 eight of the twenty-five states had repealed their primary laws, and presidential candidates often bypassed those primaries that remained.

In 1948 former Minnesota governor Harold E. Stassen almost captured the Republican nomination when he won the Wisconsin, Nebraska, and Pennsylvania primaries. He then lost to Sen. Robert A. Taft in the latter's home state of Ohio and to Gov. Thomas E. Dewey of New York, the eventual nominee, in Oregon.

Although Stassen's strategy did not succeed, his race renewed interest in the process. A few states reinstated primaries in time for the 1952 election.

In the 1950s and 1960s presidential nomination politics evolved into a mixed system. Candidates restricted their public campaign to a few primaries that would supplement other strengths, such as fund-raising ability, endorsements, control of state and local machines, regional and ideological distinctiveness, and skill in negotiating with other political forces. In many cases the nomination was settled only during negotiations at the summer convention.

The major function of primaries under the mixed system was to allow the candidate to demonstrate an ability to campaign and to appeal to voters. Primaries were a rough test of electability. In 1968, for example, Richard Nixon used a string of primary victories to show that he was not a loser with the voters, despite losses in the 1960 presidential and 1962 California gubernatorial campaigns.

Under the mixed system a candidate who dominated the primary season could lose the nomination if enough state party organizations rallied behind other candidates. For example, Vice President Hubert H. Humphrey won the Democratic nomination in 1968 even though he had not entered a single primary. That nomination, won at a bitterly contested national convention shaken by violent antiwar protests, led the Democrats to institute a series of delegate selection reforms that opened up primaries and caucuses to citizen participation and sharply reduced the party influence in the nomination process.

In the wake of these reforms the number of presidential primaries mushroomed. Between 1968 and 1976 they nearly doubled, increasing from sixteen to thirty, and that number has increased further in recent years. Most state party leaders felt that the adoption of a presidential primary was the easiest way to provide the openness the Democratic rules required and thereby avoid a challenge to their delegates at the next national convention.

The need to campaign in many states raises the financial bar for prospective nominees. In 1996, for example, magazine publisher Steve Forbes spent more than $25 million of his own money to contest the Republican nomination. He won only two primaries but forced the eventual Republican nominee, Sen. Robert J. Dole, to spend heavily on primary campaigns, which depleted his war chest for the general election.

Although the proliferation of primaries gives voters the opportunity to influence the choice of their parties' candidates, the number of people who participate is still small. Less than one-fourth of party members typically vote in primaries, and less than one-tenth participate in most caucuses. In 2000, the last election cycle in which both parties had contested nominations, 14.05 million Democratic voters participated in forty primaries. Some 17.16 million Republicans participated in forty-three primaries. Only 55.3 percent of the nation's voting-age population cast ballots in the 2004 general election for president, although it was the highest percentage since 1968.

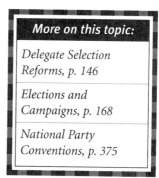

More on this topic:

Delegate Selection Reforms, p. 146

Elections and Campaigns, p. 168

National Party Conventions, p. 375

Presidential Nominating
Campaign Lengths, 1968–2004

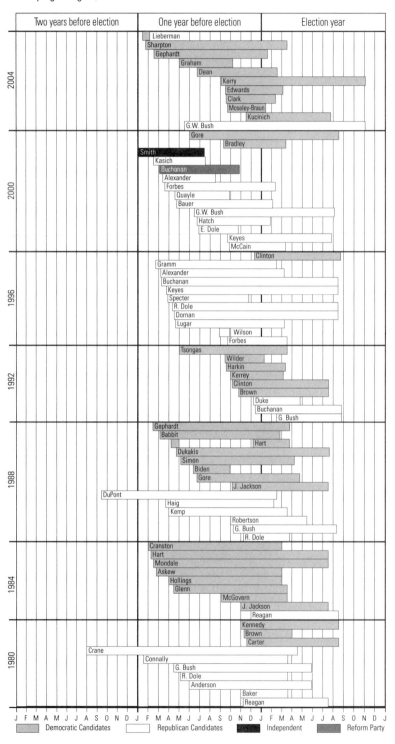

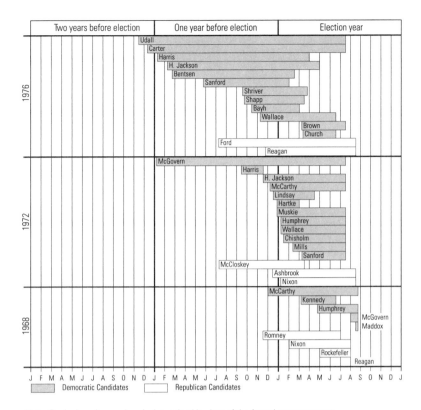

	Two years before election	One year before election	Election year

Democratic Candidates   Republican Candidates

Note: Beginning of campaigns is determined by date of the formal announcement.

Sources: 1968–1984: Congressional Quarterly, *Elections '80* (Washington, D.C.: Congressional Quarterly, 1980), and Congressional Quarterly, *Congressional Quarterly's Guide to U.S. Elections,* 2d ed. (Washington, D.C.: Congressional Quarterly, 1985), 387; 1988–1996: *Congressional Quarterly Weekly Report* (1987), 2732; (1988), 1894, 1896, 1899; (1991), 3735; (1992), 66, 361, 556, 633, 1086; (1995), 2, 13, 15, 3025, 3606; (1996), 641, 716; 2000, 2004: compiled by the editors from news reports, various sources.

Proclamations and Endorsements

Presidential proclamations are unique documents in that they illustrate the president's role as chief of state unlike most other forms of presidential communication. Since proclamations are in essence a formal announcement by the president to the nation, one distinguishing characteristic is that they begin with an introduction similar to that used by the British monarch:

BY THE PRESIDENT OF THE
UNITED STATES OF AMERICA
A PROCLAMATION

After the announcement, the president then lays out the authority and rationale involved with his proclamation, stating for each point, "WHEREAS." Ceremonially presenting his decision or order, the president then states, "NOW THEREFORE, I, [President's Name], President of the United States of America . . ." and the text of what the president is proclaiming. Like many legal documents, the president's signing of the proclamation is witnessed, usually by the secretary of state, who holds the official seal of the United States. The proclamation usually ends with "IN WITNESS WHEREOF, I have hereunto set my hand and caused the Seal of the United States of America to be affixed," followed by the place and date the proclamation was signed, spelled out including the year of the independence of the republic.

The president serves as the ceremonial leader of the nation. A presidential proclamation or endorsement is a national stamp of approval for cultural events, national monuments, public works projects, charity drives, interest groups, and special weeks and days. Such proclamations promote national concern and awareness of worthy organizations and causes by showing that the president attaches importance to the object of the proclamation.

Often presidents highlight their recognition of a charity, organization, or movement by inviting its leaders to the White House. Such an invitation is a further measure of the group's perceived importance.

Presidential proclamations and endorsements give an event, cause, group, or monument a place in the national consciousness. They also emphasize the unity of the United States and can inspire patriotic sentiment. For example, a new hydroelectric dam is said to be not just a source of power for a particular region, but an engineering feat and a symbol of American industrial might and technological ingenuity. The work of a charitable organization, such as the American Red Cross, is praised as an example of the nation's caring spirit.

Presidential endorsements are in great demand by organizations and charities. In most cases the White House staff must choose which groups will receive an official presidential proclamation. Many of the causes presidents endorse from year to year are determined by precedent. The United Way, Easter Seals, American Cancer Society, and many others receive annual presidential endorsements. Yet the number and type of causes that receive presidential recognition also may reflect the incumbent's political interests. For example, Ronald Reagan's frequent endorsement of charities was consistent with his goal of promoting an increase in the nation's charitable giving as a partial alternative to federal spending on social programs.

Presidents traditionally have issued statements celebrating official holidays, such as Memorial Day and Thanksgiving, and unofficial holidays, such as St. Patrick's Day. In September 2002 George W. Bush proclaimed September 11 "Patriot Day" in remembrance of the terrorist attacks a year earlier. Congress had asked for such a designation. George Washington was the first president to proclaim a national holiday. In response to a congressional recommendation, he declared that a national day of thanksgiving should be observed on Thursday, November 26, 1789. This proclamation contributed to the development of the Thanksgiving holiday now observed in the United States. Presidents, however, cannot formally establish an official federal holiday without an act of Congress.

Now, therefore, I do recommend and assign Thursday, the 26th day of November next, to be devoted by the people of these States to the service of that great and glorious Being who is the beneficent author of all the good that was, that is, or that will be. . . .

—George Washington, Thanksgiving Proclamation, October 3, 1789

More on this topic:

Chief of State, p. 86

Prosecutor, Special *See* INDEPENDENT COUNSEL.

Public Opinion and the Presidency

Political analysts and presidents themselves have long recognized that presidential success rests largely on favorable public opinion. "Public sentiment is everything," Abraham Lincoln once said. "With public sentiment, nothing can fail, without it nothing can succeed."

The achievements and popularity of presidents are determined not just by legislation won and lost, foreign policy developments, and economic conditions, but also by presidents' ability to set a political tone, instill trust and confidence among the people, offer a vision of the future, and cre-

In a room across from the Oval Office, President Lyndon B. Johnson set up charts displaying his private polls before the 1964 election.
Source: Library of Congress

ate a national consensus. The power of the presidency is the power to persuade. Especially in the modern era, presidents must communicate directly with the voters and build a strong base of support among them if they are to be able to influence Congress, retain control of their political party, and win reelection.

Fortunately for presidents, their office provides many advantages and resources in the battle for public opinion: the historical aura and stately trappings of the institution; the huge corps of White House aides; and the clear statement in the Constitution that there can be only one chief executive at a time.

Perhaps even more important, however, are the deep psychological bonds between Americans and their presidents. Although these bonds can be strained as a result of specific events, they are a foundation for the president's relationship with the people. The chief executive is the single most visible figure in American life, the only government official who represents the entire population and the first political figure children learn about. For the average citizen the president is a symbol of the nation, and the office is a vital stabilizing force that inspires awe.

Still, although these advantages set the president apart in the eyes of the people, none of them guarantees public support. Support is something that presidents and other political leaders must work to build. But before they can begin effectively to build or strengthen their popular backing, presidents must seek to learn citizens' thoughts about the events of the day.

In the first century and more of the presidency, the methods available to presidents for gauging public opinion directly were limited. Most often, chief executives looked to state and local party organizations, which provided the most regular and reliable information about political attitudes. Other sources of information about the mood of the country were public demonstrations, newspaper editorials, and letters, as well as Congress.

USA TODAY/Gallup Poll of the Public: Who do you regard as the greatest United States president?

Poll Results

	Feb. 07	Feb. 05	Nov. 03	Apr. 03	Feb. 99
Abraham Lincoln	18%	14%	17%	15%	18%
Ronald Reagan	16	20	13	10	12
John Kennedy	14	12	17	13	12
Bill Clinton	13	15	9	11	12
Franklin Roosevelt	9	12	11	9	9
George Washington	7	5	7	7	12
Harry Truman	3	2	3	4	4
George W. Bush	2	5	3	11	--
Theodore Roosevelt	2	2	3	2	3
Dwight Eisenhower	2	1	2	1	2
Thomas Jefferson	2	2	3	2	2
Jimmy Carter	2	3	3	3	3
Gerald Ford	1	—	—	—	—
George H. W. Bush	1	1	2	2	5
Richard Nixon	—	1	1	1	2
Other	1	1	2	2	1
None	1	1	—	1	1
No opinion	6	3	4	6	2

Those methods are still in use today, but they have largely been superseded by increasingly sophisticated public opinion polling, which has become a vital factor in every presidency. Polling data are often sketchy and contradictory, but at least they reduce the uncertainty under which the president operates.

Franklin D. Roosevelt was the first president to use polling data regularly to interpret the public's reactions to the political and policy actions of the administration. As the likelihood of U.S. involvement in World War II grew in the late 1930s, Roosevelt received advice from George Gallup, the founder of modern polling, on how to frame his rhetoric on possible U.S. involvement.

Lyndon B. Johnson was the first president to hire a pollster, Albert Cantril, for the White House staff. Throughout his term Johnson kept track of a steady stream of polling data from every state. When faced with growing opposition to the Vietnam War, Johnson pointed to polls showing majority support for his military effort. Similarly, Richard Nixon said polls showed there was a "silent majority" of Americans opposed to vocal antiwar demonstrators.

Polling became a permanent part of White House staff activity with the elections of Jimmy Carter and Ronald Reagan. Sometimes the tactic backfired on the user—such as when Carter, on the basis of polling data, gave a speech warning of a "crisis of confidence" in the nation, which was widely criticized. The Reagan administration installed a comprehensive polling program that enabled it to steer policy debates according to day-to-day shifts in the popular mood.

Independent polling data also provide a barometer of the president's standing with the public. The most important of these polls is the monthly Gallup survey, which since 1945 has asked members of the public whether they approve or disapprove of the way the president has been handling his job.

The Gallup surveys and other data suggest that there is a natural rhythm to a president's popularity while in office. The president's standing tends to decline throughout most of the four-year term in office, with temporary increases after important international events and at the beginning of a reelection campaign or the end of the term.

Presidential approval ratings can vary widely. Polling support for the incumbent has ranged from 22 percent for Truman in early 1952 during the Korean War, to almost 92 percent in 1945 after the surrender of Japan ending World War II. Approval ratings can shift rapidly, as they did in late 1991 when concern over the recession cut George H. W. Bush's support from its record high level to below 50 percent.

George W. Bush's popularity took a major leap upward after the terrorist attacks of September 11, 2001. On the eve of the attacks Bush's job approval rating stood at 51 percent, the low mark of his almost nine-month tenure as president, according to a Gallup poll taken September 7–10. The next Gallup poll, taken September 14–15, revealed that the president's job approval rating had

soared to 86 percent. A week later, after a presidential address from Capitol Hill, Bush's approval rating stood at an unprecedented 90 percent. This "rally effect," whereby the public tends to offer support for presidents during times of foreign policy crisis, is historically short lived. Bush's job approval rating has declined steadily since September 11, 2001. With the Iraq War continuing and no end in sight, Bush's approval rating reached the 30s in mid-2006 and has remained there into 2007.

In general, though, popular backing for the White House erodes steadily during a four-year term and normally falls even lower during an incumbent's second term. One reason for the decline is the unusually high level of support given to new presidents during their "honeymoon period" after the inauguration. Another cause is the voters' seemingly inevitable disappointment that the bold promises of an election campaign cannot be achieved.

> **We're going to win this election because our values and our priorities do not shift because of the latest public opinion poll. We're going to win because we've got an optimistic and hopeful agenda.**
>
> —*George W. Bush,* Remarks at a Montana Victory 2006 Rally in Billings, November 2, 2006

Within that broad downward trend, domestic issues and foreign affairs can play differing roles in causing changes in the president's standing. Domestic issues perhaps provide a more durable base of popularity than foreign affairs. Foreign policy events can provide a dramatic but fleeting opportunity for presidents to increase their popular support.

On the domestic front, voters are concerned chiefly with so-called pocketbook issues. Presidents are usually only as popular as economic conditions allow; periods of high unemployment or inflation are almost certain to undermine their standing. Some political analysts have suggested that the chief factor determining a first-term president's chances for reelection is whether the average personal income of voters rose or declined during the year before the election.

In foreign affairs, however, almost every major event is likely to increase a president's public backing, at least over the short term, even if the result of the event is not a positive one for the president. Americans have a strong inclination to "rally 'round the flag"—and the president—during times of international stress. The public's willingness to back a president in times of international crisis is almost complete, with approval ratings usually rising after a presidential display of military or diplomatic activity.

But even if their popularity will inevitably decline, presidents have a wide range of techniques and resources available to them to try to build their public support. "The selling of the president" has become a major aspect of the modern White House, as presidents and their aides try to use the media, interest groups, political parties, and speeches to reach the people, both during election campaigns and over the next four years.

New methods of communication have enabled recent presidents to adopt a strategy of going directly to the public to mobilize support. Particularly since the early 1960s, presidents have made frequent use of televised speeches to address the American people and ask for their support in dealing with some issue. In addition, presidents, as the prime news subject in the country, have at their disposal a vast publicity machine. Continual publicity is widely acknowledged as a critical aspect of presidential politics.

Chief executives also can mobilize support by taking advantage of the ceremonial aspect of the presidency—the symbolism and rhetorical flourishes that can strike an emotional chord and touch patriotic sentiments among Americans. When they travel or make major speeches, presidents frequently are portrayed as the embodiment of the national interest and the living symbol of the nation. The presidency is a form of national theater in which the chief executive is the most visible and important actor on the stage. Presidents since Washington have understood this, but its impact has been even greater since the dawn of the television age.

With his years of experience as a movie actor, Reagan was the master of using the media and the ceremonial aspect of his office to reach the voters. Each of his public appearances was a carefully choreographed, minutely scripted performance that conveyed a feeling of optimism and confidence—a feeling that in many cases was considerably more important than the substance of what he might be saying.

With the rise of White House media strategies and the "imperial presidency," as it is sometimes described, other forms of mobilizing public support have become less important. This is particularly true of political parties, which for more than a century were the chief forces in selecting and supporting the president. In recent decades the parties have declined in significance both for the president and for presidential candidates. As a result, someone like Jimmy Carter could arrive in the White House in 1977 stressing his lack of obligation to the Democratic Party. That gave him the independence to pursue his own policies, but it also deprived him of a network of support and institutional alliances when his public support weakened.

As presidential reliance on parties has declined, chief executives have stepped up their efforts to reach interest groups, which are organizations dedicated to advancing a single issue or a relatively narrow range of issues. Presidents recognize that they can no longer rely on traditional political alignments in the promotion of their legislative agenda and executive programs and realize they must seek, issue by issue, the endorsement of coalitions.

Beginning in the Nixon administration, the White House institutionalized its relationships with interest groups through the establishment of the Office of Public Liaison. A critical part of that office's function is to invite leaders of interest groups from across the country to the White House, where they meet with the president and other top officials. The hope is that the group leaders will then return home to spread the administration's message and put pressure on Congress to support the president's positions.

If their efforts to build mass support are successful, presidents can then use their popularity as an important tool for attaining public policy goals. Presidents use information about their level of public support to persuade Congress to go along with their proposals for foreign and domestic policies.

Especially regarding issues on which the public has not formed strong opinions, presidents can shape the views of many people simply by speaking out. An example is George H. W. Bush's speeches about Iraq's invasion of Kuwait, condemning the actions of Iraqi leader Saddam Hussein. The public's deep-seated desire to support its president gives the chief executive opportunities for moving the population. Several surveys have shown that the public is more willing to support an initiative if it knows the president favors the proposal.

Political scientists suggest that presidential efforts to "go public" have at least partly replaced negotiation with other powerful leaders in Washington as a means of achieving presidential goals. By referring to the public's general support for the president and its backing for specific presidential policies, the White House takes the initiative away from Congress in deciding whether to support or oppose a policy. Instead, lawmakers are given the choice of supporting the president's agenda or facing the wrath of voters back home.

Still, the link between presidential approval ratings and support of the White House on Capitol Hill is not clear. Although some scholars and others have argued that high support ratings help presidents get their way with Congress, the record of postwar presidents suggests that the relationship is indirect and that other factors influence the willingness of political leaders to follow the president.

There are many examples of the link between presidential popularity—or the lack of it—and congressional action. For example, Congress went along with Reagan's budget, tax, and military policies during the height of his popularity but started to distance itself from the president when his public standing weakened. Similarly, Congress cut off funds for the Vietnam War as Nixon's popularity plunged.

But, particularly when the administration and congressional majorities are of different parties, the president may not be able to take advantage of high approval ratings to control legislation. Despite George H. W. Bush's record approval ratings in early 1991, for example, congressional Democrats successfully resisted administration efforts to cut the capital gains tax. Moreover, the rise of split-ticket voting has reduced presidents' ability to threaten revenge against opposing legislators. With the notable exception of Reagan's 1980 victory, which helped to sweep in a Republican majority in the Senate, not many congressional candidates in recent elections have been able to ride on presidential coattails. The midterm elections of 2002—in which George W. Bush's popularity and his willingness to campaign for GOP candidates appeared to help Republicans take back control of the Senate and make gains in the House—were another exception, although Bush himself was not on the ballot that year. Still, in most recent elections many voters have seemed willing to support both a president and lawmakers who strongly oppose that president's policies.

The increased emphasis on polling and public opinion management by presidents and other political leaders has important long-term implications. But experts are divided over whether such techniques promote or damage democracy.

On the positive side, regular polling makes presidents more responsive to the wishes of the electorate than infrequent elections ever could. Presidential actions that are influenced by polls and the need to appeal to the public represent a kind of ongoing election campaign. Polls also provide a "scientific" picture of the political landscape that is more comprehensive than that provided by any other tool.

But other political analysts warn that modern techniques of public opinion polling actually stifle public expression and encourage presidents and other politicians to focus on their short-term popularity rather than the long-term needs of the nation. Presidents now may think they can "manage" popular demands so effectively that they avoid taking difficult or controversial steps to address real problems.

Moreover, say critics, polling and the sophisticated use of the mass media to manage public opinion have the effect of shifting politics from the group to the individual, at the presidential and other levels. Before polls and television, presidents were forced to obtain support by negotiating and building alliances with other political leaders and groups representing important parts of society. By being able to reach out directly to millions of people, presidents no longer have to do the work of building consensus among the other institutions of democracy. Chief executives thus deprive themselves of the core of support they may need when the ever-changing winds of public opinion blow against them.

Qualifications of the President and Vice President

The Constitution sets only a few specific requirements for the highest executive offices. To serve as either president or vice president, a person must be at least thirty-five years old and a native-born citizen of the United States, and must have lived in the United States for the previous fourteen years. In practice, the constitutional qualifications have rarely if ever been a significant factor in determining who becomes president. But other personal and political characteristics, though not specifically required in the Constitution or in law, have proved over the years to be minimum standards that must be met by anyone with realistic hopes of being considered for the highest offices in the land.

The Constitutional Convention came late to the idea of setting specific qualifications for the president. The reason that delegates did not set presidential qualifications earlier was that most had assumed throughout the convention that the president would be selected by Congress. One of the consistent principles of the convention was that the qualifications for an office had to be stated only if there were no specific qualifications for those who would choose the person to fill that office. Because the qualifications of members of Congress were specified, it was not necessary to spell out the president's qualifications. Presumably members of Congress would not choose a president who was not qualified to be in Congress.

Once the delegates began to shift toward another method of choosing the president—ultimately, they settled on an ELECTORAL COLLEGE selected by the states—it became necessary to think again about setting qualifications for the presidency. On September 7, 1787, the convention unanimously approved the qualifications proposed by the Committee on Postponed Matters.

Each element of the qualifications had a reason behind it. The minimum age, for example, was based on the belief that age brings maturity. Moreover, the framers reasoned, setting a minimum age would ensure that candidates had a political and personal record that would offer a substantial basis for voters to assess their fitness for office.

The residency and citizenship requirements probably were shaped largely by current political considerations. By specifying that the president had to have lived in the United States for the past fourteen years, for example, the framers excluded British sympathizers who had fled the country during the Revolution. Similarly, exclusion of those who were not born in America or who were not citizens at the time of the adoption of the Constitution ensured that there would be no move to invite a foreign monarch to assume the presidency, as some feared might happen.

One significant qualification the delegates decided not to adopt involved property. Many states had requirements that officeholders also be property owners, and the convention at one point agreed to have a property requirement for all executive, judicial, and legislative officials. Many delegates and others at the time assumed that only people who already owned property, particularly land, would be responsible and trustworthy enough to hold public office. The convention never actually rejected that view. Instead, delegates did not adopt a property standard because of the practical difficulties in deciding how much property a president should be required to have.

The convention's system for selecting a vice president—the candidate with the second highest number of votes in the Electoral College—seemingly assumed that the vice president would meet the same minimum qualifications as the president. The Constitution, however, did not address the issue of vice-presidential qualifications. The Twelfth Amendment, which established the current method of selecting a vice president, specified that the holder of that office must have the same qualifications as the chief executive.

In the two centuries since the Constitution was adopted, the specified qualifications for the president have almost never come into play. Few politicians are likely to have the stature and political support even to consider a run for the White House before they reach their mid-thirties. Occasionally, regret will be voiced that some distinguished foreign-born citizen is ineligible to be considered for his adopted country's highest office, but there has never been a significant movement to alter the requirement of native birth.

> *No Person except a natural born Citizen, or a Citizen of the United States, at the time of the Adoption of this Constitution, shall be eligible to the Office of President; neither shall any person be eligible to that Office who shall not have attained to the Age of thirty five Years, and been fourteen Years a Resident within the United States.*
>
> —*Constitution of the United States,* Article II, Section 1, Clause 5

More on this topic:

Article II, p. 16

Background of Presidents, p. 26

Electoral College, p. 185

Quayle, Dan

James Danforth Quayle III (1947–), called "Dan" since childhood, was born on February 4, 1947, into a prominent Indiana family. His maternal grandfather was Eugene C. Pulliam, a conservative Indiana newspaper publisher who amassed a fortune of close to $1 billion.

In 1965 Quayle enrolled in DePauw University, a small liberal arts college in Greencastle, Indiana, where he compiled a mediocre academic record. Upon graduation in 1969 he lost his student defer-

Dan Quayle
Source: NASA

ment and became eligible for the military draft. He secured a place in the Indiana National Guard, which made military service in Vietnam unlikely.

While serving in the National Guard one weekend a month, Quayle attended Indiana University Law School at night and held a series of jobs in Indiana state government. He graduated from law school in 1974 and opened a law practice in Huntington. He also was the associate publisher of the family-owned *Huntington Herald-Press*.

In 1976 Quayle defeated an eight-term incumbent Democrat, Edward Roush, for a seat in the U.S. House of Representatives. He served two terms in the House before defeating incumbent Democrat Birch Bayh for a Senate seat.

Quayle performed in the Senate with greater diligence than he had shown during his four years in the House and was easily reelected in 1986.

In August 1988 the Republican presidential nominee, George H.W. Bush, surprised the nation by naming Quayle, who was only forty-one, as his running mate. Within hours of the announcement Quayle became the subject of controversy. Journalists focused on his decision to enter the National Guard rather than risk being drafted. The action seemed to conflict with his hawkish posture in Congress. It also appeared that Quayle had used his family's influence to avoid having to serve in Vietnam. Negative reports also pointed to his unimpressive academic record and his apparent use of family influence to gain admittance to law school. The media's portrait of a wealthy underachiever who used family connections to further his career threatened to damage Bush's election chances. Some Republicans advised Bush to withdraw Quayle's nomination, but Bush stuck by his choice.

National polls in the months after the convention showed that Quayle was hurting Bush's popularity. It was generally held that Democratic vice-presidential nominee Lloyd M. Bentsen Jr. defeated Quayle in their one televised debate. Nevertheless, in the election Bush and Quayle defeated Massachusetts governor Michael S. Dukakis and Bentsen by a vote of 426–111 in the Electoral College.

As vice president, Quayle served Bush as a policy adviser, a liaison with Congress, and an emissary to foreign countries. He also chaired the White House Council on Competitiveness and the National Space Council.

Quayle was a hero to many conservatives for his attacks on bureaucratic red tape and regulation and for his vocal campaign for family values. Quayle survived attempts to drop him as Bush's 1992 running mate, but, against the backdrop of a troubled economy, the Bush-Quayle ticket was defeated in November.

After leaving the vice presidency Quayle returned to Indiana, where he worked on a book and gave speeches, often to groups associated with the GOP's conservative wing. In 1995, after assembling a campaign team for a possible run at the 1996 Republican presidential nomination, Quayle pulled out of the crowded race, dissuaded, analysts said, by polling data and poor fund-raising prospects. He made an unsuccessful bid for the 2000 Republican presidential nomination, dropping out in 1999. Dan Quayle currently resides in Arizona and is the only living former vice president never to have been nominated by his party for president.

More on this topic:

Bush, George H.W., p. 52

Campaign Debates, p. 68

Vice President, p. 539

R

Ratings of Presidents *See* PRESIDENTIAL GREATNESS.

Reagan, Nancy

Nancy Reagan (1923–) was the second wife of Ronald Reagan, who served as president from 1981 to 1989. Nancy was one of the most controversial first ladies. She was both praised and faulted for her fierce loyalty to her husband and her desire to protect his image.

Born Anne Frances Robbins and nicknamed "Nancy," she was the daughter of an auto salesman and a stage actress. Her father left the family shortly after she was born, and her mother, determined to pursue a stage career, left young Nancy with relatives. She lived until age six with an aunt in Washington, D.C. In 1929 her mother married a Chicago physician, and Nancy went to live with them. She was legally adopted at age fourteen and became Nancy Davis. She attended a private high school in Chicago and Smith College in Massachusetts.

Like her mother, Nancy decided to become an actress. In 1943 she began her stage career and in 1949 moved to Hollywood to break into movies. There she met Ronald Reagan, then president of the Screen Actors Guild, who cleared her of a baseless charge of communist associations. The couple married on March 4, 1952, and Nancy largely abandoned her acting career, returning to the screen for only brief intervals. She made her last movie in 1954. Nancy returned to the public eye, however, when Ronald entered politics. After serving two terms as governor of California, he became president in 1981.

As first lady, Nancy initially stated her intention to stay out of the limelight and take care of her husband, on whom she had a great influence. Her first two years in the White House were stormy,

After first lady Nancy Reagan was criticized for projecting a superficial, materialistic image, she attempted to repair her reputation by working on several charitable causes. In 1983 she launched "Just say no," a nationwide antidrug campaign.
Source: The White House

however. She was criticized for her fashionable wardrobe, her rich friends, and the general image of luxury that she projected. Gradually, Nancy began to improve her public image by actively supporting anti–drug abuse programs and other charitable causes. By the end of her husband's first term Nancy had largely repaired her image.

During Reagan's second term Nancy came under fire again for her cool relationship with Soviet first lady Raisa Gorbachev, her use of gowns that were provided to her free of charge by leading fashion designers, and her reported antipathy toward Vice President George H. W. Bush and his wife, Barbara.

The issue that raised the most controversy was Nancy's behind-the-scenes influence on White House politics, particularly personnel decisions. She displayed an iron will in protecting the interests of her more easygoing husband. Several White House insiders attested to her power to remove people she thought were a liability to him. Some commentators remarked that presidential policies known to be pushed by Nancy, such as the firing of Chief of Staff Donald T. Regan and the aggressive pursuit of better relations with the Soviet Union, were among the smarter political moves made by the president during his tenure in office. But many people saw Nancy Reagan as a manipulator, who was willing to sacrifice anyone or any policy to protect her husband's place in history.

In 1989, after two terms in the White House, the Reagans retired to California. Nancy, the only first lady to publish an autobiography before entering the White House, later wrote a second book entitled *My Turn: The Memoirs of Nancy Reagan,* an account of her Washington years that also attempted to answer her critics. On May 16, 2002, the Reagans were awarded the Congressional Gold Medal, presented by President George W. Bush and congressional leaders at a Capitol Hill ceremony. A few months later on July 9, 2002, Mrs. Reagan was presented with the Presidential Medal of Freedom.

During the state funeral proceedings for President Reagan in June 2004, Nancy Reagan captured the hearts of a worldwide audience as she accompanied the body of her late husband with her military escort, Maj. Gen. Galen B. Jackman, from California to Washington, D.C., and finally back to California, where President Reagan rests in Simi Valley. In opposition to the policies of President George W. Bush, Mrs. Reagan continues to support stem-cell research, believing that it may lead to successful treatments for Alzheimer's disease, the ailment that afflicted President Reagan after he left office.

More on this topic:

First Ladies, p. 219

Reagan, Ronald, p. 437

Reagan, Ronald

Source: Pete Souza, The White House

Ronald Wilson Reagan (1911–2004) was the oldest person ever to serve as president. He left office in January 1989 a few weeks before his seventy-eighth birthday. Reagan remained popular throughout most of his eight years in office, despite a severe recession during his first term, the Iran-contra affair during his second term, and a rapidly expanding federal budget deficit. His ability to deliver speeches skillfully and appeal to audiences at orchestrated public appearances helped to shape a positive public perception of him and earned him the epithet the Great Communicator.

Reagan was born on February 6, 1911, in Tampico, Illinois. His father was a shoe salesman. He graduated from Eureka College near Peoria, Illinois, in 1932 with a degree in economics and sociology. After college Reagan worked as a sports announcer for radio stations in Davenport and Des Moines, Iowa. During a trip to California in 1937 he took a movie screen test that launched a twenty-eight-year acting career in which he made fifty-five movies. Reagan married Jane Wyman, an actress, on January 24, 1940. They divorced in 1948. Reagan then married another actress, Nancy Davis, on March 4, 1952.

In 1942 Reagan entered the U.S. Army Air Corps as a second lieutenant and was assigned to make training films. He was discharged in 1945 with the rank of captain. After the war he continued to act in movies but devoted an increasing share of his time to film industry politics. In 1947 he was elected president of the Screen Actors Guild, a labor union representing Hollywood actors. He held that office until 1952 and was reelected to a one-year term in 1959.

Political Career

In 1964 Reagan made a televised campaign speech on behalf of Republican presidential candidate Barry Goldwater. The speech established Reagan as a spokesman for the conservative wing of the Republican Party. He received the 1966 Republican nomination for governor of California after winning almost 65 percent of the vote in a five-candidate primary election. He then defeated incumbent Democrat Edmund G. Brown and was easily elected to a second term in 1970.

After declining to run for a third term as governor in 1974, Reagan began campaigning for the presidency. Despite facing an incumbent president, Gerald R. Ford, Reagan came close to winning the 1976 Republican presidential nomination. When Ford lost the election to Democrat Jimmy Carter, Reagan became the favorite to receive the Republican nomination in 1980.

During the next four years Reagan campaigned for Republican candidates and raised money for his 1980 campaign. He was upset in the Iowa caucuses by George H. W. Bush but recovered with a win in the New Hampshire primary. Reagan went on to win all but four of the remaining Republican primaries. He then defeated incumbent Jimmy Carter in the general election by a vote of 489–49 in the Electoral College.

Presidency

On March 30, 1981, less than three months after he became president, Reagan was shot as he was leaving the Washington Hilton Hotel, where he had delivered a speech. The assailant, John Hinckley Jr., fired six shots at Reagan with a .22-caliber pistol. One bullet struck Reagan in the chest and lodged in his left lung. He was rushed to a nearby hospital where surgeons removed the bullet. He became the first incumbent president to be wounded by an assassin and survive. Hinckley was found not guilty by reason of insanity and placed in St. Elizabeth's Hospital in Washington, D.C.

In 1981 the president pushed a large tax cut through Congress, along with increases in the defense budget and decreases in funding for many domestic programs. Reagan claimed that the tax cut would produce an economic boom that would reduce unemployment and ultimately produce tax revenues that would balance the federal budget. However, a severe recession that began in late 1981 increased unemployment to post–Great Depression highs.

In early 1983 the economy began to recover. Unlike economic recoveries during the 1970s the expansion was not accompanied by high inflation. In the 1984 presidential election, with the economy prospering, Reagan overwhelmed his Democratic challenger, former vice president Walter F. Mondale, by a vote of 525–13 in the Electoral College. The economic expansion continued through the end of Reagan's term.

Although most Americans were satisfied with the economy during the Reagan years, critics pointed out that low-income groups had fared poorly, the U.S. trade position had weakened, and the government had built up huge budget deficits. The last of these problems was particularly troublesome to Reagan, because he had promised to balance the federal budget. When Reagan entered office in 1981, the budget deficit was $78.9 billion. By 1986 it stood at $221.2 billion. The national debt had risen from a little over $1 trillion in 1981 to more than $2 trillion in 1986. In response, Reagan and the Democratic Congress enacted the Gramm-Rudman-Hollings amendment in 1985. It mandated across-the-board spending cuts if the president and Congress could not agree on budget reductions that would limit the deficit to specified yearly targets.

We've done our part. And as I walk off into the city streets, a final word to the men and women of the Reagan revolution, the men and women across America who for 8 years did the work that brought America back. My friends: We did it. We weren't just marking time. We made a difference. We made the city stronger, we made the city freer, and we left her in good hands. All in all, not bad, not bad at all.

—Ronald Reagan, Farewell Address to the Nation, January 11, 1989

In foreign affairs, the first five years of Reagan's presidency were characterized by hard-line anticommunist speeches and efforts to block communist influence in developing countries. Reagan supported military aid to the anticommunist Nicaraguan rebels known as the contras, who were fighting to overthrow the Marxist regime in their country. He also backed aid to anticommunist guerrillas fighting in Angola and Cambodia, and Afghan rebels fighting Soviet forces that had invaded Afghanistan in 1979. In 1983 Reagan sent U.S. troops to Grenada to overthrow the Marxist government and bring stability to the tiny Caribbean island.

With the rise of Mikhail Gorbachev as the leader of the Soviet Union in 1985, the president began developing a working relationship with the Soviet leader. During his last three years in office Reagan held five summits with Gorbachev and signed a treaty banning intermediate-range nuclear missiles in Europe.

Reagan also took actions to strike back at terrorists in the Middle East, including a 1986 bombing raid on Libya in retaliation for Libyan support of terrorism. Reagan's antiterrorist stance was undercut late in 1986 when it was disclosed that the president had approved arms sales to Iran that appeared to be aimed at securing the release of American hostages in Lebanon held by pro-Iranian extremists. Reagan denied that the sale was an arms-for-hostages swap, which would have contradicted his policy not to negotiate with terrorists, but the evidence suggested otherwise.

Investigation revealed that members of Reagan's staff had used some of the profits from the Iran arms sales to aid the contras fighting a repressive regime in Nicaragua, despite a congressional ban then in force against supplying the contras with aid. The scandal led to the resignation of several administration officials and to strong criticism of the way Reagan ran his White House. The Tower Commission, appointed by the president to investigate the IRAN-CONTRA AFFAIR, issued a report in 1987 that was highly critical of the president's detached management style, which allowed his aides to operate without his knowledge. Special congressional investigating committees and an independent counsel also leveled blunt criticism at Reagan.

Despite the Iran-contra affair, the public's personal affection for Reagan and the strong economy that had prevailed since 1983 contributed to his high approval ratings as he left office. After leaving the White House he established a home in Bel Air, California, and continued to speak frequently in support of Republican causes and charitable organizations. In November 1994 Reagan, in a touching handwritten note to the American people, announced that he had been diagnosed with Alzheimer's disease. He said he hoped his experience would help to raise the nation's awareness about this debilitating disease. In 2002 the Reagans were awarded the Congressional Gold Medal. President George W. Bush and congressional leaders presented it to Nancy Reagan at a Capitol Hill ceremony.

President Reagan passed away at his Bel Air, California, home on June 5, 2004, after falling ill with pneumonia. The fortieth president received a state funeral and was laid to rest at the Ronald Reagan Presidential Library and Museum in Simi Valley, California.

More on this topic:

Assassinations and Assaults, p. 19

Background of Presidents, p. 26

Elections Chronology, p. 174

Iran-Contra Affair, p. 294

Reagan, Nancy, p. 435

Reconstruction

The Reconstruction era that followed the Civil War was an important one in the development of the presidency. From 1865 to 1876, political conflicts over the policies toward the defeated southern states led the nation close to the impeachment of a president. The political deal that ended the period helped to shape national and presidential politics for nearly sixty years.

The end of the Civil War left the nation almost as divided as it had been before the conflict. Concerns about punishment of the rebel states, the status of the freed slaves, and economic development were the principal sources of disagreement.

The process of reintegrating the former Confederacy into the Union was called Reconstruction. It would have been difficult even if the president who had led the North to victory had lived to

The bill in effect proposes a discrimination against large numbers of intelligent, worthy, and patriotic foreigners, and in favor of the Negro, to whom, after long years of bondage, the avenues to freedom and intelligence have just now been suddenly opened. He must of necessity, from his previous unfortunate condition of servitude, be less informed as to the nature and character of our institutions than he who, coming from abroad, has, to some extent at least, familiarized himself with the principles of a Government to which he voluntarily intrusts "life, liberty, and the pursuit of happiness."

—Andrew Johnson, *Veto of the Civil Rights Bill Message to the Senate,* March 27, 1866

After the Civil War, Andrew Johnson pledged to continue Lincoln's plan for Reconstruction even though Congress found the policies unacceptable. Seeking to build his political strength, Johnson toured the country in 1866. In this woodcut—published in 1868 in J.T. Trowbridge's book A Picture of the Desolated States—Johnson speaks from a railroad coach platform.
Source: Library of Congress

oversee it. But the assassination of Abraham Lincoln shortly after the end of the war brought to power a little-known and little-respected border state politician, Andrew Johnson.

Immediately upon assuming office, Johnson came into conflict with the radical northern Republicans who controlled Congress. He intended to continue Lincoln's plan for Reconstruction "with malice toward none." But leaders of Congress were intent both on punishing the former rebel states and on establishing political institutions that would respect the rights of former slaves. Johnson, who chafed at the idea of the South as a conquered country, attempted to put together a coalition of moderates from all parts of the nation to bring about a quick reconciliation.

The elections of 1866 gave control of Congress to the Radical Republicans, who set about imposing harsh military rule in the South and stripping Johnson of most of his power. Within the atmosphere of intense political conflict a dispute arose between Johnson and Congress over appointment powers. It led to a drive for IMPEACHMENT that fell only one Senate vote short of success.

The Republican majority in Congress continued to support its strict Reconstruction policy under President Ulysses S. Grant. The election to determine Grant's successor, however, led to the end of the era. In the 1876 election Republican Rutherford B. Hayes faced Democrat Samuel J. Tilden, who was widely thought to have a chance to capture the White House in the wake of the scandals that had plagued the Grant administration. Tilden won the popular vote but fell just short of a majority in the Electoral College because of the disputed status of electors from several states.

More on this topic:
Grant, Ulysses S., p. 235
Hayes, Rutherford B., p. 249
Impeachment, p. 273
Johnson, Andrew, p. 307

Congress dealt with the problem by setting up an electoral commission. At this point a deal was apparently struck under which southern Democratic leaders agreed to give the election to Hayes in return for a promise to end military rule in the South. Both sides kept their part of the bargain, and President Hayes ordered removal of troops from the South. This act virtually ended any attempt in the South to enforce the Fourteenth Amendment to the Constitution, which had guaranteed civil and political rights to the former slaves. The agreement also set the outlines of political alignment for many years to come. Republicans benefited from a virtual lock on the presidency, and white southern Democrats were given a free hand to solidify their own regional power and deprive blacks of their civil rights.

Religion and the Presidency

For all its profound impact on American life, religion has only occasionally played a major public role in shaping the presidency as an institution.

Although presidents take their oath of office with their hand resting on the Bible, the Constitution specifically bars the imposition of religious oaths or tests on the president and other federal officeholders. In deciding to exclude religion as a formal requirement of office, the nation's founders broke with the prevailing practice in most states at that time. Some state constitutions required an adherence to Christianity as a condition for serving as governor, while others specified allegiance to Protestant Christianity. Some of those attending the Constitutional Convention thought that it was not necessary to prohibit a religious test, but the provision was included anyway.

Given the overwhelmingly Protestant character of the United States in the nineteenth century, inclusion of a formal religious requirement would have been unnecessary—only those of that creed had any political chance at all of aspiring to the White House. It was not until the heavy waves of immigration of the late nineteenth and early twentieth centuries, which brought millions of Roman Catholics and Jews to America, that people outside the Protestant tradition began to acquire significant political power.

The first major non-Protestant presidential candidate was Gov. Alfred E. Smith of New York, who ran on the Democratic ticket in 1928. Smith, a Catholic, had strong support from ethnic groups and urban political machines. But his Catholicism was the target of religious slurs throughout his campaign, and his religion and support for repeal of Prohibition made him an object of intense suspicion in the traditionally Democratic South. Although Smith lost in a landslide, his strength among urban ethnic minorities presaged the emergence of the New Deal coalition put together by Franklin D. Roosevelt, of which Catholics were a major element.

Another test of religious tolerance and the ability of a Catholic to run for president came in 1960. At that time Sen. John F. Kennedy of Massachusetts appeared to have a strong chance for the nomination, but many people wondered whether his Catholicism would be an obstacle. Particularly in the South, some people worried that a Catholic president might somehow subordinate the nation to orders from the pope in Rome.

Kennedy's handling of the religious question in the primary campaign was shrewd and would be repeated in the fall campaign. He framed the question as one of tolerance, which put his opponents on the defensive. He frequently stated his commitment to the separation of church and state and said that a president who violated that separation would be committing both an impeachable offense and a sin against God. The decisive battle came in the primary in West Virginia, an overwhelmingly Protestant state. Kennedy's easy win there over Sen. Hubert H. Humphrey of Minnesota cleared the way for his nomination. In the general election campaign against Vice President Richard Nixon, Kennedy's strong support from Catholics may have provided the margin for his razor-thin victory.

After Kennedy, the religion of presidential candidates ceased to be a major consideration, at least for those of Christian denominations. Although no other Catholics had become major-party presidential nominees by 1992, several were important contenders for the Democratic nomination, and three were vice-presidential nominees of the party. In 1988 the fact that Gov. Michael S. Dukakis of Massachusetts was Greek Orthodox evoked virtually no discussion during his campaign for the Democratic nomination and in the general election. For non-Christians, however, religion is still perceived by some as a barrier to candidacy.

The Almighty God has blessed our land in many ways. He has given our people stout hearts and strong arms with which to strike mighty blows for freedom and truth. He has given to our country a faith which has become the hope of all peoples in an anguished world.

—Franklin D. Roosevelt, *Fourth Inaugural Address,* January 20, 1945

Religion has remained an important factor in presidential politics because of the increased political prominence of evangelical Christians, particularly Protestants. This group, which traditionally had avoided political involvement, became a political factor of rising significance during the 1970s and 1980s. Some presidential candidates have had success in mobilizing evangelical Christians, a particularly important voting bloc in the South. Jimmy Carter, for example, reached out to fellow "born again" Christians, who provided pivotal support for him in carrying some southern states. Ronald Reagan received help from the increasingly organized Christian Right, which strongly supported his opposition to abortion and endorsement of conservative moral values, even though he was not a frequent churchgoer. The Reverend Jesse Jackson unsuccessfully sought the Democratic nomination in 1984 and 1988. In 1988 Pat Robertson, a prominent Christian broadcaster, made an unsuccessful bid for the Republican presidential nomination. At the 1992 and 1996 presidential nominating conventions the Robertson-led Christian Coalition strongly influenced the GOP platform, forcing adoption of conservative planks, including a stand against abortion. Political analysts later concluded that this action alienated moderate Republicans and turned some to the Democrats in the general election.

> **More on this topic:**
>
> *Background of Presidents,*
> *p. 26*
>
> *Interest Groups and the*
> *Presidency, p. 290*
>
> *Oath of Office, p. 393*
>
> *Qualifications of the*
> *President and Vice*
> *President, p. 432*
>
> *Speeches and Rhetoric,*
> *p. 466*

George W. Bush won the support of many Christian conservatives in the 2000 election. As president, Bush established the Office of Faith-Based and Community Initiatives in the White House. The new office sparked criticism from people concerned about the effort to develop policies that would provide government funding for religious organizations involved in charitable and other public services. In December 2002 Bush, bypassing Congress, issued an executive order that gave religious charities equal treatment when applying for federal social service money.

Religion has played a key role in presidential rhetoric throughout the life of the Republic. References to Divine Providence occur regularly in the speeches and messages of many nineteenth-century presidents. In the twentieth century, religion is almost absent in official presidential communications such as messages to Congress, but it has remained an important tool presidents use in the art of public persuasion. Franklin D. Roosevelt appealed to the public's religious faith as a way to link the righteousness of America's struggle against fascism to the principles of Judeo-Christian values. In 1944, with American troops still engaged in raging battles in both Europe and the Pacific, Roosevelt ended one of his famous fireside chats with a prayer that included, "And now, may the blessing of God Almighty rest upon this whole land; may He give us light to guide us, courage to support us, charity to unite us, now and forevermore. Amen."

During the ideological struggle of the cold war, inclusion of prayer in rhetoric continued. A notable example was Dwight D. Eisenhower's asking the audience to bow their heads as he read a prayer before beginning his official inaugural address. During times of relative peace, references to God remain common, and it is has become almost a standard procedure that presidents end addresses to the nation with some acknowledgement of a creator, usually in an effort to associate a common national goal or struggle with the work of God. Among recent presidents this is commonly heard as "May God bless America."

Removal of President, Vice President   *See* DISABILITY AMENDMENT; IMPEACHMENT; SUCCESSION.

Republican Party   *See* POLITICAL PARTIES.

Rockefeller, Nelson A.

Nelson A. Rockefeller.
Source: The White House

Nelson Aldrich Rockefeller (1908–1979) served as vice president under Gerald R. Ford from December 1974 to January 1977. Ford and Rockefeller were the only president–vice president team to hold office without being elected.

Nelson was born into one of the country's wealthiest families. His paternal grandfather was John D. Rockefeller, the billionaire philanthropist who founded Standard Oil. In 1930 Nelson graduated from Dartmouth College and was named to the Phi Beta Kappa honor society, despite suffering from dyslexia. He then helped to manage the numerous holdings of the Rockefeller family. From 1935 to 1940 he served as director of the Standard Oil subsidiary in Venezuela, where he developed an interest in Latin American affairs.

In 1940 President Franklin D. Roosevelt appointed Rockefeller to head the Office for Coordination of Commercial and Cultural Relations between the American Republics (later renamed the Office of Inter-American Affairs). In 1944 Rockefeller became assistant secretary of state for Latin American affairs. He resigned in 1945 after clashing with other State Department officials. In 1950 he returned to government when President Harry S. Truman appointed him to chair the Advisory Board on International Development. When the president did not commit himself to act on the board's proposals, Rockefeller resigned in 1951.

Rockefeller supported Dwight D. Eisenhower's successful bid for the presidency in 1952, and in 1953 Eisenhower appointed him undersecretary of the newly created Department of Health, Education, and Welfare. In 1954 Rockefeller became special assistant to the president for foreign affairs, but he resigned in 1955 after conflicts with Secretary of State John Foster Dulles. From 1953 to 1958 Rockefeller chaired Eisenhower's Advisory Committee on Government Organization, which studied ways to reorganize the government.

Rockefeller was elected governor of New York as a Republican in 1958. In this office he supported civil rights legislation, urban renewal, and an expanded state university system. He was reelected governor in 1962, 1966, and 1970, resigning in December 1973 before his final term expired.

Rockefeller wanted to be president and unsuccessfully sought the Republican nomination for all three presidential elections held in the 1960s. Although he had conservative views on many issues, including law enforcement and military spending, he was hindered by the fact that many conservatives perceived him as a liberal.

On August 20, 1974, President Gerald R. Ford, who had succeeded to the presidency from the vice presidency after the resignation of President Richard Nixon, nominated Rockefeller for vice president. Under the Twenty-fifth Amendment Rockefeller's appointment had to be approved by both houses of Congress. The confirmation hearings lasted throughout the fall as committees examined the nominee's vast financial holdings for conflicts of interest. Finally, on December 19, 1974, he was sworn in as the forty-first vice president.

More on this topic:

Ford, Gerald R., p. 224

Seals of Office, p. 456

Vice President, p. 539

Rockefeller chaired several boards and commissions as vice president, including a commission set up to investigate the Central Intelligence Agency. At Ford's request Rockefeller did not run for vice president in 1976, because Ford believed he could attract more votes in the Republican primaries without him. Nevertheless, the vice president remained loyal to Ford. He delivered the speech nominating Sen. Robert J. Dole of Kansas as the Republican vice-presidential nominee and campaigned for the Ford-Dole ticket.

After leaving the vice presidency in 1977, Rockefeller returned to New York to manage various family business and philanthropic enterprises. He died of a heart attack on January 26, 1979.

Roosevelt Corollary *See* ROOSEVELT, THEODORE.

Roosevelt, Eleanor

Anna Eleanor Roosevelt (1884–1962) was the wife of President Franklin D. Roosevelt. Her public visibility, advocacy of causes, frequent travel, and independent political activism redefined the role of first lady.

Eleanor was born into a prominent New York family. Both of her parents died when she was a child, and she was raised by a strict great-aunt. In 1902 Eleanor met Franklin Delano Roosevelt, a distant cousin. They married on March 17, 1905. Their wedding date was set for the convenience of Eleanor's uncle, President Theodore Roosevelt, who gave the bride away. The couple had six children, one of whom died in infancy.

Called "first lady of the world," Eleanor Roosevelt redefined the role. She was an outspoken critic of racial discrimination and pushed strongly for women's rights. The first of the first ladies to fly, she traveled extensively throughout the country and overseas, visiting poor inner-city neighborhoods or cheering U.S. troops. Here she kneels, second row center, among women reporters in 1933.
Source: FDR Library

Eleanor was a shy young woman with a serious disposition. Franklin's urbane friends made her feel inadequate, and her mother-in-law, Sara Delano Roosevelt, was a domineering woman who largely ran Eleanor's household. Not until she was in her thirties did Eleanor begin to emerge from her shell. A series of events—including a move away from Sara to Washington, exposure to the capital's politics, the discovery of her husband's affair with her social secretary, and finally Franklin's polio attack in 1921—combined to draw her into public life. Knowing that she could help further Franklin's political career, she learned to make public appearances and to participate in politics.

When Roosevelt became president in 1933, Eleanor threw herself into the job of first lady. She traveled throughout the country, visiting coal mines, impoverished Appalachian farms, and poor inner-city neighborhoods. During World War II she made many trips overseas to cheer U.S. troops. She was the first of the nation's first ladies to fly, and she advocated air travel when many Americans were still afraid of it.

Eleanor adopted a variety of causes. She called for programs to assist the young and the rural poor. An advocate of women's rights, she was influential in the selection of the first female cabinet member, Secretary of Labor Frances Perkins, and helped to expand government employment opportunities for women. She was an outspoken critic of racial discrimination, symbolized in her public resignation from the Daughters of the American Revolution because of the group's racially discriminatory policies, and she pushed for better job opportunities for blacks.

Eleanor made wide use of the media. She held regular news conferences, made frequent radio broadcasts, wrote magazine articles, delivered public lectures, and began her own daily newspaper column. She publicly denied influencing the president, but she regularly discussed her political views with him and was an important adviser in many decisions.

> **More on this topic:**
>
> *First Ladies, p. 219*
>
> *Roosevelt, Franklin D., below*

Eleanor's time as first lady ended with the death of Franklin Roosevelt on April 12, 1945, but she remained active on the national political scene. Named as a delegate to the new United Nations in 1946, she was instrumental in writing the Universal Declaration of Human Rights. She actively supported the presidential bids of Adlai E. Stevenson II in 1952 and 1956 and continued to speak in favor of equal rights in American society.

In 1962 she was seriously ill with bone marrow tuberculosis and deteriorated rapidly. The woman who was called "first lady of the world" died on November 7 at her home in New York. She was buried next to her husband on their Hyde Park estate.

Roosevelt, Franklin D.

Source: FDR Library

Franklin Delano Roosevelt (1882–1945) served more than twelve years as president and was the only president to be elected more than twice. He died in office shortly after the beginning of his fourth term. Roosevelt faced two major challenges during his presidency—the Great Depression and World War II. He is credited with advancing policies that led the nation out of the Great Depression and with overseeing the Allied war effort that resulted in the defeat of Germany and Japan in 1945.

Roosevelt was born into a wealthy family on January 30, 1882, in Hyde Park, New York. His father, James Roosevelt, was a lawyer and railroad executive who had inherited a fortune. Franklin graduated from Harvard University in 1903, but stayed a year longer to study history and economics as a graduate student. He then studied law at Columbia University from 1904 until 1907 but left without graduating when he passed the bar. Roosevelt married Anna Eleanor Roosevelt, a fifth cousin, on March 17, 1905. They had six children, one of

Most Americans associate December 7, 1941, the day Roosevelt asserted would "live in infamy," as the date on which the Japanese navy bombed Pearl Harbor. The president's address to Congress the next morning, in which he asked for a declaration of war against Japan, also included a comprehensive list of other targets that were also attacked by Japan. The president told the Congress,

- Yesterday the Japanese Government also launched an attack against Malaya.
- Last night Japanese forces attacked Hong Kong.
- Last night Japanese forces attacked Guam.
- Last night Japanese forces attacked the Philippine Islands.
- Last night the Japanese attacked Wake Island.
- And this morning the Japanese attacked Midway Island.

—*Franklin D. Roosevelt,* Address to Congress Requesting a Declaration of War against Japan, December 8, 1941

Ironically, the attacks against American and British interests in Asia and the Pacific came the day after Roosevelt sent a letter to Japanese Emperor Hirohito in which he stated

I address myself to Your Majesty at this moment in the fervent hope that Your Majesty may, as I am doing, give thought in this definite emergency to ways of dispelling the dark clouds.

—*Franklin D. Roosevelt,* Appeal to Emperor Hirohito to Avoid War in the Pacific, December 6, 1941

whom died in infancy. Eleanor Roosevelt set a new standard for first ladies, promoting numerous social causes and serving as her husband's representative at many functions.

Political Career

Roosevelt was elected to the New York senate as a Democrat in 1910. He was reelected in 1912 but gave up his seat in 1913 when President Woodrow Wilson appointed him assistant secretary of the navy. After war broke out in Europe in 1914 Roosevelt argued for greater military preparedness. Near the end of the war he developed a plan to hinder German submarine attacks. His "North Sea Mine Barrage," a 240-mile cordon of antisubmarine mines in the Atlantic, reduced shipping losses.

In 1920 Roosevelt resigned from the Navy Department when the Democratic Party nominated him as the vice-presidential running mate of James M. Cox. Democrats hoped that the young politician with the famous name could boost the ticket, but Cox and Roosevelt were badly beaten by Republicans Warren G. Harding and Calvin Coolidge.

In 1921 Roosevelt was stricken with poliomyelitis and was left severely handicapped. Over a period of years he partially rehabilitated himself, building up his strength so that he was able to walk short distances with the aid of crutches and braces. On June 26, 1924, Roosevelt returned to national politics when he delivered a speech at the Democratic national convention in New York City. Roosevelt's courageous appearance on crutches at Madison Square Garden increased his popularity.

The Democratic Party nominated Roosevelt for governor of New York in 1928. Questions about his physical ability were dispelled by his vigorous campaigning. He went on to win the election despite the victory in New York of Republican presidential candidate Herbert C. Hoover. As governor, Roosevelt gave tax relief to New York's farmers and lowered the cost of public utilities to consumers. He was reelected in a landslide in 1930. During his second term he concentrated on easing the suffering caused by the Great Depression.

Roosevelt's success as governor led to his nomination for president in 1932. During the campaign Roosevelt radiated confidence and outlined his recovery program, which he called the "New Deal." In the election Roosevelt outpolled President Hoover by more than seven million votes and won 472–59 in the Electoral College. Many voters blamed Hoover for the severity of the depression.

Presidency

Roosevelt took office at the low point of the depression. Most of the nation's banks were closed, industrial production was about half of what it had been in 1928, and as many as fifteen million people were unemployed. He worked with the new Democratic Congress to enact many New Deal bills during the productive opening period of his presidency, known as the FIRST HUNDRED DAYS. He declared a four-day bank holiday to stop panic withdrawals, abandoned the gold standard, increased government loans to farmers and homeowners, and created federal insurance for bank deposits. At Roosevelt's urging, Congress created the Civilian Conservation Corps, which employed tens of thousands of people on conservation projects, and passed the Federal Emergency Relief Act, which provided grants to state and local governments for aid to the unemployed.

Roosevelt promoted his policies through "fireside chats," radio addresses to the nation from the White House. A second wave of New Deal programs, including Social

Security, unemployment insurance, and federal aid to dependent children, was passed in 1934 and 1935. Roosevelt's New Deal successes made him a popular president. He defeated Kansas governor Alfred M. Landon in 1936 in one of the largest landslides in presidential election history.

In 1937 Roosevelt suffered a major political defeat when he proposed to expand the Supreme Court from nine to as many as fifteen justices. Roosevelt had been frustrated by the conservative Court, which had struck down several of his New Deal measures. If the Court were expanded he could appoint justices who would accept his policies. Neither the public nor Congress, however, would go along with Roosevelt's Court-packing scheme.

In 1940 Roosevelt ran for an unprecedented third term against the progressive Republican nominee, Wendell L. Willkie of Indiana. Roosevelt defeated Willkie by a vote of 449–82 in the Electoral College. His popular margin of victory was less than that four years earlier, however, in part because some voters objected to Roosevelt's disregard of the unwritten rule that presidents should serve no more than two terms.

In September 1939 Germany, under Adolf Hitler, had invaded Poland, starting World War II in Europe. Despite strong neutralist sentiment among members of Congress and the general public, Roosevelt recognized that U.S. national security depended on Great Britain's survival. He promised to keep the United States out of the fighting, but attempted to aid Britain and other Allied nations in every way short of going to war. In March 1941 Roosevelt persuaded Congress to pass the Lend-Lease Act, which gave the president the power to supply weapons and equipment to "any country whose defense the president deems vital to the defense of the United States." In September of that year Roosevelt ordered U.S. warships protecting supply convoys bound for Great Britain to attack German vessels on sight. Thus Roosevelt engaged the United States in an undeclared naval war months before the nation formally entered the war.

On December 7, 1941, the Japanese launched a surprise attack against the U.S. fleet at Pearl Harbor, Hawaii. The next day Roosevelt asked Congress for and received a declaration of war on Japan. Congress declared war on Germany and Italy on December 11. Roosevelt oversaw the development of military strategy and met often with British prime minister Winston Churchill. Roosevelt and Churchill met with Soviet leader Joseph Stalin at Tehran in 1943 and at Yalta in 1945. At these meetings the leaders of the three Allied nations discussed wartime strategy and also planned for the postwar order. At Yalta, Roosevelt secured a Soviet promise to enter the war against Japan when Germany was defeated in return for territorial concessions in Asia. The Allies also scheduled a conference in 1945 to establish the United Nations and agreed to allow occupied countries to construct new governments based on free elections after the war. Many historians have criticized Roosevelt for being too trusting of Stalin, who established communist puppet states in eastern Europe after the war.

Although the strain of the wartime presidency had weakened Roosevelt, he ran for a fourth term in 1944. Roosevelt defeated his fourth Republican opponent, New York governor Thomas E. Dewey, by a vote of 432–99 in the Electoral College.

In April 1945, after returning from Yalta, Roosevelt went to his vacation home in Warm Springs, Georgia, for a rest. On April 12 he collapsed from a cerebral hemorrhage and died a few hours later. That same day in Washington, Vice President Harry S. Truman was sworn in as president. The world mourned the dead president as a train carried his body back to Washington to lie in state at the White House. The train then resumed its journey north to Roosevelt's Hyde Park home, where he was buried.

More on this topic:

Brownlow Committee, p. 33

Court-Packing Plan, p. 127

Elections Chronology, p. 174

First Hundred Days, p. 218

Great Depression, p. 237

Japanese American Internment, p. 303

New Deal, p. 383

Roosevelt, Eleanor, p. 444

World War II, p. 588

Roosevelt, Theodore

Source: Library of Congress

Theodore Roosevelt (1858–1919) dominated U.S. politics during the opening decade of the twentieth century. He was the first person to be elected to his own term as president after serving out the term of an incumbent who had died in office. At the age of forty-two he also was the youngest person ever to serve as president.

Roosevelt was born on October 27, 1858, in New York City. His father was a wealthy New York City banker and merchant. Throughout his boyhood he suffered from asthma and other illnesses. When he was thirteen he began a program of vigorous physical exercise that turned him into a robust young man. Roosevelt entered Harvard in 1876. He graduated in 1880 and was elected to the Phi Beta Kappa honor society. He then enrolled in Columbia Law School but dropped out after a year of study. He married Alice Hathaway Lee in 1880 on his twenty-second birthday.

Roosevelt was elected to the New York legislature at the age of twenty-three. He was reelected in 1882 and 1883 but declined to seek another term after his wife and his mother died within hours of each other on February 14, 1884. From 1884 to 1886 Roosevelt sought refuge from his grief in the Dakota Territory, where he managed a ranch and served for a period as a deputy sheriff. He returned to New York in 1886 and married his childhood friend Edith Kermit Carow later that year. They settled down at Sagamore Hill, in Oyster Bay, Long Island. There he wrote books on American history and life in the West.

In 1889 President Benjamin Harrison appointed Roosevelt U.S. civil service commissioner. He was reappointed in 1893 by Democrat Grover Cleveland and served until 1895. As commissioner, Roosevelt revised civil service exams, doubled the number of government positions subject to examination, and increased government job opportunities for women.

Roosevelt moved to Washington, D.C., in 1897 when President William McKinley appointed him assistant secretary of the navy. On February 25, 1898, with Navy Secretary John Long absent from the capital, Roosevelt ordered the Pacific fleet to go to Hong Kong and prepare to destroy the Spanish fleet stationed in the Pacific in the event of a U.S. declaration of war against Spain. In issuing the order Roosevelt overstepped his authority, but when Commodore George Dewey defeated the Spanish fleet in the battle of Manila Bay on May 1, 1898, Roosevelt's action was vindicated.

Soon after the United States declared war, Roosevelt resigned from the Navy Department so he could fight in Cuba. He secured the rank of lieutenant colonel and organized a regiment of cavalry that came to be known as the Rough Riders. Although the importance of the Rough Riders to the U.S. victory over the Spanish in Cuba became exaggerated, Roosevelt showed his courage in leading his regiment in a charge up one of the San Juan Hills overlooking Santiago.

Roosevelt's exploits in Cuba made him a celebrity in the United States. In November 1898 he was elected governor of New York. The political independence Roosevelt exerted as governor disturbed the power brokers of his state's Republican Party. In 1900 they hoped to get rid of Roosevelt by promoting him as a candidate for vice president. Although Roosevelt declared he did not want the job, he was nominated on the ticket with President McKinley. Mark Hanna, the Republican national chairman, warned his colleagues, "Don't any of you realize that there's only one life between this madman and the White House?" On September 6, 1901, President McKinley was shot in

Buffalo, New York. Doctors initially thought McKinley would recover, but he died on September 14. Later in the day Roosevelt took the oath of office.

Presidency

Despite retaining McKinley's cabinet, Roosevelt promoted his own policies, which included measures to curb abuses by big business. He directed Attorney General Philander Knox to prepare an antitrust suit against Northern Securities Company, a giant railroad trust. The suit was won in 1904 when the Supreme Court ruled that the company should be dissolved. Although the Roosevelt administration initiated fewer antitrust suits than the Taft administration that followed it, Roosevelt became known as the trust-busting president.

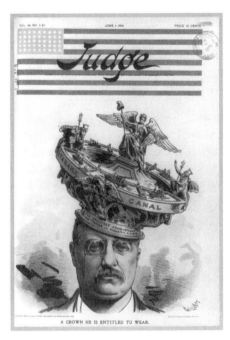

Theodore Roosevelt wearing ornate allegorical crown of Panama Canal, "the greatest achievement for trade in modern times."
Source: Library of Congress

Roosevelt's most famous act during his first term was his acquisition of land for the Panama Canal. Colombia owned Panama, and in August 1903 the Colombian senate refused to give the United States the rights to a canal zone six miles wide. Determined to build the canal, Roosevelt supported a revolution in Panama that overthrew Colombian rule with the help of the U.S. Navy. The new Panamanian government agreed to lease the zone to the United States, and the building of the canal began.

In the 1904 presidential election Roosevelt ran against New York judge Alton B. Parker. Roosevelt lost the South, but he received over 56 percent of the popular vote, swept the North and West, and easily won in the Electoral College 336–140. During his second term Roosevelt championed many pieces of reform legislation, including the Pure Food and Drug Act, the Meat Inspection Act, and the Hepburn Act, which empowered the government to set railroad rates. Roosevelt also continued the conservationist activities begun during his first term. In late 1904 Roosevelt issued the Roosevelt Corollary to the Monroe Doctrine, which said that the United States would intervene in Latin America to prevent European nations from interfering there. The next year he put the corollary into practice by taking control of the Santo Domingo customhouses to guarantee that country's European debts. In 1905 he mediated an agreement ending the Russo-Japanese War and was awarded the Nobel Peace Prize for his efforts. In the face of congressional opposition Roosevelt also sent the U.S. fleet on a world cruise that lasted from late 1907 to early 1909. The show of strength was intended to impress other nations, especially Japan, with U.S. resolve to play an active role in world affairs.

Former President

Roosevelt's friend and secretary of war, William Howard Taft, was elected president in 1908 with Roosevelt's backing. By 1910, however, Roosevelt had become alienated from Taft, who he felt had abandoned his policies. In 1912 Roosevelt wanted the Republican nomination for president. He won most of the primaries, but the Republican national convention in Chicago was controlled by

More on this topic:
Elections Chronology, p. 174
Historic Milestones of the Presidency, p. 253
Square Deal, p. 471
Stewardship Theory, p. 482
Third Parties, p. 498
Travel, p. 513
White House, p. 573

supporters of President Taft, who received the nomination. Roosevelt supporters organized the Progressive Party and persuaded Roosevelt to run. The party was dubbed the "Bull Moose" Party, because Roosevelt declared that he felt "as fit as a bull moose."

On October 14, 1912, while campaigning in Milwaukee, Roosevelt was shot in the chest by an assailant. He insisted on giving a scheduled speech, which lasted almost an hour. He was then rushed from the amazed crowd to a hospital. Taft and Democratic candidate Woodrow Wilson stopped their campaigns while Roosevelt recovered; the former president was delivering speeches again within two weeks. Roosevelt's heroic campaigning, however, could not overcome the split he had caused among Republicans. In the election second-place Roosevelt and third-place Taft together received over a million more votes than Wilson, but with his opposition divided, Wilson finished first.

The Progressives asked Roosevelt to run for president again in 1916, but Roosevelt declined and supported Republican Charles Evans Hughes, who lost to President Wilson. During World War I Roosevelt was a leading Republican spokesman and likely would have been his party's candidate for president in 1920 had he lived. He was hospitalized in November 1918 with a severe attack of rheumatism. He returned to Sagamore Hill for Christmas but remained ill. He died in his sleep on January 6, 1919, from an arterial blood clot.

Rose Garden *See* WHITE HOUSE.

Rumsfeld, Donald H.

Source: Library of Congress

Donald H. Rumsfeld (1932–) had a lengthy career in federal service, including two stints as secretary of defense. (He was both the youngest and the oldest person to hold that position.) Rumsfeld was born in Chicago and graduated from Princeton University in 1954. He served in the U.S. Navy from 1954 to 1957 as an aviator and a flight instructor, after which he served in the reserves.

Rumsfeld arrived in Washington, D.C., in 1957 as an administrative assistant on Capitol Hill. He worked for Rep. David Dennison of Ohio, a Republican, and then served on the staff of Rep. Robert Griffin of Michigan, also a Republican. He later worked for an investment banking firm before winning election in 1962 to a U.S. House seat from Illinois. He was reelected to three more terms. In 1969 he resigned from Congress to work for President Richard Nixon. His posts included director of the Office of Economic Opportunity and director of the

Economic Stabilization Program. In 1973 he went to Brussels as U.S. ambassador to the North Atlantic Treaty Organization.

Already an old Washington hand, Rumsfeld returned to the nation's capital in 1974 as chairman of President Gerald R. Ford's transition team. He served as White House chief of staff until 1975 and became defense secretary that year. When Rumsfeld left the chief of staff job, his deputy, Richard B. Cheney—who later served as vice president in George W. Bush's administration while Rumsfeld returned as defense secretary—took over.

Rumsfeld entered the private sector in 1977, working as chief executive officer, president, and then chairman of the pharmaceutical company G. D. Searle. Also in 1977 he was awarded the Presidential Medal of Freedom, the country's highest civilian honor. He later served as chairman and chief executive officer of the technology firm General Instrument Corporation. While in that position he served on various federal commissions.

After winning the White House in 2000, George W. Bush tapped Rumsfeld to come back to the Pentagon for another appointment as defense secretary. Rumsfeld took up his post in 2001, just months before the September 11 terrorist attacks, which struck the Defense Department's Pentagon headquarters and the World Trade Center in New York City. Before September 11, Rumsfeld had argued for shifting resources, and even cutting active personnel, for the sake of the modernization of weaponry and the development of a new generation of high-tech weapons. These arguments were muted in the immediate aftermath of the attacks; to fund the WAR ON TERRORISM Congress increased defense spending.

As the administration fought the war on terrorism, including overthrowing and replacing the government of Afghanistan and preparing for a possible invasion of Iraq, Rumsfeld's daily televised news briefings made him something of a celebrity. Viewed as a hawk on Iraq, Rumsfeld was a major proponent of American military action, even on a unilateral basis, to overthrow the regime of Iraqi dictator Saddam Hussein. A "coalition of the willing," which most notably included Great Britain but not France, Russia, and Germany, eventually aided the U.S. effort in Iraq, and the war began on March 19, 2003, when Hussein failed to meet a U.S. deadline to step down from power.

Although Hussein's regime fell quickly, the occupation in Iraq dragged on and the situation on the ground worsened. Rumsfeld began to face harsh criticism for lack of appropriate planning for the postwar occupation including the decision to disband the Iraqi army, leaving thousands of unemployed armed men throughout Iraq. As looting and violence broke out across the country, Rumsfeld's decision to prosecute the war with troop and material strength far below what was cautioned by some military experts was also called into question. In December 2004, while taking questions from troops deployed to Iraq, Rumsfeld was asked why soldiers had to dig through trash dumps looking for armor to weld onto their vehicles, Rumsfeld's answer was, "As you know, you go to war with the army you have, not the army you might want." This response further exasperated his critics.

Another issue that arose on Rumsfeld's watch was the treatment of "unlawful combatants" and others considered prisoners of war. The most notorious of these alleged abuses of prisoner rights occurred at the Abu Ghraib prison west of Baghdad and included sleep deprivation, water boarding, and aggravation of existing injuries. Many other accounts of activities at Abu Ghraib alleged torture and led to a diminishing of the United States' reputation throughout the world. Among the evidence were photographs leaked to the press, showing humiliating treatment of prisoners at the hands of American military personnel.

> *Don once famously said, "There are known knowns; there are known unknowns; and there are unknown unknowns." Well, Mr. Secretary, here is a known known: Your service has made America stronger and made America a safer nation.*
>
> —*George W. Bush,* Remarks on the Resignation of Secretary of Defense Donald H. Rumsfeld and the Nomination of Robert M. Gates To Be Secretary of Defense, November 8, 2006

More on this topic:

Defense Department,
p. 144

Iraq War, p. 296

War on Terrorism,
p. 554

Calls for Rumsfeld's resignation, though first seriously called for after the Abu Ghraib abuses were uncovered, gained new momentum in early 2006 when a coalition of retired generals publicly questioned his strategic competence. President Bush steadfastly supported his defense secretary, and only days before the 2006 midterm elections, the president insisted that Rumsfeld would remain in office through the remainder of his term. But on November 8, 2006, the day after the Republican Party lost both houses of Congress in a major electoral defeat, Bush announced Rumsfeld's resignation. At the time of his resignation on December 18, 2006, Rumsfeld was the second longest serving secretary of defense, behind Robert McNamara.

Salary and Perquisites

The president of the United States makes $400,000 a year, a regal salary by the standards of most Americans but very low compared with that of most top corporate executives. Like other executives, the nation's chief executive also receives perquisites, or perks—those extras such as limousines, vacation homes, and generous pensions that make the job easier and more appealing. For the most part, Americans do not mind footing the bill for the president's salary and perks, because whatever they think of a particular president, they take pride in the presidency.

Salary

Some of the framers of the Constitution, worried that the president of the new Republic would become too powerful, thought this official should receive little or no pay. Benjamin Franklin, arguing that the love of money lay at the root of all political evil, proposed that the president receive "no salary, stipend, fee or reward" beyond what was necessary for expenses. This idea was not adopted, however. Article II, Section 1, of the Constitution states that the president shall receive "a compensation" and stipulates that it is not to be "increased or diminished" while the president is in office. Congress determines the amount of the president's compensation.

The First Congress, in 1789, set the president's salary at $25,000 a year, in those times a princely sum. The first president, George Washington, perhaps mindful of the framers' fears, declined the money. It then took Congress the better part of a century to increase the president's salary. The first increase, to $50,000 a year, came in 1873 during the term of Ulysses S. Grant and placed the president squarely among the highest paid executives in the world. As the presidency grew in importance, the president's salary also grew, although not nearly as fast as inflation. Raises were few and

In addition to an annual $400,000 salary and the rent-free White House mansion, presidents receive perks such as limousines and helicopters to transport them and their families.
Source: The White House

far between. In 1969 the president's salary went from $100,000 a year, set in 1949, to $200,000 a year—far less in spending power than the salaries paid to early presidents. In 1999 Congress passed and President Bill Clinton signed legislation that doubled the president's salary to $400,000, effective upon the inauguration of the next president.

Congress also has recognized the president's growing need for extra funds to cover expenses. In 1906 it added a yearly travel allowance of $25,000 to the president's regular salary of $50,000 a year. In 1949 Congress replaced the travel allowance with a general expense account of $50,000 to supplement the president's salary. In 1969 the president began receiving an annual $100,000 travel allowance and a $12,000 entertainment allowance, in addition to a $200,000 salary. The president pays taxes on the salary, now $400,000, but not on the official expense account. The White House Office receives an annual $100,000 allowance that covers travel, among other things, and an entertainment allowance of $19,000.

Many presidents have been independently wealthy. Indeed, most recent presidents were millionaires. John F. Kennedy followed the example of George Washington by declining to accept his salary.

Perquisites

George Washington set a standard with elements of formality and pomp, but most early presidents adopted a more humble style. It was considered far more important to be born in a log cabin than to exhibit aristocratic tendencies in office. For political as well as financial reasons, most early presidents lived a more spartan existence than had Washington. Early presidents sometimes brought their own furniture to the White House to make themselves more comfortable. Most found themselves without pensions or other benefits when they retired. Presidents still pay their own personal grocery bills, but the federal government now pays for state dinners and most other official expenses. The modern president lives amid luxury at the White House, travels in special limousines and jets, and is attended to by aides and servants.

One of the president's most valuable perquisites, the WHITE HOUSE, is a rent-free mansion that comes with a large staff and a smaller group of personal servants hired by the first family at government expense. Along with the adjoining Eisenhower Executive Office Building, it offers a wealth of conveniences and luxuries such as a movie theater, a heated swimming pool, a gymnasium, tennis courts, a bowling alley, and a library. For more basic needs, a barbershop and small medical and dental clinics are available. (For serious medical treatment, free care is provided at military hospitals.) A newly elected president receives funds to redecorate the White House, which recent presidents have tended to supplement with private donations.

When presidents want to get away without traveling far, they can summon a helicopter or limousine to take them, along with family members, to the nearby presidential retreat at CAMP DAVID. The government also foots the bill when presidents travel to and from their personal vacation homes.

Daily and Family Life

The White House's travel allowance does not begin to cover the expenses of transporting the president, the first family, and staff members; many of these expenses are absorbed by the agencies that provide the transport. For long-distance trips the president uses the official presidential jet, AIR FORCE ONE, part of a fleet of aircraft maintained especially for the chief executive. For shorter travel the president has several soundproof helicopters. And for local trips a dozen limousines are available; a new addition in 2001 was a Cadillac DeVille first used at George W. Bush's inauguration.

As with travel, the president's entertainment expenses far exceed the $19,000 annual entertainment allowance and are absorbed by the various agencies that contribute to events. The State Department, for example, pays for all state banquets and receptions. At most White House social affairs military bands entertain the president and guests at the expense of the Defense Department. Distinguished performers who entertain White House guests usually consider the honor of being chosen payment enough.

There is no way to compute precisely the value of all these presidential perquisites. One set of perks that can be quantified is the president's pension and other retirement benefits. Before 1958 presidents retired without a pension and often suffered financial hardships. The Former Presidents Act of 1958 gave the president a lifetime pension of $25,000 a year and an additional $50,000 a year for office and staff.

Since 1958 Congress has steadily increased these pensions and allowances. Former presidents now receive an annual pension equal to the salary of a cabinet secretary ($184,900 when Bill Clinton left the White House in 2001), and a president's widow receives a $20,000 annual pension. In addition, FORMER PRESIDENTS are given a generous stipend to make the transition to private life, an annual allowance to maintain staff and an office, and other fringe benefits.

According to the General Services Administration, the five then-living former presidents—Gerald R. Ford, Jimmy Carter, Ronald Reagan, George H. W. Bush, and Bill Clinton—and the widow of Lyndon B. Johnson received more than $2.5 million in fiscal 2001 in pensions and expense accounts.

Vice President's Salary and Perquisites

The vice presidency was traditionally an obscure office with far fewer benefits than those enjoyed by the president. Since the mid-1970s the range of benefits available to vice presidents has grown. When Congress in 1789 set the first presidential salary at $25,000 a year, it gave the vice president only $5,000 a year. In 2001 the vice president earned a salary of $186,300 a year and received an annual expense account of $10,000. The vice president has an office in the Eisenhower Executive Office Building, smaller offices within the White House and on Capitol Hill, a large staff, and access to limousines and jets. Since 1977 the second family has lived in an official VICE-PRESIDENTIAL RESIDENCE on the grounds of the U.S. Naval Observatory in Washington, D.C.

More on this topic:

Air Force One, *p. 8*

Camp David, p. 67

Former Presidents, p. 226

Vice-Presidential Residence, p. 546

White House, p. 573

Seals of Office

Seals of office.
Source: The White House

Visitors to the Oval Office who happen to look up will see on the ceiling a proud eagle embossed in a concave medallion. Around the outside of the medallion are the words: "Seal of the President of the United States." The eagle is protected by a shield of red, white, and blue and holds in its mouth a banner with the familiar phrase "e pluribus unum" (Latin for "out of many, one"). In one talon it clutches a sheaf of arrows to symbolize military strength; in the other talon it holds a peace branch. Fifty stars representing the states surround it.

Eagles have been pictured on coins, seals, and flags since antiquity, perhaps because of their ferocity and regal appearance. In 1782 Congress proclaimed the American bald eagle the national emblem of the United States. Rutherford B. Hayes (1877–1881) was the first president to use an eagle as the official presidential seal. Theodore Roosevelt added the circular border with the words in 1903. Harry S. Truman had the circle of stars representing the states of the union added in 1945 and had the orientation of the eagle changed so that it faced the olive branches instead of the arrows. This was explained to mean that the United States favors peace. Extra stars are inserted when new states join the Union. The seal shows up in many places, from the imposing medallion in the Oval Office ceiling to the covers of matchbooks offered on AIR FORCE ONE, the president's airplane.

The vice-presidential seal looks much like the presidential seal but with-

out the circle of stars around the eagle. In 1975 Vice President Nelson A. Rockefeller had the seal redesigned to enlarge the eagle within the circle and make it look more like the eagle on the presidential seal. It was hoped that this would reflect the improved status of the number two job.

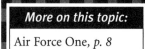

More on this topic:

Air Force One, *p. 8*

For the American eagle on the Presidential seal holds in his talons both the olive branch of peace and the arrows of military might. On the ceiling in the Presidential office, constructed many years ago, that eagle is facing the arrows of war on its left. But on the newer carpet on the floor . . . that eagle is now facing the olive branch of peace. And it is that spirit, the spirit of both preparedness and peace, that this Nation today is stronger than ever before. . . .

—*John F. Kennedy,* Address at the University of Maine, October 19, 1963

Secret Service

Everywhere presidents go they are accompanied by a crew of dark-suited, athletic-looking men and women outfitted with earphones and walkie-talkies. Their eyes never stop tracking the scene in search of anything threatening. As most Americans know, they are Secret Service agents, the most

visible employees of the agency responsible for the safety of presidents and their families. After the terrorist attacks on the United States of September 11, 2001, the Secret Service introduced additional measures to protect the president.

The Secret Service moved from the Treasury Department to the new HOMELAND SECURITY DEPARTMENT on March 1, 2003. The new department was created in the wake of the 2001 terrorist attacks. The Secret Service is really two agencies in one: it protects the president and certain others in public life, including the vice president, and it also investigates financial crimes and the counterfeiting of currency, an espe-

Surrounded by Secret Service agents, President George W. Bush rides in a bullet-proof limousine during the annual St. Patrick's Day parade in downtown Chicago, Illinois, March 16, 2002.
Source: Reuters

cially serious problem in 1865 when the agency was set up by President Abraham Lincoln. In its early years the Secret Service investigated other federal crimes as well, and even gathered intelligence. The Federal Bureau of Investigation and Central Intelligence Agency later took on those tasks, but investigation of counterfeiting and financial crimes remains the responsibility of the Secret Service. The service attempts to break counterfeiting rings before fake bills go into circulation. It also investigates forgeries of government checks and scrip, such as food stamps.

The service did not begin to protect presidents until after William McKinley's assassination in 1901. Two agents were assigned to McKinley's successor in office, Theodore Roosevelt. By 1989 the service's White House detail was seventy agents strong. Over the years Secret Service protection has been extended to cover the president's family and a long list of others in public life: the vice president and his family, retired presidents and their families (including children under sixteen), widows of presidents (unless they have remarried), presidents-elect, the principal presidential candidates and their wives, foreign heads of state, and anyone else the president designates.

The Secret Service employs approximately 2,100 special agents, 1,200 Uniformed Division officers, and approximately 1,700 other technical, professional, and administrative support personnel. A small but growing number of women are entering this traditionally male profession. To be admitted to the special agent training program, an applicant must be between the ages of twenty-one and thirty-five, must pass a physical exam and security check, and must do well in interviews. Those who meet the requirements are trained in investigative techniques, the use of guns, hand-to-hand combat, evasive driving, emergency medical procedures, and the psychology of criminals.

The Secret Service does everything possible to make the White House the safest place on earth. Agents stand guard inside and outside every room the president occupies, except when the president retreats to the family quarters. Agents constantly monitor the White House and the surrounding grounds with hidden television cameras and electronic sensors. They test the air for poisonous gases and bacteria, and they mingle with any visiting tourists to keep a close watch on them. The service even monitors air traffic in the skies around the White House and is prepared to shoot down a threatening plane.

For presidential forays outside the White House, Secret Service agents form a protective shield around the president while constantly watching for threats. They scan crowds in search of suspicious behavior: a man wearing an overcoat on a warm day, a person holding a newspaper in an odd way, a woman too eager to get close to the president, a face that keeps reappearing in different places.

The agents around the president are only a small, visible part of an elaborate network of protection that the Secret Service activates whenever the president travels. Before a trip, agents check a "watch list" of potentially threatening people who live where the president is going, and they check with local police to supplement the list. All such people are watched throughout the presidential visit. Agents check the route of the president's motorcade for potential sniper posts and places to hide bombs. Sharpshooters are stationed along motorcade routes and on rooftops of buildings near where a president will be speaking outdoors. If the president is to appear indoors, agents use trained dogs to sniff out bombs, and they set up metal detectors to check all audience members as they enter.

The best efforts of the Secret Service to protect presidents have not been enough in some cases. As Lyndon B. Johnson observed, "All a man needs is a willingness to trade his life for mine." President John F. Kennedy's assassin, Lee Harvey Oswald, was not listed in the Secret Service's files of dangerous persons, nor were any of the other assassins and would-be assassins of leaders protected by the service since then. Would-be assassins twice missed Gerald R. Ford, and Ronald Reagan survived a bullet wound in the chest.

When all precautions fail, agents are taught to risk their lives in the line of duty. In Dallas in 1963 agent Rufus W. Youngblood covered Vice President Lyndon Johnson with his own body to protect Johnson from the gunfire that killed Kennedy. Videotapes of the 1981 attempt on President Reagan show agent Timothy J. McCarthy walking directly toward the assailant, John Hinckley Jr., with arms and legs spread wide. Like Reagan, McCarthy was shot but recovered.

The element of risk and the possibility of heroism lend glamour to the work of Secret Service agents. Yet the job also entails much tension and even boredom. Leaders and their aides naturally chafe at the unrelenting protection and sometimes try to evade their protectors. The public, too, occasionally resents the agents' aggressive protection measures.

> **More on this topic:**
>
> *Assassinations and Assaults, p. 19*
>
> *Homeland Security Department, p. 260*
>
> *White House, p. 573*

Senate Election of the Vice President

In the event that none of the vice-presidential candidates receives a majority of the ELECTORAL COLLEGE vote, the task of choosing the vice president falls to the Senate. Under the Twelfth Amendment the Senate must choose between the two contenders who received the most electoral votes. Two-thirds of the Senate must be present for the vote, but a simple majority of the Senate membership is enough for election.

The Senate has chosen a vice president only once, in 1837. Martin Van Buren was elected president that year with 170 of 294 electoral votes. However, his running mate, Richard M. Johnson of Kentucky, received only 147 electoral votes—one less than a majority. A group of twenty-three Virginia electors who supported Van Buren boycotted Johnson because he was known to have kept a succession of black mistresses. The remainder of the electoral votes was split among three candidates, with Francis Granger, a Whig from New York, having the most. Required to choose between Johnson and Granger, the Senate voted on party lines, electing Johnson on a 33–16 vote.

> **More on this topic:**
>
> Electoral College, p. 185
>
> Van Buren, Martin, p. 530

The party-line vote leaves one to wonder what would have happened if the Whigs had controlled the Senate. If they had, it is conceivable that the president would have been from one party, his vice president from another.

And given the requirement for a quorum of two-thirds before the Senate would vote on the vice president, what would happen if a party's senators boycotted the Senate chamber? These questions may be answered only if and when the Senate is again asked to choose the vice president.

Senatorial Courtesy

Senatorial courtesy is an unwritten tradition by which the Senate refuses to confirm a nomination to an office within a particular state unless the nominee has been approved by the senators of the president's party from that state. A senator typically invokes the rule of courtesy by stating that the nominee is "personally obnoxious" to him or her. This may mean that the senator and the nominee are personal or political foes, or simply that the senator has another candidate for the post.

The unwritten courtesy rule primarily affects nominations of judges to federal district courts and certain other courts, U.S. attorneys, federal marshals, and other officials based locally.

Senatorial courtesy was practiced as early as 1789. During the First Congress the Senate rejected George Washington's nominee to a post in the Port of Savannah out of courtesy to the two Georgia senators, who had a candidate of their own. Washington yielded, nominating the senators' choice. The tradition declined in importance as positions once filled by patronage were brought into the civil service.

> *Q: Mr. President, I believe we mentioned a while ago the rejection of Martin Hutchinson. I wonder if you have any comment on the four rejections by the Senate?*
>
> **THE PRESIDENT: No, I have no comment. Senatorial courtesy still works.**
>
> —Harry S. Truman, News Conference, August 10, 1950

> **More on this topic:**
>
> Appointment and Removal Power, p. 9
>
> Congress and the Presidency, p. 111
>
> Courts and the President, p. 128

Although the custom is sometimes violated, senators usually respect the wishes of their colleagues because they want other senators to do the same when individuals are nominated from their states. Presidents usually respect the tradition as well to maintain good relations with the Senate, at least when it comes to "advice and consent" for their nominees. (See also APPOINTMENT AND REMOVAL POWER.)

Another aspect of senatorial courtesy, widely observed in recent years, enables a single senator to temporarily delay action on a nomination by placing a "hold" on it. Usually the leadership of the senator's party will honor the hold. The senator may be waiting for written answers to questions or other information; when it is received he or she releases the hold.

Separation of Powers

One of the principles underlying the system of government created by the Constitution is the separation of powers. This principle seeks to ensure that clear lines divide the executive, legislative, and judicial branches, especially in terms of membership and to a lesser extent in terms of authority. As long as the branches of government are kept separate, the system of checks and balances is supposed to keep any one branch from becoming a threat to liberty and democratic government.

The Constitution's framers were familiar with the theory, explained most clearly in the writings of the French political philosopher Montesquieu, that to preserve liberty, government should be designed to incorporate the principle of separation of powers. In his work *L'Esprit des Lois*, Montesquieu had written: "When the legislative and executive powers are united in the same person, or in the same body of magistracy, there can be no liberty."

The separation of powers did not require a strict division of labor in which each branch of government would be assigned exclusive power over certain areas. Indeed, the Constitution assigns few powers to the federal government that are not shared by two or more branches. Rather, by separation of powers the Constitution's framers meant something more like "separated institutions," in which the membership of one branch does not overlap with or exert control over the other.

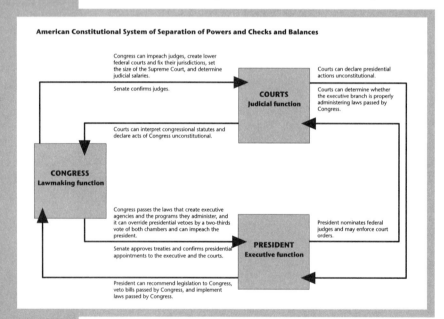

American Constitutional System of Separation of Powers and Checks and Balances

Congress can impeach judges, create lower federal courts and fix their jurisdictions, set the size of the Supreme Court, and determine judicial salaries.

Senate confirms judges.

Courts can declare presidential actions unconstitutional.

COURTS
Judicial function

Courts can determine whether the executive branch is properly administering laws passed by Congress.

Courts can interpret congressional statutes and declare acts of Congress unconstitutional.

CONGRESS
Lawmaking function

Congress passes the laws that create executive agencies and the programs they administer, and it can override presidential vetoes by a two-thirds vote of both chambers and can impeach the president.

Senate approves treaties and confirms presidential appointments to the executive and the courts.

President nominates federal judges and may enforce court orders.

PRESIDENT
Executive function

President can recommend legislation to Congress, veto bills passed by Congress, and implement laws passed by Congress.

The Constitution contains two main provisions designed to ensure the separation of powers. The first prohibits Congress from altering the salary of an incumbent president. By this provision the framers hoped to prevent the legislative branch from infringing on presidents' independence by lowering or delaying their salary, or from trying to reward or entice them with the prospect of higher pay.

The second provision prohibits simultaneous membership in the legislative and executive branches. Under this rule a member of Congress must resign his or her seat before assuming a post in the cabinet or elsewhere in the administration, and vice versa. The goal of this provision was to prevent the executive branch from trying to increase its power by "bribing" members of Congress to vote its way in return for powerful jobs and additional government pay. The prohibition is an important one, because it has effectively precluded the possibility that the United States might adopt a parliamentary system like that of Great Britain, where members of Parliament may hold posts as government ministers.

Another aspect of the Constitution that maintains the separation between the executive and legislative branches is the different schedules by which the president and members of Congress are selected. Members of the House are elected every two years and senators every six, while presidents are chosen on a four-year cycle.

This cycle has an important effect on the president's political relations with Congress. Because the entire membership of the House and one-third of the Senate are up for reelection every two years, members of Congress must face the voters during midterm elections when the presidency is not contested. Although successful presidential candidates have sometimes been able to ensure a majority for their party in Congress—the "coattail effect"—the president's party usually loses seats in the midterm elections. By incorporating an election cycle of midterm elections, the framers of the Constitution were helping to ensure that coordination between the two branches would not be too close.

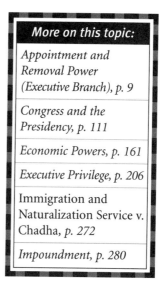

More on this topic:

Appointment and Removal Power (Executive Branch), p. 9

Congress and the Presidency, p. 111

Economic Powers, p. 161

Executive Privilege, p. 206

Immigration and Naturalization Service v. Chadha, *p. 272*

Impoundment, p. 280

In modern times many elections have resulted in divided government, in which the president's party fails to win a majority in one or both houses of Congress. Until 1992, when Democrat Bill Clinton won the White House and the Democrats retained control of Congress, there had been only one other time in the previous twenty years when American voters had chosen one-party rule for the executive and legislative branches. That was during Jimmy Carter's administration (1977–1981). After the 2000 elections Republicans held the White House and both houses of Congress for several months until the Senate switched back to Democratic control when a GOP senator, James Jeffords of Vermont, became an independent and voted with the Democrats to control the chamber. In the 2002 midterm elections Republicans again won a narrow Senate majority, leading to GOP control of both the executive and legislative branches.

The ambiguity of constitutional wording has caused the actual separation between the legislative and executive branches to vary historically. During most of the nineteenth century the dominant view was that presidents ought to scrupulously respect the preeminence of Congress in law making. Yet by modern standards appeals to Congress are considered integral to the president's involvement in the legislative process.

Also in the early years there were debates over the constitutionality of a president's public threat to veto a bill. When a president warned before a bill was passed that he would try to kill it, many people felt that he was intruding into the legislative process. The fear was that allowing the president to have an impact on congressional deliberations would amount to stripping Congress of its power to write laws. In later years it became accepted that a president has the authority to issue veto threats, although some administrations preferred to have such warnings issued by a cabinet official rather than the president himself.

Another gray area in the separation of the branches occurs in the doctrine of EXECUTIVE PRIVILEGE. It holds that the president and other executive officials have the right to withhold sensitive information from Congress or the courts on the grounds that the president needs to be able to communicate in confidence with White House aides and advisers. Congress, however, maintains that it has a legitimate "right to know" about executive business.

Arguments over executive privilege came to a head during the investigation of the Watergate scandal in the Nixon administration. At issue was an attempt by the independent counsel ap-

More on this topic:

Legislative Veto, p. 333

Line-Item Veto, p. 340

Signing Statements, p. 463

Unitary Executive Theory, p. 524

Veto Power, p. 533

War Powers, p. 555

War Powers Act of 1973, p. 560

pointed to investigate the Watergate crimes to obtain secret tape recordings made of Richard Nixon's conversations in the Oval Office. When Nixon refused to turn over the tapes, invoking executive privilege, the case was brought before the Supreme Court. Although the Court ruled against Nixon and ordered him to turn over the tapes, its decision also recognized the concept of executive privilege for the first time.

The Constitution is ambiguous about the office of the vice presidency. The vice president is clearly part of the executive branch, because this official stands ready to assume the presidency at a moment's notice. At the same time, the vice president serves as president of the Senate, which is obviously a legislative position. The lack of clarity over the position of the vice president vis-à-vis the separation of powers has been a factor in relegating the office to obscurity and impotence, at least until recent decades.

Sherman, James S.

James S. Sherman.
Source: Library of Congress

James Schoolcraft Sherman (1855–1912) served as vice president under Republican William Howard Taft from 1909 to 1912. He was the only vice president to die before election day after being nominated for a second term.

Sherman graduated from Hamilton College in Clinton, New York, in 1878. He stayed another year to earn a law degree and then joined a law firm in Utica, New York. Despite being raised in a Democratic family, Sherman chose to enter politics as a Republican. In 1884 he was elected mayor of Utica. Two years later he won a seat in the U.S. House of Representatives, where he served from 1887 to 1891 and from 1893 to 1909. As a member of Congress, Sherman was known best for his amiability and his parliamentary skills. House leaders frequently called on him to preside over debates.

In 1908 Sherman was nominated for vice president on the ticket with Taft. During the campaign Sherman was accused of financial misconduct. Edmund Burke, a California lawyer, claimed that he and Sherman had obtained tens of thousands of acres of Indian land in New Mexico at bargain prices through bribery and Sherman's influence as chairman of the House Committee on Indian Affairs. The Democrats, however, did not press the scandal issue, and the Republicans denounced the unproven charges. Taft and Sherman easily defeated William Jennings Bryan and John W. Kern by a vote of 321–162 in the Electoral College.

As vice president, Sherman was able to do what he did best—preside over a legislative body. He was not a confidant of Taft, who did not like his vice president's ties to New York's Republican machine politicians. Early in their term, however, the two men shared a regular golf game and became friendlier.

Even before becoming vice president, Sherman suffered from Bright's disease, a kidney ailment. He became seriously ill in the spring of 1908, but recovered in time to accept the vice-presidential nomination. During his vice presidency he experienced occasional periods of illness. Nevertheless, he was renominated in 1912 along with Taft. In the fall of that year he became ill, and on October 30 he died of complications caused by his kidney condition.

Because the election was just six days away, the Republican Party did not have time to choose a replacement for Sherman. His death, however, did not affect the outcome of the election. Democrat Woodrow Wilson swept to victory when Theodore Roosevelt's third-party candidacy split the Republican vote.

More on this topic:

Taft, William Howard, p. 490

Vice President, p. 539

Signing Statements

A signing statement is a written comment issued by a president at the time of signing legislation. Often signing statements merely comment on the bill signed, saying that it is good legislation or meets some pressing needs.

More controversial signing statements involve claims by presidents that they believe some part of the legislation is unconstitutional and therefore they intend to ignore it or to implement it only in ways they believe are constitutional. Critics argue that the proper presidential action is either to veto the legislation (Constitution, Article I, Section 7) or to "faithfully execute" the laws (Constitution, Article II, Section 3).

Several sources trace signing statements back to James Monroe. Monroe's path-breaking message informed Congress on January 17, 1822, that he had resolved what he saw as a confusion in an act passed by Congress intended "to reduce and fix the military peace establishment of the United States," in a way that he thought was consistent with his constitutional authority.

Even more forcefully, Monroe sent another message dated April 6, 1822 (that refers to his January 17, 1822, message as having "imperfectly explained" his concerns). In this message he pointed out that the law Congress had passed would have results he thought were nonsensical. "Such a construction would not only be subversive of the obvious principles of the Constitution, but utterly inconsistent with the spirit of the law itself."

Other early statements of presidential reservations over signed legislation came from Andrew Jackson, John Tyler, James K. Polk, and Ulysses S. Grant. In May 1830 Andrew Jackson wrote a message to the House noting his understanding of the limits of an appropriation passed by Congress for surveys and internal improvements by stating, "the phraseology of the section which appropriates the sum of $8,000 for the road from Detroit to Chicago may be construed to authorize the application of the appropriation for the continuance of the road beyond the limits of the Territory of Michigan. I desire to be understood as having approved this bill with the understanding that the road authorized by this section is not to be extended beyond the limits of the said Territory." President Tyler issued a prototypical "reluctant" signing statement, in which he signed a piece of legislation concerning legislative apportionment

> **Such a construction would not only be subversive of the obvious principles of the Constitution, but utterly inconsistent with the spirit of the law itself.**
>
> —*James Monroe,* Message to the House of Representatives, April 6, 1822

while announcing, for the record, that he thought it was unconstitutional. James Polk in 1848 similarly warned that although he was signing legislation that established a government in the Oregon territory that prohibited slavery, he would not have signed similar legislation that involved New Mexico and California south of the "Missouri Compromise Line."

Presidential signing statements came to widespread public notice in 2006. In an article published on April 30, 2006, the *Boston Globe* wrote that "President Bush has quietly claimed the authority to disobey more than 750 laws enacted since he took office." In a clarification issued on May 4, 2006, the *Globe* noted that Bush had not really challenged 750 bills (which would have implied 750 signing statements) but "claimed the authority to bypass more than 750 statutes, which were provisions contained in about 125 bills." As of early 2007, Bush had issued some 140 separate statements asserting that he would enforce laws only in a fashion consistent with his understanding of the separation of powers. Reacting to the way Bush has used signing statements, an American Bar Association (ABA) "Blue Ribbon Task Force" found in July 2006 that these presidential assertions of constitutional authority "undermine the rule of law and our constitutional system of separation of powers." In August 2006 the ABA House of Delegates endorsed the task force report that these were a "misuse" of signing statements.

> **More on this topic:**
>
> *Congress and the Presidency, p. 111*
>
> *Separation of Powers, p. 460*
>
> *Unitary Executive Theory, p. 524*
>
> *Veto Power, p. 533*

Bill Clinton issued almost 400 signing statements, far more than George W. Bush, but the latter's use of these statements has generated controversy because of the kind of signing statements issued. In one frequently used phrase, George W. Bush has routinely asserted that he will not act contrary to the constitutional provisions that direct the president to "supervise the unitary executive branch." This formulation can be found first in a signing statement issued by Ronald Reagan, and it was repeated several times by George H. W. Bush. Basically, President Bush has asserted that Congress cannot pass a law that undercuts the constitutionally granted authorities of the president.

An important legal statement in support of the use of signing statements was developed by Bernard Nussbaum, counsel to President Clinton in 1993. Nussbaum stated that the Department of Justice had advised three prior presidents that the Constitution provided authority to decline to enforce a clearly unconstitutional law.

Smith, Alfred E.

Alfred E. Smith.
Source: Library of Congress

Alfred E. Smith (1873–1944), a popular Democratic governor of New York during the 1920s, lost the 1928 presidential election to Republican Herbert C. Hoover. The grandson of Irish immigrants, Al Smith became the first Catholic to run for president on a major-party ticket. Not until John F. Kennedy's election in 1960 would a Catholic become president. Smith was a product of Tammany Hall, the Democratic machine that controlled politics in New York City, but he stayed clear of the corruption associated with machine politics. A witty and skillful speaker with a pronounced New York accent, Smith was known as "the Happy Warrior," a title given him in 1928 by another Democrat from New York, who later became his political rival—Franklin D. Roosevelt.

Smith's rise to prominence was the fulfillment of the American dream. He was raised in poverty on the Lower East Side of Manhattan. He quit school before the age of thirteen to help support his widowed mother by working long hours in a fish market. Smith rose through the ranks of Tammany Hall and by 1911 had gone from subpoena server to the New York general assembly, where he eventually was elected Speaker. He served as governor of New

York during most of the 1920s, combining social welfare concerns with a talent for tough, practical administration. As governor he streamlined the state government bureaucracy and pushed through a program of reforms to help the working class.

Smith lost his party's nomination for president in 1924 after a long and bitter convention battle that divided the Democrats along sectional lines. Representing the northeastern urban bloc, Smith opposed Prohibition and favored a strong repudiation of the Ku Klux Klan, a group that appealed to those who feared Catholics, Jews, immigrants, and blacks. William G. McAdoo of California, representing rural Democrats from the South and West, favored Prohibition and sought to downplay the Klan issue. Smith and McAdoo battled for nine days and 103 ballots before the nomination went to an obscure compromise candidate, John W. Davis, virtually assuring a victory for Calvin Coolidge in the general election.

Smith's Catholicism and opposition to Prohibition were divisive again in 1928 when he won the Democratic nomination and went on to be defeated overwhelmingly by conservative Republican Herbert Hoover. Two popular campaign slogans reflected the concerns raised about Smith: "A vote for Smith is a vote for the Pope" and "Rum, Romanism and Ruin." Another important factor in Hoover's landslide was the economic prosperity the nation was enjoying under the Republicans. Smith, running with Sen. Joseph Robinson of Arkansas, called for measures that presaged Roosevelt's New Deal—public works, farm relief, worker protections, and regulation of banking and industry. Hoover carried forty states with 21.4 million popular votes, while Smith carried only eight states with 15.0 million popular votes. Still, Smith's campaign put the Democrats in position to add urban voters to their coalition in future years.

After his defeat in 1928 Smith retired from politics to become head of the company that was planning and would operate the Empire State Building. He returned to the political arena in 1932 with an unsuccessful attempt to block the nomination of his former ally, Roosevelt. Smith was not included in the government after Roosevelt's election, and he supported the president's Republican challengers in 1936 and 1940, arguing that Roosevelt had gone too far toward socialism.

> **More on this topic:**
>
> *Religion and the Presidency, p. 441*

Spanish-American War of 1898

The Spanish-American War of 1898, in which the United States quickly defeated Spain, broadened U.S. international obligations and expanded the power of the presidency. It demonstrated that the United States was ready to assume a wider role in global affairs.

In 1895 a rebellion against Spanish rule erupted in Cuba. For some Americans the Cuban crisis offered an opportunity to flex American muscle against a European power and extend U.S. influence. Other Americans, aroused by inflammatory reports in the press of Spanish atrocities in Cuba, wished to rescue the island's inhabitants from Spanish tyranny. This combination of forces resulted in a popular crusade in the United States to aid Cuban independence.

President Grover Cleveland resisted the temptation to satisfy the nation's appetite for war with Spain during the last two years of his second term. William McKinley entered office in 1897 similarly determined to avoid war. After the mysterious sinking of the U.S. battleship *Maine* in Havana harbor in February 1898, however, McKinley could no longer resist congressional pressure and public opinion. On April 11, 1898, he asked Congress to approve armed intervention in Cuba. Spain had already agreed to most of the U.S. demands for a settlement of the Cuban crisis, but on April 25 Congress passed a declaration of war authorizing the president to use military force to expel Spain from the island. The declaration was adopted by the Senate 42–35 and by the House 310–6.

Destruction of the U.S. battleship Maine in Havana Harbor, February 15, 1898.
Source: Library of Congress

Although U.S. ground forces were poorly equipped, trained, and commanded, superior American naval power enabled the United States to oust the Spanish from Cuba, Puerto Rico, and the Philippines. The brevity of the war, the ease with which it was won, and the popularity of the conflict made McKinley's job as commander in chief an easy one. The issue of what to do with the Philippines afterwards was more controversial. McKinley decided to take possession of the islands and, as he later told a group of clergymen, "uplift and civilize and Christianize" the Filipinos.

On December 10, 1898, Spain signed a treaty in which it gave up control of Cuba and ceded the Philippines along with Puerto Rico and Guam to the United States. In spite of news that Philippine insurgents had taken up arms for independence against U.S. forces, the Senate approved the treaty after a month of debate by a vote of 57–27, only one vote more than the necessary two-thirds majority. For the first time a president and Congress had acquired territory for the United States outside the North American continent through war.

The Filipino rebellion against U.S. rule ended after three years with the defeat of the insurgents. The bloody conflict in the Philippines cost more American lives and money than the Spanish-American War.

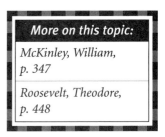

More on this topic:

McKinley, William,
p. 347

Roosevelt, Theodore,
p. 448

Speeches and Rhetoric

The presidency, Theodore Roosevelt once said, is a "bully pulpit." That phrase has come to symbolize one of the most important aspects of a president's power—the ability to use words and images, as well as actions, to set the direction of American politics and government.

Public speaking is one of the most important ties between the president and the public. For many people their most vivid memory of a president is of a speech, particularly one they heard in person or one delivered on some dramatic occasion.

Speech making has become an especially important tool of presidents in recent decades. Presidents make many more speeches now than they used to, and through television they can reach vastly greater audiences than ever before. Today, when they are frequently unable to rely on traditional bases of support such as Congress, party organizations, the print media, or the bureaucracy, presidents must depend on their ability to move the people directly with words.

Chief executives also have become more sophisticated in their use of oratory. Every president has a staff of speech writers who produce a torrent of appropriate remarks for every occasion. The president regularly meets with reporters and other media representatives, gives speeches on television and radio, addresses large crowds and groups, holds informal meetings with leaders of interest groups, travels abroad to meet foreign leaders, and attends events that feature celebrities.

In addition, presidents and their aides have learned how to make extremely effective use of the nonverbal aspects of their public appearances. What presidents say is often less important than how they say it. The potency of presidential remarks lies not just in their content but in the ceremonial way in which they are delivered.

Presidents bask in the regal splendor of the office whenever they make a public appearance. The lectern usually bears a presidential seal on the front, and flags hang somewhere within the audience's frame of vision. Standing alongside the president is usually a line of dignitaries who look on with respect and even reverence. The distance between the president and the audience increases the sense of the chief executive's lofty status.

Speech making has not always been a vital aspect of the presidency, however. Until the twentieth century, presidents seldom spoke out on policy issues, and their rhetoric was not a major force in swaying public opinion. Presidents usually confined their public appeals to written messages and addressed only matters of broad national interest.

As he did in so many other aspects of his office, George Washington set the precedent for the presidential approach to speech making. Like the other founders of the nation, Washington had fears about the dangers of democratic or "mob" rule and knew the importance of avoiding rhetorical excess. The same impulse that led the founders to set limits on democratic rule also encouraged early presidents to take great care to avoid demagoguery.

Presidents' sense of the limits of rhetoric began with Washington's first inaugural address. Dropping plans to issue a detailed list of policy recommendations, Washington instead delivered a general lecture on virtue and the need for guidance from God and the Constitution. Concerned that future presidents might exploit the possibilities for regal ceremony, he gave only the briefest of addresses at his second inauguration.

Although political debates during the nation's first century were frequently divisive and bitter, presidents generally sought to restrain their rhetoric and limit their appeals to the public as a whole. Most people believed that the custom of limiting public remarks was a good idea, because it would undermine the president's dignity for him to appear in person to appeal for mass support.

Presidents issued a variety of written proclamations and policy statements, but these were directed more at other political leaders and well-educated people than at the general public. Inaugural addresses rarely touched on specific policy issues, and for more than a century presidents delivered their constitutionally required State of the Union messages in writing rather than in person before members of Congress.

A major exception to the limited role of presidential rhetoric was Abraham Lincoln, who is generally seen as one of the best of presidential writers. Although some of Lincoln's addresses were important to his governing, he nevertheless avoided commenting on important issues in public. Even his Gettysburg Address, which is one of the best-known speeches in U.S. history, was a brief, low-key talk that attracted little notice at the time.

The continuing prejudice against presidential public speaking was shown by the fate of Lincoln's successor, Andrew Johnson, who sought to shore up his weak political support by making a speaking tour of the nation. The effort was widely criticized, and it may have added force to the nearly successful attempt to impeach him.

Although Woodrow Wilson might be said to have begun the modern era of presidential leadership, with his direct appeals to the American and foreign publics for support for the League of Nations, it was Franklin D. Roosevelt who truly transformed the presidential approach to speech making and political rhetoric in general. With the help of radio, which had reached millions of American homes by the time he took office, Roosevelt shifted the style of political speaking from

With the assistance of radio and his frequent "fireside chats," Franklin D. Roosevelt redefined the character of the president's communication with the American public. He explained the depression and the war in simple terms so that all listeners could understand.
Source: National Archives

bombastic to conversational and intimate. At the same time he transformed the role of the president from an executive responsible for a limited set of issues to a rhetorical leader on a wide range of topics. Most notably, Roosevelt delivered a series of "fireside chats" over the radio that identified him with everyday concerns.

Since Roosevelt's time, every president has come to rely heavily on oratory, making speeches a daily fact of life for chief executives. Two presidents have stood out in the history of recent presidential rhetoric—John F. Kennedy and Ronald Reagan.

Many consider Kennedy to be the founder of modern presidential speech making. Kennedy attained the presidency partly because of his polished television performances, particularly during debates with Richard Nixon. Once in office he used his wit and ease with the camera to charm the public and disarm his opponents.

Two of Kennedy's speeches were particularly memorable because of both their substance and the way they seemed to symbolize the hopes and ideals of a generation. One was his inaugural address, perhaps the most dramatic in history, in which he charged Americans to "ask not what your country can do for you—ask what you can do for your country." The other was a speech given in June 1963, when Kennedy visited West Berlin. There, under the shadow of the wall erected by the Soviet Union to seal off the East German communist regime, he said, "Ich bin ein Berliner"—a classic statement of U.S. resolve to defend the tiny island of freedom against Soviet pressure.

Reagan, who had honed his public appearance skills as a movie actor, television host, and corporate spokesman, proved so successful in speaking directly to the public that he was dubbed the Great Communicator. He was not particularly effective in extemporaneous settings, such as press conferences, where critics frequently accused him of making embarrassing errors of fact. But Reagan and his aides proved to be masters of the well-scripted presidential appearance, restoring the pomp and ceremony to the office and celebrating American icons, from the Statue of Liberty to the ordinary citizens Reagan hailed as "heroes" during his State of the Union addresses. Reagan was able to use his rhetoric about liberty and opportunity to instill a sense of national optimism in many people. He also was able to offer comfort in times of crisis, as when he gave a moving tribute to those killed in the explosion of the space shuttle *Challenger* in 1985.

Although recent presidents have varied substantially in their speaking abilities, all are required by their office and leadership needs to deliver certain common types of addresses. Political scientists have identified at least six different categories of presidential speeches. These categories are important because they reflect the ways in which and the reasons why the president communicates with the public. Each type of speech is directed toward achieving a particular goal and determines the appropriate rhetoric and speaking style for the president to use.

Ceremonial Speeches

As the symbolic embodiment of the nation, the president represents the United States in international affairs and in events designed to underscore the country's unity and progress. Perhaps the most important ceremonial speech of a president is the inaugural address, in which the president can set the tone for the administration and indicate the kind of moral leadership the people can expect. The inaugural address also is an important symbol of the reunification of the nation after the partisan election campaign. Other ceremonial speeches can be initiatory, such as at the signing of a piece of legislation; honorific, such as at a college commencement; or celebratory, such as at the ceremony recognizing the one hundredth anniversary of the Statue of Liberty in 1986.

> *In this present crisis, government is not the solution to our problem; government is the problem.*
>
> **—Ronald Reagan,** *Inaugural Address,* January 20, 1981

Official State Speeches

Although the president makes other state speeches, such as addresses to foreign parliaments or to the United Nations, by far the most significant is the STATE OF THE UNION ADDRESS. This constitutionally mandated message, now given as a speech to Congress after being delivered for many years in written form, is a major event in presidential leadership. It often serves as the forum at which presidents unveil their most important policy initiatives. Lyndon B. Johnson's Great Society program and Reagan's proposals for cuts in taxes and spending, to name just a few, were each the theme of a State of the Union speech.

General Persuasive Speeches

Although most presidential speeches seek to encourage a favorable environment for the president's approach to government, some are specifically directed toward mobilizing public support for a policy. Perhaps the most dramatic example of this was Woodrow Wilson's intensive effort to win public backing for Senate approval of the League of Nations treaty. He traveled more than eight thousand miles and delivered thirty-seven speeches in a month, until he suffered a stroke. In spite of his effort the Senate rejected the treaty. With the aid of television Reagan was far more successful during 1981, when he gave a series of speeches urging his economic program. Flooded with letters and telephone calls from the public demanding support of the president, Congress approved most of Reagan's proposals that year.

Moralistic Speeches

At other times presidents seek to persuade the public to set aside personal concerns and act in the interests of the nation by, for example, supporting the war against illegal drugs or curbing energy use. Like a high school football coach, the president seeks to infuse the people with zeal for achieving some great goal. Such speeches were common in the early days of the nation, when presidents often spoke in general about the principles of republican government.

> *Two thousand years ago the proudest boast was "civis Romanus sum." Today, in the world of freedom, the proudest boast is "Ich bin ein Berliner."*
>
> **—John F. Kennedy,** *Remarks in the Rudolph Wilde Platz, Berlin,* June 26, 1963

Crisis Speeches

The president is the focal point of the nation during times of crisis. A president's speech at such a time can mobilize the nation almost instantly, as did Franklin Roosevelt's call for war against Japan and Germany after the bombing

of Pearl Harbor. At other times a crisis speech must comfort a worried nation. Five days after President John Kennedy's assassination, for example, Lyndon Johnson delivered an address that reassured the nation of the government's stability and his own ability to govern. George W. Bush spoke to a joint session of Congress in the aftermath of the terrorist attacks of September 11, 2001. The speech received bipartisan acclaim from members of Congress and the general public and established the agenda for a wide-ranging war on international terrorism.

We last met in an hour of shock and suffering. In four short months, our Nation has comforted the victims, begun to rebuild New York and the Pentagon, rallied a great coalition, captured, arrested, and rid the world of thousands of terrorists, destroyed Afghanistan's terrorist training camps, saved a people from starvation, and freed a country from brutal oppression.

—**George W. Bush,** *Address before a Joint Session of the Congress on the State of the Union,* January 29, 2002

Addresses to Specific Groups

Presidents have spent increasing amounts of time in recent decades addressing groups that represent particular interests or parts of society, such as business organizations or civil rights supporters. These speeches can strengthen the president's support among segments of the public and help to build coalitions to achieve legislative or other goals. Most groups are flattered to have the president speak to their convention, even if the speech is only televised by satellite. By focusing on a specific group, the president can offer remarks tailored to that particular constituency without unnecessarily antagonizing other groups that might have conflicting needs but whose support the president wants to keep.

All these types of speeches, and other sorts of written and oral comments by the president, help to provide the chief executive with one of the most important advantages of the office—the ability to shape the terms of political discourse in the nation. The president's rhetoric can play a major role in determining the ways in which political issues are discussed.

Twentieth-century presidents also made effective use of catchy names to describe their programs. Among these were Square Deal (Theodore Roosevelt), New Freedom (Wilson), New Deal (Franklin Roosevelt), New Frontier (Kennedy), Great Society (Lyndon Johnson), and New Federalism (Nixon and Reagan). Such names can give the president's program a sense of coherence and completeness, even if they also create false expectations about what the president's policies can accomplish.

Although the emphasis on speaking and rhetoric in recent decades has had many advantages for presidents, political analysts are divided over whether the "rhetorical presidency" is a good thing for the American system of government. Proponents of the increased reliance on speeches and other direct appeals to the public say they help to bring the political process into the open. Because presidents are such compelling figures, what they say attracts wide attention and makes politics more accessible.

But critics point out that because presidents' remarks are so widely covered, chief executives have a natural tendency to be cautious. That caution can drain public politics of any meaningful content. In addition, critics point out that presidents have become almost totally reliant on speechwriters to produce the vast amount of public utterances they must deliver. Presidents may be reduced to reading prepared remarks rather than mastering the issues. Finally, increased presidential communications do not appear to have improved Americans' rather weak understanding of most public policy issues or to have given citizens confidence that the president and other leaders care about their needs and concerns.

More on this topic:

Farewell Addresses, p. 210

Inauguration, p. 282

Media and the Presidency, p. 355

Press Conferences, p. 416

State of the Union Address, p. 479

Spoils System *See* PATRONAGE.

Square Deal

Theodore Roosevelt came to the presidency in 1901 emboldened by the forces propelling the Progressive era, a period of urban and middle-class protest against the excesses of industrialization and unrestrained capitalism that had caused the agrarian revolts of the late nineteenth century. The national mood was for industrial reform and for changes in government institutions that, as historian Richard Hofstadter wrote, "affected in a striking way . . . the whole tone of American political life." Roosevelt's performance as president brought about that kind of change: it made the chief executive's most important political relationship the one with the American people, not with his party or Congress.

Roosevelt called his domestic policy, which centered on progressive principles and reform, the Square Deal. He proclaimed that the proper function of government was to maintain a "just balance" between management and labor, between producer and consumer, and between the extremists on both ends of the American political spectrum. As he put it, his legislative program was designed to "subordinate the big corporation to the public welfare." To achieve passage of his program, Roosevelt had to combat the vested interests in his own Republican Party and those who opposed much of his progressive agenda. As a way of overcoming congressional opposition Roosevelt went public. He used the press to appeal directly to the people for passage of reformist measures such as the Hepburn Act, which enhanced the powers of the Interstate Commerce Commission to regulate the railroads. Roosevelt signed the Hepburn Act into law in 1906. It and similar legislation such as the Pure Food and Drug Act and the Meat Inspection Act set the stage for the antitrust activism that characterized the succeeding Taft administration. They marked a major expansion of federal administrative power and were an important first step away from the laissez faire approach that had characterized government-business relationships and toward greater regulation of the nation's business practices.

The Square Deal was important for more than its reform achievements, however, for it came to define the role of the modern president as the arbiter of societal fairness and as the chief formulator of public policy and the domestic agenda reflecting that fairness standard. Since Roosevelt, other chief executives have chosen similar phrases (New Deal, Fair Deal, Great Society) to capture the essence of the philosophies underlying their programs.

> **More on this topic:**
>
> *Fair Deal, p. 209*
>
> *Great Society, p. 238*
>
> *New Deal, p. 383*
>
> *New Frontier, p. 386*
>
> *Roosevelt, Theodore, p. 448*

Staff

Modern presidents have a supporting staff that numbers in the thousands, known collectively as the EXECUTIVE OFFICE OF THE PRESIDENT (EOP). Of the various offices and councils within the EOP, perhaps the most important and surely the closest to the president is the White House Office.

Although the entire EOP does the president's business, the White House staff consists of the president's most intimate and trusted advisers—the members of the presidential establishment who are the most loyal to the president. This group oversees the political and policy interests of the administration. The centralization of executive power within the White House over the years has come at the expense of the cabinet secretaries.

A White House staff that knows the president's needs and desires and has political savvy can be a tremendous asset. It can advance the president's programs and avoid pitfalls that could undermine the president's credibility and policies. Indeed, presidential success or failure often depends on the ability and the effectiveness of the White House staff. For example, the vision and skill of President John F. Kennedy's staff were very important to his legislative success. Similarly, in the early days of Lyndon B. Johnson's administration, the ability of his staff to deal with Congress was crucial in implementing his Great Society program. The disorganization and inexperience of President Jimmy Carter's staff, on the other hand, undermined his chances to achieve much in Congress. And it was the staff's failure to anticipate problems adequately and protect the president's interests that led to the Watergate affair, which destroyed the presidency of Richard Nixon, and to the Iran-contra affair, which haunted and weakened Ronald Reagan's second term.

Staff Structure

Unlike other parts of the EOP, the White House staff is not institutionalized and can change in size and form to suit a president's managerial style. Congress has been careful not to impose any structure on it. Members of the White House staff are appointed solely by the president and are not subject to Senate confirmation. Staff members have no government status and no tenure in their positions; they serve at the president's pleasure and can be dismissed at any time for any reason. Indeed, the staff structures, offices, titles, and functions of the White House Office can change whenever the president wishes.

Chief of Staff

The most important position in the present-day White House is CHIEF OF STAFF. It is the job of the chief of staff to ensure that the White House is operating smoothly, efficiently, and swiftly. The chief also wields great influence as head gatekeeper to the president, reviewing all papers and visitors and funneling as many as possible around the president. Sherman Adams in the Eisenhower administration and H. R. Haldeman in the Nixon administration were very effective in this role.

Although most chiefs of staff will deny it, they also are involved in policy making. The chief of staff also must function as the hatchet wielder who handles staff reprimands or dismissals for the president, as well as the scapegoat when things go wrong.

Special Counsel

The special counsel is the White House's lawyer. This staff member provides legal advice on a variety of topics, reviews legislation before it is sent to Congress, and, since the Watergate affair, ensures the proper behavior of the presidential staff. The office has often provided presidents with a place to install valuable aides.

Policy Advisers

The NATIONAL SECURITY ADVISER is the president's primary adviser on foreign policy. The job originally was seen as largely administrative: overseeing the National Security Council and coordinating the various elements of the foreign policy establishment. Given the central position of the national security adviser in the policy process, presidents began turning to them for advice as well as coordination.

The domestic policy adviser has responsibilities that parallel those of the national security adviser: coordinating domestic policy making and serving as an adviser on domestic policy and problems. The adviser settles disputes between domestic agencies and uses information and advice from them to formulate legislative proposals. The domestic adviser has not been as influential or effective a coordinator as the national security adviser. Because a larger number of agencies and constituencies, many of them powerful and active, are concerned with domestic issues, the domestic adviser cannot exercise the same degree of control as the national security adviser.

Liaison Offices

Several offices in the modern White House are concerned with its links with the world outside its gates. The White House Communications Office is concerned with the news. It both manages the administration's relations with the news media and manages the news itself. The office tries to communicate the administration's point of view, using press releases, interviews, mailings, and other techniques to promote the president's side of a story. The Communications Office also includes the White House speechwriting operation; the Media Affairs Office, which deals with media outlets outside Washington; and the Office of the Press Secretary, which manages the administration's relations with the news media.

The presidential speechwriters compose the addresses, statements, and messages the president delivers to Congress and the general public, both at home and abroad. Because words define policy, speechwriters also may have a role in policy making. Indeed, in the Roosevelt, Truman, and Kennedy administrations speechwriters were policy advisers as well.

The press secretary is regarded as the voice of the administration, someone whose words are taken to represent the president's position. Press secretaries also may become policy advisers, as James C. Hagerty did in the Eisenhower administration.

The White House also maintains offices to facilitate communication with various groups. One of the most important of these is the Legislative Affairs Office, which tries to maintain a two-way flow of communication between the White House and Congress. Staff members present the president's positions to Congress and try to win support for them. The office also is a channel through which Congress can talk to the president. The Legislative Affairs staff keeps the president informed on the mood in Congress and the chances of success there. The staff must know when and to what degree direct presidential involvement is needed to save a bill.

Another such office is the Public Liaison Office. Its goal is to build support for the administration's policies among the general public. Members of staff contact groups to educate them about the administration's goals and actions. Other White House liaison offices maintain ties with various specific constituency groups, such as women and minorities.

Presidential Personnel Office

The Presidential Personnel Office locates potential officeholders, checks on their qualifications, and conducts interviews. Along with the Office of the Counsel to the President, the Presidential Personnel Office arranges for background checks, often conducted by the Federal Bureau of Investigation. If all is in order, the office presents the nominee to the president for approval and submission to the Senate, if necessary. It also might brief the appointee on the questions he or she may face on Capitol Hill.

Growth of Staff

The White House Office today is an institutionalized bureaucracy with several hundred employees and a multimillion-dollar budget. Of the many factors leading to its greater size and responsibility in modern times, perhaps the most important is the public's tendency to expect the president to address all the country's problems, from national defense and economic recession to drug addiction and disease. The president can respond only by appointing more staff to deal with these expectations. A larger presidential staff has been needed to coordinate policy within the executive branch, as problems and the policies to deal with them now often spill across departmental divisions. Impatience with a slow federal bureaucracy also has contributed to staff growth.

Other factors in the growth of the White House office include increases in congressional staffs, which have led to corresponding increases in presidential staff (and vice versa). Also, the White House staff has grown as its contacts with numerous interest groups have increased. Finally, a sophisticated public relations staff, complete with pollsters, has been added to manage the image of the presidency.

The White House bureaucracy has become a permanent fixture of U.S. politics, but it is a relatively modern development. Early presidents had little or no staff to assist them, and what staff did exist was strictly clerical. There were no specialized or resident policy advisers, speechwriters, or liaison personnel. Believing that presidents should take care of their own business, Congress did not specifically appropriate funds for staff until 1857, when it provided an allowance of $2,500 for a presidential secretary.

Presidents who wanted more help were forced to hire it themselves and to pay for it out of their own pockets. George Washington, for example, hired his nephew to assist him in 1792 and paid him $300 a year from his own funds. Given the limitations of the presidential pocket, as well as the small size of the government as a whole, the White House staff necessarily remained quite small throughout the nineteenth century. Presidents generally made more use of their cabinet as advisers than they do today.

To some extent, however, the small size of these staffs is misleading. Historically, presidents have resorted to "detailing," or borrowing, personnel from the executive departments to carry out various tasks. A president who needed assistance might requisition an aide or two from the War Department or State Department. Moreover, some presidents placed trusted advisers in positions within the executive branch to keep them available.

Although the use of "detailees" was a great asset to presidents, the growing demands of the presidency required more in-house advisers who were not encumbered by even minimal duties elsewhere. As the nation and the government grew in the early twentieth century, the need for a larger presidential staff became more acute.

Staff Reforms

The modern staff system was established during the administration of Franklin D. Roosevelt. Like his predecessors, Roosevelt regularly borrowed help from elsewhere in the executive branch, using at least a hundred detailees each year. Unlike his predecessors, however, he concluded that such arrangements were hopelessly inadequate. As an activist president faced with an unprecedented economic crisis, he decided to change things. He believed that dealing with the nation's problems required a larger permanent staff that worked solely for him.

Roosevelt found support for his staff reforms in the work of the Committee on Administrative Management, popularly called the BROWN-LOW COMMITTEE for its chairman, Louis Brownlow. The

The White House staff consists of the president's most trusted and loyal advisers. Although FDR's staff remained small, unstructured, and free of specific titles, the role of Harry Hopkins, special assistant to the president, resembled that of today's chief of staff.
Source: FDR Library

committee concluded that "the President needs help" and recommended the creation of additional staff positions.

In 1939 Congress approved most of the Brownlow Committee's proposals. Congress authorized Roosevelt to hire new staff assistants and to undertake a partial reorganization of the executive branch. On September 8, 1939, Roosevelt issued Executive Order 8248 creating the Executive Office of the President. This order represented the birth of the modern presidency, including the modern White House Office staff.

Staff Expansion

President Harry S. Truman came into office distrustful of a large staff and fearful that it would impede his interaction with his cabinet and the rest of the government. But he quickly found that his plan to reduce the White House staff to its pre–World War II size was impossible.

With Europe in ruins the United States was the leader in the international community. At home, the difficulties of restoring the economy to a peacetime status and repairing the dislocations caused by war created economic and political tensions for the federal government. The result was increasing pressure on the Truman administration, which inevitably led to a staff size that exceeded that of the Roosevelt years.

Truman created the position of assistant to the president, a direct forerunner of the chief of staff. The first hint of the future role of staff members as policy advocates also came during the Truman administration. Truman's special counsel, Clark Clifford, was a strong representative of liberal positions.

During the Truman administration Congress created two other bodies within the EOP to assist the president: the NATIONAL SECURITY COUNCIL and the Council of Economic Advisers.

Under Dwight D. Eisenhower the staff grew in both size and complexity. As a general and a career military officer, Eisenhower recognized the benefits of a properly structured staff. Reacting to what he saw as confusion within the Roosevelt and Truman administrations, Eisenhower established a more highly structured and diversified staff than those of his predecessors.

Eisenhower's staff included many of the elements found under Truman. He added a formal congressional liaison office to deal with Congress and openly lobby for the president's position on Capitol Hill. He also created the positions of staff secretary and secretary to the cabinet to improve the flow of paperwork through the channels of the administration.

In another major staff change Eisenhower expanded the role of the assistant to the president to that of a chief of staff. Sherman Adams's influence in this job was unprecedented for a White House staff member and paved the way for powerful chiefs of staff in the future.

Policy Advocates

The White House staff continued to expand under John Kennedy, who also used many more detailees from other agencies than his predecessor. But the most significant development in the staff during the Kennedy administration was not the increase in its size, but the growth in its responsibilities and influence. Kennedy's staff became involved in policy making to an unprecedented degree and began to acquire larger staffs to assist them. Kennedy was in fact beginning to pull policy making, and therefore power, out of the executive departments and concentrate it within the White House.

The influence of the White House staff continued to grow during the Johnson administration. Concentration of power in the White House was reinforced by Johnson's dominant personality, which led him to extend his control as much as possible. Later, the public outcry against his conduct of the Vietnam War caused him to withdraw into the sanctuary of the White House, relying on his staff even more.

The major structural development during the Johnson administration was the creation of a domestic policy staff within the White House. The notion of a domestic policy adviser was not new, but now for the first time it was established as a separate position with a small staff of its own.

Nixon Staff

The Nixon years saw the creation of a domestic council, a counterpart to the National Security Council, to deal with domestic policies. Nixon also established a White House communications office, separate from the existing press office, to function as a public relations arm of the White House. The cornerstone of Nixon's White House staff was the position of chief of staff, a job he gave to the ruthlessly effective H. R. Haldeman.

Under Nixon the White House Office grew into a small bureaucracy, in which some assistants to the president rarely, if ever, saw him. Nixon could not hope to supervise his staff; the staff had to control itself. At the same time Nixon's staff had an enormous amount of power, to the extent that the White House largely became the government, relegating much of the regular government to a role of secondary importance. An increasing number of decisions and details formerly left to the executive departments were taken over by the White House staff.

The staff's power, its zeal in serving Nixon, and its lack of outside supervision contributed to the political and legal excesses known collectively as the WATERGATE AFFAIR. The scandal cost many staff members, including Haldeman and chief domestic adviser John D. Ehrlichman, their positions and eventually drove Nixon from the White House.

Post-Watergate Staff

The perceived power of Nixon's staff, with its close shielding of the president and the abuses stemming from its blind loyalty, led to protests about the increasing authority gathered within the White House. Partly in response, Presidents Ford and Carter tried to create staff structures that avoided the excesses of the Nixon White House.

Both wanted more openness and increased the number of staff members who had ready access to the Oval Office. Ford downplayed the role of the chief of staff; Carter tried to eliminate it altogether, giving himself the role of staff coordinator. Neither plan worked. Finding themselves bogged down in details and having to settle disputes of authority among aides, both Ford and Carter turned to a chief of staff and reimposed hierarchy upon the White House.

Recent Staffs

Just as Ford and Carter organized their staffs partly in reaction to Nixon's experience, Ronald Reagan built a staff with one eye on the problems faced by his immediate predecessors. His staff was carefully structured to work out policy details at lower levels; only the most important questions and broad outlines of policy were taken to the president. Reagan removed himself from the minutiae of governing perhaps more than any other president in the modern era. Reagan's detachment and the resulting independence of the staff came under much criticism during investigations of the IRAN-CONTRA AFFAIR.

Innovations during the Reagan presidency included a special office to coordinate policies with public opinion, a cabinet secretariat to work with the cabinet departments, and an office of political affairs to work with outside political elements.

In contrast to Reagan, George H. W. Bush was seen as a president very much engaged in the work of his administration. After years of public service, Bush enjoyed the demands of governing. To assist him, he placed old and trusted friends in important cabinet posts and filled top positions in the White House with members of his campaign team.

Bush gave his cabinet a greater policy role than his predecessor had, but power tended to gravitate toward the White House staff, in particular toward John H. Sununu, Bush's first chief of staff. Partly because of his interest in foreign affairs and partly because of the enormous global changes taking place, Bush found himself preoccupied with foreign policy; consequently Sununu, along with several cabinet members, picked up the slack on domestic policy. But Sununu became a political liability when he came to be identified with public dissatisfaction with Bush's economic and domestic programs, as well as with several political gaffes by the White House. Sununu left the White House near the beginning of the 1992 presidential campaign.

Bill Clinton staffed his White House largely with old friends and campaign workers, but he brought in some seasoned Washington veterans when the going got rough. The Clinton White House had a collegial, consensus-building style of decision making with as many as ten advisers enjoying walk-in privileges to the Oval Office. Policy tended to be made by groups assembled to deal with specific issues, giving rise to the criticism of government by "ad-hocracy." While offering great flexibility in dealing with issues, this arrangement tended toward disorganization and often gave the impression of a White House in disarray and out of control. Clinton had to rework his staff system several times in his first two years to improve its efficiency. Midway through his second term Clinton's staff was working smoothly and efficiently. That the staff's operation reflected both Clinton's enormous energy and his tendency to move restlessly from problem to problem proved once again that the administration inevitably reflects the president who operates it.

George W. Bush eliminated or reduced certain offices and added others, based on his policy interests and political inclinations. Among his first acts he eliminated the White House Office on Women's Initiatives and Outreach and added the Office of Faith-Based and Community Initiatives to the staff. To deal with the threat of terrorism Bush added the Office of Homeland Security, which later became the basis for a full-fledged cabinet department. Another new office, established by executive order in January 2003, was the Office of Global Communications, headed by Tucker Eskew. The office, created at a time of international tensions, was designed to spread the president's messages to people around the world. The most recent unit added was the Privacy and Civil Liberties Oversight Board, created by the Intelligence Reform and Terrorism Prevention Act of 2004. With operations

> *First, let me say I take full responsibility for my own actions and for those of my administration. As angry as I may be about activities undertaken without my knowledge, I am still accountable for those activities. As disappointed as I may be in some who served me, I'm still the one who must answer to the American people for this behavior. And as personally distasteful as I find secret bank accounts and diverted funds—well, as the Navy would say, this happened on my watch.*
>
> **—Ronald Reagan,** *Address to the Nation on the Iran Arms and Contra Aid Controversy,* March 4, 1987

More on this topic:

Brownlow Committee, p. 33

Chief of Staff, p. 84

Executive Office of the President, p. 200

CLOSER LOOK ◉

The BUCK STOPS here!

Harry S. Truman famously kept a placard on his desk in the Oval Office that read, "The BUCK STOPS Here!" It was a statement that illustrated the fact that all decisions made by White House staff are ultimately the president's. Knowing this, presidents have devised different approaches in how they organize their staffs. Kennedy, Carter, and Clinton were known for their "spokes in a wheel" design. In this system, staff members are encouraged to deliberate and communicate directly with the president, who acts as the hub of a wheel. The benefit of this sort of arrangement is that it can lead to a wealth of information flowing toward the president, enhancing his ability to make informed decisions. On the other hand, it can lead to excessive micromanagement. Nixon, Reagan, and George W. Bush are known for a more hierarchical structure in which they had to rely on gatekeepers to control the flow of information to the president. This approach, however, can lead to the president's being out of the loop on what his staff is doing and is cited as a contribution to staff scandals such as the Iran-contra affair.

beginning in 2006, the board's mission is to ensure that civil liberties are protected and considered during the enforcement of laws related to the prevention of terrorism.

State Department

The State Department is the president's primary instrument of negotiation with foreign countries and an important source of information, analysis, and advice on foreign relations. The department is headed by the secretary of state, who is responsible for the overall direction, coordination, and supervision of U.S. foreign relations and for the interdepartmental activities of the U.S. government overseas.

The secretary of state is a statutory member of the National Security Council and is fourth in line for succession to the presidency after the vice president, the Speaker of the House, and the president pro tempore of the Senate. Most observers regard the secretary of state as the highest-ranking cabinet member.

Although the State Department has far-flung responsibilities, it has remained one of the smallest departments in the cabinet. About one-third of its approximately 28,000 employees serve domestically. Of the two-thirds serving abroad, slightly more than one-third are American citizens, and the rest are foreign nationals. Americans employed by the department are members of either the civil service or the foreign service. Those in the civil service generally do not serve abroad, whereas foreign service personnel spend about 60 percent of their period of service in foreign countries.

The present-day Department of State had its beginnings in 1781, when Congress established a Department of Foreign Affairs, which was redesignated as the Department of State in September 1789. During Secretary Thomas Jefferson's tenure (1789–1793) the department consisted of five clerks, two messengers, and a part-time translator of French. It maintained legations in London and Paris, a diplomatic agency in The Hague, and two consular missions. Only ten persons were added to the staff in the ensuing thirty years.

At the end of the nineteenth century the United States began to upgrade the quality and status of its diplomats in response to the nation's growing involvement in international trade and politics. Presidents increasingly relied on the State Department for information, analysis, and staff support.

With World War II and the emergence of the United States as the most powerful nation on earth, presidents needed greater support for their foreign policy decision making. The United States saw itself as an international leader and the protector of the noncommunist world. In the postwar years it entered into numerous alliances and mutual defense agreements, distributed massive amounts of military and economic aid, hosted the United Nations, and actively participated in most international organizations. This new U.S. involvement in world affairs multiplied the president's foreign policy responsibilities. An expanded bureaucracy was required to administer the growing number of U.S. programs and activities overseas and to provide the president with the information and analysis needed for constructing effective foreign policies.

As a result, the State Department increased in size, and other departments and agencies were created or expanded to furnish military, economic, scientific, and intelligence-gathering expertise that the State Department was not equipped to provide. Even though the State Department lost its exclusive role in foreign policy making and became one player among many in the field, it remains preeminent in the area of negotiations and the daily administration of foreign policy.

The secretary of state is assisted by a deputy secretary and five under secretaries (political affairs; economic, business, and agricultural affairs; global affairs; arms control and international security affairs; and management). Also attached to the secretary's office are posts such as the U.S. ambassador to the United Nations, several ambassadors-at-large who undertake special missions, the chief of protocol, and the Policy Planning Staff.

Primary responsibility for developing policy rests with the six regional bureaus: European and Canadian Affairs, African Affairs, East Asian and Pacific Affairs, Inter-American Affairs, Near Eastern Affairs, and South Asian Affairs. These are headed by assistant secretaries who advise the secretary on U.S. policies toward countries within their regional jurisdiction.

The Bureau of International Organization Affairs manages U.S. participation in the United Nations and its system of programs and agencies. The bureau also deals with certain international problems, such as food production, air traffic safety, communications, health, human rights, education, and the environment.

Other State Department bureaus are divided by function. They include the Bureau of Economic and Business Affairs; the Bureau of Intelligence and Research; the Bureau of Democracy, Human Rights, and Labor; and the Political-Military Affairs Bureau. The Bureau of Consular Affairs, under the direction of an assistant secretary, helps Americans who travel or live abroad. Its Passport Services office issues more than four million passports a year.

The United States has diplomatic relations with 160 countries. In some smaller countries where the United States does not maintain a mission, official contacts are channeled through embassies in neighboring countries or the United Nations. Ambassadors are the personal representatives of the president as well as representatives of the Department of State and all other federal agencies. They have full responsibility for the implementation of U.S. foreign policy by most U.S. government personnel within their country of assignment, except those under military commands.

> **More on this topic:**
>
> Bureaucracy, p. 44
>
> Cabinet, p. 60
>
> Diplomatic Powers, p. 149

State of the Union Address

Vice President Richard B. Cheney and Speaker of the House Dennis Hastert, R-Ill., applaud President George W. Bush as he presents his State of the Union address in January 2003. Bush's popularity had dropped below 60 percent for the first time since the terrorist attacks in September 2001, in part because of rising skepticism about his economic policy and the risks of invading Iraq.
Source: Reuters

The Constitution requires the president to report on the "state of the nation": "He shall from time to time give to the Congress Information on the State of the Union, and recommend to their Consideration such Measures as he shall judge necessary and expedient." Since early in the twentieth century presidents have addressed a joint session of Congress to assess the nation's problems and achievements and to propose policies.

George Washington began the practice of delivering the State of the Union address in person to Congress. But Thomas Jefferson, believing that it was too similar to the British monarch's practice of delivering a "Speech from the Throne," opted to send a written message every year instead. For more than one hundred years, until Woodrow Wilson, presidents contented themselves with a written message.

Since Wilson's decision to deliver his message in person, the annual State of the Union speech has become a major event in presidential leadership and congressional relations. Delivered before a joint session of Congress, the Supreme Court, and the cabinet, these addresses survey the range of budget and other policies the administration plans to pursue in the coming year.

Lenny Skutnik receiving applause during the 1982 State of the Union Address.
Source: The Washington Post

It has become routine for presidents to mention ordinary Americans by name and then recognize their attendance at State of the Union addresses. This practice is relatively new, however. The first president to do this was Ronald Reagan. In 1982 Reagan invited Lenny Skutnik to sit with the first lady. Skutnik was a hero who came to the aid of victims of an air crash in the icy waters of the Potomac River and was cited by Reagan as exemplifying the spirit of heroism that made America great. Since then, all presidents have used this strategy of connecting real-life drama to the spectacle of politics, and speech-writers have termed these people "Skutniks." Throughout the years there have been many famous Skutniks. Bill Clinton was one himself when acknowledged by President George H. W. Bush in 1990 for his work in setting national education goals. Rosa Parks, Sammy Sosa, and Hank Aaron have also been recognized.

Presidents also use State of the Union speeches to announce major new initiatives. Lyndon B. Johnson's Great Society program; Richard Nixon's Vietnam, "New Federalism," and economic programs; Jimmy Carter's energy, tax reform, and foreign policy initiatives; and Ronald Reagan's tax cut and spending cut proposals were all outlined in State of the Union addresses. George H. W. Bush's 1992 address, coming at a time when his approval rating was the lowest of his presidency, was seen as the opening volley in his reelection campaign. Bill Clinton in 1994 set a get-tough agenda for health care, welfare, and crime reforms. George W. Bush's 2002 address, just months after the terrorist attacks of September 11, 2001, highlighted international dangers, including those posed by the "axis of evil"—Iran, Iraq, and North Korea. In 2003 Bush used his address to mobilize public support for the invasion of Iraq, erroneously claiming that Saddam Hussein had tried to acquire uranium from Niger. In the beginning of his second term in 2005, Bush focused on promoting his agenda to privatize the Social Security system, a proposal that Congress ultimately never embraced.

Recent presidents have invited guests to attend the speech and sit in the first lady's gallery box—people generally selected to illustrate the president's messages. In 2007 guests seated in First Lady Laura Bush's box included a member of the military, an entrepreneur businesswoman, a Georgetown and NBA basketball star, and a hero who saved a man from being hit by a New York subway train.

The annual speech is one of the high points of the ceremonial presidency. Speaking before virtually every powerful official in Washington, with the vice president and Speaker of the House in the background on the podium, the president is presented as an awe-inspiring figure standing at the pinnacle of the political system. So potent is the president's aura that some members of Congress come hours early to the speech in the hope of securing a center-aisle seat, just so they can be seen on television shaking hands with the chief executive as that figure strides to the podium.

State of the Union speeches can have their pitfalls, however. Because of the pressure of time, programs sometimes are announced in the speech before they have been thoroughly planned and developed. There is a danger that the address will arouse false expectations and cause eventual disappointment. Many of President Johnson's Great Society programs, for example, were in their very early stages when announced in the State of the Union address. The gap between Johnson's rhetoric and the reality of the programs contributed to later disillusionment with them.

More on this topic:

Article II, p. 16

Congress and the Presidency, p. 111

Speeches and Rhetoric, p. 466

Stevenson, Adlai E.

Adlai Ewing Stevenson (1835–1914), a powerful Democratic leader from Illinois, served as vice president during Grover Cleveland's second term from 1893 to 1897. He was the grandfather of Adlai E. Stevenson II, who was the Democratic nominee for president in 1952 and 1956.

Stevenson moved to Bloomington, Illinois, from Kentucky when he was sixteen. He taught school and took some college courses but never earned a degree. While teaching, he studied law and was admitted to the bar in 1858. That year he opened a successful law office in Metamora, Illinois.

While practicing law, Stevenson became active in the Democratic Party. He was elected to the U.S. House of Representatives in 1874 but was defeated for reelection in 1876. He won his seat back in 1878 and served one term before returning to his law practice.

In 1885 President Grover Cleveland appointed Stevenson first assistant postmaster. In this office he was in charge of firing postmasters appointed by the previous Republican administrations. Although Stevenson was known for his tact and amiability, he made many enemies while firing tens of thousands of people and earned the nickname of the "Headsman." Cleveland appointed Stevenson to the Supreme Court in 1889, but the Republican majority in the Senate refused to confirm the nomination of a man who had just fired tens of thousands of their fellow party members.

Stevenson went to the 1892 Democratic national convention as the chairman of the Illinois delegation. There he received the party's nomination for vice president. With Stevenson on the ticket, Illinois voted for a Democratic presidential candidate for the first time since 1856. Cleveland and Stevenson defeated Republican incumbent Benjamin Harrison and vice-presidential candidate Whitelaw Reid by a vote of 277–145 in the Electoral College.

As vice president, Stevenson was regarded as a good presiding officer of the Senate. Although he and Cleveland maintained a friendly relationship, Stevenson was not a close adviser. In July 1893, when Cleveland secretly underwent surgery for mouth cancer, Stevenson was not even informed.

In 1900 Stevenson again received the Democratic nomination for vice president on a ticket with William Jennings Bryan, but they were defeated by incumbent William McKinley and vice-presidential nominee Theodore Roosevelt. The Illinois Democratic Party honored the aging Stevenson with its nomination for governor in 1908. He lost to Republican Charles Deneen in a close election. After this defeat Stevenson retired from politics.

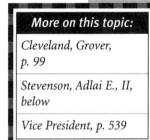

More on this topic:

Cleveland, Grover, p. 99

Stevenson, Adlai E., II, below

Vice President, p. 539

Stevenson, Adlai E., II

Gov. Adlai E. Stevenson II of Illinois (1900–1965), a liberal Democrat known for his eloquent campaign oratory and principled stands on issues, twice lost the race for the presidency to an enormously popular Republican, Gen. Dwight D. Eisenhower. In 1952 and again in 1956 Americans overwhelmingly preferred the dignified, grandfatherly World War II general to Stevenson. To many historians it later appeared that no Democrat could have defeated Eisenhower, given his personal popularity and the nation's weariness with the Democrats after the Roosevelt and Truman years.

Stevenson came from a prominent Illinois family. His grandfather, also named Adlai, had been vice president during the 1890s under Democrat Grover Cleveland. A lawyer, Stevenson had worked in the Navy and State Departments during Franklin D. Roosevelt's administration before his election as governor of Illinois in 1949. Stevenson was a popular governor with an ambitious program of social reforms. Despite incumbent president Harry Truman's attempt to recruit him for the presidential race early in 1952, Stevenson insisted until the last minute that he wanted to run again for governor. He won the 1952 Democratic presidential nomination on the third ballot, defeating Sen. Estes Kefauver of Tennessee, who had come to the convention with more delegates.

Stevenson's 1952 campaign was a call to arms for liberals and reformers. Years later, Democrats would recall that the campaign had inspired the generation that would come to power under President John F. Kennedy. Stevenson and his running mate, Sen. John Sparkman of Alabama, did not attempt to attack Eisenhower; most of their rhetoric was directed instead at Eisenhower's controversial running mate, Richard Nixon. Nixon, in turn, called Stevenson a naive idealist who was soft on communism. The Eisenhower-Nixon ticket won the 1952 election decisively and went on

Adlai E. Stevenson displayed evidence of Soviet missile bases in Cuba during a UN meeting held on October 25, 1962. Stevenson challenged his Soviet counterpart to deny the evidence, reminding him, "You are in the courtroom of world opinion right now."
Source: U.S. Department of State

to defeat Stevenson and Kefauver even more thoroughly in 1956.

After a belated and half-hearted attempt to win the Democratic nomination once again in 1960, Stevenson hoped that Kennedy would appoint him secretary of state, a position that would have allowed Stevenson to use his expertise in foreign affairs. Never a Kennedy insider, Stevenson was offered instead the less desirable job of ambassador to the United Nations, which he accepted and held from 1961 until his death four and a half years later. In that capacity Stevenson again moved to center stage during the 1962 Cuban missile crisis, but he was often frustrated in his attempts to promote world peace. Stevenson was remembered by his detractors as an indecisive, unrealistic politician not to be trusted with high office. His supporters saw him as a leader whose intellectual depth and self-deprecating wit raised him far above the common run of politicians.

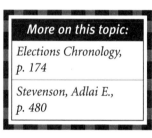

> **More on this topic:**
>
> *Elections Chronology,*
> p. 174
>
> *Stevenson, Adlai E.,*
> p. 480

Stewardship Theory

One of the bases of Theodore Roosevelt's successful presidency was his expansive view of the authority of the president. Roosevelt argued that the restrictive view of the power of his office had rendered the U.S. political system impotent and subject to special interests. To counter this trend, he developed the idea of the president as a "steward" of the people, who would be "bound actively and affirmatively to do all he could for the people, and not to content himself" with a limited conception of the office. Roosevelt believed the executive power was limited only by the actual wording of the Constitution and the laws. Constitutional silence, he held, left far greater scope for presidential action than previous presidents had believed.

> *I declined to adopt the view that what was imperatively necessary for the Nation could not be done by the President unless he could find some specific authorization to do it. My belief was that it was not only his right but his duty to do anything that the needs of the Nation demanded unless such action was forbidden by the Constitution or by the laws.*
>
> **—Theodore Roosevelt,** Theodore
> Roosevelt: An Autobiography by Theodore
> Roosevelt, 1913

Roosevelt's stewardship model of the executive office accepted the essential characteristics of the system of checks and balances among the three branches. By reviving a nationalist spirit, he sought to strengthen the prevailing constitutional order and prepare it to address the problems of an industrial society. His view was a marked contrast to that of his hand-picked successor, William Howard Taft, who held that the president should not exercise any power that was not clearly tied to a specific constitutional authority.

> **More on this topic:**
>
> *Roosevelt, Theodore,*
> p. 448

Succession

The Constitution provides that the vice president shall assume the powers and duties of the chief executive in the event the president dies, resigns, becomes disabled, or is removed from office. The delegates to the Constitutional Convention anticipated well. As of 2007 eight presidents had died in office and one had resigned under threat of impeachment. All were duly succeeded by their vice presidents.

- John Tyler became president when William Henry Harrison died of an illness just one month after his inauguration in 1841.
- Millard Fillmore succeeded to the presidency in 1850 when Zachary Taylor died of natural causes during the second year of his term.
- Andrew Johnson became president when Abraham Lincoln was assassinated in 1865, just six weeks after the start of his second term.
- Chester A. Arthur became president in 1881 after the death of James A. Garfield, who was assassinated near the start of his term.
- In 1901 an assassin killed William McKinley. Theodore Roosevelt served the remaining three and a half years of McKinley's term and was elected president in 1904.
- Warren G. Harding died of natural causes in 1923 with nineteen months left in his term. He was succeeded by Calvin Coolidge, who in 1924 won election to a full term as president.
- Franklin D. Roosevelt died of natural causes three months after the start of his fourth term in 1945 and was succeeded by Harry S. Truman. Truman was elected president in 1948.
- Lyndon B. Johnson was sworn in as president in 1963 barely an hour after John F. Kennedy was assassinated with fourteen months remaining in his term. Johnson was elected president in his own right in 1964.
- Under threat of imminent impeachment and removal, Richard Nixon resigned in 1974, after serving less than two years of his second term. Gerald R. Ford became president. In 1976 Ford was nominated for a full term in his own right but was narrowly defeated in the general election.

Vacancies have occurred in the vice presidency on eighteen occasions—nine of them when the vice president succeeded to the presidency. Seven other vice presidents died in office, and two resigned.

Although the Constitution provided for succession, it was silent on many issues concerning implementation. Was the vice president to be sworn in as president or simply to serve in an acting capacity? Was the vice president to serve out the president's term or to hold the office only until a new president could be selected at a special election? What would happen if the presidency and vice presidency fell vacant at the same time?

These were not idle questions. Assassination attempts, impeachment proceedings, and illness made succession an active concern in twenty of the nation's first forty-two presidencies. As a result, many of the questions surrounding succession have been answered through precedent, constitutional amendment, and law.

On November 22, 1963, barely an hour after President Kennedy was assassinated in Dallas, Texas, Vice President Lyndon B. Johnson, with his wife, Lady Bird, (left) and Jacqueline Kennedy (right) looking on, took the oath of office aboard Air Force One.
Source: LBJ Library

Full Succession

The question of whether the vice president would succeed to the office of president or only perform the president's duties was resolved the first time the presidency became vacant. That occurred in 1841, when William Henry Harrison died shortly after his inauguration. Initially some members of Harrison's cabinet thought Vice President Tyler would only become acting president. But Tyler had different thoughts. He quickly took the oath of office as president, delivered an inaugural speech of sorts, declared his intention to serve out the remainder of Harrison's term, and moved into the White House.

Tyler's decisiveness prevailed in a constitutionally and politically uncertain situation. His action set a precedent that Fillmore nine years later and future vice presidents were able to follow without controversy. Not until the Twenty-fifth Amendment was ratified in 1967, however, did the Constitution explicitly state the vice president's right to full succession.

Line of Succession

The Constitution also did not set a line of succession that extended past the vice president, but instead left that task to Congress.

The Second Congress passed the Succession Act of 1792, which called for a special election if a double vacancy occurred. In the interim the president pro tempore of the Senate (or if there were none, the Speaker of the House) would serve as interim president. In 1886 Congress replaced that law with a new one that located the line of succession in the president's cabinet in the order in which the departments were created, beginning with the secretary of state.

This law remained in place until 1947 when, at Truman's request, Congress enacted a new law. Truman had succeeded to the presidency after Franklin Roosevelt died in 1945. Had Truman died in office he would have been succeeded, under the 1886 law, by the secretary of state, an official Truman himself had appointed. Truman argued that in a democracy the power to choose a successor should not lie solely with the chief executive.

The 1947 law set the line of succession that is still in effect today: vice president, Speaker of the House, president pro tempore of the Senate, secretary of state, secretary of the Treasury, secretary of defense, attorney general, and, in order, the secretaries of interior, agriculture, commerce, labor, health and human services, housing and urban development, transportation, energy, education, veterans affairs, and homeland security.

Remarkably, the nation by 2007 had never experienced a presidential term in which both the president and the vice president died. As a result, the statutory line of succession has never been invoked.

Vice-Presidential Vacancies

Although the Constitution provided for the vice president to succeed the president if the chief executive died or otherwise left office, it made no provision to fill vacancies in the vice presidency. Such vacancies could occur either when the vice president succeeded to the presidency or when the vice president himself died, resigned, or was impeached and removed from office.

Despite frequent vacancies in the office, a mechanism to name a successor vice president did not become part of the Constitution until 1967, when the Twenty-fifth Amendment was ratified. That amendment authorized the president to nominate, and Congress to confirm, a new vice president whenever the office became vacant.

Before 1967 sixteen vice-presidential vacancies had occurred—eight of them because the vice president succeeded to the presidency. In addition, seven vice presidents died in office. They were George Clinton (1812), Elbridge Gerry (1814), William R. King (1853), Henry Wilson (1875),

Thomas A. Hendricks (1885), Garret A. Hobart (1899), and James S. Sherman (1912). Two vice presidents—John C. Calhoun and Spiro T. Agnew—resigned.

The importance of having a successor standing ready to become president became clear at the end of World War II, when Truman served for the first three and a half years of the nuclear age with no vice president. The possibility that a vice president would not be available to succeed to the presidency was not regarded as intolerable, however, until after the assassination of President Kennedy on November 22, 1963.

During the fourteen months remaining in Kennedy's term, the two men in line to succeed Lyndon Johnson were aged and ill members of Congress, House Speaker John W. McCormack of Massachusetts and the president pro tempore of the Senate, Carl Hayden of Arizona. As legal scholar John D. Feerick noted, "Neither had been chosen for his position with an eye toward possible succession to the presidency, and neither was viewed by the public as a person of presidential stature."

Less than three weeks after Kennedy's death, Democratic senator Birch Bayh proposed a constitutional amendment that empowered the president to nominate a vice president when the office became vacant. A majority of both houses of Congress would have to confirm the nomination before the new vice president could take office. (The proposal also established a mechanism for replacing a disabled president; see DISABILITY AMENDMENT.) The Twenty-fifth Amendment was approved by Congress in 1965 and ratified in 1967. Six years later Gerald R. Ford became the first nonelected vice president in U.S. history.

Ford Nomination

On October 10, 1973, Vice President Spiro Agnew resigned as part of a plea bargain that allowed him to avoid prosecution on most of the charges of bribery and income tax evasion that the Justice Department was preparing to bring against him. Two days later President Nixon nominated Gerald Ford for the post. The House Republican leader was popular with legislators of both parties. Although Ford was reportedly not Nixon's first choice, the president, by then deeply entangled in the Watergate affair, wanted to avoid a prolonged confirmation battle and possible defeat.

Ford's nomination prompted the most extensive investigation into the background of a nominee for government office that had been conducted up to that time. Personnel from the Federal Bureau of Investigation, Internal Revenue Service, Library of Congress, General Accounting Office, and various congressional committees pored over Ford's public career, tax returns, medical records, campaign finance reports, bank accounts, and payroll records. Nothing seriously detrimental was uncovered.

Although some legislators argued about the proper criteria to use in evaluating a president's nominee for vice president, a majority in Congress apparently agreed with Senator Bayh. The author of the Twenty-fifth Amendment contended that Congress should defer to the president in the selection of a vice president except when defects in character, competence, or integrity made a nominee unacceptable.

The Senate confirmed Ford by a vote of 92–3 on November 26. The House confirmed him 387–35 on December 6. Immediately after that vote Chief Justice Warren E. Burger administered the vice-presidential oath of office to Ford before a joint session of Congress. The entire confirmation process, from nomination to swearing in, had lasted seven weeks.

Rockefeller Nomination

Gerald Ford served only eight months as vice president. When President Nixon resigned on August 9, 1974, Ford became president, and the vice presidency was once again vacant.

Ford's succession posed an early test for the legitimacy of the vice-presidential appointment process. Not only was Ford, in a sense, the "handpicked" choice of his discredited predecessor, but his own nomination of a new vice president would mean that for the first time the nation would be led by an unelected president and an unelected vice president.

On August 20 Ford announced his nomination of New York governor Nelson A. Rockefeller to fill the vacancy in the vice presidency. Rockefeller was a national leader of demonstrated competence in the fields of administration, urban problems, and foreign affairs, and his nomination was met with acclaim from both the press and the public.

Rockefeller's confirmation took four months. He may have caused some of the delay himself by announcing that he would not campaign in the 1974 congressional elections until his nomination had been confirmed. Congress, led by Democrats who had little desire to see Rockefeller on the campaign trail, responded by dragging its feet. Hearings also were slowed by revelations that Rockefeller had given substantial cash gifts to several aides and may have financed the writing of a critical biography of his Democratic opponent in the 1970 gubernatorial election.

Prodded by Ford and apparently persuaded that Rockefeller had not used his vast wealth improperly, Congress finally acted. On December 10 the Senate voted 90–7 to confirm Rockefeller. The House voted 287–128 in Rockefeller's favor on December 19. Like Ford, Rockefeller was sworn in immediately after the House vote.

Other Contingencies

A combination of legislation, constitutional amendments, and political party rules cover a variety of circumstances under which a president-elect or presidential candidate must be replaced.

The Twentieth Amendment, which became part of the Constitution in 1933, dealt with some of these issues. It states that if the president-elect dies the vice president-

---

CLOSER LOOK

Presidential addresses to a joint session of Congress such as the State of the Union address are events attended by all major officers of the United States. This includes, but is not limited to, the Speaker of the House, the vice president, Supreme Court justices, the Joint Chiefs of Staff, and the heads of executive departments and agencies. With every person eligible to become president under the Presidential Succession Act of 1947 in attendance, the United States could find itself without any president if a tragedy such as a terrorist attack destroyed the House chamber. To ensure the continuation of government, an eligible cabinet-level secretary does not attend the speech. To the right is a list of persons who did not attend the State of the Union address and would have become president if such a tragedy had occurred.

DEPARTMENT HEADS IN PRESIDENTIAL LINE OF SUCCESSION WHO DID NOT ATTEND THE PRESIDENT'S STATE OF THE UNION ADDRESS

1984	Secretary Samuel R. Pierce Jr.	Housing and Urban Development
1985	Secretary Malcolm Baldrige	Commerce
1986	Secretary John Block	Agriculture
1987	Secretary Richard Lyng	Agriculture
1988	Secretary Donald P. Hodel	Interior
1989	NONE	
1990	Secretary Edward J. Derwinski	Veterans Affairs
1991	Secretary Manuel Lujan	Interior
1992	Secretary Ed Madigan	Agriculture
1993	Secretary Bruce Babbitt	Interior
1994	Secretary Mike Espy	Agriculture
1995	Secretary Federico Pena	Transportation
1996	Secretary Donna Shalala	Health and Human Services
1997	Secretary Dan Glickman	Agriculture
1998	Secretary Bill Daley	Commerce
1999	Secretary Andrew W. Cuomo	Housing and Urban Development
2000	Secretary Bill Richardson	Energy
2001	Secretary Anthony Principi	Veterans Affairs
2002	Secretary Gale Norton	Interior
2003	Attorney General John Ashcroft and Justice and Transportation Secretary Norman Mineta	
2004	Secretary Donald Evans	Commerce
2005	Secretary Donald Evans	Commerce
2006	Secretary Jim Nicholson	Veterans Affairs
2007	Attorney General Alberto Gonzales	Justice

elect becomes president at the beginning of the term. It also stipulates that if a president-elect either has not been chosen or fails to qualify by inauguration day the vice president–elect shall serve as acting president until a president is named.

The amendment also authorized Congress to provide for a situation in which neither a president nor a vice president is chosen by inauguration day. Congress did so in 1947, stipulating that the Speaker of the House would become acting president, followed by the other officials listed in the line of succession. Since enactment, these provisions of the amendment have never been needed.

Party rules govern what would happen if a presidential or vice-presidential candidate were to die or resign between the time of nomination, usually July or August, and mid-December, when the Electoral College meets. Republican Party rules provide that the party's national committee would meet to choose a replacement.

The Democratic National Committee also was responsible for choosing a replacement nominee until 1984 when the responsibility was given to the national nominating convention's "superdelegates." (Superdelegates are elected and party officials.) In 1972 the Democratic National Committee was called upon to name a replacement for vice-presidential nominee Thomas F. Eagleton, who had withdrawn from the race.

What would happen if the presidential candidate who had won a majority of electoral votes died or withdrew before January 6, the day Congress counts the electoral votes? The Twentieth Amendment left it to Congress to legislate for this possibility. But Congress never has done so.

The wisdom of our fathers, foreseeing even the most dire possibilities, made sure that the Government should never be imperiled because of the uncertainty of human life. Men may die, but the fabrics of our free institutions remain unshaken.

—**Chester A. Arthur,** Address upon Assuming the Office of President of the United States, **September 22, 1881**

> **More on this topic:**
>
> *Disability Amendment,* p. 154
>
> *Historic Milestones of the Presidency,* p. 253
>
> *Vice President,* p. 539

Summit Meetings

Presidents are responsible for the conduct of diplomacy, but presidents rarely met with foreign leaders until World War II. The difficulties of travel, the isolated location of the United States, and the traditional belief that presidents should stay close to their duties in the capital prevented presidents from acting as their own negotiators.

Today the American public takes for granted meetings between the president and other world leaders. Jet travel and modern communications allow presidents to see other world leaders anywhere around the globe without losing touch with Washington. These "summit meetings" are generally regarded as a useful tool of presidential foreign policy making. Presidents have found that a highly publicized summit tends to raise their public approval rating.

The Constitution does not specifically sanction the president's authority to meet with other world leaders. The constitutional power to appoint, send, and receive ambassadors and to negotiate treaties, however, clearly establishes the president's right to conduct diplomatic negotiations personally.

Winston Churchill is credited with coining the term *summit.* In 1953 he used the word when he called for a conference between the leaders of the Soviet Union and the Western powers. The media picked up the term and used it to describe the Geneva conference between Soviet and Western leaders in 1955. After Geneva, meetings between national leaders came to be called summits. The

One event that often takes place during a summit meeting is a state dinner. These formal events are integral to the diplomatic process and reflect the president's role as chief of state. Often at these dinners, the president says a few words reflecting the issues that brought leaders together in talks, and at the conclusion of his remarks the president offers a toast of appreciation and hope for a warm and mutually respectful relationship between the two countries. Here Richard Nixon is seen joining Chinese premier Chou En-lai in a toast pictured above.

term is now used to distinguish between meetings attended by heads of government and meetings between foreign ministers or lower-level officials.

The most famous summit meetings were those between the U.S. president and the leader of the Soviet Union. Between Franklin D. Roosevelt's presidency and the demise of the Soviet Union in 1991 every president met with a Soviet leader at least once. These meetings often were associated with arms control negotiations. Some summits, like those held in Moscow in 1972, in Vienna in 1979, and in Washington in 1987, have been used as the occasion for signing an arms control agreement. Soviet-American summits gave the leaders of the two countries with massive nuclear arsenals a chance to assess each other and clarify their goals and intentions. Superpower summits, therefore, were seen as a means of reducing the chances of a miscalculation that could lead to war.

Since the end of the cold war and the breakup of the Soviet Union into many independent nations, American presidents have continued to meet and sign arms agreements with the new leadership. However, these summits seem less extraordinary to most observers. Greater emphasis has been placed on meetings between presidents and the leaders of the large industrialized democracies with which the United States has most of its trade and economic relations. Every year since 1975 the president has met collectively with the leaders of the so-called Group of Seven (G-7) nations. Besides the United States, the other nations of the group are Canada, France, Germany, Great Britain, Italy, Japan, and, starting in 1998, Russia. The name has been changed to GROUP OF EIGHT.

Despite its popular appeal, summit diplomacy can be ineffective and even counterproductive. Diplomatic historian Elmer Plischke has pointed out numerous disadvantages and risks of summit meetings in his book *Diplomat in Chief.* Plischke notes that the extensive media attention given summits may distort their substance or raise public expectations of improved relations with another country beyond what is warranted. The spontaneity possible at summits may yield agreements that have not received proper scrutiny. Summits also may distract presidents from their other duties, place presidents in a location where it is difficult to ensure their safety, and cause physical strain that could threaten the president's health. Because the success of a summit depends on the performance of the president, relations with other countries may be harmed if the president is inexperienced or inadequately prepared.

President Carter, center, shakes hands with Egyptian president Anwar Sadat (left) and Israeli prime minister Menachem Begin (right) at the signing of the 1979 Mideast Peace Treaty, otherwise known as the Camp David Accords.
Source: Bill Fitz-Patrick, The White House

Moreover, if diplomacy with another country is grounded on the personal relationship between a president and that country's leader, relations may suffer when one of them leaves office.

Despite these dangers a summit meeting has the potential to be a valuable diplomatic tool. According to Plischke, by becoming personally acquainted a president and a foreign leader may reduce tensions, clarify national interests, and establish mutual respect. Close personal friendship between a president and a foreign leader may bring about improved relations between the two countries. Summits allow presidents to focus national attention on specific issues and to improve public understanding of them. Because foreign leaders can be sure that they are dealing with the wielder of foreign policy power, and because presidents are empowered to make shifts in policy, summits can break diplomatic impasses quickly. Summit meetings also may produce broad agreements that can resolve differences or lead to specific agreements worked out later by officials.

> **More on this topic:**
>
> *Camp David, p. 67*
>
> *Chief of State, p. 86*
>
> *Diplomatic Powers, p. 149*
>
> *Group of Eight, p. 239*

It is in that spirit, the spirit of '76, that I ask you to rise and join me in a toast to Chairman Mao, to Premier Chou, to the people of our two countries, and to the hope of our children that peace and harmony can be the legacy of our generation to theirs.

—*Richard Nixon,* Toasts of the President and Premier Chou En-lai of China at a Banquet Honoring the Premier in Peking, February 25, 1972

Supreme Court *See* COURTS AND THE PRESIDENT.

Taft, William Howard

William Howard Taft (1857–1930) was born in Cincinnati, Ohio, on September 15, 1857. His father was Alphonso Taft, a prominent lawyer who served as secretary of war and attorney general under Ulysses S. Grant. William excelled as a scholar and an athlete in high school. He enrolled at Yale University in 1874 and graduated four years later, second in his class.

Taft returned to Cincinnati, where he studied law in his father's office and at the Cincinnati Law School. He gained admission to the bar in 1880. He practiced law and served briefly as assistant prosecutor of Hamilton County, Ohio, and collector of internal revenue for his Ohio district. Taft married Helen Herron on June 19, 1886.

After serving on the Ohio state superior court and as U.S. solicitor general, Taft was appointed judge of the Sixth U.S. Circuit Court in 1892 by President Benjamin Harrison. In 1900 President William McKinley appointed Taft president of the U.S. Philippine Commission, which was charged with establishing a government on the islands. Taft was reluctant to leave his judgeship, but McKinley persuaded him to go to the Philippines by offering him an eventual appointment to the Supreme Court. He expected to be in the Philippines only a short time, but in 1901 McKinley appointed him governor general of the islands. Taft reorganized the Filipino court system; improved roads, harbors, and schools; and encouraged limited self-government. While in the Philippines he twice refused appointment to the Supreme Court, the position he coveted most, because he did not want to abandon the people of the islands. In 1904, however, he accepted an appointment as sec-

Source: Library of Congress

retary of war, made by President Theodore Roosevelt, with the condition that he could continue supervising U.S. policy toward the Philippines.

As secretary of war, Taft visited the Panama Canal site in 1904, served as temporary provisional governor of Cuba in 1906, and oversaw relief efforts after the 1906 San Francisco earthquake. By 1908 Taft's wide government experience, his close friendship with Roosevelt, and his administrative abilities made him the front-runner for the Republican presidential nomination. He was not anxious to run but was persuaded to do so by Roosevelt, Republican Party leaders, and his wife. He won the nomination at the 1908 Republican national convention in Chicago on the first ballot. In the election he defeated Democrat William Jennings Bryan in the Electoral College 321–162.

Upon entering office Taft urged Congress to reduce tariffs, a step favored by progressive Republicans. The president angered this group, however, when he signed the Payne-Aldrich Tariff Act of 1909. The act reduced tariff rates by amounts that most progressives considered insignificant.

Taft showed strong leadership in his pursuit of antitrust cases. His administration brought ninety antitrust suits in four years, compared with forty-four brought during Roosevelt's seven-year presidency. The Standard Oil and American Tobacco companies were among those broken up by the Taft administration. Taft also backed the passage of the Sixteenth Amendment, which authorized a federal income tax.

In foreign affairs Taft instituted a policy that came to be known as "dollar diplomacy." This policy sought to use investments and trade to expand U.S. influence abroad, especially in Latin America. Taft also was willing to use force to maintain order and to protect U.S. business interests in Latin America. He dispatched troops to Honduras in 1911 and to Nicaragua in 1910 and again in 1912 to protect American lives and property threatened by revolution. These interventions contributed to Latin American resentment toward the United States.

By 1910 former president Theodore Roosevelt had become disaffected with Taft because of what he considered Taft's conservative departures from progressive policies toward big business and the environment. In 1912 Taft was nominated by the Republican Party for reelection. Roosevelt, who had won most of the Republican primaries that year, protested that he had not received a fair chance to win the nomination at the Republican national convention, which had been controlled by Taft supporters. Roosevelt then launched a third-party candidacy that doomed Taft's reelection bid. Roosevelt and Taft split the Republican vote, allowing Democrat Woodrow Wilson to capture the presidency. Taft finished in third place with just eight electoral votes.

When Taft's term expired, he accepted a professorship of law at Yale University. In 1913 he was elected president of the American Bar Association. During World War I President Wilson named him joint chairman of the War Labor Board, which resolved wartime labor disputes. The election

CLOSER LOOK

Source: Library of Congress

William Howard Taft is the only person to serve both as president and as chief justice of the United States. In many ways, Taft's legacy in American history was established as much from the bench as it was from the Oval Office. As chief justice, Taft wrote the opinion of the Court in *Myers v. United States,* which set a judicial precedent putting to rest the question of whether a president can remove an appointed executive branch official. Taft argued that Article II of the Constitution implies that presidents can remove executive branch officials since the president is responsible to make sure "laws are faithfully executed." To properly execute their office, presidents must be able to control their subordinates.

More on this topic:

Courts and the President,
p. 128

Elections Chronology,
p. 174

Myers v. United States,
p. 370

of Taft's friend and fellow Republican Warren G. Harding to the presidency in 1920 opened the door to a Supreme Court appointment for the former president. When Chief Justice Edward White died on May 19, 1921, Harding chose Taft to take his place. Taft was a capable chief justice who usually rendered moderately conservative opinions. He improved the efficiency of the judicial system and fought successfully for passage of the Judiciary Act of 1925, which increased the Supreme Court's discretion in choosing which cases to accept.

Taft resigned as chief justice on February 3, 1930, because of his weak heart. He died in Washington, D.C., on March 8 of that year from heart failure. Taft's oldest son, Robert Alphonso Taft, became one of the most powerful Republicans in the Senate during the late 1940s and early 1950s and was considered as a possible presidential candidate in 1940, 1948, and 1952.

Taylor, Zachary

Source: Library of Congress

Like George Washington, Andrew Jackson, and William Henry Harrison, Zachary Taylor (1784–1850) rose to the presidency after becoming a military hero. Like Harrison, Taylor died early in his term. He served just sixteen months, the second shortest term in presidential history after Harrison's one month in office.

Taylor was born into a prominent family of Virginia planters related to both James Madison and Robert E. Lee. Shortly before Zachary's birth, the Taylors left Virginia to establish a farm near Louisville, Kentucky. Zachary, the third of nine children, was born en route on November 24, 1784, at a friend's home in Orange County, Virginia.

In 1808, at the age of twenty-three, Taylor was commissioned as a lieutenant in the army. Two years later he married Margaret Mackall Smith. Taylor participated in William Henry Harrison's Indian campaigns in the Indiana Territory and fought in the Ohio Valley during the War of 1812. He then rose through the ranks while serving in a series of garrison posts on the frontier. In 1837 he was assigned to Florida, where the army was fighting the Seminole Indians. On Christmas Day of that year his troops defeated the Seminoles in a major battle that earned him a promotion to brigadier general.

In 1841 Taylor was given command of the southern division of the army and reassigned to Baton Rouge, Louisiana, where he bought a large plantation. When the United States annexed Texas in 1845, President James K. Polk ordered Taylor to defend it against a Mexican invasion. In January 1846 Polk instructed the general to take the provocative step of deploying his forces on territory claimed by Mexico between the Nueces River and the Rio Grande. When Mexico declared war and launched an attack against Taylor's army, the general invaded Mexico and won a series of quick victories at Palo Alto, Resaca de la Palma, and Monterrey.

Polk recognized that Taylor's heroism made him an attractive Whig presidential candidate and maneuvered to prevent further boosts to the general's reputation. The president ordered Taylor to command a small force of five thousand troops in northern Mexico, while Gen. Winfield Scott was given the more glamorous duty of leading an expedition to capture Mexico City. Taylor's soldiers, however, routed a Mexican force of twenty thousand at Buena Vista in February 1847. The victory made Taylor a hero in the United States, and, as Polk had feared, the Whig Party sought to capitalize on the popularity engulfing "Old Rough and Ready" by offering him its nomination for president.

Taylor declared that he disliked partisan politics and preferred to run without party affiliation. He eventually accepted the Whig nomination but announced that he thought of himself as a national candidate rather than a Whig. In the election Taylor defeated the Democratic candidate, Lewis Cass, by a close electoral vote of 163–127. Martin Van Buren's third-party candidacy contributed to Taylor's victory by splitting New York's Democratic vote, allowing Taylor to capture the state's thirty-six electoral votes that would have given Cass a majority.

Taylor took office without prior political experience. At Taylor's inauguration Polk found the general to be "exceedingly ignorant of public affairs." Despite this handicap, Taylor refused to be just a Whig figurehead. Among his proposals were greater government aid for agriculture and the development of a transcontinental railroad.

The major issue confronting Taylor was whether slavery would be allowed to exist in the West where territories soon would be seeking statehood. Southerners feared that new states entering the Union, particularly California, would outlaw slavery and upset the balance in Congress between slave and free states. Congressional leaders, led by Henry Clay of Kentucky, attempted to legislate a compromise that would satisfy both the North and the South. Taylor supported the right of states to decide for themselves whether they would permit slavery. He encouraged New Mexico and California to apply for statehood and declared that he would oppose the compromise plan being developed by Congress.

Although Taylor was a slave-owning southerner, he believed the Union must be held together. He warned southern leaders that if their states rebelled against federal authority, he would use the army to enforce the law and preserve the Union.

Taylor never had to veto a congressional compromise plan or confront the secession of southern states. On the Fourth of July, 1850, after eating heavily during long, hot outdoor ceremonies at the Washington Monument, he became seriously ill. He died in the White House on July 9 at the age of sixty-five. His vice president, Millard Fillmore, succeeded to the presidency and threw executive support behind the Compromise of 1850, which held the Union together temporarily by making concessions to the South in return for California's entrance into the Union as a free state.

> **More on this topic:**
>
> *Death of the President, p. 142*
>
> *Fillmore, Millard, p. 217*
>
> *Mexican-American War of 1846, p. 361*

Teapot Dome Scandal

The worst scandal of the scandal-racked administration of Warren G. Harding was known as the Teapot Dome. The conspiracy among high government officials may have contributed indirectly to Harding's death after less than three years in office. Revelations after his death helped to shape the historical judgment of Harding as one of the most incompetent and corrupt of all presidents.

Harding was a genial and passive figure who gave other Republican political figures—particularly those from his home state of Ohio—a free hand in abusing their government positions for

Who Says a Watched Pot Never Boils?

Source: Library of Congress

personal gain. Among those who took advantage of the situation was Secretary of the Interior Albert B. Fall. Fall entered into a corrupt bargain with the oil companies of Edward L. Doheny and Harry F. Sinclair to turn over to them valuable petroleum deposits that President Wilson had reserved for future use by the navy.

Under the secret agreement, the Elk Hill oil reserve in California was leased to Doheny, while the Teapot Dome reserve in Wyoming, after which the scandal was named, was leased to Sinclair. Fall personally received at least $100,000 from Doheny and $300,000 from Sinclair.

Although the Teapot Dome conspiracy was not fully revealed until after Harding's death, evidence of it and other abuses of office began coming to light early in 1923. The emerging accounts of corruption were devastating to Harding, who did not personally participate in or profit from the conspiracy. He complained bitterly about his "goddamned friends," and his sadness and feelings of betrayal probably helped to bring about his sudden death during a western trip that summer.

Investigations by a Senate committee led Harding's successor, Calvin Coolidge, to appoint a special commission to initiate prosecutions. The resulting trials and legal maneuvering lasted for almost six years, after which Fall was sentenced to a year in jail and a $100,000 fine, and Sinclair was sentenced to six months in jail. Doheny was acquitted, however, even though Fall had been convicted of taking a bribe from him.

> **More on this topic:**
>
> *Ethics, p. 195*
>
> *Harding, Warren G., p. 245*

Tennessee Valley Authority

One of the most important accomplishments of Franklin D. Roosevelt's New Deal was the creation of the Tennessee Valley Authority (TVA). This massive project continues today to provide electrical power and flood control to a large portion of the South.

The TVA was established by Congress in 1933, during the depths of the Great Depression. People had long recognized that the rivers of the Tennessee Valley were an enormous untapped resource for hydroelectric power, as well as a regular flood threat to many communities. The political impetus to act on this, however, had been lacking until Roosevelt included a TVA program in his New Deal.

By harnessing the rivers to produce electrical power and to control floods, the project was able to bring progress to an area that previously had suffered from underdevelopment and poverty. In addition, the TVA solidified Roosevelt's political support in the South.

Today the TVA is an independent corporate agency of the federal government, charged with developing the resources of the Tennessee Valley region. It serves people living in an area of 91,000 square miles in seven states—Alabama, Georgia, Kentucky, Mississippi, North Carolina, Tennessee, and Virginia. The TVA is responsible for providing flood control and improving navigation on the

Tennessee River, supplying power, and promoting economic development.

The TVA power system is the nation's largest, serving more than eight million consumers through about 160 municipal and cooperative power distributors. The power system has been self-supporting from revenues from power sales, but other TVA programs, such as flood control, have been funded by Congress.

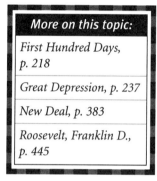

More on this topic:

First Hundred Days, p. 218

Great Depression, p. 237

New Deal, p. 383

Roosevelt, Franklin D., p. 445

Hydroelectric dam in the Tennessee Valley Authority system
Source: National Archives

Term of Office

The president is elected for a four-year term. The fixed term, historian Daniel Boorstin has written, "remains one of the most significant if least celebrated features of the office. It expressed the Framers' confidence—which history has justified—in the civility of American politics."

Before 1951 presidents were eligible to run for reelection as often as they liked, but until Franklin D. Roosevelt ran for and won an unprecedented third term in 1940 and a fourth term in 1944, no president had sought more than two consecutive terms in office.

Roosevelt's victories sparked adoption of the Twenty-second Amendment in 1951. The amendment prohibits any person from being elected president more than two times. It also prevents successor presidents from being elected more than once if they have served more than two years of a departed president's four-year term. (If they serve two years or less of an unexpired term, they may be elected two times on their own, for a maximum tenure of ten years.)

A president's term begins with INAUGURATION at noon on January 20 after the November election. Until the Twentieth Amendment was ratified in 1933 presidents were not inaugurated until March 4, leaving a four-month hiatus between the election and the inauguration. The briefer period established by the amendment shortened the period in which the nation had, in effect, two presidents—the outgoing president and an incoming president-elect. Yet the amendment allowed time for an orderly TRANSITION PERIOD between the old and the new administrations.

Presidents generally enter office accompanied by an aura of good feeling. Even in a close, bitterly contested election, supporters and opponents alike in Congress and elsewhere traditionally express hopes for cooperation, respect, and goodwill. This closing of ranks is seen in the boost in popularity that presidents enjoy immediately after taking office. The HONEYMOON PERIOD rarely lasts beyond a few months, however, and presidents need to act quickly after taking office if they are to reap the benefits of initial congressional and popular goodwill.

A reverse phenomenon takes hold toward the end of a presidential term. Whether the president is seeking reelection or is retiring, Congress is less willing to respond to presidential requests during this LAME-DUCK period.

Besides Franklin Roosevelt, who served as president for slightly more than twelve years, through 2001 twelve presidents served one full term, ten served less than a full term, eleven served two full terms, and seven served for more than four years but less than eight years.

Among presidents who served two full terms, Grover Cleveland is the only one to have served two nonconsecutive terms.

Two-Term Tradition

Delegates to the Constitutional Convention did not decide how long the president's term would be and whether the executive would be eligible for reelection until they determined how the president would be selected. One early plan favored by the delegates called for Congress to elect the president to a single seven-year term. Delegates valued eligibility for reelection because of the incentive to excellent performance it offered the president. However, reelection was considered incompatible with legislative selection, for fear that a president would use political patronage and ply legislators with favors in an effort to win additional terms. Ultimately the delegates adopted a plan under which the president would be chosen by an ELECTORAL COLLEGE for a four-year term with no limit on reelection.

George Washington stepped down from the presidency voluntarily after two terms, saying in his farewell address that he had done so not as a matter of principle but because he longed for "the shade of retirement."

Thomas Jefferson was the first president to argue that no president should serve more than two terms. "If some termination to the services of the Chief Magistrate be not fixed by the Constitution, or supplied by practice, his office ... will in fact become for life, and history shows how easily that degenerates into an inheritance," Jefferson wrote to the Vermont legislature in 1807, declining its request that he run for a third term.

Much to the dismay of Republicans who cried, "No third term," President Franklin Roosevelt won a third term in 1940 and then a fourth in 1944. He died just three months after the January 1945 inauguration.
Source: FDR Library

Jefferson's defense of a two-term limit took root quickly. Indeed, the Whig Party and many Democrats soon argued for a one-term limit. Andrew Jackson was the last president until Abraham Lincoln to be elected to two terms, and even Jackson said he would prefer a constitutional amendment barring more than one six-year presidential term.

Of the first thirty presidents (Washington to Herbert C. Hoover), twenty served one term or less, and the issue of a third term arose only occasionally. Ulysses S. Grant in 1876 and Woodrow Wilson in 1920 probably would have liked to serve another four years, but both were too unpopular at the end of their second terms even to be renominated by their political parties.

Theodore Roosevelt's situation was more complicated. He had succeeded to the presidency upon the assassination of William McKinley, serving all but six months of McKinley's term. In

1904 he won the presidential election in his own right. But in 1908 he declined certain renomination and almost certain reelection, calling the two-term limit a "wise custom."

Four years later, Roosevelt ran for president again, first as a Republican, then as a third-party candidate. He was unsuccessful. That he had refused a "third cup of coffee" in 1908, Roosevelt said, did not mean that he never intended to drink coffee again. "I meant, of course, a third consecutive term."

Breaking with Custom

As early as 1937 Franklin Roosevelt announced that he did not plan to seek a third term in 1940. But as his second term wore on he became increasingly frustrated by congressional resistance to his policies and programs. In 1939 World War II broke out in Europe, and there was little hope that the United States would be able to remain aloof from the fray. Waiting until the Democratic convention in July 1940, Roosevelt finally signaled his willingness to be renominated. The delegates overwhelmingly approved.

Polls showed that the public was deeply divided over the propriety of Roosevelt's candidacy. Republicans took up the cry of "no third term" on behalf of their nominee, Wendell Willkie. Roosevelt won the election, but his popular vote margin was five million, compared with eleven million in 1936.

In 1944, with the United States and its allies nearing victory in the war, Roosevelt won another term, this time by three million votes. Roosevelt was ill at the time of his fourth election and died barely three months after the inauguration.

The Twenty-Second Amendment

Congress had always been unhappy with the Constitution's failure to restrict the number of terms a president might serve. From 1789 to 1947, 270 resolutions to limit the president's tenure were introduced in the House and Senate, 60 of them after 1928. But the Roosevelt years added a partisan dimension to this long-standing concern.

In the midterm elections of 1946 the Republicans, who had been driven from power with Roosevelt's first election in 1932, regained control of both chambers of Congress. Less than three months after Congress convened in 1947, Republicans pushed through a constitutional amendment limiting the president to two full terms (or one full term if he had served more than half of his predecessor's term).

The proposed Twenty-second Amendment received a mixed response from the states. But after three years and eleven months the requisite three-fourths of the states had ratified the amendment, and it was declared part of the Constitution on February 17, 1951. (Only the Twenty-seventh Amendment took longer to ratify.)

Effects Untested

So few presidents have served even two full terms since the Twenty-second Amendment was enacted that its effects on the modern presidency are hard to measure.

John F. Kennedy was assassinated in the third year of his first term. His successor, Lyndon B. Johnson, was eligible to run for two full terms on his own. But Johnson's political unpopularity in 1968 led him to abandon his attempt to win a second full term.

Richard Nixon was elected to a second full term in 1972, but his role in the Watergate scandal forced him to resign less than two years later. Gerald R. Ford served more than half of Nixon's term, which limited him to only one elected term as president. But Ford failed to win even that. The candidate who defeated him in 1976, Jimmy Carter, was defeated in turn by Ronald Reagan in 1980. Reagan was reelected in 1984 and served until the end of his second term in 1989.

Dwight D. Eisenhower, the first president to whom the amendment applied, would have liked to run for a third term in 1960, according to John Eisenhower, his son and deputy chief of staff. While president, Eisenhower expressed "deep reservations" about the two-term limit.

Reagan was the second president to be denied the opportunity to run for re-election by the Twenty-second Amendment. During his second term he campaigned for a constitutional amendment that would repeal the two-term limit (although not in such a way as to apply to him). Reagan, who remained one of the twentieth century's most popular presidents throughout his two terms, argued that the voters should not be denied the opportunity to extend a president's tenure for as long as they liked. Critics warned of the danger of an overly personal presidency.

By the way, in a few weeks a new film opens: "Rambo III." You remember, in the first movie Rambo took over a town. In the second, he single-handedly defeated several Communist armies. And now in the third Rambo film, they say he really gets tough. Almost makes me wish I could serve a third term.

—**Ronald Reagan,** Remarks at the Annual Republican Congressional Fund-raising Dinner, May 11, 1988

The third president to feel the effects of the amendment was Bill Clinton, a Democrat elected president in 1992 and 1996 who served two full terms. Clinton survived being impeached by the House (he was acquitted by the Senate) and retained both his critics and his champions through the end of his presidency.

Some presidents have proposed that the president be limited to a single term but that the term be extended to six years. Advocates, including Jackson, Lyndon Johnson, and Carter, have claimed that a single six-year term would free the president from the political pressures of re-election and grant the administration more time to accomplish its long-term goals. Opponents have noted that under a six-year term an unpopular president would serve two more years than under the current system and a popular president two fewer years.

More on this topic:
Electoral College, p. 185
Honeymoon Period, p. 262
Inauguration, p. 282
Lame Duck, p. 328
Transition Period, p. 510

Third Parties

Although the United States has a two-party system, third parties often have entered the electoral fray. Third parties are usually of short duration. Most are formed in times of intense conflict, and their base of support is often regional rather than national. Whenever and wherever they emerge, they are a sign of dissatisfaction with the two major POLITICAL PARTIES.

Third parties seldom win a sizable share of the votes cast for president. Since 1832 third-party or independent candidates have won more than 20 percent of the popular vote only twice. They have won more than 10 percent of the popular vote only eight times. But third parties occasionally have influenced elections despite their small share of the vote. For example, in 1848 the Liberty Party, a movement dedicated to the abolition of slavery, received less than 3 percent of the popular vote and no electoral votes. Yet the party drained enough votes from the Whig Party to guarantee the election of Democratic candidate James K. Polk.

From time to time there have been fears that a third-party presidential candidate would attract enough votes to throw the election into the House of Representatives. When none of the presidential candidates wins a majority of the votes in the Electoral College, the election automatically goes to the House for decision. For example, in 1968 when Alabama governor George C. Wallace ran as the standard bearer of the American Independent Party, it was feared that he would win enough southern states to deny either of the major-party candidates a victory in the Electoral College. But the Republican candidate, Richard Nixon, managed to outpoll Wallace in several

Third parties often signal the public's dissatisfaction with the two major parties. In 1968 Alabama governor George Wallace left the Democratic Party to form the American Independent Party. His supporters included blue-collar workers who were fed up with what they saw as the liberal ideology of the Democrats.

Source: Congressional Quarterly

southern states and win a solid majority in the Electoral College.

Third parties also exert influence by publicizing important issues or options that the major parties have ignored. Because the major parties do not want to lose support to third parties, they may adopt positions they otherwise might not have taken up.

Some observers view third parties as a threat to the stability of the democratic system in the United States. Others see them as a vital element in expressing minority sentiments and as a testing ground for new ideas and policies.

Types of Third Parties

Political scientist James Q. Wilson has identified four types of third parties: ideological, one-issue, economic protest, and factional parties.

Ideological Parties

Ideological parties, according to Wilson, have a "comprehensive view of American society and government that is radically different from that of the established parties." They can be found at both ends of the political spectrum and include in the present day the Socialist, Green, and Libertarian Parties. Although ideological parties appeal to a narrow base of support, they have proved to be the most enduring type of third party, largely because of the ideological commitment of their members. In the 2000 election Ralph Nader, the Green candidate, took 2.7 percent of the vote. Nader's role became a key topic for political pundits because of the close contest between Republican George W. Bush and Democrat Al Gore.

One-Issue Parties

Dissatisfaction with the major parties often centers on their stance on a particular issue. Therefore, many third parties have formed around a single policy concern, such as slavery, states' rights, currency, opposition to immigration, abortion, and even hostility to lawyers. Once the issue ceases to be of importance, the basis for the party's existence disappears.

Because most issues provoke intense feelings for a relatively short period of time—or, if they persist, eventually are addressed adequately by the major parties—one-issue parties tend to be short-lived. One exception is the Prohibition Party, which has run a presidential candidate in each election since its founding in 1869. It is the longest-running third party in U.S. history. Although primarily dedicated to banning the sale of liquor, the party was closely linked to the early feminist movement. Indeed, it was the first party to endorse women's suffrage.

Economic Protest Parties

Economic protest parties evolve in opposition to depressed economic conditions. A sour economy, for example, prompted formation of the People's Party, better known as the Populists. In 1891 the Populists nominated presidential and vice-presidential candidates at a national convention in Cincinnati. Calling for free coinage of silver (the country was then on a gold standard), the party won 8.5 percent of the popular vote in the 1892 presidential election.

○ **CLOSER LOOK**

Third-party candidates for president have sometimes played the role of spoiler in elections by taking votes from one candidate and allowing another who might lose to squeeze out a plurality. A famous example was Theodore Roosevelt's 1912 candidacy, which split the Republican vote between Roosevelt and William Howard Taft, resulting in the election of Woodrow Wilson with 41.8 percent of the vote.

Ralph Nader's candidacy in 2000 is another example. Nader received only 2.7 percent of the vote, but his 97,488 votes in Florida would have been more than enough to give Al Gore the state—and the presidency, assuming that Nader voters would instead have cast their votes for the more ideologically similar Al Gore. By contrast, many political scientists believe that the candidacy of H. Ross Perot did not affect the outcome of the 1992 election. Exit polling suggested that Perot took a significant number of votes away from both George H. W. Bush and Clinton. At the same time, Perot brought to the polls additional voters who otherwise would not have voted.

Four years later, however, the Democrats embraced many of the Populists' issues and nominated William Jennings Bryan on a free-silver platform. Populists ran in presidential elections through 1908 but with no appreciable accumulation of support.

In 1992 independent candidate H. Ross Perot rode a tide of discontent with the nation's budget deficit, among other issues, to an 18.9 percent vote share. In 1995 Perot formed the Reform Party and ran as its presidential nominee in the 1996 election. Economic good times had eroded much of his appeal, however, and he won less than half the vote share of his 1992 run. By 2000 the Reform Party had been torn by factional fights. Patrick J. Buchanan, who had run for president as a Republican in 1992 and 1996, ran under the Reform Party banner and took less than 1 percent of the vote.

Factional Parties

Factional parties evolve from a split in one of the major parties. According to Wilson, they usually form to protest "the identity and philosophy of the major party's presidential candidate." In the twentieth century factional parties drew the most votes of any type of third party.

The most successful was the Progressive Party, formed in 1912 to support the candidacy of former president Theodore Roosevelt after he lost the Republican nomination to President William Howard Taft. In November Roosevelt won 27.5 percent of the popular vote to Taft's 23.2 percent, but both men lost to Democrat Woodrow Wilson. When Roosevelt later defected from the Progressives, the party disintegrated.

In 1924 Sen. Robert M. La Follette split off from the Republican Party and revived the Progressive Party label. The liberal La Follette went on to receive 16.6 percent of the popular vote. But when he died in 1925 the party again collapsed.

SIGNIFICANT THIRD-PARTY PRESIDENTIAL CANDIDATES, 1824–2004

Year	Candidate	Party	Percentage of popular vote received	Electoral votes received
1824	Henry Clay	Democratic-Republican	13	37
	William Crawford	Democratic-Republican	11	41
1836	Hugh White	Whig	10	26
1848	Martin Van Buren	Free Soil	10	0
1856	Millard Fillmore	Whig-American	22	8
1860	John C. Breckinridge	Southern Democrat	18	72
	John Bell	Constitutional Union	13	39
1912	Theodore Roosevelt	Progressive	27	88
1924	Robert M. LaFollette	Progressive	17	13
1968	George C. Wallace	American Independent	14	46
1992	H. Ross Perot	Independent	19	0

SOURCE: *Congressional Quarterly's Guide to U.S. Elections*, 4th ed. (Washington, D.C.: CQ Press, 2001).
NOTE: Only candidates who received at least 10 percent of the popular vote are listed. There were no significant third-party candidates prior to 1824.

The Progressives reemerged briefly in 1948, this time splitting off from the liberal wing of the Democratic Party. But the third party with more impact that year was the States' Rights Party, formed by southerners who walked out of the Democratic national convention in opposition to President Harry S. Truman's civil rights program. Led by South Carolina governor J. Strom Thurmond, the party captured four southern states and thirty-nine electoral votes.

Civil rights was again the issue in 1968, when Governor George Wallace bolted from the Democratic Party to form the American Independent Party. Wallace was supported by many whites, especially blue-collar workers who were fed up with civil rights activism, antiwar demonstrations, urban riots, and what they saw as the liberal ideology of the Democratic Party. Wallace won 13.5 percent of the popular vote and forty-six electoral votes.

In 1980 Illinois representative John B. Anderson formed the National Unity Campaign as the vehicle for his independent candidacy after he failed to win the Republican nomination. Anderson received a lot of attention but only 6.6 percent of the popular vote and no electoral votes.

Obstacles to Success

Third parties face considerable legal, political, and cultural barriers. Often voters do not cast their ballots for third parties because of their loyalty to a major party. Indeed, loyal members tend to work within their party to promote change. They leave the party only as a last resort.

Often voters disillusioned with their party simply do not vote. When third parties prosper, voter participation declines nationwide. People with weak party allegiances, such as new voters, are more likely to vote for third-party candidates.

The fact that third parties have little chance of winning further diminishes their support. Indeed, people often feel that a vote for a third party is a wasted vote. Many people also have the sense that third parties are somehow illegitimate, a belief that the major parties try to encourage.

The legal barriers facing third parties may seem daunting. To appear on the election ballots in the fifty states and the District of Columbia, third parties must pass a series of hurdles, including petition requirements, filing deadlines, and fees. The requirements vary from state to state.

The 1974 Federal Election Campaign Act also has been a barrier to third-party presidential candidates. The act allows major-party candidates to receive public funds during the campaign. But third parties are allowed public funds only after the election is over and only if they appear on the ballot in at least ten states and receive at least 5 percent of the popular vote nationwide.

Receiving public funds after the campaign has ended puts third-party candidates at a significant disadvantage. Not only is the money not available when it is most needed, but valuable time must be spent on fund raising rather than on other campaign activities. Fund raising itself is more difficult because third parties do not have the organizational structure or expertise of the major parties.

Third parties also are at a disadvantage because their party organizations are weaker than those of the major parties, and their candidates are usually less experienced and less known to the public. Also important, third-party candidates receive less free media coverage than the major-party candidates.

More on this topic:
Bryan, William Jennings, p. 33
La Follette, Robert M., p. 326
Perot, H. Ross, p. 400
Political Parties, p. 407
Roosevelt, Theodore, p. 448
Wallace, George C., p. 550

The U.S. political culture is not particularly conducive to third parties. The American political tradition of moderation, consensus, and compromise does not lead to the formation of vigorous and persistent third-party movements.

Thurmond, J. Strom

In 1948, very early in his long political career, J. Strom Thurmond (1902–2003) of South Carolina ran for president as the candidate of the Dixiecrats, a group of southern Democrats who did not like their party's endorsement of civil rights legislation. Thurmond captured four southern states (Alabama, Louisiana, Mississippi, and South Carolina), thirty-nine electoral votes (including one in Tennessee even though the state went Democratic), and more than 22 percent of the popular vote in the South.

Thurmond's appeal, however, was entirely regional; nationally he received only 2.4 percent of the popular vote that year. Democrat Harry S. Truman won the election in spite of the Dixiecrats. Thurmond, who was governor of South Carolina during the 1948 election, was elected to the Senate in 1954 as a write-in candidate, and on May 27, 1997, during his seventh term, he became the longest serving member of the Senate. He also was the oldest person to ever serve as a member of Congress. He celebrated his hundredth birthday in 2002 while still serving in the Senate, and finally left that body at the end of his term in January 2003. A veteran opponent of civil rights legislation known for his courtly manner, physical fitness, and political toughness, Thurmond switched parties to become a Republican in 1964, as the Democrats' hold on the South began to weaken.

In an unexpected throwback to his segregationist past, Thurmond indirectly caused the downfall of a Republican Senate leader in late 2002. At a party to celebrate Thurmond's hundredth birthday, Trent Lott, R-Miss., who was scheduled to resume the role of majority leader when the GOP retook control of the Senate in 2003 after the 2002 midterm elections, praised Thurmond for his presidential campaign and said, "I want to say this about my state: When Strom Thurmond ran for president, we voted for him. We're proud of it. And if the rest of the country had followed our lead, we wouldn't have had all these problems over all these years, either." Because Thurmond ran on a segregationist platform, Lott's remarks were widely interpreted to mean he still favored the racial policies of an earlier time. Although he apologized several times for the comments and insisted they did not reflect his thinking in 2002, Lott's ability to lead the party was fatally compromised, and he stepped down as majority-leader-to-be at the end of 2002.

The Dixiecrats' defection from the Democratic Party in 1948 marked the opening of the struggle over civil rights that culminated in the 1960s. The seeds of the breakaway movement were planted the year before when the President's Committee on Civil Rights issued a report calling for the protection of the rights of all minorities. After delegates to the 1948 Democratic national convention rejected a states' rights plank and adopted instead a civil rights plank, the southern segrega-

Sen. Strom Thurmond, R-S.C., the only senator to reach age one hundred, celebrated at a party hosted by President George W. Bush at the White House in December 2002. Behind Thurmond are Bush, Sen. Trent Lott, R-Miss., Thurmond's daughter Julie Thurmond Whitmer, and Thurmond's wife Nancy. After a forty-eight-year Senate career, Senator Thurmond retired to his hometown of Edgefield, S.C., in January 2003.

Source: Reuters

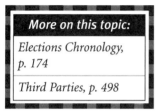

tionists walked out of the convention and formed the States' Rights Party, known informally as the Dixiecrats. They held their own convention in Birmingham, Alabama, and nominated Thurmond for president and Mississippi governor Fielding L. Wright for vice president. Truman survived the Dixiecrat defection, as well as a defection by left-wing Democrats supporting Henry A. Wallace, to defeat Republican Thomas E. Dewey by a narrow margin. The Dixiecrats may have helped Truman by inspiring northern liberals to go to the polls.

Thurmond joined the Republican Party in 1964 because, he said, the Democrats were leading the nation toward socialism. That year the conservative Republican candidate, Barry Goldwater, reflected Thurmond's outlook much more closely than did Democratic nominee Lyndon B. Johnson. In the Senate during the 1950s and 1960s Thurmond became a master of obstructionist tactics against civil rights legislation. In one legendary episode he wrestled another senator to the floor in an attempt to prevent action on a civil rights bill. But as blacks gained political power in his state, Thurmond softened his stance and insisted that he served all constituents equally, pointing out that he had been the first southern senator to hire a black professional staff member and had sponsored the South's first black federal judge. As chairman of the Senate Judiciary Committee from 1981 to 1987 Thurmond shifted his focus from civil rights to other causes, including revision of the criminal code and support of the death penalty.

> **More on this topic:**
>
> *Elections Chronology,* p. 174
>
> *Third Parties,* p. 498

Q: Mr. President, would you care to clear up some things on what you said or didn't say, about whether the electoral votes that were won by Governor Thurmond should be voted for the Governor, or for the successful Democratic—

THE PRESIDENT: I said nothing about it. But I don't want the Dixiecrat vote. We won without New York and without the solid South, and I am proud of that.

—**Harry S. Truman,** News Conference, December 2, 1948

Tilden, Samuel J.

Samuel J. Tilden.
Source: Library of Congress

Samuel Jones Tilden (1814–1886) lost the 1876 presidential election in a manner unique in U.S. history. Tilden, a Democrat and former governor of New York, won a majority of the popular vote in his race against Republican Rutherford B. Hayes. By the end of election day everyone thought Tilden had won. The electoral vote count was close, however, and the electoral votes of four states were called into question the next day. A special commission was set up to resolve the resulting constitutional crisis, which some people feared would lead to civil war. After weeks of maneuvering, the Republicans won the presidency through backroom bargaining with southern Democrats who wanted to end the Republicans' post–Civil War Reconstruction program. The Republicans agreed to pull federal troops out of the South and to continue rebuilding the region in exchange for the election of Hayes. The agreement paved the way for Democratic Party control of the South and for the racially discriminatory "Jim Crow" laws that disenfranchised blacks for most of the next century.

More on this topic:

Elections Chronology,
p. 174

Electoral College, p. 185

Hayes, Rutherford B.,
p. 249

Reconstruction, p. 439

The outcome of the 1876 election was perhaps the most controversial in U.S. history and had a significant impact on the country's political landscape. Although Tilden believed the presidency had been stolen from him through chicanery, there were charges of corruption on both sides in the unstable political climate that followed the Civil War. In the three southern states where electoral votes were in dispute—Florida, Louisiana, and South Carolina—elections had been chaotic, as Republicans fought to get blacks to the polls and Democrats used intimidation and bribery to keep them away. Tilden's own views on the racial question were not radical; he had sided with the antislavery wing of the New York Democratic Party before the war but opposed the inclusion of blacks in state governments after the war.

Tilden believed himself to be the rightful heir to the presidency after the 1876 election, but the Democrats did not nominate him to run again. A wealthy bachelor, he left a large bequest for the establishment of what is now the New York Public Library in New York City.

Titles of the President and Vice President

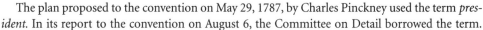

When the delegates to the Constitutional Convention decided on a single person to head the executive branch, they did not immediately consider the question of what formal title that person should have. During the first two months of their deliberations, the delegates usually referred to the head of the executive branch as the "national executive," "supreme executive," or "governor."

The plan proposed to the convention on May 29, 1787, by Charles Pinckney used the term *president*. In its report to the convention on August 6, the Committee on Detail borrowed the term. The title had been used for the presiding officer of Congress and many other legislative bodies, including the convention itself. It was familiar and unthreatening to delegates who feared they might be creating a new monarchy or tyranny. Once proposed by the committee, *president* was accepted without debate by the convention.

The most superlatively ridiculous thing I ever heard of.

—**Thomas Jefferson,** reacting to the news that Adams had proposed the title "His Highness, the President of the United States, and protector of their Liberties," July 29, 1789. Quoted in The Papers of Thomas Jefferson (Princeton: Princeton University Press, 1958), XV, pp. 315–316.

Even after approval of the Constitution and after George Washington's election as the first chief executive, there was still some uncertainty about the title of the office. A committee of the House of Representatives suggested simply "the president of the United States," as in the Constitution. But the Senate in May 1789, at the behest of Vice President John Adams, rejected the House report. Adams believed that "titles and politically inspired elegance were essential aspects of strong government," and supported the title "His Highness, the President of the United States, and protector of their Liberties."

Washington was annoyed by the whole question and was put out with Adams's attempt to give him such an elaborate title. It was soon agreed that "president of the United States" was good enough.

Although the delegates to the Constitutional Convention left ambiguities about the vice president's role as successor to the president and devoted little attention to the issue, the title of the office was adopted from the Latin word *vice* meaning "in place of."

Tompkins, Daniel D.

Daniel D. Tompkins (1774–1825) served two full terms as vice president under James Monroe from 1817 to 1825. Tompkins had the political credentials to make a run for the presidency in his own right, but a financial scandal damaged his reputation and forced him to focus his energies on his defense instead of on political advancement.

Tompkins graduated from Columbia College in 1795 and was admitted to the bar two years later. He enjoyed a brilliant early career in New York state politics. Tompkins served in the New York assembly, the U.S. House of Representatives, and the New York Supreme Court. In 1807 he was elected governor of New York, a post he held until he became vice president in 1817.

As governor, Tompkins was one of the few leaders in the Northeast who supported the War of 1812. He borrowed millions of dollars and oversaw the disbursement of funds to pay troops and buy supplies. During his ten years as New York's chief executive, Tompkins also worked for prison reform, better treatment of Indians, and the abolition of slavery in his state. In 1814 President James Madison offered him the post of secretary of state, but he declined the appointment to remain governor of New York.

Tompkins was interested in the presidential nomination in 1816, but he was forced to settle for the vice presidency because Madison supported Secretary of State James Monroe. The Monroe-Tompkins ticket was elected easily.

During Tompkins's first term he was accused of mismanaging New York's finances while he was governor during the war. Tompkins denied the charges and resolved to fight them. Despite the financial scandal hanging over his head, he was again chosen by the Democratic-Republican Party as its candidate for vice president in 1820. Monroe and Tompkins won with only one Electoral College vote cast against them. Throughout his second term Tompkins remained preoccupied with his financial problems. He declined to travel to the capital for the inauguration and instead took the oath of office in a private ceremony in New York. In 1823, at his request, the Senate chose a president pro tempore to preside over its deliberations; Tompkins never again led that body.

When his term ended in 1825 Tompkins made no attempt to run for another office. Weakened by the stress of the scandal and his heavy drinking, he died a year later. After his death, audits finally revealed that New York actually owed him money. His descendants were paid $92,000 by the state.

> **More on this topic:**
>
> *Monroe, James, p. 366*
>
> *Vice President, p. 539*

Tonkin Gulf Resolution

The Tonkin Gulf Resolution was passed almost unanimously by Congress in 1964. It granted the president broad authority over decisions related to the war in Vietnam. The resolution was intended to unify support of presidential action. For President Lyndon B. Johnson, however, it represented advance congressional authorization for almost any decision he made with regard to Vietnam. Therefore, Johnson never sought congressional approval for any policy or strategy decision about the Vietnam War, except for the appropriations bills necessary to continue U.S. military involvement in Southeast Asia.

The resolution stemmed from an incident that occurred on August 2, 1964. The U.S. destroyer *Maddox,* which the navy said was on a routine mission in the Tonkin Gulf off the coast of North Vietnam, was attacked by North Vietnamese patrol boats. Two nights later the *Maddox* and a second destroyer, the *C. Turner Joy,* reported a second patrol boat attack. Neither ship was damaged. Johnson responded to the incidents by ordering U.S. warplanes to bomb North Vietnamese bases for torpedo boats.

Johnson informed Congress that U.S. ships had been attacked and asked both houses to pass a resolution empowering him to respond to further North Vietnamese aggression. The administration depicted the incidents as unprovoked acts of belligerence. On August 7 Congress passed the Tonkin Gulf resolution by votes of 88–2 in the Senate and 416–0 in the House. The resolution said,

"Congress approves and supports the determination of the President as Commander-in-Chief, to take all necessary measures to repel any armed attack against the forces of the United States and to prevent further aggression." It also declared that the United States was "prepared, as the President determines, to take all necessary steps, including the use of armed force, to assist any member or protocol state of the Southeast Asia Collective Defense Treaty requesting assistance in defense of its freedom."

> *This resolution confirms and reinforces powers of the Presidency. I pledge to all Americans to use those powers with all the wisdom and judgment God grants to me.*
>
> **—Lyndon B. Johnson,** *Remarks upon Signing Joint Resolution of the Maintenance of Peace and Security in Southeast Asia,* **August 10, 1964**

The debate on the resolution demonstrated that members of Congress understood that it gave the president great authority to prosecute the war. By overwhelmingly passing the resolution, Congress was following the practice set during the previous decade of deferring to the president's judgment in national security matters in the name of expediency and unity.

The Tonkin Gulf resolution has been described by historians as a "blank check" for presidential war making in Southeast Asia. Members of the Johnson administration and the president himself frequently cited the resolution as evidence of congressional approval for the widening of the war in Vietnam.

Investigations by the Senate Foreign Relations Committee in 1968 revealed that the Johnson administration had deceived Congress. Records and testimony showed that the *Maddox* had been gathering sensitive information within North Vietnam's territorial waters, and the administration knew that such a mission could draw an attack. Moreover, evidence suggested that the second attack had never been confirmed. Nervous U.S. sailors, struggling in conditions of poor visibility, may have imagined it. Nevertheless, it was presented to Congress as a fact.

The 1968 revelations about the Tonkin Gulf incidents and growing congressional discontent with the war led to the repeal of the Tonkin Gulf resolution on December 31, 1970. The repeal provision was added to a foreign military sales bill, which was signed by President Richard Nixon on January 12, 1971. The measure was largely symbolic and had no effect on Nixon's continuing prosecution of the war. The Nixon administration claimed that the president's power as commander in chief gave him the authority to carry on the war.

> **More on this topic:**
>
> *Constitutional Powers and Provisions, p. 119*
>
> *Vietnam War, p. 546*
>
> *War Powers, p. 555*
>
> *War Powers Act of 1973, p. 560*

Tower Commission *See* IRAN-CONTRA AFFAIR.

Trade Policy

The Constitution gives Congress the power "to regulate Commerce with foreign Nations." Therefore, the rules governing foreign trade are set by legislation. Since the Great Depression, however, trade legislation has contained broad grants of power to the president. The president may shape trade policy through international negotiations and the implementation of tariffs and other trade barriers designed to force foreign countries to open up their markets to U.S. products.

Congress has granted the executive broad trade powers because only the president has the authority to negotiate with foreign governments. When Congress in 1934 adopted the strategy of pursuing mutual reductions in tariffs through international negotiations, it had to turn to the president to carry out those negotiations.

In addition, Congress wanted to isolate U.S. trade policy from pressures for protectionism from specific industries. Because members of Congress have to be concerned with the economic conditions in their states and districts, protectionist sentiment has tended to be stronger in Congress than in the executive branch. If a single industry predominates in a congressional district, that district's representative often will support protectionist measures for that industry. By giving the president extensive trade powers, members of Congress can lobby for their constituents' industries while allowing the president to pursue free trade for the nation.

Throughout much of U.S. history the national economy had benefited from trade surpluses. In 1981, however, the U.S. trade position began to decline rapidly as U.S. exports failed to keep pace with imports. The next year U.S. trade dropped into deficit, where it has remained. The persistence of the trade deficit has created much public pressure for higher barriers to imports.

Thomas Jefferson, depicted here as being robbed by King George and Napoleon, found himself in 1805 in the middle of the war between England and France. The cartoon symbolizes the war's effect on U.S. trade.
Source: Houghton Library, Harvard University

Protectionism

The primary trade question that presidents must address is whether to pursue free trade or to erect barriers that protect U.S. industries but ultimately risk reducing the overall flow of trade. Economists agree that the ideal trade environment for enhancing international prosperity is one in which nations can trade goods and services without trade barriers, such as tariffs, import quotas, embargoes, and strict licensing procedures for importing goods. Yet even the most ardent advocates of free trade recognize that the threat of protectionism is the most effective negotiating tool the government has to convince other nations to end their own unfair trading practices. Appeals for protection for specific industries often have diverted national policy from the ideal of free trade. Nevertheless, since 1934, even when Congress has enacted bills to protect specific industries or to pry open foreign markets, policy makers have maintained a consensus that the U.S. economy benefits from free trade.

Throughout U.S. history, tariffs have been a contentious political issue. The nation's first Treasury secretary, Alexander Hamilton, supported high tariffs, which he hoped would nurture the infant industries of the Northeast. The tariffs enacted during the Federalist era remained in effect when Thomas Jefferson took power in 1800, although the pro-agrarian Democratic-Republicans favored trade policies that enhanced the ability of farmers to sell their products overseas.

During most of the nineteenth century the industrial and commercial interests of the North bickered with the agricultural interests of the South over national tariff policy. Because the South was dependent on foreign markets for its agricultural products, it opposed tariffs that could trig-

ger a retaliatory response from its foreign customers. In addition, tariffs raised the price of many goods the South needed to buy from foreign countries. The intersectional tensions over trade policy led to the nullification crisis in South Carolina in 1832. After Congress passed a high tariff bill in 1832, the South Carolina legislature passed an ordinance declaring the tariff void in that state. President Andrew Jackson, determined to assert federal authority, threatened to enforce the law in South Carolina with federal troops. Hostilities were averted when Jackson and South Carolina leaders accepted a compromise tariff.

For the rest of the nineteenth century tariffs remained high as the generally pro-tariff Republican Party dominated national politics. With the election of Woodrow Wilson in 1913, tariff policy was reversed. That year, with President Wilson's strong support, Congress enacted the Underwood-Simmons Tariff Act, which sharply cut tariffs. Wilson saw tariff reduction as a way to help American consumers, limit the influence of powerful pro-business lobbyists, and stimulate competition.

U.S. participation in World War I rekindled "America first" sentiments in the United States that led to a postwar return of high tariffs. The Tariff Act of 1921 and the Fordney-McCumber Act of 1922, both supported by Republican president Warren G. Harding, returned tariffs to roughly their pre-1913 levels.

When the Great Depression began in 1929, the governments of the major industrialized nations reacted by erecting trade barriers to protect their domestic industries. In 1930 Congress passed the Smoot-Hawley Act, which established the highest tariffs ever levied in the United States. The trade war of the early 1930s left trade between nations a small fraction of what it had been. Protectionist measures meant the world had to dig out of the depression without the benefits of international trade.

You implement that NAFTA, the Mexican trade agreement, where they pay people a dollar an hour, have no health care, no retirement, no pollution controls, et cetera, et cetera, et cetera, and you're going to hear a giant sucking sound of jobs being pulled out of this country right at a time when we need the tax base to pay the debt and pay down the interest on the debt and get our house back in order.

—H. Ross Perot, *Presidential Debate in East Lansing, Michigan,* October 19, 1992

International Trade Negotiations

The Great Depression forced Congress and the president to reconsider the country's position on trade. President Franklin D. Roosevelt proposed to stimulate trade by negotiating mutual reductions in tariffs with U.S. trading partners. Roosevelt asked Congress to delegate to him the authority to reduce U.S. tariffs up to 50 percent in return for equal tariff concessions by other nations. Congress delegated this power to the president in the Trade Agreements Act of 1934. Armed with the new authority, the Roosevelt administration negotiated bilateral agreements that cut tariffs and increased the flow of trade. The resulting greater access to foreign markets helped to stimulate the U.S. economy. After the initial success of Roosevelt's negotiations, congressional grants of authority to the president to negotiate mutual tariff reductions became a regular feature of U.S. trade policy.

In 1947 President Harry S. Truman sought to institutionalize talks to reduce international protectionism. That year, the United States and twenty-three other nations signed the General Agreement on Tariffs and Trade (GATT). In the years that followed, most noncommunist nations signed the agreement.

Since 1947 GATT signatories have held eight rounds of multinational trade negotiations. The eighth (Uruguay) round was completed in 1994. Signed by more than one hundred nations, this breakthrough agreement provided for tariffs to be reduced on most manufactured items by an average of one-third. The accord also lowered barriers on agricultural products and provided protection for intellectual property rights. And it established the World Trade Organization (WTO), which, some critics charged, would harm U.S. sovereignty in trade because Washington could not veto WTO's dispute resolution procedures. Supporters said that because of the relatively open U.S. trading posture, Americans were more apt to be the injured parties in trade disputes. They argued that enhancing GATT's enforcement procedures would help American exporters. After heavy lobbying by President Bill Clinton, Congress passed the measure, and it was signed into law in December 1994.

Recent presidents also have pursued trade agreements outside of GATT, including bilateral pacts on specific trade disputes with important trading partners such as Japan and the North American Free Trade Agreement (NAFTA) with Canada and Mexico. Congressional approval of NAFTA ranked as one of President Clinton's most important victories in 1993. But to quiet critics, Clinton promised to negotiate "side agreements" with Mexico over issues such as environmental protection and labor conditions.

Clinton was unsuccessful, however, in obtaining renewal of "fast track" authority, which allows a president to negotiate a trade agreement and then submit for Congress's approval comprehensive, nonamendable legislation that implements the agreement. In 2002 President George W. Bush experienced greater success in this area when Congress finally granted him fast track authority. The action gave Bush new powers to negotiate the proposed Free Trade Area of the Americas and to try to open other international markets. The current authority is set to expire on July 1, 2007.

In 1993 President Bill Clinton successfully mobilized popular support to win passage of the North American Free Trade Agreement, despite opposition from members of his own party and its labor supporters.

> **More on this topic:**
>
> *Economic Powers, p. 161*
>
> *Executive Agreements, p. 198*

Trade Representative, Office of the U.S.

The Office of the Special Representative for Trade Negotiations was established in 1963 in response to a presidential need for expertise on the increasingly complex issues of international trade. It was redesignated the Office of the U.S. Trade Representative in 1980.

The U.S. trade representative (USTR), a cabinet-level official with the rank of ambassador, is directly responsible to the president and Congress. The USTR is confirmed by the Senate and testifies before congressional committees.

The USTR develops and coordinates U.S. trade policy and is the president's chief adviser on international trade issues. The USTR also acts as the nation's chief negotiator at international trade agreement talks, including World Trade Organization (WTO) negotiations.

Because the trade position of the United States deteriorated greatly during the 1980s, the USTR's activities have received increasing public and media attention. Before 1980 the United States almost always ran a trade surplus. Since then, the U.S. trade balance has fallen deeply into deficit as imports have exceeded exports by tens of billions of dollars.

Under these conditions, the U.S. trade representatives serving under Presidents Ronald Reagan and George H. W. Bush were expected to pry open markets in foreign countries that engage in protectionist trade practices, while fending off congressional demands for protectionism that violated the administrations' commitment to low tariffs and free trade. Although the trade representatives made some progress in opening up foreign markets, the persistent U.S. trade deficit fueled public and congressional demands for tougher trade policies. Under President Bill Clinton, China's most-favored-nation trade status was renewed despite criticism from human rights groups about Beijing's continued suppression of political dissidents. Clinton's successor, George W. Bush, continued to push for free trade on most fronts. Yet on one front, steel, he dug in his heels. In 2002 he imposed tariffs of up to 30 percent over three years on most steel imports—a move viewed as helping Republicans in steel-producing states.

More on this topic:

Cabinet, p. 60

Executive Office of the President, p. 200

Trade Policy, p. 506

Transition Period

In the approximately eleven weeks that elapse between the election and the inauguration, new presidents must turn their concentration from campaigning to governing. Some of a president's most far-reaching decisions take place during this transition period—decisions that determine the possibilities and limits of the new administration. Selecting top aides, setting a management style, determining budget and legislative priorities, and assuming foreign policy leadership are just a few of the tasks a new president must confront.

Almost as soon as the election ballots have been counted, the news fills with reports and speculation on likely cabinet selections and the managerial style of the new president. The president-elect and incoming staff receive a battery of briefings on matters ranging from budget deficits to nuclear strategy. How the new president and staff handle themselves during the transition period can be crucial in determining what kind of HONEYMOON PERIOD the administration is likely to have with Congress and the public.

The transition period is also a rare celebration of a stable democracy based on parties that differ on specific policies but achieve consensus on the most important matters of state. Transitions rarely involve active recriminations by either political party, and almost never is there struggle over the legitimacy of the electoral outcome.

The cost of the transition has grown as the executive branch has grown bigger and more complicated. In 1952 Dwight D. Eisenhower and a transition team of one hundred spent $400,000, all of it private funding, on preparations to take over the reins of government.

Franklin D. Roosevelt and Herbert Hoover in a convertible automobile on the way to the U.S. Captitol for Roosevelt's inauguration, March 4, 1933.
Source: Library of Congress

Richard Nixon was the first president-elect to receive public money; he used $500,000 in appropriated funds and another $1 million in private funding to finance his transition activities in 1968 and early 1969. In 1988 and early 1989 George H.W. Bush and a team of three hundred spent $3.5 million in public funds on talent searches, policy deliberations, and public relations activities. Separate public funds are used for inaugural ceremonies. Bill Clinton also received $3.5 million for the transition. Clinton's team of 450 spent a total of $8.3 million, $4.8 million of which was privately funded. In 2000–2001 George W. Bush's team of eight hundred—faced with a shortened transition because of disputed election results in Florida—spent a total of $8.5 million, $4.3 million of which was private funds.

Perhaps the most important matter the president-elect must address is selecting STAFF, members of the CABINET, and other officials. The men and women chosen to fill the upper levels of the BUREAUCRACY and the White House staff, along with the management style of the new administration, set the tone for the president's tenure in office and play a major role in the administration's success or failure.

The president is responsible for appointing some 5,200 people to a federal bureaucracy of about 2.7 million. New presidents often choose close associates to fill top White House positions and cabinet positions. Other sources of staff for both the White House and the rest of the federal bureaucracy are business leaders, academic figures, representatives of constituency groups served by the various departments, party leaders, and occasionally, if the election has been very close, opposition figures.

Loyalty to the president is a major consideration in naming top White House aides and cabinet members. Unlike many other presidents, Richard Nixon in his first term and Jimmy Carter did not maintain control over middle-level appointments in the executive branch. Both presidents later concluded that the departments were "captured" by career bureaucrats and the interest groups connected with the agencies.

Presidents-elect usually promise to involve cabinet members in the decision-making process, but a strong White House staff can reduce the influence of the cabinet. Dwight Eisenhower was the last president to have anything like a true cabinet government. Many recent presidents, determined to control the bureaucracy, have relied more on a White House staff with a strong CHIEF OF STAFF.

The outgoing administration briefs the president-elect and the incoming team, but the differences between the two sides often block meaningful exchanges. The meeting between the incoming and outgoing presidents is usually cordial, but new executives are often reluctant to take much advice. Harry S. Truman said he thought the advice he offered to Eisenhower on staffing "went into one ear and out the other." Carter reported that Ronald Reagan was inattentive during their Oval Office meeting. The Reagan transition team's cooperation with other agencies, such as the Office of Management and Budget, was more sustained.

The outgoing administration prepares a budget for the next fiscal year, which the incoming administration may amend. In addition, the outgoing president often delivers a farewell address to draw attention to major problems facing the nation. George Washington's call for limited foreign engagements remains the most famous of FAREWELL ADDRESSES. Prominent recent addresses include Eisenhower's warning about the "military-industrial complex" and Carter's plea for recognition of environmental and economic limits.

More on this topic:
Bureaucracy, p. 44
Cabinet, p. 60
Chief of Staff, p. 84
Farewell Addresses, p. 210
Honeymoon Period, p. 262
Staff, p. 471

Transportation Department

The Department of Transportation (DOT) is responsible for a coordinated national transportation policy. Under its jurisdiction are highway planning, development, and construction; urban mass transit; railroads; and aviation.

Integration and coordination of policies for the various modes of transportation—long a goal of Congress and the executive branch—remained elusive until the mid-1960s. Efforts to end what President John F. Kennedy called "a chaotic patchwork of inconsistent and often obsolete legislation" were hindered by the fact that each mode of transportation had some vested interest in existing policies, regulations, and legislation. Moreover, each had its own advocates in the administration and Congress who tended to oppose any changes that would alter these advantages, while often proposing changes designed to improve their own situation.

President Lyndon B. Johnson nevertheless pursued the idea of establishing a cabinet-level department of transportation, and Congress agreed in 1966. As the president requested, Congress excluded from the new department all economic regulatory and rate-setting activities conducted by existing federal agencies.

The final legislation substantially weakened the powers proposed for the secretary of transportation, effectively denying the secretary independent authority to coordinate or revise existing federal transportation policies and programs. The bill approved by Congress established the secretary chiefly as an administrator of existing policies and programs. The department officially began operation in 1967.

It became involved in a variety of national issues affecting transportation in the next years. In 1970 DOT and the Department of Defense cooperated in a project called Military Assistance to Safety in Traffic. The 1970 Airport and Airways Development Act provided for a long-term airport/airway development project under the auspices of DOT but strictly supervised by Congress.

During Jimmy Carter's administration Congress enacted legislation to deregulate the airline, railroad, and trucking industries. The new laws, for which DOT was the major overseer, pared away years of federal regulations that threatened the health of the industries and, in many cases, resulted in higher consumer costs. Deregulation continued under Ronald Reagan with the sale of Conrail, the freight rail system.

Under Samuel K. Skinner, George H. W. Bush's secretary of transportation, the federal government's strategy involved giving states greater flexibility but fewer federal funds for aviation, highway, and mass transit programs. Both Skinner and Federico F. Peña, who served as secretary under President Bill Clinton, focused attention on reviving the troubled airline industry.

In early 1995 Peña announced a reorganization plan that would consolidate the department into three agencies based on transportation over land, at sea, and in the air. Reorganization continued under Peña's successor, Rodney Slater.

George W. Bush selected Norman Y. Mineta as secretary, noteworthy for being a Democrat in Bush's cabinet. After the terrorist attacks of September 11, 2001, against the United States, the department saw a new focus on aviation safety and the movement of two DOT units, the Transportation Security Administration and the U.S. Coast Guard, to the new Homeland Security Department. The secretary of transportation oversees the work of the department's operating administrations.

The principal mission of the Federal Aviation Administration is to promote aviation safety while ensuring efficient use of the nation's navigable air space.

The Federal Highway Administration is responsible for administering the federal aid program for highways, as well as several highway safety programs. The National Highway Traffic Safety Administration covers motor vehicle and traffic safety programs. The Federal Transit Administration provides financial and planning assistance to the nation's public transit systems. The Federal Railroad Administration's principal duties include issuing standards and regulations designed to improve rail safety.

The Saint Lawrence Seaway Development Corporation operates and maintains that part of the St. Lawrence Seaway between Montreal and Lake Erie. The Maritime Administration is responsible for programs to develop, promote, and operate the U.S. merchant marine.

The Research and Special Programs Administration is responsible for, among other things, hazardous material safety, pipeline safety, transportation emergency preparedness, and research and development activities.

The Bureau of Transportation Statistics compiles, analyzes, and makes accessible information on the nation's transportation systems.

Among the many duties the new department will have, several deserve very special notice.

— To improve the safety in every means of transportation, safety of our automobiles, our trains, our planes, and our ships.

— To bring new technology to every mode of transportation by supporting and promoting research and development.

— To solve our most pressing transportation problems.

—Lyndon B. Johnson, Remarks upon Signing Bill Creating a Department of Transportation, October 15, 1966

More on this topic:

Bureaucracy, p. 44

Cabinet, p. 60

Travel

Presidents travel within the United States to stay in touch with the nation, to promote their programs, and to campaign for reelection. Foreign trips allow them to meet with other heads of state and to project power and importance. Jet travel now permits presidents to go almost anywhere at any time. A modern president can hop from city to city giving speeches and arrive back at the White House in time for bed. Presidents are especially drawn to foreign travel, which allows them to star in diplomatic dramas as the world watches.

Theodore Roosevelt was the first president to venture abroad, sailing to Panama on an American ship and, except for a few hours, remaining within U.S. waters. Woodrow Wilson became the first president to cross the seas when he attended the Paris Peace Conference after World War I. The next president to venture abroad was Franklin D. Roosevelt, who journeyed to Morocco in 1943 for a wartime conference. Dwight D. Eisenhower's 1959 goodwill tour around the world is recognized as the first presidential trip in which favorable publicity was a primary object.

Richard Nixon was the first American president to travel to communist China. His 1972 visit with Chinese leaders was widely applauded and symbolized a new beginning for U.S.-Chinese relations. Here Nixon and his wife, Pat, visit the Great Wall.
Source: Library of Congress

Foreign trips often boost a president's popularity and historic standing. Richard Nixon's visit to China in 1972, for example, was widely applauded as a bold move. Nixon's meeting with Chinese leaders signaled a new beginning for U.S.-Chinese relations, which had been hostile since the communists came to power in 1949.

The stakes are high for presidents who travel abroad, and sometimes the results are negative. Wilson was criticized severely for neglecting domestic issues and staying away too long during the World War I peace conference. A state visit to Japan in 1992 failed to bring George H. W. Bush the trade concessions he was seeking and left him vulnerable to charges that he was running away from problems at home just as his reelection campaign was beginning.

Whatever the outcome of a presidential trip, it is bound to be expensive and to require complex planning. Wherever presidents fly, AIR FORCE ONE, their official jet, is usually accompanied by at least two large jets—a backup plane and a communications plane. Sometimes a large cargo plane carrying the chief executive's bullet-proof limousine precedes the presidential entourage. Presidents are accompanied on their travels by staff, sometimes by family members, and by a flock of news reporters. (See SALARY AND PERQUISITES.)

> **More on this topic:**
>
> Air Force One, *p. 8*
>
> *Salary and Perquisites, p. 453*

Treasury Department

Source: Bureau of Engraving

The Treasury Department is in charge of the nation's finances. It is among the most powerful of the executive departments. Its secretary is officially the second-ranking cabinet officer, after the secretary of state.

The department's primary function is to manage the monetary resources of the United States. Among other responsibilities, it regulates national banks, assesses and collects income taxes and customs duties, manufactures coins and bills, determines international economic policy, reports the federal government's financial transactions, conducts international and domestic economic research, and enforces tax and tariff laws.

The department's secretaries have usually numbered among presidents' closest advisers. For example, when George H. W. Bush entered the White House he chose longtime friend and campaign adviser Nicholas F. Brady to head the Treasury Department. Bill Clinton chose the well-respected Texas senator Lloyd M. Bentsen Jr. When Bentsen resigned, Clinton chose as his successor Robert E. Rubin, who previously had coordinated the administration's overall economic policy as head of the National Economic Council. But George W. Bush's choice, former Alcoa chairman Paul H. O'Neill, was not seen as one of Bush's closest advisers. He resigned in late 2002 and was replaced by CSX Corporation head John Snow who held the position until 2006. Currently the Treasury Department is headed by Henry M. Paulson Jr., a former executive with Goldman Sachs.

Background

One of the oldest cabinet departments, Treasury was established by the first session of Congress on September 2, 1789. Yet many of its functions were carried out before the signing of the Declaration of Independence; the Continental Congress issued paper money to finance the Revolutionary War and appointed joint treasurers to oversee the effort.

The Republic's finances, however, remained in disarray until September 1789 when President George Washington appointed Alexander Hamilton to be the first secretary of the Treasury. Hamilton's shrewd financial policies resulted in confidence in the Bank of the United States, which issued money in the government's name. As Treasury's first secretary, Hamilton established a precedent for advising the president.

Treasury's authority expanded considerably during the Civil War. The loss of customs revenues from the seceded southern states led to the establishment of the Bureau of Internal Revenue, as well as the printing of paper currency and the institution of a national banking system.

The growth of international trade after World War I and World War II resulted in a central role for Treasury in the 1944 Bretton Woods Conference, which established the International Monetary Fund and the postwar monetary system.

Many federal functions that originally resided in Treasury have been transferred over the years to other departments. For example, Treasury administered the Postal Service until 1829. The Bureau of the Budget was transferred from Treasury to the Executive Office of the President in 1939. And the U.S. SECRET SERVICE and U.S. Customs Service were transferred to the new Department of Homeland Security in 2003.

Organization

The secretary of the Treasury is assisted by a deputy secretary and two under secretaries for domestic finance and international affairs. The Office of the Treasurer of the United States originally was responsible for the receipt and custody of government funds, but over the years these duties have been dispersed throughout various Treasury bureaus. Today, the treasurer oversees the operations of the department's Bureau of Engraving and Printing and the U.S. Mint.

The Office of the Comptroller of the Currency is an integral part of the national banking system. The comptroller oversees the execution of laws related to nationally chartered banks and promulgates rules and regulations governing their operations.

Of all the bureaus within the department, perhaps none is better known than the Internal Revenue Service (IRS), the bureau responsible for collecting most taxes. The IRS today is the largest of Treasury bureaus, employing more than 100,000 people in Washington, D.C., and throughout the country.

The Bureau of Alcohol, Tobacco, Firearms and Explosives enforces federal firearms and explosives laws, as well as those requiring excise taxes on alcoholic substances and regulating the tobacco industry.

The Bureau of Engraving and Printing designs and prints a large variety of security products, including all paper currency; U.S. postage; customs and revenue stamps; Treasury bills, notes, and bonds; permits; and certificates of award. It is the largest printer of security documents in the world, printing more than forty billion annually.

The Financial Management Service issues $1.2 trillion annually in Treasury checks or electronic fund transfer payments for federal salaries and wages; payments to suppliers of goods and services to the government; income tax refunds; and payments under major government programs, such as Social Security and veterans' benefits.

The principal function of the U.S. Mint is to produce coins and medals; it also has custody over Treasury gold and silver bullion.

The Bureau of the Public Debt's responsibilities include managing the public debt and issuing U.S. securities.

The Office of Thrift Supervision oversees federal and state-chartered thrift institutions. It was created in 1989 as part of the sweeping overhaul of laws governing the savings and loan industry that followed the failure of numerous institutions.

> **More on this topic:**
>
> *Bureaucracy, p. 44*
>
> *Cabinet, p. 60*
>
> *Hamilton, Alexander, p. 243*
>
> *Secret Service, p. 457*

Treaty Power

The authors of the Constitution devoted only one clause to explaining how treaties were to be made. Article II, Section 2, Clause 2 declares that the president "shall have Power, by and with the Advice and Consent of the Senate, to make Treaties, provided two-thirds of the Senators present concur." This concise statement sets up a classic division of power between the legislative and executive branches. The primary responsibility for conducting treaty negotiations is a presidential duty. The president, however, cannot conclude a treaty without first getting the consent of the Senate and probably will be deterred from negotiating a treaty that the Senate is unlikely to approve.

Nevertheless, the executive branch has established itself as the dominant branch in treaty making. As the sole organ of communication with foreign countries, commander in chief of the armed forces, and head of the foreign policy bureaucracy, the president has the means to control the treaty-making process. The president decides what treaties to negotiate, chooses the negotiators, develops the negotiating strategy, and submits completed draft treaties to the Senate for approval. Thus the president has the power of initiative over a treaty throughout the treaty-making process.

Treaty-Making Power

In the eighteenth century, treaties were considered to be the primary tool of foreign policy, and the framers of the Constitution deliberated extensively on how treaties should be made. Under the Articles of Confederation the treaty power was completely entrusted to Congress. But the framers of the Constitution recognized that the president could conduct treaty negotiations with more speed and secrecy than a large body like Congress.

The ambiguity of the language in the Constitution describing the treaty-making power raised questions about how treaties would be made. It was clear that both the president and the Senate had a role in treaty making, but the form of the Senate's advice on treaty matters and its influence over negotiations were matters that had to be worked out in practice.

President George Washington's initial interpretation of the treaty-making clause was that "advice" meant he was to seek Senate opinions in person before his representatives began talks with foreign governments. On August 21, 1789, Washington questioned the Senate in its chambers about a treaty to be negotiated with the Creek Indians. After some debate the Senate decided to postpone its response to Washington's questions until the following week. Washington, who had expected an immediate reply, returned on Monday, August 24, and received answers to his questions, but he was apparently angered by the Senate's indecisiveness. He never again went to the Senate for advice before treaty negotiations.

Had Washington established a presidential precedent of consulting with the Senate, that body's role in treaty making would likely have been greater. Subsequent presidents agreed with Washington that the advice and consent of the Senate were best obtained from a distance. Several twentieth-century presidents, including Woodrow Wilson and Harry S. Truman, went to the Senate to propose or lobby for a treaty, but no president has ever returned to the Senate chamber to seek direct advice on treaty matters. Moreover, up to the end of James Madison's administration in 1817 the names of treaty negotiators were referred to the Senate for confirmation. The Senate repeatedly protested subsequent presidents' neglect of this practice.

Washington's handling of the important Jay Treaty of 1794, which avoided war with Great Britain, showed that he had abandoned his initial interpretation of the Constitution's treaty-making clause. During the early years of his presidency Washington had written to the Senate for advice on treaty matters before and during negotiations. In preparation for the Jay Treaty talks, however, Washington only submitted the appointment of his negotiator, Chief Justice John Jay, to the Senate for approval. He withheld from the Senate Jay's instructions, and the talks were held in London without Senate involvement.

Rather than challenging the president's power to negotiate a treaty on his own, the Senate responded by amending the Jay Treaty. Washington accepted the Senate's power to do this, and after initial protests, the British ratified the amended treaty. The Jay Treaty established a process of treaty making that was followed by later presidents and Senates.

Washington's actions established the power of the executive branch to make treaties on its own before submitting them for Senate approval. In its landmark decision in the 1936 case of UNITED STATES V. CURTISS-WRIGHT EXPORT CORP., the Supreme Court ruled that "the president ... alone negotiates. Into the field of negotiation the Senate cannot intrude, and Congress itself is powerless to invade it."

The Treaty-Making Process

The first step in making a treaty is negotiating with a foreign power. This stage is controlled by the president. Regardless of congressional protests or encouragement, the president and the president's representatives cannot be constrained from holding treaty talks with another country.

Once U.S. negotiators have agreed on the terms of a treaty with a foreign government, the president must decide whether to submit the draft to the Senate for consideration. If it appears that Senate opposition to a treaty will make approval unlikely, the president may decide to withdraw the treaty to avoid a political defeat. Also, international events may change the president's mind about a treaty. President Jimmy Carter came to such a conclusion after the Soviet Union invaded Afghanistan in December 1979. He withdrew the SALT II treaty from Senate consideration to protest the Soviet presence in that country, although before the invasion he had pressed the Senate to approve the treaty.

If the president submits a treaty to the Senate for consideration, the Constitution requires that a two-thirds majority of senators voting be in favor of the treaty for it to be approved. The Senate does not have to approve or reject a treaty in the form in which it has been negotiated. Senators may attach amendments to a treaty that require the president to renegotiate its terms with the other signatories before they grant their approval. In effect, then, when the Senate gives its consent on condition that its amendments are accepted by the negotiating partner of the United States, it is rejecting the treaty while outlining a revision to which it grants its consent in advance. Presidents in turn may decide not to renegotiate if they believe the amendments make the treaty undesirable.

On September 7, 1977, President Jimmy Carter (seated left) and Panamanian leader Brig. Gen. Omar Torrijos Herrera (right) signed the treaty that transferred control of the Panama Canal to Panama after the year 2000.
Source: Jimmy Carter Library

The Senate also has the power to add nonbinding reservations to a treaty before approving it. This option can be used when the Senate agrees to the basic terms of a treaty but wishes to state its interpretation of the document to prevent ambiguity and to influence the treaty's implementation.

The president—not the Senate, as commonly believed—has the final power of ratification. Once the Senate has approved a treaty, it does not become law until the president ratifies it. If the president decides to ratify a treaty the Senate has approved, an exchange of ratifications occurs between the signatories. Then the treaty is promulgated—that is, officially proclaimed to be law—by the president.

After the Senate approves a treaty and the president ratifies it, legislation may be required to fulfill its intent. Such treaties are referred to as "non-self-executing." For example, the Migratory Bird Treaty of 1916 between the United States and Canada pledged the two nations to make and implement laws to protect migratory birds. Treaties that require the appropriation of funds or the enactment of criminal laws for their implementation also would be non-self-executing, because these tasks can be accomplished only through laws made by Congress.

Approval Record

The Senate has approved without changes about 90 percent of the treaties submitted to it. This apparent Senate acquiescence to the executive branch on treaty matters is not as striking as it seems. Presidents often have withdrawn from consideration treaties that risked Senate rejection. Other

treaties were neither approved nor rejected by the Senate but instead were left without action in political limbo. For example, the 1949 Genocide Treaty, which instructed signers to prevent and punish the crime of genocide, was not approved by the Senate until 1986, thirty-seven years after Truman submitted it to that body.

The 1972 ABM Treaty was signed by the United States and the Soviet Union at a much different time, in a vastly different world. One of the signatories, the Soviet Union, no longer exists, and neither does the hostility that once led both our countries to keep thousands of nuclear weapons on hair trigger alert, pointed at each other.

—*George W. Bush, Remarks Announcing the United States' Withdrawal from the Anti-Ballistic Missile Treaty, December 13, 2001*

Many more pacts that could have taken the form of treaties were concluded as less formal EXECUTIVE AGREEMENTS between the president and a foreign government. Executive agreements do not require Senate approval. During the twentieth century, presidents made increasing use of executive agreements with other nations as a way of avoiding the formal approval process for treaties.

Although the Senate's approval record has been overwhelmingly favorable, there have been significant exceptions. The best-known rejection of a treaty was the Senate's refusal in 1920 to approve the Treaty of Versailles, which ended World War I and established the League of Nations. President Woodrow Wilson campaigned vigorously but unsuccessfully for approval of the completed treaty; his failure to include the Senate in the treaty-making process contributed to its defeat.

Termination of Treaties

Although Article VI, Clause 2 of the Constitution declares that treaties are the "supreme Law of the Land," the federal government is not legally constrained from terminating a treaty through agreement with the other party, in response to the other party's violations of the treaty, or for any other reason. It is unclear, however, which branch has the authority to terminate a treaty. The Constitution provides no guidelines as to who determines that a treaty should be revoked. Both the president and Congress at various times have claimed the power to end treaties.

In 1979 this issue was brought before the Supreme Court when the Carter administration terminated the 1954 Mutual Defense Treaty with the Republic of China (Taiwan) as part of the process of establishing formal relations with the People's Republic of China (PRC). Because the president cannot ratify a treaty without Senate consent, his authority to unilaterally revoke an existing treaty was uncertain.

Republican senator Barry Goldwater of Arizona and twenty-three other members of Congress objected to Carter's termination of the treaty and brought suit against the president to prevent it. The Supreme Court ruled 7–2 in favor of the president's authority to terminate the treaty on his own. Four justices said that the termination of the treaty was a political issue that the executive and legislative branches would have to resolve themselves.

An administration's attitude toward treaties can be a reflection of its view of foreign policy in general. For example, George W. Bush's administration pursued a more aggressive and unilateralist foreign policy than some previous administrations. Early in his presidency Bush opted out of some high-profile international pacts such as the 1972 Antiballistic Missile Treaty and the Kyoto global warming protocol.

Treaties and State Law

One weakness of the Articles of Confederation that the Constitutional Convention was determined to correct was the dependence on the states to implement treaties. Congress had the power to make treaties with other countries, but it could not force the states to recognize treaty provisions as law. As a result, several states had violated certain articles of the Peace Treaty of 1783 with

Great Britain. The convention's answer to this problem was Article VI, Clause 2 of the Constitution, which states that "all Treaties made, or which shall be made, under the Authority of the United States, shall be the supreme Law of the Land; and the Judges in every State shall be bound thereby, any Thing in the Constitution or Laws of any State to the Contrary notwithstanding."

Chief Justice John Marshall interpreted this clause in his opinion in the case of *Foster v. Neilson* in 1829. He confirmed that any treaty or portion of a treaty that did not require legislation to fulfill its provisions was binding on the states and had force equal to federal law. Therefore, although Congress may have to enact legislation to carry out acts stipulated by a treaty, any self-executing treaty or part of a treaty automatically attains the status of a law and is enforceable by the courts.

> **More on this topic:**
>
> *Constitutional Powers and Provisions, p. 119*
>
> *Diplomatic Powers, p. 149*
>
> *Executive Agreements, p. 198*
>
> United States v. Curtiss-Wright Export Corp., p. 528

Truman, Harry S.

Source: Harry S. Truman Library

Harry S. Truman (1884–1972) was born in Lamar, Missouri, on May 8, 1884. His father was a mule trader. The boy's parents wanted to give him a middle name in honor of a grandfather but could not decide between grandfathers Anderson Shippe Truman and Solomon Young. Consequently they gave him the middle initial *S,* which stood for nothing.

After living in several Missouri towns, the Trumans settled in Independence, near Kansas City. Harry graduated from high school and then held a succession of jobs, including mailroom clerk, bank teller, and bookkeeper. He wanted to go to college, but he and his family could not afford it. In 1906 Truman took over the management of his grandmother's 600-acre farm. He succeeded at farming and became active in local politics.

During World War I Truman served with distinction as commander of an artillery battery. He attained the rank of major before leaving the service in 1919. That year, on June 28, he married Elizabeth (Bess) Wallace, whom he had known since childhood.

Political Career

Upon returning to Missouri, Truman opened a haberdashery in Kansas City with a war buddy. When the store failed in 1922 he entered politics. During most of the 1920s and early 1930s Truman held local elective administrative posts. He also became an ally of Kansas City political boss Tom Pendergast. Despite Truman's ties to Pendergast and the Kansas City political machine, he gained a reputation for honesty.

In 1934 Truman was elected to the U.S. Senate. He supported President Franklin D. Roosevelt's New Deal legislation and was reelected to the Senate in 1940. During his second term Truman

In most surveys of historians used to rank the country's presidents, Harry S. Truman is usually ranked near the top as a "near great" president. This was not apparent when Truman left office in 1953. In 1952 Truman's name appeared on the New Hampshire primary ballot, but he lost to Estes Kefauver, and on March 29 he announced he would not seek an additional term. Just over a month before he left office, his job approval rating was in the low 30s, up from the mid 20s, due largely to the unpopularity of the Korean War, his dismissal of General MacArthur, and corruption among some staffers. The turnaround of Truman's legacy is due to many policies he advocated that strengthened the country as it entered the second half of the twentieth century. Among his accomplishments, some of the most notable were the Truman Doctrine, the Marshall Plan, NATO, the United Nations, the Berlin Airlift, and his efforts to break ground to promote civil rights.

backed Roosevelt's efforts to aid the Allies before the entry of the United States into World War II.

In 1944 the Democratic Party was set to nominate Roosevelt for his fourth term, but the vice-presidential nomination remained in doubt. Vice President Henry Wallace had alienated many Democratic Party leaders, who considered him too liberal. Acting on the suggestion of his advisers, Roosevelt dropped Wallace in favor of Truman. Roosevelt and Truman then defeated Republicans Thomas E. Dewey and John W. Bricker in the general election.

Presidency

Truman served just eighty-two days as vice president. On April 12, 1945, he was informed by First Lady Eleanor Roosevelt that the president had died of a cerebral hemorrhage. Later in the day Truman took the oath of office.

World events forced Truman to become an expert in foreign affairs. His first priority was winning World War II. On May 7, 1945, Germany surrendered to the Allies. In July Truman traveled to Potsdam, Germany, to discuss the composition of the postwar world with British prime minister Winston Churchill and Soviet premier Joseph Stalin. There the three leaders agreed to divide Germany and its capital, Berlin, into occupation zones.

While at Potsdam, Truman was informed that the United States had successfully tested an atomic bomb. He approved atomic bomb attacks on Japanese cities to hasten the end of the war. On August 6, 1945, the United States dropped an atomic bomb on Hiroshima that killed eighty thousand people. Three days later another atomic bomb destroyed the city of Nagasaki. On September 2 Japan officially surrendered. Truman's decision to use atomic weapons has been debated by many scholars, some of whom believe Japan might have been willing to surrender even if the bombs had not been used.

After the war, differences between the United States and Soviet Union quickly developed into a "cold war." The United States objected in particular to the Soviet Union's creation of communist governments in the East European states it had occupied while pushing Nazi forces back into Germany. Truman resolved to contain Soviet expansion. In March 1947 he proclaimed the Truman Doctrine and asked Congress for $400 million in economic and military aid to prevent Greece and Turkey from falling to communist insurgents. The Truman Doctrine declared that the United States would aid governments threatened by communist subversion. Later that year Truman and Secretary of State George Marshall asked Congress to dramatically expand foreign aid by approving the Marshall Plan, a multibillion-dollar program to rebuild the economies of Western Europe. Congress gave its approval in 1948, and the Marshall Plan became one of the foremost successes of Truman's presidency.

Later in 1948 the Soviet Union closed passage between western Germany and Berlin, which was located within the Soviet occupation zone. Truman used a massive airlift to supply the parts of the city that were administered by Britain, France, and the United States. The Soviet Union had hoped to force the United States and its western allies to give up control of their part of Berlin, but Truman's airlift broke the blockade and the Soviets backed down.

In domestic policy Truman developed a plan to extend Franklin Roosevelt's New Deal, which the new president called the FAIR DEAL. Republicans and conservative Democrats in Congress, however, blocked many of his proposals. He also unsuccessfully backed progressive civil rights legislation. In 1947 Congress overrode Truman's veto of the Taft-Hartley Act, which he claimed unfairly weakened the bargaining power of unions. Five years later he seized and operated steel mills shut

down by a strike during the Korean War, a move that the Supreme Court declared unconstitutional. Truman battled postwar inflation with the modest tools at his disposal, but Congress rejected his proposals for more sweeping price-control legislation, and inflation continued to be the most troublesome domestic problem during Truman's presidency.

In 1948 Truman ran for reelection against Thomas E. Dewey. Public opinion polls indicated that Dewey would win easily. Truman, however, used a cross-country, whistle-stop campaign to take his message to the people. In the election he scored a surprise victory, defeating Dewey 303–189 in the Electoral College.

Truman's second term was dominated by the Korean War. On June 24, 1950, troops from communist North Korea invaded South Korea. Truman sent U.S. troops to Korea under the auspices of the United Nations (UN). UN forces pushed the North Koreans out of South Korea and drove into North Korea. Communist China entered the war on the side of the North Koreans in late 1950 and pushed UN forces back into South Korea. Eventually, the war became deadlocked near the boundary that had divided the two Koreas before the war. Truman was unable to attain a negotiated peace during his presidency. In 1951 Truman fired Gen. Douglas MacArthur, commander of UN forces in Korea, for insubordination. MacArthur enjoyed a large following among the American public, and Truman's popularity sank in response.

During Truman's years in office the country became consumed with paranoia over the issue of communist subversion. Sen. Joseph R. McCarthy, a Republican from Wisconsin, led a group of legislators who claimed that communists had infiltrated the U.S. government, especially the State Department. Truman denounced McCarthy but was unable to rally support against the senator, despite the lack of evidence to back up McCarthy's claims. After Truman retired, McCarthy became chairman of a Senate investigative subcommittee and accused many citizens of procommunist activities until he was censured by the Senate in 1954.

On March 29, 1952, Truman announced that he would not run for reelection. After leaving office he returned to his home in Independence, Missouri. He remained active during his retirement, commenting on political developments and overseeing construction of the Truman Library near his home. He died on December 26, 1972, in Kansas City.

> *I believe that it must be the policy of the United States to support free peoples who are resisting attempted subjugation by armed minorities or by outside pressures.*
>
> *I believe that we must assist free peoples to work out their own destinies in their own way.*
>
> *I believe that our help should be primarily through economic and financial aid which is essential to economic stability and orderly political processes.*
>
> **—Harry S. Truman,** *Special Message to the Congress on Greece and Turkey: The Truman Doctrine,* March 12, 1947

More on this topic:

Doctrines, Presidential, p. 155

Elections Chronology, p. 174

Fair Deal, p. 209

Korean War, p. 323

World War II, p. 588

Tyler, John

John Tyler (1790–1862) became the first vice president to succeed to the presidency when William Henry Harrison died after just one month in office. The Constitution did not specify whether a vice president was to become president upon the death of an incumbent or merely to assume the duties of the office. Tyler set an important precedent by assuming the presidency's title and all of its power.

Tyler was born on March 29, 1790, in Charles City County, Virginia. His father was a prominent planter who had served as governor of the state. John attended the College of William and Mary in Williamsburg, Virginia, graduating in 1807 when he was just seventeen. He then studied law under his father and was admitted to the bar two years later.

John Tyler

Source: Library of Congress

In 1811 Tyler was elected to the Virginia House of Delegates as a Jeffersonian Democratic-Republican. He was reelected five times and remained in office through 1816. During the War of 1812 he served briefly as captain of a Virginia militia company but saw no action. He married Letitia Christian in 1813 on his twenty-third birthday. In November 1816 he was elected to the U.S. House of Representatives, but he retired from Congress in 1821, citing poor health. During his early political career Tyler was noted for his support of slavery and states' rights.

In 1823 Tyler was again elected to the Virginia House of Delegates, where he served until he was elected governor in 1825. After he resigned the governorship in 1827 he won a seat in the U.S. Senate, which he held until 1836.

As a senator, Tyler promoted the compromise tariffs that eased the nullification crisis in South Carolina in 1832. Although he doubted that the states could legally nullify federal laws, he vigorously opposed President Andrew Jackson's threats to use force against South Carolina. In 1836 Tyler resigned his Senate seat after a disagreement with the Virginia legislature.

Tyler's unhappiness with Jackson and the Democratic Party on several issues led him to join the Whig Party, despite the antislavery and nationalistic positions of many of its leaders. As one of several regional Whig vice-presidential candidates in 1836, Tyler received forty-seven electoral votes. Democrats Martin Van Buren and Richard Johnson won the presidency and vice presidency, respectively.

The Whigs nominated Tyler as the vice-presidential running mate of William Henry Harrison (nicknamed "Old Tippecanoe") in 1840. The Whigs shunned policy issues and promoted their candidates through parties, parades, songs, and catchy slogans such as "Tippecanoe and Tyler too." The Whig ticket easily defeated President Martin Van Buren, whose popularity had been damaged by an economic depression.

Tyler appeared destined to have a small role in the Harrison administration. Daniel Webster, Henry Clay, and other Whig leaders planned to have considerable influence over the aging Harrison, so there would be little place for Tyler, whose views in any case were outside the Whig mainstream. However, Tyler was thrust into the presidency when Harrison died on April 4, 1841, after only one month in office.

For the first time in our history the person elected to the Vice-Presidency of the United States, by the happening of a contingency provided for in the Constitution, has had devolved upon him the Presidential office.

—*John Tyler*, Address Upon Assuming the Office of President of the United States, April 9, 1841

As president, Tyler pursued an independent policy course. He opposed the major goals of the Whig leadership, including the national bank, high tariffs, and federally funded internal improvements. As a result, he was disowned by the Whig Party while still president.

Letitia Tyler died in the White House in 1842 after an extended illness. Several months after her death Tyler became infatuated with Julia Gardiner, a young socialite from New York. After a year of courtship they were married in New York on June 26, 1844. Tyler had fifteen children—eight by his first wife and seven by his second wife—the most of any president.

Tyler made U.S. acquisition of Texas, which had declared its independence from Mexico in 1836, a primary goal of his presidency. He oversaw the negotiation of a treaty of annexation with

Texas in early 1844. On April 22 of that year he submitted the treaty to the Senate for approval. The Senate, however, rejected the treaty on June 8.

Tyler wished to run for reelection in 1844, but neither of the major political parties wanted to nominate him. He therefore organized a new party dedicated to states' rights and the annexation of Texas. He gave up his candidacy when the Democrats nominated James K. Polk, who also advocated annexation of Texas.

On December 4 Tyler, now a lame-duck president, sent his last State of the Union message to Congress. In it he proposed that the Texas annexation treaty be approved by a simple majority of both houses instead of a two-thirds vote by the Senate, which he would not have been able to obtain. The proposal was controversial because annexation of Texas would have implications for the slavery issue and also because such a method of granting congressional consent would ignore the constitutional provision requiring a two-thirds vote by the Senate for approval of treaties. The House passed the joint resolution by a vote of 120–98 on January 25, 1845, and the Senate followed suit by a vote of 27–25 on February 27, 1845. Tyler's strategy had worked, and an important legislative precedent had been set. Tyler signed the bill into law on March 1, three days before leaving office.

When his term expired, Tyler retired to his Virginia estate where he remained an outspoken advocate of southern interests. In early 1861 he presided over the Washington Peace Conference, an eleventh-hour attempt to resolve sectional differences and avoid civil war. When Virginia seceded, he pledged his loyalty to the South. In November 1861 Tyler was elected to the new Confederate Congress in Richmond, Virginia. He died in a Richmond hotel room on January 18, 1862, before he could take his seat.

More on this topic:

Death of the President,
p. 142

Harrison, William Henry,
p. 248

Oath of Office, p. 393

Succession, p. 483

Veto Power, p. 533

Vice President, p. 539

Unitary Executive Theory

The theory of the unitary executive in American politics is a controversial conception of presidential power. It implies that all executive authority in the United States rests with the president and is beyond the reach of the other branches, in particular Congress. The theory is rooted in a reaction to congressional attempts to oversee elements of the executive branch, for example, by mandating actions to be taken by executive branch officials or by creating independent agencies or counsels outside of the president's direct control. Many such attempts at congressional oversight arose in response to the Watergate affair and the perception that the Nixon administration was attempting to build what historian Arthur Schlesinger called an "imperial presidency," where the president would dominate the other branches while surrounded by a dedicated and loyal staff.

Proponents of the unitary executive believe that independent counsels are inherently unconstitutional because they exert executive-style authority but are not subordinate to the president. In addition, independent regulatory agencies, it is argued, are limited in their ability to sue or mandate actions among other executive branch departments or agencies because doing so would in essence pit the president against himself. For example, under George W. Bush, the Justice Department decided that the Environmental Protection Agency (EPA) could not sue components of the Defense Department for breaking EPA guidelines, because doing so would in essence involve only the president as both the plaintiff and defendant in the suit.

The constitutional basis of the theory of the unitary executive is rooted in two clauses in Article II: the "vesting clause" and the "take care clause." The vesting clause states, "The executive Power shall be vested in a President of the United States of America," meaning that the institution is aggregated in the hands of one unitary actor. The take care clause reads, "he shall take Care that the Laws be faithfully executed," interpreted by proponents of the unitary executive to mean that only the president has the power to enforce law and administer the executive branch.

The notion of the unitary executive has become the subject of debate in recent years, especially during George W. Bush's administration. Bush has sought to expand his interpretation of presidential powers by citing the theory, particularly in his use of SIGNING STATEMENTS. The use of these statements, issued to accompany legislation signed into law, is not unique to the Bush administration. However, Bush has used these statements with noted frequency as a way to declare that he will interpret the law, "in a manner consistent with the President's constitutional authority to supervise the unitary executive branch." The idea that the president can unilaterally interpret the law based on his conception of the constitutionality of enacted statute has been debated. Proponents of the legislative branch's right to influence the execution of laws is rooted in Article I, Section 8's elastic clause. In it, Congress is granted the authority to, "make all Laws which shall be necessary and proper for carrying into Execution [its various enumerated powers]."

The Supreme Court has not heard a case that specifically challenges the notion of the unitary executive, although a number of cases have addressed individual tenants of the theory. According to the Court's 1926 ruling in *Myers v. United States,* Article II of the Constitution implies the president does have the power to remove executive branch officials as a necessary component of his ability to effectively manage the executive branch, a core idea of the "unitary executive" theory. However, in 1988 the Supreme Court ruled 7–1 in *Morrison v. Olson* that the Independent Counsel Act was constitutional, even though proponents of the unitary executive insist that prosecutors must be subordinate to the president.

More on this topic:
Article II, p. 16
Bureaucracy, p. 44
Constitutional Powers and Provisions, p. 119
Separation of Powers, p. 460
Signing Statements, p. 463

The United Nations

The United Nations (UN) was established in 1945 as a world body that would promote international peace and security and the welfare of the world's peoples. All of its member nations send delegations to UN headquarters in New York City. Each nation has one vote in the General Assembly. Presidents appoint the U.S. ambassador to the UN with the advice and consent of the Senate.

The primary responsibility for the peace and security function of the United Nations resides with the Security Council, a committee of fifteen nations. The council attempts to use peaceful measures to prevent aggression. If nonmilitary actions fail or are inappropriate, the Security Council may vote to use military force.

CLOSER LOOK

President George W. Bush signs a bill into law from the Bush ranch in Crawford, Texas.
Source: AP

President George W. Bush's use of signing statements has generated significant debate over the notion of the unitary executive. In these statements, the president makes the claim that he will "construe" various provisions of the legislation he is signing into law in a "manner consistent" with various constitutional prerogatives he interprets to be found in Article II. One of the most controversial signing statements was issued on December 30, 2005, when President Bush signed into law H.R. 2863. This legislation, sponsored by Republican senator John McCain of Arizona, sought to ban inhuman or degrading treatment of prisoners by U.S. armed forces. Feeling that elements of the law intruded on his power as commander in chief, President Bush included in his signing statement the proviso that he would construe a section of the law "consistent with the President's constitutional authority as Commander in Chief."

UN General Assembly
Source: AP

A Security Council decision to use military force or to create a detachment of military observers requires unanimous approval of its members. The United States, Russia, Great Britain, France, and the People's Republic of China are permanent members of the Security Council. These nations hold a veto over Security Council resolutions. The other ten slots on the committee are filled on a rotating basis by the other members of the UN.

The relevance of the UN peacekeeping role during the cold war was limited. A mission supported by the United States would almost always be opposed by the Soviet Union, and vice versa. Nevertheless, the Security Council sanctioned limited peacekeeping missions in places such as the Congo, Cyprus, Indonesia, West New Guinea, and the border between India and Pakistan, when the interests of the United States and the Soviet Union converged.

Presidents have often promoted UN peacekeeping missions, and, when appropriate, they have offered the services of the U.S. military to those missions. The advantages that UN peacekeeping missions have over unilateral U.S. action in many regions are that UN peacekeeping forces are less threatening to local nations, the economic costs to the United States are decreased, and a UN peacekeeping force can promote a spirit of international accountability and cooperation in solving a particular regional problem.

During the late 1980s and early 1990s the status of UN-sponsored peacekeeping forces was enhanced when UN peacekeepers were awarded the 1988 Nobel Peace Prize. The Soviet Union and the United States advocated the use of UN peacekeeping troops to monitor negotiated settlements of several regional conflicts. The UN created new peacekeeping forces to oversee peace accords in Afghanistan, Angola, Cambodia, and Yugoslavia, and sent other armed missions to Somalia and Haiti.

The American people look upon the United Nations not as a temporary expedient but as a permanent partnership—a partnership among the peoples of the world for their common peace and common well-being.

—*Harry S. Truman,* Address in New York City at the Opening Session of the UN General Assembly, October 23, 1946

The most contentious issue in the Senate debate in 1945 on U.S. membership in the UN was who had the power to commit U.S. forces to Security Council military operations. The Senate did not want to hand the president exclusive authority to furnish troops to the UN. Such a power would have allowed the president to commit the United States to UN military operations without the congressional consent required by a declaration of war.

The United Nations Participation Act of 1945 outlined the rules under which U.S. forces could be placed at the disposal of the United Nations: "The President is authorized to negotiate a special agreement or agreements with the Security Council which shall be subject to the approval of the Congress by appropriate Act or joint resolution, providing for the numbers and types of armed forces, their degree of readiness and general location, and the nature of

facilities and assistance, including rights of passage, to be made available to the Security Council on its call for the purpose of maintaining international peace and security."

Presidents therefore are expressly prohibited by the Participation Act from unilaterally concluding an agreement with the Security Council under their powers to negotiate treaties, execute the laws, or defend the United States. In other words, presidents cannot legally aid or commit U.S. forces to UN peacekeeping missions without an approving congressional resolution.

On several occasions the UN has sanctioned the use of military force far beyond keeping the peace. In response to the North Korean invasion of South Korea in 1950, the Security Council authorized member nations to come to the aid of South Korea. Because the Soviet Union was boycotting the Security Council to protest the exclusion of communist China from the council, it was not present to exercise its veto when the council voted.

Section 6 of the United Nations Participation Act required President Harry S. Truman to secure congressional approval of the agreement between the United States and the Security Council that provided for the use of U.S. forces. But no such agreement was ever negotiated. Truman based the U.S. intervention in Korea on his powers as commander in chief and the Security Council's call to UN member nations to render assistance to South Korea.

All the world now faces a test and the United Nations a difficult and defining moment. Are Security Council resolutions to be honored and enforced or cast aside without consequence? Will the United Nations serve the purpose of its founding, or will it be irrelevant?

—George W. Bush, Address to the UN General Assembly in New York City, September 12, 2002

In 1990 and 1991 the UN Security Council became a focal point of efforts to resist Iraq's invasion of Kuwait. President George H. W. Bush gained the support of the members of the council (including the Soviet Union) for a strategy of ejecting Iraqi occupation troops from Kuwait if they were not withdrawn. The UN Security Council resolution authorizing force against Iraq strengthened the president's position both in the international community and with Congress, which subsequently voted to approve the use of military force. In early 1991 a U.S.-led coalition defeated Iraqi forces and liberated Kuwait. But the expanded use of UN peacekeepers and the potential for more aggressive use of these forces, including U.S. troops, caused renewed congressional criticism and calls for restriction of U.S. participation in peacekeeping operations. Conservative Republicans, led by North Carolina senator Jesse Helms, chairman of the Senate Foreign Relations Committee, also threatened to cut off funding to the international body, demanding internal reforms of its bureaucracy. Late in the Clinton presidency, Congress, the president, and the United Nations reached an agreement that addressed some of the critics' concerns and committed the United States to paying most of its debt to the UN.

The United Nations was in the spotlight again in 2002 and 2003, as the George W. Bush administration sought UN approval for military action against Iraq. In the fall of 2002 the administration, after a concerted lobbying effort, succeeded in winning unanimous Security Council passage of a resolution calling for tough UN weapons inspections in Iraq and basically giving Iraq a last chance to disarm. By early 2003, as the Bush administration pushed for military action against Iraq, some nations agreed with Bush that the Iraqis were not disarming and that imminent military action was necessary. Other nations, though, including France, disagreed with the U.S. approach, preferring instead to give weapons inspectors more time.

More on this topic:
Iraq War, p. 296
Korean War, p. 323
Persian Gulf War, p. 401
War Powers Act of 1973, p. 560

But it became increasingly clear that the Bush administration would attack Iraq, with or without UN backing. In March 2003 the administration opted against seeking another Security Council vote after it became clear that a second resolution, to authorize war, would not pass. The attack on Iraq began on March 19, and within three weeks the regime of Iraqi dictator Saddam Hussein fell, although in 2007 the United States continues to occupy Iraq in an attempt to establish order among factions and insurgents opposed to America's presence. (See also IRAQ WAR.)

United States v. Curtiss-Wright Export Corp.

The Supreme Court usually has avoided ruling on disputes between the president and Congress that involve foreign affairs. But when the Court has acted, it has tended to support the president's claims to power. The most important and often cited Supreme Court decision dealing with the president's foreign affairs powers is *United States v. Curtiss-Wright Export Corp.*, delivered in 1936.

In 1934 Congress passed a law empowering the president to stop U.S. shipments of arms to warring nations. When President Franklin D. Roosevelt imposed an embargo on Bolivia under this law, the Curtiss-Wright Export Corporation was prohibited from shipping aircraft armaments to that country. The corporation conspired to send arms to Bolivia in spite of the embargo, but its activities were discovered. In court Curtiss-Wright's lawyers argued that Congress's delegation of power to the president was unconstitutional.

By a 7–1 vote the Supreme Court held that while Congress could not delegate its law-making authority over internal affairs, it could do so with respect to foreign affairs. Justice George Sutherland, delivering the opinion of the Court, explained:

> We are here dealing not alone with an authority vested in the President by an exertion of legislative power, but with such an authority plus the very delicate, plenary, and exclusive power of the president as the sole organ of the federal government in the field of international relations—a power which does not require as a basis for its exercise an act of Congress.... It is quite apparent that if, in the maintenance of our international relations, embarrassment—perhaps serious embarrassment—is to be avoided and success for our aims achieved, congressional legislation which is to be made effective through negotiation and inquiry in the international field must often accord to the President a degree of discretion and freedom from statutory restriction which would not be admissible were domestic affairs alone involved.

United States v. Curtiss-Wright was a landmark decision because, as historian Arthur M. Schlesinger Jr. observed, "The Court thus did in foreign policy what it had been reluctant to do in domestic policy: it affirmed the existence of an inherent, independent and superior presidential power, not derived from the Constitution and not requiring legislation as the basis for its exercise." Sutherland's statements supporting vast presidential foreign affairs powers were contained in the decision's *dicta* (legal observations not essential to the main issues of the case). Nevertheless, they continue to have great influence over conceptions of the president's constitutional power in foreign relations.

Now, Therefore, I, Franklin D. Roosevelt, President of the United States of America, acting under and by virtue of the authority conferred in me by the said joint resolution of Congress, do hereby declare and proclaim that I have found that the prohibition of the sale of arms and munitions of war in the United States to those countries now engaged in armed conflict in the Chaco may contribute to the reestablishment of peace between those countries.

—*Franklin D. Roosevelt*, Proclamation 2087—Forbidding the Shipment of Arms to the Combatants in the Chaco, May 28, 1934

More on this topic:

Courts and the President, p. 128

Treaty Power, p. 515

United States v. Nixon

The landmark Supreme Court decision *United States v. Nixon* strengthened the powers of the presidency at the same time that it contributed to the resignation of a president. The ruling, issued on July 24, 1974, affirmed for the first time the constitutional right of presidents to keep secret certain communications they have with advisers, a right known as EXECUTIVE PRIVILEGE. But the Court said that the privilege was not absolute and that President Richard Nixon would have to release some tape recordings of conversations, which Nixon argued were covered by executive privilege. The tapes demonstrated that Nixon had played an active part in the WATERGATE AFFAIR. On August 9, 1974, he became the first president to resign from office.

The scandals that brought Nixon down began when employees of Nixon's reelection campaign committee were arrested in 1972 for breaking into the Democratic Party campaign headquarters at the Watergate complex in Washington, D.C. During congressional hearings on the scandals in 1973, an administration official revealed that Nixon had recorded his conversations with aides in the Oval Office. The Supreme Court ruling resulted from the efforts of the special prosecutor appointed to investigate the Watergate scandal to obtain some of the tapes.

In March 1974 a grand jury acting on evidence presented by the special prosecutor indicted seven administration officials for conspiracy to cover up the Watergate burglary. The grand jury named Nixon as an "unindicted coconspirator." The district judge who was to try the seven Nixon officials ordered Nixon to turn

Source: Courtesy of the Swann Collection of Caricature and Cartoon, Library of Congress

over the tapes, arguing that they were relevant to the upcoming trial. When Nixon refused to produce the tapes, the issue moved with unusual speed to the Supreme Court.

The Court's decision was unanimous. It rejected Nixon's arguments that procedural rules had been violated, that executive privilege was absolute, and that, even if it was not, the president alone should decide when to apply it. Chief Justice Warren E. Burger, Nixon's first appointee to the

Court, wrote that executive privilege is conditional, not absolute, and that in disputed cases the right of a president to confidentiality must be weighed against the public's right to know. When there is a dispute, the Court said, the judicial branch of government shall decide.

Having established that disputes over executive privilege must be decided case by case in the courts, the Supreme Court ruled that the tapes should be released. Although the president's need for confidentiality was important, the Court said, in this case it was outweighed by the need of the courts to obtain evidence relevant to a criminal prosecution. "The very integrity of the judicial system and public confidence in the system depend on full disclosure of all the facts," Burger wrote.

Nixon surrendered the tapes, and they revealed that he had acted to obstruct the criminal investigation of the Watergate burglary within days of its occurrence. This revelation cost Nixon his few remaining defenders in Congress. It became clear that the president would be impeached by the House and convicted by the Senate if he did not resign.

> *This principle of confidentiality of Presidential conversations is at stake in the question of these tapes. I must and I shall oppose any efforts to destroy this principle, which is so vital to the conduct of this great office.*
>
> —*Richard Nixon,* Address to the Nation about the Watergate Investigations, August 15, 1973

More on this topic:

Executive Privilege, p. 206

Separation of Powers, p. 460

Watergate Affair, p. 567

V

Van Buren, Martin

Martin Van Buren (1782–1862) was a skillful Democratic politician who was elected president after serving as secretary of state and vice president under Andrew Jackson. Van Buren failed to win reelection when the country became mired in a depression during his term.

Van Buren was born on December 5, 1782, in Kinderhook, New York. His father was a farmer and tavern keeper who had fought in the American Revolution. Despite having received only a rudimentary education as a child, Martin began studying law under a local lawyer when he was only fourteen. He moved to New York City in 1801 and continued his law studies. Admitted to the bar in 1803, he returned to Kinderhook and opened a law practice. Van Buren married his distant cousin Hannah Hoes on February 21, 1807. She died in 1819 before her husband attained national prominence, and he never remarried.

In 1808 Van Buren moved to Hudson, New York. He began his rapid rise to power in New York politics in 1812 when he was elected to the state senate. He was appointed state attorney general in 1815 and retained his Senate seat while serving in that post. By 1820 Van Buren had become a leader of the New York political machine.

In 1821 the New York legislature elected Van Buren to the U.S. Senate as a member of the Democratic-Republican Party. He was reelected in 1827. While serving in the Senate, Van Buren was one of the most vocal critics of President John Quincy Adams.

Van Buren's rise to the presidency was aided by his association with Andrew Jackson. By 1827 Van Buren had become Jackson's most powerful supporter from the Northeast. In 1828 Van Buren resigned from the Senate to help Jackson's presidential campaign in New York by running for governor. Jackson was elected president, and Van Buren won the governorship, but Van Buren resigned after only three months to become Jackson's secretary of state.

As secretary of state, Van Buren was the most influential member of Jackson's cabinet. He became a successful diplomat respected by foreign governments and continued to be Jackson's principal political adviser. In 1831 Van Buren further endeared himself to Jackson when he concurred with Jackson's defense of Peggy Eaton, the wife of Secretary of War John Eaton; she had been rejected by Washington society for her alleged past promiscuity. Soon after the Eaton affair Van Buren resigned from his office to allow Jackson to reconstruct his entire cabinet free of supporters of Van Buren's political rival, Vice President John C. Calhoun. In 1832 Van Buren replaced Calhoun as Jackson's vice-presidential running mate. The Jackson-Van Buren team was elected easily.

In 1836, with President Jackson's backing, Van Buren received the Democratic presidential nomination. The Whig Party, believing that no single candidate had a good chance to beat Van Buren, nominated several regional candidates, hoping to divide the electoral vote and force the election into the House of Representatives. Van Buren won a majority of the popular and the electoral vote.

Van Buren pledged at his inauguration to continue the policies of Jackson, and he reappointed Jackson's cabinet. The former president's economic policies, however, contributed to the depression that dominated Van Buren's presidency. In 1832 Jackson had vetoed the bill to recharter the national bank. Without the central control provided by that bank, many state and local banks engaged in wild speculation that led to financial disaster.

In 1837 overspeculation and a natural downturn in the business cycle caused many banks and businesses to fail. While unemployment soared, Van Buren followed the conventional economic wisdom of the period by cutting government expenditures. But these restrictive fiscal policies only deepened the depression.

On the issue of slavery Van Buren promoted the moderate course of allowing slavery to continue where it existed but blocking its extension. His opposition to U.S. annexation of Texas, which would have added another slave state to the Union, avoided conflict with Mexico but cost him support in the South and West and damaged his relationship with Andrew Jackson.

Van Buren also had to deal with conflict on the U.S. border with Canada. He refused to support a movement by some U.S. citizens to aid a Canadian attempt to overthrow British rule in Canada. He defused the crisis by issuing a neutrality proclamation and sending Gen. Winfield Scott to Buffalo to enforce the peace. In 1839 a dispute developed over the uncertain legal boundary between Maine and Canada. Maine's governor, John Fairfield, called up a force of Maine militia and was preparing to fight the Canadians over the issue when Van Buren intervened by negotiating an agreement with the British ambassador to the United States.

In 1840 Van Buren was renominated unanimously by the Democratic Party, but Whig William Henry Harrison was a formidable opponent. Harrison was a national hero for his Indian-fighting exploits before and during the War of 1812, and he was portrayed as the candidate of the common people who was truer to Jacksonian principles than Van Buren was. Although Van Buren won 47 percent of the popular vote, Harrison trounced him in the Electoral College 234–60. Van Buren even failed to win his home state of New York.

Despite his defeat in 1840 Van Buren did not retire from presidential politics. He attempted to run for his party's nomination again in 1844, but he was defeated by dark-horse candidate James K. Polk, who outflanked Van Buren by openly advocating the U.S. annexation of Texas. In 1848 Van Buren ran for president as the candidate of the new antislavery Free Soil Party. His long-shot candidacy split the Democratic vote in New York, helping Whig Zachary Taylor win the state and defeat Democrat Lewis Cass by a vote of 163–127 in the Electoral College. Van Buren died on July 24, 1862, at his home in Kinderhook.

> **More on this topic:**
>
> *Jackson, Andrew, p. 300*
>
> *Vice President, p. 539*

Veterans Affairs Department

The Department of Veterans Affairs administers programs to benefit veterans and their families, including disability compensation, pensions, education and rehabilitation, medical care, home loan assistance, and national cemeteries. As of early 2007 the department reported that its vast health care system included 154 hospitals, over 875 ambulatory care and community-based outpatient clinics, 136 nursing homes, 43 domiciliaries (facilities that provide temporary nursing supervision), and 88 comprehensive home care programs. Its education programs have interacted with nearly every institution of higher education in the nation. And it operates 123 national cemeteries. The department also has significant ties to the U.S. housing and banking industries through its program to guarantee home loans for veterans.

Laws to benefit military veterans date back to colonial times. Early legislation emphasized pensions, with direct medical and hospital care provided by states and localities. In 1811 Congress authorized the first medical facility for veterans.

Congress greatly expanded veterans' benefits after the United States entered WORLD WAR I in 1917, establishing disability compensation, insurance for servicemen and veterans, a family allotment program for servicemen, and vocational rehabilitation for the disabled.

I've said before that America's debt to those who would fight for her defense doesn't end the day the uniform comes off.

—**Ronald Reagan,** Remarks at the National Defense University on Signing the Department of Veterans Affairs Act, October 25, 1988

Responsibilities for veterans were divided among various departments and agencies, which eventually proved unwieldy. In 1921 Congress consolidated some of the programs in a new U.S. Veterans' Bureau, but other agencies were still administering veterans' programs. In 1930 Congress authorized the integration of these programs into a single Veterans Administration (VA).

VA facilities and programs were significantly enlarged after WORLD WAR II and continued to grow after the KOREAN WAR and VIETNAM WAR. Sentiment grew for a separate cabinet-level department; proponents argued that VA programs for veterans and their families and survivors touched the lives of about one-third of the nation's population. Giving the agency a seat in the cabinet would enhance its access to the president and improve its ability to defend itself during budget decisions, supporters maintained. They argued that giving the VA cabinet status also would allow better coordination of policy with other departments.

Bills to elevate the VA to cabinet status were introduced in at least seventeen successive Congresses. Finally, fifty-eight years after the VA was created, legislation establishing the VA as the Department of Veterans Affairs was signed into law in 1988. The action was taken despite a nonpartisan, congressionally mandated report that found little evidence that such a move would improve government services for veterans.

The department came into being in March 1989, making it the fourteenth executive department and the fifth to be created since 1953.

Like in its forerunner, the Veterans Administration, Veterans Department programs are administered by three organizations within the department: the Veterans Health Administration, the Veterans Benefits Administration, and the National Cemetery System. Also in the department is a Board of Veterans' Appeals. The board's decisions on veterans' appeals on such issues as disability benefits, educational benefits, and loan eligibility are final, but they can be appealed to the U.S. Court of Appeals for Veterans' Claims.

More on this topic:

Korean War, p. 323

Vietnam War, p. 546

World War I, p. 586

World War II, p. 588

Veto Power

The power to reject, or veto, legislation passed by both houses of Congress is the presidency's most potent defensive weapon in its relations with the legislative branch. Just the threat of a veto can be a powerful tool in persuading Congress to drop or revise legislation or to negotiate with the administration.

Although Congress can override the president's action, it rarely happens. A two-thirds vote of each house is required to override a veto, and the president usually can round up the support of at least one-third plus one member of a House or Senate quorum to block an override.

From 1789 through 2002, presidents vetoed 2,551 bills, and Congress overrode only 106. President Woodrow Wilson once said that the veto made the president "a third branch of the legislature."

Constitutional Debate

The framers of the Constitution wanted to make sure that the new national executive would have some way to check legislative power. Many criticized the Articles of Confederation for their failure to provide for an executive strong enough to administer the laws and resist legislative tyranny.

The concept of a veto (Latin for "I forbid") was not new. It had been used in ancient Rome by the plebeians to protect the common people against the excesses of the aristocrats who dominated the senate. It later emerged in medieval Europe as a royal check on newly developing legislatures. It also had been used closer to home. A few state constitutions, such as that of Massachusetts, contained some form of executive veto, but it was not a widespread practice.

BORN TO COMMAND.

OF VETO MEMORY.

HAD I BEEN CONSULTED.

KING ANDREW THE FIRST.

For President Andrew Jackson, the veto became an instrument of political and constitutional power. In this 1833 cartoon, "King Andrew the First" is depicted as a tyrant trampling the Constitution, a book, "Judiciary of the U[nited] States," and the watchwords Virtue, Liberty, *and* Independence.
Source: Library of Congress

Virtually every plan for the new constitution contained some form of executive check on laws passed by Congress. In the debate over the procedure, opponents, such as Thomas Jefferson,

PRESIDENTIAL VETOES, GEORGE WASHINGTON TO GEORGE W. BUSH

Years	President	Total vetoes	Regular vetoes	Pocket vetoes	Vetoes overridden	Veto success rate
1789–1797	George Washington	2	2	0	0	100.0%
1797–1801	John Adams	0	0	0	0	—
1801–1809	Thomas Jefferson	0	0	0	0	—
1809–1817	James Madison	7	5	2	0	100.0
1817–1825	James Monroe	1	1	0	0	100.0
1825–1829	John Quincy Adams	0	0	0	0	—
1829–1837	Andrew Jackson	12	5	7	0	100.0
1837–1841	Martin Van Buren	1	0	1	0	—
1841–1841	William H. Harrison	0	0	0	0	—
1841–1845	John Tyler	10	6	4	1	83.3
1845–1849	James K. Polk	3	2	1	0	100.0
1849–1850	Zachary Taylor	0	0	0	0	—
1850–1853	Millard Fillmore	0	0	0	0	—
1853–1857	Franklin Pierce	9	9	0	5	44.4
1857–1861	James Buchanan	7	4	3	0	100.0
1861–1865	Abraham Lincoln	7	2	5	0	100.0
1865–1869	Andrew Johnson	29	21	8	15	28.6
1869–1877	Ulysses S. Grant	93	45	48	4	91.1
1877–1881	Rutherford B. Hayes	13	12	1	1	91.7
1881–1881	James A. Garfield	0	0	0	0	—
1881–1885	Chester A. Arthur	12	4	8	1	75.0
1885–1889	Grover Cleveland	414	304	110	2	99.3
1889–1893	Benjamin Harrison	44	19	25	1	94.7
1893–1897	Grover Cleveland	170	42	128	5	88.1
1897–1901	William McKinley	42	6	36	0	100.0
1901–1909	Theodore Roosevelt	82	42	40	1	97.6
1909–1913	William H. Taft	39	30	9	1	96.7
1913–1921	Woodrow Wilson	44	33	11	6	81.8
1921–1923	Warren G. Harding	6	5	1	0	100.0
1923–1929	Calvin Coolidge	50	20	30	4	80.0
1929–1933	Herbert C. Hoover	37	21	16	3	85.7
1933–1945	Franklin D. Roosevelt	635	372	263	9	97.6
1945–1953	Harry S. Truman	250	180	70	12	93.3
1953–1961	Dwight D. Eisenhower	181	73	108	2	97.3
1961–1963	John F. Kennedy	21	12	9	0	100.0
1963–1969	Lyndon B. Johnson	30	16	14	0	100.0
1969–1974	Richard Nixon	43	26	17	7	73.1
1974–1977	Gerald R. Ford	66	48	18	12	75.0
1977–1981	Jimmy Carter	31	13	18	2	84.6
1981–1989	Ronald Reagan	78	39	39	9	77.8
1989–1993	George Bush	46	27	19[a]	1	96.3
1993–2001	Bill Clinton	38	37	1	2	94.6
2001–	George W. Bush[b]	2	2	0	0	100.0

SOURCE: Lyn Ragsdale, *Vital Statistics on the Presidency: Washington to Clinton,* 2d ed. (Washington, D.C.: Congressional Quarterly, 1998); Michael Nelson, ed., *Guide to the Presidency,* 3d ed. (Washington, D.C.: CQ Press, 2002). Data from 2003 to 2006 compiled by Gerhard Peters, The American Presidency Project.

a. Two pocket vetoes were not recognized by Congress, which passed subsequent legislation that did not encounter vetoes.
b. Through May 2007.

argued that Congress alone represented the people and that the veto might undermine democratic values and thwart majority rule.

But James Madison insisted in the *Federalist* that only by giving each branch some control over the others could power be restrained and rights and liberties protected. Alexander Hamilton argued that unrestrained majorities were as dangerous as unchecked elites. And the majority of the framers agreed with these supporters of the veto. (See CONSTITUTIONAL POWERS AND PROVISIONS.)

Veto and Override Procedures

The Constitution gives the president three choices upon being presented with legislation passed by Congress: approve the bill and sign it into law; veto the bill by returning it to the chamber where it originated within ten days of passage (not counting Sundays); or, finally, do nothing.

If the president does nothing, the bill automatically becomes law after ten days. This provision prevents presidents from killing legislation through simple inaction. The exception to this rule occurs when Congress presents a bill and then adjourns before the required ten days have elapsed. The Constitution provides that under these circumstances the bill automatically dies. Some controversy surrounds this procedure, which is known as a "pocket veto," because of disagreement over what constitutes congressional adjournment.

If the president vetoes a bill and returns it to Congress and the legislature fails to act, the bill dies. However, if a two-thirds majority in each house passes the vetoed bill once again, it becomes law despite presidential disapproval. This is called overriding the veto. The Supreme Court ruled in 1919 that two-thirds of a quorum—which in both houses of Congress is a majority of the total membership—rather than two-thirds of the total membership is enough for an override. Barring an override, Congress can either rewrite the legislation to meet presidential objections or simply drop the issue.

Bills vetoed by the president normally are sent back to Congress accompanied by a message stating the reasons for the president's opposition. Sometimes the reasons cite constitutional problems, at other times political or issue differences between the branches, but at all times veto messages are aimed at pressing the president's views on the bill in question. Whatever their other purposes, veto messages are political statements and are directed toward Congress and also to the public at large. In this sense, then, the messages become additional resources in the president's effort to influence public policy. (See also CONGRESS AND THE PRESIDENCY.)

Historic Use

Early presidents abided by the prevailing view that Congress best represented the public will, and therefore they vetoed very few bills. When they did resort to a veto, it was almost always because they thought the bill was unconstitutional. The notion that a president should veto a bill simply because it was objectionable was not yet widely accepted.

This narrow view of the president's power to veto legislation changed significantly under President Andrew Jackson. Jackson was a strong party loyalist who quickly entered into warfare with his congressional foes, and the veto in his hands became an instrument of political as well as constitutional power. In eight years Jackson issued twelve vetoes, more than those issued by his six predecessors combined, and none of his vetoes was overridden. Jackson's best-known veto was of a bill to recharter the Second Bank of the United States, which he considered a creature of special interests.

Whig presidents after Jackson, while professing allegiance to their party's doctrine of congressional supremacy, also proved surprisingly firm when challenged by Congress. President John Tyler's veto of a tariff bill in 1843 brought on the first attempt by Congress to impeach a president. That effort failed, and Tyler's successors showed equally notable bursts of independence. Even so, only forty-nine bills were vetoed between 1829 and 1865.

The period between the Civil War and the late 1890s was a time of sharp partisan and regional controversies, dramatic social and economic changes, and disputes over the proper role of government. Presidents and Congress were increasingly at odds. Although Congress generally was the dominant branch, there were dramatic increases in presidential use of the veto.

When President Andrew Johnson vetoed a bill to protect the rights of freedmen, Congress passed the measure over his veto—the first time Congress had overridden the president's veto on a major issue. Several other measures were passed over Johnson's veto as well. When Johnson refused to abide by a law, passed over his veto, that forbade presidents from firing political appointees without congressional approval, the House voted to impeach him. Johnson was acquitted in the Senate by only one vote. The law in dispute was later repealed.

Most of the vetoes during the rest of the nineteenth century were aimed at "private" bills, measures passed by Congress to benefit specific individuals, companies, or municipalities. Most private bills during the late 1800s provided pensions for Civil War veterans, but many were fraudulent or excessive claims that often were passed late in the congressional session. Bills of a type that previous presidents had signed routinely were now being vetoed.

Modern Presidents

Franklin D. Roosevelt used the veto more vigorously than any other president and crafted the threat of the veto into his legislative strategy. He was the first president to use the veto against major tax legislation. Roosevelt in many ways created the modern presidency, in which the veto became yet another instrument of executive influence.

Presidents Harry S. Truman and Dwight D. Eisenhower continued to make extensive use of the veto. Truman used it to safeguard labor against industry and agriculture. Eisenhower used the veto and the veto threat to defeat or limit social programs favored by the Democrats, who controlled Congress during six of his eight years in office.

Democrats John F. Kennedy and Lyndon B. Johnson, blessed with friendly majorities in Congress, seldom used the veto, but Republicans Richard Nixon and Gerald R. Ford fared differently. Both Nixon and Ford had to deal with a Democratic Congress, so the veto, by necessity, became central to their legislative strategies.

Nixon successfully used the veto to block several major bills he saw as inflationary. But because the success of the veto is tied to a president's overall strength, Nixon's political troubles eventually weakened his influence within Congress as well as his national popularity. He lost an important battle in the ongoing struggle over executive and legislative powers when Congress voted to override his veto of the War Powers Act in 1973.

Ford, despite his severe political weakness of being an unelected chief executive succeeding a disgraced president, used the veto frequently and to great effect. He also used the threat of a veto to derail a consumer protection bill that was popular in both chambers.

Jimmy Carter, like Kennedy and Johnson, relied on the veto less frequently because his fellow Democrats dominated Congress. Nevertheless, in 1980 Carter became the first president since Truman to suffer an override at the hands of his own party. Only a handful of senators and representatives voted to sustain his veto of a bill eliminating the import fees that Carter had imposed on foreign oil. Later in the year Congress overrode another of Carter's vetoes.

Ronald Reagan frequently used or threatened to use the veto on budget-related matters and on foreign policy issues. His great popularity with the voters in his first term often was enough to deter congressional action, and his veto of a 1981 continuing appropriations bill proved so potent that Congress reworked the measure to his satisfaction. But in one of the severest blows to Reagan's presidency, Congress in 1986 overrode the president's veto of a measure imposing economic sanctions against South Africa. The vote was the first override of a veto on a major foreign policy issue since the 1973 War Powers Act. Reagan found it harder to use veto threats to his advantage after the 1986 elections, when the Democrats regained control of the Senate and Reagan faced a solidly Democratic Congress.

George Bush, like his Republican predecessors, used the veto to block measures that he thought would expand the role of government and went against his budget priorities. He used the veto threat not only to kill legislation but also to stimulate serious bargaining, thereby serving his penchant for negotiation rather than confrontation.

Bill Clinton vetoed no bills during his first two years in office, but in 1994 Republicans gained control of both houses of Congress and began an energetic campaign to reshape government. Clinton signed his first veto on June 7, 1995, rejecting a bill that cut spending of funds already appropriated for that fiscal year. The veto, which Congress did not override, began a struggle between Clinton and congressional Republicans for control of the federal budget. After several more vetoes and the closing down of government operations for a brief period, Clinton emerged the winner, with the support of the majority of Americans, in the 1995–1996 budget battle with the Republican-controlled Congress. After that, Clinton made frequent use of the veto threat to kill or modify legislation.

Over the first five and a half years of his administration George W. Bush did not veto any legislation. In early 2001 the Republicans controlled the House and had a slim margin in the Senate, with fifty votes and the ability of Vice President Cheney to break ties. The Democrats took narrow control of the Senate several months into Bush's presidency after Vermont senator James Jeffords left the Republican Party to become an independent and caucus with the Democrats. After scoring gains in the 2002 midterm elections, Republicans regained control of the Senate in January 2003 and following the 2004 elections maintained their control over both houses. Enjoying unified government, President Bush did not issue his first veto until July 19, 2006, when he rejected the Stem Cell Research Enhancement Act.

Throughout the rest of 2006, Bush did not veto any additional legislation, but after the November 2006 midterm elections resulting in Democratic control of both houses of Congress, ideological differences between the president and congressional Democrats on a variety of issues, including the direction of the Iraq war and tax cuts, has set the stage for increased use of the veto in the president's last two years in office. Bush's second veto came on May 1, 2007, when he rejected a supplemental appropriations bill for continuing the Iraq war. Democratic leaders in Congress had added language to the bill that would set a timetable for the withdrawal of U.S. troops. An override attempt failed the next day.

Veto Decision

It is very difficult for Congress to override a presidential veto in the face of heavy lobbying by the White House. In fact, sometimes the congressional leadership does not even bother to schedule a vote to override. Still, presidents most often use the veto as their weapon of last resort.

The president makes the decision to veto in conjunction with a varying combination of the White House staff, the heads of interested federal departments, the director of the Office of Management and Budget, important legislators of the president's own party in Congress, and—when their interests are seriously affected—state and local officials, interest groups, and private citizens.

The decision may be easy if a bill is diametrically opposed to the president's program or philosophy. But many are close calls, and the president and White House advisers must weigh the provisions of the bill they support against those they oppose.

In most cases, both sides would prefer to avoid a showdown over legislation. This reluctance makes the threat of a veto a useful bargaining tool for presidents. They can use the threat very effectively to shape, alter, or deter legislation before it reaches their desk. Normally, most members of Congress would rather compromise with the president than face the task of trying to round up the votes to override a veto.

Congress's Tools

Congress has several methods for undermining vetoes or threats of vetoes made by even popular presidents. Because, according to the Constitution, the president must accept or veto whole bills, members of Congress often add amendments, known as riders, to major legislation. Even though such a rider might be on a subject completely different from the rest of the legislation or create "pork barrel" spending, the president would be reluctant to use the veto because of the importance of the rest of the bill. (See LINE-ITEM VETO.)

To make matters more complicated, Congress in the 1980s relied on massive omnibus (or catch-all) bills to pass the budget, to appropriate funds, and to levy new taxes simultaneously. Several times President Reagan had to accept omnibus bills containing programs or provisions he detested simply because he needed other spending contained in the same bill. A prime example was the Boland Amendment, a provision restricting U.S. aid to rebels opposing the government of Nicaragua, which was tacked onto a 1984 appropriations bill.

Congress also tended to wait until late in each session to pass critical spending bills. This practice narrowed the president's options because a veto might not be feasible if Congress had adjourned and the funds needed to run the federal government were contained in the legislation.

Members of Congress may try to provoke a veto for political purposes, especially when the executive branch is controlled by one political party and the legislative branch by the other. They may pass a bill they know the president will veto and then make use of the veto decision in opposing the president during the next election.

A president cannot always depend on fellow party members in Congress for support on veto threats or even during override battles, because most members do not want to be seen by their constituents as mere rubber stamps for the president's wishes. This is especially true when the bill in question benefits a member's district or state, as when Congress overrode Reagan's vetoes on water treatment and highway bills in 1987. So popular were both measures that Republicans abandoned the president in droves.

Pocket Vetoes

Controversy has long surrounded the pocket veto—or, more to the point, the issue of when it can be used. Under the Constitution the president must return a vetoed bill to Congress within ten days. Otherwise, the bill automatically becomes a law—with one exception. The Constitution states that a bill does not become law if "Congress by their adjournment prevent its return." In such a case presidents can "pocket" the bill, because they do not have an opportunity to return it to Congress, along with their objections, for further consideration. This provision was intended to prevent Congress from passing legislation objectionable to the president and then quickly adjourning so the president could not veto the bill.

Roughly 40 percent of all vetoes have been pocket vetoes. President James Madison was the first to use the pocket veto, but this type of veto did not become common until after the Civil War.

Although the pocket veto has been used frequently, a controversy still exists over the question of what constitutes an adjournment by Congress. This is an

⊙ **CLOSER LOOK**

The veto power of the president, in and of itself, does little to promote the president's desired policy outcomes. What makes the president's power to veto important in shaping policy is when he preemptively threatens to use his veto power before legislation even reaches his desk. This often leads to bargaining between the executive and legislative branches, resulting in policy outcomes that are a compromise between the positions of the two branches. Andrew Jackson revolutionized presidential power with his very public, defiant, and outspoken veto threats. Presidents throughout history have followed Jackson's lead, sometimes to humorous effect, as in the case of Ronald Reagan on many occasions.

And if they try to do anything about that third tax cut, I sleep with a veto pen under my pillow.

—*Ronald Reagan,* Remarks at a Fundraising Dinner Honoring Former Representative John M. Ashbrook in Ashland, Ohio, May 9, 1983

important question because if the president is able to return a vetoed bill, the pocket veto is not permissible. In the 1929 *Pocket Veto Case,* the Supreme Court ruled that President Calvin Coolidge could pocket veto a bill passed just before a four-month recess. The justices ruled that the term *adjournment* applied to any break in the congressional calendar that prevented the return of a bill within the required ten-day period, in this case adjournment between sessions.

To close this apparent loophole, Congress began to appoint "agents" to receive presidential veto messages while members were away, in theory negating a president's claim for a pocket veto. The practice of appointing agents was upheld by the Supreme Court in 1938, effectively restricting pocket vetoes to final adjournment.

The issue lay dormant until 1970, when Nixon pocket-vetoed a medical training bill during a six-day congressional recess. The bill had passed both chambers by nearly unanimous votes, indicating that Congress would have overridden a regular veto. A suit was filed, and in 1974 a federal appeals court ruled that Nixon had improperly used his pocket veto power. A second case decided by the same court in 1976 broadened the ruling to prohibit the president from pocket-vetoing a bill during adjournments between sessions of the same Congress. In both cases the court ruled that the pocket veto was invalid because the two chambers had appointed agents to receive veto messages.

Despite these rulings, Reagan in 1981 and again in 1983 pocket-vetoed bills between sessions of Congress. In 1985 a federal appeals court ruled against Reagan's use of the pocket veto between sessions of a Congress. The case was appealed to the Supreme Court, but the issue was left unresolved when the Court in 1987 declared that the case was moot.

Insisting that a pocket veto was in order any time Congress adjourned for more than three days, President George H. W. Bush in 1989 pocket-vetoed a minor measure while Congress was taking its August recess. It was the first pocket veto within a session since Nixon's in 1970. Bush pocket-vetoed another bill during Congress's August 1991 recess, but because of questions raised by the federal appeals court opinions, Bush said he was returning the vetoed bill with his objections to the clerk of the House. Bush claimed another pocket veto in December 1991 at the end of the first session of a Congress, but congressional experts disputed it.

House legislation to limit use of the pocket veto to final adjournment after a two-year Congress stalled in 1990 before it reached the House floor.

> *In 1985 it was while addressing you that I warned the would-be tax hikers in Congress that I had my veto pen at the ready and dared them to make my day.*
>
> **—Ronald Reagan,** *Remarks at a White House Briefing for Members of the American Business Conference,* March 23, 1988

More on this topic:

Congress and the Presidency, p. 111

Constitutional Powers and Provisions, p. 119

Line-Item Veto, p. 340

Signing Statements, p. 463

Vice President

Throughout much of its history the office of the vice president has held little esteem and been the subject of much ridicule. Benjamin Franklin once quipped that the vice president should be addressed as "Your Superfluous Excellency." Daniel Webster, when offered the vice-presidential slot on the 1848 Whig Party ticket, declined, saying, "I do not propose to be buried until I am dead."

Constitutionally, the vice presidency was born weak and has not grown much stronger. But lost in all the laughter is an appreciation of the importance—throughout U.S. history and growing in recent years—of the position the vice presidency occupies in the U.S. political system.

The vice presidency is most significant when it provides a successor to the president. Nine vice presidents, more than one-fifth of those who have served in the office, have become president through SUCCESSION when the incumbent chief executive died or resigned. Collectively, they led the nation for forty-two years.

Recognition of the importance of having a vice president standing by at all times prompted Congress in 1965 to pass the Twenty-fifth Amendment, which established a procedure for filling vice-presidential vacancies. The amendment, ratified by the states in 1967, stated unequivocally the right of the vice president, in the event of a presidential death, resignation, or impeachment, to serve as president for the unexpired balance of the term. It also established a mechanism by which the vice president could take over if the president were disabled.

In addition to the role of presidential successor, the vice presidency also serves as an important political springboard. Although only five vice presidents actually have been elected president—George H. W. Bush was the first one since 1836 to be elected directly to the presidency—the modern vice president is not only a presumptive candidate for president but the presumptive front-runner as well. Seventeen of twenty-two twentieth-century vice presidents went on to seek the presidency.

Recent changes in the vice presidency have made the office more substantial. The vice presidency has become "institutionalized" so that it is organizationally larger and more complex than in the past. Certain kinds of vice-presidential activities now are taken for granted, including regular private meetings with the president and attendance at many other important presidential meetings, membership on the National Security Council, full national security briefings, frequent diplomatic missions, public advocacy of the president's leadership and programs, and party leadership.

History

The vice presidency was invented late in the Constitutional Convention, not because the delegates saw any need for such an office, but rather as a means of perfecting the arrangements they had made for presidential election and succession and, to some degree, for Senate leadership. The office's only ongoing responsibility was to preside over the Senate, casting tie-breaking votes.

The most important duty of the vice president was to stand by as successor to the presidency in the event of the president's death, impeachment, resignation, or "inability to discharge the Powers and Duties" of the office. But the Constitution was vague about what all that meant or how succession would be carried out. Moreover, by giving the office both legislative and executive responsibilities, the Constitution deprived the vice presidency of solid moorings in either Congress or the presidency.

John Adams was the first person to be elected vice president. Despite Adams's views to the contrary, the vice presidency was at a peak of influence when he served. Because the Senate was small and still relatively unorganized, Adams was able to cast twenty-nine tie-breaking votes (still the record) and also to guide its agenda and intervene in debate. Adams was respected and sometimes consulted on diplomatic and other matters by President George Washington.

Adams was elected president in 1796, and Thomas Jefferson, who gained the second highest number of votes, was elected vice president. Because they were from opposing parties—Federalist and Democratic-Republican, respectively—there was little interaction between the two, except on formal occasions.

To avoid such split-party administrations, in the 1800 election each party nominated a complete ticket, instructing its electors to cast their two votes for its presidential and vice-presidential candidates. Jefferson and his running mate, Aaron Burr, ended up with an equal number of votes for president. The election was thrown into the House of Representatives, which eventually chose Jefferson to be president and Burr to be vice president.

The 1800 election highlighted not only problems in the election process but also what was to become an enduring characteristic of the vice presidency: its use as a device for balancing the ticket. Burr, a New Yorker, had been placed on his party's ticket with Jefferson of Virginia to balance the Virginia and New York wings of the party.

In 1804 motions were made in Congress to abolish the vice presidency rather than continue it in a form degraded from its original constitutional status as the position awarded to the second most qualified person to be president. Instead, the Twelfth Amendment was added to the Constitution, providing for separate votes for president and vice president.

Nineteenth Century

The development of political parties and the enactment of the Twelfth Amendment sent an already constitutionally weak vice presidency into a tailspin that lasted until the end of the nineteenth century.

Party leaders, not presidential candidates—who often were not even present at national nominating conventions and who, if present, were expected to be seen and not heard—chose the nominees for vice president. This did little to foster trust or respect between the two once they were in office.

This tension was aggravated by the criteria that party leaders applied to vice-presidential selection. The nominee had to placate the region or faction of the party that had been most dissatisfied with the presidential nomination, a situation that led to numerous New York–Virginia, North-South, Stalwart-Progressive, and other such pairings. The nominee frequently was expected to carry a swing state in the general election where the presidential candidate was not popular.

Ticket balancing placed such a stigma on the office that many politicians were unwilling to accept a nomination. Those who did and were elected found that fresh political problems four years later invariably led party leaders to balance the ticket differently. No first-term vice president in the nineteenth century ever was renominated for a second term by a party convention. Nor, after Vice President Martin Van Buren in 1836, was any nineteenth-century vice president elected or even nominated for president.

In addition, the vice president's role as Senate leader, which most vice presidents had spent considerable time performing, became more ceremonial as the Senate grew more organized and took greater charge of its own affairs.

Not surprisingly, then, the nineteenth-century vice presidents made up a virtual rogues' gallery of personal and political failures. Because the office was so unappealing, an unusual number of the politicians who could be induced to run for vice president were old and in bad health (six died in office). Some became embroiled in financial scandals, others in personal scandals. Some even publicly expressed their dislike for the president.

Naturally, there were exceptions. Some presidents often sought the informal advice of their vice presidents and used them as effective advocates of administration policy in the Senate. Even in those administrations, however, the vice president was not invited to cabinet meetings or entrusted with important tasks.

In one area of vice-presidential responsibility, the nineteenth century witnessed a giant step forward: presidential succession. After the death of William Henry Harrison in 1841, Vice President John Tyler set the precedent of a vice president assuming not only the office of president but also the balance of the president's term.

Early Twentieth Century

The rise of national news media (specifically mass-circulation magazines and newspaper wire services), a new style of active presidential campaigning, and changes in the vice-presidential nominating process enhanced the status of the vice presidency during the first half of the twentieth century.

In 1900 Republican Theodore Roosevelt became the first vice-presidential candidate to campaign vigorously nationwide. The national reputation that Roosevelt gained through travel and the media stood him in good stead when he succeeded to the presidency after President William McKinley was assassinated in 1901. Unlike his predecessors who had assumed the presidency upon the death of the incumbent, Roosevelt was nominated by his party to run for a full term as president in 1904.

In another change from nineteenth-century practice, beginning in 1912 every first-term vice president who had sought a second term has been nominated for reelection (as of 2003).

The enhanced political status of the vice presidency soon began to make it more attractive to at least some able and experienced political leaders. With somewhat more talent to offer, some vice presidents were given greater responsibilities by the presidents they served.

Several presidents included their vice presidents in cabinet meetings, as has every president since Franklin D. Roosevelt. In addition, Franklin Roosevelt's first vice president, John Nance Garner, served as an important liaison from the president to Congress. It was Garner's suggestion that led to the practice, which later presidents followed, of meeting weekly with congressional leaders. Garner also undertook a goodwill mission to Mexico at Roosevelt's request, another innovation that virtually all later administrations continued. Roosevelt and Garner eventually had a falling-out, however, which set the stage for Roosevelt to take control of the choice of his running mate in 1940.

The involvement of the vice presidency in executive branch activities continued to grow, as the vice president sat with the cabinet, advised the president, and traveled abroad as an administration emissary.

Yet the office remained fundamentally weak, as was all too obvious when Vice President Harry S. Truman was thrust into the presidency after Roosevelt's death in 1945. Truman was at best dimly aware of the existence of the atomic bomb, the Allies' plans for the post–World War II world, and the serious deterioration of Roosevelt's health. He later said that in his eighty-two days as vice president he had seen the president perhaps twice outside of cabinet meetings.

Postwar Period

Truman's lack of preparation, and the challenges he soon faced in dealing with the cold war and the nuclear weapons competition between the United States and the Soviet Union, heightened public concern that the vice presidency be occupied by leaders ready and able to step into the presidency at a moment's notice.

As a result, most modern presidential candidates have paid considerable attention to experience, ability, and political compatibility in selecting their running mates. Presidential nominees realize that voters now care more about competence and loyalty—a vice-presidential candidate's ability to succeed to the presidency efficiently and to carry on the departed president's policies faithfully—than about having all the regions of the country or factions of the party represented on the ticket.

Once in office, modern presidents also keep their vice presidents informed about matters of state. In 1949, at Truman's request, the vice president was made a statutory member of the NATIONAL SECURITY COUNCIL. Vice presidents also receive full national security briefings as a matter of course.

As a further means of reassuring the American people, most presidents now encourage the vice presidents to stay active and in the public eye. Vice presidents travel abroad, meet regularly with the cabinet, and serve to some extent as legislative liaison from the president to Congress. They serve as advocates of their administration's policies, leadership, and party.

Expanded Resources

Since the 1960s vice presidents have accumulated greater institutional resources to help them fulfill their more extensive duties. Lyndon B. Johnson, the vice president to John F. Kennedy, gained for the vice presidency an impressive suite of offices in what is now the Eisenhower Executive Office Building, adjacent to the White House. Spiro T. Agnew, Richard Nixon's vice president, won a line item in the executive budget, freeing vice presidents from their earlier dependence on Congress for office space and operating funds.

Even more significant institutional gains were made by Gerald R. Ford and Nelson A. Rockefeller, the two vice presidents who were appointed under the Twenty-fifth Amendment and whose agreements to serve were urgently required by their presidents for political reasons. As vice president, Ford persuaded President Richard Nixon to increase dramatically his

On December 6, 1973, Gerald R. Ford was sworn in as vice president by Chief Justice Warren Burger before a joint session of Congress, with President Richard Nixon (right) in attendance. Ford replaced Spiro Agnew, who had resigned.
Source: Gerald R. Ford Library

budget for hiring staff. Rockefeller secured a weekly place on President Ford's calendar for a private meeting. He also increased the perquisites of the vice presidency, obtaining everything from a better airplane to serve as *Air Force Two* to an official residence—the Admiral's House at the Naval Observatory. He also called for the seal for the office to be redesigned. (The old seal showed an eagle at rest; the new one an eagle with its wings spread, with a claw full of arrows and a starburst at its head.)

Walter F. Mondale, Jimmy Carter's vice president, participated in the first nationally televised debate between vice-presidential candidates during the 1976 campaign. He won authorization to attend all presidential meetings, full access to the flow of papers to and from the president, and an office in the West Wing of the White House. More important, perhaps, Mondale demonstrated that the vice president could serve the president as a valued adviser on virtually all matters of politics and public policy.

George H. W. Bush, as Ronald Reagan's vice president; Dan Quayle, as Bush's vice president; and Al Gore, as Bill Clinton's vice president, benefited from many of the institutional gains in both role and resources that their recent predecessors had won. And Richard B. Cheney, George W. Bush's vice president, appeared to exercise substantial clout in the White House. But it is important to keep in mind that to a large extent the role and resources enjoyed by the vice president are delegated at the discretion of the president and can be revoked. The activities and influence of individual vice presidents continue to vary considerably from administration to administration.

Modern Roles

The many roles that modern vice presidents perform can be grouped into four categories: constitutional, statutory, advisory, and representative.

Constitutional Roles

The original Constitution assigned two roles to the vice president. One of these was to serve as president of the Senate, voting only to break ties. Modern vice presidents spend little time per-

forming this role. The powers of the presiding officer are largely ceremonial, and tie votes are rare. George H. W. Bush cast seven tie-breaking votes in his eight years as vice president, but Quayle cast none. When the Senate is closely divided between parties, in eras such as the 1990s and early 2000s, though, the tie-breaking authority can still be significant. Gore broke ties on two measures that were crucial to the Clinton administration's economic agenda during his first year in office. When the Senate was deadlocked with fifty Republicans and fifty Democrats in January 2001, Cheney cast the votes that gave Republicans control of the Senate's leadership and committees.

The Constitution also states that the vice president will succeed to the presidency in the event of the president's death, resignation, removal, or disability. Nine vice presidents—John Tyler, Millard Fillmore, Andrew Johnson, Chester A. Arthur, Theodore Roosevelt, Calvin Coolidge, Harry Truman, Lyndon Johnson, and Gerald Ford—have become president by succession.

Under the provisions of the Twenty-fifth Amendment, the vice president is the central figure in determining whether a president is disabled. Moreover, while a president is disabled, the vice president assumes the full powers and duties of the office as acting president. How this works is another matter. In 1981, after President Reagan was shot and taken into surgery, a move to consider whether to declare the president disabled and to transfer power to Vice President Bush was headed off by some presidential aides who were fearful of confusing the nation and making the president look weak. Bush himself remained silent.

In 1985 presidential power actually was transferred to Bush while Reagan was undergoing surgery. Eager not to offend the president or his aides with even the slightest hint of activity, Bush played tennis and chatted with friends at the vice-presidential residence during his eight hours as acting president. In 2002 George W. Bush transferred presidential powers to Vice President Cheney before undergoing a colonoscopy. The president resumed power more than two hours later.

Statutory Roles

In contrast to the presidency, to which numerous responsibilities have been assigned by law, the vice presidency has only two statutory roles: member of the National Security Council (NSC) and member of the Board of Regents of the Smithsonian Institution. While the latter role is inconsequential, membership on the NSC seems important, but it is less so than meets the eye.

Few presidents have wanted to feel obliged to involve the vice president in important foreign policy deliberations. As a result, most have either called a limited number of NSC meetings or used them as forums to announce, rather than make, policy.

Advisory Roles

Modern vice presidents serve as advisers to the president, whether as a cabinet member, commission chair, or senior adviser.

A few of the earlier vice presidents and every vice president since Garner have attended cabinet meetings. For all its symbolic value, however, cabinet membership has seldom been a position of real influence for the vice president. One reason is that cabinet meetings themselves have become less important in recent years. In addition, most vice presidents have felt bound to remain virtually silent at such meetings, listening to the discussions of presidents, department heads, and others who are responsible for administering the executive branch.

Dwight Eisenhower was the first president to appoint a vice president to chair a presidential commission, a practice that most of his successors have followed. Far from being a boon to the vice presidency, most commission assignments have been burdensome. Typically, presidents have created commissions to symbolize their concern for an issue or constituency; they have named their vice presidents as chairs because the vice presidency is a visible and prestigious office and because they have wanted to convince the public that the vice president is actively involved in the business of government. Seldom, however, have presidents entrusted vice-presidential commissions with substantive powers and responsibilities. But there have been some exceptions. Quayle, for example, as chairman of the President's Council on Competitiveness, reportedly played an influential role in mediating disputes between government agencies and those objecting to government regulations. Gore chaired the National Performance Review Commission, an effort to "reinvent government" that, among other suggestions, proposed a reduction of 252,000 government jobs. (See also COMMISSIONS, PRESIDENTIAL.)

Most recent presidents have turned to their vice presidents for advice on matters about which they are knowledgeable or experienced. For example, Reagan made good use in foreign policy of George H. W. Bush's experience as director of the Central Intelligence Agency, ambassador to the United Nations, and chief U.S. diplomat in China. Bush in turn called on Quayle, a former member of the House and Senate, for advice on political and congressional strategy, as Clinton did with Gore. Indeed, during Clinton's first year in office Gore became one of his closest advisers. Cheney was a key adviser to George W. Bush on foreign policy and other issues.

Representative Roles

In recent years presidents have had their vice presidents represent their administrations to a variety of constituencies.

Within the government, the modern vice president serves as a liaison from the president to Congress. Since 1933 twelve of fifteen vice presidents have had experience as members of Congress, and seven of these served presidents who lacked legislative experience themselves. Vice presidents are frequently used to pass information and advice between Congress and the president, working in conjunction with the White House staff's team of legislative lobbyists. The vice president's suite in the Capitol building provides a convenient setting for such discussions and "head counts" for votes on pending legislation. (See also CONGRESS AND THE PRESIDENCY.)

Garner was the first vice president to make an official trip abroad, and Nixon was the one who set the precedent of extensive vice-presidential travel. Many, perhaps most, special envoy assignments have been almost entirely symbolic in nature—the president simply wished to demonstrate goodwill toward a nation without having to undertake a trip personally. But sometimes the vice president has carried an important message to a foreign government, affirmed U.S. support for a beleaguered regime, or negotiated on a small diplomatic matter. Even relatively inconsequential trips are of political value to vice presidents, who gain more press coverage than usual while they are abroad and reinforce their image among voters as knowledgeable world leaders.

Modern vice presidents most frequently are seen in their role as defender of the president's policies to a variety of public audiences, including interest groups, the news media, state and local party organizations, and the general public. This role offers significant political benefits to the vice president who performs it well. It builds trust for the vice president with the president and the White House staff, endears the vice president to the party faithful, and increases the vice president's political visibility. Taken together, these benefits usually give the vice president the inside track for a subsequent presidential nomination.

The role of administration defender has its pitfalls, too. Vice presidents may appear to be narrow, divisive figures, especially

More on this topic:
Commissions, Presidential, p. 110
Congress and the Presidency, p. 111
National Security Council, p. 381
Succession, p. 483
Vice-Presidential Residence, p. 546

when defending the administration involves attacking its critics, as Vice Presidents Nixon and Agnew did with great fervor. In addition, vice presidents may come to seem weak and parrotlike, always defending the ideas of another while submerging their own thoughts and expertise. Vice presidents also may feel compelled to defend policies with which they profoundly disagree.

Vice Presidential Residence

The White House has been the official residence of presidents for about two hundred years, but not until 1974 did Congress give the vice president a permanent home. The cost of making a series of vice presidents' private homes secure had become greater than the expense of maintaining

At the urging of Vice President Nelson A. Rockefeller, the federal government designated this house on the grounds of the U.S. Naval Observatory as the official vice-presidential residence.

a single home for the vice president. Known originally as the Admiral's House, the mansion that became the vice-presidential residence was completed in 1893 for the superintendent of the Naval Observatory. Between 1928 and 1974 it was the home of the chief of naval operations. The navy still owns and maintains the house and supplies its staff.

The white brick Queen Anne–style house stands on the grounds of the Naval Observatory on Massachusetts Avenue in the northwest quadrant of Washington, D.C. It has a covered entrance, a curving veranda, a three-story Romanesque tower, and a steep roof of gray slate with dormer windows inset. The house required extensive renovations when Congress claimed it for the vice president in 1974.

The first vice president to whom the house was available was Gerald R. Ford. Betty Ford had just begun to plan her decorating scheme for the house when her husband became president in August 1974. The next vice president, Nelson A. Rockefeller, lived in a home owned by his family on prestigious Foxhall Road while he and his wife supervised the ongoing renovations and contributed several valuable pieces of art and furniture to the official residence. Vice President Walter F. Mondale, his wife, Joan, and their three children became the first full-time residents of the home. Joan Mondale made it a showcase for works of contemporary American artists, and the Mondales established a library of books by and about vice presidents.

Vietnam War

The Vietnam War was one of the most painful experiences in American history. During the 1960s and early 1970s the United States engaged in an undeclared war in Southeast Asia. The purpose of the war was to block communist expansion and defend South Vietnam from attacks by communist North Vietnam and South Vietnamese communist rebels who hoped to unify Vietnam under communist rule. Despite the deployment of hundreds of thousands of troops and the use of modern airpower, the U.S. military could not break the will of the communists to continue fighting. Meanwhile, disagreement over the morality and necessity of the war divided the American people and led to much social protest and debate. In 1973 the last U.S. combat troops were withdrawn from South Vietnam. More than fifty thousand American troops had been killed in the war.

Development of the War

No single president was entirely responsible for U.S. participation in the war in Vietnam. A succession of presidents gradually increased U.S. military involvement in Southeast Asia during the 1950s and 1960s.

In 1954 Vietnamese revolutionary forces defeated the French, who had controlled the region as a colonial power. President Dwight D. Eisenhower had continued the Truman administration's policy of sending aid to the French, but Eisenhower refused to intervene militarily to prevent a French defeat. After the French departed, Vietnam was temporarily partitioned, with the communist government of Ho Chi Minh ruling the North and anticommunists in Saigon controlling the South. Eisenhower ignored the scheduled reunification election in 1956 because he feared the communists would win and take over the entire country. Instead, he supported the noncommunist regime in the South.

The North Vietnamese and communist rebels in the South known as Viet Cong launched a guerrilla war in an effort to achieve reunification through force. Eisenhower avoided direct U.S. military involvement in Vietnam, although he increased economic and military aid to the Saigon government and sent a small number of American advisers.

President John F. Kennedy, fearing the collapse of the Saigon government, responded to South Vietnamese requests for greater assistance. He sent additional military advisers and counterinsurgency troops to South Vietnam. Before he was assassinated in November 1963, Kennedy had assigned 16,500 U.S. military personnel to Vietnam.

President Lyndon B. Johnson continued to increase U.S. involvement in the widening war. After North Vietnamese patrol boats allegedly attacked U.S. ships in the Gulf of Tonkin in August 1964, Congress, at the president's urging, passed by a nearly unanimous vote the TONKIN GULF RESOLUTION, which granted the president broad authority to wage war in Vietnam. Armed with this congressional sanction and fearing a communist takeover, Johnson ordered the first regular U.S. combat troops to Vietnam in 1965. By 1968 Johnson had increased U.S. troop strength in Vietnam to 500,000. The massive deployment of U.S. troops, however, could not stamp out communist resistance. As U.S. casualties mounted, the war and President Johnson became increasingly unpopular. The communists' massive Tet offensive early in 1968, although militarily unsuccessful, caused many Americans to lose confidence that the war could be won. On March 31, 1968, President Johnson surprised the nation by announcing that he would not run for another term as president.

This famous caricature shows President Lyndon Johnson displaying his gall bladder scar, drawn by the artist in the shape of South Vietnam. Drawing by David Levine.

Reprinted with permission from New York Review of Books.

President Richard Nixon inherited the war when he took office in January 1969. He began slowly withdrawing U.S. forces from Vietnam. His goal was to free the United States from the Vietnam quagmire while achieving "peace with honor." He hoped to do this through a policy of "Vietnamization," the gradual transfer of the responsibility for defend-

The Vietnam Veterans Memorial, a highly reflective black granite wall, is inscribed with a chronological listing of the more than 58,000 casualties, missing in action, and prisoners of war from the Vietnam War.
Source: R. Michael Jenkins, Congressional Quarterly

ing South Vietnam from U.S. forces to South Vietnamese forces. Nevertheless, to many Americans Nixon was moving too slowly. In 1970, even as U.S. forces were being withdrawn from Southeast Asia, Nixon secretly ordered U.S. forces into Cambodia to attack communist sanctuaries. When Nixon announced the operation on April 30, 1970, college campuses around the United States erupted in protest against the expansion of the war. Four student demonstrators were killed by National Guard troops at Kent State University in Ohio, and more than sixty thousand protesters marched on Washington.

In January 1973 the United States and North Vietnam signed a peace accord. The North Vietnamese returned U.S. prisoners of war and agreed that the South Vietnamese regime would remain in power. In return, the United States withdrew its forces from Vietnam and allowed North Vietnamese army units already in South Vietnam to remain there. Without U.S. support, however, South Vietnam was unable to defend itself against a 1975 North Vietnamese offensive that resulted in the fall of Saigon. Although Nixon had promised the South Vietnamese government that the United States would intervene if communist forces threatened to conquer the South, Nixon had resigned the presidency in 1974, and both Congress and the American public firmly opposed further involvement in Southeast Asia.

Congressional Backlash

The Vietnam War, like the Korean War, was a presidential war. Decision making about goals and strategy in Vietnam was dominated by the executive branch with little input from Congress. Neither Johnson nor Nixon sought congressional approval for their war decisions after 1965. Nevertheless, Congress continually voted in favor of military appropriations and the draft, without which Johnson and Nixon could not have carried on the war for long. Once troops and matériel had been committed to battle, most members of Congress believed denying U.S. forces the money and reinforcements they needed to wage the war would be seen as unpatriotic.

Congress did not begin to assert its war powers until 1969, when it recognized that the growing number of U.S. casualties in Vietnam, the fading prospects that the war could be won, and doubts about the morality of U.S. involvement had begun to turn the American public against the war. In that year the Senate passed the National Commitments Resolution, which, although it lacked the force of law, expressed the Senate's feeling that a national commitment "results only from affirmative action taken by the legislative and executive branches." Later that year Congress adopted an amendment supported by Nixon that prohibited the use of U.S. ground forces in Laos and Thailand.

During the early 1970s momentum continued to build for legislation that would restore Congress's role in the foreign policy process. Nixon undertook a series of controversial military actions without consulting Congress that underscored the legislative branch's inability to affect policy. He provided air support for South Vietnam's 1971 invasion of Laos, ordered North Vietnam's

Haiphong harbor mined in May 1972, and launched massive bombing raids against North Vietnam in December 1972. Furthermore, Nixon's "secret" war in Cambodia in 1970, the publication of the Pentagon Papers in 1971 (which disclosed the deceptive practices of the executive branch during the 1960s), and the revelations about secret national security commitments uncovered by a Senate Foreign Relations subcommittee contributed to the growing perception on the part of lawmakers that executive branch secrecy was out of control.

After three years of work and debate, Congress's attempts to construct a bill that would reestablish its powers over foreign policy and national security culminated in the passage of the War Powers Act in 1973. This act attempted to limit the president's war powers, most notably by restricting the length of time a president could deploy U.S. forces in an area of hostilities without congressional consent.

More on this topic:

Johnson, Lyndon B., p. 309

Nixon, Richard, p. 388

Tonkin Gulf Resolution, p. 505

War Powers Act of 1973, p. 560

Wallace, George C.

Gov. George Corley Wallace (1914–1998) of Alabama made his mark on national politics first as a militant opponent of the civil rights movement and then as a contender for the presidency in the 1960s and 1970s. As an independent candidate in the close election of 1968, Wallace ran one of the strongest third-party campaigns of the twentieth century, although not strong enough to deadlock the election as had been feared. Wallace began his long career as Alabama governor with the cry "Segregation forever!" but he muted his racist rhetoric over the years to suit changing political realities. In May 1972, while campaigning in Maryland for the Democratic presidential nomination, Wallace was shot and paralyzed below the waist by a deranged would-be assassin. In later years Wallace continued his political career from a wheelchair, displaying the determination that earlier had earned him the nickname "Fighting Judge."

Although he modified his message over the years, Wallace always played the role of the outsider doing battle on behalf of the "average man" against an establishment of uncaring, elitist bureaucrats and politicians in Washington. In the tradition of the southern demagogue, he railed against "pointy-headed professors," "federal judges playing God," and the "intellectual morons" who ran the government even though they did not know "how to park their bicycles straight." About politicians in the traditional mold, he said, "There's not a dime's worth of difference in any of 'em, national Democrats or national Republicans." Wallace delivered his political harangues at rallies that featured American flags, loud country-western music, and attractive young women passing contribution buckets.

Wallace grew up in rural Alabama in a poor but not destitute family. By the time he had graduated from law school and served as an air force flight engineer in World War II, his ambition was fixed: to become governor of his state. During most of his years in the state legislature (1947–1953), Wallace was a protégé of Gov. Jim Folsom, a moderate on racial issues. But as state circuit judge (1953–1959), Wallace adopted the outspoken segregationist stance that brought him national attention as a four-term governor (1963–1967,

Gov. George Wallace attempting to block integration at the University of Alabama.
Source: Library of Congress

1971–1979, and 1983–1987). His first wife, Lurleen Wallace, succeeded him in office in 1967 but died a year later.

In one of his best-known efforts to thwart desegregation, Wallace in July 1963 stood in the doorway of the University of Alabama to block the entry of two newly admitted black students. His symbolic protest duly recorded by the television cameras, Wallace stepped aside while federal troops escorted the students in. Wallace's popularity in Alabama outlived his losing fight against desegregation. During his last campaign for governor in 1983, he renounced his segregationist past and said he hoped people of both races could live together in harmony.

Wallace's undisputed hold on the Alabama statehouse gave him a base from which to stage presidential campaigns, an activity he appeared to relish more than the job of governing. In 1964 Wallace received one-third or more of the vote against Lyndon B. Johnson in three Democratic primaries before withdrawing. That campaign was a warm-up for the third-party race of 1968, when Wallace's "law and order" message as the candidate of the American Independent Party appealed to many Americans distressed by race riots, anti–Vietnam War protests, and the rising crime rate. As the close race between Republican Richard Nixon and Democrat Hubert H. Humphrey went down to the wire, Wallace's perceived strength raised fears that he would end up as the power broker if the winner had to be decided in the House of Representatives. Nixon won the election by a narrow margin, and Wallace took only five states. He won 13.5 percent of the popular vote and forty-six electoral votes, an impressive third-party showing in historical terms but a disappointment for the candidate. Wallace's campaign had been hurt by the bellicose views of his running mate, Gen. Curtis LeMay, who had advocated bombing North Vietnam "back to the Stone Age," and by an effective effort by organized labor to keep workers within the Democratic fold.

Wallace returned to the Democratic Party in 1972, running in the presidential primaries. He had amassed a larger popular vote than any other candidate when he was shot on May 15 by Arthur Bremer in a shopping center in Laurel,

More on this topic:

Elections Chronology, p. 174

Third Parties, p. 498

Maryland. Wallace attempted a comeback in the 1976 Democratic presidential primaries, but his physical limitations interfered: The candidate who had strutted the stage gesturing and hurling invective was forced to speak from a wheelchair bolted into place behind a bullet-proof lectern. This, combined with the success of a moderate southerner, Jimmy Carter of Georgia, put an end to Wallace's presidential hopes.

Wallace, Henry A.

Henry A. Wallace.
Source: Library of Congress

Henry Agard Wallace (1888–1965) served as Franklin D. Roosevelt's second vice president from 1941 to 1945. The vice presidency was the only office to which the Iowa native was ever elected. He was dropped from the Democratic ticket in 1944 in favor of Harry S. Truman. Four years later, Wallace ran an unsuccessful third-party candidacy for the presidency against Truman.

Wallace was the son of Henry C. Wallace, who had served as secretary of agriculture under Warren G. Harding and Calvin Coolidge. The younger Wallace graduated in 1910 from Iowa State University in Ames with a degree in animal husbandry. After college he worked as a writer and editor on his father's magazine, *Wallaces' Farmer,* one of the most influential agricultural journals in the United States.

Despite his father's Republican affiliation, Wallace left the party during the late 1920s. Franklin Roosevelt appointed him secretary of agriculture in 1933. In 1940 a rift developed between Roosevelt and Vice President John Nance Garner that caused Roosevelt and other Democratic leaders to look for a new vice-presidential candidate. During Wallace's two terms as secretary of agriculture he had supported almost all of the president's programs. This loyalty and Wallace's popularity in farm states led Roosevelt to support him as Garner's replacement. Many Democrats, however, were suspicious of Wallace's liberalism and his unconventional personal philosophy, which was influenced by Eastern religions and mysticism. Nevertheless, Roosevelt insisted on Wallace, and he was nominated. The Democratic running mates easily defeated Republicans Wendell L. Willkie and Charles L. McNary by a vote of 449–82 in the Electoral College.

Wallace was an active vice president. He made goodwill tours of Latin America, China, and Soviet Asia, and headed the Board of Economic Warfare during World War II, becoming the only vice president ever to hold an administrative position. He also became an outspoken supporter of an internationalist post–World War II foreign policy in which the United States would cooperate closely with the Soviet Union and provide economic assistance to poor nations.

By 1944 Wallace's liberal views had alienated many Democratic leaders, who urged Roosevelt to drop him from the ticket. Roosevelt said he wanted to keep Wallace but would accept either Supreme Court justice William O. Douglas or Sen. Harry Truman of Missouri. This lukewarm endorsement ended Wallace's chances for a second term, and Truman was nominated instead. Roosevelt and Truman then defeated Thomas E. Dewey and William W. Bricker in the general election.

Even after being dropped from the ticket, Wallace campaigned hard for Roosevelt and Truman. Roosevelt rewarded him by naming him secretary of commerce in 1945. After Roosevelt died in April of that year, Wallace became concerned that President Truman would abandon Roosevelt's policy of friendship toward the Soviet Union. When Wallace spoke out against Truman's tough policy toward the Soviets in September 1946, Truman fired him.

On December 29, 1947, Wallace announced his intention to run for the presidency as the candidate of the Progressive Party. Wallace's candidacy hurt Truman's chances of being elected in 1948, because southern Democrats also had formed a separate party and nominated Sen. J. Strom Thurmond of South Carolina to run for president. The endorsement of Wallace by the American Communist Party, however, undercut his credibility. Wallace received barely more than 2 percent of the popular vote and no electoral votes, while Truman overcame the divisions within his party to win the election.

After his defeat Wallace retired to his farm in South Salem, New York. By 1952 Wallace's attitude toward the Soviet Union had undergone a transformation, and he published a book, *Why I Was Wrong*, to explain his new distrust of the Soviet Union.

More on this topic:

*Roosevelt, Franklin D.,
p. 445*

Vice President, p. 539

War of 1812

The War of 1812 between the United States and Great Britain was the first declared war in U.S. history. American sentiment for war with the British had been aroused by Britain's seizure of American commercial ships and their crews, charges that the British were supplying arms to hostile Indians on the frontier, and some Americans' desire to acquire foreign territory in Canada and Florida. The leading advocates of the war were members of Congress from the South and West. These "War Hawks" represented areas that were troubled by Indian attacks and falling agricultural prices. In contrast, the Federalist merchants of the Northeast, who were making large profits on export shipments that avoided capture, were against the war. They feared that war would interfere with trade much more than did sporadic British seizures of their ships.

Although President James Madison had tried to resolve disputes with the British diplomatically, he eventually was persuaded that the nation must go to war to protect its rights. On June 1, 1812, the president asked Congress for a declaration of war. Madison, like Thomas Jefferson, believed that Congress should decide whether the nation went to war. In his address to lawmakers asking for a declaration of war, Madison called war making a "solemn question which the Constitution wisely confides to the legislative department of the Government." The declaration was passed 79–49 by the House and 19–13 by the Senate. Members of Congress from the South and the West prevailed over their colleagues from the Northeast.

Published during the vicious presidential campaign of 1828, in which Andrew Jackson defeated incumbent John Quincy Adams, this political cartoon warned the voter: "Jackson is to be president and you will be hanged." It referred to various stiff disciplinary measures taken by "Old Hickory" when he was a general, particularly during the War of 1812.

The United States, however, was militarily unprepared. The small U.S. Navy was outmatched, and the army had difficulty recruiting volunteers. In the Northeast there was talk of secession, and the governors of Massachusetts, Rhode Island, and Connecticut refused to authorize the use of their state militias. The U.S. war effort was hampered by Madison's inability to unify the country and rally citizens behind a set of goals to be achieved by the war. After the war started, Congress even failed to appropriate a sufficient amount of money to fund the military.

U.S. forces suffered a string of humiliating defeats, including the capture of Washington, D.C., by the British in August 1814. A British force of fewer than five thousand troops moved unchecked up the Chesapeake Bay and marched with little resistance into the heart of Washington, burning the Capitol, the White House, the Navy Yard, and most other public buildings in the city.

After the British forces withdrew from the capital, Congress assembled to reconsider the war effort. Yet, with the army still below needed strength and enlistments falling off, Congress failed to agree on a conscription bill proposed by James Monroe, Madison's secretary of war and state. Fortunately, the Treaty of Ghent ending the war was signed on December 24, 1814. Before the news of the treaty reached New Orleans, however, Gen. Andrew Jackson's militia inflicted a stunning defeat on British regulars attacking the city on January 8, 1815. More than two thousand British troops were killed or wounded, while Jackson's force suffered only about forty casualties. This victory restored some of the nation's pride. The war had proven that a president's ability to wage a successful war depended on wide public support for the war and the cooperation of Congress.

> *Our enemy is powerful in men and in money, on the land and on the water. Availing himself of fortuitous advantages, he is aiming with his undivided force a deadly blow at our growing prosperity, perhaps at our national existence.*
>
> —*James Madison,* Sixth Annual Message, September 20, 1814

More on this topic:

Jackson, Andrew, p. 300

Madison, James, p. 350

War on Terrorism

In response to the terrorist attacks of September 11, 2001, on the United States, President George W. Bush announced that his administration would prosecute a comprehensive "war on terrorism." The commander in chief received immediate cooperation and support from Congress. With little debate or controversy, it passed a $40 billion emergency appropriation and a resolution authorizing the use of force against terrorist organizations and the nations that support them. Congress also passed a controversial counterterrorism bill that expanded the national government's powers of surveillance and detention. Reports of a sweeping intelligence order authorizing covert actions by the Central Intelligence Agency (CIA) against Osama bin Laden and the al Qaeda organization, with extraordinary cooperation between the CIA and military units, were not greeted with the usual suspicion and congressional investigations.

A war on terrorism raises questions about war powers: what exactly is the legal and constitutional status of this kind of conflict? And with whom, or what, is the nation at war? With the terrorists, or with the countries that assist them, or both?

To the world, Bush defined the sides in the conflict sharply: either you are with us or you are with the terrorists. When the Taliban government of Afghanistan refused to arrest the al Qaeda leadership and dismantle the al Qaeda training camps, it became the target of retaliation and antiterrorist operations. The U.S. operation in Afghanistan turned almost immediately to the defeat of the Afghan government, which brought the United States much closer to a formal war.

If the same reasoning and response were applied to other countries that harbor and finance terrorist organizations, a long-term military campaign against international terrorism could involve the United States in numerous conflicts that would be, in form and fact, wars.

In his January 2002 State of the Union address Bush took a step in this direction; he singled out Iraq, Iran, and North Korea for their development of weapons of mass destruction and support for international terrorism. He declared that the United States would vigorously oppose this "axis of evil." In the fall of 2002 Bush won congressional approval to use military force against Iraq and its leader, Saddam Hussein. The United Nations Security Council also acted in the fall of 2002, supporting tough weapons inspections in Iraq and effectively giving that country one last chance to disarm. On March 19, 2003, the United States, rejecting pleas from some UN countries to continue to support inspections and a diplomatic solution to the problem of Iraqi disarmament, began a military campaign against Iraq. Hussein's regime fell within three weeks, but soon afterward an insurgency movement sprang up in opposition to the American occupation. The violence continued into 2007, growing more complicated as domestic factions, split on religious grounds, began to battle for control of the American-sponsored democratic government. The continued presence of U.S. forces in Iraq became increasingly unpopular among the American people throughout 2005 and 2006 and was a major factor in the loss of both houses of Congress by the Republican Party in the 2006 midterm elections. In 2007 pressure began mounting for a withdrawal of U.S. forces and a renewed commitment to secure Afghanistan from a resurgent Taliban.

I can hear you. I can hear you. The rest of the world hears you. And the people who knocked these buildings down will hear all of us soon.

—*George W. Bush,* Remarks to Police, Firemen, and Rescue Workers at the World Trade Center Site in New York City, September 14, 2001

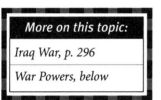

More on this topic:

Iraq War, p. 296

War Powers, below

War Powers

The framers of the Constitution distrusted both executive and military power and believed the potential for tyranny was great when the two were combined. The delegates to the Constitutional Convention were determined to restrain military power. Their main instrument for accomplishing this goal was the separation of powers. They therefore rejected a proposal to grant the president the authority to declare war and divided the war-making power between the executive and Congress.

Nevertheless, the framers were practical people who recognized that they must not cripple their young nation's ability to defend itself, especially against sudden attack. While many war powers, including the decision to go to war, could be given to Congress, command of U.S. forces during a conflict required the unified and flexible leadership that only a single person could provide. As Alexander Hamilton noted, "Of all the cares or concerns of government, the direction of war most peculiarly demands those qualities which distinguish the exercise of power by a single hand." The framers therefore assigned the power of commander in chief to the presidency and took comfort in the certainty that George Washington would be the first person to hold that office. Article II, Section 2, of the Constitution states: "The President shall be Commander in Chief of the Army and Navy of the United States, and of the Militia of the several States, when called into the actual Service of the United States." This statement is all the Constitution says about the president's war-making power.

Because the precise authority of the office of commander in chief was left undefined, presidents have been able to argue that they possess any power or duty traditionally associated with the office of supreme military commander, rather than just the single function of commanding the armed forces. Consequently, almost any action that improves the nation's defenses in peacetime or helps it prevail over an enemy in wartime without usurping the power of the other branches or violating the law can be justified under a broad interpretation of the commander-in-chief clause.

The framers did not, however, regard war making as a function to be dominated by the executive branch. In contrast to the single phrase designating the president as commander in chief, the clause outlining Congress's war powers is detailed and specific. Article I, Section 8, Clauses 11–16, of the Constitution grants Congress the authority:

> To declare War, grant Letters of Marque and Reprisal, and make Rules concerning Captures on Land and Water; To raise and support Armies …; To provide and maintain a Navy; To make Rules for the Government and Regulation of the land and naval Forces; To provide for calling forth the Militia to execute the Laws of the Union, suppress Insurrections and repel Invasions; To provide for organizing, arming and disciplining the Militia, and for governing such Part of them as may be employed in the Service of the United States, reserving to the States respectively, the Appointment of the Officers, and the Authority of training the Militia according to the discipline prescribed by Congress.

As Congress's enumerated war powers indicate, the framers intended Congress to have authority over the raising, equipping, and organizing of the armed forces; the president would direct the military in times of war. A president seeking to become a military dictator would be hindered by Congress's power to raise, equip, and organize an army and navy. Presidents might wish to fight a war, but without Congress's support they would lack the necessary tools to do so. Conversely, Congress's ability to legislate a war would be restricted by the president's command of the military during hostilities and authority to negotiate treaties.

Power to Declare and End War

Although Congress's power to raise armies and fund wars and the president's command of the military in times of war are unquestioned, the authority over the decision of when and where to employ military force has been the subject of conflict between the executive and legislative branches.

By giving Congress the power to declare war, the framers sought to ensure that the decision to risk American lives in the defense of the United States or in pursuit of its perceived interests would be made by the democratically elected representatives closest to the people who would be called upon to fight and die.

Despite the hundreds of military actions by U.S. troops overseas, Congress has made a formal declaration of war only five times:

- The War of 1812 against Great Britain
- The Mexican-American War in 1846
- The Spanish-American War in 1898
- World War I in 1917
- World War II in 1941

The delegates to the Constitutional Convention, however, did not expect Congress to authorize every use of military force. They knew that speed and secrecy, which only a single decision maker could provide, were essential to the safety of the nation if it came under attack.

The constitutional distribution of authority over the decision to go to war seems clear. Congress decides when to go to war unless the United States is attacked, in which case the president defends the nation. Yet this simple formula is full of ambiguities. How is war to be defined? Are there military missions short of war that the president can order without congressional authorization? May the president order an attack to preempt an assault from a potential enemy? May the president order U.S. forces to invade the territory of a neutral nation in pursuit of enemy forces? May the president incite an attack through actions that a potential enemy will regard as provocative? The legislative and executive branches were left to battle over these and other ambiguities of war powers. When presidents have believed that a war or military action was necessary, they usually have found ways to maneuver the nation into a conflict.

As commander in chief, presidents have the power to order the military to stop fighting or to withdraw from an area of conflict. In addition, their sole authority to negotiate treaties gives them the power to conclude an armistice with an enemy. If Congress has declared war, however, the president cannot unilaterally end the legal state of war that exists. Congress must take some action that overturns its declaration of war. Usually this action is accomplished through Senate ratification of a treaty negotiated by the president ending the war and establishing peaceful relations with the enemy nation. Congress also may formally end a state of war by repealing its declaration of war.

On December 7, 1941, the Japanese launched a surprise attack against the U.S. fleet at Pearl Harbor, Hawaii. The next day President Roosevelt asked for and received a declaration of war from Congress. Wearing a black armband for those killed, FDR holds the signed documents.
Source: Library of Congress

After the September 11, 2001, terrorist attacks on the United States, President George W. Bush faced a new kind of war, a WAR ON TERRORISM. This effort, as well as the ongoing U.S. military campaign in Iraq, raised new questions about definitions of war and enemies. (See also IRAQ WAR.)

Development of Presidential War Powers

The Civil War, World War I, and World War II demonstrated that a strong president willing to interpret the commander-in-chief power broadly is in the best position to lead the military, unite the American people, and focus the efforts of the nation on victory when war threatens its security.

The Constitution's assignment of the office of commander in chief to the president created the basis for presidential war powers, but a more precise outline of these powers had to evolve through events. Most early presidents held a narrow view of their role as commander in chief, similar to Hamilton's description of the president as the nation's "first general or admiral." Gradually, however, the commander-in-chief power grew. The Civil War and the two world wars provided the most dramatic boosts to presidential authority.

Presidential war powers expanded during these national security emergencies because the flexibility, secrecy, speed, and unity of command associated with the president were seen as crucial to the defense of the United States. According to political scientist Edward S. Corwin, "The principal canons of constitutional interpretation are in wartime set aside so far as concerns both the scope of national power and the capacity of the President to gather unto himself all constitutionally available powers in order the more effectively to focus them upon the task of the hour." Presidential actions that would have raised a storm of protest in peacetime were accepted in the name of necessity when the security of the nation was at stake.

This is not to say that when wartime emergencies were over presidents continued to wield great power as if an emergency still existed. Rather, every extension of presidential power set a precedent to which a future president could refer when an emergency of similar gravity appeared. Woodrow Wilson's expansion of presidential war power paved the way for Franklin D. Roosevelt's extraordinary wartime authority, just as Wilson had referred to Lincoln's exercise of power to justify his own.

Until late in the Vietnam War, the expansion of the president's war powers usually had been accomplished with Congress's approval and often with its active support. Congress validated many of Lincoln's actions, passed legislation delegating sweeping wartime powers to both Wilson and Franklin Roosevelt, and acquiesced in the accumulation of power by presidents after World War II. Although the Supreme Court has occasionally ruled against exercises of presidential war power, it seldom has done so when a war was in progress and often has refused to disapprove presidential actions on the grounds that they are political matters that should be resolved between the executive and legislative branches. Moreover, as the Court's approval of the internment of Americans of Japanese descent during World War II demonstrates, the Court has recognized the authority of the president acting in concert with Congress to take virtually any action in response to a grave national emergency.

After World War II, differences between the United States and the Soviet Union brought on the cold war, a state of continuous international tension that contributed to increased presidential control over national security policy. The specter of an aggressive Soviet Union pushing out wherever the West failed to resist made Congress reluctant to impose restrictions on executive action. A consensus developed that because presidents had both the capacity to act immediately and access to the most detailed and reliable information, they alone were suited to direct foreign and military policy. Their status as leaders of the free world and caretakers of the U.S. nuclear arsenal, the most devastating military force ever built, contributed to their unchallenged authority.

Presidential commander-in-chief authority continued to expand until the late 1960s and early 1970s, when Congress reacted to the executive branch's abuses of power by attempting to reassert its role in national security affairs. Although the executive branch still dominates national security policy, Congress has scrutinized national security affairs closely and has been able to restrict presidential policies on a variety of issues, including funding for selected weapons systems and military aid to allied nations and guerrilla organizations.

In 1973 Congress enacted the WAR POWERS ACT over the veto of President Richard Nixon. The act attempts to set a sixty-day limit on any presidential commitment of U.S. troops to hostilities abroad, or to situations where hostilities might be imminent, without specific congressional authorization.

Military Commander

The commander-in-chief clause gives presidents clear authority to command the military as the nation's first general and admiral. Presidents order troops into battle, approve major strategic decisions, and keep a watchful eye on the progress of any military campaign. Most presidents since World War II have even regarded specific tactical decisions related to certain military operations to be among their responsibilities as commander in chief.

In making the president the commander in chief, the framers attempted to ensure that civilian authority would always direct the armed forces. Military leaders who might use their authority over the army and navy to accumulate political power or enhance their personal reputation would be subordinate to the president, who was elected by the entire country and was responsible for the welfare of all the people. Designating the president as commander in chief also aided effective military leadership by establishing a single leader at the top of the military hierarchy.

The degree to which presidents have become involved in the direction of military operations has varied according to their own military expertise and the circumstances of the military situation. Once troops have been committed to battle, presidents usually have delegated authority for battlefield strategy to their generals and admirals. The Constitution, however, does not prohibit a president from taking direct command of troops in the field.

The tendency of presidents to become involved in planning the details of military actions increased with the advent of the nuclear age. Nuclear weapons created an environment of constant danger in which any use of U.S. armed forces could escalate into a global nuclear confrontation. Consequently, modern presidents have seldom been willing to order a military operation without personally overseeing its execution.

Sophisticated communication technologies also have contributed to presidential involvement in military operations by facilitating contact between the president and local military commanders. For example, in April 1988 the pilot of a navy aircraft patrolling the Persian Gulf observed Iranian gunboats attacking a set of oil rigs. Because U.S. forces in the Persian Gulf were authorized to respond to attacks only on American aircraft, ships, and facilities, the pilot radioed his aircraft carrier for permission to attack the Iranian vessels. The pilot's request was transmitted up the chain of command from the aircraft carrier commander to the admiral in charge of the naval task force. Then the request was relayed via satellite through the chief of the U.S. Central Command in Florida to the chairman of the Joint Chiefs of Staff and the secretary of defense at the Pentagon, who called President Ronald Reagan. The president authorized U.S. planes to bomb the Iranian gunboats, and the order was relayed back through the chain of command to navy pilots, who moved to attack only three minutes after permission had been requested.

Command of Nuclear Weapons

Despite the unlikely prospect of a modern president ever leading U.S. troops into battle, the realities of nuclear warfare have made the president the nation's "first soldier." The decision to use nuclear weapons or to delegate the authority to use them to local military commanders is entirely the president's. Presidential authority over the nation's nuclear arsenal is derived from the commander-in-chief power and the need to make the decision to use nuclear weapons with speed and secrecy.

A decision that has to be made so quickly must be assigned to a single individual with indisputable authority. The nature of nuclear weapons, which can be delivered with little warning, requires presidential control over them.

In theory, a first-strike nuclear attack by the United States against another nation would be illegal without a congressional declaration of war, because such an attack would be an initiation of hostilities on an unprecedented scale. Few observers, however, believe there is a significant chance that a U.S. president would purposely order a nuclear strike unless the United States, U.S. forces, or close U.S. allies were under a nuclear or massive conventional attack. Consequently, most scenarios for the use of nuclear weapons by the president without congressional approval can be justified on the grounds that the president is responsible for defending the United States.

Regardless of the nuclear decision-making role to which Congress might be entitled under a strict interpretation of the Constitution, the demands of secrecy and speed that accompany crisis decision making in the nuclear age disqualify Congress from taking part in decisions to use nuclear weapons, except through consultation in advance of potential crises. No president could tentatively make the decision to launch nuclear weapons, then present the plan to Congress for approval. Command over nuclear weapons, therefore, gives the president the actual power to destroy the world. Yet if a president ordered a surprise nuclear attack during peacetime when no crisis existed, it is likely that such an order would be questioned and resisted by civilian and military advisers.

President as Defense Manager

Before World War II the United States maintained a small peacetime defense establishment. The isolation and size of the nation rendered it nearly immune to serious invasions by the armies of Europe. This geographic advantage and the early antimilitaristic tradition of the United States

worked against the maintenance of large standing armies. When the United States found itself in a war, it mobilized troops until the war was over, after which the armed forces demobilized.

After World War II a national consensus developed that the United States should adopt an internationalist defense policy designed to contain the expansion of communism and block the military strength of the Soviet Union. The expanded defense commitments of the United States and its rivalry with the Soviet Union caused the United States to maintain for the first time in its history a huge peacetime military establishment.

> *No President wants to be a war President, but I am one. Not because the United States chose war, but because an enemy chose to attack us.*
>
> *—George W. Bush, Remarks at a Luncheon for Congressional Candidate Jeff Lamberti and Iowa Victory 2006 in Des Moines, Iowa, October 26, 2006*

Although the Constitution gives Congress the complete authority to raise and equip an army and navy, much of the task of administering the defense bureaucracy and maintaining the nation's defenses in the post–World War II era has been delegated to or assumed by the president and the executive branch. The growth in the size and activities of the military and the perception that nuclear weapons and the cold war had created a condition of constant emergency combined to legitimize the president's role as defense manager. Presidents function not just as the commander in chief in wartime but also as the manager of the routine operations and preparations of the military in peacetime.

More on this topic:

Iraq War, p. 296

Nuclear Command Procedures, p. 391

Vietnam War, p. 546

War on Terrorism, p. 554

War Powers Act of 1973, below

Presidents and their advisers prepare the defense budget, formulate military personnel and recruitment policy, oversee the development and purchase of new weapons, and manage the deployment of forces around the globe. Congress must ratify these policies through legislative and budgetary powers, but the executive branch dominates military policy.

War Powers Act of 1973

In November 1973 Congress passed the War Powers Act over President Richard Nixon's veto. The law attempted to limit the president's power to deploy and maintain U.S. forces in an area of hostilities without congressional consent. Congress was motivated to pass the law by the presidential actions that had committed the United States to the war in Vietnam.

The passage of the Tonkin Gulf Resolution in 1964 with only two senators dissenting and Congress's continuing approval of presidential budget and troop requests allowed the administrations of Lyndon B. Johnson and Richard Nixon to pursue a costly war. The results of the Vietnam War belied the assumption that the executive branch, with its superior intelligence resources, its unity of command, and its ability to act quickly, should decide when and how the nation should go to war. With passage of the War Powers Act, Congress attempted to ensure that it would have a decision-making role in matters of war and peace. The bill's preamble stated that its purpose was "to fulfill the intent of the framers of the Constitution of the United States and ensure that the collective judgement of both the Congress and the President will apply to the introduction of U.S. armed forces into hostilities, wherein situations where imminent involvement in hostilities is clearly indicated by the circumstances, and the continued use of such forces in hostilities or in such situations."

The most important and controversial provisions of the legislation outlined the situations under which presidents could commit troops, permitted Congress at any time by a majority vote of both houses to order the president to disengage troops involved in an undeclared war, and required presents to withdraw armed forces from a conflict within sixty days—ninety if the president certified that further military action was necessary to disengage U.S. military personnel from a conflict safely—unless Congress specifically authorized its continuation. The act also urged the president to consult with Congress "in every possible instance" before ordering U.S. forces into hostilities or into a situation where hostilities might be imminent.

Passage of the bill was heralded by its supporters as a major step in reasserting Congress's war-making powers. On October 24, 1973, President Nixon vetoed the bill, saying that it violated the Constitution because it placed unconstitutional restrictions on the flexibility of the president to defend the United States and that it was not in the best interests of the nation. On November 7, the House, by a vote of 284–135, and Senate, by a vote of 75–18, overrode the president's veto. The override was made possible in part by the Watergate affair, which had weakened Nixon's support in Congress.

Since the passage of the War Powers Act, presidents have used military force on many occasions. Several of these actions, such as President Gerald R. Ford's evacuation of Saigon, Danang, and Phnom Penh in 1975, were uncontroversial and received the general approval of Congress. In most of the military operations undertaken since 1973, however, presidents have violated at least the spirit of the law and committed the military to hostilities with no or minimal consultation of Congress. Indeed, since passage of the act in 1973, neither congressional action nor the automatic sixty- to ninety-day time limit has forced a president to disengage U.S. troops from a conflict.

Critics of the act have continued to question its constitutionality. Presidents generally have appeared undaunted by the act's potential to limit their use of U.S. armed forces. During Ronald Reagan's deployment of marines in Lebanon in 1982 and 1983, the prospect of the use of the War Powers Act resulted in a formal compromise between the legislative and executive branches on the limits of a military operation. Yet, even in this case the compromise favored the president, and it had little effect on his eventual decision to withdraw the troops. In January 1991 President George H. W. Bush asked for congressional support for his effort to drive the Iraqis out of Kuwait. Congress explicitly "authorized" offensive action under the War Powers Act while limiting that action to the terms of a UN Security Council resolution authorizing UN members to use all necessary means to restore the sovereignty of Kuwait. Bush, however, denied the validity of the War Powers Act and denied that congressional authorization was constitutionally required.

> **Consistent with the War Powers Resolution, I now inform you that pursuant to my authority as Commander in Chief, I directed U.S. Armed Forces to commence combat operations on January 16, 1991, against Iraqi forces and military targets in Iraq and Kuwait.**
>
> **—George H. W. Bush,** Letter to Congressional Leaders on the Persian Gulf Conflict, January 18, 1991

During Bill Clinton's first year in office the debate over war powers was renewed, as the White House and Congress clashed over U.S. policy toward global trouble spots. Much of the criticism arose from the operation in Somalia to relieve a famine caused mainly by a civil war. Six months after Clinton's inauguration, twenty-three UN peacekeepers were killed by one of the warring factions. As a result, U.S. warplanes and troops were involved in a retaliatory strike. The UN, with Clinton's approval, then shifted its mission to one of subduing the armed factions and rebuilding the nation's political order. In October 1993 eighteen U.S. Rangers were killed and eighty were wounded in an assault on one such faction. The new UN policy raised the possibility of extensive U.S. action and potential losses in an area remote from the nation's interests. Clinton's policies were battered, but his war powers remained intact. In the aftermath, congressional leaders initiated a review of Congress's role in committing U.S. troops abroad. Most lawmakers agreed that the War Powers Act was badly flawed and unworkable, but they could reach no consensus on what to do about it. The Clinton administration also had to deal with Congress on the question of sending troops to the Balkans. In 1999 a federal judge dismissed a lawsuit filed against Clinton by a group of congressional lawmakers who charged the president with having violated the War Powers Act by continuing a U.S. bombing campaign in Yugoslavia. The case made its way to the Supreme Court, which in 2000 ruled against the lawmakers.

For the George W. Bush administration, war with Iraq loomed as a major question in 2002 and early 2003. In the fall of 2002, Bush sought, and eventually received, congressional authorization to use military force against Saddam Hussein's regime. Also that fall, the UN Security Council voted unanimously for tough weapons inspections against Iraq, in effect giving the regime of Iraqi leader Saddam Hussein a last chance to disarm. By early 2003, however, the Bush administration faced difficulties in convincing the UN of the need for quick military action against Iraq; some countries preferred to give the weapons inspectors more time. In March 2003, after dismissing pleas for more time for inspections and widespread protests from some major powers and allies such as France, Russia, and China, and other countries, President Bush authorized the initiation of a U.S. military campaign against Iraq. In early 2007, by which time the war in Iraq had continued for almost four years and the Democratic Party had gained control over both houses of Congress in the 2006 midterm elections, pressure began to mount on the Bush administration to find an expedient way to end U.S. troop commitments in Iraq. Many members of Congress began to suggest that the original authorization for war could be rescinded, creating the potential for a showdown between the president and Congress over the issue of war powers.

More on this topic:

Tonkin Gulf Resolution, p. 505

Vietnam War, p. 546

War Powers, p. 555

Warren Commission

On November 22, 1963, President John F. Kennedy was assassinated in Dallas, Texas. Police quickly arrested Lee Harvey Oswald and charged him with the crime. Preliminary investigations determined that Oswald had shot the president with a rifle from a window of the Texas School Book Depository building as Kennedy drove through Dallas in a motorcade. Two days later, on November 24, Jack Ruby, a Dallas nightclub owner, shot Oswald to death as he was being transferred from one Dallas jail to another.

Confusing physical evidence, Oswald's murder, and other suspicious facts raised the possibility that a conspiracy was responsible for Kennedy's assassination. On November 29 President Lyndon B. Johnson appointed Chief Justice Earl Warren head of a commission charged with determining the truth about the assassination. The President's Commission on the Assassination of President Kennedy became known as the Warren Commission. Johnson selected Warren carefully, noting in his memoirs that Warren's "personal integrity" would assure a credible conclusion.

The Warren Commission was given a staff of twenty-seven. In addition to Warren, the other members of the commission were Sen. Richard B. Russell of Georgia; Sen. John Sherman Cooper of Kentucky; Rep. Hale Boggs of Louisiana; Rep. Gerald R. Ford of Michigan; Allen W. Dulles, former director of the Central Intelligence Agency (CIA); and John J. McCloy, former president of the World Bank and adviser to Kennedy.

The commission and its staff reviewed reports by the Federal Bureau of Investigation (FBI) and other law enforcement agencies. In addition to its private meetings, the commission heard directly from 94 witnesses in closed testimony. Its legal staff heard testimony from 395 others and received 61 sworn affidavits.

One of the suspicious circumstances of the assassination was that several shots were fired at the president in a very short time. It was theoretically possible for Oswald to have done all the shooting, but such marksmanship seemed to some investigators to be beyond his abilities. In addition, the angles of the bullet wounds suggested to some that a second assassin must have participated in the shooting.

Throughout the investigatory process, the Warren Commission found itself divided on whether President Kennedy and Texas governor John B. Connally (who also was shot in the attack) were hit by the same bullet. If they were not, it was much more likely that a second assassin had fired a shot or shots.

The bipartisan presidential commission appointed to investigate John F. Kennedy's assassination held its first meeting December 5, 1963, just two weeks after the event. Pictured (left to right) are Allen W. Dulles, Rep. Hale Boggs of Louisiana, Sen. John Sherman Cooper of Kentucky, Chief Justice Earl Warren, Sen. Richard Russell of Georgia, John J. McCloy, and Rep. Gerald R. Ford of Michigan.
Source: AP

Because the commission remained divided up to its final days, some chapters of the final report of the Warren Commission went through as many as twenty drafts. Finally, in seeking unanimity, the commission entered into a debate over adjectives. One commissioner wanted the report to state that there was *compelling* evidence that the same bullet had hit both Kennedy and Connally. The commission finally compromised on the adjective *persuasive*.

In its final report, which was presented to Johnson on September 24, 1964, the commission unanimously concluded that Lee Harvey Oswald was the sole assassin and dismissed the possibility that he was part of a wider conspiracy. The report asserted that the commission had investigated and disproved twenty-two myths and rumors concerning such things as the number, origin, and direction of the shots; the number of assassins; and the possible connections between Oswald and the FBI, the CIA, and the Soviet and Cuban governments. The commission failed to identify Oswald's motive, but cited his unstable and hostile personality as a factor. The report criticized the FBI and the Secret Service for inadequately protecting the president and for poorly coordinating their information.

Over time the Warren Report aroused great public controversy. Critics have charged that films of the incident, autopsy photographs, and x-rays contradict the commission's findings. Many contend that the Warren Commission did not look deeply enough into the possibility that the Soviets, the Cubans, U.S. intelligence agencies, organized crime, or several other groups could have planned and carried out the assassination. To deflate the many conspiracy theories, which were rekindled by the 1991 movie *JFK*, a law was enacted in 1992 to create a commission to review and make public documents related to the assassination and investigations.

More on this topic:

Assassinations and Assaults, p. 19

Commissions, Presidential, p. 110

Kennedy, John F., p. 318

Zapruder Film, p. 593

Washington, George

Source: Library of Congress

George Washington (1732–1799) was the first president of the United States and the leading figure of the American Revolution. He led the new nation through many of its early trials, and his actions during his eight years as president established numerous precedents that gave shape to the office of the presidency.

Washington was born on February 22, 1732, in Westmoreland County, Virginia, to a wealthy family that owned several plantations. He was tutored and attended school on an irregular basis from ages seven to fifteen, but had no formal education beyond grammar school. By the time he reached his early teens he was already a skilled woodsman, tobacco planter, and surveyor.

Washington began a frontier military career in 1753 as a major in the Virginia militia. In 1755 he was appointed aide-de-camp to Maj. Gen. Edward Braddock. After several years of service in the French and Indian War in which he achieved the rank of colonel, Washington resigned in 1758 to run for the Virginia House of Burgesses. He served there for nine years.

Washington married Martha Dandridge Custis on January 6, 1759. She was a wealthy widow, who added fifteen thousand acres to Washington's estate.

Revolutionary War

As tensions mounted between Great Britain and the colonies, Washington became deeply involved in the patriot cause. In 1774 he attended the First Continental Convention in Philadelphia as a delegate from Virginia. Afterward, he returned to Virginia and began training militia forces using his own money. On June 16, 1775, he accepted a commission from the Second Continental Convention as the commanding general of the Continental army.

As a general, Washington's inspirational and administrative abilities were more notable than his military knowledge. He made several tactical blunders during the war, including the deployment of part of his army in an exposed position on Long Island in 1776, which resulted in the loss of five thousand troops and the British capture of New York City. Despite his lack of experience in commanding large forces, Washington showed flashes of strategic brilliance. His army won celebrated triumphs at Boston, Trenton, Princeton, and Yorktown. Nevertheless, Washington's skill at inspiring loyalty and holding his army together, as exemplified during the harsh winter of 1777–1778 at Valley Forge, Pennsylvania, was more important to the success of the revolution than his tactical abilities.

After the defeat of the British at Yorktown in 1781, discontent within the Continental army became the biggest threat to the young nation. Many soldiers believed that Congress had not paid them adequately. In May 1782 Washington angrily rejected a proposal by one of his officers that he allow himself to be crowned king.

In March 1783 a more serious threat to republican government emerged. Many officers were considering using the army to depose Congress and set up their own government. Washington addressed an assembly of his officers on March 15 in Newburgh, New York, and persuaded them to give up their plan and support Congress.

With the war officially ended by the Treaty of Paris, signed on September 3, 1783, Washington retired to Mount Vernon, his Virginia estate. He managed his plantation until 1787, when he agreed to accept an appointment as one of Virginia's delegates to the Constitutional Convention in Philadelphia. His presence lent legitimacy to the convention, and its delegates unanimously elected him presiding officer. After a long summer of debate during which Washington said little, the convention agreed on a new Constitution. Washington and his fellow delegates signed the document on September 17, 1787.

Presidency

Washington was the inevitable choice of his nation to be the first president under the new Constitution. He alone had the reputation needed to transcend sectional and ideological conflicts. In early 1789 presidential electors unanimously elected Washington president. After a triumphant overland journey from Mount Vernon to New York City, Washington took the oath of office on April 30, 1789.

During Washington's first term Congress passed the Bill of Rights, and the states that had not yet ratified the Constitution did so. In an attempt to inspire confidence in the federal government and to establish a spirit of national unity, Washington toured the northern states in late 1789 and the southern states in the spring of 1791. Mindful of the problems caused by the weakness of the federal government under the Articles of Confederation, Washington was careful throughout his presidency to assert the primacy of the federal government over the states.

Washington was usually deferential toward Congress; for example, he believed that the president should veto a bill only if it was unconstitutional. He often made decisions after listening to his two most important and eloquent advisers, Secretary of State Thomas Jefferson and Secretary of the Treasury Alexander Hamilton, debate an issue. Although Washington tried to be impartial, he usually agreed with Hamilton on important issues. In particular, he backed Hamilton's plans to have the federal government assume the wartime debts of the states and to establish a national bank. After much debate Congress passed both measures. Washington signed the debt assumption bill in 1790 and the bank bill in 1791.

Washington's primary goal in foreign policy was to maintain the neutrality of the United States in the war between France and Great Britain, which began in 1793. He believed that the new nation had to avoid entangling alliances if it was to survive. Jefferson urged that the United States aid France, which had helped the colonies to defeat the British in the Revolutionary War, but Washington rejected his counsel. The president issued a neutrality proclamation on April 22, 1793, which declared that the United States would be "friendly and impartial" toward the belligerents. At the end of 1793 Jefferson resigned over his disputes with Washington. The next year Congress passed the Neutrality Act of 1794, which endorsed Washington's policy. In 1795 Washington signed the Jay Treaty with Great Britain. The agreement, which had been negotiated in London by Chief Justice John Jay, increased commerce between the two nations and settled several disputes. The treaty was highly unpopular, however, with pro-French Democratic-Republicans.

During his presidency Washington strove to avoid partisan politics, because he believed that political factions could destroy the unity of the nation. In his famous Farewell Address published on September 17, 1796, he cautioned against partisanship as well as foreign influence and permanent alliances. Despite his efforts to prevent the development of parties, before his presidency

It is our true policy to steer clear of permanent alliances with any portion of the foreign world, so far, I mean, as we are now at liberty to do it.

—**George Washington,** Farewell Address, September 17, 1796

More on this topic:

Congress and the
Presidency, p. 111

Diplomatic Powers,
p. 149

Farewell Addresses, p. 210

Neutrality Proclamation
of 1793, p. 382

Term of Office, p. 495

Whiskey Rebellion, p. 572

ended, two factions had already emerged in American politics: the Federalists, with whom Washington most closely identified, led by Alexander Hamilton and Vice President John Adams, and the Democratic-Republicans, led by Thomas Jefferson and House member James Madison.

In 1796 Washington refused to consider running for a third term. He spent the last years of his life managing his estate and entertaining friends. In 1799, when war seemed imminent with France, President John Adams asked Washington to become lieutenant general and commander in chief of the army. Washington accepted on the condition that he would not have to take active command of the forces except in an emergency. War with France was averted, and Washington's retirement was not disturbed. On December 12, 1799, after riding about his estate on a cold day, he suddenly fell ill, probably with pneumonia. His condition deteriorated rapidly, and he died on December 14 at Mount Vernon.

Washington, Martha

Martha Washington.
Source: National Portrait Gallery

Martha Dandridge Custis Washington (1731–1802) was the wife of George Washington and the first "first lady" of the United States. Her father was a small plantation owner and member of the Virginia aristocracy. Martha was schooled in the social graces but apparently had little formal education.

In 1749 Martha met and married Col. Daniel Parke Custis, son of a wealthy Virginia planter. Custis, by whom Martha had four children (two of whom died in infancy), was twice her age. He died in November 1756, leaving a considerable estate to Martha that made her very wealthy.

George Washington probably had met Martha before her husband's death. Shortly afterward he came to pay his respects to the widow. Courtship followed, and although many historians have argued that she was not Washington's first love, the pair married in 1759. Martha added her estate to George's plantation, Mount Vernon, where the Washingtons lived. The years until 1775 were spent tending to the plantation. The couple produced no children of their own.

With the onset of the American Revolution in 1775, George left Mount Vernon to lead the American army. Martha spent the summers of the war at Mount Vernon, but each winter, when the armies paused in their struggle, she joined her husband in camp.

After George became president in 1789 Martha moved with him to New York, the temporary capital of the new nation. She found her life as first lady (although the term did not yet exist) to be restrictive: "I live a very dull life here.... I think I am more like a state prisoner than anything else."

Martha was a pleasant and engaging hostess who generally enjoyed entertaining. As the initial first lady, she set precedents followed by her successors, such as the regular Friday afternoon parties for ladies and the custom of opening the White House to all visitors on New Year's Day. The latter practice survived until it was discontinued by the Hoovers in 1931.

George and Martha retired to Mount Vernon in 1797. "Lady Washington" lived quietly at her home until her death on May 22, 1802. She was buried on the plantation's grounds next to George, who had died two and a half years earlier.

More on this topic:

First Ladies, p. 219

Washington, George, p. 564

Watergate Affair

Bob Woodward, left, and Carl Bernstein, Washington Post *reporters, broke many of the Watergate stories that eventually led to President Nixon's resignation on August 9, 1974.*
Source: Washington Post

The Watergate affair was perhaps the greatest political scandal in U.S. history. It severely damaged the American public's confidence in government and led to the conviction of many top government officials and the resignation of President Richard Nixon under the threat of imminent impeachment.

The Burglary

The scandal is named for a prominent apartment-office-hotel complex in Washington, D.C., that housed the offices of the Democratic National Committee (DNC) in 1972. At 2:30 a.m. on June 17 of that year, District of Columbia police caught five men in the act of burglarizing the DNC offices. The burglars carried walkie-talkies and photographic and electronic eavesdropping equipment. It later was disclosed that, among other things, they intended to replace a faulty tap on the telephone of the Democratic Party's national chairman, Lawrence F. O'Brien, and install a bugging device nearby.

Four of the burglars became known as "the Cubans." They were Bernard L. Barker, Virgilio R. Gonzalez, Eugenio R. Martinez, and Frank Sturgis, all from Miami and identified with Cuban groups bitterly opposed to Fidel Castro, the communist leader of Cuba. They had ties to the Central Intelligence Agency (CIA), as did the fifth burglar, James W. McCord Jr. He was a former agent of the CIA and the Federal Bureau of Investigation (FBI). At the time of the burglary he was the director of security for the Committee to Re-Elect the President, Nixon's campaign organization, known by some as CRP or CREEP. Two others were later linked to the burglary: E. Howard Hunt, a former CIA agent who was working as a consultant to the White House, and G. Gordon Liddy, a former FBI agent who was working for CREEP.

The Cover-up

The Nixon administration and reelection campaign immediately denied any knowledge of or involvement in the break-in. John N. Mitchell, who had served as Nixon's attorney general from

1969 until he resigned in 1972 to manage Nixon's reelection campaign, claimed the day after the burglary, "McCord and the other four men arrested in Democratic headquarters Saturday were not operating on our behalf or with our consent in the alleged bugging." Ronald L. Ziegler, the White House press secretary, dismissed the break-in as a "third-rate burglary." At a press conference on June 22 Nixon said, "This kind of activity … has no place in the electoral process. And, as Mr. Ziegler has stated, the White House has no involvement whatever in this particular incident." In November Nixon was overwhelmingly reelected; few voters paid much attention to the Watergate burglary.

Hunt, Liddy, and the five burglars were convicted on charges of burglary, conspiracy, and illegal wiretapping on January 30, 1973, in U.S. District Court in Washington, D.C. Presiding over the trial was Judge John J. Sirica, who maintained throughout the proceedings that he believed the burglary conspiracy went beyond the seven defendants. By early 1973 investigative articles begun in 1972 by *Washington Post* reporters Bob Woodward and Carl Bernstein were focusing public attention on the Watergate burglary, its origins, and its aftermath. Reacting to the continuing emergence of disturbing details related to the Watergate break-in and investigation, the Senate on February 7, 1973, voted unanimously to establish the Select Committee on Presidential Campaign Activities. The committee was charged with investigating the "unethical activities" that occurred during the 1972 campaign and election.

On March 23 Sirica released a letter from McCord in which McCord stated that senior officials in CREEP and the White House were involved in the burglary, that the defendants had been pressured to plead guilty, and that perjury had been committed at the trial.

In an address on April 30, 1973, the president accepted "responsibility" for the Watergate events but denied any advance knowledge of them or involvement in their cover-up. Two of the president's closest aides, H. R. Haldeman and John D. Ehrlichman, were forced to resign because of their involvement in the widening pattern of political sabotage and cover-up that was being revealed by the Watergate investigations. Nixon directed the new attorney general, Elliot Richardson, to appoint an independent counsel to investigate Watergate. Richardson chose Archibald Cox, a Harvard University law professor who had served in the Kennedy and Johnson administrations.

The Watergate Hearings

During the summer of 1973 the nationally telecast Senate Watergate hearings revealed to the American public the sordid details of the administration's misconduct, and public support for the president began to erode. John W. Dean III, who had served as White House counsel until he was fired on April 30, 1973, delivered five days of testimony beginning on June 25. Dean became the first witness to publicly accuse the president of direct involvement in the cover-up. Dean charged, among other things, that Nixon had approved clemency offers for the Watergate defendants and that he knew of attempts to pay them in return for their silence.

Nixon repeatedly professed ignorance of CREEP and White House involvement in Watergate, but his claims were contradicted by testimony in the criminal trials of his associates, in investigations by the Senate Watergate committee (chaired by Sen. Sam Ervin of North Carolina), and in staff studies by the House Judiciary Committee. Testimony revealed the existence of a special White House investigative unit known as the "Plumbers," which used tactics such as harassment to "plug leaks" in the administration.

The Watergate scandal weakened the power of the presidency and brought a resurgence of congressional power. In the midst of the Watergate hearings Congress passed the WAR POWERS ACT OF 1973, designed to limit the executive's ability to exercise war-making powers unilaterally, without the knowledge or consent of Congress. Although Nixon vetoed the bill, Congress overrode the veto.

The Tapes

Despite Dean's testimony and mounting evidence that large-scale wrongdoing had been committed by the Nixon administration, there was no hard evidence that the president had been involved in the cover-up of Watergate. On July 16, 1973, however, Alexander Butterfield, a former White House aide, revealed that a secret taping system, intended to preserve all presidential conversations for posterity, had been installed in the Oval Office and other presidential offices. The tapes presumably could confirm Dean's allegations. Late in July the U.S. District Court decided unanimously that the president should turn over sixty-four tapes of White House conversations that independent counsel Cox had sought to subpoena.

Nixon objected, claiming that he did not have to turn the tapes over because of EXECUTIVE PRIVILEGE. This concept holds that the private conversations and deliberations of the executive branch should not be subject to the scrutiny of the other branches of government. The administration appealed the decision to the U.S. Court of Appeals, but that court upheld the ruling directing Nixon to surrender the tapes. The president then offered Cox a compromise—he would provide transcripts of certain tapes if Cox agreed not to subpoena additional tapes or documents. Cox rejected the compromise offer. On Saturday, October 20, 1973, Nixon directed Attorney General Richardson to fire Cox, but Richardson refused and also resigned. Deputy Attorney General William Ruckelshaus also chose to resign rather than carry out the order. Finally, the third-ranking Justice Department official, Solicitor General Robert H. Bork, acting as attorney general, fired Cox. This sequence of events, which became known as the "Saturday night massacre," prompted swift adverse public reaction and a movement in Congress to impeach Nixon. In February 1974 the House Judiciary Committee began to hold hearings on possible impeachment charges.

Cox's successor, Leon Jaworski, continued to vigorously prosecute the Watergate conspirators. On March 1, 1974, the Watergate grand jury indicted top Nixon aides H.R. Haldeman, John Ehrlichman, John Mitchell, and Charles Colson on charges of conspiring to cover up Watergate. All four were later convicted and spent time in prison. The grand jury named Nixon as an unindicted co-conspirator.

> *To continue to fight through the months ahead for my personal vindication would almost totally absorb the time and attention of both the President and the Congress in a period when our entire focus should be on the great issues of peace abroad and prosperity without inflation at home. Therefore, I shall resign the Presidency effective at noon tomorrow. Vice President Ford will be sworn in as President at that hour in this office.*
>
> *—Richard Nixon, Address to the Nation Announcing Decision to Resign the Office of President of the United States, August 8, 1974*

United States v. Nixon

President Nixon's only hope for remaining in office until the end of his term hinged on whether the Supreme Court would rule that he had to turn over the tapes. On July 24, 1974, the Court ruled in *United States v. Nixon* that the president would have to surrender the tapes. The decision said that the concept of executive privilege had some constitutional validity. In this specific case, however, the justices ruled that executive privilege was superseded by the "demands of due process of law in the fair administration of criminal justice."

On July 27, 29, and 30 the House Judiciary Committee by wide margins approved three articles of impeachment—for obstruction of justice, abuse of presidential power, and contempt of Congress. Ten of the seventeen Republicans on the thirty-eight-member committee voted against all the articles.

Nixon handed over many tapes voluntarily, and these tapes provided substantial damning evidence. During the first week of August he complied with the Supreme Court's ruling and turned over more tapes. Among these was the so-called smoking gun tape of June 23, 1972. During the

More on this topic:

Executive Privilege,
p. 206

Nixon, Richard, p. 388

United States v. Nixon,
p. 528

War Powers Act of 1973,
p. 560

conversation recorded on that tape, Haldeman told Nixon that campaign manager Mitchell had approved the burglary. Nixon then ordered that the FBI be told not to go any further into the case. This taped conversation made it clear that, contrary to Nixon's repeated claims of innocence, the president had indeed been involved in the cover-up virtually since it began.

With the president's part in Watergate demonstrated beyond doubt by this evidence of presidential wrongdoing, his remaining support in Congress evaporated. Even the ten Republicans on the House Judiciary Committee who had voted against impeachment called for Nixon's resignation or impeachment. The charges ultimately brought against Nixon asserted that he had engaged in a "course of conduct" designed to obstruct justice in the Watergate case, and that in establishing the Plumbers and through other actions and inaction he had failed to uphold the law. On August 9, 1974, faced with his imminent impeachment, Nixon resigned as president.

Nixon was succeeded by Gerald R. Ford, who had been appointed by Nixon to replace Vice President Spiro T. Agnew in 1973. Agnew had resigned after he was linked to a bribery scandal unrelated to Watergate, which had taken place before he became vice president. On September 8, 1974, Ford announced his controversial decision to pardon Nixon for all federal crimes he "committed or may have committed or taken part in" while in office.

Weaver, James B.

James B. Weaver.
Source: Library of Congress

James B. Weaver (1833–1912) ran for president in 1892 as the candidate of the People's Party, better known as the Populists. A protest movement primarily made up of farmers who had grown tired of waiting for the Democrats and Republicans to respond to their concerns, the Populists called for vigorous government action to curb the power of big business and improve the economic lot of agricultural and industrial workers. Weaver won 8.5 percent of the popular vote, a distant third after the losing Republican candidate, Benjamin Harrison. Democrat Grover Cleveland won the election. Although their party faded from existence, the Populists influenced the direction of the Democratic Party, and some of their ideas became reality.

Weaver lent an aura of dignity to a movement that had a reputation for passionate radicalism. A lawyer and Republican politician in Des Moines, Iowa, before the Civil War, he fought for the Union and attained the rank of brigadier general. After the war he was elected to the House of Representatives as a member of the Greenback Party, a forerunner of the Populists. The Greenbacks, who were allied with the Democrats, called for the government to issue paper money as a means of increasing the supply of capital and boosting farm prices. In 1880 Weaver toured the country as the presidential candidate of the Greenbacks, gaining campaign experience but few votes. He returned to the House for most of the next decade.

The creation of the People's Party at a conference in St. Louis early in 1892 was the culmination of years of political organizing and agitation by farm and labor groups. Farm prices had declined since the Civil War. But while farmers and workers frequently endured hard times, the power of banks and big corporations had grown. At the party's national convention in Omaha in the summer of 1892, delegates adopted a defiant platform that described the United States as a nation where "the fruits of the toil of millions are boldly stolen to build up colossal fortunes for a few." The platform called for free and unlimited coinage of silver to increase the money supply, nationalization of the railroads, a graduated income tax, and laws to curtail monopolies.

Weaver campaigned actively and endured heavy abuse in the South because of his Civil War allegiance to the Union. His running mate, James G. Field of Virginia, a Confederate officer, fared better there. But southern Democrats successfully deflected the Populists' appeal by adopting Populist rhetoric and ideas while proclaiming themselves the party of the white man. Weaver's ticket was strongest in silver-mining states (Nevada, Colorado, Wyoming) and in midwestern farm states (Kansas, Nebraska, the Dakotas). The Populists did not draw many votes from urban workers, a failure that dashed their hopes of building a coalition strong enough to supplant the Democratic Party. The People's Party began to disintegrate within a few years of the 1892 election, and Weaver urged fellow Populists to join forces with the Democrats. In 1896 he campaigned for Democrat William Jennings Bryan, who made the Populists' free-silver plank the centerpiece of his losing campaign against Republican William McKinley.

More on this topic:

Third Parties, p. 498

Wheeler, William A.

William Almon Wheeler (1819–1887) was vice president under Rutherford B. Hayes from 1877 to 1881. The little-known Wheeler, who had served five terms in the U.S. House of Representatives, was one of the most obscure vice presidents of the nineteenth century.

Wheeler attended the University of Vermont, but financial problems forced him to leave college before graduating. He returned to his home in Malone, New York, where he studied under the tutelage of a local lawyer. He was admitted to the New York bar in 1845. Wheeler served as district attorney of Franklin County, as a Whig representative to the New York legislature, and as a bank manager before being elected to the U.S. House of Representatives in 1861. Like many northern Whigs, Wheeler had switched to the Republican Party in the mid-1850s. He served in the House from 1861 to 1863 and from 1869 to 1877.

Wheeler's outstanding characteristic was his scrupulous honesty. He demonstrated this quality during the "Salary Grab" of 1873 in which Congress voted itself a 50 percent pay raise and back pay of $5,000. Wheeler voted against the measure, and when it was passed he returned the back pay.

When Wheeler's name was put into contention for the vice presidency at the 1876 Republican national convention, he was virtually unknown. Earlier in the year when someone had suggested a Hayes-Wheeler ticket, Hayes commented in a letter to his wife, "Who is Wheeler?" Wheeler received the vice-presidential

Campaign banner for the 1876 Republican presidential ticket with portraits of Rutherford B. Hayes and William A. Wheeler.
Source: Library of Congress

nomination because he was from the electorally important state of New York, he had a spotless reputation, and the convention delegates were anxious to go home.

The election of 1876 involved the uncontroversial Wheeler in one of the most intense political controversies in American history. Although Hayes and Wheeler received a minority of the popular vote and their Democratic opponents appeared to win the Electoral College, Republican leaders challenged the election results in several southern states. After months of political maneuvers and backroom deals, a congressionally appointed electoral commission ruled in favor of Hayes and Wheeler.

Wheeler was a conscientious presiding officer of the Senate, but he had little enthusiasm for his office. Although Hayes had never met Wheeler before 1876, they became close friends during their time in office. The widowed vice president spent many evenings at the White House with Hayes and his wife, Lucy. At the end of his term as vice president, he quietly retired to Malone, where he lived the last six years of his life.

More on this topic:

Hayes, Rutherford B., p. 249

Vice President, p. 539

Whiskey Rebellion

The Whiskey Rebellion was a major crisis in the presidency of George Washington and an important incident in shaping and demonstrating the constitutional powers of the president.

The crisis began in 1792, when Washington was confronted by whiskey manufacturers in western Pennsylvania who refused to pay federal taxes on their liquor. Washington first responded by sending a message to the distillers commanding them both to start paying taxes on their product and to stop using violence to prevent enforcement of the law. He also appointed the first presidential commission, composed of a group of distinguished citizens, to study the issue.

Washington believed he had to respond quickly and strongly to the whiskey makers' defiance. If he did not put down the rebellion quickly, he feared it would give the impression the new federal government was weak. So he ordered the governors of Pennsylvania, Maryland, New Jersey, and Virginia to supply the federal government with fifteen thousand militia.

As the nation's greatest general, Washington was expected to assume command of the troops in the field. This he did, despite the opinion of some of the delegates to the Constitutional Convention that the president, although commander in chief, should be specifically barred from leading troops into battle. Washington's appearance at the head of a large army was enough to quell the Whiskey Rebellion, and Washington never had to order his soldiers into combat.

In the wake of the confrontation, Washington also made the first presidential use of the pardon power granted by the Constitution. His granting of a full and absolute pardon to the whiskey rebels helped to bring the matter to a close and restore law and order in western Pennsylvania.

> *Whereas it is in my judgment necessary under the circumstances ... to take measures for calling forth the militia in order to ... cause the laws to be duly executed; and I have accordingly determined so to do, feeling the deepest regret for the occasion, but withal the most solemn conviction that the essential interests of the Union demand it.*
>
> **—George Washington,** Proclamation, August 7, 1794

More on this topic:

Law Enforcement Powers, p. 330

Pardon Power, p. 395

Washington, George, p. 564

Whiskey Ring Scandal

The administration of Ulysses S. Grant was plagued by many scandals and abuses of federal office for private gain. The most dramatic and damaging of these cases involved the evasion of internal revenue taxes on distillers of liquor—the so-called Whiskey Ring.

The ring was a conspiracy of revenue officials and politicians to defraud the government of tax money. It included the collector of internal revenue in St. Louis, Gen. John A. McDonald, along with Treasury officials and President Grant's private secretary, Gen. Orville E. Babcock. The conspiracy was uncovered by a newspaper, the *St. Louis Democrat*. Acting on information about the ring, Secretary of the Treasury Benjamin H. Bristow broke up the illicit activity. He used special agents who were not part of the Treasury Department in order to maintain secrecy and not tip off the suspects. Acting on May 10, 1875, the agents raided a number of locations around the United States, including Missouri, Illinois, and Wisconsin. Hundreds were arrested, eventually leading to the conviction of 110 people and the recapture of over $3 million in taxes.

Perhaps the most politically damaging aspect of the case was the way in which Grant responded to it. In the aftermath of the raids, Grant proclaimed, "Let no guilty man escape," but his reputation was tarnished as he tried to protect Babcock, preparing a deposition in his favor that led to Babcock's acquittal on charges connected with the case. Harming Grant's image more were allega-

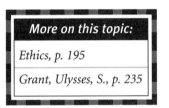

More on this topic:

Ethics, p. 195

Grant, Ulysses, S., p. 235

tions that some of the illegally gained tax proceeds were diverted to strengthen Republican election campaigns, including Grant's 1872 reelection. Although Bristow sought to break up the ring and bring its members to justice, for his efforts, Bristow was effectively forced out of the cabinet.

In the differing ways in which Grant treated Babcock and Bristow after the ring was exposed, historians have seen a clear mark of the moral laxity of Grant's administration. Grant rewarded Babcock by appointing him federal inspector of lighthouses. Bristow was forced to return to private life.

White House

The White House, home of every U.S. president except George Washington, is the oldest and best-known government building in the nation. Almost every visitor to the capital passes by to look at the gleaming white sandstone structure at 1600 Pennsylvania Avenue, with its curving porticoes, stately columns, and manicured lawns behind a six-foot iron fence.

The White House has been remodeled, redecorated, and restored many times during its two hundred years. Twice its insides were gutted entirely and rebuilt, first after the British burned the building in 1814, and again in the late 1940s when it had become structurally unsound. The original walls still stand, and many of the original rooms have been reproduced. By 1992, the bicentennial of the laying of its cornerstone, the White House had become not only a home for presidents but a carefully tended museum of the nation's history.

Early History

George Washington lived in New York and then Philadelphia while in office, but he participated in the planning for the presidential home to be built in the new federal city. Working with the French engineer and architect Pierre Charles L'Enfant, the city's chief planner, Washington helped to choose the site for the house and appointed three commissioners to conduct a contest to select an architect to design it. Thomas Jefferson submitted a plan, as did many others. The winner was

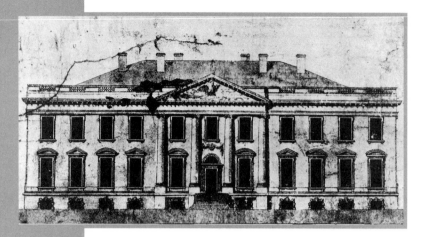

In 1792 master builder James Hoban won the competition for architect of the White House with this original design.
Source: Library of Congress

James Hoban, a self-taught master builder from Ireland.

Hoban designed a simple, three-story boxlike building with the harmonious proportions of late-eighteenth-century Georgian architecture. His interior plan included a large entrance hall with a spacious ceremonial room on the east end of the building balanced by a formal dining room on the west end. These are now the East Room, where the president holds press conferences and official ceremonies, and the State Dining Room. Three smaller drawing rooms, the Green, Blue, and Red Rooms, lined the long hallway that joined the two larger rooms. Hoban's plan for these rooms on the first floor, also called the state floor, has not been changed much over the years in spite of the many renovations the White House has undergone.

When its cornerstone was laid on October 13, 1792, the White House had not yet acquired its official name. L'Enfant insisted on calling it the President's Palace, while Washington preferred the more democratic President's House. Others spoke of it as the Executive Mansion. Once the house was completed, its painted white sandstone walls inspired a new name, the White House. This name had taken hold by the end of the administration of James Madison in 1817; in 1901 Theodore Roosevelt issued an executive order changing the official name of the president's residence from the Executive Mansion to the White House.

It took almost ten years and about $240,000 to complete the White House. In an effort to cut costs, Washington instructed Hoban to eliminate the third floor. (A third floor finally was built in 1927). Much work remained to be done when President John Adams and his wife, Abigail, became the first residents of the White House in 1800. Only six rooms were usable, the plaster was still wet, firewood for heat was scarce, there were no indoor bathrooms, and water had to be carried to the house from a park five blocks away.

Renovations

Thomas Jefferson, the second occupant of the White House, worked with his architect Benjamin Henry Latrobe to complete and add to the new residence. Latrobe built pavilions onto the building's east and west ends. Under Latrobe's direction, Dolley Madison, wife of President James Madison, oversaw the repairs and elegant decorating of some of the state rooms, financed by a $26,000 appropriation by Congress.

Dolley Madison lived to see her improvements destroyed during the WAR OF 1812. In 1814 British soldiers invaded Washington and burned the White House, Capitol, and other buildings. The interior of the White House was gutted, but the exterior walls remained, blackened by smoke and flames. When the White House's occupants fled the approaching British troops, Dolley Madison managed to take with her the full-length portrait of George Washington painted by Gilbert Stuart. Hoban supervised the rebuilding of the White House, which was completed in 1817 in time to accommodate a new president, James Monroe.

A cutaway view of the White House—with the South Portico in the foreground—reveals the mansion's interior. Visitors who take the public guided tour walk along the glass-enclosed colonnade to the Ground Floor Corridor, climb the stairs to the State Floor, visit four state reception rooms and the State Dining Room, then depart by way of the North Entrance.
Source: Library of Congress

Ground Floor		State Floor	
G_1	Library	$^*F_1$	East Room
$^*G_2$	Ground Floor Corridor	$^*F_2$	Green Room
G_3	Vermeil room	$^*F_3$	Blue Room
G_4	China Room	F_4	South Portico
G_5	Diplomatic Reception Room	$^*F_5$	Red Room
G_6	Map Room	$^*F_6$	State Dining Room
		F_7	Family Dining Room
		$^*F_8$	Cross Hall
		$^*F_9$	Entrance Hall

President George W. Bush jokes with reporters August 2, 2006, during the last day of operation of the James S. Brady Press Briefing Room before it undergoes a renovation. On stage with the president are, from left: Joe Lockhart, Dee Dee Myers, Marlin Fitzwater, Tony Snow, Ron Nessen, James Brady and his wife Sarah Brady.
Source: The White House

By the time Richard Nixon became president, the White House faced an increasing demand to produce television news about the executive branch. In 1970 Nixon ordered the construction of the White House Press Briefing Room above the mansion's swimming pool room between the West Wing and the residence. The quarters were cramped but had easy access to the Rose Garden so that journalists could quickly attend outdoor events and briefings. In the 1980s President Reagan had the blue decor and theater seats added, and in 2000, in honor of James Brady who was seriously wounded in the assassination attempt on Reagan, the room was renamed the James S. Brady Press Briefing Room. In 2006 and 2007 the briefing room underwent renovations to accommodate the cables and electronic equipment that had literally made the briefing room a cramped fire hazard in recent years.

With $20,000 appropriated by Congress, Monroe bought elegant French Empire furniture for the White House. He supplemented what he bought by selling to the government items he had collected while serving as U.S. ambassador to France. Furnishings from the Monroe administration, particularly pieces made by French cabinetmaker Pierre-Antoine Bellange, form the core of the White House historic collection. In 1824, during Monroe's second term, Hoban built a semicircular portico with Ionic columns two stories tall onto the south side of the White House. A few years later he finished work on the North Portico, a porte cochere or carriage porch.

During the rest of the nineteenth century the White House was decorated and redecorated, acquiring modern amenities along the way. The first iron pipes for running water were installed in 1833, and a stove replaced open fireplaces for cooking in 1850. In 1891 the White House was wired for electricity.

The most extensive White House renovation since the 1814 fire took place during the administration of Theodore Roosevelt. A new white brick West Wing was built on the ground floor to provide more office space for the president, his staff, and the press. A corresponding new East Wing had a portico that could hold five hundred guests. Colonial furnishings replaced the Victorian appointments in the state rooms on the first floor. New floors and modern plumbing, heating, and wiring also were installed. A third story was built onto the White House in 1927, adding eighteen new rooms for guests, servants, and storage.

In 1948 engineers warned that the White House was structurally unsound, so it was rebuilt for a second time. Like in 1814 the entire inside was gutted while the original walls were left standing. President Harry S. Truman and his family moved across the street to BLAIR HOUSE from November 1948 to March 1952 while workers tore out and rebuilt the interior of the White House. The rebuilt interior included new foundations, two newly excavated basements, a steel frame, fireproofing, and air-conditioning. Interior details were faithfully restored, and bits of wood, brick, and stone that could not be saved were sold as "relic kits." In the spring of 1952 Truman showed off the results of the $5.4 million renovation in the first televised tour of the White House.

Jacqueline Kennedy, wife of John F. Kennedy, led a second televised tour in 1962 and oversaw a new round of renovations as well. Jacqueline Kennedy emphasized the importance of the White House as a showcase for authentic early American paintings, furniture, and antiques. In the same spirit, Lyndon B. Johnson set up a Committee for the Preservation of the White House and hired a permanent curator to tend the White House collection.

The main rooms on the ground and state floors were redone once again during the administration of Richard Nixon in the early 1970s. A decade later, Ronald Reagan and his wife Nancy raised more than $1 million in private funds to redecorate the second and third floors. In preparation for the 1992 White House bicentennial, workers in 1980 began the slow process of chemically removing 175 years' worth of whitewash and paint from the outer walls and repairing the delicate sandstone carvings beneath. The cleaning exposed some of the black scorch marks left by the 1814 fire.

The White House Today

The White House has four floors: ground, first (state), second, and third. The ground floor opens onto the South Portico and can be seen only from the south side of the house, which faces the Ellipse. It includes the Oval Office, staff and press offices, and several historic rooms. The five state rooms, those used for official entertainment, are on the first floor, which opens onto the main North Portico entrance facing Pennsylvania Avenue. The president and the president's family live on the second floor, which also contains historic rooms, such as the Lincoln Bedroom; the third floor has extra family rooms, guest rooms, and storage areas.

Visiting leaders attending a state dinner at the White House are greeted at the North Portico entrance on Pennsylvania Avenue and proceed to the Diplomatic Reception Room on the ground floor. One of Hoban's three oval rooms, it opens onto the South Portico. Jacqueline Kennedy redecorated the rooms with historic furnishings and papered the curving walls with a print from the 1830s that shows a series of American scenes.

Also on the ground floor are the Vermeil and China Rooms and the Library. The Vermeil, or gold, Room displays a collection of gilded silver and portraits of seven first ladies. The China Room holds a collection of chinaware begun in the 1880s and added to by almost every administration since then. The Library has a collection of books on American history.

Much of the official entertaining is conducted on the first, or state, floor of the White House in five state rooms: the East Room, Green Room, Blue Room, Red Room, and State Dining Room. Perhaps the most famous of these is the elegantly furnished white and gold East Room, where White House press conferences are sometimes held. This large, high-ceilinged room is paneled with intricately carved white-painted wood and lit by three cut-glass chandeliers. Its furnishings include a grand piano donated by the Steinway Company in the 1930s that has gilded legs shaped like American eagles. On the wall is the full-length Gilbert Stuart portrait of Washington that was rescued by Dolley Madison. In addition to news conferences, the East Room is used for large gatherings such as bill-signing ceremonies, receptions, concerts, and even funerals. Seven presidents have lain in state here, including Abraham Lincoln, Franklin D. Roosevelt, and John F. Kennedy.

The Blue Room, the best known of Hoban's three oval rooms, was first decorated in blue by Thomas Jefferson and is used for receptions. The Red Room, a parlor, has red satin wallpaper and contains early American furniture upholstered in red. The walls of the Green Room, which is used for small receptions and teas, are covered in green silk. The elegant State Dining Room has floor-to-ceiling windows and carved woodwork. The mantel over the fireplace is inscribed with a passage from a letter John Adams wrote to his wife in 1800 on his second night in the White House: "I Pray to Heaven to Bestow the best of blessings on This House and on All that shall hereafter Inhabit it. May none but Honest and Wise Men ever rule under this Roof."

The president and the president's family have their living quarters on the second floor of the White House. Here they try to make a private home within this most public of houses. The east half of the second floor also contains some historic rooms, including the Lincoln Bedroom, where President Lincoln signed the Emancipation Proclamation in 1863. The room has housed the desk Lincoln used for that historic act and a large rosewood bed thought to have been purchased by his wife, Mary Todd Lincoln, in 1861. Lincoln used the room as an office but probably never slept in the bed. Lincoln is said to have been especially fond of the portrait of Andrew Jackson that hangs in the room.

The East and West Wings on the ground floor of the White House, added in 1902, have been remodeled many times. Many of the White House support staff, including the Uniformed Secret Service and the president's military aides, have their offices in the East Wing.

The focal point of the White House, the Oval Office, is located in the West Wing along with the Cabinet Room, other presidential staff offices, press offices, and a press briefing room. In his formal office the president conducts business and meets with visiting leaders. Presidents change the decor of the Oval Office to suit their personal tastes, except for the presidential seal in the ceiling and the U.S. and president's flags hanging behind the desk. The Oval Office overlooks the eighteenth-century-style Rose Garden, where the president receives guests and conducts ceremonies in good weather.

The mansion is defended by security systems and filled with SECRET SERVICE agents. Plainclothes agents, dressed in business suits and identifiable by small lapel pins, circulate through the White House and guard the president around the clock. Uniformed agents patrol the White House grounds and staff the small white guardhouses along the perimeter of the grounds.

The White House grounds are protected by an elaborate security system that includes electronic sensors, video equipment, and buried seismic sensors. Uniformed guards regularly check the grounds from observation points on the roof of the White House and the Treasury Building next door. The Secret Service even monitors the air space above the White House and is ready to respond with antiaircraft missiles should a plane refuse to heed its warnings to stay clear. In 1995, after several bizarre assaults on the White House late in the preceding year, President Bill Clinton allowed the Secret Service to close the portion of Pennsylvania Avenue near the mansion to vehicular traffic for security purposes. After the September 11, 2001, terrorist attacks on the United States more security precautions went into effect. Public tours of the White House were suspended—some groups, including student groups, eventually were permitted back—and a section of E Street near the building was temporarily closed.

One of the most secret and secure areas of the White House is the Situation Room, the president's communications center. Located under the Oval Office in the basement of the West Wing, this room is run by a twenty-five-person staff of communications experts from the U.S. Army Signal Corps. Twenty-four hours a day they operate the Signal Board, which links the White House with the Pentagon, the State Department, and intelligence facilities. The famous Washington-to-Moscow hotline is not found in the White House, however. It is part of the National Military Command Center at the Pentagon.

More on this topic:
Blair House, p. 31
Salary and Perquisites, p. 453
Secret Service, p. 457
War of 1812, p. 553

Whitewater Investigation

Bill Clinton began his last year in the White House as he had ended his first, facing an ongoing investigation by an independent counsel into the business and political relationships in which he and his wife, Hillary Rodham Clinton, were involved in Arkansas in the 1980s. The Clintons consistently denied any wrongdoing, but, under the glare of unrelenting media attention and political pressure from Capitol Hill, the president had agreed in 1994 to the appointment of an independent counsel.

Specifically, the counsel looked into the investment by the Clintons in the failed Whitewater Development Company real estate venture in Arkansas in 1978 and their relationship with James B. McDougal and his then-wife, Susan. McDougal was the manager of the unsuccessful land project and the former owner of Madison Guaranty Savings and Loan, which, after a series of risky real estate loans and personal loans to Little Rock political insiders, had failed in 1989 at an estimated cost of $68 million to the nation's taxpayers. A major focus of the counsel's probe was whether money from Madison Guaranty improperly ended up in Whitewater bank accounts or was used to help retire debts from Clinton's 1984 gubernatorial campaign. Hillary Clinton, while an attorney with the Rose Law Firm in Little Rock, had represented the failed thrift before state legislators.

The counsel took over the investigation from the Justice Department. In November 1993 Attorney General Janet Reno had assigned a team of department investigators to follow a recommendation from lawyers for the Resolution Trust Company, the agency in charge of failed thrifts. These lawyers suggested that the Justice Department begin a criminal investigation into whether the Clintons and other prominent Arkansans had benefited from misuse of depositor funds at Madison.

Clinton at first resisted the appointment of a special prosecutor, despite intense pressure from Republicans in Congress and from the news media. Clinton's job approval rating was low because of a series of missteps early in his first year in office, and he had little personal support on Capitol Hill. Even though he and Reno maintained that the ongoing investigation by the Justice Department was sufficient, when prominent Democrats joined Republicans in calling for a special counsel, Clinton gave in to their demands on January 12, 1994. Perhaps he hoped that the action would quiet congressional critics and allow work to begin on his legislative agenda.

Although the law providing for the judicial appointment of an independent counsel had expired at the end of 1992, the reauthorization legislation was still pending in Congress in early 1994. But the attorney general was authorized under other statutes to appoint independent counsels. On January 20, 1994, Reno named as independent counsel Robert B. Fiske Jr., a Wall Street lawyer, former U.S. attorney in New York, and a Republican.

> *Biggest bogus issue in modern American politics—classic. It was a fraud from the get-go, and a lot of the people that were propagating it knew it was a fraud. And in that sense, people will look at this years from now and be amazed that anybody rode it as hard as they did for as long as they did.*
>
> **—William J. Clinton,** *Interview with Dan Rather of CBS News, December 18, 2000*

In June 1994 Fiske reported that his investigation had not found that "officials had acted with the intent to corruptly influence" the Resolution Trust Corporation investigation of Madison's collapse.

A year earlier, on June 20, 1993, Vincent Foster, the deputy White House counsel and a colleague of Mrs. Clinton's from the Rose Law Firm, had committed suicide. Among his other duties, Foster had handled Whitewater matters for the White House. His suicide deepened outsiders' suspicions that the Clintons had something to hide. After months of pressure by Republicans (who previously had raised partisan objections to Fiske's findings), Foster's death, and the disclosure that Treasury Department officials and White House staff had discussed the Whitewater and Madison probe, the banking committees of both the House of Representatives and the Senate began hearings on Whitewater. Shortly thereafter Fiske was dismissed; a judicial panel had ruled that he was technically an administration appointee. The judges replaced him with Kenneth W. Starr, a former Republican solicitor general.

Starr approached the investigation with a new vigor and quickly secured various guilty pleas or convictions in a Little Rock federal court. He obtained an indictment of Jim Guy Tucker, then-governor of Arkansas, on charges stemming from Whitewater. Tucker was later convicted. In a separate case, Webster Hubbell, a friend of and adviser to the Clintons, a former senior partner of the first lady at the Rose Law Firm, and one of Clinton's top appointees to the Justice Department, pleaded guilty to embezzlement, mail fraud, and tax evasion. Although unrelated to Whitewater, Hubbell's involvement in Arkansas politics and his business and personal relationships with the Clintons and Foster created a fertile ground for conspiracy theorists that Whitewater was just the tip of a sinister iceberg.

Hillary Clinton's high political profile in Washington, a position that angered some Republicans and traditionalists in both parties, almost inevitably made her the major focus of both the Starr and congressional probes. Her earlier professional relationship with Madison Guaranty provided a legal justification. Even though a report prepared for the Resolution Trust Corporation concluded that the Clintons had correctly claimed that they had been only passive investors in Whitewater, by mid-1995, with Republican majorities controlling both houses of Congress, some journalistic accounts differed and the investigation intensified. A Senate committee began hearings in July, again probing Foster's death. Despite Fiske's early finding that Foster's death had nothing to do with Whitewater and that his papers were not mishandled after his death, Starr and the Senate committee seemed to ignore this conclusion and pressed on with separate probes. (Nearly two and a half years later, Fiske's original conclusion would be found justified.)

In August 1995 the McDougals were indicted by a federal grand jury in Little Rock for arranging fraudulent loans through Madison Guaranty. The Senate committee subsequently voted to subpoena White House notes taken in a 1993 meeting over Whitewater; the full Senate voted to support the subpoena. After first claiming executive privilege, in December 1995 the White House released the notes, which appeared to demonstrate no clear evidence of any wrongdoing.

In early 1996 Mrs. Clinton was subpoenaed to testify before the Whitewater grand jury in Little Rock, becoming the first first lady ever to do so. Later in the year President Clinton was ordered to testify in the trial of the McDougals and Tucker, which he did by videotape. The text was sealed. Both Jim and Susan McDougal and Tucker were found guilty. (Susan McDougal, subpoenaed after her conviction to testify at a Whitewater grand jury considering related matters, refused to testify on September 4, 1996, and was sentenced to jail for contempt. She served the maximum eighteen months. Her former husband, after serving part of a prison sentence, died on March 8, 1998.)

The Senate Whitewater Committee released its final report on June 18, 1996, with the Republican majority and Democratic minority each issuing reports. The Republicans concluded that Hillary Clinton and some White House officials had obstructed a federal investigation into Whitewater and the Clintons' involvement. The Democratic report exonerated her.

As 1997 ended, Starr gained a six-month extension for the Whitewater grand jury, continuing the term until two years after its first meeting. Starr told the presiding judge in Little Rock that the extension would be "strongly in the public's interest." Press reports noted at the time that Starr had, up to that date, spent more than $30 million investigating the Clintons and Whitewater.

In January 1998 Attorney General Reno approved Starr's request to investigate whether President Clinton had urged a former White House intern, Monica Lewinsky, to commit perjury in her deposition in the Paula Jones sexual harassment case in Arkansas—Lewinsky was testifying about an alleged sexual relationship with Clinton. Lewinsky's conversations about Clinton had been taped by Linda Tripp, a friend who also had worked in the White House before moving to the Pentagon. Later that month, U.S. District Court judge Susan Webber Wright ruled that all evidence relating to Lewinsky be excluded from the Jones case. Wright dismissed the Jones case on April 1, but Starr persisted in his investigation of Lewinsky. When physical evidence emerged to substantiate the relationship with Lewinsky, Clinton was forced to admit to having "inappropriate" sexual contact with her. That admission opened him to charges of perjury and obstruction of justice, which formed the basis of his impeachment in December 1998 and trial in January–February 1999, in which he was acquitted.

Meanwhile, the independent counsel's probe into Whitewater continued. Starr was succeeded as independent counsel by Robert W. Ray. In September 2000 Ray—like Robert Fiske before him—reported that evidence was insufficient to show criminal wrongdoing in the Whitewater case by either President Clinton or his wife.

Ray, however, continued the independent counsel's criminal investigation into the perjury and obstruction of justice charges that had formed the basis of Clinton's impeachment. To forestall further legal action against him, Clinton reached an agreement with Ray on January 19, 2001, his penultimate day in office. Clinton admitted to having given false testimony under oath, agreed to pay a $25,000 fine, and accepted a five-year suspension of his Arkansas law license. In return, the independent counsel terminated all legal action.

More on this topic:

Clinton, Bill, p. 101

Clinton v. Jones, p. 101

Clinton, Hillary, p. 106

Independent Counsel, p. 284

Willkie, Wendell L.

Wendell L. Willkie (1892–1944) was one of four Republicans defeated in presidential elections by Franklin D. Roosevelt, perhaps the most popular Democratic president in U.S. history. In the election of 1940 Willkie won 44.8 percent of the popular vote to Roosevelt's 54.7 percent, coming closer than Herbert C. Hoover or Alf Landon had done in earlier elections. A utility executive new to electoral politics, Willkie attacked Roosevelt's economic programs and accused him of undemocratic behavior for seeking a third term in defiance of tradition. (The Twenty-second Amendment to the Constitution, which limits presidents to two terms, was ratified in 1951.) But in spite of growing dissatisfaction with Roosevelt, the widening war in Europe made Americans fearful of change.

Willkie grew up in an intellectually inclined, politically liberal family in the small town of Elwood, Indiana. As a young lawyer, he participated in Democratic Party politics and admired Woodrow Wilson, the Democratic president from 1913 to 1921. Willkie made his reputation, however, as a critic of the Roosevelt administration during the 1930s. As a spokesman for a large private utility company, Willkie fought the creation of the Tennessee Valley Authority (TVA), a federally owned power company. When his attempt failed, Willkie continued his public agitation against New Deal policies he considered harmful to business and the economy as a whole.

Willkie's nomination on the sixth ballot at the 1940 Republican convention, overtaking front-runners Thomas E. Dewey of New York and Sen. Robert A. Taft of Ohio, stands out in the history of political conventions. "Nothing exactly like it has ever happened before in American politics," *Newsweek* magazine reported. "Willkie had never held public office or even sought it. Virtually a neophyte in politics, he had entered no primaries, made no deals, organized no campaign." Helped along by business supporters and a friendly press, Willkie's candidacy was promoted at the convention by thousands of letters and telegrams sent by a series of fan clubs across the country. Willkie's outgoing personality and his willingness to campaign among the convention delegates contributed as well.

During the general election Willkie hammered away at Roosevelt for his "socialistic" economic policies and "warmongering" tactics, forcing the president to pledge that he would not involve the United States in "foreign wars" except in the case of a direct attack. Yet after the election Willkie broke decisively with isolationist Republicans. He spent the war years developing and promoting his utopian ideas for a postwar peace accord among all nations, set out in a 1943 bestseller entitled *One World.* Willkie's bid for the Republican nomination in 1944 was stopped short by Dewey. Willkie died less than a month before Roosevelt won reelection for the last time in November 1944.

> **More on this topic:**
>
> *National Party Conventions, p. 375*

Wilson, Edith

Edith Bolling Galt Wilson (1872–1961) was the second wife of President Woodrow Wilson. Many historians believe that after Wilson suffered a stroke late in his presidency, Edith exercised more influence over national affairs than any other first lady in history.

At the age of twenty-four Edith married Norman Galt, an older man who was a jeweler in Washington, D.C. In 1908 Galt died suddenly, leaving his store to his wife. She managed the business and lived well, often making trips to Europe.

Edith Wilson.
Source: Library of Congress

In March 1915 Edith was introduced to Woodrow Wilson by Wilson's cousin, Helen Bones. Wilson's first wife, Ellen, had died in August 1914. A romance rapidly developed between Edith and Woodrow. After hesitating briefly because of the possible political consequences of Wilson marrying too soon after Ellen's death, they were wed quietly at Edith's home on December 18, 1915. Wilson suffered no political fallout, and he was reelected president in 1916.

Self-assured and decisive, the new Mrs. Wilson proved to be an important assistant to the president, working as his personal secretary. Nevertheless, she was not particularly interested in politics and denounced the women's suffrage movement as "unladylike." When the United States entered World War I, Edith tried to set an example for the country by observing the various meatless and gasless days, sewing items for the Red Cross, curtailing entertainment, and using sheep instead of human labor to keep the White House lawn trimmed.

In October 1919, while battling the Senate for ratification of the Treaty of Versailles after the war, Wilson suffered a stroke that left him mostly paralyzed. Edith immediately stepped in to shield her husband. She screened all visitors, and for a time almost no one saw Wilson except her. Exactly how much power she wielded and how long she held it are questions that have fascinated historians. Critics then and now have argued that she functioned as the acting president and essentially ran the country for the balance of Wilson's term. Edith claimed that her "regency" lasted but a few weeks and that Woodrow made the important decisions.

Sick and disillusioned, Woodrow Wilson lived only three years after leaving the White House. Edith survived him by almost thirty-eight years. During that time she traveled widely, participated in Democratic politics, wrote her memoirs, and served as a director of the Woodrow Wilson Foundation. She died of heart disease in 1961 and was buried with Woodrow in Washington National Cathedral.

More on this topic:

Disability Amendment, p. 154

First Ladies, p. 219

Wilson, Woodrow, p. 583

Wilson, Henry

Henry Wilson (1812–1875) rose from humble Massachusetts beginnings to become a powerful Civil War–era senator and Ulysses S. Grant's second vice president. Wilson served from 1873 to 1875, dying in office.

Wilson was born Jeremiah Jones Colbath. He spent most of his youth as an indentured servant to a farmer. When he had earned his freedom at age twenty-one, he changed his name to Henry Wilson. He then learned the shoemaking trade and expanded a small business into a large shoe factory that made him wealthy.

In 1840 Wilson was elected as a Whig to the Massachusetts legislature, where he served for most of the next twelve years. He left the Whig Party in 1848 because of its indecisiveness on slavery. He helped form the Free Soil Party and edited the *Boston Republican,* a party organ, from 1848 to 1851. He joined the ultraconservative American (Know-Nothing) Party in 1854 but left it in 1855 for the new Republican Party.

Henry Wilson.
Source: Library of Congress

Wilson served in the Senate from 1855 until 1873. There he made many enemies among southern members of Congress because of his strong attacks on slavery. During the Civil War he served as chairman of the Senate Committee on Military Affairs. He earned praise for his effective legislative leadership in raising and equipping the Union Army. After the war he backed the harsh Reconstruction plan of the Radical Republicans and voted for Andrew Johnson's impeachment in 1868.

Wilson was nominated to be President Ulysses S. Grant's vice-presidential running mate in 1872. Like the previous vice president, Schuyler Colfax, Wilson had been involved in the Crédit Mobilier scandal. A few weeks before the 1872 election the *New York Sun* broke the story that several members of Congress, including Wilson, were involved in the bribery scheme. Wilson, however, claimed that he had returned his twenty Crédit Mobilier shares before he reaped any profit from them. Although it was not until several months after the election that Wilson was exonerated by the congressional committees investigating the scandal, his troubles did not affect the election's outcome. President Grant easily won reelection.

Shortly after the election Wilson suffered a stroke. When he recovered, he claimed to be in good health but was unable to preside effectively over the Senate. On November 22, 1875, he died from a second stroke with a year and a half left in his term.

More on this topic:

Grant, Ulysses S., p. 235

Vice President, p. 539

Wilson, Woodrow

Source: Library of Congress

Woodrow Wilson (1856–1924) was one of the most intellectually brilliant presidents and the only one to earn a doctoral degree. During his two terms he pushed many reform measures through Congress and guided the United States through World War I. A stroke left him incapacitated during much of the last year and a half of his presidency, so that he was unable to achieve his foremost goal—U.S. entry into the League of Nations.

Wilson was born on December 28, 1856, in Staunton, Virginia. He was the son of a Presbyterian minister. When Wilson was two, his family moved to Augusta, Georgia, where he witnessed the destructive effects of the Civil War.

Wilson, who was originally named Thomas Woodrow, dropped his first name as a young adult. He enrolled in Davidson College near Charlotte, North Carolina, in 1873. Before the end of the school year, illness forced him to withdraw. Two years later he entered Princeton University. There he earned recognition as a debater and decided not to become a minister. After graduation in 1879 he attended the University of Virginia law school, but in 1880 poor health again forced him to leave school. He studied law independently and was admitted to the bar in 1882. He briefly practiced law in Atlanta but quit the profession in 1883 to enroll in Johns Hopkins University as a graduate student of history and government.

Educator and Governor

At Johns Hopkins, Wilson distinguished himself as a scholar. On June 24, 1885, he married Ellen Louise Axson. He was awarded his doctoral degree in 1886 and then taught at Bryn Mawr College near Philadelphia and Wesleyan University in Middletown, Connecticut. In 1890 he accepted a professorship at Princeton University. Two years later Princeton's trustees unanimously elected him president of the university.

At Princeton, Wilson became known as a crusader for democratic principles in education. New Jersey's Democratic Party leaders proposed to Wilson that he run for governor in 1910. Once elected, party leaders expected to be able to control the politically inexperienced Wilson, even though he accepted the nomination on the condition that he would not have to fulfill any promises of patronage. He resigned from Princeton and was elected governor.

Once in office Wilson quickly demonstrated that he was his own boss. He implemented a series of reforms that attracted national attention, including laws establishing direct primaries, workers' compensation, and antitrust measures. His efforts also led to improved regulation of utilities and the reorganization of the public school system. By 1912 Democrats were considering him as a potential presidential candidate.

Wilson entered the 1912 Democratic national convention as an underdog to House Speaker Champ Clark. Although Clark led Wilson in the early ballots, he could not muster a majority. On the fourteenth ballot Democratic patriarch William Jennings Bryan abandoned Clark to support Wilson, who was nominated on the forty-sixth ballot.

Wilson's election to the presidency was virtually sealed when Theodore Roosevelt split the Republican Party by running for president as the candidate of the Progressive Party. Of the 15 million votes cast, Wilson received only 6.3 million, but Republicans divided their votes between Roosevelt and President William Howard Taft. Wilson received 435 electoral votes, while Roosevelt and Taft received 88 and 8 votes, respectively.

Presidency

Once he assumed office Wilson quickly demonstrated his independence and innovation. He delivered his State of the Union address to Congress in person on April 8, 1913, which no president had done since John Adams. He also established weekly press conferences.

Wilson fulfilled a campaign promise to lower tariffs by signing the Underwood Tariff Act of 1913. The act cut tariff rates to their lowest levels since before the Civil War. At Wilson's urging, Congress passed the Federal Reserve Act of 1913, which created a system of regional federal banks to regulate currency and the banking industry. He backed the creation of the Federal Trade Commission in 1914 to ensure fair business practices. That year he also signed the Clayton Anti-Trust Act, which strengthened the government's powers to break up monopolies. In 1916 Congress passed the Adamson Act at Wilson's request, which established the eight-hour day for railroad workers.

When World War I began in 1914, Wilson announced that the United States would stay out of the European conflict. German submarines, however, were not observing U.S. neutrality. In May 1915 a German submarine sank the British passenger ship *Lusitania* with more than one hundred Americans aboard. Wilson protested the incident, and the Germans agreed not to prey on passenger ships.

In 1916 Wilson did not have the luxury of facing a divided Republican Party as he had in 1912. The Republicans united behind Supreme Court justice Charles Evans Hughes. In one of the closest presidential elections in history, Wilson defeated Hughes 277–254 in the Electoral College.

In January 1917 Germany announced it would attack any ship passing through a wide zone in the Atlantic. Wilson responded to the submarine offensive by breaking diplomatic relations with Germany on February 3. When the Germans continued their submarine warfare, Wilson asked Congress on April 2, 1917, to declare war. Within four days both houses had overwhelmingly passed the declaration. Congress delegated broad powers to Wilson to build an army and wage war. He pushed the Selective Service Act through Congress, took control of the railroads, established the War Industries Board to oversee the economy, and ordered other emergency measures.

With the addition of U.S. troops on the Allied side, Germany was defeated. An armistice was signed on November 11, 1918. Wilson hoped to implement a plan for territorial adjustment and maintenance of world peace once the war was over. The basis of this plan was his "Fourteen Points," which included arms reductions, freedom of the seas, and removal of trade barriers.

In December 1918 Wilson sailed to France to attend the Versailles peace conference. Europeans hailed the American president as a hero, and he dominated the conference. Nevertheless, he was forced to make concessions to European leaders to gain their approval of his Fourteen Points and the League of Nations. The treaty produced by the conference imposed a harsh peace on Germany that included heavy war reparations and the loss of its colonies.

Wilson submitted the Treaty of Versailles to the Senate for approval on July 10, 1919, but a group of senators led by Republican Henry Cabot Lodge of Massachusetts objected to the provision within the treaty establishing the League of Nations. They would not vote for the treaty without attaching reservations that Wilson believed undercut the agreement. On September 4, 1919, Wilson began a speaking tour designed to mobilize public support for the treaty. After delivering speeches in twenty-nine cities, Wilson became ill on September 26 in Pueblo, Colorado, and was forced to cancel the rest of his trip. He returned to Washington, D.C., where he suffered a severe stroke on October 2.

The stroke incapacitated the president for several months, and he never fully recovered his strength. The Senate, meanwhile, debated the Versailles treaty. Wilson refused to compromise with Lodge to gain its passage. The Senate rejected the treaty on November 19, 1919. Exactly four months later the Senate again voted it down. Wilson declared that the 1920 presidential contest between Republican Warren G. Harding, who opposed the treaty, and Democrat James M. Cox, who supported it, should be considered a public forum on the treaty. Voters overwhelmingly elected Harding. Wilson's fight for the League of Nations was finished.

More on this topic:

Elections Chronology, p. 174

Historic Milestones of the Presidency, p. 253

New Freedom, p. 385

Wilson, Edith, p. 581

World War I, p. 586

When Wilson left office he retired to his home in Washington, D.C. He lived in near seclusion until his death on February 3, 1924, from another stroke. His first wife, Ellen, had died on August 6, 1914, in the White House. On December 18, 1915, Wilson had married Edith Bolling Galt, a forty-three-year-old widow. After Wilson suffered his stroke in 1919, Edith restricted access to her husband. He conducted much of his presidential business during his recovery through Edith. Historians have speculated that she may have made many presidential decisions for her husband.

World War I

Soldiers returning from World War I parading through arch on street in Minneapolis.
Source: Library of Congress

World War I brought the first involvement of the United States in an overseas war of massive scale. The war, which began in 1914, pitted the Allies (Great Britain, France, and Russia) against the Central Powers (Germany and Austria-Hungary). The entry of the United States into the war on the side of the Allies in 1917 led to the most dramatic expansion of presidential powers since the Civil War.

The American people saw the war in Europe as a distant and senseless conflict between corrupt European powers. During his first term President Woodrow Wilson shared the opinion of the American people that the United States should remain neutral. However, when German submarines began sinking U.S. vessels in the Atlantic, the United States could not completely distance itself from the war. Beginning in 1915 German attacks against U.S. vessels or ships on which Americans were passengers threatened to push the United States into the war. Each crisis, however, was resolved through diplomacy until January 31, 1917, when the Germans announced they would begin an all-out submarine campaign against ships headed for Allied ports. In response, Wilson broke diplomatic ties with Germany on February 3.

American sentiment to join the Allies was bolstered by the publication of the "Zimmermann telegram" on March 1. This was a message from the German foreign minister to the German ambassador to Mexico instructing him to propose a German-Mexican alliance against the United States should the latter enter the war against Germany.

Wilson decided to ask for a declaration of war on March 20, 1917. He delivered a stirring war message to Congress on April 2, saying that the United States would make the world "safe for democracy." Congress passed the war resolution, and Wilson signed it on April 6.

Wilson's War Powers

Like Abraham Lincoln during the Civil War, Wilson wielded powers during wartime that far exceeded those of peacetime presidents. The basis for Wilson's power differed from that of Lincoln's, however, in that Lincoln had taken emergency actions independently of Congress, while Congress handed Wilson most of his expanded war-making authority.

We have no selfish ends to serve. We desire no conquest, no dominion. We seek no indemnities for ourselves, no material compensation for the sacrifices we shall freely make. We are but one of the champions of the rights of mankind. We shall be satisfied when those rights have been made as secure as the faith and the freedom of nations can make them.

—Woodrow Wilson, Address to a Joint Session of Congress: "We Must Accept War," April 2, 1917

Lawmakers gave Wilson total control of the military, discretion to fight subversion and espionage, and unprecedented authority over industries and the allocation of scarce resources. For example, the Lever Food and Fuel Act gave the president "full authority to undertake any steps necessary" for the conservation of food resources. In addition, the Overman Act gave the president power to reorganize the executive branch. Congress was willing to delegate power to Wilson because most members believed that the urgency of the war required unified direction of all operations and resources related to the war effort.

Many delegations of authority to the president simply stated their objectives and left Wilson to decide how to achieve them. He commandeered plants and mines, requisitioned supplies, fixed prices, seized and operated the nation's transportation and communications networks, and managed the production and distribution of foodstuffs. In essence, Congress did more than give Wilson broad discretion in implementing its laws, it abdicated legislative power to him for the duration of the war.

Allied Victory

The 1917 Bolshevik revolution in Russia led to the Russian withdrawal from the war and the conclusion of a separate peace with the Central Powers in early 1918.

After World War I, a feeling of uneasiness about surrendering national sovereignty to the League of Nations was widespread. In this cartoon President Wilson offers the peace dove an olive branch while she asks, "Isn't this a stick?"

Relieved from fighting a two-front war, the Central Powers launched a massive offensive against British and French troops. But the entry of U.S. forces into the war helped to stabilize French and British lines. In August the Allies launched a counteroffensive that drove back the Germans. Realizing they no longer had a chance to win the war, the Germans sued for peace on terms favorable to the Allies. On November 11, 1918, an armistice was signed ending the war. As many as 10 million combatants had died from wounds and disease. About 116,000 Americans died in the war, and another 200,000 were wounded.

With the end of the war, Wilson hoped to engineer an enlightened peace based on his Fourteen Points, which included arms reductions, free trade, and freedom of navigation. In December 1918 he sailed to France to attend the Versailles peace conference. There he was hailed as a hero, and his Fourteen Points were the basis of the conference. Nevertheless, he was forced to make concessions to European leaders to gain their support for his Fourteen Points and the establishment of a League of Nations. The Versailles treaty imposed heavy war reparations on Germany and took away its colonies. Resentment over the harsh terms of the treaty fueled a German desire for vindication that was a contributing cause of World War II.

Wilson submitted the Treaty of Versailles to the Senate for approval on July 10, 1919. But a group of senators objected to the provision establishing the League of Nations. They refused to support the treaty without attaching reservations that Wilson believed nullified the agreement. Wilson launched a speaking tour in September 1919 to put pressure on the Senate to approve the treaty, but a severe stroke in October incapacitated him. The treaty remained unratified, and the United States did not become a member of the League of Nations.

More on this topic:
Treaty Power, p. 515
War Powers, p. 555
Wilson, Woodrow, p. 583

World War II

World War II transformed the United States into a dominant world power and set the stage for the cold war between the United States and the Soviet Union. The war also led to the expansion of the president's war powers. Like Woodrow Wilson during World War I, President Franklin D. Roosevelt was delegated vast powers by Congress to manage the economy and direct the war effort. But Roosevelt went further than Wilson in asserting a right to take any action he deemed necessary to win the war.

World War II began with Germany's invasion of Poland on September 1, 1939. By the end of 1940 the German Nazis and their allies controlled most of Europe, with Great Britain the only significant power resisting them. In the summer of 1941 Nazi leader Adolf Hitler widened the war by invading the Soviet Union. Meanwhile, the Japanese were pursuing their own expansionist goals in China and elsewhere in East Asia.

During World War II FDR made several trips overseas to confer with Allied leaders about military strategy and the composition of the post-war world. In February 1945 Roosevelt (center) conferred with Winston Churchill (left) and Joseph Stalin (right) at Yalta in the Crimea.
Source: National Archives

Undeclared War

Like in World War I, the United States initially attempted to stay out of the conflict. Roosevelt, however, recognized that U.S. interests were directly threatened by German and Japanese military successes. He continued to pledge to keep the United States out of the war, while doing everything possible to aid Great Britain.

Roosevelt's war powers were tightly restrained during the 1930s by the prevailing mood of isolationism in Congress and among the American people. Congress had enacted various laws designed to keep the United States out of the conflicts brewing in Europe and Asia. Even after the Nazis' aggressive intentions had become obvious, Roosevelt had to maneuver the country toward active support of Great Britain and the other Allies.

In September 1940 Roosevelt gave Great Britain fifty "overage" destroyers in return for the right to lease certain British territory in the western Atlantic for U.S. naval and air bases. Roosevelt's destroyer deal was accomplished through an executive agreement—a legally binding pact between the president and the British government—rather than through a Senate-approved treaty. The trade violated at least two congressional statutes, but Roosevelt's attorney general, Robert Jackson, asserted that the president had acted legally under his authority as commander in chief to "dispose" of the armed forces.

On March 11, 1941, Congress passed the Lend-Lease Act. It authorized the president to manufacture any defense article and to "sell, transfer title to, exchange, lease, lend or otherwise dispose of" the defense articles to the "government of any country whose defense the President deems vital to the defense of the United States." The act gave the president the power to aid the Allied cause as he saw fit by virtually any means short of using the armed forces.

Yet Roosevelt did use the armed forces to aid the Allied cause despite the absence of any congressional sanction for acts of war. After Germany occupied Denmark in April 1941, Roosevelt ordered U.S. troops to be stationed in Greenland. Three months later, U.S. forces occupied Iceland. Both moves were made without consulting Congress. By the summer of 1941 U.S. naval vessels under presidential orders were escorting Allied convoys across the Atlantic. After the USS *Greer* exchanged shots with a German submarine on September 4, the president declared that henceforth U.S. warships providing protection to supply convoys bound for Britain would be under orders to attack Axis vessels on sight. Thus three months before Congress declared war, Roosevelt had maneuvered the nation into an undeclared naval war in the Atlantic.

The world will note that the first atomic bomb was dropped on Hiroshima, a military base. That was because we wished in this first attack to avoid, insofar as possible, the killing of civilians.

—**Harry S. Truman,** Radio Report to the American People on the Potsdam Conference, August 9, 1945

Roosevelt's "Dictatorship"

Expecting the United States to enter the war soon and fearing the power of the U.S. Pacific fleet, the Japanese attacked the U.S. base at Pearl Harbor, Hawaii, on December 7, 1941. The attack shook the nation out of its isolationist mood. Roosevelt immediately asked for and received a declaration of war against Japan. A declaration of war against Germany followed.

The U.S. entry into World War II was accompanied by the concentration of virtually all war powers in the president's hands. Congress delegated vast authority to the president to prosecute the war, as it had done during World War I. Although Roosevelt saw the wisdom of obtaining Congress's approval for controversial actions, he was far more assertive than Wilson in using his commander-in-chief power to establish complete control over the war effort.

Roosevelt created dozens of executive regulatory agencies that were not based on a specific statute, such as the Office of Emergency Management, Board of Economic Warfare, National War Labor Board, Office of Defense Transportation, and War Production Board. Anything remotely connected to the nation's war effort, including national resources and economic activity, was regulated by these war management agencies, which were responsible only to the president.

In September 1942 Roosevelt even declared in an address that if Congress failed to repeal certain provisions contained in the Emergency Price Control Act of 1942, he would repeal them himself in the interest of national security. Such a presidential act would have been unconstitutional, but Congress responded to Roosevelt's threat by repealing the provisions.

Winning the War

With the entry of the United States into the war on the Allied side, the tide of the war turned against the Axis powers. The huge industrial strength, large population, and insulated location of the United States enabled it to carry on a war against both the Germans and the Japanese. In the Pacific, the United States recovered from the attack on Pearl Harbor, captured Japanese-held islands in the South Pacific, and began "island hopping" north toward Japan. In Europe, the United States cooperated with Great Britain and the Soviet Union against the Nazis. In 1944 British and American troops invaded France and began pushing toward Germany. Meanwhile, Russian forces drove back German armies on the eastern front.

The war in Europe ended on May 8, 1945, with Germany's surrender. In August U.S. warplanes dropped two atomic bombs

More on this topic:

Emergency Powers, p. 188

Japanese American Internment, p. 303

Roosevelt, Franklin D., p. 445

Truman, Harry S., p. 519

War Powers, p. 555

on the Japanese cities of Hiroshima and Nagasaki, with devastating results. Japan surrendered to the United States on September 2, 1945.

Meanwhile, Roosevelt had died on April 12, 1945. President Harry S. Truman followed through with Roosevelt's efforts to establish a United Nations organization with the aim of preventing war. The organization was established, but growing differences between the United States and the Soviet Union about the shape of the postwar world led to a cold war that precluded cooperation between the two nations during the postwar period.

Youngstown Sheet and Tube Co. v. Sawyer

During wartime a government sometimes seizes property of its citizens that it deems vital to the war effort. Congress traditionally has passed legislation governing the seizure of property belonging to U.S. citizens. Before and during World War I, Congress empowered the president to seize transportation and communications systems if such actions became necessary. President Woodrow Wilson used these laws to take over railroad, telephone, and telegraph operations, which were returned to civilian control after the war. Similarly, President Franklin D. Roosevelt was authorized by the War Labor Disputes Act of 1943 to seize industries important to the war effort that were in danger of being shut down by labor disputes.

Presidents, however, have sometimes seized property without waiting for congressional authorization. Abraham Lincoln personally directed the army to take control of telegraph lines during the Civil War, and Roosevelt took control of several strike-threatened industries before Congress passed the War Labor Disputes Act.

The courts generally have rejected the notion that presidents have inherent EMERGENCY POWERS that authorize them to seize private property. The most famous court case dealing with this issue was *Youngstown Sheet and Tube Co. v. Sawyer,* also known as the *Steel Seizure Case.* In this case the Supreme Court ruled that President Harry S. Truman did not have the authority to seize steel mills about to be closed by strikes despite the ongoing Korean War.

The United Steelworkers threatened to strike on April 9, 1952. Truman believed the strike would damage the Korean War effort by causing steel shortages. On April 8 he directed Secretary of Commerce Charles Sawyer to seize and operate the steel mills. Truman conceded in his report to

Also known as the **Steel Seizure Case,** *this Supreme Court case ruled that President Truman did not have the authority to seize steel mills, about to be closed, even if their closing would damage the Korean War effort.*

Source: Library of Congress

Congress that it had the authority to countermand his directive, but Congress failed to approve or reject the president's action.

The steel companies brought suit against the government to stop the president's action. The case quickly reached the Supreme Court, where by a vote of 6–3 Truman's action was declared unconstitutional. The Court claimed that the president had usurped Congress's lawmaking power. It cited several acts in which Congress had set up procedures for responding to strikes, which Truman had ignored. In the debate on one of these laws, the Taft-Hartley Act of 1947, Congress had considered empowering the government to seize an industry to prevent strikes but had refused to include such a provision in the law. Truman, therefore, had not just taken action without congressional approval; he had taken an action that Congress had rejected.

In a concurring opinion Justice William O. Douglas explained:

> There can be no doubt that the emergency which caused the president to seize these steel plants was one that bore heavily on the country. But the emergency did not create power; it merely marked an occasion when power should be exercised. And the fact that it was necessary that measures be taken to keep steel in production does not mean that the President, rather than the Congress, had the constitutional authority to act.

More on this topic:
Courts and the President, p. 128
Emergency Powers, p. 188
Korean War, p. 323
Truman, Harry S., p. 519

In an era of rapidly expanding presidential power, the *Steel Seizure Case,* as presidential scholar Clinton Rossiter observed, "revived, for the moment, the notion that Presidents were subject to congressional limitations in foreign affairs."

Z

Zapruder Film

President and Mrs. Kennedy in motorcade, Dallas, Texas, November 22, 1963.
Source: Library of Congress

The Zapruder film, which was made available commercially on video in 1998, is recognized as the infamous documentation of President John F. Kennedy's assassination. Abraham Zapruder, one of many people watching the presidential motorcade in Dallas, Texas, on November 22, 1963, filmed it with his 8 mm home movie camera.

Zapruder began filming when the motorcade came within the limited range of his lens. Kennedy was waving and smiling to the crowd, his wife, Jacqueline, beside him and Texas governor John Connally and his wife, Nellie, sitting just in front of them in the limousine's rear seat. The car disappeared momentarily behind a shade tree, and when it emerged Zapruder heard what he thought was a firecracker, then another. He kept his camera trained on the president for, it would later be determined, 8.3 seconds or 152 frames. The film would show in explicit detail Kennedy being mortally wounded and the onlookers' shocked reactions.

More on this topic:

Assassinations and Assaults, p. 19

Kennedy, John F., p. 318

Warren Commission, p. 562

A reporter from *Life* magazine learned of Zapruder's historic film later that day as the world media descended on Dallas. The reporter arranged to buy all publication and broadcast rights to it for $150,000. Copies had already been turned over to the Federal Bureau of Investigation and the Dallas Police Department. Zapruder gave the original to *Life,* which used still frames from the film in its issue on the assassination and in many other issues. *Life's* editors steadfastly refused to allow the film to be shown in its entirety, fearing that its full impact would exacerbate the tragedy and delay the nation's healing. In 1970, after Zapruder's death, *Life* returned the film to his family and waived all rights to it.

The WARREN COMMISSION, appointed by Kennedy's successor, Lyndon B. Johnson, to ascertain what happened in Dallas, made extensive use of Zapruder's film, as well as those of two other amateur movie makers situated at different vantage points, to determine the precise course of events at the time of the killing and the speed of the president's vehicle (11.2 miles per hour when the shots were fired), and to examine the full range of ballistic evidence. The film helped commission members to reach the conclusion, perhaps its most important, that Lee Harvey Oswald was the sole assassin, firing the mortal shots from a sixth-floor window in the Texas School Book Depository.

Reference Material

U.S. Presidents and Vice Presidents

Backgrounds of U.S. Presidents, 1789–2007

Summary of Presidential Elections, 1789–2004

Party Affiliations in Congress and the Presidency

Presidential Cabinets, 1789–2007

U.S. Government Organization Chart

Federal Internet Gateways and Search Engines

Constitution of the United States

U.S. Presidents and Vice Presidents

President and political party	Born	Died	Age at inauguration	Native of	from	Term of service	Elected Vice president
George Washington (F)	1732	1799	57	Va.	Va.	April 30, 1789–March 4, 1793	John Adams
George Washington (F)			61			March 4, 1793–March 4, 1797	John Adams
John Adams (F)	1735	1826	61	Mass.	Mass.	March 4, 1797–March 4, 1801	Thomas Jefferson
Thomas Jefferson (DR)	1743	1826	57	Va.	Va.	March 4, 1801–March 4, 1805	Aaron Burr
Thomas Jefferson (DR)			61			March 4, 1805–March 4, 1809	George Clinton
James Madison (DR)	1751	1836	57	Va.	Va.	March 4, 1809–March 4, 1813	George Clinton
James Madison (DR)			61			March 4, 1813–March 4, 1817	Elbridge Gerry
James Monroe (DR)	1758	1831	58	Va.	Va.	March 4, 1817–March 4, 1821	Daniel D. Tompkins
James Monroe (DR)			62			March 4, 1821–March 4, 1825	Daniel D. Tompkins
John Q. Adams (DR)	1767	1848	57	Mass.	Mass.	March 4, 1825–March 4, 1829	John C. Calhoun
Andrew Jackson (D)	1767	1845	61	S.C.	Tenn.	March 4, 1829–March 4, 1833	John C. Calhoun
Andrew Jackson (D)			65			March 4, 1833–March 4, 1837	Martin Van Buren
Martin Van Buren (D)	1782	1862	54	N.Y.	N.Y.	March 4, 1837–March 4, 1841	Richard M. Johnson
W. H. Harrison (W)	1773	1841	68	Va.	Ohio	March 4, 1841–April 4, 1841	John Tyler
John Tyler (W)	1790	1862	51	Va.	Va.	April 6, 1841–March 4, 1845	
James K. Polk (D)	1795	1849	49	N.C.	Tenn.	March 4, 1845–March 4, 1849	George M. Dallas
Zachary Taylor (W)	1784	1850	64	Va.	La.	March 4, 1849–July 9, 1850	Millard Fillmore
Millard Fillmore (W)	1800	1874	50	N.Y.	N.Y.	July 10, 1850–March 4, 1853	
Franklin Pierce (D)	1804	1869	48	N.H.	N.H.	March 4, 1853–March 4, 1857	William R. King
James Buchanan (D)	1791	1868	65	Pa.	Pa.	March 4, 1857–March 4, 1861	John C. Breckinridge
Abraham Lincoln (R)	1809	1865	52	Ky.	Ill.	March 4, 1861–March 4, 1865	Hannibal Hamlin
Abraham Lincoln (R)			56			March 4, 1865–April 15, 1865	Andrew Johnson
Andrew Johnson (R)	1808	1875	56	N.C.	Tenn.	April 15, 1865–March 4, 1869	
Ulysses S. Grant (R)	1822	1885	46	Ohio	Ill.	March 4, 1869–March 4, 1873	Schuyler Colfax
Ulysses S. Grant (R)			50			March 4, 1873–March 4, 1877	Henry Wilson
Rutherford B. Hayes (R)	1822	1893	54	Ohio	Ohio	March 4, 1877–March 4, 1881	William A. Wheeler
James A. Garfield (R)	1831	1881	49	Ohio	Ohio	March 4, 1881–Sept. 19, 1881	Chester A. Arthur
Chester A. Arthur (R)	1830	1886	50	Vt.	N.Y.	Sept. 20, 1881–March 4, 1885	
Grover Cleveland (D)	1837	1908	47	N.J.	N.Y.	March 4, 1885–March 4, 1889	Thomas A. Hendricks
Benjamin Harrison (R)	1833	1901	55	Ohio	Ind.	March 4, 1889–March 4, 1893	Levi P. Morton
Grover Cleveland (D)	1837	1908	55	N.J.	N.Y.	March 4, 1893–March 4, 1897	Adlai E. Stevenson
William McKinley (R)	1843	1901	54	Ohio	Ohio	March 4, 1897–March 4, 1901	Garret A. Hobart
William McKinley (R)			58			March 4, 1901–Sept. 14, 1901	Theodore Roosevelt
Theodore Roosevelt (R)	1858	1919	42	N.Y.	N.Y.	Sept. 14, 1901–March 4, 1905	
Theodore Roosevelt (R)			46			March 4, 1905–March 4, 1909	Charles W. Fairbanks
William H. Taft (R)	1857	1930	51	Ohio	Ohio	March 4, 1909–March 4, 1913	James S. Sherman
Woodrow Wilson (D)	1856	1924	56	Va.	N.J.	March 4, 1913–March 4, 1917	Thomas R. Marshall
Woodrow Wilson (D)			60			March 4, 1917–March 4, 1921	Thomas R. Marshall
Warren G. Harding (R)	1865	1923	55	Ohio	Ohio	March 4, 1921–Aug. 2, 1923	Calvin Coolidge
Calvin Coolidge (R)	1872	1933	51	Vt.	Mass.	Aug. 3, 1923–March 4, 1925	
Calvin Coolidge (R)			52			March 4, 1925–March 4, 1929	Charles G. Dawes
Herbert Hoover (R)	1874	1964	54	Iowa	Calif.	March 4, 1929–March 4, 1933	Charles Curtis
Franklin D. Roosevelt (D)	1882	1945	51	N.Y.	N.Y.	March 4, 1933–Jan. 20, 1937	John N. Garner
Franklin D. Roosevelt (D)			55			Jan. 20, 1937–Jan. 20, 1941	John N. Garner
Franklin D. Roosevelt (D)			59			Jan. 20, 1941–Jan. 20, 1945	Henry A. Wallace
Franklin D. Roosevelt (D)			63			Jan. 20, 1945–April 12, 1945	Harry S. Truman

U.S. Presidents and Vice Presidents *(Continued)*

President and political party	Born	Died	Age at inauguration	Native of	Native from	Term of service	Elected Vice president
Harry S. Truman (D)	1884	1972	60	Mo.	Mo.	April 12, 1945–Jan. 20, 1949	
Harry S. Truman (D)			64			Jan. 20, 1949–Jan. 20, 1953	Alben W. Barkley
Dwight D. Eisenhower (R)	1890	1969	62	Texas	N.Y.	Jan. 20, 1953–Jan. 20, 1957	Richard Nixon
Dwight D. Eisenhower (R)			66		Pa.	Jan. 20, 1957–Jan. 20, 1961	Richard Nixon
John F. Kennedy (D)	1917	1963	43	Mass.	Mass.	Jan. 20, 1961–Nov. 22, 1963	Lyndon B. Johnson
Lyndon B. Johnson (D)	1908	1973	55	Texas	Texas	Nov. 22, 1963–Jan. 20, 1965	
Lyndon B. Johnson (D)			56			Jan. 20, 1965–Jan. 20, 1969	Hubert H. Humphrey
Richard Nixon (R)	1913	1994	56	Calif.	N.Y.	Jan. 20, 1969–Jan. 20, 1973	Spiro T. Agnew
Richard Nixon (R)			60		Calif.	Jan. 20, 1973–Aug. 9, 1974	Spiro T. Agnew
							Gerald R. Ford
Gerald R. Ford (R)	1913	2006	61	Neb.	Mich.	Aug. 9, 1974–Jan. 20, 1977	Nelson A. Rockefeller
Jimmy Carter (D)	1924		52	Ga.	Ga.	Jan. 20, 1977–Jan. 20, 1981	Walter F. Mondale
Ronald Reagan (R)	1911	2004	69	Ill.	Calif.	Jan. 20, 1981–Jan. 20, 1985	George H. W. Bush
Ronald Reagan (R)			73			Jan. 20, 1985–Jan. 20, 1989	George H. W. Bush
George H. W. Bush (R)	1924		64	Mass.	Texas	Jan. 20, 1989–Jan. 20, 1993	Dan Quayle
Bill Clinton (D)	1946		46	Ark.	Ark.	Jan. 20, 1993–Jan. 20, 1997	Albert Gore Jr.
Bill Clinton (D)			50			Jan. 20, 1997–Jan. 20, 2001	Albert Gore, Jr.
George W. Bush (R)	1946		54	Texas	Texas	Jan. 20, 2001–Jan. 20, 2005	Richard B. Cheney
George W. Bush (R)			58			Jan. 20, 2005–	Richard B. Cheney

SOURCES: *Presidential Elections 1789–1992* (Washington, D.C.: Congressional Quarterly, 1995), 8; www.whitehouse.gov/president/gwbbio.html.

NOTE: D—Democrat; DR—Democratic-Republican; F—Federalist; R—Republican; W—Whig.

Backgrounds of U.S. Presidents, 1789–2007

President	Age at first political office	First political office	Last political office[a]	Age at becoming president	State of residence[b]	Father's occupation	Higher education[c]	Occupation
1. Washington (1789–1797)	17	County surveyor	Commander in chief	57	Va.	Farmer	None	Farmer, surveyor
2. Adams, J. (1797–1801)	39	Surveyor of highways	Vice president	61	Mass.	Farmer	Harvard	Farmer, lawyer
3. Jefferson (1801–1809)	26	State legislator	Vice president	58	Va.	Farmer	William and Mary	Farmer, lawyer
4. Madison (1809–1817)	25	State legislator	Secretary of state	58	Va.	Farmer	Princeton	Farmer
5. Monroe (1817–1825)	24	State legislator	Secretary of state	59	Va.	Farmer	William and Mary	Lawyer, farmer
6. Adams, J. Q. (1825–1829)	27	Minister to Netherlands	Secretary of state	58	Mass.	Farmer, lawyer	Harvard	Lawyer
7. Jackson (1829–1837)	21	Prosecuting attorney	U.S. Senate	62	Tenn.	Farmer	None	Lawyer
8. Van Buren (1837–1841)	30	Surrogate of county	Vice president	55	N.Y.	Tavern keeper	None	Lawyer
9. Harrison, W. H. (1841)	26	Territorial delegate to Congress	Minister to Colombia	68	Ind.	Farmer	Hampden-Sydney	Military
10. Tyler (1841–1845)	21	State legislator	Vice president	51	Va.	Planter, lawyer	William and Mary	Lawyer
11. Polk (1845–1849)	28	State legislator	Governor	50	Tenn.	Surveyor	U. of North Carolina	Lawyer
12. Taylor (1849–1850)	—	None	a	65	Ky.	Collector of internal revenue	None	Military
13. Fillmore (1850–1853)	28	State legislator	Vice president	50	N.Y.	Farmer	None	Lawyer
14. Pierce (1853–1857)	25	State legislator	U.S. district attorney	48	N.H.	General	Bowdoin	Lawyer
15. Buchanan (1857–1861)	22	Assistant county prosecutor	Minister to Great Britain	65	Pa.	Farmer	Dickinson	Lawyer
16. Lincoln (1861–1865)	25	State legislator	U.S. House of Representatives	52	Ill.	Farmer, carpenter	None	Lawyer
17. Johnson, A. (1865–1869)	20	City alderman	Vice president	57	Tenn.	Janitor-porter	None	Tailor
18. Grant (1869–1877)	—	None	a	47	Ohio	Tanner	West Point	Military
19. Hayes (1877–1881)	36	City solicitor	Governor	55	Ohio	Farmer	Kenyon	Lawyer
20. Garfield (1881)	28	State legislator	U.S. Senate	50	Ohio	Canal worker	Williams	Educator, lawyer

Backgrounds of U.S. Presidents, 1789–2007 *(Continued)*

President	Age at first political office	First political office	Last political office[a]	Age at becoming president	State of residence[b]	Father's occupation	Higher education[c]	Occupation
21. Arthur (1881–1885)	31	State engineer	Vice president	51	N.Y.	Minister	Union	Lawyer
22. Cleveland (1885–1889)	26	Assistant district attorney	Governor	48	N.Y.	Minister	None	Lawyer
23. Harrison, B. (1889–1893)	24	City attorney	U.S. Senate	56	Ind.	Military	Miami of Ohio	Lawyer
24. Cleveland (1893–1897)			President	56				
25. McKinley (1897–1901)	26	Prosecuting attorney	Governor	54	Ohio	Ironmonger	Allegheny	Lawyer
26. Roosevelt, T. (1901–1909)	24	State legislator	Vice president	42	N.Y.	Businessman	Harvard	Lawyer, author
27. Taft (1909–1913)	24	Assistant prosecuting attorney	Secretary of war	52	Ohio	Lawyer	Yale	Lawyer
28. Wilson (1913–1921)	54	Governor	Governor	56	N.J.	Minister	Princeton	Educator
29. Harding (1921–1923)	35	State legislator	U.S. Senate	56	Ohio	Physician, editor	Ohio Central	Newspaper editor
30. Coolidge (1923–1929)	26	City councilman	Vice president	51	Mass.	Storekeeper	Amherst	Lawyer
31. Hoover (1929–1933)	43	Relief and food administrator	Secretary of commerce	55	Calif.	Blacksmith	Stanford	Mining engineer
32. Roosevelt, F. (1933–1945)	28	State legislator	Governor	49	N.Y.	Businessman, landowner	Harvard	Lawyer
33. Truman (1945–1953)	38	County judge (commissioner)	Vice president	61	Mo.	Farmer, livestock owner	None	Clerk, store
34. Eisenhower (1953–1961)	—	None	[a]	63	Kan.	Mechanic	West Point	Military
35. Kennedy (1961–1963)	29	U.S. House of Representatives	U.S. Senate	43	Mass.	Businessman	Harvard	Newspaper reporter
36. Johnson, L. (1963–1969)	28	U.S. House of Representatives	Vice president	55	Texas	Farmer, real estate	Southwest Texas State Teacher's College	Educator
37. Nixon (1969–1974)	34	U. S. House of Representatives	Vice president	56	Calif.	Streetcar conductor	Whittier	Lawyer

Backgrounds of U.S. Presidents, 1789–2007 *(Continued)*

President	Age at first political office	First political office	Last political office[a]	Age at becoming president	State of residence[b]	Father's occupation	Higher education[c]	Occupation
38. Ford (1974–1977)	36	U.S. House of Representatives	Vice president	61	Mich.	Businessman	U. of Michigan	Lawyer
39. Carter (1977–1981)	38	County Board of Education	Governor	52	Ga.	Farmer, businessman	U.S. Naval Academy	Farmer, businessman
40. Reagan (1981–1989)	55	Governor	Governor	69	Calif.	Shoe salesman	Eureka	Entertainer
41. G. Bush (1989–1993)	42	U.S. House of Representatives	Vice president	64	Texas	Businessman, U.S. senator	Yale	Businessman
42. Clinton (1993–2001)	30	State attorney general	Governor	46	Ark.	Salesman	Georgetown	Lawyer
43. G.W. Bush (2001–)	48	Governor	Governor	54	Texas	Businessman, 41st U.S. president	Yale	Businessman

SOURCE: Richard A. Watson and Norman C. Thomas, *The Politics of the Presidency,* 3d ed. (Washington, D.C.: CQ Press, 1993).

a This category refers to the last civilian office held before the presidency. Taylor, Grant, and Eisenhower had served as generals before becoming president.

b The state is where the president spent his important adult years, not necessarily where he was born.

c Refers to undergraduate education.

Summary of Presidential Elections, 1789–2004

Year	No. of states	Candidates	Party	Electoral vote	Popular vote	
1789[a]	10	**George Washington**	**Fed.**	**69**	—[b]	
		John Adams	Fed.	34		
1792[a]	15	**George Washington**	**Fed.**	**132**	—[b]	
		John Adams	Fed.	77		
1796[a]	16	**John Adams**	**Fed.**	**71**	—[b]	
		Thomas Jefferson	Dem.-Rep.	68		
1800[a]	16	**Thomas Jefferson**	**Dem.-Rep.**	**73**	—[b]	
		Aaron Burr	Dem.-Rep.	73		
		John Adams	Fed.	65		
		Charles Cotesworth Pinckney	Fed.	64		
1804	17	**Thomas Jefferson** *George Clinton*	**Dem.-Rep.**	**162**	—[b]	
		Charles Cotesworth Pinckney *Rufus King*	Fed.	64		
1808	17	**James Madison** *George Clinton*	**Dem.-Rep.**	**122**	—[b]	
		Charles Cotesworth Pinckney *Rufus King*	Fed.	64		
1812	18	**James Madison** *Elbridge Gerry*	**Dem.-Rep.**	**128**	—[b]	
		George Clinton *Jared Ingersoll*	Fed.	89		
1816	19	**James Monroe** *Daniel D. Tompkins*	**Dem.-Rep.**	**183**	—[b]	
		Rufus King *John Howard*	Fed.	34		
1820	24	**James Monroe** *Daniel D. Tompkins*	**Dem.-Rep.**	**231**[c]	—[b]	
1824[d]	24	**John Quincy Adams** *John C. Calhoun*	**Dem.-Rep.**	**99**	**113,122**	**(30.9%)**
		Andrew Jackson *Nathan Sanford*	Dem.-Rep.	84	151,271	(41.3%)
1828	24	**Andrew Jackson** *John C. Calhoun*	**Dem.-Rep.**	**178**	**642,553**	**(56.0%)**
		John Quincy Adams *Richard Rush*	Nat.-Rep.	83	500,897	(43.6%)
1832[e]	24	**Andrew Jackson** *Martin Van Buren*	**Dem.**	**219**	**701,780**	**(54.2%)**
		Henry Clay *John Sergeant*	Nat.-Rep.	49	484,205	(37.4%)
1836[f]	26	**Martin Van Buren** *Richard M. Johnson*	**Dem.**	**170**	**764,176**	**(50.8%)**
		William Henry Harrison *Francis Granger*	Whig	73	550,816	(36.6%)

Summary of Presidential Elections, 1789–2004 *(Continued)*

Year	No. of states	Candidates	Party	Electoral vote	Popular vote
1840	26	**William Henry Harrison** *John Tyler*	**Whig**	**234**	**1,275,390 (52.9%)**
		Martin Van Buren *Richard M. Johnson*	Dem.	60	1,128,854 (46.8%)
1844	26	**James K. Polk** *George M. Dallas*	**Dem.**	**170**	**1,339,494 (49.5%)**
		Henry Clay *Theodore Frelinghuysen*	Whig	105	1,300,004 (48.1%)
1848	30	**Zachary Taylor** *Millard Fillmore*	**Whig**	**163**	**1,361,393 (47.3%)**
		Lewis Cass *William O. Butler*	Dem.	127	1,223,460 (42.5%)
1852	31	**Franklin Pierce** *William R. King*	**Dem.**	**254**	**1,607,510 (50.8%)**
		Winfield Scott *William A. Graham*	Whig	42	1,386,942 (43.9%)
1856[g]	31	**James Buchanan** *John C. Breckinridge*	**Dem.**	**174**	**1,836,072 (45.3%)**
		John C. Fremont *William L. Dayton*	Rep.	114	1,342,345 (33.1%)
1860[h]	33	**Abraham Lincoln** *Hannibal Hamlin*	**Rep.**	**180**	**1,865,908 (39.8%)**
		Stephen A. Douglas *Herschel V. Johnson*	Dem.	12	1,380,202 (29.5%)
1864[i]	36	**Abraham Lincoln** *Andrew Johnson*	**Rep.**	**212**	**2,218,388 (55.0%)**
		George B. McClellan *George H. Pendleton*	Dem.	21	1,812,807 (45.0%)
1868[j]	37	**Ulysses S. Grant** *Schuyler Colfax*	**Rep.**	**214**	**3,013,650 (52.7%)**
		Horatio Seymour *Francis P. Blair Jr.*	Dem.	80	2,708,744 (47.3%)
1872	37	**Ulysses S. Grant** *Henry Wilson*	**Rep.**	**286**	**3,598,235 (55.6%)**
		Horace Greeley *Benjamin Gratz Brown*	Dem.	—[k]	2,834,761 (43.8%)
1876	38	**Rutherford B. Hayes** *William A. Wheeler*	**Rep.**	**185**	**4,034,311 (47.9%)**
		Samuel J. Tilden *Thomas A. Hendricks*	Dem.	184	4,288,546 (51.0%)
1880	38	**James A. Garfield** *Chester A. Arthur*	**Rep.**	**214**	**4,446,158 (48.3%)**
		Winfield S. Hancock *William H. English*	Dem.	155	4,444,260 (48.2%)
1884	38	**Grover Cleveland** *Thomas A. Hendricks*	**Dem.**	**219**	**4,874,621 (48.5%)**
		James G. Blaine *John A. Logan*	Rep.	182	4,848,936 (48.2%)

Summary of Presidential Elections, 1789–2004 *(Continued)*

Year	No. of states	Candidates	Party	Electoral vote	Popular vote
1888	38	**Benjamin Harrison** *Levi P. Morton*	**Rep.**	**233**	**5,443,892 (47.8%)**
		Grover Cleveland *Allen G. Thurman*	Dem.	168	5,534,488 (48.6%)
1892[l]	44	**Grover Cleveland** *Adlai E. Stevenson*	**Dem.**	**277**	**5,551,883 (46.1%)**
		Benjamin Harrison *Whitelaw Reid*	Rep.	145	5,179,244 (43.0%)
1896	45	**William McKinley** *Garret A. Hobart*	**Rep.**	**271**	**7,108,480 (51.0%)**
		William J. Bryan *Arthur Sewall*	Dem.	176	6,511,495 (46.7%)
1900	45	**William McKinley** *Theodore Roosevelt*	**Rep.**	**292**	**7,218,039 (51.7%)**
		William J. Bryan *Adlai E. Stevenson*	Dem.	155	6,358,345 (45.5%)
1904	45	**Theodore Roosevelt** *Charles W. Fairbanks*	**Rep.**	**336**	**7,626,593 (56.4%)**
		Alton B. Parker *Henry G. Davis*	Dem.	140	5,028,898 (37.6%)
1908	46	**William Howard Taft** *James S. Sherman*	**Rep.**	**321**	**7,676,258 (51.6%)**
		William J. Bryan *John W. Kern*	Dem.	162	6,406,801 (43.0%)
1912[m]	48	**Woodrow Wilson** *Thomas R. Marshall*	**Dem.**	**435**	**6,293,152 (41.8%)**
		William Howard Taft *James S. Sherman*	Rep.	8	3,486,333 (23.2%)
1916	48	**Woodrow Wilson** *Thomas R. Marshall*	**Dem.**	**277**	**9,126,300 (49.2%)**
		Charles E. Hughes *Charles W. Fairbanks*	Rep.	254	8,546,789 (46.1%)
1920	48	**Warren G. Harding** *Calvin Coolidge*	**Rep.**	**404**	**16,133,314 (60.3%)**
		James M. Cox *Franklin D. Roosevelt*	Dem.	127	9,140,884 (34.2%)
1924[n]	48	**Calvin Coolidge** *Charles G. Dawes*	**Rep.**	**382**	**15,717,553 (54.1%)**
		John W. Davis *Charles W. Bryan*	Dem.	136	8,386,169 (28.8%)
1928	48	**Herbert C. Hoover** *Charles Curtis*	**Rep.**	**444**	**21,411,991 (58.2%)**
		Alfred E. Smith *Joseph T. Robinson*	Dem.	87	15,000,185 (40.8%)
1932	48	**Franklin D. Roosevelt** *John N. Garner*	**Dem.**	**472**	**22,825,016 (57.4%)**
		Herbert C. Hoover *Charles Curtis*	Rep.	59	15,758,397 (39.6%)

Summary of Presidential Elections, 1789–2004 *(Continued)*

Year	No. of states	Candidates	Party	Electoral vote	Popular vote
1936	48	**Franklin D. Roosevelt**	**Dem.**	**523**	**27,747,636 (60.8%)**
		John N. Garner			
		Alfred M. Landon	Rep.	8	16,679,543 (36.5%)
		Frank Knox			
1940	48	**Franklin D. Roosevelt**	**Dem.**	**449**	**27,263,448 (54.7%)**
		Henry A. Wallace			
		Wendell L. Willkie	Rep.	82	22,336,260 (44.8%)
		Charles L. McNary			
1944	48	**Franklin D. Roosevelt**	**Dem.**	**432**	**25,611,936 (53.4%)**
		Harry S. Truman			
		Thomas E. Dewey	Rep.	99	22,013,372 (45.9%)
		John W. Bricker			
1948[o]	48	**Harry S. Truman**	**Dem.**	**303**	**24,105,587 (49.5%)**
		Alben W. Barkley			
		Thomas E. Dewey	Rep.	198	21,970,017 (45.1%)
		Earl Warren			
1952	48	**Dwight D. Eisenhower**	**Rep.**	**442**	**33,936,137 (55.1%)**
		Richard M. Nixon			
		Adlai E. Stevenson II	Dem.	89	27,314,649 (44.4%)
		John J. Sparkman			
1956[p]	48	**Dwight D. Eisenhower**	**Rep.**	**457**	**35,585,245 (57.4%)**
		Richard M. Nixon			
		Adlai E. Stevenson II	Dem.	73	26,030,172 (42.0%)
		Estes Kefauver			
1960[q]	50	**John F. Kennedy**	**Dem.**	**303**	**34,221,344 (49.7%)**
		Lyndon B. Johnson			
		Richard Nixon	Rep.	219	34,106,671 (49.5%)
		Henry Cabot Lodge			
1964	50*	**Lyndon B. Johnson**	**Dem.**	**486**	**43,126,584 (61.1%)**
		Hubert H. Humphrey			
		Barry Goldwater	Rep.	52	27,177,838 (38.5%)
		William E. Miller			
1968[r]	50*	**Richard Nixon**	**Rep.**	**301**	**31,785,148 (43.4%)**
		Spiro T. Agnew			
		Hubert H. Humphrey	Dem.	191	31,274,503 (42.7%)
		Edmund S. Muskie			
1972[s]	50*	**Richard Nixon**	**Rep.**	**520**	**47,170,179 (60.7%)**
		Spiro T. Agnew			
		George McGovern	Dem.	17	29,171,791 (37.5%)
		Sargent Shriver			
1976[t]	50*	**Jimmy Carter**	**Dem.**	**297**	**40,830,763 (50.1%)**
		Walter F. Mondale			
		Gerald R. Ford	Rep.	240	39,147,793 (48.0%)
		Robert Dole			
1980	50*	**Ronald Reagan**	**Rep.**	**489**	**43,904,153 (50.7%)**
		George Bush			
		Jimmy Carter	Dem.	49	35,483,883 (41.0%)
		Walter F. Mondale			

Summary of Presidential Elections, 1789–2004 *(Continued)*

Year	No. of states	Candidates	Party	Electoral vote	Popular vote
1984	50*	**Ronald Reagan** *George Bush*	**Rep.**	525	**54,455,074 (58.8%)**
		Walter F. Mondale *Geraldine Ferraro*	Dem.	13	37,577,137 (40.6%)
1988[u]	50*	**George Bush** *Dan Quayle*	**Rep.**	426	**48,881,278 (53.4%)**
		Michael S. Dukakis *Lloyd Bentsen*	Dem.	111	41,805,374 (45.6%)
1992	50*	**Bill Clinton** *Al Gore*	**Dem.**	370	**44,908,233 (43.0%)**
		George Bush *Dan Quayle*	Rep.	168	39,102,282 (37.4%)
1996	50*	**Bill Clinton** *Al Gore*	**Dem.**	379	**47,402,357 (49.2%)**
		Robert Dole *Jack Kemp*	Rep.	159	39,198,755 (40.7%)
2000[v]	50*	**George W. Bush** *Richard B. Cheney*	**Rep.**	271	**50,455,156 (47.9%)**
		Al Gore *Joseph I. Lieberman*	Dem.	266	50,992,335 (48.4%)
2004[w]	50*	**George W. Bush** *Richard B. Cheney*	**Rep.**	286	**50,455,156 (47.9%)**
		John F. Kerry *John Edwards*	Dem.	251	50,992,335 (48.4%)

SOURCES: Harold W. Stanley and Richard G. Niemi, *Vital Statistics on American Politics*, 5th ed. (Washington, D.C.: CQ Press, 1995), Table 3-13; 1996 data, Richard M. Scammon, Alice V. McGillvray, and Rhodes Cook, *America Votes 22* (Washington, D.C.: Congressional Quarterly, 1998), 9.

NOTES: In the elections of 1789, 1792, 1796, and 1800, each candidate ran for the office of president. The candidate with the second highest number of electoral votes became vice president. For elections after 1800, italic indicates vice-presidential candidates. Dem.-Rep.—Democratic-Republican; Fed.—Federalist; Nat.-Rep.—National-Republican; Dem.—Democratic; Rep.—Republican. a. Elections of 1789–1800 were held under rules that did not allow separate voting for president and vice president. b. Popular vote returns are not shown before 1824 because consistent, reliable data are not available. c. Monroe ran unopposed. One electoral vote was cast for John Adams and Richard Stockton, who were not candidates. d. 1824: All four candidates represented Democratic-Republican factions. William H. Crawford received 41 electoral votes, and Henry Clay received 37 votes. Since no candidate received a majority, the election was decided (in Adams's favor) by the House of Representatives. e. 1832: Two electoral votes were not cast. f. 1836: Other Whig candidates receiving electoral votes were Hugh L. White, who received 26 votes, and Daniel Webster, who received 14 votes. g. 1856: Millard Fillmore, Whig-American, received 8 electoral votes. h. 1860: John C. Breckinridge, Southern Democrat, received 72 electoral votes. John Bell, Constitutional Union, received 39 electoral votes. i. 1864: Eighty-one electoral votes were not cast. j. 1868: Twenty-three electoral votes were not cast. k. 1872: Horace Greeley, Democrat, died after the election. In the electoral college, Democratic electoral votes went to Thomas Hendricks, 42 votes; Benjamin Gratz Brown, 18 votes; Charles J. Jenkins, 2 votes; and David Davis, 1 vote. Seventeen electoral votes were not cast. l. 1892: James B. Weaver, People's Party, received 22 electoral votes. m. 1912: Theodore Roosevelt, Progressive Party, received 86 electoral votes. n. 1924: Robert M. La Follette, Progressive Party, received 13 electoral votes. o. 1948: J. Strom Thurmond, States' Rights Party, received 39 electoral votes. p. 1956: Walter B. Jones, Democrat, received 1 electoral vote. q. 1960: Harry Flood Byrd, Democrat, received 15 electoral votes. r. 1968: George C. Wallace, American Independent Party, received 46 electoral votes. s. 1972: John Hospers, Libertarian Party, received 1 electoral vote. t. 1976: Ronald Reagan, Republican, received 1 electoral vote. u. 1988: Lloyd Bentsen, the Democratic vice-presidential nominee, received 1 electoral vote for president, and Michael S. Dukakis received 1 electoral vote for vice-president from an elector in West Virginia. v. 2000: One elector from the District of Columbia pledged to Albert Gore, Jr. and Joseph Lieberman abstained from voting. w. 2004: John Edwards, the Democratic vice-presidential nominee, received 1 electoral vote for president from an unknown elector in Minnesota.
*Fifty states plus the District of Columbia.

Party Affiliations in Congress and the Presidency

Year	Congress	HOUSE		SENATE		President
		Majority party	Principal minority party	Majority party	Principal minority party	
2007–2009	110th	D–233	R–202	D–49[3]	R–49	R (G.W. Bush)
2005–2007	109th	R–232	D–202	R–55	D–44[2]	R (G.W. Bush)
2003–2005	108th	R–229	D–204	R–51	D–48[2]	R (G.W. Bush)
2001–2003	107th	R–221	D–212	D–50	R–50[1]	R (G.W. Bush)
1999–2001	106th	R–222	D–211	R–55	D–45	D (Clinton)
1997–1999	105th	R–227	D–207	R–55	D–45	D (Clinton)
1995–1997	104th	R–231	D–203	R–53	D–47	D (Clinton)
1993–1995	103rd	D–258	R–176	D–57	R–43	D (Clinton)
1991–1993	102nd	D–267	R–167	D–56	R–44	R (Bush)
1989–1991	101st	D–259	R–174	D–55	R–45	R (Bush)
1987–1989	100th	D–258	R–177	D–55	R–45	R (Reagan)
1985–1987	99th	D–252	R–182	R–53	D–47	R (Reagan)
1983–1985	98th	D–269	R–165	R–54	D–46	R (Reagan)
1981–1983	97th	D–243	R–192	R–53	D–46	R (Reagan)
1979–1981	96th	D–276	R–157	D–58	R–41	D (Carter)
1977–1979	95th	D–292	R–143	D–61	R–38	D (Carter)
1975–1977	94th	D–291	R–144	D–60	R–37	R (Ford)
1973–1975	93rd	D–239	R–192	D–56	R–42	R (Ford) R (Nixon)
1971–1973	92nd	D–254	R–180	D–54	R–44	R (Nixon)
1969–1971	91st	D–243	R–192	D–57	R–43	R (Nixon)
1967–1969	90th	D–247	R–187	D–64	R–36	D (L. Johnson)
1965–1967	89th	D–295	R–140	D–68	R–32	D (L. Johnson)
1963–1965	88th	D–258	R–177	D–67	R–33	D (L. Johnson) D (Kennedy)
1961–1963	87th	D–263	R–174	D–65	R–35	D (Kennedy)
1959–1961	86th	D–283	R–153	D–64	R–34	R (Eisenhower)
1957–1959	85th	D–233	R–200	D–49	R–47	R (Eisenhower)
1955–1957	84th	D–232	R–203	D–48	R–47	R (Eisenhower)
1953–1955	83rd	R–221	D–211	R–48	D–47	R (Eisenhower)
1951–1953	82nd	D–234	R–199	D–49	R–47	D (Truman)
1949–1951	81st	D–263	R–171	D–54	R–42	D (Truman)
1947–1949	80th	R–245	D–188	R–51	D–45	D (Truman)
1945–1947	79th	D–242	R–190	D–56	R–38	D (Truman)
1943–1945	78th	D–218	R–208	D–58	R–37	D (F. Roosevelt)
1941–1943	77th	D–268	R–162	D–66	R–28	D (F. Roosevelt)
1939–1941	76th	D–261	R–164	D–69	R–23	D (F. Roosevelt)
1937–1939	75th	D–331	R–89	D–76	R–16	D (F. Roosevelt)
1935–1937	74th	D–319	R–103	D–69	R–25	D (F. Roosevelt)
1933–1935	73rd	D–310	R–117	D–60	R–35	D (F. Roosevelt)
1931–1933	72nd	D–220	R–214	R–48	D–47	R (Hoover)
1929–1931	71st	R–267	D–167	R–56	D–39	R (Hoover)
1927–1929	70th	R–237	D–195	R–49	D–46	R (Coolidge)
1925–1927	69th	R–247	D–183	R–56	D–39	R (Coolidge)
1923–1925	68th	R–225	D–205	R–51	D–43	R (Coolidge)

Party Affiliations in Congress and the Presidency *(Continued)*

Year	Congress	HOUSE Majority party	HOUSE Principal minority party	SENATE Majority party	SENATE Principal minority party	President
1921–1923	67th	R–301	D–131	R–59	D–37	R (Harding)
1919–1921	66th	R–240	D–190	R–49	D–47	D (Wilson)
1917–1919	65th	D–216	R–210	D–53	R–42	D (Wilson)
1915–1917	64th	D–230	R–196	D–56	R–40	D (Wilson)
1913–1915	63rd	D–291	R–127	D–51	R–44	D (Wilson)
1911–1913	62nd	D–228	R–161	R–51	D–41	R (Taft)
1909–1911	61st	R–219	D–172	R–61	D–32	R (Taft)
1907–1909	60th	R–222	D–164	R–61	D–31	R (T. Roosevelt)
1905–1907	59th	R–250	D–136	R–57	D–33	R (T. Roosevelt)
1903–1905	58th	R–208	D–178	R–57	D–33	R (T. Roosevelt)
1901–1903	57th	R–197	D–151	R–55	D–31	R (T. Roosevelt)
						R (McKinley)
1899–1901	56th	R–185	D–163	R–53	D–26	R (McKinley)
1897–1899	55th	R–204	D–113	R–47	D–34	R (McKinley)
1895–1897	54th	R–244	D–105	R–43	D–39	D (Cleveland)
1893–1895	53rd	D–218	R–127	D–44	R–38	D (Cleveland)
1891–1893	52nd	D–235	R–88	R–47	D–39	R (B. Harrison)
1889–1891	51st	R–166	D–159	R–39	D–37	R (B. Harrison)
1887–1889	50th	D–169	R–152	R–39	D–37	D (Cleveland)
1885–1887	49th	D–183	R–140	R–43	D–34	D (Cleveland)
1883–1885	48th	D–197	R–118	R–38	D–36	R (Arthur)
1881–1883	47th	R–147	D–135	R–37	D–37	R (Arthur)
						R (Garfield)
1879–1881	46th	D–149	R–130	D–42	R–33	R (Hayes)
1877–1879	45th	D–153	R–140	R–39	D–36	R (Hayes)
1875–1877	44th	D–169	R–109	R–45	D–29	R (Grant)
1873–1875	43rd	R–194	D–92	R–49	D–19	R (Grant)
1871–1873	42nd	R–134	D–104	R–52	D–17	R (Grant)
1869–1871	41st	R–149	D–63	R–56	D–11	R (Grant)
1867–1869	40th	R–143	D–49	R–42	D–11	R (A. Johnson)
1865–1867	39th	U–149	D–42	U–42	D–10	R (A. Johnson)
						R (Lincoln)
1863–1865	38th	R–102	D–75	R–36	D–9	R (Lincoln)
1861–1863	37th	R–105	D–43	R–31	D–10	R (Lincoln)
1859–1861	36th	R–114	D–92	D–36	R–26	D (Buchanan)
1857–1859	35th	D–118	R–92	D–36	R–20	D (Buchanan)
1855–1857	34th	R–108	D–83	D–40	R–15	D (Pierce)
1853–1855	33rd	D–159	W–71	D–38	W–22	D (Pierce)
1851–1853	32nd	D–140	W–88	D–35	W–24	W (Fillmore)
1849–1851	31st	D–112	W–109	D–35	W–25	W (Fillmore)
						W (Taylor)
1847–1849	30th	W–115	D–108	D–36	W–21	D (Polk)
1845–1847	29th	D–143	W–77	D–31	W–25	D (Polk)
1843–1845	28th	D–142	W–79	W–28	D–25	W (Tyler)

Party Affiliations in Congress and the Presidency *(Continued)*

| Year | Congress | HOUSE | | SENATE | | President |
		Majority party	Principal minority party	Majority party	Principal minority party	
1841–1843	27th	W–133	D–102	W–28	D–22	W (Tyler)
						W (W. Harrison)
1839–1841	26th	D–124	W–118	D–28	W–22	D (Van Buren)
1837–1839	25th	D–108	W–107	D–30	W–18	D (Van Buren)
1835–1837	24th	D–145	W–98	D–27	W–25	D (Jackson)
1833–1835	23rd	D–147	AM–53	D–20	NR–20	D (Jackson)
1831–1833	22nd	D–141	NR–58	D–25	NR–21	D (Jackson)
1829–1831	21st	D–139	NR–74	D–26	NR–22	DR (Jackson)
1827–1829	20th	J–119	AD–94	J–28	AD–20	DR (John Q. Adams)
1825–1827	19th	AD–105	J–97	AD–26	J–20	DR (John Q. Adams)
1823–1825	18th	DR–187	F–26	DR–44	F–4	DR (Monroe)
1821–1823	17th	DR–158	F–25	DR–44	F–4	DR (Monroe)
1819–1821	16th	DR–156	F–27	DR–35	F–7	DR (Monroe)
1817–1819	15th	DR–141	F–42	DR–34	F–10	DR (Monroe)
1815–1817	14th	DR–117	F–65	DR–25	F–11	DR (Madison)
1813–1815	13th	DR–112	F–68	DR–27	F–9	DR (Madison)
1811–1813	12th	DR–108	F–36	DR–30	F–6	DR (Madison)
1809–1811	11th	DR–94	F–48	DR–28	F–6	DR (Madison)
1807–1809	10th	DR–118	F–24	DR–28	F–6	DR (Jefferson)
1805–1807	9th	DR–116	F–25	DR–27	F–7	DR (Jefferson)
1803–1805	8th	DR–102	F–39	DR–25	F–9	DR (Jefferson)
1801–1803	7th	DR–69	F–36	DR–18	F–13	DR (Jefferson)
1799–1801	6th	F–64	DR–42	F–19	DR–13	F (John Adams)
1797–1799	5th	F–58	DR–48	F–20	DR–12	F (John Adams)
1795–1797	4th	F–54	DR–52	F–19	DR–13	F (Washington)
1793–1795	3rd	DR–57	F–48	F–17	DR–13	F (Washington)
1791–1793	2nd	F–37	DR–33	F–16	DR–13	F (Washington)
1789–1791	1st	Ad–38	Op–26	Ad–17	Op–9	F (Washington)

SOURCES: *Congressional Quarterly Weekly Report,* selected issues; U.S. Bureau of the Census, *Historical Statistics of the United States, Colonial Times to 1970* (Washington, D.C.: Government Printing Office, 1975); *Official Congressional Directory,* selected years; and Harold Stanley and Richard G. Niemi, *Vital Statistics on American Politics, 1997–1998* (Washington, D.C: Congressional Quarterly, 1998), Table 1–9.

NOTE: Key to abbreviations: Ad—Administration; AM—Anti-Masonic; D—Democratic; DR—Democratic-Republican; F—Federalist; J—Jacksonian; NR—National Republican; Op—Opposition; R—Republican; U—Unionist; W—Whig. Figures are for the beginning of the first session of each Congress.

1. The November 2000 Senate elections resulted in a 50–50 split between Republicans and Democrats in that chamber. On June 5, 2001, Republican Sen. James Jeffords of Vermont left the Republican Party to become an Independent. However, he caucused with the Democrats giving them a 51–49 majority and allowing them to take control of the chamber organization and schedule and the committees.

2. In the 108th and 109th Congresses, independent Sen. James Jeffords of Vermont caucused with the Democratic Party

3. In the November 2006 Senate elections, Sen. Joseph Lieberman of Connecticut was re-elected as an independent and in the 110th Congress is considered an Independent Democrat. Sen. Bernard Sanders of Vermont was elected as an independent. Both Senators caucus with the Democratic Party giving the Democrats 51 votes and control of the Senate.

Presidential Cabinets, 1789–2007

Following is a list of cabinet members by administration from George Washington to George W. Bush. Included are dates of service. The list does not include those who served in ad interim appointments.

George Washington, 1789–1797

Secretary of State
Thomas Jefferson
March 22, 1790–Dec. 31, 1793
Edmund Randolph
Jan. 2, 1794–Aug. 20, 1795
Timothy Pickering
Dec. 10, 1795–May 12, 1800

Secretary of the Treasury
Alexander Hamilton
Sept. 11, 1789–Jan. 31, 1795
Oliver Wolcott Jr.
Feb. 3, 1795–Dec. 31, 1800

Secretary of War
Henry Knox
Sept. 12, 1789–Dec. 31, 1794
Timothy Pickering
Jan. 2–Dec. 10, 1795
James McHenry
Jan. 27, 1796–May 13, 1800

Attorney General
Edmund Randolph
Sept. 26, 1789–Jan. 2, 1794
William Bradford
Jan. 27, 1794–Aug. 23, 1795
Charles Lee
Dec. 10, 1795–Feb. 18, 1801

Postmaster General
Samuel Osgood
Sept. 26, 1789–Aug. 18, 1791
Timothy Pickering
Aug. 19, 1791–Jan. 2, 1795
Joseph Habersham
July 1, 1795–Nov. 2, 1801

John Adams, 1797–1801

Secretary of State
Timothy Pickering
Dec. 10, 1795–May 12, 1800
John Marshall
June 6, 1800–Feb. 4, 1801

Secretary of the Treasury
Oliver Wolcott Jr.
Feb. 3, 1795–Dec. 31, 1800
Samuel Dexter
Jan. 1–May 13, 1801

Secretary of War
James McHenry
Jan. 27, 1796–May 13, 1800
Samuel Dexter
May 13–Dec. 31, 1800

Attorney General
Charles Lee
Dec. 10, 1795–Feb. 18, 1801

Postmaster General
Joseph Habersham
July 1, 1795–Nov. 2, 1801

Secretary of the Navy
Benjamin Stoddert
June 18, 1798–March 31, 1801

Thomas Jefferson, 1801–1809

Secretary of State
James Madison
May 2, 1801–March 3, 1809

Secretary of the Treasury
Samuel Dexter
Jan. 1–May 13, 1801
Albert Gallatin
May 14, 1801–Feb. 8, 1814

Secretary of War
Henry Dearborn
March 5, 1801–March 7, 1809

Attorney General
Levi Lincoln
March 5, 1801–March 3, 1805
John C. Breckinridge
Aug. 7, 1805–Dec. 14, 1806
Caesar Augustus Rodney
Jan. 20, 1807–Dec. 11, 1811

Postmaster General
Joseph Habersham
July 1, 1795–Nov. 2, 1801
Gideon Granger
Nov. 28, 1801–Feb. 25, 1814

Secretary of the Navy
Benjamin Stoddert
June 18, 1798–March 31, 1801
Robert Smith
July 27, 1801–March 7, 1809

James Madison, 1809–1817

Secretary of State
Robert Smith
March 6, 1809–April 1, 1811
James Monroe
April 6, 1811–Sept. 30, 1814,
Feb. 28, 1815–March 3, 1817

Secretary of the Treasury
Albert Gallatin
May 14, 1801–Feb. 8, 1814
George Washington Campbell
Feb. 9–Oct. 5, 1814
Alexander James Dallas
Oct. 6, 1814–Oct. 21, 1816
William Harris Crawford
Oct. 22, 1816–March 6, 1825

Secretary of War
William Eustis
March 7, 1809–Jan. 13, 1813
John Armstrong
Jan. 13, 1813–Sept. 27, 1814
James Monroe
Oct. 1, 1814–Feb. 28, 1815
William Harris Crawford
Aug. 1, 1815–Oct. 22, 1816

Attorney General
Caesar Augustus Rodney
Jan. 20, 1807–Dec. 11, 1811
William Pinkney
Dec. 11, 1811–Feb. 10, 1814
Richard Rush
Feb. 10, 1814–Nov. 13, 1817

Postmaster General
Gideon Granger
Nov. 28, 1801–Feb. 25, 1814
Return Jonathan Meigs Jr.
April 11, 1814–June 30, 1823

Secretary of the Navy
Robert Smith
July 27, 1801–March 7, 1809
Paul Hamilton
May 15, 1809–Dec. 31, 1812
William Jones
Jan. 19, 1813–Dec. 1, 1814
Benjamin Williams Crowninshield
Jan. 16, 1815–Sept. 30, 1818

Presidential Cabinets, 1789–2007 *(Continued)*

James Monroe, 1817–1825

Secretary of State
John Quincy Adams
Sept. 22, 1817–March 3, 1825

Secretary of the Treasury
William Harris Crawford
Oct. 22, 1816–March 6, 1825

Secretary of War
John C. Calhoun
Oct. 8, 1817–March 7, 1825

Attorney General
Richard Rush
Feb. 10, 1814–Nov. 13, 1817
William Wirt
Nov. 13, 1817–March 3, 1829

Postmaster General
Return Jonathan Meigs Jr.
April 11, 1814–June 30, 1823
John McLean
July 1, 1823–March 9, 1829

Secretary of the Navy
Benjamin Williams Crowninshield
Jan. 16, 1815–Sept. 30, 1818
Smith Thompson
Jan. 1, 1819–Aug. 31, 1823
Samuel Lewis Southard
Sept. 16, 1823–March 3, 1829

John Quincy Adams, 1825–1829

Secretary of State
Henry Clay
March 7, 1825–March 3, 1829

Secretary of the Treasury
Richard Rush
March 7, 1825–March 5, 1829

Secretary of War
James Barbour
March 7, 1825–May 23, 1828
Peter Buell Porter
May 26, 1828–March 9, 1829

Attorney General
William Wirt
Nov. 13, 1817–March 3, 1829

Postmaster General
John McLean
July 1, 1823–March 9, 1829

Secretary of the Navy
Samuel Lewis Southard
Sept. 16, 1823–March 3, 1829

Andrew Jackson, 1829–1837

Secretary of State
Martin Van Buren
March 28, 1829–March 23, 1831
Edward Livingston
May 24, 1831–May 29, 1833
Louis McLane
May 29, 1833–June 30, 1834
John Forsyth
July 1, 1834–March 3, 1841

Secretary of the Treasury
Samuel Delucenna Ingham
March 6, 1829–June 20, 1831
Louis McLane
Aug. 8, 1831–May 28, 1833
William John Duane
May 29–Sept. 22, 1833
Roger B. Taney
Sept. 23, 1833–June 25, 1834
Levi Woodbury
July 1, 1834–March 3, 1841

Secretary of War
John Henry Eaton
March 9, 1829–June 18, 1831
Lewis Cass
Aug. 1, 1831–Oct. 5, 1836

Attorney General
John Macpherson Berrien
March 9, 1829–July 20, 1831
Roger B. Taney
July 20, 1831–Sept. 23, 1833
Benjamin Franklin Butler
Nov. 15, 1833–Sept. 1, 1838

Postmaster General
John McLean
July 1, 1823–March 9, 1829
William Taylor Barry
April 6, 1829–April 30, 1835
Amos Kendall
May 1, 1835–May 25, 1840

Secretary of the Navy
John Branch
March 9, 1829–May 12, 1831
Levi Woodbury
May 23, 1831–June 30, 1834

Mahlon Dickerson
July 1, 1834–June 30, 1838

Martin Van Buren, 1837–1841

Secretary of State
John Forsyth
July 1, 1834–March 3, 1841

Secretary of the Treasury
Levi Woodbury
July 1, 1834–March 3, 1841

Secretary of War
Joel Roberts Poinsett
March 7, 1837–March 5, 1841

Attorney General
Benjamin Franklin Butler
Nov. 15, 1833–Sept. 1, 1838
Felix Grundy
Sept. 1, 1838–Dec. 1, 1839
Henry Dilworth Gilpin
Jan. 11, 1840–March 4, 1841

Postmaster General
Amos Kendall
May 1, 1835–May 25, 1840
John Milton Niles
May 26, 1840–March 3, 1841

Secretary of the Navy
Mahlon Dickerson
July 1, 1834–June 30, 1838
James Kirke Paulding
July 1, 1838–March 3, 1841

William Henry Harrison, 1841

Secretary of State
Daniel Webster
March 6, 1841–May 8, 1843,
July 23, 1850–Oct. 24, 1852

Secretary of the Treasury
Thomas Ewing
March 4–Sept. 11, 1841

Secretary of War
John Bell
March 5–Sept. 13, 1841

Attorney General
John Jordan Crittenden
March 5–Sept. 13, 1841,
July 22, 1850– March 3, 1853

Postmaster General
Francis Granger
March 8–Sept. 13, 1841

Secretary of the Navy
George Edmund Badger
March 6–Sept. 11, 1841

John Tyler, 1841–1845

Secretary of State
Daniel Webster
March 6, 1841–May 8, 1843,
July 23, 1850–Oct. 24, 1852
Abel Parker Upshur
July 24, 1843–Feb. 28, 1844
John C. Calhoun
April 1, 1844–March 10, 1845

Secretary of the Treasury
Thomas Ewing
March 4–Sept. 11, 1841
Walter Forward
Sept. 13, 1841–March 1, 1843
John Canfield Spencer
March 8, 1843–May 2, 1844
George Mortimer Bibb
July 4, 1844–March 7, 1845

Secretary of War
John Bell
March 5–Sept. 13, 1841
John Canfield Spencer
Oct. 12, 1841–March 3, 1843
James Madison Porter
March 8, 1843–Jan. 30, 1844
William Wilkins
Feb. 15, 1844–March 4, 1845

Attorney General
John Jordan Crittenden
March 5–Sept. 13, 1841,
July 22, 1850–March 3, 1853
Hugh Swinton Legare
Sept. 13, 1841–June 20, 1843
John Nelson
July 1, 1843–March 3, 1845

Postmaster General
Francis Granger
March 8–Sept. 13, 1841
Charles Anderson Wickliffe
Oct. 13, 1841–March 6, 1845

Secretary of the Navy
George Edmund Badger
March 6–Sept. 11, 1841
Abel Parker Upshur
Oct. 11, 1841–July 23, 1843
David Henshaw
July 24, 1843–Feb. 18, 1844
Thomas Walker Gilmer
Feb. 19–Feb. 28, 1844
John Young Mason
March 26, 1844–March 10, 1845,
Sept. 10, 1846–March 7, 1849

James K. Polk, 1845–1849

Secretary of State
John C. Calhoun
April 1, 1844–March 10, 1845
James Buchanan
March 10, 1845–March 7, 1849

Secretary of the Treasury
George Mortimer Bibb
July 4, 1844–March 7, 1845
Robert John Walker
March 8, 1845–March 5, 1849

Secretary of War
William Wilkins
Feb. 15, 1844–March 4, 1845
William Learned Marcy
March 6, 1845–March 4, 1849

Attorney General
John Nelson
July 1, 1843–March 3, 1845
John Young Mason
March 11, 1845–Sept. 9, 1846
Nathan Clifford
Oct. 17, 1846–March 17, 1848
Isaac Toucey
June 21, 1848–March 3, 1849

Postmaster General
Charles Anderson Wickliffe
Oct. 13, 1841–March 6, 1845
Cave Johnson
March 7, 1845–March 5, 1849

Secretary of the Navy
John Young Mason
March 26, 1844–March 10, 1845,
Sept. 10, 1846–March 7, 1849

George Bancroft
March 11, 1845–Sept. 9, 1846

Zachary Taylor, 1849–1850

Secretary of State
James Buchanan
March 10, 1845–March 7, 1849
John Middleton Clayton
March 8, 1849–July 22, 1850

Secretary of the Treasury
Robert John Walker
March 8, 1845–March 5, 1849
William Morris Meredith
March 8, 1849–July 22, 1850

Secretary of War
William Learned Marcy
March 6, 1845–March 4, 1849
George Washington Crawford
March 8, 1849–July 23, 1850

Attorney General
Isaac Toucey
June 21, 1848–March 3, 1849
Reverdy Johnson
March 8, 1849–July 20, 1850

Postmaster General
Cave Johnson
March 7, 1845–March 5, 1849
Jacob Collamer
March 8, 1849–July 22, 1850

Secretary of the Navy
John Young Mason
March 26, 1844–March 10, 1845,
Sept. 10, 1846–March 7, 1849
William Ballard Preston
March 8, 1849–July 22, 1850

Secretary of the Interior
Thomas Ewing
March 8, 1849–July 22, 1850

Millard Fillmore, 1850–1853

Secretary of State
John Middleton Clayton
March 8, 1849–July 22, 1850
Daniel Webster
March 6, 1841–May 8, 1843,
July 23, 1850–Oct. 24, 1852

Edward Everett
Nov. 6, 1852–March 3, 1853

Secretary of the Treasury
William Morris Meredith
March 8, 1849–July 22, 1850
Thomas Corwin
July 23, 1850–March 6, 1853

Secretary of War
George W. Crawford
March 8, 1849–July 23, 1850
Charles Magill Conrad
Aug. 15, 1850–March 7, 1853
Attorney General
Reverdy Johnson
March 8, 1849–July 20, 1850
John Jordan Crittenden
March 5–Sept. 13, 1841,
July 22, 1850–March 3, 1853

Postmaster General
Jacob Collamer
March 8, 1849–July 22, 1850
Nathan Kelsey Hall
July 23, 1850–Sept. 13, 1852
Samuel Dickinson Hubbard
Sept. 14, 1852–March 7, 1853

Secretary of the Navy
William Ballard Preston
March 8, 1849–July 22, 1850
William Alexander Graham
Aug. 2, 1850–July 25, 1852
John Pendleton Kennedy
July 26, 1852–March 7, 1853

Secretary of the Interior
Thomas Ewing
March 8, 1849–July 22, 1850
Thomas McKean Thompson McKennan
Aug. 15–Aug. 26, 1850
Alexander Hugh Holmes Stuart
Sept. 12, 1850–March 7, 1853

Franklin Pierce, 1853–1857

Secretary of State
William Learned Marcy
March 8, 1853–March 6, 1857

Secretary of the Treasury
Thomas Corwin
July 23, 1850–March 6, 1853

James Guthrie
March 7, 1853–March 6, 1857

Secretary of War
Charles Magill Conrad
Aug. 15, 1850–March 7, 1853
Jefferson Davis
March 7, 1853–March 6, 1857

Attorney General
John Jordan Crittenden
March 5–Sept. 13, 1841,
July 22, 1850–March 3, 1853
Caleb Cushing
March 7, 1853–March 3, 1857

Postmaster General
Samuel Dickinson Hubbard
Sept. 14, 1852–March 7, 1853
James Campbell
March 8, 1853–March 6, 1857

Secretary of the Navy
John Pendleton Kennedy
July 26, 1852–March 7, 1853
James Cochran Dobbin
March 8, 1853–March 6, 1857

Secretary of the Interior
Alexander Hugh Holmes Stuart
Sept. 12, 1850–March 7, 1853
Robert McClelland
March 8, 1853–March 9, 1857

James Buchanan, 1857–1861

Secretary of State
William Learned Marcy
March 8, 1853–March 6, 1857
Lewis Cass
March 6, 1857–Dec. 14, 1860
Jeremiah Sullivan Black
Dec. 17, 1860–March 5, 1861

Secretary of the Treasury
James Guthrie
March 7, 1853–March 6, 1857
Howell Cobb
March 7, 1857–Dec. 8, 1860
Philip Francis Thomas
Dec. 12, 1860–Jan. 14, 1861
John Adams Dix
Jan. 15–March 6, 1861

Secretary of War
John Buchanan Floyd
March 6, 1857–Dec. 29, 1860

Joseph Holt
Jan. 18–March 5, 1861

Attorney General
Caleb Cushing
March 7, 1853–March 3, 1857
Jeremiah Sullivan Black
March 6, 1857–Dec. 17, 1860
Edwin Stanton
Dec. 20, 1860–March 3, 1861

Postmaster General
James Campbell
March 8, 1853–March 6, 1857
Aaron Venable Brown
March 7, 1857–March 8, 1859
Joseph Holt
March 14, 1859–Dec. 31, 1860
Horatio King
Feb. 12–March 9, 1861

Secretary of the Navy
James Cochran Dobbin
March 8, 1853–March 6, 1857
Isaac Toucey
March 7, 1857–March 6, 1861

Secretary of the Interior
Robert McClelland
March 8, 1853–March 9, 1857
Jacob Thompson
March 10, 1857–Jan. 8, 1861

Abraham Lincoln, 1861–1865

Secretary of State
Jeremiah Sullivan Black
Dec. 17, 1860–March 5, 1861
William Henry Seward
March 6, 1861–March 4, 1869

Secretary of the Treasury
John Adams Dix
Jan. 15–March 6, 1861
Salmon P. Chase
March 7, 1861–June 30, 1864
William Pitt Fessenden
July 5, 1864–March 3, 1865
Hugh McCulloch
March 9, 1865–March 3, 1869,
Oct. 31, 1884–March 7, 1885

Secretary of War
Joseph Holt
Jan. 18–March 5, 1861

Simon Cameron
March 5, 1861–Jan. 14, 1862
Edwin Stanton
Jan. 20, 1862–May 28, 1868

Attorney General
Edwin Stanton
Dec. 20, 1860–March 3, 1861
Edward Bates
March 5, 1861–Sept. 1864
James Speed
Dec. 2, 1864–July 17, 1866

Postmaster General
Horatio King
Feb. 12–March 9, 1861
Montgomery Blair
March 9, 1861–Sept. 30, 1864
William Dennison Jr.
Oct. 1, 1864–July 16, 1866

Secretary of the Navy
Isaac Toucey
March 7, 1857–March 6, 1861
Gideon Welles
March 7, 1861–March 3, 1869

Secretary of the Interior
Caleb Blood Smith
March 5, 1861–Dec. 31, 1862
John Palmer Usher
Jan. 1, 1863–May 15, 1865

Andrew Johnson, 1865–1869

Secretary of State
William Henry Seward
March 6, 1861–March 4, 1869

Secretary of the Treasury
Hugh McCulloch
March 9, 1865–March 3, 1869,
Oct. 31, 1884–March 7, 1885

Secretary of War
Edwin Stanton
Jan. 20, 1862–May 28, 1868
John McAllister Schofield
June 1, 1868–March 13, 1869

Attorney General
James Speed
Dec. 2, 1864–July 17, 1866
Henry Stanberry
July 23, 1866–March 12, 1868

William Maxwell Evarts
July 15, 1868–March 3, 1869

Postmaster General
William Dennison Jr.
Oct. 1, 1864–July 16, 1866
Alexander Williams Randall
July 25, 1866–March 4, 1869

Secretary of the Navy
Gideon Welles
March 7, 1861–March 3, 1869

Secretary of the Interior
John Palmer Usher
Jan. 1, 1863–May 15, 1865
James Harlan
May 15, 1865–Aug. 31, 1866
Orville Hickman Browning
Sept. 1, 1866–March 4, 1869

Ulysses S. Grant, 1869–1877

Secretary of State
William Henry Seward
March 6, 1861–March 4, 1869
Elihu Benjamin Washburne
March 5–March 16, 1869
Hamilton Fish
March 17, 1869–March 12, 1877

Secretary of the Treasury
Hugh McCulloch
March 9, 1865–March 3, 1869,
Oct. 31, 1884–March 7, 1885
George Sewel Boutwell
March 12, 1869–March 16, 1873
William Adams Richardson
March 17, 1873–June 3, 1874
Benjamin Helm Bristow
June 4, 1874–June 20, 1876
Lot Myrick Morrill
July 7, 1876–March 9, 1877

Secretary of War
John McAllister Schofield
June 1, 1868–March 13, 1869
John Aaron Rawlins
March 13–Sept. 6, 1869
William Tecumseh Sherman
Sept. 11–Oct. 25, 1869
William Worth Belknap
Oct. 25, 1869–March 2, 1876
Alphonso Taft
March 8–May 22, 1876

James Donald Cameron
May 22, 1876–March 3, 1877

Attorney General
Ebenezer Rockwood Hoar
March 5, 1869–June 23, 1870
Amos Tappan Akerman
June 23, 1870–Jan. 10, 1872
George Henry Williams
Jan. 10, 1872–May 15, 1875
Edwards Pierrepont
May 15, 1875–May 22, 1876
Alphonso Taft
May 22, 1876–March 11, 1877

Postmaster General
John Angel James Creswell
March 6, 1869–July 6, 1874
James William Marshall
July 7–Aug. 31, 1874
Marshall Jewell
Sept. 1, 1874–July 12, 1876
James Noble Tyner
July 13, 1876–March 12, 1877

Secretary of the Navy
Adolph Edward Borie
March 9–June 25, 1869
George Maxwell Robeson
June 26, 1869–March 12, 1877

Secretary of the Interior
Jacob Dolson Cox
March 5, 1869–Oct. 31, 1870
Columbus Delano
Nov. 1, 1870–Sept. 30, 1875
Zachariah Chandler
Oct. 19, 1875–March 11, 1877

Rutherford B. Hayes, 1877–1881

Secretary of State
Hamilton Fish
March 17, 1869–March 12, 1877
William Maxwell Evarts
March 12, 1877–March 7, 1881

Secretary of the Treasury
Lot Myrick Morrill
July 7, 1876–March 9, 1877
John Sherman
March 10, 1877–March 3, 1881

Secretary of War
James Donald Cameron

Presidential Cabinets, 1789–2007 *(Continued)*

May 22, 1876–March 3, 1877
George Washington McCrary
  March 12, 1877–Dec. 10, 1879
Alexander Ramsey
  Dec. 10, 1879–March 5, 1881

Attorney General
Alphonso Taft
  May 22, 1876–March 11, 1877
Charles Devens
  March 12, 1877–March 6, 1881

Postmaster General
James Noble Tyner
  July 13, 1876–March 12, 1877
David McKendree Key
  March 13, 1877–Aug. 24, 1880
Horace Maynard
  Aug. 25, 1880–March 7, 1881

Secretary of the Navy
George Maxwell Robeson
  June 26, 1869–March 12, 1877
Richard Wigginton Thompson
  March 13, 1877–Dec. 20, 1880
Nathan Goff Jr.
  Jan. 7–March 6, 1881

Secretary of the Interior
Zachariah Chandler
  Oct. 19, 1875–March 11, 1877
Carl Schurz
  March 12, 1877–March 7, 1881

James A. Garfield, 1881

Secretary of State
William Maxwell Evarts
  March 12, 1877–March 7, 1881
James G. Blaine
  March 7–Dec. 19, 1881,
  March 7, 1889–June 4, 1892

Secretary of the Treasury
William Windom
  March 8–Nov. 13, 1881,
  March 7, 1889–Jan. 29, 1891

Secretary of War
Alexander Ramsey
  Dec. 10, 1879–March 5, 1881
Robert Todd Lincoln
  March 5, 1881–March 5, 1885

Attorney General
Charles Devens
  March 12, 1877–March 6, 1881
Wayne MacVeagh
  March 7–Oct. 24, 1881

Postmaster General
Horace Maynard
  Aug. 25, 1880–March 7, 1881
Thomas Lemuel James
  March 8, 1881–Jan. 4, 1882

Secretary of the Navy
Nathan Goff Jr.
  Jan. 7–March 6, 1881
William Henry Hunt
  March 7, 1881–April 16, 1882

Secretary of the Interior
Carl Schurz
  March 12, 1877–March 7, 1881
Samuel Jordan Kirkwood
  March 8, 1881–April 17, 1882

Chester A. Arthur, 1881–1885

Secretary of State
James G. Blaine
  March 7–Dec. 19, 1881,
  March 7, 1889–June 4, 1892
Frederick Theodore Frelinghuysen
  Dec. 19, 1881–March 6, 1885

Secretary of the Treasury
William Windom
  March 8–Nov. 13, 1881,
  March 7, 1889–Jan. 29, 1891
Charles James Folger
  Nov. 14, 1881–Sept. 4, 1884
Walter Quintin Gresham
  Sept. 5–Oct. 30, 1884
Hugh McCulloch
  March 9, 1865–March 3, 1869,
  Oct. 31, 1884–March 7, 1885

Secretary of War
Robert Todd Lincoln
  March 5, 1881–March 5, 1885

Attorney General
Wayne MacVeagh
  March 7–Oct. 24, 1881
Benjamin Harris Brewster
  Jan. 2, 1882–March 5, 1885

Postmaster General
Thomas Lemuel James
  March 8, 1881–Jan. 4, 1882
Timothy Otis Howe
  Jan. 5, 1882–March 25, 1883
Walter Quintin Gresham
  April 11, 1883–Sept. 24, 1884
Frank Hatton
  Oct. 15, 1884–March 6, 1885

Secretary of the Navy
William Henry Hunt
  March 7, 1881–April 16, 1882
William Eaton Chandler
  April 16, 1882–March 6, 1885

Secretary of the Interior
Samuel Jordan Kirkwood
  March 8, 1881–April 17, 1882
Henry Moore Teller
  April 18, 1882–March 3, 1885

Grover Cleveland, 1885–1889

Secretary of State
Frederick Theodore Frelinghuysen
  Dec. 19, 1881–March 6, 1885
Thomas Francis Bayard Sr.
  March 7, 1885–March 6, 1889

Secretary of the Treasury
Hugh McCulloch
  March 9, 1865–March 3, 1869,
  Oct. 31, 1884–March 7, 1885
Daniel Manning
  March 8, 1885–March 31, 1887
Charles Stebbins Fairchild
  April 1, 1887–March 6, 1889

Secretary of War
Robert Todd Lincoln
  March 5, 1881–March 5, 1885
William Crowninshield Endicott
  March 5, 1885–March 5, 1889

Attorney General
Benjamin Harris Brewster
  Jan. 2, 1882–March 5, 1885
Augustus Hill Garland
  March 6, 1885–March 5, 1889

Postmaster General
Frank Hatton
  Oct. 15, 1884–March 6, 1885

William Freeman Vilas
March 7, 1885–Jan. 16, 1888
Donald McDonald Dickinson
Jan. 17, 1888–March 5, 1889

Secretary of the Navy
William Eaton Chandler
April 16, 1882–March 6, 1885
William Collins Whitney
March 7, 1885–March 5, 1889

Secretary of the Interior
Lucius Quintus Cincinnatus Lamar
March 6, 1885–Jan. 10, 1888
William Freeman Vilas
Jan. 16, 1888–March 6, 1889

Secretary of Agriculture
Norman Jay Colman
Feb. 15–March 6, 1889

Benjamin Harrison, 1889–1893

Secretary of State
Thomas Francis Bayard Sr.
March 7, 1885–March 6, 1889
James G. Blaine
March 7–Dec. 19, 1881,
March 7, 1889–June 4, 1892
John Watson Foster
June 29, 1892–Feb. 23, 1893

Secretary of the Treasury
Charles Stebbins Fairchild
April 1, 1887–March 6, 1889
William Windom
March 8–Nov. 13, 1881,
March 7, 1889–Jan. 29, 1891
Charles Foster
Feb. 25, 1891–March 6, 1893

Secretary of War
William Crowninshield Endicott
March 5, 1885–March 5, 1889
Redfield Proctor
March 5, 1889–Nov. 5, 1891
Stephen Benton Elkins
Dec. 17, 1891–March 5, 1893

Attorney General
Augustus Hill Garland
March 6, 1885–March 5, 1889
William Henry Harrison Miller
March 5, 1889–March 6, 1893

Postmaster General
Donald McDonald Dickinson
Jan. 17, 1888–March 5, 1889
John Wanamaker
March 6, 1889–March 7, 1893

Secretary of the Navy
William Collins Whitney
March 7, 1885–March 5, 1889
Benjamin Franklin Tracy
March 6, 1889–March 6, 1893

Secretary of the Interior
William Freeman Vilas
Jan. 16, 1888–March 6, 1889
John Willock Noble
March 7, 1889–March 6, 1893

Secretary of Agriculture
Norman Jay Colman
Feb. 15–March 6, 1889
Jeremiah McLain Rusk
March 6, 1889–March 6, 1893

Grover Cleveland, 1893–1897

Secretary of State
Walter Quintin Gresham
March 7, 1893–May 28, 1895
Richard Olney
June 10, 1895–March 5, 1897

Secretary of the Treasury
Charles Foster
Feb. 25, 1891–March 6, 1893
John Griffin Carlisle
March 7, 1893–March 5, 1897

Secretary of War
Stephen Benton Elkins
Dec. 17, 1891–March 5, 1893
Daniel Scott Lamont
March 5, 1893–March 5, 1897

Attorney General
William Henry Harrison Miller
March 5, 1889–March 6, 1893
Richard Olney
March 6, 1893–June 7, 1895
Judson Harmon
June 8, 1895–March 5, 1897

Postmaster General
John Wanamaker
March 6, 1889–March 7, 1893

Wilson Shannon Bissel
March 8, 1893–April 3, 1895
William Lyne Wilson
April 4, 1895–March 5, 1897

Secretary of the Navy
Benjamin Franklin Tracy
March 6, 1889–March 6, 1893
Hilary Abner Herbert
March 7, 1893–March 5, 1897

Secretary of the Interior
John Willock Noble
March 7, 1889–March 6, 1893
Hoke Smith
March 6, 1893–Sept. 1, 1896
David Rowland Francis
Sept. 3, 1896–March 5, 1897

Secretary of Agriculture
Jeremiah McLain Rusk
March 6, 1889–March 6, 1893
Julius Sterling Morton
March 7, 1893–March 5, 1897

William McKinley, 1897–1901

Secretary of State
Richard Olney
June 10, 1895–March 5, 1897
John Sherman
March 6, 1897–April 27, 1898
William Rufus Day
April 28–Sept. 16, 1898
John Milton Hay
Sept. 30, 1898–July 1, 1905

Secretary of the Treasury
John Griffin Carlisle
March 7, 1893–March 5, 1897
Lyman Judson Gage
March 6, 1897–Jan. 31, 1902

Secretary of War
Daniel Scott Lamont
March 5, 1893–March 5, 1897
Russell Alexander Alger
March 5, 1897–Aug. 1, 1899
Elihu Root
Aug. 1, 1899–Jan. 31, 1904

Attorney General
Judson Harmon
June 8, 1895–March 5, 1897
Joseph McKenna
March 5, 1897–Jan. 25, 1898

Presidential Cabinets, 1789–2007 *(Continued)*

John William Griggs
> *June 25, 1898–March 29, 1901*

Philander Chase Knox
> *April 5, 1901–June 30, 1904*

Postmaster General

William Lyne Wilson
> *April 4, 1895–March 5, 1897*

James Albert Gary
> *March 6, 1897–April 22, 1898*

Charles Emory Smith
> *April 23, 1898–Jan. 14, 1902*

Secretary of the Navy

Hilary Abner Herbert
> *March 7, 1893–March 5, 1897*

John Davis Long
> *March 6, 1897–April 30, 1902*

Secretary of the Interior

David Rowland Francis
> *Sept. 3, 1896–March 5, 1897*

Cornelius Newton Bliss
> *March 6, 1897–Feb. 19, 1899*

Ethan Allen Hitchcock
> *Feb. 20, 1899–March 4, 1907*

Secretary of Agriculture

Julius Sterling Morton
> *March 7, 1893–March 5, 1897*

James Wilson
> *March 6, 1897–March 5, 1913*

Theodore Roosevelt, 1901–1909

Secretary of State

John Milton Hay
> *Sept. 30, 1898–July 1, 1905*

Elihu Root
> *July 19, 1905–Jan. 27, 1909*

Robert Bacon
> *Jan. 27–March 5, 1909*

Secretary of the Treasury

Lyman Judson Gage
> *March 6, 1897–Jan. 31, 1902*

Leslie Mortier Shaw
> *Feb. 1, 1902–March 3, 1907*

George Bruce Cortelyou
> *March 4, 1907–March 7, 1909*

Secretary of War

Elihu Root
> *Aug. 1, 1899–Jan. 31, 1904*

William Howard Taft
> *Feb. 1, 1904–June 30, 1908*

Luke Edward Wright
> *July 1, 1908–March 11, 1909*

Attorney General

Philander Chase Knox
> *April 5, 1901–June 30, 1904*

William Henry Moody
> *July 1, 1904–Dec. 17, 1906*

Charles Joseph Bonaparte
> *Dec. 17, 1906–March 4, 1909*

Postmaster General

Charles Emory Smith
> *April 23, 1898–Jan. 14, 1902*

Henry Clay Payne
> *Jan. 15, 1902–Oct. 4, 1904*

Robert John Wynne
> *Oct. 10, 1904–March 4, 1905*

George Bruce Cortelyou
> *March 7, 1905–March 3, 1907*

George von Lengerke Meyer
> *March 4, 1907–March 5, 1909*

Secretary of the Navy

John Davis Long
> *March 6, 1897–April 30, 1902*

William Henry Moody
> *May 1, 1902–June 30, 1904*

Paul Morton
> *July 1, 1904–July 1, 1905*

Charles Joseph Bonaparte
> *July 1, 1905–Dec. 16, 1906*

Victor Howard Metcalf
> *Dec. 17, 1906–Nov. 30, 1908*

Truman Handy Newberry
> *Dec. 1, 1908–March 5, 1909*

Secretary of the Interior

Ethan Allen Hitchcock
> *Feb. 20, 1899–March 4, 1907*

James Rudolph Garfield
> *March 5, 1907–March 5, 1909*

Secretary of Agriculture

James Wilson
> *March 6, 1897–March 5, 1913*

Secretary of Commerce and Labor

George Bruce Cortelyou
> *Feb. 18, 1903–June 30, 1904*

Victor Howard Metcalf
> *July 1, 1904–Dec. 16, 1906*

Oscar Solomon Straus
> *Dec. 17, 1906–March 5, 1909*

William Howard Taft, 1909–1913

Secretary of State

Robert Bacon
> *Jan. 27–March 5, 1909*

Philander Chase Knox
> *March 6, 1909–March 5, 1913*

Secretary of the Treasury

George Bruce Cortelyou
> *March 4, 1907–March 7, 1909*

Franklin MacVeagh
> *March 8, 1909–March 5, 1913*

Secretary of War

Luke Edward Wright
> *July 1, 1908–March 11, 1909*

Jacob McGavock Dickinson
> *March 12, 1909–May 21, 1911*

Henry Lewis Stimson
> *May 22, 1911–March 4, 1913,*
> *July 10, 1940–Sept. 21, 1945*

Attorney General

Charles Joseph Bonaparte
> *Dec. 17, 1906–March 4, 1909*

George Woodward Wickersham
> *March 5, 1909–March 5, 1913*

Postmaster General

George von Lengerke Meyer
> *March 4, 1907–March 5, 1909*

Frank Harris Hitchcock
> *March 6, 1909–March 4, 1913*

Secretary of the Navy

Truman Handy Newberry
> *Dec. 1, 1908–March 5, 1909*

George von Lengerke Meyer
> *March 6, 1909–March 4, 1913*

Secretary of the Interior

James Rudolph Garfield
> *March 5, 1907–March 5, 1909*

Richard Achilles Ballinger
> *March 6, 1909–March 12, 1911*

Walter Lowrie Fisher
> *March 13, 1911–March 5, 1913*

Secretary of Agriculture

James Wilson
> *March 6, 1897–March 5, 1913*

Secretary of Commerce and Labor
Oscar Solomon Straus
Dec. 17, 1906–March 5, 1909
Charles Nagel
March 6, 1909–March 4, 1913

Woodrow Wilson, 1913–1921

Secretary of State
Philander Chase Knox
March 6, 1909–March 5, 1913
William Jennings Bryan
March 5, 1913–June 9, 1915
Robert Lansing
June 24, 1915–Feb. 13, 1920
Bainbridge Colby
March 23, 1920–March 4, 1921

Secretary of the Treasury
Franklin MacVeagh
March 8, 1909–March 5, 1913
William Gibbs McAdoo
March 6, 1913–Dec. 15, 1918
Carter Glass
Dec. 16, 1918–Feb. 1, 1920
David Franklin Houston
Feb. 2, 1920–March 3, 1921

Secretary of War
Henry Lewis Stimson
May 22, 1911–March 4, 1913,
July 10, 1940–Sept. 21, 1945
Lindley Miller Garrison
March 5, 1913–Feb. 10, 1916
Newton Diehl Baker
March 9, 1916–March 4, 1921

Attorney General
George W. Wickersham
March 5, 1909–March 5, 1913
James Clark McReynolds
March 5, 1913–Aug. 29, 1914
Thomas Watt Gregory
Sept. 3, 1914–March 4, 1919
Alexander Mitchell Palmer
March 5, 1919–March 5, 1921

Postmaster General
Frank Harris Hitchcock
March 6, 1909–March 4, 1913
Albert Sidney Burleson
March 5, 1913–March 4, 1921

Secretary of the Navy
George von Lengerke Meyer
March 6, 1909–March 4, 1913
Josephus Daniels
March 5, 1913–March 5, 1921

Secretary of the Interior
Walter Lowrie Fisher
March 13, 1911–March 5, 1913
Franklin Knight Lane
March 6, 1913–Feb. 29, 1920
John Barton Payne
March 15, 1920–March 4, 1921

Secretary of Agriculture
James Wilson
March 6, 1897–March 5, 1913
David Franklin Houston
March 6, 1913–Feb. 2, 1920
Edwin Thomas Meredith
Feb. 2, 1920–March 4, 1921

Secretary of Commerce
Charles Nagel
March 6, 1909–March 4, 1913
William Cox Redfield
March 5, 1913–Oct. 31, 1919
Joshua Willis Alexander
Dec. 16, 1919–March 4, 1921

Secretary of Labor
William Bauchop Wilson
March 4, 1913–March 4, 1921

Warren G. Harding, 1921–1923

Secretary of State
Bainbridge Colby
March 23, 1920–March 4, 1921
Charles Evans Hughes
March 5, 1921–March 4, 1925

Secretary of the Treasury
David Houston
Feb. 2, 1920–March 3, 1921
Andrew William Mellon
March 4, 1921–Feb. 12, 1932

Secretary of War
Newton Diehl Baker
March 9, 1916–March 4, 1921
John Wingate Weeks
March 5, 1921–Oct. 13, 1925

Attorney General
Alexander Mitchell Palmer
March 5, 1919–March 5, 1921
Harry Micajah Daugherty
March 5, 1921–March 28, 1924

Postmaster General
Albert Sidney Burleson
March 5, 1913–March 4, 1921
William Harrison Hays
March 5, 1921–March 3, 1922
Hubert Work
March 4, 1922–March 4, 1923
Harry Stewart New
March 4, 1923–March 5, 1929

Secretary of the Navy
Josephus Daniels
March 5, 1913–March 5, 1921
Edwin Denby
March 6, 1921–March 10, 1924

Secretary of the Interior
John Barton Payne
March 15, 1920–March 4, 1921
Albert Bacon Fall
March 5, 1921–March 4, 1923
Hubert Work
March 5, 1923–July 24, 1928

Secretary of Agriculture
Edwin Thomas Meredith
Feb. 2, 1920–March 4, 1921
Henry Wallace
March 5, 1921–Oct. 25, 1924

Secretary of Commerce
Joshua Willis Alexander
Dec. 16, 1919–March 4, 1921
Herbert Clark Hoover
March 5, 1921–Aug. 21, 1928

Secretary of Labor
William Bauchop Wilson
March 4, 1913–March 4, 1921
James John Davis
March 5, 1921–Nov. 30, 1930

Calvin Coolidge, 1923–1929

Secretary of State
Charles Evans Hughes
March 5, 1921–March 4, 1925
Frank Billings Kellogg
March 5, 1925–March 28, 1929

Presidential Cabinets, 1789–2007 *(Continued)*

Secretary of the Treasury
Andrew William Mellon
  March 4, 1921–Feb. 12, 1932

Secretary of War
John Wingate Weeks
  March 5, 1921–Oct. 13, 1925
Dwight Filley Davis
  Oct. 14, 1925–March 5, 1929

Attorney General
Harry Micajah Daugherty
  March 5, 1921–March 28, 1924
Harlan Fiske Stone
  April 7, 1924–March 2, 1925
John Garibaldi Sargent
  March 17, 1925–March 5, 1929

Postmaster General
Harry Stewart New
  March 4, 1923–March 5, 1929

Secretary of the Navy
Edwin Denby
  March 6, 1921–March 10, 1924
Curtis Dwight Wilbur
  March 19, 1924–March 4, 1929

Secretary of the Interior
Hubert Work
  March 5, 1923–July 24, 1928
Roy Owen West
  July 25, 1928–March 4, 1929

Secretary of Agriculture
Henry Wallace
  March 5, 1921–Oct. 25, 1924
Howard Mason Gore
  Nov. 22, 1924–March 4, 1925
William Marion Jardine
  March 5, 1925–March 4, 1929

Secretary of Commerce
Herbert C. Hoover
  March 5, 1921–Aug. 21, 1928
William Fairfield Whiting
  Aug. 22, 1928–March 4, 1929

Secretary of Labor
James John Davis
  March 5, 1921–Nov. 30, 1930

Herbert C. Hoover, 1929–1933

Secretary of State
Frank Billings Kellogg
  March 5, 1925–March 28, 1929

Henry Lewis Stimson
  March 28, 1929–March 4, 1933

Secretary of the Treasury
Andrew William Mellon
  March 4, 1921–Feb. 12, 1932
Ogden Livingston Mills
  Feb. 13, 1932–March 4, 1933

Secretary of War
Dwight Filley Davis
  Oct. 14, 1925–March 5, 1929
James William Good
  March 6–Nov. 18, 1929
Patrick Jay Hurley
  Dec. 9, 1929–March 3, 1933

Attorney General
John Garibaldi Sargent
  March 17, 1925–March 5, 1929
William DeWitt Mitchell
  March 5, 1929–March 3, 1933

Postmaster General
Harry Stewart New
  March 4, 1923–March 5, 1929
Walter Folger Brown
  March 5, 1929–March 5, 1933

Secretary of the Navy
Curtis Dwight Wilbur
  March 19, 1924–March 4, 1929
Charles Francis Adams
  March 5, 1929–March 4, 1933

Secretary of the Interior
Roy Owen West
  July 25, 1928–March 4, 1929
Ray Lyman Wilbur
  March 5, 1929–March 4, 1933

Secretary of Agriculture
William Marion Jardine
  March 5, 1925–March 4, 1929
Arthur Mastick Hyde
  March 6, 1929–March 4, 1933

Secretary of Commerce
William Fairfield Whiting
  Aug. 22, 1928–March 4, 1929
Robert Patterson Lamont
  March 5, 1929–Aug. 7, 1932
Roy Dikeman Chapin
  Aug. 8, 1932–March 3, 1933

Secretary of Labor
James John Davis
  March 5, 1921–Nov. 30, 1930
William Nuckles Doak
  Dec. 9, 1930–March 4, 1933

Franklin D. Roosevelt, 1933–1945

Secretary of State
Cordell Hull
  March 4, 1933–Nov. 30, 1944
Edward Reilly Stettinius Jr.
  Dec. 1, 1944–June 27, 1945

Secretary of the Treasury
William Hartman Woodin
  March 5–Dec. 31, 1933
Henry Morgenthau Jr.
  Jan. 1, 1934–July 22, 1945

Secretary of War
George Henry Dern
  March 4, 1933–Aug. 27, 1936
Harry Hines Woodring
  Sept. 25, 1936–June 20, 1940
Henry Lewis Stimson
  *May 22, 1911–March 4, 1913,
  July 10, 1940–Sept. 21, 1945*

Attorney General
Homer Stille Cummings
  March 4, 1933–Jan. 2, 1939
Francis William Murphy
  Jan. 17, 1939–Jan. 18, 1940
Robert Houghwout Jackson
  Jan. 18, 1940–July 10, 1941
Francis Beverley Biddle
  Sept. 15, 1941–June 30, 1945

Postmaster General
James Aloysius Farley
  March 6, 1933–Aug. 31, 1940
Frank Comerford Walker
  Sept. 11, 1940–June 30, 1945

Secretary of the Navy
Claude Augustus Swanson
  March 4, 1933–July 7, 1939
Charles Edison
  Jan. 2–June 24, 1940
William Franklin "Frank" Knox
  July 11, 1940–April 28, 1944
James V. Forrestal
  May 19, 1944–Sept. 17, 1947

Secretary of the Interior
Harold LeClair Ickes
March 4, 1933–Feb. 15, 1946

Secretary of Agriculture
Henry A. Wallace
March 4, 1933–Sept. 4, 1940
Claude Raymond Wickard
Sept. 5, 1940–June 29, 1945

Secretary of Commerce
Daniel Calhoun Roper
March 4, 1933–Dec. 23, 1938
Harry Hopkins
Dec. 24, 1938–Sept. 18, 1940
Jesse Holman Jones
Sept. 19, 1940–March 1, 1945
Henry A. Wallace
March 2, 1945–Sept. 20, 1946

Secretary of Labor
Frances Perkins
March 4, 1933–June 30, 1945

Harry S. Truman, 1945–1953

Secretary of State
Edward Reilly Stettinius Jr.
Dec. 1, 1944–June 27, 1945
James Francis Byrnes
July 3, 1945–Jan. 21, 1947
George C. Marshall
Jan. 21, 1947–Jan. 20, 1949
Dean Acheson
Jan. 21, 1949–Jan. 20, 1953

Secretary of the Treasury
Henry Morgenthau Jr.
Jan. 1, 1934–July 22, 1945
Frederick Moore Vinson
July 23, 1945–June 23, 1946
John Wesley Snyder
June 25, 1946–Jan. 20, 1953

Secretary of War
Henry Lewis Stimson
May 22, 1911–March 4, 1913,
July 10, 1940–Sept. 21, 1945
Robert Porter Patterson
Sept. 27, 1945–July 18, 1947
Kenneth Claiborne Royall
July 19–Sept. 17, 1947

Secretary of Defense
James Vincent Forrestal
Sept. 17, 1947–March 27, 1949
Louis Arthur Johnson
March 28, 1949–Sept. 19, 1950
George Catlett Marshall
Sept. 21, 1950–Sept. 12, 1951
Robert Abercrombie Lovett
Sept. 17, 1951–Jan. 20, 1953

Attorney General
Francis Beverley Biddle
Sept. 15, 1941–June 30, 1945
Thomas Campbell Clark
July 1, 1945–Aug. 24, 1949
James Howard McGrath
Aug. 24, 1949–April 7, 1952
James Patrick McGranery
May 27, 1952–Jan. 20, 1953

Postmaster General
Frank Comerford Walker
Sept. 11, 1940–June 30, 1945
Robert Emmet Hannegan
July 1, 1945–Dec. 15, 1947
Jesse Monroe Donaldson
Dec. 16, 1947–Jan. 20, 1953

Secretary of the Navy
James V. Forrestal
May 19, 1944–Sept. 17, 1947

Secretary of the Interior
Harold LeClair Ickes
March 4, 1933–Feb. 15, 1946
Julius Albert Krug
March 18, 1946–Dec. 1, 1949
Oscar Littleton Chapman
Dec. 1, 1949–Jan. 20, 1953

Secretary of Agriculture
Claude Raymond Wickard
Sept. 5, 1940–June 29, 1945
Clinton Presba Anderson
June 30, 1945–May 10, 1948
Charles Franklin Brannan
June 2, 1948–Jan. 20, 1953

Secretary of Commerce
Henry A. Wallace
March 2, 1945–Sept. 20, 1946
W. Averell Harriman
Oct. 7, 1946–April 22, 1948
Charles Sawyer
May 6, 1948–Jan. 20, 1953

Secretary of Labor
Frances Perkins
March 4, 1933–June 30, 1945
Lewis Baxter Schwellenbach
July 1, 1945–June 10, 1948
Maurice Joseph Tobin
Aug. 13, 1948–Jan. 20, 1953

Dwight D. Eisenhower, 1953–1961

Secretary of State
John Foster Dulles
Jan. 21, 1953–April 22, 1959
Christian Archibald Herter
April 22, 1959–Jan. 20, 1961

Secretary of the Treasury
George Magoffin Humphrey
Jan. 21, 1953–July 29, 1957
Robert Bernard Anderson
July 29, 1957–Jan. 20, 1961

Secretary of Defense
Charles Erwin Wilson
Jan. 28, 1953–Oct. 8, 1957
Neil Hosler McElroy
Oct. 9, 1957–Dec. 1, 1959
Thomas Sovereign Gates Jr.
Dec. 2, 1959–Jan. 20, 1961

Attorney General
Herbert Brownell Jr.
Jan. 21, 1953–Nov. 8, 1957
William Pierce Rogers
Nov. 8, 1957–Jan. 1961

Postmaster General
Arthur Summerfield
Jan. 21, 1953–Jan. 20, 1961

Secretary of the Interior
Douglas McKay
Jan. 21, 1953–April 15, 1956
Fred Andrew Seaton
June 8, 1956–Jan. 20, 1961

Secretary of Agriculture
Ezra Taft Benson
Jan. 21, 1953–Jan. 20, 1961

Secretary of Commerce
Charles Sinclair Weeks
Jan. 21, 1953–Nov. 10, 1958
Frederick Henry Mueller
Aug. 10, 1959–Jan. 19, 1961

Presidential Cabinets, 1789–2007 *(Continued)*

Secretary of Labor
Martin Patrick Durkin
Jan. 21–Sept. 10, 1953
James Paul Mitchell
Oct. 9, 1953–Jan. 20, 1961

**Secretary of Health, Education
and Welfare**
Oveta Culp Hobby
April 11, 1953–July 31, 1955
Marion Bayard Folsom
Aug. 1, 1955–July 31, 1958
Arthur Sherwood Flemming
Aug. 1, 1958–Jan. 19, 1961

John F. Kennedy, 1961–1963

Secretary of State
David Dean Rusk
Jan. 21, 1961–Jan. 20, 1969

Secretary of the Treasury
C. Douglas Dillon
Jan. 21, 1961–April 1, 1965

Secretary of Defense
Robert S. McNamara
Jan. 21, 1961–Feb. 29, 1968

Attorney General
Robert F. Kennedy
Jan. 21, 1961–Sept. 3, 1964

Postmaster General
James Edward Day
Jan. 21, 1961–Aug. 9, 1963
John A. Gronouski Jr.
Sept. 30, 1963–Nov. 2, 1965

Secretary of the Interior
Stewart Lee Udall
Jan. 21, 1961–Jan. 20, 1969

Secretary of Agriculture
Orville Lothrop Freeman
Jan. 21, 1961–Jan. 20, 1969

Secretary of Commerce
Luther Hartwell Hodges
Jan. 21, 1961–Jan. 15, 1965

Secretary of Labor
Arthur Joseph Goldberg
Jan. 21, 1961–Sept. 20, 1962
William Willard Wirtz
Sept. 25, 1962–Jan. 20, 1969

**Secretary of Health, Education
and Welfare**
Abraham Alexander Ribicoff
Jan. 21, 1961–July 13, 1962
Anthony Joseph Celebrezze
July 31, 1962–Aug. 17, 1965

Lyndon B. Johnson, 1963–1969

Secretary of State
David Dean Rusk
Jan. 21, 1961–Jan. 20, 1969

Secretary of the Treasury
C. Douglas Dillon
Jan. 21, 1961–April 1, 1965
Henry Hamill Fowler
April 1, 1965–Dec. 20, 1968
Joseph Walker Barr
Dec. 21, 1968–Jan. 20, 1969

Secretary of Defense
Robert S. McNamara
Jan. 21, 1961–Feb. 29, 1968
Clark McAdams Clifford
March 1, 1968–Jan. 20, 1969

Attorney General
Robert F. Kennedy
Jan. 21, 1961–Sept. 3, 1964
Nicholas de Belleville Katzenbach
Feb. 11, 1965–Oct. 2, 1966
William Ramsey Clark
March 2, 1967–Jan. 20, 1969

Postmaster General
John A. Gronouski Jr.
Sept. 30, 1963–Nov. 2, 1965
Lawrence Francis O'Brien
Nov. 3, 1965–April 26, 1968
William Marvin Watson
April 26, 1968–Jan. 20, 1969

Secretary of the Interior
Stewart Lee Udall
Jan. 21, 1961–Jan. 20, 1969

Secretary of Agriculture
Orville Lothrop Freeman
Jan. 21, 1961–Jan. 20, 1969

Secretary of Commerce
Luther Hartwell Hodges
Jan. 21, 1961–Jan. 15, 1965
John Thomas Connor
Jan. 18, 1965–Jan. 31, 1967

Alexander Buel Trowbridge
June 14, 1967–March 1, 1968
Cyrus Rowlett Smith
March 6, 1968–Jan. 19, 1969

Secretary of Labor
William Willard Wirtz
Sept. 25, 1962–Jan. 20, 1969

**Secretary of Health, Education
and Welfare**
Anthony Joseph Celebrezze
July 31, 1962–Aug. 17, 1965
John William Gardner
Aug. 18, 1965–March 1, 1968
Wilbur Joseph Cohen
May 16, 1968–Jan. 20, 1969

**Secretary of Housing and
Urban Development**
Robert Clifton Weaver
Jan. 18, 1966–Dec. 3, 1968

Secretary of Transportation
Alan Stephenson Boyd
Jan. 23, 1967–Jan. 20, 1969

Richard Nixon, 1969–1974

Secretary of State
William Pierce Rogers
Jan. 22, 1969–Sept. 3, 1973
Henry Alfred Kissinger
Sept. 22, 1973–Jan. 20, 1977

Secretary of the Treasury
David Matthew Kennedy
Jan. 22, 1969–Feb. 10, 1971
John Bowden Connally
Feb. 11, 1971–June 12, 1972
George Pratt Shultz
June 12, 1972–May 8, 1974
William Edward Simon
May 8, 1974–Jan. 20, 1977

Secretary of Defense
Melvin Robert Laird
Jan. 22, 1969–Jan. 29, 1973
Elliot Lee Richardson
Jan. 30–May 24, 1973
James Rodney Schlesinger
July 2, 1973–Nov. 19, 1975

Attorney General
John Newton Mitchell
Jan. 21, 1969–March 1, 1972

Richard Gordon Kleindienst
June 12, 1972–May 24, 1973
Elliot Lee Richardson
May 25–Oct. 20, 1973
William Bart Saxbe
Jan. 4, 1974–Feb. 3, 1975

Postmaster General
Winton Malcolm Blount
Jan. 22, 1969–Jan. 12, 1971

Secretary of the Interior
Walter Joseph Hickel
Jan. 24, 1969–Nov. 25, 1970
Rogers Clark Ballard Morton
Jan. 29, 1971–April 30, 1975

Secretary of Agriculture
Clifford Morris Hardin
Jan. 21, 1969–Nov. 17, 1971
Earl Lauer Butz
Dec. 2, 1971–Oct. 4, 1976

Secretary of Commerce
Maurice Hubert Stans
Jan. 21, 1969–Feb. 15, 1972
Peter George Peterson
Feb. 29, 1972–Feb. 1, 1973
Frederick Baily Dent
Feb. 2, 1973–March 26, 1975

Secretary of Labor
George Pratt Shultz
Jan. 22, 1969–July 1, 1970
James Day Hodgson
July 2, 1970–Feb. 1, 1973
Peter Joseph Brennan
Feb. 2, 1973–March 15, 1975

**Secretary of Health, Education
and Welfare**
Robert Hutchinson Finch
Jan. 21, 1969–June 23, 1970
Elliot Lee Richardson
June 24, 1970–Jan. 29, 1973
Caspar Willard Weinberger
Feb. 12, 1973–Aug. 8, 1975

**Secretary of Housing and
Urban Development**
George Wilcken Romney
Jan. 20, 1969–Feb. 2, 1973
James Thomas Lynn
Feb. 2, 1973–Feb. 10, 1975

Secretary of Transportation
John Anthony Volpe
Jan. 22, 1969–Feb. 1, 1973
Claude Stout Brinegar
Feb. 2, 1973–Feb. 1, 1975

Gerald R. Ford, 1974–1977

Secretary of State
Henry Alfred Kissinger
Sept. 22, 1973–Jan. 20, 1977

Secretary of the Treasury
William Edward Simon
May 8, 1974–Jan. 20, 1977

Secretary of Defense
James Rodney Schlesinger
July 2, 1973–Nov. 19, 1975
Donald Henry Rumsfeld
Nov. 20, 1975–Jan. 20, 1977

Attorney General
William Bart Saxbe
Jan. 4, 1974–Feb. 3, 1975
Edward Hirsh Levi
Feb. 6, 1975–Jan. 20, 1977

Secretary of the Interior
Rogers Clark Ballard Morton
Jan. 29, 1971–April 30, 1975
Stanley Knapp Hathaway
June 12–Oct. 9, 1975
Thomas Savig Kleppe
Oct. 17, 1975–Jan. 20, 1977

Secretary of Agriculture
Earl Lauer Butz
Dec. 2, 1971–Oct. 4, 1976
John Albert Knebel
Nov. 4, 1976–Jan. 20, 1977

Secretary of Commerce
Frederick Baily Dent
Feb. 2, 1973–March 26, 1975
Rogers Clark Ballard Morton
May 1, 1975–Feb. 2, 1976
Elliot Lee Richardson
Feb. 2, 1976–Jan. 20, 1977

Secretary of Labor
Peter Joseph Brennan
Feb. 2, 1973–March 15, 1975
John Thomas Dunlop
March 18, 1975–Jan. 31, 1976

William Julian Usery Jr.
Feb. 10, 1976–Jan. 20, 1977

**Secretary of Health, Education
and Welfare**
Caspar Willard Weinberger
Feb. 12, 1973–Aug. 8, 1975
Forrest David Mathews
Aug. 8, 1975–Jan. 20, 1977

**Secretary of Housing and
Urban Development**
James Thomas Lynn
Feb. 2, 1973–Feb. 10, 1975
Carla Anderson Hills
March 10, 1975–Jan. 20, 1977

Secretary of Transportation
Claude Stout Brinegar
Feb. 2, 1973–Feb. 1, 1975
William Thaddeus Coleman Jr.
March 7, 1975–Jan. 20, 1977

Jimmy Carter 1977–1981

Secretary of State
Cyrus Roberts Vance
Jan. 23, 1977–April 28, 1980
Edmund Sixtus Muskie
May 8, 1980–Jan. 18, 1981

Secretary of the Treasury
Werner Michael Blumenthal
Jan. 23, 1977–Aug. 4, 1979
George William Miller
Aug. 7, 1979–Jan. 20, 1981

Secretary of Defense
Harold Brown
Jan. 21, 1977–Jan. 20, 1981

Attorney General
Griffin Boyette Bell
Jan. 26, 1977–Aug. 16, 1979
Benjamin Richard Civiletti
Aug. 16, 1979–Jan. 19, 1981

Secretary of the Interior
Cecil Dale Andrus
Jan. 23, 1977–Jan. 20, 1981

Secretary of Agriculture
Robert Selmer Bergland
Jan. 23, 1977–Jan. 20, 1981

Presidential Cabinets, 1789–2007 *(Continued)*

Secretary of Commerce
Juanita Morris Kreps
Jan. 23, 1977–Oct. 31, 1979
Philip M. Klutznick
Jan. 9, 1980–Jan. 19, 1981

Secretary of Labor
Fred Ray Marshall
Jan. 27, 1977–Jan. 20, 1981

**Secretary of Health, Education
and Welfare**
Joseph Anthony Califano Jr.
Jan. 25, 1977–Aug. 3, 1979
Patricia Roberts Harris
Aug. 3, 1979–May 4, 1980

Secretary of Health and Human Services
Patricia Roberts Harris
May 4, 1980–Jan. 20, 1981

**Secretary of Housing and
Urban Development**
Patricia Roberts Harris
Jan. 23, 1977–Aug. 3, 1979
Maurice Edwin "Moon" Landrieu
Sept. 24, 1979–Jan. 20, 1981

Secretary of Transportation
Brockman "Brock" Adams
Jan. 23, 1977–July 22, 1979
Neil Goldschmidt
July 27, 1979–Jan. 20, 1981

Secretary of Energy
James Rodney Schlesinger
Aug. 6, 1977–Aug. 23, 1979
Charles William Duncan Jr.
Aug. 24, 1979–Jan. 20, 1981

Secretary of Education
Shirley Mount Hufstedler
Dec. 6, 1979–Jan. 19, 1981

Ronald Reagan, 1981–1989

Secretary of State
Alexander Meigs Haig Jr.
Jan. 22, 1981–July 5, 1982
George Pratt Shultz
July 16, 1982–Jan. 20, 1989

Secretary of the Treasury
Donald Thomas Regan
Jan. 22, 1981–Feb. 1, 1985

James Addison Baker III
Feb. 4, 1985–Aug. 17, 1988
Nicholas Frederick Brady
Sept. 16, 1988–Jan. 19, 1993

Secretary of Defense
Caspar Willard Weinberger
Jan. 21, 1981–Nov. 21, 1987
Frank Charles Carlucci
Nov. 23, 1987–Jan. 20, 1989

Attorney General
William French Smith
Jan. 23, 1981–Feb. 24, 1985
Edwin Meese III
Feb. 25, 1985–Aug. 12, 1988
Richard Lewis Thornburgh
Aug. 12, 1988–Aug. 9, 1991

Secretary of the Interior
James Gaius Watt
Jan. 23, 1981–Nov. 8, 1983
William Patrick Clark
Nov. 18, 1983–Feb. 7, 1985
Donald Paul Hodel
Feb. 8, 1985–Jan. 20, 1989

Secretary of Agriculture
John Rusling Block
Jan. 23, 1981–Feb. 14, 1986
Richard Edmund Lyng
March 7, 1986–Jan. 20, 1989

Secretary of Commerce
Malcolm Baldrige
Jan. 20, 1981–July 25, 1987
Calvin William Verity Jr.
Oct. 19, 1987–Jan. 20, 1989

Secretary of Labor
Raymond James Donovan
Feb. 4, 1981–March 15, 1985
William Emerson Brock III
April 29, 1985–Oct. 31, 1987
Ann Dore McLaughlin
Dec. 17, 1987–Jan. 20, 1989

Secretary of Health and Human Services
Richard Schultz Schweiker
Jan. 22, 1981–Feb. 3, 1983
Margaret Mary O'Shaughnessy Heckler
March 9, 1983–Dec. 13, 1985
Otis Ray Bowen
Dec. 13, 1985–Jan. 20, 1989

**Secretary of Housing and
Urban Development**
Samuel Riley Pierce Jr.
Jan. 23, 1981–Jan. 20, 1989

Secretary of Transportation
Andrew Lindsay "Drew" Lewis Jr.
Jan. 23, 1981–Feb. 1, 1983
Elizabeth Hanford Dole
Feb. 7, 1983–Sept. 30, 1987
James Horace Burnley IV
Dec. 3, 1987–Jan. 30, 1989

Secretary of Energy
James Burrows Edwards
Jan. 23, 1981–Nov. 5, 1982
Donald Paul Hodel
Nov. 5, 1982–Feb. 7, 1985
John Stewart Herrington
Feb. 11, 1985–Jan. 20, 1989

Secretary of Education
Terrel Howard Bell
Jan. 23, 1981–Dec. 31, 1984
William John Bennett
Feb. 6, 1985–Sept. 20, 1988
Lauro Fred Cavazos
Sept. 20, 1988–Dec. 12, 1990

George Bush, 1989–1993

Secretary of State
James Addison Baker III
Jan. 27, 1989–Aug. 23, 1992
Lawrence Sidney Eagleburger
Dec. 8, 1992–Jan. 19, 1993

Secretary of the Treasury
Nicholas Frederick Brady
Sept. 16, 1988–Jan. 19, 1993

Secretary of Defense
Richard Bruce Cheney
March 21, 1989–Jan. 20, 1993

Attorney General
Richard Lewis Thornburgh
Aug. 12, 1988–Aug. 9, 1991
William Pelham Barr
Nov. 26, 1991–Jan. 15, 1993

Secretary of the Interior
Manuel Lujan Jr.
Feb. 8, 1989–Jan. 20, 1993

Presidential Cabinets, 1789–2007 *(Continued)*

Secretary of Agriculture
Clayton Keith Yeutter
Feb. 16, 1989–March 1, 1991
Edward Rell Madigan
March 12, 1991–Jan. 20, 1993

Secretary of Commerce
Robert Adam Mosbacher
Feb. 3, 1989–Jan. 15, 1992
Barbara Hackman Franklin
Feb. 27, 1992–Jan. 20, 1993

Secretary of Labor
Elizabeth Hanford Dole
Jan. 30, 1989–Nov. 23, 1990
Lynn Morley Martin
Feb. 22, 1991–Jan. 20, 1993

Secretary of Health and Human Services
Louis Wade Sullivan
March 10, 1989–Jan. 20, 1993

**Secretary of Housing and
Urban Development**
Jack French Kemp
Feb. 13, 1989–Jan. 20, 1993

Secretary of Transportation
Samuel Knox Skinner
Feb. 6, 1989–Dec. 16, 1991
Andrew Hill Card Jr.
Feb. 24, 1992–Jan. 20, 1993

Secretary of Energy
James David Watkins
March 9, 1989–Jan. 20, 1993

Secretary of Education
Lauro Fred Cavazos
Sept. 20, 1988–Dec. 12, 1990
Lamar Alexander
March 22, 1991–Jan. 20, 1993

Secretary of Veterans Affairs
Edward Joseph Derwinski
March 15, 1989–Sept. 26, 1992

Bill Clinton, 1993–2001

Secretary of State
Warren Christopher
Jan. 22, 1993–Jan. 20, 1997
Madeleine K. Albright
Jan. 23, 1997–Jan. 20, 2001

Secretary of the Treasury
Lloyd Bentsen
Jan. 22, 1993–Dec. 22, 1994
Robert E. Rubin
Jan. 19, 1995–July 2, 1999
Lawrence H. Summers
July 2, 1999–Jan. 20, 2001

Secretary of Defense
Les Aspin
Jan. 22, 1993–Feb. 2, 1994
William J. Perry
Feb. 3, 1994–Jan. 22, 1997
William S. Cohen
Jan. 24, 1997–Jan. 20, 2001

Attorney General
Janet Reno
March 12, 1993–Jan. 20, 2001

Secretary of the Interior
Bruce Edward Babbit
Jan. 22, 1993–Jan. 2, 2001

Secretary of Agriculture
Mike Espy
Jan. 22, 1993–Dec. 31, 1994
Dan Glickman
March 30, 1995–Jan. 19, 2001

Secretary of Commerce
Ronald H. Brown
Jan. 22, 1993–April 3, 1996
William M. Daley
Jan. 30, 1997–July 19, 2000
Norman Y. Mineta
July 21, 2000–Jan. 19, 2001

Secretary of Labor
Robert B. Reich
Jan. 22, 1993–Jan. 10, 1997
Alexis Herman
May 1, 1997–Jan. 20, 2001

Secretary of Health and Human Services
Donna E. Shalala
Jan. 22, 1993–Jan. 20, 2001

**Secretary of Housing
and Urban Development**
Henry G. Cisneros
Jan. 22, 1993–Jan. 17, 1997
Andrew M. Cuomo
Jan. 29, 1997–Jan. 20, 2001

Secretary of Transportation
Frederico F. Peña
Jan. 22, 1993–Feb. 14, 1997
Rodney Slater
Feb. 14, 1997–Jan. 20, 2001

Secretary of Energy
Hazel R. O'Leary
Jan. 22, 1993–Jan. 20, 1997
Frederico F. Peña
March 12, 1997–June 30, 1998
Bill Richardson
July 31, 1998–Jan. 20, 2001

Secretary of Education
Richard W. Riley
Jan. 22, 1993–Jan. 20, 2001

Secretary of Veterans Affairs
Jesse Brown
Jan. 22, 1993–July 1, 1997
Togo D. West Jr.
April 28, 1998–July 24, 2000

George W. Bush, 2001–

Secretary of State
Colin Powell
Jan. 20, 2001–Jan. 20, 2005
Condoleezza Rice
Jan. 26, 2005–

Secretary of the Treasury
Paul O'Neill
Jan. 20, 2001–Dec. 6, 2002
John Snow
Jan. 13, 2003–June 30, 2006
Henry M. Paulson
July 10, 2006–

Secretary of Defense
Donald Rumsfeld
Jan. 20, 2001–Dec. 18, 2006
Robert M. Gates
Dec. 18, 2006–

Attorney General
John Ashcroft
Feb. 1, 2001–Feb. 3, 2005
Alberto Gonzales
Feb. 3, 2005–

Secretary of the Interior
Gale Norton
Jan. 31, 2001–Mar. 31, 2006

Presidential Cabinets, 1789–2007 *(Continued)*

Dirk Kempthorne
May 26, 2006–

Secretary of Agriculture
Ann M. Veneman
Jan. 20, 2001–Jan. 20, 2005
Mike Johanns
Jan. 21, 2005–

Secretary of Commerce
Don Evans
Jan. 20, 2001–Feb. 7, 2005
Carlos M. Gutierrez
Feb. 7, 2005–

Secretary of Labor
Elaine Chao
Jan. 31, 2001–

Secretary of Health and Human Services
Tommy Thompson
Feb. 2, 2001–Jan. 26, 2005

Michael Leavitt
Jan. 26, 2005–

Secretary of Housing and Urban Development
Mel Martinez
Jan. 24, 2001–Dec. 12, 2003
Alphonso Jackson
Mar. 31, 2004–

Secretary of Transportation
Norman Mineta
Jan. 25, 2001–July 7, 2006
Mary Peters
Sep. 30, 2006–

Secretary of Energy
Spencer Abraham
Jan. 20, 2001–Feb. 1, 2005
Samuel Bodman
Feb. 1, 2005–

Secretary of Education
Roderick Paige
Jan. 24, 2001–Jan. 20, 2005
Margaret Spellings
Jan. 20, 2005–

Secretary of Veterans Affairs
Anthony Principi
Jan. 24, 2001–Jan. 26, 2005
James Nicholson
Jan. 26, 2005–

Secretary of Homeland Security
Tom Ridge
Jan. 24, 2003–Feb. 1, 2005
Michael Chertoff
Feb. 15, 2005–

THE GOVERNMENT OF THE UNITED STATES

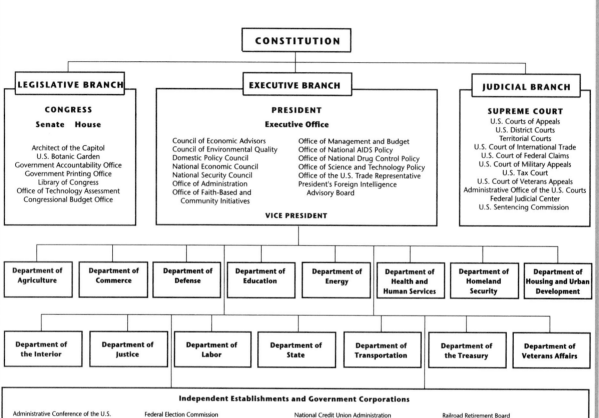

CONSTITUTION

LEGISLATIVE BRANCH

CONGRESS

Senate   House

Architect of the Capitol
U.S. Botanic Garden
Government Accountability Office
Government Printing Office
Library of Congress
Office of Technology Assessment
Congressional Budget Office

EXECUTIVE BRANCH

PRESIDENT

Executive Office

Council of Economic Advisors
Council of Environmental Quality
Domestic Policy Council
National Economic Council
National Security Council
Office of Administration
Office of Faith-Based and
    Community Initiatives

Office of Management and Budget
Office of National AIDS Policy
Office of National Drug Control Policy
Office of Science and Technology Policy
Office of the U.S. Trade Representative
President's Foreign Intelligence
    Advisory Board

VICE PRESIDENT

JUDICIAL BRANCH

SUPREME COURT

U.S. Courts of Appeals
U.S. District Courts
Territorial Courts
U.S. Court of International Trade
U.S. Court of Federal Claims
U.S. Court of Military Appeals
U.S. Tax Court
U.S. Court of Veterans Appeals
Administrative Office of the U.S. Courts
Federal Judicial Center
U.S. Sentencing Commission

| Department of Agriculture | Department of Commerce | Department of Defense | Department of Education | Department of Energy | Department of Health and Human Services | Department of Homeland Security | Department of Housing and Urban Development |

| Department of the Interior | Department of Justice | Department of Labor | Department of State | Department of Transportation | Department of the Treasury | Department of Veterans Affairs |

Independent Establishments and Government Corporations

Administrative Conference of the U.S.
American Battle Monuments Commission
Appalachian Regional Commission
African Development Foundation
Central Intelligence Agency
Commission on Civil Rights
Commission of Fine Arts
Commodity Futures Trading Commission
Consumer Product Safety Commission
Corporation for National Service
Defense Nuclear Facilities Safety Board
Environmental Protection Agency
Equal Employment Opportunity Commission
Export-Import Bank of the U.S.
Farm Credit Administration
Federal Communications Commission
Federal Deposit Insurance Corporation

Federal Election Commission
Federal Emergency Management Agency
Federal Housing Finance Board
Federal Labor Relations Authority
Federal Maritime Commission
Federal Mediation and Conciliation Service
Federal Mine Safety and Health Review Commission
Federal Reserve System
Federal Retirement Thrift Investment Board
Federal Trade Commission
General Services Administration
Inter-American Foundation
Legal Services Corporation
Merit Systems Protection Board
National Aeronautics and Space Administration
National Archives and Records Administration
National Capital Planning Commission

National Credit Union Administration
National Foundation on the Arts and the Humanities
National Labor Relations Board
National Mediation Board
National Railroad Passenger Corporation (Amtrak)
National Science Foundation
National Transportation Safety Board
Nuclear Regulatory Commission
Occupational Safety and Health Review Commission
Office of Government Ethics
Office of Personnel Management
Office of Special Counsel
Panama Canal Commission
Peace Corps
Pennsylvania Avenue Development Corporation
Pension Benefit Guaranty Corporation
Postal Rate Commission

Railroad Retirement Board
Securities and Exchange Commission
Selective Service System
Small Business Administration
Smithsonian Institution
Social Security Administration
State Justice Institute
Tennessee Valley Authority
Trade and Development Agency
U.S. Arms Control and Disarmament Agency
U.S. Information Agency
U.S. Institute of Peace
U.S. International Development Cooperation Agency
U.S. International Trade Commission
U.S. Postal Service

Federal Internet Gateways and Search Engines

The federal government operates thousands of Internet sites that offer free access to transcripts of presidential speeches, the full texts of bills introduced in Congress, health information, consumer publications about everything from buying a house to helping your child learn to read, and more.

It's often easiest to find specific government information by starting at a federal gateway or search engine. These sites offer seamless entry to the vast resources the federal government offers online. The sites described below are some of the best federal gateways and search engines currently available.

Federal Government Resources on the Web

http://www.lib.umich.edu/govdocs/federal.html

This site, which is operated by the University of Michigan Documents Center, offers a superb collection of annotated links to federal government sites. The links are divided into nearly twenty broad categories such as agency directories and Web sites, laws and Constitution, executive branch, executive orders, legislative branch, regulations, and historic documents.

GPO Access

http://www.access.gpo.gov/su_docs/index.html

GPO Access, which is operated by the Government Printing Office, offers the full texts of a huge range of documents from the executive, legislative, and judicial branches of government. Some of the highlights include the texts of all bills introduced in Congress, the *Congressional Record,* the federal budget, the *Federal Register,* the U.S. Code, the *Code of Federal Regulations,* the *Weekly Compilation of Presidential Documents,* and electronic versions of the *Statistical Abstract of the United States* and the *United States Government Manual.*

The White House

http://www.whitehouse.gov/government/
independent-agencies.html

The White House provides this page, which has links to sites operated by dozens of federal agencies and commissions. They include the Agency for International Development, Ballistic Missile Defense Organization, Chemical Safety and Hazard Investigations Board, Commission on Civil Rights, Environmental Protection Agency, Immigration and Natu-

---

Federal Job Information Available Online

Federal job seekers have a new tool in their quest for employment: Internet sites and bulletin board systems (BBSs) that offer free federal job information.

The major site is USAJOBS, which is operated by the U.S. Office of Personnel Management. USAJOBS offers listings of federal job openings across the United States and overseas, information about how to apply for a federal job, the optional application form for federal employment, a list of Federal Job Information Centers, details about student work programs, and other information.

USAJOBS is provided in three slightly different versions depending on which access method is used: the World Wide Web (WWW), FTP, or Telnet and BBS (the Telnet and BBS versions are identical). One of notable difference is that with the WWW site, users can apply online for federal jobs. The WWW site and the Telnet version also allow users to search databases of federal job openings. Users can search by series number, job title, state, and grade level.

Here are the site's various addresses:
To access WWW: *http://www.usajobs.opm.gov*
To access Telnet: *telnet://fjob.mail.opm.gov*
To access FTP: *ftp://ftp.fjob.mail.opm.gov*
  Login: anonymous
  Password: your e-mail address
To access BBS: 912-757-3100
Voice: 912-757-3090

---

ralization Service, International Labor Organization, National Commission on Libraries and Information Science, and National Endowment for the Humanities, among many others.

Google: Uncle Sam

http://www.google.com/unclesam

Uncle Sam is a subset of the popular Google search engine. It only searches Web sites operated by government agencies, although both federal and state sites are included.

U.S. Government Documents Ready Reference Collection

http://www.columbia.edu/cu/lweb/indiv/dsc/readyref.html

This site lists the federal government documents that are most frequently requested at the Columbia University Libraries. Most of the listings include links to electronic versions of the documents. The listings are divided by topics such as census and demographics, education, environment, foreign countries, health and social services, and military.

LSU Libraries Federal Agencies Directory

http://www.lib.lsu.edu/gov/fedgov.html

This directory is a partnership between Louisiana State University and the Federal Depository Library Program. It provides links to Web sites operated by federal agencies, departments, boards, commissions, and committees that are listed in the *United States Government Manual*. The links are not annotated.

Doc-Law Web Agency Index

http://www.washlaw.edu/doclaw/executive5m.html

The Washington University School of Law operates this handy site. Besides providing links to the home pages of federal agency Web sites, for many agencies it also provides direct links to pages with publications, organizational charts, forms, opinions, manuals, and directories. There also are direct links to libraries operated by many federal agencies.

FirstGov

http://firstgov.gov

FirstGov is the official gateway and search engine for federal and state government information. The main part of the site is separated into areas that provide links to information for citizens, businesses, and governments. It also has an index of federal and state government Web sites, e-mail addresses and telephone numbers for federal agencies and departments, a variety of federal forms, and the texts of laws and regulations.

Constitution of the United States

We the People of the United States, in Order to form a more perfect Union, establish Justice, insure domestic Tranquility, provide for the common defence, promote the general Welfare, and secure the Blessings of Liberty to ourselves and our Posterity, do ordain and establish this Constitution for the United States of America.

ARTICLE I

Section 1. All legislative Powers herein granted shall be vested in a Congress of the United States, which shall consist of a Senate and House of Representatives.

Section 2. The House of Representatives shall be composed of Members chosen every second Year by the People of the several States, and the Electors in each State shall have the Qualifications requisite for Electors of the most numerous Branch of the State Legislature.

No Person shall be a Representative who shall not have attained to the age of twenty five Years, and been seven Years a Citizen of the United States, and who shall not, when elected, be an Inhabitant of that State in which he shall be chosen.

[Representatives and direct Taxes shall be apportioned among the several States which may be included within this Union, according to their respective Numbers, which shall be determined by adding to the whole Number of free Persons, including those bound to Service for a Term of Years, and excluding Indians not taxed, three fifths of all other Persons.][1] The actual Enumeration shall be made within three Years after the first Meeting of the Congress of the United States, and within every subsequent Term of ten Years, in such Manner as they shall by Law direct. The Number of Representatives shall not exceed one for every thirty Thousand, but each State shall have at Least one Representative; and until such enumeration shall be made, the State of New Hampshire shall be entitled to chuse three, Massachusetts eight, Rhode-Island and Providence Plantations one, Connecticut five, New-York six, New Jersey four, Pennsylvania eight, Delaware one, Maryland six, Virginia ten, North Carolina five, South Carolina five, and Georgia three.

When vacancies happen in the Representation from any State, the Executive Authority thereof shall issue Writs of Election to fill such Vacancies.

The House of Representatives shall chuse their Speaker and other Officers; and shall have the sole Power of Impeachment.

Section 3. The Senate of the United States shall be composed of two Senators from each State, [chosen by the Legislature thereof,][2] for six Years; and each Senator shall have one Vote.

Immediately after they shall be assembled in Consequence of the first Election, they shall be divided as equally as may be into three Classes. The Seats of the Senators of the first Class shall be vacated at the Expiration of the second Year, of the second Class at the Expiration of the fourth Year, and of the third Class at the Expiration of the sixth Year, so that one third may be chosen every second Year; [and if Vacancies happen by Resignation, or otherwise, during the Recess of the Legislature of any State, the Executive thereof may make temporary Appointments until the next Meeting of the Legislature, which shall then fill such Vacancies.][3]

No Person shall be a Senator who shall not have attained to the Age of thirty Years, and been nine Years a Citizen of the United States, and who shall not, when elected, be an Inhabitant of that State for which he shall be chosen.

The Vice President of the United States shall be President of the Senate, but shall have no Vote, unless they be equally divided.

The Senate shall chuse their other Officers, and also a President pro tempore, in the Absence of the Vice President, or when he shall exercise the Office of President of the United States.

The Senate shall have the sole Power to try all Impeachments. When sitting for that Purpose, they shall be on Oath or Affirmation. When the President of the United States is tried, the Chief Justice shall preside: And no Person shall be convicted without the Concurrence of two thirds of the Members present.

Judgment in Cases of Impeachment shall not extend further than to removal from Office, and disqualification to hold and enjoy any Office of honor, Trust or Profit under the United States: but the Party convicted shall nevertheless be liable and subject to Indictment, Trial, Judgment and Punishment, according to Law.

Section 4. The Times, Places and Manner of holding Elections for Senators and Representatives, shall be prescribed in each State by the Legislature thereof; but the Congress may at any time by Law make or alter such Regulations, except as to the Places of chusing Senators.

The Congress shall assemble at least once in every Year, and such Meeting shall [be on the first Monday in December],[4] unless they shall by Law appoint a different Day.

Section 5. Each House shall be the Judge of the Elections, Returns and Qualifications of its own Members, and a Majority of each shall constitute a Quorum to do Business; but a smaller Number may adjourn from day to day, and may be authorized to compel the Attendance of absent Members, in such Manner, and under such Penalties as each House may provide.

Each House may determine the Rules of its Proceedings, punish its Members for disorderly Behaviour, and, with the Concurrence of two thirds, expel a Member.

Each House shall keep a Journal of its Proceedings, and from time to time publish the same, excepting such Parts as may in their Judgment require Secrecy; and the Yeas and Nays of the Members of either House on any question shall, at the Desire of one fifth of those Present, be entered on the Journal.

Neither House, during the Session of Congress, shall, without the Consent of the other, adjourn for more than three days, nor to any other Place than that in which the two Houses shall be sitting.

Section 6. The Senators and Representatives shall receive a Compensation for their Services, to be ascertained by Law, and paid out of the Treasury of the United States. They shall in all Cases, except Treason, Felony and Breach of the Peace, be privileged from Arrest during their Attendance at the Session of their respective Houses, and in going to and returning from the same; and for any Speech or Debate in either House, they shall not be questioned in any other Place.

No Senator or Representative shall, during the Time for which he was elected, be appointed to any civil Office under the Authority of the United States, which shall have been created, or the Emoluments whereof shall have been encreased during such time; and no Person holding any Office under the United States, shall be a Member of either House during his Continuance in Office.

Section 7. All Bills for raising Revenue shall originate in the House of Representatives; but the Senate may propose or concur with Amendments as on other Bills.

Every Bill which shall have passed the House of Representatives and the Senate, shall, before it become a Law, be presented to the President of the United States; If he approve he shall sign it, but if not he shall return it, with his Objections to that House in which it shall have originated, who shall enter the Objections at large on their Journal, and proceed to reconsider it. If after such Reconsideration two thirds of that House shall agree to pass the Bill, it shall be sent, together with the Objections, to the other House, by which it shall likewise be reconsidered, and if approved by two thirds of that House, it shall become a Law. But in all such Cases the Votes of both Houses shall be determined by yeas and Nays, and the Names of the Persons voting for and against the Bill shall be entered on the Journal of each House respectively. If any Bill shall not be returned by the President within ten Days (Sundays excepted) after it shall have been presented to him, the Same shall be a Law, in like Manner as if he had signed it, unless the Congress by their Adjournment prevent its Return, in which Case it shall not be a Law.

Every Order, Resolution, or Vote to which the Concurrence of the Senate and House of Representatives may be necessary (except on a question of Adjournment) shall be presented to the President of the United States; and before the Same shall take Effect, shall be approved by him, or being disapproved by him, shall be repassed by two thirds of the Senate and House of Representatives, according to the Rules and Limitations prescribed in the Case of a Bill.

Section 8. The Congress shall have Power To lay and collect Taxes, Duties, Imposts and Excises, to pay the Debts and provide for the common Defence and general Welfare of the United States; but all Duties, Imposts and Excises shall be uniform throughout the United States;

To borrow Money on the credit of the United States;

To regulate Commerce with foreign Nations, and among the several States, and with the Indian Tribes;

To establish an uniform Rule of Naturalization, and uniform Laws on the subject of Bankruptcies throughout the United States;

To coin Money, regulate the Value thereof, and of foreign Coin, and fix the Standard of Weights and Measures;

To provide for the Punishment of counterfeiting the Securities and current Coin of the United States;

To establish Post Offices and post Roads;

To promote the Progress of Science and useful Arts, by securing for limited Times to Authors and Inventors the exclusive Right to their respective Writings and Discoveries;

To constitute Tribunals inferior to the supreme Court;

To define and punish Piracies and Felonies committed on the high Seas, and Offences against the Law of Nations;

To declare War, grant Letters of Marque and Reprisal, and make Rules concerning Captures on Land and Water;

To raise and support Armies, but no Appropriation of Money to that Use shall be for a longer Term than two Years;

To provide and maintain a Navy;

To make Rules for the Government and Regulation of the land and naval Forces;

To provide for calling forth the Militia to execute the Laws of the Union, suppress Insurrections and repel Invasions;

To provide for organizing, arming, and disciplining, the Militia, and for governing such Part of them as may be employed in the Service of the United States, reserving to the States respectively, the Appointment of the Officers, and the Authority of training the Militia according to the discipline prescribed by Congress;

To exercise exclusive Legislation in all Cases whatso-ever, over such District (not exceeding ten Miles square) as may, by Cession of particular States, and the Acceptance of Congress, become the Seat of the Government of the United States, and to exercise like Authority over all Places purchased by the Consent of the Legislature of the State in which the Same shall be, for the Erection of Forts, Magazines, Arsenals, dock-Yards, and other needful Buildings;—And

To make all Laws which shall be necessary and proper for carrying into Execution the foregoing Powers, and all other Powers vested by this Constitution in the Government of the United States, or in any Department or Officer thereof.

Section 9. The Migration or Importation of such Persons as any of the States now existing shall think proper to admit, shall not be prohibited by the Congress prior to the Year one thousand eight hundred and eight, but a Tax or duty may be imposed on such Importation, not exceeding ten dollars for each Person.

The Privilege of the Writ of Habeas Corpus shall not be suspended, unless when in Cases of Rebellion or Invasion the public Safety may require it.

No Bill of Attainder or ex post facto Law shall be passed.

No Capitation, or other direct, Tax shall be laid, unless in Proportion to the Census or Enumeration herein before directed to be taken.[5]

No Tax or Duty shall be laid on Articles exported from any State.

No Preference shall be given by any Regulation of Commerce or Revenue to the Ports of one State over those of another; nor shall Vessels bound to, or from, one State, be obliged to enter, clear, or pay Duties in another.

No Money shall be drawn from the Treasury, but in Consequence of Appropriations made by Law; and a regular Statement and Account of the Receipts and Expenditures of all public Money shall be published from time to time.

No Title of Nobility shall be granted by the United States: And no Person holding any Office of Profit or Trust under them, shall, without the Consent of the Congress, accept of any present, Emolument, Office, or Title, of any kind whatever, from any King, Prince, or foreign State.

Section 10. No State shall enter into any Treaty, Alliance, or Confederation; grant Letters of Marque and Reprisal; coin Money; emit Bills of Credit; make any Thing but gold and silver Coin a Tender in Payment of Debts; pass any Bill of Attainder, ex post facto Law, or Law impairing the Obligation of Contracts, or grant any Title of Nobility.

No State shall, without the Consent of the Congress, lay any Imposts or Duties on Imports or Exports, except what may be absolutely necessary for executing it's inspection Laws: and the net Produce of all Duties and Imposts, laid by any State on Imports or Exports, shall be for the Use of the Treasury of the United States; and all such Laws shall be subject to the Revision and Controul of the Congress.

No State shall, without the Consent of Congress, lay any Duty of Tonnage, keep Troops, or Ships of War in time of Peace, enter into any Agreement or Compact with another State, or with a foreign Power, or engage in War, unless actually invaded, or in such imminent Danger as will not admit of delay.

ARTICLE II

Section 1. The executive Power shall be vested in a President of the United States of America. He shall hold his Office during the Term of four Years, and, together with the Vice President, chosen for the same Term, be elected, as follows

Each State shall appoint, in such Manner as the Legislature thereof may direct, a Number of Electors, equal to the whole Number of Senators and Representatives to which the State may be entitled in the Congress: but no Senator or Representative, or Person holding an Office of Trust or Profit under the United States, shall be appointed an Elector.

[The Electors shall meet in their respective States, and vote by Ballot for two Persons, of whom one at least shall not be an Inhabitant of the same State with themselves. And they shall make a List of all the Persons voted for, and of the Number of Votes for each; which List they shall sign and certify, and transmit sealed to the Seat of the Government of the United States, directed to the President of the Senate. The President of the Senate shall, in the Presence of the Senate and House of Representatives, open all the Certificates, and the Votes shall then be counted. The Person having the greatest Number of Votes shall be the President, if such Number be a Majority of the whole Number of Electors appointed; and if there be more than one who have such Majority, and have an equal Number of Votes, then the House of Representatives shall immediately chuse by Ballot one of them for President; and if no Person have a Majority, then from the five highest on the list the said House shall in like Manner chuse the President. But in chusing the President, the Votes shall be taken by States, the Representation from each State having one Vote; A quorum for this Purpose shall consist of a Member or Members from two thirds of the States, and a Majority of all the States shall be necessary to a Choice. In every Case, after the Choice of the President, the Person having the greatest Number of Votes of the Electors shall be the Vice President. But if there should remain two or more who have equal Votes, the Senate shall chuse from them by Ballot the Vice President.][6]

The Congress may determine the Time of chusing the Electors, and the Day on which they shall give their Votes; which Day shall be the same throughout the United States.

No Person except a natural born Citizen, or a Citizen of the United States, at the time of the Adoption of this Constitution, shall be eligible to the Office of President; neither shall any Person be eligible to that Office who shall not have attained to the Age of thirty five Years, and been fourteen Years a Resident within the United States.

In Case of the Removal of the President from Office, or of his Death, Resignation, or Inability to discharge the Powers and Duties of the said Office,[7] the Same shall devolve on the Vice President, and the Congress may by Law provide for the Case of Removal, Death, Resignation or Inability, both of the President and Vice President, declaring what Officer shall then act as President, and such Officer shall act accordingly, until the Disability be removed, or a President shall be elected.

The President shall, at stated Times, receive for his Services, a Compensation, which shall neither be encreased nor diminished during the Period for which he shall have been elected, and he shall not receive within that Period any other Emolument from the United States, or any of them.

Before he enter on the Execution of his Office, he shall take the following Oath or Affirmation:—"I do solemnly swear (or affirm) that I will faithfully execute the Office of President of the United States, and will to the best of my Ability, preserve, protect and defend the Constitution of the United States."

Section 2. The President shall be Commander in Chief of the Army and Navy of the United States, and of the Militia of the several States, when called into the actual Service of the United States; he may require the Opinion, in writing, of the principal Officer in each of the executive Departments, upon any Subject relating to the Duties of their respective Offices, and he shall have Power to grant Reprieves and Pardons for Offences against the United States, except in Cases of Impeachment.

He shall have Power, by and with the Advice and Consent of the Senate, to make Treaties, provided two thirds of the Senators present concur; and he shall nominate, and by and with the Advice and Consent of the Senate, shall appoint Ambassadors, other public Ministers and Consuls, Judges of the supreme Court, and all other Officers of the United States, whose Appointments are not herein otherwise provided for, and which shall be established by Law: but the Congress may by Law vest the Appointment of such inferior Officers, as they think proper, in the President alone, in the Courts of Law, or in the Heads of Departments.

The President shall have Power to fill up all Vacancies that may happen during the Recess of the Senate, by grant-ing Commissions which shall expire at the End of their next Session.

Section 3. He shall from time to time give to the Congress Information of the State of the Union, and recommend to their Consideration such Measures as he shall judge necessary and expedient; he may, on extraordinary Occasions, convene both Houses, or either of them, and in Case of Disagreement between them, with Respect to the Time of Adjournment, he may adjourn them to such Time as he shall think proper; he shall receive Ambassadors and other public Ministers; he shall take Care that the Laws be faithfully executed, and shall Commission all the Officers of the United States.

Section 4. The President, Vice President and all civil Officers of the United States, shall be removed from Office on Impeachment for, and Conviction of, Treason, Bribery, or other high Crimes and Misdemeanors.

Section 1. The judicial Power of the United States, shall be vested in one supreme Court, and in such inferior Courts as the Congress may from time to time ordain and establish. The Judges, both of the supreme and inferior Courts, shall hold their Offices during good Behaviour, and shall, at stated Times, receive for their Services, a Compensation, which shall not be diminished during their Continuance in Office.

Section 2. The judicial Power shall extend to all Cases, in Law and Equity, arising under this Constitution, the Laws of the United States, and Treaties made, or which shall be made, under their Authority; —to all Cases affecting Ambassadors, other public Ministers and Consuls; —to all Cases of admiralty and maritime Jurisdiction; —to Controversies to which the United States shall be a Party; —to Controversies between two or more States; —between a State and Citizens of another State; —between Citizens of different States; —between Citizens of the same State claiming Lands under Grants of different States, and between a State, or the Citizens thereof, and foreign States, Citizens or Subjects.[8]

In all Cases affecting Ambassadors, other public Ministers and Consuls, and those in which a State shall be Party, the supreme Court shall have original Jurisdiction. In all the other Cases before mentioned, the supreme Court shall have appellate Jurisdiction, both as to Law and Fact, with such Exceptions, and under such Regulations as the Congress shall make.

The Trial of all Crimes, except in Cases of Impeachment, shall be by Jury; and such Trial shall be held in the State where the said Crimes shall have been committed; but when not committed within any State, the Trial shall be at such Place or Places as the Congress may by Law have directed.

Section 3. Treason against the United States, shall consist only in levying War against them, or in adhering to their Enemies, giving them Aid and Comfort. No Person shall be convicted of Treason unless on the Testimony of two Witnesses to the same overt Act, or on Confession in open Court.

The Congress shall have Power to declare the Punishment of Treason, but no Attainder of Treason shall work Corruption of Blood, or Forfeiture except during the Life of the Person attainted.

ARTICLE IV

Section 1. Full Faith and Credit shall be given in each State to the public Acts, Records, and judicial Proceedings of every other State. And the Congress may by general Laws prescribe the Manner in which such Acts, Records and Proceedings shall be proved, and the Effect thereof.

Section 2. The Citizens of each State shall be entitled to all Privileges and Immunities of Citizens in the several States.

A Person charged in any State with Treason, Felony, or other Crime, who shall flee from Justice, and be found in another State, shall on Demand of the executive Authority of the State from which he fled, be delivered up, to be removed to the State having Jurisdiction of the Crime.

[No Person held to Service or Labour in one State, under the Laws thereof, escaping into another, shall, in Consequence of any Law or Regulation therein, be discharged from such Service or Labour, but shall be delivered up on Claim of the Party to whom such Service or Labour may be due.][9]

Section 3. New States may be admitted by the Congress into this Union; but no new State shall be formed or erected within the Jurisdiction of any other State; nor any State be formed by the Junction of two or more States, or Parts of States, without the Consent of the Legislatures of the States concerned as well as of the Congress.

The Congress shall have Power to dispose of and make all needful Rules and Regulations respecting the Territory or other Property belonging to the United States; and nothing in this Constitution shall be so construed as to Prejudice any Claims of the United States, or of any particular State.

Section 4. The United States shall guarantee to every State in this Union a Republican Form of Government, and shall protect each of them against Invasion; and on Application of the

Legislature, or of the Executive (when the Legislature cannot be convened) against domestic Violence.

ARTICLE V

The Congress, whenever two thirds of both Houses shall deem it necessary, shall propose Amendments to this Constitution, or, on the Application of the Legislatures of two thirds of the several States, shall call a Convention for proposing Amendments, which, in either Case, shall be valid to all Intents and Purposes, as Part of this Constitution, when ratified by the Legislatures of three fourths of the several States, or by Conventions in three fourths thereof, as the one or the other Mode of Ratification may be proposed by the Congress; Provided [that no Amendment which may be made prior to the Year One thousand eight hundred and eight shall in any Manner affect the first and fourth Clauses in the Ninth Section of the first Article; and][10] that no State, without its Consent, shall be deprived of its equal Suffrage in the Senate.

ARTICLE VI

All Debts contracted and Engagements entered into, before the Adoption of this Constitution, shall be as valid against the United States under this Constitution, as under the Confederation.

This Constitution, and the Laws of the United States which shall be made in Pursuance thereof; and all Treaties made, or which shall be made, under the Authority of the United States, shall be the supreme Law of the Land; and the Judges in every State shall be bound thereby, any Thing in the Constitution or Laws of any State to the Contrary notwithstanding.

The Senators and Representatives before mentioned, and the Members of the several State Legislatures, and all executive and judicial Officers, both of the United States and of the several States, shall be bound by Oath or Affirmation, to support this Constitution; but no religious Test shall ever be required as a Qualification to any Office or public Trust under the United States.

ARTICLE VII

The Ratification of the Conventions of nine States, shall be sufficient for the Establishment of this Constitution between the States so ratifying the Same.

Done in Convention by the Unanimous Consent of the States present the Seventeenth Day of September in the Year of our Lord one thousand seven hundred and Eighty seven and of the Independence of the United States of America the Twelfth. IN WITNESS whereof We have hereunto subscribed our Names,

George Washington,
President and deputy from Virginia.

[The language of the original Constitution, not including the Amendments, was adopted by a convention of the states on September 17, 1787, and was subsequently ratified by the states on the following dates: Delaware, December 7, 1787; Pennsylvania, December 12, 1787; New Jersey, December 18, 1787; Georgia, January 2, 1788; Connecticut, January 9, 1788; Massachusetts, February 6, 1788; Maryland, April 28, 1788; South Carolina, May 23, 1788; New Hampshire, June 21, 1788.

Ratification was completed on June 21, 1788.

The Constitution subsequently was ratified by Virginia, June 25, 1788; New York, July 26, 1788; North Carolina, November 21, 1789; Rhode Island, May 29, 1790; and Vermont, January 10, 1791.]

AMENDMENTS

Amendment I
(First ten amendments ratified December 15, 1791.)
Congress shall make no law respecting an establishment of religion, or prohibiting the free ex-

ercise thereof; or abridging the freedom of speech, or of the press; or the right of the people peaceably to assemble, and to petition the Government for a redress of grievances.

Amendment II

A well regulated Militia, being necessary to the security of a free State, the right of the people to keep and bear Arms, shall not be infringed.

Amendment III

No Soldier shall, in time of peace be quartered in any house, without the consent of the Owner, nor in time of war, but in a manner to be prescribed by law.

Amendment IV

The right of the people to be secure in their persons, houses, papers, and effects, against unreasonable searches and seizures, shall not be violated, and no Warrants shall issue, but upon probable cause, supported by Oath or affirmation, and particularly describing the place to be searched, and the persons or things to be seized.

Amendment V

No person shall be held to answer for a capital, or otherwise infamous crime, unless on a presentment or indictment of a Grand Jury, except in cases arising in the land or naval forces, or in the Militia, when in actual service in time of War or public danger; nor shall any person be subject for the same offence to be twice put in jeopardy of life or limb; nor shall be compelled in any criminal case to be a witness against himself, nor be deprived of life, liberty, or property, without due process of law; nor shall private property be taken for public use, without just compensation.

Amendment VI

In all criminal prosecutions, the accused shall enjoy the right to a speedy and public trial, by an impartial jury of the State and district wherein the crime shall have been committed, which district shall have been previously ascertained by law, and to be informed of the nature and cause of the accusation; to be confronted with the witnesses against him; to have compulsory process for obtaining witnesses in his favor, and to have the Assistance of Counsel for his defence.

Amendment VII

In Suits at common law, where the value in controversy shall exceed twenty dollars, the right of trial by jury shall be preserved, and no fact tried by a jury, shall be otherwise re-examined in any Court of the United States, than according to the rules of the common law.

Amendment VIII

Excessive bail shall not be required, nor excessive fines imposed, nor cruel and unusual punishments inflicted.

Amendment IX

The enumeration in the Constitution, of certain rights, shall not be construed to deny or disparage others retained by the people.

Amendment X

The powers not delegated to the United States by the Constitution, nor prohibited by it to the States, are reserved to the States respectively, or to the people.

Amendment XI (Ratified February 7, 1795)

The Judicial power of the United States shall not be construed to extend to any suit in law or equity, commenced or prosecuted against one of the United States by Citizens of another State, or by Citizens or Subjects of any Foreign State.

Amendment XII (Ratified June 15, 1804)

The Electors shall meet in their respective states and vote by ballot for President and Vice-President, one of whom, at least, shall not be an inhabitant of the same state with themselves; they shall name in their ballots the person voted for as President, and in distinct ballots the person voted for as Vice-President, and they shall make distinct lists of all persons voted for as President, and of all persons voted for as Vice-President, and of the number of votes for each, which lists they shall sign and certify, and transmit sealed to the seat of the government of the United States, directed to the President of the Senate; — The President of the Senate shall, in the presence of the Senate and House of Representatives, open all the certificates and the votes shall then be counted; — The person having the greatest number of votes for President, shall be the President, if such number be a majority of the whole number of Electors appointed; and if no person have such majority, then from the persons having the highest numbers not exceeding three on the list of those voted for as President, the House of Representatives shall choose immediately, by ballot, the President. But in choosing the President, the votes shall be taken by states, the representation from each state having one vote; a quorum for this purpose shall consist of a member or members from two-thirds of the states, and a majority of all the states shall be necessary to a choice. [And if the House of Representatives shall not choose a President whenever the right of choice shall devolve upon them, before the fourth day of March next following, then the Vice-President shall act as President, as in the case of the death or other constitutional disability of the President. —][11] The person having the greatest number of votes as Vice-President, shall be the Vice-President, if such number be a majority of the whole number of Electors appointed, and if no person have a majority, then from the two highest numbers on the list, the Senate shall choose the Vice-President; a quorum for the purpose shall consist of two-thirds of the whole number of Senators, and a majority of the whole number shall be necessary to a choice. But no person constitutionally ineligible to the office of President shall be eligible to that of Vice-President of the United States.

Amendment XIII (Ratified December 6, 1865)

Section 1. Neither slavery nor involuntary servitude, except as a punishment for crime whereof the party shall have been duly convicted, shall exist within the United States, or any place subject to their jurisdiction.

Section 2. Congress shall have power to enforce this article by appropriate legislation.

Amendment XIV (Ratified July 9, 1868)

Section 1. All persons born or naturalized in the United States, and subject to the jurisdiction thereof, are citizens of the United States and of the State wherein they reside. No State shall make or enforce any law which shall abridge the privileges or immunities of citizens of the United States; nor shall any State deprive any person of life, liberty, or property, without due process of law; nor deny to any person within its jurisdiction the equal protection of the laws.

Section 2. Representatives shall be apportioned among the several States according to their respective numbers, counting the whole number of persons in each State, excluding Indians not taxed. But when the right to vote at any election for the choice of electors for President and Vice President of the United States, Representatives in Congress, the Executive and Judicial officers of a State, or the members of the Legislature thereof, is denied to any of the male inhabitants of such State, being twenty-one years of age,[12] and citizens of the United States, or in any way abridged, except for participation in rebellion, or other crime, the basis of representation therein shall be reduced in the proportion which the number of such male citizens shall bear to the whole number of male citizens twenty-one years of age in such State.

Section 3. No person shall be a Senator or Representative in Congress, or elector of President and Vice President, or hold any office, civil or military, under the United States, or under any State, who, having previously taken an oath, as a member of Congress, or as an officer of the United States, or as a member of any State legislature, or as an executive or judicial officer of any State, to support the Constitution of the United States, shall have engaged in insurrection or rebellion against the same, or given aid or comfort to the enemies thereof. But Congress may by a vote of two-thirds of each House, remove such disability.

Section 4. The validity of the public debt of the United States, authorized by law, including debts incurred for payment of pensions and bounties for services in suppressing insurrection or rebellion, shall not be questioned. But neither the United States nor any State shall assume or pay any debt or obligation incurred in aid of insurrection or rebellion against the United States, or any claim for the loss or emancipation of any slave; but all such debts, obligations and claims shall be held illegal and void.

Section 5. The Congress shall have power to enforce, by appropriate legislation, the provisions of this article.

Amendment XV *(Ratified February 3, 1870)*

Section 1. The right of citizens of the United States to vote shall not be denied or abridged by the United States or by any State on account of race, color, or previous condition of servitude.

Section 2. The Congress shall have power to enforce this article by appropriate legislation.

Amendment XVI *(Ratified February 3, 1913)*

The Congress shall have power to lay and collect taxes on incomes, from whatever source derived, without apportionment among the several States, and without regard to any census or enumeration.

Amendment XVII *(Ratified April 8, 1913)*

The Senate of the United States shall be composed of two Senators from each State, elected by the people thereof, for six years; and each Senator shall have one vote. The electors in each State shall have the qualifications requisite for electors of the most numerous branch of the State legislatures.

When vacancies happen in the representation of any State in the Senate, the executive authority of such State shall issue writs of election to fill such vacancies: *Provided,* That the legislature of any State may empower the executive thereof to make temporary appointments until the people fill the vacancies by election as the legislature may direct.

This amendment shall not be so construed as to affect the election or term of any Senator chosen before it becomes valid as part of the Constitution.

[Amendment XVIII *(Ratified January 16, 1919)*

Section 1. After one year from the ratification of this article the manufacture, sale, or transportation of intoxicating liquors within, the importation thereof into, or the exportation thereof from the United States and all territory subject to the jurisdiction thereof for beverage purposes is hereby prohibited.

Section 2. The Congress and the several States shall have concurrent power to enforce this article by appropriate legislation.

Section 3. This article shall be inoperative unless it shall have been ratified as an amendment to the Constitution by the legislatures of the several States, as provided in the Constitution, within seven years from the date of the submission hereof to the States by the Congress.][13]

Amendment XIX (Ratified August 18, 1920)

The right of citizens of the United States to vote shall not be denied or abridged by the United States or by any State on account of sex.

Congress shall have power to enforce this article by appropriate legislation.

Amendment XX (Ratified January 23, 1933)

Section 1. The terms of the President and Vice President shall end at noon on the 20th day of January, and the terms of Senators and Representatives at noon on the 3d day of January, of the years in which such terms would have ended if this article had not been ratified; and the terms of their successors shall then begin.

Section 2. The Congress shall assemble at least once in every year, and such meeting shall begin at noon on the 3d day of January, unless they shall by law appoint a different day.

Section 3.[14] If, at the time fixed for the beginning of the term of the President, the President elect shall have died, the Vice President elect shall become President. If a President shall not have been chosen before the time fixed for the beginning of his term, or if the President elect shall have failed to qualify, then the Vice President elect shall act as President until a President shall have qualified; and the Congress may by law provide for the case wherein neither a President elect nor a Vice President elect shall have qualified, declaring who shall then act as President, or the manner in which one who is to act shall be selected, and such person shall act accordingly until a President or Vice President shall have qualified.

Section 4. The Congress may by law provide for the case of the death of any of the persons from whom the House of Representatives may choose a President whenever the right of choice shall have devolved upon them, and for the case of the death of any of the persons from whom the Senate may choose a Vice President whenever the right of choice shall have devolved upon them.

Section 5. Sections 1 and 2 shall take effect on the 15th day of October following the ratification of this article.

Section 6. This article shall be inoperative unless it shall have been ratified as an amendment to the Constitution by the legislatures of three-fourths of the several States within seven years from the date of its submission.

Amendment XXI (Ratified December 5, 1933)

Section 1. The eighteenth article of amendment to the Constitution of the United States is hereby repealed.

Section 2. The transportation or importation into any State, Territory, or possession of the United States for delivery or use therein of intoxicating liquors, in violation of the laws thereof, is hereby prohibited.

Section 3. This article shall be inoperative unless it shall have been ratified as an amendment to the Constitution by conventions in the several States, as provided in the Constitution, within seven years from the date of the submission hereof to the States by the Congress.

Amendment XXII (Ratified February 27, 1951)

Section 1. No person shall be elected to the office of the President more than twice, and no person who has held the office of President, or acted as President, for more than two years of a term to which some other person was elected President shall be elected to the office of the President more than once. But this Article shall not apply to any person holding the office of President when this Article was proposed by the Congress, and shall not prevent any person who may be holding the office of President, or acting as President, during the term within which this Article becomes operative from holding the office of President or acting as President during the remainder of such term.

Section 2. This article shall be inoperative unless it shall have been ratified as an amendment to the Constitution by the legislatures of three-fourths of the several States within seven years from the date of its submission to the States by the Congress.

Amendment XXIII (Ratified March 29, 1961)

Section 1. The District constituting the seat of Government of the United States shall appoint in such manner as the Congress may direct:

A number of electors of President and Vice President equal to the whole number of Senators and Representatives in Congress to which the District would be entitled if it were a State, but in no event more than the least populous State; they shall be in addition to those appointed by the States, but they shall be considered, for the purposes of the election of President and Vice President, to be electors appointed by a State; and they shall meet in the District and perform such duties as provided by the twelfth article of amendment.

Section 2. The Congress shall have power to enforce this article by appropriate legislation.

Amendment XXIV (Ratified January 23, 1964)

Section 1. The right of citizens of the United States to vote in any primary or other election for President or Vice President, for electors for President or Vice President, or for Senator or Representative in Congress, shall not be denied or abridged by the United States or any State by reason of failure to pay any poll tax or other tax.

Section 2. The Congress shall have power to enforce this article by appropriate legislation.

Amendment XXV (Ratified February 10, 1967)

Section 1. In case of the removal of the President from office or of his death or resignation, the Vice President shall become President.

Section 2. Whenever there is a vacancy in the office of the Vice President, the President shall nominate a Vice President who shall take office upon confirmation by a majority vote of both Houses of Congress.

Section 3. Whenever the President transmits to the President pro tempore of the Senate and the Speaker of the House of Representatives his written declaration that he is unable to discharge the powers and duties of his office, and until he transmits to them a written declaration to the contrary, such powers and duties shall be discharged by the Vice President as Acting President.

Section 4. Whenever the Vice President and a majority of either the principal officers of the executive departments or of such other body as Congress may by law provide, transmit to the President pro tempore of the Senate and the Speaker of the House of Representatives their written declaration that the President is unable to discharge the powers and duties of his office, the Vice President shall immediately assume the powers and duties of the office as Acting President.

Thereafter, when the President transmits to the President pro tempore of the Senate and the Speaker of the House of Representatives his written declaration that no inability exists, he shall resume the powers and duties of his office unless the Vice President and a majority of either the principal officers of the executive departments or of such other body as Congress may by law provide, transmit within four days to the President pro tempore of the Senate and the Speaker of the House of Representatives their written declaration that the President is unable to discharge the powers and duties of his office. Thereupon Congress shall decide the issue, assembling within forty-eight hours for that purpose if not in session. If the Congress, within twenty-one days after receipt of the latter written declaration, or, if Congress is not in session, within twenty-one days after Congress is required to assemble, determines by two-thirds vote of both Houses that the President is unable to discharge the powers and duties of his office, the Vice President shall continue to discharge the same as Acting President; otherwise, the President shall resume the powers and duties of his office.

Amendment XXVI (Ratified July 1, 1971)

Section 1. The right of citizens of the United States, who are eighteen years of age or older, to vote shall not be denied or abridged by the United States or by any State on account of age.

Section 2. The Congress shall have power to enforce this article by appropriate legislation.

Amendment XXVII (Ratified May 7, 1992)

No law varying the compensation for the services of the Senators and Representatives shall take effect, until an election of Representatives shall have intervened.

SOURCE: U.S. Congress, House, Committee on the Judiciary, *The Constitution of the United States of America, as Amended,* 100th Cong., 1st sess., 1987, H Doc 100–94.

NOTES:

1. The part in brackets was changed by section 2 of the Fourteenth Amendment.
2. The part in brackets was changed by the first paragraph of the Seventeenth Amendment.
3. The part in brackets was changed by the second paragraph of the Seventeenth Amendment.
4. The part in brackets was changed by section 2 of the Twentieth Amendment.
5. The Sixteenth Amendment gave Congress the power to tax incomes.
6. The material in brackets was superseded by the Twelfth Amendment.
7. This provision was affected by the Twenty-fifth Amendment.
8. These clauses were affected by the Eleventh Amendment.
9. This paragraph was superseded by the Thirteenth Amendment.
10. Obsolete.
11. The part in brackets was superseded by section 3 of the Twentieth Amendment.
12. See the Nineteenth and Twenty-sixth Amendments.
13. This amendment was repealed by section 1 of the Twenty-first Amendment.
14. See the Twenty-fifth Amendment.

Selected Bibliography

Abbott, Philip. *Strong Presidents: A Theory of Leadership.* Knoxville: University of Tennessee Press, 1996.

Aberbach, Joel D., and Mark A. Petersen. *The Executive Branch.* Oxford: Oxford University Press, 2005.

Adams, Abigail, and John Adams. *The Book of Abigail and John: Selected Letters of the Adams Family, 1762–1784.* Edited by L. H. Butterfield et al. Cambridge, Mass.: Harvard University Press, 1975.

Alexander, Herbert E., and Anthony Corrado. *Financing the 1992 Election.* Boulder: Westview, 1995.

Ambrosius, Lloyd E. *Woodrow Wilson and the American Diplomatic Tradition: The Treaty Fight in Perspective.* New York: Cambridge University Press, 1990.

Anderson, Judith I. *William Howard Taft: An Intimate History.* New York: Norton, 1981.

Arnold, Peri E. *Making the Managerial Presidency.* Princeton: Princeton University Press, 1986.

Baker, Jean H. *Mary Todd Lincoln: A Biography.* New York: Norton, 1989.

Barbash, Fred. *The Founding: A Dramatic Account of the Writing of the Constitution.* New York: Linden Press/Simon and Schuster, 1987.

Barber, James David. *The Presidential Character.* 4th ed. Englewood Cliffs, N.J.: Prentice Hall, 1992.

Barber, James David, ed. *Choosing the President.* Englewood Cliffs, N.J.: Prentice Hall, 1974.

Beard, Charles, A. *An Economic Interpretation of the Constitution.* New York: Macmillan, 1913.

Beer, Samuel. "Federalism, Nationalism, and Democracy in America." *American Political Science Review.* March, 1978.

Bennett, Anthony J. *The American President's Cabinet: From Kennedy to Bush.* New York: St Martin's Press, 1996.

Berman, Larry. *The Office of Management and Budget and the Presidency, 1921–1979.* Princeton: Princeton University Press, 1979.

———. *Planning a Tragedy: The Americanization of the War in Vietnam.* New York: Norton, 1982.

———. *No Peace, No Honor: Nixon, Kissinger, and Betrayal in Vietnam.* New York: Free Press, 2001.

Berry, Jeffrey. *The Interest Group Society.* Boston: Little, Brown, 1984.

Bond, Jon R., and Richard Fleisher. *Polarized Politics: Congress and the President in a Partisan Era.* Washington, D.C.: CQ Press, 2000.

———. *The President in the Legislative Arena.* Chicago: University of Chicago Press, 1990.

Bowen, Catherine Drinker. *Miracle at Philadelphia.* Boston: Little, Brown, 1966.

Bradlee, Benjamin C. *Conversations with Kennedy.* New York: Norton, 1984.

Burke, John P. *The Institutional Presidency: Organizing the White House from FDR to Clinton.* Baltimore: Johns Hopkins University Press, 2000.

Burke, John P., and Fred I Greenstein. *How Presidents Test Reality: Decisions on Vietnam, 1954 and 1964.* New York: The Russell Sage Foundation, 1989.

Burns, James MacGregor. *Presidential Government: The Crucible of Leadership.* Boston: Houghton Mifflin, 1965.

Cameron, Charles M. *Veto Bargaining: Presidents and the Politics of Negative Powers.* Cambridge: Cambridge University Press, 2000.

Campbell, Angus, Philip E. Converse, Warren E. Miller, and Donald E. Stokes. *The American Voter.* New York: Wiley, 1960.

Cannon, Lou. *President Reagan: A Role of a Lifetime.* Rev. ed. New York: Public Affairs, 2000.

Caro, Robert A. *Means of Ascent: The Years of Lyndon Johnson.* New York: Knopf, 1990.

———. *The Path to Power: The Years of Lyndon Johnson.* New York: Knopf, 1982.

Ceaser, James. *Presidential Selection: Theory and Development.* Princeton: Princeton University Press, 1979.

Clinton, William J. *My Life.* New York: Vintage, 2005.

Cohen, Jeffrey E. *The Politics of the U.S. Cabinet: Representation in the Executive Branch, 1789–1984.* Pittsburgh: University of Pittsburgh Press, 1988.

———. *Presidential Responsiveness and Public Policy-Making: The Public and the Policies that Presidents Choose.* Ann Arbor: University of Michigan Press, 1997.

Collier, Christopher, and James Lincoln Collier. *Decision in Philadelphia: The Constitutional Convention of 1787.* New York: Ballantine, 1986.

Conley, Patricia H. *Presidential Mandates: How Elections Shape the National Agenda.* Chicago: University of Chicago Press, 2001.

Congressional Quarterly. *National Party Conventions, 1831–2004.* Washington, D.C.: CQ Press, 2005.

Cordtz, Dan. "The Imperial Lifestyle of the U. S. President." *Fortune.* October 1973.

Cornwell, Elmer. *Presidential Leadership of Public Opinion.* Bloomington: Indiana University Press, 1965.

Corwin, Edward S. *The President: Office and Powers.* 4th ed. New York: New York University Press, 1984.

Crabb, Cecil V., Jr., and Pat M. Holt. *Invitation to Struggle: Congress, the President, and Foreign Policy.* 4th ed. Washington, D.C.: CQ Press, 1991.

Crabb, Cecil V., Jr., and Kevin V. Mulcahy. *American National Security: A Presidential Perspective.* Pacific Grove, Calif.: Brooks/Cole, 1991.

Cunningham, Noble E., Jr. *In Pursuit of Reason: The Life of Thomas Jefferson.* Baton Rouge: Louisiana State University Press, 1987.

Davis, James W. *National Conventions in an Age of Party Reform.* Westport, Conn.: Greenwood Press, 1983.

DeWitt, David Miller. *Impeachment and Trial of Andrew Johnson.* New York: Macmillan, 1903.

Downs, Anthony. *Inside Bureaucracy.* Boston: Little, Brown, 1967.

Drew, Elizabeth. *Politics and Money: The New Road to Corruption.* New York: Macmillan, 1983.

Edelman, Murray. *The Symbolic Uses of Politics.* Urbana: University of Illinois Press, 1985.

Edwards, George C., III. *The Public Presidency: The Pursuit of Popular Support.* New York: St. Martin's, 1983.

Edwards, George C., III, and Stephen J. Wayne. *Presidential Leadership.* 7th ed. New York: Wadsworth, 2005.

Farrand, Max, ed. *The Records of the Federal Convention of 1787.* New Haven: Yale University Press, 1913.

Feerick, John D. *From Falling Hands: The Story of Presidential Succession.* New York: Fordham University Press, 1975.

Fehrenbacher, Don E. *Lincoln in Text and Context: Collected Essays.* Stanford: Stanford University Press, 1987.

Fenno, Richard F., Jr. *The President's Cabinet.* New York: Vintage, 1958.

Fesler, James W., and Donald F. Kettl. *The Politics of the Administrative Process.* 2d ed. Chatham, N.J.: Chatham House, 1996.

Fishel, Jeff. *Presidents and Promises: From Campaign Pledge to Presidential Performance.* Washington, D.C.: CQ Press, 1985.

Fisher, Louis. *Constitutional Conflicts between Congress and the President.* 4th ed. Lawrence: University Press of Kansas, 1997.

———. *Military Tribunals and Presidential Power: American Revolution to the War on Terrorism.* Lawrence: University Press of Kansas, 2005.

———. *The Politics of Shared Power: Congress and the Executive.* 4th ed. College Station: Texas A&M Press, 2000.

———. *Presidential Spending Power.* Princeton: Princeton University Press, 1975.

Flexner, James Thomas. *Washington: The Indispensable Man.* Boston: Little, Brown, 1974.

Ford, Gerald. "On the Threshold of the White House." *Atlantic Monthly.* July 1974.

Friedel, Frank. *Franklin D. Roosevelt: Rendezvous With Destiny.* Boston: Little, Brown, 1991.

George, Alexander, and Juliette George. *Woodrow Wilson and Colonel House: A Personality Study.* New York: John Day, 1956.

Golden, Marissa Martino. *What Motivates Bureaucrats? Politics and Administration during the Reagan Years.* New York: Columbia University Press, 2000.

Goldstein, Joel K. *The Modern American Vice Presidency.* Princeton: Princeton University Press, 1982.

Gordon, George J. *Public Administration in America.* 2d ed. New York: St. Martin's, 1982.

Gould, Lewis L. *The Presidency of William McKinley.* Lawrence: University Press of Kansas, 1981.

Graber, Doris A. *Mass Media and American Politics.* 7th ed. Washington, D.C.: CQ Press, 2005.

Greenstein, Fred I. *The Hidden-Hand Presidency: Eisenhower as Leader.* New York: Basic Books, 1982.

———. *Presidential Difference: Leadership Style from FDR to George W. Bush. 2nd ed.* Princeton: Princeton University Press, 2004.

Grossman, Michael Baruch, and Martha Joynt Kumar. Portraying the President: The White House and the News Media. Baltimore: Johns Hopkins University Press, 1981.

Halberstam, David. *The Best and the Brightest.* New York: Random House, 1972.

Hamilton, Alexander, John Jay, and James Madison. *The Federalist.* Introduction by Edward Gaylord Bourne. New York: Tudor, 1937.

Harbaugh, William H. *The Life and Times of Theodore Roosevelt.* Rev. ed. New York: Oxford University Press, 1975.

Hargreaves, Mary W. *The Presidency of John Quincy Adams.* Lexington: University Press of Kentucky, 1985.

Hargrove, Erwin C. *Presidential Leadership: Personality and Political Style.* New York: Macmillan, 1966.

———. *Jimmy Carter as President: Leadership and the Politics of the Public Good.* Baton Rouge: Louisiana State University Press,.1988.

Hargrove, Erwin C., and Michael Nelson. *Presidents, Politics, and Policy.* New York: Knopf, 1984.

Harmel, Robert, ed. *Presidents and Their Parties: Leadership or Neglect?* New York: Praeger, 1984.

Hart, John. *The Presidential Branch.* 2d ed. Chatham, N.J.: Chatham House, 1995.

Harvey, Donald R. *The Civil Service Commission.* New York: Praeger, 1970.

Heard, Alexander, and Michael Nelson, eds. *Presidential Selection.* Durham, N.C.: Duke University Press, 1987.

Heclo, Hugh. *A Government of Strangers.* Washington, D.C.: Brookings, 1977.

Heclo, Hugh, and Lester M. Salamon, eds. *The Illusion of Presidential Government.* Boulder: Westview, 1981.

Henry, Nicholas. *Public Administration and Public Affairs.* Englewood Cliffs, N.J.: Prentice Hall, 1975.

Hess, Stephen. *Organizing the Presidency.* 3d ed. Washington, D.C.: Brookings, 2002.

———. *The Washington Reporters.* Washington, D.C.: Brookings, 1981.

Hinckley, Barbara. *The Symbolic Presidency: How Presidents Portray Themselves.* New York: Routledge, 1990.

Hodgson, Godfrey. *All Things to All Men: The False Promise of the Modern American Presidency.* New York: Simon and Schuster, 1980.

Hult, Karen, and Charles Walcott. *Governing the White House: From Hoover through LBJ.* Lawrence: University of Kansas Press, 1995.

Hutson, James H., ed. *Supplement to Max Farrand's The Records of the Federal Convention of 1787.* New Haven: Yale University Press, 1987.

———. *John Adams and the Diplomacy of the American Revolution.* Lexington: University Press of Kentucky, 1980.

Hyland, Pat. *Presidential Libraries and Museums: An Illustrated Guide.* Washington, D.C.: Congressional Quarterly, 1995.

Jacobs, Lawrence J., and Robert Y. Shapiro. *Politicians Don't Pander: Political Manipulation and the Loss of Democratic Responsiveness.* Chicago: University of Chicago Press, 2000.

Jenson, Amy La Follette. *The White House and Its Thirty-three Families.* New York: McGraw-Hill, 1962.

Johnson, Donald B., and Jack L. Walker, eds. *The Dynamics of the American Presidency.* New York: Wiley, 1964.

Jones, Charles O. *The Presidency in a Separated System.* 2nd ed. Washington, DC: Brookings Institution Press, 2005.

Kaiser, Frederick M. *Presidential Protection: Assassinations, Assaults, and Secret Service Protective Procedures.* Washington, D.C.: Congressional Research Service, 1981.

Kallenbach, Joseph E. *The American Chief Executive: The Presidency and the Governorship.* New York: Harper and Row, 1966.

Kenyon, Cecelia M., ed. *The Antifederalists.* Indianapolis: Bobbs-Merrill, 1966.

Kernell, Samuel. *Going Public: New Strategies of Presidential Leadership.* 4th ed. Washington, D.C.: CQ Press, 2006.

Kernell, Samuel, and Samuel L. Popkin, eds. *Chief of Staff: Twenty-Five Years of Managing the Presidency.* Berkeley: University of California Press, 1986.

Kessel, John H. *Presidential Parties.* Homewood, Ill.: Dorsey, 1984.

Ketchum, Ralph. *James Madison: A Biography.* Charlottesville: University Press of Virginia, 1990.

Kilian, Michael, and Arnold Sawislak. *Who Runs Washington?* New York: St. Martin's, 1982.

King, Anthony, ed. *Both Ends of the Avenue: The Presidency, the Executive Branch, and Congress in the 1980's.* Washington, D.C.: American Enterprise Institute, 1983.

Krehbiel, Keith. *Pivotal Politics: A Theory of U.S. Lawmaking.* Chicago: University of Chicago Press, 1998.

Kurtz, Howard. *Spin Cycle: Inside the Clinton Propaganda Machine.* New York: Free Press, 1998.

Landy, Marc, ed. *Modern Presidents and the Presidency.* Lexington, Mass.: Lexington Books, 1985.

Langston, Thomas S. *With Reverence and Contempt: How Americans Think About Their President.* Baltimore: Johns Hopkins University Press, 1995.

Laski, Harold J. *The American Presidency: An Interpretation.* New York: Harper and Row, 1940.

Lawford, Valentine. "The Presidential Yacht U.S.S. Sequoia." *Architectural Digest.* January 1983.

LeLoup, Lance T., and Steven Shull. *The President and Congress.* Boston: Allyn and Bacon, 1999.

Light, Paul C. *The President's Agenda: Domestic Policy Choice from Kennedy to Reagan.* 2d rev. ed. Baltimore: Johns Hopkins University Press, 1991.

———. *The True Size of Government.* Washington, D.C.: Brookings, 1999.

———. *Vice-Presidential Power: Advice and Influence in the White House.* Baltimore: Johns Hopkins University Press, 1984.

Lowi, Theodore J. *The Personal President: Power Invested, Promise Unfulfilled.* Ithaca, N.Y.: Cornell University Press, 1985.

Mackenzie, G. Calvin. *The In-and-Outers: Presidential Appointees and Transient Government in Washington.* Baltimore: Johns Hopkins University Press, 1987.

Mackenzie, G. Calvin., ed. *The Politics of Presidential Appointments.* New York: Free Press, 1981.

———. *Innocent Until Nominated: The Breakdown of the Presidential Appointments Process.* Washington, D.C.: Brookings, 2001.

Macy, John W., Bruce Adams, and J. Jackson Walter. *America's Unelected Government: Appointing the President's Team.* Cambridge, Mass.: Ballinger, 1983.

Magleby, David B., ed. *Financing the 2000 Election.* Washington, D.C.: Brookings, 2002.

Maltese, John Anthony. *The Selling of Supreme Court Nominees.* Baltimore: Johns Hopkins University Press, 1995.

Mann, Thomas E., ed. *A Question of Balance: The President, the Congress, and Foreign Policy.* Washington, D. C.: Brookings, 1990.

Martin, Janet M. *The Presidency and Women: Promise, Performance and Illusion.* College Station: Texas A&M University Press, 2003.

Mayer, Kenneth R. *With the Stroke of a Pen: Executive Orders and Presidential Power.* Princeton: Princeton University Press, 2001.

Mayhew, David. *Divided We Govern: Party Control, Lawmaking, and Investigations, 1946–2002.* New Haven: Yale University Press, 2nd ed. 2005.

McCullough, David. *Truman.* New York: Simon and Schuster, 1992.

McFeely, William S. *Grant: A Biography.* Newton, CT: American Political Biography Press, 1996.

McMahon, Kevin J. *Reconsidering Roosevelt on Race: How The Presidency Paved the Road to Brown.* Chicago: University of Chicago Presw, 2004.

McPherson, James M. *Abraham Lincoln and the Second American Revolution.* New York: Oxford University Press, 1991.

Mee, Charles L., Jr. *The Genius of the People.* New York: Harper and Row, 1987.

Meier, Kenneth J. *Politics and the Bureaucracy: Policymaking in the Fourth Branch of Government.* 4th ed. Fort Worth: Harcourt College Publishers, 2000.

Milkis, Sidney M. *Political Parties, American Democracy, and the Constitution.* Baltimore: Johns Hopkins University Press, 1999.

———. *The President and the Parties: The Transformation of the American Party System Since the New Deal.* New York: Oxford University Press, 1993.

Milkis, Sidney M., and Michael Nelson. *The American Presidency: Origins and Development, 1776–1998.* 4th ed. Washington, D.C.: CQ Press, 2003.

Mueller, John. *War, Presidents and Public Opinion.* New York: Wiley, 1973.

Nathan, Richard P. *The Plot That Failed.* New York: Wiley, 1975.

Nelson, Michael. *The Evolving Presidency: Addresses, Cases, Letters, Reports, Resolutions, Essays, Transcripts, and Other Landmark Documents, 1787–1998.* Washington, D.C.: CQ Press, 1999.

———. *A Heartbeat Away.* New York: Unwin Hyman, 1988.

———. "Constitutional Qualifications for the President." *Presidential Studies Quarterly 17* (spring 1987): 383–399.

Nelson, Michael, ed. *The Presidency and the Political System*, 8th ed. Washington, D.C.: CQ Press, 2005.

———. *The Elections of 1996*. Washington, D.C.: CQ Press, 1997.

———. *The Elections of 2000*. Washington, D.C.: CQ Press, 2001.

———. *Guide to the Presidency*. 4th ed. Washington, D.C.: CQ Press, 2007.

Neustadt, Richard E. *Presidential Power and the Modern Presidents: The Politics of Leadership from Roosevelt to Reagan*. Rev. ed. New York: Free Press, 1991.

Nixon, Richard M. *RN: Memoirs of Richard Nixon*. New York: Simon and Schuster, 1990.

Pach, Chester J., Jr., and Elmo Richardson. *The Presidency of Dwight D. Eisenhower*. Rev. ed. Lawrence: University Press of Kansas, 1991.

Patterson, Bradley H., Jr. *The White House Staff: Inside the West Wing and Beyond*. Washington, D.C.: Brookings, 2000.

Pessen, Edward. *The Log Cabin Myth: The Social Backgrounds of the Presidents*. New Haven: Yale University Press, 1984.

Peters, William. *A More Perfect Union: The Making of the United States Constitution*. New York: Crown, 1987.

Peterson, Mark A. *Legislating Together: The White House and Capitol Hill from Eisenhower to Reagan*. Cambridge, Mass.: Harvard University Press, 1990.

Pfiffner, James P., ed. *The Managerial Presidency*. 2nd ed. College Station: Texas A&M University Press, 1999.

Pfiffner, James P., and Roger Davidson, eds. *Understanding the Presidency*. 4th ed. New York: Pearson Longman, 2007.

Pious, Richard M. *The American Presidency*. New York: Basic Books, 1979.

Plischke, Elmer. *Diplomat in Chief: The President at the Summit*. New York: Praeger, 1986.

Polsby, Nelson, W., ed. *The Modern Presidency*. Lanham, Md.: University Press of America, 1973.

Porter, Roger B. *Presidential Decision Making: The Economic Policy Board*. New York: Cambridge University Press, 1980.

Posner, Richard A. *An Affair of State: The Investigation, Impeachment, and Trial of President Clinton*. Cambridge, Mass.: Harvard University Press, 1999.

Reagan, Ronald. *An American Life*. New York: Simon and Schuster, 1990.

Reedy, George. *The Twilight of the Presidency*. New York: New American Library, 1970.

Remini, Robert V. *The Life of Andrew Jackson*. New York: Viking Penguin, 1990.

Renshon, Stanley A. *High Hopes: The Clinton Presidency and the Politics of Ambition*. New York: Routledge, 1998.

Richardson, James D. *Messages and Papers of the Presidents*. 2 vols. Washington, D.C.: Bureau of National Literature and Art, 1903.

Rockman, Bert A. *The Leadership Question: The Presidency and the American Political System*. New York: Praeger, 1984.

Rose, Richard. *The Postmodern President: George Bush Meets the World*. 2d ed. Chatham, N.J.: Chatham House, 1991.

Roseboom, Eugene H., and Alfred E. Eckes Jr. *A History of Presidential Elections: From George Washington to Jimmy Carter*. 4th ed. New York: Macmillan, 1979.

Ross, Irwin. *The Loneliest Campaign: The Truman Victory of 1948*. New York: New American Library, 1968.

Rossiter, Clinton. *The American Presidency*. Baltimore: Johns Hopkins University Press, 1987.

———. *Constitutional Dictatorship*. Princeton: Princeton University Press, 1948.

Rowan, Carl T., and David M. Mazie. "Shield Against Assassins: The Secret Service." *Reader's Digest*. April 1982.

Rozell, Mark J. *Executive Privilege: The Dilemmas of Secrecy and Accountability*. Baltimore: Johns Hopkins University Press, 1994.

Rudalevige, Andrew C. *Managing the President's Program: Presidential Leadership and Legislative Policy Formulation*. Princeton: Princeton University Press, 2002.

Sabato, Larry J. *The Rise of Political Consultants*. New York: Basic Books, 1981.

Schick, Allen. *The Federal Budget: Politics, Policy, Process*. Washington, D.C.: Brookings, 1995.

Schlesinger, Arthur M., Jr.. *The Imperial Presidency*. Rev. ed. Boston: Replica Books, 1998.

———. *A Thousand Days*. New York: Fawcett, 1967.

Schwartz, Barry. *George Washington: The Making of an American Symbol*. Ithaca, N.Y.: Cornell University Press, 1987.

Scigliano, Robert. *The Supreme Court and the Presidency*. New York: Free Press, 1971.

Seager, Robert, II. *And Tyler Too: A Biography of John and Julia Gardiner Tyler*. New York: McGraw-Hill, 1963.

Seligman, Lester G., and Cary R. Covington. *The Coalitional Presidency*. Chicago: Dorsey, 1989.

Shafer, Byron E. *Quiet Revolution: The Struggle for the Democratic Party and the Shaping of Post-Reform Politics.* New York: Russell Sage Foundation, 1983.

Sherrill, Robert. *Why They Call It Politics.* 4th ed. New York: Harcourt Brace Jovanovich, 1984.

Sickels, Robert J. *Presidential Transactions.* Englewood Cliffs, N.J.: Prentice Hall, 1974.

Sifrey, Micah L. *Spoiling for a Fight: Third-Party Politics in America.* New York: Routledge, 2002.

Skowronek, Stephen. *The Politics Presidents Make: Leadership from John Adams to Bill Clinton.* Cambridge, Mass.: Belknap Press, 1997.

Smith, Gene. *When the Cheering Stopped: The Last Years of Woodrow Wilson.* New York: William Morrow, 1971.

Smith, Hedrick. *The Power Game: How Washington Works.* New York: Random House, 1988.

Speakes, Larry, with Robert Pack. *Speaking Out: The Reagan Presidency from Inside the White House.* New York: Scribner's, 1988.

Spitzer, Robert J. *President and Congress: Executive Harmony at the Crossroads of American Government.* New York: McGraw-Hill, 1993.

———. *The Presidential Veto: Touchstone of the American Presidency.* Albany: State University of New York Press, 1988.

Stein, Herbert. *Presidential Economics: The Making of Economic Policy from Roosevelt to Reagan and Beyond.* 2d rev. ed. Washington, D.C.: American Enterprise Institute, 1988.

Stuckey, Mary E. *Defining Americans: The Presidency and National Identity.* Lawrence: University Press of Kansas, 2004.

Sundquist, James L. *Constitutional Reform and Effective Government.* Rev. ed. Washington, D.C.: Brookings, 1992.

Thach, Charles C., Jr. *The Creation of the Presidency, 1775–1789.* Baltimore: Johns Hopkins University Press, 1969.

Thomas, Norman C., and Joseph A. Pika. *The Politics of the Presidency.* 4th ed. Washington, D.C.: CQ Press, 1997.

Thompson, Kenneth W., ed. *The Ford Presidency: Twenty-two Intimate Perspectives of Gerald R. Ford.* Lanham, Md.: University Press of America, 1988.

Thurber, James A., ed. *Rivals for Power: Presidential-Congressional Relations.* Washington, D.C.: CQ Press, 1996.

Trefousse, Hans L. *Andrew Johnson: A Biography.* New York: Norton, 1991.

Truman, Harry S. *The Autobiography of Harry S. Truman.* Edited by Robert H. Ferrell. Boulder: University Press of Colorado, 1980.

———. *1945, Year of Decisions.* New York: Signet, 1955.

Tugwell, Rexford. *How They Became President.* New York: Simon and Schuster, 1968.

Tulis, Jeffrey. *The Rhetorical Presidency.* Princeton: Princeton University Press, 1984.

Tutchings, Terrence R. *Rhetoric and Reality: Presidential Commissions and the Making of Public Policy.* Boulder: Westview, 1979.

Warshaw, Shirley Anne. *The Domestic Presidency: Policy Making in the White House.* Boston: Allyn and Bacon, 1997.

Wayne, Stephen J. *The Legislative Presidency.* New York: Harper and Row, 1978.

———. *The Road to the White House, 2000: The Politics of Presidential Elections.* New York: St. Martin's, 2001.

Wead, Doug. *Conversations with the President: George Bush in His Own Words.* Washington, D.C.: Regnery Gateway, 1990.

Weko, Thomas J. *The Politicizing Presidency: The White House Personnel Office.* Lawrence: University Press of Kansas, 1995.

Wetterau, Bruce. *The Presidential Medal of Freedom: Winners and Their Achievements.* Washington, D.C.: Congressional Quarterly, 1996.

White, Theodore H. *The Making of the President, 1960.* New York: Atheneum Publishers, 1961.

———. *Breach of Faith: The Fall of Richard Nixon.* New York: Atheneum Publishers, 1975.

White House Historical Association. *The Living White House.* 7th rev. ed. Washington, D.C.: White House Historical Association, 1982.

Wildavsky, Aaron, and Naomi Caiden. *The New Politics of the Budgetary Process.* 4th ed. New York: HarperCollins, 2001.

Williams, Irving G. *The Rise of the Vice Presidency.* Washington, D.C.: Public Affairs Press, 1956.

Wilson, James Q. *Bureaucracy: What Government Agencies Do and Why They Do It.* New York: Basic Books, 2000.

Wilson, James Q., and John DiIulio, Jr. *American Government.* 11th ed. Boston: Houghton Mifflin Co., 2007.

Wilson, Woodrow. *Constitutional Government in the United States.* New York: Columbia University Press, 1908.

Witcover, Jules. *Crapshoot: Rolling the Dice on the Vice Presidency.* New York: Crown, 1992.

Wood, Gordon S. *The Creation of the American Republic, 1776–1787*. Chapel Hill: University of North Carolina Press, 1969.

Yalof, David Alistair. *Pursuit of Justices: Presidential Politics and the Selection of Supreme Court Nominees*. Chicago: University of Chicago Press, 1999.

Youngs, William T. *Eleanor Roosevelt: A Personal and Public Life*. Boston: Little, Brown, 1984.

Index

President's names and primary coverage are indicated by bold typeface.

Abraham, Spencer, 194
Abu Ghraib, 451–452
Accountability for Intelligence Activities Act of 1980, 82
Acheson, Dean, 324
Adams, Abigail, *1*, 1–2, 4, 220, 574
Adams, John, 1, *2*, **2–4**
    appointments, 4, 248
    background, 28
    cabinet, 62
    election of 1789, 3, 174–175
    election of 1796, 17, 175, 305
    father-son presidents, 4
    as Federalist, 566
    France, dispute with, 3
    presidential title preference, 504
    press, relationship with, 356
    rating by historians, 413
    veto power of, 534
    as vice president, 2, 3, 540
    White House and, 574, 577
    XYZ affair and, 232
Adams, John Quincy, 1, *4*, **4–5**, *553*
    appointments, 98
    background, 27–28, 29
    election of 1824, 5, 6, 98, 118, 119, 133, 176, 186, 302
    father-son presidents, 4
    presidential anthem, 242
    as secretary of state, 5, 367–368
    support of Jackson, 301
    Treaty of Ghent, 4–5
    in U.S. House of Representatives, 5, 226
    veto power of, 534
    vice president, 66–67
Adams, Sherman, 84, 196, 472, 475
Adams Memorial Foundation, 4
Adamson Act of 1916, 584
Adams-Onis Treaty of 1819, 5
Administration, Office of, 204
Administration on Aging, 252
Adversarial press, 357
Advisory committees or councils, 62
    Council on Executive Organization, 443
Afghanistan, 56, 191, 297, 554
AFL-CIO, 405
Agency for Toxic Substances and Disease Registry, 252

Age requirement for president, 433
Agnew, Spiro T., *6*, 6–7, 181, 391
    resignation, 7, 181, 223, 225, 485, 570
    as vice president, 6–7, 543, 546
Agriculture Adjustment Act of 1933, 219, 385
Agriculture Department (USDA), 7–8, 64
    law enforcement powers, 331
Air Force One, 8–9, *9*, 22, 455, 513
Air Force Two, 543
Airport and Airways Development Act of 1970, 512
Akerson, George, 356, 418
Alaska, 308
Alaska Airlines v. Brock (1987), 273
Alcohol, Tobacco, Firearms and Explosives, Bureau of (ATF), 211, 515
Aldrich Commission, 110
Ali, Muhammad, 415
Alien and Sedition Acts, 3, 305
Allen, Lewis F., 99
Alliance for Progress, 319
Altged, John P., 100
American Bar Association, 491
American Conservative Union, 36
American Independent Party, 187, 498, 500, 501. *See also* Wallace, George C.
American (Know-Nothing) Party, 30, 35, 218, 337, 583
American Printing House for the Blind, 166
American Railway Union, 143
American Revolution, 564–565
Ames, Aldrich, 82
Ames, Oakes, 109
Amistad case (1841), 5
Amnesty. *See* Pardon power
Anderson, John B., 183, 501
Anti-Deficiency Acts, 281
Anti-Masonic Party, 217, 378
Antitrust activities, 471, 491
Appointment and removal power, 9–15
    agency and department heads, 399–400
    ambassadors, 123, 152
    appointment process, 10–14
    background, 9–10
    bureaucracy and, 48
    Cabinet, 10
    ceremonial duties and, 86–87
    CIA director, 80
    commissions, 110–111

constitutional power for, 120
constraints, 11
court decisions on, 14–15
diplomatic personnel, 152–153
factors in, 10–11, 517
Federal Reserve Board, 161, 215
Humphrey's Executor v. United States (1935), 15, 269, 288, 370
judicial nominations, 130–132
Justice Department and, 332–333
Myers v. United States (1926), 14–15, 18, 269, 276, 370
patronage and, 116
personnel system, 13–14
Policy and Supporting Positions book listing openings, 399
of president, 400
Senate role, 10, 12–13, 459
transition period and, 510–511
Wiener v. United States (1958), 15, 269
Approval rating, 428–429
Arab oil embargo, 194, 390
Arctic National Wildlife Refuge, 194
Aristide, Jean-Bertrand, 79, 103
Armed Services Committee and Defense Department, 145
Arms control. *See* Diplomatic powers
Arms shipment to warring nations. *See United States v. Curtiss-Wright Export Corp.*
Arthur, Chester A., *15*, **15–16**
background, 28
death of, 16
oath of office and, 394
succeeds Garfield, 15, 16, 21, 230, 483, 544
veto power of, 534
as vice president, 369
as widower, 15, 27
Articles. *See* Constitution
Ashcroft, John, 65, 315
Assassinations and assaults, 19–25. *See also specific president*
assaults, 23–24
effects of, 19–20
Garfield, 16, 21, 31, 142
Jackson, 302
Kennedy (J.F.), 22, 24, 142–143, 309, 310, 319–320, 547, 593–594. *See also* Warren Commission
Lincoln, *20*, 20–21, 98, 142, 230, 307, 339
McKinley, 21–22, 24, 142, 347, 349, 448–449, 541–542
presidential security, 24–25, 457–458
Reagan, 23, 438, 458
statistics, 20
Truman, 31

Atzerodt, George, 20
Axson, Ellen Louise, 584

Babcock, Orville E., 237, 573
Background of presidents, 26–29
common profile, 27
differences of, 27–29
presidential qualifications, 17, 26, 432–433
similarities in, 26–27
Bailey, Thomas A., 414
Baker, Howard H., Jr., 85
Baker, James A., III, 85
Balanced Budget and Emergency Deficit Control Act of 1985, 41
Ballot, election, *58*
Bank Holiday Proclamation, 219
Banking Act of 1933, 191, 384
Banking industry, 384
Bank of the United States, 255, 514
Barker, Bernard L., 567
Barkley, Alben W., *29*, 29–30
Bartlett, Dan, 270
Bates, Edward, *188*
Bayh, Birch, 155, 434, 485
Bay of Pigs, 319, 386–387
Beer, Samuel, 178–179
Begin, Menachem, 68, 79, 80, *488*
Belknap, William W., 237, 280
Bell, John, 30, 32, 159, 177, 337, 500
Bell, Terrill, 166
Bellange, Pierre-Antoine, 576
Bentsen, Lloyd M., Jr.
defeat of G.H.W. Bush in senate race, 52
as secretary of Treasury, 514
vice-presidential campaign debates, 69–70
Berger, Samuel R. "Sandy", 380
Berle, Adolph A., Jr., 323
Berlin airlift, 520
Berlin Wall, Kennedy speech at, 151
Bernanke, Benjamin, 215
Bernstein, Carl, 357, *567*, 568
Betty Ford Center for Drug and Alcohol Rehabilitation, 224
Biden, Joseph R., Jr., 169
Bill of Rights, 407, 565
bin Laden, Osama, 191, 242, 554
Bipartisan Campaign Reform Act of 2002, 76, 212, 406
Birchard, Sardis, 250
Black, Hugo, 303
Black, Jeremiah S., 131
Blackmun, Harry, 132
Blaine, James G., 21, 30–31, 247
election of 1876, 250
election of 1884, 99–100, 253

Republican convention of 1880, 16, 230
Blair, Francis Preston, 31, 109, 323
Blair, Montgomery, *188*
Blair House, 31, *32*, 576
Blanco, Kathleen, 270
Blount, William, 280
Blue ribbon commissions, 82, 111, 313
Boggs, Hale, 562, *563*
BOGSAT, 13
Boland, Edward P., 294
Boland Amendments, 294, 538
Bolten, Joshua B., *84*, 85, 86
Bonaparte, Charles J., 211
Bones, Helen, 582
Boorstin, Daniel, 495
Booth, John Wilkes, 20, *20*, 25, 98, 307, 339
Border and Transportation Security, 261
Bork, Robert H., 131, 132, 284, 569
Bouvier, Jacqueline Lee. *See* Kennedy, Jacqueline
Bowles, Erskine, 85, 86
Braddock, Edward, 564
Bradley, Bill, 235
Bradley, Omar, 324
Brady, James, 23, 419, 576, *576*
Brady, John R., 21
Brady, Nicholas F., 514
Brady, Sarah, *576*
Brady bill, 103
Brandeis, Louis D., 131
Breckinridge, John C., 30, *32*, 32–33, 159, 176–177, 337–338, 500
Bremer, Arthur, 551
Bremer, L. Paul, 297
Presidential Medal of Freedom and, 416
Bretton Woods Conference of 1944, 514
Breyer, Stephen G., 101, 132
Brezhnev, Leonid, 79, 390
Bricker, John W., 148, 199, 520
Bristow, Benjamin H., 573
Bristow, Joseph L., 353–354
Britton, Nan, 246
Brown, Edmund G., 389, 437
Brown, Jerry, 102
Brown, Michael, 261, 270–271
Brownlow, Louis D., 33, 204, 474
Brownlow Committee, 13, 33, 111, 204, 264, 474–475
Bryan, Charles W., 141
Bryan, William Jennings, 33–34, *34*, 348
election 1900, 481
election 1908, 462, 491
nomination of 1896, 100, 260, 571

nomination of 1912, 584
third-party politics and, 500
Brzezinski, Zbigniew, 380
Buchanan, James, *35,* **35–36**
  appointments, 140
  bachelor status, 27, 36, 137, 322
  background, 28
  election of 1856, 218
  as ex-president, 226
  judicial nominations, 131
  national party convention of 1852, 404
  veto power of, 534
  vice president, 32
Buchanan, Patrick, 500
Buckley, James L., 36
Buckley v. Valeo (1976), 36–37, 72–73, 212
Budget and Accounting Act of 1921, 40, 114
Budget and Impoundment Control Act of 1974, 41, 281–282
Budget Committees, House and Senate, 41
Budget Enforcement Act of 1990, 42
Budget process, 37–43, 120
  background, 37–38, 40
  congressional role, 39, 280, 281–282
  Defense Department and, 144–146
  deficits and surpluses, 38
  executive influence, 39–40
  federal deficit and, 38, 40–43
  fiscal year, 38
  Gramm-Rudman-Hollings bill, 41–42
  president's budget, 38–39, 114, 164
  reforms, 40–43
  summits, 39–40
Bulganin, Nikolai, 168
Bull Moose Party. *See* Progressive Party
Bureaucracy, 44–50. *See also* Brownlow Committee; Hoover commissions; Personnel Management, Office of
  agencies, 44–45
  appointment/approval, 10
  budget process and, 40–43
  departments, 44
  government corporations, 45
  growth of, 45–47
  presidential and congressional agencies, 45
  presidents and, 47–50, 510–511
Bureau of Citizenship and Immigration Services (BCIS), 261
Bureau of Engraving and Printing, 515
Bureau of Labor Statistics, 328
Bureau of Prisons, 331
Bureau of the Budget, 40, 201, 352
Burger, Warren E., 131, 273, 485, 529, *543*

Burke, Edmund, 462
Burr, Aaron, 3, *50,* 50–51, 175–176, 186, 540
  duel with Hamilton, 50, 51, 243, 244, 280, 380
  election of 1800, 50, 254, 305, 407–408
Bush, Barbara, *51,* 51–52, 222–223, *227*
Bush, George H. W., *52,* **52–54,** *227, 261, 419*
  appointments, 12, 83, 85, 512, 514
  background, 27–28, 51–52
  budget director, 353
  budget process and, 38, 39–40
  cabinet, 65
  campaign debates, 69, 71, 216
  commander in chief and, 124
  election 1980, 53
  election 1984, 53, 366
  election 1988, 53
  election 1992, 53, 102, 183
  Energy Department and, 194
  as ex-president, 105, 226, *227,* 228
  family and friends, 137
  father-son presidents, 4
  Gulf War, 81, 296–297, 527, 561
  Hatch Act and, 95
  honeymoon period, 262
  international trade, 509
  Iran-contra affair and, 285, 295–296
  judicial nominations, 131
  library of, 336
  marriage, 51
  national security adviser, 380
  Persian Gulf War, 401–403
  personnel and, 14
  pitching baseballs, ceremonial, 90
  poor economic conditions and, 161
  press, relationship with, 357
  public opinion, 428, 430, 431
  religion, 27
  Republican National Committee chair, 52
  rest and recreation, 136
  staff, 476–477
  State of the Union addresses, 480
  transition funds for, 510
  travel abroad, 513
  veto power of, 40, 95, 534, 537, 539
  as vice president, 155, 183, 540, 543, 545
  vice president of, 434, 545
  war powers, 561
  work habits, 135
Bush, George W., *54,* **54–56,** 67, *113, 160, 286,* 298, *313, 358, 417, 479, 502, 525, 576*

  appointments, 14, 18, 85, 93, 451, 512, 514
  background, 26, 27–28
  budget director, 353
  budget process and, 43
  cabinet, 61, 65, *65*
  campaign debates, 69, 71
  campaign financing, 71, 73, 74
  CIA and, 81
  commander in chief, 124
  Congress and, 114
  counsel to the president, 127
  court challenge over 2000 presidential election, 57–59
  election of 2000, 53, 69, 83, 184–185, 186–187, 235, 410
  election of 2004, 56, 69, 70–71, 74, 77, 84, 320, 321
  emergency powers, 122
  Energy Department and, 194
  ethics and, 196
  Executive Office of the President and, 205
  executive privilege, 206–207
  family and friends, 137
  father-son presidents, 4
  health, 155
  homeland security and, 191, 205, 260–262
  honeymoon period, 262, 263
  Hurricane Katrina, 269, 270–271
  inauguration, 283, 455
  interest groups and, 291
  international trade, 165, 509, 510
  Iraq War, 296–299, 403, 527, 537, 555, 562. *See also* Iraq War
  judicial nominations, 132
  Justice Department, 315
  library of, 336
  mid-term elections and, 364
  national security advisor, 380
  pardon power, 396
  party leadership and, 397
  pitching baseballs, ceremonial, 90
  presidential commissions and, 110–111
  Presidential Medal of Freedom and, 415–416
  presidential oath, 18
  press, relationship with, 358
  proclamations, 426
  public opinion, 364, 428–429, 431
  religion and, 27, 442
  reorganization control, 50
  rest and recreation, 137
  September 11 attacks. *See* September 11 attacks
  signing statements, 463–464, 525

staff, 477
State of the Union Address, 341, 480, 554–555
tax cuts and, 43, 165
terrorism. *See* Terrorism
transition funds for, 510
U.N. and, 527
USDA and, 8
veto power of, 534, 537
vice president of, 82–84, 543, 544, 545
war powers, 557, 562
work habits, 135
Bush, Jeb, 53, 58
Bush, Jenna, 57, 138
Bush, Laura, 56–57, *57*, 138, 223, *358*
Bush, Prescott, 52
Bush v. Gore (2000), 57–59, 128, 184, 235
Bush Doctrine, 156–157
Business-Industry Political Action Committee (BIPAC), 405
Butler, William, 217
Butterfield, Alexander, 569
Buttons, campaign, *173*, *496*
Byrd, Harry F., 181

C. Turner Joy (destroyer), 505
Cabinet, 44, 60–66
  of Bush, George W., *65*
  economic management and, 162
  interest groups, role with, 292
  members, 65–66
  modern, 62, 63–65
  nineteenth century, 62–63
  origins, 61–62
  rankings in, 514
  role of, 60–61, 322
  room, 60
  as transition period issue, 510, 511
  vice president and, 541, 542, 544
Cabinet secretariat, 64
Calabresi, Steven G., 414
Calhoun, John C., *66*, 66–67, 176, 302, 531
  cabinet and, 322
  Congress and the presidency, 113
  resignation, 485
  War Hawks and, 351
Campaign buttons, *173*, *496*
Campaign debates, *68*, 68–71, *173*, 180–181, 182, 216
  prenomination, 71
  televised, 70, 389
  vice-presidential, 69–71, 235
Campaign financing, 36–37, 71–77, 170, 182. *See also* Federal Election Commission (FEC); Political action committees (PACs)

advertising expenses, 73
cartoon, *37*
disclosure statements, 197
general campaign, 74–76
landmark law in 2002, 172
party strength and, 77
polling and other professional services, 73
primaries, 73–74
public money, 72–73
reform of, 36–37, 76–77
Section 527 groups, 77
staff salaries, 73
statistics, 2000 candidates, 71
third parties and, 501
travel and headquarters expenses, 73
violations, 196
Campaigns. *See* Elections and campaigns
Camp David, 67–68, 136, 455
Camp David Accords, 68, 79
Candidates. *See* Elections and campaigns; *specific individuals*
Cantril, Albert, 428
Capitol Hill. *See* Congress and the presidency
Card, Andrew H., Jr., *84*, 85, 86
Carswell, G. Harrold, 131
Carter, Amy, 138
Carter, Billy, 138
Carter, Jimmy, 77–79, *78*, *227*, *488*, *517*
  amnesty for Vietnam War draft evaders, 121
  appointments, 49, 85, 123, 130
  background, 28
  cabinet, 61, 64–65
  campaign debates, 68–69
  Camp David Accords, 68
  counsel to the president, 127
  Democratic Congress and, 461
  economic conditions and, 161
  Education Department and, 166
  election of 1976, 77–78, 169–170, 182, 226
  election of 1980, 79, 182–183, 437
  emergency powers, 189
  Energy Department plan, 194
  ethics and, 196, 197
  Executive Office of the President and, 205
  as ex-president, 226, 228
  family and friends, 138, 139
  farewell address, 210
  on federal bureaucracy, 47
  inauguration, 283
  interests groups and, 293
  Justice Department and, 314
  library of, *335*, 336

Mutual Defense Treaty of 1954, 518
national party convention of 1976, 379
national security advisor, 380
Nobel Peace Prize and, 79
pardon power, 396
party leadership and, 398
personnel difficulties, 14
polling data and, 428
presidential security and, 25
public opinion, 430
religion and, 27, 442
rest and recreation, 137
SALT II treaty, 123, 517
six-year term proposal and, 498
staff, 472
State of the Union addresses, 480
veto power of, 534, 536
vice president, 365–366
work habits, 134–135
Carter, Rosalynn, 79–80, *80*, 221–222, *227*
Carter Center, *335*
Carter Doctrine, 156
Cartoons and caricatures
  Adams, John Quincy, *553*
  campaign financing, *37*
  Court-Packing Plan, *127*
  Jackson, Andrew, *118*, *533*, *553*
  Jefferson, Thomas, *507*
  Johnson (L. B.) and Vietnam, *547*
  Roosevelt (F. D.), New Deal, *384*
  spoils system, *91*
  Steel Seizure case, *592*
  Teapot Dome Scandal, *494*
  United States v. Nixon (1974), *206*, *529*
  Wilson, Woodrow, *587*
Case Act of 1972, 199
Casey, William, 294
Cass, Lewis, 35, 140, 217, 404, 411, 493, 532
Castro, Fidel, 82, 567
Caucuses, political, 170, 375, 421–422. *See also* Delegate selection reforms; Primaries
  nature of, 421–422
CEA. *See* Economic Advisers, Council of
Centers for Disease Control and Prevention (CDC), 252
Central Intelligence Agency (CIA), 80–82, 286
  Bay of Pigs and, 319
  DHS and, 261
  director, and National Security Council, 381
  illegal activities, 81–82

National Commission on Terrorist
Attacks (9/11 Commission) and,
374
war or terrorism, 554
Watergate and, 53, 567
Ceremonial duties
as chief of state, 86–87
effect on public opinion, 429–430,
467
speeches, 469
State of the Union address, 19, 480
Cermak, Anton J., 23
Chadha, Jagdish Rai, 272–273
Challenger (space shuttle), 468
Chase, Salmon P., 21, *188*, 308
Chase, Samuel, 279
Checks and balances. *See* Separation of
powers
Cheney, Lynne, 82, 83
Cheney, Richard, 55, 82–84, *83*, 85,
479
Energy Task Force (2001) and, 207
Government Accountability Office,
lawsuit with, 206–207
Halliburton (company) and, 196
Libby, I. Lewis "Scooter" and, 196
as vice president, 155, 185, 537, 543,
544, 545
vice-presidential campaign debates,
70–71
Cheney v. U.S. District Court (2004),
207
Chertoff, Michael, 261, 270
Chief executive, 17, 119–120
Chief justice of the United States, 394
Chief of staff, 84–86, 472, 511
Chief of state, 86–91, 124
background, 86
burdens of, 89–90
ceremonial duties, 86–87
dangers of deference, 90–91
enhancement of power, 87–88
foreign policy role, 88–89, 149–151
partisan politics and, 89
Children and Families, Administration
for, 252
China, People's Republic of, 79, 390
"most favored nation" principle and,
510
Mutual Defense Treaty of 1954 and,
518
"open door" trade policy, 348
Chinn, Julia, 312
Chou En-lai, *488*
Christian Coalition, 441
Church, Frank P., 81–82
Churchill, Winston, 447, 487, 520, *588*
CIA. *See* Central Intelligence Agency

Citizenship and Immigration, Bureau
of, 261
Citizenship requirement for president
and vice-president, 433
Civil Aeronautics Act of 1938, 385
Civil Aeronautics Administration, 110
Civilian Conservation Corps, *163*, 219,
446
Civil Liberties Act of 1988, 304
Civil Rights Act of 1964, 239, 262, 310,
387
Civil rights and schools, 166
Civil Rights Commission, 287
Civil service, 91–95
background, 93–94
chief executive and, 10
competitive, 92
excepted service, 93
Garfield assassination and, 91, 94
senior executives, 93
separate merit systems, 93
Civil Service Commission, 33, 46, 94
Civil service reform, 94, 251
patronage and, 399
Civil Service Reform Act of 1978, 94
Civil War, 95–96, 338
Grant's involvement, 235
Hayes and, 250
Lincoln's war powers, 96–97, 558
road to conflict, 95–96
state secessions and, 177
Union victory, 97–98
Claiborne, William C.C., 342
Clark, Champ, *584*
Classification of government
documents, 205–206
Clay, Henry, *98*, 98–99, 522
Congress and the presidency, 113
death of, 218
election of 1824, 5, 6, 119, 133, 176,
302, 500
election of 1832, 98, 302, 379
election of 1844, 99, 140, 412
Fillmore and, 217
Monroe Doctrine and, 156
slavery compromise and, 218, 493
War Hawks and, 351
Clayton Anti-Trust Act of 1914, 386, 584
Clean Air Act of 1990, 195
Clean Water Act of 1987, 195
Clemency power, 120–121
Clement, Paul D., *316*
Cleveland, Frances Folsom, 100, 220
Cleveland, Grover, *99*, **99–100,** 178,
226
appointments, 448, 480
background, 28
conservatism of, 408

election of 1884, 31, 99–100
election of 1888, 100, 186, 247, 369
election of 1892, 100, 246, 247–248,
481, 570
farewell address, 210
judicial nominations, 131
law enforcement powers and, 330
marriage, 27, 137
Pullman strike and, 143
rating by historians, 413
removal power and, 14
Secret Service and, 24
Spanish-American relations and, 465
surgery of, 481
terms of office, 496
veto power of, 534
vice presidents, 252–253, 480, 481
Clifford, Clark, 127, 475
Clinton, Bill, *101,* **101–105,** *227, 360,*
509
appointments, 12, 85, 512, 514
assassination attempts, 24
background, 28
budgets, 42–43, 164–165
bureaucratic control, 49–50
cabinet, 65
campaign debates, 69
campaign financing, 73, 75–76, 196,
285
character questions, 169, 184, 580
CIA and, 82
Congress and, 114
counsel to the president, 127
Defense Department budget and,
145–146
election of 1992, 53, 183–184, 410,
461
election of 1996, 108, 157, 158
Energy Department and, 194
ethics and, 196
eulogizes Nixon, 87
Executive Office of the President and,
205
executive orders, 293
as ex-president, 105, *227,* 228, 455
family and friends, 138, 139
first term, 102–104
foreign policy and, 103–104, 105
Hatch Act and, 95
honeymoon period, 262, 263
impeachment trial, 19, 103, 104, 114,
195, 259, 273, 278–279, 335
inauguration, 283
interest groups and, 291, 292, 293
international trade, 165, 509, 510
Iraq and, 297
joint chiefs and, 145
judicial nominations, 131, 132

Kennedy (J. F.) and, *103*
law enforcement powers and, *332*
law practice, 28
library of, 335–336
line-item veto and, 340–341
midterm elections and, 363
national party convention of 1988, 378
national security adviser, 380
Oklahoma City bombing and, 88
pardon power and, 105, 121, 196, 396
Pennsylvania Avenue, closing, 24, 578
personnel and, 14
political career, 102
Presidential Medal of Freedom and, 415
press, relationship with, 357–358
religion and, 27
rest and recreation, 136, 137
salary, 454
second term, 104–105
signing statements and, 464
staff, 477
State of the Union addresses, 480
tax cut bills and, 165
transitions funds for, 510
two-term limit and, 498
U.N. and, 527
USDA reorganization, 8
veto power of, 42, 43, 103, 534, 537
vice president, 102, 234–235, 545
war powers, 561–562
Whitewater investigation, 578–580
work habits, 135
Clinton, Chelsea, 102, 137, 227
Clinton, DeWitt, 106, 233, 351
Clinton, George, 105–106, *106*, 484
Clinton, Hillary Rodham, 101, 106–108, *107*, 139, 223, *227*
health care and, 103, 107
presidential campaign (2008), 29, 108
as Senator, 105, 108
Whitewater investigation and, 278, 578, 579, 580
Clinton, Roger, 138
Clinton v. City of New York (1998), 341
Clinton v. Jones (1997), 101, 128
Coast Guard, U.S., 260, 262
homeland security and, 50, 512
Colbath, Jeremiah Jones, 583
Cold war, 167, 520, 526, 558
Coleman, Norm, 366
Colfax, Schuyler, *108*, 108–109, 237, 280
Collazo, Oscar, 25
Colson, Charles, 569
Columbia (space shuttle), *192*
Commander in chief, 123–124
growth of, 558–559

law enforcement powers, 330
limits on, 243
Lincoln and, 255–256
nuclear weapons and, 391–392
Polk and, 255
Roosevelt (F. D.) and, 588, 589
war powers, 123–124, 506, 555–556
Commerce Department, 64, 109–110
Commissions, presidential, 45, 110–111, 544–545. *See also* Hoover commissions
vice presidents and, 544–545
Committee to Re-elect the President, 284, 567, 568
Commodities Exchange Authority, 289
Communications Office, White House, 473
Communism, 520. *See also* Cold war
Compromise of 1850, 99, 217–218, 405, 493
Comptroller of the Currency, Office of, 515
Confederate States of America, 96, 140, 177
Conference for Progressive Political Action, 327
Conflicts of interest, 197
Congress and the presidency, 111–117
appointments, 12–13, 18
budget process, 39–40
congressional role, 117
counterterrorism, 554–555
executive lobbying, 112–113
executive orders, 117, 206
executive privilege, 206–207
legislative leader, 112
pardon power, 18
patronage, 116
president's program, 114–115
public appeals, 116
veto power, 116–117
war powers, 96–97, 506, 555–556, 560
Congressional Budget and Impoundment Control Act of 1974, 41, 281–282, 334
Congressional Budget Office, 39, 41
Congressional Caucus (King Caucus), 118–119, 176
Conkling, Roscoe, 16, 230, 256, 369
Connally, John B., 22, 563, *593*
Connally, Tom, 324
Constitution, *119. See also* Constitutional amendments
appointment and removal power, 9–10, 120
Article I, 18, 525
Article II, 9, 16–19, 62, 119–124, 525
budgeting, 120

chief executive, 17, 119–120
chief of state, 124
clemency, 120–121
commander in chief, 123–124
congressional caucus and, 118–119
courts and, 128–132
diplomatic powers, 149–153
economic powers, 161
electoral college and, 117
emergency powers, 122, 365
executive agreements, 123, 198–199
executive orders, 121–122, 205
Federalist Papers and, 213–214
foreign affairs, 122–123, 149–153
founders signing their names, *119*
law enforcement, 120, 330–331
legislative powers, 121
legislative veto and, 334
line-item veto and, 341
Madison and, 350–351
national bank, 372–373
oath and office, 17–18, 393–394
pardon power, 395
power and provisions, 119–124
presidential disability, 154–155
qualifications for president, 17, 26, 432–433
recognitions and appointments, 123, 152–153
religion and, 441
salary and perquisites, 453
separation of powers, 460–462
stewardship theory and, 482
succession, 483
term of office and, 496, 497
treaties, 18, 515, 516, 519
veto, 121, 533, 535
vice president and, 539, 540
"Virginia Plan" and, 351
war powers, 123–124, 555–560
Constitutional amendments
Bill of Rights, 407, 565
Twelfth, 17, 19, 51, 176, 186, 254, 408, 458, 541
Thirteenth, 188
Fourteenth, 58, 440
Fifteenth, 235
Sixteenth, 491
Twentieth, 19, 328–329, 486–487, 495
Twenty-second, 19, 258, 329, 495, 497, 498
Twenty-third, 19
Twenty-fifth, 19, 182, 225, 392, 443, 540, 543, 544
Constitutional Union Party, 30, 32, 159, 176–177, 500
Consumer Product Safety Commission, 289

Consumer protection, 289
Continental Congress, 350
Continental congresses, 232, 244, 248, 564
Continuing resolutions, 43
Contract with America, 42
line-item veto and, 340
Conventions. *See* National party conventions
Coolidge, Calvin, *125*, **125–126**
appointments, 27, 552
background, 28
on burdens of presidency, 89
election of 1920, 446
election of 1924, 327, 465
inauguration, 284
national party convention of 1920, 378
pocket veto and, 539
on right to strike, 125
succeeds Harding, 126, 483, 544
Teapot Dome prosecutions and, 494
veto power of, 534
vice presidents, 141
work habits, 135
Coolidge, Grace, 125
Cooper, John Sherman, 562, *563*
Corrupt Practices Acts, 212
Corwin, Edward S., 150, 557
Council of Economic Advisers, 160–161, 475
Council of Environmental Quality, 203
Counsel to the president, 126–127
Court-packing plan, *127*, 127–128, 385, 447
Courts and the president, 128–132
appointments, 130–132
defining the limits, 101, 129–130
executive agreements and, 199
executive orders and, 205
Judiciary Act of 1925, 492
law enforcement power and, 333
legislative veto and, 334
line-item veto and, 340–341
Pullman strike of 1894, 143
segregation outlawed, 331
treaty termination power, 518
Cox, Archibald, 277, 284, 568, 569
Cox, James M., 125, 246, 446, 585
Crawford, William H., 5, 6, 98, 118, 119, 132–133, 176, 302, 500
Credentials committee, 376–377
Crédit Mobilier scandal, 31, 109, 230, 237, 280, 583
CREEP. *See* Committee to Re-elect the President
Cronin, Thomas E., 61

CRP. *See* Committee to Re-elect the President
Cuba
EXCOMM meeting on missile crisis, *201*
Taft and, 491
Cuban missile crisis, 81, 319
Currie, Betty, 279
Curtis, Charles, 133, 231
Curtiss-Wright Export Corp., 528
Custis, Daniel Parke, 566
Custis, Martha Dandridge, 564, *566*, 566–567
Customs Service, U.S., 260, 261, 289, 514
Cutler, Lloyd, 127
Czolgosz, Leon, 21–22, 25, 349

Daily and family life, 134–139
president's workday, 134–135
rest and recreation, 135–137
Dallas, Alexander, 139
Dallas, George M., *139*, 139–140
Dana, Francis, 4
Daniels, Mitchell E., 353
Darman, Richard, 353
Darrow, Clarence, 34
Daugherty, Harry, 246
Davis, David, 364
Davis, Henry G., 209
Davis, Jefferson, 32, 96, *140*, 140–141
Davis, John W., 141, 327, 379, 465
election of 1924, 126
Davis, Lanny J., 127
Davis, Nancy. *See* Reagan, Nancy
Davis, Sarah Taylor, 140
Davis, Warren, 23
Dawes, Charles G., *141*, 141–142
Dawes, William, 141
Dawes Plan, 141
Dean, John W., III, 568, 569
Death of the president, 142–143. *See also* Assassinations and assaults; Succession
Deaver, Michael D., 197–198
Debates. *See* Campaign debates
Debs, Eugene V., *143*, 143–144
Declaration of Independence, 305
Defense Analysis Center, 144
Defense Department, 11, 64, 144–146
creation of, 144
law enforcement powers and, 331
presidential command, 145–146
Deficit, federal
Bush (G.W.) term and, 38
Eisenhower to G.W. Bush, 38
Great Society/Vietnam War costs, 40

Reagan term and, 41–42
reduction, 103
de Gaulle, Charles, 32
DeLay, Tom, *113*
Delegate selection reforms, 146–148, 171, 375, 376
Delegates to national conventions, 171, 375
Democratic Leadership Council, 102
Democratic National Committee, 75–76
Democratic Party, 408. *See also* Political parties
campaign finance allegations, 75
campaign financing (1860–2004), 75
Commission on Party Structure and Delegate Selection, 346
delegate selection reforms, 146–148, 376
interest groups and, 291
national party convention of 1832, 378–379
national party convention of 1848, 35
national party convention of 1856, 32
national party convention of 1932, 30
national party convention of 1936, 30
national party convention of 1940, *376*
national party convention of 1948, 30
national party convention of 1972, 346
national party convention of 2000, 74, 171
Democratic-Republican Party, 2, 5, 50, 98, 106
Congressional Caucus and, 118–119, 176
election of 1816, 132
election of 1820, 505
election of 1824, 132, 133, 500
Jefferson and, 407, 507
National Gazette, 356
role of, 407
Democratic Study Group, 344
Denby, Edwin, 246
Deneen, Charles, 481
Department of Defense Reorganization Act of 1958, 144
Departments, executive, 44. *See also* Cabinet; *specific departments*
size of, selected years, 64
Deportation, 272–273
Depression. *See* Great Depression
Desegregation, 192, 387
Little Rock, Arkansas (1957), *331*
Dewey, George, 348, 448
Dewey, Thomas E., *148*, 148–149, 447, 581
election of 1944, 179, 378, 447, 520

election of 1948, 30, 179, 423, 503, 521
de Wolfe, Florence Kling, 246
DHS. *See* Homeland Security Department
Dickenson, Charles, 301
Dillinger, John, 211
Dimmick, Mary Scott Lord, 248
Dingley Tariff Act of 1897, 348
Diplomatic powers, 149–153
  presidential doctrines and, 155–157
  staff, 478–479
  termination of relations, 153
Director of National Intelligence (DNI), 81, *374*, 374–375
Dirksen, Everett McKinley, *111*
Disability amendment (25th), 154–155
Dixiecrats, 179, 502, 503
Doctrines, presidential, 155–157
Doheny, Edward L., 494
Dole, Elizabeth, *157*
Dole, Robert J., *157*, 157–158
  campaign debates, 69
  election of 1976, 366
  election of 1996, 104, 400, 423
  Presidential Medal of Freedom and, 158, 415
  Rockefeller and, 444
  vice-presidential campaign debates, 69
Dollar diplomacy, 491
Domestic affairs, and public opinion, 429
Domestic Policy Council, 202, 373
Domestic policy staff, 476
Domestic unrest, 192
Donelson, Andrew J., 322
Douglas, Stephen A., 30, 32, *158*, 158–159, 176–177
  Kansas-Nebraska Act and, 35, 337, 405
  national party convention of 1852, 404
  national party convention of 1860, 379
Douglas, William O., 552, 592
Dred Scott decision (1857), 35–36
Drug abuse, 203
Drug Enforcement Agency (DEA), 211
Duberstein, Kenneth, 85
Dukakis, Michael S.
  election of 1988, 53, 70
  as governor, 321
  national party convention of 1988, 102, 378
  religion and, 441
Dulles, Allen W., 562, *563*
Dulles, John Foster, 443
Duncan v. Kahanamoku (1946), 355

Eagleton, Thomas E., 182, 346, 487
Early, Stephen T., 356, 418
Eaton, John H., 66, 322, 531
Eaton, Peggy, 531
Economic Advisers, Council of, 160–161, 202
Economic Opportunity, Office of, 83, 286–287
Economic policy, 239–240
  emergency powers and, 191–192
  Hamilton's, 244
  independent regulatory agencies and, 288–289
  international role of, 239–240, 488
  Trading with the Enemy Act of 1917, 191, 193
Economic Policy Council, 374
Economic powers, 161–165. *See also* Monetary policy; New Deal
  fiscal policy, 164
  international role, 165
  limitations on, 161–162
  management and, 162–163
Economic protest parties, 499–500
Economic Stabilization Act of 1970, 192
Education Department, 44, 49, 61, 64, 65, 293
  history of, 165–166
Edwards, John, 71
Ehrlichman, John D., 476, 568, 569
Eisenhower, Dwight D., *167*, **167–168**, *357*
  Air Force One and, 9
  ancestry, 26
  appointments, 13, 85, 204, 443
  cabinet, 64
  Camp David and, 68
  Congress and, 115
  election of 1952, 179–180, 481
  emergency powers and, 192
  ethics and, 196
  Executive Office Building and, 200
  Executive Office of the President and, 204
  executive privilege and, 206
  as ex-president, 226
  family and friends, 138
  farewell address, 210
  Federal Security Agency reorganization, 251
  good will tour, 513
  health, 154, 251
  honeymoon period, 262
  Hoover commission and, 265
  impoundments, 281
  judicial nominations, 131
  Korean War and, 168, 325

library of, 336
military experience, 26, 28
national party convention of 1952, 379
National Security Council and, 381
pardon power, 395
party affiliation of, 408
press, relationship with, 357
press conferences, 416
rating by historians, 414
religion and, 442
removal power, 269
rest and recreation, *135*, 136
staff, 475
summits and, 168
transition funds for, 510
two-term limit and, 498
veto power of, 534, 536
vice president, 544
Vietnam War and, 547
as war hero, 167
work habits, 135
Eisenhower, John, 498
Eisenhower, Mamie, 167, 221
Eisenhower, Milton, 138
Eisenhower Doctrine, 156
Eisenhower Executive Office Building, 455
Elders, Joycelyn, 11
Election ballot, *58*
Elections and campaigns, 168–174. *See also* Federal Election Commission; National party conventions; Primaries
1789, 3, 174–175
1796, 118, 175, 301, 305, 540
1800, 3, 4, 50–51, 118–119, 175–176, 186, 254, 305, 407–408, 540
1804, 106, 306
1808, 306, 351
1812, 233, 351
1816, 132, 367, 505
1820, 367
1824, 5, 6, 98, 118, 119, 133, 176, 186, 300
1828, 176, 302
1832, 98, 302, 378–379, 531
1836, 248, 302, 311, 459, 522, 531
1840, 312, 522, 532
1844, 99, 139–140, 217, 302, 378, 411–412, 523, 532
1848, 217, 363, 493, 498, 532
1852, 218, 404–405
1856, 32, 35, 218
1860, 30, 32, 36, 96, 158–159, 176–177, 337–338, 379, 408
1864, 345–346
1868, 109, 235, 379
1872, *27*, 237, 584

1876, 177–178, 186, 250–251, 440, 503–504, 571–572
1880, 16, 230, 237, 379
1884, 30, 31, 99–100
1888, 100, 186, 247, 369
1892, 100, 246, 247–248, 348, 369, 481, 570–571
1896, 34, 100, 260, 348, 370
1900, 34, 143, 349, 541–542
1904, 34, 143, 209, 449
1908, 34, 143, 449, 462, 491
1912, 34, 143, 178, 327, 353, 449–450, 463, 500, 584
1916, 209, 267, 354, 379, 450, 585
1920, 125, 246, 446, 585
1924, 126, 326–327, 379, 465, 500
1928, 133, 264, 465
1932, 133, 178–179, 231, 264, 329, 408, 446
1936, 329, 447
1938, 95
1940, 379, 447, 581
1944, 148, 179, 378, 447, 520
1948, 30, 148–149, 179, 377, 423, 501, 502–503, 521, 553
1952, 167–168, 179–180, 379, 389, 481
1956, 309, 482
1960, 180–181, 310, 319, 379, 389
1964, 181, 233, 268, 310–311, 551
1968, 6–7, 146, 181–182, 187, 268, 314, 343, 344, 389, 423, 450, 501, 551
1972, 7, 182, 268, 346, 390, 551, 567
1976, 77–78, 157, 182, *224*, 226, 366, 379, 437, 552
1980, 53, 79, 157, 182–183, 366, 437, 501
1984, 53, 183, 216, 366, 438
1988, 53, 157, *291*
1992, 53, 102, 183–184, 234–235, 400, 410, 461, 500
1994, 363
1996, 104, 157–158, 196, 235, 400, 423, 500
1998, 364
2000, 14, 53–54, 55–56, 57–59, 83, 184–185, 235, 410, 423, 499, 500
2004, 56, 69, 70–71, 74, 75, 76–77, 84, 320, 321, 423
chronology, 174–185
controversy, 57–59
exploratory stage, 169–170
financial holdings disclosure, 197
midterm elections, 363–364, 555
presidential nomination, 171–173
requirements, 169
third-party candidates, 500. *See also* Third parties

vice-presidential candidates, 539–540
Electoral college
background, 17, 185–187, 252, 433, 496
campaign strategy and, 172
Constitution and, 173–174, 185, 186
election of 1876, 250–251
election of 2000 and, 184
executive power and, 253
"faithless electors" and, 186
formula of delegate allocation, 375–376
qualifications for president and vice president, 17, 433
Twelfth Amendment and, 458
Electoral Count Act of 1887, 58
Elementary and Secondary Education Act, 239
Elizabeth II, Queen, 32
Emancipation Proclamation, 97, 187–188, 256, 338, 577
Embargo Act of 1807, 4, 306
Emergency Banking Bill, 219
Emergency Farm Mortgage Act, 219
Emergency powers, 96–97, 122, 130, 188–193. *See also* War powers
Congress and, 193
domestic unrest, 192
economic crises, 191–192
Eisenhower and, 192
Japanese American internment, 303–304
limits on, 193
Lincoln and, 189–190
martial law and, 354
Milligan, Ex parte (1866), 190, 355, 364–365
natural disasters, 192–193
Nixon and, 192
Roosevelt (F.D.) and, 190–191, 303–304
supplemental appropriations, 193
terrorism, 191
wartime, 189–191
Wilson and, 585, 586–587
World Wars, 190, 588–589
Youngstown Sheet and Tube Co. v. Sawyer (1952), 191, 591–592
Emergency Preparedness and Response, 261
Emergency Price Control Act of 1942, 589
EMILY's List, 405
Employment Act of 1946, 114, 160
Employment and Training Administration, 328

Employment Standards Administration, 328
Endorsements, presidential, 426
Energy Department, 49, 61, 64, 193–195
Energy Information Administration, 194–195
Energy Research and Development Administration, 194
Energy Security and Assurance Program, 194
English, William H., 16
Engraving, Bureau of, 515
Environmental Measurements Laboratory, 194
Environmental Protection Agency (EPA), 195, 286, 287, 288
creation of, 203
Environmental Quality, Council on, 203
Envoys, presidential, 153
EOP. *See* Executive Office of the President
Equal Employment Opportunity Commission, 310
Equal Rights Amendment, 222, 223
Ervin, Sam, 568
Eskew, Tucker, 477
Espionage Act of 1917, 144
Espy, Mike, 8, 196
Ethics, 195–198
media manipulation and, 359
Ethics in Government Act of 1978, 12, 284, 314
independent counsel law, 197, 284–286, 314
Ethics Reform Act of 1989, 197
Evans, Donald, *65*
Executive agreements, 123, 198–199
defined, 198
Louisiana Purchase and, 123, 342
Texas annexation and, 362
treaty power and, 123, 152, 518
Executive branch. *See* Bureaucracy
Executive Office Buildings, 200
Executive Office of the President, 45, 114–115, 200–205, 471
administrative staff, 204
budget and, 164
bureaucracy and, 48
cabinet and, 61
creation of, 200–201, 204–205, 265, 475
Economic Advisers, Council on, 202, 373
Environmental Quality, Council on, 203
executive power and, 16–17, 253–254

Hoover commissions and, 264–265
independent executive agencies, 286–287
Management and Budget, Office of, 201–202
National Drug Control Policy Office, 203
National Security Council, 202
Policy Development Office and, 202
presidential staff, 10, 471–472
president's budget, 38–39
Roosevelt (F.D.) and, 204
senior executives, 93
U.S. Trade Representative, Office of the, and, 202
Vice President, Office of, 203
White House Office, 200, 201
Executive orders, 117, 121–122, 205–206, 293, 303
bureaucracy and, 48
commissions, 111
presidential libraries and, 336
White House name and, 574
Executive privilege, 206–207
separation of powers and, 461–462
Watergate affair and, 130, 277, 528–529, 569–570
Executive Residence, 203
Exit polls, 185

Factional parties, 500–501
Fairbanks, Charles W., 208, 208–209, 354
Fair Deal, 209–210, 386, 520
Fairfield, John, 531
Fair Labor Standards Act of 1938, 385
Fall, Albert B., 246, 494
Family life, 134–139
Famine Emergency Commission, 264
Fannie Mae, 267
Farewell addresses, 210, 511, 565
Farm Credit Act, 219
Fast track authority, trade policy, 509
FEC. See Federal Election Commission
The Fed. See Federal Reserve System
Federal Advisory Committee Act (1972), 207
Federal Agriculture Improvement and Reform Act of 1996 (FAIR), 8
Federal Bureau of Investigation (FBI), 24, 47, 211, 316
law enforcement powers, 331
National Commission on Terrorist Attacks (9/11 Commission) and, 374
Federal Communications Commission, 287

Federal Deposit Insurance Corporation, 289
Federal Election Campaign Act of 1971, 212
Federal Election Campaign Act of 1974, 334, 501
Federal Election Commission (FEC), 172
background, 212–213
Buckley v. Valeo (1976), 36–37
campaign finance abuses, 75–76
campaign finance reform, 76–77, 212–213
financial disclosure reports, 172
functions of, 73
matching funds, 74
McConnell v. FEC (2003), 76
Federal Emergency Management Agency (FEMA), 50, 260–261, 270–271
Federal Emergency Relief Act, 219, 446
Federal Energy Administration, 194
Federal Energy Regulatory Commission, 195
Federal Highway Administration, 512
Federal Home Loan Bank Board, 289
Federal Home Loan Mortgage Corporation (Freddie Mac), 267
Federal Housing Administration (FHA), 267
Federal Housing Enterprise Oversight, 267
Federalist Papers, 213, 244, 351
advisers councils, 62
background, 213–214
foreign government recognition, 152
on veto power, 535
Federalist Party, 3, 35, 98, 174
congressional caucus system and, 118–119
executive power philosophy, 254
Hamilton and, 243–244, 305, 407
Jefferson and, 51
Federal Law Enforcement Training Center, 262
Federal National Mortgage Association (Fannie Mae), 267
Federal Power Commission, 289
Federal Railroad Administration, 512
Federal Register, 371
executive orders and, 206
Federal Register, Office of the, 371
Federal Reserve Act of 1913, 386
Federal Reserve Act of 1914, 373, 584
Federal Reserve Banks, 215
Federal Reserve Board, 162, 215, 287
Federal Reserve System (The Fed), 110, 214–216, 289, 373
Federal Security Agency, 251

Federal Trade Commission, 15, 287, 289, 584
appointment and removal power and, 333
law enforcement powers and, 331
Federal Trade Commission Act, 386
Federal Transit Administration, 512
Feerick, John D., 485
Feingold, Russell D., 76, 213
Ferraro, Geraldine A., 29, 53, 183, 216, 216–217, 366
Field, James G., 571
Fielding, Fred, 127
Fifteenth Amendment, 235
Fillmore, Millard, 35, 217, 217–218
background, 28
Compromise of 1850 and, 218
election of 1848, 217
election of 1856, 500
as ex-president, 226
Japan initiative, 405
succeeds Taylor, 218, 483, 493, 544
veto power of, 534
Financial Management Service, 515
Financing. See Campaign financing
First Hundred Days. See Hundred Days
First ladies, 219–223. See also specific first lady by name
early, 220
first elective office of, 105
twentieth century, 220–223
weddings in White House and, 136
First National Bank of the United States, 372
Fiscal policy, 164, 216
Fish, Hamilton, 235
Fiske, Robert B., Jr., 285, 579–580
Fitzwater, Martin, 576
Fleischer, Ari, 358, 419
Folsom, Frances. See Cleveland, Frances Folsom
Folsom, Jim, 551
Food and Drug Administration, 7, 46, 251, 252, 288
Food Stamp Program, 8
Forbes, Charles, 246
Forbes, Malcolm S., Jr. (Steve), 74, 423
Ford, Betty, 222, 223–224, 224, 227, 278, 546
Ford, Gerald R., 224, 224–226, 227, 278, 543, 563
appointments, 83, 85, 451
assassination attempts, 23, 25, 226, 458
background, 28
Bush (G.H.W.) and, 52–53
cabinet, 64
campaign debates, 68–69

CIA investigation, 82
death of, 226
election of 1976, 77–78, 157, 226, 366, 437
Energy Department plan, 194
Executive Office of the President and, 205
as ex-president, 227–228
family and friends, 138
Hatch Act and, 95
honeymoon period, 262
on impeachment, 274
interest groups and, 292
Justice Department and, 314
law practice, 28
legislative veto and, 334
library of, 336
Mayaguez and, 225–226
national party convention of 1976, 379
national security adviser, 380
pardon of Nixon, 78, 121, 182, 225, 330, 391, 395, 396, 570
poor economic conditions and, 161
rest and recreation, 137
Rockefeller and, 443–444
Secret Service and, 458
succeeds Nixon, 443, 483, 485, 543, 570
veto power of, 95, 534, 536
as vice president, 7, 182, 223, 443, 543, 546
vice president nomination, 485
war powers, 561
Warren Commission, 562, *563*
work habits, 135
Ford, Susan, 138
Fordney-McCumber Act of 1922, 246, 508
Foreign affairs, 122–123. *See also United States v. Curtiss-Wright Export Corp.*
chief of state and, 88–89, 254
diplomatic powers, 149–153
executive agreements and, 123, 198–199
presidential dominance of, 150–151
public opinion and, 299, 429
recognition power and, 152–153
summit meetings, 487–489
treaty powers, 122–123, 152, 516
Foreign Intelligence, Committee on, 153
Forest Service, 46
Former presidents, 226–228, *227*
benefits of, 226–228
perquisites, 455
Former Presidents Act of 1958, 227, 455
Fortas, Abe, 131
Foster, Henry, 11
Foster, Vincent, 127, 579–580

Foster v. Neilson (1829), 519
Fourteen Points, 585, 587. *See also* Wilson, Woodrow; World War I
Fourteenth Amendment, 58, 440
Fourth branch, 44
Framers, constitutional. *See Federalist Papers*
France, 3
Frankfurter, Felix, 131, 303
Franklin, Benjamin, 2, 453, 539
Franks, Tommy, 416
Fraser, Donald, 146
Freddie Mac, 267
Freeman, Orville, 365
Free Soil Party, 404, 500, 532, 583
Frelinghusyen, Theodore, 140
Fremont, John C., 32, 35
election of 1856, 218
Fromme, Lynette "Squeaky", 23, 25, 226
Fugitive Slave Act, 35, 218

G-7 (Group of Seven), 488
G-8 (Group of Eight), 239–240, 488
Gallaudet University, 166
Gallup, George, 330, 428
Gallup surveys, 428
Galt, Norman, 582
Garfield, Abram, 229
Garfield, Eliza, 229
Garfield, James A., *229*, **229–231**
appointments, 30, 31, 369
assassination, 16, 21, 25, 31, 142
background, 28
civil service reform and, 46, 399
death of, 15, 16
nomination, presidential, 237
presidential disability and, 154
religion, 27
veto power of, 534
vice presidents, 369
Garner, John Nance, 133, 231, *231*, 542, 545, 552
General Accounting Office, 40
Cheney lawsuit with, 206–207
General Agreement on Tariffs and Trade (GATT), 508–509
General Services Administration, 286, 371
Genêt, Edmund, 151, 152
Geneva Conference, 487
Geneva Convention, 242–243
Genocide Treaty (1949), 518
Gerry, Elbridge, *232*, 232–233, 484
Gerrymander, 232, 233
Gettysburg Address, 87, 338, 467
Ghent, Treaty of, 5, 352, 554
Gingrich, Newt, 196
Ginnie Mae, 267

Ginsburg, Ruth Bader, 131
Glass-Steagall Banking Act, 219
Global Communications, Office of, 477
Goldwater, Barry M., 181, *233*, 233–234, 268, 310, *517*
Mutual Defense Treaty of 1954 and, 518
Reagan and, 437
Thurmond and, 503
Gompers, Samuel, 125
Gonzales, Alberto R., *126*, 127, 315
González, Elián, 315, *332*
Gonzalez, Virgilio R., 567
Gorbachev, Mikhail, 438
Gorbachev, Raisa, 436
Gore, Al, 184, *234*, 234–235
budgets, 42
campaign debates, 69
campaign financing, 71, 75–76, 196, 285
court challenge over 2000 presidential election, 57–59
election of 2000, 53, 55, 57–59, 184–185, 186–187, 410, 499
environmental protection, 195, 234, 235
inauguration, 283
An Inconvenient Truth, 235
rest and recreation, 137
as vice president, 49–50, 102, 543, 544, 545
vice-presidential campaign debates, 70
Gore, Albert, Sr., 234
Government Accountability Office, 206–207
Government Ethics, Office of, 197, 404
Government National Mortgage Association (Ginnie Mae), 267
Government operations. *See* Bureaucracy
Government Printing Office, 45
Graham, William Alexander, 322
Gramm-Rudman-Hollings bill, 41–42, 438
Granger, Francis, 459
Granger, Gordon, 188
Grant, Julia, 220, 236
Grant, Ulysses S., *27*, *96*, *235*, 235–237
appointments, 16, 490
background, 28
Civil War and, 97
election of 1864, 345
as ex-president, 226
family and friends, 139
judicial nominations, 131
memorial to, 361
military experience, 26, 235–236, 338

national party convention of 1880, 379

rating by historians, 413

Reconstruction era and, 440

salary, 453

Tenure of Office Act and, 276

veto power of, 534

vice presidents, 108–109, 584

as war hero, 167

Whiskey Ring scandal, 195, 237, 573

Gray, L. Patrick, 211

Great Communicator, 258–259, 468

Great Depression, 7, 121, 126, 127, 237–238, *238*

  background, 237–238

  economic management and, 162–163

  election of 1932, 133

  Hoover's presidency and, 264

  Roosevelt (F.D.) and, 114, 189, 219

  trade policy and, 506

Great Society, 114, 181, 238–239, 311, 469, 470

  budget deficit and, 40

  HHS and, 251

  Labor Department and, 328

Greeley, Horace, 237

Greenback Party, 570

Green Party, 499

Greenspan, Alan, 215

Grenada invasion, 438

Group of Eight (G-8), 239–240, 488

Group of Seven (G-7), 488

Guadalupe Hidalgo, Treaty of, 362, 412

Guam Doctrine, 156

Guantanamo Bay detainees, 242

Guiteau, Charles J., 16, 25, 94, 230, 399

Gulf War, 81, 83, 183, 296–297, 401–403, 527, 561

Gulf War Syndrome, 403

Gulick, Luther, 204

Habeas corpus, 242, 255

  martial law and, 354

  suspension of by confederate Davis, 141

  suspension of by Lincoln, 189–190

Hadley, Stephen, 380

Hagerty, James C., 418, 473

Hagin, Joe, *84*

Haig, Alexander, Jr., 85, 155

"Hail to the Chief," 241–242, *242*

Haldeman, H.R., 84, 85, 472, 476, 568, 569, 570

Half-Breed faction, Republican Party, 16, 230

Halliburton (company), 196

Hamdan v. Rumsfeld (2006), 242–243

Hamilton, Alexander, *63, 210, 243,* 243–244, 351

  Adams and, 174

  advisory councils, 62

  duel with Burr, 51, 243, 244

  on executive power, 383

  Federalist Papers, 213–214

  Federalist Party and, 407, 566

  foreign policy, 254

  on impeachment, 274

  national bank and, 372

  Neutrality Proclamation of 1973, 383

  on pardon power, 395–396

  as secretary of Treasury, 62, 112, 305, 398, 514, 565

  support of Jefferson, 305

  tariff policy preference, 507

  on veto power, 535

  on war power, 555, 557

Hamilton, Lee H., 295

Hamlin, Hannibal, 244–245, *245*

Hance, Kent, 54

Hancock, Winfield Scott, 16, 230

Hanna, Mark, *72,* 349, 448

Harding, Warren G., *245,* **245–246**

  appointments, 27, 141, 264, 267, 492, 493–494, 552

  background, 28

  death, 125, 142, 494

  election of 1920, 446, 585

  family and friends, 139

  pardon power, 144

  rating by historians, 413

  Teapot Dome scandal, 139, 195, 246, 493–494

  trade policy and, 508

  veto power of, 534

  vice president, 125

Harrison, Anna Symmes, 249

Harrison, Benjamin, **246–248,** *247*

  appointments, 30, 31, 448, 490

  background, 27, 28

  death, 17

  election of 1888, 100, 186

  election of 1892, 100, 246, 247–248, 369, 481, 570

  inauguration, 249

  veto power of, 534

  vice presidents, 369

  work habits, 135

Harrison, Benjamin (elder), 247, 248

Harrison, Caroline Lavinia Scott, 247

Harrison, John Scott, 249

Harrison, Mary Scott Lord Dimmick, 248

Harrison, William Henry, 246, *248,* **248–249**

  background, 27, 28

death, 142, *142,* 251, 255, 521

election of 1840, 312, 522, 532

inauguration, 249, 283, 284

veto power of, 534

vice president, 521, 541

War of 1812, 352

Hart, Gary, 71, 169, 216, 346, 366

Hatch, Carl, 95

Hatch Act, 95, 399

Hawaii, 348

Hay, John, 348

Hayden, Carl, *154,* 485

Hayden, Michael, *81*

Hayes, Lucy Ware Webb, 250, 572

Hayes, Rutherford B., *177,* **249–251,** *250, 571*

  background, 28

  compromise of 1876, 177–178

  election of 1876, 177, 186, 440, 503

  fires Arthur, 16

  library of, 335–336

  seal of office and, 456

  veto power of, 534

  vice president, 571–572

Haynsworth, Clement, 131

Health, Education, and Welfare Department (HEW), 251–252, 443

Health and Human Services Department (HHS), 11, 64, 251–252, 288

Health Care Financing Administration, 252

Health Resources and Services Administration, 252

Hearst, William Randolph, 267

Heclo, Hugh, 49

Helms, Jesse, 13, 527

Hendricks, Thomas A., 252–253, 485

Henry, Lou, 263

Hepburn Act, 471

Herrera, Omar Torrijos, *517*

HHS. *See* Health and Human Services Department

Highway Beautification Act of 1965, 222

Hill, Isaac, 323

Hinckley, John W., Jr., 23–24, 25, 438, 458

Hiroshima, Japan, 520, 589–590

Historians' ratings of the presidents, 413–414

Historic milestones of the presidency, 253–259

  creation of strong presidency, 253

  election of 1800, 118–119, 254, 540

  impeachment of Clinton, 259

  impeachment of Johnson (A.), 256

  Jacksonian philosophy and, 254–255

  Kennedy's personal presidency, 258

Lincoln's wartime powers, 255–256
patronage issues, 256
Polk and executive authority, 255
Reagan administrative presidency, 259
Roosevelt's (F.D.) One Hundred
  Days, 258
Roosevelt (T.) and executive authority,
  256–257
succession issues, 255
Washington's defining presidential
  role, 253–254
Watergate affair, 258
Wilson and popular leadership, 257
Hitler, Adolf, 447, 588
Hoar, Ebenezer R., 131
Hoban, James, 574, 576, 577
Hobart, Garret A., 259–260, 348, 485
Ho Chi Minh, 547
Hodges, Albert, 96
Hofstadter, Richard, 471
Homeland Security Department
  (DHS), 260–262
creation of, 43, 50, 61, 65, 191, 201,
  331, 477
Critical Infrastructure Assurance
  Office and, 110
Customs Service and, 260, 261, 514
Defense Analysis Center and, 144
DNI and, 375
Energy Department and, 195
FBI and, 211
FEMA and, 56
functions of, 50, 81, 331
Hurricane Katrina, 270–271
Justice Department and, 313
law enforcement powers and, 331
National BW (biological weapons)
  Defense Analysis Center, 144
Secret Service and, 50, 457, 514
size of, 64
Transportation Department and, 512
USDA and, 8
Honeymoon period, 102–103, 218–219,
  225, 262–263, 360, 495, 510
Hoover, Herbert, 263, **263–264,** 510
ancestry, 26
appointments of, 267
background, 27, 28
Commerce Department and, 109–110
education, 28
election of 1928, 464, 465
election of 1932, 178–179, 231, 329,
  408, 446
as ex-president, 226
Great Depression and, 161, 219,
  237–238, 408
impeachment attempts, 280
judicial nominations, 131

legislative veto and, 333
library of, 336
veto power of, 534
vice president, 133
work habits, 135
Hoover, J. Edgar, 47, 211, *211,* 316
Hoover, Lou, 221
Hoover commissions, 13, 110, 264–266
Hopkins, Harry, 139, 323, *474*
Hornblower, William B., 131
House, Edward M., 138–139, 323, *323*
House of Representatives
election decisions, 51, 117, 174,
  181–182, 407–408, 498, 540
election of 1824, 5, 98, 176, 302
ethics and, 196–197
Judiciary Committee, impeachment
  proceedings and, 274, 277, 279,
  570
Twenty-fifth Amendment, 155
Un-American Activities Committee,
  179
Ways and Means Committee, 164
Housing and Urban Development
  Department (HUD), 64, 196,
  266–267
Howard University, 166
Howe, Louis M., 139, 323
Hubbard, Allan, *160,* 373
Hubbell, Webster, 139, 579
Huerta, Victoriano, 152
Hughes, Charles Evans, 209, 267, *267*
election of 1916, 267, 354, 379, 585
support of T. Roosevelt, 450
Washington Disarmament
  Conference, 246
Hughes, Howard, 138
Hughes, Karen, 358, 419
Hughes, Sarah, 22, 309, 310
Humphrey, Hubert H., 6, 7, *268,*
  268–269, 346, 365
election of 1960, 180
election of 1968, 146, 181–182, 343,
  344, 389, 420, 423, 551
Humphrey, Muriel, 268
Humphrey, William E., 269
Humphrey's Executor v. United States
  (1935), 15, 269, 288, 370
Hundred Days, 121, 238, 258, 384, 446
Roosevelt (F.D.) and, 218–219
Hunt, E. Howard, 567, 568
Hunt, James B., Jr., 146
Hurricane Katrina, 56, 261, 269–271,
  270
Hussein, Saddam, 56, 401–403
death of, 299
disarming regime of, 124, 157,
  296–299, 527, 555, 562

Ideological parties, 499
Immigration and Nationality Act of
  1952, 272
Immigration and Naturalization
  Service (INS), 260, 261, *332*
*Immigration and Naturalization Service
  v. Chadha* (1983), 272–273, 334
Impeachment, 10–11, 273–280
Clinton proceedings, 103, 104, 114,
  184, 195, 259, 278–279
constitutional origins, 274
Johnson's appointment powers and,
  256, 275–276, 308, 440
Johnson's Senate trial, *276*
Nixon case, 276–278, 391, 569–570
procedures, 274–275
veto power and, 535, 536
Impoundment, 41, 280–282
Inaugural addresses
Kennedy, 468
Lincoln, 338
Washington, 467
Inauguration, 249, 282–284, 495. *See
  also* Oath of office
Bush (G.W.), 284, 455
Carter, 283
Clinton, 283
Coolidge, 284
Harrison (B.), 249
Harrison (W.H.), 249, 283, 284
inaugural parades, 283
Kennedy, 258, 283, 284
Polk, 284
Reagan, 283
Roosevelt (F.D.), 283–284
Washington, 282
Independent counsel, 10, 196, 197,
  284–286, 314. *See also* Watergate
  affair; Whitewater investigation
Independent executive agencies, 44–45,
  195, 286–287, 288. *See also specific
  agencies*
National Archives and Records
  Administration, 371–372
Independent regulatory agencies,
  44–45, 287–290. *See also specific
  agencies*
Federal Election Commission, 212
growth of regulation, 288–289
methods of regulation, 289–290
unitary executive theory and, 524
Indian Health Service, 252
Information Analysis and
  Infrastructure Protection, 261
Ingersoll, Jared, 233
Inouye, Daniel K., 295
Intelligence community, 80

Intelligence Czar, 81
Intelligence Oversight Board, 153
Intelligence Reform and Terrorism
    Prevention Act (2004), 81, 374,
    477
Inter-American Conference, 247
Interest groups and the presidency,
    290–293
    vice president and, 545
Interior Department, 64, 293–294
Internal Revenue Service (IRS), 515
International Monetary Fund, 514
International Security Assistance and
    Arms Control Act of 1976, 334
Internment. *See* Japanese American
    internment
Interstate Commerce Commission, 194,
    288–289, 471
Iran, war on terrorism and, 554
Iran-contra affair, 53, 285, 294–296,
    314, 382, 439
    Reagan's staff and, *296*, 476
Iranian hostage crisis, 79, 153, 182
Iraq, 124, 157, 185. *See also* Hussein,
    Saddam
    Civil War, 298–299
    "coalition of the willing" and, 451
    defense spending and, 146
    Operation Iraqi Freedom, 562
Iraq Study Group, 299
Iraq War, 56, 296–299, 555, 562
    background, 403
    budget deficit and, 43
    U.N. and, 527
Iron triangles, 48–49
Issue networks, 49
Item veto. *See* Line-item veto

Jackman, Galen B., 436
Jackson, Andrew, *23, 300,* **300–302,**
    533, 553
    administrative system of, 46
    appointments, 35, 248, 530
    assassination attempt on, 23, 25, 302
    background, 28, 29
    cabinet, 63, 322
    cartoon, *533*
    Congress and, 113
    declares martial law, 302, 355
    election of 1824, 5, 6, 98, 119, 133,
        176, 302
    election of 1828, 176, 300
    election of 1832, 99
    executive philosophy, 18, 254–255
    as ex-president, 226
    farewell address, 210
    Johnson (R.) and, 311
    judicial nominations, 130

military career, 300, 301, 352, 554
national bank and, 373
national party convention of 1832,
    379
nullification crisis and, 508
partisan press and, 356
party leadership and, 397
presidential anthem, 242
rating by historians, 413–414
recognition power, 153
rise of two-party system and, 408
six-year proposal and, 498
spoils system, 30, 93–94, 397, 399
Supreme Court and, 130
two-term limit and, 496
veto power of, 373, 534, 535, 538
vice presidents, 66–67, 530
War of 1812 and, 352
as widower, 27
Jackson, Andrew (elder), 300
Jackson, Elizabeth, 300, 301
Jackson, Jesse, 441
Jackson, Rachel, 301
Jackson, Robert, 300, 301, 588
James Brady Press Briefing Room, 576,
    576
Japan, trade with, 405
Japanese American internment, *303,*
    303–304, *304*
    executive order for, 205
Jaworski, Leon, 284, 569
Jay, John, 516, 565
    Federalist Papers and, 213, 244, 351
Jay Treaty of 1794, 206, 516, 565
Jefferson, Martha, 305
Jefferson, Thomas, *63,* **304–308,** *305,*
    507
    Adams (J.) and, 4
    appointments, 131, 351, 398
    background, 28
    Congress and, 112–113, 115
    Democratic-Republican Party and,
        407–408, 566
    design for the White House, 573, 574,
        577
    election of 1796, 17, 118, 175, 305
    election of 1800, 3, 50–51, 175–176,
        254, 305, 407–408
    election of 1804, 106, 306
    electoral college and, 185
    as ex-president, 226
    federal government, 244
    foreign policy and, 151
    impoundments, 281
    judicial nominations, 130
    Louisiana Purchase, 123, 341–342,
        367
    Madison and, 350–352

memorials to, 361
Monroe and, 366–368
national bank and, 372
Neutrality Proclamation of 1793, 383
partisan press and, 356
party leadership and, 397
presidency, 305–306
rating by historians, 413–414
religion and, 27
as secretary of state, 62, 112, 305, 478,
    565
State of the Union address, 479
two-term tradition and, 496
on veto power, 533, 535
veto power of, 534
as vice president, 540
vice presidents, 50, 105
as widower, 27
Jeffords, James, 185, 461, 537
"Jim Crow" laws, 503
Johnson, Andrew, *276, 307,* **307–308,**
    339, 440
    assassination plot against, 20
    background, 28
    education, 28
    election of 1836, 312
    impeachment trial, 18, 256, 273,
        275–276
    impeachment vote, 308
    pardon power, 33, 396
    press, relationship with, 356
    Reconstruction era and, 439–440
    removal power and, 14
    speaking tour, 467
    succeeds Lincoln, 21, 244, 307, 483,
        544
    veto power of, 534, 536
Johnson, Eliza, 307
Johnson, John B., 266
Johnson, Lady Bird, 22, 221–222,
    308–309, *309, 483*
Johnson, Lucy Baines, 138
Johnson, Lynda Bird, 138
Johnson, Lyndon B., *111, 154,*
    309–311, *310, 408, 483, 547*
    appointments, 11, 225
    background, 26, 28
    budget control, 49
    cabinet, 64
    Congress and, 114, 115
    election of 1960, 180, 310, 319
    election of 1964, 181, 233, 268,
        310–311
    election of 1968, 343, 344
    emergency powers, 189
    ethics and, 197
    Executive Office of the President and,
        204–205

executive orders, 122, 197, 205
family and friends, 138
Great Society programs, 40, 238–239, 251, *251*, 480
honeymoon period, 262
impoundments, 281
interest groups and, 291
judicial nominations, 131
Kennedy's New Frontier programs and, 387
Labor Department and, 328
library of, 336
memorial to, 361
oath of office, 22, 394
Office of Economic Opportunity, 286–287
personnel and, 13
polling data and, 428
presidential commissions and, 110
presidential disability and, 154
Presidential Medal of Freedom and, 415
press, relationship with, 357
public appeals, 116
rest and recreation, 136
six-year term proposal and, 498
staff, 472, 475–476
succeeds Kennedy, 483, 544
Tonkin Gulf Resolution, 124, 505–506, 547
Transportation Department and, 511–512
veto power of, 534, 536
as vice president, 542–543
vice presidents, 268–269, 343, 346
Vietnam War and, 311, 547, 548, 560
White House preservation and, 576
work habits, 135
Johnson, Richard M., 133, 311–312, 459, 522
Johnson, Sam Houston, 138
Joint Chiefs of Staff, 145, 312–313
National Security Council and, 381
Jones, Paula Corbin, 101, 104, 278, 580
Jonkman, Bartel, 225
Jordan, Hamilton, 85, 419
Journalists. *See* Media and the presidency
Judicial Watch, 207
Judiciary Act of 1789, 314
Judiciary Act of 1925, 492
Justice Department, 313–316
appointment and removal powers and, 196, 332–333
background, 314–315
Homeland Security Department and, 211

independent regulatory agencies and, 524
organization, 315–316
prosecutor guidelines, 286
September 11 attacks and, 211
size of, 64
solicitor general, 315
U.S. Bureau of Prisons and, 331
Watergate affair and, 211

Kansas-Nebraska Act of 1854, 35, 337, 404
Kassebaum, Nancy Landon, 330
Kefauver, Estes, 319, 344, 481
Kemp, Jack
election of 1996, 157
vice-presidential campaign debates, 70
Kendall, Amos, 46, 323
Kennedy, Caroline, 138
Kennedy, Edward M., 79, 182
Kennedy, Jacqueline, 222, *317*, 317–318, *483, 593*
Air Force One design, 9
JFK's assassination and, 22, 318
White House renovation and, 317, 576
Kennedy, John F., *68, 318,* **318–320**, *386, 408, 593*
Air Force One and, 9
appointments, 347
assassination, 22, 24, 25, 142–143, 309, 310, 318, 319–320, 387, 593–594. *See also* Warren Commission
background, 27, 28
cabinet, 64
campaign debates, 68
Clinton and, *103*
Congress and, 115
counsel to the president, 127
Cuban missile crisis, 81
election of 1960, 180–181, 310, 379
ethics and, 197
Executive Office of the President and, 204
executive orders, 205
family and friends, 138
foreign policy and, 49, 149, 151
HUD and, 266
impoundments, 281
inaugural address, 468
inauguration, 258, *282, 283,* 284
law enforcement powers, 120, 330, 331
library of, 336
New Frontier program, 386–387
Peace Corps and, 153

personnel and, 13
presidential disability and, 154–155
Presidential Medal of Freedom and, 415
press, relationship with, 357, 416
rating by historians, 413
religion and, 27, 441
rest and recreation, 136
speeches of, 468
staff, 475
tax cuts and, 165
television and, 142–143
veto power of, 534, 536
vice president, 542–543
Vietnam War and, 547
White House and, 577
work habits, 135
Kennedy, John F., Jr., 138
Kennedy, Joseph P., 318
Kennedy, Robert F., 138, 394
assassination of, 23
election of 1960, 180
election of 1968, 181, 268, 343, 344
Kern, John W., 56, 462
Kerry, John, 69, 70, 77, 185, *320,* 320–321
Keynote address, 377
Khrushchev, Nikita, 168, 389
King, Martin Luther, Jr., 192
King, Rufus, 106, 367
King, William R., 321–322, 484
King Caucus, 118–119, 378
Kirkpatrick, Jeane, 123
Kissinger, Henry, 347, 380, 382
Kitchen cabinet, 63, 322–323
Kleberg, Richard, 309
Know-Nothing Party, 30, 35, 218, 337, 582
Knox, Frank, 330
Knox, Henry, *63*
Knox, Philander, 449
Korean War, 168, 190, 323–325, 521
Korematsu v. United States (1944), 303–304
Kuwait, invasion of, 401–403
Kyoto global warming protocol, 518

Labor Department, 64, 109, 327–328
law enforcement powers, 331
Lafitte, Jean, 301
La Follette, Philip Fox, 327
La Follette, Robert M., *326,* 326–327
election of 1924, 500
La Follette, Robert M., Jr., 327
Lake, Anthony, 12, 380
Lame duck, 328–329, 496
Lance, Bert, 78, 139, 196
Landon, Alfred, *329,* 329–330, 447

Latrobe, Benjamin Henry, 574
Law enforcement powers, 120, 330–333.
    See also Justice Department
  Agriculture Department and, 331
  Defense Department and, 331
  desegregation, 1957, *331*
  FBI and, 331
  Federal Trade Commission and, 331
  growth of, 332–333
  Labor Department and, 331
  Securities and Exchange Commission
    and, 311
  sources of, 330–331
Lawrence, Richard, 23, *23*, 25, 302
Lazear, Ed, *160*
Lazio, Rick, 108, 223
Leadership PACs, 405
League of Nations, 18, 246, 469, 585, 587
Lee, Arthur, 2
Lee, Elizabeth Blair, 31
Lee, Robert E., 97, 188, 236, 338
Legislative branch, 111–117
  budget process and, 39, 80, 281–282
  diplomatic powers, 149–150
  impeachment and, 19, 274–275
  Washington and, 254
Legislative powers. *See* Congress and
  the presidency; Veto power
Legislative proposals to Congress, 121
Legislative veto, 117, 272–273, 333–334
LeMay, Curtis, 551
Lend-Lease Act of 1941, 447, 588
L'Enfant, Pierre Charles, 573, 574
Lenroot, Irvine L., 125
Lever Food and Fuel Act, 587
Lewinsky, Monica S., 101, 104, 184,
  195, 278–279, 286, 580
Liaison Office. *See* Public Liaison,
  Office of
Libby, I. Lewis "Scooter", 84, 196
Libertarian Party, 499
Liberty Party, 498
Libraries, 227, 335–336
  Carter Center, *335*
  executive order and, 336
  at National Archives, 372
  New York Public Library, 504
  U.S. Postal Service stamp and, *336*
Libya, 438
Liddy, G. Gordon, 567, 568
Lieberman, Joseph, 55
  vice-presidential campaign debates,
    70
Lincoln, Abraham, *20*, **188**, **336–339**,
  337
  antiwar press and, 356
  assassination, 20–21, 25, 98, 142, 230,
    307, 339, 577

background, 28
cabinet, 63
Congress and, 113
Douglas and, 158
early career, 337–338
education, 28
election of 1860, 30, 32, 36, 96, 159,
  176–177, 408
Emancipation Proclamation,
  187–188
emergency powers, 96–97, 113, 122,
  189, 255–256, 354, 364
Gettysburg Address, 87
inauguration, 284
judicial nominations, 130
martial law and, 354–355
McClellan and, 345, *345*
memorials to, 360–361
pardon power, 396
party leadership and, 397
patronage and, 94
presidency, 338–339
rating by historians, 413–414
religion and, 27
rhetoric of, 467
Secret Service and, 457
Supreme Court and, 130
veto power of, 534
vice presidents, 244–245, 275
war powers, 189–190, 558
White House and, 577
on writ of habeas corpus, 97
Lincoln, Edward, 339
Lincoln, Mary Todd, 220, *339*, 339–340,
  577
Lincoln, Nancy, 336
Lincoln, Robert, 340
Lincoln, Tad, 340
Lincoln, Thomas, 336
Lincoln, Willie, 339
Lindgren, James, 414
Lindsey, Lawrence, 374
Line-item veto, 340–341, 538
Line-item Veto Act, 340–341
Lipshutz, Robert J., 127
Livingston, Robert, 306, 342, 367
Lobbying. *See also* Interest groups and
  the presidency; Political action
  committees
  executive, 112–113, 115–116
  restrictions on, 197–198
  White House officials, 197–198
Lockhart, Joseph, 358, 419
Lodge, Henry Cabot, 18, 180, 310,
  585
Loewy, Raymond, 9
Logan, John A., 253
Long, John, 448

Lott, Trent, 502, *502*
Louisiana Purchase, 123, 294, 306,
  341–342
  map of, *342*
  Monroe and, 367
Louis XVI, king of France, 151
Lowell, Robert, 344
Luciano, Lucky, 148
MacArthur, Douglas, 167, 323–324,
  324, 521
MacFarlane, Robert, 294
Maddox, USS, 505, 506
Madison, Dolley, 220, *349*, 349–350,
  351, 574, 577
Madison, James, 349, *350*, **350–352**
  appointments, 4, 132, 139, 367
  background, 27, 28
  cabinet, 62
  as Democratic-Republican, 566
  election of 1808, 306, 351
  election of 1812, 351
  on executive power, 383
  as ex-president, 226
  Federalist Papers and, 213, 244
  on impeachment, 274
  Jefferson and, 350–352, 566
  judicial nominations, 131
  national bank and, 372
  Neutrality Proclamation of 1791,
    383
  recognition power, 152
  veto power of, 534, 538
  vice presidents, 105, 106, 232, 233
  "Virginia Plan" and, 351
  war powers, 553–554
Mahoney, George, 6
Maine, USS, 465, *466*
Management and Budget, Office of
  (OMB), 201–202, 352–353
  authority of, 205
  budget directors of, 353
  budget process and, 39
  scope of, 40, 537
Mansfield, Mike, *111*
Manson, Charles, 226
Manson family, 23, 25
Marcy, William, 404
Maritime Administration, 512
Marshall, George, 520
Marshall, John, 131, 279, 519
  appointed chief justice, 4
  Burr trial, 51
  foreign policy communications and,
    151
  XYZ affair and, 232
Marshall, Thomas R., 154, 209, *353*
  disability of president and, 354
  as vice president, 353–354

Marshall, Thurgood, 37, 131
Marshall Plan, 179, 520
Martial law, 189–190, 354–355
Martinez, Eugenio R., 567
Matching funds, 74
Mayaguez (U.S. merchant ship),
    225–226, 381
McAdoo, William G., 379, 465
McCain, John, 55, 525
    campaign debates, 71
    campaign finance reform and, 76, 213
McCain-Feingold Reform Act of 2002,
    76, 212–213, 406
McCardle, Eliza, 307
McCarthy, Eugene J., 36, 146, 181, *343*,
    343–344
McCarthy, Joseph R., 521
McCarthy, Timothy J., 458
McClellan, George B., 97, 307, 338, *345*,
    345–346
McClellan, Scott, *419*
McCloy, John J., 562, *563*
McConnell, Mike, 375
McConnell, Mitch, 76
McConnell v. FEC (2003), 76
McCord, James W., Jr., 567, 568
McCormack, John W., *154*, 485
McCulloch v. Maryland (1819), 373
McCullough, David, 361
McCurry, Michael, 358, *419*
McDonald, John A., 573
McDougal, James B., 578, 580
McDougal, Susan, 580
McGovern, George S., 146, 346–347
    election of 1972, 7, 182, 268, 390
McGovern-Fraser Commission, 146
McIntosh, Caroline, 218
McKinley, Ida Saxton, *72*, 348
McKinley, William, *72*, *347*, **347–349**
    appointments, 448, 490
    assassination, 21–22, 25, 142, 349,
        448–449
    background, 28
    election of 1896, 34, 259, 370
    election of 1900, 34, 348–349, 481
    martial law and, 355
    oath of office, 394
    press as watchdog and, 356
    Secret Service and, 262
    Spanish-American War and, 465–466
    veto power of, 534
    vice president, 542
McKinley Tariff Act of 1890, 247, 348
McLarty, Thomas F. "Mack", III, 85, 86
McLaughlin, John, 375
McNary, Charles L., 552
Meat Inspection Act, 471

Media and the presidency, 355–360. *See
    also* Public appeals
    bypassing, 356–358
    conflict, 357
    as element of elections, 172
    partisan press, 356
    press corps, 355, 357–358
    Roosevelt (Eleanor) use of, 445
    third parties and, 501
    vice president and, 545
    war on terrorism and, 358
    White House correspondents, 358–359
Medicaid, 239, 251, 252
Medicare, 42, 239, 251, 252
Meehan, Martin T., 76, 213
Meese, Edwin, III, 12, 196, 295, 314
Memorials, presidential, 360–361
Merchant marine, U.S., 512
Meredith, James, 120, 330
Merit Systems Protection Board, 92, 94
Merriam, Charles E., 204
Merryman, Ex parte (1861), 190
Mexican-American War of 1846,
    235–236, 255, 294, 361–363, *362*
    Davis (Jefferson) and, 140
    Pierce and, 404
    Polk and, 362, 412
Midnight appointments, 4
Midterm elections, 329, 363–364, 363t,
    461, 555
Miers, Harriet, 127
Migratory Bird Treaty of 1916, 517
Mikva, Abner J., 127
Military Assistance to Safety in Traffic,
    512
Military Commission Act (2006), 243
"Military-industrial complex," 168
Military rule during Reconstruction,
    440
Military tribunals, 242–243
Miller, William E., 268
Milligan, Ex parte (1866), 190, 355,
    364–365
Milligan, Lambdin P., 364
Milosevic, Slobodan, 105
Mine Safety and Health
    Administration, 328
Mineta, Norman Y., 512
Missouri Compromise of 1820, 36, 367,
    405
Mitchell, John N., 314, 567–568, 569, 570
Moley, Raymond, 323
Mondale, Joan, 546
Mondale, Walter, *365*, 365–366
    campaign debates, 69, 71
    election of 1980, 53, 183, 365
    election of 1984, 53, 172, 183, 216,
        365, 366, 438

as vice president, 366, 543, 546
Monetary policy, 163, 214–216. *See also*
    Federal Reserve System
Monroe, Elizabeth Kortright, 366
Monroe, James, 366–368, *367*
    appointments, 5, 66, 132
    background, 28
    election of 1816, 367
    election of 1820, 367
    as ex-president, 226
    inauguration, 249
    Louisiana Purchase and, 306, 342, 367
    as secretary of state, 367
    signing statements and, 463
    support of Jackson, 301
    veto power of, 534
    vice president, 504–505
    White House and, 574, 576
Monroe Doctrine, 5, 155–156, 368–369,
    449
Montesquieu, 460
Monticello, 306
Moore, Sara Jane, 23, 25, 226
Morgan, Edward D., 15
Morris, Gouverneur, 253
Morrison v. Olson (1988), 525
Morse, Samuel, 284
Morton, Levi P., 16, *369*, 369–370
"Most favored nation" principle, 510
Mount Rushmore, *256*, 360–361, *361*
Muckraking, 356
Mugwumps, 99
Murphy, Francis, 303
Muskie, Edmund S., 7, *296*, 346
Mutual Defense Treaty of 1954, 518
Myers, Dee Dee, 358, *419*, *576*
Myers, Frank, 370
Myers v. United States (1926), 14–15,
    18, 269, 276, 370, 525

Nader, Ralph, 499, 500
NAFTA. *See* North American Free
    Trade Agreement
Nagin, Ray, 269, 270
Napoleon I, emperor, 51, 306, *507*
    Louisiana Purchase and, 342, 367
Nast, Thomas, 91
National Aeronautics and Space
    Administration (NASA), 286, *286*,
    287
National Archives, 58, 335–336,
    371–372
National Bank, 67, 372–373
National Book Festival, 223
National Bureau of Standards, 110
National Commission on Terrorist
    Attacks Upon the United States
    (9/11 Commission), 110–111

National Communications Center, 144
National Defense Authorization Act of 1992, 313
National Domestic Preparedness Office, 211
National Drug Control Policy, Office of, 203
National Economic Council (NEC), 202, 373–374
National Environmental Policy Act of 1969, 203
National Gazette, 356
National Guard troops, 192, *331*
National Highway Traffic Safety Administration, 289, 512
National Industrial Recovery Act of 1933, 219, 385
National Infrastructure Protection Center, 211
National Institute for Literacy, 166
National Institutes of Health (NIH), 252
National Intelligence, Office of the Director of, 374–375
National Labor Relations Act of 1935, 384
National Labor Relations Board, 287, 289
National Military Command Center, 578
National Monetary Commission, 373
National party conventions, 170–171, 375–379. *See also* Primaries
1844, 139–140, 411–412, 532
1848, 140
1852, 218, 404
1860, 159, 244–245, 337–338, 379
1878, 247
1880, 230, 237
1892, 348, 481
1912, 491, 584
1920, 125, 246, 378
1924, 465
1936, 330, 378
1940, 581
1944, 148
1964, 233, 268
1968, 181, 268, 344, 420
development of, 378–379
events of, 376–378
National Performance Review, 50
National Progressive Republican League. *See* Progressive Party
National Republican Party, 99, 378, 408
National Response Plan, 270
National Rifle Association, 405
National Security Act of 1947, 144, 260, 374, 381
National security adviser, 380, 381

National Security Council, 144, 202, 381–382, 475
State Department and, 478
vice president and, 542, 544
National Technical Institute for the Deaf, 166
National Traffic Safety Administration, 512
National Union Party, 245, 307
National Unity Campaign, 501
NATO. *See* North Atlantic Treaty Organization
Natural disasters, 192–193
Naval Observatory, 203, 455, 543, 546, *546*
Negroponte, John, 374–375
Nehru, Jawaharlal, 32
Nessen, Ron, *576*
Neustadt, Richard E., 111
Neutrality Act of 1974, 383
Neutrality Proclamation of 1793, 382–383, 565
New Deal, 46–47, 114, 129, 178–179, 238, 383–385
coalition of disparate groups and, 385
court-packing plan, 127–128, 385, 447
Emergency Banking Bill and, 219
Executive Office of the President and, 204–205
Hatch Act and, 95
independent regulatory agencies and, 288, 289, 385
law enforcement and, 332
Supreme Court and, 127–128
New Executive Office Building, 200
New Federalism, 470
New Freedom, 385–386, 470
New Frontier, 239, 386–387, 470
New Hampshire, as first primary, 344, 421
New Nationalism, 385–386
New Orleans, 269–270
News conferences, 356–357, 359, 416–417. *See also* Media and the Presidency
Eisenhower, *357*
televised live, 357
New York Civil Liberties Union, 36
Nichols, Roy F., 118
9/11 Commission, 110–111, 211, 374
Nixon, Donald, 138
Nixon, Julie, 138
Nixon, Pat, *278*, 387–388, *388*, *513*
Nixon, Richard, *68*, *278*, *388*, **388–391**, *488*, *513*, 528–529, *543*. *See also* Watergate affair
appointments, 52, 85, 130, 450–451
background, 28, 29
budget process and, 37–38

budget reform and, 40–41
cabinet, 64
on cabinet functions, 61
campaign debates, 68, 180–181
campaign financing, 36, 72
cartoon, *United States v. Nixon* (1974), *206*, *529*
Checkers speech, 180, 387, 389
China trip, 513
CIA and, 82
commander in chief and, 124
dangers of deference and, 90
domestic policy and, 430
election of 1952, 179–180
election of 1960, 180–181, 310, 319
election of 1968, 6, 181–182, 268, 314, 423, 498–499, 551
election of 1972, 7, 182, 346, 347
election of 1974, 363
emergency powers, 192
Energy Department and, 194
environmental quality and, 203
eulogizes Eisenhower, 87
Executive Office of the President and, 205
executive orders, 48, 205
executive privilege and, 461–462, 569–570
as ex-president, 227
family and friends, 138
farewell address, 210
honeymoon period, 262
impeachment effort against, 273, 276–278
impoundments, 41, 280, 281
judicial nominations, 130, 131
law practice, 28
library of, 335–336
Management and Budget, Office of, 352
national security adviser, 380
pardon of, 78, 121, 182, 225, 330, 391, 395, 396, 570
patronage and, 399
personnel difficulties, 14
political career, 389
presidency, 389–391
presidential disability and, 154
Presidential Medal of Freedom and, 415
press, relationship with, 357, 359, 416
Press Briefing Room, 576
press conferences, 416
reorganization control, 49
resignation, 225, 227, 258, 277, 391
rest and recreation, 136
Science and Technology Policy, Office of, 202
staff, 476

State of the Union Address, 480
transition funds for, 510
veto power of, 534, 536, 539
as vice president, 180, 545, 546
vice presidents, 223, 225, 543
Vietnam War and, 547–548, 560
War Powers Act of 1973, 558, 560, 561
White House renovation and, 576
work habits, 135
Nixon, Tricia, 138
Nixon, Walter L., Jr., 275
Nixon Doctrine, 156
Nobel Peace Prize
Carter, 79
Dawes, Charles, 141
Roosevelt (T.), *150*, 449
Nofziger, Lyn, 197–198
Nolan, Beth, 127
Nominating process, 171, 377–378. *See also* Caucuses, political; National party conventions; Primaries
political party decline and, 409
Non-Intercourse Act of 1809, 306
North, Oliver L., 285, 294, 295, 296, 382
North American Aerospace Defense Command (NORAD), 392
North American Free Trade Agreement (NAFTA), 103, 165, 235, 509
North Atlantic Treaty Organization (NATO), 167, 179, 199
North Korea, 554
Nuclear command procedures, 391–392, 559
Nuclear Incident Response Team, 195
Nuclear Regulatory Commission, 289
Nullification crisis, 67, 508, 522
Nunn, Sam, 145
Nussbaum, Bernard, 127, 464

Oath of office, 86, 282, *282*, 393–394. *See also* Inauguration
Washington, *394*
Obama, Barack, 29, *422*
O'Brien, Lawrence F., 567
Occupational Safety and Health Administration (OSHA), 288, 328
O'Connor, John, 216
O'Connor, Sandra Day, *129*, 131, 223
Office of Faith-Based and Community Initiatives, 442, 477
Office of Health Homes and Lead Hazard Control, 267
Office of the American Workplace, 328
Office of the Director of National Intelligence (DNI), 81
Oklahoma City bombing, 88
Old Executive Office Building, 200, *200*

OMB. *See* Management and Budget, Office of
Onassis, Aristotle, 318
One Hundred Days. *See* Hundred Days
O'Neill, Paul H., 514
O'Neill, Thomas P. "Tip", 217
One-issue parties, 499
Operation Desert Fox, 297
Operation Desert Storm, *401*, *402*, 402–403
Operation Enduring Freedom, 191, 297
Operation Iraqi Freedom. *See* Iraq War
OPM. *See* Personnel Management, Office of
Oregon Territory, 412
Oswald, Lee Harvey, 22, 24, 25, 319–320, 458, 594. *See also* Warren Commission
Oval Office, 576, 577–578
Overman Act, 587

PACs. *See* Political action committees
Panama Canal, 79, 257, 449, *517*
Panama invasion, 83
Pan American Union, 247
Panetta, Leon, 85, 86
Panic of 1893, 100
Pardon of Nixon. *See* Nixon, Richard
Pardon power, 33, 395–396
Clinton and, 105, 121, 196, 396
constitutional provision, 18, 120–121, 330, 395
Washington and, 396, 572
Parker, Alton B., 34, 209, 449
Parker, John J., 131
Parties. *See* Political parties
Party leader, 89, 396–398
Patel, Marilyn Hall, 304
Patriot Act. *See* U.S.A. Patriot Act
Patriot Day, 426
Patronage, 91, 398–400
background, 397, 398–399
Bell and, 30
Brownlow Committee and, 33
bureaucracy and, 10
Congress and, 116
decline of, 399–400
Hayes and, 256
interest groups and, 292
Jackson and, 30, 46, 176
political parties and, 411
president and, 116
Paulson, Henry M., 514
Payne-Aldrich Tariff Act of 1909, 491
Peace Corps, 319, 387
Peace dividend, 145
Peace Treaty of 1783, 518–519
Peckham, Wheeler H., 131

Pelosi, Nancy, *113*, 409
Peña, Federico F., 512
Pendergast, Tom, 519
Pendleton, George H., 94, 307
Pendleton Reform Act of 1883, 10, 16, 46, 91, 94, 100, 399
Pension and Welfare Benefits Administration, 328
Pentagon, *145*, 578. *See also* Defense Department
Pentagon Papers, 357
People's Party, 100, 570, 571. *See also* Populist Party
Perino, Dana, 419
Perkins, Frances, 327–328, *328*, 445
Perot, H. Ross, 400, *400*
campaign debates, 69, 235
election of 1992, 102, 184, 500
election of 1996, 158, 500
Perry, Matthew, 218, 405
Persian Gulf War. *See* Gulf War
Person, Wilton, 85
Personnel Management, Office of (OPM), 94, 404–405
competitive civil service and, 92
Philippines, 348, 490
A Picture of the Desolated States (Trowbridge), *440*
Pierce, Franklin, 32, *404*, **404–405**
appointments, 35, 140, 252
background, 28
election of 1852, 218
as ex-president, 226
Kansas-Nebraska Act and, 35
oath of office, 393
veto power of, 534
vice presidents, 321–322
Pierce, Jane, 404, 405
Pinckney, Charles C., 106, 175, 306, 351
on impeachment, 274
titles of president and vice president, 504
XYZ affair and, 232
Pinckney, Thomas, 175
Plame, Valerie, 84
Platform committee, 377
Plischke, Elmer, 488, 489
Plum book, 399
Pocket veto, 121, 535, 538–539
Pocket Veto Case (1929), 539
Podesta, John, 85, 86
Poindexter, John, 285, 294, 295, 296
Policy advisers, 472–473, 475–476
Policy and Supporting Positions (book on openings for presidential appointments), 399
Policy Development, Office of, 202, 373

Political action committees (PACs), 74–75, 170, 405–406
  regulation of, 406
  types of, 405–406
Political Activities Act of 1939, 95
Political parties, 407–411. *See also* Third parties; *specific party names*
  decline of, 409–410
  emergence of, 407–408
  organization, 410–411
  party leader, 89
  separation of power, 461
  two-party system, 408–409
Polk, James K., *411*, **411–412**
  appointments, 35, 404
  background, 28
  election of 1844, 99, 302, 523, 532
  election of 1848, 498
  executive power and, 255
  inauguration, 249, 284
  judicial nominations, 131
  Mexican War and, 361, 362–363, 492
  national party convention of 1844, 379
  oath of office, 394
  presidential anthem, 242
  rating by historians, 413–414
  veto power of, 534
  vice presidents, 139
  war powers and, 362
  work habits, 135
Polk, Sarah Childress, 411
Polling data, 330, 427–431
  criticism of, 431
  rise of, 428
Popular leadership, *257*
"Popular sovereignty," 158
Populist Party, 34, 499–500, 570, 571
Portman, Rob, 353
Posse Comitatus Act (1878), 271
Postal Reorganization Act of 1970, 399
Postal Service, U.S., 11, 399
  creation of, 46
  presidential libraries stamp and, *336*
  scandals of, 16
Powell, Colin, *65*, 145
Powell, Jody, 419
Powell, Lewis Thorton, 20
Powers, Abigail, 218
Presidential greatness, 413–414
Presidential Medal of Freedom, *415*, 415–416
Presidential Personnel Office, 473
Presidential proclamations. *See* Executive orders
Presidential Rank Awards, 403
President pro tempore of the Senate, 155, 485

President's Committee on Civil Rights, 502
Press Briefing Room, 576, *576*
Press conferences, 359, 416–417. *See also* Media and the presidency; News conferences
Press corps. *See* Media and the presidency
Press secretary, presidential, 418–419, 473
  creation of the position, 356
  image management and, 359
  role in modern times, 357–358
Primaries, 379, 420–425. *See also* Delegate selection reforms
  campaigns and, 169
  development of, 326, 422–423
  national political conventions and, 375, 379
  presidential, 1912-2004, 147
  proliferation of, 147–148
  schedule, 170
  schedule for 2008, 421
  types of, 420–421
Prize Cases (1863), 97, 189
Proclamations, presidential, 426
Profile, of presidents, 28
Progressive Party
  La Follette and, 326, 327, 500
  Roosevelt (T.) and, 143, 178, 267, 327, 450, 500, 584
  Wallace (H.A.) and, 553
Prohibition Party, 499
Property ownership as qualification to hold office, 433
Proportional representation of delegates, 146
Prosecutor, special. *See* Independent counsel
Protests, *290*
Public appeals, 116, 466, 467–468, 470
  media use by Eleanor Roosevelt, 445
  Square Deal, 471
Public campaign funding program, 72–74
Public Credit Act of 1869, 236
Public Health Service, 251, 252
Public Liaison, Office of, 292, 430, 473
Public opinion and the presidency, 427–431
  approval ratings, 428–429
  ceremonial duties and, 429–430
  communication methods and, 429
  issues and, 429
  polling data, 427–431
Public speaking. *See* Speeches and rhetoric
Pullman Strike of 1894, 100, 143, 192

Pure Food and Drug Act, 471
Putin, Vladimir, 32

al Qaeda, 191, 299, 554. *See also* Terrorism
Qualifications of president and vice president, 17, 26, 432–433
Qualifications Review Board, 403
Qualities, presidential, 413–414
Quayle, Dan, 433–434
  election of 1988, 53
  as vice president, 543, 544, 545
  vice-presidential campaign debates, 69–70
Quinn, Jack, 127

Radical Republicans, 188, 276, 307–308, 583
  Reconstruction and, 440
Radio, 357
  Roosevelt (F.D.) and, *468*
Randolph, Edmund, *63*, 351
Ratings of presidents (by historians), 413–414
Ray, Robert W., 104, 279, 286, 580
Reagan, Nancy, *183*, 222, *227*, 435–436, *436*, *480*, 576
  antidrug campaign and, 436
  influence on White House politics, 436
  Presidential Medal of Freedom and, 415, 436
Reagan, Ronald, 182–183, *183*, *227*, *296*, *437*, **437–439**
  acting and, 28, 437, 468
  administration, 409
  Alzheimer's disease and, 436, 437
  anticommunist moves of, 438
  appointments, 12, 85, 123
  assassination attempt, 23–24, 25, 438, 458
  background, 27, 29, 437
  budget director, 353
  budget process and, 38, 41
  bureaucratic control, 49, 259
  cabinet, 61, 65
  campaign debates, 69, 71
  charities, endorsement of, 426
  Congress and, 115
  Congressional Gold Medal, 439
  death of, 439
  Education Department, 49, 166
  election of 1980, 53, 79, 182–183, 366, 437
  election of 1984, 53, 183, 366, 438
  Energy Department and, 49, 194
  EPA and, 195
  ethics and, 196

Executive Office of the President and, 205
executive orders, 48, 205
as ex-president, 228
family and friends, 137
as the Great Communicator, 437
inauguration, 283
interest groups and, 291, 293
international trade policy, 509
Iran-contra affair, 285, 294–296, 382, 439
Joint Chiefs of Staff and, 313
judicial nominations, 130, 131
Justice Department and, 314
legislative veto of, 334
library of, 335–336, 439
national convention of 1976, 377
National Security Council reliance, 382
O'Connor appointment, *129*
party leadership and, 398
political career, 437
polling data and, 428
presidency, 438–439
presidential disability and, 155
presidential security and, 24–25
press, relationship and, 357, 359
Press Briefing Room, 576
press conferences, 416
public appeals, 116, 468, 469
public opinion, 429–430, 431
religion and, 27, 442
rest and recreation, 136
speeches of, 468
staff, 14, 476
State of the Union addresses, 480
summits with Gorbachev, 438
Supreme Court and, 130
tax cuts and, 165
two-term limit and, 498
USDA and, 8
on veterans, 532
veto power of, 534, 536, 538, 539
vice president, 53, 545
war powers, 559, 561
White House renovation and, 576
work habits, 135
Reagan Doctrine, 156
Recess appointments, 10
Recognition power, 123, 152–153
Reconstruction, 98, 236, 237, 250–251, 339, 439–440, *440*, 503
Reconstruction Act of 1867, 308
Reform Party, 74, 400, 500
1996 election, 158
Regan, Donald, 85
Rehnquist, William H., 104, 130, 279
Reid, Whitelaw, 481

Reinventing Government initiative, 235
Religion and the presidency, 441–442
evangelical Christians and, 442
Kennedy (J. F.) and, 441
Smith (A. E.) and, 441
Removal of the president or vice president. *See also* Impeachment; Succession
disability amendment (25th), 154–155
Removal power, 14–15, 268. *See also* Appointment and removal power
Reno, Janet, 285, 315, *332*
Democratic campaign financing, illegal, 76, 196
Fiske appointment by, 285
Whitewater investigation, 578, 580
Reprieves. *See* Pardon power
Republican Party. *See also* Political parties
campaign finance allegations, 76
campaign financing (1860–2004), 75
delegate selection reforms, 376
election of 1860, 177, 337–338, 408
election of 1872, *27*
high tariff policy of, 508
interest groups and, 291
national party convention of 1900, 348
national party convention of 2000, 55, 74, 171
rise of, 408–409
Stalwarts vs. Half-Breeds, 16
Republic of China (Taiwan), 518
Requirements, presidential candidates, 26
Research and Special Programs Administration, 512
Residency requirement for president and vice-president, 433
Resignation. *See also* Succession
Agnew, 7, 182
Calhoun, 67
Nixon, 52, 182, 443
Resolution Trust Corp., 579, 580
Revere, Paul, 141
Revolving-door reform, 197–198
Rhetoric. *See* Speeches and rhetoric
Rhetorical presidency, 257
Rice, Condoleezza, *67*, 380, *380*, 382
Rich, Denise, 396
Rich, Marc, 105, 396
Richards, Ann, 53, 55
Richardson, Elliot, 284, 568, 569
Ridge, Thomas J., 260, *261*
Robards, Lewis, 301
Robards, Rachel Donelson, 301

Robbins, Anne Frances. *See* Reagan, Nancy
Roberts, Owen J., 128
Robertson, Pat, *291*, 441
Robinson, Joseph, 133, 465
Rockefeller, John D., 443
Rockefeller, Nelson A., 181, *443*, 443–444
seal of office, 456
as vice president, 53, 225, 444, 543, 546
vice-presidential nomination, 443, 485–486
Rodham, Hugh, 105
Rogers, William P., 380
Roosevelt, Alice Hathaway Lee, 448
Roosevelt, Edith, 221, 448
Roosevelt, Eleanor, 221, *221*, *408*, *444*, 444–445
Roosevelt, Franklin D., *163*, *179*, *445*, **445–447**, *474*, *510*, *557*, *588*
agencies, 251
Air Force One and, 8
ancestry, 26
appointments, 85, 130, 310, 318, 443, 552
assassination attempt, 23
background, 27, 28
Brownlow Committee, 33, 111
Bureau of the Budget and, 40
cabinet, 63, 323
cartoon, *384*
Congress and, 114, 115
counsel to the president, 126–127
court-packing plan, 127–128, 129, 385, 447
death, 142, 447
Eisenhower and, 167
election of 1920, 125, 446
election of 1932, 133, 178–179, 231, 329, 408, 446
election of 1936, 329–330, 447
election of 1940, 447
election of 1944, 148, 179, 447, 520
emergency powers, 189, 190, 191, 303–304
executive agreements, 199
Executive Office of the President and, 201, 204
executive orders, 204, 205
family and friends, 139, 445
foreign affairs powers, 528
Hatch Act and, 95, 399
health, 446
Hundred Days, 121, 218–219, 238, 258, 384
impoundments, 281
inauguration, 249, 283–284

independent regulatory agencies and, 288, 289
interest groups and, 291
international trade, 508
judicial nominations, 131
legislative veto and, 334
library of, 335–336
martial law and, 355
memorial to, *360*, 361
national party convention of 1936, 378
New Deal, 46–47, 383–385, 446–447
oath of office, 394
party leadership and, 397
pitching baseballs, ceremonial, 90
political career, 446
presidency, 446–447
press, relationship with, 356–357
press conferences, 416
public appeals of, 116, 446, 467–468
public opinion of, 428
rating by historians, 413–414
religion and, 441, 442
removal power and, 15, 268
rest and recreation, 136, 447
Shangri-La (Camp David) and, 68
staff, 13, 474–475
summit meetings, 447, 488
term of office and, 496, *496*, 497
travel abroad, 513
TVA, 494
veto power of, 534, 536
vice presidents, 231, 378, 542, 552–553
war powers, 190–191, 557–558
White House and, 577
work habits, 135
World War II and, 588–590
Roosevelt, James, 445
Roosevelt, Sara Delano, 444
Roosevelt, Theodore, *150*, *448*, **448–450**, *449*
ancestry, 26
appointments, 27, 490–491
background, 27, 28, 448
campaign financing reform, 212
Congress and, 113, 115
death, 450
election of 1900, 34, 448, 481
election of 1904, 449
election of 1912, 143, 178, 267, 326–327, 450, 491, 500, 584
on executive authority, 129
executive power, 256–257
family and friends, 137, *137*, 444
inauguration, 249
La Follette and, 326–327

Monroe Doctrine and, 156, 449
New Nationalism program, 385–386
oath of office, 394
party leadership and, 397, 450
presidential commissions and, 110
press, relationship with, 356
rating by historians, 414
rest and recreation, 137
seal of office and, 456
Square Deal, 471
stewardship theory and, 482
succeeds McKinley, 448–449, 483, 544
sworn in as president, 22, 449
travel abroad, 513
two-term tradition and, 496–497, *497*
veto power of, 534
vice president, 208
as vice president, 349, 481, 541–542
White House and, 576
White House renovation and, 574
work habits, 135
Roosevelt corollary, 156, 369, 449. *See also* Roosevelt, Theodore
Rose Garden. *See* White House
Rosenman, Samuel I., 127
Ross, Edmund G., 308
Rossiter, Clinton, 88, 161, 219, 592
Rubin, Robert E., 374, 514
Ruby, Jack, 22, 320. *See also* Warren Commission
Ruckelshaus, William, 284, 569
Rudman, Warren B., 41
Rudolph, Lucretia, 230
Ruff, Charles F.C., 126, 127
Rules committee, 377
Rumsfeld, Donald, 23, 65, *65*, 83, 85, *313*, 374, 450, *450*–452
background, 450
Defense Department budget and, 145–146
Presidential Medal of Freedom, 451
resignation, 452
Rural Electrification Administration, 194
Rush, Benjamin, 4, 248
Rush, Richard, 66
Rush-Bagot Agreement of 1817, 367
Rusk, Dean, 22
Russell, Richard B., 562, *563*
Russia, 4
Russo-Japanese War, 257, 449
Rutledge, John, 131
Ryan, Thelma Catherine (Pat). *See* Nixon, Pat

Sacred Cow, 9
Sadat, Anwar, 68, 79, 80, *488*

Presidential Medal of Freedom and, 415
Saint Lawrence Seaway Development Corporation, 512
Salary and perquisites, 453–455
president's perquisites, *454*, 454–455
president's salary, 453–454
vice president, 455
Salinger, Pierre, 418
SALT. *See* Strategic Arms Limitation Treaty
Sanderson, James, 241
Saturday night massacre, 277, 284, 569–570
Sawyer, Charles, 591
Saxton, Ida. *See* McKinley, Ida Saxton
Schlesinger, Arthur M., Jr., 219, 325, 414, 524, 528
Schlesinger, Arthur M., Sr., 413–414
Schwarzenegger, Arnold, 17
Schwiker, Richard, 377
Science and Technology Policy, Office of, 202–203, 261
Scott, Caroline Lavinia, 247
Scott, Winfield, 218, 322, 362, 412, 531
election of 1852, 404
Mexico City capture, 493
Scowcroft, Brent, 380
Seals of office, 456, *456*
Second National Bank of the United States, 373
Secretary of Defense, Office of, 144
Secret Service, 24, 50, 134, 261–262, *457*, 457–458, 578
protection of ex-presidents, 227
protection of first family, 138
Securities and Exchange Commission, 287, 289
appointment and removal power and, 333
law enforcement powers and, 311
Security, 24–25. *See also* Secret Service
Security and Exchange Commission, 196
Security Council, U.N., 525–527
Iraq weapons inspection, 297, 527
Sedition Act, 3, 356
Selective Service Act, 585
Seminole Indians, 492
Senate
appointment power, 9–10, 12–13
election of the vice president, 117, 186, 458–459
ethics and, 196–197
Foreign Relations Committee, 506
judicial nominations, 131, 132
treaties, 516

Senatorial courtesy, 13, 459
Senior Executive Service, 93, 266
Separation of powers, 111–112,
    460–462
  checks and balances, *460*
  treaty powers and, 515–519
  war powers and, 558
September 11 attacks, 56, 88. *See also*
    U.S.A. Patriot Act of 2001
  attorney general and, 65
  Bush Doctrine and, 156, 297–299
  CIA and, 81, 82, 211
  economic effect of, 43
  FBI and, 211
  Patriot Day, declared, 426
  September 14, as national day of
      remembrance, 87
  vice president and, 84
  White House security, effect on, 24
Seward, William H., 20, *188*, 308, 339
Seymour, Horatio, 15, 109, 236, 379
Shays, Christopher, 76, 213
Sherman, James S., *462*, 462–463, 485
Sherman, William T., 97, 338, 345
Sherman Antitrust Act of 1890, 247
Sherman Silver Purchase Act, 100, 247
Shriver, R. Sargent, Jr., 182, 346
Sierra Club suit against Cheney, 207
Signal Board, 578
Signing statements, 463–464
Sinclair, Harry F., 494
Single Integrated Operational Plan
    (SIOP), 391–392
Sirica, John J., 568
Situation Room, White House, 578
Sixteenth Amendment, 491
Skelton, Martha Wayles, 305
Skinner, Samuel, 85, 512
Skutnik, Lenny, *480*
Slater, Rodney, 512
Smith, Abigail. *See* Adams, Abigail
Smith, Adam, 162
Smith, Alfred, *464*, 464–465
  election of 1928, 133, 264
  election of 1932, 231
  national party convention of 1924,
      379
  religion and, 441
Smith, Caleb B., *188*
Smith, Rosalynn. *See* Carter, Rosalynn
Smithsonian Institution, 544
Smoot-Hawley Act of 1930, 261, 264,
    508
Snow, John, 514
Snow, Tony, 358, 419, *419, 576*
Social Democratic Party, 143
Socialist Labor Party, 143

Socialist Party, 143, 499
Social policy, independent regulatory
    agencies and, 289
Social Security Act of 1935, 384
Social Security Administration, 251
Soft money, 71, 73, 75, 406
  restrictions, 76–77, 212–213
Somalia, 561
Sorenson, Theodore, 127
Southeast Asia Collective Defense
    Treaty, 506
Spanish-American War of 1898, 347,
    348, 448, 465–466
Sparkman, John, 481
Speaker of the House, 155, 485, 487
Speakes, Larry, 419
Special counsel, 472, 475. *See also*
    Independent counsel
  counsel to the president, 126–127
Specter, Arlen, 193
Speeches and rhetoric, 466–470
  ceremonial speeches, 469
  crisis speeches, 469–470
  general persuasive speeches, 469
  moralistic speeches, 469
  program themes, 470
  to specific groups, 470
  televised speeches, 429
Speechwriters, 466, 470
Spencer, John C., 131
Spoils systems, 30, 91, 93–94, 397, 399.
    See also Patronage
  cartoons and caricatures, *91*
Square Deal, 471
Stabilization policy, economic, 163
Staff, 471–478. *See also* Appointment
    and removal power
  appointment/approval of, 10
  Brownlow Committee and, 33
  cabinet and, 61
  chief of, 83, 84–86, 472, 511
  Congress and, 115
  growth of, 473–478
  liaison offices, 473
  policy advisers, 472
  structure, 266
  as transition period issue, 510, 511
Stalin, Joseph, 168, 447, 520, *588*
Stalwarts, Republican Party, 16, 21, 231
Stamp Act of 1765, 2
Stanton, Edwin M., 14, 18, *188*, 276
Starr, Kenneth, 101, 104, 184, 278–279,
    285, 286, 579, 580
Stassen, Harold E., 423
State Department, 64, 478–479
State of the Union address, 19, 39, 469,
    479–480, 584

  economic powers, 161
  purposes of, 112
States' Rights Party, 377, 501, 502–503
Stealth PACs, 406
Steelman, John Roy, 85
*Steel Seizure case. See Youngstown Sheet
    and Tube Co. v. Sawyer* (1952)
Steiger, William A., 83
Stem-cell research, 436
Stem Cell Research Enhancement Act
    (proposed), 537
Stevens, John Paul, 59, 101, 341
Stevenson, Adlai E., 480–481
Stevenson, Adlai E., II, 180, 319,
    481–482, *482*
  election of 1952, 168, 379, 445,
      481–482
  election of 1956, 481–482
  Kefauver and, 481
Stewardship theory, 482
Stockdale, James, 70
Stockman, David, 353
Strategic Arms Limitation Treaty
    (SALT), 79, 123, 517
Stuart, Gilbert, 220, 349, 574, 577
Sturgis, Frank, 567
Subpoena, *285*
Succession, 69, 255, 483–487
  disability and, 154–155, 485
  full, 484
  line of, 144, 478, 484
  party rules and, 487
  Twentieth Amendment and, 486–487
  Twenty-fifth Amendment and, 484
  vice president and, 539–540
Succession Act of 1792, 484
Succession Act of 1947, 392, 484
Suez crisis, 168
Summit meetings, 153, 487–489
  economic, 165
Sununu, John H., 85, 477
Super-delegates, 146, 487
Superfund law, 195
Supply-side economics, 157
Supreme Court. *See* Courts and the
    president
Supreme Court cases. *See also* Court-
    packing plan; Watergate affair
  Alaska Airlines v. Brock (1987), 273
  Buckley v. Valeo (1976), 36–37, 72–73,
      212
  Bush v. Gore (2000), 57–59, 128, 184,
      235
  Cheney v. U.S. District Court (2004),
      207
  Clinton v. Jones (1997), 101, 128
  Dred Scott decision (1857), 35–36

Duncan v. Kahanamoku (1946), 355
Foster v. Neilson (1829), 519
Hamdan v. Rumsfeld (2006), 242–243
Humphrey's Executor v. United States (1935), 15, 269, 288, 370
Immigration and Naturalization Service v. Chadha (1983), 272–273, 334
Japanese American internment, 303–304
Justice Department and, 315
Korematsu v. United States (1944), 303–304
McConnell v. FEC (2003), 76
McCulloch v. Maryland (1819), 373
Merryman, Ex parte (1861), 190
Milligan, Ex parte (1866), 190, 355, 364–365
Morrison v. Olson (1988), 525
Myers v. United States (1926), 14–15, 18, 269, 525
Pocket Veto Case (1929), 539
Prize Cases (1863), 97, 189
United States v. Belmont (1936), 199
United States v. Curtiss-Wright Export Corp. (1936), 129, 516, 528
United States v. Nixon (1974), 206, 528–529, 569–570
veto power and, 535, 539
war powers, 558, 562
Wiener v. United States (1958), 15, 269
Youngstown Sheet and Tube Co. v. Sawyer (1952), 191, 325, 591–592
Sutherland, George, 129, 528
Symmes, Anna, 249

Taft, Helen, 221, 490
Taft, Robert A., 379, 423, 492, 582
Taft, William Howard, 490–492, *491*
  appointments, 267
  on appointments, 11
  background, 27, 28, 490
  Congress and, 113
  election of 1908, 34, 327, 449, 491
  election of 1912, 143, 178, 245, 353, 491, 500, 584
  inauguration, 249
  pitching first baseball, *87, 91*
  Roosevelt (T.) endorsement of, 209
  stewardship theory and, 482
  as Supreme Court Justice, 129, 226, 370, 492
  veto power of, 534
  vice president, 462, 463
Taft-Hartley Labor Act of 1947, 191, 520, 592
Taiwan, 518

Talleyrand, Charles Maurice de, 3, 232
Taney, Roger B., 131, 190, 323
Tariff Act of 1921, 508
Tariff Act of 1930. *See* Smoot-Hawley Act
Tariff Commission, 289
Tariffs, 302, 348, 507–508. *See also* Trade policy
  General Agreement on Tariffs and Trade, 508–509
  reform legislation, 386
Taxation. *See also* Economic powers
  budget growth and, 46–47
  campaign financing and, 72
  presidential power and, 164–165
Taylor, Claudia Alta. *See* Johnson, Lady Bird
Taylor, Margaret Mackall Smith, 492
Taylor, Zachary, *492,* **492–493**
  background, 28, 492
  Compromise of 1850, 218
  death, 142, 218, 493
  election of 1844, 217
  election of 1848, 99, 492, 532
  Grant and, 235
  inauguration, 249
  military experience, 26–27, 167, 362, 412, 492–493
  veto power of, 534
  vice presidents, 217
Teapot Dome scandal, 139, 195, 246, 493–494, *494*
Tecumseh (Shawnee chief), 248
Television. *See also* Media and the presidency
  Kennedy assassination/funeral, 142–143
  political party decline and, 409, 410
  public appeals and, 116, 466–467, 468
  use of, by president, 258, 355, 357
Tenet, George, *67*
  Presidential Medal of Freedom and, 415–416
Tennessee Valley Authority (TVA), 384, 494–495, 582
Tenure of Office Act of 1867, 14, 275, 276, 308
Term of office, 495–498
  honeymoon period, 495
  inauguration, 282–284, 495
  lame duck period, 496
  six-year term proposal, 498
  transition period, 495
  Twentieth Amendment and, 328
  Twenty-second Amendment and, 497

two-term tradition, 496–497
Terrorism, 56. *See also* Homeland Security Department (DHS); September 11 attacks
  Bush (G.W.) and, 122, 156–157, 201
  CIA and, 81
  domestic, crime of, 193
  media and, 358
  military tribunals, 242–243
  Rumsfeld and, 451
  Summit meetings and, 240
  war on, 191, 451, 554–555
Texas
  annexation of, 5, 198, 412, 492, 522–523
  Mexican-American War of 1846 and, 361–362
  Republic of, recognition, 153
Thatcher, Margaret, 32
Thieu, Nguyen Van, 390
Third parties, 172, 498–501. *See also* Political parties; *specific parties*
  election of 1824, 118, 119, 176, 187, 302
  election of 1836, 248, 312, 459, 531, 532
  election of 1856, 35, 218
  election of 1860, 30, 32, 96, 159, 177, 408
  election of 1892, 100, 570–571
  election of 1912, 143, 178, 327, 463
  election of 1924, 327, 500
  election of 1948, 179, 377, 501
  election of 1968, 6, 187, 268
  election of 1992, 102, 184, 400
  types of, 499–501
Thirteenth Amendment, 188
Thomas, Clarence, 131
Thomson, Charles, *175*
Thornburgh, Richard, 315
Thurman, Allen G., 369
Thurmond, J. Strom, 179, 377, 501, *502,* 502–503, 553
Tilden, Samuel J., 440, *503,* 503–504
  compromise of 1876, 177–178, 186, 250
  election of 1876, 253
  New York Public Library and, 504
Tippecanoe, 248, 249
Titles of president and vice president, 504
Tocqueville, Alexis de, 290
Todd, John, 349
Todd, Mary. *See* Lincoln, Mary Todd
Tompkins, Daniel D., 504–505
Tonkin Gulf Resolution, 124, 505–506, 547, 560
Torresola, Griselio, 25

Tower, John, 12, 66
  Iran-contra affair and, 295, *296*
Tower Commission. *See* Iran-contra
  affair
Trade Agreements Act of 1934, 508
Trade policy, 506–509
  Constitution and, 506
  economic summits and, 165
  fast track authority, 509
  international negotiations, 508–509
  "open door" policy toward China, 348
  protectionism, 507–508
Trade Representative, Office of U.S.,
  110, 202, 509–510
Trading with the Enemy Act of 1917,
  191, 193
Transcontinental railroad, 493
Transition period, 495, 510–511
Transportation Department, 64, 110,
  511–512
Transportation Security Administration
  (TSA), 261, 512
Transportation Statistics, Bureau of,
  512
Travel, 513
  vice-presidential, 545
Treason, 51, 97
Treasurer of the United States, Office
  of, 515
Treasury Department, 110, 514–515.
  See also Secret Service
  background, 514
  creation of, 40
  law enforcement powers, 331
  size of, 64
Treaties. *See* Executive agreements;
  specific treaty (e.g., Ghent, Treaty of)
Treaty power, 122–123, 152, 515–519
  executive agreements and, 152
  ratification of, 517
  Senate advisory role in, 516
  Senate approval of, 517–518
  state law and, 518–519
  termination of, 518
Triangulation policy, 104
Tripp, Linda, 101, 278, 580
Trowbridge, J. T., 440
Truman, Anderson Shippe, 519
Truman, Bess, 221, 519
Truman, Harry S., *251, 324, 519,*
  519–521
  Air Force One and, 8–9
  appointments, 13, 85, 265, 266, 443,
    552–553
  assassination attempt, 23, 24, 25, 31
  background, 28, 29, 519
  Blair House residence, 31, 576
  cabinet, 63–64

as commander in chief, 521
Congress and, 115, 209–210
counsel to the president, 127
creates chief of staff, 85
education, 28, 29
Eisenhower and, 167
election of 1946, 552
election of 1948, 148–149, 502
emergency powers, 122
ethics and, 196
Executive Office of the President and,
  204
executive orders, 205
as ex-president, 226
Fair Deal, 209–210
family and friends, 139
Famine Emergency Commission and,
  264
Hoover commission, 265, 266
impoundments, 281
international trade, 508
Korean War and, 323–324, 527
library of, 336, 521
National Security Act of 1947 and,
  260
Old Executive Office Building and, 200
political career, 519–521
presidency, 520–521
Presidential Medal of Freedom and,
  415
public opinion, 428
rating by historians, 413–414
rest and recreation, 136
staff, 475
steel mills seizure, 129, 190–191, 325,
  591–592
succeeds F. D. Roosevelt, 179, 447,
  483, 520, 542, 544, 590
veto power of, 534, 536
vice president, 29–30, 484, 520
White House and, 576
work habits, 135
Truman Doctrine, 156, 520
Tsongas, Paul, 102, 321
Tucker, Jim Guy, 579, 580
Tugwell, Rexford G., 323
Tumulty, Joseph P., 356, 418
Twelfth Amendment, 17, 19, 51, 174,
  176, 186, 254, 408, 433, 458, 541
Twentieth Amendment, 19, 328, 487,
  495
Twenty-second Amendment, 19, 258,
  329, 495, 498
Twenty-third Amendment, 19
Twenty-fifth Amendment, 19, 154, 182,
  225, 392, 443, 540, 543
Two-term tradition, 496–497
Tyler, John, 521–523, *522*

appointments, 67, 322
background, 27, 28
election of 1836, 522
election of 1840, 522
executive agreement, 198
as ex-president, 226, 523
impeachment effort against, 280
judicial nominations, 131
Mexican War of 1846, 362
oath of office and, 394
succeeds W. H. Harrison, 17, 255, 483,
  484, 521, 522, 544
veto power of, 534, 535
as vice president, 249, 312, 541
Tyler, Julia, 220, 242, 522
Tyler, Letitia Christian, 522

Ulysses, Hiram. *See* Grant, Ulysses S.
Underwood-Simmons Tariff Act of
  1913, 508
Underwood Tariff Act of 1913, 584
Uniform Code of Military Justice,
  242–243
Union Pacific Railroad, 31, 109, 280
Unitary executive theory, 524–525
United Nations, 525–527. *See also*
  Security Council, U.N.
  Cold war, 526
  creation of, 590
  General Assembly room, *526*
  Gulf War, 401–402, 527
  Iraq War, 527, 562
  Korean War and, 323–324, 521, 527
  Stevenson, Adlai E., II and, 482
  U.S. war powers and, 562
United Nations Participation Act of
  1945, 526–527
United States v. Belmont (1936), 199
*United States v. Curtiss-Wright Export
  Corp.* (1936), 129, 516, 528
United States v. Nixon (1974), 206,
  528–529, 569–570
  cartoon, *206, 529*
United States Government Manual, 203
United We Stand America, 400
Unit rule, 146
Uruguay Round, GATT negotiations,
  508
U.S. Mint, 515
U.S. Trade Representative, Office of,
  202, 509–510
U.S.A. Patriot Act of 2001, 193, 211,
  315, 332
U.S.A. Patriot Act of 2006, 193
USDA. *See* Agriculture Department
U-2 spy plane, 168

Van Buren, Hannah Hoes, 530

Van Buren, Martin, 530–532
ancestry, 26
as cabinet member, 323
election of 1828, 176
election of 1836, 248, 302, 312, 459, 522
election of 1840, 133
election of 1848, 500
as ex-president, 226
national party convention of 1844, 411–412
party leadership and, 176, 397
on presidency, 88
presidential anthem, 242
third-party candidacy 1848, 493
veto power of, 534
as vice president, 541
vice presidents, 311
as widower, 27
Vandenburg, Arthur H., 225
Versailles, Treaty of, 18, 246, 518, 582, 585
Veterans Affairs Department, 61, 64, 532–533
Veterans' Employment and Training Services, 328
Veto power, 116–117, 121, 533–539. See also Legislative veto; Line-item veto
Congress and, 538
constitutional debate on, 533, 535
deciding to use, 537–538
Fair Deal and, 209
historic use of, 535–536
national bank and, 373
override procedures of, 535, 537–538
separation of power and, 461
vetoes by presidents, 534, 536–537
Vice president, 539–546. See also Twelfth Amendment
advisory roles for, 544–545
constitutional roles for, 543–544
enhanced status of, 541–542
executive lobbying and, 115
expanded resources for, 542–543
history of, 540–541
modern roles for, 543–546
nineteenth century, 541
Office of, 543
postwar period, 542
qualifications of, 17, 26, 432–433
representative roles for, 545–546
as Senate leader, 3, 541
separation of power and, 462
statutory roles for, 544
succession and, 17, 539–540
ticket balancing and, 540, 541
title of, 504
twentieth century, 541–542

vacancies in, 484–485
Vice-presidential residence, 203, 455, 543, 546, *546*
"Vietnamization," 154
Vietnam Veterans Memorial, *548*
Vietnam War, 181, 546–549. *See also* Johnson, Lyndon B.
Agnew as spokesman for, 7
budget deficit and, 40
Congress and, 548–549
demonstrations against and federal troops, 192
development of, 547–548
election of 1968 and, 181, 268, 343, 344
interests groups and, 293
Justice Department and, 314
LeMay and, 551
Mondale and, 365
Nixon and, 389–390, 428
Nixon Doctrine and, 156
Pentagon Papers and, 357
presidential-congressional relations and, 114
presidential oath of office and, 394
public opinion, 311
Tonkin Gulf resolution, 124, 505–506, 547, 560
Veterans Affairs Department and, 532
war powers and, 558
Voting Rights Act, 239

Wade, Ben, 276
Wagner Act of 1935, 192, 384
Waite, Morrison R., *177*
Walker Tariff Act of 1846, 412
Wallace, George C., 6, 181, 187, 268, 498–499, *499*, 500, 550–551, *551*. See also American Independent Party
Wallace, Henry A., 179, 378, *493*, 520, 552–553
election of 1948, 503
Wallace, Lurleen, 551
Wallas, Graham, 239
Walsh, Lawrence E., 285, 295–296
War Hawks, 66, 98, 311, 321, 351
War Labor Board, 491
War Labor Disputes Act of 1943, 591
War of 1812, 4–5, 248, 311, 492, 505, 553–554
Madison and, 351–352
War on Poverty, 239
War on Terrorism. *See* Terrorism
War powers, 555–560. *See also* Defense Department
Bush (G. H. W.) and, 124
Bush (G. W.) and, 124, 191, 557
Civil War, 96–97, 188

commander in chief and, 123–124, 558–559
Congress and, 117, 124, 555–556
development of, 557–558
Emancipation Proclamation, 188
legislative veto and, 334
limits on, 190–191
nuclear weapons and, 391–392, 559
Polk and, 362
president as defense manager and, 559–560
Roosevelt (F. D.) and, 190–191
terrorism, 554–555
Truman and, 190–191
Wilson and, 190–191
World War I, 586–587
World War II, 588–589
War Powers Act of 1973, 536, 537, 549, 558, 560–562
background, 560–561
War Powers Resolution of 1973, 334
Warren, Earl, 22, 110, 131, 562, *563*
election of 1948, 30, 148
Warren, William, 223
Warren Commission, 22, 110, 225, 320, 562–563
Zapruder film and, 594
Washington, George, *63*, *175*, *210*, *394*, *564*, **564–566**
appointments, 4, 243–244, 305, 367
background, 26, 28
cabinet, 62
as commander in chief, 555
Congress and, 112, 118
education, 28
election of 1789, 174–175
election of 1792, 174
executive privilege and, 206
as ex-president, 226
farewell address, 210, *210*, 565
inaugural address, 467
inauguration, 249, 282
judicial nominations, 131
memorials to, 360
Neutrality Proclamation of 1973, 382–383
oath of office, 394
pardon power, 396, 572
patronage and, 398
perquisites, 454
presidency, 124, 565–566
presidential anthem, 242
presidential proclamation and, 426
presidential title and, 504
rating by historians, 413–414
recognition power, 152
retirement of, 566
Revolutionary War and, 564–565

salary, 453
speech-making approach, 467
staff, 46, 474
State of the Union address, 479
treaty power interpretation, 516
two-term tradition and, 496
veto power of, 534
Whiskey Rebellion and, 572
White House and, 574
Washington, Martha, 564, *566*, 566–567
Washington, Treaty of, 1871, 236–237
Washington Disarmament Conference, 1921, 246
Washington Peace Conference, 523
Watergate affair, 36, 195
   burglary segment, 507
   cover-up of, 507–508
   effects of, 64, 182, 197
   executive privilege and, 206
   FBI and, 211
   Federal Election Commission and, 212
   Ford and, 224, 225
   hearings, 568–569
   independent counsel and, 284. *See also* Saturday night massacre
   midterm elections and, 363
   Nixon and, 227, 314, 390–391
   Nixon impeachment effort, 131, 276–278
   Nixon Library and, 335
   politicians and political advisers, 234
   as presidential milestone, 258
   separation of power and, 461–462
   subpoena, *285*
   tapes, 128, 130, 569
   United States v. Nixon (1974), 206, 528–529, 569–570
   White House staff after, 476
Watkins, James D., 194
Watson, Jack H., Jr., 85
Weaver, James B., 100, *570*, 570–571
Weaver, Robert C., 11
Webster, Daniel, 218, 522, 539
Weinberger, Casper W., 296
Weiner v. United States (1958), 269
Weizmann, Chaim, 32
Welch, Laura. *See* Bush, Laura
Weld, William, 13
Welfare, political parties and, 409
Welles, Gideon, *188*
Wellstone, Paul, 366
West Wing of White House, offices in, 203
Wheeler, William A., *571*, 571–572

Whigs, 30, 99, 248–249, 312, 337. *See also* National Republican Party
   disintegration of party, 218
   election of 1836, 500
   Fillmore and, 217
   national party convention of 1831, 378
   Tyler and, 522
Whiskey Rebellion, 396, 572
Whiskey Ring scandal, 195, 237, 573
Whistle blowers, 92
White, Edward, 492
White, Hugh, 500
White, Theodore H., 181
White House, *60*, 317, 455, 573–578, *574, 575*
   cabinet room, 60
   conferences, 111
   correspondents, 359
   daily and family life in, 134–139, 455
   diagram of, *575*
   early history, 573–574
   Press Briefing Room, 576, *576*
   renovations, 576–578
   security in, 24, 578
   Signal Board, 578
   Situation Room, 578
   staff, 471–478
   today, 576–578
   weddings in, 136
White House Office, 201
   Executive Office of the President, 200
White House staff, 61, 134. *See also* Staff
Whitewater investigation, 103, 108, 578–580
   Clinton (H.R.) and, 108
   closure of, 184
   independent counsel and, 285
   Justice Department and, 314
Wiener, Myron, 269
Wiener v. United States (1958), 15
Wilkie, Wendall L., 148, 447, 552, 581
   national party convention of 1940, 379
   term limits and, 497
Wilkinson, James, 51
William J. Clinton Foundation, 105
Williams, James D., 247
Wills, Mark, 270
Wilson, Edith, 221, 581–582, *582*, 585
Wilson, Ellen, 221, 582, 585
Wilson, Henry, *27*, 237, 484, 582–583
Wilson, James, 253
Wilson, James Q., 499
Wilson, Joe, 84
Wilson, Valerie Plame, 84

Wilson, Woodrow, *323, 583*, **583–585**, 587, *587*. *See also* Versailles, Treaty of
   appointments, 34, 446
   background, 28, 29
   cabinet, 63, 323
   Congress and, 113, 115
   Council of National Defense, 63
   education, 28
   election of 1912, 143, 178, 353, 450, 491, 500
   election of 1916, 209, 267, 354
   emergency powers, 190
   family and friends, 138–139
   New Freedom program, 385–386
   party leadership and, 397
   popular leadership and, 257
   presidential commissions and, 110
   presidential disability and, 154
   press, relationship with, 356
   press conferences, 416
   public appeals of, 467
   rating by historians, 413–414
   recognition power, 152
   removal power, 269, 370
   State of the Union addresses, 479, 584
   tariff policy, 508
   travel criticized, 513
   on veto power, 533
   veto power of, 534
   war powers, 190–191, 557–558, 586–587
Wirt, William, 378
Wolcott, Alexander, 131
Women's suffrage, 499
Woodward, Bob, 357, *567*, 568
Woodward, George W., 131
Works Projects Administration (WPA), 399
World Trade Organization (WTO), 508, 509
World War I, 190, *586*, 586–587
   Wilson and, 586–587
World War II, 190, 588–590
   Allied victory, 587
   Eisenhower and, 167
   reparations, 141
Wright, Fielding L., 503
Wright, Silas, 139–140
Wright, Susan Webber, 580
Wyman, Jane, 437
Wythe, George, 304

XYZ affair, 3, 232

Yarborough, Ralph, 52
Yellowstone National Park, *293*